This book is dedicated to my wife and best friend, Nancy, with love.

– PK

This book is dedicated to my wife, Punam, and my two daughters,
Carolyn and Allison, with much love and thanks.

– KLK

About the Authors

Philip Kotler

Philip Kotler *is one of the world's leading authorities on marketing. He is the S. C. Johnson & Son Distinguished Professor of International Marketing at the Kellogg School of Management, Northwestern University. He received his master's degree at the University of Chicago and his Ph.D. at MIT, both in economics. He did postdoctoral work in mathematics at Harvard University and in behavioral science at the University of Chicago.*

*Dr. Kotler is the coauthor of **Principles of Marketing** and **Marketing: An Introduction.** His **Strategic Marketing for Nonprofit Organizations,** now in its seventh edition, is the best seller in that specialized area. Dr. Kotler's other books include **Marketing Models; The New Competition; Marketing Professional Services; Strategic Marketing for Educational Institutions; Marketing for Health Care Organizations; Marketing Congregations; High Visibility; Social Marketing; Marketing Places; The Marketing of Nations; Marketing for Hospitality and Tourism; Standing Room Only—Strategies for Marketing the Performing Arts; Museum Strategy and Marketing; Marketing Moves; Kotler on Marketing; Lateral Marketing: Ten Deadly Marketing Sins;** and **Corporate Social Responsibility.***

*In addition, he has published more than one hundred articles in leading journals, including the **Harvard Business Review, Sloan Management Review, Business Horizons, California Management Review,** the **Journal of Marketing,** the **Journal of Marketing Research, Management Science,** the **Journal of Business Strategy,** and **Futurist.** He is the only three-time winner of the coveted Alpha Kappa Psi award for the best annual article published in the **Journal of Marketing.***

Professor Kotler was the first recipient of the American Marketing Association's (AMA) Distinguished Marketing Educator Award (1985). The European Association of Marketing Consultants and Sales Trainers awarded him their Prize for Marketing Excellence. He was chosen as the Leader in Marketing Thought by the Academic Members of the AMA in a 1975 survey. He also received the 1978 Paul Converse Award of the AMA, honoring his original contribution to marketing. In 1995, the Sales and Marketing Executives International (SMEI) named him Marketer of the Year. In 2002, Professor Kotler received the Distinguished Educator Award from the Academy of Marketing Science. He has received honorary doctoral degrees from Stockholm University, the University of Zurich, Athens University of Economics and Business, DePaul University, the Cracow School of Business and Economics, Groupe H.E.C. in Paris, the Budapest School of Economic Science and Public Administration, and the University of Economics and Business Administration in Vienna.

Professor Kotler has been a consultant to many major U.S. and foreign companies, including IBM, General Electric, AT&T, Honeywell, Bank of America, Merck, SAS Airlines, Michelin, and others in the areas of marketing strategy and planning, marketing organization, and international marketing.

He has been Chairman of the College of Marketing of the Institute of Management Sciences, a Director of the American Marketing Association, a Trustee of the Marketing Science Institute, a Director of the MAC Group, a member of the Yankelovich Advisory Board, and a member of the Copernicus Advisory Board. He was a member of the Board of Governors of the School of the Art Institute of Chicago and a member of the Advisory Board of the Drucker Foundation. He has traveled extensively throughout Europe, Asia, and South America, advising and lecturing to many companies about global marketing opportunities.

Marketing Management

14e

Global Edition

PHILIP KOTLER
Northwestern University

KEVIN LANE KELLER
Dartmouth College

PEARSON

Boston   Columbus   Indianapolis   New York   San Francisco   Upper Saddle River
Amsterdam   Cape Town   Du   London   Madrid   Milan   Munich   Paris   Montreal   Toronto
Delhi   Mexico City   Sao   l   Singapore   Taipei   Tokyo

Editorial Director: Sally Yagan
Editor in Chief: Eric Svendsen
Executive Editor: Melissa Sabella
Senior Acquisitions Editor, Global Edition:
Steven Jackson
Development Editor: Elisa Adams
Director of Editorial Services: Ashley Santora
Editorial Project Manager: Kierra Bloom
Editorial Assistant: Elizabeth Scarpa
Director of Marketing: Patrice Lumuba Jones
Senior Marketing Manager: Anne Fahlgren
Marketing Manager, International: Dean Erasmus

Senior Managing Editor: Judy Leale
Production Project Manager: Ann Pulido
Senior Operations Supervisor: Arnold Vila
Creative Director: John Christiano
Senior Art Director: Blair Brown
Text Designer: Blair Brown
Cover Designers: Blair Brown and Jodi Notowitz
Lead Media Project Manager: Lisa Rinaldi
Editorial Media Project Manager: Denise Vaughn
Full-Service Project Management: Sharon
Anderson/BookMasters, Inc.
Cover Printer: Courier Kendallville

Pearson Education Limited
Edinburgh Gate
Harlow
Essex CM20 2JE
England

and Associated Companies throughout the world

Visit us on the World Wide Web at:
www.pearsoned.co.uk

© Pearson Education Limited 2012

ISBN 13: 978-0-273-75336-0
ISBN 10: 0-273-75336-3

British Library Cataloguing-in-Publication Data
A catalogue record for this book is available from the British Library

10 9 8 7 6 5 4
15 14 13

Typeset in 9.5/11.5, Minion by Integra
Printed and bound by Courier/Kendallville in The United States of America

Kevin Lane Keller *is widely recognized as one of the top marketing academics of the last 25 years. He is the E. B. Osborn Professor of Marketing at the Tuck School of Business at Dartmouth College. Professor Keller has degrees from Cornell, Carnegie-Mellon, and Duke universities. At Dartmouth, he teaches MBA courses on marketing management and strategic brand management and lectures in executive programs on those topics.*

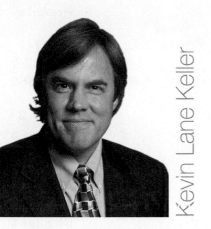

Previously, Professor Keller was on the faculty of the Graduate School of Business at Stanford University, where he also served as the head of the marketing group. Additionally, he has been on the marketing faculty at the University of California at Berkeley and the University of North Carolina at Chapel Hill, been a visiting professor at Duke University and the Australian Graduate School of Management, and has two years of industry experience as Marketing Consultant for Bank of America.

*Professor Keller's general area of expertise lies in marketing strategy and planning, and branding. His specific research interest is in how understanding theories and concepts related to consumer behavior can improve marketing strategies. His research has been published in three of the major marketing journals—the **Journal of Marketing,** the **Journal of Marketing Research,** and the **Journal of Consumer Research.** He also has served on the Editorial Review Boards of those journals. With over ninety published papers, his research has been extensively cited and has received numerous awards.*

*Professor Keller is acknowledged as one of the international leaders in the study of brands and branding. His textbook on those subjects, **Strategic Brand Management,** has been adopted at top business schools and leading firms around the world and has been heralded as the "bible of branding."*

Actively involved with industry, he has worked on a host of different types of marketing projects. He has served as a consultant and advisor to marketers for some of the world's most successful brands, including Accenture, American Express, Disney, Ford, Intel, Levi Strauss, Procter & Gamble, and Samsung. Additional brand consulting activities have been with other top companies such as Allstate, Beiersdorf (Nivea), BlueCross BlueShield, Campbell's, Colgate, Eli Lilly, ExxonMobil, General Mills, GfK, Goodyear, Intuit, Johnson & Johnson, Kodak, L.L.Bean, Mayo Clinic, Nordstrom, Ocean Spray, Red Hat, SAB Miller, Shell Oil, Starbucks, Unilever, and Young & Rubicam. He has also served as an academic trustee for the Marketing Science Institute.

A popular and highly sought-after speaker, he has made speeches and conducted marketing seminars to top executives in a variety of forums. Some of his senior management and marketing training clients have included such diverse business organizations as Cisco, Coca-Cola, Deutsche Telekom, GE, Google, IBM, Macy's, Microsoft, Nestle, Novartis, and Wyeth. He has lectured all over the world, from Seoul to Johannesburg, from Sydney to Stockholm, and from Sao Paulo to Mumbai. He has served as keynote speaker at conferences with hundreds to thousands of participants.

An avid sports, music, and film enthusiast, in his so-called spare time, he has helped to manage and market, as well as serve as executive producer for, one of Australia's great rock and roll treasures, The Church, as well as American power-pop legends Dwight Twilley and Tommy Keene. Additionally, he is the Principal Investor and Marketing Advisor for Second Motion Records. He is also on the Board of Directors for The Doug Flutie, Jr. Foundation for Autism and the Montshire Museum of Science. Professor Keller lives in Etna, NH, with his wife, Punam (also a Tuck marketing professor), and his two daughters, Carolyn and Allison.

Brief Contents

Contents

Preface

What's New in the 14th Edition

The overriding goal of the revision for the 14th edition of *Marketing Management* was to create as comprehensive, current, and engaging MBA marketing textbook as possible. Where appropriate, new material was added, old material was updated, and no longer relevant or necessary material was deleted. *Marketing Management,* 14th edition, allows those instructors who have used the 13th edition to build on what they have learned and done while at the same time offering a text that is unsurpassed in breadth, depth, and relevance for students experiencing *Marketing Management* for the first time.

The successful across-chapter reorganization into eight parts that began with the 12th edition of *Marketing Management* has been preserved, as well as many of the favorably received within-chapter features that have been introduced through the years, such as topical chapter openers, in-text boxes highlighting noteworthy companies or issues, and the Marketing Insight and Marketing Memo boxes that provide in-depth conceptual and practical commentary.

Significant changes to the 14th edition include:

- Brand new opening vignettes for each chapter set the stage for the chapter material to follow. By covering topical brands or companies, the vignettes are great classroom discussion starters.
- Almost half of the in-text boxes are new. These boxes provide vivid illustrations of chapter concepts using actual companies and situations. The boxes cover a variety of products, services, and markets, and many have accompanying illustrations in the form of ads or product shots.
- The end-of-chapter section now includes two Marketing in Action mini-cases highlighting innovative, insightful marketing accomplishments by leading organizations. Each case includes questions that promote classroom discussion and analysis.
- Dramatic changes in the marketing environment have occurred in recent years—in particular, the economic, natural, and technological environments. Throughout the new edition, these three areas are addressed, sometimes via new subsections in chapters, with emphasis on marketing during economic downturns and recessions, the rise of sustainability and "green" marketing, and the increased development of computing power, the Internet, and mobile phones. These new marketing realities make it more important than ever for marketers to be holistic in what they do, the overriding theme of this text.
- Chapter 19, on personal communications, received a significant update with much new material to reflect the changing social media landscape and communications environment.
- Forecasting has been moved to Chapter 3 where it fits well with the material on the marketing environment.
- Chapter 5 was re-titled as "Creating Long-Term Loyalty Relationships" to better reflect its stronger area of emphasis.
- Chapters 10 and 11 were reorganized and material swapped. Chapter 11 was also re-titled as "Competitive Dynamics" to acknowledge the significant material added on marketing in an economic downturn.

What Is *Marketing Management* All About?

Marketing Management is the leading marketing text because its content and organization consistently reflect changes in marketing theory and practice. The very first edition of *Marketing Management,* published in 1967, introduced the concept that companies must be customer-and-market driven. But there was little mention of what have now become fundamental topics such as segmentation, targeting, and positioning. Concepts such as brand equity, customer value analysis, database marketing, e-commerce, value networks, hybrid channels, supply chain management, and integrated marketing communications were not even part of the marketing vocabulary then. *Marketing Management* continues to reflect the changes in the marketing discipline over the past 40 years.

Firms now sell goods and services through a variety of direct and indirect channels. Mass advertising is not nearly as effective as it was, so marketers are exploring new forms of communication, such as experiential, entertainment, and viral marketing. Customers are telling companies what types of product or services they want and when, where, and how they want to buy them. They are increasingly reporting to other consumers what they think of specific companies and products—using e-mail, blogs, podcasts, and other digital media to do so. Company messages are becoming a smaller fraction of the total "conversation" about products and services.

In response, companies have shifted gears from managing product portfolios to managing *customer* portfolios, compiling databases on individual customers so they can understand them better and construct individualized offerings and messages. They are doing less product and service standardization and more niching and customization. They are replacing monologues with customer dialogues. They are improving their methods of measuring customer profitability and customer lifetime value. They are intent on measuring the return on their marketing investment and its impact on shareholder value. They are also concerned with the ethical and social implications of their marketing decisions.

As companies change, so does their marketing organization. Marketing is no longer a company department charged with a limited number of tasks—it is a company-wide undertaking. It drives the company's vision, mission, and strategic planning. Marketing includes decisions like who the company wants as its customers, which of their needs to satisfy, what products and services to offer, what prices to set, what communications to send and receive, what channels of distribution to use, and what partnerships to develop. Marketing succeeds only when all departments work together to achieve goals: when engineering designs the right products; finance furnishes the required funds; purchasing buys high-quality materials; production makes high-quality products on time; and accounting measures the profitability of different customers, products, and areas.

To address all these different shifts, good marketers are practicing holistic marketing. *Holistic marketing* is the development, design, and implementation of marketing programs, processes, and activities that recognize the breadth and interdependencies of today's marketing environment. Four key dimensions of holistic marketing are:

1. *Internal marketing*—ensuring everyone in the organization embraces appropriate marketing principles, especially senior management.

2. *Integrated marketing*—ensuring that multiple means of creating, delivering, and communicating value are employed and combined in the best way.

3. *Relationship marketing*—having rich, multifaceted relationships with customers, channel members, and other marketing partners.

4. *Performance marketing*—understanding returns to the business from marketing activities and programs, as well as addressing broader concerns and their legal, ethical, social, and environmental effects.

These four dimensions are woven throughout the book and at times spelled out explicitly. The text specifically addresses the following tasks that constitute modern marketing management in the 21st century:

1. Developing marketing strategies and plans

2. Capturing marketing insights and performance

3. Connecting with customers

4. Building strong brands

5. Shaping the market offerings

6. Delivering and communicating value

7. Creating successful long-term growth

What Makes *Marketing Management* the Marketing Leader?

Marketing is of interest to everyone, whether they are marketing goods, services, properties, persons, places, events, information, ideas, or organizations. As it has maintained its respected position among students, educators, and businesspeople, *Marketing Management* has kept up-to-date and contemporary. Students (and instructors) feel that the book is talking directly to them in terms of both content and delivery.

Marketing Management owes its marketplace success to its ability to maximize three dimensions that characterize the best marketing texts—depth, breadth, and relevance—as measured by the following criteria:

- **Depth.**   Does the book have solid academic grounding? Does it contain important theoretical concepts, models, and frameworks? Does it provide conceptual guidance to solve practical problems?
- **Breadth.**   Does the book cover all the right topics? Does it provide the proper amount of emphasis on those topics?
- **Relevance.**   Does the book engage the reader? Is it interesting to read? Does it have lots of compelling examples?

The 14th edition builds on the fundamental strengths of past editions that collectively distinguish it from all other marketing management texts:

- **Managerial Orientation.**   The book focuses on the major decisions that marketing managers and top management face in their efforts to harmonize the organization's objectives, capabilities, and resources with marketplace needs and opportunities.
- **Analytical Approach.**   *Marketing Management* presents conceptual tools and frameworks for analyzing recurring problems in marketing management. Cases and examples illustrate effective marketing principles, strategies, and practices.
- **Multidisciplinary Perspective.**   The book draws on the rich findings of various scientific disciplines—economics, behavioral science, management theory, and mathematics—for fundamental concepts and tools directly applicable to marketing challenges.
- **Universal Applications.**   The book applies strategic thinking to the complete spectrum of marketing: products, services, persons, places, information, ideas and causes; consumer and business markets; profit and nonprofit organizations; domestic and foreign companies; small and large firms; manufacturing and intermediary businesses; and low- and high-tech industries.
- **Comprehensive and Balanced Coverage.**   *Marketing Management* covers all the topics an informed marketing manager needs to understand to execute strategic, tactical, and administrative marketing.

Student Supplements

mymarketinglab

Mymarketinglab gives you the opportunity to test yourself on key concepts and skills, track your progress through the course and use the personalized study plan activities—all to help you achieve success in the classroom.

Features include:

- **Personalized Study Plans**—Pre- and post-tests with remediation activities directed to help you understand and apply the concepts where you need the most help.

- *Interactive Elements*—A wealth of hands-on activities and exercises let you experience and learn actively.
- *Current Events Articles*—Concise, highly relevant articles about the latest marketing related news with thought provoking short essay questions.
- *Critical Thinking Challenge Question*—These questions measure core critical-thinking skills through the context of marketing applications. To answer these questions, you will need to recognize assumptions, evaluate arguments, identify relevant issues, draw inferences, spot logical flaws, and recognize similarities between arguments. Knowledge of marketing content picked up through the text and the class will help you zero in on the correct issues, but you will still need to exercise critical judgment in order to get the correct answer.

Marketing Management Video Gallery

Make your classroom "newsworthy." Pearson Education has updated the Marketing Management video library for the 14th edition. A full library of video segments accompany this edition featuring issue-focused footage such as interviews with top executives, objective reporting by real news anchors, industry research analysts, and marketing and advertising campaign experts. A full video guide, including synopses, discussion questions, and teaching suggestions, is available (online) to accompany the video library.

The Marketing Plan Handbook, 4th edition, with Marketing Plan Pro

Marketing Plan Pro is a highly rated commercial software program that guides you through the entire marketing plan process. The software is totally interactive and features 10 sample marketing plans, step-by-step guides, and customizable charts. Customize your marketing plan to fit your marketing needs by following easy-to-use plan wizards. Follow the clearly outlined steps from strategy to implementation. Click to print, and your text, spreadsheet, and charts come together to create a powerful marketing plan. The new *The Marketing Plan Handbook,* by Marian Burk Wood, supplements the in-text marketing plan material with an in-depth guide to what student marketers really need to know. A structured learning process leads to a complete and actionable marketing plan. Also included are timely, real-world examples that illustrate key points, sample marketing plans, and Internet resources.

Acknowledgments

The 14th edition bears the imprint of many people. *From Phil Kotler:* My colleagues and associates at the Kellogg School of Management at Northwestern University continue to have an important impact on my thinking: Nidhi Agrawal, Eric T. Anderson, James C. Anderson, Robert C. Blattberg, Miguel C. Brendl, Bobby J. Calder, Gregory S. Carpenter, Alex Chernev, Anne T. Coughlan, David Gal, Kent Grayson, Karsten Hansen, Dipak C. Jain, Lakshman Krishnamurti, Angela Lee, Vincent Nijs, Yi Qian, Mohanbir S. Sawhney, Louis W. Stern, Brian Sternthal, Alice M. Tybout, and Andris A. Zoltners. I also want to thank the S. C. Johnson Family for the generous support of my chair at the Kellogg School. Completing the Northwestern team are my former Deans, Donald P. Jacobs and Dipak Jain, and my present Dean, Sally Blount for providing generous support for my research and writing.

Several former faculty members of the marketing department had a great influence on my thinking when I first joined the Kellogg marketing faculty, specifically Richard M. Clewett, Ralph Westfall, Harper W. Boyd, and Sidney J. Levy. I also want to acknowledge Gary Armstrong for our work on *Principles of Marketing* and *Marketing - An Introduction.*

I am indebted to the following coauthors of international editions of *Marketing Management* and *Principles of Marketing* who have taught me a great deal as we worked together to adapt marketing management thinking to the problems of different nations:

- Swee-Hoon Ang and Siew-Meng Leong, National University of Singapore
- Chin-Tiong Tan, Singapore Management University
- Friedhelm W. Bliemel, Universitat Kaiserslautern (Germany)
- Linden Brown; Stewart Adam, Deakin University; Suzan Burton, Macquarie Graduate School of Management; and Sara Denize, University of Western Sydney (Australia)
- Bernard Dubois, Groupe HEC School of Management (France); and Delphine Manceau, ESCP-EAP European School of Management
- John Saunders, Loughborough University and Veronica Wong, Warwick University (United Kingdom)
- Jacob Hornick, Tel Aviv University (Israel)
- Walter Giorgio Scott, Universita Cattolica del Sacro Cuore (Italy)
- Peggy Cunningham, Queen's University (Canada)

I also want to acknowledge how much I have learned from working with coauthors on more specialized marketing subjects: Alan Andreasen, Christer Asplund, Paul N. Bloom, John Bowen, Roberta C. Clarke, Karen Fox, David Gertner, Michael Hamlin, Thomas Hayes, Donald Haider, Hooi Den Hua, Dipak Jain, Somkid Jatusripitak, Hermawan Kartajaya, Neil Kotler, Nancy Lee, Sandra Liu, Suvit Maesincee, James Maken, Waldemar Pfoertsch, Gustave Rath, Irving Rein, Eduardo Roberto, Joanne Scheff, Norman Shawchuck, Joel Shalowitz, Ben Shields, Francois Simon, Robert Stevens, Martin Stoller, Fernando Trias de Bes, Bruce Wrenn, and David Young.

My overriding debt continues to be to my lovely wife, Nancy, who provided me with the time, support, and inspiration needed to prepare this edition. It is truly our book.

From Kevin Lane Keller: I continually benefit from the wisdom of my marketing colleagues at Tuck—Punam Keller, Scott Neslin, Kusum Ailawadi, Praveen Kopalle, Jackie Luan, Peter Golder, Ellie Kyung, Fred Webster, Gert Assmus, and John Farley—as well as the leadership of Dean Paul Danos. I also gratefully acknowledge the invaluable research and teaching contributions from my faculty colleagues and collaborators through the years. I owe a considerable debt of gratitude to Duke University's Jim Bettman and Rick Staelin for helping to get my academic career started and serving as positive role models to this day. I am also appreciative of all that I have learned from working with many industry executives who have generously shared their insights and experiences. With this 14th edition, I received some extremely helpful research assistance from two former Tuck MBAs—Jeff Davidson and Lowey Sichol—who were as accurate, thorough, dependable, and cheerful as you could possibly imagine. Alison Pearson provided superb administrative support. Finally, I give special thanks to Punam, my wife, and Carolyn and Allison, my daughters, who make it all happen and make it all worthwhile.

We are indebted to the following colleagues at other universities who reviewed this new edition:

- Jennifer Barr, Richard Stockton College
- Lawrence Kenneth Duke, Drexel University LeBow College of Business
- Barbara S. Faries, Mission College, Santa Clara, CA
- William E. Fillner, Hiram College
- Frank J. Franzak, Virginia Commonwealth University
- Robert Galka, De Paul University
- Albert N. Greco, Fordham University
- John A. Hobbs, University of Oklahoma
- Brian Larson, Widener University
- Anthony Racka, Oakland Community College, Auburn Hills, MI
- Jamie Ressler, Palm Beach Atlantic University
- James E. Shapiro, University of New Haven
- George David Shows, Louisiana Tech University

We would also like to thank colleagues who have reviewed previous editions of *Marketing Management*:

Homero Aguirre, TAMIU
Alan Au, University of Hong Kong
Hiram Barksdale, University of Georgia
Boris Becker, Oregon State University
Sandy Becker, Rutgers University
Parimal Bhagat, Indiana University of Pennsylvania
Sunil Bhatla, Case Western Reserve University
Michael Bruce, Anderson University
Frederic Brunel, Boston University
John Burnett, University of Denver
Lisa Cain, University of California at Berkeley and Mills College
Surjit Chhabra, DePaul University
Yun Chu, Frostburg State University
Dennis Clayson, University of Northern Iowa
Bob Cline, University of Iowa
Brent Cunningham, Jacksonville State University
Hugh Daubek, Purdue University
John Deighton, University of Chicago
Kathleen Dominick, Rider University
Tad Duffy, Golden Gate University
Mohan Dutta, Purdue University
Barbara Dyer, University of North Carolina at Greensboro

Jackkie Eastman, Valdosta State University
Steve Edison, University of Arkansas–Little Rock
Alton Erdem, University of Houston at Clear Lake
Elizabeth Evans, Concordia University
Barb Finer, Suffolk University
Chic Fojtik, Pepperdine University
Renee Foster, Delta State University
Ralph Gaedeke, California State University, Sacramento
Robert Galka, De Paul University
Betsy Gelb, University of Houston at Clear Lake
Dennis Gensch, University of Wisconsin, Milwaukee
David Georgoff, Florida Atlantic University
Rashi Glazer, University of California, Berkeley
Bill Gray, Keller Graduate School of Management
Barbara Gross, California State University at Northridge
Lewis Hershey, Fayetteville State University
Thomas Hewett, Kaplan University
Mary Higby, University of Detroit–Mercy
Arun Jain, State University of New York, Buffalo
Michelle Kunz, Morehead State University
Eric Langer, Johns Hopkins University
Even Lanseng, Norwegian School of Management
Ron Lennon, Barry University
Michael Lodato, California Lutheran University
Henry Loehr, Pfeiffer University–Charlotte
Bart Macchiette, Plymouth University
Susan Mann, Bluefield State College
Charles Martin, Wichita State University
H. Lee Matthews, Ohio State University
Paul McDevitt, University of Illinois at Springfield
Mary Ann McGrath, Loyola University, Chicago
John McKeever, University of Houston
Kenneth P. Mead, Central Connecticut State University
Henry Metzner, University of Missouri, Rolla
Robert Mika, Monmouth University
Mark Mitchell, Coastal Carolina University
Francis Mulhern, Northwestern University
Pat Murphy, University of Notre Dame
Jim Murrow, Drury College
Zhou Nan, University of Hong Kong
Nicholas Nugent, Boston College
Nnamdi Osakwe, Bryant & Stratton College
Donald Outland, University of Texas, Austin

Albert Page, University of Illinois, Chicago

Young-Hoon Park, Cornell University

Koen Pauwels, Dartmouth College

Lisa Klein Pearo, Cornell University

Keith Penney, Webster University

Patricia Perry, University of Alabama

Mike Powell, North Georgia College and State University

Hank Pruden, Golden Gate University

Christopher Puto, Arizona State University

Abe Qstin, Lakeland University

Lopo Rego, University of Iowa

Richard Rexeisen, University of St. Thomas

William Rice, California State University–Fresno

Scott D. Roberts, Northern Arizona University

Bill Robinson, Purdue University

Robert Roe, University of Wyoming

Jan Napoleon Saykiewicz, Duquesne University

Larry Schramm, Oakland University

Alex Sharland, Hofstra University

Dean Siewers, Rochester Institute of Technology

Anusorn Singhapakdi, Old Dominion University

Jim Skertich, Upper Iowa University

Allen Smith, Florida Atlantic University

Joe Spencer, Anderson University

Mark Spriggs, University of St. Thomas

Nancy Stephens, Arizona State University

Michael Swenso, Brigham Young University, Marriott School

Thomas Tellefsen, The College of Staten Island–CUNY

Daniel Turner, University of Washington

Sean Valentine, University of Wyoming

Ann Veeck, West Michigan University

R. Venkatesh, University of Pittsburgh

Edward Volchok, Stevens Institute of Management

D. J. Wasmer, St. Mary-of-the-Woods College

Zac Williams, Mississippi State University

Greg Wood, Canisius College

Kevin Zeng Zhou, University of Hong Kong

A warm welcome and many thanks to the following people who contributed to the global case studies developed for the 14th edition:

Mairead Brady, Trinity College

John R. Brooks, Jr., Houston Baptist University

Sylvain Charlebois, University of Regina

Geoffrey da Silva, Temasek Business School

Malcolm Goodman, Durham University

Torben Hansen, Copenhagen Business School

Abraham Koshy, Sanjeev Tripathi, and Abhishek, Indian Institute of Management Ahmedabad

Peter Ling, Edith Cowan University

Marianne Marando, Seneca College

Lu Taihong, Sun Yat-Sen University

The talented staff at Pearson Education deserves praise for their role in shaping the 14th edition. We want to thank our editor, Melissa Sabella, for her contribution to this revision. We also want to thank our project manager, Kierra Bloom, for making sure everything was moving along and falling into place in such a personable way, both with regard to the book and supplements. We benefited greatly from the superb editorial help of Elisa Adams, who lent her considerable talents as a development editor to this edition. We also want to acknowledge the fine production work of Ann Pulido, the creative design work of Blair Brown, and the editorial assistance of Elizabeth Scarpa. We thank Denise Vaughn for her work on the media package. We also thank our marketing manager, Anne Fahlgren.

Philip Kotler

S. C. Johnson Distinguished Professor of International Marketing
Kellogg School of Management
Northwestern University
Evanston, Illinois

Kevin Lane Keller

E. B. Osborn Professor of Marketing
Tuck School of Business
Dartmouth College
Hanover, New Hampshire

Pearson wishes to thank and acknowledge the following people for their work on the Global Edition:

Dr. Naila Aaijaz, Faculty of Entrepreneurship and Business, University Malaysia Kelantan, Malaysia

John Allee, Senior Lecturer Marketing, The American University of Sharjah, United Arab Emirates

Dr. Samar M. Baqer, Assistant Professor, Department of Management and Marketing, Kuwait University, Kuwait

Dr. Mohsen A. Bagnied, Associate Professor, Division of Business and Economics, American University of Kuwait, Kuwait

Professor Richard Beswick, Lecturer, University of Applied Sciences, Switzerland

Dr. Yoosuf A. Cader, Associate Professor (Marketing), Researcher in Marketing and Knowledge Management, College of Business, Zayed University, Abu Dhabi, United Arab Emirates

Dr. Efthymios Constantinides, Assistant Professor, School of Management and Governance University of Twente, The Netherlands

Professor Dr. Mohamed Dahlan Bin Ibrahim, Faculty of Entrepreneurship & Business, University Malaysia Ketalan, Malaysia

Huldan Dereli, Assistant Professor, School of Advanced Vocational Studies, Istanbul Bilgi University, Turkey

Dr. Frances Ekwulugo, Senior Lecturer, Westminster Business School, The University of Westminster, UK

Prof. Dr. Michael A. Grund, Head of Center for Marketing, HWZ University of Applied Sciences in Business Administration Zurich, Switzerland

Ali Zakaria El Hallak, Interactive Manager - Nokia KSA & Yemen, Wundermann Middle East

Dr. Hooi Den Huan, Director, Nanyang Technopreneurship Center, Nanyang Technological University, Singapore

Bhooma Janakiramanan, Research Associate, Centre for Applied Research, SIM University Singapore

Peter B. Mason, Instructor of Marketing, School of Business and Management, American University of Sharjah, United Arab Emirates

Jan Møller Jensen, Associate Professor, Department of Marketing and Management, University of Southern Denmark, Denmark

K. Raja Kumar K. Kathiravelu, Lecturer, Department of Marketing, University Tunku Abdul Rahman, Malaysia

Winnie Leow Chye Huang, Senior Lecturer, Marketing and Retail, Singapore Polytechnic Business School, Singapore

Leung Chi-hong, Teaching Fellow, Department of Management and Marketing, The Hong Kong Polytechnic University, Hong Kong

Dr. Leung Lai-cheung, Leo, Senior Teaching Fellow, Department of Marketing and International Business, Lingnan University, Hong Kong

Gary Lin Guo Xin, School of Business, Temasek Polytechnic, Singapore

Sue Lou, School of Business, Temasek Polytechnic, Singapore

Maha Mourad, Assistant Professor of Marketing, School of Business, American University in Cairo, Egypt

Reena Ng Su Eng, School of Business, Temasek Polytechnic, Singapore

Steven Ng Chee Kuen, School of Business, Temasek Polytechnic, Singapore

Christian D. Pentz, Lecturer, Department of Business Management, Stellenbosch University, South Africa

Susan Scoffield, Senior Lecturer in Marketing, Department of Business & Management, Manchester Metropolitan University, UK

Philip Siow Khing Shing, School of Business, Temasek Polytechnic, Singapore

Dr. Joseph A. Sy-Changco, Assistant Professor, Faculty of Business Administration, University of Macau, China

Yeong Wai Mun, Mandy, University Tunku Abdul Rahman, Malaysia

Dr. Che Aniza Binti Che Wel, Senior Lecturer, Faculty of Economics and Management, University Kebangsaan Malaysia, Malaysia

In This Chapter, We Will Address the Following Questions

1. Why is marketing important?

2. What is the scope of marketing?

3. What are some core marketing concepts?

4. How has marketing management changed in recent years?

5. What are the tasks necessary for successful marketing management?

One of the key factors in Barack Obama's victory in the 2008 U.S. presidential election was a well-designed and well-executed marketing program.

Defining Marketing for the 21st Century

Formally or informally, people and organizations engage in a vast number of activities we could call marketing. Good marketing has become increasingly vital for success. But what constitutes good marketing is constantly evolving and changing. The election of Barack Obama as the 44th President of the United States was attributed, in part, to the adoption of new marketing practices.

 *The "Obama for America" presidential campaign combined a charismatic politician, a powerful message of hope, and a thoroughly integrated modern marketing program. The marketing plan needed to accomplish two very different goals: expand the electorate via broader messages while targeting very specific audiences. Multimedia tactics combined offline and online media, as well as free and paid media. When research* showed that the more voters learned about Obama, the more they identified with him, the campaign added long-form videos to traditional print, broadcast, and outdoor ads. The Obama team—aided by its agency GMMB—also put the Internet at the heart of the campaign, letting it serve as the "central nervous system" for PR, advertising, advance work, fund-raising, and organizing in all 50 states. Their guiding philosophy was to "build online tools to help people self-organize and then get out of their way." Technology was a means to "empower people to do what they were interested in doing in the first place." Although social media like Facebook, Meetup, YouTube, and Twitter were crucial, perhaps Obama's most powerful digital tool was a massive 13.5 million–name e-mail list. What were the results of these online efforts? About $500 million (most in sums of less than $100) was raised online from 3 million donors; 35,000 groups organized through the Web site, My.BarackObama.com; 1,800 videos posted to YouTube; the creation of Facebook's most popular page; and, of course, the election of the next President of the United States.[1]*

Good marketing is no accident, but a result of careful planning and execution using state-of-the-art tools and techniques. It becomes both an art and a science as marketers strive to find creative new solutions to often-complex challenges amid profound changes in the 21st century marketing environment. In this book, we describe how top marketers balance discipline and imagination to address these new marketing realities. In the first chapter, we lay the foundation by reviewing important marketing concepts, tools, frameworks, and issues.

The Importance of Marketing

The first decade of the 21st century challenged firms to prosper financially and even survive in the face of an unforgiving economic environment. Marketing is playing a key role in addressing those challenges. Finance, operations, accounting, and other business functions won't really matter without sufficient demand for products and services so the firm can make a profit. In other words, there must be a top line for there to be a bottom line. Thus financial success often depends on marketing ability.

Marketing's broader importance extends to society as a whole. Marketing has helped introduce and gain acceptance of new products that have eased or enriched people's lives. It can inspire enhancements in existing products as marketers innovate to improve their position in the marketplace. Successful marketing builds demand for products and services, which, in turn, creates jobs. By contributing to the bottom line, successful marketing also allows firms to more fully engage in socially responsible activities.[2]

CEOs recognize the role of marketing in building strong brands and a loyal customer base, intangible assets that contribute heavily to the value of a firm. Consumer goods makers, health care insurers, nonprofit organizations, and industrial product manufacturers all trumpet their latest marketing achievements. Many now have a chief marketing officer (CMO) to put marketing on a more equal footing with other C-level executives such as the chief financial officer (CFO) or chief information officer (CIO).[3]

Making the right marketing decisions isn't always easy. One survey of more than a thousand senior marketing and sales executives revealed that although 83 percent felt that marketing and sales capabilities were a top priority for their organization's success, in rating their actual marketing effectiveness, only 6 percent felt that they were doing an "extremely good" job.[4]

Marketers must decide what features to design into a new product or service, what prices to set, where to sell products or offer services, and how much to spend on advertising, sales, the Internet, or mobile marketing. They must make those decisions in an Internet-fueled environment where consumers, competition, technology, and economic forces change rapidly, and the consequences of the marketer's words and actions can quickly multiply.

Domino's   When two employees in Conover, North Carolina, posted a YouTube video showing themselves preparing sandwiches while putting cheese up their noses and violating other health-code standards, Domino's learned an important lesson about PR and brand communications in a modern era. Once it found the employees—who claimed the video was just a gag and the sandwiches were never delivered—the company fired them. In just a few days, however, there had been more than a million downloads of the video and a wave of negative publicity. When research showed that perception of quality for the brand had turned from positive to negative in that short time, the firm aggressively took action through social media such as Twitter, YouTube, and others.[5]

As Domino's learned, in an era of connectivity, it is important to respond swiftly and decisively. While marketers were coming to grips with this increasingly wired world, the economic recession of 2008–2009 brought budget cuts and intense pressure from senior management to make every marketing dollar count. More than ever, marketers need to understand and adapt to the latest marketplace developments. At greatest risk are firms that fail to carefully monitor their customers and competitors, continuously improve their value offerings and marketing strategies, or satisfy their employees, stockholders, suppliers, and channel partners in the process.

After a distasteful video was posted online by two employees, Domino's Pizza learned a valuable lesson about the power of social media.

Skillful marketing is a never-ending pursuit. Consider how some top firms drive business:

- OfficeMax promoted a new line of products by professional organizer Peter Walsh with Web videos and in-store events featuring local experts demonstrating his OfficeMax-branded organizing system.
- eBay promoted its "Let's Make a Daily Deal" holiday promotion by recreating the famous 1970s TV game show *Let's Make a Deal* in Times Square, adding an online component so people outside New York City could play.
- Johnson & Johnson launched BabyCenter.com to help new parents. Its success is thought to have contributed to subscription slumps experienced by parenting magazines.

Good marketers are always seeking new ways to satisfy customers and beat competition.[6]

The Scope of Marketing

To prepare to be a marketer, you need to understand what marketing is, how it works, who does it, and what is marketed.

What Is Marketing?

Marketing is about identifying and meeting human and social needs. One of the shortest good definitions of marketing is "meeting needs profitably." When eBay recognized that people were unable to locate some of the items they desired most, it created an online auction clearinghouse. When IKEA noticed that people wanted good furnishings at substantially lower prices, it created knockdown furniture. These two firms demonstrated marketing savvy and turned a private or social need into a profitable business opportunity.

The American Marketing Association offers the following formal definition: *Marketing is the activity, set of institutions, and processes for creating, communicating, delivering, and exchanging offerings that have value for customers, clients, partners, and society at large.*[7] Coping with these exchange processes calls for a considerable amount of work and skill. *Marketing management* takes place when at least one party to a potential exchange thinks about the means of achieving desired responses from other parties. Thus we see **marketing management** as *the art and science of choosing target markets and getting, keeping, and growing customers through creating, delivering, and communicating superior customer value.*

We can distinguish between a social and a managerial definition of marketing. A social definition shows the role marketing plays in society; for example, one marketer has said that marketing's role is to "deliver a higher standard of living." Here is a social definition that serves our purpose: *Marketing is a societal process by which individuals and groups obtain what they need and want through creating, offering, and freely exchanging products and services of value with others.*

Managers sometimes think of marketing as "the art of selling products," but many people are surprised when they hear that selling is *not* the most important part of marketing! Selling is only the tip of the marketing iceberg. Peter Drucker, a leading management theorist, puts it this way:

> There will always, one can assume, be need for some selling. But the aim of marketing is to make selling superfluous. The aim of marketing is to know and understand the customer so well that the product or service fits him and sells itself. Ideally, marketing should result in a customer who is ready to buy. All that should be needed then is to make the product or service available.[8]

When Nintendo designed its Wii game system, when Canon launched its ELPH digital camera line, and when Toyota introduced its Prius hybrid automobile, these manufacturers were swamped with orders because they had designed the right product, based on doing careful marketing homework.

What Is Marketed?

Marketers market 10 main types of entities: goods, services, events, experiences, persons, places, properties, organizations, information, and ideas. Let's take a quick look at these categories.

GOODS Physical goods constitute the bulk of most countries' production and marketing efforts. Each year, U.S. companies market billions of fresh, canned, bagged, and frozen food products and millions of cars, refrigerators, televisions, machines, and other mainstays of a modern economy.

SERVICES As economies advance, a growing proportion of their activities focuses on the production of services. The U.S. economy today produces a 70–30 services-to-goods mix. Services include the work of airlines, hotels, car rental firms, barbers and beauticians, maintenance and repair people, and accountants, bankers, lawyers, engineers, doctors, software programmers, and management consultants. Many market offerings mix goods and services, such as a fast-food meal.

EVENTS Marketers promote time-based events, such as major trade shows, artistic performances, and company anniversaries. Global sporting events such as the Olympics and the World Cup are promoted aggressively to both companies and fans.

The Rolling Stones have done a masterful job of marketing their rebellious form of rock and roll to audiences of all ages.

EXPERIENCES By orchestrating several services and goods, a firm can create, stage, and market experiences. Walt Disney World's Magic Kingdom allows customers to visit a fairy kingdom, a pirate ship, or a haunted house. There is also a market for customized experiences, such as a week at a baseball camp with retired baseball greats, a four-day rock and roll fantasy camp, or a climb up Mount Everest.[9]

PERSONS Artists, musicians, CEOs, physicians, high-profile lawyers and financiers, and other professionals all get help from celebrity marketers.[10] Some people have done a masterful job of marketing themselves—David Beckham, Oprah Winfrey, and the Rolling Stones. Management consultant Tom Peters, a master at self-branding, has advised each person to become a "brand."

PLACES Cities, states, regions, and whole nations compete to attract tourists, residents, factories, and company headquarters.[11] Place marketers include economic development specialists, real estate agents, commercial banks, local business associations, and advertising and public relations agencies. The Las Vegas Convention & Visitors Authority succeeded with its provocative ad campaign, "What Happens Here, Stays Here," portraying Las Vegas as "an adult playground." In the recession of 2008, however, convention attendance declined. Concerned about its potentially out-of-step racy reputation, the Authority took out a full-page *BusinessWeek* ad to defend its ability to host serious business meetings. Unfortunately, the 2009 summer box office blockbuster *The Hangover*, set in a debauched Las Vegas, likely did not help the city position itself as a choice business and tourist destination.[12]

PROPERTIES Properties are intangible rights of ownership to either real property (real estate) or financial property (stocks and bonds). They are bought and sold, and these exchanges require marketing. Real estate agents work for property owners or sellers, or they buy and sell residential or commercial real estate. Investment companies and banks market securities to both institutional and individual investors.

ORGANIZATIONS Organizations work to build a strong, favorable, and unique image in the minds of their target publics. In the United Kingdom, Tesco's "Every Little Helps" marketing program reflects the food marketer's attention to detail in everything it does, within the store and in the community and environment. The campaign has vaulted Tesco to the top of the UK supermarket chain industry. Universities, museums, performing arts organizations, corporations, and nonprofits all use marketing to boost their public images and compete for audiences and funds.

INFORMATION The production, packaging, and distribution of information are major industries.[13] Information is essentially what books, schools, and universities produce, market, and distribute at a price to parents, students, and communities. The former CEO of Siemens Medical

For a city like Las Vegas that thrives on tourism, good marketing is essential.

Solutions USA, Tom McCausland, says, "[our product] is not necessarily an X-ray or an MRI, but information. Our business is really health care information technology, and our end product is really an electronic patient record: information on lab tests, pathology, and drugs as well as voice dictation."[14]

IDEAS Every market offering includes a basic idea. Charles Revson of Revlon once observed: "In the factory we make cosmetics; in the drugstore we sell hope." Products and services are platforms for delivering some idea or benefit. Social marketers are busy promoting such ideas as "Friends Don't Let Friends Drive Drunk" and "A Mind Is a Terrible Thing to Waste."

Who Markets?

MARKETERS AND PROSPECTS A **marketer** is someone who seeks a response—attention, a purchase, a vote, a donation—from another party, called the **prospect**. If two parties are seeking to sell something to each other, we call them both marketers.

One of the most important areas of marketing is the work that social marketers do to promote socially desirable behaviors.

Marketers are skilled at stimulating demand for their products, but that's a limited view of what they do. Just as production and logistics professionals are responsible for supply management, marketers are responsible for demand management. They seek to influence the level, timing, and composition of demand to meet the organization's objectives. Eight demand states are possible:

1. *Negative demand*—Consumers dislike the product and may even pay to avoid it.
2. *Nonexistent demand*—Consumers may be unaware of or uninterested in the product.
3. *Latent demand*—Consumers may share a strong need that cannot be satisfied by an existing product.
4. *Declining demand*—Consumers begin to buy the product less frequently or not at all.
5. *Irregular demand*—Consumer purchases vary on a seasonal, monthly, weekly, daily, or even hourly basis.
6. *Full demand*—Consumers are adequately buying all products put into the marketplace.
7. *Overfull demand*—More consumers would like to buy the product than can be satisfied.
8. *Unwholesome demand*—Consumers may be attracted to products that have undesirable social consequences.

In each case, marketers must identify the underlying cause(s) of the demand state and determine a plan of action to shift demand to a more desired state.

MARKETS Traditionally, a "market" was a physical place where buyers and sellers gathered to buy and sell goods. Economists describe a *market* as a collection of buyers and sellers who transact over a particular product or product class (such as the housing market or the grain market).

Five basic markets and their connecting flows are shown in △ Figure 1.1. Manufacturers go to resource markets (raw material markets, labor markets, money markets), buy resources and turn them into goods and services, and sell finished products to intermediaries, who sell them to consumers. Consumers sell their labor and receive money with which they pay for goods and services. The government collects tax revenues to buy goods from resource, manufacturer, and intermediary markets and uses these goods and services to provide public services. Each nation's economy, and the global economy, consists of interacting sets of markets linked through exchange processes.

Marketers use the term **market** to cover various groupings of customers. They view sellers as constituting the industry and buyers as constituting the market. They talk about need markets (the diet-seeking market), product markets (the shoe market), demographic markets (the youth market), and geographic markets (the Chinese market); or they extend the concept to cover voter markets, labor markets, and donor markets, for instance.

△ Figure 1.2 shows the relationship between the industry and the market. Sellers and buyers are connected by four flows. Sellers send goods and services and communications such as ads and direct mail to the market; in return they receive money and information such as customer attitudes and sales data. The inner loop shows an exchange of money for goods and services; the outer loop shows an exchange of information.

|Fig. 1.1| △

Structure of Flows in a Modern Exchange Economy

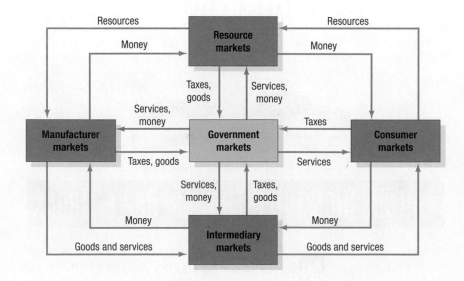

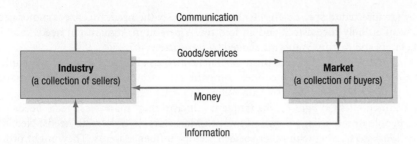

|Fig. 1.2| △

A Simple Marketing System

KEY CUSTOMER MARKETS Consider the following key customer markets: consumer, business, global, and nonprofit.

Consumer Markets Companies selling mass consumer goods and services such as juices, cosmetics, athletic shoes, and air travel spend a great deal of time establishing a strong brand image by developing a superior product and packaging, ensuring its availability, and backing it with engaging communications and reliable service.

Business Markets Companies selling business goods and services often face well-informed professional buyers skilled at evaluating competitive offerings. Business buyers buy goods to make or resell a product to others at a profit. Business marketers must demonstrate how their products will help achieve higher revenue or lower costs. Advertising can play a role, but the sales force, the price, and the company's reputation may play a greater one.

Global Markets Companies in the global marketplace must decide which countries to enter; how to enter each (as an exporter, licenser, joint venture partner, contract manufacturer, or solo manufacturer); how to adapt product and service features to each country; how to price products in different countries; and how to design communications for different cultures. They face different requirements for buying and disposing of property; cultural, language, legal and political differences; and currency fluctuations. Yet, the payoff can be huge.

Nonprofit and Governmental Markets Companies selling to nonprofit organizations with limited purchasing power such as churches, universities, charitable organizations, and government agencies need to price carefully. Lower selling prices affect the features and quality the seller can build into the offering. Much government purchasing calls for bids, and buyers often focus on practical solutions and favor the lowest bid in the absence of extenuating factors.[15]

MARKETPLACES, MARKETSPACES, AND METAMARKETS The *marketplace* is physical, such as a store you shop in; the *marketspace* is digital, as when you shop on the Internet.[16] Northwestern University's Mohan Sawhney has proposed the concept of a *metamarket* to describe a cluster of complementary products and services closely related in the minds of consumers, but spread across a diverse set of industries.

Metamarkets are the result of marketers packaging a system that simplifies carrying out these related product/service activities. The automobile metamarket consists of automobile manufacturers, new and used car dealers, financing companies, insurance companies, mechanics, spare parts dealers, service shops, auto magazines, classified auto ads in newspapers, and auto sites on the Internet.

A car buyer will engage many parts of this metamarket, creating an opportunity for *metamediaries* to assist him or her in moving seamlessly through them. Edmund's (www.edmunds.com) lets a car buyer find the stated features and prices of different automobiles and easily click to other sites to search for the lowest-price dealer for financing, accessories, and used cars. Metamediaries also serve other metamarkets, such as home ownership, parenting and baby care, and weddings.[17]

Core Marketing Concepts

To understand the marketing function, we need to understand the following core set of concepts.

Needs, Wants, and Demands

Needs are the basic human requirements such as for air, food, water, clothing, and shelter. Humans also have strong needs for recreation, education, and entertainment. These needs become *wants* when they are directed to specific objects that might satisfy the need. A U.S. consumer needs food but may want a Philly cheesesteak and an iced tea. A person in Afghanistan needs food but may want rice, lamb, and carrots. Wants are shaped by our society.

Demands are wants for specific products backed by an ability to pay. Many people want a Mercedes; only a few are able to buy one. Companies must measure not only how many people want their product, but also how many are willing and able to buy it.

These distinctions shed light on the frequent criticism that "marketers create needs" or "marketers get people to buy things they don't want." Marketers do not create needs: Needs preexist marketers. Marketers, along with other societal factors, influence wants. They might promote the idea that a Mercedes would satisfy a person's need for social status. They do not, however, create the need for social status.

Some customers have needs of which they are not fully conscious or that they cannot articulate. What does it mean when the customer asks for a "powerful" lawn mower or a "peaceful" hotel? The marketer must probe further. We can distinguish five types of needs:

1. Stated needs (The customer wants an inexpensive car.)
2. Real needs (The customer wants a car whose operating cost, not initial price, is low.)
3. Unstated needs (The customer expects good service from the dealer.)
4. Delight needs (The customer would like the dealer to include an onboard GPS navigation system.)
5. Secret needs (The customer wants friends to see him or her as a savvy consumer.)

Responding only to the stated need may shortchange the customer.[18] Consumers did not know much about cellular phones when they were first introduced, and Nokia and Ericsson fought to shape consumer perceptions of them. To gain an edge, companies must help customers learn what they want.

Target Markets, Positioning, and Segmentation

Not everyone likes the same cereal, restaurant, college, or movie. Therefore, marketers start by dividing the market into segments. They identify and profile distinct groups of buyers who might prefer or require varying product and service mixes by examining demographic, psychographic, and behavioral differences among buyers.

After identifying market segments, the marketer decides which present the greatest opportunities—which are its *target markets*. For each, the firm develops a *market offering* that it *positions* in the minds of the target buyers as delivering some central benefit(s). Volvo develops its cars for buyers to whom safety is a major concern, positioning its vehicles as the safest a customer can buy.

Offerings and Brands

Companies address customer needs by putting forth a **value proposition**, a set of benefits that satisfy those needs. The intangible value proposition is made physical by an *offering*, which can be a combination of products, services, information, and experiences.

A *brand* is an offering from a known source. A brand name such as McDonald's carries many associations in people's minds that make up its image: hamburgers, cleanliness, convenience, courteous service, and golden arches. All companies strive to build a brand image with as many strong, favorable, and unique brand associations as possible.

Value and Satisfaction

The buyer chooses the offerings he or she perceives to deliver the most *value*, the sum of the tangible and intangible benefits and costs to her. Value, a central marketing concept, is primarily a combination of quality, service, and price (qsp), called the *customer value triad*. Value perceptions increase with quality and service but decrease with price.

We can think of marketing as the identification, creation, communication, delivery, and monitoring of customer value. *Satisfaction* reflects a person's judgment of a product's perceived performance in relationship to expectations. If the performance falls short of expectations, the customer is disappointed. If it matches expectations, the customer is satisfied. If it exceeds them, the customer is delighted.

Marketing Channels

To reach a target market, the marketer uses three kinds of marketing channels. *Communication channels* deliver and receive messages from target buyers and include newspapers, magazines, radio, television, mail, telephone, billboards, posters, fliers, CDs, audiotapes, and the Internet. Beyond these, firms communicate through the look of their retail stores and Web sites and other media. Marketers are increasingly adding dialogue channels such as e-mail, blogs, and toll-free numbers to familiar monologue channels such as ads.

The marketer uses *distribution channels* to display, sell, or deliver the physical product or service(s) to the buyer or user. These channels may be direct via the Internet, mail, or mobile phone or telephone, or indirect with distributors, wholesalers, retailers, and agents as intermediaries.

To carry out transactions with potential buyers, the marketer also uses *service channels* that include warehouses, transportation companies, banks, and insurance companies. Marketers clearly face a design challenge in choosing the best mix of communication, distribution, and service channels for their offerings.

Supply Chain

The supply chain is a longer channel stretching from raw materials to components to finished products carried to final buyers. The supply chain for coffee may start with Ethiopian farmers who plant, tend, and pick the coffee beans, selling their harvest to wholesalers or perhaps a Fair Trade cooperative. If sold through the cooperative, the coffee is washed, dried, and packaged for shipment by an Alternative Trading Organization (ATO) that pays a minimum of $1.26 a pound. The ATO transports the coffee to the developing world where it can sell it directly or via retail channels. Each company captures only a certain percentage of the total value generated by the supply chain's value delivery system. When a company acquires competitors or expands upstream or downstream, its aim is to capture a higher percentage of supply chain value.

Competition

Competition includes all the actual and potential rival offerings and substitutes a buyer might consider. An automobile manufacturer can buy steel from U.S. Steel in the United States, from a foreign firm in Japan or Korea, or from a minimill such as Nucor at a cost savings, or it can buy aluminum for certain parts from Alcoa to reduce the car's weight, or engineered plastics from Saudi Basic Industries Corporation (SABIC) instead of steel. Clearly, U.S. Steel would be thinking too narrowly about its competition if it thought only of other integrated steel companies. In the long run, U.S. Steel is more likely to be hurt by substitute products than by other steel companies.

Marketing Environment

The marketing environment consists of the task environment and the broad environment. The *task environment* includes the actors engaged in producing, distributing, and promoting the offering. These are the company, suppliers, distributors, dealers, and target customers. In the supplier group are material suppliers and service suppliers, such as marketing research agencies, advertising agencies, banking and insurance companies, transportation companies, and telecommunications companies. Distributors and dealers include agents, brokers, manufacturer representatives, and others who facilitate finding and selling to customers.

The *broad environment* consists of six components: demographic environment, economic environment, social-cultural environment, natural environment, technological environment, and political-legal environment. Marketers must pay close attention to the trends and developments in these and adjust their marketing strategies as needed. New opportunities are constantly emerging that await the right marketing savvy and ingenuity. Here are two good examples.

TerraCycle   After finding that some of his friend's indoor herbal plants flourished with a fertilizer made by feeding table scraps to red wiggler worms in a composting bin, TerraCycle founder Tom Szaky came up with an idea for a business. TerraCycle is devoted to "upcycling," finding new ways to use nonrecyclable waste materials. Plastic bags become sturdy totes, yogurt cups become plant holders, and cookie wrappers become notebook covers, all distributed by major retailers such as Home Depot, Whole Foods, and Walmart. The firm also has partnerships with Kraft, Target, Honest Tea, Stonyfield Farms, and others. Schools, churches, wineries, and nonprofits provide space to store donated used bottles, corks, and candy wrappers. For each item collected, TerraCycle makes a donation to a charity (typically 2 cents).[19] ▭

Allrecipes.com   Allrecipes.com has cooked up a winning online formula by blending recipes posted by individuals with those provided by corporations promoting their own products like Kraft cheese or Campbell's Soup. After almost a 50 percent increase in site visits and unique visitors in 2009, the Web site overtook the Food Network's recipe site as the market leader. With tens of thousands of posted recipes, it thrives on people's willingness to share recipes and the satisfaction they feel if their recipe becomes popular with others. The viral nature of the site's success is obvious—it doesn't spend any money on advertising! Users tend to think of it as "their" site—not something with a big company behind it.[20] ▭

The New Marketing Realities

We can say with some confidence that the marketplace isn't what it used to be. It is dramatically different from what it was even 10 years ago.

Major Societal Forces

Today, major, and sometimes interlinking, societal forces have created new marketing behaviors, opportunities, and challenges. Here are 12 key ones.

- *Network information technology.* The digital revolution has created an Information Age that promises to lead to more accurate levels of production, more targeted communications, and more relevant pricing.
- *Globalization.* Technological advances in transportation, shipping, and communication have made it easier for companies to market in, and consumers to buy from, almost any country in the world. International travel has continued to grow as more people work and play in other countries.
- *Deregulation.* Many countries have deregulated industries to create greater competition and growth opportunities. In the United States, laws restricting financial services, telecommunications, and electric utilities have all been loosened in the spirit of greater competition.
- *Privatization.* Many countries have converted public companies to private ownership and management to increase their efficiency, such as the massive telecom company Telefónica CTC in Chile and the international airline British Airways in the United Kingdom.
- *Heightened competition.* Intense competition among domestic and foreign brands raises marketing costs and shrinks profit margins. Brand manufacturers are further buffeted by powerful retailers that market their own store brands. Many strong brands have become megabrands and extended into a wide variety of related product categories, presenting a significant competitive threat.
- *Industry convergence.* Industry boundaries are blurring as companies recognize new opportunities at the intersection of two or more industries. The computing and consumer electronics industries are converging, for example, as Apple, Sony, and Samsung release a stream of entertainment devices from MP3 players to plasma TVs and camcorders. Digital technology fuels this massive convergence.[21]
- *Retail transformation.* Store-based retailers face competition from catalog houses; direct-mail firms; newspaper, magazine, and TV direct-to-customer ads; home shopping TV; and e-commerce. In response, entrepreneurial retailers are building entertainment into

Modern retailers increasingly emphasize in-store experiences for their customers, as does Dick's Sporting Goods.

their stores with coffee bars, demonstrations, and performances, marketing an "experience" rather than a product assortment. Dick's Sporting Goods has grown from a single bait-and-tackle store in Binghamton, New York, into a 300-store sporting goods retailer in 30 states. Part of its success springs from the interactive features of its stores. Customers can test golf clubs in indoor ranges, sample shoes on its footwear track, and shoot bows in its archery range.[22]

- **Disintermediation.** The amazing success of early dot-coms such as AOL, Amazon.com, Yahoo!, eBay, E*TRADE, and others created *disintermediation* in the delivery of products and services by intervening in the traditional flow of goods through distribution channels. These firms struck terror into the hearts of established manufacturers and retailers. In response, traditional companies engaged in *reintermediation* and became "brick-and-click" retailers, adding online services to their offerings. Some became stronger contenders than pure-click firms, because they had a larger pool of resources to work with and established brand names.

- **Consumer buying power.** In part, due to disintermediation via the Internet, consumers have substantially increased their buying power. From the home, office, or mobile phone, they can compare product prices and features and order goods online from anywhere in the world 24 hours a day, 7 days a week, bypassing limited local offerings and realizing significant price savings. Even business buyers can run a *reverse auction* in which sellers compete to capture their business. They can readily join others to aggregate their purchases and achieve deeper volume discounts.

- **Consumer information.** Consumers can collect information in as much breadth and depth as they want about practically anything. They can access online encyclopedias, dictionaries, medical information, movie ratings, consumer reports, newspapers, and other information sources in many languages from anywhere in the world. Personal connections and user-generated content thrive on social media such as Facebook, Flickr (photos), Del.icio.us (links), Digg (news stories), Wikipedia (encyclopedia articles), and YouTube (video).[23] Social networking sites—such as Dogster for dog lovers, TripAdvisor for ardent travelers, and Moterus for bikers—bring together consumers with a common interest. At CarSpace.com auto enthusiasts talk about chrome rims, the latest BMW model, and where to find a great local mechanic.[24]

- **Consumer participation.** Consumers have found an amplified voice to influence peer and public opinion. In recognition, companies are inviting them to participate in designing and even marketing offerings to heighten their sense of connection and ownership. Consumers see their favorite companies as workshops from which they can draw out the offerings they want.

- **Consumer resistance.** Many customers today feel there are fewer real product differences, so they show less brand loyalty and become more price- and quality-sensitive in their search for value, and less tolerant about undesired marketing. A Yankelovich study found record levels of marketing resistance from consumers; a majority reported negative opinions about marketing and advertising and said they avoid products they feel are over-marketed.[25]

New Company Capabilities

These major societal forces create complex challenges for marketers, but they have also generated a new set of capabilities to help companies cope and respond.

- *Marketers can use the Internet as a powerful information and sales channel.* The Internet augments marketers' geographical reach to inform customers and promote products worldwide. A Web site can list products and services, history, business philosophy, job opportunities, and other information of interest. In 2006, a Montgomery, Alabama, flea market gained national popularity when owner Sammy Stephens's rap-style advertisement spread virally through the Internet. Created for $1,500, the advertisement was viewed more than 100,000 times on YouTube and landed Stephens on *The Ellen DeGeneres Show*. Stephens now sells T-shirts, ring tones, and other branded merchandise through his Web site, advises retailers about advertising, and hosts hundreds of visitors from all over the world at his store each month.[26]

- *Marketers can collect fuller and richer information about markets, customers, prospects, and competitors.* Marketers can conduct fresh marketing research by using the Internet to arrange focus groups, send out questionnaires, and gather primary data in several other ways. They can assemble information about individual customers' purchases, preferences, demographics, and profitability. The drugstore chain CVS uses loyalty-card data to better understand what consumers purchase, the frequency of store visits, and other buying preferences. Its ExtraCare program netted an extra 30 million shoppers and $12 billion a year in revenue across 4,000 stores.[27]

- *Marketers can tap into social media to amplify their brand message.* Marketers can feed information and updates to consumers via blogs and other postings, support online communities, and create their own stops on the Internet superhighway. Dell Corporation's @DellOutlet Twitter account has more than 600,000 followers. Between 2007 and June 2009, Dell took in more than $2 million in revenue from coupons provided through Twitter, and another $1 million from people who started at Twitter and went on to buy a new computer on the company's Web site.[28]

- *Marketers can facilitate and speed external communication among customers.* Marketers can also create or benefit from online and offline "buzz" through brand advocates and user

Sammy Stephen's viral video helped his flea market receive unprecedented attention.

communities. Word-of-mouth marketing agency BzzAgent has assembled a nationwide volunteer army of 600,000 consumers who join promotional programs for products and services they deem worth talking about.[29] In 2005, Dunkin' Donuts hired BzzAgent to help launch a new espresso beverage, Latte Lite. Three thousand trained volunteers (called BzzAgents) in 12 test markets experienced the Latte Lite, formed their opinions, engaged in natural conversations about the product, and reported back to BzzAgent via the company's reporting interface. After four weeks, product sales had increased by more than 15 percent in test markets.[30]

- *Marketers can send ads, coupons, samples, and information to customers who have requested them or given the company permission to send them.* Micro-target marketing and two-way communication are easier thanks to the proliferation of special-interest magazines, TV channels, and Internet newsgroups. Extranets linking suppliers and distributors let firms send and receive information, place orders, and make payments more efficiently. The company can also interact with each customer individually to *personalize* messages, services, and the relationship.

- *Marketers can reach consumers on the move with mobile marketing.* Using GPS technology, marketers can pinpoint consumers' exact location and send them messages at the mall with coupons good only that day, a reminder of an item on their wish list, and a relevant perk (buy this book today and get a free coffee at the bookstore's coffee shop). Location-based advertising is attractive because it reaches consumers closer to the point of sale. Firms can also advertise on video iPods and reach consumers on their cell phones through mobile marketing.[31]

- *Companies can make and sell individually differentiated goods.* Thanks to advances in factory customization, computer technology, and database marketing software, customers can buy M&M candies, TABASCO jugs, or Maker's Mark bottles with their names on them; Wheaties boxes or Jones soda cans with their picture on the front; and Heinz ketchup bottles with customized messages.[32] BMW's technology allows buyers to design their own car models from among 350 variations, with 500 options, 90 exterior colors, and 170 trims. The company claims that 80 percent of the cars bought in Europe and up to 30 percent bought in the United States are built to order.

- *Companies can improve purchasing, recruiting, training, and internal and external communications.* Firms can recruit new employees online, and many have Internet training products for their employees, dealers, and agents. Retailer Patagonia has joined Walt Disney, General Motors, and McDonald's in embracing corporate blogging to communicate with the public and employees. Patagonia's The Cleanest Line posts environmental news, reports the results of its sponsored athletes, and posts pictures and descriptions of employees' favorite outdoor locations.[33]

- *Companies can facilitate and speed up internal communication among their employees by using the Internet as a private intranet.* Employees can query one another, seek advice, and download or upload needed information from and to the company's main computer. Seeking a single online employee portal that transcended business units, General Motors launched a platform called mySocrates in 2006 consisting of announcements, news, links, and historical information. GM credits the portal with $17.4 million in cost savings to date.[34]

- *Companies can improve their cost efficiency by skillful use of the Internet.* Corporate buyers can achieve substantial savings by using the Internet to compare sellers' prices and purchase materials at auction, or by posting their own terms in reverse auctions. Companies can improve logistics and operations to reap substantial cost savings while improving accuracy and service quality.

Marketing in Practice

Not surprisingly, these new marketing forces and capabilities have profoundly changed marketing management. In theory, the marketing *planning* process consists of analyzing marketing opportunities, selecting target markets, designing marketing strategies, developing marketing programs, and managing the marketing effort.

Companies are increasingly allowing customers to customize their products, such as with personalized messages on the front labels of Heinz ketchup bottles.

In practice, however, in the highly competitive marketplaces that are more often the norm, marketing planning is more fluid and is continually refreshed.

Companies must always be moving forward with marketing programs, innovating products and services, staying in touch with customer needs, and seeking new advantages rather than relying on past strengths. This is especially true of incorporating the Internet into marketing plans. Marketers must try to balance increased spending on search advertising, social media, direct e-mail, and text/SMS marketing efforts with appropriate spending on traditional marketing communications. But they must do so in tough economic times, when accountability has become a top priority and returns on investment are expected from every marketing activity. "Marketing Insight: Marketing in an Age of Turbulence" offers some recommendations for adjusting to new marketing realities.

Marketing Insight

Marketing in an Age of Turbulence

The severe economic recession of 2008–2009 caused marketers to rethink best practices of management. Philip Kotler and John Caslione see management entering a new Age of Turbulence in which chaos, risk, and uncertainty characterize many industries, markets, and companies. According to them, turbulence is the new normal, punctuated by periodic and intermittent spurts of prosperity and downturn—including extended downturns amounting to recession, or even depression. They see many new challenges in the foreseeable future, and unlike past recessions, there may be no assurance that a return to past management practices would ever be successful again.

According to Kotler and Caslione, marketers should always be ready to activate automatic responses when turbulence whips up and chaos reigns in. They recommend marketers keep these eight factors in mind as they create "*chaotics* marketing strategies."

1. *Secure your market share from core customer segments.* This is not a time to get greedy, so get your core customer segments firmly secured, and be prepared to ward off attacks from competitors seeking your most profitable and loyal customers.

2. *Push aggressively for greater market share from competitors.* All companies fight for market share, and in turbulent and chaotic times, many have been weakened. Slashing marketing budgets and sales travel expenses is a sure sign a competitor is buckling under pressure. Push aggressively to add to your core customer segments at the expense of your weakened competitors.

3. *Research customers more now, because their needs and wants are in flux.* Everyone is under pressure during times of turbulence and chaos, and all customers—even those in your core segments whom you know so well—are changing. Stay close to them as never before. Research them more than ever. Don't find yourself using old, tried-and-true marketing messages that no longer resonate with them.

4. *Minimally maintain, but seek to increase, your marketing budget.* With your competitors aggressively marketing to your core customers, this is the worst time to think about cutting anything in your marketing budget that targets them. In fact, you need to add to it, or take money away from forays into totally new customer segments. It's time to secure the home front.

5. *Focus on all that's safe and emphasize core values.* When turbulence is scaring everyone in the market, most customers flee to higher ground. They need to feel the safety and security of your company and your products and services. Do everything possible to tell them that continuing to do business with you is safe, and to sell them products and services that keep making them feel safe.

6. *Drop programs that aren't working for you quickly.* Your marketing budgets will always be scrutinized, in good times and bad times. If anyone is to cut one of your programs, let it be you, before anyone else spots any ineffective ones. If you're not watching, rest assured someone else is, including your peers whose budgets couldn't be protected from the axe.

7. *Don't discount your best brands.* Discounting your established and most successful brands tells the market two things: your prices were too high before, and your products won't be worth the price in the future once the discounts are gone. If you want to appeal to more frugal customers, create a new brand with lower prices. This lets value-conscious customers stay close to you, without alienating those still willing to pay for your higher-priced brands. Once the turbulence subsides, you may consider discontinuing the value product line—or not.

8. *Save the strong; lose the weak.* In turbulent markets, your strongest brands and products must become even stronger. There's no time or money to be wasted on marginal brands or products that lack strong value propositions and a solid customer base. Appeal to safety and value to reinforce strong brands and product and service offerings. Remember, your brands can never be strong enough, especially against the waves of a turbulent economy.

Source: Based on Philip Kotler and John A. Caslione, *Chaotics: The Business and Marketing in the Age of Turbulence* (New York: AMACOM, 2009) pp. 151–153.

THE NEW CMO The rapidly changing marketing environment is putting even greater demands on marketing executives. A well-publicized survey revealed that the average CMO tenure at U.S. companies is about 28 months, well below the average tenure of CEOs (54 months) or other C-level positions. One explanation is that the role of marketing—and thus management expectations—varies widely among firms. Harvard's Gail McGovern and John Quelch find tremendous variability in CMO responsibilities and job descriptions.[35]

Another challenge CMOs face is that the success factors for top marketers are many and varied. CMOs must have strong quantitative skills but also well-honed qualitative skills; they must have an independent, entrepreneurial attitude but also work in close harmony with other departments such as sales; and they must capture the "voice" and point of view of consumers yet have a keen bottom-line understanding of how marketing creates value within their organization.[36] One survey asked 200 senior level marketing executives which innate and learned qualities were most important; here are their answers:[37]

- **Innate Qualities**
  - Risk taker
  - Willingness to make decisions
  - Problem-solving ability
  - Change agent
  - Results-oriented
- **Learned Qualities**
  - Global experience
  - Multichannel expertise
  - Cross-industry experience
  - Digital focus
  - Operational knowledge

Perhaps the most important role for any CMO is to infuse a customer perspective and orientation in business decisions affecting any customer *touch point* (where a customer directly or indirectly interacts with the company in some form). The CMO of lodging franchisor Choice Hotels International, Chris Malone, is responsible for directing virtually all customer-facing efforts for the firm, including:[38]

- Advertising, loyalty programs, and direct response;
- Guiding the company's central reservations systems, including its call centers, Web site, and relationships with outside travel vendors such as Travelocity and Orbitz; and
- Heading up the company's global group sales efforts with organizations such as AAA, AARP, and professional sports teams.

MARKETING IN THE ORGANIZATION Although an effective CMO is crucial, increasingly marketing is *not* done only by the marketing department. Because marketing must affect every aspect of the customer experience, marketers must properly manage all possible touch points—store layouts, package designs, product functions, employee training, and shipping and logistics methods. Marketing must also be influential in key general management activities, such as product innovation and new-business development. To create a strong marketing organization, marketers must think like executives in other departments, and executives in other departments must think more like marketers.[39]

As the late David Packard of Hewlett-Packard observed, "Marketing is far too important to leave to the marketing department." Companies now know that every employee has an impact on the customer and must see the customer as the source of the company's prosperity. So they're beginning to emphasize interdepartmental teamwork to manage key processes. They're emphasizing the smooth management of core business processes, such as new-product realization, customer acquisition and retention, and order fulfillment.

Company Orientation Toward the Marketplace

Given these new marketing realities, what philosophy should guide a company's marketing efforts? Increasingly, marketers operate consistent with the holistic marketing concept. Let's first review the evolution of earlier marketing ideas.

The Production Concept

The **production concept** is one of the oldest concepts in business. It holds that consumers prefer products that are widely available and inexpensive. Managers of production-oriented businesses concentrate on achieving high production efficiency, low costs, and mass distribution. This orientation makes sense in developing countries such as China, where the largest PC manufacturer, Legend (principal owner of Lenovo Group), and domestic appliances giant Haier take advantage of the country's huge and inexpensive labor pool to dominate the market. Marketers also use the production concept when they want to expand the market.[40]

The Product Concept

The **product concept** proposes that consumers favor products offering the most quality, performance, or innovative features. However, managers are sometimes caught in a love affair with their products. They might commit the "better-mousetrap" fallacy, believing a better product will by itself lead people to beat a path to their door. A new or improved product will not necessarily be successful unless it's priced, distributed, advertised, and sold properly.

The Selling Concept

The **selling concept** holds that consumers and businesses, if left alone, won't buy enough of the organization's products. It is practiced most aggressively with unsought goods—goods buyers don't normally think of buying such as insurance and cemetery plots—and when firms with overcapacity aim to sell what they make, rather than make what the market wants. Marketing based on hard selling is risky. It assumes customers coaxed into buying a product not only won't return or bad-mouth it or complain to consumer organizations but might even buy it again.

The Marketing Concept

The **marketing concept** emerged in the mid-1950s[41] as a customer-centered, sense-and-respond philosophy. The job is to find not the right customers for your products, but the right products for your customers. Dell doesn't prepare a perfect computer for its target market. Rather, it provides product platforms on which each person customizes the features he or she desires in the computer.

The marketing concept holds that the key to achieving organizational goals is being more effective than competitors in creating, delivering, and communicating superior customer value to your target markets. Harvard's Theodore Levitt drew a perceptive contrast between the selling and marketing concepts:

> Selling focuses on the needs of the seller; marketing on the needs of the buyer. Selling is preoccupied with the seller's need to convert his product into cash; marketing with the idea of satisfying the needs of the customer by means of the product and the whole cluster of things associated with creating, delivering, and finally consuming it.[42]

Several scholars found that companies embracing the marketing concept at that time achieved superior performance.[43]

The Holistic Marketing Concept

Without question, the trends and forces that have defined the first decade of the 21st century are leading business firms to a new set of beliefs and practices. "Marketing Memo: Marketing Right and Wrong" suggests where companies go wrong—and how they can get it right—in their marketing.

The **holistic marketing** concept is based on the development, design, and implementation of marketing programs, processes, and activities that recognize their breadth and interdependencies. Holistic marketing acknowledges that everything matters in marketing—and that a broad, integrated perspective is often necessary.

Holistic marketing thus recognizes and reconciles the scope and complexities of marketing activities. △ Figure 1.3 provides a schematic overview of four broad components characterizing holistic marketing: relationship marketing, integrated marketing, internal marketing, and performance marketing. We'll examine these major themes throughout this book. Successful companies keep their marketing changing with the changes in their marketplace—and marketspace.

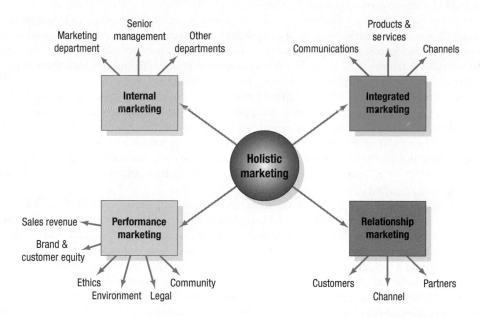

|Fig. 1.3| △

Holistic Marketing
Dimensions

---

marketing Memo

Marketing Right and Wrong

The Ten Deadly Sins of Marketing	The Ten Commandments of Marketing
1. The company is not sufficiently market focused and customer driven.	1. The company segments the market, chooses the best segments, and develops a strong position in each chosen segment.
2. The company does not fully understand its target customers.	2. The company maps its customers' needs, perceptions, preferences, and behavior and motivates its stakeholders to obsess about serving and satisfying the customers.
3. The company needs to better define and monitor its competitors.	3. The company knows its major competitors and their strengths and weaknesses.
4. The company has not properly managed its relationships with its stakeholders.	4. The company builds partners out of its stakeholders and generously rewards them.
5. The company is not good at finding new opportunities.	5. The company develops systems for identifying opportunities, ranking them, and choosing the best ones.
6. The company's marketing plans and planning process are deficient.	6. The company manages a marketing planning system that leads to insightful long-term and short-term plans.
7. The company's product and service policies need tightening.	7. The company exercises strong control over its product and service mix.
8. The company's brand-building and communications skills are weak.	8. The company builds strong brands by using the most cost-effective communication and promotion tools.
9. The company is not well organized to carry on effective and efficient marketing.	9. The company builds marketing leadership and a team spirit among its various departments.
10. The company has not made maximum use of technology.	10. The company constantly adds technology that gives it a competitive advantage in the marketplace.

Source: Adapted from Philip Kotler, *Ten Deadly Marketing Sins* (Hoboken, NJ: John Wiley & Sons, 2004) pp. 10, 145–148.

Relationship Marketing

Increasingly, a key goal of marketing is to develop deep, enduring relationships with people and organizations that directly or indirectly affect the success of the firm's marketing activities. **Relationship marketing** aims to build mutually satisfying long-term relationships with key constituents in order to earn and retain their business.[44]

Four key constituents for relationship marketing are customers, employees, marketing partners (channels, suppliers, distributors, dealers, agencies), and members of the financial community (shareholders, investors, analysts). Marketers must create prosperity among all these constituents and balance the returns to all key stakeholders. To develop strong relationships with them requires understanding their capabilities and resources, needs, goals, and desires.

The ultimate outcome of relationship marketing is a unique company asset called a **marketing network**, consisting of the company and its supporting stakeholders—customers, employees, suppliers, distributors, retailers, and others—with whom it has built mutually profitable business relationships. The operating principle is simple: build an effective network of relationships with key stakeholders, and profits will follow.[45] Thus more companies are choosing to own brands rather than physical assets and are subcontracting activities to firms that can do them better and more cheaply, while retaining core activities at home.

Companies are also shaping separate offers, services, and messages to *individual customers*, based on information about past transactions, demographics, psychographics, and media and distribution preferences. By focusing on their most profitable customers, products, and channels, these firms hope to achieve profitable growth, capturing a larger share of each customer's expenditures by building high customer loyalty. They estimate individual customer lifetime value and design their market offerings and prices to make a profit over the customer's lifetime.

These activities fall under what Columbia Business School professor Larry Selden and his wife and business consulting partner, Yoko Sugiura Selden, call "customer centricity." The Seldens offer the Royal Bank of Canada as an example.

Royal Bank of Canada   Thinking of its business in terms of customer segments rather than product segments, Royal Bank of Canada (RBC) has put each of its roughly 11 million clients into meaningful segments whose profitability it can measure. In the process, it discovered a sizable subsegment of customers hidden within its broader categories of "wealth preservers" and "wealth accumulators." Dubbed "snowbirds," these individuals spent a number of months each winter in Florida, where they were experiencing difficulties establishing credit as well as missing their Canadian communities, particularly the familiarity of the French-Canadian accent and fluency in French. To meet their unique needs, RBC created a Canadian banking experience in Florida.[46]

Because attracting a new customer may cost five times as much as retaining an existing one, relationship marketing also emphasizes customer retention. Companies build customer share by offering a larger variety of goods to existing customers, training employees in cross-selling and upselling. Marketing must skillfully conduct not only customer relationship management (CRM), but partner relationship management (PRM) as well. Companies are deepening their partnering arrangements with key suppliers and distributors, seeing them as partners in delivering value to final customers so everybody benefits.

Integrated Marketing

Integrated marketing occurs when the marketer devises marketing activities and assembles marketing programs to create, communicate, and deliver value for consumers such that "the whole is greater than the sum of its parts." Two key themes are that (1) many different marketing activities can create, communicate, and deliver value and (2) marketers should design and implement any one marketing activity with all other activities in mind. When a hospital buys an MRI from General Electric's Medical Systems division, for instance, it expects good installation, maintenance, and training services to go with the purchase.

All company communications also must be integrated. Using an integrated communication strategy means choosing communication options that reinforce and complement each other. A marketer might selectively employ television, radio, and print advertising, public relations and events, and PR and Web site communications so each contributes on its own as well as improving the effectiveness of the others. Each must also deliver a consistent brand message at every contact.

When BMW launched the modernized MINI Cooper in 2002, it employed an integrated marketing strategy in the United States that included a broad mix of media: billboards, posters, Internet, print, PR, product placement, and grassroots campaigns. Many were linked to a cleverly designed Web site with product and dealer information. The car was placed atop Ford Excursion SUVs at 21 auto shows across the United States, was used as seats in a sports stadium, and appeared in *Playboy* magazine as a centerfold. The imaginative integrated campaign built a six-month waiting list for the MINI Cooper.

The company must also develop an integrated channel strategy. It should assess each channel option for its direct effect on product sales and brand equity, as well as its indirect effect through interactions with other channel options. Marketers must weigh the trade-off between having too many channels (leading to conflict among channel members and/or a lack of support) and too few (resulting in market opportunities being overlooked).

Online marketing activities are increasingly prominent in building brands and sales. Created for $300,000 and no additional promotional expense, the Carnival Connections site made it easy for cruise fans to compare notes on destinations and onboard entertainment from casinos to conga lines. In a few short months, 2,000 of the site's 13,000 registered users planned trips aboard Carnival's 22 ships, generating an estimated $1.6 million in revenue for the company.[47]

Internal Marketing

Internal marketing, an element of holistic marketing, is the task of hiring, training, and motivating able employees who want to serve customers well. It ensures that everyone in the organization embraces appropriate marketing principles, especially senior management. Smart marketers recognize that marketing activities *within* the company can be as important—or even more important—than those directed outside the company. It makes no sense to promise excellent service before the company's staff is ready to provide it.

Snowshoe Mountain
Snowshoe Mountain in Snowshoe, West Virginia, embarked on a marketing program to better brand the ski resort with a promise of an "authentic, rustic and engaging wilderness experience." In launching a branding initiative to define their goals and articulate what they wanted the Snowshoe Mountain

To improve its guests' experiences, Snowshoe Mountain ski resort engages in a series of internal marketing activities to build its brand promise with employees.

brand to represent to visitors, the resort's marketers started inside. They incorporated the new brand promise in a 40-page brand book that contained the history of the resort and a list of seven attitude words that characterized how employees should interact with guests. On-mountain messaging and signs also reminded employees to deliver on the brand promise. All new hires received a brand presentation from the director of marketing to help them better understand the brand and become effective advocates.[48] ▱

Marketing is no longer the responsibility of a single department—it is a company-wide undertaking that drives the company's vision, mission, and strategic planning.[49] It succeeds only when all departments work together to achieve customer goals (see ▱ Table 1.1): when engineering designs the right products, finance furnishes the right amount of funding, purchasing buys the right materials, production makes the right products in the right time horizon, and accounting measures profitability in the right ways. Such interdepartmental harmony can only truly coalesce, however, when management clearly communicates a vision of how the company's marketing orientation and philosophy serve customers. The following example highlights some of the potential challenge in integrating marketing:

> The marketing vice president of a major European airline wants to increase the airline's traffic share. His strategy is to build up customer satisfaction by providing better food, cleaner cabins, better-trained cabin crews, and lower fares, yet he has no authority in these matters. The catering department chooses food that keeps food costs down; the maintenance department uses inexpensive cleaning services; the human resources department hires people without regard to whether they are naturally friendly; the finance department sets the fares. Because these departments generally take a cost or production point of view, the vice president of marketing is stymied in his efforts to create an integrated marketing program.

Internal marketing requires vertical alignment with senior management and horizontal alignment with other departments, so everyone understands, appreciates, and supports the marketing effort.

Performance Marketing

Performance marketing requires understanding the financial and nonfinancial returns to business and society from marketing activities and programs. Top marketers are increasingly going beyond sales revenue to examine the marketing scorecard and interpret what is happening to market share, customer loss rate, customer satisfaction, product quality, and other measures. They are also considering the legal, ethical, social, and environmental effects of marketing activities and programs.

FINANCIAL ACCOUNTABILITY Marketers are increasingly asked to justify their investments in financial and profitability terms, as well as in terms of building the brand and growing the customer base.[50] They're employing a broader variety of financial measures to assess the direct and indirect value their marketing efforts create and recognizing that much of their firms' market value comes from intangible assets, particularly brands, customer base, employees, distributor and supplier relations, and intellectual capital. Marketing metrics can help firms quantify and compare their marketing performance along a broad set of dimensions. Marketing research and statistical analysis assess the financial efficiency and effectiveness of different marketing activities. Finally, firms can employ processes and systems to make sure they maximize the value from analyzing these different metrics.

SOCIAL RESPONSIBILITY MARKETING Because the effects of marketing extend beyond the company and the customer to society as a whole, marketers must consider the ethical, environmental, legal, and social context of their role and activities.[51]

The organization's task is thus to determine the needs, wants, and interests of target markets and satisfy them more effectively and efficiently than competitors while preserving or enhancing consumers' and society's long-term well-being. LG Electronics, Toshiba, and NEC Display Solutions

TABLE 1.1 Assessing Which Company Departments Are Customer-Minded

R&D
- They spend time meeting customers and listening to their problems.
- They welcome the involvement of marketing, manufacturing, and other departments to each new project.
- They benchmark competitors' products and seek "best of class" solutions.
- They solicit customer reactions and suggestions as the project progresses.
- They continuously improve and refine the product on the basis of market feedback.

Purchasing
- They proactively search for the best suppliers.
- They build long-term relationships with fewer but more reliable, high-quality suppliers.
- They don't compromise quality for price savings.

Manufacturing
- They invite customers to visit and tour their plants.
- They visit customer plants.
- They willingly work overtime to meet promised delivery schedules.
- They continuously search for ways to produce goods faster and/or at lower cost.
- They continuously improve product quality, aiming for zero defects.
- They meet customer requirements for "customization" where possible.

Marketing
- They study customer needs and wants in well-defined market segments.
- They allocate marketing effort in relation to the long-run profit potential of the targeted segments.
- They develop winning offers for each target segment.
- They measure company image and customer satisfaction on a continuous basis.
- They continuously gather and evaluate ideas for new products, product improvements, and services.
- They urge all company departments and employees to be customer centered.

Sales
- They have specialized knowledge of the customer's industry.
- They strive to give the customer "the best solution."
- They make only promises that they can keep.
- They feed back customers' needs and ideas to those in charge of product development.
- They serve the same customers for a long period of time.

Logistics
- They set a high standard for service delivery time and meet this standard consistently.
- They operate a knowledgeable and friendly customer service department that can answer questions, handle complaints, and resolve problems in a satisfactory and timely manner.

Accounting
- They prepare periodic "profitability" reports by product, market segment, geographic areas (regions, sales territories), order sizes, channels, and individual customers.
- They prepare invoices tailored to customer needs and answer customer queries courteously and quickly.

Finance
- They understand and support marketing expenditures (e.g., image advertising) that produce long-term customer preference and loyalty.
- They tailor the financial package to the customer's financial requirements.
- They make quick decisions on customer creditworthiness.

Public Relations
- They send out favorable news about the company and "damage control" unfavorable news.
- They act as an internal customer and public advocate for better company policies and practices.

Source: ©Philip Kotler, *Kotler on Marketing* (New York: Free Press, 1999), pp. 21–22. Reprinted with permission of The Free Press, a Division of Simon & Schuster Adult Publishing Group. Copyright © 1999 by Philip Kotler. All rights reserved.

TABLE 1.2	Corporate Social Initiatives	
Type	**Description**	**Example**
Corporate social marketing	Supporting behavior change campaigns	McDonald's promotion of a statewide childhood immunization campaign in Oklahoma
Cause marketing	Promoting social issues through efforts such as sponsorships, licensing agreements, and advertising	McDonald's sponsorship of Forest (a gorilla) at Sydney's Zoo—a 10-year sponsorship commitment, aimed at preserving this endangered species
Cause-related marketing	Donating a percentage of revenues to a specific cause based on the revenue occurring during the announced period of support	McDonald's earmarking of $1 for Ronald McDonald Children's Charities from the sale of every Big Mac and pizza sold on McHappy Day
Corporate philanthropy	Making gifts of money, goods, or time to help nonprofit organizations, groups, or individuals	McDonald's contributions to Ronald McDonald House Charities
Corporate community involvement	Providing in-kind or volunteer services in the community	McDonald's catering meals for firefighters in the December 1997 bushfires in Australia
Socially responsible business practices	Adapting and conducting business practices that protect the environment and human and animal rights	McDonald's requirement that suppliers increase the amount of living space for laying hens on factory farms

Source: Philip Kotler and Nancy Lee, *Corporate Social Responsibility: Doing the Most Good for Your Company and Your Cause* (Hoboken, NJ: Wiley, 2004). Copyright © 2005 by Philip Kotler and Nancy Lee. Used by permission of John Wiley & Sons, Inc.

Ben & Jerry's "triple bottom line" business philosophy is based on monitoring the environmental and social effects of its actions in addition to the profits from the sale of its products.

offer electronic recycling programs, for instance, often providing consumers with prepaid postage to return old items. Retailers such as Office Depot, Best Buy, and AT&T offer similar programs in their stores.

Table 1.2 displays some different types of corporate social initiatives, illustrated by McDonald's.[52]

As goods become more commoditized, and consumers grow more socially conscious, some companies—including The Body Shop, Timberland, and Patagonia—incorporate social responsibility as a way to differentiate themselves from competitors, build consumer preference, and achieve notable sales and profit gains. When they founded Ben & Jerry's, Ben Cohen and Jerry Greenfield embraced the performance marketing concept by dividing the traditional financial bottom line into a "double bottom line" that also measured the environmental impact of their products and processes. That later expanded into a "triple bottom line," to represent the social impacts, negative and positive, of the firm's entire range of business activities.[53]

Stonyfield Farm   Social responsibility has been at the core of Stonyfield Farm—makers of all-natural organic yogurts—from the start. Stonyfield's suppliers eschew the productivity practices of agribusiness, including the use of antibiotics, growth hormones, pesticides, and fertilizers. After calculating the amount of energy used to run its plant, Stonyfield decided to make an equivalent investment in environmental projects such as reforestation and wind farms. The company dropped plastic lids on its yogurt, saving about a million pounds of plastic a year, and added on-package messages about global warming, the perils of hormones, and genetically modified foods. It makes low-fat versions of its products, and adds cultures or dietary supplements to help the immune system fight off illness. The attitudes and beliefs Stonyfield adopted have not hurt its financial performance as it has become the number-three yogurt brand in the United States.[54]

Updating The Four Ps

McCarthy classified various marketing activities into *marketing-mix* tools of four broad kinds, which he called *the four Ps* of marketing: product, price, place, and promotion.[55] The marketing variables under each P are shown in △ Figure 1.4.

Given the breadth, complexity, and richness of marketing, however—as exemplified by holistic marketing—clearly these four Ps are not the whole story anymore. If we update them to reflect the holistic marketing concept, we arrive at a more representative set that encompasses modern marketing realities: people, processes, programs, and performance, as in △ Figure 1.5.

People reflects, in part, internal marketing and the fact that employees are critical to marketing success. Marketing will only be as good as the people inside the organization. It also reflects the fact that marketers must view consumers as people to understand their lives more broadly, and not just as they shop for and consume products and services.

Processes reflects all the creativity, discipline, and structure brought to marketing management. Marketers must avoid ad hoc planning and decision making and ensure that state-of-the-art marketing ideas and concepts play an appropriate role in all they do. Only by instituting the right set of processes to guide activities and programs can a firm engage in mutually beneficial long-term relationships. Another important set of processes guides the firm in imaginatively generating insights and breakthrough products, services, and marketing activities.

Programs reflects all the firm's consumer-directed activities. It encompasses the old four Ps as well as a range of other marketing activities that might not fit as neatly into the old view of marketing. Regardless of whether they are online or offline, traditional or nontraditional, these activities must be integrated such that their whole is greater than the sum of their parts and they accomplish multiple objectives for the firm.

|Fig. 1.4| △

The Four P
Components of the
Marketing Mix

|Fig. 1.5| △

The Evolution
of Marketing
Management

We define *performance* as in holistic marketing, to capture the range of possible outcome measures that have financial and nonfinancial implications (profitability as well as brand and customer equity), and implications beyond the company itself (social responsibility, legal, ethical, and community related).

Finally, these new four Ps actually apply to *all* disciplines within the company, and by thinking this way, managers grow more closely aligned with the rest of the company.

Marketing Management Tasks

With the holistic marketing philosophy as a backdrop, we can identify a specific set of tasks that make up successful marketing management and marketing leadership. We'll use the following situation to illustrate these tasks in the context of the plan of the book. (The "Marketing Memo: Marketers' Frequently Asked Questions" is a good checklist for the questions marketing managers ask, all of which we examine in this book.)

> Zeus Inc. (name disguised) operates in several industries, including chemicals, cameras, and film. The company is organized into SBUs. Corporate management is considering what to do with its Atlas camera division, which produces a range of 35mm and digital cameras. Although Zeus has a sizable share and is producing revenue, the 35mm market is rapidly declining. In the much faster-growing digital camera segment, Zeus faces strong competition and has been slow to gain sales. Zeus's corporate management wants Atlas's marketing group to produce a strong turnaround plan for the division.

Developing Marketing Strategies and Plans

The first task facing Atlas is to identify its potential long-run opportunities, given its market experience and core competencies (see Chapter 2). Atlas can design its cameras with better features. It can make a line of video cameras, or it can use its core competency in optics to design a line of binoculars and telescopes. Whichever direction it chooses, it must develop concrete marketing plans that specify the marketing strategy and tactics going forward.

Capturing Marketing Insights

Atlas needs a reliable marketing information system to closely monitor its marketing environment so it can continually assess market potential and forecast demand. Its microenvironment consists of all the players who affect its ability to produce and sell cameras—suppliers, marketing intermediaries, customers, and competitors. Its macroenvironment includes demographic, economic, physical, technological, political-legal, and social-cultural forces that affect sales and profits (see Chapter 3).

Atlas also needs a dependable marketing research system. To transform strategy into programs, marketing managers must make basic decisions about their expenditures, activities, and budget

marketing Memo — Marketers' Frequently Asked Questions

1. How can we spot and choose the right market segment(s)?
2. How can we differentiate our offerings?
3. How should we respond to customers who buy on price?
4. How can we compete against lower-cost, lower-price competitors?
5. How far can we go in customizing our offering for each customer?
6. How can we grow our business?
7. How can we build stronger brands?
8. How can we reduce the cost of customer acquisition?
9. How can we keep our customers loyal longer?
10. How can we tell which customers are more important?
11. How can we measure the payback from advertising, sales promotion, and public relations?
12. How can we improve sales force productivity?
13. How can we establish multiple channels and yet manage channel conflict?
14. How can we get the other company departments to be more customer-oriented?

allocations. They may use sales-response functions that show how the amount of money spent in each application will affect sales and profits (see Chapter 4).

Connecting with Customers

Atlas must consider how to best create value for its chosen target markets and develop strong, profitable, long-term relationships with customers (see Chapter 5). To do so, it needs to understand consumer markets (see Chapter 6). Who buys cameras, and why? What features and prices are they looking for, and where do they shop? Atlas also sells cameras to business markets, including large corporations, professional firms, retailers, and government agencies (see Chapter 7), where purchasing agents or buying committees make the decisions. Atlas needs to gain a full understanding of how organizational buyers buy. It needs a sales force well trained in presenting product benefits.

Atlas will not want to market to all possible customers. It must divide the market into major market segments, evaluate each one, and target those it can best serve (see Chapter 8).

Building Strong Brands

Atlas must understand the strengths and weaknesses of the Zeus brand as customers see it (see Chapter 9). Is its 35mm film heritage a handicap in the digital camera market? Suppose Atlas decides to focus on the consumer market and develop a positioning strategy (see Chapter 10). Should it position itself as the "Cadillac" brand, offering superior cameras at a premium price with excellent service and strong advertising? Should it build a simple, low-priced camera aimed at more price-conscious consumers? Or something in between?

Atlas must also pay close attention to competitors (see Chapter 11), anticipating their moves and knowing how to react quickly and decisively. It may want to initiate some surprise moves, in which case it needs to anticipate how its competitors will respond.

Shaping the Market Offerings

At the heart of the marketing program is the product—the firm's tangible offering to the market, which includes the product quality, design, features, and packaging (see Chapter 12). To gain a competitive advantage, Atlas may provide leasing, delivery, repair, and training as part of its product offering (see Chapter 13).

A critical marketing decision relates to price (see Chapter 14). Atlas must decide on wholesale and retail prices, discounts, allowances, and credit terms. Its price should match well with the offer's perceived value; otherwise, buyers will turn to competitors' products.

Delivering Value

Atlas must also determine how to properly deliver to the target market the value embodied in its products and services. Channel activities include those the company undertakes to make the product accessible and available to target customers (see Chapter 15). Atlas must identify, recruit, and link various marketing facilitators to supply its products and services efficiently to the target market. It must understand the various types of retailers, wholesalers, and physical-distribution firms and how they make their decisions (see Chapter 16).

Communicating Value

Atlas must also adequately communicate to the target market the value embodied by its products and services. It will need an integrated marketing communication program that maximizes the individual and collective contribution of all communication activities (see Chapter 17). Atlas needs to set up mass communication programs consisting of advertising, sales promotion, events, and public relations (see Chapter 18). It also needs to plan more personal communications, in the form of direct and interactive marketing, as well as hire, train, and motivate salespeople (see Chapter 19).

Creating Successful Long-Term Growth

Based on its product positioning, Atlas must initiate new-product development, testing, and launching as part of its long-term view (see Chapter 20). The strategy should take into account changing global opportunities and challenges (see Chapter 21).

Finally, Atlas must build a marketing organization capable of implementing the marketing plan (see Chapter 22). Because surprises and disappointments can occur as marketing plans unfold, Atlas will need feedback and control to understand the efficiency and effectiveness of its marketing activities and how it can improve them.[56]

Summary

1. Marketing is an organizational function and a set of processes for creating, communicating, and delivering value to customers and for managing customer relationships in ways that benefit the organization and its stakeholders. Marketing management is the art and science of choosing target markets and getting, keeping, and growing customers through creating, delivering, and communicating superior customer value.

2. Marketers are skilled at managing demand: they seek to influence its level, timing, and composition for goods, services, events, experiences, persons, places, properties, organizations, information, and ideas. They also operate in four different marketplaces: consumer, business, global, and nonprofit.

3. Marketing is not done only by the marketing department. It needs to affect every aspect of the customer experience. To create a strong marketing organization, marketers must think like executives in other departments, and executives in other departments must think more like marketers.

4. Today's marketplace is fundamentally different as a result of major societal forces that have resulted in many new consumer and company capabilities. These forces have created new opportunities and challenges and changed marketing management significantly as companies seek new ways to achieve marketing excellence.

5. There are five competing concepts under which organizations can choose to conduct their business: the production concept, the product concept, the selling concept, the marketing concept, and the holistic marketing concept. The first three are of limited use today.

6. The holistic marketing concept is based on the development, design, and implementation of marketing programs, processes, and activities that recognize their breadth and interdependencies. Holistic marketing recognizes that everything matters in marketing and that a broad, integrated perspective is often necessary. Four components of holistic marketing are relationship marketing, integrated marketing, internal marketing, and socially responsible marketing.

7. The set of tasks necessary for successful marketing management includes developing marketing strategies and plans, capturing marketing insights, connecting with customers, building strong brands, shaping the market offerings, delivering and communicating value, and creating long-term growth.

Applications

Marketing Debate
Does Marketing Create or Satisfy Needs?

Marketing has often been defined in terms of satisfying customers' needs and wants. Critics, however, maintain that marketing goes beyond that and creates needs and wants that did not exist before. They feel marketers encourage consumers to spend more money than they should on goods and services they do not really need.

Take a position: Marketing shapes consumer needs and wants *versus* Marketing merely reflects the needs and wants of consumers.

Marketing Discussion
Shifts in Marketing

Consider the broad shifts in marketing. Do any themes emerge in them? Can you relate the shifts to the major societal forces? Which force has contributed to which shift?

Marketing Excellence

>>Nike

Nike hit the ground running in 1962. Originally known as Blue Ribbon Sports, the company focused on providing high-quality running shoes designed for athletes by athletes. Founder Philip Knight believed high-tech shoes for runners could be manufactured at competitive prices if imported from abroad. Nike's commitment to designing innovative footwear for serious athletes helped it build a cult following among U.S. consumers.

Nike believed in a "pyramid of influence" in which the preferences of a small percentage of top athletes influenced the product and brand choices of others. From the start its marketing campaigns featured accomplished athletes. Runner Steve Prefontaine, the first spokesperson, had an irreverent attitude that matched the company's spirit.

In 1985, Nike signed up then-rookie guard Michael Jordan as a spokesperson. Jordan was still an up-and-comer, but he personified superior performance. Nike's bet paid off—the Air Jordan line of basketball shoes flew off the shelves and revenues hit over $100 million in the first year alone. As one reporter stated, "Few marketers have so reliably been able to identify and sign athletes who transcend their sports to such great effect."

In 1988, Nike aired the first ads in its $20 million "Just Do It" ad campaign. The campaign, which ultimately featured 12 TV spots in all, subtly challenged a generation of athletic enthusiasts to chase their goals. It was a natural manifestation of Nike's attitude of self-empowerment through sports.

As Nike began expanding overseas to Europe, it found that its U.S.-style ads were seen as too aggressive. Nike realized it had to "authenticate" its brand in Europe, so it focused on soccer (known as football outside the United States) and became active as a sponsor of youth leagues, local clubs, and national teams. However, for Nike to build authenticity among the soccer audience, consumers had to see professional athletes using its product, especially athletes who won. Nike's big break came in 1994 when the Brazilian team (the only national team for which Nike had any real sponsorship) won the World Cup. That victory transformed Nike's image in Europe from a sneaker company into a brand that represented emotion, allegiance, and identification. It also helped launch Nike into other international markets over the next decade, and by 2003, overseas revenues surpassed U.S. revenues for the first time.

In 2007, Nike acquired Umbro, a British maker of soccer-related footwear, apparel, and equipment. The acquisition helped boost Nike's presence in soccer as the company became the sole supplier of uniforms to over 100 professional soccer teams around the world.

Nike focused its efforts on international markets, especially China, during the 2008 Summer Olympics in Beijing. Although Nike's rival, Adidas, was the official sponsor of the Olympic Games, Nike received special permission from the International Olympic Committee to run Nike ads featuring Olympic athletes during the games. In addition, Nike sponsored several teams and athletes, including most of the Chinese teams and 11 of the 12 high-profile members on the United States men's basketball teams. That year, sales in the Asian region grew 15 percent to $3.3 billion and Nike's international divisions grew to 53 percent of the company's revenue. Some believed Nike's marketing strategy during the Olympics was more effective than Adidas's Olympic sponsorship.

In addition to expanding the brand overseas, Nike successfully entered new athletic footwear, apparel, and equipment product categories by using endorsements from high-profile athletes and consumer outreach programs. The Nike Golf brand, endorsed by Tiger Woods, has changed the way professional golfers dress. Tiger's powerful influence on the game and his Nike emblazoned style have turned the greens at the majors into "golf's fashion runway." In addition, Nike has used the superstar to help build its relationship with consumers. In 2009, it launched a Tiger Web Talkback session at nikegolf.com, where fans could ask questions and hear Tiger talk about golf. The session was part of a nationwide Nike Golf consumer experience day, which included equipment demos, long-drive contests, and in-store specials.

In tennis, Nike has aligned with Maria Sharapova, Roger Federer, and Rafael Nadal to push its line of tennis clothing and gear. Some called the famous 2008 Wimbledon match between Roger Federer and Rafael Nadal—both dressed in swooshes from head to toe—a five-hour Nike commercial valued at $10.6 million.

Nike teamed up with seven-time Tour de France champion Lance Armstrong not only to sell Nike products but also to help Armstrong's LIVESTRONG campaign. Nike designed, manufactured, and sold over 70 million yellow LIVESTRONG bracelets, netting $80 million for the Lance Armstrong Foundation. It also featured Armstrong's message of survival, willpower, and giving in a series of Nike commercials.

To promote its line of basketball shoes and apparel, Nike continues to feature basketball superstars such as Kobe Bryant and LeBron James. In addition, it formed a partnership with Foot Locker to create a new chain of stores, House of Hoops by Foot Locker, which offers only basketball products by Nike brands such as Converse and Jordan.

Recently, Nike's lead in the running category has grown to 60 percent market share thanks to its exclusive partnership with Apple. Nike+ (Plus) technology includes a sensor that runners put into their running shoes and a receiver, which fits into an iPod, iTouch, or iPhone. When the athlete goes for a run or hits the gym, the receiver captures his or her mileage, calories burned, and pace and stores it until the information is downloaded. Nike+ is now considered the world's largest running club.

In 2008 and 2009, Nike+ hosted the Human Race 10K, the largest and only global virtual race in the world. The event, designed to celebrate running, drew 780,000 participants in 2008 and surpassed that number in 2009. To participate, runners register online, gear up with Nike+ technology, and hit the road on race day, running any 10K route they choose at any time during the day. Once the data is downloaded from the Nike+ receiver, each runner's official time is posted and can be compared to the times of runners from around the world.

Like many companies, Nike is trying to make its company and products more eco-friendly. However, unlike many companies, Nike does not promote its efforts. One brand consultant explained, "Nike has always been about winning. How is sustainability relevant to its brand?" Nike executives agree that promoting an eco-friendly message would distract from its slick high-tech image, so efforts like recycling old shoes into new shoes are kept quiet.

Today, Nike dominates the athletic footwear market with a 31 percent market share globally and a 50 percent market share in the United States. Swooshes abound on everything from wristwatches to skateboards to swimming caps. The firm's long-term strategy focuses on basketball, running, football, women's fitness, men's training, and sports culture. As a result of its successful expansion across geographic markets and product categories, Nike is the top athletic apparel and footwear manufacturer in the world, with corporate fiscal 2009 revenues exceeding $19 billion.

Questions

1. What are the pros, cons, and risks associated with Nike's core marketing strategy?

2. If you were Adidas, how would you compete with Nike?

Sources: Justin Ewers and Tim Smart, "A Designer Swooshes In," *U.S. News & World Report,* January 26, 2004, p. 12; "Corporate Media Executive of the Year," *Delaney Report,* January 12, 2004, p. 1; Barbara Lippert, "Game Changers: Inside the Three Greatest Ad Campaigns of the Past Three Decades," *Adweek,* November 17, 2008; "10 Top Nontraditional Campaigns," *Advertising Age,* December 22, 2003, p. 24; Chris Zook and James Allen, "Growth Outside the Core," *Harvard Business Review,* December 2003, p. 66; Jeremy Mullman, "NIKE; What Slowdown? Swoosh Rides Games to New High," *Advertising Age,* October 20, 2008, p. 34; Allison Kaplan, "Look Just Like Tiger (until you swing)," *America's Intelligence Wire,* August 9, 2009; Reena Jana and Burt Helm, "Nike Goes Green, Very Quietly," *BusinessWeek,* June 22, 2009.

Marketing Excellence

>>Google

In 1998, two Stanford University PhD students, Larry Page and Sergey Brin, founded a search engine company and named it Google. The name plays on the number *googol*—1 followed by 100 zeroes—and refers to the massive quantity of data available online that the company helps users find. Google's corporate mission is "To organize the world's information and make it universally accessible and useful." From the beginning, Google has strived to be one of the "good guys" in the corporate world, supporting a touchy-feely work environment, strong ethics, and a famous founding credo: "Don't be evil."

The company has become the market leader for search engines through its business focus and constant innovation. As Google grew into a primary destination for Web users searching for information online, it attracted a host of online advertisers. These advertisers drove Google's revenue by buying "search ads," little text-based boxes shown alongside search results that advertisers pay for only when users click on them. Google's search ad program, called AdWords, sells space on its search pages to ads linked with specific keywords. Google auctions off the keyword ads, with prime keywords and page locations going to the highest bidder. Google recently added a program called AdSense, which allows any Web site to display targeted Google ads related to the content of its site. Web site publishers earn money every time visitors click on these ads.

In addition to offering prime online "real estate" for advertisers, Google adds value by providing tools to better target their ads and better understand the effectiveness of their marketing. Google Analytics, free to Google's advertisers, provides a custom report, or dashboard, detailing how Internet users found the site, what ads they saw and/or clicked on, how they behaved while there, and how much traffic was generated. Google client Discount Tire was able to identify where visitors encountered problems that led them to abandon a purchase midstream. After modifying its site and updating its keyword search campaign, Discount Tire measured a 14 percent increase in sales within a week.

With its ability to deploy data that enable up-to-the-minute improvements in a Web marketing program, Google supports a style of marketing in which the advertising resources and budget can be constantly monitored and optimized. Google calls this approach "marketing asset management," implying that advertising should be managed like assets in a portfolio depending on the market conditions. Rather than following a marketing plan developed months in advance, companies use the real-time data collected on their campaigns to optimize the campaign's effectiveness and be more responsive to the market.

Over the past decade, Google has expanded far beyond its search capabilities with numerous other services, applications, and tools. It creates and distributes its products for free, which in turn provide new opportunities for the firm to sell additional targeted advertising space. Since 97 percent of Google's revenues come from online advertising, new advertising space is critical to the company's growth.

Google's wide range of products and services fall into five categories: desktop products, mobile products, Web products, hardware products, and other products. *Desktop products* include both stand-alone applications such as Google Earth (a virtual globe that uses satellite imagery and aerial photography), Google Chrome (a Web browser), and Google Video/YouTube (Google acquired the video hosting site YouTube in 2006 for $1.65 billion), or desktop extensions such as Google Toolbar (a browser toolbar). *Mobile products* include all Google products available for mobile devices. *Web products* are broken down into the following subsets—advertising (e.g., AdWorks, DoubleClick, Click-to-Call), communications and publishing (e.g., Google Docs, Google Calendar, Google Gadgets, Wave), development (e.g., Android, Google Code), mapping (e.g., Google Sky, Google Maps), Search (e.g., Google Dictionary, Google Alerts, Google Scholar), and statistics (e.g., Google Trends, Google Analytics).

Google's stage of development starts within Google Labs, which lists new products available for testing. It next moves to beta status, where invited users test early prototypes. Once the product is fully tested and ready to be released to the general public, it moves into the gold stage as a core Google product. Google Voice, for example, is in the beta stage. It provides consumers with one Google phone number, which then connects to the user's home, office, and cell numbers. The user decides which phones ring, based on who calls. Due to Google Voice's complexity and popularity, users can sign up only by invitation.

Google has not spent a lot of money on traditional advertising. Recent efforts have targeted Microsoft consumers with appeals to use Google's "cloud computing" applications instead of Microsoft Office or Windows. By "Going Google," a user can access all of his or her documents and applications via a Web browser instead of owning the physical infrastructure and software. In addition, in 2009 Google launched its first-ever television commercial for Google Chrome, an alternative to Microsoft's Internet Explorer Web browser.

Google is also betting big in the mobile category. With its 2008 launch of Android, a mobile operating system, Google went head-to-head with Apple's iPhone. Although many still prefer Apple's platform, even critics have praised Android's benefits. Most importantly, Android is free, open sourced, and backed by a multimillion-dollar investment. That means Google wants its partners to help build and design Android over the years. In addition, the iPhone is available only through AT&T in the United States, while most of AT&T's competitors support Android phones. If Google influences millions of new consumers to use smart phones, it could make billions in mobile advertising. One analyst stated that Google "is trying to get ahead of the curve with these initiatives so when [mobile advertising] becomes mainstream, Google will be one of the major players, and display is a key growth area for Google."

Google's goal is to reach as many people as possible on the Web—whether by PC or by phone. The more users on the Web, the more advertising Google can sell. Google's new products also accomplish this goal and make the Web a more personalized experience. One program allows users to mark their current position on Google Maps, click the local tab, and receive information about local restaurants, bars, and entertainment venues.

Google has enjoyed great success as a company and a brand since its launch. When it experienced an hour-long outage in 2009, worldwide Internet traffic decreased by 5 percent. In 2009, Google held a 65 percent market share in search in the United States, significantly greater than second place Yahoo!'s 20 percent market share. Globally, Google held a more dominant lead with 89 percent market share versus Yahoo!'s 5 percent and MSN's 3 percent. Google's revenues topped $21 billion in 2008, and the company was ranked the most powerful brand in the world with a brand value of $86 billion.

Questions

1. With a portfolio as diverse as Google's, what are the company's core brand values?

2. What's next for Google? Is it doing the right thing taking on Microsoft with the concept of cloud computing, and Apple in the fight for smart phones?

Sources: www.google.com; Catherine P. Taylor, "Google Flex," *Adweek*, March 20, 2006, cover story; Richard Karpinski, "Keywords, Analytics Help Define User Lifetime Value," *Advertising Age*, April 24, 2006, p. S2; Danny Gorog, "Survival Guide," *Herald Sun*, March 29, 2006; Julie Schlosser, "Google," *Fortune*, October 31, 2005, pp. 168–69; Jefferson Graham, "Google's Profit Sails Past Expectations," *USA Today*, October 21, 2005; Dan Frommer, "BrandZ Top 100 2008 Report"; "Google's Android Mobile Platform Is Getting Huge," *Advertising Age*, October 8, 2009; Rita Chang, "Google Set for Richer Advertising on Smartphones," *Advertising Age*, October 5, 2009.

Chapter 2

In This Chapter, We Will Address the Following Questions

1. How does marketing affect customer value?

2. How is strategic planning carried out at different levels of the organization?

3. What does a marketing plan include?

Yahoo! faces many strategic challenges as it attempts to fend off competition from Google and others.

YAHOO!

NOW THE INTERNET HAS A PERSONALITY. YOURS.

It's Y!ou

Developing Marketing Strategies and Plans

Key ingredients of the marketing management process are insightful, creative strategies and plans that can guide marketing activities. Developing the right marketing strategy over time requires a blend of discipline and flexibility. Firms must stick to a strategy but also constantly improve it. They must also develop strategies for a range of products and services within the organization.

Founded in 1994 by Web-surfing Stanford University grad students, Yahoo! grew from a tiny upstart surrounded by Silicon Valley heavyweights to a powerful force in Internet media. Yahoo! worked hard to be more than just a search engine. The company proudly proclaims it is "The only place anyone needs to go to find anything, communicate with anyone, or buy anything." Its range of services includes e-mail, news, weather, music, photos, games, shopping, auctions, and travel. A large percentage of revenues comes from advertising, but the company also profits from subscription services such as online personal ads, premium e-mail, and small-business services. Although Yahoo! strives to achieve a competitive advantage over rival Google with its vast array of original content, Google's ascension to the runaway leader in search, e-mail, and related services has made it a darling with advertisers. Yahoo!'s acquisition of photo-sharing service Flickr, social bookmark manager Del.icio.us, and online video editing site Jumpcut strengthened its capabilities. Yahoo! has also continued to grow globally in Europe and Asia, helped in part by the acquisition of Kelkoo, a European comparison-shopping site, for $579 million, and of 46 percent of Alibaba, a Chinese e-commerce company, for $1 billion in cash. Discussions with Microsoft about a possible merger culminated in a 10-year deal in June 2009 that gave Microsoft full access to the Yahoo! search engine, to be used in future Microsoft projects for its own search engine, Bing. CEO Carol Bartz faced many questions, however, about how Yahoo! should best move forward.[1]

This chapter begins by examining some of the strategic marketing implications in creating customer value. We'll look at several perspectives on planning and describe how to draw up a formal marketing plan.

Marketing and Customer Value

The task of any business is to deliver customer value at a profit. In a hypercompetitive economy with increasingly informed buyers faced with abundant choices, a company can win only by fine-tuning the value delivery process and choosing, providing, and communicating superior value.

The Value Delivery Process

The traditional view of marketing is that the firm makes something and then sells it, with marketing taking place in the selling process. Companies that subscribe to this view have the best chance of succeeding in economies marked by goods shortages where consumers are not fussy about quality, features, or style—for example, basic staple goods in developing markets.

This traditional view will not work, however, in economies with many different types of people, each with individual wants, perceptions, preferences, and buying criteria. The smart competitor must design and deliver offerings for well-defined target markets. This realization inspired a new view of business processes that places marketing at the *beginning* of planning. Instead of emphasizing making and selling, companies now see themselves as part of a value delivery process.

We can divide the value creation and delivery sequence into three phases.[2] First, *choosing the value* represents the "homework" marketing must do before any product exists. Marketers must segment the market, select the appropriate target, and develop the offering's value positioning. The formula "segmentation, targeting, positioning (STP)" is the essence of strategic marketing. The second phase is *providing the value.* Marketing must determine specific product features, prices, and distribution. The task in the third phase is *communicating the value* by utilizing the sales force, Internet, advertising, and any other communication tools to announce and promote the product. The value delivery process begins before there is a product and continues through development and after launch. Each phase has cost implications.

The Value Chain

Harvard's Michael Porter has proposed the **value chain** as a tool for identifying ways to create more customer value.[3] According to this model, every firm is a synthesis of activities performed to design, produce, market, deliver, and support its product. The value chain identifies nine strategically relevant activities—five primary and four support activities—that create value and cost in a specific business.

The *primary activities* are (1) inbound logistics, or bringing materials into the business; (2) operations, or converting materials into final products; (3) outbound logistics, or shipping out final products; (4) marketing, which includes sales; and (5) service. Specialized departments handle the *support activities*—(1) procurement, (2) technology development, (3) human resource management, and (4) firm infrastructure. (Infrastructure covers the costs of general management, planning, finance, accounting, legal, and government affairs.)

The firm's task is to examine its costs and performance in each value-creating activity and look for ways to improve it. Managers should estimate competitors' costs and performances as *benchmarks* against which to compare their own. And they should go further and study the "best of class" practices of the world's best companies. We can identify best-practice companies by consulting customers, suppliers, distributors, financial analysts, trade associations, and magazines to see whom they rate as doing the best job. Even the best companies can benchmark, against other industries if necessary, to improve their performance. To support its corporate goal to be more innovative, GE has benchmarked against P&G as well as developing its own best practices.[4]

The firm's success depends not only on how well each department performs its work, but also on how well the company coordinates departmental activities to conduct *core business processes*.[5] These processes include:

- *The market-sensing process.* All the activities in gathering and acting upon information about the market
- *The new-offering realization process.* All the activities in researching, developing, and launching new high-quality offerings quickly and within budget
- *The customer acquisition process.* All the activities in defining target markets and prospecting for new customers
- *The customer relationship management process.* All the activities in building deeper understanding, relationships, and offerings to individual customers
- *The fulfillment management process.* All the activities in receiving and approving orders, shipping the goods on time, and collecting payment

Strong companies are reengineering their work flows and building cross-functional teams to be responsible for each process.[6] At Xerox, a Customer Operations Group links sales, shipping, installation, service, and billing so these activities flow smoothly into one another. Winning companies excel at managing core business processes through cross-functional teams. AT&T, LexisNexis, and Pratt & Whitney have reorganized their employees into cross-functional teams; cross-functional teams exist in nonprofit and government organizations as well.

To be successful, a firm also needs to look for competitive advantages beyond its own operations, into the value chains of suppliers, distributors, and customers. Many companies today have

Pratt & Whitney employs cross-functional employee teams to build its products, such as this 4000 series aircraft engine.

partnered with specific suppliers and distributors to create a superior **value delivery network**, also called a **supply chain**.

Sony In May 2009, Sony announced it would cut its number of suppliers in half over the next two years (to 1,200), increasing the volume of parts and materials from each and thus reducing unit costs and overall procurement spending. Some stock analysts received the news positively as evidence of the company's commitment to restructuring. Others were less optimistic, such as Mizuho Investors Securities analyst Nobuo Kurahashi: "I'm not sure how effective this is because it's just operational streamlining and wouldn't simply push up earnings or bear fruit immediately."[7]

Core Competencies

Traditionally, companies owned and controlled most of the resources that entered their businesses—labor power, materials, machines, information, and energy—but many today outsource less-critical resources if they can obtain better quality or lower cost.

The key, then, is to own and nurture the resources and competencies that make up the *essence* of the business. Many textile, chemical, and computer/electronic product firms do not manufacture their own products because offshore manufacturers are more competent in this task. Instead, they focus on product design and development and marketing, their core competencies. A **core competency** has three characteristics: (1) It is a source of competitive advantage and makes a significant contribution to perceived customer benefits. (2) It has applications in a wide variety of markets. (3) It is difficult for competitors to imitate.[8]

Competitive advantage also accrues to companies that possess *distinctive capabilities* or excellence in broader business processes. Wharton's George Day sees market-driven organizations as excelling in three distinctive capabilities: market sensing, customer linking, and channel bonding.[9] In terms of market sensing, he believes tremendous opportunities and threats often begin as "weak signals" from the "periphery" of a business.[10] He offers a systematic process for developing peripheral vision, and practical tools and strategies for building "vigilant organizations" attuned to changes in the environment, by asking three questions each related to learning from the past, evaluating the present, and envisioning the future.

Competitive advantage ultimately derives from how well the company has fitted its core competencies and distinctive capabilities into tightly interlocking "activity systems." Competitors find it hard to imitate Southwest Airlines, Walmart, and IKEA because they are unable to copy their activity systems.

Business realignment may be necessary to maximize core competencies. It has three steps: (1) (re)defining the business concept or "big idea", (2) (re)shaping the business scope, and (3) (re)positioning the company's brand identity. Consider what Kodak is doing to realign its business.

Kodak With the advent of the digital era and the capacity to store, share, and print photos using PCs, Kodak faces more competition than ever, in-store and online. In 2004, after being bumped from the Dow Jones Industrial Average where it had held a spot for more than 70 years, the company started the painful process of transformation. It began by expanding its line of digital cameras, printers, and other equipment, and it also set out to increase market share in the lucrative medical imaging business. Making shifts is not without challenges, however. The company eliminated almost 30,000 jobs between 2004 and 2007 and acquired a string of companies for its graphics communications unit. In 2006, Kodak announced it would outsource the making of its digital cameras. Not only must Kodak convince consumers to buy its digital cameras and home printers, but it also must become known as the most convenient and affordable way to process digital images. So far, it faces steep competition from Sony, Canon, and Hewlett-Packard.[11]

Kodak has installed thousands of its Picture Kiosks to allow customers to print digital photos or scan existing photos when, where, and how they want.

A Holistic Marketing Orientation and Customer Value

One view of holistic marketing sees it as "integrating the value exploration, value creation, and value delivery activities with the purpose of building long-term, mutually satisfying relationships and coprosperity among key stakeholders."[12] Holistic marketers thus succeed by managing a superior value chain that delivers a high level of product quality, service, and speed. They achieve profitable growth by expanding customer share, building customer loyalty, and capturing customer lifetime value. Holistic marketers address three key management questions:

1. **Value exploration**—How a company identifies new value opportunities
2. **Value creation**—How a company efficiently creates more promising new value offerings
3. **Value delivery**—How a company uses its capabilities and infrastructure to deliver the new value offerings more efficiently

The Central Role of Strategic Planning

Successful marketing thus requires capabilities such as understanding, creating, delivering, capturing, and sustaining customer value. Only a select group of companies have historically stood out as master marketers (see 🔲 Table 2.1). These companies focus on the customer and are organized to respond effectively to changing customer needs. They all have well-staffed marketing departments, and their other departments accept that the customer is king.

To ensure they select and execute the right activities, marketers must give priority to strategic planning in three key areas: (1) managing a company's businesses as an investment portfolio, (2) assessing each business's strength by considering the market's growth rate and the company's position and fit in that market, and (3) establishing a strategy. The company must develop a game plan for achieving each business's long-run objectives.

Most large companies consist of four organizational levels: (1) corporate, (2) division, (3) business unit, and (4) product. Corporate headquarters is responsible for designing a corporate strategic plan to guide the whole enterprise; it makes decisions on the amount of resources to allocate to each division, as well as on which businesses to start or eliminate. Each division establishes a plan covering the allocation of funds to each business unit within the division. Each business unit develops a strategic plan to carry that business unit into a profitable future. Finally, each product level (product line, brand) develops a marketing plan for achieving its objectives.

The **marketing plan** is the central instrument for directing and coordinating the marketing effort. It operates at two levels: strategic and tactical. The **strategic marketing plan** lays out the

TABLE 2.I Some Examples of Master Marketers		
Amazon.com	Electrolux	Progressive Insurance
Bang & Olufsen	Enterprise Rent-A-Car	Ritz-Carlton
Barnes & Noble	Google	Samsung
Best Buy	Harley-Davidson	Sony
BMW	Honda	Southwest Airlines
Borders	IKEA	Starbucks
Canon	LEGO	Target
Caterpillar	McDonald's	Tesco
Club Med	Nike	Toyota
Costco	Nokia	Virgin
Disney	Nordstrom	Walmart
eBay	Procter & Gamble	Whole Foods

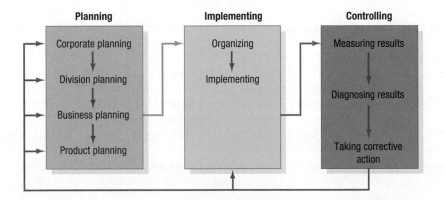

|Fig. 2.1| ▲

The Strategic
Planning,
Implementation, and
Control Processes

target markets and the firm's value proposition, based on an analysis of the best market opportunities. The **tactical marketing plan** specifies the marketing tactics, including product features, promotion, merchandising, pricing, sales channels, and service. The complete planning, implementation, and control cycle of strategic planning is shown in ▲ Figure 2.1. Next, we consider planning at each of these four levels of the organization.

Corporate and Division Strategic Planning

Some corporations give their business units freedom to set their own sales and profit goals and strategies. Others set goals for their business units but let them develop their own strategies. Still others set the goals and participate in developing individual business unit strategies.

All corporate headquarters undertake four planning activities:

1. Defining the corporate mission
2. Establishing strategic business units
3. Assigning resources to each strategic business unit
4. Assessing growth opportunities

We'll briefly look at each process.

Defining the Corporate Mission

An organization exists to accomplish something: to make cars, lend money, provide a night's lodging. Over time, the mission may change, to take advantage of new opportunities or respond to new market conditions. Amazon.com changed its mission from being the world's largest online bookstore to aspiring to become the world's largest online store; eBay changed from running online auctions for collectors to running online auctions of all kinds of goods; and Dunkin' Donuts switched its emphasis from doughnuts to coffee.

To define its mission, a company should address Peter Drucker's classic questions:[13] What is our business? Who is the customer? What is of value to the customer? What will our business be? What should our business be? These simple-sounding questions are among the most difficult a company will ever have to answer. Successful companies continuously raise and answer them.

Organizations develop **mission statements** to share with managers, employees, and (in many cases) customers. A clear, thoughtful mission statement provides a shared sense of purpose, direction, and opportunity.

Mission statements are at their best when they reflect a vision, an almost "impossible dream" that provides direction for the next 10 to 20 years. Sony's former president, Akio Morita, wanted everyone to have access to "personal portable sound," so his company created the Walkman and portable CD player. Fred Smith wanted to deliver mail anywhere in the United States before 10:30 AM the next day, so he created FedEx.

Good mission statements have five major characteristics.

1. *They focus on a limited number of goals.* The statement "We want to produce the highest-quality products, offer the most service, achieve the widest distribution, and sell at the lowest prices" claims too much.
2. *They stress the company's major policies and values.* They narrow the range of individual discretion so employees act consistently on important issues.
3. *They define the major competitive spheres within which the company will operate.* 🖵 Table 2.2 summarizes some key competitive dimensions for mission statements.
4. *They take a long-term view.* Management should change the mission only when it ceases to be relevant.
5. *They are as short, memorable, and meaningful as possible.* Marketing consultant Guy Kawasaki advocates developing three- to four-word corporate mantras rather than mission statements, like "Enriching Women's Lives" for Mary Kay.[14]

Compare the rather vague mission statements on the left with Google's mission statement and philosophy on the right:

To build total brand value by innovating to deliver customer value and customer leadership faster, better, and more completely than our competition. We build brands and make the world a little happier by bringing our best to you.	**Google Mission** To organize the world's information and make it universally accessible and useful. **Google Philosophy** Never settle for the best. 1. Focus on the user and all else will follow. 2. It's best to do one thing really, really well. 3. Fast is better than slow. 4. Democracy on the Web works. 5. You don't need to be at your desk to need an answer. 6. You can make money without doing evil. 7. There is always more information out there. 8. The need for information crosses all borders. 9. You can be serious without a suit. 10. Great just isn't good enough.[15]

TABLE 2.2	Defining Competitive Territory and Boundaries in Mission Statements

- **Industry.** *Some companies operate in only one industry; some only in a set of related industries; some only in industrial goods, consumer goods, or services; and some in any industry.*
  - Caterpillar focuses on the industrial market; John Deere operates in the industrial and consumer markets.

- **Products and applications.** *Firms define the range of products and applications they will supply.*
  - St. Jude Medical is "dedicated to developing medical technology and services that put more control in the hands of physicians, and that advance the practice of medicine and contribute to successful outcomes for every patient."

- **Competence.** *The firm identifies the range of technological and other core competencies it will master and leverage.*
  - Japan's NEC has built its core competencies in computing, communications, and components to support production of laptop computers, television receivers, and handheld telephones.

- **Market segment.** *The type of market or customers a company will serve is the market segment.*
  - Aston Martin makes only high-performance sports cars. Gerber serves primarily the baby market.

- **Vertical.** *The vertical sphere is the number of channel levels, from raw material to final product and distribution, in which a company will participate.*
  - At one extreme are companies with a large vertical scope. American Apparel dyes, designs, sews, markets, and distributes its line of clothing apparel out of a single building in downtown Los Angeles.
  - At the other extreme are "hollow corporations," which outsource the production of nearly all goods and services to suppliers. Metro International prints 34 free local newspaper editions in 16 countries. It employs few reporters and owns no printing presses; instead it purchases its articles from other news sources and outsources all its printing and much of its distribution to third parties.[16]

- **Geographical.** *The range of regions, countries, or country groups in which a company will operate defines its geographical sphere.*
  - Some companies operate in a specific city or state. Others are multinationals like Deutsche Post DHL and Royal Dutch/Shell, which each operate in more than 100 countries.

Establishing Strategic Business Units

Companies often define themselves in terms of products: They are in the "auto business" or the "clothing business." *Market definitions* of a business, however, describe the business as a customer-satisfying process. Products are transient; basic needs and customer groups endure forever. Transportation is a need: the horse and carriage, automobile, railroad, airline, ship, and truck are products that meet that need.

Viewing businesses in terms of customer needs can suggest additional growth opportunities. Table 2.3 lists companies that have moved from a product to a market definition of their business. It highlights the difference between a target market definition and a strategic market definition.

A *target market definition* tends to focus on selling a product or service to a current market. Pepsi could define its target market as everyone who drinks carbonated soft drinks, and competitors would therefore be other carbonated soft drink companies. A *strategic market definition*, however, also focuses on the potential market. If Pepsi considered everyone who might drink something to quench their thirst, its competition would include noncarbonated soft drinks, bottled water, fruit juices, tea, and coffee. To better compete, Pepsi might decide to sell additional beverages with promising growth rates.

A business can define itself in terms of three dimensions: customer groups, customer needs, and technology.[17] Consider a small company that defines its business as designing incandescent lighting

American Apparel is a fully vertically integrated company that conducts all its business from its Los Angeles, California, location.

systems for television studios. Its customer group is television studios; the customer need is lighting; the technology is incandescent lighting. The company might want to expand to make lighting for homes, factories, and offices, or it could supply other services television studios need, such as heating, ventilation, or air conditioning. It could design other lighting technologies for television

TABLE 2.3 🖛 Product-Oriented versus Market-Oriented Definitions of a Business

Company	Product Definition	Market Definition
Union Pacific Railroad	We run a railroad.	We are a people-and-goods mover.
Xerox	We make copying equipment.	We help improve office productivity.
Hess Corporation	We sell gasoline.	We supply energy.
Paramount Pictures	We make movies.	We market entertainment.
Encyclopaedia Britannica	We sell encyclopedias.	We distribute information.
Carrier	We make air conditioners and furnaces.	We provide climate control in the home.

HANDBAGS CLOTHING SHOES IN OUR SHOPS AND ONLINE AT KATESPADE.COM

The Kate Spade brand allows Liz Claiborne to attract a more youthful customer.

studios, such as infrared or ultraviolet lighting or perhaps environmentally friendly "green" fluorescent bulbs.

Large companies normally manage quite different businesses, each requiring its own strategy. At one time, General Electric classified its businesses into 49 **strategic business units (SBUs)**. An SBU has three characteristics:

1. It is a single business, or a collection of related businesses, that can be planned separately from the rest of the company.
2. It has its own set of competitors.
3. It has a manager responsible for strategic planning and profit performance, who controls most of the factors affecting profit.

The purpose of identifying the company's strategic business units is to develop separate strategies and assign appropriate funding. Senior management knows its portfolio of businesses usually includes a number of "yesterday's has-beens" as well as "tomorrow's breadwinners."[18] Liz Claiborne has put more emphasis on some of its younger businesses such as Juicy Couture, Lucky Brand Jeans, Mexx, and Kate Spade while selling businesses without the same buzz (Ellen Tracy, Sigrid Olsen, and Laundry). Campbell Soup has out-paced the stock market for close to a decade by developing or keeping only products that ranked number one or number two in the categories of simple meals, baked snacks, and veggie-based drinks and that had a strong emphasis on value, nutrition, and convenience.[19]

Dubai World Home to the world's tallest building and one of the largest shopping malls, Dubai boasts a skyline that rises dramatically from the desert. The United Arab Emirates' economy is supported by four sectors: tourism, financial services, international shipping, and real estate. As the leading local developer, Dubai World manages a portfolio of government investments in all four sectors (see ▭ Table 2.4). The economic recession of 2008–2009 hit the Emirates hard. Tourism declined and income from real estate plummeted. On the artificial island of Palm Jumeirah, luxury homes that had commanded over $626 per square foot in 2007 were selling for $191 by August 2010. In late 2009 the Dubai government asked creditors to restructure its debt. Tough negotiations with foreign banks followed. By October 2010, there was good news. According to the International Monetary Fund (IMF), Dubai's economy was set to grow by 0.5 percent in 2010. The growth was largely due to an increase in trade and the logistics-related part of Dubai's business, which has traditionally been a source of strength. The ability to negotiate and the strengths of conglomerate diversification may have helped Dubai weather its financial crisis.[20] ▭

TABLE 2.4 ▭	Dubai Word Business Units

Dubai World is a global holding company that operates in four strategic areas: logistics, marine, urban development, and financial services. Its portfolio includes:

- DP World—international marine terminal (port) operations
- Drydocks World—ship building and repair
- Dubai Maritime City—a multipurpose maritime hub, including yachting and luxury residences (under construction)
- Economic Zones World—worldwide management of free zones and special economic zones
- Istithmar World—global private equity investments in consumer, industrial, financial services, aerospace, and real estate
- Limitless—a real estate development company (combined with Nakheel on July 3, 2010)
- Nakheel—real estate development and tourism

Assigning Resources to Each SBU[21]

Once it has defined SBUs, management must decide how to allocate corporate resources to each. Several portfolio-planning models provide ways to make investment decisions. The GE/McKinsey Matrix classifies each SBU by the extent of its competitive advantage and the attractiveness of its industry. Management can decide to grow, "harvest" or draw cash from, or hold on to the business. Another model, BCG's Growth-Share Matrix, uses relative market share and annual rate of market growth as criteria to make investment decisions, classifying SBUs as dogs, cash cows, question marks, and stars.

Portfolio-planning models like these have fallen out of favor as oversimplified and subjective. Newer methods rely on shareholder value analysis, and on whether the market value of a company is greater with an SBU or without it (whether it is sold or spun off). These value calculations assess the potential of a business based on growth opportunities from global expansion, repositioning or retargeting, and strategic outsourcing.

Assessing Growth Opportunities

Assessing growth opportunities includes planning new businesses, downsizing, and terminating older businesses. If there is a gap between future desired sales and projected sales, corporate management will need to develop or acquire new businesses to fill it.

▲ Figure 2.2 illustrates this strategic-planning gap for a major manufacturer of blank compact disks called Musicale (name disguised). The lowest curve projects the expected sales over the next five years from the current business portfolio. The highest describes desired sales over the same period. Evidently, the company wants to grow much faster than its current businesses will permit. How can it fill the strategic-planning gap?

The first option is to identify opportunities for growth within current businesses (intensive opportunities). The second is to identify opportunities to build or acquire businesses related to

|Fig. 2.2| ▲

The Strategic-Planning Gap

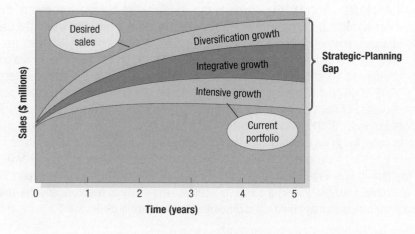

current businesses (integrative opportunities). The third is to identify opportunities to add attractive unrelated businesses (diversification opportunities).

INTENSIVE GROWTH Corporate management's first course of action should be a review of opportunities for improving existing businesses. One useful framework for detecting new intensive-growth opportunities is a "product-market expansion grid." It considers the strategic growth opportunities for a firm in terms of current and new products and markets.

The company first considers whether it could gain more market share with its current products in their current markets, using a *market-penetration strategy*. Next it considers whether it can find or develop new markets for its current products, in a *market-development strategy*. Then it considers whether it can develop new products of potential interest to its current markets with a *product development strategy*. Later the firm will also review opportunities to develop new products for new markets in a *diversification strategy*. Consider how Nespresso has employed growth opportunities.

NESPRESSO

In 1986, Nestlé launched Nespresso with the aim of enabling anyone to create the perfect cup of espresso coffee. With an average annual growth rate of 30 percent since 2000, Nespresso has become one of the key drivers of Nestlé's success and is now available in 50 countries. Driven by the idea of delivering high-quality espresso coffee at home or at work, Nespresso pioneered the development of a coffee capsule system. There are three main reasons for its success: First, Nespresso uses the highest-quality coffee, selected from the top 1 percent of coffee beans worldwide. Second, it uses excellent machines, fulfilling different customer needs as well as guaranteeing high-quality coffee and ease of use. Third, it provides delightful customer service via the Internet, boutiques, and call centers. More than 7 million members of the Nespresso club keep in touch with the company and are the key for future growth as ambassadors of the brand. Nespresso's growth strategy is supported by a growing product line of seasonal coffee varieties, accessories, and chocolates; B2B partnerships with hotels (e.g. Ritz-Carlton, Kempinski) and airlines (e.g. Lufthansa, Emirates); and a commitment to sustainability through capsule recycling and partnership with a rainforest alliance. And the growth continues: In August 2010 Nespresso opened its 200th boutique worldwide in Shanghai, where revenues were expected to exceed $3 billion in 2010. Every minute, more than 10,000 cups of Nespresso coffee are enjoyed by customers worldwide.[22]

Nespresso pioneered the idea of delivering high quality coffee at home or work and has become one of Nestlé's most successful brands.

So how might Musicale use these three major intensive growth strategies to increase its sales? It could try to encourage its current customers to buy more by demonstrating the benefits of using compact disks for data storage in addition to music storage. It could try to attract competitors' customers if it noticed major weaknesses in their products or marketing programs. Finally, Musicale could try to convince nonusers of compact disks to start using them.

How can Musicale use a market-development strategy? First, it might try to identify potential user groups in the current sales areas. If it has been selling compact disks only to consumer markets, it might go after office and factory markets. Second, it might seek additional distribution channels by adding mass merchandising or online channels. Third, the company might sell in new locations in its home country or abroad.

Management should also consider new-product possibilities. Musicale could develop new features, such as additional data storage capabilities or greater durability. It could offer the CD at two or more quality levels, or it could research an alternative technology such as flash drives.

These intensive growth strategies offer several ways to grow. Still, that growth may not be enough, and management must also look for integrative growth opportunities.

INTEGRATIVE GROWTH A business can increase sales and profits through backward, forward, or horizontal integration within its industry. Merck has gone beyond developing and selling prescription pharmaceuticals. It formed joint ventures in 1989 with Johnson & Johnson to sell over-the-counter pharmaceuticals; in 1991 with DuPont to expand basic research, and in 2000 with Schering-Plough to develop and market new prescription medicines. In 1997, Merck and Rhône-Poulenc S.A. (now Sanofi-Aventis S.A.) combined their animal health and poultry genetics businesses to form Merial Limited, a fully integrated animal health company. Finally, Merck purchased Medco, a mail-order pharmaceutical distributor, in 2003 and Sirna Therapeutics in 2006.

Horizontal mergers and alliances don't always work out. The merger between Sears and Kmart didn't solve either retailer's problems.[23] Media companies, however, have long reaped the benefits of integrative growth. Here's how one business writer explains the potential NBC could reap from its merger with Vivendi Universal Entertainment to become NBC Universal. Although it's a far-fetched example, it gets across the possibilities inherent in this growth strategy:[24]

> [When] the hit movie *Fast & Furious* 4 (produced by Universal Pictures) comes to television, it would air on Bravo (owned by NBC) or USA Network (owned by Universal), followed by the inevitable bid to make the movie into a TV series (by Universal Television Group), with the pilot being picked up by NBC. The show then begins airing on Hulu.com (owned in part by NBC), and ultimately leads to the creation of a popular amusement-park attraction at Universal Studios.

In today's highly integrated media world, NBC Universal may take a successful movie franchise such as *Fast & Furious* and leverage it across all its businesses, including its Universal Studios theme park.

How might Musicale achieve integrative growth? The company might acquire one or more of its suppliers, such as plastic material producers, to gain more control or generate more profit through backward integration. It might acquire some wholesalers or retailers, especially if they are highly profitable, in forward integration. Finally, Musicale might acquire one or more competitors, provided the government does not bar this horizontal integration. However, these new sources may still not deliver the desired sales volume. In that case, the company must consider diversification.

DIVERSIFICATION GROWTH   Diversification growth makes sense when good opportunities exist outside the present businesses—the industry is highly attractive and the company has the right mix of business strengths to succeed. From its origins as an animated film producer, The Walt Disney Company has moved into licensing characters for merchandised goods, publishing general interest fiction books under the Hyperion imprint, entering the broadcast industry with its own Disney Channel as well as ABC and ESPN, developing theme parks and vacation and resort properties, and offering cruise and commercial theatre experiences.

Several types of diversification are possible for Musicale. First, the company could choose a concentric strategy and seek new products that have technological or marketing synergies with existing product lines, though appealing to a different group of customers. It might start a laser disk manufacturing operation, because it knows how to manufacture compact discs. Second, it might use a horizontal strategy to search for unrelated new products that appeal to current customers. Musicale might produce compact disc cases, for example, though they require a different manufacturing process. Finally, the company might seek new businesses that have no relationship to its current technology, products, or markets, adopting a conglomerate strategy to consider making application software or personal organizers.

DOWNSIZING AND DIVESTING OLDER BUSINESSES Companies must carefully prune, harvest, or divest tired old businesses to release needed resources for other uses and reduce costs. To focus on its travel and credit card operations, American Express in 2005 spun off American Express Financial Advisors, which provided insurance, mutual funds, investment advice, and brokerage and asset management services (it was renamed Ameriprise Financial).

Organization and Organizational Culture

Strategic planning happens within the context of the organization. A company's **organization** consists of its structures, policies, and corporate culture, all of which can become dysfunctional in a rapidly changing business environment. Whereas managers can change structures and policies (though with difficulty), the company's culture is very hard to change. Yet adapting the culture is often the key to successfully implementing a new strategy.

What exactly is a **corporate culture**? Some define it as "the shared experiences, stories, beliefs, and norms that characterize an organization." Walk into any company and the first thing that strikes you is the corporate culture—the way people dress, talk to one another, and greet customers. When Mark Hurd became CEO of HP, one of his goals was to reinvigorate the famous "HP Way," a benevolent but hard-nosed corporate culture that rewarded employees amply but expected teamwork, growth, and profits in return.[25]

A customer-centric culture can affect all aspects of an organization. Sometimes corporate culture develops organically and is transmitted directly from the CEO's personality and habits to the company employees. Mike Lazaridis, president and co-CEO of BlackBerry producer Research In Motion, is a scientist in his own right, winning an Academy Award for technical achievement in film. He has hosted a weekly, innovation-centered "Vision Series" at company headquarters that focuses on new research and company goals. As he states, "I think we have a culture of innovation here, and [engineers] have absolute access to me. I live a life that tries to promote innovation."[26]

Marketing Innovation

Innovation in marketing is critical. Imaginative ideas on strategy exist in many places within a company.[27] Senior management should identify and encourage fresh ideas from three underrepresented groups: employees with youthful or diverse perspectives, employees far removed from company headquarters, and employees new to the industry. Each group can challenge company orthodoxy and stimulate new ideas.

German-based Reckitt Benckiser has been an innovator in the staid household cleaning products industry by generating 40 percent of sales from products under three years old. Its multinational staff is encouraged to dig deep into consumer habits and is well rewarded for excellent performance. "Marketing Insight: Creating Innovative Marketing" describes how some leading companies approach innovation.

Firms develop strategy by identifying and selecting among different views of the future. The Royal Dutch/Shell Group has pioneered **scenario analysis**, which develops plausible representations of a firm's possible future using assumptions about forces driving the market and different uncertainties. Managers think through each scenario with the question, "What will we do if it happens?" adopt one scenario as the most probable, and watch for signposts that might confirm or disconfirm it.[28] Consider the challenges faced by the movie industry.

Marketing Insight

Creating Innovative Marketing

When IBM surveyed top CEOs and government leaders about their priorities, business-model innovation and coming up with unique ways of doing things scored high. IBM's own drive for business-model innovation led to much collaboration, both within IBM itself and externally with companies, governments, and educational institutions. CEO Samuel Palmisano noted how the breakthrough Cell processor, based on the company's Power architecture, would not have happened without collaboration with Sony and Nintendo, as well as competitors Toshiba and Microsoft.

Procter & Gamble (P&G) similarly has made it a goal for 50 percent of new products to come from outside P&G's labs—from inventors, scientists, and suppliers whose new-product ideas can be developed in-house.

Business guru Jim Collins's research emphasizes the importance of systematic, broad-based innovation: "Always looking for the one big breakthrough, the one big idea, is contrary to what we found: To build a truly great company, it's decision upon decision, action upon action, day upon day, month upon month. . . . It's cumulative momentum and no one decision defines a great company." He cites the success of Walt Disney with theme parks and Walmart with retailing as examples of companies that were successful after having executed against a big idea brilliantly over such a long period of time.

Northwestern's Mohanbir Sawhney and his colleagues outline 12 dimensions of business innovation that make up the "innovation radar" (see ▭ Table 2.5) and suggest that business innovation is about increasing customer *value*, not just creating new *things*; comes in many flavors and can take place on any dimension of a business system; and is systematic and requires careful consideration of all aspects of a business.

Finally, to find breakthrough ideas, some companies find ways to immerse a range of employees in solving marketing problems. Samsung's Value Innovation Program (VIP) isolates product development teams of engineers, designers, and planners with a timetable and end date in the company's center just south of Seoul, Korea, while 50 specialists help guide their activities. To help make tough trade-offs, team members draw "value curves" that rank attributes such as a product's sound or picture quality on a scale from 1 to 5. To develop a new car, BMW similarly mobilizes specialists in engineering, design, production, marketing, purchasing, and finance at its Research and Innovation Center or Project House.

Sources: Steve Hamm, "Innovation: The View from the Top," *BusinessWeek*, April 3, 2006, pp. 52–53; Jena McGregor, "The World's Most Innovative Companies," *BusinessWeek*, April 24, 2006, pp. 63–74; Rich Karlgard, "Digital Rules," *Forbes*, March 13, 2006, p. 31; Jennifer Rooney and Jim Collins, "Being Great Is *Not* Just a Matter of Big Ideas," *Point*, June 2006, p. 20; Moon Ihlwan, "Camp Samsung," *BusinessWeek*, July 3, 2006, pp. 46–47; Mohanbir Sawhney, Robert C. Wolcott, and Inigo Arroniz, "The 12 Different Ways for Companies to Innovate," *MIT Sloan Management Review* (Spring 2006), pp. 75–85.

TABLE 2.5 ▭ The 12 Dimensions of Business Innovation		
Dimension	**Definition**	**Examples**
Offerings (WHAT)	Develop innovative new products or services.	• Gillette MACH3 Turbo Razor • Apple iPod music player and iTunes music service
Platform	Use common components or building blocks to create derivative offerings.	• General Motors OnStar telematics platform • Disney animated movies
Solutions	Create integrated and customized offerings that solve end-to-end customer problems.	• UPS logistics services Supply Chain Solutions • DuPont Building Innovations for construction
Customers (WHO)	Discover unmet customer needs or identify underserved customer segments.	• Enterprise Rent-A-Car focus on replacement car renters • Green Mountain Energy focus on "green power"
Customer Experience	Redesign customer interactions across all touch points and all moments of contact.	• Washington Mutual Occasio retail banking concept • Cabela's "store as entertainment experience" concept

(Continued)

Value Capture	Redefine how company gets paid or create innovative new revenue streams.	• Google paid search • Blockbuster revenue sharing with movie distributors
Processes (HOW)	Redesign core operating processes to improve efficiency and effectiveness.	• Toyota Production System for operations • General Electric Design for Six Sigma (DFSS)
Organization	Change form, function, or activity scope of the firm.	• Cisco partner-centric networked virtual organization • Procter & Gamble front-back hybrid organization for customer focus
Supply Chain	Think differently about sourcing and fulfillment.	• Moen ProjectNet for collaborative design with suppliers • General Motors Celta use of integrated supply and online sales
Presence (WHERE)	Create new distribution channels or innovative points of presence, including the places where offerings can be bought or used by customers.	• Starbucks music CD sales in coffee stores • Diebold RemoteTeller System for banking
Networking	Create network-centric intelligent and integrated offerings.	• Otis Remote Elevator Monitoring service • Department of Defense Network-Centric Warfare
Brand	Leverage a brand into new domains.	• Virgin Group "branded venture capital" • Yahoo! as a lifestyle brand

Source: Mohanbir Sawhney, Robert C. Wolcott, and Inigo Arroniz, "The 12 Different Ways for Companies to Innovate," *MIT Sloan Management Review* (Spring 2006), p. 78. © 2006 by Massachusetts Institute of Technology. All rights reserved. Distributed by Tribune Media Services.

Movie Industry The success of Netflix (see Chapter 15) and the ease of watching longer-form entertainment or playing games on broadband Internet helped produce a 6.8 percent decrease in DVD sales—one that experts believe will continue. The recent emergence of Redbox and its thousands of kiosks renting movies for $1 a day poses yet another threat to the movie business and DVD sales. Film studios clearly need to prepare for the day when films are primarily sold not through physical distribution but through satellite and cable companies' video-on-demand services. Although studios make 70 percent on a typical $4.99 cable viewing versus 30 percent on the sale of a DVD, sales of DVDs still generate 70 percent of film profits. To increase electronic distribution without destroying their DVD business, studios are experimenting with new approaches. Some, such as Warner Bros., are releasing a DVD at the same time as online and cable versions of a movie. Disney has emphasized its parent-friendly Disney-branded films, which generate higher DVD sales and are easy to cross-promote at the company's theme parks, on its TV channels, and in its stores. Paramount chose to debut *Jackass 2.5* on Blockbuster's site for free to create buzz and interest. Film studios are considering all possible scenarios as they rethink their business model in a world where the DVD no longer will reign as king.[29]

The easy availability of rentals from Redbox kiosks has film studios rethinking their pricing and distribution strategies.

Business Unit Strategic Planning

The business unit strategic-planning process consists of the steps shown in ▲ Figure 2.3. We examine each step in the sections that follow.

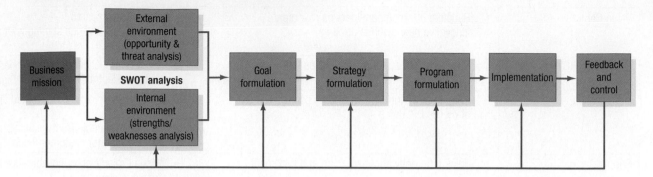

|Fig. 2.3| ▲

The Business Unit
Strategic-Planning
Process

The Business Mission

Each business unit needs to define its specific mission within the broader company mission. Thus, a television-studio-lighting-equipment company might define its mission as, "To target major television studios and become their vendor of choice for lighting technologies that represent the most advanced and reliable studio lighting arrangements." Notice this mission does not attempt to win business from smaller television studios, offer the lowest price, or venture into nonlighting products.

SWOT Analysis

The overall evaluation of a company's strengths, weaknesses, opportunities, and threats is called SWOT analysis. It's a way of monitoring the external and internal marketing environment.

EXTERNAL ENVIRONMENT (OPPORTUNITY AND THREAT) ANALYSIS A business unit must monitor key *macroenvironment forces* and significant *microenvironment factors* that affect its ability to earn profits. It should set up a marketing intelligence system to track trends and important developments and any related opportunities and threats.

Good marketing is the art of finding, developing, and profiting from these opportunities.[30] A **marketing opportunity** is an area of buyer need and interest that a company has a high probability of profitably satisfying.[31] There are three main sources of market opportunities. The first is to offer something that is in short supply. This requires little marketing talent, as the need is fairly obvious. The second is to supply an existing product or service in a new or superior way. How? The *problem detection method* asks consumers for their suggestions, the *ideal method* has them imagine an ideal version of the product or service, and the *consumption chain method* asks them to chart their steps in acquiring, using, and disposing of a product. This last method often leads to a totally new product or service.

Marketers need to be good at spotting opportunities. Consider the following:

- *A company may benefit from converging industry trends and introduce hybrid products or services that are new to the market.* Major cell manufacturers have released phones with digital photo and video capabilities, and Global Positioning Systems (GPS).
- *A company may make a buying process more convenient or efficient.* Consumers can use the Internet to find more books than ever and search for the lowest price with a few clicks.
- *A company can meet the need for more information and advice.* Angie's List connects individuals with local home improvement contractors and doctors that have been reviewed by others.
- *A company can customize a product or service.* Timberland allows customers to choose colors for different sections of their boots, add initials or numbers to their boots, and choose different stitching and embroidery.
- *A company can introduce a new capability.* Consumers can create and edit digital "iMovies" with the iMac and upload them to an Apple Web server or Web site such as YouTube to share with friends around the world.
- *A company may be able to deliver a product or service faster.* FedEx discovered a way to deliver mail and packages much more quickly than the U.S. Post Office.
- *A company may be able to offer a product at a much lower price.* Pharmaceutical firms have created generic versions of brand-name drugs, and mail-order drug companies often sell for less.

(a) Opportunity Matrix

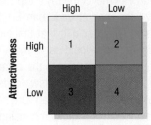

1. Company develops more powerful lighting system
2. Company develops device to measure energy efficiency of any lighting system
3. Company develops device to measure illumination level
4. Company develops software program to teach lighting fundamentals to TV studio personnel

(b) Threat Matrix

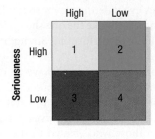

1. Competitor develops superior lighting system
2. Major prolonged economic depression
3. Higher costs
4. Legislation to reduce number of TV studio licenses

|Fig. 2.4| ▲

Opportunity and Threat Matrices

To evaluate opportunities, companies can use **market opportunity analysis (MOA)** to ask questions like:

1. Can we articulate the benefits convincingly to a defined target market(s)?
2. Can we locate the target market(s) and reach them with cost-effective media and trade channels?
3. Does our company possess or have access to the critical capabilities and resources we need to deliver the customer benefits?
4. Can we deliver the benefits better than any actual or potential competitors?
5. Will the financial rate of return meet or exceed our required threshold for investment?

In the opportunity matrix in ▲ Figure 2.4 (a), the best marketing opportunities facing the TV-lighting-equipment company appear in the upper-left cell (#1). The opportunities in the lower-right cell (#4) are too minor to consider. The opportunities in the upper-right cell (#2) and the lower-left cell (#3) are worth monitoring in the event that any improve in attractiveness and potential.

An **environmental threat** is a challenge posed by an unfavorable trend or development that, in the absence of defensive marketing action, would lead to lower sales or profit. Figure 2.4 (b) illustrates the threat matrix facing the TV-lighting-equipment company. The threats in the upper-left cell are major, because they have a high probability of occurrence and can seriously hurt the company. To deal with them, the company needs contingency plans. The threats in the lower-right cell are minor and can be ignored. The firm will want to carefully monitor threats in the upper-right and lower-left cells in the event they grow more serious.

INTERNAL ENVIRONMENT (STRENGTHS AND WEAKNESSES) ANALYSIS It's one thing to find attractive opportunities, and another to be able to take advantage of them. Each business needs to evaluate its internal strengths and weaknesses.

Loan Bright
At the Web site of Loan Bright, an online mortgage company, potential homebuyers can get a personalized list of lenders and available terms. At first, Loan Bright made its money by selling the homebuyer data to high-end mortgage lenders, including Wells Fargo Home Mortgage, Bank of America Mortgage, and Chase Home Mortgage. These firms turned the data into leads for their sales teams. But worrisome internal issues arose. For

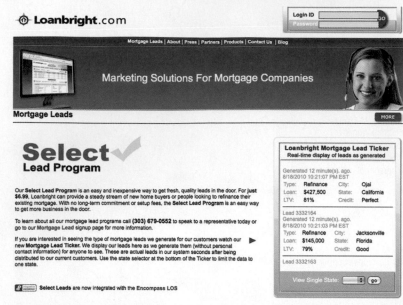

On the basis of a SWOT analysis, online mortgage company Loan Bright changed the focus of their marketing efforts to target individual loan officers.

one thing, Loan Bright had to please every one of its big clients, yet each was becoming tougher to satisfy, eating up time and resources. The company's top managers gathered to analyze the market and Loan Bright's strengths and weaknesses. They decided that instead of serving a few choice clients, they would serve many more individual loan officers who responded to the company's Google ads and only wanted to buy a few leads. The switch required revamping the way Loan Bright salespeople brought in new business, including using a one-page contract instead of the old 12-page contract, and creating a separate customer service department.[32]

Businesses can evaluate their own strengths and weaknesses by using a form like the one shown in "Marketing Memo: Checklist for Performing Strengths/Weaknesses Analysis."

Clearly, the business doesn't have to correct *all* its weaknesses, nor should it gloat about all its strengths. The big question is whether it should limit itself to those opportunities for which it possesses the required strengths, or consider those that might require it to find or develop new strengths. Managers at Texas Instruments (TI) were split between those who wanted to stick to industrial electronics, where TI has clear strength, and those who wanted to continue introducing consumer products, where TI lacks some required marketing strengths.

Goal Formulation

Once the company has performed a SWOT analysis, it can proceed to **goal formulation,** developing specific goals for the planning period. Goals are objectives that are specific with respect to magnitude and time.

Most business units pursue a mix of objectives, including profitability, sales growth, market share improvement, risk containment, innovation, and reputation. The business unit sets these objectives and then manages by objectives (MBO). For an MBO system to work, the unit's objectives must meet four criteria:

1. *They must be arranged hierarchically, from most to least important.* The business unit's key objective for the period may be to increase the rate of return on investment. Managers can increase profit by increasing revenue and reducing expenses. They can grow revenue, in turn, by increasing market share and prices.
2. *Objectives should be quantitative whenever possible.* The objective "to increase the return on investment (ROI)" is better stated as the goal "to increase ROI to 15 percent within two years."
3. *Goals should be realistic.* Goals should arise from an analysis of the business unit's opportunities and strengths, not from wishful thinking.
4. *Objectives must be consistent.* It's not possible to maximize sales and profits simultaneously.

Other important trade-offs include short-term profit versus long-term growth, deep penetration of existing markets versus development of new markets, profit goals versus nonprofit goals, and high growth versus low risk. Each choice calls for a different marketing strategy.[33]

Many believe adopting the goal of strong market share growth may mean foregoing strong short-term profits. Volkswagen has 15 times the annual revenue of Porsche—but Porsche's profit margins are seven times bigger than Volkswagen's. Other successful companies such as Google, Microsoft, and Samsung have maximized profitability *and* growth.

Strategic Formulation

Goals indicate what a business unit wants to achieve; **strategy** is a game plan for getting there. Every business must design a strategy for achieving its goals, consisting of a *marketing strategy* and a compatible *technology strategy* and *sourcing strategy.*

PORTER'S GENERIC STRATEGIES   Michael Porter has proposed three generic strategies that provide a good starting point for strategic thinking: overall cost leadership, differentiation, and focus.[34]

- *Overall cost leadership.* Firms work to achieve the lowest production and distribution costs so they can underprice competitors and win market share. They need less skill in marketing. The problem is that other firms will usually compete with still-lower costs and hurt the firm that rested its whole future on cost.
- *Differentiation.* The business concentrates on achieving superior performance in an important customer benefit area valued by a large part of the market. The firm seeking quality leadership, for example, must make products with the best components, put them together expertly, inspect them carefully, and effectively communicate their quality.
- *Focus.* The business focuses on one or more narrow market segments, gets to know them intimately, and pursues either cost leadership or differentiation within the target segment.

Customers can travel virtually anywhere in the world via flights on Star Alliance airlines.

The online air travel industry provides a good example of these three strategies: Travelocity is pursuing a differentiation strategy by offering the most comprehensive range of services to the traveler; Lowestfare is pursuing a lowest-cost strategy; and Last Minute is pursuing a niche strategy by focusing on travelers who have the flexibility to travel on very short notice. Some companies use a hybrid approach.

According to Porter, firms directing the same strategy to the same target market constitute a **strategic group**.[35] The firm that carries out that strategy best will make the most profits. Circuit City went out of business because it did not stand out in the consumer electronics industry as lowest in cost, highest in perceived value, or best in serving some market segment.

Porter draws a distinction between operational effectiveness and strategy. Competitors can quickly copy the operationally effective company using benchmarking and other tools, thus diminishing the advantage of operational effectiveness. Porter defines strategy as "the creation of a unique and valuable position involving a different set of activities." A company can claim it has a strategy when it "performs different activities from rivals or performs similar activities in different ways."

STRATEGIC ALLIANCES   Even giant companies—AT&T, Philips, and Nokia—often cannot achieve leadership, either nationally or globally, without forming alliances with domestic or multinational companies that complement or leverage their capabilities and resources.

Just doing business in another country may require the firm to license its product, form a joint venture with a local firm, or buy from local suppliers to meet "domestic content" requirements. Many firms have developed global strategic networks, and victory is going to those who build the better global network. The Star Alliance brings together 21 airlines, including Lufthansa, United Airlines, Singapore Airlines, Air New Zealand, and South Africa Airways, in a huge global partnership that allows travelers to make nearly seamless connections to hundreds of destinations.

Many strategic alliances take the form of marketing alliances. These fall into four major categories.

1. *Product or service alliances*—One company licenses another to produce its product, or two companies jointly market their complementary products or a new product. The credit card industry is a complicated combination of cards jointly marketed by banks such as Bank of America, credit card companies such as Visa, and affinity companies such as Alaska Airlines.
2. *Promotional alliances*—One company agrees to carry a promotion for another company's product or service. McDonald's teamed up with Disney for 10 years to offer products related to current Disney films as part of its meals for children.
3. *Logistics alliances*—One company offers logistical services for another company's product. Warner Music Group and Sub Pop Records created the Alternative Distribution Alliance (ADA) in 1993 as a joint venture to distribute and manufacture records owned by independent labels. ADA is the leading "indie" distribution company in the United States for both physical and digital product.
4. *Pricing collaborations*—One or more companies join in a special pricing collaboration. Hotel and rental car companies often offer mutual price discounts.

Checklist for Performing Strengths/Weaknesses Analysis

	Performance					Importance		
	Major Strength	Minor Strength	Neutral	Minor Weakness	Major Weakness	High	Med.	Low
Marketing								
1. Company reputation	____	____	____	____	____	____	____	____
2. Market share	____	____	____	____	____	____	____	____
3. Customer satisfaction	____	____	____	____	____	____	____	____
4. Customer retention	____	____	____	____	____	____	____	____
5. Product quality	____	____	____	____	____	____	____	____
6. Service quality	____	____	____	____	____	____	____	____
7. Pricing effectiveness	____	____	____	____	____	____	____	____
8. Distribution effectiveness	____	____	____	____	____	____	____	____
9. Promotion effectiveness	____	____	____	____	____	____	____	____
10. Sales force effectiveness	____	____	____	____	____	____	____	____
11. Innovation effectiveness	____	____	____	____	____	____	____	____
12. Geographical coverage	____	____	____	____	____	____	____	____
Finance								
13. Cost or availability of capital	____	____	____	____	____	____	____	____
14. Cash flow	____	____	____	____	____	____	____	____
15. Financial stability	____	____	____	____	____	____	____	____
Manufacturing								
16. Facilities	____	____	____	____	____	____	____	____
17. Economies of scale	____	____	____	____	____	____	____	____
18. Capacity	____	____	____	____	____	____	____	____
19. Able, dedicated workforce	____	____	____	____	____	____	____	____
20. Ability to produce on time	____	____	____	____	____	____	____	____
21. Technical manufacturing skill	____	____	____	____	____	____	____	____
Organization								
22. Visionary, capable leadership	____	____	____	____	____	____	____	____
23. Dedicated employees	____	____	____	____	____	____	____	____
24. Entrepreneurial orientation	____	____	____	____	____	____	____	____
25. Flexible or responsive	____	____	____	____	____	____	____	____

Companies need to give creative thought to finding partners that might complement their strengths and offset their weaknesses. Well-managed alliances allow companies to obtain a greater sales impact at lower cost. To keep their strategic alliances thriving, corporations have begun to develop organizational structures to support them, and many have come to view the ability to form and manage partnerships as core skills called **partner relationship management (PRM)**.[36]

Both pharmaceutical and biotech companies are starting to make partnership a core competency. It's estimated that nearly 700 such partnerships were formed in 2007 alone.[37] After years of growth through acquisition and buying interests in two dozen companies, the world's biggest wireless telecom operator, Vodafone, has looked outside the company for partners to help it leverage its existing assets.[38]

Vodafone
To spur more innovation and growth, Vodafone has embraced open source software and open platforms that allow it to tap into the creativity and skills of others. With its Web portal called Betavine, amateur or professional software developers can create and test their latest mobile applications on any network, not just Vodafone's. While

these developers retain intellectual property rights, Vodafone gains early exposure to the latest trends and ensures that innovations are compatible with its network. Some of the new apps include real-time train arrivals and departures, movie show times, and an Amazon.com widget with personalized details. With 289 million customers in 27 countries, the $35 billion company hasn't had trouble finding help from interested corporate partners either. Dell has collaborated with Vodafone to design laptops and low-priced netbooks with built-in wireless broadband access over Vodafone's networks. ▭

Vodafone has actively partnered with a number of other firms to help drive its innovation.

Program Formulation and Implementation

Even a great marketing strategy can be sabotaged by poor implementation. If the unit has decided to attain technological leadership, it must strengthen its R&D department, gather technological intelligence, develop leading-edge products, train its technical sales force, and communicate its technological leadership.

Once they have formulated marketing programs, marketers must estimate their costs. Is participating in a particular trade show worth it? Will a specific sales contest pay for itself? Will hiring another salesperson contribute to the bottom line? Activity-based cost accounting (ABC)—described in greater detail in Chapter 5—can help determine whether each marketing program is likely to produce sufficient results to justify its cost.[39]

Today's businesses recognize that unless they nurture other stakeholders—customers, employees, suppliers, distributors—they may never earn sufficient profits for the stockholders. A company might aim to delight its customers, perform well for its employees, and deliver a threshold level of satisfaction to its suppliers. In setting these levels, it must not violate any stakeholder group's sense of fairness about the treatment it is receiving relative to the others.[40]

A dynamic relationship connects the stakeholder groups. A smart company creates a high level of employee satisfaction, which leads to higher effort, which leads to higher-quality products and services, which creates higher customer satisfaction, which leads to more repeat business, which leads to higher growth and profits, which leads to high stockholder satisfaction, which leads to more investment, and so on. This virtuous circle spells profits and growth.

According to McKinsey & Company, strategy is only one of seven elements—all of which start with the letter s—in successful business practice.[41] The first three—strategy, structure, and systems—are considered the "hardware" of success. The next four—style, skills, staff, and shared values—are the "software."

The first "soft" element, *style*, means company employees share a common way of thinking and behaving. The second, *skills*, means employees have the skills needed to carry out the company's strategy. *Staffing* means the company has hired able people, trained them well, and assigned them to the right jobs. The fourth element, *shared values*, means employees share the same guiding values. When these elements are present, companies are usually more successful at strategy implementation.[42]

Feedback and Control

A company's strategic fit with the environment will inevitably erode, because the market environment changes faster than the company's seven Ss. Thus, a company might remain efficient yet lose effectiveness. Peter Drucker pointed out that it is more important to "do the right thing"—to be effective—than "to do things right"—to be efficient. The most successful companies, however, excel at both.

Once an organization fails to respond to a changed environment, it becomes increasingly hard to recapture its lost position. Consider KB Toys. Founded in 1922 as a candy wholesaler, the company successfully reinvented itself many times, first by shifting its focus to discounted toys and then by anticipating the growth of shopping malls. The firm became the second-largest toy retailer in the world but ultimately crumbled due to competition from big-box retailers and its failed acquisition of eToys. The company declared bankruptcy in 1994 but reemerged in the late 1990s—only to again file bankruptcy and liquidate its assets in late 2008.

Organizations, especially large ones, are subject to inertia. It's difficult to change one part without adjusting everything else. Yet, organizations can be changed through strong leadership, preferably in advance of a crisis. The key to organizational health is willingness to examine the changing environment and adopt new goals and behaviors.

Product Planning: The Nature and Contents of a Marketing Plan

Working within the plans set by the levels above them, product managers come up with a marketing plan for individual products, lines, brands, channels, or customer groups. Each product level, whether product line or brand, must develop a marketing plan for achieving its goals. A **marketing plan** is a written document that summarizes what the marketer has learned about the marketplace and indicates how the firm plans to reach its marketing objectives.[43] It contains tactical guidelines for the marketing programs and financial allocations over the planning period.[44]

A marketing plan is one of the most important outputs of the marketing process. It provides direction and focus for a brand, product, or company. Nonprofit organizations use marketing plans to guide their fund-raising and outreach efforts, and government agencies use them to build public awareness of nutrition and stimulate tourism.

More limited in scope than a business plan, the marketing plan documents how the organization will achieve its strategic objectives through specific marketing strategies and tactics, with the customer as the starting point. It is also linked to the plans of other departments. Suppose a marketing plan calls for selling 200,000 units annually. The production department must gear up to make that many units, finance must arrange funding to cover the expenses, human resources must be ready to hire and train staff, and so on. Without the appropriate level of organizational support and resources, no marketing plan can succeed.

Marketing plans are becoming more customer- and competitor-oriented, better reasoned, and more realistic. They draw more inputs from all the functional areas and are team-developed. Planning is becoming a continuous process to respond to rapidly changing market conditions. The most frequently cited shortcomings of current marketing plans, according to marketing executives, are lack of realism, insufficient competitive analysis, and a short-run focus. (See "Marketing Memo: Marketing Plan Criteria" for some guideline questions to ask in developing marketing plans.)

Although the exact length and layout varies from company to company, most marketing plans cover one year in anywhere from 5 to 50 pages. Smaller businesses may create shorter or less formal marketing plans, whereas corporations generally require highly structured documents. To guide implementation effectively, every part of the plan must be described in considerable detail. Sometimes a company will post its marketing plan on an internal Web site so everyone can consult specific sections and collaborate on changes. A marketing plan usually contains the following sections.

- *Executive summary and table of contents.* The marketing plan should open with a table of contents and brief summary for senior management of the main goals and recommendations.
- *Situation analysis.* This section presents relevant background data on sales, costs, the market, competitors, and the various forces in the macroenvironment. How do we define the market, how big is it, and how fast is it growing? What are the relevant trends and critical issues? Firms will use all this information to carry out a SWOT analysis.
- *Marketing strategy.* Here the marketing manager defines the mission, marketing and financial objectives, and needs the market offering is intended to satisfy as well as its competitive positioning. All this requires inputs from other areas, such as purchasing, manufacturing, sales, finance, and human resources.
- *Financial projections.* Financial projections include a sales forecast, an expense forecast, and a break-even analysis. On the revenue side is forecasted sales volume by month and product category, and on the expense side the expected costs of marketing, broken down into finer categories. The break-even analysis estimates how many units the firm must sell monthly (or how many years it will take) to offset its monthly fixed costs and average per-unit variable costs.

A more complex method of estimating profit is **risk analysis**. Here we obtain three estimates (optimistic, pessimistic, and most likely) for each uncertain variable affecting profitability, under an assumed marketing environment and marketing strategy for the planning period. The

Marketing Plan Criteria

Here are some questions to ask in evaluating a marketing plan.

1. *Is the plan simple?* Is it easy to understand and act on? Does it communicate its content clearly and practically?

2. *Is the plan specific?* Are its objectives concrete and measurable? Does it include specific actions and activities, each with specific dates of completion, specific persons responsible, and specific budgets?

3. *Is the plan realistic?* Are the sales goals, expense budgets, and milestone dates realistic? Has a frank and honest self-critique been conducted to raise possible concerns and objections?

4. *Is the plan complete?* Does it include all the necessary elements? Does it have the right breadth and depth?

Source: Adapted from Tim Berry and Doug Wilson, *On Target: The Book on Marketing Plans* (Eugene, OR: Palo Alto Software, 2000).

computer simulates possible outcomes and computes a distribution showing the range of possible rates of returns and their probabilities.[45]

- *Implementation controls.* The last section outlines the controls for monitoring and adjusting implementation of the plan. Typically, it spells out the goals and budget for each month or quarter, so management can review each period's results and take corrective action as needed. Some organizations include contingency plans.

The Role of Research

To develop innovative products, successful strategies, and action programs, marketers need up-to-date information about the environment, the competition, and the selected market segments. Often, analysis of internal data is the starting point for assessing the current marketing situation, supplemented by marketing intelligence and research investigating the overall market, the competition, key issues, threats, and opportunities. As the plan is put into effect, marketers use research to measure progress toward objectives and identify areas for improvement.

Finally, marketing research helps marketers learn more about their customers' requirements, expectations, perceptions, satisfaction, and loyalty. Thus, the marketing plan should outline what marketing research will be conducted and when, as well as how the findings will be applied.

The Role of Relationships

Although the marketing plan shows how the company will establish and maintain profitable customer relationships, it also affects both internal and external relationships. First, it influences how marketing personnel work with each other and with other departments to deliver value and satisfy customers. Second, it affects how the company works with suppliers, distributors, and partners to achieve the plan's objectives. Third, it influences the company's dealings with other stakeholders, including government regulators, the media, and the community at large. Marketers must consider all these relationships when developing a marketing plan.

From Marketing Plan to Marketing Action

Most companies create yearly marketing plans. Marketers start planning well in advance of the implementation date to allow time for marketing research, analysis, management review, and coordination between departments. As each action program begins, they monitor ongoing results, investigate any deviation from plans, and take corrective steps as needed. Some prepare contingency plans; marketers must be ready to update and adapt marketing plans at any time.

The marketing plan should define how progress toward objectives will be measured. Managers typically use budgets, schedules, and marketing metrics for monitoring and evaluating results.

With budgets, they can compare planned expenditures with actual expenditures for a given period. Schedules allow management to see when tasks were supposed to be completed and when they actually were. Marketing metrics track actual outcomes of marketing programs to see whether the company is moving forward toward its objectives.

Summary

1. The value delivery process includes choosing (or identifying), providing (or delivering), and communicating superior value. The value chain is a tool for identifying key activities that create value and costs in a specific business.

2. Strong companies develop superior capabilities in managing core business processes such as new-product realization, inventory management, and customer acquisition and retention. Managing these core processes effectively means creating a marketing network in which the company works closely with all parties in the production and distribution chain, from suppliers of raw materials to retail distributors. Companies no longer compete—marketing networks do.

3. According to one view, holistic marketing maximizes value exploration by understanding the relationships between the customer's cognitive space, the company's competence space, and the collaborator's resource space; maximizes value creation by identifying new customer benefits from the customer's cognitive space, utilizing core competencies from its business domain, and selecting and managing business partners from its collaborative networks; and maximizes value delivery by becoming proficient at customer relationship management, internal resource management, and business partnership management.

4. Market-oriented strategic planning is the managerial process of developing and maintaining a viable fit between the organization's objectives, skills, and resources and its changing market opportunities. The aim of strategic planning is to shape the company's businesses and products so they yield target profits and growth. Strategic planning takes place at four levels: corporate, division, business unit, and product.

5. The corporate strategy establishes the framework within which the divisions and business units prepare their strategic plans. Setting a corporate strategy means defining the corporate mission, establishing strategic business units (SBUs), assigning resources to each, and assessing growth opportunities.

6. Strategic planning for individual businesses includes defining the business mission, analyzing external opportunities and threats, analyzing internal strengths and weaknesses, formulating goals, formulating strategy, formulating supporting programs, implementing the programs, and gathering feedback and exercising control.

7. Each product level within a business unit must develop a marketing plan for achieving its goals. The marketing plan is one of the most important outputs of the marketing process.

Applications

Marketing Debate
What Good Is a Mission Statement?

Mission statements are often the product of much deliberation and discussion. At the same time, critics claim they sometimes lack "teeth" and specificity, or do not vary much from firm to firm and make the same empty promises.

Take a position: Mission statements are critical to a successful marketing organization *versus* Mission statements rarely provide useful marketing value.

Marketing Discussion
Marketing Planning

Consider Porter's value chain and the holistic marketing orientation model. What implications do they have for marketing planning? How would you structure a marketing plan to incorporate some of their concepts?

Marketing Excellence

>>Cisco

Cisco Systems is the worldwide leading supplier of networking equipment for the Internet. The company sells hardware (routers and switches), software, and services that make most of the Internet work. Cisco was founded in 1984 by a husband and wife team who worked in the computer operations department at Stanford University. They named the company cisco—with a lowercase *c*, short for San Francisco, and developed a logo that resembled the Golden Gate Bridge, which they frequently traveled.

Cisco went public in 1990 and the two founders left the company shortly thereafter, due to conflicting interests with the new president and CEO. Over the next decade, the company grew exponentially, led by new-product launches such as patented routers, switches, platforms, and modems—which significantly contributed to the backbone of the Internet. Cisco opened its first international offices in London and France in 1991 and has opened a number of new international offices since then. During the 1990s, Cisco acquired and successfully integrated 49 companies into its core business. As a result, the company's market capitalization grew faster than for any company in history—from $1 billion to $300 billion between 1991 and 1999. In March 2000, Cisco became the most valuable company in the world, with market capitalization peaking at $582 billion or $82 per share.

By the end of the 20th century, although the company was extremely successful, brand awareness was low—Cisco was known to many for its stock price rather than for what it actually did. Cisco developed partnerships with Sony, Matsushita, and US West to co-brand its modems with the Cisco logo in hopes of building its name recognition and brand value. In addition, the company launched its first television spots as part of a campaign entitled "Are You Ready?" In the ads, children and adults from around the world delivered facts about the power of the Internet and challenged viewers to ponder, "Are You Ready?"

Surviving the Internet bust, the company reorganized in 2001 into 11 new technology groups and a marketing organization, which planned to communicate the company's product line and competitive advantages better than it had in the past. In 2003, Cisco introduced a new marketing message, "This Is the Power of the Network. Now." The international campaign targeted corporate executives and highlighted Cisco's critical role in a complicated, technological system by using a soft-sell approach. Television commercials explained how Cisco's systems change people's lives around the world and an eight-page print ad spread didn't mention Cisco's name until the third page. Marilyn Mersereau, Cisco's vice president of corporate marketing, explained, "Clever advertising involves the reader in something that's thought-provoking and provocative and doesn't slam the brand name into you from the first page."

The year 2003 brought new opportunities as Cisco entered the consumer segment with the acquisition of Linksys, a home and small-office network gear maker. By 2004, Cisco offered several home entertainment solutions, including wireless capabilities for music, printing, video, and more. Since previous marketing strategies had targeted corporate and IT decision makers, the company launched a rebranding campaign in 2006, to increase awareness among consumers and help increase the overall value of Cisco's brand. "The Human Network" campaign tried to "humanize" the technology giant by repositioning it as more than just a supplier of switches and routers and communicating its critical role in connecting people through technology. The initial results were positive. Cisco's revenues increased 41 percent from 2006 to 2008, led by sales increases in both home and business use. By the end of 2008, Cisco's revenue topped $39.5 billion and *BusinessWeek* ranked it the 18th biggest global brand.

With its entrance into the consumer market, Cisco has had to develop unique ways to connect with consumers. One recent development is *Cisco Connected Sports,* a platform that turns sports stadiums into digitally connected interactive venues. The company already has transformed the Dallas Cowboys, New York Yankees, Kansas City Royals, Toronto Blue Jays, and Miami Dolphins stadiums into "the ultimate fan experience" and plans to add more teams to its portfolio. Fans can virtually meet the players through Telepresence, a videoconferencing system. Digital displays throughout the stadium allow fans to pull up scores from other games, order food, and view local traffic. In addition, HD flat-screen televisions throughout the stadium ensure that fans never miss a play—even in the restroom.

Today, Cisco continues to acquire companies—including 40 between 2004 and 2009—that help it expand into newer markets such as consumer electronics, business collaboration software, and computer servers. These acquisitions align with Cisco's goal of increasing overall Internet traffic, which ultimately drives demand for its networking hardware products. However, by entering into these new markets, Cisco has gained new competitors such as Microsoft, IBM, and Hewlett-Packard. To compete against them, it reaches out to both consumers and businesses in its advertising efforts, including tapping into social media such as Facebook, Twitter, and blogs.

Questions

1. How is building a brand in a business-to-business context different from doing so in the consumer market?

2. Is Cisco's plan to reach out to consumers a viable one? Why or why not?

Sources: Marguerite Reardon, "Cisco Spends Millions on Becoming Household Name." *CNET,* October 5, 2006; Michelle Kessler, "Tech Giants Build Bridge to Consumers." *USA Today,* March 13, 2006; Marla Matzer, "Cisco Faces the Masses." *Los Angeles Times,* August 20, 1998; David R. Baker, "New Ad Campaign for Cisco." *San Francisco Chronicle,* February 18, 2003; Bobby White, "Expanding into Consumer Electronics, Cisco Aims to Jazz Up Its Stodgy Image," *Wall Street Journal,* September 6, 2006, p. B1; Burt Helm, "Best Global Brands" *BusinessWeek,* September 18, 2008; Ashlee Vance, "Cisco Buys Norwegian Firm for $3 Billion." *New York Times,* October 1, 2009; Jennifer Leggio, "10 Fortune 500 Companies Doing Social Media Right." *ZDNet,* September 28, 2009.

Marketing Excellence

>>Intel

Intel makes the microprocessors found in 80 percent of the world's personal computers. Today, it is one of the most valuable brands in the world, with revenues exceeding $37 billion. In the early days, however, Intel microprocessors were known simply by their engineering numbers, such as "80386" or "80486." Since numbers can't be trademarked, competitors came out with their own "486" chips and Intel had no way to distinguish itself. Nor could consumers see Intel's products, buried deep inside their PCs. Thus, Intel had a hard time convincing consumers to pay more for its high-performance products.

As a result, Intel created the quintessential ingredient-branding marketing campaign and made history. It chose a name for its latest microprocessor introduction that could be trademarked, Pentium, and launched the "Intel Inside" campaign to build brand awareness of its whole family of microprocessors. This campaign helped move the Intel brand name outside the PC and into the minds of consumers. In order to execute the new brand strategy, it was essential that the computer manufacturers who used Intel processors support the program. Intel gave them significant rebates when they included the Intel logo in their PC ads or when they placed the "Intel Inside" sticker on the outside of their PCs and laptops.

The company created several effective and identifiable marketing campaigns in the late 1990s to become a recognizable and well-liked ingredient brand name. The "Bunny People" series featured Intel technicians dressed in brightly colored contamination suits as they danced to disco music inside a processor facility. Intel also used the famous Blue Man Group in its commercials for Pentium III and Pentium IV.

In 2003, Intel launched Centrino, a platform that included a new microprocessor, an extended battery, and wireless capabilities. The company launched a multimillion-dollar media effort around the new platform called "Unwired," which urged the wired world to "Unwire. Untangle. Unburden. Uncompromise. Unstress." "Unwired" helped the company generate $2 billion in revenue during the first nine months of the campaign.

As the PC industry slowed in the mid-2000s, Intel sought opportunities in new growth areas such as home entertainment and mobile devices. It launched two new platforms: Viiv (rhymes with "five") aimed at home entertainment enthusiasts, and Centrino Duo mobile. In addition, the company created a $2 billion global marketing campaign to help reposition Intel from a brainy microprocessor company to a "warm and fuzzy company" that offered solutions for consumers as well. As part of the campaign, Intel's new slogan "Leap Ahead" replaced the familiar "Intel Inside" campaign that had become synonymous with the Intel brand, and a new logo was created.

In 2007, Intel created the Classmate PC—a small, kid-friendly, durable, and affordable Intel processor–based computer intended for children in remote regions of the world. It was part of an initiative called Intel Learning Series, intended to help expand education in technology throughout the world.

The following year, Intel launched the Atom processor, the company's smallest processor to date, designed for mobile Internet devices, netbooks, and nettops such as the Classmate PC. Also that year, Intel introduced its most advanced microprocessor, the Intel Core i7, which focused on the needs for video, 3-D gaming, and advanced computer activities. Both processors became an instant hit. The Atom, smaller than a grain of rice, ideally powered the growing market of netbooks—mobile, light computers that weighed as little as 13 ounces. Intel sold more than 20 million Atom processors for netbooks in its first year alone and 28 million in its second year. Some analysts predict that when the Atom processor taps into the smart phone and cell phone markets, Intel could sell hundreds of millions of units in a very short amount of time.

Intel's most recent ad campaign aimed to improve the company's brand awareness was entitled "Sponsors of Tomorrow." The commercials highlighted Intel's role in changing the future of technology and took a humorous tone. In one, a middle-aged man wearing his company ID tag struts through the cafeteria as fellow employees scream, grope, and beg for his autograph. The screen reads, "Ajay Bhatt, co-inventor of the U.S.B." as the employee (played by an actor) winks at a fan. The ad ends with the line, "Our superheroes aren't like your superheroes."

As Intel's superheroes continue to create powerful microprocessors for smaller and more mobile devices, the company's brand value continues to grow, as does its influence on the future of technology.

Questions

1. Discuss how Intel changed ingredient-marketing history. What did it do so well in those initial marketing campaigns?

2. Evaluate Intel's more recent marketing efforts. Did they lose something by dropping the "Intel Inside" tagline or not?

Sources: Cliff Edwards, "Intel Everywhere?" *BusinessWeek,* March 8, 2004, pp. 56–62; Scott Van Camp, "ReadMe.1st," *Brandweek,* February 23, 2004, p. 17; "How to Become a Superbrand," *Marketing,* January 8, 2004, p. 15; Roger Slavens, "Pam Pollace, VP-Director, Corporate Marketing Group, Intel Corp," *BtoB,* December 8, 2003, p. 19; Kenneth Hein, "Study: New Brand Names Not Making Their Mark," *Brandweek,* December 8, 2003, p. 12; Heather Clancy, "Intel Thinking Outside the Box," *Computer Reseller News,* November 24, 2003, p. 14; Cynthia L. Webb, "A Chip Off the Old Recovery?" *Washingtonpost.com,* October 15, 2003; "Intel Launches Second Phase of Centrino Ads," *Technology Advertising & Branding Report,* October 6, 2003; David Kirkpatrick, "At Intel, Speed Isn't Everything," *Fortune,* February 9, 2004, p. 34; Don Clark. "Intel to Overhaul Marketing in Bid to Go Beyond PCs," *Wall Street Journal,* December 30, 2005; Stephanie Clifford, "Tech Company's Campaign to Burnish Its Brand," *New York Times,* May 6, 2009, p. B7; Tim Bajarin, "Intel Makes Moves in Mobility," *PC Magazine,* October 5, 2009.

Sample Marketing Plan | Pegasus Sports International*

1.0 Executive Summary

Pegasus Sports International is a start-up aftermarket inline skating accessory manufacturer. In addition to the aftermarket products, Pegasus is developing SkateTours, a service that takes clients out, in conjunction with a local skate shop, and provides them with an afternoon of skating using inline skates and some of Pegasus' other accessories such as SkateSails. The aftermarket skate accessory market has been largely ignored. Although there are several major manufacturers of the skates themselves, the accessory market has not been addressed. This provides Pegasus with an extraordinary opportunity for market growth. Skating is a booming sport. Currently, most of the skating is recreational. There are, however, a growing number of skating competitions, including team-oriented competitions such as skate hockey as well as individual competitions such as speed skate racing. Pegasus will work to grow these markets and develop the skate transportation market, a more utilitarian use of skating. Several of Pegasus' currently developed products have patents pending, and local market research indicates that there is great demand for these products. Pegasus will achieve fast, significant market penetration through a solid business model, long-range planning, and a strong management team that is able to execute this exciting opportunity. The three principals on the management team have over 30 years of combined personal and industry experience. This extensive experience provides Pegasus with the empirical information as well as the passion to provide the skating market with much-needed aftermarket products. Pegasus will sell its products initially through its Web site. This "Dell" direct-to-the-consumer approach will allow Pegasus to achieve higher margins and maintain a close relationship with the customers, which is essential for producing products that have a true market demand. By the end of the year, Pegasus will have also developed relationships with different skate shops and will begin to sell some of its products through retailers.

2.0 Situation Analysis

Pegasus is entering its first year of operation. Its products have been well received, and marketing will be key to the development of brand and product awareness as well as the growth of the customer base. Pegasus International offers several different aftermarket skating accessories, serving the growing inline skating industry.

2.1 Market Summary

Pegasus possesses good information about the market and knows a great deal about the common attributes of the most prized customer. This information will be leveraged to better understand who is served, what their specific needs are, and how Pegasus can better communicate with them.

Target Markets

- Recreational
- Fitness
- Speed
- Hockey
- Extreme

2.1.1 Market Demographics

The profile for the typical Pegasus customer consists of the following geographic, demographic, and behavior factors:

Geographics

- Pegasus has no set geographic target area. By leveraging the expansive reach of the Internet and multiple delivery services, Pegasus can serve both domestic and international customers.
- The total targeted population is 31 million users.

| TABLE 2.1 | Target Market Forecast |

Target Market Forecast

Potential Customers	Growth	2011	2012	2013	2014	2015	CAGR*
Recreational	10%	19,142,500	21,056,750	23,162,425	25,478,668	28,026,535	10.00%
Fitness	15%	6,820,000	7,843,000	9,019,450	10,372,368	11,928,223	15.00%
Speed	10%	387,500	426,250	468,875	515,763	567,339	10.00%
Hockey	6%	2,480,000	2,628,800	2,786,528	2,953,720	3,130,943	6.00%
Extreme	4%	2,170,000	2,256,800	2,347,072	2,440,955	2,538,593	4.00%
Total	10.48%	31,000,000	34,211,600	37,784,350	41,761,474	46,191,633	10.48%

*Compound Annual Growth Rate

Source: Adapted from a sample plan provided by and copyrighted by Palo Alto Software, Inc. Find more complete sample marketing plans at www.mplans.com. Reprinted by permission of Palo Alto Software.

Demographics

- There is an almost equal ratio between male and female users.
- Ages 13–46, with 48% clustering around ages 23–34. The recreational users tend to cover the widest age range, including young users through active adults. The fitness users tend to be ages 20–40. The speed users tend to be in their late twenties and early thirties. The hockey players are generally in their teens through their early twenties. The extreme segment is of similar age to the hockey players.
- Of the users who are over 20, 65% have an undergraduate degree or substantial undergraduate coursework.
- The adult users have a median personal income of $47,000.

Behavior Factors

- Users enjoy fitness activities not as a means for a healthy life, but as an intrinsically enjoyable activity in itself.
- Users spend money on gear, typically sports equipment.
- Users have active lifestyles that include some sort of recreation at least two to three times a week.

2.1.2 Market Needs

Pegasus is providing the skating community with a wide range of accessories for all variations of skating. The company seeks to fulfill the following benefits that are important to its customers:

- **Quality craftsmanship.** The customers work hard for their money and do not enjoy spending it on disposable products that work for only a year or two.
- **Well-thought-out designs.** The skating market has not been addressed by well-thought-out products that serve skaters' needs. Pegasus' industry experience and personal dedication to the sport will provide it with the needed information to produce insightfully designed products.   .
- **Customer service.** Exemplary service is required to build a sustainable business that has a loyal customer base.

2.1.3 Market Trends

Pegasus will distinguish itself by marketing products not previously available to skaters. The emphasis in the past has been to sell skates and very few replacement parts. The number of skaters is not restricted to any one single country, continent, or age group, so there is a world market. Pegasus has products for virtually every group of skaters. The fastest-growing segment of this sport is the fitness skater. Therefore, the marketing is being directed toward this group. BladeBoots will enable users to enter establishments without having to remove their skates. BladeBoots will be aimed at the recreational skater, the largest segment. SkateAids, on the other hand, are great for everyone.

The sport of skating will also grow through SkateSailing. This sport is primarily for the medium-to-advanced skater, and its growth potential is tremendous. The sails that Pegasus has manufactured have been sold in Europe, following a pattern similar to windsurfing. Windsailing originated in Santa Monica but did not take off until it had already grown big in Europe.

Another trend is group skating. More and more groups are getting together on skating excursions in cities all over the world. For example, San Francisco has night group skating that attracts hundreds of people. The market trends are showing continued growth in all directions of skating.

2.1.4 Market Growth

With the price of skates going down due to competition by so many skate companies, the market has had steady growth throughout the world, although sales had slowed down in some markets. The growth statistics for 2007 were estimated to be over 35 million units. More and more people are discovering—and in many cases rediscovering—the health benefits and fun of skating.

2.2 SWOT Analysis

The following SWOT analysis captures the key strengths and weaknesses within the company and describes the opportunities and threats facing Pegasus.

2.2.1 Strengths

- In-depth industry experience and insight
- Creative, yet practical product designers
- The use of a highly efficient, flexible business model utilizing direct customer sales and distribution

2.2.2 Weaknesses

- The reliance on outside capital necessary to grow the business
- A lack of retailers who can work face-to-face with the customer to generate brand and product awareness
- The difficulty of developing brand awareness as a start-up company

2.2.3 Opportunities

- Participation within a growing industry
- Decreased product costs through economy of scale
- The ability to leverage other industry participants' marketing efforts to help grow the general market

2.2.4 Threats

- Future/potential competition from an already established market participant
- A slump in the economy that could have a negative effect on people's spending of discretionary income on fitness/recreational products
- The release of a study that calls into question the safety of skating or the inability to prevent major skating-induced traumas

2.3 Competition

Pegasus Sports International is forming its own market. Although there are a few companies that do make sails and foils that a few skaters are using, Pegasus is the only brand that is truly designed for and by skaters. The few competitors' sails on the market are not designed for skating, but for windsurfing or for skateboards. In the case of foils, storage and carrying are not practical. There are different indirect competitors who are manufacturers of the actual skates. After many years in the market, these companies have yet to become direct competitors by manufacturing accessories for the skates that they make.

2.4 Product Offering

Pegasus Sports International now offers several products:

- The first product that has been developed is BladeBoots, a cover for the wheels and frame of inline skates, which allows skaters to enter places that normally would not allow them in with skates on. BladeBoots come with a small pouch and belt that converts to a well-designed skate carrier.

- The second product is SkateSails. These sails are specifically designed for use while skating. Feedback that Pegasus has received from skaters indicates skatesailing could become a very popular sport. Trademarking this product is currently in progress.

- The third product, SkateAid, will be in production by the end of the year. Other ideas for products are under development, but will not be disclosed until Pegasus can protect them through pending patent applications.

2.5 Keys to Success

The keys to success are designing and producing products that meet market demand. In addition, Pegasus must ensure total customer satisfaction. If these keys to success are achieved, it will become a profitable, sustainable company.

2.6 Critical Issues

As a start-up business, Pegasus is still in the early stages. The critical issues are for Pegasus to:

- Establish itself as the premier skating accessory company.
- Pursue controlled growth that dictates that payroll expenses will never exceed the revenue base. This will help protect against recessions.
- Constantly monitor customer satisfaction, ensuring that the growth strategy will never compromise service and satisfaction levels.

3.0 Marketing Strategy

The key to the marketing strategy is focusing on the speed, health and fitness, and recreational skaters. Pegasus can cover about 80% of the skating market because it produces products geared toward each segment. Pegasus is able to address all of the different segments within the market because, although each segment is distinct in terms of its users and equipment, its products are useful to all of the different segments.

3.1 Mission

Pegasus Sports International's mission is to provide the customer with the finest skating accessories available. "We exist to attract and maintain customers. With a strict adherence to this maxim, success will be ensured. Our services and products will exceed the expectations of the customers."

3.2 Marketing Objectives

- Maintain positive, strong growth each quarter (notwithstanding seasonal sales patterns).
- Achieve a steady increase in market penetration.
- Decrease customer acquisition costs by 1.5% per quarter.

3.3 Financial Objectives

- Increase the profit margin by 1% per quarter through efficiency and economy-of-scale gains.
- Maintain a significant research and development budget (as a percentage relative to sales) to spur future product developments.
- Achieve a double- to triple-digit growth rate for the first three years.

3.4 Target Markets

With a world skating market of over 31 million that is steadily growing (statistics released by the Sporting Goods Manufacturers Association), the niche has been created. Pegasus' aim is to expand this market by promoting SkateSailing, a new sport that is popular in both Santa Monica and Venice Beach in California. The Sporting Goods Manufacturers Association survey indicates that skating now has more participation than football, softball, skiing, and snowboarding combined. The breakdown of participation in skating is as follows: 1+% speed (growing), 8% hockey (declining), 7% extreme/aggressive (declining), 22% fitness (nearly 7 million—the fastest growing), and 61% recreational (first-timers). Pegasus' products are targeting the fitness and recreational groups, because they are the fastest growing. These groups are gearing themselves toward health and fitness, and combined, they can easily grow to 85% (or 26 million) of the market in the next five years.

3.5 Positioning

Pegasus will position itself as the premier aftermarket skating accessory company. This positioning will be achieved by leveraging Pegasus' competitive edge: industry experience and passion. Pegasus is a skating company formed by skaters for skaters. Its management is able to use its vast experience and personal passion for the sport to develop innovative, useful accessories for a broad range of skaters.

3.6 Strategies

The single objective is to position Pegasus as the premier skating accessory manufacturer, serving the domestic market as well as the international market. The marketing strategy will seek to first create customer awareness concerning the offered products and services and then develop the customer base. The message that Pegasus will seek to communicate is that it offers the best-designed, most useful skating accessories. This message will be communicated through a variety of methods. The first will be the Pegasus Web site, which will provide a rich source of product information and offer consumers the opportunity to purchase. A lot of time and money will be invested in the site to provide the customer with the perception of total professionalism and utility for Pegasus' products and services.

The second marketing method will be advertisements placed in numerous industry magazines. The skating industry is supported by several different glossy magazines designed to promote the industry as a whole. In addition, a number of smaller periodicals serve the smaller market segments within the skating industry. The last method of communication is the use of printed sales literature. The two previously mentioned marketing methods will create demand for the sales literature, which will be sent out to customers. The cost of the sales literature will be fairly minimal, because it will use the already-compiled information from the Web site.

3.7 Marketing Program

Pegasus' marketing program is comprised of the following approaches to pricing, distribution, advertising and promotion, and customer service.

- **Pricing.** This will be based on a per-product retail price.
- **Distribution.** Initially, Pegasus will use a direct-to-consumer distribution model. Over time, it will use retailers as well.
- **Advertising and promotion.** Several different methods will be used for the advertising effort.
- **Customer service.** Pegasus will strive to achieve benchmarked levels of customer care.

3.8 Marketing Research

Pegasus is blessed with the good fortune of being located in the center of the skating world: Venice, California. It will be able to leverage this opportune location by working with many of the different skaters that live in the area. Pegasus was able to test all of its products not only with its principals, who are accomplished skaters, but also with the many other dedicated and "newbie" users located in Venice. The extensive product testing by a wide variety of users provided Pegasus with valuable product feedback and has led to several design improvements.

4.0 Financials

This section will offer the financial overview of Pegasus related to marketing activities. Pegasus will address break-even analysis, sales forecasts, expense forecast, and indicate how these activities link to the marketing strategy.

4.1 Break-Even Analysis

The break-even analysis indicates that $7,760 will be required in monthly sales revenue to reach the break-even point.

TABLE 4.1	Break-Even Analysis
Break-Even Analysis:	
Monthly Units Break-Even	62
Monthly Sales Break-Even	$ 7,760
Assumptions:	
Average Per-Unit Revenue	$125.62
Average Per-Unit Variable Cost	$ 22.61
Estimated Monthly Fixed Cost	$ 6,363

4.2 Sales Forecast

Pegasus feels that the sales forecast figures are conservative. It will steadily increase sales as the advertising budget allows. Although the target market forecast (Table 2.1) listed all of the potential customers divided into separate groups, the sales forecast groups customers into two categories: recreational and competitive. Reducing the number of categories allows the reader to quickly discern information, making the chart more functional.

Monthly Sales Forecast

TABLE 4.2	Sales Forecast		
Sales Forecast			
Sales	**2011**	**2012**	**2013**
Recreational	$455,740	$598,877	$687,765
Competitive	$ 72,918	$ 95,820	$110,042
Total Sales	$528,658	$694,697	$797,807
Direct Cost of Sales	**2011**	**2012**	**2013**
Recreational	$ 82,033	$107,798	$123,798
Competitive	$ 13,125	$ 17,248	$ 19,808
Subtotal Cost of Sales	$ 95,158	$125,046	$143,606

4.3 Expense Forecast

The expense forecast will be used as a tool to keep the department on target and provide indicators when corrections/modifications are needed for the proper implementation of the marketing plan.

Milestones

TABLE 4.3 　Milestones

	Plan				
Milestones	Start Date	End Date	Budget	Manager	Department
Marketing plan completion	1/1/11	2/1/11	$ 0	Stan	Marketing
Web site completion	1/1/11	3/15/11	$20,400	outside firm	Marketing
Advertising campaign #1	1/1/11	6/30/11	$ 3,500	Stan	Marketing
Advertising campaign #2	3/1/11	12/30/11	$ 4,550	Stan	Marketing
Development of the retail channel	1/1/11	11/30/11	$ 0	Stan	Marketing
Totals			$28,450		

Monthly Expense Budget

TABLE 4.4 　Marketing Expense Budget

Marketing Expense Budget	2011	2012	2013
Web Site	$ 25,000	$ 8,000	$ 10,000
Advertisements	$ 8,050	$ 15,000	$ 20,000
Printed Material	$ 1,725	$ 2,000	$ 3,000
Total Sales and Marketing Expenses	$ 34,775	$ 25,000	$ 33,000
Percent of Sales	6.58%	3.60%	4.14%
Contribution Margin	$398,725	$544,652	$621,202
Contribution Margin/Sales	75.42%	78.40%	77.86%

5.0 Controls

The purpose of Pegasus' marketing plan is to serve as a guide for the organization. The following areas will be monitored to gauge performance:

- Revenue: monthly and annual
- Expenses: monthly and annual
- Customer satisfaction
- New-product development

5.1 Implementation

The following milestones identify the key marketing programs. It is important to accomplish each one on time and on budget.

5.2 Marketing Organization

Stan Blade will be responsible for the marketing activities.

5.3 Contingency Planning

Difficulties and Risks

- Problems generating visibility, a function of being an Internet-based start-up organization
- An entry into the market by an already-established market competitor

Worst-Case Risks

- Determining that the business cannot support itself on an ongoing basis
- Having to liquidate equipment or intellectual capital to cover liabilities

The severe economic recession that began in 2008 led many firms to cut their prices and use sales to try to retain customers.

In This Chapter, We Will Address the Following Questions

1. What are the components of a modern marketing information system?

2. What are useful internal records for such a system?

3. What makes up a marketing intelligence system?

4. What are some influential macroenvironment developments?

5. How can companies accurately measure and forecast demand?

Collecting Information and Forecasting Demand

Making marketing decisions in a fast-changing world is both an art and a science. To provide context, insight, and inspiration for marketing decision making, companies must possess comprehensive, up-to-date information about macro trends, as well as about micro effects particular to their business. Holistic marketers recognize that the marketing environment is constantly presenting new opportunities and threats, and they understand the importance of continuously monitoring, forecasting, and adapting to that environment.

 The severe credit crunch and economic slowdown of 2008–2009 brought profound changes in consumer behavior as shoppers cut and reallocated spending. Sales of discretionary purchases like toys, apparel, jewelry, and home furnishings dropped. Sales of luxury brands like Mercedes—driven for years by free-spending baby boomers—declined by a staggering one-third.

Meanwhile, brands that offered simple, affordable solutions prospered. General Mills's revenues from such favorites as Cheerios, Wheaties, Progresso soup, and Hamburger Helper rose. Consumers also changed how and where they shopped, and sales of low-priced private label brands soared. Virtually all marketers were asking themselves whether a new age of prudence and frugality had emerged and, if so, what would be the appropriate response.

Firms are adjusting the way they do business for more reasons than just the economy. Virtually every industry has been touched by dramatic shifts in the technological, demographic, social-cultural, natural, and political-legal environments. In this chapter, we consider how firms can develop processes to identify and track important macroenvironment trends. We also outline how marketers can develop good sales forecasts. Chapter 4 will review how they conduct more customized research on specific marketing problems.

Components of a Modern Marketing Information System

The major responsibility for identifying significant marketplace changes falls to the company's marketers. Marketers have two advantages for the task: disciplined methods for collecting information, and time spent interacting with customers and observing competitors and other outside groups. Some firms have marketing information systems that provide rich detail about buyer wants, preferences, and behavior.

DuPont DuPont commissioned marketing studies to uncover personal pillow behavior for its Dacron Polyester unit, which supplies filling to pillow makers and sells its own Comforel brand. One challenge is that people don't give up their old pillows: 37 percent of one sample described their relationship with their pillow as being like that of "an old married couple," and an additional 13 percent said their pillow was like a "childhood friend." Respondents fell into distinct groups in terms of pillow behavior: stackers (23 percent), plumpers (20 percent), rollers or folders (16 percent), cuddlers (16 percent), and smashers, who pound their pillows into a more comfy shape (10 percent). Women were more likely to plump, men to fold. The prevalence of stackers led the company to sell more pillows packaged as pairs, as well as to market different levels of softness or firmness.[1]

Marketers also have extensive information about how consumption patterns vary across and within countries. On a per capita basis, for example, the Swiss consume the most chocolate, the Czechs the most beer, the Portuguese the most wine, and the Greeks the most cigarettes. Table 3.1 summarizes these and other comparisons across countries. Consider regional differences within the United States: Seattle's residents buy more toothbrushes per person than in any other U.S. city, people in Salt Lake City eat more candy bars, New Orleans residents use more ketchup, and people in Miami drink more prune juice.[2]

TABLE 3.1   A Global Profile of Extremes

Highest fertility rate	Niger	6.88 children per woman
Highest education expenditure as percent of GDP	Kiribati	17.8% of GDP
Highest number of mobile phone subscribers	China	547,286,000
Largest number of airports	United States	14,951 airports
Highest military expenditure as percent of GDP	Oman	11.40% of GDP
Largest refugee population	Pakistan	21,075,000 people
Highest divorce rate	Aruba	4.4 divorces per 1,000 population
Highest color TV ownership per 100 households	United Arab Emirates	99.7 TVs
Mobile telephone subscribers per capita	Lithuania	138.1 subscribers per 100 people
Highest cinema attendance	India	1,473,400,000 cinema visits
Biggest beer drinkers per capita	Czech Republic	81.9 litres per capita
Biggest wine drinkers per capita	Portugal	33.1 litres per capita
Highest number of smokers per capita	Greece	8.2 cigarettes per person per day
Highest GDP per person	Luxembourg	$87,490
Largest aid donors as % of GDP	Sweden	1.03% of GDP
Most economically dependent on agriculture	Liberia	66% of GDP
Highest population in workforce	Cayman Islands	69.20%
Highest percent of women in workforce	Belarus	53.30%
Most crowded road networks	Qatar	283.6 vehicle per km of road
Most deaths in road accidents	South Africa	31 killed per 100,000 population
Most tourist arrivals	France	79,083,000
Highest life expectancy	Andorra	83.5 years
Highest diabetes rate	United Arab Emirates	19.5% of population aged 20–79

Source: *CIA World Fact Book,* https://www.cia.gov/library/publications/the-world-factbook/geos/xx.html, accessed July 24, 2009; *The Economist's Pocket World in Figures,* 2009 edition, www.economist.com.

A well-researched and well-executed marketing campaign for the state of Michigan increased tourism and state tax revenue.

Companies with superior information can choose their markets better, develop better offerings, and execute better marketing planning. The Michigan Economic Development Corporation (MEDC) studied the demographic information of its visitors and those of competing Midwestern cities to create a new marketing message and tourism campaign. The information helped MEDC attract 3.8 million new trips to Michigan, $805 million in new visitor spending, and $56 million in incremental state tax revenue over the period 2004–2008.[3]

Every firm must organize and distribute a continuous flow of information to its marketing managers. A **marketing information system (MIS)** consists of people, equipment, and procedures to gather, sort, analyze, evaluate, and distribute needed, timely, and accurate information to marketing decision makers. It relies on internal company records, marketing intelligence activities, and marketing research. We'll discuss the first two components here, and the third one in the next chapter.

The company's marketing information system should be a mixture of what managers think they need, what they really need, and what is economically feasible. An internal MIS committee can interview a cross-section of marketing managers to discover their information needs. 🖥 Table 3.2 displays some useful questions to ask them.

TABLE 3.2 🖥 Information Needs Probes
1. What decisions do you regularly make?
2. What information do you need to make these decisions?
3. What information do you regularly get?
4. What special studies do you periodically request?
5. What information would you want that you are not getting now?
6. What information would you want daily? Weekly? Monthly? Yearly?
7. What online or offline newsletters, briefings, blogs, reports, or magazines would you like to see on a regular basis?
8. What topics would you like to be kept informed of?
9. What data analysis and reporting programs would you want?
10. What are the four most helpful improvements that could be made in the present marketing information system?

Internal Records

To spot important opportunities and potential problems, marketing managers rely on internal reports of orders, sales, prices, costs, inventory levels, receivables, and payables.

The Order-to-Payment Cycle

The heart of the internal records system is the order-to-payment cycle. Sales representatives, dealers, and customers send orders to the firm. The sales department prepares invoices, transmits copies to various departments, and back-orders out-of-stock items. Shipped items generate shipping and billing documents that go to various departments. Because customers favor firms that can promise timely delivery, companies need to perform these steps quickly and accurately. Many use the Internet and extranets to improve the speed, accuracy, and efficiency of the order-to-payment cycle.

Fossil Group   Fossil Group Australia designs and distributes accessories and apparel globally. Its account executives lacked the latest information about pricing and inventory while taking wholesale orders. High demand items were often out of stock, creating problem for retailers. After the firm deployed a mobile sales solution that connected account executives with current inventory data, the number of sales tied up in back orders fell 80 percent. The company can now provide retailers with actual inventory levels and ship orders in hours instead of days.[4]

Sales Information Systems

Marketing managers need timely and accurate reports on current sales. Walmart operates a sales and inventory data warehouse that captures data on every item for every customer, every store, every day and refreshes it every hour. Consider the experience of Panasonic.

Panasonic   Panasonic makes digital cameras, plasma televisions, and other consumer electronics. After missing revenue goals, the company decided to adopt a vendor-managed inventory solution. Inventory distribution then came in line with consumption, and availability of products to customers jumped from 70 percent to 95 percent. The average weeks that product supply sat in Panasonic's channels went from 25 weeks to just 5 weeks within a year, and unit sales of the targeted plasma television rose from 20,000 to approximately 100,000. Best Buy, the initial retailer covered by the vendor-managed inventory model, has since elevated Panasonic from a Tier 3 Supplier to a Tier 1 "Go-To" Brand for plasma televisions.[5]

Panasonic's new vendor-managed inventory system met with marketplace success, including from retailers.

Companies that make good use of "cookies," records of Web site usage stored on personal browsers, are smart users of targeted marketing. Many consumers are happy to cooperate: A recent survey showed that 49 percent of individuals agreed cookies are important to them when using the Internet. Not only do they *not* delete cookies, but they also expect customized marketing appeals and deals once they accept them.

Companies must carefully interpret the sales data, however, so as not to draw the wrong conclusions. Michael Dell gave this illustration: "If you have three yellow Mustangs sitting on a dealer's lot and a customer wants a red one, the salesman may be really good at figuring out how to sell the yellow Mustang. So the yellow Mustang gets sold, and a signal gets sent back to the factory that, hey, people want yellow Mustangs."[6]

Databases, Data Warehousing, and Data Mining

Companies organize their information into customer, product, and salesperson databases—and then combine their data. The customer database will contain every customer's name, address, past transactions, and sometimes even demographics and psychographics (activities, interests, and opinions). Instead of sending a mass "carpet bombing" mailing of a new offer to every customer in its database, a company will rank its customers according to factors such as purchase recency, frequency, and monetary value (RFM) and send the offer to only the highest-scoring customers. Besides saving on mailing expenses, such manipulation of data can often achieve a double-digit response rate.

Companies make these data easily accessible to their decision makers. Analysts can "mine" the data and garner fresh insights into neglected customer segments, recent customer trends, and other useful information. Managers can cross-tabulate customer information with product and salesperson information to yield still-deeper insights. Using in-house technology, Wells Fargo can track and analyze every bank transaction made by its 10 million retail customers—whether at ATMs, at bank branches, or online. When it combines transaction data with personal information provided by customers, Wells Fargo can come up with targeted offerings to coincide with a customer's life-changing event. As a result, compared with the industry average of 2.2 products per customer, Wells Fargo sells 4 products.[7] Best Buy is also taking advantage of these new rich databases.

Best Buy   Best Buy has assembled a 15-plus terabyte database with seven years of data on 75 million households. It captures information about every interaction—from phone calls and mouse clicks to delivery and rebate-check addresses—and then deploys sophisticated algorithms to classify over three-quarters of its customers, or more than 100 million individuals, into profiled categories such as "Buzz" (the young technology buff), "Jill" (the suburban soccer mom), "Barry" (the wealthy professional guy), and "Ray" (the family man). The firm also applies a customer lifetime value model that measures transaction-level profitability and factors in customer behaviors that increase or decrease the value of the relationship. Knowing so much about consumers allows Best Buy to employ precision marketing and customer-triggered incentive programs with positive response rates.[8]

Best Buy uses a massive database to develop profiles with which to classify its customers.

Marketing Intelligence

The Marketing Intelligence System

A **marketing intelligence system** is a set of procedures and sources that managers use to obtain everyday information about developments in the marketing environment. The internal records system supplies *results* data, but the marketing intelligence system supplies *happenings* data. Marketing managers collect marketing intelligence in a variety of different ways, such as by reading books, newspapers, and trade publications; talking to customers, suppliers, and distributors; monitoring social media on the Internet; and meeting with other company managers.

Before the Internet, sometimes you just had to go out in the field, literally, and watch the competition. This is what oil and gas entrepreneur T. Boone Pickens did. Describing how he learned about a rival's drilling activity, Pickens recalls, "We would have someone who would watch [the rival's] drilling floor from a half mile away with field glasses. Our competitor didn't like it but there wasn't anything they could do about it. Our spotters would watch the joints and drill pipe. They would count them; each [drill] joint was 30 feet long. By adding up all the joints, you would be able to tally the depth of the well." Pickens knew that the deeper well, the more costly it would be for his rival to get the oil or gas up to the surface, and this information provided him with an immediate competitive advantage.[9]

Marketing intelligence gathering must be legal and ethical. In 2006, the private intelligence firm Diligence paid auditor KPMG $1.7 million for having illegally infiltrated it to acquire an audit of a Bermuda-based investment firm for a Russian conglomerate. Diligence's cofounder posed as a British intelligence officer and convinced a member of the audit team to share confidential documents.[10]

A company can take eight possible actions to improve the quantity and quality of its marketing intelligence. After describing the first seven, we devote special attention to the eighth, collecting marketing intelligence on the Internet.

- **_Train and motivate the sales force to spot and report new developments._** The company must "sell" its sales force on their importance as intelligence gatherers. Grace Performance Chemicals, a division of W. R. Grace, supplies materials and chemicals to the construction and packaging industries. Its sales reps were instructed to observe the innovative ways customers used its products in order to suggest possible new products. Some were using Grace water-proofing materials to soundproof their cars and patch boots and tents. Seven new-product ideas emerged, worth millions in sales.[11]

- **_Motivate distributors, retailers, and other intermediaries to pass along important intelligence._** Marketing intermediaries are often closer to the customer and competition and can offer helpful insights. ConAgra has initiated a study with some of its retailers such as Safeway, Kroger, and Walmart to study how and why people buy its foods. Finding that shoppers who bought their Orville Redenbacher and Act II brands of popcorn tended to also buy Coke, ConAgra worked with the retailers to develop in-store displays for both products. Combining retailers' data with its own qualitative insights, ConAgra learned that many mothers switched to time-saving meals and snacks when school started. It launched its "Seasons of Mom" campaign to help grocers adjust to seasonal shifts in household needs.[12]

- **_Hire external experts to collect intelligence._** Many companies hire specialists to gather marketing intelligence.[13] Service providers and retailers send mystery shoppers to their stores to assess cleanliness of facilities, product quality, and the way employees treat customers. Health care facilities' use of mystery patients has led to improved estimates of wait times, better explanations of medical procedures, and less-stressful programming on the waiting room TV.[14]

- **_Network internally and externally._** The firm can purchase competitors' products, attend open houses and trade shows, read competitors' published reports, attend stockholders' meetings, talk to employees, collect competitors' ads, consult with suppliers, and look up news stories about competitors.

- **_Set up a customer advisory panel._** Members of advisory panels might include the company's largest, most outspoken, most sophisticated, or most representative customers. For example, GlaxoSmithKline sponsors an online community devoted to weight loss and says it is learning far more than it could have gleamed from focus groups on topics from packaging its weight-loss pill to where to place in-store marketing.[15]

- **_Take advantage of government-related data resources._** The U.S. Census Bureau provides an in-depth look at the population swings, demographic groups, regional migrations, and changing family structure of the estimated 304,059,724 people in the United States (as of July 1, 2008). Census marketer Nielsen Claritas cross-references census figures with consumer surveys and its own grassroots research for clients such as The Weather Channel, BMW, and Sovereign Bank. Partnering with "list houses" that provide customer phone and address information, Nielsen Claritas can help firms select and purchase mailing lists with specific clusters.[16]

- **_Purchase information from outside research firms and vendors._** Well-known data suppliers include firms such as the A.C. Nielsen Company and Information Resources Inc. They collect information about product sales in a variety of categories and consumer exposure to various media. They also gather consumer-panel data much more cheaply than marketers manage on their own. Biz360 and its online content partners, for example, provide real-time coverage and analysis of news media and consumer opinion information from over 70,000 traditional and social media sources (print, broadcast, Web sites, blogs, and message boards).[17]

Collecting Marketing Intelligence on the Internet

Thanks to the explosion of outlets available on the Internet, online customer review boards, discussion forums, chat rooms, and blogs can distribute one customer's experiences or evaluation to other potential buyers and, of course, to marketers seeking information about the consumers and the competition. There are five main ways marketers can research competitors' product strengths and weaknesses online.[18]

- **Independent customer goods and service review forums.** Independent forums include Web sites such as Epinions.com, RateItAll.com, ConsumerReview.com, and Bizrate.com. Bizrate.com collects millions of consumer reviews of stores and products each year from two sources: its 1.3 million volunteer members, and feedback from stores that allow Bizrate.com to collect it directly from their customers as they make purchases.
- **Distributor or sales agent feedback sites.** Feedback sites offer positive and negative product or service reviews, but the stores or distributors have built the sites themselves. Amazon.com offers an interactive feedback opportunity through which buyers, readers, editors, and others can review all products on the site, especially books. Elance.com is an online professional services provider that allows contractors to describe their experience and level of satisfaction with subcontractors.
- **Combo sites offering customer reviews and expert opinions.** Combination sites are concentrated in financial services and high-tech products that require professional knowledge. ZDNet.com, an online advisor on technology products, offers customer comments and evaluations based on ease of use, features, and stability, along with expert reviews. The advantage is that a product supplier can compare experts' opinions with those of consumers.
- **Customer complaint sites.** Customer complaint forums are designed mainly for dissatisfied customers. PlanetFeedback.com allows customers to voice unfavorable experiences with specific companies. Another site, Complaints.com, lets customers vent their frustrations with particular firms or offerings.
- **Public blogs.** Tens of millions of blogs and social networks exist online, offering personal opinions, reviews, ratings, and recommendations on virtually any topic—and their numbers continue to grow. Firms such as Nielsen's BuzzMetrics and Scout Labs analyze blogs and social networks to provide insights into consumer sentiment.

Communicating and Acting on Marketing Intelligence

In some companies, the staff scans the Internet and major publications, abstracts relevant news, and disseminates a news bulletin to marketing managers. The competitive intelligence function works best when it is closely coordinated with the decision-making process.[19]

Ticket broker StubHub monitors online activity so that when confusion arose over a rainout at a New York Yankees game, for instance, it was able to respond quickly.

Given the speed of the Internet, it is important to act quickly on information gleaned online. Here are two companies that benefited from a proactive approach to online information:[20]

- When ticket broker StubHub detected a sudden surge of negative sentiment about its brand after confusion arose about refunds for a rain-delayed Yankees–Red Sox game, it jumped in to offer appropriate discounts and credits. The director of customer service observed, "This [episode] is a canary in a coal mine for us."
- When Coke's monitoring software spotted a Twitter post that went to 10,000 followers from an upset consumer who couldn't redeem a prize from a MyCoke rewards program, Coke quickly posted an apology on his Twitter profile and offered to help resolve the situation. After the consumer got the prize, he changed his Twitter avatar to a photo of himself holding a Coke bottle.

Analyzing the Macroenvironment

Successful companies recognize and respond profitably to unmet needs and trends.

Needs and Trends

Enterprising individuals and companies manage to create new solutions to unmet needs. Dockers was created to meet the needs of baby boomers who could no longer fit into their jeans and wanted a physically and psychologically comfortable pair of pants. Let's distinguish among fads, trends, and megatrends.

- A **fad** is "unpredictable, short-lived, and without social, economic, and political significance." A company can cash in on a fad such as Crocs clogs, Elmo TMX dolls, and Pokémon gifts and toys, but getting it right requires luck and good timing.[21]
- A direction or sequence of events with momentum and durability, a **trend** is more predictable and durable than a fad; trends reveal the shape of the future and can provide strategic direction. A trend toward health and nutrition awareness has brought increased government regulation and negative publicity for firms seen as peddling unhealthy food. Macaroni Grill revamped its menu to include more low-calorie and low-fat offerings after a wave of bad press: *The Today Show* called its chicken and artichoke sandwich "the calorie equivalent of 16 Fudgesicles," and in its annual list of unhealthy restaurant dishes, *Men's Health* declared its 1,630 calorie dessert ravioli the "worst dessert in America."[22]
- A **megatrend** is a "large social, economic, political, and technological change [that] is slow to form, and once in place, influences us for some time—between seven and ten years, or longer."[23]
- To help marketers spot cultural shifts that might bring new opportunities or threats, several firms offer social-cultural forecasts. The Yankelovich Monitor interviews 2,500 people nationally each year and has tracked 35 social value and lifestyle trends since 1971, such as "anti-bigness," "mysticism," "living for today," "away from possessions," and "sensuousness." A new market opportunity doesn't guarantee success, of course, even if the new product is technically feasible. Market research is necessary to determine an opportunity's profit potential.

Identifying the Major Forces

The end of the first decade of the new century brought a series of new challenges: the steep decline of the stock market, which affected savings, investment, and retirement funds; increasing unemployment; corporate scandals; stronger indications of global warming and other signs of deterioration in the national environment; and of course, the rise of terrorism. These dramatic events were accompanied by the continuation of many existing trends that have already profoundly influenced the global landscape.[24]

Firms must monitor six major forces in the broad environment: demographic, economic, social-cultural, natural, technological, and political-legal. We'll describe them separately, but remember that their interactions will lead to new opportunities and threats. For example, explosive population growth (demographic) leads to more resource depletion and pollution (natural), which leads consumers to call for more laws (political-legal), which stimulate new technological solutions and products (technological) that, if they are affordable (economic), may actually change attitudes and behavior (social-cultural).

The Demographic Environment

Demographic developments often move at a fairly predictable pace. The main one marketers monitor is *population,* including the size and growth rate of population in cities, regions, and nations; age distribution and ethnic mix; educational levels; household patterns; and regional characteristics and movements.

WORLDWIDE POPULATION GROWTH World population growth is explosive: Earth's population totaled 6.8 billion in 2010 and will exceed 9 billion by 2040.[25] Table 3.3 offers an interesting perspective.[26]

Population growth is highest in countries and communities that can least afford it. Developing regions of the world currently account for 84 percent of the world population and are growing at 1 percent to 2 percent per year; the population in developed countries is growing at only 0.3 percent.[27] In developing countries, modern medicine is lowering the death rate, but the birthrate remains fairly stable.

A growing population does not mean growing markets unless there is sufficient purchasing power. Care and education of children can raise the standard of living but are nearly impossible to accomplish in most developing countries. Nonetheless, companies that carefully analyze these markets can find major opportunities. Sometimes the lessons from developing markets are helping businesses in developed markets. See "Marketing Insight: Finding Gold at the Bottom of the Pyramid."

POPULATION AGE MIX Mexico has a very young population and rapid population growth. At the other extreme is Italy, with one of the world's oldest populations. Milk, diapers, school supplies, and toys will be more important products in Mexico than in Italy.

There is a global trend toward an aging population. In 1950, there were only 131 million people 65 and older; in 1995, their number had almost tripled to 371 million. By 2050, one of ten people worldwide will be 65 or older. In the United States, boomers—those born between 1946 and 1964—represent a market of some 36 million, about 12 percent of the population. By 2011, the 65-and-over population will be growing faster than the population as a whole in each of the 50 states.[28]

Marketers generally divide the population into six age groups: preschool children, school-age children, teens, young adults age 20 to 40, middle-aged adults 40 to 65, and older adults 65 and

TABLE 3.3 ▭   The World as a Village
If the world were a village of 100 people:
• 61 villagers would be Asian (of that, 20 would be Chinese and 17 would be Indian), 14 would be African, 11 would be European, 8 would be Latin or South American, 5 would be North American, and only one of the villagers would be from Australia, Oceania, or Antarctica.
• At least 18 villagers would be unable to read or write but 33 would have cellular phones and 16 would be online on the Internet.
• 18 villagers would be under 10 years of age and 11 would be over 60 years old. There would be an equal number of males and females.
• There would be 18 cars in the village.
• 63 villagers would have inadequate sanitation.
• 32 villagers would be Christians, 20 would be Muslims, 14 would be Hindus, 6 would be Buddhists, 16 would be non-religious, and the remaining 12 would be members of other religions.
• 30 villagers would be unemployed or underemployed, while of those 70 who would work, 28 would work in agriculture (primary sector), 14 would work in industry (secondary sector), and the remaining 28 would work in the service sector (tertiary sector).
• 53 villagers would live on less than two U.S. dollars a day. One villager would have AIDS, 26 villagers would smoke, and 14 villagers would be obese.
• By the end of a year, one villager would die and two new villagers would be born so the population would climb to 101.

Source: David J. Smith and Shelagh Armstrong, *If the World Were a Village: A Book About the World's People,* 2nd ed. (Tonawanda, NY: Kids Can Press, 2002).

Marketing Insight

Finding Gold at the Bottom of the Pyramid

Business writer C.K. Prahalad believes much innovation can come from developments in emerging markets such as China and India. He estimates there are 5 billion unserved and underserved people at the so-called "bottom of the pyramid." One study showed that 4 billion people live on $2 or less a day. Firms operating in those markets have had to learn how to do more with less.

In Bangalore, India, Narayana Hrudayalaya Hospital charges a flat fee of $1,500 for heart bypass surgery that costs 50 times as much in the United States. The hospital has low labor and operating expenses and an assembly-line view of care that has specialists focus on their own area. The approach works—the hospital's mortality rates are half those of U.S. hospitals. Narayana also operates on hundreds of infants for free and profitably insures 2.5 million poor Indians against serious illness for 11 cents a month.

Overseas firms are also finding creative solutions in developing countries. In Brazil, India, Eastern Europe, and other markets, Microsoft launched its pay-as-you-go FlexGo program, which allows users to pre-pay to use a fully loaded PC only for as long as wanted or needed without having to pay the full price the PC would normally command. When the payment runs out, the PC stops operating and the user prepays again to restart it.

Other firms find "reverse innovation" advantages by developing products in countries like China and India and then distributing them globally. After GE successfully introduced a $1,000 handheld electro-cardiogram device for rural India and a portable, PC-based ultrasound

machine for rural China, it began to sell them in the United States. Nestlé repositioned its low-fat Maggi brand dried noodles—a popular, low-priced meal for rural Pakistan and India—as a budget-friendly health food in Australia and New Zealand.

Sources: C.K. Prahalad, *The Fortune at the Bottom of the Pyramid* (Upper Saddle River, NJ: Wharton School Publishing, 2010); Bill Breen, "C.K. Prahalad: Pyramid Schemer," *Fast Company*, March 2007, p. 79; Pete Engardio, "Business Prophet: How C.K. Prahalad Is Changing the Way CEOs Think," *BusinessWeek*, January 23, 2006, pp. 68–73; Reena Jane, "Inspiration from Emerging Economies," *BusinessWeek*, March 23 and 30, 2009, pp. 38–41; Jeffrey R. Immelt, Vijay Govindarajan, and Chris Trimble, "How GE Is Disrupting Itself," *Harvard Business Review*, October 2009, pp. 56–65; Peter J. Williamson and Ming Zeng, "Value-for-Money Strategies for Recessionary Times," *Harvard Business Review*, March 2009, pp. 66–74.

older. Some marketers focus on **cohorts**, groups of individuals born during the same time period who travel through life together. The defining moments they experience as they come of age and become adults (roughly ages 17 through 24) can stay with them for a lifetime and influence their values, preferences, and buying behaviors.

ETHNIC AND OTHER MARKETS Ethnic and racial diversity varies across countries. At one extreme is Japan, where almost everyone is Japanese; at the other is the United States, where nearly 25 million people—more than 9 percent of the population—were born in another country. As of the 2000 census, the U.S. population was 72 percent White, 13 percent African American, and 11 percent Hispanic. The Hispanic population has been growing fast and is expected to make up 18.9 percent of the population by 2020; its largest subgroups are of Mexican (5.4 percent), Puerto Rican (1.1 percent), and Cuban (0.4 percent) descent. Asian Americans constituted 3.8 percent of the U.S. population; Chinese are the largest group, followed by Filipinos, Japanese, Asian Indians, and Koreans, in that order.

The growth of the Hispanic population represents a major shift in the nation's center of gravity. Hispanics made up half of all new workers in the past decade and will account for 25 percent of workers in two generations. Despite lagging family incomes, their disposable income has grown twice as fast as the rest of the population and could reach $1.2 trillion by 2012. From the food U.S. consumers eat, to the clothing, music, and cars they buy, Hispanics are having a huge impact.

Companies are scrambling to refine their products and marketing to reach this fastest-growing and most influential consumer group:[29] Research by Hispanic media giant Univision suggests 70 percent of Spanish-language viewers are more likely to buy a product when it's advertised in Spanish. Fisher-Price, recognizing that many Hispanic mothers did not grow up with its brand, shifted away from appeals to their heritage. Instead, its ads emphasize the joy of mother and child playing together with Fisher-Price toys.[30]

Several food, clothing, and furniture companies have directed products and promotions to one or more ethnic groups.[31] Yet marketers must not overgeneralize. Within each ethnic group are consumers quite different from each other.[32] For instance, a 2005 Yankelovich Monitor Multicultural Marketing study separated the African American market into six sociobehavioral segments: Emulators, Seekers, Reachers, Attainers, Elites, and Conservers. The largest and perhaps most influential are the Reachers (24 percent) and Attainers (27 percent), with very different needs. Reachers, around 40, are slowly working toward the American dream. Often single parents caring for elderly relatives, they have a median income of $28,000 and seek the greatest value for their money. Attainers have a more defined sense of self and solid plans for the future. Their median income is $55,000, and they want ideas and information to improve their quality of life.[33]

Diversity goes beyond ethnic and racial markets. More than 51 million U.S. consumers have disabilities, and they constitute a market for home delivery companies, such as Peapod, and for various drugstore chains.

EDUCATIONAL GROUPS The population in any society falls into five educational groups: illiterates, high school dropouts, high school diplomas, college degrees, and professional degrees. Over two-thirds of the world's 785 million illiterate adults are found in only eight countries (India, China, Bangladesh, Pakistan, Nigeria, Ethiopia, Indonesia, and Egypt); of all illiterate adults in the world, two-thirds are women.[34] The United States has one of the world's highest percentages of college-educated citizens: 54 percent of those 25 years or older have had "some college or more," 28 percent have bachelor's degrees, and 10 percent have advanced degrees. The large number of educated people in the United States drives strong demand for high-quality books, magazines, and travel, and creates a high supply of skills.

HOUSEHOLD PATTERNS The traditional household consists of a husband, wife, and children (and sometimes grandparents). Yet by 2010, only one in five U.S. households will consist of a married couple with children under 18. Other households are single live-alones (27 percent), single-parent families (8 percent), childless married couples and empty nesters (32 percent), living with nonrelatives only (5 percent), and other family structures (8 percent).[35]

More people are divorcing or separating, choosing not to marry, marrying later, or marrying without intending to have children. Each group has distinctive needs and buying habits. The single, separated, widowed, and divorced may need smaller apartments; inexpensive and smaller appliances, furniture, and furnishings; and smaller-size food packages.[36]

Nontraditional households are growing more rapidly than traditional households. Academics and marketing experts estimate that the gay and lesbian population ranges between 4 percent and 8 percent of the total U.S. population, higher in urban areas.[37] Even so-called traditional households have experienced change. Boomer dads marry later than their fathers or grandfathers did, shop more, and are much more active in raising their kids. To appeal to them, the maker of the high-concept Bugaboo stroller designed a model with a sleek look and dirt bike–style tires. Dyson, the high-end vacuum company, is appealing to dads' inner geek by focusing on the machine's revolutionary technology. Before Dyson entered the U.S. market, men weren't even on the radar for vacuum cleaner sales. Now they make up 40 percent of Dyson's customers.[38]

The Economic Environment

The available purchasing power in an economy depends on current income, prices, savings, debt, and credit availability. As the recent economic downturn vividly demonstrated, trends affecting purchasing power can have a strong impact on business, especially for companies whose products are geared to high-income and price-sensitive consumers.

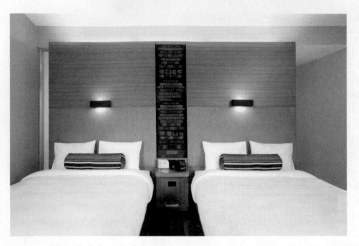

Starwood's Aloft hotel chain blends urban chic with affordable prices.

CONSUMER PSYCHOLOGY Did new consumer spending patterns during the 2008–2009 recession reflect short-term, temporary adjustments or long-term, permanent changes?[39] Some experts believed the recession had fundamentally shaken consumers' faith in the economy and their personal financial situations. "Mindless" spending would be out; willingness to comparison shop, haggle, and use discounts would become the norm. Others maintained tighter spending reflected a mere economic constraint and not a fundamental behavioral change. Thus, consumers' aspirations would stay the same, and spending would resume when the economy improves.

Identifying the more likely long-term scenario—especially with the coveted 18- to 34-year-old age group—would help to direct how marketers spend their money. After six months of research and development in the baby boomer market, Starwood launched a "style at a steal" initiative to offer affordable but stylish hotel alternatives to its high-end W, Sheraton, and Westin chains. Targeting an audience seeking both thrift and luxury, it introduced two new low-cost chains: Aloft, designed to reflect the urban cool of loft apartments, and Element, suites with every "element" of modern daily lives, including healthy food choices and spa-like bathrooms.[40]

INCOME DISTRIBUTION There are four types of industrial structures: *subsistence economies* like Papua New Guinea, with few opportunities for marketers; *raw-material-exporting economies* like Democratic Republic of Congo (copper) and Saudi Arabia (oil), with good markets for equipment, tools, supplies, and luxury goods for the rich; *industrializing economies* like India, Egypt, and the Philippines, where a new rich class and a growing middle class demand new types of goods; and *industrial economies* like Western Europe, with rich markets for all sorts of goods.

Marketers often distinguish countries using five income-distribution patterns: (1) very low incomes; (2) mostly low incomes; (3) very low, very high incomes; (4) low, medium, high incomes; and (5) mostly medium incomes. Consider the market for the Lamborghini, an automobile costing more than $150,000. The market would be very small in countries with type 1 or 2 income patterns. One of the largest single markets for Lamborghinis is Portugal (income pattern 3)—one of the poorer countries in Western Europe, but with enough wealthy families to afford expensive cars.

INCOME, SAVINGS, DEBT, AND CREDIT Consumer expenditures are affected by income levels, savings rates, debt practices, and credit availability. U.S. consumers have a high debt-to-income ratio, which slows expenditures on housing and large-ticket items. When credit became scarcer in the recession, especially to lower-income borrowers, consumer borrowing dropped for the first time in two decades. The financial meltdown that led to this contraction was due to overly liberal credit policies that allowed consumers to buy homes and other items they could really not afford. Marketers wanted every possible sale, banks wanted to earn interest on loans, and near financial ruin resulted.

An economic issue of increasing importance is the migration of manufacturers and service jobs offshore. From India, Infosys provides outsourcing services for Cisco, Nordstrom, Microsoft, and others. The 25,000 employees the fast-growing $4 billion company hires every year receive technical, team, and communication training in Infosys's $120 million facility outside Bangalore.[41]

The Sociocultural Environment

From our sociocultural environment we absorb, almost unconsciously, a world view that defines our relationships to ourselves, others, organizations, society, nature, and the universe.

- *Views of ourselves.* In the United States during the 1960s and 1970s, "pleasure seekers" sought fun, change, and escape. Others sought "self-realization." Today, some are adopting more conservative behaviors and ambitions (see ▭ Table 3.4 for favorite consumer leisure-time activities and how they have changed, or not, in recent years).
- *Views of others.* People are concerned about the homeless, crime and victims, and other social problems. At the same time, they seek those like themselves for long-lasting relationships, suggesting a growing market for social-support products and services such as health clubs, cruises, and religious activity as well as "social surrogates" like television, video games, and social networking sites.

TABLE 3.4   Favorite Leisure-Time Activities

	1995	2008
	%	%
Reading	28	30
TV watching	25	24
Spending time with family/kids	12	20
Going to movies	8	8
Fishing	10	7
Computer activities	2	7
Gardening	9	5
Renting movies	5	5
Walking	8	6
Exercise (aerobics, weights)	2	8

Source: Harris Interactive, "Spontaneous, Unaided Responses to: 'What Are Your Two or Three Most Favorite Leisure-Time Activities?'"
http://www.harrisinteractive.com/harris_poll/index.asp?PID=980. Base: All Adults.

- *Views of organizations.* After a wave of layoffs and corporate scandals, organizational loyalty has declined.[42] Companies need new ways to win back consumer and employee confidence. They need to ensure they are good corporate citizens and that their consumer messages are honest.[43]
- *Views of society.* Some people defend society (preservers), some run it (makers), some take what they can from it (takers), some want to change it (changers), some are looking for something deeper (seekers), and still others want to leave it (escapers).[44] Consumption patterns often reflect these social attitudes. Makers are high achievers who eat, dress, and live well. Changers usually live more frugally, drive smaller cars, and wear simpler clothes. Escapers and seekers are a major market for movies, music, surfing, and camping.
- *Views of nature.* Business has responded to increased awareness of nature's fragility and finiteness by producing wider varieties of camping, hiking, boating, and fishing gear such as boots, tents, backpacks, and accessories.
- *Views of the universe.* Most U.S. citizens are monotheistic, although religious conviction and practice have waned through the years or been redirected into an interest in evangelical movements or Eastern religions, mysticism, the occult, and the human potential movement.

Other cultural characteristics of interest to marketers are the high persistence of core cultural values and the existence of subcultures. Let's look at both.

HIGH PERSISTENCE OF CORE CULTURAL VALUES Most people in the United States still believe in working, getting married, giving to charity, and being honest. *Core beliefs* and values are passed from parents to children and reinforced by social institutions—schools, churches, businesses, and governments. *Secondary beliefs* and values are more open to change. Believing in the institution of marriage is a core belief; believing people should marry early is a secondary belief.

Marketers have some chance of changing secondary values, but little chance of changing core values. The nonprofit organization Mothers Against Drunk Drivers (MADD) does not try to stop the sale of alcohol but promotes lower legal blood-alcohol levels for driving and limited operating hours for businesses that sell alcohol.

Although core values are fairly persistent, cultural swings do take place. In the 1960s, hippies, the Beatles, Elvis Presley, and other cultural phenomena had a major impact on hairstyles, clothing, sexual norms, and life goals. Today's young people are influenced by new heroes and activities: the alternative rock band Green Day, the NBA's LeBron James, and snowboarder and skateboarder Shaun White.

Young people may be influenced by a diverse range of heroes, from basketball player LeBron James to punk-rock band Green Day.

EXISTENCE OF SUBCULTURES Each society contains **subcultures**, groups with shared values, beliefs, preferences, and behaviors emerging from their special life experiences or circumstances. Marketers have always loved teenagers because they are trendsetters in fashion, music, entertainment, ideas, and attitudes. Attract someone as a teen, and you will likely keep the person as a customer later in life. Frito-Lay, which draws 15 percent of its sales from teens, noted a rise in chip snacking by grown-ups. "We think it's because we brought them in as teenagers," said Frito-Lay's marketing director.[45]

The Natural Environment

In Western Europe, "green" parties have pressed for public action to reduce industrial pollution. In the United States, experts have documented ecological deterioration, and watchdog groups such as the Sierra Club and Friends of the Earth carry these concerns into political and social action.

Environmental regulations hit certain industries hard. Steel companies and public utilities have invested billions of dollars in pollution-control equipment and environmentally friendly fuels, making hybrid cars, low-flow toilets and showers, organic foods, and green office buildings every-day realities. Opportunities await those who can reconcile prosperity with environmental protection. Consider these solutions to concerns about air quality:[46]

- Nearly a quarter of the carbon dioxide that makes up about 80 percent of all greenhouse gases comes from electrical power plants. Dublin-based Airtricity operates wind farms in the United States and the United Kingdom that offer cheaper and greener electricity.
- Transportation is second only to electricity generation as a contributor to global warming, accounting for roughly a fifth of carbon emissions. Vancouver-based Westport Innovations developed a conversion technology—high-pressure direct injection—that allows diesel engines to run on cleaner-burning liquid natural gas, reducing greenhouse emissions by a fourth.

Actor and environmental activist Ed Begley Jr. examines a solar oven.

- Due to millions of rural cooking fires, parts of Southern Asia suffer extremely poor air quality. A person cooking over an open wood or kerosene fire inhales the equivalent of two packs of cigarettes a day. Illinois-based Sun Ovens International makes family-sized and institutional solar ovens that use mirrors to redirect the sun's rays into an insulated box. Used in 130 countries, the oven both saves money and reduces greenhouse gas emissions.

Corporate environmentalism recognizes the need to integrate environmental issues into the firm's strategic plans. Trends in the natural environment for marketers to be aware of include the shortage of raw materials, especially water; the increased cost of energy; increased pollution levels; and the changing role of governments. (See also "Marketing Insight: The Green Marketing Revolution.")[47]

- The earth's raw materials consist of the infinite, the finite renewable, and the finite nonrenewable. Firms whose products require *finite nonrenewable resources*—oil, coal, platinum, zinc, silver—face substantial cost increases as depletion approaches. Firms that can develop substitute materials have an excellent opportunity.
- One finite nonrenewable resource, oil, has created serious problems for the world economy. As oil prices soar, companies search for practical means to harness solar, nuclear, wind, and other alternative energies.
- Some industrial activity will inevitably damage the natural environment, creating a large market for pollution-control solutions such as scrubbers, recycling centers, and landfill systems as well as for alternative ways to produce and package goods.
- Many poor nations are doing little about pollution, lacking the funds or the political will. It is in the richer nations' interest to help them control their pollution, but even richer nations today lack the necessary funds.

The Technological Environment

It is the essence of market capitalism to be dynamic and tolerate the creative destructiveness of technology as the price of progress. Transistors hurt the vacuum-tube industry, and autos hurt the railroads. Television hurt the newspapers, and the Internet hurt them both.

When old industries fight or ignore new technologies, their businesses decline. Tower Records had ample warning that its music retail business would be hurt by Internet downloads of music (as well as the growing number of discount music retailers). Its failure to respond led to the liquidation of all its domestic physical stores in 2006.

Marketing Insight

The Green Marketing Revolution

Consumers' environmental concerns are real. Gallup polls reveal the percentage of U.S. adults who believe global warming will pose a serious threat during their lifetime has increased from 25 percent in 1998 to 40 percent in 2008. A Mediamark Research & Intelligence study in 2008 found that almost two-thirds of U.S. men and women stated that "preserving the environment as a guiding principle in your life" was "very important." A *Washington Post*/ABC News/ Stanford University poll in 2007 found that 94 percent of respondents were "willing" to "personally change some of the things you do in order to improve the environment," with 50 percent saying they were "very willing."

Converting this concern into concerted consumer action on the environment, however, will be a longer-term process. A 2008 TNS survey found that only 26 percent of Americans said they were "actively seeking environmentally friendly products." A 2008 Gallup poll found that only 28 percent of respondents claimed to have made "major changes" in their own shopping and living habits over the past five years to protect the environment. Other research reported that consumers were more concerned with closer to home environmental issues such as water pollution in rivers and lakes than broader issues such as global warming. As is often the case, behavioral change is following attitudinal change for consumers.

Nevertheless, as research by GfK Roper Consulting shows, consumer expectations as to corporate behavior with the environment have significantly changed, and in many cases these expectations are higher than the demands they place on themselves. Consumers vary, however, in their environmental sensitivity and can be categorized into five groups based on their degree of commitment (see △ Figure 3.1). Interestingly, although some marketers assume that younger people are more concerned about the environment than older consumers, some research suggests that older consumers actually take their eco-responsibilities more seriously.

In the past, the "green marketing" programs launched by companies around specific products were not always entirely successful for several possible reasons. Consumers might have thought that the product was inferior because it was green, or that it was not even really green to begin with. Those green products that were successful, however, persuaded consumers that they were acting in their own and society's long-run interest at the same time. Some examples were organic foods that were seen as healthier, tastier, and safer, and energy-efficient appliances that were seen as costing less to run.

There are some expert recommendations as to how to avoid "green marketing myopia" by focusing on consumer value positioning, calibration of consumer knowledge, and the credibility of product claims. One challenge with green marketing is the difficulty consumers have in understanding the environmental benefits of products, leading to many accusations of "greenwashing" where products are not nearly as green and environmentally beneficial as their marketing might suggest.

Although there have been green products emphasizing their natural benefits for years—Tom's of Maine, Burt's Bees, Stonyfield Farm, and Seventh Generation to name just a few—products offering environmental benefits are becoming more mainstream. Part of the success of Clorox Green Works cleaning products and household cleaning products, launched in January 2008, was that it found the sweet spot of a target market wanting to take smaller steps toward a greener lifestyle

---

|Fig. 3.1| △

Consumer Environmental Segments

Source: GfK Roper Green Gauge® 2007, GfK Roper Consulting, New York, NY.

- *Genuine Greens* (15%): This segment is the most likely to think and act green. Some may be true environmental activists, but most probably fall more under the category of strong advocates. This group sees few barriers to behaving green and may be open to partnering with marketers on environmental initiatives.

- *Not Me Greens* (18%): This segment expresses very pro-green attitudes, but its behaviors are only moderate, perhaps because these people perceive lots of barriers to living green. There may be a sense among this group that the issue is too big for them to handle, and they may need encouragement to take action.

- *Go-with-the-Flow Greens* (17%): This group engages in some green behaviors—mostly the "easy" ones such as recycling. But being green is not a priority for them, and they seem to take the path of least resistance. This group may only take action when it's convenient for them.

- *Dream Greens* (13%): This segment cares a great deal about the environment, but doesn't seem to have the knowledge or resources to take action. This group may offer the greatest opportunity to act green if given the chance.

- *Business First Greens* (23%): This segment's perspective is that the environment is not a huge concern and that business and industry is doing its part to help. This may explain why they don't feel the need to take action themselves—even as they cite lots of barriers to doing so.

- *Mean Greens* (13%): This group claims to be knowledgeable about environmental issues, but does not express pro-green attitudes or behaviors. Indeed, it is practically hostile toward pro-environmental ideas. This segment has chosen to reject prevailing notions about environmental protection and may even be viewed as a potential threat to green initiatives.

and matched that with a green product with a very modest price premium and sold through a grassroots marketing program.

Environmental concerns are affecting how virtually every major company does their business: Walt Disney Corp. has pledged to reduce its solid waste by 2013, conserve millions of gallons of water, invest in renewable energy, and become completely carbon neutral (reaching 50 percent of that goal by 2012); Best Buy has expanded its recycling program for electronics; Caterpillar announced plans to reduce the GHG emissions of its entire product line by 20 percent by 2020; and Whole Foods, a leader among national supermarket chains in selling certified "organic food" already, cofounded a partnership to reduce emissions from grocery refrigerators and offsets 100 percent of its electricity use with renewable energy via wind-energy credits.

Toyota, HP, IKEA, Procter & Gamble, and Walmart have all been linked to high-profile environmental and sustainability programs. Some other marketers, fearing harsh scrutiny or unrealistic expectations, keep a lower profile. Even though Nike uses recycled sneakers in its soles of new shoes, they chose not to publicize that fact so that they can keep their focus on performance and winning. The rules of the game in green marketing are changing rapidly as both consumers and companies respond to problems and proposed solutions to the significant environmental problems that exist.

Sources: Jerry Adler, "Going Green," *Newsweek*, July 17, 2006, pp. 43–52; Jacquelyn A. Ottman, Edwin R. Stafford, and Cathy L. Hartman, "Avoiding Green Marketing Myopia," *Environment* (June 2006): 22–36; Jill Meredith Ginsberg and Paul N. Bloom, "Choosing the Right Green Marketing Strategy," *MIT Sloan Management Review* (Fall 2004): 79–84; Jacquelyn Ottman, *Green Marketing: Opportunity for Innovation,* 2nd ed. (New York: BookSurge Publishing, 2004); Mark Dolliver, "Deflating a Myth,"*Brandweek*, May 12, 2008, pp. 30–31; "Winner: Corporate Sustainability, Walt Disney Worldwide," *Travel and Leisure*, November 2009, p. 106; "The Greenest Big Companies in America, *Newsweek*, September 28, 2009, pp. 34–53; Sarah Mahoney, "Best Buy Connects Green with Thrift," *Media Post News: Marketing Daily*, January 28, 2009; Reena Jana, "Nike Quietly Goes Green," *BusinessWeek*, June 11, 2009.

Clorox's Green Works has been a huge market hit by combining environmental benefits with affordability.

Major new technologies stimulate the economy's growth rate. Unfortunately, between innovations, an economy can stagnate. Minor innovations fill the gap—new supermarket products such as frozen waffles, body washes, and energy bars might pop up—but while lower risk, they can also divert research effort away from major breakthroughs.

Innovation's long-run consequences are not always foreseeable. The contraceptive pill reduced family size and thus increased discretionary incomes, also raising spending on vacation travel, durable goods, and luxury items. Cell phones, video games, and the Internet are reducing attention to traditional media, as well as face-to-face social interaction as people listen to music or watch a movie on their cell phones.

Marketers should monitor the following technology trends: the accelerating pace of change, unlimited opportunities for innovation, varying R&D budgets, and increased regulation of technological change.

ACCELERATING PACE OF CHANGE More ideas than ever are in the works, and the time between idea and implementation is shrinking. So is the time between introduction and peak production. Apple ramped up in seven years to sell a staggering 220 million iPods worldwide by September 2009.

UNLIMITED OPPORTUNITIES FOR INNOVATION Some of the most exciting work today is taking place in biotechnology, computers, microelectronics, telecommunications, robotics, and designer materials. Researchers are working on AIDS vaccines, safer contraceptives, and nonfattening foods. They are developing new classes of antibiotics to fight ultra-resistant infections, superheating furnaces to reduce trash to raw materials, and building miniature water-treatment plants for remote locations.[48]

Text messaging is profoundly changing how consumers choose to communicate.

VARYING R&D BUDGETS A growing portion of U.S. R&D expenditures goes to the development as opposed to the research side, raising concerns about whether the United States can maintain its lead in basic science. Many companies put their money into copying competitors' products and making minor feature and style improvements. Even basic research companies such as Dow Chemical, Bell Laboratories, and Pfizer are proceeding cautiously, and more consortiums than single companies are directing research efforts toward major breakthroughs.

INCREASED REGULATION OF TECHNOLOGICAL CHANGE Government has expanded its agencies' powers to investigate and ban potentially unsafe products. In the United States, the Food and Drug Administration (FDA) must approve all drugs before they can be sold. Safety and health regulations have increased for food, automobiles, clothing, electrical appliances, and construction.

The Political-Legal Environment

The political and legal environment consists of laws, government agencies, and pressure groups that influence various organizations and individuals. Sometimes these laws create new business opportunities. Mandatory recycling laws have boosted the recycling industry and launched dozens of new companies making new products from recycled materials. Two major trends are the increase in business legislation and the growth of special-interest groups.

INCREASE IN BUSINESS LEGISLATION Business legislation is intended to protect companies from unfair competition, protect consumers from unfair business practices, protect society from unbridled business behavior, and charge businesses with the social costs of their products or production processes. Each new law may also have the unintended effect of sapping initiative and slowing growth.

The European Commission has established new laws covering competitive behavior, product standards, product liability, and commercial transactions for the 27 member nations of the European Union. The United States has many consumer protection laws covering competition, product safety and liability, fair trade and credit practices, and packaging and labeling, but many countries' laws are stronger.[49] Norway bans several forms of sales promotion—trading stamps, contests, and premiums—as inappropriate or unfair. Thailand requires food processors selling national brands to market low-price brands also, so low-income consumers can find economy brands. In India, food companies need special approval to launch duplicate brands, such as another cola drink or brand of rice. As more transactions take place in cyberspace, marketers must establish new ways to do business ethically.

GROWTH OF SPECIAL-INTEREST GROUPS Political action committees (PACs) lobby government officials and pressure business executives to respect the rights of consumers, women, senior citizens, minorities, and gays and lesbians. Insurance companies directly or indirectly affect the design of smoke detectors; scientific groups affect the design of spray products. Many companies have established public affairs departments to deal with these groups and issues. The **consumerist movement** organized citizens and government to strengthen the rights and powers of buyers in relationship to sellers. Consumerists have won the right to know the real cost of a loan, the true cost per standard unit of competing brands (unit pricing), the basic ingredients and true benefits of a product, and the nutritional quality and freshness of food.

Privacy issues and identity theft will remain public policy hot buttons as long as consumers are willing to swap personal information for customized products—from marketers they trust.[50] Consumers worry they will be robbed or cheated; that private information will be used against them; that they will be bombarded by solicitations; and that children will be targeted.[51] Wise companies establish consumer affairs departments to formulate policies and resolve complaints.

Forecasting and Demand Measurement

Understanding the marketing environment and conducting marketing research (described in Chapter 4) can help to identify marketing opportunities. The company must then measure and forecast the size, growth, and profit potential of each new opportunity. Sales forecasts prepared by marketing are used by finance to raise cash for investment and operations; by manufacturing to establish capacity and output; by purchasing to acquire the right amount of supplies; and by human resources to hire the needed workers. If the forecast is off the mark, the company will face excess or inadequate inventory. Since it's based on estimates of demand, managers need to define what they mean by market demand. Although DuPont's Performance Materials group knows DuPont Tyvek has 70 percent of the $100 million market for air-barrier membranes, they see greater opportunity with more products and services to tap into the entire $7 billion U.S. home construction market.[52]

The Measures of Market Demand

Companies can prepare as many as 90 different types of demand estimates for six different product levels, five space levels, and three time periods (see △ Figure 3.2). Each demand measure serves a specific purpose. A company might forecast short-run demand to order raw materials, plan production, and borrow cash. It might forecast regional demand to decide whether to set up regional distribution.

There are many productive ways to break down the market:

- The **potential market** is the set of consumers with a sufficient level of interest in a market offer. However, their interest is not enough to define a market unless they also have sufficient income and access to the product.
- The **available market** is the set of consumers who have interest, income, *and* access to a particular offer. The company or government may restrict sales to certain groups; a particular state might ban motorcycle sales to anyone under 21 years of age. Eligible adults constitute the *qualified available market*—the set of consumers who have interest, income, access, and qualifications for the market offer.
- The **target market** is the part of the qualified available market the company decides to pursue. The company might concentrate its marketing and distribution effort on the East Coast.
- The **penetrated market** is the set of consumers who are buying the company's product.

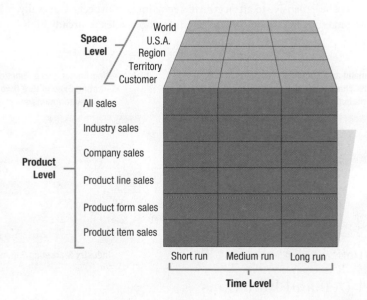

|Fig. 3.2| △

Ninety Types of
Demand Measurement
(6 × 5 × 3)

These definitions are a useful tool for market planning. If the company isn't satisfied with its current sales, it can try to attract a larger percentage of buyers from its target market. It can lower the qualifications for potential buyers. It can expand its available market by opening distribution elsewhere or lowering its price, or it can reposition itself in the minds of its customers.

A Vocabulary for Demand Measurement

The major concepts in demand measurement are market demand and company demand. Within each, we distinguish among a demand function, a sales forecast, and a potential.

MARKET DEMAND   The marketer's first step in evaluating marketing opportunities is to estimate total market demand. **Market demand** for a product is the total volume that would be bought by a defined customer group in a defined geographical area in a defined time period in a defined marketing environment under a defined marketing program.

Market demand is not a fixed number, but rather a function of the stated conditions. For this reason, we call it the *market demand function*. Its dependence on underlying conditions is illustrated in △ Figure 3.3(a). The horizontal axis shows different possible levels of industry marketing expenditure in a given time period. The vertical axis shows the resulting demand level. The curve represents the estimated market demand associated with varying levels of marketing expenditure.

Some base sales—called the *market minimum* and labeled Q_1 in the figure—would take place without any demand-stimulating expenditures. Higher marketing expenditures would yield higher levels of demand, first at an increasing rate, then at a decreasing rate. Take fruit juices. Given the indirect competition they face from other types of beverages, we would expect increased marketing expenditures to help fruit juice products stand out and increase demand and sales. Marketing expenditures beyond a certain level would not stimulate much further demand, suggesting an upper limit called the *market potential* and labeled Q_2 in the figure.

The distance between the market minimum and the market potential shows the overall *marketing sensitivity of demand*. We can think of two extreme types of markets, the expansible and the nonexpansible. An *expansible market*, such as the market for racquetball playing, is very much affected in size by the level of industry marketing expenditures. In terms of Figure 3.3(a), the distance between Q_1 and Q_2 is relatively large. A *nonexpansible market*—for example, the market for weekly trash or garbage removal—is *not* much affected by the level of marketing expenditures; the distance between Q_1 and Q_2 is relatively small. Organizations selling in a nonexpansible market must accept the market's size—the level of *primary demand* for the product class—and direct their efforts toward winning a larger **market share** for their product, that is, a higher level of selective demand for their product.

It pays to compare the current and potential levels of market demand. The result is the **market-penetration index**. A low index indicates substantial growth potential for all the firms. A high index suggests it will be expensive to attract the few remaining prospects. Generally, price competition increases and margins fall when the market-penetration index is already high.

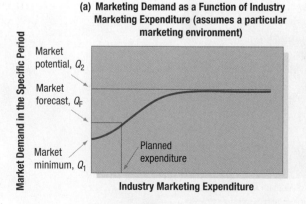

(a) Marketing Demand as a Function of Industry Marketing Expenditure (assumes a particular marketing environment)

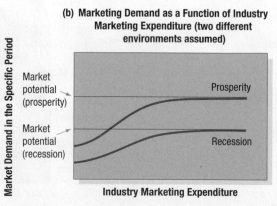

(b) Marketing Demand as a Function of Industry Marketing Expenditure (two different environments assumed)

|Fig. 3.3| △ Market Demand Functions

Comparing current and potential market shares yields a firm's **share-penetration index**. If this index is low, the company can greatly expand its share. Holding it back could be low brand awareness, low availability, benefit deficiencies, or high price. A firm should calculate the share-penetration increases from removing each factor, to see which investments produce the greatest improvement.[53]

Remember the market demand function is not a picture of market demand over time. Rather, it shows alternative current forecasts of market demand associated with possible levels of industry marketing effort.

MARKET FORECAST Only one level of industry marketing expenditure will actually occur. The market demand corresponding to this level is called the **market forecast**.

MARKET POTENTIAL The market forecast shows *expected* market demand, not maximum market demand. For the latter, we need to visualize the level of market demand resulting from a very high level of industry marketing expenditure, where further increases in marketing effort would have little effect. **Market potential** is the limit approached by market demand as industry marketing expenditures approach infinity for a given marketing environment.

The phrase "for a given market environment" is crucial. Consider the market potential for automobiles. It's higher during prosperity than during a recession. The dependence of market potential on the environment is illustrated in △ Figure 3.3(b). Market analysts distinguish between the position of the market demand function and movement along it. Companies cannot do anything about the position of the market demand function, which is determined by the marketing environment. However, they influence their particular location on the function when they decide how much to spend on marketing.

Companies interested in market potential have a special interest in the **product-penetration percentage**, the percentage of ownership or use of a product or service in a population. Companies assume that the lower the product-penetration percentage, the higher the market potential, although this also assumes everyone will eventually be in the market for every product.

COMPANY DEMAND **Company demand** is the company's estimated share of market demand at alternative levels of company marketing effort in a given time period. It depends on how the company's products, services, prices, and communications are perceived relative to the competitors'. Other things equal, the company's market share depends on the relative scale and effectiveness of its market expenditures. Marketing model builders have developed sales response functions to measure how a company's sales are affected by its marketing expenditure level, marketing mix, and marketing effectiveness.[54]

COMPANY SALES FORECAST Once marketers have estimated company demand, their next task is to choose a level of marketing effort. The **company sales forecast** is the expected level of company sales based on a chosen marketing plan and an assumed marketing environment.

We represent the company sales forecast graphically with sales on the vertical axis and marketing effort on the horizontal axis, as in Figure 3.3. We often hear that the company should develop its marketing plan on the basis of its sales forecast. This forecast-to-plan sequence is valid if *forecast* means an estimate of national economic activity, or if company demand is nonexpansible. The sequence is not valid, however, where market demand is expansible or where *forecast* means an estimate of company sales. The company sales forecast does not establish a basis for deciding what to spend on marketing. On the contrary, the sales forecast is the result of an assumed marketing expenditure plan.

Two other concepts are important here. A **sales quota** is the sales goal set for a product line, company division, or sales representative. It is primarily a managerial device for defining and stimulating sales effort, often set slightly higher than estimated sales to stretch the sales force's effort.

A **sales budget** is a conservative estimate of the expected volume of sales, primarily for making current purchasing, production, and cash flow decisions. It's based on the need to avoid excessive risk and is generally set slightly lower than the sales forecast.

COMPANY SALES POTENTIAL **Company sales potential** is the sales limit approached by company demand as company marketing effort increases relative to that of competitors. The absolute limit of company demand is, of course, the market potential. The two would be equal if the company got 100 percent of the market. In most cases, company sales potential is less than the market potential, even when company marketing expenditures increase considerably. Each competitor has a hard core of loyal buyers unresponsive to other companies' efforts to woo them.

Estimating Current Demand

We are now ready to examine practical methods for estimating current market demand. Marketing executives want to estimate total market potential, area market potential, and total industry sales and market shares.

TOTAL MARKET POTENTIAL **Total market potential** is the maximum sales available to all firms in an industry during a given period, under a given level of industry marketing effort and environmental conditions. A common way to estimate total market potential is to multiply the potential number of buyers by the average quantity each purchases, times the price.

If 100 million people buy books each year, and the average book buyer buys three books a year at an average price of $20 each, then the total market potential for books is $6 billion (100 million $\times$ 3 $\times$ $20). The most difficult component to estimate is the number of buyers. We can always start with the total population in the nation, say, 261 million people. Next we eliminate groups that obviously would not buy the product. Assume illiterate people and children under 12 don't buy books and constitute 20 percent of the population. This means 80 percent of the population, or 209 million people, are in the potentials pool. Further research might tell us that people of low income and low education don't buy books, and they constitute over 30 percent of the potentials pool. Eliminating them, we arrive at a prospect pool of approximately 146.3 million book buyers. We use this number to calculate total market potential.

A variation on this method is the *chain-ratio method*, which multiplies a base number by several adjusting percentages. Suppose a brewery is interested in estimating the market potential for a new light beer especially designed to accompany food. It can make an estimate with the following calculation:

| Demand for the new light beer | = Population | $\times$ | Personal discretionary income per capita | $\times$ | Average percentage of discretionary income spent on food | $\times$ | Average percentage of amount spent on food that is spent on beverages | $\times$ | Average percentage of amount spent on beverages that is spent on alcoholic beverages | $\times$ | Average percentage of amount spent on alcoholic beverages that is spent on beer | $\times$ | Expected percentage of amount spent on beer that will be spent on light beer |

AREA MARKET POTENTIAL Because companies must allocate their marketing budget optimally among their best territories, they need to estimate the market potential of different cities, states, and nations. Two major methods are the market-buildup method, used primarily by business marketers, and the multiple-factor index method, used primarily by consumer marketers.

Market-Buildup Method The **market-buildup method** calls for identifying all the potential buyers in each market and estimating their potential purchases. It produces accurate results if we have a list of all potential buyers and a good estimate of what each will buy. Unfortunately, this information is not always easy to gather.

Consider a machine-tool company that wants to estimate the area market potential for its wood lathe in the Boston area. Its first step is to identify all potential buyers of wood lathes in the area, primarily manufacturing establishments that shape or ream wood as part of their operations. The company could compile a list from a directory of all manufacturing establishments in the area. Then it could estimate the number of lathes each industry might purchase, based on the number of lathes per thousand employees or per $1 million of sales in that industry.

An efficient method of estimating area market potentials makes use of the *North American Industry Classification System (NAICS)*, developed by the U.S. Bureau of the Census in conjunction with the Canadian and Mexican governments.[55] The NAICS classifies all manufacturing into 20 major industry sectors and further breaks each sector into a six-digit, hierarchical structure as follows.

51	Industry sector (information)	
513	Industry subsector (broadcasting and telecommunications)	
5133	Industry group (telecommunications)	
51332	Industry (wireless telecommunications carriers, except satellite)	
513321	National industry (U.S. paging)	

For each six-digit NAICS number, a company can purchase CD-ROMs of business directories that provide complete company profiles of millions of establishments, subclassified by location, number of employees, annual sales, and net worth.

To use the NAICS, the lathe manufacturer must first determine the six-digit NAICS codes that represent products whose manufacturers are likely to require lathe machines. To get a full picture of all six-digit NAICS industries that might use lathes, the company can (1) determine past customers' NAICS codes; (2) go through the NAICS manual and check off all the six-digit industries that might have an interest in lathes; (3) mail questionnaires to a wide range of companies inquiring about their interest in wood lathes.

The company's next task is to determine an appropriate base for estimating the number of lathes each industry will use. Suppose customer industry sales are the most appropriate base. Once the company estimates the rate of lathe ownership relative to the customer industry's sales, it can compute the market potential.

Multiple-Factor Index Method Like business marketers, consumer companies also need to estimate area market potentials, but since their customers are too numerous to list they commonly use a straightforward index. A drug manufacturer might assume the market potential for drugs is directly related to population size. If the state of Virginia has 2.55 percent of the U.S. population, Virginia might be a market for 2.55 percent of total drugs sold.

A single factor is rarely a complete indicator of sales opportunity. Regional drug sales are also influenced by per capita income and the number of physicians per 10,000 people. Thus, it makes sense to develop a multiple-factor index and assign each factor a specific weight. Suppose Virginia has 2.00 percent of U.S. disposable personal income, 1.96 percent of U.S. retail sales, and 2.28 percent of U.S. population, and the respective weights are 0.5, 0.3, and 0.2. The buying-power index for Virginia is then 2.04 [0.5(2.00) + 0.3(1.96) + 0.2(2.28)]. Thus 2.04 percent of the nation's drug sales (not 2.28 percent) might be expected to take place in Virginia.

The weights in the buying-power index are somewhat arbitrary, and companies can assign others if appropriate. A manufacturer might adjust the market potential for additional factors, such as competitors' presence, local promotional costs, seasonal factors, and market idiosyncrasies.

Many companies compute area indexes to allocate marketing resources. Suppose the drug company is reviewing the six cities listed in Table 3.5. The first two columns show its percentage of U.S. brand and category sales in these six cities. Column 3 shows the **brand development index** (**BDI**), the index of brand sales to category sales. Seattle has a BDI of 114 because the brand is

TABLE 3.5 Calculating the Brand Development Index (BDI)

Territory	(a) Percent of U.S. Brand Sales	(b) Percent of U.S. Category Sales	BDI (a ÷ b) × 100
Seattle	3.09	2.71	114
Portland	6.74	10.41	65
Boston	3.49	3.85	91
Toledo	.97	.81	120
Chicago	1.13	.81	140
Baltimore	3.12	3.00	104

relatively more developed than the category in Seattle. Portland's BDI is 65, which means the brand is relatively underdeveloped there.

Normally, the lower the BDI, the higher the market opportunity, in that there is room to grow the brand. Other marketers would argue instead that marketing funds should go into the brand's *strongest* markets, where it might be important to reinforce loyalty or more easily capture additional brand share. Investment decisions should be based on the potential to grow brand sales. Feeling it was underperforming in a high-potential market, Anheuser-Busch targeted the growing Hispanic population in Texas with a number of special marketing activities. Cross-promotions with Budweiser and Clamato tomato clam cocktail (to mix the popular Michiladas drink), sponsorship of the Esta Noche Toca concert series, and support of Latin music acts with three-on-three soccer tournaments helped drive higher sales.[56]

After the company decides on the city-by-city allocation of its budget, it can refine each city allocation down to census tracts or zip+4 code centers. *Census tracts* are small, locally defined statistical areas in metropolitan areas and some other counties. They generally have stable boundaries and a population of about 4,000. Zip+4 code centers (designed by the U.S. Post Office) are a little larger than neighborhoods. Data on population size, median family income, and other characteristics are available for these geographical units. Using other sources such as loyalty card data, Mediabrands's Geomentum targets "hyper-local" sectors of zip codes, city blocks, or even individual households with ad messages delivered via interactive TV, zoned editions of newspapers, Yellow Pages, outdoor media, and local Internet searches.[57]

INDUSTRY SALES AND MARKET SHARES Besides estimating total potential and area potential, a company needs to know the actual industry sales taking place in its market. This means identifying competitors and estimating their sales.

The industry trade association will often collect and publish total industry sales, although it usually does not list individual company sales separately. With this information, however, each company can evaluate its own performance against the industry's. If a company's sales are increasing by 5 percent a year and industry sales are increasing by 10 percent, the company is losing its relative standing in the industry.

Another way to estimate sales is to buy reports from a marketing research firm that audits total sales and brand sales. Nielsen Media Research audits retail sales in various supermarket and drugstore product categories. A company can purchase this information and compare its performance to the total industry or any competitor to see whether it is gaining or losing share, overall or brand by brand. Because distributors typically will not supply information about how much of competitors' products they are selling, business-to-business marketers operate with less knowledge of their market share results.

Estimating Future Demand

The few products or services that lend themselves to easy forecasting generally enjoy an absolute level or a fairly constant trend, and competition that is either nonexistent (public utilities) or stable (pure oligopolies). In most markets, in contrast, good forecasting is a key factor in success.

Companies commonly prepare a macroeconomic forecast first, followed by an industry forecast, followed by a company sales forecast. The macroeconomic forecast projects inflation, unemployment, interest rates, consumer spending, business investment, government expenditures, net exports, and other variables. The end result is a forecast of gross domestic product (GDP), which the firm uses, along with other environmental indicators, to forecast industry sales. The company derives its sales forecast by assuming it will win a certain market share.

How do firms develop their forecasts? They may create their own or buy forecasts from outside sources such as marketing research firms, which interview customers, distributors, and other knowledgeable parties. Specialized forecasting firms produce long-range forecasts of particular macroenvironmental components, such as population, natural resources, and technology. Examples are IHS Global Insight (a merger of Data Resources and Wharton Econometric Forecasting Associates), Forrester Research, and the Gartner Group. Futurist research firms produce speculative scenarios; three such firms are the Institute for the Future, Hudson Institute, and the Futures Group.

All forecasts are built on one of three information bases: what people say, what people do, or what people have done. Using what people say requires surveying buyers' intentions, composites of sales force opinions, and expert opinion. Building a forecast on what people do means putting the product into a test market to measure buyer response. To use the final basis—what people have done—firms analyze records of past buying behavior or use time-series analysis or statistical demand analysis.

SURVEY OF BUYERS' INTENTIONS **Forecasting** is the art of anticipating what buyers are likely to do under a given set of conditions. For major consumer durables such as appliances, research organizations conduct periodic surveys of consumer buying intentions, ask questions like *Do you intend to buy an automobile within the next six months?* and put the answers on a **purchase probability scale:**

0.00	0.20	0.40	0.60	0.80	1.00
No chance	Slight possibility	Fair possibility	Good possibility	High possibility	Certain

Surveys also inquire into consumers' present and future personal finances and expectations about the economy. They combine bits of information into a consumer confidence measure (Conference Board) or a consumer sentiment measure (Survey Research Center of the University of Michigan).

For business buying, research firms can carry out buyer-intention surveys for plant, equipment, and materials, usually falling within a 10 percent margin of error. These surveys are useful in estimating demand for industrial products, consumer durables, product purchases where advanced planning is required, and new products. Their value increases to the extent that buyers are few, the cost of reaching them is low, and they have clear intentions they willingly disclose and implement.

COMPOSITE OF SALES FORCE OPINIONS When buyer interviewing is impractical, the company may ask its sales representatives to estimate their future sales. Few companies use these estimates without making some adjustments, however. Sales representatives might be pessimistic or optimistic, they might not know how their company's marketing plans will influence future sales in their territory, and they might deliberately underestimate demand so the company will set a low sales quota. To encourage better estimating, the company could offer incentives or assistance, such as information about marketing plans or past forecasts compared to actual sales.

Sales force forecasts yield a number of benefits. Sales reps might have better insight into developing trends than any other group, and forecasting might give them greater confidence in their sales quotas and more incentive to achieve them. A "grassroots" forecasting procedure provides detailed estimates broken down by product, territory, customer, and sales rep.

EXPERT OPINION Companies can also obtain forecasts from experts, including dealers, distributors, suppliers, marketing consultants, and trade associations. Dealer estimates are subject to the same strengths and weaknesses as sales force estimates. Many companies buy economic and industry forecasts from well-known economic-forecasting firms that have more data available and more forecasting expertise.

Occasionally, companies will invite a group of experts to prepare a forecast. The experts exchange views and produce an estimate as a group (*group-discussion method*) or individually, in which case another analyst might combine them into a single estimate (*pooling of individual estimates*). Further rounds of estimating and refining follow (the Delphi method).[58]

PAST-SALES ANALYSIS Firms can develop sales forecasts on the basis of past sales. *Time-series analysis* breaks past time series into four components (trend, cycle, seasonal, and erratic) and projects them into the future. *Exponential smoothing* projects the next period's sales by combining an average of past sales and the most recent sales, giving more weight to the latter. *Statistical demand analysis* measures the impact of a set of causal factors (such as income, marketing expenditures, and price) on the sales level. Finally, *econometric analysis* builds sets of equations that describe a system and statistically derives the different parameters that make up the equations statistically.

MARKET-TEST METHOD When buyers don't plan their purchases carefully, or experts are unavailable or unreliable, a direct-market test can help forecast new-product sales or established product sales in a new distribution channel or territory. (We discuss market testing in detail in Chapter 20.)

Summary

1. To carry out their analysis, planning, implementation, and control responsibilities, marketing managers need a marketing information system (MIS). The role of the MIS is to assess the managers' information needs, develop the needed information, and distribute that information in a timely manner.

2. An MIS has three components: (a) an internal records system, which includes information on the order-to-payment cycle and sales information systems; (b) a marketing intelligence system, a set of procedures and sources used by managers to obtain everyday information about pertinent developments in the marketing environment; and (c) a marketing research system that allows for the systematic design, collection, analysis, and reporting of data and findings relevant to a specific marketing situation.

3. Marketers find many opportunities by identifying trends (directions or sequences of events that have some momentum and durability) and megatrends (major social, economic, political, and technological changes that have long-lasting influence).

4. Within the rapidly changing global picture, marketers must monitor six major environmental forces: demographic, economic, social-cultural, natural, technological, and political-legal.

5. In the demographic environment, marketers must be aware of worldwide population growth; changing mixes of age, ethnic composition, and educational levels; the rise of nontraditional families; and large geographic shifts in population.

6. In the economic arena, marketers need to focus on income distribution and levels of savings, debt, and credit availability.

7. In the social-cultural arena, marketers must understand people's views of themselves, others, organizations, society, nature, and the universe. They must market products that correspond to society's core and secondary values and address the needs of different subcultures within a society.

8. In the natural environment, marketers need to be aware of the public's increased concern about the health of the environment. Many marketers are now embracing sustainability and green marketing programs that provide better environmental solutions as a result.

9. In the technological arena, marketers should take account of the accelerating pace of technological change, opportunities for innovation, varying R&D budgets, and the increased governmental regulation brought about by technological change.

10. In the political-legal environment, marketers must work within the many laws regulating business practices and with various special-interest groups.

11. There are two types of demand: market demand and company demand. To estimate current demand, companies attempt to determine total market potential, area market potential, industry sales, and market share. To estimate future demand, companies survey buyers' intentions, solicit their sales force's input, gather expert opinions, analyze past sales, or engage in market testing. Mathematical models, advanced statistical techniques, and computerized data collection procedures are essential to all types of demand and sales forecasting.

Applications

Marketing Debate
Is Consumer Behavior More a Function of a Person's Age or Generation?

One of the widely debated issues in developing marketing programs that target certain age groups is how much consumers change over time. Some marketers maintain that age differences are critical and that the needs and wants of a 25-year-old in 2010 are not that different from those of a 25-year-old in 1980. Others argue that cohort and generation effects are critical, and that marketing programs must therefore suit the times.

Take a position: Age differences are fundamentally more important than cohort effects *versus* Cohort effects can dominate age differences.

Marketing Discussion
Age Targeting

What brands and products do you feel successfully "speak to you" and effectively target your age group? Why? Which ones do not? What could they do better?

Marketing Excellence

>>Microsoft

Microsoft is the world's most successful software company. The company was founded by Bill Gates and Paul Allen in 1975 with the original mission of having "a computer on every desk and in every home, running Microsoft software." Since then, Microsoft has grown to become the third most valuable brand in the world through strategic marketing and aggressive growth tactics.

Microsoft's first significant success occurred in the early 1980s with the creation of the DOS operating system for IBM computers. The company used this initial success with IBM to sell software to other manufacturers, quickly making Microsoft a major player in the industry. Initial advertising efforts focused on communicating the company's range of products from DOS to the launch of Excel and Windows—all under a unified "Microsoft" look.

Microsoft went public in 1986 and grew tremendously over the next decade as the Windows operating system and Microsoft Office took off. In 1990, Microsoft launched a completely revamped version of its operating system and named it Windows 3.0. Windows 3.0 offered an improved set of Windows icons and applications like File Manager and Program Manager that are still used today. It was an instant success; Microsoft sold more than 10 million copies of the software within two years—a phenomenon in those days. In addition, Windows 3.0 became the first operating system to be preinstalled on certain PCs, marking a major milestone in the industry and for Microsoft.

Throughout the 1990s, Microsoft's communication efforts convinced businesses that its software was not only the best choice for business but also that it needed to be upgraded frequently. Microsoft spent millions of dollars in magazine advertising and received endorsements from the top computer magazines in the industry, making Microsoft Windows and Office the must-have software of its time. Microsoft successfully launched Windows 95 in 1995 and Windows 98 in 1998, using the slogan, "Where Do You Want to Go Today?" The slogan didn't push individual products but rather the company itself, which could help empower companies and consumers alike.

During the late 1990s, Microsoft entered the notorious "browser wars" as companies struggled to find their place during the Internet boom. In 1995, Netscape launched its Navigator browser over the Internet. Realizing what a good product Netscape had, Microsoft launched the first version of its own browser, Internet Explorer, later that same year. By 1997, Netscape held a 72 percent share and Exploror an 18 percent share. Five years later, however, Netscape's share had fallen to 4 percent.

During those five years, Microsoft took three major steps to overtake the competition. First, it bundled Internet Explorer with its Office product, which included Excel, Word, and PowerPoint. Automatically, consumers who wanted MS Office became Explorer users as well. Second, Microsoft partnered with AOL, which opened the doors to 5 million new consumers almost overnight. And, finally, Microsoft used its deep pockets to ensure that Internet Explorer was available free, essentially "cutting off Netscape's air supply." These efforts, however, were not without controversy. Microsoft faced antitrust charges in 1998 and numerous lawsuits based on its marketing tactics, and some perceived that it was monopolizing the industry.

Charges aside, the company's stock took off, peaking in 1999 at $60 per share. Microsoft released Windows 2000 in 2000 and Windows XP in 2001. It also launched Xbox in 2001, marking the company's entrance into the multibillion-dollar gaming industry.

Over the next several years, Microsoft's stock price dipped by over $40 a share as consumers waited for the next operating system and Apple made a significant comeback with several new Mac computers, the iPod, the iPhone, and iTunes. Microsoft launched the Vista operating system in 2007 to great expectations; however, it was plagued with bugs and problems.

As the recession worsened in 2008, the company found itself in a bind. Its brand image was tarnished from years of Apple's successful "Get a Mac" campaign, a series of commercials that featured a smart, creative, easygoing Mac character alongside a geeky, virus-prone, uptight PC character. In addition, consumers and analysts continued to slam Vista for its poor performance.

In response, Microsoft created a campaign entitled "Windows. Life Without Walls" to help turn its image around. The company focused on how cost effective computers with its software were, a message that resonated well in the recession. It launched a series of commercials boasting "I'm a PC" that began with a Microsoft employee (looking very similar to the PC character from the Apple ads) stating, "Hello, I'm a PC and I've been made into a stereotype." The commercials, which highlighted a wide variety of individuals who prided themselves on being PC owners, helped improve employee morale and customer loyalty.

Microsoft opened a handful of retail stores—similar to Apple stores—in 2009. "The purpose of opening these stores is to create deeper engagement with consumers and continue to learn firsthand about what they want and how they buy," Microsoft said in a statement.

Today, the company offers a wide range of software and home entertainment products. In the ongoing browser wars, Internet Explorer holds a 66 percent market share compared to Firefox's 22 percent and Safari's 8 percent. In 2009, Microsoft launched a new search engine called Bing, which challenges Google's dominant position in the marketplace and claims to give better search results. Microsoft's most profitable products continue to be Microsoft Windows and Microsoft Office, which bring in approximately 90 percent of the company's $60 billion in revenue.

Questions

1. Evaluate Microsoft's strategy in good and poor economic times.

2. Discuss the pros and cons of Microsoft's most recent "I'm a PC" campaign. Is Microsoft doing a good thing by acknowledging Apple's campaign in its own marketing message? Why or why not?

Sources: Burt Helm, "Best Global Brands," *BusinessWeek,* September 18, 2008; Stuart Elliot, "Microsoft Takes a User-Friendly Approach to Selling Its Image in a New Global Campaign," *New York Times,* November 11, 1994; "Todd Bishop, "The Rest of the Motto," *Seattle Post Intelligencer,* September 23, 2004; Devin Leonard, "Hey PC, Who Taught You to Fight Back?" *New York Times,* August 30, 2009; Suzanne Vranica and Robert A. Guth, "Microsoft Enlists Jerry Seinfeld in Its Ad Battle Against Apple," *Wall Street Journal,* August 21, 2008, p. A1; Stuart Elliott, "Echoing the Campaign of a Rival, Microsoft Aims to Redefine 'I'm a PC,'" *New York Times,* September 18, 2008, p. C4; John Furguson, "From Cola Wars to Computer Wars—Microsoft Misses Again," *BN Branding,* April 4, 2009.

Marketing Excellence

>>Ferrero

Ferrero is an Italian confectionery company, privately owned by the Ferrero family. Lauded in Reputation Institute's 2009 survey as "the most reputable company in the world," Ferrero holds 7.3 percent of the world's chocolate market and is the leader in Western Europe with a 13.2 percent share. Its revenue in fiscal year 2008 was $8.2 billion, an 8.2 percent rise from the previous year, and the company employs more than 21,000 people in 18 factories worldwide.

The story of this remarkable company begins in 1946 with a small patisserie in Alba, Italy. There, Pietro Ferrero invented a 50 percent hazelnut, 50 percent cocoa confection. Because taxes on cacao beans were extremely high in post–World War II Italy, pure chocolate was not readily available. Alba was known for the production of hazelnuts, and Ferrero's cheaply produced *pasta gianduja* block, made from readily available ingredients, suitably satisfied consumers' cravings for sweet foods. The product was a hit, and by 1951 the Ferrero family had decided to turn the *pasta gianduja* block into a creamy spread. By 1951 Ferrero was marketing this as *Supercrema*. In 1963, Pietro's son Michele—by now CEO—modified the recipe and marketed it as the immensely popular Nutella. Ferrero now sells more than 67,000 jars of Nutella a year in Italy alone. While it offers a limited product range, Ferrero's offerings are nonetheless consumable at all times of day, from breakfast (Nutella) to dessert (Ferrero Rocher) and any time in between (Kinder chocolates—Bueno and Surprise—and the ever-popular Tic Tac). The emphasis is on *quality*, and it is certainly part of the key to Ferrero's success.

Ferrero began expanding into Europe in 1956 by setting up a factory in Germany, where chocolate was extremely popular. This early understanding of global trends allowed the company to swiftly expand into the French, Australian, Canadian, Asian, Puerto Rican, Ecuadorian, and finally the U.S. markets.

In 1974, Ferrero established operations in Australia with the mission of delighting customers with unique products of the highest quality and integrity and contributing to the well-being of employers, customers, and the company.

The firm concentrates on meeting high standards; thus it manufactures only in places where it is sure it can deliver consistent quality and where a secure retail supply chain means it will never let consumers down. Managing Director of Ferrero Australia, Rocco Perna, believes that nothing the company does should compromise its consumer relationships, and that if such a risk does exist, the product should not be made available. He points out that only top-quality, locally sourced ingredients are used in Ferrero's products, with the exception of cacao and hazelnut.

Ferrero's focus on consumers is accompanied by its emphasis on quality, integrity, product innovation, and passion. The company strives to understand market preferences. Ferrero Australia does extensive testing of its products in the Australian market before bringing them to market. First, it carries out internal taste testing to see whether consumers rate the product to the same high standards of the company. Then Ferrero conducts market testing in one state before going national. Ferrero test-marketed three products in the Kinder line in Victoria for two years before nationally marketing them. By understanding the insights of the market, Ferrero has ensured constant growth since the 1940s.

The company again demonstrated its understanding of consumer markets in its forays into the Indian market. Leading up to the holiday of Deepavali in 2010, the company marketed Ferrero Rocher in gift packs as a lower-calorie alternative to traditional Indian milk sweets in up-market circles.

The company also started to use new media strategies in its product development. To promote Tic Tac, Ferrero Australia launched a Facebook page and an iPhone application, which allowed the company to engage with customers online. Based on feedback, Ferrero was able to introduce two new products to the Tic Tac line: the limited edition Bold! and a larger 24-gram pack. These were available in two new flavors: Apple Sour and Mint.

Ferrero also used the Internet to reach out to parents and children. In 2003, in addition to the small, collectible figurine inside the Kinder Surprise egg, the company inserted a small slip of paper containing a Magicode that allowed children to play an online Surprise game featuring Kinder characters. In 2010, Ferrero drew attention to its commitment to quality by launching its first boutique store online, www.ferreroboutique.com.au, which sells a range of premium gifts priced from $45 to $360 and gift boxes for special occasions. These gift boxes contain chocolates from the Ferrero Rocher line, including the traditional praline chocolate, the dark chocolate Ferrero Rondnoir, and the white chocolate Raffaello. Corporate gifts are also available.

Ferrero uses its marketing insights to promote sales. The company's 2010 promotion of Nutella included sponsorship of the Football Federation of Australia and the Socceroos, the Australian national soccer team, and was one of the biggest sponsorship exercises in the history of the brand. It also emphasized that Nutella was one of Australia's best-known and most-loved brands, by associating it with a sport that most Australians enjoy. The sponsorship program resulted in an increase of Nutella's household penetration from 15.1 to 16.3 percent.

Ferrero also has to think strategically in order to broaden its market share in other ways. In January 2010, Ferrero announced that it did not intend to challenge Kraft Food's takeover of British confectioner Cadbury. Ferrero announced on January 14, 2010 that the debts and job cuts that would have been required to accommodate this move, ostensibly considered in order to improve market reach, were not justified. Instead, the company aimed to introduce "fresh" products, using newer technologies, in order to improve its reach into South American and Asian markets. By not overdiversifying, Ferrero has maintained its ability to focus on its commitment to a small number of high-quality products.

Finally, Ferrero Australia has also engaged in many community programs, such as a food bank that distributes food and grocery industry donations to welfare agencies to feed the hungry. It also supports Brainwave, a charity supporting pediatric neuroscience. The company introduced the pink Tic Tac in celebration of Pink Ribbon Month to support breast cancer research and awareness along with the National Breast Cancer Foundation (NBCF). Ferrero also supports the abolition of child labor and forest conservation methods. It purchases cacao only from suppliers who grow and process without using child labor, and it purchases palm oil only from countries and areas not known for deforestation. Ferrero has been combating the issue of childhood obesity since 2008 by emphasizing Nutella's role in a healthy and well-balanced breakfast and pledging not to target children in its advertisements.

Questions

1. Evaluate Ferrero Australia's decision to open an online boutique. Will this have any impact on the company's other business segments?

2. How can Ferrero use new technology to market its products better?

Sources: Klaus Kneale, "World's Most Reputable Companies," *Forbes*, May 6, 2009, www.forbes.com/2009/05/06/world-reputable-companies-leadership-reputation-table.html; Armorel Kenna, "Ferrero Won't Make Takeover Bid for Cadbury to Challenge Kraft," *Bloomberg BusinessWeek*, January 25, 2010, www.businessweek.com/news/2010-01-25/ferrero-won-t-make-takeover-bid-for-cadbury-to-challenge-kraft.html; Ferrero, www.ferrero.com.au; *FlowerAdvisor*, www.floweradvisor.co.in/.

Chapter 4

In This Chapter, We Will Address the Following Questions

1. What constitutes good marketing research?

2. What are the best metrics for measuring marketing productivity?

3. How can marketers assess their return on investment of marketing expenditures?

Insightful consumer research helped Kimberly-Clark improve its Huggies diapers and gain share in the market.

Conducting Marketing Research

Good marketers need insights to help them interpret past performance as well as plan future activities. To make the best possible tactical decisions in the short run and strategic decisions in the long run, they need timely, accurate, and actionable information about consumers, competition, and their brands. Discovering a consumer insight and understanding its marketing implications can often lead to a successful product launch or spur the growth of a brand.

 A series of novel consumer innovations through the years—including Kleenex facial tissues, Kotex feminine napkins, and others—have transformed Kimberly-Clark from a paper mill company to a consumer products powerhouse. Among the company's recent successes was Huggies Supreme Natural Fit, named one of the most successful new product launches in 2007. Nearly three years of research and design were invested in the creation of the new diaper. After assembling a sample of new mothers from different parts of the country with different income backgrounds and ethnicities, Kimberly-Clark's marketers conducted in-home interviews and placed motion-activated cameras in homes to learn about diaper-changing routines. Seeing new moms constantly struggle to straighten a squirming baby's legs when putting on a diaper led to the insight that the new diaper also needed to be shaped to better follow the curves of a baby's body. Because mothers said they wanted their older babies to feel like they weren't wearing a diaper, the new diaper also had to be thinner with a closer fit, so new polymers cut the width of the imbedded absorbent by 16 percent and stretch was added to the back waistband. When research also revealed that moms often used the cartoon graphics on another diaper to distract the baby during a diaper change, more active images of Disney-licensed Winnie the Pooh characters were added. The successful launch of the research-inspired innovation boosted Kimberly-Clark's market share by one to two percentage points and significantly contributed to the company's $4 billion-plus sales in diapers that year.[1]

In this chapter, we review the steps in the marketing research process. We also consider how marketers can develop effective metrics for measuring marketing productivity.

The Marketing Research System

Marketing managers often commission formal marketing studies of specific problems and opportunities. They may request a market survey, a product-preference test, a sales forecast by region, or an advertising evaluation. It's the job of the marketing researcher to produce insight into the customer's attitudes and buying behavior. **Marketing insights** provide diagnostic information about how and why we observe certain effects in the marketplace, and what that means to marketers.[2]

Good marketing insights often form the basis of successful marketing programs. When an extensive consumer research study of U.S. retail shoppers by Walmart revealed that the store's key competitive advantages were the functional benefit of "offers low prices" and the emotional benefit of "makes me feel like a smart shopper," its marketers used those insights to develop their "Save Money, Live Better" campaign. Gillette's Venus razor has become the most successful female shaving line ever—holding more than 50 percent of the global women's shaving market—as a result of insightful consumer research that led to product design, packaging, and advertising cues that better satisfied female shaving needs.[3]

Venus Razor   As part of a $300 million budget for the development of its first razor designed solely for women, Gillette conducted extensive consumer research and performed numerous market tests. The razor, called Venus, was a marked departure from previous women's razor designs, which had essentially been colored or repackaged versions of men's razors. After research revealed that women change their grip on a razor about 30 times during each shaving session, Gillette designed the Venus with a wide, sculpted rubberized handle offering superior grip and control, and an oval-shaped blade in a storage case that could stick to shower walls. Research also indicated that women were reluctant to leave the shower in order to replace a dull blade, so the case was made to hold spare blade cartridges. When Gillette research later revealed four distinct segments of women shavers—perfect shave seekers (no missed hairs), skin pamperers, pragmatic functionalists, and EZ seekers—the company designed Venus products for each of them.

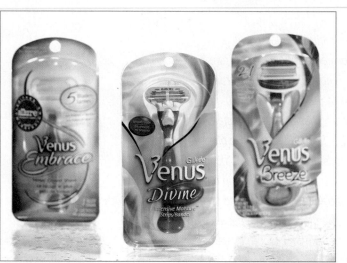

Extensive consumer research was crucial to the success of Gillette's Venus series of razors designed exclusively for women.

Gaining marketing insights is crucial for marketing success. If marketers lack consumer insights, they often get in trouble. When Tropicana redesigned its orange juice packaging, dropping the iconic image of an orange skewered by a straw, it failed to adequately test for consumer reactions, with disastrous results. Sales dropped by 20 percent, and Tropicana reinstated the old package design after only a few months.[4]

We define **marketing research** as the systematic design, collection, analysis, and reporting of data and findings relevant to a specific marketing situation facing the company. Spending on marketing research topped $28 billion globally in 2009, according to ESOMAR, the world association of opinion and market research professionals.[5] Most large companies have their own marketing research departments, which often play crucial roles within the organization. Procter & Gamble's Consumer & Market Knowledge (CMK) market research function has dedicated CMK groups working for P&G businesses around the world to improve both their brand strategies and program execution, as well as a relatively smaller, centralized corporate CMK group that focuses on a variety of big-picture concerns that transcend any specific line of business.

Marketing research, however, is not limited to large companies with big budgets and marketing research departments. Often at much smaller companies, everyone carries out marketing research—including the customers. Small companies can also hire the services of a marketing research firm or conduct research in creative and affordable ways, such as:

1. *Engaging students or professors to design and carry out projects*—Companies such as American Express, Booz Allen Hamilton, GE, Hilton Hotels, IBM, Mars, Price Chopper, and Whirlpool engage in "crowdcasting" and are sponsors of competitions such as the Innovation Challenge, where top MBA students compete in teams. The payoff to the students is experience and visibility; the payoff to the companies is a fresh sets of eyes to solve problems at a fraction of what consultants would charge.[6]
2. *Using the Internet*—A company can collect considerable information at very little cost by examining competitors' Web sites, monitoring chat rooms, and accessing published data.
3. *Checking out rivals*—Many small businesses, such as restaurants, hotels, or specialty retailers, routinely visit competitors to learn about changes they have made.
4. *Tapping into marketing partner expertise*—Marketing research firms, ad agencies, distributors, and other marketing partners may be able to share relevant market knowledge they have accumulated. Those partners targeting small or medium-sized businesses may be especially

helpful. For example, to promote more shipping to China, UPS conducted several in-depth surveys of the Chinese market to portray its complexities but also its opportunities for even small and medium-sized businesses.[7]

Most companies use a combination of marketing research resources to study their industries, competitors, audiences, and channel strategies. Companies normally budget marketing research at 1 percent to 2 percent of company sales and spend a large percentage of that on the services of outside firms. Marketing research firms fall into three categories:

1. *Syndicated-service research firms*—These firms gather consumer and trade information, which they sell for a fee. Examples include the Nielsen Company, Kantar Group, Westat, and IRI.
2. *Custom marketing research firms*—These firms are hired to carry out specific projects. They design the study and report the findings.
3. *Specialty-line marketing research firms*—These firms provide specialized research services. The best example is the field-service firm, which sells field interviewing services to other firms.

To take advantage of all these different resources and practices, good marketers adopt a formal marketing research process.

The Marketing Research Process

Effective marketing research follows the six steps shown in ▲ Figure 4.1. We illustrate them in the following situation.[8]

> American Airlines (AA) was one of the first companies to install phone handsets on its planes. Now it's reviewing many new ideas, especially to cater to its first-class passengers on very long flights, mainly businesspeople whose high-priced tickets pay most of the freight. Among these ideas are: (1) an Internet connection primarily for e-mail but with some limited access to Web pages, (2) 24 channels of satellite cable TV, and (3) a 50-CD audio system that lets each passenger create a customized in-flight play list. The marketing research manager was assigned to investigate how first-class passengers would rate these services, specifically the Internet connection, and how much extra they would be willing to pay for it. One source estimates revenues of $70 billion from in-flight Internet access over 10 years, if enough first-class passengers paid $25. AA could thus recover its costs in a reasonable time. Making the connection available would cost the airline $90,000 per plane.[9]

Step 1: Define the Problem, the Decision Alternatives, and the Research Objectives

Marketing managers must be careful not to define the problem too broadly or too narrowly for the marketing researcher. A marketing manager who says, "Find out everything you can about first-class air travelers' needs," will collect a lot of unnecessary information. One who says, "Find out whether enough passengers aboard a B747 flying direct between Chicago and Tokyo would be willing to pay $25 for an Internet connection for American Airlines to break even in one year on the cost of offering this service," is taking too narrow a view of the problem.

The marketing researcher might even ask, "Why does the Internet connection have to be priced at $25 as opposed to $15, $35, or some other price? Why does American have to break even on the cost of the service, especially if it attracts new customers?" Another relevant question to ask is, "How important is it to be first in the market, and how long can the company sustain its lead?"

The marketing manager and marketing researcher agreed to define the problem as follows: "Will offering an in-flight Internet service create enough incremental preference and profit for American Airlines to justify its cost against other possible investments in service enhancements American might make?" To help in designing the research, management should first spell out the decisions it might face and then work backward. Suppose management outlines these decisions: (1) Should American offer an Internet connection? (2) If so, should we offer the service to first-class only, or

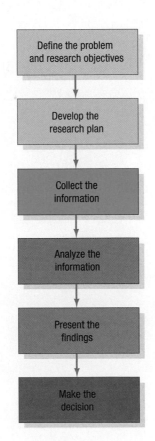

|Fig. 4.1| ▲

The Marketing Research Process

An airline looking to add in-flight Internet service would need to conduct careful consumer research.

include business class, and possibly economy class? (3) What price(s) should we charge? (4) On what types of planes and lengths of trips should we offer the service?

Now management and marketing researchers are ready to set specific research objectives: (1) What types of first-class passengers would respond most to using an in-flight Internet service? (2) How many first-class passengers are likely to use the Internet service at different price levels? (3) How many extra first-class passengers might choose American because of this new service? (4) How much long-term goodwill will this service add to American Airlines' image? (5) How important is Internet service to first-class passengers relative to other services, such as a power plug or enhanced entertainment?

Not all research projects can be this specific. Some research is *exploratory*—its goal is to shed light on the real nature of the problem and to suggest possible solutions or new ideas. Some research is *descriptive*—it seeks to quantify demand, such as how many first-class passengers would purchase in-flight Internet service at $25. Some research is *causal*—its purpose is to test a cause-and-effect relationship.

Step 2: Develop the Research Plan

The second stage of marketing research is where we develop the most efficient plan for gathering the needed information and what that will cost. Suppose American made a prior estimate that launching in-flight Internet service would yield a long-term profit of $50,000. If the manager believes that doing the marketing research will lead to an improved pricing and promotional plan and a long-term profit of $90,000, he should be willing to spend up to $40,000 on this research. If the research will cost more than $40,000, it's not worth doing.[10]

To design a research plan, we need to make decisions about the data sources, research approaches, research instruments, sampling plan, and contact methods.

DATA SOURCES The researcher can gather secondary data, primary data, or both. *Secondary data* are data that were collected for another purpose and already exist somewhere. *Primary data* are data freshly gathered for a specific purpose or for a specific research project.

Researchers usually start their investigation by examining some of the rich variety of low-cost and readily available secondary data, to see whether they can partly or wholly solve the problem without collecting costly primary data. For instance, auto advertisers looking to get a better return on their online car ads might purchase a copy of J.D. Power and Associates' semiannual Power Auto Online Media Study, a survey that gives insights into who buys specific brands and where on the Web advertisers can find them.[11]

When the needed data don't exist or are dated, inaccurate, incomplete, or unreliable, the researcher will need to collect primary data. Most marketing research projects do include some primary-data collection.

RESEARCH APPROACHES Marketers collect primary data in five main ways: through observation, focus groups, surveys, behavioral data, and experiments.

Observational Research Researchers can gather fresh data by observing the relevant actors and settings unobtrusively as they shop or consume products.[12] Sometimes they equip consumers with pagers and instruct them to write down what they're doing whenever prompted, or they hold informal interview sessions at a café or bar. Photographs can also provide a wealth of detailed information.

Ethnographic research is a particular observational research approach that uses concepts and tools from anthropology and other social science disciplines to provide deep cultural understanding of how people live and work.[13] The goal is to immerse the researcher into consumers' lives to uncover unarticulated desires that might not surface in any other form of research.[14] Firms such as Fujitsu Laboratories, Herman Miller, IBM, Intel, Steelcase, and Xerox have embraced ethnographic research to design breakthrough products. Here are three specific examples.

- Bank of America's ethnographic research that followed female baby boomers at home and while they shopped yielded two insights—women rounded up financial transactions because it was more convenient, and those with children found it difficult to save. Subsequent research led to the launch of "Keep the Change," a debit card program that rounded purchases up to the nearest dollar amount and automatically transferred the added difference from a checking to a savings account. Since the launch, 2.5 million customers have signed up for the program, opening 800,000 new checking accounts and 3 million new savings accounts in the process.[15]

- To boost sagging sales for its Orville Redenbacher popcorn, ConAgra spent nine months observing families in their homes and assembling their weekly diaries of how they felt about various snacks. In reviewing the results, ConAgra found a key insight: the essence of popcorn was that it was a "facilitator of interaction." Four nationwide TV ads followed with the tagline, "Spending Time Together: That's the Power of Orville Redenbacher."[16]

- When package design firm 4sight, Inc., was hired by PepsiCo to come up with a new design for Gatorade's 64-ounce package, its team initially assumed the package functioned as a "family pack" to be used for multiple servings to multiple users in the household. In watching moms in their homes, however, team members were surprised to find them taking the jug out of the refrigerator—for example, after a hard workout—and chugging it right there on the spot! That insight led to a totally different package design, one that could be easily gripped and grabbed.[17]

Ethnographic research isn't limited to consumer companies in developed markets. In a business-to-business setting, GE's ethnographic research into the plastic-fiber industry revealed to the firm that it wasn't in a commodity business driven by price, as it had assumed. Instead it was in an artisanal industry, with customers who wanted collaborations at the earliest stages of development. GE completely reoriented the way it interacted with the companies in the industry as a result. In developing markets, ethnographic research also can be very useful, especially in far-flung rural areas, given that marketers often do not know these consumers as well.[18]

The American Airlines researchers might meander around first-class lounges to hear how travelers talk about the different carriers and their features or sit next to passengers on planes. They can fly on competitors' planes to observe in-flight service.

Focus Group Research A **focus group** is a gathering of 6 to 10 people carefully selected by researchers based on certain

Ethnographic research with female baby boomers helped Bank of America launch its well-received "Keep the Change" program.

demographic, psychographic, or other considerations and brought together to discuss various topics of interest at length. Participants are normally paid a small sum for attending. A professional research moderator provides questions and probes based on the marketing managers' discussion guide or agenda. In focus groups, moderators try to discern consumers' real motivations and why they say and do certain things. They typically record the sessions, and marketing managers often remain behind two-way mirrors in the next room. To allow for more in-depth discussion with participants, focus groups are trending smaller in size.[19]

Focus-group research is a useful exploratory step, but researchers must avoid generalizing from focus-group participants to the whole market, because the sample size is too small and the sample is not drawn randomly. Some marketers feel the research setting is too contrived and prefer to seek other means of collecting information that they believe are less artificial. "Marketing Memo: Conducting Informative Focus Groups" has some practical tips to improve the quality of focus groups.

In the American Airlines research, the moderator might start with a broad question, such as, "How do you feel about first-class air travel?" Questions then move to how people view the different airlines, different existing services, different proposed services, and specifically, Internet service.

marketing Memo

Conducting Informative Focus Groups

Focus groups allow marketers to observe how and why consumers accept or reject concepts, ideas, or any specific notion. The key to using focus groups successfully is to *listen and observe.* Marketers should eliminate their own biases as much as possible. Although many useful insights can emerge from thoughtfully run focus groups, questions can arise about their validity, especially in today's complex marketing environment.

There are many challenges to conducting a good focus group. Some researchers believe consumers have been so bombarded with ads, they unconsciously (or perhaps cynically) parrot back what they've already heard instead of what they really think. There's always a concern that participants are just trying to maintain their self-image and public persona or have a need to identify with the other members of the group. Participants also may not be willing to acknowledge in public—or may not even recognize—their behavior patterns and motivations. And the "loudmouth" or "know-it-all" problem often crops up when one highly opinionated person drowns out the rest of the group. Getting the right participants is crucial, but it may be expensive to recruit qualified subjects who meet the sampling criteria ($3,000 to $5,000 per group).

Even when marketers use multiple focus groups, it may be difficult to generalize the results to a broader population. For example, within the United States, focus-group findings often vary from region to region. One firm specializing in focus-group research claimed the best city to conduct groups was Minneapolis, because there it could get a sample of fairly well-educated people who were honest and forthcoming with their opinions. Many marketers interpret focus groups in New York and other northeastern cities carefully, because the people in these areas tend to be highly critical and generally don't report that they like much.

Participants must feel as relaxed as possible and strongly motivated to be truthful. Physical surroundings can be crucial to achieving the right atmosphere. At one agency an executive noted, "We wondered why people always seemed grumpy and negative—people were resistant to any idea we showed them." Finally in one session a fight broke out between participants. The problem was the room itself: cramped, stifling, forbidding. "It was a cross between a hospital room and a police interrogation room." To fix the problem, the agency gave the room a makeover. Other firms are adapting the look of the room to fit the theme of the topic—such as designing the room to look like a playroom when speaking to children.

To allow for more interactivity among focus group members, some researchers are incorporating pre-session homework assignments such as diaries, photography, and videography. An area of increasing interest is online focus groups. These may cost less than a fourth of a traditional, in-person focus group. Online focus groups also offer the advantages of being less intrusive, allowing geographically diverse subjects to participate, and yielding fast results. They are useful at collecting reactions to focused topics such as a specific new product concept.

Proponents of traditional focus groups, on the other hand, maintain that in-person focus groups allow marketers to be immersed in the research process, get a close-up look to people's emotional and physical reactions, and ensure that sensitive materials are not leaked. Marketers can also make spontaneous adjustments to the flow of discussion and delve deeply into more complex topics, such as alternative creative concepts for a new ad campaign.

Regardless of the particular form it takes, the beauty of a focus group, as one marketing executive noted, is that "It's still the most cost-effective, quickest, dirtiest way to get information in rapid time on an idea." In analyzing the pros and cons, Wharton's Americus Reed might have said it best: "A focus group is like a chain saw. If you know what you're doing, it's very useful and effective. If you don't, you could lose a limb."

Sources: Naomi R. Henderson, "Beyond Top of Mind," *Marketing Research* (September 1, 2005); Rebecca Harris, "Do Focus Groups Have a Future?" *Marketing,* June 6, 2005, p. 17; Linda Tischler, "Every Move You Make," *Fast Company,* April 2004, pp. 73–75; Alison Stein Wellner, "The New Science of Focus Groups," *American Demographics,* March 2003, pp. 29–33; Dennis Rook, "Out-of-Focus Groups," *Marketing Research* 15, no. 2 (Summer 2003), p. 11; Dennis W. Rook, "Loss of Vision: Focus Groups Fail to Connect Theory, Current Practice," *Marketing News,* September 15, 2003, p. 40; Sarah Jeffrey Kasner, "Fistfights and Feng Shui," *Boston Globe,* July 21, 2001; Piet Levy, "In With the Old, In Spite of the New," *Marketing News,* May 30, 2009, p. 19.

Survey Research Companies undertake surveys to assess people's knowledge, beliefs, preferences, and satisfaction and to measure these magnitudes in the general population. A company such as American Airlines might prepare its own survey instrument to gather the information it needs, or it might add questions to an omnibus survey that carries the questions of several companies, at a much lower cost. It can also pose the questions to an ongoing consumer panel run by itself or another company. It may do a mall intercept study by having researchers approach people in a shopping mall and ask them questions.

As we'll discuss in more detail later in this chapter, many marketers are taking their surveys online where they can easily develop, administer, and collect e-mail and Web-based questionnaires. However they conduct their surveys—online, by phone, or in person—companies must feel the information they're getting from the mounds of data makes it all worthwhile. San Francisco–based Wells Fargo bank collects more than 50,000 customer surveys each month through its bank branches. It has used customers' comments to begin more stringent new wait-time standards designed to improve customer satisfaction.

Of course, by putting out so many surveys each month, companies may run the risk of creating "survey burnout" and seeing response rates plummet. Keeping a survey short and simple and contacting customers no more than once a month are two keys to drawing people into the data collection effort. Offering incentives is another way companies get consumers to respond. Both Gap and Jack in the Box offer coupons for discount merchandise or the chance to win a cash prize.[20]

BEHAVIORAL RESEARCH Customers leave traces of their purchasing behavior in store scanning data, catalog purchases, and customer databases. Marketers can learn much by analyzing these data. Actual purchases reflect consumers' preferences and often are more reliable than statements they offer to market researchers. For example, grocery shopping data show that high-income people don't necessarily buy the more expensive brands, contrary to what they might state in interviews; and many low-income people buy some expensive brands. And as Chapter 3 described, there is a wealth of online data to collect from consumers. Clearly, American Airlines can learn many useful things about its passengers by analyzing ticket purchase records and online behavior.

EXPERIMENTAL RESEARCH The most scientifically valid research is **experimental research**, designed to capture cause-and-effect relationships by eliminating competing explanations of the observed findings. If the experiment is well designed and executed, research and marketing managers can have confidence in the conclusions. Experiments call for selecting matched groups of subjects, subjecting them to different treatments, controlling extraneous variables, and checking whether observed response differences are statistically significant. If we

An important marketing research tool is focus groups.

can eliminate or control extraneous factors, we can relate the observed effects to the variations in the treatments or stimuli.

American Airlines might introduce in-flight Internet service on one of its regular flights from Chicago to Tokyo and charge $25 one week and $15 the next week. If the plane carried approximately the same number of first-class passengers each week and the particular weeks made no difference, the airline could relate any significant difference in the number of passengers using the service to the different prices charged.

RESEARCH INSTRUMENTS Marketing researchers have a choice of three main research instruments in collecting primary data: questionnaires, qualitative measures, and technological devices.

Questionnaires A **questionnaire** consists of a set of questions presented to respondents. Because of its flexibility, it is by far the most common instrument used to collect primary data. Researchers need to carefully develop, test, and debug questionnaires before administering them on a large scale. The form, wording, and sequence of the questions can all influence the responses. *Closed-end questions* specify all the possible answers and provide answers that are easier to interpret and tabulate. *Open-end questions* allow respondents to answer in their own words and often reveal more about how people think. They are especially useful in exploratory research, where the researcher is looking for insight into how people think rather than measuring how many people think a certain way. 📖 Table 4.1 provides examples of both types of questions; also see "Marketing Memo: Questionnaire Dos and Don'ts."

Qualitative Measures Some marketers prefer more qualitative methods for gauging consumer opinion, because consumer actions don't always match their answers to survey questions. *Qualitative research techniques* are relatively unstructured measurement approaches that permit a range of possible responses. Their variety is limited only by the creativity of the marketing researcher.

Because of the freedom it affords both researchers in their probes and consumers in their responses, qualitative research can often be an especially useful first step in exploring consumers' brand and product perceptions. It is indirect in nature, so consumers may be less guarded and reveal more about themselves in the process.

Qualitative research does have its drawbacks. Marketers must temper the in-depth insights that emerge with the fact that the samples are often very small and may not necessarily generalize to broader populations. And different researchers examining the same qualitative results may draw very different conclusions.

---

marketing Memo

Questionnaire Dos and Don'ts

1. *Ensure that questions are without bias.* Don't lead the respondent into an answer.

2. *Make the questions as simple as possible.* Questions that include multiple ideas or two questions in one will confuse respondents.

3. *Make the questions specific.* Sometimes it's advisable to add memory cues. For example, be specific with time periods.

4. *Avoid jargon or shorthand.* Avoid trade jargon, acronyms, and initials not in everyday use.

5. *Steer clear of sophisticated or uncommon words.* Use only words in common speech.

6. *Avoid ambiguous words.* Words such as "*usually*" or "*frequently*" have no specific meaning.

7. *Avoid questions with a negative in them.* It is better to say, "Do you ever . . . ?" than "Do you never . . . ?"

8. *Avoid hypothetical questions.* It's difficult to answer questions about imaginary situations. Answers aren't necessarily reliable.

9. *Do not use words that could be misheard.* This is especially important when administering the interview over the telephone. "What is your opinion of sects?" could yield interesting but not necessarily relevant answers.

10. *Desensitize questions by using response bands.* To ask people their age or ask companies about employee turnover rates, offer a range of response bands instead of precise numbers.

11. *Ensure that fixed responses do not overlap.* Categories used in fixed-response questions should be distinct and not overlap.

12. *Allow for the answer "other" in fixed-response questions.* Precoded answers should always allow for a response other than those listed.

Source: Adapted from Paul Hague and Peter Jackson, *Market Research: A Guide to Planning, Methodology, and Evaluation* (London: Kogan Page, 1999). See also, Hans Baumgartner and Jan-Benedict E. M. Steenkamp, "Response Styles in Marketing Research: A Cross-National Investigation," *Journal of Marketing Research* (May 2001), pp. 143–56.

TABLE 4.1   Types of Questions

Name	Description	Example
A. Closed-End Questions		
Dichotomous	A question with two possible answers	In arranging this trip, did you personally phone American? Yes No
Multiple choice	A question with three or more answers	With whom are you traveling on this flight? ☐ No one ☐ Children only ☐ Spouse ☐ Business associates/friends/relatives ☐ Spouse and children ☐ An organized tour group
Likert scale	A statement with which the respondent shows the amount of agreement/ disagreement	Small airlines generally give better service than large ones. Strongly Disagree Neither Agree Strongly disagree agree nor agree disagree 1_____ 2_____ 3_____ 4_____ 5_____
Semantic differential	A scale connecting two bipolar words. The respondent selects the point that represents his or her opinion.	American Airlines Large _____ Small Experienced _____ Inexperienced Modern _____ Old-fashioned
Importance scale	A scale that rates the importance of some attribute	Airline in-flight service to me is Extremely Very Somewhat Not very Not at all important important important important important 1_____ 2_____ 3_____ 4_____ 5_____
Rating scale	A scale that rates some attribute from "poor" to "excellent"	American in-flight service is Excellent Very Good Good Fair Poor 1_____ 2_____ 3_____ 4_____ 5_____
Intention-to-buy scale	A scale that describes the respondent's intention to buy	If an in-flight telephone were available on a long flight, I would Definitely Probably Not sure Probably Definitely buy buy not buy not buy 1_____ 2_____ 3_____ 4_____ 5_____
B. Open-End Questions		
Completely unstructured	A question that respondents can answer in an almost unlimited number of ways	What is your opinion of American Airlines?
Word association	Words are presented, one at a time, and respondents mention the first word that comes to mind.	What is the first word that comes to your mind when you hear the following? Airline_____ American_____ Travel_____
Sentence completion	An incomplete sentence is presented and respondents complete the sentence.	When I choose an airline, the most important consideration in my decision is _____ .
Story completion	An incomplete story is presented, and respondents are asked to complete it.	"I flew American a few days ago. I noticed that the exterior and interior of the plane had very bright colors. This aroused in me the following thoughts and feelings . . . ." Now complete the story.
Picture	A picture of two characters is presented, with one making a statement. Respondents are asked to identify with the other and fill in the empty balloon.	
Thematic Apperception Test (TAT)	A picture is presented and respondents are asked to make up a story about what they think is happening or may happen in the picture.	

Nevertheless, there is increasing interest in using qualitative methods. "Marketing Insight: Getting into the Heads of Consumers" describes the pioneering ZMET approach. Some other popular qualitative research approaches to get inside consumers' minds and find out what they think or feel about brands and products include:[21]

1. **Word associations**—Ask subjects what words come to mind when they hear the brand's name. "What does the Timex name mean to you? Tell me what comes to mind when you think of Timex watches." The primary purpose of free-association tasks is to identify the range of possible brand associations in consumers' minds.

2. **Projective techniques**—Give people an incomplete stimulus and ask them to complete it, or give them an ambiguous stimulus and ask them to make sense of it. One approach is "bubble exercises" in which empty bubbles, like those found in cartoons, appear in scenes of people buying or using certain products or services. Subjects fill in the bubble, indicating what they believe is happening or being said. Another technique is comparison tasks in which people compare brands to people, countries, animals, activities, fabrics, occupations, cars, magazines, vegetables, nationalities, or even other brands.

3. **Visualization**—Visualization requires people to create a collage from magazine photos or drawings to depict their perceptions.

Marketing Insight

Getting into the Heads of Consumers

Harvard Business School marketing professor Gerald Zaltman, with some of his research colleagues, has developed an in-depth methodology to uncover what consumers truly think and feel about products, services, brands, and other things. The basic assumption behind the Zaltman Metaphor Elicitation Technique (ZMET) is that most thoughts and feelings are unconscious and shaped by a set of "deep metaphors." **Deep metaphors** are basic frames or orientations that consumers have toward the world around them. Largely unconscious and universal, they recast everything someone thinks, hears, says, or does. According to Zaltman, there are seven main metaphors:

1. *Balance:* justice equilibrium and the interplay of elements;
2. *Transformation:* changes in substance and circumstance;
3. *Journey:* the meeting of past, present, and future;
4. *Container:* inclusion, exclusion, and other boundaries;
5. *Connection:* the need to relate to oneself and others;
6. *Resource:* acquisitions and their consequences; and
7. *Control:* sense of mastery, vulnerability, and well-being

The ZMET technique works by first asking participants in advance to select a minimum of 12 images from their own sources (magazines,

catalogs, family photo albums) to represent their thoughts and feelings about the research topic. In a one-on-one interview, the study administrator uses advanced interview techniques to explore the images with the participant and reveal hidden meanings. Finally, the participants use a computer program to create a collage with these images that communicates their subconscious thoughts and feelings about the topic. The results often profoundly influence marketing actions, as the following three examples illustrate:

- In a ZMET study about pantyhose for marketers at DuPont, some respondents' pictures showed fence posts encased in plastic wrap or steel bands strangling trees, suggesting that pantyhose are tight and inconvenient. But another picture showed tall flowers in a vase, suggesting that the product made a woman feel thin, tall, and sexy. The "love-hate" relationship in these and other pictures suggested a more complicated product relationship than the DuPont marketers had assumed.

- A ZMET study of Nestlé Crunch revealed that—besides the obvious associations to a small indulgence in a busy world, a source of quick energy, and something that just tasted good—the candy bar was also seen as a powerful reminder of pleasant childhood memories.

- When Motorola conducted a ZMET study of a proposed new security system, study participants selected images of what they felt when they were secure. The Motorola researchers were struck by how many images of dogs showed up, suggesting that it might be appropriate to position the product as a companion.

Sources: Gerald Zaltman and Lindsay Zaltman, *Marketing Metaphoria: What Deep Metaphors Reveal About the Minds of Consumers* (Boston: Harvard Business School Press, 2008); Daniel H. Pink, "Metaphor Marketing," *Fast Company*, March/April 1998, pp. 214–29; Brad Wieners, "Getting Inside—Way Inside—Your Customer's Head," *Business 2.0*, April 2003, pp. 54–55; Glenn L. Christensen and Jerry C. Olson, "Mapping Consumers' Mental Models with ZMET," *Psychology & Marketing* 19, no. 6 (June 2002), pp. 477–502; Emily Eakin, "Penetrating the Mind by Metaphor," *New York Times*, February 23, 2002.

4. **Brand personification**—Ask subjects what kind of person they think of when the brand is mentioned: "If the brand were to come alive as a person, what would it be like, what would it do, where would it live, what would it wear, who would it talk to if it went to a party (and what would it talk about)?" For example, the John Deere brand might make someone think of a rugged Midwestern male who is hardworking and trustworthy. The brand personality delivers a picture of the more human qualities of the brand.

5. **Laddering**—A series of increasingly more specific "why" questions can reveal consumer motivation and consumers' deeper, more abstract goals. Ask why someone wants to buy a Nokia cell phone. "They look well built" (attribute). "Why is it important that the phone be well built?" "It suggests Nokia is reliable" (a functional benefit). "Why is reliability important?" "Because my colleagues or family can be sure to reach me" (an emotional benefit). "Why must you be available to them at all times?" "I can help them if they're in trouble" (brand essence). The brand makes this person feel like a Good Samaritan, ready to help others.

Marketers don't necessarily have to choose between qualitative and quantitative measures, however, and many marketers use both approaches, recognizing that their pros and cons can offset each other. For example, companies can recruit someone from an online panel to participate in an in-home use test in which the subject is sent a product and told to capture his or her reactions and intentions with both a video diary and an online survey.[22]

Technological Devices There has been much interest in recent years in various technological devices. Galvanometers can measure the interest or emotions aroused by exposure to a specific ad or picture. The tachistoscope flashes an ad to a subject with an exposure interval that may range from less than one hundredth of a second to several seconds. After each exposure, the respondent describes everything he or she recalls. Eye cameras study respondents' eye movements to see where their eyes land first, how long they linger on a given item, and so on.

Technology has now advanced to such a degree that marketers can use devices such as skin sensors, brain wave scanners, and full body scanners to get consumer responses.[23] Some researchers study eye movements and brain activity of Web surfers to see which ads grab their attention.[24] "Marketing Insight: Understanding Brain Science" provides a glimpse into some new marketing research frontiers studying the brain.

Technology has replaced the diaries that participants in media surveys used to keep. Audiometers attached to television sets in participating homes now record when the set is on and to which channel it is tuned. Electronic devices can record the number of radio programs a person is exposed to during the day, or, using Global Positioning System (GPS) technology, how many billboards a person may walk or drive by during a day.

SAMPLING PLAN After deciding on the research approach and instruments, the marketing researcher must design a sampling plan. This calls for three decisions:

1. **Sampling unit: Whom should we survey?** In the American Airlines survey, should the sampling unit consist only of first-class business travelers, first-class vacation travelers, or both? Should it include travelers under age 18? Both traveler and spouse? Once they have determined the sampling unit, marketers must develop a sampling frame so everyone in the target population has an equal or known chance of being sampled.

2. **Sample size: How many people should we survey?** Large samples give more reliable results, but it's not necessary to sample the entire target population to achieve reliable results. Samples of less than 1 percent of a population can often provide good reliability, with a credible sampling procedure.

3. **Sampling procedure: How should we choose the respondents?** Probability sampling allows marketers to calculate confidence limits for sampling error and makes the sample more representative. Thus, after choosing the sample, marketers could conclude that "the interval five to seven trips per year has 95 chances in 100 of containing the true number of trips taken annually by first-class passengers flying between Chicago and Tokyo."

CONTACT METHODS Now the marketing researcher must decide how to contact the subjects: by mail, by telephone, in person, or online.

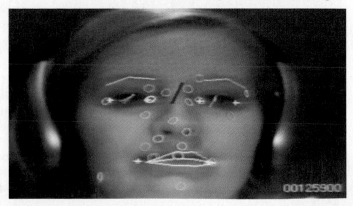

Using sophisticated equipment and methods, neuroscience researchers are studying how brain activity is affected by consumer marketing.

Marketing Insight

Understanding Brain Science

As an alternative to traditional consumer research, some researchers have begun to develop sophisticated techniques from neuroscience that monitor brain activity to better gauge consumer responses to marketing. The term *neuromarketing* describes brain research on the effect of marketing stimuli. Firms with names such as NeuroFocus and EmSense are using EEG (electroencephalograph) technology to correlate brand activity with physiological cues such as skin temperature or eye movement and thus gauge how people react to ads.

Researchers studying the brain have found different results from conventional research methods. One group of researchers at UCLA used functional magnetic resonance imaging (fMRI) to measure how consumers' brains responded to 2006's Super Bowl advertisements. They found that the ads for which subjects displayed the highest brain activity were different from the ads with the highest stated preferences. Other research found little effect from product placement unless the products in question played an integral role in the storyline.

One major research finding to emerge from neurological consumer research is that many purchase decisions appear to be characterized less by the logical weighing of variables and more "as a largely unconscious habitual process, as distinct from the rational, conscious, information-processing model of economists and traditional marketing textbooks." Even basic decisions, such as the purchase of gasoline, seem to be influenced by brain activity at the subrational level.

Neurological research has been used to measure the type of emotional response consumers exhibit when presented with marketing stimuli. A group of researchers in England used an EEG to monitor cognitive functions related to memory recall and attentiveness for 12 different regions of the brain as subjects were exposed to advertising. Brain wave activity in different regions indicated different emotional responses. For example, heightened activity in the left prefrontal cortex is characteristic of an "approach" response to an ad and indicates an attraction to the stimulus. In contrast, a spike in brain activity in the right prefrontal cortex is indicative of a strong revulsion to the stimulus. In yet another part of the brain, the degree of memory formation activity correlates with purchase intent. Other research has shown that people activate different regions of the brain in assessing the personality traits of people than they do when assessing brands.

By adding neurological techniques to their research arsenal, marketers are trying to move toward a more complete picture of what goes on inside consumers' heads. Although it may be able to offer different insights from conventional techniques, neurological research at this point is very costly, running as much as $100,000 or even more per project. Given the complexity of the human brain, however, many researchers caution that neurological research should not form the sole basis for marketing decisions. These research activities have not been universally accepted. The measurement devices to capture brain activity can be highly obtrusive, such as with skull caps studded with electrodes, creating artificial exposure conditions. Others question whether they offer unambiguous implications for marketing strategy. Brian Knutson, a professor of neuroscience and psychology at Stanford University, compares the use of EEG to "standing outside a baseball stadium and listening to the crowd to figure out what happened." Other critics worry that if the methods do become successful, they will only lead to more marketing manipulation by companies. Despite all this controversy, marketers' endless pursuit of deeper insights about consumers' response to marketing virtually guarantees continued interest in neuromarketing.

Sources: Carolyn Yoon, Angela H. Gutchess, Fred Feinberg, and Thad A. Polk, "A Functional Magnetic Resonance Imaging Study of Neural Dissociations between Brand and Person Judgments," *Journal of Consumer Research* 33 (June 2006), pp. 31–40; Daryl Travis, "Tap Buyers' Emotions for Marketing Success," *Marketing News*, February 1, 2006, pp. 21–22; Deborah L. Vence, "Pick Someone's Brain," *Marketing News*, May 1, 2006, pp. 11–13; Martin Lindstrom, *Buyology: Truth and Lies About Why We Buy* (New York: Doubleday, 2008); Tom Abate, "Coming to a Marketer Near You: Brain Scanning," *San Francisco Chronicle*, May 19, 2008; Brian Sternberg, "How Couch Potatoes Watch TV Could Hold Clues for Advertisers," *Boston Globe*, September 6, 2009, pp. G1, G3.

Mail Contacts The *mail questionnaire* is one way to reach people who would not give personal interviews or whose responses might be biased or distorted by the interviewers. Mail questionnaires require simple and clearly worded questions. Unfortunately, the response rate is usually low or slow.

Telephone Contacts *Telephone interviewing* is a good method for gathering information quickly; the interviewer is also able to clarify questions if respondents do not understand them. Interviews must be brief and not too personal. Although the response rate has typically been higher than for mailed questionnaires, telephone interviewing in the United States is getting more difficult because of consumers' growing antipathy toward telemarketers.

In late 2003, Congress passed legislation allowing the Federal Trade Commission to restrict telemarketing calls through its "Do Not Call" registry. By mid-2010, consumers had registered over 200 million phone numbers. Marketing research firms are exempt from the ruling, but given the increasingly widespread resistance to telemarketing, it undoubtedly reduces the effectiveness of telephone surveys as a marketing research method in the United States.

In other parts of the world, such restrictive legislation does not exist. Because mobile phone penetration in Africa has risen from just 1 in 50 people in 2000 to almost one-third of the population in 2008, cell phones in Africa are used to convene focus groups in rural areas and to interact via text messages.[25]

Personal Contacts *Personal interviewing* is the most versatile method. The interviewer can ask more questions and record additional observations about the respondent, such as dress and body language. At the same time, however, personal interviewing is the most expensive method, is subject to interviewer bias, and requires more administrative planning and supervision. Personal interviewing takes two forms. In *arranged interviews*, marketers contact respondents for an appointment and often offer a small payment or incentive. In *intercept interviews*, researchers stop people at a shopping mall or busy street corner and request an interview on the spot. Intercept interviews must be quick, and they run the risk of including nonprobability samples.

In parts of the developing world such as Africa, the widespread penetration of cell phones allows them to be used to conduct marketing research.

Online Contacts An approach of increasing importance, the Internet offers many ways to do research. A company can embed a questionnaire on its Web site and offer an incentive to answer it, or it can place a banner on a frequently visited site such as Yahoo!, inviting people to answer some questions and possibly win a prize. Online product testing, in which companies float trial balloons for new products, is also growing and providing information much faster than traditional new-product marketing research techniques. Here is how one small business is using the Internet to conduct research on new-product development.

Local Motors The Web site of Local Motors of Wareham, Massachusetts, a small-scale automaker, lets anyone upload design ideas. The site occasionally hosts competitions for cash prizes of up to $10,000 in which registered members—who include trained design engineers and transportation experts—vote on the designs they like best, or other decisions related to building the autos and running the company. The winning ideas are then incorporated in the cars Local Motors builds. Members remain involved after the competitions, offering criticism and suggestions throughout the cars' development. Local Motors has been diligent about building its car design community by marketing the site on other sites that attract design enthusiasts and experts. To make sure outside contributors do not seek compensation if their ideas are adopted, Local Motors requires members of its online community to sign a lengthy legal agreement.[26]

Marketers can also host a real-time consumer panel or virtual focus group or sponsor a chat room, bulletin board, or blog and introduce questions from time to time. They can ask customers to brainstorm or have followers of the company on Twitter rate an idea. Online communities and networks of customers serve as a resource for a wide variety of companies. Insights from Kraft-sponsored online communities helped the company develop its popular line of 100-calorie snacks.[27] Here are two other examples.

- Del Monte tapped into its 400-member, handpicked online community called "I Love My Dog" when it was considering a new breakfast treat for dogs. The consensus request was for something with a bacon-and-egg taste and an extra dose of vitamins and minerals. Continuing to work with the online community throughout the product development, the company introduced fortified "Snausage Breakfast Bites" in half the time usually required to launch a new product.[28]

- InterContinental Hotel Groups uses both surveys and communities to gather data on customer satisfaction. Online surveys provide actionable and speedy results to correct customer service issues; the online community provides a sounding board for more in-depth, longer-term research objectives.[29]

Online research was estimated to make up 33 percent of all survey-based research in 2006, and Internet-based questionnaires also accounted for nearly one-third of U.S. spending on market research surveys in the same year.[30] There are many other means to use the Internet as a research tool. The company can learn about individuals who visit its site by tracking how they *clickstream* through the Web site and move to other sites. It can post different prices, use different headlines, and offer different product features on different Web sites or at different times to learn the relative effectiveness of its offerings.

Yet, as popular as online research methods are, smart companies are choosing to use them to augment rather than replace more traditional methods. At Kraft Foods, online research is a supplement to traditional research, said Seth Diamond, director of consumer insights and strategy. "Online is not a solution in and of itself to all of our business challenges," he said, "but it does expand our toolkit."[31]

There are a number of pros and cons to online research.[32] Here are some advantages:

- *Online research is inexpensive.* A typical e-mail survey can cost between 20 percent and 50 percent less than what a conventional survey costs, and return rates can be as high as 50 percent.
- *Online research is fast.* Online surveys are fast because the survey can automatically direct respondents to applicable questions and transmit results immediately. One estimate says an online survey can generate 75 percent to 80 percent of the targeted response in 48 hours, compared to a telephone survey that can require 70 days to obtain 150 interviews.
- *People tend to be honest and thoughtful online.* People may be more open about their opinions when they can respond privately and not to another person whom they feel might be judging them, especially on sensitive topics (such as, "how often do you bathe or shower?"). Because they choose when and where they take the survey and how much time to devote to each question, they may be more relaxed, introspective, and candid.
- *Online research is versatile.* Increased broadband penetration offers online research even more flexibility and capabilities. For instance, virtual reality software lets visitors inspect 3-D models of products such as cameras, cars, and medical equipment and manipulate product characteristics. Even at the basic tactile level, online surveys can make answering a questionnaire easier and more fun than paper-and-pencil versions. Online community blogs allow customer participants to interact with each other.

Some disadvantages include:

- *Samples can be small and skewed.* Some 40 percent of households were without broadband Internet access in the United States in 2009; the percentage is even higher among lower-income groups, in rural areas, and in most parts of Asia, Latin America, and Central and Eastern Europe, where socioeconomic and education levels also differ.[33] Although it's certain that more and more people will go online, online market researchers must find creative ways to reach population segments on the other side of the "digital divide." One option is to combine offline sources with online findings. Providing temporary Internet access at locations such as malls and recreation centers is another strategy. Some research firms use statistical models to fill in the gaps in market research left by offline consumer segments.
- *Online panels and communities can suffer from excessive turnover.* Members may become bored with the company's efforts and flee. Or perhaps even worse, they may stay but only half-heartedly participate. Panel and community organizers are taking steps to address the quality of the panel and the data they provide by raising recruiting standards, downplaying incentives, and carefully monitoring participation and engagement levels. New features, events, and other activities must be constantly added to keep members interested and engaged.[34]
- *Online market research can suffer from technological problems and inconsistencies.* Problems can arise with online surveys because browser software varies. The Web designer's final product may look very different on the research subject's screen.

Online researchers have also begun to use text messaging in various ways—to conduct a chat with a respondent, to probe more deeply with a member of an online focus group, or to direct respondents to a Web site.[35] Text messaging is also a useful way to get teenagers to open up on topics.

Step 3: Collect the Information

The data collection phase of marketing research is generally the most expensive and the most prone to error. Marketers may conduct surveys in homes, over the phone, via the Internet, or at a central interviewing location like a shopping mall. Four major problems arise in surveys. Some respondents will be away from home or otherwise inaccessible and must be contacted again or replaced. Other respondents will refuse to cooperate. Still others will give biased or dishonest answers. Finally, some interviewers will be biased or dishonest.

Internationally, one of the biggest obstacles to collecting information is the need to achieve consistency.[36] Latin American respondents may be uncomfortable with the impersonal nature of the Internet and need interactive elements in a survey so they feel they're talking to a real person. Respondents in Asia, on the other hand, may feel more pressure to conform and may therefore not be as forthcoming in focus groups as online. Sometimes the solution may be as simple as ensuring the right language is used.

Leica Surveying and Engineering   When Leica Surveying and Engineering, a global provider of high-end surveying and measurement equipment, sought to gather competitive intelligence in its industry, it initially deployed surveys only in English, because the company's business was typically conducted in English, even across several different European countries. However, the response rate was dismal, even though the sample comprised individuals who had an affinity with the company. Closer review showed that the in-country sales representatives conducted business in their native languages. Consequently, the company redeployed its survey in various languages, such as Spanish and German, and the response rate doubled almost overnight.[37]

Step 4: Analyze the Information

The next-to-last step in the process is to extract findings by tabulating the data and developing summary measures. The researchers now compute averages and measures of dispersion for the major variables and apply some advanced statistical techniques and decision models in the hope of discovering additional findings. They may test different hypotheses and theories, applying sensitivity analysis to test assumptions and the strength of the conclusions.

Step 5: Present the Findings

As the last step, the researcher presents findings relevant to the major marketing decisions facing management. Researchers increasingly are being asked to play a more proactive, consulting role in translating data and information into insights and recommendations.[38] They're also considering ways to present research findings in as understandable and compelling a fashion as possible. "Marketing Insight: Bringing Marketing Research to Life with Personas" describes an approach that some researchers are using to maximize the impact of their consumer research findings.

The main survey findings for the American Airlines case showed that:

1. Passengers' chief reason for using in-flight Internet service would be to stay connected and receive and send e-mails. Some would also pass the time surfing the Web. This entertainment capability would require expensive broadband Internet access, but passengers stated they would be able to charge the cost and their companies would pay.
2. At $25, about 5 out of 10 first-class passengers would use Internet service during a flight; about 6 would use it at $15. Thus, a fee of $15 would produce less revenue ($90 = 6 × $15) than $25 ($125 = 5 × $25). Assuming the same flight takes place 365 days a year, American could collect $45,625 (= $125 × 365) annually. Given an investment of $90,000, it would take two years to break even.
3. Offering in-flight Internet service would strengthen the public's image of American Airlines as an innovative and progressive airline. American would gain some new passengers and customer goodwill.

Step 6: Make the Decision

The American Airlines managers who commissioned the research need to weigh the evidence. If their confidence in the findings is low, they may decide against introducing the in-flight Internet service. If they are predisposed to launching the service, the findings support their inclination.

Marketing Insight

Bringing Marketing Research to Life with Personas

To bring all the information and insights they have gained about their target market to life, some researchers are employing personas. *Personas* are detailed profiles of one, or perhaps a few, hypothetical target market consumers, imagined in terms of demographic, psychographic, geographic, or other descriptive attitudinal or behavioral information. Researchers may use photos, images, names, or short bios to help convey the particulars of the persona.

The rationale behind personas is to provide exemplars or archetypes of how the target customer looks, acts, and feels that are as true-to-life as possible, to ensure marketers within the organization fully understand and appreciate their target market and therefore incorporate a target-customer point of view in all their marketing decision making. Consider some applications:

- Chrysler designed rooms for two fictional characters—28-year-old single male Roberto Moore and 30-year-old pharmaceutical rep Jenny Sieverson—and decorated them to reflect the personality, lifestyles, and brand choices of these key targets for the Dodge Caliber and Jeep Compass.

- Specialty tool and equipment maker Campbell Hausfeld relied on the many retailers it supplied, including Home Depot and Lowe's, to help it keep in touch with consumers. After developing eight consumer profiles, including a female do-it-yourselfer and an elderly consumer, the firm was able to successfully launch new products such as drills that weighed less or that included a level for picture hanging.

- Unilever's biggest and most successful hair-care launch, for Sunsilk, was aided by insights into the target consumer the company dubbed "Katie." The Katie persona outlined the twenty-something female's hair-care needs, but also her perceptions and attitudes and the way she dealt with her everyday life "dramas."

Although personas provide vivid information to aid marketing decision making, marketers also have to be careful to not overgeneralize. Any target market may have a range of consumers who vary along a number of key dimensions. To accommodate these potential differences, researchers sometimes employ two to six personas. Best Buy used multiple personas to help redesign and relaunch GeekSquad.com, the online site of its fast-growing national computer-support service. Using quantitative, qualitative, and observational research, the firm developed five online customer personas to guide its Web redesign efforts:

- "Jill"—a suburban mom who uses technology and her computer daily and depends on the Geek Squad as an outsourced service akin to a landscape or plumber.

- "Charlie"—a 50-plus male who is curious about and interested in technology but needs an unintimidating guide.

- "Daryl"—a technologically savvy hands-on experimenter who occasionally needs a helping hand with his tech projects.

- "Luis"—a time-pressed small-business owner whose primary goal is to complete tasks as expediently as possible.

- "Nick"—a prospective Geek Squad agent who views the site critically and needs to be challenged.

To satisfy Charlie, a prominent 911 button was added to the upper right-hand corner in case a crisis arose, but to satisfy Nick, Best Buy created a whole channel devoted to geek information.

Sources: Dale Buss, "Reflections of Reality," *Point* (June 2006), pp. 10–11; Todd Wasserman, "Unilever, Whirlpool Get Personal with Personas," *Brandweek,* September 18, 2006, p. 13; Daniel B. Honigman, "Persona-fication," *Marketing News,* April 1, 2008, p. 8. Rick Roth, "Take Back Control of the Purchase," *Advertising Age,* September 3, 2007, p. 13. Lisa Sanders, "Major Marketers Get Wise to the Power of Assigning Personas," *Advertising Age,* April 9, 2007, p. 36.

They may even decide to study the issues further and do more research. The decision is theirs, but rigorously done research provides them with insight into the problem (see 🖳 Table 4.2).[39]

Some organizations use marketing decision support systems to help their marketing managers make better decisions. MIT's John Little defines a **marketing decision support system (MDSS)** as a coordinated collection of data, systems, tools, and techniques, with supporting software and hardware, by which an organization gathers and interprets relevant information from business and environment and turns it into a basis for marketing action.[40] Once a year, *Marketing News* lists hundreds of current marketing and sales software programs that assist in designing marketing research studies, segmenting markets, setting prices and advertising budgets, analyzing media, and planning sales force activity.[41]

Overcoming Barriers to the Use of Marketing Research

In spite of the rapid growth of marketing research, many companies still fail to use it sufficiently or correctly.[42] They may not understand what all marketing research is capable of and not provide the

To better understand what people thought of Cheetos snacks, researchers dressed up as the brand's Chester Cheetah character and interacted with consumers in the street.

TABLE 4.2 🖿	The Seven Characteristics of Good Marketing Research
1. Scientific method	Effective marketing research uses the principles of the scientific method: careful observation, formulation of hypotheses, prediction, and testing.
2. Research creativity	In an award-winning research study to reposition Cheetos snacks, researchers dressed up in a brand mascot Chester Cheetah suit and walked around the streets of San Francisco. The response the character encountered led to the realization that even adults loved the fun and playfulness of Cheetos. The resulting repositioning led to a double-digit sales increase despite a tough business environment.[43]
3. Multiple methods	Marketing researchers shy away from overreliance on any one method. They also recognize the value of using two or three methods to increase confidence in the results.
4. Interdependence of models and data	Marketing researchers recognize that data are interpreted from underlying models that guide the type of information sought.
5. Value and cost of information	Marketing researchers show concern for estimating the value of information against its cost. Costs are typically easy to determine, but the value of research is harder to quantify. It depends on the reliability and validity of the findings and management's willingness to accept and act on those findings.
6. Healthy skepticism	Marketing researchers show a healthy skepticism toward glib assumptions made by managers about how a market works. They are alert to the problems caused by "marketing myths."
7. Ethical marketing	Marketing research benefits both the sponsoring company and its customers. The misuse of marketing research can harm or annoy consumers, increasing resentment at what consumers regard as an invasion of their privacy or a disguised sales pitch.

researcher the right problem definition and information from which to work. They may also have unrealistic expectations about what researchers can offer. Failure to use marketing research properly has led to numerous gaffes, including the following historic one.

Star Wars   In the 1970s, a successful marketing research executive left General Foods to try a daring gambit: bringing market research to Hollywood, to give film studios access to the same research that had spurred General Foods's success. A major film studio handed him a science fiction film proposal and asked him to research and predict its success or failure. His views would inform the studio's decision about whether to back the film. The research executive concluded the film would fail. For one, he argued, Watergate had made the United States less trusting of institutions and, as a result, its citizens in the 1970s prized realism and authenticity over science fiction. This particular film also had the word "*war*" in its title; he reasoned that viewers, suffering from post-Vietnam hangover, would stay away in droves. The film was *Star Wars*, which eventually grossed over $4.3 billion in box office receipts alone. What this researcher delivered was information, not insight. He failed to study the

Improperly conducted and interpreted consumer research almost killed Star Wars, one of the most successful film franchises of all time.

script itself, to see that it was a fundamentally human story—of love, conflict, loss, and redemption—that happened to play out against the backdrop of space.[44]

Measuring Marketing Productivity

Marketers are facing increased pressure to provide clear, quantifiable evidence to senior management as to how their marketing expenditures help the firm to achieve its goals and financial objectives. Although we can easily quantify marketing expenses and investments as inputs in the short run, the resulting outputs such as broader brand awareness, enhanced brand image, greater customer loyalty, and improved new product prospects may take months or even years to manifest themselves. Moreover, a whole host of internal changes within the organization and external changes in the marketing environment may coincide with the marketing expenditures, making it hard to isolate the effects of any particular marketing activity.[45]

Nevertheless, an important task of marketing research is to assess the efficiency and effectiveness of marketing activities. In one survey, 65 percent of marketers indicated that return on marketing investment was a concern.[46] A recent survey of the nation's leading technology Chief Marketing Officers revealed that over 80 percent of the companies surveyed expressed dissatisfaction with their ability to benchmark their marketing program's business impact and value.[47]

Marketing research can help address this increased need for accountability. Two complementary approaches to measuring marketing productivity are: (1) *marketing metrics* to assess marketing effects and (2) *marketing-mix modeling* to estimate causal relationships and measure how marketing activity affects outcomes. *Marketing dashboards* are a structured way to disseminate the insights gleaned from these two approaches within the organization.

Marketing Metrics

Marketers employ a wide variety of measures to assess marketing effects.[48] **Marketing metrics** is the set of measures that helps them quantify, compare, and interpret their marketing performance. Here is how two marketing executives look at marketing metrics to better understand marketing ROI at their companies: [49]

- The CMO of Mary Kay , Rhonda Shasteen, focuses on four long-term brand strength metrics—market awareness, consideration, trial, and 12-month beauty consultant productivity—as well as a number of short-term program-specific metrics like ad impressions, Web site traffic, and purchase conversion.
- The Virgin America VP of marketing, Porter Gale, looks at a broad set of online metrics—cost per acquisition, cost per click, and cost per thousand page impressions (CPM). She also looks at total dollars driven by natural and paid search and online display advertising as well as tracking results and other metrics from the offline world.

There are many different marketing measures; marketers choose one or more based on the particular issue they face or the problem they must solve. An advocate of simple, relevant metrics, the University of Virginia's Paul Farris draws an analogy to the way a Boeing 747 jet pilot decides what information to use from the vast array of instruments in the cockpit to fly the plane:[50]

Aircraft pilots have protocols. When they are sitting on the tarmac warming their engines waiting to take off, they are looking at certain things. When they are taxiing, they look at others. When they are in flight, they look at still others. There is a sequence of knowing when to pay attention to which metrics, which lets them have their cake and eat it too, in terms of the simplicity and complexity trade-off.

London Business School's Tim Ambler suggests that if firms think they are already measuring marketing performance adequately, they should ask themselves five questions:[51]

1. Do you routinely research consumer behavior (retention, acquisition, usage) and why consumers behave that way (awareness, satisfaction, perceived quality)?
2. Do you routinely report the results of this research to the board in a format integrated with financial marketing metrics?
3. In those reports, do you compare the results with the levels previously forecasted in the business plans?
4. Do you also compare them with the levels achieved by your key competitor using the same indicators?
5. Do you adjust short-term performance according to the change in your marketing-based asset(s)?

Ambler says firms must give priority to measuring and reporting marketing performance through marketing metrics. He believes they can split evaluation into two parts: (1) short-term results and (2) changes in brand equity. Short-term results often reflect profit-and-loss concerns as shown by sales turnover, shareholder value, or some combination of the two. Brand-equity measures could include customer awareness, attitudes, and behaviors; market share; relative price premium; number of complaints; distribution and availability; total number of customers; perceived quality, and loyalty and retention.[52]

Companies can also monitor an extensive set of internal metrics, such as innovation. For example, 3M tracks the proportion of sales resulting from its recent innovations. Ambler also recommends developing employee measures and metrics, arguing that "end users are the ultimate customers, but your own staff are your first; you need to measure the health of the internal market." Table 4.3 summarizes a list of popular internal and external marketing metrics from Ambler's survey in the United Kingdom.[53]

Carefully measuring the effects of a marketing activity or program helps ensure managers make the right decisions going forward. Seeking greater engagement with younger consumers, Servus Credit Union in Alberta, Canada, launched its "Young & Free Alberta" program featuring a competition to find a youth spokesperson for Alberta. To connect with young Albertans, Kelsey MacDonald, the 2010 winner, works with Servus to create daily blogs, post entertaining and educational videos at YoungFreeAlberta.com, and maintain a Facebook and Twitter presence.

TABLE 4.3 Sample Marketing Metrics	
I. External	**II. Internal**
Awareness	Awareness of goals
Market share (volume or value)	Commitment to goals
Relative price (market share value/volume)	Active innovation support
Number of complaints (level of dissatisfaction)	Resource adequacy
Consumer satisfaction	Staffing/skill levels
Distribution/availability	Desire to learn
Total number of customers	Willingness to change
Perceived quality/esteem	Freedom to fail
Loyalty/retention	Autonomy
Relative perceived quality	Relative employee satisfaction

Source: Tim Ambler, "What Does Marketing Success Look Like?" *Marketing Management* (Spring 2001), pp. 13–18. Reprinted with permission from Marketing Management, published by the American Marketing Association.

Canada's Servus Credit Union used research to validate the effects of the spokesperson for its Young & Free Alberta Spokester program. Kelsey MacDonald, shown here, was the 2010 contest winner.

Kelsey also attends events throughout Alberta where she interacts with the 17- to 25-year-old crowd in order to better understand their financial needs. Research validated the campaign's success, with more than 107 million impressions to the program generated through various forms of media and thousands of new accounts opened.[54]

Marketing-Mix Modeling

Marketing accountability also means that marketers must more precisely estimate the effects of different marketing investments. *Marketing-mix models* analyze data from a variety of sources, such as retailer scanner data, company shipment data, pricing, media, and promotion spending data, to understand more precisely the effects of specific marketing activities.[55] To deepen understanding, marketers can conduct multivariate analyses, such as regression analysis, to sort through how each marketing element influences marketing outcomes such as brand sales or market share.[56]

Especially popular with packaged-goods marketers such as Procter & Gamble, Clorox, and Colgate, the findings from marketing-mix modeling help allocate or reallocate expenditures. Analyses explore which part of ad budgets are wasted, what optimal spending levels are, and what minimum investment levels should be.[57]

Although marketing-mix modeling helps to isolate effects, it is less effective at assessing how different marketing elements work in combination. Wharton's Dave Reibstein also notes three other shortcomings:[58]

- Marketing-mix modeling focuses on incremental growth instead of baseline sales or long-term effects.
- The integration of important metrics such as customer satisfaction, awareness, and brand equity into marketing-mix modeling is limited.
- Marketing-mix modeling generally fails to incorporate metrics related to competitors, the trade, or the sales force (the average business spends far more on the sales force and trade promotion than on advertising or consumer promotion).

Marketing Dashboards

Firms are also employing organizational processes and systems to make sure they maximize the value of all these different metrics. Management can assemble a summary set of relevant internal and external measures in a *marketing dashboard* for synthesis and interpretation. Marketing dashboards are like the instrument panel in a car or plane, visually displaying real-time indicators to ensure proper functioning. They are only as good as the information on which they're based, but sophisticated visualization tools are helping bring data alive to improve understanding and analysis.[59]

Some companies are also appointing marketing controllers to review budget items and expenses. Increasingly, these controllers are using business intelligence software to create digital versions of marketing dashboards that aggregate data from disparate internal and external sources.

As input to the marketing dashboard, companies should include two key market-based scorecards that reflect performance and provide possible early warning signals.

- A **customer-performance scorecard** records how well the company is doing year after year on such customer-based measures as those shown in 🖼 Table 4.4. Management should set target goals for each measure and take action when results get out of bounds.
- A **stakeholder-performance scorecard** tracks the satisfaction of various constituencies who have a critical interest in and impact on the company's performance: employees, suppliers, banks, distributors, retailers, and stockholders. Again, management should take action when one or more groups register increased or above-norm levels of dissatisfaction.[60]

Some executives worry that they'll miss the big picture if they focus too much on a set of numbers on a dashboard. Some critics are concerned about privacy and the pressure the technique places on employees. But most experts feel the rewards offset the risks.[61] "Marketing Insight: Marketing Dashboards to Improve Effectiveness and Efficiency" provides practical advice about the development of these marketing tools.

TABLE 4.4	Sample Customer-Performance Scorecard Measures
• Percentage of new customers to average number of customers
• Percentage of lost customers to average number of customers
• Percentage of win-back customers to average number of customers
• Percentage of customers falling into very dissatisfied, dissatisfied, neutral, satisfied, and very satisfied categories
• Percentage of customers who say they would repurchase the product
• Percentage of customers who say they would recommend the product to others
• Percentage of target market customers who have brand awareness or recall
• Percentage of customers who say that the company's product is the most preferred in its category
• Percentage of customers who correctly identify the brand's intended positioning and differentiation
• Average perception of company's product quality relative to chief competitor
• Average perception of company's service quality relative to chief competitor

Marketing Insight

Marketing Dashboards to Improve Effectiveness and Efficiency

Marketing consultant Pat LaPointe sees marketing dashboards as providing all the up-to-the-minute information necessary to run the business operations for a company—such as sales versus forecast, distribution channel effectiveness, brand equity evolution, and human capital development. According to LaPointe, an effective dashboard will focus thinking, improve internal communications, and reveal where marketing investments are paying off and where they aren't.

LaPointe observes four common measurement "pathways" marketers are pursuing today (see △ Figure 4.2).

- The *customer metrics pathway* looks at how prospects become customers, from awareness to preference to trial to repeat purchase, or some less linear model. This area also examines how the customer experience contributes to the perception of value and competitive advantage.

- The *unit metrics pathway* reflects what marketers know about sales of product/service units—how much is sold by product line and/or by geography; the marketing cost per unit sold as an efficiency yardstick; and where and how margin is optimized in terms of characteristics of the product line or distribution channel.

|Fig. 4.2| △

Marketing Measurement Pathway

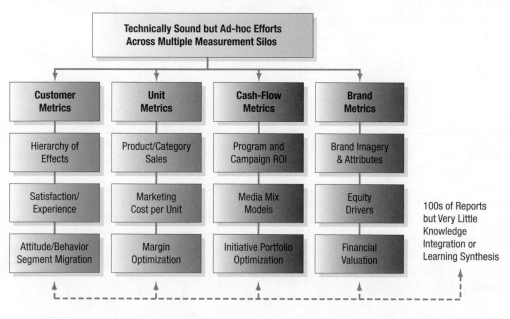

(continued)

|Fig. 4.3| △

Example of a Marketing Dashboard

Source: Adapted from Patrick LaPointe, *Marketing by the Dashboard Light—How to Get More Insight, Foresight, and Accountability from Your Marketing Investments.* © 2005, Patrick LaPointe.

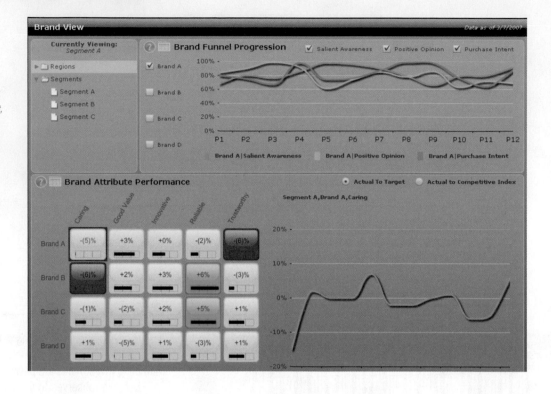

- The *cash-flow metrics pathway* focuses on how well marketing expenditures are achieving short-term returns. Program and campaign ROI models measure the immediate impact or net present value of profits expected from a given investment.

- The *brand metrics pathway* tracks the development of the longer-term impact of marketing through brand equity measures that assess both the perceptual health of the brand from customer and prospective customer perspectives as well as the overall financial health of the brand.

LaPointe feels a marketing dashboard can present insights from all the pathways in a graphically related view that helps management see subtle links between them. A well-constructed dashboard can have a series of tabs that allow the user to toggle easily between different "families" of metrics organized by customer, product, experience, brand, channels, efficiency, organizational development, or macroenvironmental factors. Each tab presents the three or four most insightful metrics, with data filtered by business unit, geography, or customer segment based on the users' needs. (See Figure △ 4.3 for a sample brand metrics page.)

Ideally, the number of metrics presented in the marketing dashboard would be reduced to a handful of key drivers over time. Meanwhile, the process of developing and refining the marketing dashboard will undoubtedly raise and resolve many key questions about the business.

Source: Adapted from Pat LaPointe, *Marketing by the Dashboard Light*, Association of National Advertisers, 2005, www.MarketingNPV.com. Based in part on related prior research by Don Schultz.

Summary

1. Companies can conduct their own marketing research or hire other companies to do it for them. Good marketing research is characterized by the scientific method, creativity, multiple research methods, accurate model building, cost-benefit analysis, healthy skepticism, and an ethical focus.

2. The marketing research process consists of defining the problem, decision alternatives; and research objectives; developing the research plan; collecting the information; analyzing the information; presenting the findings to management; and making the decision.

3. In conducting research, firms must decide whether to collect their own data or use data that already exist. They must also choose a research approach (observational, focus group, survey, behavioral data, or experimental) and research instruments (questionnaire, qualitative measures, or technological devices). In addition, they must decide on a sampling plan and contact methods (by mail, by phone, in person, or online).

4. Two complementary approaches to measuring marketing productivity are: (1) marketing metrics to assess marketing effects and (2) marketing-mix modeling to estimate causal relationships and measure how marketing activity affects outcomes. Marketing dashboards are a structured way to disseminate the insights gleaned from these two approaches within the organization.

Applications

Marketing Debate
What Is the Best Type of Marketing Research?

Many market researchers have their favorite research approaches or techniques, although different researchers often have different preferences. Some researchers maintain that the only way to really learn about consumers or brands is through in-depth, qualitative research. Others contend that the only legitimate and defensible form of marketing research uses quantitative measures.

Take a position: The best marketing research is quantitative in nature *versus* The best marketing research is qualitative in nature.

Marketing Discussion
Survey Quality

When was the last time you participated in a survey? How helpful do you think the information you provided was? How could the research have been done differently to make it more effective?

Marketing Excellence

>>IDEO

IDEO is the largest design consultancy firm in the United States. The company has created some of the most recognizable design icons of the technology age, including the first laptop computer, the first mouse (for Apple), the Palm V PDA, and the TiVo digital video recorder. Beyond its high-tech wizardry, the company has designed household items such as the Swiffer Sweeper and the Crest Neat Squeeze toothpaste tube, both for Procter & Gamble. IDEO's diverse roster of clients includes AT&T, Bank of America, Ford Motor Company, PepsiCo, Nike, Marriott, Caterpillar, Eli Lilly, Lufthansa, Prada, and the Mayo Clinic.

IDEO's success is predicated on an approach called "design thinking" based on a "human-centered methodology." The company strives to design products that consumers actively want because they offer a superior experience and solve a problem. In order to achieve these consumer-friendly solutions, IDEO tries to uncover deep insights through a variety of human-centered research methods. These studies help the firm better understand how consumers purchase, interact with, use, and even dispose of products. This customer-focused approach has run counter to the prevailing wisdom of many high-tech firms that focus more on their own capabilities when designing products. David Blakely, head of IDEO's technology group, explained, "Tech companies design from the inside out, whereas we design from the outside in so that we can put customers first."

IDEO employs a number of other observational methods to conduct "deep dives" into consumer behavior. The company's "human factors" team shadows consumers, takes pictures or videos of them during product purchase or use occasions, and conducts in-depth interviews with them to further evaluate their experiences. Another method is called "behavioral mapping," which creates a photographic log of people within a certain area like an airline departure lounge, a hospital waiting room, or a food court at a shopping mall over a period of days to gauge how the experience can be improved. A third method relies on "camera journals" that participants keep, in which they record their visual impressions of a given product or category. IDEO also invites consumers to use "storytelling" techniques to share personal narratives, videos, skits, or even animations about their experiences with a product or service.

Prototyping has also contributed to IDEO's success. It takes place throughout the design process so individuals can test out, experience, and improve upon each level of development. IDEO encourages its clients, even senior executives, to participate in the research so they get a sense of the actual consumer experience with their product or service. AT&T executives, for example, were sent on a scavenger hunt designed to test the company's location software for its mMode mobile phones. The executives soon realized the software was not user-friendly. One resorted to calling his wife so she could use Google to help him find an item on the list. IDEO helped AT&T redesign the interface to be more intuitive for the average user.

IDEO helped apparel-maker Warnaco improve sales by having its designers shadow eight women as they shopped for lingerie. The "shop-alongs" revealed that most consumers had a negative buying experience. They had difficulty locating the lingerie section in the department store and finding the right size in the overcrowded display, and they felt the fitting rooms were too small. IDEO developed a new six-stage merchandising environment that included larger fitting rooms, "concierges" to give shoppers information, and improved displays. Warnaco implemented this plan with the help of the department stores.

In another example, Marriott hired IDEO to help make its Courtyard by Marriott hotels more appealing to younger guests. IDEO conducted interviews and observed guests in the hotel's lounges, lobbies, and restaurants. Its research revealed that younger guests were turned off by the lack of activity in the hotel's public places, the lack of technology offered, and the poor food options. As a result, Courtyard by Marriott changed its furniture and decor to be more warm, comfortable, and inviting. The hotel added advanced technology options throughout its lobbies and lounges, such as flat-screen TVs and free Wi-Fi. Marriott converted the breakfast buffets to 24/7 coffee-shop-style cafés, where guests can quickly grab a gourmet coffee drink and healthy bite to eat any time. And Courtyard created new outdoor hangout spots with sound speakers and fire pits. After the renovations, Courtyard by Marriott changed its tagline to "Courtyard. It's a New Stay."

IDEO's novel consumer-led approach to design has led to countless success stories and awards for its clients and for the firm itself. The most important result for IDEO's designs is that they solve a usability problem for clients. The company goes "broad and deep" to achieve this goal. Since its founding, it has been issued over 1,000 patents, and in 2008 the company generated $120 million in revenues.

Questions

1. Why has IDEO been so successful? What is the most difficult challenge it faces in conducting its research and designing its products?

2. In the end, IDEO creates great solutions for companies that then receive all the credit. Should IDEO try to create more brand awareness for itself? Why or why not?

Sources: Lisa Chamberlain, "Going off the Beaten Path for New Design Ideas," *New York Times*, March 12, 2006; Chris Taylor, "School of Bright Ideas," *Time*, March 6, 2005, p. A8; Scott Morrison, "Sharp Focus Gives Design Group the Edge," *Financial Times*, February 17, 2005, p. 8; Bruce Nussbaum, "The Power of Design," *BusinessWeek*, May 17, 2004, p. 86; Teressa Iezzi, "Innovate, But Do It for Consumers," *Advertising Age*, September 11, 2006; Barbara De Lollis, "Marriott Perks Up Courtyard with Edgier, More Social Style," *USA Today*, April 1, 2008; Tim Brown, "Change by Design," *BusinessWeek*, October 5, 2009, pp. 54–56.

Marketing Excellence

>>Intuit

Intuit develops and sells financial and tax solution software for consumers and small to medium-sized businesses. The company was founded in 1983 by a former Procter & Gamble employee, Scott Cook, and a Stanford University programmer, Tom Proulx, after Cook realized there must be a better way to automate his bill-paying process. For over 25 years, Intuit's mission has been to "revolutionize people's lives by solving their important business and financial management problems."

Intuit launched its first product, Quicken, in 1984 and struggled to survive during those first years. After some favorable reviews in the trade journals and an effective print advertising campaign, the company got its first break. By 1988, Quicken was the best-selling finance product on the market. In 1992, the company launched QuickBooks, a bookkeeping and payroll software product for small businesses, and went public the following year.

Intuit grew quickly in the early 1990s, thanks to the success of Quicken, QuickBooks, and TurboTax, a tax preparation software program. Intuit's products did something for small businesses that more complicated accounting packages didn't: they solved finance and tax problems in a simple, easy-to-use manner. Intuit had recognized correctly that simplicity was the key, not in-depth accounting analysis. By 1995, the firm held a 70 percent market share, and Microsoft tried to purchase it for $2 billion. However, the Justice Department blocked the deal as anticompetitive and the buyout collapsed.

From 1995 to 1997, Intuit's stock tumbled 72 percent and forced the company to refocus its strategic efforts. It turned to the growing power of the Internet, online banking capabilities, and valuable input from its customers to develop new product versions, which in turn improved the company's stock value and market position throughout the 2000s.

Intuit spends a significant amount of time and money—approximately 20 percent of net revenues—on consumer research each year. It is critical for Intuit to know exactly how customers use and feel about their products due to the fast-paced nature of technology, shifting consumer needs, and the competitiveness of its industry. Intuit conducts several levels of research and invites consumers and businesses to participate in a variety of ways.

During a *Site Visit,* Intuit researchers visit the individual's home or office to observe and learn exactly how its products are used and can be improved in the true work environment. A *Lab Study* invites consumers to one of Intuit's U.S. research labs to test out new products and ideas. During a *Remote Study,* consumers are interviewed over the phone and often asked to view new design concepts over the Internet. The company also conducts an ongoing extensive research study with the Institute for the Future, to learn more about the future trends affecting small businesses. Intuit uses what it learns not only to produce improved versions of its products each year, but also to better understand the next generation of financial and tax software, such as solutions for mobile devices.

Demand for Intuit's products is seasonal, and its marketing efforts are typically concentrated around tax preparation time—November through April. During that time, Intuit develops promotions with original equipment manufacturers (OEMs) and major retailers. It promotes its products through a number of marketing efforts including direct mail, Web marketing, print, radio, and television ads.

While Intuit's marketing campaigns have evolved over the years, it was clear early on that positive word of mouth and exceptional customer service are its most effective marketing tools. Harry Pforzheimer, chief communications officer and marketing leader, explained, "It's a little harder to measure but when you know that roughly eight out of

10 customers bought your product because of word-of-mouth that's a pretty powerful tool . . . So engaging with our customers directly is part of our DNA and communicating with customers on a timely basis is critical. And that timely basis now is instantaneous."

Recently, Intuit has increased its presence on social media Web sites such as Twitter, Facebook, and LinkedIn. Just 12 weeks after the firm integrated a small-business Web site with these social networks, sales of QuickBooks increased 57 percent. To measure the viral success of this site, Intuit identified bloggers who either wrote their own stories or picked up stories originally posted by a few influential bloggers who were given a special preview. Intuit classified each blog post according to *velocity* (whether it took a month or happened in a few days), *share of voice* (how much talk occurred in the blogosphere), *voice quality* (what was said and how positive or negative it was), and *sentiment* (how meaningful the comments were).

In 2008, Intuit earned $3.1 billion in revenue, primarily from Quicken, QuickBooks, and TurboTax sales. The company now employs over 8,000 people, mostly in the United States, and is planning to expand internationally. It continues to acquire companies, such as personal finance Web site Mint.com in 2009, that will help it in growth areas such as solutions for mobile devices. Intuit believes that expanding its mobile solutions will encourage younger consumers to turn to the company for their finance and tax software. Growth will also come from previous Microsoft Money customers. In 2009, Microsoft announced it would discontinue its Money product line after an 18-year battle with Quicken. The victory was a rare win against the software giant and one that should provide great opportunity for Intuit.

Questions

1. Elaborate on Intuit's use of customer research. Why did it work so well for the company?

2. Could anything go wrong for Intuit now that it has beaten out Microsoft? Why or why not?

3. How should Intuit gauge the results of its research among younger consumers with mobile devices?

Sources: Intuit, *2008 Annual Report*; Karen E. Klein, "The Face of Entrepreneurship in 2017," *BusinessWeek*, January 31, 2007; Intuit, "Intuit Study: Next-Gen Artisans Fuel New Entrepreneurial Economy," February 13, 2008; Michael Bush, "How PR Chiefs Have Shifted Toward Center of Marketing Departments," *Advertising Age*, September 21, 2009; Jon Swartz, "More Marketers Use Social Networking to Reach Customers," *USA Today*, August 28, 2009; Mark Johnson and Joe Sinfield, "Focusing on Consumer Needs Is Not Enough," *Advertising Age*, April 28, 2008; "Intuit CEO Sees Growth in Mobile, Global Markets," *Associated Press*, September 23, 2009.

Chapter 5

In This Chapter, We Will Address the Following Questions

1. What are customer value, satisfaction, and loyalty, and how can companies deliver them?

2. What is the lifetime value of customers, and how can marketers maximize it?

3. How can companies attract and retain the right customers and cultivate strong customer relationships?

4. What are the pros and cons of database marketing?

Harrah's Total Rewards loyalty program has significantly increased customer value to the firm.

Creating Long-term Loyalty Relationships

Today, companies face their toughest competition ever. Moving from a product-and-sales philosophy to a holistic marketing philosophy, however, gives them a better chance of outperforming the competition. The cornerstone of a well-conceived holistic marketing orientation is strong customer relationships. Marketers must connect with customers—informing, engaging, and maybe even energizing them in the process. Customer-centered companies are adept at building customer relationships, not just products; they are skilled in market engineering, not just product engineering. A pioneer in customer relationship management techniques is Harrah's Entertainment.

 In 1997, Harrah's Entertainment, in Las Vegas, launched a pioneering loyalty program that pulled all customer data into a centralized warehouse and provided sophisticated analysis to better understand the value of the investments the casino made in its customers. Harrah's has over 10 million active members in its Total Rewards loyalty program, a system it has fine-tuned to achieve near-real-time analysis: As customers interact with slot machines, check into casinos, or buy meals, they receive reward offers—food vouchers or gambling credits, for example—based on the predictive analyses. The company has now identified hundreds of highly specific customer segments, and by targeting offers to each of them, it can almost double its share of customers' gaming budgets and generate $6.4 billion annually (80 percent of its gaming revenue). Harrah's dramatically cut back its traditional ad spending, largely replacing it with direct mail and e-mail—a good customer may receive as many as 150 pieces in a year. Data from the Total Rewards program even influenced Harrah's decision to buy Caesars Entertainment, when company research revealed that most of Harrah's customers who visited Las Vegas without staying at a Harrah's-owned hotel were going to Caesars Palace. Harrah's latest loyalty innovation is a mobile marketing program that sends time-based and location-based offers to customers' mobile devices in real time.[1]

As Harrah's experience shows, successful marketers are those who carefully manage their customer base. In this chapter, we spell out in detail the ways they can go about winning customers and beating competitors. The answer lies largely in doing a better job of meeting or exceeding customer expectations.

Building Customer Value, Satisfaction, and Loyalty

Creating loyal customers is at the heart of every business.[2] As marketing experts Don Peppers and Martha Rogers say:[3]

> The only value your company will ever create is the value that comes from customers—the ones you have now and the ones you will have in the future. Businesses succeed by getting, keeping, and growing customers. Customers are the only reason you build factories, hire employees, schedule meetings, lay fiber-optic lines, or engage in any business activity. Without customers, you don't have a business.

|Fig. 5.1| △

Traditional
Organization versus
Modern Customer-
Oriented Company
Organization

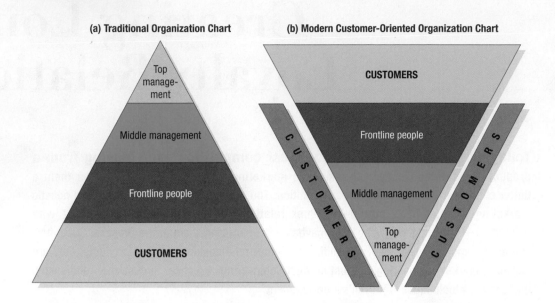

(a) Traditional Organization Chart

Top management

Middle management

Frontline people

CUSTOMERS

(b) Modern Customer-Oriented Organization Chart

CUSTOMERS

Frontline people

Middle management

Top management

CUSTOMERS (along sides)

Managers who believe the customer is the company's only true "profit center" consider the traditional organization chart in △ Figure 5.1(a)—a pyramid with the president at the top, management in the middle, and frontline people and customers at the bottom—obsolete.[4]

Successful marketing companies invert the chart as in Figure 5.1(b). At the top are customers; next in importance are frontline people who meet, serve, and satisfy customers; under them are the middle managers, whose job is to support the frontline people so they can serve customers well; and at the base is top management, whose job is to hire and support good middle managers. We have added customers along the sides of Figure 5.1(b) to indicate that managers at every level must be personally involved in knowing, meeting, and serving customers.

Some companies have been founded with the customer-on-top business model, and customer advocacy has been their strategy—and competitive advantage—all along. With the rise of digital technologies such as the Internet, increasingly informed consumers today expect companies to do more than connect with them, more than satisfy them, and even more than delight them. They expect companies to *listen* and *respond* to them.[5]

When Office Depot added customer reviews to its Web site in 2008, revenue and sales conversion increased significantly. The company also incorporated review-related terms to its paid search advertising campaign. As a result of these efforts, Web site revenue and the number of new buyers visiting the site both increased by more than 150 percent.[6]

Customer Perceived Value

Consumers are better educated and informed than ever, and they have the tools to verify companies' claims and seek out superior alternatives.[7]

When certain business decisions led to a deterioration of customer service, Dell's founder Michael Dell took decisive action.

Dell   Dell rode to success by offering low-priced computers, logistical efficiency, and after-sales service. The firm's maniacal focus on low costs has been a key ingredient in its success. When the company shifted its customer-service call centers to India and the Philippines to cut costs, however, understaffing frequently led to 30-minute waits for customers. Almost half the calls required at least one transfer. To discourage customer calls, Dell even removed its toll-free service number from its Web site. With customer satisfaction slipping, and competitors matching its product quality and prices *and* offering improved service, Dell's market share and stock price both declined sharply. Dell ended up hiring more North American call center employees. "The team was managing cost instead of managing service and quality," Michael Dell confesses.[8]

How then do customers ultimately make choices? They tend to be value maximizers, within the bounds of search costs and limited knowledge, mobility, and income. Customers estimate which offer they believe—for whatever reason—will deliver the most perceived value and act on it (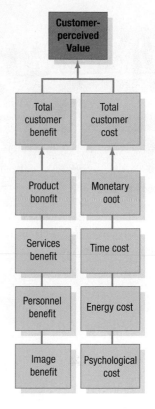 Figure 5.2). Whether the offer lives up to expectation affects customer satisfaction and the probability that the customer will purchase the product again. In one 2008 survey asking U.S. consumers "Does [Brand X] give good value for what you pay?" the highest scoring brands included Craftsman tools, Discovery Channel, History Channel, Google, and Rubbermaid.[9]

Customer-perceived value (CPV) is the difference between the prospective customer's evaluation of all the benefits and all the costs of an offering and the perceived alternatives. **Total customer benefit** is the perceived monetary value of the bundle of economic, functional, and psychological benefits customers expect from a given market offering because of the product, service, people, and image. **Total customer cost** is the perceived bundle of costs customers expect to incur in evaluating, obtaining, using, and disposing of the given market offering, including monetary, time, energy, and psychological costs.

Customer-perceived value is thus based on the difference between benefits the customer gets and costs he or she assumes for different choices. The marketer can increase the value of the customer offering by raising economic, functional, or emotional benefits and/or reducing one or more costs. The customer choosing between two value offerings, V1 and V2, will favor V1 if the ratio V1:V2 is larger than one, favor V2 if the ratio is smaller than one, and be indifferent if the ratio equals one.

APPLYING VALUE CONCEPTS Suppose the buyer for a large construction company wants to buy a tractor for residential construction from either Caterpillar or Komatsu. He wants the tractor to deliver certain levels of reliability, durability, performance, and resale value. The competing salespeople carefully describe their respective offers. The buyer decides Caterpillar has greater product benefits based on his perceptions of those attributes. He also perceives differences in the accompanying services—delivery, training, and maintenance—and decides Caterpillar provides better service as well as more knowledgeable and responsive staff. Finally, he places higher value on Caterpillar's corporate image and reputation. He adds up all the economic, functional, and psychological benefits from these four sources—product, services, personnel, and image—and perceives Caterpillar as delivering greater customer benefits.

Does he buy the Caterpillar tractor? Not necessarily. He also examines his total cost of transacting with Caterpillar versus Komatsu, which consists of more than money. As Adam Smith observed over two centuries ago in *The Wealth of Nations*, "The real price of anything is the toil and trouble of acquiring it." Total customer cost also includes the buyer's time, energy, and psychological costs expended in product acquisition, usage, maintenance, ownership, and disposal. The buyer evaluates these elements together with the monetary cost to form a total customer cost. Then he considers whether Caterpillar's total customer cost is too high compared to total customer benefits. If it is, he might choose Komatsu. The buyer will choose whichever source delivers the highest perceived value.

Now let's use this decision-making theory to help Caterpillar succeed in selling to this buyer. Caterpillar can improve its offer in three ways. First, it can increase total customer benefit by improving economic, functional, and psychological benefits of its product, services, people, and/or image. Second, it can reduce the buyer's nonmonetary costs by reducing the time, energy, and psychological investment. Third, it can reduce its product's monetary cost to the buyer.

Suppose Caterpillar concludes the buyer sees its offer as worth $20,000. Further, suppose Caterpillar's cost of producing the tractor is $14,000. This means Caterpillar's offer generates $6,000 over its cost, so the firm needs to charge between $14,000 and $20,000. If it charges less than $14,000, it won't cover its costs; if it charges more, it will price itself out of the market.

Caterpillar's price will determine how much value it delivers to the buyer and how much flows to Caterpillar. If it charges $19,000, it is creating $1,000 of customer perceived value and keeping $5,000 for itself. The lower Caterpillar sets its price, the higher the customer perceived value and, therefore, the higher the customer's incentive to purchase. To win the sale, the firm must offer more customer perceived value than Komatsu does.[10] Caterpillar is well aware of the importance of taking a broad view of customer value.

|Fig. 5.2|

Determinants of Customer-Perceived Value

 Caterpillar Caterpillar has become a leading firm by maximizing total customer value in the construction-equipment industry, despite challenges from a number of able competitors such as John Deere, Case, Komatsu, Volvo, and Hitachi. First, Caterpillar produces high-performance equipment known for reliability and durability—key purchase

Caterpillar's market success is partly a result of how well the firm creates customer value.

considerations in heavy industrial equipment. The firm also makes it easy for customers to find the right product by providing a full line of construction equipment and a wide range of financial terms. Caterpillar maintains the largest number of independent construction-equipment dealers in the industry. These dealers all carry a complete line of Caterpillar products and are typically better trained and perform more reliably than competitors' dealers. Caterpillar has also built a worldwide parts and service system second to none in the industry. Customers recognize all the value Caterpillar creates in its offerings, allowing the firm to command a premium price 10 percent to 20 percent higher than competitors. Caterpillar's biggest challenges are a reenergized Komatsu, which has made a strong push in China, and some supply chain issues in introducing new products.[11]

Very often, managers conduct a **customer value analysis** to reveal the company's strengths and weaknesses relative to those of various competitors. The steps in this analysis are:

1. *Identify the major attributes and benefits customers value.* Customers are asked what attributes, benefits, and performance levels they look for in choosing a product and vendors. Attributes and benefits should be defined broadly to encompass all the inputs to customers' decisions.
2. *Assess the quantitative importance of the different attributes and benefits.* Customers are asked to rate the importance of different attributes and benefits. If their ratings diverge too much, the marketer should cluster them into different segments.
3. *Assess the company's and competitors' performances on the different customer values against their rated importance.* Customers describe where they see the company's and competitors' performances on each attribute and benefit.
4. *Examine how customers in a specific segment rate the company's performance against a specific major competitor on an individual attribute or benefit basis.* If the company's offer exceeds the competitor's offer on all important attributes and benefits, the company can charge a higher price (thereby earning higher profits), or it can charge the same price and gain more market share.
5. *Monitor customer values over time.* The company must periodically redo its studies of customer values and competitors' standings as the economy, technology, and features change.

CHOICE PROCESSES AND IMPLICATIONS Some marketers might argue the process we have described is too rational. Suppose the customer chooses the Komatsu tractor. How can we explain this choice? Here are three possibilities.

1. *The buyer might be under orders to buy at the lowest price.* The Caterpillar salesperson's task is then to convince the buyer's manager that buying on price alone will result in lower long-term profits and customer value.
2. *The buyer will retire before the company realizes the Komatsu tractor is more expensive to operate.* The buyer will look good in the short run; he is maximizing personal benefit. The Caterpillar salesperson's task is to convince other people in the customer company that Caterpillar delivers greater customer value.
3. *The buyer enjoys a long-term friendship with the Komatsu salesperson.* In this case, Caterpillar's salesperson needs to show the buyer that the Komatsu tractor will draw complaints from the tractor operators when they discover its high fuel cost and need for frequent repairs.

The point is clear: Buyers operate under various constraints and occasionally make choices that give more weight to their personal benefit than to the company's benefit.

Customer-perceived value is a useful framework that applies to many situations and yields rich insights. It suggests that the seller must assess the total customer benefit and total customer cost associated with each competitor's offer in order to know how his or her offer rates in the buyer's mind. It also implies that the seller at a disadvantage has two alternatives: increase total customer benefit or decrease total customer cost. The former calls for strengthening or augmenting the economical, functional, and psychological benefits of the offering's product, services, personnel, and image. The latter calls for reducing the buyer's costs by reducing the price or cost of ownership and maintenance, simplifying the ordering and delivery process, or absorbing some buyer risk by offering a warranty.[12]

DELIVERING HIGH CUSTOMER VALUE Consumers have varying degrees of loyalty to specific brands, stores, and companies. Oliver defines **loyalty** as "a deeply held commitment to rebuy or repatronize a preferred product or service in the future despite situational influences and marketing efforts having the potential to cause switching behavior."[13] ▭ Table 5.1 displays brands with the greatest degree of customer loyalty according to one 2010 survey.[14]

The **value proposition** consists of the whole cluster of benefits the company promises to deliver; it is more than the core positioning of the offering. For example, Volvo's core positioning has been "safety," but the buyer is promised more than just a safe car; other benefits include good performance, design, and safety for the environment. The value proposition is thus a promise about the experience customers can expect from the company's market offering and their relationship with the supplier. Whether the promise is kept depends on the company's ability to manage its value delivery system.[15] The **value delivery system** includes all the experiences the customer will have on the way to obtaining and using the offering. At the heart of a good value delivery system is a set of core business processes that help deliver distinctive consumer value.[16]

TABLE 5.1 ▭ Top 25 Brands in Customer Loyalty			
Brand	**Category**	**Rankings**	
		2010	**2009**
Apple iPhone	Wireless Handset	1	1
Clairol (hair color)	Hair Color	2	NA
Samsung	Wireless Handset	3	2
Mary Kay	Cosmetics (Mass Merchandiser)	4	7
Grey Goose	Vodka	5	6
Clinique (cosmetics: Luxury)	Cosmetics (Luxury)	6	19
AVIS	Car Rental	7	8
Walmart	Retail Store (Discount)	8	5
Google	Search Engine	9	3
Amazon.com	Online Book/Music	10	10
Bing	Search Engine	11	NA
J. Crew	Retail Store (Apparel)	12	23
AT&T Wireless	Wireless Phone	13	123
Discover Card	Credit Card	14	121
Verizon Wireless	Wireless Phone	15	21
Intercontinental Hotels	Hotel (Luxury)	16	103
Cheerios	Breakfast Cereal: Kids	17	71
Dunkin' Donuts	Coffee	18	54
Home Depot	Retail Store (Home Improvement)	19	192
Domino's Pizza	Pizza	20	156
Barilla	Pasta Sauce	21	NA
Canon	MFP Copier	22	44
Nike	Athletic Footwear	23	178
Coors Light	Beer (Light)	24	63
Acer	Computer (Netbook)	25	NA

Source: "2010 Brand Keys Customer Loyalty Leaders List," www.brandkeys.com.

THE FIRST CAR TO STOP TRAFFIC. AND ITSELF.

INTRODUCING THE NEW VOLVO XC60 WITH CITY SAFETY.

Eighty years of safety innovation have come to this. You're looking at a car that can actually stop itself. City Safety comes standard, which means the XC60 will apply its own brakes to help avoid a low-speed collision. Coupled with available features like the Blind Spot Information System and the Collision Avoidance Package, the XC60 is the safest Volvo in the history of Volvo. All for you, from Sweden with Löv.

Starting at MSRP $32,400. volvocars.com/us

VOLVO

Volvo. for life

Although safety is Volvo's core position, the value proposition the firm offers customers includes other benefits too.

Total Customer Satisfaction

In general, **satisfaction** is a person's feelings of pleasure or disappointment that result from comparing a product's perceived performance (or outcome) to expectations.[17] If the performance falls short of expectations, the customer is dissatisfied. If it matches expectations, the customer is satisfied. If it exceeds expectations, the customer is highly satisfied or delighted.[18] Customer assessments of product performance depend on many factors, especially the type of loyalty relationship the customer has with the brand.[19] Consumers often form more favorable perceptions of a product with a brand they already feel positive about.

Although the customer-centered firm seeks to create high customer satisfaction, that is not its ultimate goal. Increasing customer satisfaction by lowering price or increasing services may result in lower profits. The company might be able to increase its profitability by means other than increased satisfaction (for example, by improving manufacturing processes or investing more in R&D). Also, the company has many stakeholders, including employees, dealers, suppliers, and stockholders. Spending more to increase customer satisfaction might divert funds from increasing the satisfaction of other "partners." Ultimately, the company must try to deliver a high level of customer satisfaction subject to also delivering acceptable levels to other stakeholders, given its total resources.[20]

How do buyers form their expectations? Expectations result from past buying experience, friends' and associates' advice, and marketers' and competitors' information and promises. If marketer raise expectations too high, the buyer is likely to be disappointed. If it sets expectations too low, it won't attract enough buyers (although it will satisfy those who do buy).[21] Some of today's most successful companies are raising expectations and delivering performances to match. Korean automaker Kia found success in the United States by launching low-cost, high-quality cars with enough reliability to offer 10-year, 100,000 mile warranties.

Monitoring Satisfaction

Many companies are systematically measuring how well they treat customers, identifying the factors shaping satisfaction, and changing operations and marketing as a result.[22]

Wise firms measure customer satisfaction regularly, because it is one key to customer retention.[23] A highly satisfied customer generally stays loyal longer, buys more as the company introduces new and upgraded products, talks favorably to others about the company and its products, pays less attention to competing brands and is less sensitive to price, offers product or service ideas to the company, and costs less to serve than new customers because transactions can become routine.[24] Greater customer satisfaction has also been linked to higher returns and lower risk in the stock market.[25]

The link between customer satisfaction and customer loyalty is not proportional, however. Suppose customer satisfaction is rated on a scale from one to five. At a very low level of satisfaction (level one), customers are likely to abandon the company and even bad-mouth it. At levels two to four, customers are fairly satisfied but still find it easy to switch when a better offer comes along. At level five, the customer is very likely to repurchase and even spread good word of mouth about the company. High satisfaction or delight creates an emotional bond with the brand or company, not just a rational preference. Xerox's senior management found its "completely satisfied" customers were six times more likely to repurchase Xerox products over the following 18 months than even its "very satisfied" customers.[26]

The company needs to recognize, however, that customers vary in how they define good performance. Good delivery could mean early delivery, on-time delivery, or order completeness, and two customers can report being "highly satisfied" for different reasons. One may be easily satisfied most of the time and the other might be hard to please but was pleased on this occasion.[27]

MEASUREMENT TECHNIQUES *Periodic surveys* can track customer satisfaction directly and ask additional questions to measure repurchase intention and the respondent's likelihood or willingness to recommend the company and brand to others. One of the nation's largest and most diversified new-home builders, Pulte Homes, wins more awards in J.D. Power's annual survey than any other by constantly measuring how well it's doing with customers and tracking them over a long period of time. Pulte surveys customers just after they buy their homes and again several years later to make sure they're still happy.[28] "Marketing Insight: Net Promoter and Customer Satisfaction" describes why some companies believe just one well-designed question is all that is necessary to assess customer satisfaction.[29]

Companies need to monitor their competitors' performance too. They can monitor their *customer loss rate* and contact those who have stopped buying or who have switched to another supplier to find out why. Finally, as described in Chapter 3, companies can hire *mystery shoppers* to pose as potential buyers and report on strong and weak points experienced in buying the company's and competitors' products. Managers themselves can enter company and competitor sales

---

Net Promoter and Customer Satisfaction

Many companies make measuring customer satisfaction a top priority, but how should they go about doing it? Bain's Frederick Reichheld suggests only one customer question really matters: "How likely is it that you would recommend this product or service to a friend or colleague?" According to Reichheld, a customer's willingness to recommend results from how well the customer is treated by frontline employees, which in turn is determined by all the functional areas that contribute to a customer's experience.[30]

Reichheld was inspired in part by the experiences of Enterprise Rent-A-Car. When the company cut its customer satisfaction survey in 1998 from 18 questions to 2—one about the quality of the rental experience and the other about the likelihood customers would rent from the company again—it found those who gave the highest ratings to their rental experience were three times as likely to rent again than those who gave the second highest rating. The firm also found that diagnostic information managers collected from dissatisfied customers helped it fine-tune its operations.

In a typical Net Promoter survey that follows Reichheld's thinking, customers are asked to rate their likelihood to recommend on a 0 to 10-point scale. Marketers then subtract *detractors* (those who gave a 0 to 6) from *promoters* (those who gave a 9 or 10) to arrive at the Net Promoter Score (NPS). Customers who rate the brand with a 7 or 8 are deemed *passively satisfied* and are not included. A typical set of NPS scores falls in the 10 percent to 30 percent range, but world-class

companies can score over 50 percent. Some firms with top NPS scores include USAA (89 percent), Apple (77 percent), Amazon.com (74 percent), Costco.com (73 percent), and Google (71 percent).

Reichheld is gaining believers. GE, American Express, and Microsoft among others have all adopted the NPS metric, and GE has tied 20 percent of its managers' bonuses to its NPS scores. When the European unit of GE Healthcare scored low, follow-up research revealed that response times to customers were a major problem. After it overhauled its call center and put more specialists in the field, GE Healthcare's Net Promoter scores jumped 10 to 15 points. BearingPoint found clients who gave it high Net Promoter scores showed the highest revenue growth.

Reichheld says he developed NPS in response to overly complicated—and thus ineffective—customer surveys. So it's not surprising that client firms praise its simplicity and strong relationship to financial performance. When Intuit applied Net Promoter to its TurboTax product, feedback revealed dissatisfaction with the software's rebate procedure. After Intuit dropped the proof-of-purchase requirement, sales jumped 6 percent.

Net Promoter is not without critics. One comprehensive academic study of 21 firms and more than 15,000 consumers in Norway failed to find any superiority of Net Promoter over other metrics such as the ACSI measure, discussed later in this chapter.

Sources: Fred Reichheld, *Ultimate Question: For Driving Good Profits and True Growth* (Cambridge, MA: Harvard Business School Press, 2006); Jena McGregor, "Would You Recommend Us?" *BusinessWeek*, January 30, 2006, pp. 94–95; Kathryn Kranhold, "Client-Satisfaction Tool Takes Root," *Wall Street Journal*, July 10, 2006; Fred Reichheld, "The One Number You Need to Grow," *Harvard Business Review*, December 2003; Tlmothy L. Keiningham, Bruce Cooil, Tor Wallin Andreassen, and Lerzan Aksoy, "A Longitudinal Examination of Net Promoter and Firm Revenue Growth," *Journal of Marketing*, 71 (July 2007), pp. 39–51; Neil A. Morgan and Lopo Leotte Rego, "The Value of Different Customer Satisfaction and Loyalty Metrics in Predicting Business Performance," *Marketing Science*, 25, no. 5 (September–October 2006), pp. 426–39; Timothy L. Keiningham, Lerzan Aksoy, Bruce Cooil, and Tor W. Andreassen, "Linking Customer Loyalty to Growth," *MIT Sloan Management Review* (Summer 2008), pp. 51–57; Timothy L. Keiningham, Lerzan Aksoy, Bruce Cooil, and Tor W. Andreassen, "Commentary on 'The Value of Different Customer Satisfaction and Loyalty Metrics in Predicting Business Performance,'" *Marketing Science*, 27, no. 3 (May–June 2008), 531–32.

situations where they are unknown and experience firsthand the treatment they receive, or they can phone their own company with questions and complaints to see how employees handle the calls.

INFLUENCE OF CUSTOMER SATISFACTION For customer-centered companies, customer satisfaction is both a goal and a marketing tool. Companies need to be especially concerned with their customer satisfaction level today because the Internet provides a tool for consumers to quickly spread both good and bad word of mouth to the rest of the world. Some customers set up their own Web sites to air grievances and galvanize protest, targeting high-profile brands such as United Airlines, Home Depot, and Mercedes-Benz.[31]

The University of Michigan's Claes Fornell has developed the American Customer Satisfaction Index (ACSI) to measure consumers' perceived satisfaction with different firms, industries, economic sectors, and national economies.[32] ⬜ Table 5.2 displays some of the 2009 leaders.

Companies that do achieve high customer satisfaction ratings make sure their target market knows it. Once they achieved number one status in their category on J.D. Power's customer satisfaction ratings, Hyundai, American Express, Medicine Shoppe (a chain pharmacy), and Alaska Airways have communicated that fact.

TABLE 5.2 ⬜	2009 ACSI Scores by Industry	
Industry	**Firm**	**Score**
Airlines	Southwest Airlines	81
Apparel	Jones Apparel	84
Automobiles & Light Vehicles	Lexus & BMW	87
Banks	Wachovia	76
Breweries	Molson Coors Brewing	83
Cable & Satellite TV	DIRECTV	71
Cellular Telephones	Nokia	74
Cigarettes	Philip Morris	79
Department & Discount Stores	Nordstrom & Kohl's	80
Energy Utilities	Sempra Energy	80
Express Delivery	FedEx	84
Fixed Line Telephone Service	Cox Communications	74
Food Manufacturing	H. J. Heinz	89
Health Insurance	Blue Cross and Blue Shield	73
Hotels	Hilton Hotels	79
Internet Brokerage	Fidelity Investments	80
Internet News & Information	MSNBC.com	76
Internet Portals & Search Engines	Google	86
Internet Travel	Expedia	77
Life Insurance	Prudential Financial	79
Personal Care & Cleaning Products	Clorox	87
Personal Computers	Apple	85
Soft Drinks	Dr Pepper Snapple	87
Supermarkets	Publix	82
Wireless Telephone Service	Verizon Wireless	74

Source: ACSI LLC, www.theacsi.org. Used with permission.

CUSTOMER COMPLAINTS Some companies think they're getting a sense of customer satisfaction by tallying complaints, but studies show that while customers are dissatisfied with their purchases about 25 percent of the time, only about 5 percent complain. The other 95 percent either feel complaining is not worth the effort or don't know how or to whom to complain. They just stop buying.[33]

Of the customers who register a complaint, 54 percent to 70 percent will do business with the organization again if their complaint is resolved. The figure goes up to a staggering 95 percent if the customer feels the complaint was resolved *quickly*. Customers whose complaints are satisfactorily resolved tell an average of 5 people about the good treatment they received.[34] The average dissatisfied customer, however, gripes to 11 people. If each of these tells still other people, the number exposed to bad word of mouth may grow exponentially.

No matter how perfectly designed and implemented a marketing program is, mistakes will happen. The best thing a company can do is make it easy for customers to complain. Suggestion forms, toll-free numbers, Web sites, and e-mail addresses allow for quick, two-way communication. The 3M Company claims that over two-thirds of its product improvement ideas come from listening to customer complaints.

Given the potential downside of having an unhappy customer, it's critical that marketers deal with negative experiences properly.[35] Beyond that, the following procedures can help to recover customer goodwill:[36]

1. Set up a 7-day, 24-hour toll-free hotline (by phone, fax, or e-mail) to receive and act on customer complaints.
2. Contact the complaining customer as quickly as possible. The slower the company is to respond, the more dissatisfaction may grow and lead to negative word of mouth.
3. Accept responsibility for the customer's disappointment; don't blame the customer.
4. Use customer service people who are empathic.
5. Resolve the complaint swiftly and to the customer's satisfaction. Some complaining customers are not looking for compensation so much as a sign that the company cares.

Product and Service Quality

Satisfaction will also depend on product and service quality. What exactly is quality? Various experts have defined it as "fitness for use," "conformance to requirements," and "freedom from variation." We will use the American Society for Quality's definition: **Quality** is the totality of features and characteristics of a product or service that bear on its ability to satisfy stated or implied needs.[37] This is clearly a customer-centered definition. We can say the seller has delivered quality whenever its product or service meets or exceeds the customers' expectations.

A company that satisfies most of its customers' needs most of the time is called a quality company, but we need to distinguish between *conformance* quality and *performance* quality (or grade). A Lexus provides higher performance quality than a Hyundai: The Lexus rides smoother, goes faster, and lasts longer. Yet both a Lexus and a Hyundai deliver the same conformance quality if all the units deliver their respective promised quality.

IMPACT OF QUALITY Product and service quality, customer satisfaction, and company profitability are intimately connected. Higher levels of quality result in higher levels of customer satisfaction, which support higher prices and (often) lower costs. Studies have shown a high correlation between relative product quality and company profitability.[38] The drive to produce goods that are superior in world markets has led some countries—and groups of countries—to recognize or award prizes to companies that exemplify the best quality practices, such as the Deming Prize in Japan, the Malcolm Baldrige National Quality Award in the United States, and the European Quality Award.

Companies that have lowered costs to cut corners have paid the price when the quality of the customer experience suffers:[39] When Northwest Airlines stopped offering free magazines, pillows, movies, and even minibags of pretzels on domestic flights, it also raised prices and reduced its flight schedule. As one frequent flier noted, "Northwest acts low cost without *being* low cost." Not surprisingly, Northwest came in last of all top U.S. airlines in both the ACS index and J.D. Power's customer satisfaction poll soon thereafter. British Airways also encountered turbulence when it became overly focused on cost cutting.

British Airways   From 1989 to 1996, British Airways was voted the world's best airline in *Business Traveler* magazine's survey. In May 1996, British Airways implemented a business efficiency plan that called for cutting costs by eliminating more than 5,000 jobs. It also sold its ground fleet services, in-flight catering operations, and landing-gear overhaul unit and scrapped its Marketplace Performance Unit, which was responsible for getting information about customer perceptions. These measures lowered employee morale and inspired the cabin staff union to go on a 72-hours strike. Customers complained about delays in baggage handling and in getting responses to their complaints. The planes also started to have technical problems, which increased customer dissatisfaction. To improve employee morale and increase customer satisfaction, the operations and customer service departments were combined to improve cooperation between the two areas, and the company put more emphasis on punctuality and baggage handling. It entered into an alliance with other airlines such as Qantas to form "one world" through which frequent flyer mileage can be accumulated or redeemed, which resulted in cost sharing at airport terminals. In 2009, British Airways was awarded "the best airline" in the world by *Business Traveller*.[40] ▱

After losing its title as the world's best airline in 1996, British Airways experienced a number of problems but they have worked hard to improve their image and earned first place in 2009.

Quality is clearly the key to value creation and customer satisfaction. Total quality is everyone's job, just as marketing is everyone's job. "Marketing Memo: Marketing and Total Quality" outlines the role of marketing in maximizing total quality for the firm.

Maximizing Customer Lifetime Value

Ultimately, marketing is the art of attracting and keeping profitable customers. Yet every company loses money on some of its customers. The well-known 80–20 rule states that 80 percent or more of the company's profits come from the top 20 percent of its customers. Some cases may be more extreme—the most profitable 20 percent of customers (on a per capita basis) may contribute as much as 150 percent to 300 percent of profitability. The least profitable 10 percent to 20 percent, on the other hand, can actually reduce profits between 50 percent to 200 percent per account, with the middle 60 percent to 70 percent breaking even.[41] The implication is that a company could improve its profits by "firing" its worst customers.

---

marketing
Memo   **Marketing and Total Quality**

Marketers play several roles in helping their companies define and deliver high-quality goods and services to target customers

- They correctly identify customers' needs and requirements.
- They communicate customer expectations properly to product designers.
- They make sure customers' orders are filled correctly and on time.
- They check that customers have received proper instructions, training, and technical assistance in the use of the product.

- They stay in touch with customers after the sale to ensure they are, and remain, satisfied.
- They gather customer ideas for product and service improvements and convey them to the appropriate departments.

When marketers do all this, they make substantial contributions to total quality management and customer satisfaction, as well as to customer and company profitability.

It's not always the company's largest customers, who can demand considerable service and deep discounts, who yield the most profit. The smallest customers pay full price and receive minimal service, but the costs of transacting with them can reduce their profitability. Midsize customers who receive good service and pay nearly full price are often the most profitable.

Customer Profitability

A **profitable customer** is a person, household, or company that over time yields a revenue stream exceeding by an acceptable amount the company's cost stream for attracting, selling, and serving that customer. Note the emphasis is on the *lifetime* stream of revenue and cost, not the profit from a particular transaction.[42] Marketers can assess customer profitability individually, by market segment, or by channel.

Many companies measure customer satisfaction, but few measure individual customer profitability.[43] Banks claim this is a difficult task, because each customer uses different banking services and the transactions are logged in different departments. However, the number of unprofitable customers in their customer base has appalled banks that have succeeded in linking customer transactions. Some report losing money on over 45 percent of their retail customers.

CUSTOMER PROFITABILITY ANALYSIS A useful type of profitability analysis is shown in △ Figure 5.3.[44] Customers are arrayed along the columns and products along the rows. Each cell contains a symbol representing the profitability of selling that product to that customer. Customer 1 is very profitable; he buys two profit-making products (P1 and P2). Customer 2 yields mixed profitability; he buys one profitable product (P1) and one unprofitable product (P3). Customer 3 is a losing customer because he buys one profitable product (P1) and two unprofitable products (P3 and P4).

What can the company do about customers 2 and 3? (1) It can raise the price of its less profitable products or eliminate them, or (2) it can try to sell customers 2 and 3 its profit-making products. Unprofitable customers who defect should not concern the company. In fact, the company should encourage them to switch to competitors.

Customer profitability analysis (CPA) is best conducted with the tools of an accounting technique called **activity-based costing (ABC)**. ABC accounting tries to identify the real costs associated with serving each customer—the costs of products and services based on the resources they consume. The company estimates all revenue coming from the customer, less all costs.

With ABC, the costs should include the cost not only of making and distributing the products and services, but also of taking phone calls from the customer, traveling to visit the customer, paying for entertainment and gifts—all the company's resources that go into serving that customer. ABC also allocates indirect costs like clerical costs, office expenses, supplies, and so on, to the activities that use them, rather than in some proportion to direct costs. Both variable and overhead costs are tagged back to each customer.

Companies that fail to measure their costs correctly are also not measuring their profit correctly and are likely to misallocate their marketing effort. The key to effectively employing ABC is to define and judge "activities" properly. One time-based solution calculates the cost of one minute of overhead and then decides how much of this cost each activity uses.[45]

Customers

Products	C₁	C₂	C₃	
P₁	+	+	+	Highly profitable product
P₂	+			Profitable product
P₃		−	−	Unprofitable product
P₄			−	Highly unprofitable product
	High-profit customer	Mixed-bag customer	Losing customer	

|Fig. 5.3| △

Customer-Product
Profitability Analysis

Measuring Customer Lifetime Value

The case for maximizing long-term customer profitability is captured in the concept of customer lifetime value.[46] **Customer lifetime value (CLV)** describes the net present value of the stream of future profits expected over the customer's lifetime purchases. The company must subtract from its expected revenues the expected costs of attracting, selling, and servicing the account of that customer, applying the appropriate discount rate (say, between 10 percent and 20 percent, depending on cost of capital and risk attitudes). Lifetime value calculations for a product or service can add up to tens of thousands of dollars or even into six figures.[47]

Many methods exist to measure CLV.[48] "Marketing Memo: Calculating Customer Lifetime Value" illustrates one. CLV calculations provide a formal quantitative framework for planning customer investment and help marketers adopt a long-term perspective. One challenge, however, is to arrive at reliable cost and revenue estimates. Marketers who use CLV concepts must also take into account the short-term, brand-building marketing activities that help increase customer loyalty.

Cultivating Customer Relationships

Companies are using information about customers to enact precision marketing designed to build strong long-term relationships.[49] Information is easy to differentiate, customize, personalize, and dispatch over networks at incredible speed.

---

marketing
Memo

Calculating Customer Lifetime Value

Researchers and practitioners have used many different approaches for modeling and estimating CLV. Columbia's Don Lehmann and Harvard's Sunil Gupta recommend the following formula to estimate the CLV for a not-yet-acquired customer:

$$CLV = \sum_{t=0}^{T} \frac{(p_t - c_t)r_t}{(1 + i)^t} - AC$$

where p_t = price paid by a consumer at time t,

c_t = direct cost of servicing the customer at time t,

i = discount rate or cost of capital for the firm,

r_t = probability of customer repeat buying or being "alive" at time t,

AC = acquisition cost,

T = time horizon for estimating CLV.

A key decision is what time horizon to use for estimating CLV. Typically, three to five years is reasonable. With this information and estimates of other variables, we can calculate CLV using spreadsheet analysis.

Gupta and Lehmann illustrate their approach by calculating the CLV of 100 customers over a 10-year period (see ▢ Table 5.3). In this example, the firm acquires 100 customers with an acquisition cost per customer of $40. Therefore, in year 0, it spends $4,000. Some of these customers defect each year. The present value of the profits from this cohort of customers over 10 years is $13,286.52. The net CLV (after deducting acquisition costs) is $9,286.52, or $92.87 per customer.

Using an infinite time horizon avoids having to select an arbitrary time horizon for calculating CLV. In the case of an infinite time horizon, if margins (price minus cost) and retention rates stay constant over time, the future CLV of an existing customer simplifies to the following:

$$CLV = \sum_{t=1}^{\infty} \frac{mr^t}{(1 + i)^t} = m\frac{r}{(1 + i - r)}$$

In other words, CLV simply becomes margin (m) times a *margin multiple* $[r/(1 + i - r)]$.

▢ Table 5.4 shows the margin multiple for various combinations of r and i and a simple way to estimate CLV of a customer. When retention rate is 80 percent and discount rate is 12 percent, the margin multiple is about two and a half. Therefore, the future CLV of an existing customer in this scenario is simply his or her annual margin multiplied by 2.5.

Sources: Sunil Gupta and Donald R. Lehmann, "Models of Customer Value," Berend Wierenga, ed., *Handbook of Marketing Decision Models* (Berlin, Germany: Springer Science and Business Media, 2007); Sunil Gupta and Donald R. Lehmann, "Customers as Assets," *Journal of Interactive Marketing* 17, no. 1 (Winter 2006), pp. 9–24; Sunil Gupta and Donald R. Lehmann, *Managing Customers as Investments* (Upper Saddle River, NJ: Wharton School Publishing, 2005); Peter Fader, Bruce Hardie, and Ka Lee, "RFM and CLV: Using Iso-Value Curves for Customer Base Analysis," *Journal of Marketing Research* 42, no. 4 (November 2005), pp. 415–30; Sunil Gupta, Donald R. Lehmann, and Jennifer Ames Stuart, "Valuing Customers," *Journal of Marketing Research* 41, no. 1 (February 2004), pp. 7–18; Werner J. Reinartz and V. Kumar, "On the Profitability of Long-Life Customers in a Noncontractual Setting: An Empirical Investigation and Implications for Marketing," *Journal of Marketing* 64 (October 2000), pp. 17–35.

TABLE 5.3 💬 A Hypothetical Example to Illustrate CLV Calculations											
	Year 0	Year 1	Year 2	Year 3	Year 4	Year 5	Year 6	Year 7	Year 8	Year 9	Year 10
Number of Customers	100	90	80	72	60	48	34	23	12	6	2
Revenue per Customer		100	110	120	125	130	135	140	142	143	145
Variable Cost per Customer		70	72	75	76	78	79	80	81	82	83
Margin per Customer		30	38	45	49	52	56	60	61	61	62
Acquisition Cost per Customer	40										
Total Cost or Profit	−4,000	2,700	3,040	3,240	2,940	2,496	1,904	1,380	732	366	124
Present Value	−4,000	2,454.55	2,512.40	2,434.26	2,008.06	1,549.82	1,074.76	708.16	341.48	155.22	47.81

TABLE 5.4 💬 Margin Multiple				
	Discount Rate			
Retention Rate	10%	12%	14%	16%
60%	1.20	1.5	1.11	1.07
70%	1.75	1.67	1.59	1.52
80%	2.67	2.50	2.35	2.22
90%	4.50	4.09	3.75	3.46

But information cuts both ways. For instance, customers now have a quick and easy means of doing comparison shopping through sites such as Bizrate.com, Shopping.com, and PriceGrabber.com. The Internet also facilitates communication between customers. Web sites such as Epinions.com and Yelp.com enable customers to share information about their experiences with various products and services. Customer empowerment has become a way of life for many companies that have had to adjust to a shift in the power with their customer relationships.

Customer Relationship Management

Customer relationship management (CRM) is the process of carefully managing detailed information about individual customers and all customer "touch points" to maximize loyalty.[50] A *customer touch point* is any occasion on which a customer encounters the brand and product—from actual experience to personal or mass communications to casual observation. For a hotel, the touch points include reservations, check-in and checkout, frequent-stay programs, room service, business services, exercise facilities, laundry service, restaurants, and bars. The Four Seasons relies on personal touches, such as a staff that always addresses guests by name, high-powered employees who understand the needs of sophisticated business travelers, and at least one best-in-region facility, such as a premier restaurant or spa.[51]

CRM enables companies to provide excellent real-time customer service through the effective use of individual account information. Based on what they know about each valued customer, companies can customize market offerings, services, programs, messages, and media. CRM is important because a major driver of company profitability is the aggregate value of the company's customer base.[52]

PERSONALIZING MARKETING The widespread usage of the Internet allows marketers to abandon the mass market practices that built brand powerhouses in the 1950s, 1960s, and 1970s for new approaches that are a throwback to marketing practices from a century ago, when merchants literally knew their customers by name. *Personalizing marketing* is about making sure the brand and its marketing are as relevant as possible to as many customers as possible—a challenge, given that no two customers are identical.

Jones Soda   Peter van Stolk founded Jones Soda on the premise that Gen Y consumers would be more accepting of a new soft drink brand if they felt they discovered it themselves. Jones Soda initially was sold only in shops that sell surfboards, snowboards, and skateboards. The Jones Soda Web site would encourage fans to send in personal photos for possible use on Jones Soda labels. Although only a small number were picked from tens of thousands of entries, the approach helped create relevance and an emotional connection. Customers could also purchase bottles with customized labels. Famous for unusual flavors such as Turkey and Gravy, Pineapple Upside Down, Berry White (a pun on singer Barry White), Purple Carrot, and Lemon Drop Dead, the company also adds pithy words of wisdom from customers under the bottle cap to create additional relevance and distinctiveness. The approach worked for a number of years— revenue grew at 15 percent to 30 percent annually—until an ill-fated foray into canned soda and selling through mass market retailers Target and Walmart resulted in some devastating financial losses and a vow to return to the company's personal-touch roots.[53]

An increasingly essential ingredient for the best relationship marketing today is the right technology. GE Plastics could not target its e-mail effectively to different customers if it were not for advances in database software. Dell could not customize computer ordering for its global corporate customers without advances in Web technology. Companies are using e-mail, Web sites, call centers, databases, and database software to foster continuous contact between company and customer.

E-commerce companies looking to attract and retain customers are discovering that personalization goes beyond creating customized information.[54] For example, the Lands' End Live Web site offers visitors the opportunity to talk with a customer service representative. Nordstrom takes a similar approach to ensure online buyers are as satisfied with the company's customer service as in-store visitors. Domino's has put the customer in charge of ordering a pizza delivery every step of the way.

Domino's   Domino's has introduced a new "build-your-own-pizza" feature on its Web site that allows customers to watch a simulated photographic version of their pizza as they select a size, choose a sauce, and add toppings. The Web site also shows exactly what the completed pizza would cost in the process. It lets customers track orders from when the pizza enters the oven to when it leaves the store. Domino's also introduced a new point-of-sale system that streamlined the logistics of online and phone orders. This system improved accuracy, increased repeat visits, and boosted revenues and processes.[55]

Companies are also recognizing the importance of the personal component to CRM and what happens once customers make actual contact with the company. Employees can create strong bonds with customers by individualizing and personalizing relationships. In essence, thoughtful companies turn their customers into clients. Here is the distinction:

> Customers may be nameless to the institution; clients cannot be nameless. Customers are served as part of the mass or as part of larger segments; clients are served on an individual basis. Customers are served by anyone who happens to be available; clients are served by the professional assigned to them.[56]

To adapt to customers' increased desire for personalization, marketers have embraced concepts such as permission marketing and one-to-one marketing.

Permission marketing, the practice of marketing to consumers only after gaining their expressed permission, is based on the premise that marketers can no longer use "interruption marketing" via mass media campaigns. According to Seth Godin, a pioneer in the technique, marketers can develop stronger consumer relationships by respecting consumers' wishes and sending messages only when they express a willingness to become more involved with the brand.[57] Godin believes permission marketing works because it is "anticipated, personal, and relevant."

Permission marketing, like other personalization approaches, presumes consumers know what they want. But in many cases, consumers have undefined, ambiguous, or conflicting preferences. "Participatory marketing" may be a more appropriate concept than permission marketing, because marketers and consumers need to work together to find out how the firm can best satisfy consumers.

Don Peppers and Martha Rogers outline a four-step framework for *one-to-one marketing* that can be adapted to CRM marketing as follows:[58]

1. *Identify your prospects and customers.* Don't go after everyone. Build, maintain, and mine a rich customer database with information from all the channels and customer touch points.
2. *Differentiate customers in terms of (1) their needs and (2) their value to your company.* Spend proportionately more effort on the most valuable customers (MVCs). Apply activity-based costing and calculate customer lifetime value. Estimate net present value of all future profits from purchases, margin levels, and referrals, less customer-specific servicing costs.
3. *Interact with individual customers to improve your knowledge about their individual needs and to build stronger relationships.* Formulate customized offerings you can communicate in a personalized way.
4. *Customize products, services, and messages to each customer.* Facilitate customer interaction through the company contact center and Web site.

One-to-one marketing is not for every company: It works best for firms that normally collect a great deal of individual customer information and carry a lot of products that can be cross-sold, need periodic replacement or upgrading, and offer high value. For others, the required investment in information collection, hardware, and software may exceed the payout. With automobiles that can cost over $100,000, Aston Martin engages in one-to-one marketing with a select group of customers. High-end dealerships offer separate owners-only clubroom sections and weekend getaways to test-drive new models.[59]

CUSTOMER EMPOWERMENT Often seen as the flag bearer for marketing best practices, P&G's former chairman, A.G. Lafley, created shockwaves with his Association of National Advertisers' speech in October 2006. "The power is with the consumer," proclaimed Lafley, and "marketers and retailers are scrambling to keep up with her. Consumers are beginning in a very real sense to own our brands and participate in their creation. We need to learn to let go." In support of his contention, Lafley pointed out how a teenager had created an animated spot for Pringles snacks that was posted on YouTube; how Pantene, the hair care products company, had created a campaign that encouraged women to cut their hair and donate the clippings to make wigs for cancer patients; and how sales of Cover Girl Outlast lipstick increased 25 percent after the firm put mirrored ads in women's restrooms asking, "Is your lipstick still on?" and ran targeted five-second TV ads with the same theme.[60]

Other marketers have begun to advocate a "bottom-up" grassroots approach to marketing, rather than the more traditional "top-down" approach in which marketers feel they are calling the shots. Burger King has launched attention-getting edgy campaigns in recent years ("Whopper Freakout," "Subservient Chicken," and "Wake Up With the King") on consumer-friendly new media such as YouTube, MySpace, video games, and iPods. Allowing the customer to take charge just makes sense for a brand whose slogan is "Have It Your Way" and whose main rival, McDonald's, already owns the more staid family market.

Marketers are helping consumers become evangelists for brands by providing them resources and opportunities to demonstrate their passion. Doritos held a contest to let consumers name their next flavor. Converse asked amateur filmmakers to submit 30-second short films that demonstrated their inspiration from the iconic sneaker brand. The best of the 1,800 submissions were showcased in the Converse Gallery Web site, and the best of the best became TV commercials. Sales of shoes via the Web site doubled in the month after the gallery's launch.[61]

Even business-to-business firms are getting into the action. PAETEC provides telecommunications services to hotels, universities, and other companies. It has grown into a $500 million company in six years, and its growth is due entirely to customer evangelism. PAETEC's primary marketing strategy: Invite current customers and key prospects to dine on PAETEC's tab and meet

Burger King's "Subservient Chicken" marketing campaign reinforced the brand's core promise of putting the customer in charge.

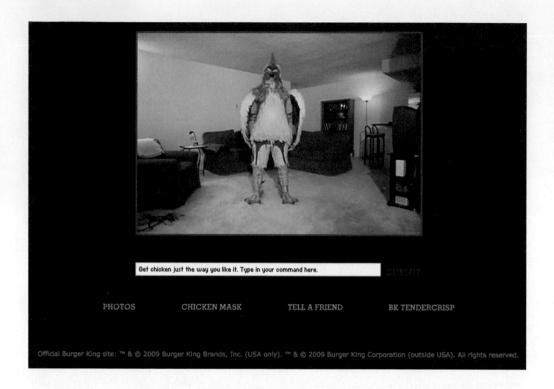

one another. No boring PowerPoint presentations here, just customers talking about their telecommunications challenges and their unfiltered experiences being PAETEC customers. Prospects are sold on the company by other customers.[62]

Although much has been made of the newly empowered consumer—in charge, setting the direction of the brand, and playing a much bigger role in how it is marketed—it's still true that only *some consumers* want to get involved with *some of the brands* they use and, even then, only *some of the time*. Consumers have lives, jobs, families, hobbies, goals, and commitments, and many things matter more to them than the brands they purchase and consume. Understanding how to best market a brand given such diversity is crucially important.

CUSTOMER REVIEWS AND RECOMMENDATIONS Although the strongest influence on consumer choice remains "recommended by relative/friend," an increasingly important decision factor is "recommendations from consumers." With increasing mistrust of some companies and their advertising, online customer ratings and reviews are playing an important role for Internet retailers such as Amazon.com and Shop.com.

Online pet food retailer PETCO actually started using consumer product ratings and reviews in e-mails and banner ads, finding the click-through rate increased considerably as a result.[63] Brick-and-mortar retailers such as Staples and Cabela's are also recognizing the power of consumer reviews and have begun to display them in their stores.[64]

Despite consumer acceptance of such reviews, however, their quality and integrity is always in question. In one famous example, over a period of seven years, the cofounder and CEO of Whole Foods Market reportedly posted more than 1,100 entries on Yahoo! Finance's online bulletin board under a pseudonym, praising his company and criticizing competitors.

Some sites offer summaries of reviews to provide a range of product evaluations. Metacritic aggregates music, game, TV, and movie reviews from leading critics—often from more than 100 publications—averaged into a single 1 to 100 score. Review sites are important in the video game industry because of the influence they wield and the product's high selling price—often $50 to $60. Some game companies tie bonuses for their developers to game scores on the more popular sites. If a major new release doesn't make the 85-plus cutoff, the publisher's stock price may even drop.[65]

Bloggers who review products or services have become important because they may have thousands of followers; blogs are often among the top links returned in online searches for certain brands or categories. A company's PR department may track popular blogs via online services such as Google alerts, BlogPulse, and Technorati. Firms also court the favor of key bloggers via free samples, advance information, and special treatment. Most bloggers disclose when they are given free samples by companies.

For smaller brands with limited media budgets, online word of mouth is critical. To generate prelaunch buzz for one of its new hot cereals, organic food maker Amy's Kitchen shipped out samples before its release to several of the 50 or so vegan, gluten-free, or vegetarian food bloggers the company tracks. When favorable reviews appeared on these blogs, the company was besieged by e-mails asking where the cereal could be bought.[66]

Negative reviews actually can be surprisingly helpful. A January 2007 Forrester study of 10,000 consumers of Amazon.com's electronics and home and garden products found that 50 percent found negative reviews helpful. Most consumers purchased the products regardless of negative comments because they felt the comments reflected personal tastes and opinions that differed from their own. Because consumers can better learn the advantages and disadvantages of products through negative reviews, fewer product returns may result, saving retailers and producers money.[67]

Online retailers often add their own recommendations, "If you like that black purse, you'll love this red blouse." One source estimated that recommendation systems contribute 10 percent to 30 percent of an online retailer's sales. Specialized software tools help online retailers facilitate customer "discovery" or unplanned purchases. When Blockbuster adopted one such system, cancellation rates fell and subscribers nearly doubled the number of movies on their order lists.[68]

At the same time, online companies need to make sure their attempts to create relationships with customers don't backfire, as when customers are bombarded by computer-generated recommendations that consistently miss the mark. Buy a lot of baby gifts on Amazon.com, and your personalized recommendations suddenly don't look so personal! E-tailers need to recognize the limitations of online personalization at the same time that they try harder to find technology and processes that really work.

Amy's Kitchen sent product samples to carefully selected bloggers to quickly spread the word about its new products.

Attracting and Retaining Customers

Companies seeking to expand their profits and sales must spend considerable time and resources searching for new customers. To generate leads, they develop ads and place them in media that will reach new prospects; send direct mail and e-mails to possible new prospects; send their salespeople to participate in trade shows where they might find new leads; purchase names from list brokers; and so on.

Different acquisition methods yield customers with varying CLVs. One study showed that customers acquired through the offer of a 35 percent discount had about one-half the long-term value of customers acquired without any discount.[69] Campaigns that target loyal customers by reinforcing the benefits they enjoy often also attract new customers. Two-thirds of the considerable growth spurred by UK mobile communication leader O2's loyalty strategy was attributed to recruitment of new customers, the remainder from reduced defection.[70]

REDUCING DEFECTION It is not enough to attract new customers; the company must also keep them and increase their business.[71] Too many companies suffer from high **customer churn** or defection. Adding customers here is like adding water to a leaking bucket.

Cellular carriers and cable TV operators are plagued by "spinners," customers who switch carriers at least three times a year looking for the best deal. Many lose 25 percent of their subscribers each year, at an estimated cost of $2 billion to $4 billion. Some of the dissatisfaction defecting customers cite comes from unmet needs and expectations, poor product/service quality and high complexity, and billing errors.[72]

To reduce the defection rate, the company must:

1. **Define and measure its retention rate.** For a magazine, subscription renewal rate is a good measure of retention. For a college, it could be first- to second-year retention rate, or class graduation rate.

2. ***Distinguish the causes of customer attrition and identify those that can be managed better.*** Not much can be done about customers who leave the region or go out of business, but much can be done about those driven away by poor service, shoddy products, or high prices.[73]

3. ***Compare the lost customer's lifetime value to the costs of reducing the defection rate.*** As long as the cost to discourage defection is lower than the lost profit, spend the money to try to retain the customer.

RETENTION DYNAMICS △ Figure 5.4 shows the main steps in attracting and retaining customers in terms of a funnel and some sample questions to measure customer progress through the funnel. The **marketing funnel** identifies the percentage of the potential target market at each stage in the decision process, from merely aware to highly loyal. Consumers must move through each stage before becoming loyal customers. Some marketers extend the funnel to include loyal customers who are brand advocates or even partners with the firm.

By calculating *conversion rates*—the percentage of customers at one stage who move to the next—the funnel allows marketers to identify any bottleneck stage or barrier to building a loyal customer franchise. If the percentage of recent users is significantly lower than triers, for instance, something might be wrong with the product or service that prevents repeat buying.

The funnel also emphasizes how important it is not just to attract new customers, but to retain and cultivate existing ones. Satisfied customers are the company's *customer relationship capital.* If the company were sold, the acquiring company would pay not only for the plant and equipment and brand name, but also for the delivered *customer base,* the number and value of customers who will do business with the new firm. Consider this data about customer retention:[74]

- Acquiring new customers can cost five times more than satisfying and retaining current ones. It requires a great deal of effort to induce satisfied customers to switch from their current suppliers.
- The average company loses 10 percent of its customers each year.
- A 5 percent reduction in the customer defection rate can increase profits by 25 percent to 85 percent, depending on the industry.
- Profit rate tends to increase over the life of the retained customer due to increased purchases, referrals, price premiums, and reduced operating costs to service.

MANAGING THE CUSTOMER BASE Customer profitability analysis and the marketing funnel help marketers decide how to manage groups of customers that vary in loyalty, profitability, and other factors.[75] A key driver of shareholder value is the aggregate value of the customer base. Winning companies improve that value by excelling at strategies like the following:

- ***Reducing the rate of customer defection.*** Selecting and training employees to be knowledgeable and friendly increases the likelihood that customers' shopping questions will be answered satisfactorily. Whole Foods, the world's largest retailer of natural and organic foods, woos customers with a commitment to market the best foods and a team concept for employees.
- ***Increasing the longevity of the customer relationship.*** The more engaged with the company, the more likely a customer is to stick around. Nearly 65 percent of new Honda purchases replace an older Honda. Drivers cited Honda's reputation for creating safe vehicles with high resale value.

|Fig. 5.4| △

The Marketing
Funnel

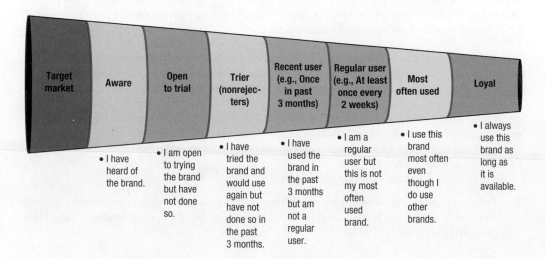

- *Enhancing the growth potential of each customer through "share of wallet," cross-selling, and up-selling.*[76] Sales from existing customers can be increased with new offerings and opportunities. Harley-Davidson sells more than motorcycles and accessories like gloves, leather jackets, helmets, and sunglasses. Its dealerships sell more than 3,000 items of clothing—some even have fitting rooms. Licensed goods sold by others range from predictable items (shot glasses, cue balls, and Zippo cigarette lighters) to the more surprising (cologne, dolls, and cell phones).
- *Making low-profit customers more profitable or terminating them.* To avoid the direct need for termination, marketers can encourage unprofitable customers to buy more or in larger quantities, forgo certain features or services, or pay higher amounts or fees.[77] Banks, phone companies, and travel agencies all now charge for once-free services to ensure minimum revenue levels. Firms can also discourage those with questionable profitability prospects. Progressive Insurance screens customers and diverts the potentially unprofitable to competitors.[78] "Free" customers who pay little or nothing and are subsidized by paying customers—as in print and online media, employment and dating services, and shopping malls—may still create useful direct and indirect network effects, however, an important function.[79]
- *Focusing disproportionate effort on high-profit customers.* The most profitable customers can be treated in a special way. Thoughtful gestures such as birthday greetings, small gifts, or invitations to special sports or arts events can send them a strong positive signal.

Building Loyalty

Creating a strong, tight connection to customers is the dream of any marketer and often the key to long-term marketing success. Companies that want to form such bonds should heed some specific considerations (see △ Figure 5.5). One set of researchers sees retention-building activities as adding financial benefits, social benefits, or structural ties.[80] The following sections explain three types of marketing activities companies are using to improve loyalty and retention.

INTERACTING WITH CUSTOMERS Listening to customers is crucial to customer relationship management. Some companies have created an ongoing mechanism that keeps their marketers permanently plugged in to frontline customer feedback.

- Deere & Company, which makes John Deere tractors and has a superb record of customer loyalty—nearly 98 percent annual retention in some product areas—has used retired employees to interview defectors and customers.[81]
- Chicken of the Sea has 80,000 members in its Mermaid Club, a core-customer group that receives special offers, health tips and articles, new product updates, and an informative e-newsletter. In return, club members provide valuable feedback on what the company is doing and thinking of doing. Feedback from club members has helped design the brand's Web site, develop messages for TV advertising, and craft the look and text on the packaging.[82]
- Build-A-Bear Workshop uses a "Cub Advisory Board" as a feedback and decision-input body. The board is made up of twenty 8- to 12-year-olds who review new-product ideas and give a "paws up or down." Many products in the stores are customer ideas.[83]

But listening is only part of the story. It is also important to be a customer advocate and, as much as possible, take the customers' side and understand their point of view.[84] USAA Insurance's legendary quality of service has led to the highest customer satisfaction in the industry. USAA subscribers will often tell stories about how the company looks out for them, even counseling them not

|Fig. 5.5| △

**Forming Strong
Customer Bonds**

- Create superior products, services, and experiences for the target market.
- Get cross-departmental participation in planning and managing the customer satisfaction and retention process.
- Integrate the "Voice of the Customer" to capture their stated and unstated needs or requirements in all business decisions.
- Organize and make accessible a database of information on individual customer needs, preferences, contacts, purchase frequency, and satisfaction.
- Make it easy for customers to reach appropriate company staff and express their needs, perceptions, and complaints.
- Assess the potential of frequency programs and club marketing programs.
- Run award programs recognizing outstanding employees.

Feedback from members of its Mermaid Club has helped Chicken of the Sea improve its marketing and customer appeal.

to take out more insurance than they need. With such levels of trust, USAA enjoys high customer loyalty and significant cross-selling opportunities.[85]

DEVELOPING LOYALTY PROGRAMS **Frequency programs (FPs)** are designed to reward customers who buy frequently and in substantial amounts.[86] They can help build long-term loyalty with high CLV customers, creating cross-selling opportunities in the process. Pioneered by the airlines, hotels, and credit card companies, FPs now exist in many other industries. Most supermarket chains offer price club cards that grant discounts on certain items.[87]

Typically, the first company to introduce a FP in an industry gains the most benefit, especially if competitors are slow to respond. After competitors react, FPs can become a financial burden to all the offering companies, but some companies are more efficient and creative in managing them. Some FPs generate rewards in a way that locks customers in and creates significant costs to switching. FPs can also produce a psychological boost and a feeling of being special and elite that customers value.[88]

Club membership programs can be open to everyone who purchases a product or service, or limited to an affinity group or those willing to pay a small fee. Although open clubs are good for building a database or snagging customers from competitors, limited-membership clubs are more powerful long-term loyalty builders. Fees and membership conditions prevent those with only a fleeting interest in a company's products from joining. These clubs attract and keep those customers responsible for the largest portion of business. Apple has a highly successful club.

Apple   Apple encourages owners of its computers to form local Apple-user groups. By 2009, there were over 700, ranging in size from fewer than 30 members to over 1,000. The groups provide Apple owners with opportunities to learn more about their computers, share ideas, and get product discounts. They sponsor special activities and events and perform community service. A visit to Apple's Web site will help a customer find a nearby user group.[89]

CREATING INSTITUTIONAL TIES The company may supply customers with special equipment or computer links that help them manage orders, payroll, and inventory. Customers are less inclined to switch to another supplier when it means high capital costs, high search costs, or the loss of loyal-customer discounts. A good example is McKesson Corporation, a leading pharmaceutical wholesaler, which invested millions of dollars in EDI (Electronic Data Interchange) capabilities to help independent pharmacies manage inventory, order-entry processes, and shelf space. Another example is Milliken & Company, which provides proprietary software programs, marketing research, sales training, and sales leads to loyal customers.

Win-Backs

Regardless of how hard companies may try, some customers inevitably become inactive or drop out. The challenge is to reactivate them through win back strategies.[90] It's often easier to reattract ex-customers (because the company knows their names and histories) than to find new ones. Exit interviews and lost-customer surveys can uncover sources of dissatisfaction and help win back only those with strong profit potential.[91]

Customer Databases and Database Marketing

Marketers must know their customers.[92] And in order to know the customer, the company must collect information and store it in a database from which to conduct database marketing. A **customer database** is an organized collection of comprehensive information about individual customers or prospects that is current, accessible, and actionable for lead generation, lead qualification, sale of a product or service, or maintenance of customer relationships. **Database marketing** is the process of building, maintaining, and using customer databases and other databases (products, suppliers, resellers) to contact, transact, and build customer relationships.

Customer Databases

Many companies confuse a customer mailing list with a customer database. A **customer mailing list** is simply a set of names, addresses, and telephone numbers. A customer database contains much more information, accumulated through customer transactions, registration information, telephone queries, cookies, and every customer contact.

Ideally, a customer database also contains the consumer's past purchases, demographics (age, income, family members, birthdays), psychographics (activities, interests, and opinions), mediagraphics (preferred media), and other useful information. The catalog company Fingerhut possesses some 1,400 pieces of information about each of the 30 million households in its massive customer database.

Ideally, a **business database** contains business customers' past purchases; past volumes, prices, and profits; buyer team member names (and ages, birthdays, hobbies, and favorite foods); status of current contracts; an estimate of the supplier's share of the customer's business; competitive suppliers; assessment of competitive strengths and weaknesses in selling and servicing the account; and relevant customer buying practices, patterns, and policies.

A Latin American unit of the Swiss pharmaceutical firm Novartis keeps data on 100,000 of Argentina's farmers, knows their crop protection chemical purchases, groups them by value, and treats each group differently.

Data Warehouses and Data Mining

Savvy companies capture information every time a customer comes into contact with any of their departments, whether it is a customer purchase, a customer-requested service call, an online query, or a mail-in rebate card.[93] Banks and credit card companies, telephone companies, catalog marketers, and many other companies have a great deal of information about their customers, including not only addresses and phone numbers, but also transactions and enhanced data on age, family size, income, and other demographic information.

These data are collected by the company's contact center and organized into a **data warehouse** where marketers can capture, query, and analyze them to draw inferences about an individual customer's needs and responses. Telemarketers can respond to customer inquiries based on a complete picture of the customer relationship, and customized marketing activities can be directed to individual customers.

---

dunnhumby   British research firm dunnhumby has increased the profitability of struggling retailers by gleaning insights from their loyalty program data and credit card transactions. The firm helped British supermarket giant Tesco tailor coupons and special discounts to its loyalty card shoppers. Tesco decided against dropping a poor-selling type of bread after dunnhumby's analysis revealed it was a "destination product" for a loyal cohort that would shop elsewhere if it disappeared. Other U.S. clients have included Kroger, Macy's, and Home Depot. For a major European catalog company, dunnhumby found that not only did shoppers with different body types prefer different clothing styles, they also shopped at different times of the year: Slimmer consumers tended to buy early in a new season, whereas larger folks tended to take fewer risks and wait until later in the season to see what would be popular.[94]

Through **data mining,** marketing statisticians can extract from the mass of data useful information about individuals, trends, and segments. Data mining uses sophisticated statistical and mathematical techniques such as cluster analysis, automatic interaction detection, predictive modeling, and neural networking. Some observers believe a proprietary database can provide a company with a significant competitive advantage.[95] See △ Figure 5.6 for some examples.

In general, companies can use their databases in five ways:

1. *To identify prospects*—Many companies generate sales leads by advertising their product or service. The ads generally contain a response feature, such as a business reply card or toll-free phone number, and the company builds its database from customer responses. It sorts through the database to identify the best prospects, then contacts them by mail or phone to try to convert them into customers.

|Fig. 5.6| △

Examples of Database Marketing

Qwest Twice a year Qwest sifts through its customer list looking for customers that have the potential to be more profitable. The company's database contains as many as 200 observations about each customer's calling patterns. By looking at demographic profiles, plus the mix of local versus long-distance calls or whether a consumer has voice mail, Qwest can estimate potential spending. Next, the company determines how much of the customer's likely telecom budget is already coming its way. Armed with that knowledge, Qwest sets a cutoff point for how much to spend on marketing to this customer.

Royal Caribbean Royal Caribbean uses its database to offer spur-of-the-moment cruise packages to fill all the berths on its ships. It focuses on retired people and single people because they are more able to make quick commitments. Fewer empty berths mean maximized profits for the cruise line.

Fingerhut The skillful use of database marketing and relationship building has made catalog house Fingerhut one of the nation's largest direct-mail marketers. Not only is its database full of demographic details such as age, marital status, and number of children, but it also tracks customers' hobbies, interests, and birthdays. Fingerhut tailors mail offers based on what each customer is likely to buy. Fingerhut stays in continuous touch with customers through regular and special promotions, such as annual sweepstakes, free gifts, and deferred billing. Now the company has applied its database marketing to its Web sites.

Mars Mars is a market leader not only in candy, but also in pet food. In Germany, Mars has compiled the names of virtually every cat-owning family by contacting veterinarians and by advertising a free booklet titled "How to Take Care of Your Cat." Those who request the booklet fill out a questionnaire, so Mars knows the cat's name, age, and birthday. Mars now sends a birthday card to each cat each year, along with a new catfood sample or money-saving coupons for Mars brands.

American Express It is no wonder that, at its secret location in Phoenix, security guards watch over American Express's 500 billion bytes of data on how its customers have used the company's 35 million green, gold, and platinum charge cards. Amex uses the database to include precisely targeted offers in its monthly mailing of millions of customer bills.

2. *To decide which customers should receive a particular offer*—Companies interested in selling, up-selling, and cross-selling set up criteria describing the ideal target customer for a particular offer. Then they search their customer databases for those who most closely resemble the ideal. By noting response rates, a company can improve its targeting precision. Following a sale, it can set up an automatic sequence of activities: One week later send a thank-you note; five weeks later send a new offer; ten weeks later (if customer has not responded) phone and offer a special discount.

3. *To deepen customer loyalty*—Companies can build interest and enthusiasm by remembering customer preferences and sending appropriate gifts, discount coupons, and interesting reading material.

4. *To reactivate customer purchases*—Automatic mailing programs (automatic marketing) can send out birthday or anniversary cards, holiday shopping reminders, or off-season promotions. The database can help the company make attractive or timely offers.

5. *To avoid serious customer mistakes*—A major bank confessed to a number of mistakes it had made by not using its customer database well. In one case, the bank charged a customer a penalty for late payment on his mortgage, failing to note he headed a company that was a major depositor in this bank. The customer quit the bank. In a second case, two different staff members of the bank phoned the same mortgage customer offering a home equity loan at different prices. Neither knew the other had made the call. In a third case, the bank gave a premium customer only standard service in another country.

The Downside of Database Marketing and CRM

Database marketing is most frequently used by business marketers and service providers that normally and easily collect a lot of customer data, like hotels, banks, airlines, and insurance, credit card, and phone companies. Other types of companies in the best position to invest in CRM are those that do a lot of cross-selling and up-selling (such as GE and Amazon.com) or whose customers have highly differentiated needs and are of highly differentiated value to the company. Packaged-goods retailers and consumer packaged-goods companies use database marketing less frequently, though some (such as Kraft, Quaker Oats, Ralston Purina, and Nabisco) have built databases for certain brands. Some businesses cited as CRM successes include Enterprise Rent-A-Car, Pioneer Hi-Bred Seeds, Fidelity Investments, Lexus, Intuit, and Capital One.[96]

Having covered the upside of database marketing, we also need to cover the downside. Five main problems can prevent a firm from effectively using CRM.

1. *Some situations are just not conducive to database management.* Building a customer database may not be worthwhile when: (1) the product is a once-in-a-lifetime purchase (a grand piano); (2) customers show little loyalty to a brand (there is lots of customer churn); (3) the unit sale is very small (a candy bar) so CLV is low; (4) the cost of gathering information is too high; and (5) there is no direct contact between the seller and ultimate buyer.

2. *Building and maintaining a customer database requires a large, well-placed investment in computer hardware, database software, analytical programs, communication links, and skilled staff.* It's difficult to collect the right data, especially to capture all the occasions of company interaction with individual customers. Deloitte Consulting found that 70 percent of firms found little or no improvement from implementing CRM because the CRM system was poorly designed, it became too expensive, users didn't make much use of it or report much benefit, and collaborators ignored the system. Sometimes companies mistakenly concentrate on customer contact processes without making corresponding changes in internal structures and systems.[97]

3. *It may be difficult to get everyone in the company to be customer oriented and use the available information.* Employees find it far easier to carry on traditional transaction marketing than to practice CRM. Effective database marketing requires managing and training employees as well as dealers and suppliers.

4. *Not all customers want a relationship with the company.* Some may resent knowing the company has collected that much personal information about them. Online companies should explain their privacy policies and give consumers the right not to have their information stored. European countries do not look favorably on database marketing and are protective of consumers' private information. The European Union passed a law handicapping the

growth of database marketing in its 27 member countries. "Marketing Insight: The Behavioral Targeting Controversy" reviews some privacy and security issues.

5. **The assumptions behind CRM may not always hold true.**[98] High-volume customers often know their value to a company and can leverage it to extract premium service and/or price discounts, so that it may not cost the firm less to serve them. Loyal customers may expect and demand more and resent any attempt to charge full prices. They may also be jealous of attention lavished on other customers. When eBay began to chase big corporate customers such as IBM, Disney, and Sears, some mom-and-pop businesses that helped build the brand felt abandoned.[99] Loyal customers also may not necessarily be the best ambassadors for the brand. One study found those who scored high on behavioral loyalty and bought a lot of a company's products were less active word-of-mouth marketers than customers who scored high on attitudinal loyalty and expressed greater commitment to the firm.

Thus, the benefits of database marketing do not come without significant costs and risks, not only in collecting the original customer data, but also in maintaining and mining them. When it works, a data warehouse yields more than it costs, but the data must be in good condition, and the discovered relationships must be valid and acceptable to consumers.

Marketing Insight

The Behavioral Targeting Controversy

The emergence of *behavioral targeting* is allowing companies to track the online behavior of target customers and find the best match between ads and prospects. Tracking an individual's Internet usage behavior relies on cookies—randomly assigned numbers, codes, and data that are stored on the user's computer hard drive and reveal which sites have been visited, the amount of time spent there, which products or pages were viewed, which search terms entered, and so on.

Most behavioral targeting is carried out by online ad networks owned by large Internet firms such as Google or AOL, as well as by some Internet service providers (ISPs). These online ad networks—such as AdBrite, which has more than 70,000 sites in its online marketplace—use cookies to track consumers' movements through all their affiliated sites. A new customer signing up with Microsoft for a free Hotmail e-mail account, for example, is required to give the company his or her name, age, gender, and zip code. Microsoft can then combine those facts with information such as observed online behavior and characteristics of the area in which the customer lives, to help advertisers better understand whether, when, and how to contact that customer. Although Microsoft must be careful to preserve consumer privacy—the company claims it won't purchase an individual's income history—it can still provide advertising clients with behavioral targeting information.

For example, Microsoft can help a DiningIn franchisee zero in on working moms aged 30 to 40 in a given neighborhood with ads designed to reach them before 10 AM when they're most likely to be planning their evening meal. Or if a person clicks on three Web sites related to auto insurance and then visits an unrelated site for sports or entertainment, auto insurance ads may show up on that site, in addition to the auto insurance sites. This practice ensures that ads are readily apparent for a potential customer likely to be in the market. Microsoft claims behavioral targeting can increase the likelihood a visitor clicks an ad by as much as 76 percent.

Proponents of behavioral targeting maintain that consumers see more relevant ads in this way. Because the ads are more effective as a result, greater ad revenue is available to support free online content. Spending on behavioral targeting is projected to grow to $4.4 billion or 8.6 percent of total online ad spending by 2012.

But consumers have significant misgivings about being tracked online by advertisers. In one 2009 U.S. survey, about two-thirds of respondents objected to the practice, including 55 percent of respondents aged 18 to 24. Two-thirds of respondents also believed laws should give people the right to know everything a Web site knows about them. Government regulators wonder whether industry self-regulation will be sufficient or legislation is needed.

Proponents of behavioral targeting maintain that many consumers lack full understanding of different tracking practices and would be less concerned if they knew exactly how it worked. Their claims of anonymity and privacy, however, have been weakened by events such as a leak at AOL of online behavioral data in 2006 for 650,000 users and overly aggressive attempts to institute data capture procedures at Facebook and various ISPs.

Sources: Elisabeth Sullivan, "Behave," *Marketing News*, September 15, 2008, pp. 12–15; Stephanie Clifford, "Two-Thirds of Americans Object to Online Tracking," *New York Times*, September 30, 2009; Jessica Mintz, "Microsoft Adds Behavioral Targeting," *Associated Press*, December 28, 2006; Becky Ebenkamp, "Behavior Issues," *Brandweek*, October 20, 2008, pp. 21–25; Brian Morrissey, "Connect the Thoughts," *Adweek Media*, June 29, 2009, pp. 10–11; Laurie Birkett, "The Cookie That Won't Crumble," *Forbes*, January 18, 2010, p. 32; Alden M. Hayashi, "How *Not* to Market on the Web," *MIT Sloan Management Review* (Winter 2010), pp. 14–15.

Summary

1. Customers are value maximizers. They form an expectation of value and act on it. Buyers will buy from the firm that they perceive to offer the highest customer-delivered value, defined as the difference between total customer benefits and total customer cost.

2. A buyer's satisfaction is a function of the product's perceived performance and the buyer's expectations. Recognizing that high satisfaction leads to high customer loyalty, companies must ensure that they meet and exceed customer expectations.

3. Losing profitable customers can dramatically affect a firm's profits. The cost of attracting a new customer is estimated to be five times the cost of keeping a current customer happy. The key to retaining customers is relationship marketing.

4. Quality is the totality of features and characteristics of a product or service that bear on its ability to satisfy stated or implied needs. Marketers play a key role in achieving high levels of total quality so that firms remain solvent and profitable.

5. Marketing managers must calculate customer lifetime values of their customer base to understand their profit implications. They must also determine ways to increase the value of the customer base.

6. Companies are also becoming skilled in customer relationship management (CRM), which focuses on developing programs to attract and retain the right customers and meeting the individual needs of those valued customers.

7. Customer relationship management often requires building a customer database and data mining to detect trends, segments, and individual needs. A number of significant risks also exist, so marketers must proceed thoughtfully.

Applications

Marketing Debate
Online versus Offline Privacy

As more firms practice relationship marketing and develop customer databases, privacy issues are emerging as an important topic. Consumers and public interest groups are scrutinizing—and sometimes criticizing—the privacy policies of firms and raising concerns about potential theft of online credit card information or other potentially sensitive or confidential financial information. Others maintain online privacy fears are unfounded and that security issues are as much a concern offline. They argue that the opportunity to steal information exists virtually everywhere, and it's up to consumers to protect their interests.

Take a position: Privacy is a bigger issue online than offline *versus* Privacy is no different online than offline.

Marketing Discussion
Using CLV

Consider customer lifetime value (CLV). Choose a business and show how you would go about developing a quantitative formulation that captures the concept. How would that business change if it totally embraced the customer equity concept and maximized CLV?

Marketing Excellence

>>Nordstrom

Nordstrom is an upscale U.S. department store chain with sales that topped $8 billion in 2009. John W. Nordstrom originally started the company as a shoe store but grew it over the years into a fashion specialty chain store selling top-quality, brand-name clothing, accessories, jewelry, cosmetics, and fragrances.

From the beginning, Nordstrom has believed in and stressed the importance of providing the highest level of customer service possible along with top-of-the-line, high-quality merchandise. As a shoe retailer, the company offered a wide range of products to fit most everyone's needs and price point. As it expanded into fashion and apparel, it maintained these goals.

Today, Nordstrom sets the standard in customer service and loyalty. In fact, the company is so well-known for this trait that urban legends of unusual acts of customer service still circulate today. One of the best-known tells how in 1975 a customer came into a Nordstrom store after Nordstrom had purchased a company called Northern Commercial Company. The customer wanted to return a

set of tires originally bought at Northern Commercial. Although Nordstrom has never carried or sold tires, it happily accepted the return and instantly provided the customer cash for his purchase.

While Nordstrom's "no questions asked" return policy remains intact today, there are many other examples of its exceptional customer service. Its sales representatives send thank-you cards to customers who shop there and have hand-delivered special orders to customers' homes. Nordstrom installed a tool called Personal Book at its registers that allow salespeople to enter and recall customers' specific preferences in order to better personalize their shopping experiences. Nordstrom also provides customers with multichannels for shopping, allowing them to buy something online and pick it up at a store within an hour.

Nordstrom's customer loyalty program, Fashion Rewards Program, rewards customers on four different levels based on their annual spending. Customers who spend $10,000 annually receive complimentary alterations, free shipping, a 24-hour fashion emergency hotline, and access to a personal concierge service. Customers at the highest rewards level ($20,000 spent annually) also receive private

shopping trips complete with prestocked dressing rooms in the customers' specific size, champagne, and live piano music; tickets to Nordstrom's runway fashion shows; and access to exclusive travel and fashion packages, including red carpet events.

This strategic and often costly customer-focus approach has reaped great benefits for the company. Not only has Nordstrom emerged over the past 100+ years as a luxury brand known for quality, trust, and service, but its customers stay loyal even in hard times. During the economic crisis in 2008 and 2009, many customers chose to shop at Nordstrom over its competitors due to their existing relationship and hassle-free return policy.

Nordstrom currently operates 112 full-line stores, 69 Nordstrom Rack clearance stores, two Jeffrey Boutiques, and one clearance store, with plans to open 50 new stores over the next 10 years. When a new store opens, Nordstrom connects with the surrounding community by hosting an opening night gala complete with live entertainment, a runway fashion show, and the ultimate shopping experience to help raise money for local charities.

As Nordstrom moves forward, the company continues to be flexible and look for new tools and means to help deepen and develop its customer-salesperson relationship.

Questions

1. How else can Nordstrom continue to provide exceptional customer service and increase brand loyalty?

2. What are Nordstrom's greatest risks, and who are its biggest competitors?

Sources: "Annual Reports," Nordstrom.com; "Company History," Nordstrom.com; Chantal Todé, "Nordstrom Loyalty Program Experience," *DMNews*, May 4, 2007; Melissa Allison and Amy Martinez, "Nordstrom's Solid December Showing Suggests Some Shoppers Eager to Spend." *Seattle Times*, January 7, 2010.

Marketing Excellence

>>Harley-Davidson

Harley-Davidson, a U.S. brand synonymous with beautiful motorbikes, inspires many to own its customized bike with iconic engine. Today the brand is sought after not only in the United States but globally too. What explains its wide global acceptance, and the strong sense of brand loyalty among Harley-Davidson motorbike owners?

Harley-Davidson dealers, ranging from the CEO to the sales staff, maintain personalized relationships with customers through face-to-face and social media contact. Knowing customers as individuals and conducting ongoing research to keep up with their changing expectations and

experiences helps Harley-Davidson to define their customers' needs better.

Current customers have told Harley-Davidson's management to keep the identity, look, and sound of the motorcycles because they are unique. Globally, customers accept the U.S. brand image as it stands. When customers' views are heard and accepted by management, customers develop greater brand loyalty, creating an extraordinary customer experience that is unique and valuable. Buying a Harley allows owners to express their individualism and freedom, connect with friends, and share a sense of comradeship through the activities of H.O.G., the company-sponsored Harley Owners Group and riding club. Owners of new Harley-Davidson motorbikes enjoy free H.O.G. membership in the first year. If renewed, members can enjoy various discounts and benefits.

Examples of events and activities that are sponsored by independent dealerships such as Harley-Davidson of Singapore can range from short rides, major destination rides, or local charity events. H.O.G. members are also invited to events such as new model launches, and riders' appreciation nights. Dealers in each country support H.O.G. members and foster positive bonding relationships among members and other dealers.

In Singapore, for instance, a community of friends ride Harley-Davidson motorcycles with a passion. "We ride 'em, and we have lots of fun! And we've been doing it since 1996 in Singapore." "To Ride and Have Fun" is a motto that all H.O.G. chapters around the world follow. Riders associate riding with other owners as a time of bonding and conveys the image of freedom and adventure.

Membership of H.O.G. has increased. Now not only men but also women, children, and families have joined H.O.G.'s many and varied group outings and activities. Harley-Davidson is a strong brand whose consumers appreciate the image of the brand by experiencing it. The desire to be associated with the Harley-Davidson brand is strong because it is linked to an aspirational life style.

For a week in June 2010, the Malaysian Highway was filled by 300 Harley-Davidson bikers from 11 countries in the first Southeast Asia Harley Owners Group (SEA H.O.G.) Rally. The rally, which also included a fund-raising activity, started in Kuala Lumpur and headed to Singapore, and back to Kuala Lumpur City Center for the Harley-Davidson Festival before heading to Krabi in Thailand.

Some H.O.G. members around the world ride in rallies every Sunday, rain or shine, displaying a strong sense of loyalty for the Harley-Davidson brand. In Hong Kong, H.O.G. members include professionals like doctors, lawyers, accountants, pilots, engineers, movie stars, and business executives. Their participation shows the strong brand loyalty among Harley-Davidson owners and the strong desire to be engaged in H.O.G. members' activities.

Proactive in people development, Harley-Davidson shares company values, philosophy, and brand experience with its staff and provides effective communication to its independent dealers. Professional training by members of the Harley-Davidson University in the U.S. encourages consistent service at every dealership. Thus Harley-Davidson's employees around the world can be confident about providing the genuine Harley-Davidson experience. Satisfied employees deliver outstanding services, which generates sustainable customer and brand loyalty, positive word of mouth, and ultimately higher company sales.

To remain competitive, Milwaukee-based Harley-Davidson has started to enlarge its customer base and successfully connect with new, younger riders by way of social media applications such as Facebook. Engaging relationships have been established with its young adults who are global fans of its Facebook page. Important feedback that Harley-Davidson's strong brand name remains appealing to the younger audience is encouraging.

Harley-Davidson has also made in-person connections with new potential riders at music festivals by using dynamometers to create an interactive experience called Jump Start, which allows novice or non riders an opportunity to feel what it's like to ride a Harley-Davidson.

In 2008, it became the leading manufacturer of motorcycles to sell to customers younger than 34 years old without changing the products too drastically or lowering its prices. Harley-Davidson merely modified some design elements for its Dark Custom series of motorcycles which consists largely of existing Harley-Davidson motorcycles but with flat black paint, much less chrome, and toned-down styling. It portrayed its heritage message of freedom, uniqueness, individual expression, and shared experience recognized by older customers.

Questions

1. What kinds of things has Harley-Davidson done well with its H.O.G. program to create an extraordinary customer experience that is unique and valuable to its members?

2. To enlarge its customer base, what kinds of things would you recommend Harley-Davidson do to cultivate long-term relationships with a younger audience, aged between 18-34?

Sources: Jill Z. McBride, "DMA2010—How Harley-Davidson Builds Champion Customers One Rider at a Time," *Colloquy*, www.colloquy.com/article_view.asp?xd=7650; Shaun Smith, "Customer Experience Management Plus: Harley-Davidson," *CustomerThink*, March 4, 2008; Smith & Co., "Customer loyalty—Increasing Customer Loyalty;" "Case Study of Harley Davidson's Business Practices," *University of Louisville*, http://cbpa.louisville.edu/bruce, http://infotechdesign.net/itd/a-case-study-of-harley-davidsons-business-practices.html; Evans Smith, MBA Candidate, Posted by Joe Alexander, Harley-Davidson, "Master H.O.G.s of Brand Loyalty," *BusinessWeek*, http://bwnt.businessweek.com/Interactive_reports/undergrad_bschool; *Harley-Davidson Hong Kong*; *Harley-Davidson Kuala Lumpur*; *Harley-Davidson Singapore*; H.O.G. Singapore, www.hogsingapore.com/events.php; H.O.G., "Garage Party," www.h-d.com/garageparty; Jay WM Wong, "Harley-Davidson Kuala Lumpur to Host First South East Asia Hog Rally 2010," www.wemotor.com/blog/2010/05/harley-davidson-kuala-lumpur-to-host-first-south-east-asia-hog-rally-2010, May 12, 2010; www.scribd.com/doc/43454855/Harley-Davidson-Case-Analysis-Essay; Eric Decker, "Harley Reaches out to the Next Generation," *Biz Times*, http://www.biztimes.com/news/2010/7/23/harley-reaches-out-to-the-next-generation/; Eric Decker, "What should Harley do Now?," *Biz Times*, http://www.biztimes.com/news/2010/7/23/what-should-harley-do-now/; "The Experimental Meaning of Harley Davidson," http://www.slideshare.net/ulrichx/storytelling-experience-economy-harley-davidson.

Chapter 6

In This Chapter, We Will Address the Following Questions

1. How do consumer characteristics influence buying behavior?

2. What major psychological processes influence consumer responses to the marketing program?

3. How do consumers make purchasing decisions?

4. In what ways do consumers stray from a deliberative, rational decision process?

LEGO has programs in place to help it stay close to its customers—especially the more devoted and loyal ones.

Analyzing Consumer Markets

The aim of marketing is to meet and satisfy target customers' needs and wants better than competitors. Marketers must have a thorough understanding of how consumers think, feel, and act and offer clear value to each and every target consumer.

 LEGO of Billund, Denmark, may have been one of the first mass customized brands. Every child who has ever had a set of the most basic LEGO blocks has built his or her own unique and amazing creations, brick by plastic brick. When LEGO decided to become a lifestyle brand and launch theme parks; its own lines of clothes, watches, and video games; and products such as Clikits craft sets designed to attract more girls to the brand franchise, it neglected its core market of five- to nine-year-old boys. Plunging profits led to layoffs of almost half its employees as the firm streamlined its brand portfolio to emphasize its core businesses. To better coordinate new product activities, LEGO revamped its organizational structure into four functional groups managing eight key areas. One group was responsible for supporting customer communities and tapping into them for product ideas. LEGO also set up what was later renamed LEGO Design byME, which let customers design, share, and build their own custom LEGO products using LEGO's freely downloadable Digital Designer 3.0 software. The creations that result can exist—and be shared with other enthusiasts— solely online, or, if customers want to build them, the software tabulates the pieces required and sends an order to LEGO's Enfield, Connecticut, warehouse. Customers can request step-by-step building guide instructions and even design their own box to store the pieces.[1]*

Successful marketing requires that companies fully connect with their customers. Adopting a holistic marketing orientation means understanding customers— gaining a 360-degree view of both their daily lives and the changes that occur during their lifetimes so the right products are always marketed to the right customers in the right way. This chapter explores individual consumer buying dynamics; the next chapter explores the buying dynamics of business buyers.

What Influences Consumer Behavior?

Consumer behavior is the study of how individuals, groups, and organizations select, buy, use, and dispose of goods, services, ideas, or experiences to satisfy their needs and wants.[2] Marketers must fully understand both the theory and reality of consumer behavior. 🖮 Table 6.1 provides a snapshot profile of U.S. consumers.

A consumer's buying behavior is influenced by cultural, social, and personal factors. Of these, cultural factors exert the broadest and deepest influence.

Cultural Factors

Culture, subculture, and social class are particularly important influences on consumer buying behavior. **Culture** is the fundamental determinant of a person's wants and behavior. Through family and other key institutions, a child growing up in the United States is exposed to values such as

TABLE 6.1   American Consumer Almanac

Expenditures		
Average U.S. outlays for goods and services in 2009		
	$	%
Housing	$16,920	34.1%
Transportation	$8,758	17.6%
Food	$6,133	12.4%
Personal insurance and pensions	$5,336	10.7%
Healthcare	$2,853	5.7%
Entertainment	$2,698	5.4%
Apparel and services	$1,881	3.8%
Cash contributions	$1,821	3.7%
Education	$945	1.9%
Miscellaneous	$808	1.6%
Personal care products and services	$588	1.2%
Alcoholic beverages	$457	.9%
Tobacco products and smoking supplies	$323	0.7%
Reading	$118	0.2%
Ownership		
Percentage of households with at least one vehicle owned or leased		77.0%
Percentage of households that own homes		67%
Percentage of households that own their homes "free and clear"		23%
Time use on an average workday for employed persons ages 25–54 with children in 2008		
Working and related activities	8.8 hours	
Sleeping	7.6 hours	
Leisure and sports	2.6 hours	
Caring for others	1.3 hours	
Eating and drinking	1.0 hours	
Household activities	1.0 hours	
Other	1.7 hours	
Monthly users' time spent in hours: Minutes per user aged 2+ years—Q1 2009		
	# of Americans	Average minutes per day spent
Watching TV in the home	285,574,000	153 minutes
Watching time-shifted TV	79,533,000	8 minutes
Using the Internet	163,110,000	29 minutes
Watching video on the Internet	131,102,000	3 minutes
Mobile subscribers watching video on a mobile phone	13,419,000	4 minutes

Sources: Bureau of Labor Statistics, *Consumer Expenditure Survey*, www.bls.gov/cex; AC Nielsen, *A2 M2 Three Screen Report*, 1st Quarter 2009, http://blog.nielsen.com/nielsenwire/wp-content/uploads/2009/05/nielsen_threescreenreport_q109.pdf.

achievement and success, activity, efficiency and practicality, progress, material comfort, individualism, freedom, external comfort, humanitarianism, and youthfulness.[3] A child growing up in another country might have a different view of self, relationship to others, and rituals. Marketers must closely attend to cultural values in every country to understand how to best market their existing products and find opportunities for new products.

Each culture consists of smaller **subcultures** that provide more specific identification and socialization for their members. Subcultures include nationalities, religions, racial groups, and geographic regions. When subcultures grow large and affluent enough, companies often design specialized marketing programs to serve them.

Virtually all human societies exhibit *social stratification*, most often in the form of **social classes**, relatively homogeneous and enduring divisions in a society, hierarchically ordered and with members who share similar values, interests, and behavior. One classic depiction of social classes in the United States defined seven ascending levels: (1) lower lowers, (2) upper lowers, (3) working class, (4) middle class, (5) upper middles, (6) lower uppers, and (7) upper uppers.[4]

Social class members show distinct product and brand preferences in many areas, including clothing, home furnishings, leisure activities, and automobiles. They also differ in media preferences; upper-class consumers often prefer magazines and books, and lower-class consumers often prefer television. Even within a category such as TV, upper-class consumers may show greater preference for news and drama, whereas lower-class consumers may lean toward reality shows and sports. There are also language differences—advertising copy and dialogue must ring true to the targeted social class.

Social Factors

In addition to cultural factors, social factors such as reference groups, family, and social roles and statuses affect our buying behavior.

REFERENCE GROUPS A person's **reference groups** are all the groups that have a direct (face-to-face) or indirect influence on their attitudes or behavior. Groups having a direct influence are called **membership groups**. Some of these are **primary groups** with whom the person interacts fairly continuously and informally, such as family, friends, neighbors, and coworkers. People also belong to **secondary groups**, such as religious, professional, and trade-union groups, which tend to be more formal and require less continuous interaction.

Reference groups influence members in at least three ways. They expose an individual to new behaviors and lifestyles, they influence attitudes and self-concept, and they create pressures for conformity that may affect product and brand choices. People are also influenced by groups to which they do *not* belong. **Aspirational groups** are those a person hopes to join; **dissociative groups** are those whose values or behavior an individual rejects.

Where reference group influence is strong, marketers must determine how to reach and influence the group's opinion leaders. An **opinion leader** is the person who offers informal advice or information about a specific product or product category, such as which of several brands is best or how a particular product may be used.[5] Opinion leaders are often highly confident, socially active, and frequent users of the category. Marketers try to reach them by identifying their demographic and psychographic characteristics, identifying the media they read, and directing messages to them.

Clothing companies such as Hot Topic, which hope to appeal to the fickle and fashion-conscious youth market, have used music in a concerted effort to monitor opinion leaders' style and behavior.

 Hot Topic With over 600 stores in malls in 49 states and Puerto Rico, Hot Topic has been hugely successful at using anti-establishment style in its fashions. The chain also sells books, comics, jewelry, CDs, records, posters, and other paraphernalia. Hot Topic's slogan, "Everything about the music," reflects its operating premise: Whether a teen is into rock, pop-punk, emo, acid rap, rave, or rockabilly—or even more obscure musical tastes—Hot Topic has the right T-shirt. To keep up with music trends, all Hot Topic staffers, from the CEO to the music-obsessed salespeople (80 percent of whom are under 25), regularly attend concerts by up-and-coming and established bands to scout who's wearing what. Each store looks more like a campus student center

Hot Topic works hard to stay on top of what's new and what matters with its core youth audience—especially in music.

than a shop—loud music plays and dark walls have bulletin boards displaying concert flyers and staff music picks. Hot Topic also hosts free acoustic shows, called Local Static, showcasing local bands and has created a music-related social network site, ShockHound.com. Hot Topic can catch trends and launch new hip clothing and hard-to-find pop culture merchandise in six to eight weeks, literally months before traditional competitors using off-shore suppliers.[6] ▭

FAMILY The family is the most important consumer buying organization in society, and family members constitute the most influential primary reference group.[7] There are two families in the buyer's life. The **family of orientation** consists of parents and siblings. From parents a person acquires an orientation toward religion, politics, and economics and a sense of personal ambition, self-worth, and love.[8] Even if the buyer no longer interacts very much with his or her parents, parental influence on behavior can be significant. Almost 40 percent of families have auto insurance with the same company as the husband's parents.

A more direct influence on everyday buying behavior is the **family of procreation**—namely, the person's spouse and children. In the United States, husband–wife engagement in purchases has traditionally varied widely by product category. The wife has usually acted as the family's main purchasing agent, especially for food, sundries, and staple clothing items. Now traditional purchasing roles are changing, and marketers would be wise to see both men and women as possible targets.

For expensive products and services such as cars, vacations, or housing, the vast majority of husbands and wives engage in joint decision making.[9] Men and women may respond differently to marketing messages, however.[10] Research has shown that women value connections and relationships with family and friends and place a higher priority on people than on companies. Men, on the other hand, relate more to competition and place a high priority on action.[11]

Marketers are taking more direct aim at women with new products such as Quaker's Nutrition for Women cereals and Crest Rejuvenating Effects toothpaste. In 2003, Sherwin-Williams launched a Dutch Boy easy-to-use "Twist and Pour" paint can targeted specifically at women. Priced $2 higher than the same paint in traditional metal containers, the new product helped the company triple its revenue.[12]

Another shift in buying patterns is an increase in the amount of dollars spent and the direct and indirect influence wielded by children and teens. Direct influence describes children's hints, requests, and demands—"I want to go to McDonald's." Indirect influence means that parents know the brands, product choices, and preferences of their children without hints or outright requests ("I think Jake and Emma would want to go to McDonald's").

Research has shown that more than two-thirds of 13- to 21-year-olds make or influence family purchase decisions on audio/video equipment, software, and vacation destinations.[13] In total, these teens and young adults spend over $120 billion a year. They report that to make sure they buy the right products, they watch what their friends say and do as much as what they see or hear in an ad or are told by a salesperson in a store.[14]

Television can be especially powerful in reaching children, and marketers are using it to target them at younger ages than ever before with product tie-ins for just about everything—Disney character pajamas, retro G.I. Joe toys and action figures, Harry Potter backpacks, and *High School Musical* playsets.

By the time children are around 2 years old, they can often recognize characters, logos, and specific brands. They can distinguish between advertising and programming by about ages 6 or 7. A year or so later, they can understand the concept of persuasive intent on the part of advertisers. By 9 or 10, they can perceive the discrepancies between message and product.[15]

ROLES AND STATUS We each participate in many groups—family, clubs, organizations. Groups often are an important source of information and help to define norms for behavior. We can define a person's position in each group in terms of role and status. A **role** consists of the activities a person is expected to perform. Each role in turn connotes a **status**. A senior vice

The Average U.S. Consumer Quiz

Listed below is a series of statements used in attitude surveys of U.S. consumers. For each statement, estimate what percent of U.S. men and women agreed with it in 2009 and write your answer, a number between 0 percent and 100 percent, in the columns to the right. Then check your results against the correct answers in the footnote.*

	Percent of Consumers Agreeing	
Statements	**% Men**	**% Women**
1. It's more important to fit in than to be different from other people.	____	____
2. Material things like the car I drive and the house I live in are really important to me.	____	____
3. Religion doesn't provide the answers to many of today's problems.	____	____
4. Businesses care more about selling me products and services that already exist rather than coming up with something that really fits my lifestyle.	____	____
5. Most of the time, the service people that I deal with don't care much about me or my needs.	____	____
6. I wish there were clearer rules about what is right and wrong.	____	____
7. I am comfortable with a certain amount of debt.	____	____
8. It is risky to buy a brand you are not familiar with.	____	____
9. I try to have as much fun as I can now and let the future take care of itself.	____	____
10. No matter how hard I try, I never seem to have enough time to do all the things I need to do.	____	____

Note:
   Results are from a nationally representative sample of 4,147 respondents surveyed in 2009.
Source: The Futures Company Yankelovich MONITOR (with permission). Copyright 2009, Yankelovich, Inc.
*Answers:

1. M = 27%, W = 20%; 2. M = 47%, W = 39%; 3. M = 53%, W = 45%; 4. M = 72%, W = 66%; 5. M = 60%, W = 57%; 6. M = 47%, W = 45%; 7. M = 54%, W = 46%; 8. M = 49%, W = 46%; 9. M = 56%, W = 63%; 10. M = 63%, W = 69%.

Source: The Futures Company/Yankelovich Monitor. Copyright 2009, Yankelovich, Inc.

president of marketing may be seen as having more status than a sales manager, and a sales manager may be seen as having more status than an office clerk. People choose products that reflect and communicate their role and their actual or desired status in society. Marketers must be aware of the status-symbol potential of products and brands.

Personal Factors

Personal characteristics that influence a buyer's decision include age and stage in the life cycle, occupation and economic circumstances, personality and self-concept, and lifestyle and values. Because many of these have a direct impact on consumer behavior, it is important for marketers to follow them closely. See how well you do with "Marketing Memo: The Average U.S. Consumer Quiz."

AGE AND STAGE IN THE LIFE CYCLE Our taste in food, clothes, furniture, and recreation is often related to our age. Consumption is also shaped by the *family life cycle* and the number, age, and gender of people in the household at any point in time. U.S. households are increasingly fragmented—the traditional family of four with a husband, wife, and two kids makes up a much smaller percentage of total households than it once did. The average U.S. household size in 2008 was 2.6 persons.[16]

In addition, *psychological* life-cycle stages may matter. Adults experience certain "passages" or "transformations" as they go through life.[17] Their behavior as they go through these passages, such as becoming a parent, is not necessarily fixed but changes with the times.

Marketers should also consider *critical life events or transitions*—marriage, childbirth, illness, relocation, divorce, first job, career change, retirement, death of a spouse—as giving rise to new needs. These should alert service providers—banks, lawyers, and marriage, employment, and bereavement counselors—to ways they can help. For example, the wedding industry attracts marketers of a whole host of products and services.

Newlyweds   Newlyweds in the United States spend a total of about $70 billion on their households in the first year after marriage—and they buy more in the first six months than an established household does in five years! Marketers know marriage often means two sets of shopping habits and brand preferences must be blended into one. Procter & Gamble, Clorox, and Colgate-Palmolive include their products in "Newlywed Kits," distributed when couples apply for a marriage license. JCPenney has identified "Starting Outs" as one of its two major customer groups. Marketers pay a premium for name lists to assist their direct marketing because, as one noted, newlywed names "are like gold."[18]

One well-defined and attractive target market for many firms is newlyweds.

OCCUPATION AND ECONOMIC CIRCUMSTANCES

Occupation also influences consumption patterns. Marketers try to identify the occupational groups that have above-average interest in their products and services and even tailor products for certain occupational groups: Computer software companies, for example, design different products for brand managers, engineers, lawyers, and physicians.

As the recent recession clearly indicated, both product and brand choice are greatly affected by economic circumstances: spendable income (level, stability, and time pattern), savings and assets (including the percentage that is liquid), debts, borrowing power, and attitudes toward spending and saving. Luxury-goods makers such as Gucci, Prada, and Burberry are vulnerable to an economic downturn. If economic indicators point to a recession, marketers can take steps to redesign, reposition, and reprice their products or introduce or increase the emphasis on discount brands so they can continue to offer value to target customers. Some firms—such as Snap Fitness—are well-positioned to take advantage of good and bad economic times to begin with.

Snap Fitness   Although some gym chains struggled in the recession—Bally's Total Fitness filed for bankruptcy twice—24-hour Snap Fitness actually expanded the number of its clubs, and its revenue doubled. The franchise chain did all this despite charging members only $35 per month with easy cancellation fees. Its secret? A no-frills approach reinforced by the motto, "Fast, Convenient, Affordable." The small gyms—only 2,500 square feet—typically have five treadmills, two stationary bikes, five elliptical machines, and weight equipment. What's important is what they *don't* have—no classes, spa rooms, on-site child care, or juice bars. Few clubs have showers, and most are staffed only 25 to 40 hours a week. The sweet spot of their target market is married 35- to 55-year-olds with kids who live nearby and are busy enough that they cannot afford more than an hour a day to go to the gym.[19]

No-frills Snap Fitness was perfectly positioned to weather the latest economic recession.

PERSONALITY AND SELF-CONCEPT

Each person has personality characteristics that influence his or her buying behavior. By **personality**, we mean a set of distinguishing human psychological traits that lead to relatively consistent and enduring responses to environmental stimuli (including buying behavior). We often describe personality in terms of such traits as self-confidence, dominance, autonomy, deference, sociability, defensiveness, and adaptability.[20]

Personality can be a useful variable in analyzing consumer brand choices. Brands also have personalities, and consumers are likely to choose brands whose personalities match their own. We define **brand personality** as the specific mix of human traits that we can attribute to a particular brand.

Stanford's Jennifer Aaker researched brand personalities and identified the following traits:[21]

1. Sincerity (down-to-earth, honest, wholesome, and cheerful)
2. Excitement (daring, spirited, imaginative, and up-to-date)
3. Competence (reliable, intelligent, and successful)
4. Sophistication (upper-class and charming)
5. Ruggedness (outdoorsy and tough)

Aaker analyzed some well-known brands and found that a number tended to be strong on one particular trait: Levi's on "ruggedness"; MTV on "excitement"; CNN on "competence"; and Campbell's on "sincerity." These brands will, in theory, attract users high on the same traits. A brand personality may have several attributes: Levi's suggests a personality that is also youthful, rebellious, authentic, and American.

A cross-cultural study exploring the generalizability of Aaker's scale outside the United States found three of the five factors applied in Japan and Spain, but a "peacefulness" dimension replaced "ruggedness" both in Japan and Spain, and a "passion" dimension emerged in Spain instead of "competence."[22] Research on brand personality in Korea revealed two culture-specific factors—"passive likeableness" and "ascendancy"—reflecting the importance of Confucian values in Korea's social and economic systems.[23]

Consumers often choose and use brands with a brand personality consistent with their *actual self-concept* (how we view ourselves), although the match may instead be based on the consumer's *ideal self-concept* (how we would like to view ourselves) or even on *others' self-concept* (how we think others see us).[24] These effects may also be more pronounced for publicly consumed products than for privately consumed goods.[25] On the other hand, consumers who are high "self-monitors"—that is, sensitive to how others see them—are more likely to choose brands whose personalities fit the consumption situation.[26] Finally, often consumers have multiple aspects of self (serious professional, caring family member, active fun-lover) that may be evoked differently in different situations or around different types of people. Some marketers carefully orchestrate brand experiences to express brand personalities. Here's how San Francisco's Joie de Vivre chain does this.[27]

Joie de Vivre
Joie de Vivre Hospitality operates a chain of boutique hotels, restaurants, and resorts in the San Francisco area. Each property's unique décor, quirky amenities, and thematic style are often loosely based on popular magazines. For example, The Hotel del Sol—a converted motel bearing a yellow exterior and surrounded by palm trees wrapped with festive lights—is described as "kind of *Martha Stewart Living* meets *Islands* magazine." The Phoenix, represented by *Rolling Stone,* is, like the magazine, described as "adventurous, hip, irreverent, funky, and young at heart." Joie de Vivre's goal is to stimulate each of the five senses in accordance with the five words chosen for each hotel. The boutique concept enables the hotels to offer personal touches, such as vitamins in place of chocolates on pillows. There's even an online personality matchmaker to help match guests to the most fitting hotels. Joie de Vivre now owns the largest number of independent hotel properties in the Bay Area.

LIFESTYLE AND VALUES People from the same subculture, social class, and occupation may lead quite different lifestyles. A **lifestyle** is a person's pattern of living in the world as expressed in activities, interests, and opinions. It portrays the "whole person" interacting with his or her environment. Marketers search for relationships between their products and lifestyle groups. A computer manufacturer might find that most computer buyers are achievement-oriented and then aim the brand more clearly at the achiever lifestyle. Here's an example of one of the latest lifestyle trends businesses are targeting.

Boutique hotel chain Joie de Vivre uniquely positions each of its properties and then offers an online matchmaker to help consumers find the hotel that best fits their interests.

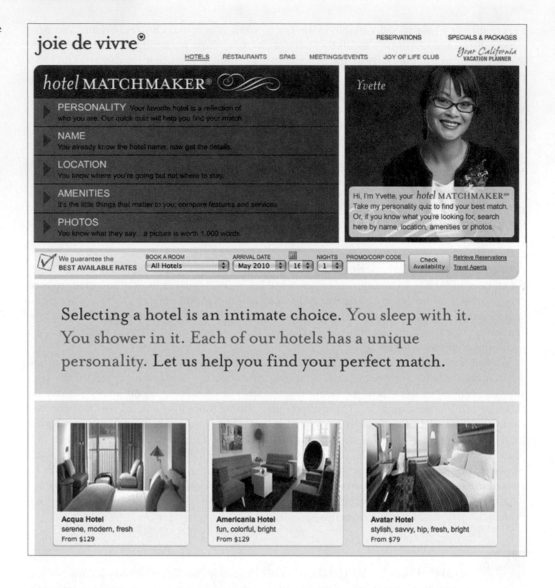

LOHAS Consumers who worry about the environment, want products to be produced in a sustainable way, and spend money to advance their personal health, development, and potential have been named "LOHAS," an acronym for *lifestyles of health and sustainability.* One estimate placed 19 percent of the adults in the United States, or 41 million people, in the LOHAS or "Cultural Creatives" category.[28] The market for LOHAS products encompasses organic foods, energy-efficient appliances and solar panels, alternative medicine, yoga tapes, and ecotourism. Taken together, these account for an estimated $209 billion market. Table 6.2 breaks the LOHAS demographic into six segments with estimated size, and product and service interests.

Lifestyles are shaped partly by whether consumers are *money constrained* or *time constrained.* Companies aiming to serve money-constrained consumers will create lower-cost products and services. By appealing to thrifty consumers, Walmart has become the largest company in the world. Its "everyday low prices" have wrung tens of billions of dollars out of the retail supply chain, passing the larger part of savings along to shoppers in the form of rock-bottom bargain prices.

Consumers who experience time famine are prone to **multitasking**, doing two or more things at the same time. They will also pay others to perform tasks because time is more important to them than money. Companies aiming to serve them will create convenient products and services for this group.

TABLE 6.2   LOHAS Market Segments

Personal Health	**Natural Lifestyles**
Natural, organic products	Indoor & outdoor furnishings
Nutritional products	Organic cleaning supplies
Integrative health care	Compact fluorescent lights
Dietary supplements	Social change philanthropy
Mind body spirit products	Apparel
U.S. Market—$110.03 billion	*U.S. Market—$10.6 billion*
Green Building	**Alternative Transportation**
Home certification	Hybrid vehicles
Energy Star appliances	Biodiesel fuel
Sustainable flooring	Car sharing programs
Renewable energy systems	*U.S. Market—$6.12 billion*
Wood alternatives	
U.S. Market—$50 billion	
Eco-Tourism	**Alternative Energy**
Eco-tourism travel	Renewable energy credits
Eco-adventure travel	Green pricing
U.S. Market—$24.17 billion	*U.S. Market—$380 million*

Source: Reprinted by permission of LOHAS, http://www.lohas.com/.

In some categories, notably food processing, companies targeting time-constrained consumers need to be aware that these very same people want to believe they're *not* operating within time constraints. Marketers call those who seek both convenience and some involvement in the cooking process the "convenience involvement segment."[29]

Hamburger Helper   Launched in 1971 in response to tough economic times, the inexpensive pasta-and-powdered mix Hamburger Helper was designed to quickly and inexpensively stretch a pound of meat into a family meal. With an estimated 44 percent of evening meals prepared in under 30 minutes and strong competition from fast-food drive-through windows, restaurant deliveries, and precooked grocery store dishes, Hamburger Helper's days of prosperity might seem numbered. Market researchers found, however, that some consumers don't want the fastest microwaveable solution possible—they also want to feel good about how they prepare a meal. In fact, on average, they prefer to use at least one pot or pan and 15 minutes of time. To remain attractive to this segment, marketers of Hamburger Helper are always introducing new flavors to tap into changing consumer taste trends. Not surprisingly, the latest economic downturn saw sales of the brand rise 9 percent in 2009.[30]

Consumer decisions are also influenced by **core values**, the belief systems that underlie attitudes and behaviors. Core values go much deeper than behavior or attitude and determine, at a basic level, people's choices and desires over the long term. Marketers who target consumers on the basis of their values believe that with appeals to people's inner selves, it is possible to influence their outer selves—their purchase behavior.

Key Psychological Processes

The starting point for understanding consumer behavior is the stimulus-response model shown in △ Figure 6.1. Marketing and environmental stimuli enter the consumer's consciousness, and a set of psychological processes combine with certain consumer characteristics to result in decision processes and purchase decisions. The marketer's task is to understand what happens in the consumer's consciousness between the arrival of the outside marketing stimuli and the ultimate purchase decisions. Four key psychological processes—motivation, perception, learning, and memory—fundamentally influence consumer responses.[31]

Motivation: Freud, Maslow, Herzberg

We all have many needs at any given time. Some needs are *biogenic*; they arise from physiological states of tension such as hunger, thirst, or discomfort. Other needs are *psychogenic*; they arise from psychological states of tension such as the need for recognition, esteem, or belonging. A need becomes a **motive** when it is aroused to a sufficient level of intensity to drive us to act. Motivation has both direction—we select one goal over another—and intensity—we pursue the goal with more or less vigor.

Three of the best-known theories of human motivation—those of Sigmund Freud, Abraham Maslow, and Frederick Herzberg—carry quite different implications for consumer analysis and marketing strategy.

FREUD'S THEORY Sigmund Freud assumed the psychological forces shaping people's behavior are largely unconscious, and that a person cannot fully understand his or her own motivations. Someone who examines specific brands will react not only to their stated capabilities, but also to other, less conscious cues such as shape, size, weight, material, color, and brand name. A technique called *laddering* lets us trace a person's motivations from the stated instrumental ones to the more terminal ones. Then the marketer can decide at what level to develop the message and appeal.[32]

Motivation researchers often collect in-depth interviews with a few dozen consumers to uncover deeper motives triggered by a product. They use various *projective techniques* such as word association, sentence completion, picture interpretation, and role playing, many pioneered by Ernest Dichter, a Viennese psychologist who settled in the United States.[33]

Today, motivational researchers continue the tradition of Freudian interpretation. Jan Callebaut identifies different motives a product can satisfy. For example, whiskey can meet the need for social relaxation, status, or fun. Different whiskey brands need to be motivationally positioned in one of these three appeals.[34] Another motivation researcher, Clotaire Rapaille, works on breaking the "code" behind product behavior.[35]

Chrysler   When Chrysler decided to offer a new sedan, it had already done a great deal of traditional market research that suggested U.S. consumers wanted excellent gas mileage, safety, and prices. However, it was only through qualitative research that Chrysler discovered what cultural anthropologist Clotaire Rapaille calls "the code"—the unconscious meaning people give to a particular market offering. First, interviewers took on the role of "a visitor from another planet," asking participants to help them understand the product in question. Then, participants told stories about the product, and finally, after a relaxation exercise, they wrote about their first experiences with it. In this way, Chrysler learned that "cookie-cutter" sedans were "off-code," and it used information from the sessions to create the PT Cruiser. With its highly distinctive retro design, this sedan was one of the most successful U.S. car launches in recent history.[36] ▭

MASLOW'S THEORY Abraham Maslow sought to explain why people are driven by particular needs at particular times.[37] His answer is that human needs are arranged in a hierarchy from most to least pressing—physiological needs, safety needs, social needs, esteem needs, and self-actualization

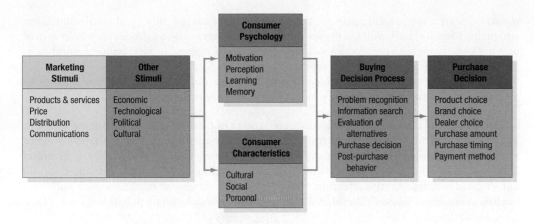

|Fig. 6.1| △

Model of Consumer Behavior

needs (see △ Figure 6.2). People will try to satisfy their most important need first and then try to satisfy the next most important. For example, a starving man (need 1) will not take an interest in the latest happenings in the art world (need 5), nor in how he is viewed by others (need 3 or 4), nor even in whether he is breathing clean air (need 2), but when he has enough food and water, the next most important need will become salient.

HERZBERG'S THEORY Frederick Herzberg developed a two-factor theory that distinguishes *dissatisfiers* (factors that cause dissatisfaction) from *satisfiers* (factors that cause satisfaction).[38] The absence of dissatisfiers is not enough to motivate a purchase; satisfiers must be present. For example, a computer that does not come with a warranty would be a dissatisfier. Yet the presence of a product warranty would not act as a satisfier or motivator of a purchase, because it is not a source of intrinsic satisfaction. Ease of use would be a satisfier.

Herzberg's theory has two implications. First, sellers should do their best to avoid dissatisfiers (for example, a poor training manual or a poor service policy). Although these things will not sell a product, they might easily unsell it. Second, the seller should identify the major satisfiers or motivators of purchase in the market and then supply them.

Perception

A motivated person is ready to act—*how* is influenced by his or her perception of the situation. In marketing, perceptions are more important than reality, because perceptions affect consumers' actual behavior. **Perception** is the process by which we select, organize, and interpret information

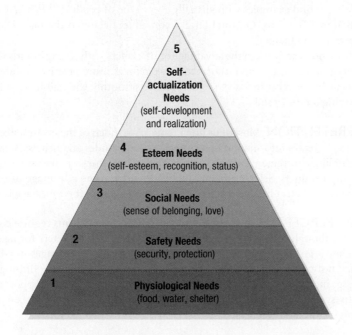

|Fig. 6.2| △

Maslow's Hierarchy of Needs

Source: A. H. Maslow, Motivation and Personality, 3rd ed. (Upper Saddle River, NJ: Prentice Hall, 1987). Printed and electronically reproduced by permission of Pearson Education, Inc., Upper Saddle River, NJ.

inputs to create a meaningful picture of the world.[39] It depends not only on physical stimuli, but also on the stimuli's relationship to the surrounding environment and on conditions within each of us. One person might perceive a fast-talking salesperson as aggressive and insincere; another, as intelligent and helpful. Each will respond to the salesperson differently.

People emerge with different perceptions of the same object because of three perceptual processes: selective attention, selective distortion, and selective retention.

SELECTIVE ATTENTION Attention is the allocation of processing capacity to some stimulus. Voluntary attention is something purposeful; involuntary attention is grabbed by someone or something. It's estimated that the average person may be exposed to over 1,500 ads or brand communications a day. Because we cannot possibly attend to all these, we screen most stimuli out—a process called **selective attention**. Selective attention means that marketers must work hard to attract consumers' notice. The real challenge is to explain which stimuli people will notice. Here are some findings:

1. *People are more likely to notice stimuli that relate to a current need.* A person who is motivated to buy a computer will notice computer ads and be less likely to notice DVD ads.
2. *People are more likely to notice stimuli they anticipate.* You are more likely to notice computers than radios in a computer store because you don't expect the store to carry radios.
3. *People are more likely to notice stimuli whose deviations are large in relationship to the normal size of the stimuli.* You are more likely to notice an ad offering $100 off the list price of a computer than one offering $5 off.

Though we screen out much, we are influenced by unexpected stimuli, such as sudden offers in the mail, over the phone, or from a salesperson. Marketers may attempt to promote their offers intrusively in order to bypass selective attention filters.

SELECTIVE DISTORTION Even noticed stimuli don't always come across in the way the senders intended. **Selective distortion** is the tendency to interpret information in a way that fits our preconceptions. Consumers will often distort information to be consistent with prior brand and product beliefs and expectations.[40]

For a stark demonstration of the power of consumer brand beliefs, consider that in "blind" taste tests, one group of consumers samples a product without knowing which brand it is, while another group knows. Invariably, the groups have different opinions, despite consuming *exactly the same product.*

When consumers report different opinions of branded and unbranded versions of identical products, it must be the case that their brand and product beliefs, created by whatever means (past experiences, marketing activity for the brand, or the like), have somehow changed their product perceptions. We can find examples with virtually every type of product.[41] When Coors changed its label from "Banquet Beer" to "Original Draft," consumers claimed the taste had changed even though the formulation had not.

Selective distortion can work to the advantage of marketers with strong brands when consumers distort neutral or ambiguous brand information to make it more positive. In other words, coffee may seem to taste better, a car may seem to drive more smoothly, the wait in a bank line may seem shorter, depending on the brand.

SELECTIVE RETENTION Most of us don't remember much of the information to which we're exposed, but we do retain information that supports our attitudes and beliefs. Because of **selective retention**, we're likely to remember good points about a product we like and forget good points about competing products. Selective retention again works to the advantage of strong brands. It also explains why marketers need to use repetition—to make sure their message is not overlooked.

SUBLIMINAL PERCEPTION The selective perception mechanisms require consumers' active engagement and thought. A topic that has fascinated armchair marketers for ages is **subliminal perception**. They argue that marketers embed covert, subliminal messages in ads or packaging. Consumers are not consciously aware of them, yet they affect behavior. Although it's clear that mental processes include many subtle subconscious effects,[42] no evidence supports the notion that marketers can systematically control consumers at that level, especially enough to change moderately important or strongly held beliefs.[43]

Learning

When we act, we learn. **Learning** induces changes in our behavior arising from experience. Most human behavior is learned, although much learning is incidental. Learning theorists believe learning is produced through the interplay of drives, stimuli, cues, responses, and reinforcement. Two popular approaches to learning are classical conditioning and operant (instrumental) conditioning.

A **drive** is a strong internal stimulus impelling action. **Cues** are minor stimuli that determine when, where, and how a person responds. Suppose you buy an HP computer. If your experience is rewarding, your response to computers and HP will be positively reinforced. Later, when you want to buy a printer, you may assume that because it makes good computers, HP also makes good printers. In other words, you *generalize* your response to similar stimuli. A countertendency to generalization is discrimination. **Discrimination** means we have learned to recognize differences in sets of similar stimuli and can adjust our responses accordingly.

Learning theory teaches marketers that they can build demand for a product by associating it with strong drives, using motivating cues, and providing positive reinforcement. A new company can enter the market by appealing to the same drives competitors use and by providing similar cues, because buyers are more likely to transfer loyalty to similar brands (generalization); or the company might design its brand to appeal to a different set of drives and offer strong cue inducements to switch (discrimination).

Some researchers prefer more active, cognitive approaches when learning depends on the inferences or interpretations consumers make about outcomes (was an unfavorable consumer experience due to a bad product, or did the consumer fail to follow instructions properly?). The **hedonic bias** occurs when people have a general tendency to attribute success to themselves and failure to external causes. Consumers are thus more likely to blame a product than themselves, putting pressure on marketers to carefully explicate product functions in well-designed packaging and labels, instructive ads and Web sites, and so on.

Emotions

Consumer response is not all cognitive and rational; much may be emotional and invoke different kinds of feelings. A brand or product may make a consumer feel proud, excited, or confident. An ad may create feelings of amusement, disgust, or wonder.

Here are two recent examples that recognize the power of emotions in consumer decision making.

- For years, specialty foam mattress leader Tempur-Pedic famously used infomercials showing that a wine glass on its mattress did not spill even as people bounced up and down on the bed. To create a stronger emotional connection, the company began a broader-based media campaign in 2007 that positioned the mattresses as a wellness brand and "the nighttime therapy for body and mind."[44]
- Reckitt Benckiser and Procter & Gamble launched advertising approaches in 2009 for Woolite and Tide, respectively, that tapped not into the detergents' performance benefits but into the emotional connection—and challenges—of laundry. Based on research showing that one in three working women recognize they ruined some of their clothes in the wash over the last year, Reckitt Benckiser launched an online and in-store "Find the Look, Keep the Look" style guide for Woolite for "finding fashion and keeping it looking fabulous without breaking the bank." Based on the premise that a detergent should do more than clean, P&G positioned new Tide Total Care as preserving clothing and keeping the "7 signs of beautiful clothes," including shape, softness, and finish.[45]

Memory

Cognitive psychologists distinguish between **short-term memory (STM)**—a temporary and limited repository of information—and **long-term memory (LTM)**—a more permanent, essentially unlimited repository. All the information and experiences we encounter as we go through life can end up in our long-term memory.

Most widely accepted views of long-term memory structure assume we form some kind of associative model.[46] For example, the **associative network memory model** views LTM as a set of nodes and links. *Nodes* are stored information connected by *links* that vary in strength. Any type of information can be stored in the memory network, including verbal, visual, abstract, and contextual.

Woolite's style guide focuses on the emotional benefits of choosing and preserving the right look in clothes for women.

A spreading activation process from node to node determines how much we retrieve and what information we can actually recall in any given situation. When a node becomes activated because we're encoding external information (when we read or hear a word or phrase) or retrieving internal information from LTM (when we think about some concept), other nodes are also activated if they're strongly enough associated with that node.

In this model, we can think of consumer brand knowledge as a node in memory with a variety of linked associations. The strength and organization of these associations will be important determinants of the information we can recall about the brand. **Brand associations** consist of all brand-related thoughts, feelings, perceptions, images, experiences, beliefs, attitudes, and so on that become linked to the brand node.

We can think of marketing as a way of making sure consumers have product and service experiences to create the right brand knowledge structures and maintain them in memory. Companies such as Procter & Gamble like to create mental maps of consumers that depict their knowledge of a particular brand in terms of the key associations likely to be triggered in a marketing setting, and their relative strength, favorability, and uniqueness to consumers. ▲ Figure 6.3 displays a very simple mental map highlighting brand beliefs for a hypothetical consumer for State Farm insurance.

|Fig. 6.3| ▲

Hypothetical State Farm Mental Map

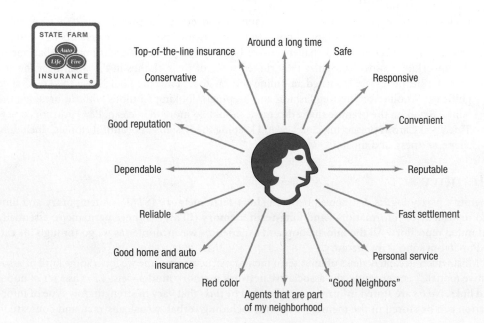

MEMORY PROCESSES Memory is a very constructive process, because we don't remember information and events completely and accurately. Often we remember bits and pieces and fill in the rest based on whatever else we know. "Marketing Insight: Made to Stick" offers some practical tips for how marketers can ensure their ideas—inside or outside the company—are remembered and have impact.

Memory encoding describes how and where information gets into memory. The strength of the resulting association depends on how much we process the information at encoding (how much we think about it, for instance) and in what way.[47] In general, the more attention we pay to the meaning of information during encoding, the stronger the resulting associations in memory will be.[48] Advertising research in a field setting suggests that high levels of repetition for an uninvolving, unpersuasive ad, for example, are unlikely to have as much sales impact as lower levels of repetition for an involving, persuasive ad.[49]

Memory retrieval is the way information gets out of memory. Three facts are important about memory retrieval.

1. The presence of *other* product information in memory can produce interference effects and cause us to either overlook or confuse new data. One marketing challenge in a category crowded with many competitors—for example, airlines, financial services, and insurance companies—is that consumers may mix up brands.

Made to Stick

Picking up on a concept first introduced by Malcolm Gladwell in his *Tipping Point* book, brothers Chip and Dan Heath set out to uncover what makes an idea sticky and catch on with an audience. Considering a wide range of ideas from diverse sources—urban legends, conspiracy theories, public policy mandates, and product design—they identified six traits that characterize all great ideas and used the acronym "SUCCES" to organize them:

1. *Simple*—find the core of any idea. Take an idea and distill it down, whittling away everything that is not essential. "Southwest Airlines is THE low-fare airline."

2. *Unexpected*—grab people's attention by surprising them. Nordstrom's customer service is legendary because it unexpectedly exceeds customer's already high expectations by going beyond helping them buy to address their personal situations—ironing shirts before meetings, keeping cars warm while they shop, or wrapping presents they actually bought at Macy's.

3. *Concrete*—make sure any idea can be easily grasped and remembered later. Boeing successfully designed the 727 airplane by giving its thousands of engineers a very specific goal—the plane had to seat 131 passengers, be able to fly nonstop from New York to Miami, and land on runway 4-22 at LaGuardia, which could not be used by large planes.

4. *Credibility*—give an idea believability. Indian overnight delivery service Safexpress was able to overcome doubts about its capabilities by describing to a Bollywood film studio how it had flawlessly delivered 69,000 copies of the latest *Harry Potter* novel to bookstores all over the country by 8 AM on the morning of its release.

5. *Emotion*—help people see the importance of an idea. Research on fact-based versus appeal-to-emotion antismoking ads has demonstrated that emotional appeals are more compelling and memorable.

6. *Stories*—empower people to use an idea through narrative. Research again shows how narratives evoke mental stimulation, and visualization of events makes recall and further learning easier.

The Heaths believe great ideas are made, not born, via these traits. One example is the Subway ad campaign starring Jared—who lost 100 pounds in three months by eating two subs a day—that helped to raise Subway's sales 18 percent in one year. According to the Heaths, the idea scores high on all six dimensions of stickiness.

1. *Simple*—weight loss
2. *Unexpected*—weight loss by eating fast food
3. *Concrete*—weight loss by eating two Subway subs daily
4. *Credibility*—a documented loss of 100 pounds
5. *Emotion*—a triumph over difficult weight problems
6. *Stories*—a personal account of how eating two Subway Subs lead to an incredible weight loss.

Sources: Chip Heath and Dan Heath, *Made to Stick: Why Some Ideas Survive and Others Die ...* (New York: Random House, 2007); Malcolm Gladwell, *The Tipping Point: How Little Things Can Make a Big Difference* (New York: Little, Brown and Company, 2000); Barbara Kiviat, "Are You Sticky?" *Time*, October 29, 2006; Justin Ewers, "Making It Stick," *U.S. News & World Report*, January 21, 2007; Mike Hofman, "Chip and Dan Heath: Marketing Made Sticky," *Inc*, January 1, 2007.

TABLE 6.3 ⬛ Understanding Consumer Behavior
Who buys our product or service?
Who makes the decision to buy the product?
Who influences the decision to buy the product?
How is the purchase decision made? Who assumes what role?
What does the customer buy? What needs must be satisfied?
Why do customers buy a particular brand?
Where do they go or look to buy the product or service?
When do they buy? Any seasonality factors?
How is our product perceived by customers?
What are customers' attitudes toward our product?
What social factors might influence the purchase decision?
Do customers' lifestyles influence their decisions?
How do personal or demographic factors influence the purchase decision?

Source: Based on figure 1.7 from George Belch and Michael Belch, *Advertising and Promotion: An Integrated Marketing Communications Perspective*, 8th ed. (Homewood, IL: Irwin, 2009).

2. The time between exposure to information and encoding has been shown generally to produce only gradual decay. Cognitive psychologists believe memory is extremely durable, so once information becomes stored in memory, its strength of association decays very slowly.[50]

3. Information may be *available* in memory but not be *accessible* for recall without the proper retrieval cues or reminders. The effectiveness of retrieval cues is one reason marketing *inside* a supermarket or any retail store is so critical—the actual product packaging, the use of in-store mini-billboard displays, and so on. The information they contain and the reminders they provide of advertising or other information already conveyed outside the store will be prime determinants of consumer decision making.

|Fig. 6.4| ▲

Five-Stage Model of the Consumer Buying Process

Problem recognition

↓

Information search

↓

Evaluation of alternatives

↓

Purchase decision

↓

Postpurchase behavior

The Buying Decision Process: The Five-Stage Model

The basic psychological processes we've reviewed play an important role in consumers' actual buying decisions.[51] ⬛ Table 6.3 provides a list of some key consumer behavior questions marketers should ask in terms of who, what, when, where, how, and why.

Smart companies try to fully understand customers' buying decision process—all the experiences in learning, choosing, using, and even disposing of a product.[52] Marketing scholars have developed a "stage model" of the process (see ▲ Figure 6.4). The consumer typically passes through five stages: problem recognition, information search, evaluation of alternatives, purchase decision, and postpurchase behavior. Clearly, the buying process starts long before the actual purchase and has consequences long afterward.[53]

Consumers don't always pass through all five stages—they may skip or reverse some. When you buy your regular brand of toothpaste, you go directly from the need to the purchase decision, skipping information search and evaluation. The model in Figure 6.4 provides a good frame of reference, however, because it captures the full range of considerations that arise when a consumer faces a highly involving new purchase.[54] Later in the chapter, we will consider other ways consumers make decisions that are less calculated.

Problem Recognition

The buying process starts when the buyer recognizes a problem or need triggered by internal or external stimuli. With an internal stimulus, one of the person's normal needs—hunger, thirst, sex—rises to a threshold level and becomes a drive. A need can also be aroused by an external stimulus. A person may admire a friend's new car or see a television ad for a Hawaiian vacation, which inspires thoughts about the possibility of making a purchase.

Marketers need to identify the circumstances that trigger a particular need by gathering information from a number of consumers. They can then develop marketing strategies that spark consumer interest. Particularly for discretionary purchases such as luxury goods, vacation packages, and entertainment options, marketers may need to increase consumer motivation so a potential purchase gets serious consideration.

Information Search

Surprisingly, consumers often search for limited amounts of information. Surveys have shown that for durables, half of all consumers look at only one store, and only 30 percent look at more than one brand of appliances. We can distinguish between two levels of engagement in the search. The milder search state is called *heightened attention*. At this level a person simply becomes more receptive to information about a product. At the next level, the person may enter an *active information search:* looking for reading material, phoning friends, going online, and visiting stores to learn about the product.

INFORMATION SOURCES Major information sources to which consumers will turn fall into four groups:
- *Personal.* Family, friends, neighbors, acquaintances
- *Commercial.* Advertising, Web sites, salespersons, dealers, packaging, displays
- *Public.* Mass media, consumer-rating organizations
- *Experiential.* Handling, examining, using the product

The relative amount and influence of these sources vary with the product category and the buyer's characteristics. Generally speaking, although consumers receive the greatest amount of information about a product from commercial—that is, marketer-dominated—sources, the most effective information often comes from personal or experiential sources, or public sources that are independent authorities.

Each source performs a different function in influencing the buying decision. Commercial sources normally perform an information function, whereas personal sources perform a legitimizing or evaluation function. For example, physicians often learn of new drugs from commercial sources but turn to other doctors for evaluations.

SEARCH DYNAMICS By gathering information, the consumer learns about competing brands and their features. The first box in △ Figure 6.5 shows the *total set* of brands available. The individual consumer will come to know a subset of these, the *awareness set*. Only some, the *consideration set*, will meet initial buying criteria. As the consumer gathers more

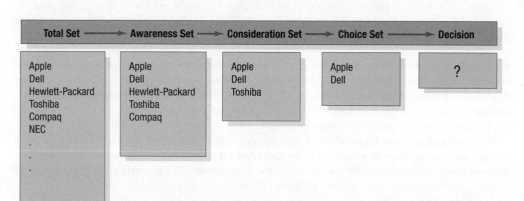

|Fig. 6.5| △

Successive Sets Involved in Consumer Decision Making

information, just a few, the *choice set,* will remain strong contenders. The consumer makes a final choice from these.[55]

Marketers need to identify the hierarchy of attributes that guide consumer decision making in order to understand different competitive forces and how these various sets get formed. This process of identifying the hierarchy is called **market partitioning**. Years ago, most car buyers first decided on the manufacturer and then on one of its car divisions (*brand-dominant hierarchy*). A buyer might favor General Motors cars and, within this set, Chevrolet. Today, many buyers decide first on the nation from which they want to buy a car (*nation-dominant hierarchy*). Buyers may first decide they want to buy a German car, then Audi, and then the A4 model of Audi.

The hierarchy of attributes also can reveal customer segments. Buyers who first decide on price are price dominant; those who first decide on the type of car (sports, passenger, hybrid) are type dominant; those who choose the brand first are brand dominant. Type/price/brand-dominant consumers make up one segment; quality/service/type buyers make up another. Each may have distinct demographics, psychographics, and mediagraphics and different awareness, consideration, and choice sets.[56]

Figure 6.5 makes it clear that a company must strategize to get its brand into the prospect's awareness, consideration, and choice sets. If a food store owner arranges yogurt first by brand (such as Dannon and Yoplait) and then by flavor within each brand, consumers will tend to select their flavors from the same brand. However, if all the strawberry yogurts are together, then all the vanilla, and so forth, consumers will probably choose which flavors they want first, and then choose the brand name they want for that particular flavor. Australian supermarkets arrange meats by the way they might be cooked, and stores use more descriptive labels, such as "a 10-minute herbed beef roast." The result is that Australians buy a greater variety of meats than U.S. shoppers, who choose from meats laid out by animal type—beef, chicken, pork, and so on.[57]

The company must also identify the other brands in the consumer's choice set so that it can plan the appropriate competitive appeals. In addition, marketers should identify the consumer's information sources and evaluate their relative importance. Asking consumers how they first heard about the brand, what information came later, and the relative importance of the different sources will help the company prepare effective communications for the target market.

Evaluation of Alternatives

How does the consumer process competitive brand information and make a final value judgment? No single process is used by all consumers, or by one consumer in all buying situations. There are several processes, and the most current models see the consumer forming judgments largely on a conscious and rational basis.

Some basic concepts will help us understand consumer evaluation processes: First, the consumer is trying to satisfy a need. Second, the consumer is looking for certain benefits from the product solution. Third, the consumer sees each product as a bundle of attributes with varying abilities to deliver the benefits. The attributes of interest to buyers vary by product—for example:

1. *Hotels*—Location, cleanliness, atmosphere, price
2. *Mouthwash*—Color, effectiveness, germ-killing capacity, taste/flavor, price
3. *Tires*—Safety, tread life, ride quality, price

Consumers will pay the most attention to attributes that deliver the sought-after benefits. We can often segment the market for a product according to attributes and benefits important to different consumer groups.

BELIEFS AND ATTITUDES Through experience and learning, people acquire beliefs and attitudes. These in turn influence buying behavior. A **belief** is a descriptive thought that a person holds about something. Just as important are **attitudes**, a person's enduring favorable or unfavorable evaluations, emotional feelings, and action tendencies toward some object or idea.[58] People have attitudes toward almost everything: religion, politics, clothes, music, food.

Attitudes put us into a frame of mind: liking or disliking an object, moving toward or away from it. They lead us to behave in a fairly consistent way toward similar objects. Because attitudes economize on energy and thought, they can be very difficult to change. As a general rule, a company is well advised to fit its product into existing attitudes rather than try to change attitudes. If beliefs and attitudes become too negative, however, more serious steps may be necessary. With a controversial ad campaign for its pizza, Domino's took drastic measures to try to change consumer attitudes.

Domino's Known more for the speed of its delivery than for the taste of its pizza, Domino's decided to address negative perceptions head on. A major communication program featured documentary-style TV ads that opened with Domino's employees at corporate headquarters reviewing written and videotaped focus group feedback from customers. The feedback contained biting and vicious comments, such as, "Domino's pizza crust to me is like cardboard" and "The sauce tastes like ketchup." After President Patrick Doyle is shown on camera stating these results were unacceptable, the ads proceeded to show Domino's chefs and executives in their test kitchens proclaiming that its pizza was new and improved with a bolder, richer sauce; a more robust cheese combination; and an herb-and-garlic-flavored crust. Many critics were stunned by the admission of the company that their number 2 ranked pizza, in effect, had been inferior for years. Others countered by noting that the new product formulation and unconventional ads were addressing a widely held, difficult-to-change negative belief that was dragging the brand down and required decisive action. Doyle summed up consumer reaction as "Most really like it, some don't. And that's OK."[59]

Recognizing consumers' solidly entrenched beliefs, Domino's launched a bold ad campaign to transform its image.

EXPECTANCY-VALUE MODEL The consumer arrives at attitudes toward various brands through an attribute evaluation procedure, developing a set of beliefs about where each brand stands on each attribute.[60] The **expectancy-value model** of attitude formation posits that consumers evaluate products and services by combining their brand beliefs—the positives and negatives—according to importance.

Suppose Linda has narrowed her choice set to four laptop computers (A, B, C, and D). Assume she's interested in four attributes: memory capacity, graphics capability, size and weight, and price. Table 6.4 shows her beliefs about how each brand rates on the four attributes. If one computer dominated the others on all the criteria, we could predict that Linda would choose it. But, as is often the case, her choice set consists of brands that vary in their appeal. If Linda wants the best memory capacity, she should buy C; if she wants the best graphics capability, she should buy A; and so on.

If we knew the weights Linda attaches to the four attributes, we could more reliably predict her laptop choice. Suppose she assigned 40 percent of the importance to the laptop's memory capacity, 30 percent to graphics capability, 20 percent to size and weight, and 10 percent to price. To find Linda's perceived value for each laptop according to the expectancy-value model, we multiply her weights by her beliefs about each computer's attributes. This computation leads to the following perceived values:

$$\text{Laptop A} = 0.4(8) + 0.3(9) + 0.2(6) + 0.1(9) = 8.0$$

$$\text{Laptop B} = 0.4(7) + 0.3(7) + 0.2(7) + 0.1(7) = 7.0$$

TABLE 6.4 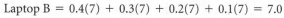 A Consumer's Brand Beliefs about Laptop Computers				
Laptop Computer	**Attribute**			
	Memory Capacity	**Graphics Capability**	**Size and Weight**	**Price**
A	8	9	6	9
B	7	7	7	7
C	10	4	3	2
D	5	3	8	5

Note: Each attribute is rated from 0 to 10, where 10 represents the highest level on that attribute. Price, however, is indexed in a reverse manner, with 10 representing the lowest price, because a consumer prefers a low price to a high price.

$$\text{Laptop C} = 0.4(10) + 0.3(4) + 0.2(3) + 0.1(2) = 6.0$$

$$\text{Laptop D} = 0.4(5) + 0.3(3) + 0.2(8) + 0.1(5) = 5.0$$

An expectancy-model formulation predicts that Linda will favor laptop A, which (at 8.0) has the highest perceived value.[61]

Suppose most laptop computer buyers form their preferences the same way. Knowing this, the marketer of laptop B, for example, could apply the following strategies to stimulate greater interest in brand B:

- *Redesign the laptop computer.* This technique is called *real repositioning*.
- *Alter beliefs about the brand.* Attempting to alter beliefs about the brand is called *psychological repositioning*.
- *Alter beliefs about competitors' brands.* This strategy, called *competitive depositioning*, makes sense when buyers mistakenly believe a competitor's brand has more quality than it actually has.
- *Alter the importance weights.* The marketer could try to persuade buyers to attach more importance to the attributes in which the brand excels.
- *Call attention to neglected attributes.* The marketer could draw buyers' attention to neglected attributes, such as styling or processing speed.
- *Shift the buyer's ideals.* The marketer could try to persuade buyers to change their ideal levels for one or more attributes.[62]

Purchase Decision

In the evaluation stage, the consumer forms preferences among the brands in the choice set and may also form an intention to buy the most preferred brand. In executing a purchase intention, the consumer may make up to five subdecisions: brand (brand A), dealer (dealer 2), quantity (one computer), timing (weekend), and payment method (credit card).

NONCOMPENSATORY MODELS OF CONSUMER CHOICE The expectancy-value model is a compensatory model, in that perceived good things about a product can help to overcome perceived bad things. But consumers often take "mental shortcuts" called **heuristics** or rules of thumb in the decision process.

With **noncompensatory models** of consumer choice, positive and negative attribute considerations don't necessarily net out. Evaluating attributes in isolation makes decision making easier for a consumer, but it also increases the likelihood that she would have made a different choice if she had deliberated in greater detail. We highlight three choice heuristics here.

1. Using the **conjunctive heuristic**, the consumer sets a minimum acceptable cutoff level for each attribute and chooses the first alternative that meets the minimum standard for all attributes. For example, if Linda decided all attributes had to rate at least 5, she would choose laptop computer B.
2. With the **lexicographic heuristic**, the consumer chooses the best brand on the basis of its perceived most important attribute. With this decision rule, Linda would choose laptop computer C.
3. Using the **elimination-by-aspects heuristic**, the consumer compares brands on an attribute selected probabilistically—where the probability of choosing an attribute is positively related to its importance—and eliminates brands that do not meet minimum acceptable cutoffs.

Our brand or product knowledge, the number and similarity of brand choices and time pressures present, and the social context (such as the need for justification to a peer or boss) all may affect whether and how we use choice heuristics.[63]

Consumers don't necessarily use only one type of choice rule. For example, they might use a noncompensatory decision rule such as the conjunctive heuristic to reduce the number of brand choices to a more manageable number, and then evaluate the remaining brands. One reason for the runaway success of the Intel Inside campaign in the 1990s was that it made the brand the first cutoff for many consumers—they would buy only a personal computer that had an Intel microprocessor. Leading personal computer makers at the time such as IBM, Dell, and Gateway had no choice but to support Intel's marketing efforts.

INTERVENING FACTORS Even if consumers form brand evaluations, two general factors can intervene between the purchase intention and the purchase decision (see △ Figure 6.6).[64] The first factor is the *attitudes of others*. The influence of another person's attitude depends on two

|Fig. 6.6| △

Steps between Evaluation of Alternatives and a Purchase Decision

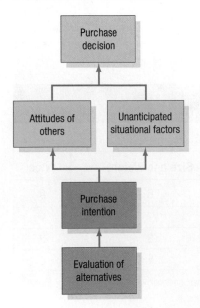

things: (1) the intensity of the other person's negative attitude toward our preferred alternative and (2) our motivation to comply with the other person's wishes.[65] The more intense the other person's negativism and the closer he or she is to us, the more we will adjust our purchase intention. The converse is also true.

Related to the attitudes of others is the role played by infomediaries' evaluations: *Consumer Reports,* which provides unbiased expert reviews of all types of products and services; J.D. Power, which provides consumer-based ratings of cars, financial services, and travel products and services; professional movie, book, and music reviewers; customer reviews of books and music on such sites as Amazon.com; and the increasing number of chat rooms, bulletin boards, blogs, and so on where people discuss products, services, and companies.

Consumers are undoubtedly influenced by these external evaluations, as evidenced by the success of a small-budget movie such as *Paranormal Activity,* which cost only $15,000 to make but grossed over $100 million at the box office in 2009 thanks to a slew of favorable reviews by moviegoers and online buzz at many Web sites.[66]

The second factor is *unanticipated situational factors* that may erupt to change the purchase intention. Linda might lose her job, some other purchase might become more urgent, or a store salesperson may turn her off. Preferences and even purchase intentions are not completely reliable predictors of purchase behavior.

A consumer's decision to modify, postpone, or avoid a purchase decision is heavily influenced by one or more types of *perceived risk*:[67]

1. ***Functional risk***—The product does not perform to expectations.
2. ***Physical risk***—The product poses a threat to the physical well-being or health of the user or others.
3. ***Financial risk***—The product is not worth the price paid.
4. ***Social risk***—The product results in embarrassment in front of others.
5. ***Psychological risk***—The product affects the mental well-being of the user.
6. ***Time risk***—The failure of the product results in an opportunity cost of finding another satisfactory product.

The degree of perceived risk varies with the amount of money at stake, the amount of attribute uncertainty, and the level of consumer self-confidence. Consumers develop routines for reducing the uncertainty and negative consequences of risk, such as avoiding decisions, gathering information from friends, and developing preferences for national brand names and warranties. Marketers must understand the factors that provoke a feeling of risk in consumers and provide information and support to reduce it.

Every year there are hit movies, such as *Paranormal Activity,* that ride a wave of buzz and favorable consumer word of mouth to box-office success.

Postpurchase Behavior

After the purchase, the consumer might experience dissonance from noticing certain disquieting features or hearing favorable things about other brands and will be alert to information that supports his or her decision. Marketing communications should supply beliefs and evaluations that reinforce the consumer's choice and help him or her feel good about the brand. The marketer's job therefore doesn't end with the purchase. Marketers must monitor postpurchase satisfaction, postpurchase actions, and postpurchase product uses and disposal.

POSTPURCHASE SATISFACTION Satisfaction is a function of the closeness between expectations and the product's perceived performance.[68] If performance falls short of expectations, the consumer is *disappointed*; if it meets expectations, the consumer is *satisfied*; if it exceeds expectations, the consumer is *delighted*. These feelings make a difference in whether the customer buys the product again and talks favorably or unfavorably about it to others.

The larger the gap between expectations and performance, the greater the dissatisfaction. Here the consumer's coping style comes into play. Some consumers magnify the gap when the product isn't perfect and are highly dissatisfied; others minimize it and are less dissatisfied.[69]

POSTPURCHASE ACTIONS A satisfied consumer is more likely to purchase the product again and will also tend to say good things about the brand to others. Dissatisfied consumers may abandon or return the product. They may seek information that confirms its high value. They may take public action by complaining to the company, going to a lawyer, or complaining to other groups (such as business, private, or government agencies). Private actions include deciding to stop buying the product (*exit option*) or warning friends (*voice option*).[70]

Chapter 5 described CRM programs designed to build long-term brand loyalty. Postpurchase communications to buyers have been shown to result in fewer product returns and order cancellations. Computer companies, for example, can send a letter to new owners congratulating them on having selected a fine computer. They can place ads showing satisfied brand owners. They can solicit customer suggestions for improvements and list the location of available services. They can write intelligible instruction booklets. They can send owners a magazine containing articles describing new computer applications. In addition, they can provide good channels for speedy redress of customer grievances.

POSTPURCHASE USES AND DISPOSAL Marketers should also monitor how buyers use and dispose of the product (△ Figure 6.7). A key driver of sales frequency is product consumption rate—the more quickly buyers consume a product, the sooner they may be back in the market to repurchase it.

Consumers may fail to replace some products soon enough because they overestimate product life.[71] One strategy to speed replacement is to tie the act of replacing the product to a certain holiday, event, or time of year.

|Fig. 6.7| △

How Customers Use or Dispose of Products

Source: Jacob Jacoby, et al., "What about Disposition?" Journal of Marketing (July 1977), p. 23. Reprinted with permission from the *Journal of Marketing*, published by the American Marketing Association.

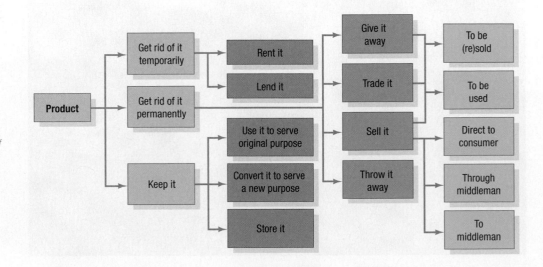

Oral B has tied toothbrush promotions to the springtime switch to daylight savings time. Another strategy is to provide consumers with better information about either (1) the time they first used the product or need to replace it or (2) its current level of performance. Batteries have built-in gauges that show how much power they have left; toothbrushes have color indicators to indicate when the bristles are worn; and so on. Perhaps the simplest way to increase usage is to learn when actual usage is lower than recommended and persuade customers that more regular usage has benefits, overcoming potential hurdles.

If consumers throw the product away, the marketer needs to know how they dispose of it, especially if—like batteries, beverage containers, electronic equipment, and disposable diapers—it can damage the environment. There also may be product opportunities in disposed products: Vintage clothing shops, such as Savers, resell 2.5 billion pounds of used clothing annually; Diamond Safety buys finely ground used tires and then makes and sells playground covers and athletic fields; and, unlike the usual potato chip maker, which discards some of the spud, Pringles converts the whole potato into dehydrated potato flakes that are rolled and cut into chips.[72]

Moderating Effects on Consumer Decision Making

The manner or path by which a consumer moves through the decision-making stages depends on several factors, including the level of involvement and extent of variety seeking, as follows.

LOW-INVOLVEMENT CONSUMER DECISION MAKING The expectancy-value model assumes a high level of **consumer involvement**, or engagement and active processing the consumer undertakes in responding to a marketing stimulus.

Richard Petty and John Cacioppo's *elaboration likelihood model*, an influential model of attitude formation and change, describes how consumers make evaluations in both low- and high-involvement circumstances.[73] There are two means of persuasion in their model: the *central route*, in which attitude formation or change stimulates much thought and is based on the consumer's diligent, rational consideration of the most important product information; and the *peripheral route*, in which attitude formation or change provokes much less thought and results from the consumer's association of a brand with either positive or negative peripheral cues. *Peripheral cues* for consumers include a celebrity endorsement, a credible source, or any object that generates positive feelings.

Consumers follow the central route only if they possess sufficient motivation, ability, and opportunity. In other words, they must want to evaluate a brand in detail, have the necessary brand and product or service knowledge in memory, and have sufficient time and the proper setting. If any of those factors is lacking, consumers tend to follow the peripheral route and consider less central, more extrinsic factors in their decisions.

We buy many products under conditions of low involvement and without significant brand differences. Consider salt. If consumers keep reaching for the same brand in this category, it may be out of habit, not strong brand loyalty. Evidence suggests we have low involvement with most low-cost, frequently purchased products.

Marketers use four techniques to try to convert a low-involvement product into one of higher

Savers takes clothes consumers no longer want and sells them to other consumers who do want them—at the right price.

involvement. First, they can link the product to an engaging issue, as when Crest linked its toothpaste to avoiding cavities. Second, they can link the product to a personal situation—for example, fruit juice makers began to include vitamins such as calcium to fortify their drinks. Third, they might design advertising to trigger strong emotions related to personal values or ego defense, as when cereal makers began to advertise to adults the heart-healthy nature of cereals and the importance of living a long time to enjoy family life. Fourth, they might add an important feature—for example, when GE lightbulbs introduced "Soft White" versions. These strategies at best raise consumer involvement from a low to a moderate level; they do not necessarily propel the consumer into highly involved buying behavior.

If consumers will have low involvement with a purchase decision regardless of what the marketer can do, they are likely to follow the peripheral route. Marketers must give consumers one or more positive cues to justify their brand choice, such as frequent ad repetition, visible sponsorships, and vigorous PR to enhance brand familiarity. Other peripheral cues that can tip the balance in favor of the brand include a beloved celebrity endorser, attractive packaging, and an appealing promotion.

VARIETY-SEEKING BUYING BEHAVIOR Some buying situations are characterized by low involvement but significant brand differences. Here consumers often do a lot of brand switching. Think about cookies. The consumer has some beliefs about cookies, chooses a brand without much evaluation, and evaluates the product during consumption. Next time, the consumer may reach for another brand out of a desire for a different taste. Brand switching occurs for the sake of variety, rather than dissatisfaction.

The market leader and the minor brands in this product category have different marketing strategies. The market leader will try to encourage habitual buying behavior by dominating the shelf space with a variety of related but different product versions, avoiding out-of-stock conditions, and sponsoring frequent reminder advertising. Challenger firms will encourage variety seeking by offering lower prices, deals, coupons, free samples, and advertising that tries to break the consumer's purchase and consumption cycle and presents reasons for trying something new.

Behavioral Decision Theory and Behavioral Economics

As you might guess from low-involvement decision making and variety-seeking, consumers don't always process information or make decisions in a deliberate, rational manner. One of the most active academic research areas in marketing over the past three decades has been *behavioral decision theory* (BDT). Behavioral decision theorists have identified many situations in which consumers make seemingly irrational choices. 🖿 Table 6.5 summarizes some provocative findings from this research.[74]

What all these and other studies reinforce is that consumer behavior is very constructive and the context of decisions really matters. Understanding how these effects show up in the marketplace can be crucial for marketers.

The work of these and other academics has also challenged predictions from economic theory and assumptions about rationality, leading to the emergence of the field of *behavioral economics*.[75] Here, we review some of the issues in three broad areas—decision heuristics, framing, and other contextual effects. "Marketing Insight: Predictably Irrational" summarizes one in-depth treatment of the topic.

Decision Heuristics

Previously we reviewed some common heuristics that occur with noncompensatory decision making. Other heuristics similarly come into play in everyday decision making when consumers forecast the likelihood of future outcomes or events.[76]

1. The **availability heuristic**—Consumers base their predictions on the quickness and ease with which a particular example of an outcome comes to mind. If an example comes to mind too easily, consumers might overestimate the likelihood of its happening. For example, a recent

TABLE 6.5 🔲 Selected Behavioral Decision Theory Findings
• Consumers are more likely to choose an alternative (a home bread maker) after a relatively inferior option (a slightly better, but significantly more expensive home bread maker) is added to the available choice set.
• Consumers are more likely to choose an alternative that appears to be a compromise in the particular choice set under consideration, even if it is not the best alternative on any one dimension.
• The choices consumers make influence their assessment of their own tastes and preferences.
• Getting people to focus their attention more on one of two considered alternatives tends to enhance the perceived attractiveness and choice probability of that alternative.
• The way consumers compare products that vary in price and perceived quality (by features or brand name) and the way those products are displayed in the store (by brand or by model type) both affect their willingness to pay more for additional features or a better-known brand.
• Consumers who think about the possibility that their purchase decisions will turn out to be wrong are more likely to choose better-known brands.
• Consumers for whom possible feelings of regret about missing an opportunity have been made more relevant are more likely to choose a product currently on sale than wait for a better sale or buy a higher-priced item.
• Consumers' choices are often influenced by subtle (and theoretically inconsequential) changes in the way alternatives are described.
• Consumers who make purchases for later consumption appear to make systematic errors in predicting their future preferences.
• Consumer's predictions of their future tastes are not accurate—they do not really know how they will feel after consuming the same flavor of yogurt or ice cream several times.
• Consumers often overestimate the duration of their overall emotional reactions to future events (moves, financial windfalls, outcomes of sporting events).
• Consumers often overestimate their future consumption, especially if there is limited availability (which may explain why Black Jack and other gums have higher sales when availability is limited to several months per year than when they are offered year round).
• In anticipating future consumption opportunities, consumers often assume they will want or need more variety than they actually do.
• Consumers are less likely to choose alternatives with product features or promotional premiums that have little or no value, even when these features and premiums are optional (like the opportunity to purchase a collector's plate) and do not reduce the actual value of the product in any way.
• Consumers are less likely to choose products selected by others for reasons they find irrelevant, even when these other reasons do not suggest anything positive or negative about the product's values.
• Consumers' interpretations and evaluations of past experiences are greatly influenced by the ending and trend of events. A positive event at the end of a service experience can color later reflections and evaluations of the experience as a whole.

product failure may lead a consumer to inflate the likelihood of a future product failure and make him more inclined to purchase a product warranty.

2. The **representativeness heuristic**—Consumers base their predictions on how representative or similar the outcome is to other examples. One reason package appearances may be so similar for different brands in the same product category is that marketers want their products to be seen as representative of the category as a whole.

Marketing Insight

Predictably Irrational

In a new book, Dan Ariely reviews some of his own research, as well as that of others, that shows that although consumers may think they are making well-reasoned, rational decisions, that is not often the case. As it turns out, a host of mental factors and unconscious cognitive biases conspire to result in seemingly irrational decision making in many different settings. Ariely believes these irrational decisions are not random but are systematic and predictable. As he says, we make the same "mistake" over and over. Some of the thought-provoking research insights he highlights include:

- When selling a new product, marketers should be sure to compare it with something consumers already know about, even if the new product is literally new-to-the-world with little direct comparisons. Consumers find it difficult to judge products in isolation and feel more comfortable if they base a new decision at least in part on a past decision.

- Consumers find the lure of "free" almost irresistible. In one experiment, consumers were offered normally high-priced Lindt chocolate truffles for 15 cents and ordinary Hershey kisses for a penny. Customers had to pick one or the other, not both. Seventy-three percent of the customers went for the truffles. When the prices were cut to 14 cents for the truffles and free for the kisses, however, 69 percent of customers went for the kisses, even though the truffles were actually a better deal.

- The "optimism bias" or "positivity illusion" is a pervasive effect that transcends gender, age, education, and nationality. People tend to overestimate their chances of experiencing a good outcome (having a successful marriage, healthy kids, or financial security) but underestimate their chances of experiencing a bad outcome (divorce, a heart attack, or a parking ticket).

In concluding his analysis, Ariely notes, "If I were to distill one main lesson from the research described in this book, it is that we are all pawns in a game whose forces we largely fail to comprehend."

Sources: Dan Ariely, *Predictably Irrational* (New York: Harper Collins, 2008; Dan Ariely, "The Curious Paradox of Optimism Bias," *BusinessWeek*, August 24 and 31, 2009, p. 48; Dan Ariely, "The End of Rational Economics," *Harvard Business Review*, July–August 2009, pp. 78–84; "A Managers Guide to Human Irrationalities," *MIT Sloan Management Review* (Winter 2009), pp. 53–59; Russ Juskalian, "Not as Rational as We Think We Are," *USA Today*, March 17, 2008; Elizabeth Kolbert, "What Was I Thinking?" *New Yorker*, February 25, 2008; David Mehegan, "Experimenting on Humans," *Boston Globe*, March 18, 2008.

3.   The **anchoring and adjustment heuristic**—Consumers arrive at an initial judgment and then adjust it based on additional information. For services marketers, a strong first impression is critical to establish a favorable anchor so subsequent experiences will be interpreted in a more favorable light.

Note that marketing managers also may use heuristics and be subject to biases in their own decision making.

Framing

Decision framing is the manner in which choices are presented to and seen by a decision maker. A $200 cell phone may not seem that expensive in the context of a set of $400 phones but may seem very expensive if those phones cost $50. Framing effects are pervasive and can be powerful.

University of Chicago professors Richard Thaler and Cass Sunstein show how marketers can influence consumer decision making through what they call the *choice architecture*—the environment in which decisions are structured and buying choices are made. According to these researchers, in the right environment, consumers can be given a "nudge" via some small feature in the environment that attracts attention and alters behavior. They maintain Nabisco is employing a smart choice architecture by offering 100-calorie snack packs, which have solid profit margins, while nudging consumers to make healthier choices.[77]

MENTAL ACCOUNTING   Researchers have found that consumers use mental accounting when they handle their money.[78] **Mental accounting** refers to the way consumers code, categorize, and evaluate financial outcomes of choices. Formally, it is "the tendency to categorize *funds* or items of value even though there is no logical *basis* for the categorization, e.g., individuals often segregate their savings into separate accounts to meet different goals even though funds from any of the accounts can be applied to any of the goals."[79]

Consider the following two scenarios:

1. Assume you spend $50 to buy a ticket for a concert.[80] As you arrive at the show, you realize you've lost your ticket. You decide to buy a replacement.
2. Assume you decided to buy a ticket to a concert at the door. As you arrive at the show, you realize somehow you lost $50 along the way. You decide to buy the ticket anyway.

Which one would you be more likely to do? Most people choose scenario 2. Although you lost the same amount in each case—$50—in the first case, you may have mentally allocated $50 for going to a concert. Buying another ticket would exceed your mental concert budget. In the second case, the money you lost did not belong to any account, so you had not yet exceeded your mental concert budget.

According to Chicago's Thaler, mental accounting is based on a set of core principles:

Mental accounting principles help predict whether consumers will or will not go to a concert after having lost a ticket or some money.

1. Consumers tend to *segregate gains*. When a seller has a product with more than one positive dimension, it's desirable to have the consumer evaluate each dimension separately. Listing multiple benefits of a large industrial product, for example, can make the sum of the parts seem greater than the whole.
2. Consumers tend to *integrate losses*. Marketers have a distinct advantage in selling something if its cost can be added to another large purchase. House buyers are more inclined to view additional expenditures favorably given the high price of buying a house.
3. Consumers tend to *integrate smaller losses with larger gains*. The "cancellation" principle might explain why withholding taxes from monthly paychecks is less aversive than large, lump-sum tax payments—the smaller withholdings are more likely to be absorbed by the larger pay amount.
4. Consumers tend to *segregate small gains from large losses*. The "silver lining" principle might explain the popularity of rebates on big-ticket purchases such as cars.

The principles of mental accounting are derived in part from prospect theory. **Prospect theory** maintains that consumers frame their decision alternatives in terms of gains and losses according to a value function. Consumers are generally loss-averse. They tend to overweight very low probabilities and underweight very high probabilities.

Summary

1. Consumer behavior is influenced by three factors: cultural (culture, subculture, and social class), social (reference groups, family, and social roles and statuses), and personal (age, stage in the life cycle, occupation, economic circumstances, lifestyle, personality, and self-concept). Research into these factors can provide clues to reach and serve consumers more effectively.

2. Four main psychological processes that affect consumer behavior are motivation, perception, learning, and memory.

3. To understand how consumers actually make buying decisions, marketers must identify who makes and has input into the buying decision; people can be initiators, influencers, deciders, buyers, or users. Different marketing campaigns might be targeted to each type of person.

4. The typical buying process consists of the following sequence of events: problem recognition, information search, evaluation of alternatives, purchase decision, and postpurchase behavior. The marketers' job is to understand the behavior at each stage. The attitudes of others, unanticipated situational factors, and perceived risk may all affect the decision to buy, as will consumers' levels of postpurchase product satisfaction, use and disposal, and the company's actions.

5. Consumers are constructive decision makers and subject to many contextual influences. They often exhibit low involvement in their decisions, using many heuristics as a result.

Applications

Marketing Debate
Is Target Marketing Ever Bad?

As marketers increasingly tailor marketing programs to target market segments, some critics have denounced these efforts as exploitive. They see the preponderance of billboards advertising cigarettes and alcohol in low-income urban areas as taking advantage of a vulnerable market segment. Critics can be especially harsh in evaluating marketing programs that target African Americans and other minority groups, claiming they often employ stereotypes and inappropriate depictions. Others counter that targeting and positioning is critical to marketing, and that these marketing programs are an attempt to be relevant to a certain consumer group.

Take a position: Targeting minorities is exploitive *versus* Targeting minorities is a sound business practice.

Marketing Discussion
Mental Accounts

What mental accounts do you have in your mind about purchasing products or services? Do you have any rules you employ in spending money? Are they different from what other people do? Do you follow Thaler's four principles in reacting to gains and losses?

Marketing Excellence

>>Disney

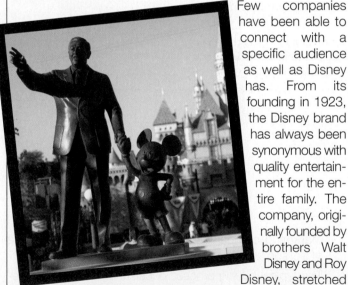

Few companies have been able to connect with a specific audience as well as Disney has. From its founding in 1923, the Disney brand has always been synonymous with quality entertainment for the entire family. The company, originally founded by brothers Walt Disney and Roy Disney, stretched the boundaries of entertainment during the 20th century to bring classic and memorable family entertainment around the world. Beginning with simple black-and-white animated cartoons, the company grew into the worldwide phenomenon that today includes theme parks, feature films, television networks, theatre productions, consumer products, and a growing online presence.

In its first two decades, Walt Disney Productions was a struggling cartoon studio that introduced the world to its most famous character ever, Mickey Mouse. Few believed in Disney's vision at the time, but the smashing success of cartoons with sound and the first-ever full-length animated film, *Snow White and the Seven Dwarfs*, in 1937 led, over the next three decades, to other animated classics including *Pinocchio*, *Bambi, Cinderella,* and *Peter Pan*, live action films such as *Mary Poppins* and *The Love Bug,* and television series like *Davy Crockett*.

When Walt Disney died in 1966, he was considered the best-known person in the world. By then the company had expanded the Disney brand into film, television, consumer products, and Disneyland in southern California, its first theme park, where families could experience the magic of Disney in real life. After Walt's death, Roy Disney took over as CEO and realized Walt's dream of opening the 24,000 acre Walt Disney World theme park in Florida. By the time of Roy's death in 1971, the two brothers had created a brand that stood for trust, fun, and entertainment that resonated with children, families, and adults through some of the most moving and iconic characters, stories, and memories of all time.

The company stumbled for a few years without the leadership of its two founding brothers. However, by the 1980s, The Walt Disney Company was back on its feet and thinking of new ways to target its core family-oriented consumers as well as expand into new areas that would reach an older audience. It launched the Disney Channel, Touchstone Pictures, and Touchstone Television. In addition, Disney featured classic films during *The Disney Sunday Night Movie* and sold classic Disney films on video at extremely low prices in order to reach a whole new generation of children. The brand continued to expand in the 1990s as Disney tapped into publishing, international theme parks, and theatrical productions that reached a variety of audiences around the world.

Today, Disney is comprised of five business segments: The Walt Disney Studios, which creates films, recording labels, and theatrical performances; Parks and Resorts, which focuses on Disney's 11 theme parks, cruise lines, and other travel-related assets; Disney Consumer Products, which sells all Disney-branded products; Media Networks, which includes Disney's television networks such as ESPN, ABC, and the Disney Channel; and Interactive Media.

Disney's greatest challenge today is to keep a 90-year-old brand relevant and current to its core audience while staying true to its heritage and core brand values. Disney's CEO Bob Iger explained, "As a brand that people seek out and trust, it opens doors to new platforms and markets, and hence to new consumers. When you deal with a company that has a great legacy, you deal with decisions and conflicts that arise from the clash of heritage versus innovation versus relevance. I'm a big believer in respect for heritage, but I'm also a big believer in the need to innovate and the need to balance that respect for heritage with a need to be relevant."

Internally, Disney has focused on the *Disney Difference* — "a value-creation dynamic based on high standards of quality and recognition that set Disney apart from its competitors." Disney leverages all aspects of its businesses and abilities to touch its audience in multiple ways, efficiently and economically. Disney's *Hannah Montana* provides an excellent example of how the company took a tween-targeted television show and moved it across its various creative divisions to become a significant franchise for the company, including millions of CD sales, video games, popular consumer products, box office movies, concerts around the world, and ongoing live performances at international Disneyland resorts like Hong Kong, India, and Russia.

Disney also uses emerging technologies to connect with its consumers in innovative ways. It was one of the first companies to begin regular podcasts of its television shows as well as release ongoing news about its products and interviews with Disney's employees, staff, and park officials. Disney's Web site provides insight into movie trailers, television clips, Broadway shows, virtual theme park experiences, and much more. And the company continues to explore ways to make Mickey Mouse and his peers more text-friendly and virtually exciting.

According to internal studies, Disney estimates that consumers spend 13 billion hours "immersed" with the Disney brand each year. Consumers around the world spend 10 billion hours watching programs on the Disney Channel, 800 million hours at Disney's resorts and theme parks, and 1.2 billion hours watching a Disney movie—at home, in the theatre, or on their computer. Today, Disney is the 63rd largest company in the world with revenues reaching nearly $38 billion in 2008.

Questions

1. What does Disney do best to connect with its core consumers?

2. What are the risks and benefits of expanding the Disney brand in new ways?

Sources: "Company History," Disney.com; "Annual Reports," Disney.com; Richard Siklosc, "The Iger Difference," Fortune, April 11, 2008; Brooks Barnes, "After Mickey's Makeover; Less Mr. Nice Guy," *New York Times*, November 4, 2009.

Marketing Excellence

>>IKEA

IKEA was founded in 1943 by a 17-year-old Swede named Ingvar Kamprad. The company, which initially sold pens, Christmas cards, and seeds from a shed on Kamprad's family farm, eventually grew into a retail titan in home furnishings and a global cultural phenomenon, what *BusinessWeek* called a "one-stop sanctuary for coolness" and "the quintessential cult brand."

IKEA inspires remarkable levels of interest and devotion from its customers. In 2008, 500 million visitors walked through IKEA stores, which are located all over the world. When a new location debuted in London in 2005, about 6,000 people arrived before the doors opened. A contest in Atlanta crowned five winners "Ambassador of Kul" (Swedish for "fun") who, in order to collect their prizes, had to live in the IKEA store for three full days before it opened, which they gladly did.

IKEA achieved this level of success by offering a unique value proposition to consumers: leading-edge Scandinavian design at extremely low prices. The company's fashionable bargains include products with unusual Swedish names such as Klippan loveseats for $279, BILLY bookcases for $60, and LACK side tables for $8. IKEA founder Kamprad, who was dyslexic, believed it was easier to remember product *names* rather than codes or numbers. The company is able to offer such low prices in part because most items come boxed and require the customer to completely assemble them at home. This strategy results in cheaper and easier transportation as well as more efficient use of store shelf space.

IKEA's vision is "to create a better everyday life for the many people." Its mission of providing value is predicated on founder Kamprad's statement that "People have very

thin wallets. We should take care of their interests." IKEA adheres to this philosophy by reducing prices across its products by 2 percent to 3 percent annually. Its focus on value also benefits the bottom line: IKEA enjoys 10 percent margins, higher than its competitors such as Target (7.7 percent) and Pier 1 Imports (5 percent). IKEA sources its products from multiple companies all over the world rather than a handful of suppliers as many furniture retailers do. This ensures the lowest price possible, and savings that are passed on to the consumer. Today, IKEA works with approximately 1,300 suppliers from 53 countries.

IKEA's stores are located a good distance from most city centers, which helps keep land costs down and taxes low. The average IKEA customer drives 50 miles round-trip to visit an IKEA store. Many stores resemble a large box with few windows and doors and are painted bright yellow and blue—Sweden's national colors. They save energy with low-wattage lightbulbs and have unusually long hours of operation; some are 24-hour stores. When a consumer walks through an IKEA store, it is a very different experience than most furniture retailers. The floor plan is designed in a one-way format, so the consumer experiences the entire store first, then can grab a shopping cart, visit the warehouse, and pick up the desired items in a flat box.

Many IKEA products are sold uniformly throughout the world, but the company also caters to local tastes.

- In China, it stocked 250,000 plastic placemats with "Year of the Rooster" themes, which quickly sold out after the holiday.

- When employees realized U.S. shoppers were buying vases as drinking glasses because they considered IKEA's regular glasses too small, the company developed larger glasses for the U.S. market.

- IKEA managers visited European and U.S. consumers in their homes and learned that Europeans generally hang their clothes, whereas U.S. shoppers prefer to store them folded. Therefore, wardrobes for the U.S. market were designed with deeper drawers.

- Visits to Hispanic households in California led IKEA to add seating and dining space in its California stores, brighten the color palettes, and hang more picture frames on the walls.

IKEA has evolved into the largest furniture retailer in the world with approximately 300 stores in 38 countries and revenues topping €21.5 billion in 2009. Its top countries in terms of sales include Germany, 16 percent; United States, 11 percent; France, 10 percent; United Kingdom, 7 percent; and Italy, 7 percent.

Questions

1. What are some of the things IKEA is doing right to reach consumers in different markets? What else could it be doing?

2. IKEA has essentially changed the way people shop for furniture. Discuss the pros and cons of this strategy.

Sources: Kerry Capell, "IKEA: How the Swedish Retailer Became a Global Cult Brand," *BusinessWeek*, November 14, 2005, p. 96; "Need a Home to Go with That Sofa?" *BusinessWeek*, November 14, 2005, p. 106; Ellen Ruppel Shell, "Buy to Last," *Atlantic*, July/August 2009; Jon Henley, "Do You Speak IKEA?" *Guardian*, February 4, 2008; IKEA, www.ikea.com.

Chapter 7

In This Chapter, We Will Address the Following Questions

From its Redwood Shores headquarters, Oracle introduces innovative marketing programs to satisfy its many business-to-business customers.

1. What is the business market, and how does it differ from the consumer market?

2. What buying situations do organizational buyers face?

3. Who participates in the business-to-business buying process?

4. How do business buyers make their decisions?

5. How can companies build strong relationships with business customers?

6. How do institutional buyers and government agencies do their buying?

Analyzing Business Markets

Business organizations do not only sell; they also buy vast quantities of raw materials, manufactured components, plant and equipment, supplies, and business services. According to the Census Bureau, there are roughly 6 million businesses with paid employees in the United States alone. To create and capture value, sellers need to understand these organizations' needs, resources, policies, and buying procedures.

Business-software giant Oracle became an industry leader by offering a whole range of products and services to satisfy customer needs for enterprise software. Known originally for its flagship database management systems, Oracle spent $30 billion in recent years to buy 56 companies, including $7.4 billion to buy Sun Microsystems, doubling the company's revenue to $24 billion and sending its stock soaring in the process.

To become a one-stop shop for all kinds of business customers, Oracle seeks to offer the widest ranges of products in the software industry. It now sells everything from server computers and data storage devices to operating systems, databases, and software for running accounting, sales, and supply-chain management. At the same time, Oracle has launched "Project Fusion" to unify its different applications, so customers can reap the benefits of consolidating many of their software needs with Oracle. Oracle's market power has sometimes raised both criticism from customers and concerns from government regulators. At the same time, its many long-time customers speak to its track record of product innovation and customer satisfaction.[1]

Some of the world's most valuable brands belong to business marketers: ABB, Caterpillar, DuPont, FedEx, GE, Hewlett-Packard, IBM, Intel, and Siemens, to name a few. Many principles of basic marketing also apply to business marketers. They need to embrace holistic marketing principles, such as building strong relationships with their customers, just like any marketer. But they also face some unique considerations in selling to other businesses. In this chapter, we will highlight some of the crucial similarities and differences for marketing in business markets.[2]

What Is Organizational Buying?

Frederick E. Webster Jr. and Yoram Wind define **organizational buying** as the decision-making process by which formal organizations establish the need for purchased products and services and identify, evaluate, and choose among alternative brands and suppliers.[3]

The Business Market versus the Consumer Market

The **business market** consists of all the organizations that acquire goods and services used in the production of other products or services that are sold, rented, or supplied to others. The major industries making up the business market are agriculture, forestry, and fisheries; mining; manufacturing; construction; transportation; communication; public utilities; banking, finance, and insurance; distribution; and services.

More dollars and items change hands in sales to business buyers than to consumers. Consider the process of producing and selling a simple pair of shoes. Hide dealers must sell hides to tanners, who sell leather to shoe manufacturers, who sell shoes to wholesalers, who sell shoes to retailers, who finally sell them to consumers. Each party in the supply chain also buys many other goods and services to support its operations.

Given the highly competitive nature of business-to-business markets, the biggest enemy to marketers here is commoditization.[4] Commoditization eats away margins and weakens customer loyalty. It can be overcome only if target customers are convinced that meaningful differences exist in the marketplace, and that the unique benefits of the firm's offerings are worth the added expense. Thus, a critical step in business-to-business marketing is to create and communicate relevant differentiation from competitors. Here is how Navistar has adjusted its marketing to reflect the economic crisis and a different customer mind-set.

Navistar Navistar sells trucks and buses under the International and IC brands. Its diverse customer base includes bookkeepers, truck drivers, insurance people, large retailers, and so on. In recent years, these customers have been trying to cope with the harsh economic realities brought on by higher fuel prices, tougher federal regulation, and increased environmental consciousness. To address these customer concerns, Navistar devised a new marketing strategy and campaign. It introduced a new lineup of trucks and engines, including the first medium-duty hybrid truck and new diesel engines. To support new product development, Navistar launched an extensive multimedia marketing campaign that included an experiential truck stop and key industry event mobile tours, outbound video e-mail, brand advertising, and an outreach program to bloggers. It even shot a short documentary-style film, *Drive and Deliver*, which showcased three long-haul truckers driving around the country making deliveries using one of Navistar's new long-haul LoneStar truck models.[5]

Navistar's innovative LoneStar truck model was featured in a short film directed by an Academy Award nominee.

Business marketers face many of the same challenges as consumer marketers. In particular, understanding their customers and what they value is of paramount importance to both. A survey of top business-to-business firms identified the following as challenges they faced:[6]

1. Understanding deep customer needs in new ways;
2. Identifying new opportunities for organic business growth;
3. Improving value management techniques and tools;
4. Calculating better marketing performance and accountability metrics;
5. Competing and growing in global markets, particularly China;
6. Countering the threat of product and service commoditization by bringing innovative offerings to market faster and moving to more competitive business models; and
7. Convincing C-level executives to embrace the marketing concept and support robust marketing programs.

Business marketers contrast sharply with consumer markets in some ways, however:

- *Fewer, larger buyers.* The business marketer normally deals with far fewer, much larger buyers than the consumer marketer does, particularly in such industries as aircraft engines and defense weapons. The fortunes of Goodyear tires, Cummins engines, Delphi control systems, and other automotive part suppliers depends on getting big contracts from just a handful of major automakers.

- *Close supplier–customer relationship.* Because of the smaller customer base and the importance and power of the larger customers, suppliers are frequently expected to customize their offerings to individual business customer needs. Through its Supplier Added Value Effort ($AVE) program, Pittsburgh-based PPG industries challenges its suppliers of maintenance, repair, and operating (MRO) goods and services to deliver on annual value-added/cost-savings proposals equaling at least 5 percent of their total annual sales to PPG. One preferred supplier submitted a suggestion to $AVE that reduced costs for a lighting project by $160,000 by negotiating discounted prices for new fixtures and fluorescent bulbs.[7] Business buyers often select suppliers that also buy from them. A paper manufacturer might buy from a chemical company that buys a considerable amount of its paper.

- *Professional purchasing.* Business goods are often purchased by trained purchasing agents, who must follow their organizations' purchasing policies, constraints, and requirements. Many of the buying instruments—for example, requests for quotations, proposals, and purchase contracts—are not typically found in consumer buying. Professional buyers spend their careers learning how to buy better. Many belong to the Institute for Supply Management, which seeks to improve professional buyers' effectiveness and status. This means business marketers must provide greater technical data about their product and its advantages over competitors' products.

- *Multiple buying influences.* More people typically influence business buying decisions. Buying committees consisting of technical experts and even senior management are common in the purchase of major goods. Business marketers need to send well-trained sales representatives and sales teams to deal with the well-trained buyers.

- *Multiple sales calls.* A study by McGraw-Hill found that it took four to four and a half calls to close an average industrial sale. In the case of capital equipment sales for large projects, it may take many attempts to fund a project, and the sales cycle—between quoting a job and delivering the product—is often measured in years.[8]

- *Derived demand.* The demand for business goods is ultimately derived from the demand for consumer goods. For this reason, the business marketer must closely monitor the buying patterns of ultimate consumers. Pittsburgh-based Consol Energy's coal business largely depends on orders from utilities and steel companies, which, in turn, depend on broader economic demand from consumers for electricity and steel-based products such as automobiles, machines, and appliances. Business buyers must also pay close attention to current and expected economic factors, such as the level of production, investment, and consumer spending and the interest rate. In a recession, they reduce their investment in plant, equipment, and inventories. Business marketers can do little to stimulate total demand in this environment. They can only fight harder to increase or maintain their share of the demand.

- *Inelastic demand.* The total demand for many business goods and services is inelastic—that is, not much affected by price changes. Shoe manufacturers are not going to buy much more leather if the price of leather falls, nor will they buy much less leather if the price rises unless they can find satisfactory substitutes. Demand is especially inelastic in the short run because producers cannot make quick changes in production methods. Demand is also inelastic for business goods that represent a small percentage of the item's total cost, such as shoelaces.

- *Fluctuating demand.* The demand for business goods and services tends to be more volatile than the demand for consumer goods and services. A given percentage increase in consumer demand can lead to a much larger percentage increase in the demand for plant and equipment necessary to produce the additional output. Economists refer to this as the *acceleration effect*. Sometimes a rise of only 10 percent in consumer demand can cause as much as a 200 percent rise in business demand for products in the next period; a 10 percent fall in consumer demand may cause a complete collapse in business demand.

- *Geographically concentrated buyers.* For years, more than half of U.S. business buyers have been concentrated in seven states: New York, California, Pennsylvania, Illinois, Ohio, New Jersey, and Michigan. The geographical concentration of producers helps to reduce selling costs. At the same time, business marketers need to monitor regional shifts of certain industries.

- *Direct purchasing.* Business buyers often buy directly from manufacturers rather than through intermediaries, especially items that are technically complex or expensive such as mainframes or aircraft.

Buying Situations

The business buyer faces many decisions in making a purchase. *How* many depends on the complexity of the problem being solved, newness of the buying requirement, number of people involved, and time required. Three types of buying situations are the straight rebuy, modified rebuy, and new task.[9]

- *Straight rebuy.* In a straight rebuy, the purchasing department reorders supplies such as office supplies and bulk chemicals on a routine basis and chooses from suppliers on an approved list. The suppliers make an effort to maintain product and service quality and often propose automatic reordering systems to save time. "Out-suppliers" attempt to offer something new or exploit dissatisfaction with a current supplier. Their goal is to get a small order and then enlarge their purchase share over time.

- *Modified rebuy.* The buyer in a modified rebuy wants to change product specifications, prices, delivery requirements, or other terms. This usually requires additional participants on both sides. The in-suppliers become nervous and want to protect the account. The out-suppliers see an opportunity to propose a better offer to gain some business.
- *New task.* A new-task purchaser buys a product or service for the first time (an office building, a new security system). The greater the cost or risk, the larger the number of participants, and the greater their information gathering—the longer the time to a decision.[10]

The business buyer makes the fewest decisions in the straight rebuy situation and the most in the new-task situation. Over time, new-buy situations become straight rebuys and routine purchase behavior.

New-task buying is the marketer's greatest opportunity and challenge. The process passes through several stages: awareness, interest, evaluation, trial, and adoption.[11] Mass media can be most important during the initial awareness stage; salespeople often have their greatest impact at the interest stage; and technical sources can be most important during the evaluation stage. Online selling efforts may be useful at all stages.

In the new-task situation, the buyer must determine product specifications, price limits, delivery terms and times, service terms, payment terms, order quantities, acceptable suppliers, and the selected supplier. Different participants influence each decision, and the order in which these decisions are made varies.

Because of the complicated selling required, many companies use a *missionary sales force* consisting of their most effective salespeople. The brand promise and the manufacturer's brand name recognition will be important in establishing trust and the customer's willingness to consider change.[12] The marketer also tries to reach as many key participants as possible and provide helpful information and assistance.

Once a customer has been acquired, in-suppliers are continually seeking ways to add value to their market offer to facilitate rebuys. Data storage leader EMC successfully acquired a series of computer software leaders to reposition the company to manage—and not just store—information, often by giving customers customized information.[13]

Customers considering dropping six or seven figures on one transaction for big-ticket goods and services want all the information they can get. One way to entice new buyers is to create a customer reference program in which satisfied existing customers act in concert with the company's sales and marketing department by agreeing to serve as references. Technology companies such as HP, Lucent, and Unisys have all employed such programs.

Business marketers are also recognizing the importance of their brand and how they must execute well in a number of areas to gain marketplace success. Boeing, which makes everything from commercial airplanes to satellites, implemented the "One Company" brand strategy to unify all its different operations with a one-brand culture. The strategy was based in part on a triple helix representation: (1) enterprising spirit (why Boeing does what it does), (2) precision performance (how Boeing gets things done), and (3) defining the future (what Boeing achieves as a company).[14] NetApp is another good example of the increased importance placed on branding in business-to-business marketing.

NetApp
NetApp is a *Fortune* 1000 company providing data management and storage solutions to medium- and large-sized clients. Despite some marketplace success, the company found its branding efforts in disarray by 2007. Several variations of its name were in use, leading to a formal name change to NetApp in 2008. Branding consultants Landor also created a new identity, architecture, nomenclature, tone of voice, and tagline ("Go further, faster.") for the brand and its new name. Messages emphasized NetApp's superior technology, innovation, and customer-centric "get things done" culture. Some of the marketing efforts supporting the brand, however, still left some things to be desired. The Web sites were called "Frankensites" because they had been worked on and modified by so many developers over a 12-year period. Web site makeovers streamlined and organized the company's presentation and made it easier to make changes and updates. The new Web site was estimated to increase sales leads from inquiries by fourfold. Investing heavily in marketing communications despite the recession, NetApp ran print and online ads and tapped into a number of social media outlets—communities and forums, bloggers, Facebook, Twitter, and YouTube.[15]

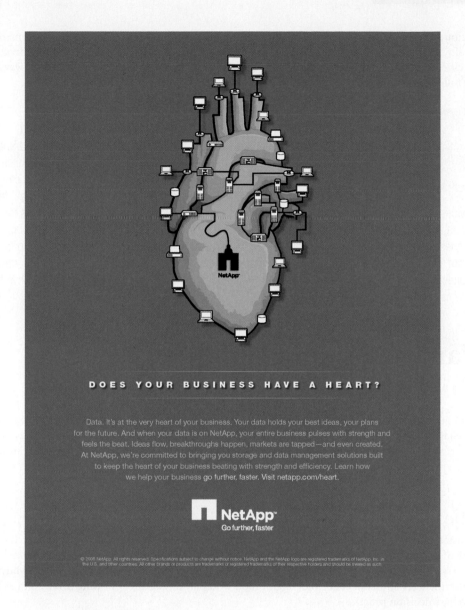

Business-to-business technology leader NetApp has made a concerted effort to build its brand through a variety of marketing communications and activities.

Systems Buying and Selling

Many business buyers prefer to buy a total problem solution from one seller. Called *systems buying*, this practice originated with government purchases of major weapons and communications systems. The government solicited bids from *prime contractors* that, if awarded the contract, would be responsible for bidding out and assembling the system's subcomponents from *second-tier contractors*. The prime contractor thus provided a turnkey solution, so-called because the buyer simply had to turn one key to get the job done.

Sellers have increasingly recognized that buyers like to purchase in this way, and many have adopted systems selling as a marketing tool. One variant of systems selling is *systems contracting*, in which a single supplier provides the buyer with its entire requirement of MRO supplies. During the contract period, the supplier also manages the customer's inventory. Shell Oil manages the oil inventories of many of its business customers and knows when they require replenishment. The customer benefits from reduced procurement and management costs and from price protection over the term of the contract. The seller benefits from lower operating costs thanks to steady demand and reduced paperwork.

Systems selling is a key industrial marketing strategy in bidding to build large-scale industrial projects such as dams, steel factories, irrigation systems, sanitation systems, pipelines, utilities, and even new towns. Customers present potential suppliers with a list of project specifications and requirements. Project engineering firms must compete on price, quality, reliability, and other attributes to win contracts. Suppliers, however, are not just at the mercy of customer demands. Ideally, they're active with customers early in the process to influence the actual development of the specifications. Or they can go beyond the specifications to offer additional value in various ways, as the following example shows.

Selling to the Indonesian Government The Indonesian government requested bids to build a cement factory near Jakarta. A U.S. firm made a proposal that included choosing the site, designing the factory, hiring the construction crews, assembling the materials and equipment, and turning over the finished factory to the Indonesian government. A Japanese firm, in outlining its proposal, included all these services, plus hiring and training the workers to run the factory, exporting the cement through its trading companies, and using the cement to build roads and new office buildings in Jakarta. Although the Japanese proposal involved more money, it won the contract. Clearly, the Japanese viewed the problem as not just building a cement factory (the narrow view of systems selling) but as contributing to Indonesia's economic development. They took the broadest view of the customer's needs, which is true systems selling.

Participants in the Business Buying Process

Who buys the trillions of dollars' worth of goods and services needed by business organizations? Purchasing agents are influential in straight-rebuy and modified-rebuy situations, whereas other department personnel are more influential in new-buy situations. Engineering personnel usually have a major influence in selecting product components, and purchasing agents dominate in selecting suppliers.[16]

The Buying Center

Webster and Wind call the decision-making unit of a buying organization *the buying center*. It consists of "all those individuals and groups who participate in the purchasing decision-making process, who share some common goals and the risks arising from the decisions."[17] The buying center includes all members of the organization who play any of the following seven roles in the purchase decision process.

1. *Initiators*—Users or others in the organization who request that something be purchased.
2. *Users*—Those who will use the product or service. In many cases, the users initiate the buying proposal and help define the product requirements.
3. *Influencers*—People who influence the buying decision, often by helping define specifications and providing information for evaluating alternatives. Technical personnel are particularly important influencers.
4. *Deciders*—People who decide on product requirements or on suppliers.
5. *Approvers*—People who authorize the proposed actions of deciders or buyers.
6. *Buyers*—People who have formal authority to select the supplier and arrange the purchase terms. Buyers may help shape product specifications, but they play their major role in selecting vendors and negotiating. In more complex purchases, buyers might include high-level managers.
7. *Gatekeepers*—People who have the power to prevent sellers or information from reaching members of the buying center. For example, purchasing agents, receptionists, and telephone operators may prevent salespersons from contacting users or deciders.

Several people can occupy a given role such as user or influencer, and one person may play multiple roles.[18] A purchasing manager, for example, often occupies the roles of buyer, influencer, and gatekeeper simultaneously: She can determine which sales reps can call on other people in the organization; what budget and other constraints to place on the purchase; and which firm will actually get the business, even though others (deciders) might select two or more potential vendors that can meet the company's requirements.

The typical buying center has a minimum of five or six members and often has dozens. Some may be outside the organization, such as government officials, consultants, technical advisors, and other members of the marketing channel. One study found that 3.5 more people on average were engaged in making a business purchase decision in 2005 than in 2001.[19]

Buying Center Influences

Buying centers usually include several participants with differing interests, authority, status, and persuasiveness, and sometimes very different decision criteria. Engineers may want to maximize the performance of the product; production people may want ease of use and reliability of supply; financial staff focus on the economics of the purchase; purchasing may be concerned with operating and replacement costs; union officials may emphasize safety issues.

Business buyers also have personal motivations, perceptions, and preferences influenced by their age, income, education, job position, personality, attitudes toward risk, and culture. Buyers definitely exhibit different buying styles. There are "keep-it-simple" buyers, "own-expert" buyers, "want-the-best" buyers, and "want-everything-done" buyers. Some younger, highly educated buyers are computer experts who conduct rigorous analyses of competitive proposals before choosing a supplier. Other buyers are "toughies" from the old school who pit competing sellers against one another, and in some companies, the purchasing powers-that-be are legendary.

Webster cautions that ultimately individuals, not organizations, make purchasing decisions.[20] Individuals are motivated by their own needs and perceptions in attempting to maximize the rewards (pay, advancement, recognition, and feelings of achievement) offered by the organization. Personal needs motivate their behavior, but organizational needs legitimate the buying process and its outcomes. Thus, businesspeople are not buying "products." They are buying solutions to two problems: the organization's economic and strategic problem, and their own personal need for individual achievement and reward. In this sense, industrial buying decisions are both "rational" and "emotional"—they serve both the organization's and the individual's needs.[21]

Research by one industrial component manufacturer found that although top executives at its small- and medium-size customers were comfortable buying from other companies, they appeared to harbor subconscious insecurities about buying the manufacturer's product. Constant changes in technology had left them concerned about internal effects within the company. Recognizing this unease, the manufacturer retooled its selling approach to emphasize more emotional appeals and how its product line actually enabled the customer's employees to improve their performance, relieving management of the complications and stress of using components.[22]

Recognizing these extrinsic, interpersonal influences, more industrial firms have put greater emphasis on strengthening their corporate brand. At one time, Emerson Electric, a global provider of power tools, compressors, electrical equipment, and engineering solutions, was a conglomerate of 60 autonomous—and sometimes anonymous—companies. A new CMO aligned the brands under a new global brand architecture and identity, allowing Emerson to achieve a broader presence so it could sell locally while leveraging its global brand name. Record sales and stock price highs soon followed.[23] SAS is another firm that recognized the importance of its corporate brand.

 SAS With sales of more than $2.3 billion and a huge "fan club" of IT customers, SAS, the business analytics software firm, seemed to be in an enviable position in 1999. Yet its image was what one industry observer called "a geek brand." In order to extend the company's reach beyond IT managers with PhDs in math or statistical analysis, the company needed to connect with C-level executives in the largest companies—the kind of people who either didn't have a clue what SAS's software was and what to do with it, or who didn't think business analytics was a strategic issue. Working with its first outside ad agency ever, SAS emerged with a new logo, a new slogan, "The Power to Know®," and a series of TV spots and print ads in

Like many business-to-business firms, software giant SAS emphasizes its corporate brand in its marketing efforts.

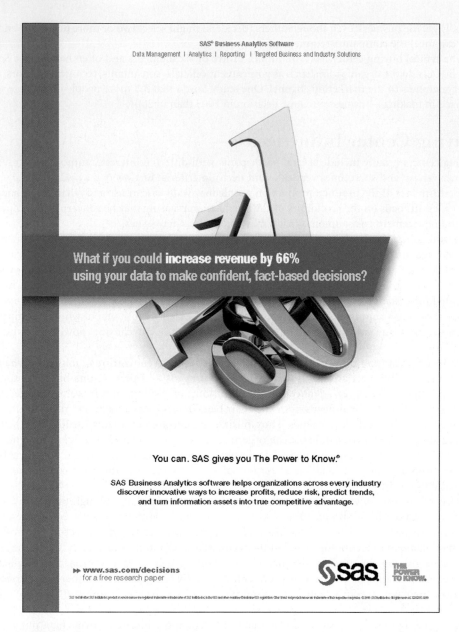

business publications such as *BusinessWeek, Forbes,* and the *Wall Street Journal.* One TV spot that exemplifies SAS's rebranding effort ran like this:

> The problem is not harvesting the new crop of e-business information. It's making sense of it. With e-intelligence from SAS, you can harness the information. And put the knowledge you need within reach. SAS. The Power to Know.

Subsequent research showed that SAS had made the transition to a mainstream business decision-making support brand and was seen as both user-friendly and necessary. Highly profitable and now one of the world's largest privately owned software companies, more than doubling its revenue stream since the brand change, SAS has met with just as much success inside the company. For 14 years, *Fortune* magazine has ranked it one of the best U.S. companies to work for; in 2010 the company was number one.[24]

Targeting Firms and Buying Centers

Successful business-to-business marketing requires that business marketers know which types of companies to focus on in their selling efforts, as well as who to concentrate on within the buying centers in those organizations.

TARGETING FIRMS As we will discuss in detail in Chapter 8, business marketers may divide the marketplace in many different ways to decide on the types of firms to which they will sell. Finding those business sectors with the greatest growth prospects, most profitable customers, and most promising opportunities for the firm is crucial, as Timken found out.

Timken When Timken, which manufactures bearings and rotaries for companies in a variety of industries, saw its net income and shareholder returns dip compared to competitors, the firm became concerned that it was not investing in the most profitable areas. To identify businesses that operated in financially attractive sectors and would be most likely to value its offerings, the company conducted an extensive market study. It revealed that some customers generated a lot of business but had little profit potential, while for others the opposite was true. As a result, Timken shifted its attention away from the auto industry and into the heavy processing, aerospace, and defense industries, and it also addressed customers that were financially unattractive or minimally attractive. A tractor manufacturer complained that Timken's bearings prices were too high for its medium-sized tractors. Timken suggested the firm look elsewhere but continued to sell bearings for the manufacturer's large tractors to the satisfaction of both sides. By adjusting its products, prices, and communications to appeal to the right types of firms, Timken experienced record revenue of $5.7 billion in 2008.[25]

Timken has fine-tuned its marketing activities to sell its specialized bearing and rotary products only to the most promising prospects.

It's also true, however, that as a slowing economy has put a stranglehold on large corporations' purchasing departments, the small and midsize business markets are offering new opportunities for suppliers. See "Marketing Insight: Big Sales to Small Businesses," for more on this important B2B market.

Marketing Insight

Big Sales to Small Businesses

Small businesses—defined as those with fewer than 500 employees—represent 99.7 percent of all employer firms and employ about half of all private-sector employees. They have generated 60 percent to 80 percent of net new jobs annually over the past decade. According to the Small Business Administration's Office of Advocacy, nearly 640,000 small businesses opened in the United States in 2007. Those new ventures all need capital equipment, technology, supplies, and services. Look beyond the United States to new ventures around the world and you have a huge and growing B-to-B market. Here's how two top companies are reaching it:

- IBM counts small to midsize customers as 20 percent of its business and has launched Express, a line of hardware, software services, and financing, for this market. IBM sells through regional reps as well as independent software vendors and resellers, and it supports its small–midsize push with millions of dollars in advertising annually, including in publications such as *American Banker* and *Inc.* The company has also directly targeted gay business owners with ads in *The Advocate* and *Out* and has partnered with nonprofits to reach racial and ethnic minority segments.

- American Express has been steadily adding new features to its credit card for small business, which some small companies use to cover hundreds of thousands of dollars a month in cash needs. It has also created a small business network called OPEN Forum to bring together various services, Web tools, and discount programs with other giants such as FedEx, JetBlue, Hertz, and Hyatt. With OPEN Forum, American Express not only allows customers to save money on common expenses, it also encourages them to do much of their recordkeeping on its Web site and gain business insights.

Small and midsize businesses present huge opportunities and huge challenges. The market is large and fragmented by industry, size, and number of years in operation. Small business owners are notably averse to long-range planning and often have an "I'll buy it when I need it" decision-making style. Here are some guidelines for selling to small businesses:

- **Don't lump small and midsize businesses together.** There's a big gap between $1 million in revenue and $50 million, or between a start-up with 10 employees and a more mature business with 100 or more employees. IBM distinguishes its offerings to small and medium-sized businesses on its common Web site for the two.

- **Do keep it simple.** Simplicity means having one supplier point of contact for all service problems, or one bill for all services and products. AT&T serves millions of small business customers (fewer than 100 employees) with services that bundle Internet, local phone, long-distance phone, data management, business networking, Web hosting, and teleconferencing.

- **Do use the Internet.** Hewlett-Packard found that time-strapped small business decision makers prefer to buy, or at least research, products and services online. So it designed a site targeted to small and midsize businesses and pulls visitors through extensive advertising, direct mail, e-mail campaigns, catalogs, and events.

- **Don't forget about direct contact.** Even if a small business owner's first point of contact is via the Internet, you still need to offer phone or face time.

- **Do provide support after the sale.** Small businesses want partners, not pitchmen. When the DeWitt Company, a 100-employee landscaping products business, purchased a large piece of machinery from Moeller, the company's president paid DeWitt's CEO a personal visit and stayed until the machine was up and running properly.

- **Do your homework.** The realities of small or midsize business management are different from those of a large corporation. Microsoft created a small, fictional executive research firm, Southridge, and baseball-style trading cards of its key decision makers to help Microsoft employees tie sales strategies to small business realities.

Sources: Based on Barnaby J. Feder, "When Goliath Comes Knocking on David's Door," *New York Times,* May 6, 2003; Jay Greene, "Small Biz: Microsoft's Next Big Thing?" *BusinessWeek,* April 21, 2003, pp. 72–73; Jennifer Gilbert, "Small but Mighty," *Sales & Marketing Management* (January 2004), pp. 30–35; www.sba.gov; www.openforum.com; www-304.ibm.com/businesscenter/smb/us/en.

In developing selling efforts, business marketers can also consider their customers' customers, or end users, if these are appropriate. Many business-to-business transactions are to firms using the products they purchase as components or ingredients in products they sell to the ultimate end users. A sharper focus on end users helped propel Thomson Reuters to greater financial heights.

Thomson Reuters Just before it acquired Reuters, global information services giant Thomson Corporation embarked on an extensive research study to better understand its ultimate customers. Thomson sold to businesses and professionals in the financial, legal, tax and accounting, scientific, and health care sectors, but it felt it knew much more about how a financial services manager made purchases for an entire department, for example, than about how individual brokers or investment bankers used Thomson data, research, and other resources to make day-to-day investment decisions for clients. Segmenting the market by these end users, rather than by purchasers, and studying how they viewed Thomson versus competitors allowed the firm to identify market segments that offered growth opportunities. To better understand these segments, Thomson conducted surveys and "day in the life" ethnographic research on how end users did their jobs. Using an approach called "three minutes," researchers combined observation with detailed interviews to understand what end users were doing three minutes before and after they used one of Thomson's products. Insights from the research helped the company develop new products and make acquisitions that led to significantly higher revenue and profits in the year that followed.[26]

TARGETING WITHIN THE BUSINESS CENTER Once it has identified the type of businesses on which to focus marketing efforts, the firm must then decide how best to sell to them. To target their efforts properly, business marketers need to figure out: Who are the major decision participants? What decisions do they influence? What is their level of influence? What evaluation criteria do they use? Consider the following example:

A company sells nonwoven disposable surgical gowns to hospitals. The hospital staff who participate in this buying decision include the vice president of purchasing, the operating-room administrator, and the surgeons. The vice president of purchasing

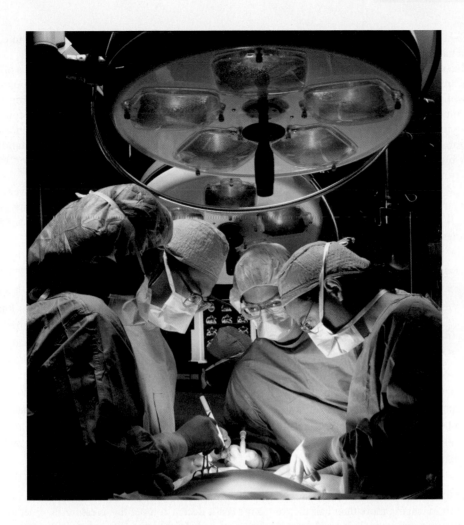

A number of different people play a role in the purchase of hospital products such as surgical gowns; all these people have their own objectives and interests.

analyzes whether the hospital should buy disposable gowns or reusable gowns. If the findings favor disposable gowns, then the operating-room administrator compares various competitors' products and prices and makes a choice. This administrator considers absorbency, antiseptic quality, design, and cost and normally buys the brand that meets functional requirements at the lowest cost. Surgeons influence the decision retroactively by reporting their satisfaction with the particular brand.

The business marketer is not likely to know exactly what kind of group dynamics take place during the decision process, although whatever information he or she can obtain about personalities and interpersonal factors is useful.

Small sellers concentrate on reaching the *key buying influencers*. Larger sellers go for *multilevel in-depth selling* to reach as many participants as possible. Their salespeople virtually "live with" high-volume customers. Companies must rely more heavily on their communications programs to reach hidden buying influences and keep current customers informed.[27]

Business marketers must periodically review their assumptions about buying center participants. For years Kodak sold X-ray film to hospital lab technicians, but research indicated that professional administrators were increasingly making purchasing decisions. Kodak revised its marketing strategy and developed new advertising to reach out to these decision makers.

The Purchasing/Procurement Process

In principle, business buyers seek to obtain the highest benefit package (economic, technical, service, and social) in relation to a market offering's costs. To make comparisons, they will try to translate all costs and benefits into monetary terms. A business buyer's incentive to purchase will be a function of the difference between perceived benefits and perceived costs.[28] The marketer's task is to construct a profitable offering that delivers superior customer value to the target buyers.

Business marketers must therefore ensure that customers fully appreciate how the firm's offerings are different and better. *Framing* occurs when customers are given a perspective or point of view that allows the firm to "put its best foot forward." Framing can be as simple as making sure customers realize all the benefits or cost savings afforded by the firm's offerings, or becoming more involved and influential in the thought process behind how customers view the economics of purchasing, owning, using, and disposing product offerings. Framing requires understanding how business customers currently think of and choose among products and services, and then determining how they *should* ideally think and choose.

Supplier diversity is a benefit that may not have a price tag but that business buyers overlook at their risk. As the CEOs of many of the country's largest companies see it, a diverse supplier base is a business imperative. Minority suppliers are the fastest-growing segment of today's business landscape.

Pfizer   One of the biggest names in pharmaceuticals, Pfizer, views its supplier-diversity program as an essential tool in connecting with customers. Chief Diversity Officer Karen Boykin-Towns directs diversity efforts that include recruitment and talent development inside the company, as well as engaging with customers and suppliers outside the company. For leadership, Pfizer also relies on a diversity and inclusion worldwide council and an infrastructure of "ambassadors" throughout the company. Pfizer concentrates its diversity efforts on women, LGBT, people with disabilities, Latino/Hispanics, Asian Pacific Islanders, U.S. Caribbeans, and African Americans. The company has spent about $700 million with 2,400 minority and women suppliers. Pfizer has even developed a mentoring program that identifies women and minority suppliers that need help growing, whether it's designing a better Web site or building a better business plan. Pfizer managers meet with the owners, often on-site, to figure out what they need.[29]

In the past, purchasing departments occupied a low position in the management hierarchy, in spite of often managing more than half the company's costs. Recent competitive pressures have led many companies to upgrade their purchasing departments and elevate administrators to vice presidential rank. These new, more strategically oriented purchasing departments have a mission to seek the best value from fewer and better suppliers. Some multinationals have even elevated them to "strategic supply departments" with responsibility for global sourcing and partnering. At Caterpillar, purchasing, inventory control, production scheduling, and traffic have been combined into one department. Here are other companies that have benefited from improving their business buying practices.

- Rio Tinto is a world leader in finding, mining, and processing the earth's mineral resources with a significant presence in North America and Australia. Coordinating with its suppliers was time consuming, so Rio Tinto embarked on an electronic commerce strategy with one key supplier. Both parties have reaped significant benefits from this new arrangement. In many cases, orders are being filled in the suppliers' warehouse within minutes of being transmitted, and the supplier is now able to take part in a pay-on-receipt program that has shortened Rio Tinto's payment cycle to around 10 days.[30]
- Mitsui & Co. Ltd is a leading Japanese trading firm that owns more than 850 companies and subsidiaries. When the firm took its purchase orders and payments transactions for one group online, it reduced the cost of purchase transactions by 50 percent and increased customer satisfaction due to greater process efficiencies.[31]
- Medline Industries, the largest privately owned manufacturer and distributor of health care products in the United States, used software to integrate its view of customer activity across online and direct sales channels. The results? The firm enhanced its product margin by 3 percent, improved customer retention by 10 percent, reduced revenue lost to pricing errors by 10 percent, and enhanced the productivity of its sales representatives by 20 percent.[32]

The upgrading of purchasing means business marketers must upgrade their sales staff to match the higher caliber of today's business buyers.

Leading mining and exploration company Rio Tinto has worked with its suppliers to streamline the way they get paid.

Stages in the Buying Process

We're ready to describe the general stages in the business buying-decision process. Patrick J. Robinson and his associates identified eight stages and called them *buyphases*.[33] The model in Table 7.1 is the *buygrid* framework.

In modified-rebuy or straight-rebuy situations, some stages are compressed or bypassed. For example, the buyer normally has a favorite supplier or a ranked list of suppliers and can skip the search and proposal solicitation stages. Here are some important considerations in each of the eight stages.

TABLE 7.1	Buygrid Framework: Major Stages (Buyphases) of the Industrial Buying Process in Relation to Major Buying Situations (Buyclasses)		

		Buyclasses		
		New Task	**Modified Rebuy**	**Straight Rebuy**
Buyphases	1. Problem recognition	Yes	Maybe	No
	2. General need description	Yes	Maybe	No
	3. Product specification	Yes	Yes	Yes
	4. Supplier search	Yes	Maybe	No
	5. Proposal solicitation	Yes	Maybe	No
	6. Supplier selection	Yes	Maybe	No
	7. Order-routine specification	Yes	Maybe	No
	8. Performance review	Yes	Yes	Yes

Problem Recognition

The buying process begins when someone in the company recognizes a problem or need that can be met by acquiring a good or service. The recognition can be triggered by internal or external stimuli. The internal stimulus might be a decision to develop a new product that requires new equipment and materials, or a machine that breaks down and requires new parts. Or purchased material turns out to be unsatisfactory and the company searches for another supplier, or lower prices or better quality. Externally, the buyer may get new ideas at a trade show, see an ad, or receive a call from a sales representative who offers a better product or a lower price. Business marketers can stimulate problem recognition by direct mail, telemarketing, and calling on prospects.

General Need Description and Product Specification

Next, the buyer determines the needed item's general characteristics and required quantity. For standard items, this is simple. For complex items, the buyer will work with others—engineers, users—to define characteristics such as reliability, durability, or price. Business marketers can help by describing how their products meet or even exceed the buyer's needs.

The buying organization now develops the item's technical specifications. Often, the company will assign a product-value-analysis engineering team to the project. *Product value analysis (PVA) is an approach to cost reduction that studies whether components can be redesigned or standardized or made by cheaper methods of production without adversely impacting product performance.* The PVA team will identify overdesigned components, for instance, that last longer than the product itself. Tightly written specifications allow the buyer to refuse components that are too expensive or that fail to meet specified standards. When HP won ISRI's first Design for Recycling Award through an application of PVA methods, it received this accolade:

> HP has worked for many years to design products that are easier to recycle. The firm operates several recycling facilities, which allows it to determine the most effective design features to facilitate product recycling. HP has developed standards that integrate clear design guidelines and checklists into every product's design process to assess and improve recyclability. Hewlett-Packard's design process includes: Using modular design to allow components to be removed, upgraded, or replaced; eliminating glues and adhesives by using, for example, snap-in features; marking plastic parts weighing more than 25g according to ISO 11469 international standards, to speed up materials identification during recycling; reducing the number and types of materials used; using single plastic polymers; using recycled plastic; using moulded-in colours and finishes instead of paint, coatings, or plating.[34]

Suppliers can use product value analysis as a tool for positioning themselves to win an account. Regardless, it is important to eliminate excessive costs. Mexican cement giant Cemex is famed for "The Cemex Way," which uses high-tech methods to squeeze out inefficiencies.[35]

Supplier Search

The buyer next tries to identify the most appropriate suppliers through trade directories, contacts with other companies, trade advertisements, trade shows, and the Internet.[36] The move to Internet purchasing has far-reaching implications for suppliers and will change the shape of purchasing for years to come.[37] Companies that purchase over the Internet are utilizing electronic marketplaces in several forms:

- *Catalog sites.* Companies can order thousands of items through electronic catalogs distributed by e-procurement software, such as Grainger's.
- *Vertical markets.* Companies buying industrial products such as plastics, steel, or chemicals or services such as logistics or media can go to specialized Web sites (called e-hubs). Plastics.com allows plastics buyers to search the best prices among thousands of plastics sellers.
- *"Pure Play" auction sites.* Ritchie Bros. Auctioneers is the world's largest industrial auctioneer, with more than 40 auction sites worldwide. It sold $3.5 billion of used and unused equipment at more than 300 unreserved auctions in 2009, including a wide range of heavy equipment, trucks, and other assets for the construction, transportation, agricultural, material handling, mining, forestry, petroleum, and marine industries. While most people prefer to bid in person at Ritchie Bros. auctions, they are also able to bid online in real time at rbauction.com—the

The world's largest industrial auctioneer, Ritchie Bros., sells a wide range of heavy equipment.

Company's multilingual Web site. In 2009, 33 percent of the bidders at Ritchie Bros. auctions bid over the Internet; online bidders purchased $830 million of equipment.[38]

- **Spot (or exchange) markets.** On spot electronic markets, prices change by the minute. ChemConnect.com is an online exchange for buyers and sellers of bulk chemicals such as benzene, and it's a B2B success in an arena littered with failed sites. First to market, it is now the biggest online exchange for chemical trading, with 1 million barrels traded daily. Customers such as Vanguard Petroleum Corp. in Houston conduct about 15 percent of their spot purchases and sales of natural gas liquids on ChemConnect's commodities trading site.
- **Private exchanges.** Hewlett-Packard, IBM, and Walmart operate private exchanges to link with specially invited groups of suppliers and partners over the Web.
- **Barter markets.** In barter markets, participants offer to trade goods or services.
- **Buying alliances.** Several companies buying the same goods can join together to form purchasing consortia to gain deeper discounts on volume purchases. TopSource is an alliance of firms in the retail and wholesale food-related businesses.

Online business buying offers several advantages: It shaves transaction costs for both buyers and suppliers, reduces time between order and delivery, consolidates purchasing systems, and forges more direct relationships between partners and buyers. On the downside, it may help to erode supplier–buyer loyalty and create potential security problems.

E-PROCUREMENT Web sites are organized around two types of e-hubs: *vertical hubs* centered on industries (plastics, steel, chemicals, paper) and *functional hubs* (logistics, media buying, advertising, energy management). In addition to using these Web sites, companies can use e-procurement in other ways:

- **Set up direct extranet links to major suppliers.** A company can set up a direct e-procurement account at Dell or Office Depot, for instance, and its employees can make their purchases this way.
- **Form buying alliances.** A number of major retailers and manufacturers such as Acosta, Ahold, Best Buy, Carrefour, Family Dollar Stores, Lowe's, Safeway, Sears, SUPERVALU, Target, Walgreens, Walmart, and Wegmans Food Markets are part of a data-sharing alliance called 1SYNC. Several auto companies (GM, Ford, Chrysler) formed Covisint for the same reason. Covisint is the leading provider of services that can integrate crucial business information and processes between partners, customers, and suppliers. The company has now also targeted health care to provide similar services.
- **Set up company buying sites.** General Electric formed the Trading Process Network (TPN), where it posts *requests for proposals (RFPs),* negotiates terms, and places orders.

Moving into e-procurement means more than acquiring software; it requires changing purchasing strategy and structure. However, the benefits are many: Aggregating purchasing across multiple departments yields larger, centrally negotiated volume discounts, a smaller purchasing staff, and less buying of substandard goods from outside the approved list of suppliers.

LEAD GENERATION The supplier's task is to ensure it is considered when customers are—or could be—in the market and searching for a supplier. Identifying good leads and converting them to sales requires the marketing and sales organizations to take a coordinated, multichannel approach to the role of trusted advisor to prospective customers. Marketing must work together with sales to define what makes a "sales ready" prospect and cooperate to send the right messages via sales calls, trade shows, online activities, PR, events, direct mail, and referrals.[39]

Marketing must find the right balance between the quantity and quality of leads. Too many leads, even of high quality, and the sales force may be overwhelmed and allow promising opportunities to fall through the cracks; too few or low-quality leads and the sales force may become frustrated or demoralized.[40] To proactively generate leads, suppliers need to know about their customers. They can obtain background information from vendors such as Dun & Bradstreet and InfoUSA or information-sharing Web sites such as Jigsaw and LinkedIn.[41]

Suppliers that lack the required production capacity or suffer from a poor reputation will be rejected. Those that qualify may be visited by the buyer's agents, who will examine the suppliers' manufacturing facilities and meet their staff. After evaluating each company, the buyer will end up with a short list of qualified suppliers. Many professional buyers have forced suppliers to change their marketing to increase their likelihood of making the cut.

Proposal Solicitation

The buyer next invites qualified suppliers to submit proposals. If the item is complex or expensive, the proposal will be written and detailed. After evaluating the proposals, the buyer will invite a few suppliers to make formal presentations.

Business marketers must be skilled in researching, writing, and presenting proposals. Written proposals should be marketing documents that describe value and benefits in customer terms. Oral presentations must inspire confidence and position the company's capabilities and resources so they stand out from the competition. Proposals and selling are often team efforts. Pittsburgh-based Cutler-Hammer developed "pods" of salespeople focused on a particular geographic region, industry, or market concentration. Salespeople can leverage the knowledge and expertise of coworkers instead of working in isolation.[42]

Supplier Selection

Before selecting a supplier, the buying center will specify and rank desired supplier attributes, often using a supplier-evaluation model such as the one in ▭ Table 7.2.

TABLE 7.2 ▭ An Example of Vendor Analysis					
Attributes	**Rating Scale**				
	Importance Weights	**Poor (1)**	**Fair (2)**	**Good (3)**	**Excellent (4)**
Price	.30				X
Supplier reputation	.20			X	
Product reliability	.30				X
Service reliability	.10		X		
Supplier flexibility	.10			X	
Total Score: .30(4) + .20(3) + .30(4) + .10(2) + .10(3) = 3.5					

To develop compelling value propositions, business marketers need to better understand how business buyers arrive at their valuations.[43] Researchers studying how business marketers assess customer value found eight different *customer value assessment (CVA)* methods. Companies tended to use the simpler methods, although the more sophisticated ones promise to produce a more accurate picture of CPV (see "Marketing Memo: Developing Compelling Customer Value Propositions").

The choice of attributes and their relative importance varies with the buying situation. Delivery reliability, price, and supplier reputation are important for routine-order products. For procedural-problem products, such as a copying machine, the three most important attributes are technical service, supplier flexibility, and product reliability. For political-problem products that stir rivalries in the organization (such as the choice of a computer system), the most important attributes are price, supplier reputation, product reliability, service reliability, and supplier flexibility.

OVERCOMING PRICE PRESSURES The buying center may attempt to negotiate with preferred suppliers for better prices and terms before making the final selection. Despite moves toward strategic sourcing, partnering, and participation in cross-functional teams, buyers still spend a large chunk of their time haggling with suppliers on price. The number of price-oriented buyers can vary by country, depending on customer preferences for different service configurations and characteristics of the customer's organization.[44]

marketing Memo

Developing Compelling Customer Value Propositions

To command price premiums in competitive B2B markets, firms must create compelling customer value propositions. The first step is to research the customer. Here are a number of productive research methods:

1. *Internal engineering assessment*—Have company engineers use laboratory tests to estimate the product's performance characteristics. Weakness: Ignores the fact that the product will have different economic value in different applications.

2. *Field value-in-use assessment*—Interview customers about how costs of using a new product compare to those of using an incumbent. The task is to assess how much each cost element is worth to the buyer.

3. *Focus-group value assessment*—Ask customers in a focus group what value they would put on potential market offerings.

4. *Direct survey questions*—Ask customers to place a direct dollar value on one or more changes in the market offering.

5. *Conjoint analysis*—Ask customers to rank their preferences for alternative market offerings or concepts. Use statistical analysis to estimate the implicit value placed on each attribute.

6. *Benchmarks*—Show customers a "benchmark" offering and then a new-market offering. Ask how much more they would pay for the new offering or how much less they would pay if certain features were removed from the benchmark offering.

7. *Compositional approach*—Ask customers to attach a monetary value to each of three alternative levels of a given attribute. Repeat for other attributes, then add the values together for any offer configuration.

8. *Importance ratings*—Ask customers to rate the importance of different attributes and their suppliers' performance on each.

Having done this research, you can specify the customer value proposition, following a number of important principles. First, clearly substantiate value claims by concretely specifying the differences between your offerings and those of competitors on the dimensions that matter most to the customer. Rockwell Automation determined the cost savings customers would realize from purchasing its pump instead of a competitor's by using industry-standard metrics of functionality and performance: kilowatt-hours spent, number of operating hours per year, and dollars per kilowatt-hour. Also, make the financial implications obvious.

Second, document the value delivered by creating written accounts of costs savings or added value that existing customers have actually captured by using your offerings. Chemical producer Akzo Nobel conducted a two-week pilot on a production reactor at a prospective customer's facility to document points-of-parity and points-of-difference of its high-purity metal organics product.

Finally, make sure the method of creating a customer value proposition is well implemented within the company, and train and reward employees for developing a compelling one. Quaker Chemical conducts training programs for its managers that include a competition to develop the best proposals.

Sources: James C. Anderson, Nirmalya Kumar, and James A. Narus, *Value Merchants: Demonstrating and Documenting Superior Value in Business Markets.* (Boston: Harvard Business School Press, 2007); James C. Anderson, James A. Narus, and Wouter van Rossum, "Customer Value Propositions in Business Markets," *Harvard Business Review,* March 2006, pp. 2–10; James C. Anderson and James A. Narus, "Business Marketing: Understanding What Customers Value," *Harvard Business Review,* November 1998, pp. 53–65.

Marketers can counter requests for a lower price in a number of ways. They may be able to show evidence that the total cost of ownership, that is, the life-cycle cost of using their product, is lower than for competitors' products. They can cite the value of the services the buyer now receives, especially if they are superior to those offered by competitors. Research shows that service support and personal interactions, as well as a supplier's know-how and ability to improve customers' time to market, can be useful differentiators in achieving key-supplier status.[45]

Improving productivity helps alleviate price pressures. Burlington Northern Santa Fe Railway has tied 30 percent of employee bonuses to improvements in the number of railcars shipped per mile.[46] Some firms are using technology to devise novel customer solutions. With Web technology and tools, Vistaprint printers can offer professional printing to small businesses that previously could not afford it.[47]

Some companies handle price-oriented buyers by setting a lower price but establishing restrictive conditions: (1) limited quantities, (2) no refunds, (3) no adjustments, and (4) no services.[48]

- Cardinal Health set up a bonus-dollars plan and gave points according to how much the customer purchased. The points could be turned in for extra goods or free consulting.
- GE is installing diagnostic sensors in its airline engines and railroad engines. It is now compensated for hours of flight or railroad travel.
- IBM is now more of a "service company aided by products" than a "product company aided by services." It can sell computer power on demand (like video on demand) as an alternative to selling computers.

Solution selling can also alleviate price pressure and comes in different forms. Here are three examples.[49]

- *Solutions to Enhance Customer Revenues.* Hendrix UTD has used its sales consultants to help farmers deliver an incremental animal weight gain of 5 percent to 10 percent over competitors.
- *Solutions to Decrease Customer Risks.* ICI Explosives formulated a safer way to ship explosives for quarries.
- *Solutions to Reduce Customer Costs.* W.W. Grainger employees work at large customer facilities to reduce materials-management costs.

More firms are seeking solutions that increase benefits and reduce costs enough to overcome any low-price concerns. Consider the following example.

Lincoln Electric   Lincoln Electric has a decades-long tradition of working with its customers to reduce costs through its Guaranteed Cost Reduction Program. When a customer insists that a Lincoln distributor lower prices to match competitors, the company and the distributor may guarantee that, during the coming year, they will find cost reductions in the customer's plant that meet or exceed the price difference between Lincoln's products and the competition's. The Holland Binkley Company, a major manufacturer of components for tractor trailers, had been purchasing Lincoln Electric welding wire for years. When Binkley began to shop around for a better price on wire, Lincoln Electric developed a package of reducing costs and working together that called for a $10,000 savings but eventually led to a six-figure savings, a growth in business, and a strong, long-term partnership between customer and supplier.[50]

Risk and gain sharing can offset price reductions that customers request. Suppose Medline, a hospital supplier, signs an agreement with Highland Park Hospital promising $350,000 in savings over the first 18 months in exchange for getting a tenfold increase in the hospital's share of supplies. If Medline achieves less than this promised savings, it will make up the difference. If Medline achieves substantially more than promised, it participates in the extra savings. To make such arrangements work, the supplier must be willing to help the customer build a historical database, reach an agreement for measuring benefits and costs, and devise a dispute resolution mechanism.

NUMBER OF SUPPLIERS Companies are increasingly reducing the number of their suppliers. Ford, Motorola, and Honeywell have cut their number of suppliers 20 percent to 80 percent. These companies want their chosen suppliers to be responsible for a larger component system, they want them to achieve continuous quality and performance improvement, and at the same time they want them to lower prices each year by a given percentage. They expect their suppliers to work closely with them during product development, and they value their suggestions.

There is even a trend toward single sourcing, though companies that use multiple sources often cite the threat of a labor strike as the biggest deterrent to single sourcing. Companies may also fear single suppliers will become too comfortable in the relationship and lose their competitive edge.

Order-Routine Specification

After selecting suppliers, the buyer negotiates the final order, listing the technical specifications, the quantity needed, the expected time of delivery, return policies, warranties, and so on. Many industrial buyers lease heavy equipment such as machinery and trucks. The lessee gains a number of advantages: the latest products, better service, the conservation of capital, and some tax advantages. The lessor often ends up with a larger net income and the chance to sell to customers that could not afford outright purchase.

In the case of maintenance, repair, and operating items, buyers are moving toward blanket contracts rather than periodic purchase orders. A blanket contract establishes a long-term relationship in which the supplier promises to resupply the buyer as needed, at agreed-upon prices, over a specified period of time. Because the seller holds the stock, blanket contracts are sometimes called *stockless purchase plans*. The buyer's computer automatically sends an order to the seller when stock is needed. This system locks suppliers in tighter with the buyer and makes it difficult for out-suppliers to break in unless the buyer becomes dissatisfied with prices, quality, or service.

Companies that fear a shortage of key materials are willing to buy and hold large inventories. They will sign long-term contracts with suppliers to ensure a steady flow of materials. DuPont, Ford, and several other major companies regard long-term supply planning as a major responsibility of their purchasing managers. For example, General Motors wants to buy from fewer suppliers, who must be willing to locate close to its plants and produce high-quality components. Business marketers are also setting up extranets with important customers to facilitate and lower the cost of transactions. Customers enter orders that are automatically transmitted to the supplier.

Some companies go further and shift the ordering responsibility to their suppliers in systems called *vendor-managed inventory* (VMI). These suppliers are privy to the customer's inventory levels and take responsibility for replenishing automatically through *continuous replenishment programs*. Plexco International AG supplies audio, lighting, and vision systems to the world's leading automakers. Its VMI program with its 40 suppliers resulted in significant time and cost savings and allowed the company to use former warehouse space for productive manufacturing activities.[51]

Performance Review

The buyer periodically reviews the performance of the chosen supplier(s) using one of three methods. The buyer may contact end users and ask for their evaluations, rate the supplier on several criteria using a weighted-score method, or aggregate the cost of poor performance to come up with adjusted costs of purchase, including price. The performance review may lead the buyer to continue, modify, or end a supplier relationship.

Many companies have set up incentive systems to reward purchasing managers for good buying performance, in much the same way sales personnel receive bonuses for good selling performance. These systems lead purchasing managers to increase pressure on sellers for the best terms.

Managing Business-to-Business Customer Relationships

To improve effectiveness and efficiency, business suppliers and customers are exploring different ways to manage their relationships.[52] Closer relationships are driven in part by supply chain management, early supplier involvement, and purchasing alliances.[53] Cultivating the right relationships with business is paramount for any holistic marketing program.

Business-to-business marketers are avoiding "spray and pray" approaches to attracting and retaining customers in favor of honing in on their targets and developing one-to-one marketing approaches. They are increasingly using online social media in the form of company blogs, online press releases, and forums or discussion groups to communicate with existing as well as prospective customers.

Tellabs   Competing with industry giants Alcatel-Lucent and Cisco Systems, Tellabs is a telecommunications equipment design and research company that provides equipment to transmit voice, video, and data across communication networks. To differentiate itself, Tellabs decided to develop a marketing campaign that would focus on tech-savvy end users of products its *customers* sold. The campaign, "Inspire the New Life," targeted telecommunication service providers to show how Tellabs understood the new generation of technology users and provided solutions to meet their needs. After research showed users were five times more likely to listen to an audio podcast than to read a white paper, and twice as likely to watch a video than listen to a podcast, Tellabs decided to use six-minute video "technology primers" instead of traditional case studies and white papers. Its videos posted on YouTube, Google Video, and the company's Web site were downloaded 100,000 times. Adding a new podcast once or twice a month, the company estimated that the campaign generated three times the exposure, for the cost, than a traditional ad-based Web campaign.[54]

"MY MOBILE KEEPS ME WORKING, KEEPS ME LIVING—KEEPS ME COMPLETELY CONNECTED."
Giulia, 27

INSPIRE GIULIA—WITH TELLABS®

This is **Giulia's life**. And her work, her fun—**everything**—depends on her **ever-reliable** mobile connection. So are you **absolutely sure** that you can give Giulia what she needs to **thrive**?

Tellabs' **experience** offers you that **certainty**. We're speeding migration to **3G** and beyond. In fact, a third of the worlds' wireless calls are made on Tellabs' customers' networks.

Now you can **unite** all of your network's disparate backhaul technologies onto a single, **cost-efficient** platform and offer unmatched **reliability** and guaranteed **QoS** with end-to-end network visibility.

inspirethenewlife.com   **tellabs®** *Inspire the new life*

Tellabs differentiates itself by its focus on the customers of its customers.

The Benefits of Vertical Coordination

Much research has advocated greater vertical coordination between buying partners and sellers, so they can transcend merely transacting and instead engage in activities that create more value for both parties.[55] Building trust is one prerequisite to healthy long-term relationships. "Marketing Insight: Establishing Corporate Trust, Credibility, and Reputation" identifies some key dimensions of such trust. Knowledge that is specific and relevant to a relationship partner is also an important factor in the strength of inter-firm ties.[56]

A number of forces influence the development of a relationship between business partners.[57] Four relevant factors are availability of alternatives, importance of supply, complexity of supply, and supply market dynamism. Based on these we can classify buyer–supplier relationships into eight categories:[58]

1. *Basic buying and selling*—These are simple, routine exchanges with moderate levels of cooperation and information exchange.
2. *Bare bones*—These relationships require more adaptation by the seller and less cooperation and information exchange.
3. *Contractual transaction*—These exchanges are defined by formal contract and generally have low levels of trust, cooperation, and interaction.
4. *Customer supply*—In this traditional custom supply situation, competition rather than cooperation is the dominant form of governance.
5. *Cooperative systems*—The partners in cooperative systems are united in operational ways, but neither demonstrates structural commitment through legal means or adaptation.
6. *Collaborative*—In collaborative exchanges, much trust and commitment lead to true partnership.

Establishing Corporate Trust, Credibility, and Reputation

Corporate credibility is the extent to which customers believe a firm can design and deliver products and services that satisfy their needs and wants. It reflects the supplier's reputation in the marketplace and is the foundation for a strong relationship.

Corporate credibility depends on three factors:

- *Corporate expertise*—the extent to which a company is seen as able to make and sell products or conduct services.

- *Corporate trustworthiness*—the extent to which a company is seen as motivated to be honest, dependable, and sensitive to customer needs.

- *Corporate likability*—the extent to which a company is seen as likable, attractive, prestigious, dynamic, and so on.

In other words, a credible firm is good at what it does; it keeps its customers' best interests in mind and is enjoyable to work with.

Trust is the willingness of a firm to rely on a business partner. It depends on a number of interpersonal and interorganizational factors, such as the firm's perceived competence, integrity, honesty, and benevolence.

Personal interactions with employees of the firm, opinions about the company as a whole, and perceptions of trust will evolve with experience. A firm is more likely to be seen as trustworthy when it:

- Provides full, honest information

- Provides employees incentives that are aligned to meet with customer needs

- Partners with customers to help them learn and help themselves

- Offers valid comparisons with competitive products

Building trust can be especially tricky in online settings, and firms often impose more stringent requirements on their online business partners than on others. Business buyers worry that they won't get products of the right quality delivered to the right place at the right time. Sellers worry about getting paid on time—or at all—and how much credit they should extend. Some firms, such as transportation and supply chain management company Ryder System, use automated credit-checking applications and online trust services to determine the creditworthiness of trading partners.

Sources: Bob Violino, "Building B2B Trust," *Computerworld*, June 17, 2002, p. 32; Richard E. Plank, David A. Reid, and Ellen Bolman Pullins, "Perceived Trust in Business-to-Business Sales: A New Measure," *Journal of Personal Selling and Sales Management* 19, no. 3 (Summer 1999), pp. 61–72; Kevin Lane Keller and David A. Aaker, "Corporate-Level Marketing: The Impact of Credibility on a Company's Brand Extensions," *Corporate Reputation Review* 1 (August 1998), pp. 356–78; Robert M. Morgan and Shelby D. Hunt, "The Commitment–Trust Theory of Relationship Marketing," *Journal of Marketing* 58, no. 3 (July 1994), pp. 20–38; Christine Moorman, Rohit Deshpande, and Gerald Zaltman, "Factors Affecting Trust in Market Research Relationships," *Journal of Marketing* 57 (January 1993), pp. 81–101; Glen Urban, "Where Are You Positioned on the Trust Dimensions?" *Don't Just Relate-Advocate: A Blueprint for Profit in the Era of Customer Power* (Upper Saddle River, NJ: Pearson Education/Wharton School Publishers, 2005).

7. *Mutually adaptive*—Buyers and sellers make many relationship-specific adaptations, but without necessarily achieving strong trust or cooperation.
8. *Customer is king*—In this close, cooperative relationship, the seller adapts to meet the customer's needs without expecting much adaptation or change in exchange.

Over time, however, relationship roles may shift or be activated under different circumstances.[59] Some needs can be satisfied with fairly basic supplier performance. Buyers then neither want nor require a close relationship with a supplier. Likewise, some suppliers may not find it worth their while to invest in customers with limited growth potential.

One study found the closest relationships between customers and suppliers arose when the supply was important to the customer and there were procurement obstacles, such as complex purchase requirements and few alternate suppliers.[60] Another study suggested that greater vertical coordination between buyer and seller through information exchange and planning is usually necessary only when high environmental uncertainty exists and specific investments (described next) are modest.[61]

Business Relationships: Risks and Opportunism

Researchers have noted that establishing a customer–supplier relationship creates tension between safeguarding (ensuring predictable solutions) and adaptation (allowing for flexibility for unanticipated events). Vertical coordination can facilitate stronger customer–seller ties but at the same time may increase the risk to the customer's and supplier's specific investments. *Specific investments* are those expenditures tailored to a particular company and value chain partner (investments in company-specific training, equipment, and operating procedures or systems).[62] They help firms grow profits and achieve their positioning.[63] Xerox worked closely with its suppliers to develop customized processes and components that reduced its copier manufacturing costs by 30 percent to 40 percent. In return, suppliers received sales and volume guarantees, an enhanced understanding of their customer's needs, and a strong position with Xerox for future sales.[64]

Specific investments, however, also entail considerable risk to both customer and supplier. Transaction theory from economics maintains that because these investments are partially sunk, they lock firms into a particular relationship. Sensitive cost and process information may need to be exchanged. A buyer may be vulnerable to holdup because of switching costs; a supplier may be more vulnerable because it has dedicated assets and/or technology/knowledge at stake. In terms of the latter risk, consider the following example.[65]

> An automobile component manufacturer wins a contract to supply an under-hood component to an original equipment manufacturer (OEM). A one-year, sole-source contract safeguards the supplier's OEM-specific investments in a dedicated production line. However, the supplier may also be obliged to work (noncontractually) as a partner with the OEM's internal engineering staff, using linked computing facilities to exchange detailed engineering information and coordinate frequent design and manufacturing changes over the term of the contract. These interactions could reduce costs and/or increase quality by improving the firm's responsiveness to marketplace changes. But they could also magnify the threat to the supplier's intellectual property.

When buyers cannot easily monitor supplier performance, the supplier might shirk or cheat and not deliver the expected value. *Opportunism* is "some form of cheating or undersupply relative to an implicit or explicit contract."[66] It may entail blatant self-serving and deliberate misrepresentation that violates contractual agreements. In creating the 1996 version of the Ford Taurus, Ford Corporation chose to outsource the whole process to one supplier, Lear Corporation. Lear committed to a contract that, for various reasons, it knew it was unable to fulfill. According to Ford, Lear missed deadlines, failed to meet weight and price objectives, and furnished parts that did not work.[67] A more passive form of opportunism might be a refusal or unwillingness to adapt to changing circumstances.

Opportunism is a concern because firms must devote resources to control and monitoring that they could otherwise allocate to more productive purposes. Contracts may become inadequate to govern supplier transactions when supplier opportunism becomes difficult to detect, when firms make specific investments in assets they cannot use elsewhere, and when contingencies are harder to anticipate. Customers and suppliers are more likely to form a joint venture (instead of signing a simple contract) when the supplier's degree of asset specificity is high, monitoring the supplier's behavior is difficult, and the supplier has a poor reputation.[68] When a supplier has a good reputation, it is more likely to avoid opportunism to protect this valuable intangible asset.

The presence of a significant future time horizon and/or strong solidarity norms typically causes customers and suppliers to strive for joint benefits. Their specific investments shift from expropriation (increased opportunism on the receiver's part) to bonding (reduced opportunism).[69]

New Technology and Business Customers

Top firms are comfortable using technology to improve the way they do business with their business-to-business customers. Here are some examples of how they are redesigning Web sites, improving search results, leveraging e-mails, engaging in social media, and launching Webinars and podcasts to improve their business performance.

- Chapman Kelly provides audit and other cost containment products to help firms reduce their health care and insurance costs. The company originally tried to acquire new customers through traditional cold calling and outbound selling techniques. After it redesigned its Web site and optimized the site's search engine so the company's name moved close to the top of relevant online searches, revenue nearly doubled.[70]
- Hewlett-Packard launched a "Technology at Work" e-mail newsletter to focus on retention of its current customers. The newsletter's content and format were based on in-depth research to find out what customers wanted. Hewlett-Packard measures the effects of the newsletter carefully and found that e-mailing product updates helped avoid inbound service calls, saving millions of dollars.[71]

Health care cost-containment service provider Chapman Kelly finds its online marketing efforts have provided bottom-line rewards.

- Emerson Process Management makes automation systems for chemical plants, oil refineries, and other types of factories. The company blog about factory automation is visited by thousand of readers who like to hear and swap factory war stories. It attracts 35,000 to 40,000 regular visitors each month, generating five to seven leads a week. Given that the systems sell for up to millions, ROI on the blog investment is immense.[72]
- Machinery manufacturer Makino builds relationships with end-user customers by hosting an ongoing series of industry-specific Webinars, producing an average of three a month. The company uses highly specialized content, such as how to get the most out of machine tools and how metal-cutting processes work, to appeal to different industries and different styles of manufacturing. Makino's database created from Webinar participants has allowed the firm to cut marketing costs and improve its effectiveness and efficiency.[73]
- Acquired by IBM in January 2008, Cognos provides business intelligence and performance management software and services to help companies manage their financial and operational performance. To increase their visibility and improve customer relations, Cognos launched BI radio, an RSS-enabled series of 30-minute podcasts released every six weeks addressing a range of topics such as marketing, leadership, business management, and "killer apps." Attracting 60,000 subscribers, the podcasts are thought to have directly or indirectly led to $7 million in deals.[74]

Institutional and Government Markets

Our discussion has concentrated largely on the buying behavior of profit-seeking companies. Much of what we have said also applies to the buying practices of institutional and government organizations. However, we want to highlight certain special features of these markets.

The **institutional market** consists of schools, hospitals, nursing homes, prisons, and other institutions that must provide goods and services to people in their care. Many of these organizations are characterized by low budgets and captive clienteles. For example, hospitals must decide what quality of food to buy for patients. The buying objective here is not profit, because the food is provided as part of the total service package; nor is cost minimization the sole objective, because poor food will cause patients to complain and hurt the hospital's reputation. The hospital purchasing agent must search for institutional-food vendors whose quality meets or exceeds a certain minimum standard and whose prices are low. In fact, many food vendors set up a separate sales division to cater to institutional buyers' special needs and characteristics. Heinz produces, packages, and prices its ketchup differently to meet the requirements of hospitals, colleges, and prisons. ARAMARK, which provides food services for stadiums, arenas, campuses, businesses, and schools, also has a competitive advantage in providing food for the nation's prisons, a direct result of refining its purchasing practices and supply chain management.

ARAMARK   Where ARAMARK once merely selected products from lists provided by potential suppliers, it now collaborates with suppliers to develop products customized to meet the needs of individual segments. In the corrections segment, quality has historically been sacrificed to meet food cost limits that operators outside the market would find impossible to work with. "When you go after business in the corrections field, you are making bids that are measured in hundredths of a cent," says John Zillmer, president of ARAMARK's Food & Support Services, "so any edge we can gain on the purchasing side is extremely valuable." ARAMARK sourced a series of protein products with unique partners at price points it never could have imagined before. These partners were unique because they understood the chemistry of proteins and knew how to lower the price while still creating a product acceptable to ARAMARK's customers, allowing ARAMARK to drive down costs. Then ARAMARK replicated this process with 163 different items formulated exclusively for corrections. Rather than reducing food costs by 1 cent or so a meal as usual, ARAMARK took 5 to 9 cents off—while maintaining or even improving quality.[75]

In most countries, government organizations are a major buyer of goods and services. They typically require suppliers to submit bids and often award the contract to the lowest bidder. In some cases, they will make allowance for superior quality or a reputation for completing contracts on time. Governments will also buy on a negotiated contract basis, primarily in complex projects with major R&D costs and risks and those where there is little competition.

A major complaint of multinationals operating in Europe is that each country shows favoritism toward its nationals despite superior offers from foreign firms. Although such practices are fairly entrenched, the European Union is attempting to remove this bias.

Because their spending decisions are subject to public review, government organizations require considerable paperwork from suppliers, who often complain about bureaucracy, regulations, decision-making delays, and frequent shifts in procurement staff. But the fact remains that the U.S. government bought goods and services valued at $220 billion in fiscal year 2009, making it the largest and therefore most potentially attractive customer in the world.

It is not just the dollar figure that is large, but the number of individual acquisitions. According to the General Services Administration Procurement Data Center, over 20 million individual contract actions are processed every year. Although most items purchased cost between $2,500 and $25,000, the government also makes purchases in the billions, many in technology.

Government decision makers often think vendors have not done their homework. Different types of agencies—defense, civilian, intelligence—have different needs, priorities, purchasing styles, and time frames. In addition, vendors do not pay enough attention to cost justification, a major activity for government procurement professionals. Companies hoping to be government contractors need to help government agencies see the bottom-line impact of products. Demonstrating useful experience and successful past performance through case studies, especially with other government organizations, can be influential.[76]

Just as companies provide government agencies with guidelines about how best to purchase and use their products, governments provide would-be suppliers with detailed guidelines describing how to sell to the government. Failure to follow the guidelines or to fill out forms and contracts correctly can create a legal nightmare.[77]

Fortunately for businesses of all sizes, the federal government has been trying to simplify the contracting procedure and make bidding more attractive. Reforms place more emphasis on buying off-the-shelf items instead of items built to the government's specs, communicating with vendors online to eliminate the massive paperwork, and giving vendors who lose a bid a "debriefing" from the appropriate government agency to increase their chances of winning the next time around.[78] More purchasing is being done online via Web-based forms, digital signatures, and electronic procurement cards (P-cards).[79] Several federal agencies that act as purchasing agents for the rest of the government have launched Web-based catalogs that allow authorized defense and civilian agencies to buy everything from medical and office supplies to clothing online. The General Services Administration, for example, not only sells stocked merchandise through its Web site but also creates direct links between buyers and contract suppliers. A good starting point for any work with the U.S. government is to make sure the company is in the Central Contractor Registration (CCR) database (www.ccr.gov), which collects, validates, stores, and disseminates data in support of agency acquisitions.[80]

In spite of these reforms, for a number of reasons many companies that sell to the government have not used a marketing orientation. Some, though, have pursued government business by establishing separate government marketing departments. Companies such as Gateway, Rockwell, Kodak, and Goodyear anticipate government needs and projects, participate in the product specification phase, gather competitive intelligence, prepare bids carefully, and produce strong communications to describe and enhance their companies' reputations.

Summary

1. Organizational buying is the decision-making process by which formal organizations establish the need for purchased products and services, then identify, evaluate, and choose among alternative brands and suppliers. The business market consists of all the organizations that acquire goods and services used in the production of other products or services that are sold, rented, or supplied to others.

2. Compared to consumer markets, business markets generally have fewer and larger buyers, a closer customer supplier relationship, and more geographically concentrated buyers. Demand in the business market is derived from demand in the consumer market and fluctuates with the business cycle. Nonetheless, the total demand for many business goods and services is quite price inelastic. Business marketers need to be aware of the role of professional purchasers and their influencers, the need for multiple sales calls, and the importance of direct purchasing, reciprocity, and leasing.

3. The buying center is the decision-making unit of a buying organization. It consists of initiators, users, influencers, deciders, approvers, buyers, and gatekeepers. To influence these parties, marketers must be aware of environmental, organizational, interpersonal, and individual factors.

4. The buying process consists of eight stages called buyphases: (1) problem recognition, (2) general need description, (3) product specification, (4) supplier search, (5) proposal solicitation, (6) supplier selection, (7) order-routine specification, and (8) performance review.

5. Business marketers must form strong bonds and relationships with their customers and provide them added value. Some customers, however, may prefer a transactional relationship. Technology is aiding the development of strong business relationships.

6. The institutional market consists of schools, hospitals, nursing homes, prisons, and other institutions that provide goods and services to people in their care. Buyers for government organizations tend to require a great deal of paperwork from their vendors and to favor open bidding and domestic companies. Suppliers must be prepared to adapt their offers to the special needs and procedures found in institutional and government markets.

Applications

Marketing Debate
How Different Is Business-to-Business Marketing?

Many business-to-business marketing executives lament the challenges of business-to-business marketing, maintaining that many traditional marketing concepts and principles do not apply. For a number of reasons, they assert that selling products and services to a company is fundamentally different from selling to individuals. Others disagree, claiming marketing theory is still valid and only requires some adaptation in marketing tactics.

Take a position: Business-to-business marketing requires a special, unique set of marketing concepts and principles *versus* Business-to-business marketing is really not that different, and the basic marketing concepts and principles apply.

Marketing Discussion
B-to-C & B-to-B Concepts

Consider some of the consumer behavior topics for business-to-consumer (B-to-C) marketing from Chapter 6. How might you apply them to business-to-business (B-to-B) settings? For example, how might noncompensatory models of choice work? Mental accounting?

Marketing Excellence

>>Accenture

Accenture began in 1942 as Administrative Accounting Group, the consulting arm of accounting firm Arthur Andersen. In 1989, it launched as a separate business unit focused on IT consulting and bearing the name Andersen Consulting. At that time, though it was earning $1 billion annually, Andersen Consulting had low brand awareness among information technology consultancies and was commonly mistaken for its accounting corpo- rate parent. To build its brand and separate itself from the accounting firm, Andersen Consulting launched the first large-scale advertising campaign in the professional services area. By the end of the decade, it was the world's largest management and technology consulting organization.

In 2000, following arbitration against its former parent, Andersen Consulting was granted its full independence from Arthur Andersen—but it had to relinquish the Andersen name. Andersen Consulting was given three months to find a name that was able to be trademarked in 47 countries, effective and inoffensive in over 200 languages, and acceptable to employees and clients—*and* that corresponded with an available URL. The effort that followed was one of the largest—and most successful— rebranding campaigns in corporate history.

As luck would have it, the company's new name came from a consultant at the company's Oslo office, who submitted "Accenture" as part of an internal name-generation initiative dubbed "Brandstorming." The consultant coined the Accenture name because it rhymed with "adventure" and connoted an "accent on the future." The name also retained the "Ac" of the original Andersen Consulting name (echoing the Ac.com Web site), which would help the firm retain some of its former brand equity. On midnight, December 31, 2000, Andersen Consulting officially adopted the Accenture name and launched a global marketing campaign targeting senior executives at

Accenture's clients and prospects, all Accenture partners and employees, the media, leading industry analysts, potential recruits, and academia.

The results of the advertising, marketing, and communications campaigns were quick and impressive. Overall, Accenture's brand equity increased 11 percent, and the number of firms inquiring about its services increased 350 percent. Awareness of Accenture's breadth and depth of services achieved 96 percent of its previous level. Globally, awareness of Accenture as a provider of management and technology consulting services was 76 percent of levels for the former Andersen Consulting name. These results enabled Accenture to successfully complete a $1.7 billion IPO in July 2001.

In 2002, Accenture unveiled a new positioning to reflect its new role as a partner to aid execution of strategy, summarized succinctly by the tagline "Innovation Delivered." This tagline was supported by the statement, "From innovation to execution, Accenture helps accelerate your vision." Accenture surveyed senior executives from different industries and countries and confirmed that they saw inability to execute and deliver on ideas as the number one barrier to success.

Accenture saw its differentiator as the ability both to provide innovative ideas—ideas grounded in business processes as well as IT—and to execute them. Competitors such as McKinsey were seen as highly specialized at developing strategy, whereas other competitors such as IBM were seen as highly skilled in technological implementation. Accenture wanted to be seen as excelling at both. As Ian Watmore, its UK chief, explained: "Unless you can provide both transformational consulting and outsourcing capability, you're not going to win. Clients expect both."

In 2002, the business climate changed. After the dot-com crash and the economic downturn, innovation was no longer enough. Executives wanted bottom-line results. As part of its new commitment to helping clients achieve their business objectives, Accenture introduced a policy whereby many of its contracts contained incentives that it realized only if specific business targets were met. For instance, a contract with British travel agent Thomas Cook was structured such that Accenture's bonus depended on five metrics, including a cost-cutting one.

In late 2003, Accenture built upon the "Innovation Delivered" theme and announced its new tagline, "High Performance. Delivered," along with a campaign that featured golf superstar Tiger Woods as spokesperson. When Accenture sought Woods out, the athlete was at the top of his game—the world's best golfer with an impeccable image. What better symbol for high performance? Accenture's message communicated that it could help

client companies become "high-performing business leaders," and the Woods endorsement drove home the importance of high performance.

Over the next six years, Accenture spent nearly $300 million in ads that mostly featured Tiger Woods, alongside slogans such as "We know what it takes to be a Tiger" and "Go on. Be a Tiger." The campaign capitalized on Woods's international appeal, ran all over the world, and became the central focus of Accenture-sponsored events such as the World Golf Championships and the Chicago Marathon.

That all changed when the scandal surrounding Tiger Woods, his extramarital affairs, and his indefinite absence from golf hit the press in late 2009. Accenture dropped Woods as a spokesperson, saying he was no longer a good fit for its brand. Indeed, focus groups showed that consumers were too distracted by the scandal to focus on Accenture's strategic message. Accenture quickly searched for a new concept that not only resonated across the world, translated appropriately into different cultures, but also cut its ties with Woods.

The result came after the firm dusted off some previous concepts, tested them with focus groups of business professionals, and launched a $50 million campaign featuring animals and the same slogan, "High Performance. Delivered." In one ad, an elephant is pictured surfing alongside copy that reads, "Who says you can't be big and nimble?" In a later ad, a lizard tries to catch a butterfly by transforming its tongue into the design of a flower. The copy stated, "If you innovate, they will come."

Today, Accenture continues to excel as a global management consulting, technology services, and outsourcing company. Its clients include 99 of the *Fortune* Global 100 and more than three-quarters of the *Fortune* Global 500. The company ended fiscal 2009 with revenues of $21.5 billion.

Questions

1. What has Accenture done well to target its B-to-B audience?

2. Has Accenture done the right thing by dropping Tiger Woods as its spokesperson? Discuss the pros and cons of its decision.

Sources: "Annual Reports," *Accenture.com*; "Lessons Learned from Top Firms' Marketing Blunders," *Management Consultant International*, December 2003, p. 1; Sean Callahan, "Tiger Tees Off in New Accenture Campaign," *BtoB Magazine*, October 13, 2003, p. 3; "Inside Accenture's Biggest UK Client," *Management Consultant International*, October 2003, pp. 1–3; "Accenture's Results Highlight Weakness of Consulting Market," *Management Consultant International*, October 2003, pp. 8–10; "Accenture Re-Branding Wins UK Plaudits," *Management Consultant International*, October 2002, p. 5; Mary Ellen Podmolik, "Accenture Turns to Tiger for Global Marketing Effort," *BtoB Magazine*, October 25, 2004; Sean Callahan, "Tiger Tees Off in New Accenture Campaign," *BtoB Magazine*, October 13, 2003; Emily Steel, "After Ditching Tiger, Accenture Tries New Game," *Wall Street Journal*, January 14, 2010.

Marketing Excellence

>>GE

General Electric (GE) is made up of five major divisions that operate in a wide range of industries: Energy (Energy, Oil & Gas, Water and Process Technologies), Technology Infrastructure (Aviation, Enterprise Solutions, Healthcare, Transportation), GE Capital (Commercial Lending & Leasing, Consumer Financing, Energy Financial Services, GE Capital Aviation Services, Real Estate Financing), NBC Commercial (Cable, Film, Networks, Parks & Resorts), and Consumer & Industrial (Appliances, Consumer Electronics, Electrical Distribution, Lighting). As a result, GE sells a diverse array of products and services from home appliances to jet engines, security systems, wind turbines, and financial services. GE's revenues topped $161 billion in 2009, making it so large that if each of its five business units were ranked separately, they all would appear in the *Fortune* 200. If GE were its own country, it would be the 50th largest in the world, ahead of Kuwait, New Zealand, and Iraq.

Thomas Edison originally founded the company as the Edison Electric Light Company in 1878. The company, which soon changed its name to General Electric, became an early pioneer in lightbulbs and electrical appliances and served the electrical needs of various industries, such as transportation, utilities, manufacturing, and broadcasting. GE became the acknowledged pioneer in business-to-business marketing in the 1950s and 1960s under the tagline "Progress Is Our Most Important Product."

As the company diversified its business-to-business product lines in the 1970s and 1980s, it created new corporate campaigns, including "Progress for People" and "We Bring Good Things to Life." In 1981, Jack Welch succeeded Reginald Jones as GE's eighth CEO. Over Welch's two decades of leadership, he helped grow GE from an "American manufacturer into a global services giant," and increased the company's market value from $12 billion in 1981 to $280 billion in 2001, making it the world's most valuable corporation at the time.

In 2003, GE and the company's new CEO, Jeffrey Immelt, faced a fresh challenge; how to promote its diversified brand with a unified global message. After extensive consumer research, the company launched a major new campaign called "Imagination at Work," which highlighted its renewed focus on innovation and new technology. The award-winning campaign promoted units such as GE Aircraft Engines, GE Medical Systems, and GE Plastics, focusing on the breadth of GE's product offerings. GE initially spent over $150 million on corporate advertising, a significant expenditure but one that created efficiencies by focusing on the core GE brand. The goal was to unify these divisions under the GE brand while giving them a voice. "When you're a company like ours, with 11 different businesses, brand is really important in pulling the identity of the company together," said former Chief Marketing Officer Beth Comstock. "Integration was important in communicating the brand across the organization and to all of our constituents."

The new integrated campaign got results. "Research indicates GE is now being associated with attributes such as being high tech, leading edge, innovative, contemporary, and creative," stated Judy Hu, GE's general manager for global advertising and branding. In addition, survey respondents continued to associate GE with some of its traditional attributes, including trust and reliability.

In 2005, the company extended the campaign with its next initiative, "Ecomagination," which highlighted the company's efforts to develop environmentally friendly "green" technologies such as solar energy, lower-emission engines, and water purification technologies. The company leveraged the "Imagination" tagline again with a 2006 campaign called "Health Care Re-Imagined" that featured innovative GE health care products for detecting, preventing, and curing diseases.

Immelt made some strategic restructuring decisions that helped the company survive the worldwide recession of 2008 and 2009 and also helped shift it even more in the B2B direction. GE moved from 11 divisions to 5 and sold off some of its consumer-focused businesses, including 51 percent of NBC Universal (sold to Comcast). This shift allowed GE to spend more resources on innovation, green initiatives, and its growing businesses such as power generation, aviation, medical-imaging, and cell technologies. GE continued to use the Ecomagination campaign and introduced "Healthymagination," which communicated its advances in medical technologies around the world.

GE's recent corporate campaigns have united its business units, but its success rests on its ability to understand the business market and the business buying process, putting itself in the shoes of its business customers. Consider its approach to pricing its aircraft engines. GE knows that purchasing an aircraft engine is a multimillion-dollar expenditure, and one that doesn't end with the purchase. Customers (the airlines) face substantial maintenance costs to meet FAA guidelines and ensure reliability of the engines. So in 1999, GE pioneered a new pricing option called "Power by the Hour." This concept gives customers an opportunity to pay a fixed fee each time they run the engine. In return, GE performs all the maintenance and guarantees the engine's reliability. When demand for air travel is uncertain, "Power by the Hour" provides GE's customers with a lower cost of ownership.

This kind of B-to-B marketing savvy has helped GE cement its top position in the *Financial Times*'s "World's Most Respected Companies" survey for years. Its understanding of the business markets, its way of doing business, and its brand marketing have kept GE's brand equity growing. Indeed, its brand equity was ranked fourth and valued at $48 billion in the 2009 Interbrand/*BusinessWeek* ranking of the "Top 100 Global Brands." "The GE brand is what connects us all and makes us so much better than the parts," Chief Marketing Officer Comstock said.

Questions

1. Discuss the importance of B-to-B marketing and a strong B-to-B brand to GE.

2. Have "Imagination at Work," "Ecomagination," and "Healthymagination" successfully communicated GE's focus on its newer endeavors? Why or why not?

Sources: Geoffrey Colvin, "What Makes GE Great?" *Fortune*, March 6, 2006, pp. 90–104; Thomas A. Stewart, "Growth as a Process," *Harvard Business Review*, June 2006, pp. 60–70; Kathryn Kranhold, "The Immelt Era, Five Years Old, Transforms GE," *Wall Street Journal*, September 11, 2006; Daniel Fisher, "GE Turns Green," *Forbes*, August 15, 2005, pp. 80– 85; John A. Byrne, "Jeff Immelt," *Fast Company*, July 2005, pp. 60–65; Rachel Layne, "GE's NBC Sale Brings Immelt Cash, Scrutiny," *BusinessWeek*, December 3, 2009.

Chapter 8

In This Chapter, We Will Address the Following Questions

1. What are the different levels of market segmentation?

2. In what ways can a company divide a market into segments?

3. What are the requirements for effective segmentation?

4. How should business markets be segmented?

5. How should a company choose the most attractive target markets?

Club Med has gone upscale to target new market segments.

Identifying Market Segments and Targets

Companies cannot connect with all customers in large, broad, or diverse markets. But they can divide such markets into groups of consumers or segments with distinct needs and wants. A company then needs to identify which market segments it can serve effectively. This decision requires a keen understanding of consumer behavior and careful strategic thinking. To develop the best marketing plans, managers need to understand what makes each segment unique and different. Identifying and satisfying the right market segments is often the key to marketing success.

One of the most famous leisure travel brands in the world, France's Club Méditerranée, better known as Club Med, has targeted several different customer groups through the years. Started in 1950 and long a pioneer in the concept of the all-inclusive resort, Club Med originally used exotic locations, bare-bones accommodations, and the advertising theme "The antidote to civilization" to target singles, young couples, and others seeking sea, sand, and a good time. Rooms did not have phones, TVs, fans, or locks on the doors. To transcend its hedonistic image and broaden its clientele, Club Med decided to add family-friendly resort locations and services in the 1970s. Depending on location, the resorts, known as villages, offer a wide range of activities, from flying-trapeze clinics to body building to snow skiing. Club Med staff are called "GOs," or Gentil Organisateurs ("gracious/nice organizers"); clients are called "GMs," or Gentils Membres ("gracious/nice guests/members"). An informal atmosphere has GOs and GMs dining, drinking, dancing, and playing together.

An attempt to move outside the leisure-travel business to become a broader services company proved ill-fated; a series of urban bar/restaurants flopped. Combined with a post-9/11 economic recession and increased competition, the failure left Club Med reeling in 2001–2002. Under the new leadership of Henri Giscard d'Estaing (son of the former president of France), the company invested hundreds of millions of dollars to move upscale and attract wealthier customers by crafting a more sophisticated image. For the firm's 60th anniversary in 2010, advertising proclaimed that Club Med was "Where Happiness Means the World," which was backed by an extensive online marketing effort.[1]

To compete more effectively, many companies are now embracing target marketing. Instead of scattering their marketing efforts, they're focusing on those consumers they have the greatest chance of satisfying.

Effective target marketing requires that marketers:

1. Identify and profile distinct groups of buyers who differ in their needs and wants (market segmentation).
2. Select one or more market segments to enter (market targeting).
3. For each target segment, establish and communicate the distinctive benefit(s) of the company's market offering (market positioning).

This chapter will focus on the first two steps. After reviewing some important branding concepts in Chapter 9, Chapter 10 discusses the third step, market positioning.

Bases for Segmenting Consumer Markets

Market segmentation divides a market into well-defined slices. A *market segment* consists of a group of customers who share a similar set of needs and wants. The marketer's task is to identify the appropriate number and nature of market segments and decide which one(s) to target.

We use two broad groups of variables to segment consumer markets. Some researchers try to define segments by looking at descriptive characteristics: geographic, demographic, and psychographic. Then they examine whether these customer segments exhibit different needs or product responses. For example, they might examine the differing attitudes of "professionals," "blue collars," and other groups toward, say, "safety" as a product benefit.

Other researchers try to define segments by looking at behavioral considerations, such as consumer responses to benefits, usage occasions, or brands. The researcher then sees whether different characteristics are associated with each consumer-response segment. For example, do people who want "quality" rather than "low price" in an automobile differ in their geographic, demographic, and psychographic makeup?

Regardless of which type of segmentation scheme we use, the key is adjusting the marketing program to recognize customer differences. The major segmentation variables—geographic, demographic, psychographic, and behavioral segmentation—are summarized in 🔲 Table 8.1.

Geographic Segmentation

Geographic segmentation divides the market into geographical units such as nations, states, regions, counties, cities, or neighborhoods. The company can operate in one or a few areas, or it can operate in all but pay attention to local variations. In that way it can tailor marketing programs to the needs and wants of local customer groups in trading areas, neighborhoods, even individual stores. In a growing trend called *grassroots marketing,* such activities concentrate on getting as close and personally relevant to individual customers as possible.

Much of Nike's initial success comes from engaging target consumers through grassroots marketing efforts such as sponsorship of local school teams, expert-conducted clinics, and provision of shoes, clothing, and equipment. Citibank provides different mixes of banking services in its branches depending on neighborhood demographics. Curves, an exercise chain aimed at middle-aged women, places paper bags where consumers can place a form asking for more information about Curves in local businesses such as ice cream shops, pizza parlors, and other places where guilt can strike the weight-conscious shopper. Retail firms such as Starbucks, Costco, Trader Joe's, and REI have all found great success emphasizing local marketing initiatives, but other types of firms have also jumped into action.[2]

Bed Bath & Beyond   Home furnishing retailer Bed Bath & Beyond's ability to cater to local tastes has fueled its phenomenal growth. The firm's managers pick 70 percent of their own merchandise, and this fierce local focus has helped the chain evolve from bed linens to the "beyond" part—products from picture frames and pot holders to imported olive oil and designer doormats. In Manhattan stores, for instance, managers are beginning to stock wall paint. You won't find paint in suburban stores, where customers can go to Home Depot or Lowe's. One manager says several customers have been surprised to find out the store is part of a national chain and not a mom-and-pop operation. For Bed Bath & Beyond, that's the ultimate compliment.[3] 🔲

More and more, regional marketing means marketing right down to a specific zip code.[4] Many companies use mapping software to pinpoint the geographic locations of their customers, learning, say, that most customers are within a 10-mile radius of the store and are further concentrated within certain zip+4 areas. By mapping the densest areas, the retailer can rely on *customer cloning,* assuming the best prospects live where most of the customers already come from.

TABLE 8.I	Major Segmentation Variables for Consumer Markets
Geographic region	Pacific Mountain, West North Central, West South Central, East North Central, East South Central, South Atlantic, Middle Atlantic, New England
City or metro size	Under 5,000; 5,000–20,000; 20,000–50,000; 50,000–100,000; 100,000–250,000; 250,000–500,000; 500,000–1,000,000; 1,000,000–4,000,000; 4,000,000+
Density	Urban, suburban, rural
Climate	Northern, southern
Demographic age	Under 6, 6–11, 12–17, 18–34, 35–49, 50–64, 64+
Family size	1–2, 3–4, 5+
Family life cycle	Young, single; young, married, no children; young, married, youngest child under 6; young; married, youngest child 6 or older; older, married, with children; older, married, no children under 18; older, single; other
Gender	Male, female
Income	Under $10,000; $10,000–$15,000; $15,000–$20,000; $20,000–$30,000; $30,000–$50,000; $50,000–$100,000; $100,000+
Occupation	Professional and technical; managers, officials, and proprietors; clerical sales; craftspeople; forepersons; operatives; farmers; retired; students; homemakers; unemployed
Education	Grade school or less; some high school; high school graduate; some college; college graduate
Religion	Catholic, Protestant, Jewish, Muslim, Hindu, other
Race	White, Black, Asian, Hispanic
Generation	Silent Generation, Baby boomers, Gen X, Gen Y
Nationality	North American, Latin American, British, French, German, Italian, Chinese, Indian, Japanese
Social class	Lower lowers, upper lowers, working class, middle class, upper middles, lower uppers, upper uppers
Psychographic lifestyle	Culture-oriented, sports-oriented, outdoor-oriented
Personality	Compulsive, gregarious, authoritarian, ambitious
Behavioral occasions	Regular occasion, special occasion
Benefits	Quality, service, economy, speed
User status	Nonuser, ex-user, potential user, first-time user, regular user
Usage rate	Light user, medium user, heavy user
Loyalty status	None, medium, strong, absolute
Readiness stage	Unaware, aware, informed interested, desirous, intending to buy
Attitude toward product	Enthusiastic, positive, indifferent, negative, hostile

Some approaches combine geographic data with demographic data to yield even richer descriptions of consumers and neighborhoods. Nielsen Claritas has developed a geoclustering approach called PRIZM (Potential Rating Index by Zip Markets) NE that classifies over half a million U.S. residential neighborhoods into 14 distinct groups and 66 distinct lifestyle segments called PRIZM Clusters.[5] The groupings take into consideration 39 factors in five broad categories: (1) education and affluence, (2) family life cycle, (3) urbanization, (4) race and ethnicity, and (5) mobility. The neighborhoods are broken down by zip code, zip+4, or census tract and block group. The clusters have descriptive titles such as *Blue Blood Estates, Winner's Circle, Hometown Retired, Shotguns and Pickups,* and *Back Country Folks.* The inhabitants in a cluster tend to lead similar lives, drive similar cars, have similar jobs, and read similar magazines. Table 8.2 has examples of four PRIZM clusters.

Marketers can use PRIZM to answer questions such as: Which geographic areas (neighborhoods or zip codes) contain our most valuable customers? How deeply have we already penetrated these segments? Which distribution channels and promotional media work best in reaching our target clusters in each area? Geoclustering captures the increasing diversity of the U.S. population.

TABLE 8.2	Examples of PRIZM clusters

- **Young Digerati.** Young Digerati are the nation's tech-savvy singles and couples living in fashionable neighborhoods on the urban fringe. Affluent, highly educated, and ethnically mixed, they live in areas typically filled with trendy apartments and condos, fitness clubs and clothing boutiques, casual restaurants, and all types of bars—from juice to coffee to microbrew.

- **Beltway Boomers.** One segment of the huge baby boomer cohort—college-educated, upper-middle-class, and home-owning—is Beltway Boomers. Like many of their peers who married late, these boomers are still raising children in comfortable suburban subdivisions and pursuing kid-centered lifestyles.

- **The Cosmopolitans.** Educated, midscale, and multiethnic, The Cosmopolitans are urbane couples in America's fast-growing cities. Concentrated in a handful of metros—such as Las Vegas, Miami, and Albuquerque—these households feature older home owners, empty nesters, and college graduates. A vibrant social scene surrounds their older homes and apartments, and residents love the nightlife and enjoy leisure-intensive lifestyles.

- **Old Milltowns.** Once-thriving mining and manufacturing towns have aged—as have the residents in Old Milltowns communities. Today, the majority of residents are retired singles and couples, living on downscaled incomes in pre-1960 homes and apartments. For leisure, they enjoy gardening, sewing, socializing at veterans clubs, and eating out at casual restaurants.

Source: *Nielsen*, www.claritas.com.

A number of organizations have applied this service to their marketing. The U.S. Army uses a custom Claritas system to help in recruiting. Sodexho Marriott uses a system to select menu offerings for its nationwide college food program. Wendy's and PETCO rely on Claritas to help decide where to put new stores. When Ace Hardware launched a customer loyalty program called the Helpful Hardware Club a few years ago, it assigned a Claritas cluster code to every one of the 7 million members. When Ace found that 12 clusters generated most of its business, it targeted them with specific promotions.[6]

Marketing to microsegments has become possible even for small organizations as database costs decline, software becomes easier to use, and data integration increases.[7] Those who favor such localized marketing see national advertising as wasteful because it is too "arm's length" and fails to address local needs. Those against local marketing argue that it drives up manufacturing and marketing costs by reducing economies of scale and magnifying logistical problems. A brand's overall image might be diluted if the product and message are different in different localities.

Demographic Segmentation

In demographic segmentation, we divide the market on variables such as age, family size, family life cycle, gender, income, occupation, education, religion, race, generation, nationality, and social class. One reason demographic variables are so popular with marketers is that they're often associated with consumer needs and wants. Another is that they're easy to measure. Even when we describe the target market in nondemographic terms (say, by personality type), we may need the link back to demographic characteristics in order to estimate the size of the market and the media we should use to reach it efficiently.

Here's how marketers have used certain demographic variables to segment markets.

AGE AND LIFE-CYCLE STAGE Consumer wants and abilities change with age. Toothpaste brands such as Crest and Colgate offer three main lines of products to target kids, adults, and older consumers. Age segmentation can be even more refined. Pampers divides its market into prenatal, new baby (0–5 months), baby (6–12 months), toddler (13–23 months), and preschooler (24 months+). Indirect age effects also operate for some products. One study of kids aged 8–12 found that 91 percent decided or influenced clothing or apparel buys, 79 percent grocery purchases, and 54 percent vacation choices, while 14 percent even made or swayed vehicle decisions.[8]

Nevertheless, age and life cycle can be tricky variables.[9] The target market for some products may be the *psychologically* young. To target 21-year-olds with its boxy Element, which company officials described as a "dorm room on wheels," Honda ran ads depicting sexy college kids partying near the car at a beach. So many baby boomers were attracted to the ads, however, that the average age of Element buyers turned out to be 42! With baby boomers seeking to stay young, Honda decided the lines between age groups were getting blurred. When it was ready to launch a new subcompact called the Fit, the firm deliberately targeted Gen Y buyers as well as their empty-nest parents.

LIFE STAGE People in the same part of the life cycle may still differ in their life stage. **Life stage** defines a person's major concern, such as going through a divorce, going into a second marriage, taking care of an older parent, deciding to cohabit with another person, deciding to buy a new home, and so on. These life stages present opportunities for marketers who can help people cope with their major concerns.

GENDER Men and women have different attitudes and behave differently, based partly on genetic makeup and partly on socialization.[10] Women tend to be more communal-minded and men more self-expressive and goal-directed; women tend to take in more of the data in their immediate environment and men to focus on the part of the environment that helps them achieve a goal. A research study examining how men and women shop found that men often need to be invited to touch a product, whereas women are likely to pick it up without prompting. Men often like to read product information; women may relate to a product on a more personal level.[11]

According to some studies, women in the United States and the United Kingdom control or influence over 80 percent of consumer goods and services, make 75 percent of the decisions about buying new homes, and purchase outright 60 percent of new cars. Gender differentiation has long been applied in clothing, hairstyling, cosmetics, and magazines. Avon, for one, has built a $6 billion–plus business selling beauty products to women. Marketers can now reach women more easily via media like Lifetime, Oxygen, and WE television networks and scores of women's magazines and Web sites; men are more easily found at ESPN, Comedy Central, Fuel, and Spike TV channels and through magazines such as *Maxim* and *Men's Health*.[12]

Some traditionally more male-oriented markets, such as the automobile industry, are beginning to recognize gender segmentation and changing the way they design and sell cars.[13] Women shop differently for cars than men; they are more interested in environmental impact, care more about interior than exterior styling, and view safety in terms of features that help drivers survive an accident rather than help avoid one.[14]

Avon's marketing is laser-focused on women.

Lessons learned from its European customers have helped Victoria's Secret to successfully target women in North America and other markets.

Victoria's Secret

Victoria's Secret, purchased by Limited Brands in 1982, has become one of the most identifiable brands in retailing through skillful marketing of women's clothing, lingerie, and beauty products. Most U.S. women a generation ago did their underwear shopping in department stores and owned few items that could be considered "lingerie." After witnessing women buying expensive lingerie as fashion items from small boutiques in Europe, Limited Brands founder Leslie Wexner felt a similar store model could work on a mass scale in the United States, though it was unlike anything the average shopper would have encountered amid the bland racks at department stores. Wexner, however, had reason to believe U.S. women would relish the opportunity to have a European-style lingerie shopping experience. "Women need underwear, but women want lingerie," he observed. Wexner's assumption proved correct: A little more than a decade after he bought the business, Victoria's Secret's average customer bought 8 to 10 bras per year, compared with the national average

of two. To enhance its upscale reputation and glamorous appeal, the brand is endorsed by high-profile supermodels in ads and fashion shows. Through the years, Victoria's Secret has often delivered 25 percent or more annual sales growth, selling through its stores, catalogs, and company Web site, and posted $5.1 billion in revenues in 2008.[15]

INCOME Income segmentation is a long-standing practice in such categories as automobiles, clothing, cosmetics, financial services, and travel. However, income does not always predict the best customers for a given product. Blue-collar workers were among the first purchasers of color television sets; it was cheaper for them to buy these sets than to go to movies and restaurants.

Many marketers are deliberately going after lower-income groups, in some cases discovering fewer competitive pressures or greater consumer loyalty.[16] Procter & Gamble launched two discount-priced brand extensions in 2005—Bounty Basic and Charmin Basic—whose success led to the introduction in 2009 of Tide Basic, although this extension was later withdrawn from the market. At the same time other marketers are finding success with premium-priced products. When Whirlpool launched a pricey Duet washer line, sales doubled their forecasts in a weak economy, due primarily to middle-class shoppers who traded up.

Increasingly, companies are finding their markets are hourglass shaped as middle-market U.S. consumers migrate toward both discount *and* premium products.[17] Companies that miss out on this new market risk being "trapped in the middle" and seeing their market share steadily decline. Recognizing that its channel strategy emphasized retailers like Sears selling primarily to the middle class, Levi-Strauss introduced premium lines such as Levi's Capital E to upscale retailers Bloomingdales and Nordstrom, and the less-expensive Signature by Levi Strauss & Co. line to mass market retailers Walmart and Target. "Marketing Insight: Trading Up, Down, and Over" describes the factors creating this trend and what it means to marketers.

Marketing Insight

Trading Up, Down, and Over

Michael Silverstein and Neil Fiske, the authors of *Trading Up*, observed an increasing number of middle-market consumers periodically trading up to what they call "New Luxury" products and services "that possess higher levels of quality, taste, and aspiration than other goods in the category but are not so expensive as to be out of reach." For example, consumers might trade up to such brands as Starbucks coffee, Aveda shampoo, or Viking ranges, depending in part on the emotional benefits they gain in the trade.

Thanks to the trading-up trend, New Luxury goods sell at higher volumes than traditional luxury goods, although priced higher than conventional middle-market items. The authors identify three main types of New Luxury products:

- *Accessible superpremium products*, such as Victoria's Secret underwear and Kettle gourmet potato chips, carry a significant premium over middle-market brands, yet consumers can readily trade up to them because they are relatively low-ticket items in affordable categories.

- *Old Luxury brand extensions* extend historically high-priced brands down-market while retaining their cachet, such as the Mercedes-Benz C-class and the American Express Blue card.

- *Masstige goods*, such as Kiehl's skin care and Kendall-Jackson wines, are priced between average middle-market brands and superpremium Old Luxury brands. They are "always based on emotions, and consumers have a much stronger emotional engagement with them than with other goods."

To trade up to brands that offer these emotional benefits, consumers often "trade down" by shopping at discounters such as Walmart and Costco for staple items or goods that confer no emotional benefit but still deliver quality and functionality. As one consumer explained in rationalizing why her kitchen boasted a Sub-Zero refrigerator, a state-of-the-art Fisher & Paykel dishwasher, and a $900 warming drawer but a giant 12-pack of Bounty paper towels from a warehouse discounter: "When it comes to this house, I didn't give in on anything. But when it comes to food shopping or cleaning products, if it's not on sale, I won't buy it."

In a subsequent book titled *Treasure Hunt*, Silverstein notes that 82 percent of U.S. consumers trade down in five or more categories (what he calls "treasure hunting"), whereas 62 percent focus on trading up in the two categories that provide the most emotional benefits. This makes the new consumer "part martyr and part hedonist," willingly sacrificing on a number of purchases in order to experience enhanced benefits from a handful of others.

Silverstein believes successful firms will offer one of two kinds of value: New Luxury or Treasure Hunting. Brands that offer opportunities to trade up, such as Coach, Victoria's Secret, Grey Goose, and Bath &

Body Works, or to trade down, such as Best Value Inn, Kohl's, Dollar General, and IKEA, are optimally positioned to deliver the value modern consumers seek. The remaining firms, occupying the middle market and lacking the economic, functional, and emotional value modern consumers are searching for, will see their market share shrink as they get "trapped in the middle." Traditional grocers and department stores are already suffering, with market share declines of 30 percent and 50 percent, respectively.

Market research firm Mintel observes that consumers have also been "trading over" by switching spending from one category to another, buying a new home theater system, say, instead of a new car. In the recent economic downturn, consumers were "making substitutions that work for recession-minded lifestyles" while still preserving a desired experience. Mintel cites as examples Starbucks VIA Ready Brew coffee, a new, home based Starbucks experience that's more affordable than coffee at one of the company's outlets, and Tide TOTALCARE, which enables users to obtain certain dry-cleaning-type results at home with prices below those of professional dry cleaners.

Sources: Michael J. Silverstein, *Treasure Hunt: Inside the Mind of the New Consumer* (New York: Portfolio, 2006); Jeff Cioletti, "Movin' on Up," *Beverage World* (June 2006), p. 20; Michael J. Silverstein and Neil Fiske, *Trading Up: The New American Luxury* (New York: Portfolio, 2003); Linda Tischler, "The Price Is Right," *Fast Company*, November 2003; Sarah Mahoney, "Top Consumer Trends: Trust, Control, . . . Playfulness," *Marketing Daily*, September 4, 2009; David Orgel, "Quality Trumps Quantity in New Product Releases," *Supermarket News*, May 25, 2009.

GENERATION Each generation or *cohort* is profoundly influenced by the times in which it grows up—the music, movies, politics, and defining events of that period. Members share the same major cultural, political, and economic experiences and have similar outlooks and values. Marketers often advertise to a cohort by using the icons and images prominent in its experiences. They also try to develop products and services that uniquely meet the particular interests or needs of a generational target. Here is how one bank targeted Gen Y consumers.

PNC's Virtual Wallet In early 2007, PNC bank hired design consultants IDEO to study Gen Y—defined by PNC as 18- to 34-year-olds—and help develop a marketing plan to appeal to them. IDEO's research found this cohort (1) didn't know how to manage money and (2) found bank Web sites clunky and awkward to use. PNC thus chose to introduce a new offering, Virtual Wallet, that combined three accounts—"Spend" (regular checking), "Reserve" (backup checking that garners interest), and "Grow" (savings)—with a slick personal finance tool. Customers can drag money from account to account on one screen. Instead of seeing a traditional ledger, they view balances on a calendar that displays estimated future cash flow based on when they are paid, when they pay bills, and their spending habits. Customers also can set a "Savings Engine" tool to transfer money to savings when they receive a paycheck and get their account balances by text messages. Despite offering subscribers financial returns that were nothing out of the ordinary, PNC was able to sign up 20,000 mostly Gen Y consumers within the first few months.[18]

Consumers have been "trading over" to Tide TOTALCARE to obtain dry-cleaning type results at home.

Although the beginning and ending birth dates of any generation are always subjective—and generalizations can mask important differences within the group—here are some general observations about the four main generation cohorts of consumers, from youngest to oldest.[19]

Millennials (or Gen Y) Born between 1979 and 1994, Millennials, also called Gen Y, number 78 million with annual spending power estimated at $187 billion. If you factor in career growth and household and family formation, and multiply by another 53 years of life expectancy, trillions of dollars in consumer spending are at stake over their life spans. It's not surprising that market researchers and advertisers are racing to get a bead on Gen Y's buying behavior.

Also known as the Echo Boomers, these consumers have been "wired" almost from birth—playing computer games, navigating the Web, downloading music, connecting with friends via instant messaging and mobile phones. They have a sense of entitlement and abundance from growing up during the economic boom and being pampered by their boomer parents. Yet they are highly socially conscious and concerned about environmental issues. They are selective, confident, and impatient.

TABLE 8.3	Profiling U.S. Generation Cohorts		
Generational Cohort	**Birth Range**	**Approximate Size**	**Defining Features**
Millennials (Gen Y)	1979–1994	78 million	Raised with relative affluence, technologically plugged in and concerned with the environment and social issues, they also have a strong sense of independence and a perceived immunity from marketing.
Gen X	1964–1978	50 million	Sometimes seen as falling between the generational cracks, they bridge the technological savvy of Gen Y with the adult realities of the baby boomers.
Baby Boomers	1946–1964	76 million	Still largely in the prime of their consumption cycle, they embrace products and lifestyles that allow them to turn back the hands of time.
Silent Generation	1925–1945	42 million	Defying their advancing age, they maintain active lives and products and marketing that help them to achieve that.

Sources: Kenneth Gronbach, "The 6 Markets You Need to Know Now," *Advertising Age*, June 2, 2008, p. 21; Geoffrey E. Meredith and Charles D. Schewe, *Managing by Defining Moments: America's 7 Generational Cohorts, Their Workplace Values, and Why Managers Should Care* (New York: Hungry Minds, 2002).

Because Gen Y members are often turned off by overt branding practices and "hard sell," marketers have tried many different approaches to reach and persuade them.[20]

1. *Online buzz*—Rock band Foo Fighters created a digital street team that sends targeted e-mail blasts to members who "get the latest news, exclusive audio/video sneak previews, tons of chances to win great Foo Fighters prizes, and become part of the Foo Fighters Family."

2. *Student ambassadors*—Red Bull enlisted college students as Red Bull Student Brand Managers to distribute samples, research drinking trends, design on-campus marketing initiatives, and write stories for student newspapers.

3. *Unconventional sports*—Chick-fil-A sponsored the National Amateur Dodgeball Association, "a recreational pursuit for nontraditional sport enthusiasts."

4. *Cool events*—Hurley, which defined itself as an authentic "Microphone for Youth" brand rooted in surf, skate, art, music, and beach cultures, became the title sponsor of the U.S. Open of Surfing. Other sponsors included Casio, Converse, Corona, Paul Mitchell, and Southwest Airlines.

Hurley reinforces its strong identification with Gen Y consumers through its sponsorship of the U.S. Open of Surfing.

5. **Computer games**—Product placement is not restricted to movies or TV: Mountain Dew, Oakley, and Harley-Davidson all made deals to put logos on Tony Hawk's *Pro Skater 3* from Activision.
6. **Videos**—Burton ensures its snowboards and riders are clearly visible in any videos that are shot.
7. **Street teams**—As part of an antismoking crusade, the American Legacy Foundation hires teens as the "Truth Squad" to hand out T-shirts, bandanas, and dog tags at teen-targeted events.

Gen X Often lost in the demographic shuffle, the 50 million or so Gen X consumers, named for a 1991 novel by Douglas Coupland, were born between 1964 and 1978. The popularity of Kurt Cobain, rock band Nirvana, and the lifestyle portrayed in the critically lauded film *Slacker* led to the use of terms like *grunge* and *slacker* to characterize Gen X teens and young adults. It was an unflattering image of a disaffected group with short attention spans and little work ethic.

Although some saw rock band Nirvana as a defining symbol of Gen X, subsequent portrayals reveal a more complex picture of this cohort.

These stereotypes slowly disappeared. Gen X was certainly raised in more challenging times, when working parents relied on day care or left "latchkey kids" on their own after school, and corporate downsizing led to the threat of layoffs and economic uncertainty. At the same time, social and racial diversity were accepted and technology rapidly changed the way people lived and worked. Although Gen Xers created new norms in educational achievement, they were also the first generation to find surpassing their parents' standard of living a serious challenge.

These realities had a profound impact. Gen Xers feel self-sufficiency and the ability to handle any circumstance are key. Technology is an enabler for them, not a barrier. Unlike the more optimistic, team-oriented Gen Yers, Gen Xers are more pragmatic and individualistic. As consumers, they are wary of hype and pitches that seem inauthentic or patronizing. Direct appeals where value is clear often works best, especially as Gen Xers become parents raising families.[21]

Baby Boomers Baby boomers are the approximately 76 million U.S. consumers born between 1946 and 1964. Though they represent a wealthy target, possessing $1.2 trillion in annual spending power and controlling three-quarters of the country's wealth, marketers often overlook them. In network television circles, because advertisers are primarily interested in 18- to 49-year-olds, viewers over 50 are referred to as "undesirables."

With many baby boomers moving into their 60s and even the last and youngest wave bearing down on 50, demand has exploded for products to turn back the hands of time. According to one survey, nearly one in five boomers was actively resisting the aging process, driven by the mantra, "Fifty is the new thirty." As they search for the fountain of youth, sales of hair replacement and hair coloring aids, health club memberships, home gym equipment, skin-tightening creams, nutritional supplements, and organic foods have all soared.

Interestingly, because so many members of the Gen Y "Echo Boomers" are living with their boomer parents, parents are being influenced by what demographers are calling a "boom-boom effect." The same products that appeal to 21-year-olds are appealing to youth-obsessed baby boomers. The multiseason success of MTV's reality show *The Osbournes,* starring heavy-metal rocker Ozzy Osbourne and his family, was fueled as much by boomer parents as by their MTV-loving kids.

Contrary to conventional marketing wisdom that brand preferences of consumers over 50 are fixed, one study found 52 percent of boomers are willing to change brands, in line with the total population. Although they love to buy things, they hate being sold to, and as one marketer noted, "You have to earn your stripes every day." But abundant opportunity exists. Boomers are also less likely to associate retirement with "the beginning of the end" and see it instead as a new chapter in their lives with new activities, interests, careers, or even relationships.[22]

Silent Generation Those born between 1925 and 1945—the "Silent Generation"—are redefining what *old age* means. To start with, many people whose chronological age puts them in this category don't see themselves as old. One survey found that 60 percent of respondents over 65 said they felt younger than their actual age. A third aged 65 to 74 said they felt 10 to 19 years younger, and one in six felt at least 20 years younger than their actual age.[23]

The hit reality show *The Osbournes* tapped into baby boomers' rock-and-roll sensibilities and their parental responsibilities.

Members of the oldest generation, the Silent Generation, take much pride in their roles as grandparents.

Consistent with what they say, many older consumers lead very active lives. As one expert noted, it is if they were having a second middle age before becoming elderly. Advertisers have learned that older consumers don't mind seeing other older consumers in ads targeting them, as long as they appear to be leading vibrant lives. But marketers have learned to avoid clichés like happy older couples riding bikes or strolling hand-in-hand on a beach at sunset.

Emphasizing their roles as grandparents is universally well-received. Many older consumers not only happily spend time with their grandkids, they often provide for their basic needs or at least occasional gifts. The founders of eBeanstalk.com, which sells children's learning toys online, thought their business would be largely driven by young consumers starting families. They were surprised to find that up to 40 percent of their customers were older consumers, mainly grandparents. These customers are very demanding, but also more willing to pay full price than their younger counterparts.[24]

RACE AND CULTURE *Multicultural marketing* is an approach recognizing that different ethnic and cultural segments have sufficiently different needs and wants to require targeted marketing activities, and that a mass market approach is not refined enough for the diversity of the marketplace. Consider that McDonald's now does 40 percent of its U.S. business with ethnic minorities. Its highly successful "I'm Lovin' It" campaign was rooted in hip-hop culture but has had an appeal that transcended race and ethnicity.[25]

The Hispanic American, African American, and Asian American markets are all growing at two to three times the rate of nonmulticultural populations, with numerous submarkets, and their buying power is expanding. Multicultural markets also vary in whether they are first and second (or more) generation, and whether they are immigrants or born and raised in the United States.

The norms, language nuances, buying habits, and business practices of multicultural markets need to be factored into the initial formulation of a marketing strategy, rather than added as an afterthought. All this diversity also has implications for marketing research; it takes careful sampling to adequately profile target markets.[26]

Multicultural marketing can result in different marketing messages, media, channels, and so on. Specialized media exists to reach virtually any cultural segment or minority group, though some companies have struggled to provide financial and management support for fully realized programs.

Fortunately, as countries become more culturally diverse, many marketing campaigns targeting a specific cultural group can spill over and positively influence others. An ad for Tide in which an African American man wearing a wedding ring was drying his son off after a bath was well regarded by both African Americans and the market as a whole.[27] Boost Mobile has leveraged a shared interest in youth culture to create a diverse customer base of young adults made up of 35 percent African Americans, 27 percent Hispanic Americans, and 32 percent Caucasians.[28]

Next, we consider issues in the three largest multicultural markets—Hispanic Americans, African Americans, and Asian Americans. 🖵 Table 8.4 lists some important facts and figures about them.[29]

Hispanic Americans Hispanic Americans have become the largest minority in the country with annual purchasing power estimated to be more than $1 trillion in 2010. By 2020, 17 percent of Americans are projected to be of Hispanic origin.

The Hispanic American market holds a wide variety of subsegments, with roughly two dozen nationalities including Cuban, Mexican, Puerto Rican, Dominican, and other Central and South American groups, and a mix of cultures, physical types, racial backgrounds, and aspirations.[30] To meet these divergent needs, Goya, the United States' largest Hispanic food company, sells 1,600 products ranging from bags of rice to ready-to-eat, frozen empanadas. The company sells 38 varieties of beans alone.[31]

Although Hispanics suffered from greater unemployment and diminished disposable income in the recession, they were still an attractive target because they had lower mortgage and credit card debt, two or more income earners, and a greater propensity to buy advertised brands.[32] Companies such as Johnson & Johnson,

TABLE 8.4 🔲 Multicultural Market Profile			
	Hispanic Americans	**Asian Americans**	**African Americans**
Estimated population—2007	46.9 million	15.2 million	40.7 million
Estimated population—2050	132.8 million	40.6 million	65.7 million
Number of minority-owned businesses in 2002	1.6 million	1.1 million	1.2 million
Revenue generated by minority-owned businesses in 2002	$222 billion	$326 billion	$89 billion
Median household income in 2007	$38,679	$66,103	$33,916
Poverty rate in 2007	21.5%	10.20%	24.50%
Percentage of those aged >25 with at least a high school education in 2008	62%	86%	82%
Number of veterans of U.S. armed forces	1,100,000	277,751	2,400,000
Median age in 2008	27.7	35.4	30.3
Percent of population under 18 years old in 2008	34%	26%	30%
Buying power—2008	$863 billion	$847 billion	$509 billion

Sources: www.selig.uga.edu. and www.census.gov.

Verizon, and General Mills all significantly increased their advertising investment in the Hispanic market during the last recession.

State Farm   After trailing its main competitor for years, State Farm decided to make its Hispanic American marketing a priority in 2008. The firm sponsored local Latino community events, soccer matches, the Latin Music Awards, and Univision's highly rated Saturday night variety show, *Sabádo Gigante*. Perhaps State Farm's most original marketing activity, however, was the support and sponsorship of a new band. Los Felinos de la Noche (The Felines of the Night), as the six men (primarily Hispanic immigrants) are called, play the percussion heavy pop-rock sound of Norteño or Northern Mexico regional music. With State Farm's support, the band recorded singles, shot music videos, and played live concerts to make a name for themselves. State Farm, however, chose a subtle approach to its sponsorship. Although the band's Web site did not display the State Farm logo or contain marketing messages, the band did praise the company for the opportunity it gave them in many of the posted interviews. The color red in the band's uniforms was meant to tie in State Farm's familiar color. Targeting first-generation Hispanics with an emotional appeal showed that State Farm understood the needs of the Hispanic community. Positively received, the campaign has been credited with helping to change opinions of that market.[33] 🔲

State Farm's musical sponsorship of the band Los Felinos de la Noche reflects the company's increased emphasis on Hispanic marketing.

Hispanic Americans often share strong family values—several generations may reside in one household—and strong roots to their original country of origin. They have a need for respect, brand loyalty, and a keen interest in product quality. Procter & Gamble's research revealed that Hispanic consumers believe "*lo barato sale caro*" ("cheap can be expensive," or in the English equivalent, "you get what you pay for"). P&G found Hispanic consumers were so value-oriented they would even do their own product tests at home. One woman was using different brands of tissues and toilet paper in different rooms and bathrooms to see which her family liked best.[34]

Marketers are reaching out to Hispanic Americans with targeted promotions, ads, and Web sites but need to be careful to capture the nuances of cultural and market trends.[35] The California Milk Processor Board (CMPB) had to change its famed "got milk?" ad campaign when targeting the Hispanic market.

Got Milk? In 2001, Hispanics represented 32.5 percent of California's total population, a number that was growing every year. They were also heavy milk drinkers, spending more on milk than any other demographic segment. Initial consumer testing of the "got milk?" ads revealed, however, that Spanish-speaking households did not find the commercials funny when translated directly to Spanish. As CMPB Executive Director Jeff Manning explained, "We found out that not having milk or rice in Hispanic households is not funny: running out of milk means you failed your family." In addition, "got milk?" translated in Spanish roughly means "Are you lactating?"

As a result, the CMPB and its Hispanic ad agency, Anita Santiago Advertising, created a series of ads focused on milk as a sacred ingredient, often using the tagline "Familia, Amor y Leche" (Family, Love, and Milk). When the campaign did use the "Got Milk?" tagline, it was left untranslated. Awareness rose among the Hispanic population, and in 2002 the CMPB tested its first Spanish-language television spot, featuring La Llorona, a mythical Hispanic character. Hispanic consumers were thrilled that the commercial understood their culture and targeted them specifically.[36]

U.S.-born Hispanic Americans also have different needs and tastes than their foreign-born counterparts and, though bilingual, often prefer to communicate in English. With two-thirds of U.S. Hispanics considered "bicultural" and comfortable with both Spanish- and English-speaking cultures, most firms choose not to risk alienating the English-speaking audience on national TV and to run Spanish-only ads just on Hispanic networks Univision, Telemundo, and Telefutura.

Some marketers such as General Motors and Toyota have used a "Spanglish" approach in their ads, mixing some Spanish naturally in with English in conversations among Hispanic families.[37] Companies such as Continental Airlines, General Mills, and Sears have recently been using mobile marketing to reach Hispanics.[38] With a mostly younger population and less access to Internet or landline service, Hispanics are much more likely to consume content on their cell phones than the general market.

African Americans African Americans have had a significant economic, social, and cultural impact on U.S. life, influencing inventions, art, music, sports, fashion, and literature. Like many cultural segments, they are deeply rooted in the U.S. landscape while also proud of their heritage and respectful of family ties.[39]

Based on survey findings, African Americans are the most fashion-conscious of all racial and ethnic groups but strongly motivated by quality and selection. They're also more likely to be influenced by their children when selecting a product for purchase, and less likely to buy unfamiliar brands. African Americans watch television and listen to the radio more than other groups, and they buy more DVDs than any other multicultural segment except Hispanics.[40]

Many companies have successfully tailored products to meet the needs of African Americans. In 1987, Hallmark Cards launched its African American–targeted Mahogany line with only 16 greeting cards; today it offers 800 cards and a line of stationery. Sara Lee Corporation's L'eggs discontinued its separate line of pantyhose for black women; now shades and styles popular among black women make up half the company's general-focus sub-brands.

Ad messages must also be seen as relevant. In a campaign for Lawry's Seasoned Salt targeting African Americans, images of soul food appeared; a campaign for Kentucky Fried Chicken showed an African American family gathered at a reunion—demonstrating an understanding of both the market's values and its lifestyle.[41]

Cigarette, liquor, and fast-food firms have been criticized for targeting urban African Americans. As one writer noted, with obesity a problem, it is disturbing that it is easier to find a fast-food restaurant than a grocery store in many black neighborhoods.[42]

Asian Americans According to the U.S. Census Bureau, "Asian" refers to people having origins in any of the original peoples of the Far East, Southeast Asia, or the Indian subcontinent. Six countries represent 79 percent of the Asian American population: China (21 percent), the Philippines

(18 percent), India (11 percent), Vietnam (10 percent), Korea (10 percent), and Japan (9 percent). The diversity of these national identities limits the effectiveness of pan-Asian marketing appeals.

The Asian American market has been called the "invisible market" because, compared to Hispanic Americans and African Americans, it has traditionally received a disproportionally small fraction of U.S. companies' total multicultural marketing expenditure.[43] Yet it is getting easier and easier to reach this market. The number of media outlets targeting Asian Americans has grown from 200 in the 1980s to between 700 and 800 by 2007.

Philadelphia-based Sovereign Bank has been successful targeting Boston's Chinese American community with a 100 percent Chinese American–staffed branch. Not only do employees speak Cantonese, they know that in financial planning for Chinese Americans it is appropriate to acknowledge the need to care for elderly parents.[44] Traditional packaged-good firms have also been getting in the act. Here is how Kraft got its start.

Kraft   Kraft's initial Asian American marketing efforts began in 2005 with an integrated marketing campaign featuring in-language ads, in-store product demos/tastings, and a Web site with recipes and tips for healthy living. Kraft's research revealed that Asian American shoppers did not want more Asian-style products from Kraft. Rather, they wanted to learn how to prepare Western-style meals using Kraft products. Kraft's marketing communications used Mandarin and Cantonese, two of the more commonly spoken dialects of Asian immigrants, and targeted immigrant moms as the cultural gatekeepers of their families at home, striking a balance between Western and Eastern cultures. One print ad used the Chinese proverb "Life has a hundred flavors" to show an array of Kraft products brightly arranged on a platter. To further connect with shoppers, Kraft deployed Chinese-speaking representatives to supermarkets. The reps conducted cooking demos of Western recipes using Kraft products, handed out product samples, and offered suggestions for convenient kid-friendly school lunches. Kraft also launched a Web site (www.krafthealthyliving.com) to promote tips for healthy eating, such as "sip your tea" for better health benefits.[45]

Kraft has actively targeted Asian Americans with its brands and products.

Asian Americans tend to be more brand-conscious than other minority groups yet are the least loyal to particular brands. They also tend to care more about what others think (for instance, whether their neighbors will approve of them) and share core values of safety and education. Comparatively affluent and well-educated, they are an attractive target for luxury brands. The most computer-literate group, Asian Americans are more likely to use the Internet on a daily basis.[46]

Lesbian, Gay, Bisexual, and Transgender (LGBT) The lesbian, gay, bisexual, and transgender (LGBT) market is estimated to make up 5 percent to 10 percent of the population and have approximately $700 billion in buying power.[47] Many firms have recently created initiatives to target this market. American Airlines created a Rainbow Team with a dedicated LGBT staff and Web site that has emphasized community-relevant services such as an event calendar of gay-themed national events. According to one survey of the gay and lesbian community, Absolut, Apple, Levi's, and Bravo and Showtime television networks are seen as among the most gay-friendly businesses.[48]

Logo, MTV's television channel for a gay and lesbian audience, has 150 advertisers in a wide variety of product categories and is available in 40 million homes. Increasingly, advertisers are using digital efforts to reach the market. Hyatt's online appeals to the LGBT community targets social sites and blogs where customers share their travel experiences.

Some firms, however, worry about backlash from organizations that will criticize or even boycott firms supporting gay and lesbian causes. Although Pepsi, Campbell's, and Wells Fargo have all experienced such boycotts, they continue to advertise to the gay community.

Psychographic Segmentation

Psychographics is the science of using psychology and demographics to better understand consumers. In *psychographic segmentation,* buyers are divided into different groups on the basis of

|Fig. 8.1| ▲

The VALS Segmentation System: An Eight-Part Typology

Source: VALS™ © Strategic Business Insights (SBI), www.strategicbusinessinsights.com/VALS. Used with permission.

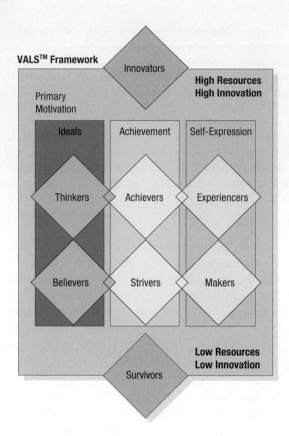

psychological/personality traits, lifestyle, or values. People within the same demographic group can exhibit very different psychographic profiles.

One of the most popular commercially available classification systems based on psychographic measurements is Strategic Business Insight's (SBI) VALS™ framework. VALS, signifying values and lifestyles, classifies U.S. adults into eight primary groups based on responses to a questionnaire featuring 4 demographic and 35 attitudinal questions. The VALS system is continually updated with new data from more than 80,000 surveys per year (see ▲ Figure 8.1). You can find out which VALS type you are by going to the SBI Web site.[49]

The main dimensions of the VALS segmentation framework are consumer motivation (the horizontal dimension) and consumer resources (the vertical dimension). Consumers are inspired by one of three primary motivations: ideals, achievement, and self-expression. Those primarily motivated by ideals are guided by knowledge and principles. Those motivated by achievement look for products and services that demonstrate success to their peers. Consumers whose motivation is self-expression desire social or physical activity, variety, and risk. Personality traits such as energy, self-confidence, intellectualism, novelty seeking, innovativeness, impulsiveness, leadership, and vanity—in conjunction with key demographics—determine an individual's resources. Different levels of resources enhance or constrain a person's expression of his or her primary motivation.

The four groups with higher resources are:

1. *Innovators*—Successful, sophisticated, active, "take-charge" people with high self-esteem. Purchases often reflect cultivated tastes for relatively upscale, niche-oriented products and services.
2. *Thinkers*—Mature, satisfied, and reflective people motivated by ideals and who value order, knowledge, and responsibility. They seek durability, functionality, and value in products.
3. *Achievers*—Successful, goal-oriented people who focus on career and family. They favor premium products that demonstrate success to their peers.
4. *Experiencers*—Young, enthusiastic, impulsive people who seek variety and excitement. They spend a comparatively high proportion of income on fashion, entertainment, and socializing.

The four groups with lower resources are:

1. *Believers*—Conservative, conventional, and traditional people with concrete beliefs. They prefer familiar, U.S.-made products and are loyal to established brands.
2. *Strivers*—Trendy and fun-loving people who are resource-constrained. They favor stylish products that emulate the purchases of those with greater material wealth.
3. *Makers*—Practical, down-to-earth, self-sufficient people who like to work with their hands. They seek U.S.-made products with a practical or functional purpose.
4. *Survivors*—Elderly, passive people concerned about change and loyal to their favorite brands.

Marketers can apply their understanding of VALS segments to marketing planning. For example, Transport Canada, the agency that operates major Canadian airports, found that Actualizers, who desire to express independence and taste, made up a disproportionate percentage of air travelers. Given that segment's profile, stores such as Sharper Image and Nature Company were expected to do well in the firm's airports.

Psychographic segmentation schemes are often customized by culture. The Japanese version of VALS, Japan VALS™, divides society into 10 consumer segments on the basis of two key concepts: life orientation (traditional ways, occupations, innovation, and self-expression) and attitudes to social change (sustaining, pragmatic, adapting, and innovating).

Behavioral Segmentation

In behavioral segmentation, marketers divide buyers into groups on the basis of their knowledge of, attitude toward, use of, or response to a product.

NEEDS AND BENEFITS Not everyone who buys a product has the same needs or wants the same benefits from it. Needs-based or benefit-based segmentation is a widely used approach because it identifies distinct market segments with clear marketing implications. Constellation Brands identified six different benefit segments in the U.S. premium wine market ($5.50 a bottle and up).[50]

*   *Enthusiast (12 percent of the market).* Skewing female, their average income is about $76,000 a year. About 3 percent are "luxury enthusiasts" who skew more male with a higher income.
*   *Image Seekers (20 percent).* The only segment that skews male, with an average age of 35. They use wine basically as a badge to say who they are, and they're willing to pay more to make sure they're getting the right bottle.
*   *Savvy Shoppers (15 percent).* They love to shop and believe they don't have to spend a lot to get a good bottle of wine. Happy to use the bargain bin.
*   *Traditionalist (16 percent).* With very traditional values, they like to buy brands they've heard of and from wineries that have been around a long time. Their average age is 50 and they are 68 percent female.
*   *Satisfied Sippers (14 percent).* Not knowing much about wine, they tend to buy the same brands. About half of what they drink is white zinfandel.
*   *Overwhelmed (23 percent).* A potentially attractive target market, they find purchasing wine confusing.

DECISION ROLES It's easy to identify the buyer for many products. In the United States, men normally choose their shaving equipment and women choose their pantyhose; but even here marketers must be careful in making targeting decisions, because buying roles change. When ICI, the giant British chemical company, discovered that women made 60 percent of decisions on the brand of household paint, it decided to advertise its Dulux brand to women.

People play five roles in a buying decision: *Initiator, Influencer, Decider, Buyer,* and *User.* For example, assume a wife initiates a purchase by requesting a new treadmill for her birthday. The husband may then seek information from many sources, including his best friend who has a treadmill and is a key influencer in what models to consider. After presenting the alternative choices to his wife, he purchases her preferred model, which ends up being used

Constellation Brands has adopted a needs-based market segmentation plan to sell its premium wines.

by the entire family. Different people are playing different roles, but all are crucial in the decision process and ultimate consumer satisfaction.

USER AND USAGE—REAL USER AND USAGE-RELATED VARIABLES Many marketers believe variables related to various aspects of users or their usage—occasions, user status, usage rate, buyer-readiness stage, and loyalty status—are good starting points for constructing market segments.

Occasions Occasions mark a time of day, week, month, year, or other well-defined temporal aspects of a consumer's life. We can distinguish buyers according to the occasions when they develop a need, purchase a product, or use a product. For example, air travel is triggered by occasions related to business, vacation, or family. Occasion segmentation can help expand product usage.

User Status Every product has its nonusers, ex-users, potential users, first-time users, and regular users. Blood banks cannot rely only on regular donors to supply blood; they must also recruit new first-time donors and contact ex-donors, each with a different marketing strategy. The key to attracting potential users, or even possibly nonusers, is understanding the reasons they are not using. Do they have deeply held attitudes, beliefs, or behaviors or just lack knowledge of the product or brand benefits and usage?

Included in the potential-user group are consumers who will become users in connection with some life stage or life event. Mothers-to-be are potential users who will turn into heavy users. Producers of infant products and services learn their names and shower them with products and ads to capture a share of their future purchases. Market-share leaders tend to focus on attracting potential users because they have the most to gain. Smaller firms focus on trying to attract current users away from the market leader.

Usage Rate We can segment markets into light, medium, and heavy product users. Heavy users are often a small slice but account for a high percentage of total consumption. Heavy beer drinkers account for 87 percent of beer consumption—almost seven times as much as light drinkers. Marketers would rather attract one heavy user than several light users. A potential problem, however, is that heavy users are often either extremely loyal to one brand or never loyal to any brand and always looking for the lowest price. They also may have less room to expand their purchase and consumption.

Buyer-Readiness Stage Some people are unaware of the product, some are aware, some are informed, some are interested, some desire the product, and some intend to buy. To help characterize how many people are at different stages and how well they have converted people from one stage to another, marketers can employ a *marketing funnel* to break down the market into different buyer-readiness stages.

The proportions of consumers at different stages make a big difference in designing the marketing program. Suppose a health agency wants to encourage women to have an annual Pap test to detect cervical cancer. At the beginning, most women may be unaware of the Pap test. The marketing effort should go into awareness-building advertising using a simple message. Later, the advertising should dramatize the benefits of the Pap test and the risks of not getting it. A special offer of a free health examination might motivate women to actually sign up for the test.

△ Figure 8.2 displays a funnel for two hypothetical brands. Compared to Brand B, Brand A performs poorly at converting one-time users to more recent users (only 46 percent convert for Brand A compared to 61 percent for Brand B). Depending on the reasons consumers didn't use again, a marketing campaign could introduce more relevant products, find more accessible retail outlets, or dispel rumors or incorrect beliefs consumers hold.

Loyalty Status Marketers usually envision four groups based on brand loyalty status:

1. *Hard-core loyals*—Consumers who buy only one brand all the time
2. *Split loyals*—Consumers who are loyal to two or three brands
3. *Shifting loyals*—Consumers who shift loyalty from one brand to another
4. *Switchers*—Consumers who show no loyalty to any brand[51]

A company can learn a great deal by analyzing degrees of brand loyalty: Hard-core loyals can help identify the products' strengths; split loyals can show the firm which brands are most competitive with its own; and by looking at customers dropping its brand, the company can learn about its marketing weaknesses and attempt to correct them. One caution: What appear to be

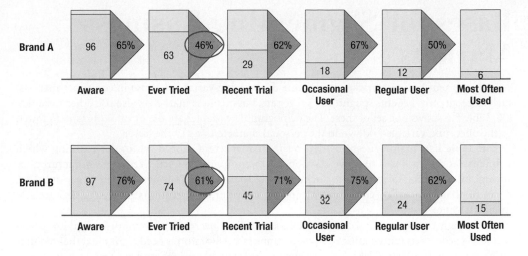

|Fig. 8.2| △

Example of Marketing Funnel

brand-loyal purchase patterns may reflect habit, indifference, a low price, a high switching cost, or the unavailability of other brands.

Attitude Five consumer attitudes about products are enthusiastic, positive, indifferent, negative, and hostile. Door-to-door workers in a political campaign use attitude to determine how much time to spend with each voter. They thank enthusiastic voters and remind them to vote, reinforce those who are positively disposed, try to win the votes of indifferent voters, and spend no time trying to change the attitudes of negative and hostile voters.

Multiple Bases Combining different behavioral bases can provide a more comprehensive and cohesive view of a market and its segments. △ Figure 8.3 depicts one possible way to break down a target market by various behavioral segmentation bases.

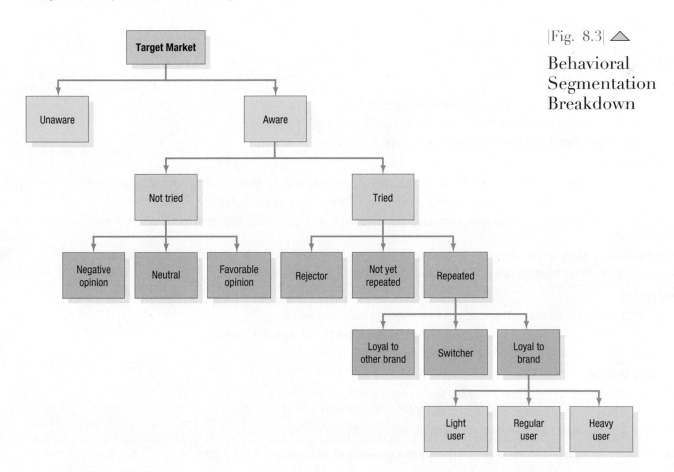

|Fig. 8.3| △

Behavioral Segmentation Breakdown

Bases for Segmenting Business Markets

We can segment business markets with some of the same variables we use in consumer markets, such as geography, benefits sought, and usage rate, but business marketers also use other variables. Table 8.5 shows one set of these. The demographic variables are the most important, followed by the operating variables—down to the personal characteristics of the buyer.

The table lists major questions that business marketers should ask in determining which segments and customers to serve. A rubber-tire company can sell tires to manufacturers of automobiles, trucks, farm tractors, forklift trucks, or aircraft. Within a chosen target industry, it can further segment by company size and set up separate operations for selling to large and small customers.

A company can segment further by purchase criteria. Government laboratories need low prices and service contracts for scientific equipment, university laboratories need equipment that requires little service, and industrial labs need equipment that is highly reliable and accurate.

Business marketers generally identify segments through a sequential process. Consider an aluminum company: The company first undertook macrosegmentation. It looked at which end-use market to serve: automobile, residential, or beverage containers. It chose the residential market, and it needed to determine the most attractive product application: semifinished material, building components, or aluminum mobile homes. Deciding to focus on building components, it considered the best customer size and chose large customers. The second stage consisted of microsegmentation. The

TABLE 8.5 Major Segmentation Variables for Business Markets

Demographic

1. *Industry:* Which industries should we serve?
2. *Company size:* What size companies should we serve?
3. *Location:* What geographical areas should we serve?

Operating Variables

4. *Technology:* What customer technologies should we focus on?
5. *User or nonuser status:* Should we serve heavy users, medium users, light users, or nonusers?
6. *Customer capabilities:* Should we serve customers needing many or few services?

Purchasing Approaches

7. *Purchasing-function organization:* Should we serve companies with a highly centralized or decentralized purchasing organization?
8. *Power structure:* Should we serve companies that are engineering dominated, financially dominated, and so on?
9. *Nature of existing relationship:* Should we serve companies with which we have strong relationships or simply go after the most desirable companies?
10. *General purchasing policies:* Should we serve companies that prefer leasing? Service contract? Systems purchases? Sealed bidding?
11. *Purchasing criteria:* Should we serve companies that are seeking quality? Service? Price?

Situational Factors

12. *Urgency:* Should we serve companies that need quick and sudden delivery or service?
13. *Specific application:* Should we focus on a certain application of our product rather than all applications?
14. *Size or order:* Should we focus on large or small orders?

Personal Characteristics

15. *Buyer-seller similarity:* Should we serve companies whose people and values are similar to ours?
16. *Attitude toward risk:* Should we serve risk-taking or risk-avoiding customers?
17. *Loyalty:* Should we serve companies that show high loyalty to their suppliers?

Source: Adapted from Thomas V. Bonoma and Benson P. Shapiro, *Segmenting the Industrial Market* (Lexington, MA: Lexington Books, 1983).

company distinguished among customers buying on price, service, or quality. Because it had a high-service profile, the firm decided to concentrate on the service-motivated segment of the market.

Business-to-business marketing experts James C. Anderson and James A. Narus have urged marketers to present flexible market offerings to all members of a segment.[52] A **flexible market offering** consists of two parts: a *naked solution* containing the product and service elements that all segment members value, and *discretionary options* that some segment members value. Each option might carry an additional charge. Siemens Electrical Apparatus Division sells metal-clad boxes to small manufacturers at prices that include free delivery and a warranty, but it also offers installation, tests, and communication peripherals as extra-cost options. Delta Airlines offers all economy passengers a seat, small snack and soft drinks and charges extra for alcoholic beverages and meals.

Market Targeting

There are many statistical techniques for developing market segments.[53] Once the firm has identified its market-segment opportunities, it must decide how many and which ones to target. Marketers are increasingly combining several variables in an effort to identify smaller, better-defined target groups. Thus, a bank may not only identify a group of wealthy retired adults but within that group distinguish several segments depending on current income, assets, savings, and risk preferences. This has led some market researchers to advocate a *needs-based market segmentation approach*, as introduced previously. Roger Best proposed the seven-step approach shown in 🖾 Table 8.6.

Delta Airlines uses flexible market offerings; it offers some products on board for free, such as soft drinks and small snacks, but charges for other items, such as meals.

Effective Segmentation Criteria

Not all segmentation schemes are useful. We could divide buyers of table salt into blond and brunette customers, but hair color is undoubtedly irrelevant to the purchase of salt. Furthermore, if all salt buyers buy the same amount of salt each month, believe all salt is the same, and would pay only one price for salt, this market is minimally segmentable from a marketing point of view.

To be useful, market segments must rate favorably on five key criteria:

- *Measurable.* The size, purchasing power, and characteristics of the segments can be measured.
- *Substantial.* The segments are large and profitable enough to serve. A segment should be the largest possible homogeneous group worth going after with a tailored marketing program. It would not pay, for example, for an automobile manufacturer to develop cars for people who are less than four feet tall.
- *Accessible.* The segments can be effectively reached and served.

TABLE 8.6 🖾 Steps in the Segmentation Process	
	Description
1. Needs-Based Segmentation	Group customers into segments based on similar needs and benefits sought by customers in solving a particular consumption problem.
2. Segment Identification	For each needs-based segment, determine which demographics, lifestyles, and usage behaviors make the segment distinct and identifiable (actionable).
3. Segment Attractiveness	Using predetermined segment attractiveness criteria (such as market growth, competitive intensity, and market access), determine the overall attractiveness of each segment.
4. Segment Profitability	Determine segment profitability.
5. Segment Positioning	For each segment, create a "value proposition" and product-price positioning strategy based on that segment's unique customer needs and characteristics.
6. Segment "Acid Test"	Create "segment storyboard" to test the attractiveness of each segment's positioning strategy.
7. Marketing-Mix Strategy	Expand segment positioning strategy to include all aspects of the marketing mix: product, price, promotion, and place.

Source: Adapted from Roger J. Best, *Market-Based Management*, 5th ed. (Upper Saddle River NJ: Prentice Hall, 2009). ©2009. Printed and electronically reproduced by permission of Pearson Education, Inc. Upper Saddle River, New Jersey.

254   PART 3   CONNECTING WITH CUSTOMERS

- *Differentiable.* The segments are conceptually distinguishable and respond differently to different marketing-mix elements and programs. If married and unmarried women respond similarly to a sale on perfume, they do not constitute separate segments.
- *Actionable.* Effective programs can be formulated for attracting and serving the segments.

Michael Porter has identified five forces that determine the intrinsic long-run attractiveness of a market or market segment: industry competitors, potential entrants, substitutes, buyers, and suppliers. The threats these forces pose are as follows:

1. *Threat of intense segment rivalry*—A segment is unattractive if it already contains numerous, strong, or aggressive competitors. It's even more unattractive if it's stable or declining, if plant capacity must be added in large increments, if fixed costs or exit barriers are high, or if competitors have high stakes in staying in the segment. These conditions will lead to frequent price wars, advertising battles, and new-product introductions and will make it expensive to compete. The cellular phone market has seen fierce competition due to segment rivalry.

2. *Threat of new entrants*—The most attractive segment is one in which entry barriers are high and exit barriers are low.[54] Few new firms can enter the industry, and poorly performing firms can easily exit. When both entry and exit barriers are high, profit potential is high, but firms face more risk because poorer-performing firms stay in and fight it out. When both entry and exit barriers are low, firms easily enter and leave the industry, and returns are stable but low. The worst case is when entry barriers are low and exit barriers are high: Here firms enter during good times but find it hard to leave during bad times. The result is chronic overcapacity and depressed earnings for all. The airline industry has low entry barriers but high exit barriers, leaving all carriers struggling during economic downturns.

3. *Threat of substitute products*—A segment is unattractive when there are actual or potential substitutes for the product. Substitutes place a limit on prices and on profits. If technology advances or competition increases in these substitute industries, prices and profits are likely to fall. Air travel has severely challenged profitability for Greyhound and Amtrak.

4. *Threat of buyers' growing bargaining power*—A segment is unattractive if buyers possess strong or growing bargaining power. The rise of retail giants such as Walmart has led some analysts to conclude that the potential profitability of packaged-goods companies will become curtailed. Buyers' bargaining power grows when they become more concentrated or organized, when the product represents a significant fraction of their costs, when the product is undifferentiated, when buyers' switching costs are low, when buyers are price-sensitive because of low profits, or when they can integrate upstream. To protect themselves, sellers might select buyers who have the least power to negotiate or switch suppliers. A better defense is developing superior offers that strong buyers cannot refuse.

5. *Threat of suppliers' growing bargaining power*—A segment is unattractive if the company's suppliers are able to raise prices or reduce quantity supplied. Suppliers tend to be powerful when they are concentrated or organized, when they can integrate downstream, when there are few substitutes, when the supplied product is an important input, and when the costs of switching suppliers are high. The best defenses are to build win-win relationships with suppliers or use multiple supply sources.

Evaluating and Selecting the Market Segments

In evaluating different market segments, the firm must look at two factors: the segment's overall attractiveness and the company's objectives and resources. How well does a potential segment score on the five criteria? Does it have characteristics that make it generally attractive, such as size, growth, profitability, scale economies, and low risk? Does investing in the segment make sense given the firm's objectives, competencies, and resources? Some attractive segments may not mesh with the company's long-run objectives, or the company may lack one or more necessary competencies to offer superior value.

Marketers have a range or continuum of possible levels of segmentation that can guide their target market decisions. As △ Figure 8.4 shows, at one end is a mass market of essentially one segment; at the other are individuals or segments of one person. Between lie multiple segments and single segments. We describe each of the four approaches next.

FULL MARKET COVERAGE With full market coverage, a firm attempts to serve all customer groups with all the products they might need. Only very large firms such as Microsoft (software

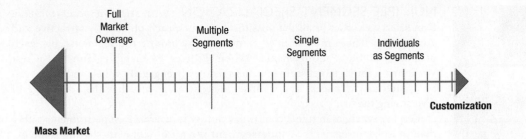

|Fig. 8.4| △

Possible Levels of Segmentation

market), General Motors (vehicle market), and Coca-Cola (nonalcoholic beverage market) can undertake a full market coverage strategy. Large firms can cover a whole market in two broad ways: through differentiated or undifferentiated marketing.

In *undifferentiated* or *mass marketing*, the firm ignores segment differences and goes after the whole market with one offer. It designs a marketing program for a product with a superior image that can be sold to the broadest number of buyers via mass distribution and mass communications. Undifferentiated marketing is appropriate when all consumers have roughly the same preferences and the market shows no natural segments. Henry Ford epitomized this strategy when he offered the Model-T Ford in one color, black.

The argument for mass marketing is that it creates the largest potential market, which leads to the lowest costs, which in turn can lead to lower prices or higher margins. The narrow product line keeps down the costs of research and development, production, inventory, transportation, marketing research, advertising, and product management. The undifferentiated communication program also reduces costs. However, many critics point to the increasing splintering of the market, and the proliferation of marketing channels and communication, which make it difficult and increasingly expensive to reach a mass audience.

When different groups of consumers have different needs and wants, marketers can define multiple segments. The company can often better design, price, disclose, and deliver the product or service and also fine-tune the marketing program and activities to better reflect competitors' marketing. In *differentiated marketing*, the firm sells different products to all the different segments of the market. Cosmetics firm Estée Lauder markets brands that appeal to women (and men) of different tastes: The flagship brand, the original Estée Lauder, appeals to older consumers; Clinique caters to middle-aged women; M.A.C. to youthful hipsters; Aveda to aromatherapy enthusiasts; and Origins to ecoconscious consumers who want cosmetics made from natural ingredients.[55] Perhaps no firm practises differentiated marketing like Burberry.

Burberry
Burberry has an authentic British heritage and it is uniquely positioned as a luxury product. Its core values—to protect, explore, and inspire—influence the company's culture and strategy. The principles of quality, function, and modern classic style are rooted in its globally recognized product portfolio: the trench coat, trademark check, and *prorsum* (a Latin phrase meaning "forward" to illustrate the innovative nature of the company) horse logo. Today, Burberry products include women's wear, menswear, nonapparel, and children's wear, with innovative outerwear as the foundation. The company has operations in markets throughout the world.

Recent changes in the global market meant that Burberry realized that the concept of "traditional" is not enough to remain competitive. As a result Burberry decided to benefit from its multi-segmentation by extending its range and re-labeled the casual component of its women's and men's apparel lines as "Burberry Brit." This range represents a younger, more laid back look with stylish separates that are perfect for everyday use, not just for formal wear. The new label is loose and unstructured and still retains the elegance of its traditional concept. Burberry also offers the more tailored "Burberry London" line that allows the company to offer more complete assortments in each segment and to target customers more effectively.[56]

Differentiated marketing typically creates more total sales than undifferentiated marketing. However, it also increases the costs of doing business. Because differentiated marketing leads to both higher sales and higher costs, no generalizations about its profitability are valid.

Although P&G initially targeted very specific segments with its Crest Whitestrips tooth-whitening product, it later expanded both its product offerings and its target markets.

MULTIPLE SEGMENT SPECIALIZATION

With *selective specialization*, a firm selects a subset of all the possible segments, each objectively attractive and appropriate. There may be little or no synergy among the segments, but each promises to be a moneymaker. When Procter & Gamble launched Crest Whitestrips, initial target segments included newly engaged women and brides-to-be as well as gay males. The multisegment strategy also has the advantage of diversifying the firm's risk.

Keeping synergies in mind, companies can try to operate in supersegments rather than in isolated segments. A **supersegment** is a set of segments sharing some exploitable similarity. For example, many symphony orchestras target people who have broad cultural interests, rather than only those who regularly attend concerts. A firm can also attempt to achieve some synergy with product or market specialization.

- With *product specialization*, the firm sells a certain product to several different market segments. A microscope manufacturer, for instance, sells to university, government, and commercial laboratories, making different instruments for each and building a strong reputation in the specific product area. The downside risk is that the product may be supplanted by an entirely new technology.
- With *market specialization*, the firm concentrates on serving many needs of a particular customer group, such as by selling an assortment of products only to university laboratories. The firm gains a strong reputation among this customer group and becomes a channel for additional products its members can use. The downside risk is that the customer group may suffer budget cuts or shrink in size.

SINGLE-SEGMENT CONCENTRATION

With single-segment concentration, the firm markets to only one particular segment. Porsche concentrates on the sports car market and Volkswagen on the small-car market—its foray into the large-car market with the Phaeton was a failure in the United States. Through concentrated marketing, the firm gains deep knowledge of the segment's needs and achieves a strong market presence. It also enjoys operating economies by specializing its production, distribution, and promotion. If it captures segment leadership, the firm can earn a high return on its investment.

A *niche* is a more narrowly defined customer group seeking a distinctive mix of benefits within a segment. Marketers usually identify niches by dividing a segment into subsegments. Whereas Hertz, Avis, Alamo, and others specialize in airport rental cars for business and leisure travelers, Enterprise has attacked the low-budget, insurance-replacement market by primarily renting to customers whose cars have been wrecked or stolen. By creating unique associations to low cost and convenience in an overlooked niche market, Enterprise has been highly profitable.

Niche marketers aim to understand their customers' needs so well that customers willingly pay a premium. Tom's of Maine was acquired by Colgate-Palmolive for $100 million in part because its all-natural personal care products and charitable donation programs appeal to consumers turned off by big businesses. The brand commands a 30 percent price premium as a result.[57]

What does an attractive niche look like? Customers have a distinct set of needs; they will pay a premium to the firm that best satisfies them; the niche is fairly small but has size, profit, and growth potential and is unlikely to attract many competitors; and the niche gains certain economies through specialization. As marketing efficiency increases, niches that were seemingly too small may become more profitable.[58] See "Marketing Insight: Chasing the Long Tail."

INDIVIDUAL MARKETING

The ultimate level of segmentation leads to "segments of one," "customized marketing," or "one-to-one marketing."[59] Today, customers are taking more individual initiative in determining what and how to buy. They log onto the Internet; look up information and evaluations of product or service offerings; conduct dialogue with suppliers, users, and product critics; and in many cases design the product they want.

Tom's of Maine has developed a very successful niche with its all-natural personal care products.

Jerry Wind and Arvind Rangaswamy see a movement toward "customerizing" the firm.[60] **Customerization** combines operationally driven mass customization with customized marketing in a way that empowers consumers to design the product and service offering of their choice. The firm no longer requires prior information about the customer, nor does it need to own manufacturing. It provides a platform and tools and "rents"

Marketing Insight

Chasing the Long Tail

The advent of online commerce, made possible by technology and epitomized by Amazon.com, eBay, iTunes, and Netflix, has led to a shift in consumer buying patterns, according to Chris Anderson, editor-in-chief of *Wired* magazine and author of *The Long Tail*.

In most markets, the distribution of product sales conforms to a curve weighted heavily to one side—the "head"—where the bulk of sales are generated by a few products. The curve falls rapidly toward zero and hovers just above it far along the X-axis—the "long tail"—where the vast majority of products generate very little sales. The mass market traditionally focused on generating "hit" products that occupy the head, disdaining the low-revenue market niches comprising the tail. The Pareto principle–based "80–20" rule—that 80 percent of a firm's revenue is generated by 20 percent of a firm's products—epitomizes this thinking.

Anderson asserts that as a result of consumers' enthusiastic adoption of the Internet as a shopping medium, the long tail holds significantly more value than before. In fact, Anderson argues, the Internet has directly contributed to the shifting of demand "down the tail, from hits to niches" in a number of product categories including music, books, clothing, and movies. According to this view, the rule that now prevails is more like "50–50," with smaller-selling products adding up to half a firm's revenue.

Anderson's long tail theory is based on three premises: (1) Lower costs of distribution make it economically easier to sell products without precise predictions of demand; (2) The more products available for sale, the greater the likelihood of tapping into latent demand for niche tastes unreachable through traditional retail channels; and (3) If enough niche tastes are aggregated, a big new market can result.

Anderson identifies two aspects of Internet shopping that support these premises. First, the increased inventory and variety afforded online permit greater choice. Second, the search costs for relevant new products are lowered due to the wealth of information online, the filtering of product recommendations based on user preferences that vendors can provide, and the word-of-mouth network of Internet users.

Some critics challenge the notion that old business paradigms have changed as much as Anderson suggests. Especially in entertainment, they say, the "head" where hits are concentrated is valuable also to consumers, not only to the content creators. One critique argued that "most hits are popular because they are of high quality," and another noted that the majority of products and services making up the long tail originate from a small concentration of online "long-tail aggregators."

Although some academic research supports the long tail theory, other research is more challenging, finding that poor recommendation systems render many very low-share products in the tail so obscure and hard to find they disappear before they can be purchased frequently enough to justify their existence. For companies selling physical products, inventory, stocking, and handling costs can outweigh any financial benefits of such products.

Sources: Chris Anderson, *The Long Tail* (New York: Hyperion, 2006); "Reading the Tail," interview with Chris Anderson, *Wired*, July 8, 2006, p. 30; "Wag the Dog: What the Long Tail Will Do," *The Economist*, July 8, 2006, p. 77; Erik Brynjolfsson, Yu "Jeffrey" Hu, and Michael D. Smith, "From Niches to Riches: Anatomy of a Long Tail," *MIT Sloan Management Review* (Summer 2006), p. 67; John Cassidy, "Going Long," *New Yorker*, July 10, 2006; www.longtail.com; "Rethinking the Long Tail Theory: How to Define 'Hits' and 'Niches,'" *Knowledge@Wharton*, September 16, 2009.

---

to customers the means to design their own products. A company is customerized when it is able to respond to individual customers by customizing its products, services, and messages on a one-to-one basis.[61]

Customization is certainly not for every company.[62] It may be very difficult to implement for complex products such as automobiles. It can also raise the cost of goods by more than the customer is willing to pay. Some customers don't know what they want until they see actual products, but they also cannot cancel the order after the company has started to work on it. The product may be hard to repair and have little sales value. In spite of this, customization has worked well for some products.

ETHICAL CHOICE OF MARKET TARGETS Marketers must target carefully to avoid consumer backlash. Some consumers resist being labeled. Singles may reject single-serve food packaging because they don't want to be reminded they are eating alone. Elderly consumers who don't feel their age may not appreciate products that label them "old."

Market targeting also can generate public controversy when marketers take unfair advantage of vulnerable groups (such as children) or disadvantaged groups (such as inner-city poor people) or promote potentially harmful products.[63] The cereal industry has been heavily criticized for marketing efforts directed toward children. Critics worry that high-powered appeals presented through the mouths of lovable animated characters will overwhelm children's defenses and lead them to want sugared cereals or poorly balanced breakfasts. Toy marketers have been similarly criticized.

Another area of concern is the millions of kids under the age of 17 who are online. Marketers have jumped online with them, offering freebies in exchange for personal information. Many have come under fire for this practice and for not clearly differentiating ads from games or entertainment. Establishing ethical and legal boundaries in marketing to children online and offline continues to be a hot topic as consumer advocates decry the commercialism they believe such marketing engenders.

Not all attempts to target children, minorities, or other special segments draw criticism. Colgate-Palmolive's Colgate Junior toothpaste has special features designed to get children to brush longer and more often. Other companies are responding to the special needs of minority segments. Black-owned ICE theaters noticed that although moviegoing by blacks has surged, there were few inner-city theaters. Starting in Chicago, ICE partnered with the black communities in which it operates theaters, using local radio stations to promote films and featuring favorite food items at concession stands.[64] Thus, the issue is not who is targeted, but how and for what. Socially responsible marketing calls for targeting that serves not only the company's interests, but also the interests of those targeted.

This is the case many companies make in marketing to the nation's preschoolers. With nearly 4 million youngsters attending some kind of organized child care, the potential market—including kids and parents—is too great to pass up. So in addition to standards such as art easels, gerbil cages, and blocks, the nation's preschools are likely to have Care Bear worksheets, Pizza Hut reading programs, and Nickelodeon magazines.

Teachers and parents are divided about the ethics of this increasing preschool marketing push. Some side with groups such as Stop Commercial Exploitation of Children, whose members feel preschoolers are incredibly susceptible to advertising and that schools' endorsements of products make children believe the product is good for them—no matter what it is. Yet many preschools and day care centers operating on tight budgets welcome the free resources.[65]

Summary

1. Target marketing includes three activities: market segmentation, market targeting, and market positioning. Market segments are large, identifiable groups within a market.

2. Two bases for segmenting consumer markets are consumer characteristics and consumer responses. The major segmentation variables for consumer markets are geographic, demographic, psychographic, and behavioral. Marketers use them singly or in combination.

3. Business marketers use all these variables along with operating variables, purchasing approaches, and situational factors.

4. To be useful, market segments must be measurable, substantial, accessible, differentiable, and actionable.

5. We can target markets at four main levels: mass, multiple segments, single (or niche) segment, and individuals.

6. A mass market targeting approach is adopted only by the biggest companies. Many companies target multiple segments defined in various ways such as various demographic groups who seek the same product benefit.

7. A niche is a more narrowly defined group. Globalization and the Internet have made niche marketing more feasible to many.

8. More companies now practice individual and mass customization. The future is likely to see more individual consumers take the initiative in designing products and brands.

9. Marketers must choose target markets in a socially responsible manner at all times.

Applications

Marketing Debate
Is Mass Marketing Dead?

With marketers increasingly adopting more and more refined market segmentation schemes—fueled by the Internet and other customization efforts—some claim mass marketing is dead. Others counter there will always be room for large brands employing marketing programs to target the mass market.

Take a position: Mass marketing is dead *versus* Mass marketing is still a viable way to build a profitable brand.

Marketing Discussion
Marketing Segmentation Schemes

Think of various product categories. In each segmentation scheme, to which segment do you feel you belong? How would marketing be more or less effective for you depending on the segment? How would you contrast demographic and behavioral segment schemes? Which one(s) do you think would be most effective for marketers trying to sell to you?

Marketing Excellence

>>HSBC

HSBC wants to be known as the "world's local bank." This tagline reflects HSBC's positioning as a globe-spanning financial institution with a unique focus on serving local markets. Originally the Hong Kong and Shanghai Banking Corporation Limited, HSBC was established in 1865 to finance the growing trade between China and the United Kingdom. It's now the second-largest bank in the world.

Despite serving over 100 million customers through 9,500 branches in 85 countries, the bank works hard to maintain a local presence and local knowledge in each area. Its fundamental operating strategy is to remain close to its customers. As HSBC's former chairman, Sir John Bond, stated, "Our position as the world's local bank enables us to approach each country uniquely, blending local knowledge with a worldwide operating platform."

Ads for the "World's Local Bank" campaign have depicted the way different cultures or people interpret the same objects or events. One TV spot showed a U.S. businessman hitting a hole-in-one during a round in Japan with his Japanese counterparts. He is surprised to find that rather than paying for a round of drinks in the clubhouse, as in the United States, by Japanese custom he must buy expensive gifts for his playing partners. In another international TV spot, a group of Chinese businessmen take a British businessman out to an elaborate dinner where live eels are presented to the diners and then served sliced and cooked. Clearly disgusted by the meal, the British businessman finishes the dish as the voice-over explains, "The English believe it's a slur on your hosts' food if you don't clear your plate." His Chinese host then orders another live eel for him as the voice-over explained, "Whereas the Chinese feel that it's questioning their generosity if you do."

HSBC demonstrated its local knowledge with marketing efforts dedicated to specific locations. In 2005 it set out to prove to jaded New Yorkers that the London-based financial behemoth was a bank with local knowledge. The company held a "New York City's Most Knowledgeable Cabbie" contest, in which the winning cabbie got paid to drive an HSBC-branded BankCab full-time for a year. HSBC customers could win, too. Any customer showing an HSBC bank card, checkbook, or bank statement was able to get a free ride in the BankCab. HSBC also ran an integrated campaign highlighting the diversity of New Yorkers, which appeared throughout the city.

More than 8,000 miles away, HSBC undertook a two-part "Support Hong Kong" campaign to revitalize a local economy hit hard by the 2003 SARS outbreak. First, HSBC delayed interest payments for personal-loan customers who worked in industries most affected by SARS (cinemas, hotels, restaurants, and travel agencies). Second, the bank offered discounts and rebates for HSBC credit card users when they shopped and dined out. More than 1,500 local merchants participated in the promotion.

HSBC also targets consumer niches with unique products and services. It found a little-known product area growing at 125 percent a year: pet insurance. The bank now distributes nationwide pet insurance to its depositors through its HSBC Insurance agency. In Malaysia, HSBC offered a "smart card" and no-frills credit cards to the underserved student segment and targeted high-value customers with special "Premium Centers" bank branches.

In order to connect with different people and communities, HSBC sponsors more than 250 cultural and sporting events with a special focus on helping the youth, growing education, and embracing communities. These sponsorships also allow the company to learn from different people and cultures around the world.

The bank pulls its worldwide businesses together under a single global brand with the "World's Local Bank" slogan. The aim is to link its international size with close relationships in each of the countries in which it operates. HSBC spends $600 million annually on global marketing, consolidated under the WPP group of agencies.

In 2006, HSBC launched a global campaign entitled "Different Values," which embraced this exact notion of multiple viewpoints and different interpretations. Print ads showed the same picture three times with a different interpretation in each. For example, an old classic car appeared three times with the words, *freedom*, *status symbol*, and *polluter*. Next to the picture reads, "The more you look at the world, the more you realize that what one person values may be different from the next." In another set of print ads, HSBC used three different pictures side by side but with the same word. For example, the word *accomplishment* is first shown on a picture of a woman winning a beauty pageant, then an astronaut walking on the moon, and finally a young child tying his sneaker. The copy reads, "The more you look at the world, the more you realize what really matters to people." Tracy Britton, head of marketing for HSBC Bank, USA, explained the strategy behind the campaign, "It encapsulates our global outlook that acknowledges and respects that people value things in very different ways. HSBC's global footprint gives us the insight and the opportunity not only to be comfortable, but confident in helping people with different values achieve what's really important to them."

HSBC earned $142 billion in sales in 2009, making it the 21st largest company in the world. It hopes its latest campaign and continued position as the "World's Local Bank" will improve its $10.5 billion brand value, which placed it 32nd on the 2009 Interbrand/*BusinessWeek* global brand rankings.

Questions

1. What are the risks and benefits of HSBC's positioning itself as the "World's Local Bank"?

2. Does HSBC's most recent campaign resonate with its target audience? Why or why not?

Sources: Carrick Mollenkamp, "HSBC Stumbles in Bid to Become Global Deal Maker," *Wall Street Journal*, October 5, 2006; Kate Nicholson, "HSBC Aims to Appear Global Yet Approachable," *Campaign*, December 2, 2005, p. 15; Deborah Orr, "New Ledger," *Forbes*, March 1, 2004, pp. 72–73; "HSBC's Global Marketing Head Explains Review Decision," *Adweek*, January 19, 2004; "Now Your Customers Can Afford to Take Fido to the Vet," *Bank Marketing* (December 2003): 47; Kenneth Hein, "HSBC Bank Rides the Coattails of Chatty Cabbies," *Brandweek*, December 1, 2003, p. 30; Sir John Bond and Stephen Green, "HSBC Strategic Overview," presentation to investors, November 27, 2003; "Lafferty Retail Banking Awards 2003," *Retail Banker International*, November 27, 2003, pp. 4–5; "Ideas that Work," *Bank Marketing* (November 2003): 10; "HSBC Enters the Global Branding Big League," *Bank Marketing International* (August 2003): 1–2; Normandy Madden, "HSBC Rolls out Post-SARS Effort," *Advertising Age*, June 16, 2003, p. 12; "www.hsbc.com" Douglas Quenqua, "HSBC Dominates Ad Pages in New York Magazine Issue." *New York Times*, October 20, 2008, pg. B.6; Kimia M. Ansari, "A Different Point of View: HSBC." *Unbound Edition*, July 10, 2009; Press release, "The Evolution of "Your Point of View." October 20, 2008; *Fortune*, Global 500; HSBC.com.

Marketing Excellence

>>BMW

BMW is the ultimate driving machine. Manufactured by the German company, Bayerische Motoren Werke AG, BMW stands for both performance and luxury. The company was founded in 1916 as an aircraft-engine manufacturer and produced engines during World War I and World War II. It evolved into a motorcycle and automobile maker by the mid-20th century, and today it is an internationally respected company and brand with €53 billion (about $76 billion) in revenues in 2008.

BMW's logo is one of the most distinct and globally recognized ever created. The signature BMW roundel *looks* like a spinning propeller blade set against a blue sky background—originally thought to be a tribute to the company's founding days as an aircraft engine manufacturer. Recently, however, a *New York Times* reporter revealed that the logo, which features the letters BMW at the top of the outer ring and a blue-and-white checkered design in the inner ring, was trademarked in 1917 and meant to show the colors of the Free State of Bavaria, where the company is headquartered.

BMW's growth exploded in the 1980s and 1990s, when it successfully targeted the growing market of baby boomers and professional yuppies who put work first and wanted a car that spoke of their success. The result: sporty sedans with exceptional performance and a brand that stood for prestige and achievement. The cars, which came in a 3, 5, or 7 Series, were basically the same design in three different sizes. The 1980s was also a time when yuppies made Beemer and Bimmer, slang terms for BMW's cars and motorcycles, popular names that are still used today. At the turn of the century, consumers' attitudes toward cars changed. Research showed that they cared less about the bragging rights of the BMW brand and instead desired a variety of design, size, price, and style choices. As a result, the company took several steps to grow its product line by targeting specific market segments, which resulted in unique premium-priced cars such as SUVs, convertibles, roadsters, and less expensive compact cars, the 1 Series. In addition, BMW redesigned its 3, 5, and 7 Series cars, making them unique in appearance yet remaining exceptional in performance. BMW's full range of cars now include the 1 Series, 3 Series, 5 Series, 6 Series, 7 Series, X3 SUV, X5 SUV, X6 SUV, Z4 (Roadster), and M. The redesign of the 7 Series, BMW's most luxurious car, targeted a group called "upper conservatives." These wealthy, traditional consumers traditionally don't like sportier cars, so BMW added an influx of electronic components such as multiple options to control the windows, seats, airflow, and lights, a push-button ignition, and night vision, all controlled by a point-and-click system called iDrive. These enhancements were created to add comfort and luxury and attract consumers away from competitors like Jaguar and Mercedes.

BMW successfully launched the X5 by targeting "upper liberals" who achieved success in the 1990s and had gone on to have children and take up extracurricular activities such as biking, golf, and skiing. These consumers needed a bigger car for their active lifestyles and growing families, so BMW created a high-performance luxury SUV. BMW refers to its SUVs as sport *activity* vehicles in order to appeal even more to these active consumers.

BMW created the lower-priced 1 Series and X3 SUV to target the "modern mainstream," a group who are also family-focused and active but had previously avoided BMWs because of the premium cost. The 1 Series reached this group with its lower price point, sporty design, and aspiration to own a luxury brand. The X3 also hit home with its smaller, less expensive SUV design.

BMW introduced convertibles and roadsters to target "post-moderns," a high-income group that continues to attract attention with more showy, flamboyant cars. BMW's 6 Series, a flashier version of the high-end 7 Series, also targeted this group.

BMW uses a wide range of advertising tactics to reach each of its target markets but has kept the tagline "The Ultimate Driving Machine" for over 35 years. During that time, U.S. sales of BMW vehicles have grown from 15,000 units in 1974 to approximately 250,000 in 2009. BMW owners are very loyal to the brand, and enthusiasts host an annual Bimmerfest each year to celebrate their cars. The company nurtures these loyal consumers and continues to research, innovate, and reach out to specific segment groups year after year.

Questions

1. What are the pros and cons to BMW's selective target marketing? What has the firm done well over the years and where could it improve?

2. BMW's sales slipped during the worldwide recession in 2008 and 2009. Is its segmentation strategy too selective? Why or why not?

Sources: Stephen Williams, "BMW Roundel: Not Born from Planes," *New York Times*, January 7, 2010; Gail Edmondson, "BMW: Crashing the Compact Market," *BusinessWeek*, June 28, 2004; Neil Boudette, "BMW's Push to Broaden Line Hits Some Bumps in the Road," *Wall Street Journal*, January 10, 2005; Boston Chapter BMW Club Car of America, boston-bmwcca.org; bmw.org, Annual Report, Company History, January 22, 2010.

Chapter 9

In This Chapter, We Will Address the Following Questions

1. What is a brand, and how does branding work?

2. What is brand equity?

3. How is brand equity built, measured, and managed?

4. What are the important brand architecture decisions in developing a branding strategy?

With a unique concept and shrewd grassroots marketing, Lululemon has attracted a loyal customer base and built a strong brand.

Creating Brand Equity

One of the most valuable intangible assets of a firm is its brands, and it is incumbent on marketing to properly manage their value. Building a strong brand is both an art and a science. It requires careful planning, a deep long-term commitment, and creatively designed and executed marketing. A strong brand commands intense consumer loyalty—at its heart is a great product or service.

 While attending yoga classes, Canadian entrepreneur Chip Wilson decided the cotton-polyester blends most fellow students wore were too uncomfortable. After designing a well-fitting, sweat-resistant black garment to sell, he also decided to open a yoga studio, and lululemon was born. The company has taken a grassroots approach to growth that creates a strong emotional connection with its customers. Before it opens a store in a new city, lululemon first identifies influential yoga instructors or other fitness teachers. In exchange for a year's worth of clothing, these yogi serve as "ambassadors," hosting students at lululemon-sponsored classes and product sales events. They also provide product design advice to the company. The cult-like devotion of lululemon's customers is evident in their willingness to pay $92 for a pair of workout pants that might cost only $60 to $70 from Nike or Under Armour. lululemon can sell as much as $1,800 worth of product per square feet in its approximately 100 stores, three times what established retailers Abercrombie & Fitch and J.Crew sell. After coping with some inventory challenges, the company is looking to expand beyond yoga-inspired athletic apparel and accessories into similar products in other sports such as running, swimming, and biking.[1]

Marketers of successful 21st-century brands must excel at the strategic brand management process. *Strategic brand management* combines the design and implementation of marketing activities and programs to build, measure, and manage brands to maximize their value. The strategic brand management process has four main steps:

- Identifying and establishing brand positioning
- Planning and implementing brand marketing
- Measuring and interpreting brand performance
- Growing and sustaining brand value deals with brand positioning.

The latter three topics are discussed in this chapter.[2] Chapter 11 reviews important concepts dealing with competitive dynamics.

What Is Brand Equity?

Perhaps the most distinctive skill of professional marketers is their ability to create, maintain, enhance, and protect brands. Established brands such as Mercedes, Sony, and Nike have commanded a price premium and elicited deep customer loyalty through the years. Newer brands such as POM Wonderful, SanDisk, and Zappos have captured the imagination of consumers and the interest of the financial community alike.

The American Marketing Association defines a **brand** as "a name, term, sign, symbol, or design, or a combination of them, intended to identify the goods or services of one seller or group of sellers and to differentiate them from those of competitors." A brand is thus a product or service whose dimensions differentiate it in some way from other products or services designed to satisfy the same need. These differences may be functional, rational, or tangible—related to product performance of the brand. They may also be more symbolic, emotional, or intangible—related to what the brand represents or means in a more abstract sense.

Branding has been around for centuries as a means to distinguish the goods of one producer from those of another.[3] The earliest signs of branding in Europe were the medieval guilds' requirement that craftspeople put trademarks on their products to protect themselves and their customers against inferior quality. In the fine arts, branding began with artists signing their works. Brands today play a number of important roles that improve consumers' lives and enhance the financial value of firms.

The Role of Brands

Brands identify the source or maker of a product and allow consumers—either individuals or organizations—to assign responsibility for its performance to a particular manufacturer or distributor. Consumers may evaluate the identical product differently depending on how it is branded. They learn about brands through past experiences with the product and its marketing program, finding out which brands satisfy their needs and which do not. As consumers' lives become more complicated, rushed, and time-starved, a brand's ability to simplify decision making and reduce risk becomes invaluable.[4]

Brands also perform valuable functions for firms.[5] First, they simplify product handling or tracing. Brands help to organize inventory and accounting records. A brand also offers the firm legal protection for unique features or aspects of the product.[6] The brand name can be protected through registered trademarks; manufacturing processes can be protected through patents; and packaging can be protected through copyrights and proprietary designs. These intellectual property rights ensure that the firm can safely invest in the brand and reap the benefits of a valuable asset.

A credible brand signals a certain level of quality so that satisfied buyers can easily choose the product again.[7] Brand loyalty provides predictability and security of demand for the firm, and it creates barriers to entry that make it difficult for other firms to enter the market. Loyalty also can translate into customer willingness to pay a higher price—often 20 percent to 25 percent more than competing brands.[8] Although competitors may duplicate manufacturing processes and product designs, they cannot easily match lasting impressions left in the minds of individuals and organizations by years of product experience and marketing activity. In this sense, branding can be a powerful means to secure a competitive advantage.[9] Sometimes marketers don't see the real importance of brand loyalty until they change a crucial element of the brand, as the now-classic tale of New Coke illustrates.

Coca-Cola learned a valuable lesson about its brand when it changed its formula without seeking sufficient consumer permission.

Coca-Cola   Battered by a nationwide series of taste-test challenges from the sweeter-tasting Pepsi-Cola, Coca-Cola decided in 1985 to replace its old formula with a sweeter variation, dubbed New Coke. Coca-Cola spent $4 million on market research. Blind taste tests showed that Coke drinkers preferred the new, sweeter formula, but the launch of New Coke provoked a national uproar. Market researchers had measured the taste but failed to measure the emotional attachment consumers had to Coca-Cola. There were angry letters, formal protests, and even lawsuit threats to force the retention of "The Real Thing." Ten weeks later, the company withdrew New Coke and reintroduced its century-old formula as "Classic Coke," a move that ironically might have given the old formula even stronger status in the marketplace.

For better or worse, branding effects are pervasive. One research study that provoked much debate about the effects of marketing on children showed that preschoolers felt identical McDonald's food items—even carrots, milk, and apple juice—tasted better when wrapped in McDonald's familiar packaging than in unmarked wrappers.[10]

To firms, brands represent enormously valuable pieces of legal property that can influence consumer behavior, be bought and sold, and provide their owner the security of sustained future revenues. Companies have paid dearly for brands in mergers or acquisitions, often justifying the price premium on the basis of the extra profits expected and the difficulty and expense of creating similar brands from scratch. Wall Street believes strong brands result in better earnings and profit performance for firms, which, in turn, create greater value for shareholders.[11]

The Scope of Branding

How do you "brand" a product? Although firms provide the impetus to brand creation through marketing programs and other activities, ultimately a brand resides in the minds of consumers. It is a perceptual entity rooted in reality but reflecting the perceptions and idiosyncrasies of consumers.

Branding is endowing products and services with the power of a brand. It's all about creating differences between products. Marketers need to teach consumers "who" the product is—by giving it a name and other brand elements to identify it—as well as what the product does and why consumers should care. Branding creates mental structures that help consumers organize their knowledge about products and services in a way that clarifies their decision making and, in the process, provides value to the firm.

For branding strategies to be successful and brand value to be created, consumers must be convinced there are meaningful differences among brands in the product or service category. Brand differences often relate to attributes or benefits of the product itself. Gillette, Merck, and 3M have led their product categories for decades, due in part to continual innovation. Other brands create competitive advantages through nonproduct-related means. Gucci, Chanel, and Louis Vuitton have become category leaders by understanding consumer motivations and desires and creating relevant and appealing images around their products.

Marketers can apply branding virtually anywhere a consumer has a choice. It's possible to brand a physical good (Ford Flex automobile, or Lipitor cholesterol medication), a service (Singapore Airlines or Blue Cross and Blue Shield medical insurance), a store (Nordstrom or Foot Locker), a person (actress Angelina Jolie or tennis player Roger Federer), a place (the city of Sydney or country of Spain), an organization (U2 or American Automobile Association), or an idea (abortion rights or free trade).[12]

Brand Yao Yao Ming, the 7'6" Chinese basketball player on the NBA's Houston Rockets, is a well-known celebrity both on and off the court. He has helped the NBA to open new markets in Asia, reportedly increasing attendance by 55 percent and drawing many Asian fans to Rockets' games. Yao has numerous endorsement deals with brands such as Tag Heuer, McDonald's, Reebok, Garmin, and Pepsi, and businesses such as the Yao Yao Restaurant and a line of Yao Monster electronics and lifestyle products leverage his popularity. Yao reportedly earns more than $100 million a year through endorsements alone. His star power in both Asia and the West is evident in the increased sales he has helped to bring in for the brands he promotes.

In part because Yao also participates in public service campaigns, the Yao brand embodies qualities such as genuineness, patriotism, humility, and sincerity. These qualities enhance both the star's likability and the brands he endorses. With his surging popularity, the basketball player has a team of professionals, collectively known as Team Yao, to manage his brand. A key challenge faced by Team Yao will be to improve and maintain the Yao brand equity as the star continues to suffer from regular foot injuries which affect his performance.[13]

Yao Ming's popularity both on and off the basketball court means that he is a good choice to endorse brands such as Pepsi, Reebok, McDonald's, and Garmin.

Defining Brand Equity

Brand equity is the added value endowed on products and services. It may be reflected in the way consumers think, feel, and act with respect to the brand, as well as in the prices, market share, and profitability the brand commands.[14]

Marketers and researchers use various perspectives to study brand equity.[15] Customer-based approaches view it from the perspective of the consumer—either an individual or an organization—and recognize that the power of a brand lies in what customers have seen, read, heard, learned, thought, and felt about the brand over time.[16]

To reinforce its luxury image, Louis Vuitton uses iconic celebrities such as legendary Rolling Stones rocker Keith Richards in print and outdoor advertising.

Customer-based brand equity is thus the differential effect brand knowledge has on consumer response to the marketing of that brand.[17] A brand has *positive* customer-based brand equity when consumers react more favorably to a product and the way it is marketed when the brand is *identified,* than when it is not identified. A brand has negative customer-based brand equity if consumers react less favorably to marketing activity for the brand under the same circumstances. There are three key ingredients of customer-based brand equity.

1. Brand equity arises from differences in consumer response. If no differences occur, the brand-name product is essentially a commodity, and competition will probably be based on price.[18]
2. Differences in response are a result of consumers' **brand knowledge**, all the thoughts, feelings, images, experiences, and beliefs associated with the brand. Brands must create strong, favorable, and unique brand associations with customers, as have Toyota *(reliability)*, Hallmark *(caring)*, and Amazon.com *(convenience)*.
3. Brand equity is reflected in perceptions, preferences, and behavior related to all aspects of the marketing of a brand. Stronger brands lead to greater revenue.[19] Table 9.1 summarizes some key benefits of brand equity.

The challenge for marketers is therefore ensuring customers have the right type of experiences with products, services, and marketing programs to create the desired brand knowledge. In an abstract sense, we can think of brand equity as providing marketers with a vital strategic "bridge" from their past to their future.[20]

TABLE 9.1	Marketing Advantages of Strong Brands	
Improved perceptions of product performance		Greater trade cooperation and support
Greater loyalty		Increased marketing communications effectiveness
Less vulnerability to competitive marketing actions		Possible licensing opportunities
Less vulnerability to marketing crises		Additional brand extension opportunities
Larger margins		Improved employee recruiting and retention
More inelastic consumer response to price increases		Greater financial market returns
More elastic consumer response to price decreases		

Marketers should also think of the marketing dollars spent on products and services each year as investments in consumer brand knowledge. The *quality* of that investment is the critical factor, not necessarily the *quantity* (beyond some threshold amount). It's actually possible to overspend on brand building, if money is not spent wisely.

Brand knowledge dictates appropriate future directions for the brand. A **brand promise** is the marketer's vision of what the brand must be and do for consumers. Consumers will decide, based on what they think and feel about the brand, where (and how) they believe the brand should go and grant permission (or not) to any marketing action or program. New-product ventures such as BENGAY aspirin, Cracker Jack cereal, Frito-Lay lemonade, Fruit of the Loom laundry detergent, and Smucker's premium ketchup all failed because consumers found them inappropriate extensions for the brand.

Virgin America
After flying for only a few years, Virgin America became an award-winning airline that passengers adore *and* that makes money. It is not unusual for the company to receive e-mails from customers saying they actually wished their flights lasted longer! Virgin America set out to reinvent the entire travel experience, starting with an easy-to-use and friendly Web site and check-in. In flight, passengers revel in Wi-Fi, spacious leather seats, mood lighting, and in-seat food and beverage ordering through touch-screen panels. Some passengers remark that Virgin America is like "flying in an iPod or nightclub." Without a national TV ad campaign, Virgin America has relied on PR, word of mouth, social media, and exemplary customer service to create an extraordinary customer experience and build the brand. As VP-marketing Porter Gale notes, "Most of the social-media engagement has been responding, listening and connecting with fans, which is important because it builds loyalty."[21]

By satisfying unmet consumer needs with a little bit of flair, Virgin America has quickly built a strong brand.

Brand Equity Models

Although marketers agree about basic branding principles, a number of models of brand equity offer some differing perspectives. Here we highlight three more-established ones.

BRANDASSET® VALUATOR Advertising agency Young and Rubicam (Y&R) developed a model of brand equity called the BrandAsset® Valuator (BAV). Based on research with almost 800,000 consumers in 51 countries, BAV compares the brand equity of thousands of brands across hundreds of different categories. There are four key components—or pillars—of brand equity, according to BAV (see ▲ Figure 9.1):

- *Energized differentiation* measures the degree to which a brand is seen as different from others, and its perceived momentum and leadership.
- *Relevance* measures the appropriateness and breadth of a brand's appeal.
- *Esteem* measures perceptions of quality and loyalty, or how well the brand is regarded and respected.
- *Knowledge* measures how aware and familiar consumers are with the brand.

Energized differentiation and relevance combine to determine *brand strength*—a leading indicator that predicts future growth and value. Esteem and knowledge together create *brand stature*, a "report card" on past performance and a current indicator of current value.

The relationships among these dimensions—a brand's "pillar pattern"—reveal much about a brand's current and future status. Energized brand strength and brand stature combine to form the *power grid*, depicting stages in the cycle of brand development in successive quadrants (see ▲ Figure 9.2). Strong new brands show higher levels of differentiation and energy than relevance, whereas both esteem and knowledge are lower still. Leadership brands show high levels on all pillars. Finally, declining brands show high knowledge—evidence of past performance—a lower level of esteem, and even lower relevance, energy, and differentiation.

|Fig. 9.1| △

BrandAsset® Valuator Model

Source: Courtesy of BrandAsset® Consulting, a division of Young & Rubicam.

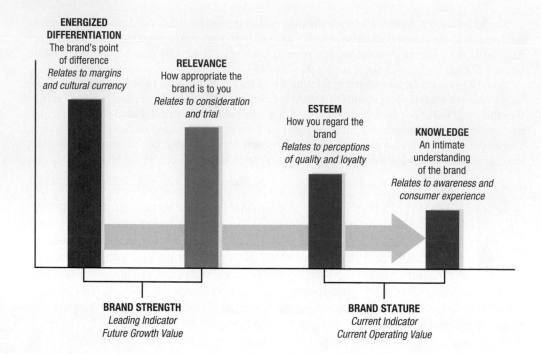

According to BAV analysis, consumers are concentrating their devotion and purchasing power on an increasingly smaller portfolio of special brands—brands with energized differentiation that keep evolving. These brands connect better with consumers—commanding greater usage loyalty and pricing power, and creating greater shareholder value. A hypothetical $10,000 invested in the top 50 energy-gaining brands grew 12 percent while the S&P 500 index lost nearly 20 percent between December 31, 2001, and June 30, 2009. Some of the latest insights from the BAV data are summarized in "Marketing Insight: Brand Bubble Trouble."

BRANDZ Marketing research consultants Millward Brown and WPP have developed the BrandZ model of brand strength, at the heart of which is the BrandDynamics pyramid. According to this model, brand building follows a series of steps (see △ Figure 9.3).

For any one brand, each person interviewed is assigned to one level of the pyramid depending on their responses to a set of questions. The BrandDynamics Pyramid shows the number of consumers who have reached each level.

* **Presence.** Active familiarity based on past trial, saliency, or knowledge of brand promise
* **Relevance.** Relevance to consumer's needs, in the right price range or in the consideration set
* **Performance.** Belief that it delivers acceptable product performance and is on the consumer's short-list
* **Advantage.** Belief that the brand has an emotional or rational advantage over other brands in the category
* **Bonding.** Rational and emotional attachments to the brand to the exclusion of most other brands

"Bonded" consumers at the top of the pyramid build stronger relationships with and spend more on the brand than those at lower levels. There are more consumers at the lower levels, so the challenge for marketers is to help them move up.

BRAND RESONANCE MODEL The brand resonance model also views brand building as an ascending series of steps, from bottom to top: (1) ensuring customers identify the brand and associate it with a specific product class or need; (2) firmly establishing the brand meaning in customers' minds by strategically linking a host of tangible and intangible brand associations; (3) eliciting the proper customer responses in terms of brand-related judgment and feelings; and (4) converting customers' brand response to an intense, active loyalty.

By plotting a representative group of brands' scores for both strength and stature, this matrix derived from the BrandAsset Valuator shows an accurate picture of a brand's status and overall performance.

|Fig. 9.2| △

The Universe of Brand Performance

Source: Young & Rubicam BrandAsset Valuator.

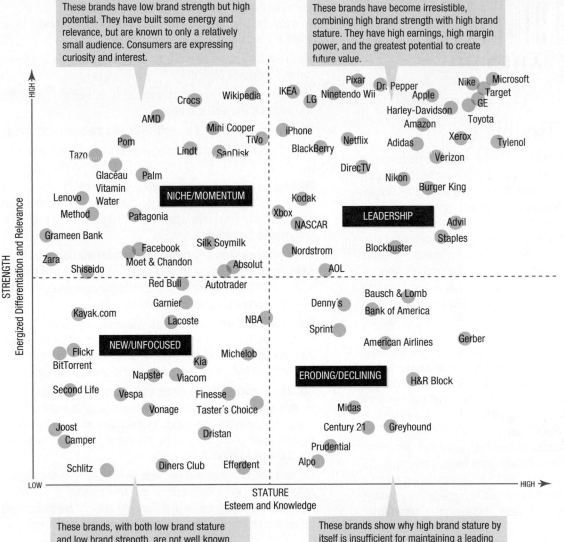

These brands have low brand strength but high potential. They have built some energy and relevance, but are known to only a relatively small audience. Consumers are expressing curiosity and interest.

These brands have become irresistible, combining high brand strength with high brand stature. They have high earnings, high margin power, and the greatest potential to create future value.

These brands, with both low brand stature and low brand strength, are not well known among the general population. Many are new entrants; others are middling brands that have lost their way.

These brands show why high brand stature by itself is insufficient for maintaining a leading position. They struggle to overcome what consumers already know about and expect from them.

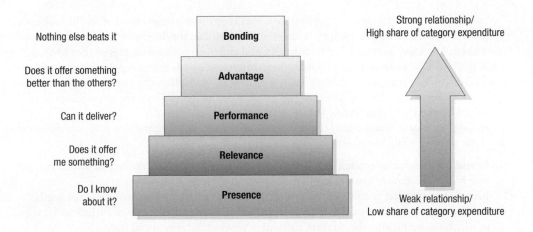

|Fig. 9.3| △

BrandDynamics™ Pyramid

Source: BrandDynamics™ Pyramid. Reprinted with permission of Millward Brown.

Nothing else beats it — **Bonding** — Strong relationship/ High share of category expenditure

Does it offer something better than the others? — **Advantage**

Can it deliver? — **Performance**

Does it offer me something? — **Relevance**

Do I know about it? — **Presence** — Weak relationship/ Low share of category expenditure

Brand Bubble Trouble

In *The Brand Bubble*, brand consultants Ed Lebar and John Gerzema use Y&R's historical BAV database to conduct a comprehensive examination of the state of brands. Beginning with data from mid-2004, they discovered several odd trends. For thousands of consumer goods and services brands, key brand value measures such as consumer "top-of-mind" awareness, trust, regard, and admiration experienced significant drops.

At the same time, however, share prices for a number of years were being driven higher by the intangible value the markets were attributing to consumer brands. Digging deeper, Lebar and Gerzema found the increase was actually due to a very few extremely strong brands such as Google, Apple, and Nike. The value created by the vast majority of brands was stagnating or falling.

The authors viewed this mismatch between the value consumers see in brands and the value the markets were ascribing to them as a recipe for disaster in two ways. At the macroeconomic level, it implied that stock prices of most consumer companies are overstated. At the microeconomic, company level, it pointed to a serious and continuing problem in brand management.

Why have consumer attitudes toward brands declined? The research identified three fundamental causes. First, there has been a proliferation of brands. New product introductions have accelerated, but many fail to register with consumers. Two, consumers expect creative "big ideas" from brands and feel they are just not getting them. Finally, due to corporate scandals, product crises, and executive misbehavior, trust in brands has plummeted.

Yet, vital brands are still being successfully built. Although all four pillars of the BAV model play a role, the strongest brands resonated with consumers in a special way. Amazon.com, Axe, Facebook, Innocent, IKEA, Land Rover, LG, LEGO, Tata, Nano, Twitter, Whole Foods, and

Zappos exhibited notable energized differentiation by communicating dynamism and creativity in ways most other brands did not.

Formally, the BAV analysis identified three factors that help define energy and the marketplace momentum it creates:

1. *Vision*—A clear direction and point of view on the world and how it can and should be changed.

2. *Invention*—An intention for the product or service to change the way people think, feel, and behave.

3. *Dynamism*—Excitement and affinity in the way the brand is presented.

The authors offer a five-step framework to infuse brands with more energy.

1. **Perform an "energy audit" on your brand.** Identify the current sources and level of energy to understand your brand's strengths and weaknesses and how well brand management aligns with the dynamics of the new marketplace.

2. **Make your brand an organizing principle for the business.** Find an essential brand idea or thought that can serve as a lens through which you define every aspect of the customer experience, including products, services, and communications.

3. **Create an energized value chain.** Make the organization's goals for the brand real for everyone; all participants must think uniquely from the perspective of the brand and understand how their own actions boost the energy level of the brand and fuel the core.

4. **Become an energy-driven enterprise.** Stakeholders need to transfer their energy and passion to their business units and functions. Once management's aspirations for the brand and business begin becoming part of the culture, the process of building an energized brand enterprise is nearly complete.

5. **Create a loop of constant reinvention.** Finally, keep the organization and its brand in a state of constant renewal. Brand managers must be keenly aware of shifts in consumers' perception and values and be ready to reshape themselves again and again.

Sources: John Gerzema and Ed Lebar, *The Brand Bubble: The Looming Crisis in Brand Value and How to Avoid It* (New York: Jossey-Bass, 2008); John Gerzema and Ed Lebar, "The Trouble with Brands," *Strategy+Business* 55 (Summer 2009).

According to this model, enacting the four steps means establishing a pyramid of six "brand building blocks" as illustrated in ▲ Figure 9.4. The model emphasizes the duality of brands—the rational route to brand building is on the left side of the pyramid and the emotional route is on the right side.[22]

MasterCard is a brand with duality, because it emphasizes both the rational advantages of the credit card—its acceptance at establishments worldwide—as well as the emotional advantages, expressed in the award-winning "Priceless" advertising campaign ("There are some things money can't buy; for everything else, there's MasterCard.").

Creating significant brand equity requires reaching the top of the brand pyramid, which occurs only if the right building blocks are put into place.

- *Brand salience* is how often and how easily customers think of the brand under various purchase or consumption situations.
- *Brand performance* is how well the product or service meets customers' functional needs.
- *Brand imagery* describes the extrinsic properties of the product or service, including the ways in which the brand attempts to meet customers' psychological or social needs.

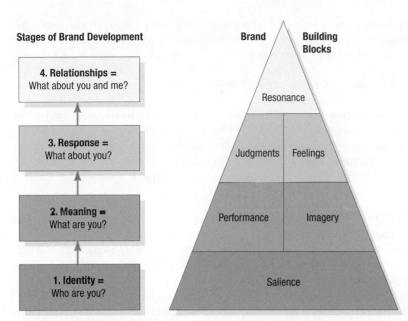

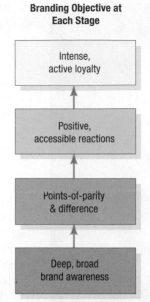

|Fig. 9.4| △

Brand Resonance
Pyramid

MasterCard's "Priceless"
campaign reinforces the emotional rewards of the brand.

- **Brand judgments** focus on customers' own personal opinions and evaluations.
- **Brand feelings** are customers' emotional responses and reactions with respect to the brand.
- **Brand resonance** describes the relationship customers have with the brand and the extent to which they feel they're "in sync" with it.

Resonance is the intensity of customers' psychological bond with the brand and the level of activity it engenders.[23] Brands with high resonance include Harley-Davidson, Apple, and eBay. Fox News has found that the higher levels of resonance and engagement its programs engender often lead to greater recall of the ads it runs.[24]

Building Brand Equity

Marketers build brand equity by creating the right brand knowledge structures with the right consumers. This process depends on *all* brand-related contacts—whether marketer-initiated or not.[25] From a marketing management perspective, however, there are three main sets of *brand equity drivers:*

1. *The initial choices for the brand elements or identities making up the brand (brand names, URLs, logos, symbols, characters, spokespeople, slogans, jingles, packages, and signage)*—Microsoft chose the name Bing for its new search engine because it felt it unambiguously conveyed search and the "aha" moment of finding what a person is looking for. It is also short, appealing, memorable, active, and effective multiculturally.[26]

The brand name 42BELOW has both direct product meaning and indirect meaning related to its New Zealand origins.

2. *The product and service and all accompanying marketing activities and supporting marketing programs*—Liz Claiborne's fastest-growing label is Juicy Couture, whose edgy, contemporary sportswear and accessories have a strong lifestyle appeal to women, men, and kids. Positioned as an affordable luxury, the brand creates its exclusive cachet via limited distribution and a somewhat risqué name and rebellious attitude.[27]

3. *Other associations indirectly transferred to the brand by linking it to some other entity (a person, place, or thing)*—The brand name of New Zealand vodka 42BELOW refers to both a latitude that runs through New Zealand and the percentage of its alcohol content. The packaging and other visual cues are designed to leverage the perceived purity of the country to communicate the positioning for the brand.[28]

Choosing Brand Elements

Brand elements are devices, which can be trademarked, that identify and differentiate the brand. Most strong brands employ multiple brand elements. Nike has the distinctive "swoosh" logo, the empowering "Just Do It" slogan, and the "Nike" name from the Greek winged goddess of victory.

Marketers should choose brand elements to build as much brand equity as possible. The test is what consumers would think or feel about the product *if* the brand element were all they knew. Based on its name alone, for instance, a consumer might expect SnackWell's products to be healthful snack foods and Panasonic Toughbook laptop computers to be durable and reliable.

BRAND ELEMENT CHOICE CRITERIA There are six criteria for choosing brand elements. The first three—memorable, meaningful, and likable—are "brand building." The latter three—transferable, adaptable, and protectable—are "defensive" and help leverage and preserve brand equity against challenges.

1. *Memorable*—How easily do consumers recall and recognize the brand element, and when—at both purchase and consumption? Short names such as Tide, Crest, and Puffs are memorable brand elements.

2. *Meaningful*—Is the brand element credible? Does it suggest the corresponding category and a product ingredient or the type of person who might use the brand? Consider the inherent meaning in names such as DieHard auto batteries, Mop & Glo floor wax, and Lean Cuisine low-calorie frozen entrees.

3. *Likable*—How aesthetically appealing is the brand element? A recent trend is for playful names that also offer a readily available URL, like Flickr photo sharing, Wakoopa social networking, and Motorola's ROKR and RAZR cell phones.[29]

4. *Transferable*—Can the brand element introduce new products in the same or different categories? Does it add to brand equity across geographic boundaries and market segments? Although initially an online book seller, Amazon.com was smart enough not to call itself "Books 'R' Us." The Amazon is famous as the world's biggest river, and the name suggests the wide variety of goods that could be shipped, an important descriptor of the diverse range of products the company now sells.

5. *Adaptable*—How adaptable and updatable is the brand element? The face of Betty Crocker has received more than seven makeovers in 87 years, and she doesn't look a day over 35!

6. *Protectable*—How legally protectable is the brand element? How competitively protectable? Names that become synonymous with product categories—such as Kleenex, Kitty Litter, Jell-O, Scotch Tape, Xerox, and Fiberglass—should retain their trademark rights and not become generic.

DEVELOPING BRAND ELEMENTS Brand elements can play a number of brand-building roles.[30] If consumers don't examine much information in making product decisions, brand elements should be easy to recall and inherently descriptive and persuasive. The likability of brand elements may also increase awareness and associations.[31] The Keebler elves reinforce home-style baking quality and a sense of magic and fun for their line of cookies; Michelin's friendly tire-shaped Bibendum helps to convey safety for the family.

Often, the less concrete brand benefits are, the more important that brand elements capture intangible characteristics. Many insurance firms use symbols of strength for their brands (the Rock of Gibraltar for Prudential and the stag for Hartford), security (the "good hands" of Allstate and the hard hat of Fireman's Fund), or some combination (the castle for Fortis).

Mountain Dew's Dew Tour is a high-energy sponsorship that reinforces the brand's credentials for the youth market.

Like brand names, slogans are an extremely efficient means to build brand equity.[32] They can function as useful "hooks" to help consumers grasp what the brand is and what makes it special, as in "Like a Good Neighbor, State Farm Is There," "Nothing Runs Like a Deere," "Citi Never Sleeps," "Every Kiss Begins with Kay" for the jeweler, and "We Try Harder" for Avis rental cars. But choosing a name with inherent meaning may make it harder to add a different meaning or update the positioning.[33]

Designing Holistic Marketing Activities

Brands are not built by advertising alone. Customers come to know a brand through a range of contacts and touch points: personal observation and use, word of mouth, interactions with company personnel, online or telephone experiences, and payment transactions. A **brand contact** is any information-bearing experience, whether positive or negative, a customer or prospect has with the brand, its product category, or its market.[34] The company must put as much effort into managing these experiences as into producing its ads.[35]

As we describe throughout this text, marketing strategy and tactics have changed dramatically.[36] Marketers are creating brand contacts and building brand equity through new avenues such as clubs and consumer communities, trade shows, event marketing, sponsorship, factory visits, public relations and press releases, and social cause marketing. Mountain Dew created the multicity Dew Tour in which athletes compete in different skateboarding, BMX, and freestyle motocross events to reach the coveted but fickle 12- to 24-year-old target market.[37]

Integrated marketing is about mixing and matching these marketing activities to maximize their individual and collective effects.[38] To achieve it, marketers need a variety of different marketing activities that consistently reinforce the brand promise. The Olive Garden has become the second-largest casual dining restaurant chain in the United States, with more than $3 billion in sales in 2010 from its more than 700 North American restaurants, in part through establishing a fully integrated marketing program.

Olive Garden goes to extraordinary lengths to live up to its brand promise of offering "the idealized Italian family meal."

The Olive Garden The Olive Garden brand promise is "the idealized Italian family meal" characterized by "fresh, simple, delicious Italian food," "complemented by a great glass of wine," served by "people who treat you like family," "in a comfortable homelike setting." To live up to that brand promise, The Olive Garden has sent more than 1,100 restaurant General Managers and team members on cultural immersion trips to Italy, launched the Culinary Institute of Tuscany in Italy to inspire new dishes and teach General Managers and team members authentic Italian cooking techniques, conducts wine training workshops for team members and in-restaurant wine sampling for guests, and is remodeling restaurants to give them a Tuscan farmhouse look. Communications include in-store, employee, and mass media messages that all reinforce the brand promise and ad slogan, "When You're Here, You're Family."[39]

We can evaluate integrated marketing activities in terms of the effectiveness and efficiency with which they affect brand awareness and create, maintain, or strengthen brand associations and image. Although Volvo may invest in R&D and engage in advertising, promotions, and other communications to reinforce its "safety" brand association, it may also sponsor events to make sure it is seen as contemporary and up-to-date. Marketing programs should be put together so the whole is greater than the sum of the parts. In other words, marketing activities should work singularly and in combination.

Leveraging Secondary Associations

The third and final way to build brand equity is, in effect, to "borrow" it. That is, create brand equity by linking the brand to other information in memory that conveys meaning to consumers (see △ Figure 9.5).

These "secondary" brand associations can link the brand to sources, such as the company itself (through branding strategies), to countries or other geographical regions (through identification of product origin), and to channels of distribution (through channel strategy), as well as to other brands (through ingredient or co-branding), characters (through licensing), spokespeople (through endorsements), sporting or cultural events (through sponsorship), or some other third-party sources (through awards or reviews).

Suppose Burton—the maker of snowboards, ski boots, bindings, clothing, and outerwear—decided to introduce a new surfboard called the "Dominator." Burton has gained over a third of the snowboard market by closely aligning itself with top professional riders and creating a strong amateur snowboarder community around the country. To support the new surfboard, Burton could leverage secondary brand knowledge in a number of ways:

- It could "sub-brand" the product, calling it "Dominator by Burton." Consumers' evaluations of the new product would be influenced by how they felt about Burton and whether they felt that such knowledge predicted the quality of a Burton surfboard.
- Burton could rely on its rural New England origins, but such a geographical location would seem to have little relevance to surfing.

|Fig. 9.5| △

Secondary Sources of Brand Knowledge

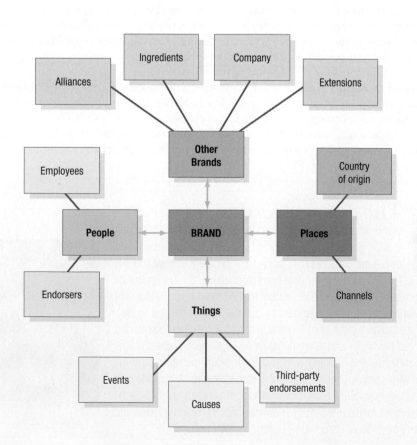

- Burton could sell through popular surf shops in the hope that its credibility would rub off on the Dominator brand.
- Burton could co-brand by identifying a strong ingredient brand for its foam or fiberglass materials (as Wilson did by incorporating Goodyear tire rubber on the soles of its Pro Staff Classic tennis shoes).
- Burton could find one or more top professional surfers to endorse the surfboard, or it could sponsor a surfing competition or even the entire Association of Surfing Professionals (ASP) World Tour.
- Burton could secure and publicize favorable ratings from third-party sources such as *Surfer* or *Surfing* magazine.

Thus, independent of the associations created by the surfboard itself, its brand name, or any other aspects of the marketing program, Burton could build equity by linking the brand to these other entities.

Internal Branding

Marketers must now "walk the walk" to deliver the brand promise. They must adopt an *internal* perspective to be sure employees and marketing partners appreciate and understand basic branding notions and how they can help—or hurt—brand equity.[40] **Internal branding** consists of activities and processes that help inform and inspire employees about brands.[41] Holistic marketers must go even further and train and encourage distributors and dealers to serve their customers well. Poorly trained dealers can ruin the best efforts to build a strong brand image.

    Brand bonding occurs when customers experience the company as delivering on its brand promise. All the customers' contacts with company employees and communications must be positive.[42] *The brand promise will not be delivered unless everyone in the company lives the brand.* Disney is so successful at internal branding that it holds seminars on the "Disney Style" for employees from other companies.

    When employees care about and believe in the brand, they're motivated to work harder and feel greater loyalty to the firm. Some important principles for internal branding are:[43]

1. ***Choose the right moment.*** Turning points are ideal opportunities to capture employees' attention and imagination. After it ran an internal branding campaign to accompany its external repositioning, "Beyond Petroleum," BP found most employees were positive about the new brand and thought the company was going in the right direction.
2. ***Link internal and external marketing.*** Internal and external messages must match. IBM's e-business campaign not only helped to change public perceptions of the company in the marketplace, it also signaled to employees that IBM was determined to be a leader in the use of Internet technology.
3. ***Bring the brand alive for employees.*** Internal communications should be informative and energizing. Miller Brewing has tapped into its brewing heritage to generate pride and passion and improve employee morale.

Brand Communities

Thanks to the Internet, companies are interested in collaborating with consumers to create value through communities built around brands. A **brand community** is a specialized community of consumers and employees whose identification and activities focus around the brand.[44] Three characteristics identify brand communities:[45]

1. A "consciousness of kind" or sense of felt connection to the brand, company, product, or other community members;
2. Shared rituals, stories, and traditions that help to convey the meaning of the community; and
3. A shared moral responsibility or duty to both the community as a whole and individual community members.

    Brand communities come in many different forms.[46] Some arise organically from brand users, such as the Atlanta MGB riders club, the Apple Newton User Group, and the Porsche Rennlist on-line discussion group. Others are company-sponsored and facilitated, such as the Club Green Kids (official kids' fan club of the Boston Celtics) and the Harley-Davidson Owner's Group (H.O.G.).

Successful brands such as Burton Snowboards have to think carefully about how to leverage their strengths with new products and markets, as well as how to "borrow" equity from other people, places, or things.

Harley-Davidson

Harley-Davidson Founded in 1903 in Milwaukee, Wisconsin, Harley-Davidson has twice narrowly escaped bankruptcy but is today one of the most recognized motor vehicle brands in the world. In dire financial straits in the 1980s, Harley desperately licensed its name to such ill-advised ventures as cigarettes and wine coolers. Although consumers loved the brand, sales were depressed by product-quality problems, so Harley began its return to greatness by improving manufacturing processes. It also developed a strong brand community in the form of an owners' club, called the Harley Owners Group (H.O.G.), which sponsors bike rallies, charity rides, and other motorcycle events and now numbers 1 million members in over 1,200 chapters. H.O.G. benefits include a magazine called *Hog Tales*, a touring handbook, emergency road service, a specially designed insurance program, theft reward service, discount hotel rates, and a Fly & Ride program enabling members to rent Harleys on vacation. The company also maintains an extensive Web site devoted to H.O.G., with information about club chapters, events, and a special members-only section.[47]

A strong brand community results in a more loyal, committed customer base. Its activities and advocacy can substitute to some degree for activities the firm would otherwise have to engage in, creating greater marketing effectiveness and efficiency.[48] A brand community can also be a constant source of inspiration and feedback for product improvements or innovations.

To better understand how brand communities work, one comprehensive study examined communities around brands as diverse as StriVectin cosmeceutical, BMW Mini auto, *Xena: Warrior Princess* television show, Jones soda, Tom Petty & the Heartbreakers rock and roll band, and Garmin GPS devices. Using multiple research methods such as "netnographic" research with online forums, participant and naturalistic observation of community activities, and in-depth

TABLE 9.2 Value Creation Practices	
SOCIAL NETWORKING	
Welcoming	Greeting new members, beckoning them into the fold, and assisting in their brand learning and community socialization.
Empathizing	Lending emotional and/or physical support to other members, including support for brand-related trials (e.g., product failure, customizing) and/or for nonbrand-related life issues (e.g., illness, death, job).
Governing	Articulating the behavioral expectations within the brand community.
IMPRESSION MANAGEMENT	
Evangelizing	Sharing the brand "good news," inspiring others to use, and preaching from the mountaintop.
Justifying	Deploying rationales generally for devoting time and effort to the brand and collectively to outsiders and marginal members in the boundary.
COMMUNITY ENGAGEMENT	
Staking	Recognizing variance within the brand community membership and marking intragroup distinction and similarity.
Milestoning	Noting seminal events in brand ownership and consumption.
Badging	Translating milestones into symbols and artifacts.
Documenting	Detailing the brand relationship journey in a narrative way, often anchored by and peppered with milestones.
BRAND USE	
Grooming	Cleaning, caring for, and maintaining the brand or systematizing optimal use patterns
Customizing	Modifying the brand to suit group-level or individual needs. This includes all efforts to change the factory specs of the product to enhance performance.
Commoditizing	Distancing/approaching the marketplace in positive or negative ways. May be directed at other members (e.g., you should sell/should not sell that) or may be directed at the firm through explicit link or through presumed monitoring of the site (e.g., you should fix this/do this/change this).

Source: Adapted from Hope Jensen Schau, Albert M. Muniz, and Eric J. Arnould, "How Brand Community Practices Create Value," *Journal of Marketing* 73 (September 2009) pp. 30–51.

TABLE 9.3	The Myths and Realities of Brand Communities
Myth: Brand community is a marketing strategy.	**Reality**: Brand community is a business strategy. The entire business model must support the community brand.
Myth: Brand communities exist to serve the business.	**Reality**: Brand communities exist to serve the people that comprise them. Brand communities are a means to an end, not the ends themselves.
Myth: Build the brand, and the community will follow.	**Reality**: Cultivate the community and the brand will grow; engineer the community and the brand will be strong.
Myth: Brand communities should be love fests for faithful brand advocates.	**Reality**: Communities are inherently political and this reality must be confronted with honesty and authenticity head-on; smart companies embrace the conflicts that make communities thrive.
Myth: Focus on opinion leaders to build a strong community.	**Reality**: Strong communities take care of all of their members; everyone in the community plays an important role.
Myth: Online social networks are the best way to build community.	**Reality**: Social networks are one community tool, but the tool is not the strategy.
Myth: Successful brand communities are tightly managed and controlled.	**Reality**: Control is an illusion; brand community success requires opening up and letting go; of and by the people, communities defy managerial control.

Sources: Susan Fournier and Lara Lee, *The Seven Deadly Sins of Brand Community,* Marketing Science Institute Special Report 08-208, 2008; Susan Fournier and Lara Lee, "Getting Brand Communities Right," *Harvard Business Review,* April 2009, pp. 105–11.

interviews with community members, the researchers found 12 value creation practices taking place. They divided them into four categories—social networking, community engagement, impression management, and brand use—summarized in ⬭ Table 9.2.

Building a positive, productive brand community requires careful thought and implementation. Branding experts Susan Fournier and Lara Lee have identified seven common myths about brand communities and suggest the reality in each case (see ⬭ Table 9.3).

Measuring Brand Equity

How do we measure brand equity? An *indirect* approach assesses potential sources of brand equity by identifying and tracking consumer brand knowledge structures.[49] A *direct* approach assesses the actual impact of brand knowledge on consumer response to different aspects of the marketing. "Marketing Insight: The Brand Value Chain" shows how to link the two approaches.[50]

Marketing Insight

The Brand Value Chain

The **brand value chain** is a structured approach to assessing the sources and outcomes of brand equity and the way marketing activities create brand value (see △ Figure 9.6). It is based on several premises.

First, brand value creation begins when the firm targets actual or potential customers by investing in a marketing program to develop the brand, including product research, development, and design; trade or intermediary support; and marketing communications. Next, we assume customers' mind-sets, buying behavior, and response to price will change as a result of the marketing program; the question is how. Finally, the investment community will consider market performance, replacement cost, and purchase price in acquisitions (among other factors) to assess shareholder value in general and the value of a brand in particular.

The model also assumes that three multipliers moderate the transfer between the marketing program and the subsequent three value stages.

• The *program multiplier* determines the marketing program's ability to affect the customer mind-set and is a function of the quality of the program investment.

• The *customer multiplier* determines the extent to which value created in the minds of customers affects market performance. This result depends on competitive superiority (how effective the quantity and quality of the marketing investment of other competing brands are), channel and other intermediary support (how much brand

|Fig. 9.6| △

Brand Value Chain

Source: Kevin Lane Keller, *Strategic Brand Management*, 3rd ed. (Upper Saddle River, NJ: Prentice Hall, 2008). Printed and electronically reproduced by permission of Pearson Education, Inc. Upper Saddle River, New Jersey.

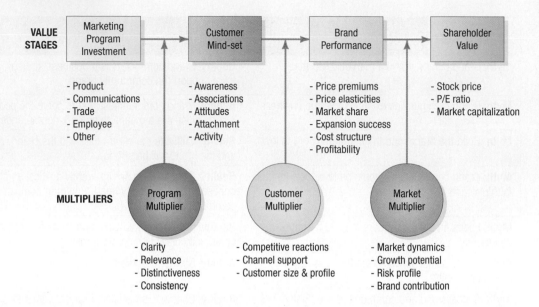

reinforcement and selling effort various marketing partners are putting forth), and customer size and profile (how many and what types of customers, profitable or not, are attracted to the brand).

- The *market multiplier* determines the extent to which the value shown by the market performance of a brand is manifested in shareholder value. It depends, in part, on the actions of financial analysts and investors.

Sources: Kevin Lane Keller and Don Lehmann, "How Do Brands Create Value," *Marketing Management* (May–June 2003), pp. 27–31. See also Marc J. Epstein and Robert A. Westbrook, "Linking Actions to Profits in Strategic Decision Making," *MIT Sloan Management Review* (Spring 2001), pp. 39–49; Rajendra K. Srivastava, Tasadduq A. Shervani, and Liam Fahey, "Market-Based Assets and Shareholder Value," *Journal of Marketing* 62, no. 1 (January 1998), pp. 2–18; Shuba Srinivasan, Marc Vanheule, and Koen Pauwels, "Mindset Metrics in Market Response Models: An Integrative Approach," *Journal of Marketing Research,* forthcoming.

The two general approaches are complementary, and marketers can employ both. In other words, for brand equity to perform a useful strategic function and guide marketing decisions, marketers need to fully understand (1) the sources of brand equity and how they affect outcomes of interest, and (2) how these sources and outcomes change, if at all, over time. Brand audits are important for the former; brand tracking for the latter.

- A **brand audit** is a consumer-focused series of procedures to assess the health of the brand, uncover its sources of brand equity, and suggest ways to improve and leverage its equity. Marketers should conduct a brand audit when setting up marketing plans and when considering shifts in strategic direction. Conducting brand audits on a regular basis, such as annually, allows marketers to keep their fingers on the pulse of their brands so they can manage them more proactively and responsively.
- **Brand-tracking studies** collect quantitative data from consumers over time to provide consistent, baseline information about how brands and marketing programs are performing. Tracking studies help us understand where, how much, and in what ways brand value is being created, to facilitate day-to-day decision making.

Marketers should distinguish brand equity from **brand valuation**, which is the job of estimating the total financial value of the brand. ▭ Table 9.4 displays the world's most valuable brands in 2009 according to one ranking.[51] In these well-known companies, brand value is typically over half the total company market capitalization. John Stuart, cofounder of Quaker Oats, said: "If this business were split up, I would give you the land and bricks and mortar, and I would take the brands and trademarks, and I would fare better than you." U.S. companies do not list brand equity on their balance sheets in part because of differences in opinion about what constitutes a good estimate. However, companies do give it a value in countries such as the United Kingdom, Hong Kong, and Australia. "Marketing Insight: What Is a Brand Worth?" reviews one popular valuation approach.

TABLE 9.4	The World's 10 Most Valuable Brands in 2009	
Rank	Brand	2009 Brand Value (Billions)
1	Coca-Cola	$68.7
2	IBM	$60.2
3	Microsoft	$56.6
4	GE	$47.8
5	Nokia	$34.9
6	McDonald's	$32.3
7	Google	$32.0
8	Toyota	$31.3
9	Intel	$30.6
10	Disney	$28.4

Source: Interbrand. Used with permission.

Marketing Insight

What Is a Brand Worth?

Top brand-management firm Interbrand has developed a model to formally estimate the dollar value of a brand. It defines brand value as the net present value of the future earnings that can be attributed to the brand alone. The firm believes marketing and financial analyses are equally important in determining the value of a brand. Its process follows five steps (see Figure 9.7 for a schematic overview):

1. **Market Segmentation**—The first step is to divide the market(s) in which the brand is sold into mutually exclusive segments that help determine variances in the brand's different customer groups.

2. **Financial Analysis**—Interbrand assesses purchase price, volume, and frequency to help calculate accurate forecasts of future brand sales and revenues. Once it has established Brand Revenues, it deducts all associated operating costs to derive earnings before interest and tax (EBIT). It also deducts the appropriate taxes and a charge for the capital employed to operate the underlying business, leaving Economic Earnings, that is, the earnings attributed to the branded business.

3. **Role of Branding**—Interbrand next attributes a proportion of Economic Earnings to the brand in each market segment, by first identifying the various drivers of demand, then determining the degree to which the brand directly influences each. The Role of Branding assessment is based on market research, client workshops, and interviews and represents the percentage of Economic Earnings the brand generates. Multiplying the Role of Branding by Economic Earnings yields Brand Earnings.

4. **Brand Strength**—Interbrand then assesses the brand's strength profile to determine the likelihood that the brand will realize forecasted Brand Earnings. This step relies on competitive benchmarking and a structured evaluation of the brand's clarity, commitment, protection, responsiveness, authenticity, relevance, differentiation, consistency, presence, and understanding. For each segment, Interbrand applies industry and brand equity metrics to determine a risk premium for the brand. The company's analysts derive the overall Brand Discount Rate by adding a brand-risk premium to the risk-free rate, represented by the yield on government bonds. The Brand Discount Rate, applied to the forecasted Brand Earnings forecast, yields the net present value of the Brand Earnings. The stronger the brand, the lower the discount rate, and vice versa.

5. **Brand Value Calculation**—Brand Value is the net present value (NPV) of the forecasted Brand Earnings, discounted by the Brand Discount Rate. The NPV calculation comprises both the forecast period and the period beyond, reflecting the ability of brands to continue generating future earnings.

Increasingly, Interbrand uses brand value assessments as a dynamic, strategic tool to identify and maximize return on brand investment across a whole host of areas.

Sources: Interbrand, the Interbrand Brand Glossary, and Interbrand's Nik Stucky and Rita Clifton.

|Fig. 9.7| △

Interbrand Brand
Valuation Method

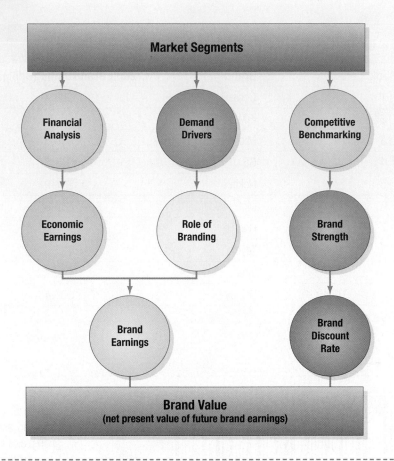

Managing Brand Equity

Because consumer responses to marketing activity depend on what they know and remember about a brand, short-term marketing actions, by changing brand knowledge, necessarily increase or decrease the long-term success of future marketing actions.

Brand Reinforcement

As a company's major enduring asset, a brand needs to be carefully managed so its value does not depreciate.[52] Many brand leaders of 70 years ago remain leaders today—Wrigley's, Coca-Cola, Heinz, and Campbell Soup—but only by constantly striving to improve their products, services, and marketing.

Marketers can reinforce brand equity by consistently conveying the brand's meaning in terms of (1) what products it represents, what core benefits it supplies, and what needs it satisfies; and (2) how the brand makes products superior, and which strong, favorable, and unique brand associations should exist in consumers' minds.[53] NIVEA, one of Europe's strongest brands, has expanded from a skin cream brand to a skin care and personal care brand through carefully designed and implemented brand extensions that reinforce the brand promise of "mild," "gentle," and "caring."

Reinforcing brand equity requires that the brand always be moving forward— in the right direction and with new and compelling offerings and ways to market them. In virtually every product category, once-prominent and admired brands—such as Fila, Oldsmobile, Polaroid, Circuit City— have fallen on hard times or gone out of business.[54]

An important part of reinforcing brands is providing consistent marketing support. Consistency doesn't mean uniformity with no changes: While there is little need to deviate from a successful position, many tactical changes may be necessary to maintain the strategic thrust and direction of the brand. When change *is* necessary, marketers should vigorously preserve and defend sources of brand equity.

Discover Communications

In the hypercompetitive marketplace of cable TV channels, having a consistently clear but evolving identity is critical. One of the most successful cable TV programmers, Discovery Communications, operates 13 channels in the United States with such signature shows as *Deadliest Catch* and *MythBusters* (Discovery Channel), *Whale Wars* (Animal Planet), and the once-popular, now-defunct *Jon & Kate Plus 8* (TLC). Positioning itself as the number one nonfiction media company in the world, Discovery Communications is dedicated "to satisfying curiosity and making a difference in people's lives with the highest quality content, services and products that entertain, engage and enlighten—inviting viewers to explore their world." For example, by recognizing that nature and animals harbor mystery and danger, Animal Planet has developed into a more aggressive and compelling brand. New channels in the works include a women's channel with Oprah Winfrey, a kid's channel in partnership with Hasbro, and a possible series of science shows with director Steven Spielberg. Discovery is also increasing its global expansion—including China and India—and now reaches more than 1.5 billion subscribers in 170 countries, generating a third of the company's revenue from overseas.[55]

Deadliest Catch has become a defining program for the Discovery Channel.

Marketers must recognize the trade-offs between activities that fortify the brand and reinforce its meaning, such as a well-received product improvement or a creatively designed ad campaign, and those that leverage or borrow from existing brand equity to reap some financial benefit, such as a short-term promotional discount.[56] At some point, failure to reinforce the brand will diminish brand awareness and weaken brand image.

Brand Revitalization

Any new development in the marketing environment can affect a brand's fortunes. Nevertheless, a number of brands have managed to make impressive comebacks in recent years.[57] After some hard times, Burberry, Fiat, and Volkswagen have all turned their brand fortunes around to varying degrees.

Often, the first thing to do in revitalizing a brand is to understand what the sources of brand equity were to begin with. Are positive associations losing their strength or uniqueness? Have negative associations become linked to the brand? Then decide whether to retain the same positioning or create a new one, and if so, which new one.

Sometimes the actual marketing program is the source of the problem, because it fails to deliver on the brand promise. Then a "back to basics" strategy may make sense. As noted previously, Harley-Davidson regained its market leadership by doing a better job of living up to customer expectations as to product performance. Eu Yan Sang did it by returning to its roots and leveraging key brand assets.

Eu Yan Sang wanted to appeal to the younger generation so it launched new products and embarked on a marketing campaign involving roadshows and cooking demonstrations.

Eu Yan Sang

Eu Yan Sang, a brand with more than 130 years of history, has come a long way since opening its first shop in 1873. The brand has succeeded in growing from a traditional Chinese medical hall to a publicly listed company with stores in Hong Kong, Malaysia, China, Macau, and Singapore.

Traditional Chinese medicine (TCM) is commonly linked to images of elderly men measuring out dried herbs and brewing bowls full of black bitter soup. Though TCM is popular with the older generation, younger consumers saw it as inconvenient. Eu Yan Sang remained stagnant with flat growth for a period of nearly 60 years. All this changed when Richard Eu took over his

family business in 1989. Knowing he had to make the brand relevant to younger consumers, Eu leveraged Eu Yan Sang's strong equity as a trusted brand and modernized it by going back to basics. Through research and development, he was able to provide innovative offerings such as ready-to-use concentrates and easy-to-swallow pills that changed the way Chinese medicine is consumed. The retail stores were also redesigned to give them a brighter and friendlier look. With the support of other marketing activities such as advertising, road shows, and cooking demonstrations, Eu Yan Sang's business has grown by leaps and bounds. Initiatives such as the Eu Yan Sang TCM clinics that combined the best of east-west health care practices help the brand stay relevant. The brand's success in revitalizing itself is evident in the numerous awards it has received. Eu Yan Sang was included in the "Best Under a Billion" companies list by *Forbes* Asia and received the Putra Brand Award, Hong Kong's Pride Award, and Singapore Brand Award.[58] ▭

In other cases, however, the old positioning is just no longer viable and a reinvention strategy is necessary. Mountain Dew completely overhauled its brand image to become a soft drink powerhouse. As its history reveals, it is often easier to revive a brand that is alive but has been more or less forgotten. Old Spice is another example.

Old Spice   One of the first mass market fragrances, Old Spice dates back to 1937. Its classic aftershave and cologne combination—with soap on a rope sometimes tossed in for good measure—was the classic Father's Day gift for baby boomers to give, but was largely irrelevant by the time Procter & Gamble acquired the brand in 1990. P&G's revitalization strategy was to abandon the old cologne business to focus on deodorants and other male grooming products. Facing tough competition from Unilever's edgy line of Axe products, the firm reverted to its classic one-two punch of product innovation and new communications to target the 12- to 34-year-old male. New product development resulted in the creation of Old Spice High Endurance, Pro Strength, and Red Zone lines of deodorants, body washes, body sprays, and shaving products. Old Spice's latest line, Ever Clear, arose from focus group participants' "good-bye letters" to their current deodorant. A technological breakthrough allowed Ever Clear to promise the protection of a dry solid without the uncomfortable waxy residue that left white streaks on clothing. All Old Spice products were backed by tongue-in-cheek advertising that stressed the brand's "experience."[59] ▭

There is obviously a continuum of revitalization strategies, with pure "back to basics" at one end, pure "reinvention" at the other, and many combinations in between. The challenge is often to change enough to attract some new customers but not enough to alienate old customers. Brand revitalization of almost any kind starts with the product.[60] General Motors's turnaround of its fading Cadillac brand was fueled by new designs that redefined its look and styling, such as the CTS sedan, XLR roadster, and ESV sport utility vehicle.[61] High-end clothing retailer Paul Stuart introduced its first ever sub-brand, the bolder, sleeker Phineas Cole, to update its conservative image for a hipper, younger demographic.[62]

Devising a Branding Strategy

A firm's **branding strategy**—often called the **brand architecture**—reflects the number and nature of both common and distinctive brand elements. Deciding how to brand new products is especially critical. A firm has three main choices:

1. It can develop new brand elements for the new product.
2. It can apply some of its existing brand elements.
3. It can use a combination of new and existing brand elements.

When a firm uses an established brand to introduce a new product, the product is called a **brand extension**. When marketers combine a new brand with an existing brand, the brand extension can also be called a **sub-brand**, such as Hershey Kisses candy, Adobe Acrobat software, Toyota Camry automobiles, and American Express Blue cards. The existing brand that gives birth to a brand extension or sub-brand is the **parent brand**. If the parent brand is already associated with multiple products through brand extensions, it can also be called a **master brand** or **family brand**.

Brand extensions fall into two general categories:[63] In a **line extension**, the parent brand covers a new product within a product category it currently serves, such as with new flavors, forms, colors, ingredients, and package sizes. Dannon has introduced several types of Dannon yogurt line extensions through the years—Fruit on the Bottom, All Natural Flavors, Dan-o-nino, and Fruit Blends. In a **category extension**, marketers use the parent brand to enter a different product category, such as Swiss Army watches. Honda has used its company name to cover such different products as automobiles, motorcycles, snowblowers, lawn mowers, marine engines, and snowmobiles. This allows the firm to advertise that it can fit "six Hondas in a two-car garage."

A **brand line** consists of all products—original as well as line and category extensions—sold under a particular brand. A **brand mix** (or brand assortment) is the set of all brand lines that a particular seller makes. Many companies are introducing **branded variants**, which are specific brand lines supplied to specific retailers or distribution channels. They result from the pressure retailers put on manufacturers to provide distinctive offerings. A camera company may supply its low-end cameras to mass merchandisers while limiting its higher-priced items to specialty camera shops. Valentino may design and supply different lines of suits and jackets to different department stores.[64]

A **licensed product** is one whose brand name has been licensed to other manufacturers that actually make the product. Corporations have seized on licensing to push their company names and images across a wide range of products—from bedding to shoes—making licensing a multibillion-dollar business.[65] Jeep's licensing program, which now has 600 products and 150 licensees, includes everything from strollers (built for a father's longer arms) to apparel (with Teflon in the denim)—as long they fit the brand's positioning of "Life without Limits." Through 400-plus dedicated Jeep shop-in-shops and 80 Jeep freestanding stores around the world, licensing revenue now exceeds $550 million in retail sales. New areas of emphasis include outdoor and travel gear, juvenile products, and sporting goods.[66]

Branding Decisions

ALTERNATIVE BRANDING STRATEGIES Today, branding is such a strong force that hardly anything goes unbranded. Assuming a firm decides to brand its products or services, it must choose which brand names to use. Three general strategies are popular:

- *Individual or separate family brand names.* Consumer packaged-goods companies have a long tradition of branding different products by different names. General Mills largely uses individual brand names, such as Bisquick, Gold Medal flour, Nature Valley granola bars, Old El Paso Mexican foods, Progresso soup, Wheaties cereal, and Yoplait yogurt. If a company produces quite different products, one blanket name is often not desirable. Swift and Company developed separate family names for its hams (Premium) and fertilizers (Vigoro). A major advantage of individual or separate family brand names is that if a product fails or appears to be of low quality, the company has not tied its reputation to it. Companies often use different brand names for different quality lines within the same product class.
- *Corporate umbrella or company brand name.* Many firms, such as Heinz and GE, use their corporate brand as an umbrella brand across their entire range of products.[67] Development costs are lower with umbrella names because there's no need to run "name" research or spend heavily on advertising to create recognition. Campbell Soup introduces new soups under its brand name with extreme simplicity and achieves instant recognition. Sales of the new product are likely to be strong if the manufacturer's name is good. Corporate-image associations of innovativeness, expertise, and trustworthiness have been shown to directly influence consumer evaluations.[68] Finally, a corporate branding strategy can lead to greater intangible value for the firm.[69]
- *Sub-brand name.* Sub-brands combine two or more of the corporate brand, family brand, or individual product brand names. Kellogg employs a sub-brand or hybrid branding strategy by combining the corporate brand with individual product brands as with Kellogg's Rice Krispies, Kellogg's Raisin Bran, and Kellogg's Corn Flakes. Many durable-goods makers such as Honda, Sony, and Hewlett-Packard use sub-brands for their products. The corporate or company name legitimizes, and the individual name individualizes, the new product.

HOUSE OF BRANDS VERSUS A BRANDED HOUSE The use of individual or separate family brand names has been referred to as a "house of brands" strategy, whereas the use of an umbrella corporate or company brand name has been referred to as a "branded house" strategy. These two branding strategies represent two ends of a brand relationship continuum. A sub-brand strategy falls somewhere between, depending on which component of the sub-brand receives more emphasis. A good example of a house of brands strategy is United Technologies.

United Technologies

UTC's brand portfolio includes Otis elevators, Carrier heaters and air conditioners, Hamilton Sundstrand aerospace and industrial, Sikorsky helicopters, Pratt & Whitney jet engines, and UTC Fire & Security systems. Most of its brands are the names of the individuals who invented the product or created the company decades ago—they have more power and are more recognizable in the business buying marketplace. The parent brand, UTC, is advertised only to small but influential audiences—the financial community and opinion leaders in New York and Washington, DC. After all, employees are more loyal to the individual companies owned by UTC. "My philosophy has always been to use the power of the trademarks of the subsidiaries to improve the recognition and brand acceptance, awareness, and respect for the parent company itself," said UTC's then-CEO George David.[70]

United Technologies' brand portfolio consists of a diverse collection of companies, products, and brands.

Two key components of virtually any branding strategy are brand portfolios and brand extensions. (Chapter 12 discusses co-branding and ingredient branding, as well as line-stretching through vertical extensions.)

Brand Portfolios

A brand can only be stretched so far, and all the segments the firm would like to target may not view the same brand equally favorably. Marketers often need multiple brands in order to pursue these multiple segments. Some other reasons for introducing multiple brands in a category include:[71]

1. Increasing shelf presence and retailer dependence in the store
2. Attracting consumers seeking variety who may otherwise have switched to another brand
3. Increasing internal competition within the firm
4. Yielding economies of scale in advertising, sales, merchandising, and physical distribution

The **brand portfolio** is the set of all brands and brand lines a particular firm offers for sale in a particular category or market segment.

Starwood Hotels & Resorts

One of the leading hotel and leisure companies in the world, Starwood Hotels & Resorts Worldwide, has 850 properties in more than 95 countries and 145,000 employees at its owned and managed properties. In its rebranding attempt to go "beyond beds," Starwood has differentiated its hotels along emotional, experiential lines. Its hotel and call center operators convey different experiences for the firm's different chains, as does the firm's advertising. This strategy emerged from a major 18-month positioning project, started in 2006, to find positions for the portfolio of brands that would establish an emotional connection with consumers. Consumer research suggested these positions for some of the brands:[72]

- *Sheraton.* With the tagline "You don't stay here, you belong," Sheraton—the largest brand—is about warm, comforting, and casual. Its core value centers on "connections," an image aided by the hotel's alliance with Yahoo!, which cofounded the Yahoo! Link@Sheraton lobby kiosks and cyber cafés.
- *Four Points by Sheraton.* For the self-sufficient traveler, Four Points strives to be honest, uncomplicated, and comfortable. The brand is all about providing a high level of comfort and little indulgences like free high-speed Internet access and bottled water. Its ads feature apple pies and talk about providing guests with "the comforts of home."

- *W.* With a brand personality defined as flirty, for the insider, and an escape, W offers guests unique experiences around the warmth of cool.
- *Westin.* Westin's emphasis on "personal, instinctive, and renewal" has led to a new sensory welcome featuring a white tea scent, signature music and lighting, and refreshing towels. Each room features Westin's own "Heavenly Beds," sold exclusively in the retail market through Nordstrom, further enhancing the brand's upscale image.

The hallmark of an optimal brand portfolio is the ability of each brand in it to maximize equity in combination with all the other brands in it. Marketers generally need to trade off market coverage with costs and profitability. If they can increase profits by dropping brands, a portfolio is too big; if they can increase profits by adding brands, it's not big enough. The basic principle in designing a brand portfolio is to maximize market coverage so no potential customers are being ignored, but minimize brand overlap so brands are not competing for customer approval. Each brand should be clearly differentiated and appealing to a sizable enough marketing segment to justify its marketing and production costs.[73]

Marketers carefully monitor brand portfolios over time to identify weak brands and kill unprofitable ones.[74] Brand lines with poorly differentiated brands are likely to be characterized by much cannibalization and require pruning.[75] There are scores of cereals, beverages, and snacks and thousands of mutual funds. Students can choose among hundreds of business schools. For the seller, this spells hypercompetition. For the buyer, it may mean too much choice.

Brands can also play a number of specific roles as part of a portfolio.

FLANKERS Flanker or "fighter" brands are positioned with respect to competitors' brands so that more important (and more profitable) *flagship brands* can retain their desired positioning. Busch Bavarian is priced and marketed to protect Anheuser-Busch's premium Budweiser; and after a difficult product launch, Celeron helped thwart AMD's competitive challenge to Intel's premium Pentium microprocessor.[76] Marketers walk a fine line in designing fighter brands, which must be neither so attractive that they take sales away from their higher-priced comparison brands nor designed so cheaply that they reflect poorly on them.

CASH COWS Some brands may be kept around despite dwindling sales because they manage to maintain their profitability with virtually no marketing support. Companies can effectively "milk" these "cash cow" brands by capitalizing on their reservoir of brand equity. Gillette still sells the older Trac II, Atra, Sensor, and Mach III brands because withdrawing them may not necessarily move customers to another Gillette brand.

LOW-END ENTRY LEVEL The role of a relatively low-priced brand in the portfolio often may be to attract customers to the brand franchise. Retailers like to feature these "traffic builders" because they are able to "trade up" customers to a higher-priced brand. BMW introduced certain models in its 3 Series automobiles in part as a means of bringing new customers into the brand franchise, with the hope of later moving them to higher-priced models when they decided to trade in their cars.

HIGH-END PRESTIGE The role of a relatively high-priced brand often is to add prestige and credibility to the entire portfolio. One analyst argued that the real value to Chevrolet of its high-performance Corvette sports car was "its ability to lure curious customers into showrooms and at the same time help improve the image of other Chevrolet cars. It does not mean a hell of a lot for GM profitability, but there is no question that it is a traffic builder."[77] Corvette's technological image and prestige cast a halo over the entire Chevrolet line.

Brand Extensions

Many firms have decided to leverage their most valuable asset by introducing a host of new products under their strongest brand names. Most new products are in fact line extensions—typically 80 percent to 90 percent in any one year. Moreover, many of the most successful new products, as rated by various sources, are extensions. Among the most successful new product brand extensions in supermarkets in 2008 were Dunkin' Donuts coffee, Progresso Light soups, and Hormel

Compleats microwave meals. Nevertheless, many new products are introduced each year as new brands. The year 2008 also saw the launch of Zyrtec allergy relief medicine, G2 thirst quencher, and Ped Egg foot files.

ADVANTAGES OF BRAND EXTENSIONS Two main advantages of brand extensions are that they can facilitate new-product acceptance and provide positive feedback to the parent brand and company.

Improved Odds of New-Product Success Consumers form expectations about a new product based on what they know about the parent brand and the extent to which they feel this information is relevant.[78] When Sony introduced a new personal computer tailored for multimedia applications, the Vaio, consumers may have felt comfortable with its anticipated performance because of their experience with and knowledge of other Sony products.

By setting up positive expectations, extensions reduce risk.[79] It also may be easier to convince retailers to stock and promote a brand extension because of anticipated increased customer demand. An introductory campaign for an extension doesn't need to create awareness of both the brand *and* the new product; it can concentrate on the new product itself.[80]

Extensions can thus reduce launch costs, important given that establishing a new brand name for a consumer packaged good in the U.S. marketplace can cost over $100 million! Extensions also can avoid the difficulty—and expense—of coming up with a new name and allow for packaging and labeling efficiencies. Similar or identical packages and labels can lower production costs for extensions and, if coordinated properly, provide more prominence in the retail store via a "billboard" effect.[81] Stouffer's offers a variety of frozen entrees with identical orange packaging that increases their visibility when they're stocked together in the freezer. With a portfolio of brand variants within a product category, consumers who want a change can switch to a different product type without having to leave the brand family.

Positive Feedback Effects Besides facilitating acceptance of new products, brand extensions can provide feedback benefits.[82] They can help to clarify the meaning of a brand and its core values or improve consumer loyalty to the company behind the extension.[83] Through their brand extensions, Crayola means "colorful arts and crafts for kids," Aunt Jemima means "breakfast foods," and Weight Watchers means "weight loss and maintenance."

Line extensions can renew interest and liking for the brand and benefit the parent brand by expanding market coverage. The goal of Kimberly-Clark's Kleenex unit is to have facial tissue in every room of the home. This philosophy has led to a wide variety of Kleenex facial tissues and packaging, including scented, ultra-soft, and lotion-impregnated tissues; boxes with drawings of dinosaurs and dogs for children's rooms; colorful, stylish designs to match living room décor; and a "man-sized" box with tissues 50 percent larger than regular Kleenex.

By defining its brand promise in terms of "colorful arts and crafts for kids," Crayola has extended beyond crayons to successfully introduce a range of different products.

A successful extension may also generate subsequent extensions.[84] During the 1970s and 1980s, Billabong established its brand credibility with the young surfing community as a designer and producer of quality surf apparel. This success permitted it to extend into other youth-oriented areas, such as snowboarding and skateboarding.

DISADVANTAGES OF BRAND EXTENSIONS On the downside, line extensions may cause the brand name to be less strongly identified with any one product.[85] Al Ries and Jack Trout call this the "line-extension trap."[86] By linking its brand to mainstream food products such as mashed potatoes, powdered milk, soups, and beverages, Cadbury ran the risk of losing its more specific meaning as a chocolate and candy brand.[87] **Brand dilution** occurs when consumers no longer associate a brand with a specific or highly similar set of products and start thinking less of the brand.

If a firm launches extensions consumers deem inappropriate, they may question the integrity of the brand or become confused or even frustrated: Which version of the product is the "right one" for them? Retailers reject many new products and brands because they don't have the shelf or display space for them. And the firm itself may become overwhelmed.

The worst possible scenario is for an extension not only to fail, but to harm the parent brand in the process. Fortunately, such events are rare. "Marketing failures," in which too few consumers were attracted to a brand, are typically much less damaging than "product failures," in which the brand fundamentally fails to live up to its promise. Even then, product failures dilute brand equity only when the extension is seen as very similar to the parent brand. The Audi 5000 car suffered from a tidal wave of negative publicity and word of mouth in the mid-1980s when it was alleged to have a "sudden acceleration" problem. The adverse publicity spilled over to the 4000 model. But the Quattro was relatively insulated, because it was distanced from the 5000 by its more distinct branding and advertising strategy.[88]

Even if sales of a brand extension are high and meet targets, the revenue may be coming from consumers switching to the extension from existing parent-brand offerings—in effect cannibalizing the parent brand. Intrabrand shifts in sales may not necessarily be undesirable if they're a form of *preemptive cannibalization*. In other words, consumers might have switched to a competing brand instead of the line extension if the extension hadn't been introduced. Tide laundry detergent maintains the same market share it had 50 years ago because of the sales contributions of its various line extensions—scented and unscented powder, tablet, liquid, and other forms.

One easily overlooked disadvantage of brand extensions is that the firm forgoes the chance to create a new brand with its own unique image and equity. Consider the advantages to Disney of having introduced adult-oriented Touchstone films, to Levi's of creating casual Dockers pants, and to Black & Decker of introducing high-end DeWALT power tools.

SUCCESS CHARACTERISTICS Marketers must judge each potential brand extension by how effectively it leverages existing brand equity from the parent brand, as well as how effectively, in turn, it contributes to the parent brand's equity.[89] Crest Whitestrips leveraged the strong reputation of Crest and dental care to provide reassurance in the teeth-whitening arena, while also reinforcing its dental authority image.

Marketers should ask a number of questions in judging the potential success of an extension.[90]

- Does the parent brand have strong equity?
- Is there a strong basis of fit?
- Will the extension have the optimal points-of-parity and points-of-difference?
- How can marketing programs enhance extension equity?
- What implications will the extension have for parent brand equity and profitability?
- How should feedback effects best be managed?

To help answer these questions, ▭ Table 9.5 offers a sample scorecard with specific weights and dimensions that users can adjust for each application.

▭ Table 9.6 lists a number of academic research findings on brand extensions.[91] One major mistake in evaluating extension opportunities is failing to take *all* consumers' brand knowledge structures into account and focusing instead on one or a few brand associations as a potential basis of fit.[92]

TABLE 9.5 Brand Extendibility Scorecard

Allocate points according to how well the new product concept rates on the specific dimensions in the following areas:

Consumer Perspectives: Desirability

10 pts. _____	Product category appeal (size, growth potential)
10 pts. _____	Equity transfer (perceived brand fit)
5 pts. _____	Perceived consumer target fit

Company Perspectives: Deliverability

10 pts. _____	Asset leverage (product technology, organizational skills, marketing effectiveness via channels and communications)
10 pts. _____	Profit potential
5 pts. _____	Launch feasibility

Competitive Perspectives: Differentiability

10 pts. _____	Comparative appeal (many advantages; few disadvantages)
10 pts. _____	Competitive response (likelihood; immunity or invulnerability from)
5 pts. _____	Legal/regulatory/institutional barriers

Brand Perspectives: Equity Feedback

10 pts. _____	Strengthens parent brand equity
10 pts. _____	Facilitates additional brand extension opportunities
5 pts. _____	Improves asset base
TOTAL _____ pts.	

TABLE 9.6 Research Insights on Brand Extensions

- Successful brand extensions occur when the parent brand is seen as having favorable associations and there is a perception of fit between the parent brand and the extension product.

- There are many bases of fit: product-related attributes and benefits, as well as nonproduct-related attributes and benefits related to common usage situations or user types.

- Depending on consumer knowledge of the categories, perceptions of fit may be based on technical or manufacturing commonalties or more surface considerations such as necessary or situational complementarity.

- High-quality brands stretch farther than average-quality brands, although both types of brands have boundaries.

- A brand that is seen as prototypical of a product category can be difficult to extend outside the category.

- Concrete attribute associations tend to be more difficult to extend than abstract benefit associations.

- Consumers may transfer associations that are positive in the original product class but become negative in the extension context.

- Consumers may infer negative associations about an extension, perhaps even based on other inferred positive associations.

- It can be difficult to extend into a product class that is seen as easy to make.

- A successful extension cannot only contribute to the parent brand image but also enable a brand to be extended even farther.

- An unsuccessful extension hurts the parent brand only when there is a strong basis of fit between the two.

- An unsuccessful extension does not prevent a firm from "backtracking" and introducing a more similar extension.

- Vertical extensions can be difficult and often require sub-branding strategies.

- The most effective advertising strategy for an extension emphasizes information about the extension (rather than reminders about the parent brand).

Source: Kevin Lane Keller, *Strategic Brand Management,* 3rd ed. (Upper Saddle River, NJ: Prentice Hall, 2008). Printed and electronically reproduced by permission of Pearson Education, Inc., Upper Saddle River, NJ.

Bic   The French company Société Bic, by emphasizing inexpensive, disposable products, was able to create markets for nonrefillable ballpoint pens in the late 1950s, disposable cigarette lighters in the early 1970s, and disposable razors in the early 1980s. It unsuccessfully tried the same strategy in marketing BIC perfumes in the United States and Europe in 1989. The perfumes—two for women ("Nuit" and "Jour") and two for men ("BIC for Men" and "BIC Sport for Men")—were packaged in quarter-ounce glass spray bottles that looked like fat cigarette lighters and sold for $5 each. The products were displayed on racks at checkout counters throughout Bic's extensive distribution channels. At the time, a Bic spokeswoman described the new products as extensions of the Bic heritage—"high quality at affordable prices, convenient to purchase, and convenient to use." The brand extension was launched with a $20 million advertising and promotion campaign containing images of stylish people enjoying themselves with the perfume and using the tagline "Paris in Your Pocket." Nevertheless, Bic was unable to overcome its lack of cachet and negative image associations, and the extension was a failure.[93]

Customer Equity

Achieving brand equity should be a top priority for any organization. "Marketing Memo: Twenty-First-Century Branding" offers some contemporary perspectives on enduring brand leadership.

---

marketing Memo

Twenty-First-Century Branding

One of the most successful marketers of the past two decades, Scott Bedbury, played a key role in the rise of both Nike and Starbucks. In his insightful book, *A New Brand World,* he offers the following branding principles:

1. *Relying on brand awareness has become marketing fool's gold.* Smart brands are more concerned with brand relevance and brand resonance.

2. *You have to know it before you can grow it.* Most brands don't know who they are, where they've been, and where they're going.

3. *Always remember the Spandex rule of brand expansion.* Just because you can, doesn't mean you should.

4. *Great brands establish enduring customer relationships.* They have more to do with emotions and trust than with footwear cushioning or the way a coffee bean is roasted.

5. *Everything matters.* Even your restroom.

6. *All brands need good parents.* Unfortunately, most brands come from troubled homes.

7. *Big is no excuse for being bad.* Truly great brands use their superhuman powers for good and place people and principles before profits.

8. *Relevance, simplicity, and humanity.* Rather than technology, these will distinguish brands in the future.

Source: Scott Bedbury, *A New Brand World* (New York: Viking Press, 2002). Copyright © 2001 by Scott Bedbury. Used by permission of Viking Penguin, a division of Penguin Group (USA) Inc.

Finally, we can relate brand equity to one other important marketing concept, **customer equity**. The aim of customer relationship management (CRM) is to produce high customer equity.[94] Although we can calculate it in different ways, one definition is "the sum of lifetime values of all customers."[95] As Chapter 5 reviewed, customer lifetime value is affected by revenue and by the costs of customer acquisition, retention, and cross-selling.[96]

- *Acquisition* depends on the number of prospects, the acquisition probability of a prospect, and acquisition spending per prospect.
- *Retention* is influenced by the retention rate and retention spending level.
- *Add-on spending* is a function of the efficiency of add-on selling, the number of add-on selling offers given to existing customers, and the response rate to new offers.

The brand equity and customer equity perspectives certainly share many common themes.[97] Both emphasize the importance of customer loyalty and the notion that we create value by having as many customers as possible pay as high a price as possible.

In practice, however, the two perspectives emphasize different things. The customer equity perspective focuses on bottom-line financial value. Its clear benefit is its quantifiable measures of financial performance. But it offers limited guidance for go-to-market strategies. It largely ignores some of the important advantages of creating a strong brand, such as the ability to attract higher-quality employees, elicit stronger support from channel and supply chain partners, and create growth opportunities through line and category extensions and licensing. The customer equity approach can overlook the "option value" of brands and their potential to affect future revenues and costs. It does not always fully account for competitive moves and countermoves, or for social network effects, word of mouth, and customer-to-customer recommendations.

Brand equity, on the other hand, tends to emphasize strategic issues in managing brands and creating and leveraging brand awareness and image with customers. It provides much practical guidance for specific marketing activities. With a focus on brands, however, managers don't always develop detailed customer analyses in terms of the brand equity they achieve or the resulting long-term profitability they create.[98] Brand equity approaches could benefit from sharper segmentation schemes afforded by customer-level analyses and more consideration of how to develop personalized, customized marketing programs for individual customers—whether individuals or organizations such as retailers. There are generally fewer financial considerations put into play with brand equity than with customer equity.

Nevertheless, both brand equity and customer equity matter. There are no brands without customers and no customers without brands. Brands serve as the "bait" that retailers and other channel intermediaries use to attract customers from whom they extract value. Customers are the tangible profit engine for brands to monetize their brand value.

Summary

1. A brand is a name, term, sign, symbol, design, or some combination of these elements, intended to identify the goods and services of one seller or group of sellers and to differentiate them from those of competitors. The different components of a brand—brand names, logos, symbols, package designs, and so on—are brand elements.

2. Brands are valuable intangible assets that offer a number of benefits to customers and firms and need to be managed carefully. The key to branding is that consumers perceive differences among brands in a product category.

3. Brand equity should be defined in terms of marketing effects uniquely attributable to a brand. That is, different outcomes result in the marketing of a product or service because of its brand, compared to the results if that same product or service was not identified by that brand.

4. Building brand equity depends on three main factors: (1) The initial choices for the brand elements or identities making up the brand; (2) the way the brand is integrated into the supporting marketing program; and (3) the associations indirectly transferred to the brand by links to some other entity (the company, country of origin, channel of distribution, or another brand).

5. Brand audits measure "where the brand has been," and tracking studies measure "where the brand is now" and whether marketing programs are having the intended effects.

6. A branding strategy identifies which brand elements a firm chooses to apply across the various products it sells. In a brand extension, a firm uses an established brand name to introduce a new product. Potential extensions must be judged by how effectively they leverage existing brand equity to a new product, as well as how effectively they contribute to the equity of the parent brand in turn.

7. Brands may expand coverage, provide protection, extend an image, or fulfill a variety of other roles for the firm. Each brand-name product must have a well-defined positioning to maximize coverage, minimize overlap, and thus optimize the portfolio.

8. Customer equity is a complementary concept to brand equity that reflects the sum of lifetime values of all customers for a brand.

Applications

Marketing Debate
Are Brand Extensions Good or Bad?

Some critics vigorously denounce the practice of brand extensions, because they feel that too often companies lose focus and consumers become confused. Other experts maintain that brand extensions are a critical growth strategy and source of revenue for the firm.

Take a position: Brand extensions can endanger brands *versus* Brand extensions are an important brand-growth strategy.

Marketing Discussion
Brand Equity Models

How can you relate the different models of brand equity in this chapter to each other? How are they similar? How are they different? Can you construct a brand-equity model that incorporates the best aspects of each model?

Marketing Excellence

>>Procter & Gamble

Procter & Gamble (P&G) began in 1837 when brothers-in-law William Procter and James Gamble, whose wives were sisters, formed a small candle and soap company. From there, P&G innovated and launched scores of revolutionary products of superior quality and value, including Ivory soap in 1882, Tide laundry detergent in 1946, Crest toothpaste with fluoride in 1955, and Pampers disposable diapers in 1961. P&G also acquired a number of companies to open the doors to new product categories. Among these were Richardson-Vicks (makers of personal care products like Pantene, Olay, and Vicks), Norwich Eaton Pharmaceuticals (makers of Pepto-Bismol), Gillette, Noxell (makers of Noxzema), Shulton's Old Spice, Max Factor, and the Iams Company.

Today, P&G is one of the most skillful marketers of consumer packaged goods in the world and holds one of the most powerful portfolios of trusted brands. The company employs 138,000 people in more than 80 countries worldwide and has total worldwide sales of more than $79 billion a year. It is the leader in 15 of the 21 product categories in which it competes, has 23 billion-dollar global brands, spends more than $2 billion annually on R&D, and serves more than 4 billion people in 180 different countries. Its sustained market leadership rests on a number of capabilities and philosophies:

- *Customer knowledge.* P&G studies its customers—both end consumers and trade partners—through continuous marketing research and intelligence gathering. It spends more than $100 million on over 10,000 formal consumer research projects every year and generates more than 3 million consumer contacts via its e-mail and phone center. It also emphasizes getting its marketers and researchers out into the field, where they can interact with consumers and retailers in their natural environment.

- *Long-term outlook.* P&G takes the time to analyze each opportunity carefully and prepare the best product, then commits itself to making this product a success. It struggled with Pringles potato chips for almost a decade before achieving market success. Recently, P&G has focused on increasing its presence in developing markets by concentrating on affordability, brand awareness, and distribution through e-commerce and high frequency stores.

- *Product innovation.* P&G is an active product innovator, devoting $2 billion annually to research and development, an impressively high amount for a packaged-goods company. It employs more science PhDs than Harvard, Berkeley, and MIT combined and applies for roughly 3,800 patents each year. Part of its innovation process is to develop brands that offer new consumer benefits. Recent innovations that created entirely new categories include Febreze, an odor-eliminating fabric spray; Dryel, a product that helps "dry-clean" clothes at home in the dryer; and Swiffer, a cleaning system that more effectively removes dust, dirt, and hair from floors and other hard surfaces.

- *Quality strategy.* P&G designs products of above-average quality and continuously improves them in ways that matter to consumers, including Tide compact detergents, Pampers Rash Guard (a diaper that treats and prevents diaper rash), and improved two-in-one shampoo and conditioner products for Pantene, Vidal Sassoon, and Pert Plus.

- *Brand extension strategy.* P&G produces its brands in several sizes and forms. This strategy gains more shelf space and prevents competitors from moving in to satisfy unmet market needs. P&G also uses its strong brand names to launch new products with instant recognition and much less advertising outlay. The Mr. Clean brand has been extended from household cleaner to bathroom cleaner, and even to a carwash system. Old Spice extended its brand from men's fragrances to deodorant. Crest successfully extended into a tooth-whitening system called Crest Whitestrips that removes surface stains from teeth in 14 days.

- *Multibrand strategy.* P&G markets several brands in the same product category, such as Luvs and Pampers diapers and Oral-B and Crest toothbrushes. Each brand meets a different consumer want and competes against specific competitors' brands. At the same time, P&G is careful not to sell too many brands and has reduced its vast array of products, sizes, flavors, and varieties in recent years to assemble a stronger brand portfolio.

- *Communication pioneer.* With its acquisition of Gillette, P&G became the nation's largest advertiser, spending over $2.3 billion a year or nearly twice as much as the number two company, General Motors Corp. P&G pioneered the power of television to create strong consumer awareness and preference. In recent years, the company has shifted more of its advertising budget to online marketing efforts and social media such as Facebook, Twitter, and blogs. These efforts help infuse stronger emotional appeals into its communications and create deeper consumer connections.

- *Aggressive sales force.* P&G's sales force has been named one of the top 25 by *Sales & Marketing Management* magazine. A key to its success is the close ties its sales force forms with retailers, notably Walmart. The 150-person team that serves the retail giant works closely with Walmart to improve both the products that go to the stores and the process by which they get there.

- *Manufacturing efficiency and cost cutting.* P&G's reputation as a great marketing company is matched by its excellence as a manufacturing company. P&G spends significant amounts developing and improving production operations to keep its costs among the lowest in the industry, allowing it to reduce the premium prices at which some of its goods sell.

- *Brand-management system.* P&G originated the brand-management system, in which one executive is responsible for each brand. The system has been copied by many competitors but not often with P&G's success. Recently, P&G modified its general management structure so each brand category is now run by a category manager with volume and profit responsibility. Although this new organization does not replace the brand-management system, it helps to sharpen strategic focus on key consumer needs and competition in the category.

P&G's accomplishments over the past 173 years have come from successfully orchestrating the myriad factors that contribute to market leadership.

Questions

1. P&G's impressive portfolio includes some of the strongest brand names in the world. What are some of the challenges and risks associated with being the market leader in so many categories?

2. With social media becoming increasingly important and fewer people watching traditional commercials on television, what does P&G need to do to maintain its strong brand images?

3. What risks do you feel P&G will face going forward?

Sources: Robert Berner, "Detergent Can Be So Much More," *BusinessWeek*, May 1, 2006, pp. 66–68; "A Post-Modern Proctoid," *The Economist*, April 15, 2006, p. 68; *P&G Fact Sheet* (December 2006); John Galvin, "The World on a String," *Point* (February 2005), pp. 13–24; Jack Neff, "P&G Kisses Up to the Boss: Consumers," *Advertising Age*, May 2, 2005, p. 18; www.pg.com; "The Nielsen Company Issues Top Ten U.S. Lists for 2008," *The Nielsen Company press release*, December 12, 2008.

Marketing Excellence

>>McDonald's

McDonald's is the world's leading hamburger fast-food chain, with over 32,000 restaurants in 118 countries. More than 75 percent of McDonald's restaurants are owned and operated by franchisees, which decreases the risk associated with expansion and ensures long-term tenants for the company. McDonald's serves 58 million people each day and promises a simple, easy, and enjoyable food experience for its customers.

The history of the McDonald's Corporation dates back to 1955 when Ray Kroc, a multimixer salesman, franchised a hamburger restaurant from the McDonald brothers, named it McDonald's, and offered simple foods such as the famous 15 cent hamburger. Kroc helped design the building, which featured red and white sides and a single golden arch to attract local attention. Ten years later, 700 McDonald's restaurants existed around the country, and the brand was on its way to becoming a household name.

During the 1960s and 1970s, Kroc led McDonald's growth domestically and internationally while pushing the importance of quality, service, cleanliness, and value. The menu expanded to include the Big Mac, Quarter Pounder, Happy Meal, Filet-O-Fish, and breakfast items like the Egg McMuffin. Kroc also understood early on that his core audience consisted of children and families. Therefore, he focused McDonald's advertising efforts at these groups and introduced Ronald McDonald in 1965 during a 60-second commercial. Soon, characters such as Grimace, the Hamburgler, and Mayor McCheese made their debut in McDonald's advertising campaigns and helped lure children into its restaurants for simple, good-tasting food, and a fun experience.

It was also during this time that McDonald's created the Ronald McDonald House, which opened in 1974 to help children with leukemia. Since then, it has expanded into a global charity effort called Ronald McDonald House Charities that strives to improve children's lives, health, and well-being through three major programs: Ronald McDonald House, Ronald McDonald Family Room, and Ronald McDonald Care Mobile.

McDonald's aggressively expanded overseas throughout the 1980s by adding locations throughout Europe, Asia, the Philippines, and Malaysia. This rapid expansion, however, led to many struggles during the 1990s and early 2000s. The company lost focus and direction, expanding by as many as 2,000 new restaurants a year. New employees weren't trained fast or well enough, all of which led to poor customer service and dirtier restaurants. New competitors popped up and the company acquired nonburger companies, Chipotle and Boston Market (which were eventually sold in 2006 and 2007). Consumer tastes changed, and new products like pizza, the Arch Deluxe, and deli sandwiches failed to connect with consumers, as did tweaks to the current menu including multiple changes to the Big Mac special sauce. Jim Skinner, McDonald's chief executive explained, "We got distracted from the most important thing: hot, high-quality food at a great value at the speed and convenience of McDonald's."

In 2003, McDonald's implemented a strategic effort called the "Plan to Win." The framework, which still exists today, helped McDonald's restaurants refocus on offering a better, higher-quality consumer experience rather than a quick and cheap fast-food option. The Plan to Win "playbook" provided strategic insight on how to improve on the company's 5 Ps—people, products, promotions, price, and place—yet allowed local restaurants to adapt to different environments and cultures. For example, McDonald's introduced a Bacon Roll breakfast sandwich in the United Kingdom, a premium M burger in France, and an egg, tomato, and pepper McPuff in China. Prices also varied slightly across the United States to better reflect different tastes in different regions.

Some food changes that helped turn the company around included offering more chicken options as beef consumption started to decline, selling milk in a bottle instead of a carton, and removing "Super Size" options after the documentary *Super Size Me* targeted McDonald's and its link to obesity. McDonald's responded to health trends and began offering premium salads as well as apple slices instead of French fries in Happy Meals as well as all-white-meat McNuggets. While many of the healthier options targeted moms and held a premium price, McDonald's introduced the $1 menu at the same time, which targeted the lower-income bracket and teenagers. Other responses included improving drive-thru service since 60 percent of McDonald's U.S. business came from drive-thrus, introducing more snack options, and refurbishing restaurants with leather seats, warmer paint colors, and flat-screen TVs. Initial results were staggering; from 2003 to 2006, the stock price increased 170 percent. Sales continued to increase through the late 2000s and topped $23.5 billion in 2008, making McDonald's one of only two companies in the Dow Jones Industrial Average whose share price rose in 2008.

McDonald's continued to flourish in 2009, led by its premium Angus burgers and its McCafé coffee line, which directly targeted competitors like Starbucks with less expensive specialty coffee drinks. McDonald's also launched a worldwide repackaging effort as a result of intense consumer research. The new packaging aimed to accomplish several tasks, including teaching consumers about McDonald's health consciousness and building awareness of its use of locally grown produce. It included bold text and full-color photographs of real ingredients like potatoes on French fry packaging and vegetables, cheese, and cooking utensils on hamburger packaging. Mary Dillon, McDonald's global chief marketing officer, explained that the goal is to "create unique personalities for our menu items by telling a story about each one."

Through the years, McDonald's has created a number of successful marketing campaigns and slogans such as "You Deserve a Break Today," "It's a Good Time for the Great Taste of McDonald's," and "Food, Folks, and Fun." Its current campaign, "I'm Lovin' It," seems on track to join the others by helping the company reach record sales and growth despite difficult economic times.

Questions

1. What are McDonald's core brand values? Have these changed over the years?

2. McDonald's did very well during the recession in the late 2000s. With the economy turning around for the better, should McDonald's change its strategy? Why or why not?

3. What risks do you feel McDonald's will face going forward?

Sources: Andrew Martin, "At McDonald's, the Happiest Meal Is Hot Profits," *New York Times*, January 10, 2009; Janet Adamy, "McDonald's Seeks Way to Keep Sizzling," *Wall Street Journal*, March 10, 2009; Matt Vella, "McDonald's Thinks About the Box," *BusinessWeek*, December 8, 2008; Jessica Wohl, "McDonald's CEO: Tough Economy, but Some 'Thawing,'" *Reuters*, April 17, 2009; "McDonald's Rolls Out New Generation of Global Packaging," *McDonald's* press release, October 28, 2008.

In This Chapter, We Will Address the Following Questions

1. How can a firm develop and establish an effective positioning in the market?

2. How do marketers identify and analyze competition?

3. How are brands successfully differentiated?

4. What are the differences in positioning and branding with a small business?

With distinctive packaging and a compelling product concept, Method has carved out a unique spot in the previously staid cleaning-products market.

Crafting the Brand Positioning

No company can win if its products and services resemble every other product and offering. As part of the strategic brand management process, each offering must represent the right kinds of things in the minds of the target market. Although successfully positioning a new product in a well-established market may seem difficult, Method Products shows that it is not impossible.

 *Named the seventh fastest-growing company in the United States by Inc. magazine back in 2006, Method Products is the brainchild of former high school buddies Eric Ryan and Adam Lowry. The company started with the realization that although cleaning and house-hold products is a huge category, taking up an entire supermarket aisle or more, it was an incredibly boring one. Ryan and Lowry designed a sleek, uncluttered dish soap con-*tainer that also had a functional advantage—the bottle, shaped like a chess piece, was built to let soap flow out the bottom, so users would never have to turn it upside down. This signature product, with its pleasant fragrance, was designed by award-winning industrial designer Karim Rashid. "The cleaning product industry is very backwards, and many of the products have a 1950s language," Rashid said, "They are cluttered with graphics, too much information, and complicated ugly forms."*

By creating a line of nontoxic, biodegradable household cleaning products with bright colors and sleek designs totally unique to the category, Method has crossed the line of $100 million in revenues with a phenomenal growth rate. Its big break came with the placement of its product in Target, known for partnering with well-known design-ers to produce stand-out products at affordable prices. Because of a limited advertising budget, the company believes its attractive packaging and innovative products must work harder to express the brand positioning. The challenge for Method now, however, is to differentiate beyond design to avoid copycats eroding the company's cachet. The company is capitalizing on growing interest in green products by emphasizing its nontoxic, nonpolluting ingredients.[1]

As the success of Method products demonstrates, a company can reap the benefits of carving out a unique position in the marketplace. Creating a compelling, well-differentiated brand position requires a keen understanding of consumer needs and wants, company capabilities, and competitive actions. It also requires disciplined but creative thinking. In this chapter, we outline a process by which marketers can uncover the most powerful brand positioning.

Developing and Establishing a Brand Positioning

All marketing strategy is built on segmentation, targeting, and positioning (STP). A company discovers different needs and groups in the marketplace, targets those it can satisfy in a supe-rior way, and then positions its offerings so the target market recognizes the company's distinctive offerings and images.

Positioning is the act of designing a company's offering and image to occupy a distinctive place in the minds of the target market.[2] The goal is to locate the brand in the minds of consumers to maximize the potential benefit to the firm. A good brand positioning helps guide marketing strategy by clarifying the brand's essence, identifying the goals it helps the consumer achieve, and showing how it does so in a unique way. Everyone in the organization should understand the brand positioning and use it as context for making decisions.

Entertainment Weekly   When publisher Scott Donaton took over *Entertainment Weekly*, he repositioned the magazine away from celebrity lifestyles to focus more directly on entertainment itself and what actually appeared on the screen, page, or CD. This updated positioning became a filter that guided the content and marketing of the magazine: "Every event, sales program, marketing initiative gets poured through that filter—the goal being to keep and enhance the things that are true to who you are; kill the things that aren't, necessarily; and create great new things that are even better expressions of who you are." Out was the glitzy annual Oscar party at Elaine's restaurant in New York City; in its place was a week-long Academy Awards program at ArcLight Theater in Hollywood showcasing all the best-pictures nominees and featuring a panel discussion with nominated screenwriters.[3]

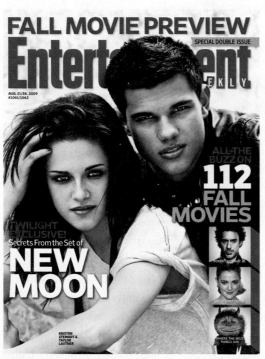

Entertainment Weekly uses its updated brand positioning to guide everything it does.

A good positioning has a "foot in the present" and a "foot in the future." It needs to be somewhat aspirational so the brand has room to grow and improve. Positioning on the basis of the current state of the market is not forward-looking enough, but, at the same time, the positioning cannot be so removed from reality that it is essentially unobtainable. The real trick in positioning is to strike just the right balance between what the brand is and what it could be.

The result of positioning is the successful creation of a *customer-focused value proposition,* a cogent reason why the target market should buy the product. Table 10.1 shows how three companies—Perdue, Volvo, and Domino's—have defined their value proposition through the years given their target customers, benefits, and prices.[4]

Positioning requires that marketers define and communicate similarities and differences between their brand and its competitors. Specifically, deciding on a positioning requires: (1) determining a frame of reference by identifying the target market and relevant competition, (2) identifying the optimal points of parity and points of difference brand associations given that frame of reference, and (3) creating a brand mantra to summarize the positioning and essence of the brand.

Determining a Competitive Frame of Reference

The **competitive frame of reference** defines which other brands a brand competes with and therefore which brands should be the focus of competitive analysis. Decisions about the competitive

TABLE 10.1   Examples of Value Propositions

Company and Product	Target Customers	Key Benefits	Price	Value Proposition
Perdue (chicken)	Quality-conscious consumers of chicken	Tenderness	10% premium	More tender golden chicken at a moderate premium price
Volvo (station wagon)	Safety-conscious upscale families	Durability and safety	20% premium	The safest, most durable wagon in which your family can ride
Domino's (pizza)	Convenience-minded pizza lovers	Delivery speed and good quality	15% premium	A good hot pizza, delivered promptly to your door, at a moderate price

frame of reference are closely linked to target market decisions. Deciding to target a certain type of consumer can define the nature of competition, because certain firms have decided to target that segment in the past (or plan to do so in the future), or because consumers in that segment may already look to certain products or brands in their purchase decisions.

IDENTIFYING COMPETITORS A good starting point in defining a competitive frame of reference for brand positioning is to determine **category membership**—the products or sets of products with which a brand competes and which function as close substitutes. It would seem a simple task for a company to identify its competitors. PepsiCo knows Coca-Cola's Dasani is a major bottled-water competitor for its Aquafina brand; Citigroup knows Bank of America is a major banking competitor; and Petsmart.com knows a major online retail competitor for pet food and supplies is Petco.com.

The range of a company's actual and potential competitors, however, can be much broader than the obvious. For a brand with explicit growth intentions to enter new markets, a broader or maybe even more aspirational competitive frame may be necessary to reflect possible future competitors. And a company is more likely to be hurt by emerging competitors or new technologies than by current competitors.

*   After having spent billions of dollars building their networks, cell phone carriers AT&T, Verizon Wireless, and Sprint face the threat of new competition emerging as a result of a number of changes in the marketplace: Skype and the growth of Wi-Fi hotspots, municipal Wi-Fi networks built by cities, dual mode phones that can easily switch networks, and the opening up of the old analog 700 MHz frequency used for UHF broadcasts.[5]
*   The energy-bar market created by PowerBar ultimately fragmented into a variety of subcategories, including those directed at specific segments (such as Luna bars for women) and some possessing specific attributes (such as the protein-laden Balance and the calorie-control bar Pria). Each represented a subcategory for which the original PowerBar was potentially not as relevant.[6]

Firms should identify their competitive frame in the most advantageous way possible. In the United Kingdom, for example, the Automobile Association positioned itself as the fourth "emergency service"—along with police, fire, and ambulance—to convey greater credibility and urgency. Consider the competitive frame adopted by Bertolli.[7]

The energy bar market has fragmented into a number of sub-categories, each appealing to different people in different situations.

Bertolli   Unilever's Bertolli, a line of frozen Italian food, experienced a steady 10 percent growth in sales through the recent economic recession, in part due to its clever positioning as "restaurant quality Italian food that you can eat at home." Targeting men and women with "discerning palates," Bertolli has aggressively innovated with a stream of high-quality new dishes to keep target customers interested. In its marketing for the brand, Bertolli deliberately chooses to go to places "appropriate for a fine dining brand but not a frozen food brand." Advertising "Spend a Night In with Bertolli," the brand has advertised during the Emmys and Golden Globes award show telecasts and hosted celebrity chef dinners in Manhattan.

We can examine competition from both an industry and a market point of view.[8] An **industry** is a group of firms offering a product or class of products that are close substitutes for one another. Marketers classify industries according to number of sellers; degree of product differentiation; presence or absence of entry, mobility, and exit barriers; cost structure; degree of vertical integration; and degree of globalization.

Using the market approach, we define *competitors* as companies that satisfy the same customer need. For example, a customer who buys a word-processing package really wants "writing ability"—a need that can also be satisfied by pencils, pens, or, in the past, typewriters. Marketers must overcome "marketing myopia" and stop defining competition in traditional category and industry terms.[9] Coca-Cola, focused on its soft drink business, missed seeing the market for coffee bars and fresh-fruit-juice bars that eventually impinged on its soft-drink business.

The market concept of competition reveals a broader set of actual and potential competitors than competition defined in just product category terms. Jeffrey F. Rayport and Bernard J. Jaworski suggest profiling a company's direct and indirect competitors by mapping the buyer's steps in obtaining and using the product. This type of analysis highlights both the opportunities and the challenges a company faces.[10] "Marketing Insight: High Growth through Value Innovation" describes how firms can tap into new markets while minimizing competition from others.

Marketing Insight

High Growth Through Value Innovation

INSEAD professors W. Chan Kim and Renée Mauborgne believe too many firms engage in "red-ocean thinking"—seeking bloody, head-to-head battles with competitors based largely on incremental improvements in cost, quality, or both. They advocate engaging in "blue-ocean thinking" by creating products and services for which there are no direct competitors. Instead of searching within the conventional boundaries of industry competition, managers should look beyond those boundaries to find unoccupied market positions that represent real value innovation.

The authors cite as one example Bert Claeys, a Belgian company that operates movie theaters, and its introduction of the 25-screen, 7,600-seat Kinepolis megaplex. Despite an industry slump, Kinepolis has thrived on a unique combination of features, such as ample and safe free parking; large screens and state-of-the-art sound and projection equipment; and roomy, comfortable, oversized seats with unobstructed views. Through smart planning and economies of scale, Bert Claeys created Kinepolis's unique cinema experience at a lower cost.

This is classic blue-ocean thinking—designing creative business ventures to positively affect both a company's cost structure and its value proposition to consumers. Cost savings result from eliminating and reducing the factors affecting traditional industry competition; value to consumers comes from introducing factors the industry has never before offered. Over time, costs drop even more as superior value leads to higher sales volume, and that generates economies of scale.

Here are other marketers that exhibit unconventional, blue-ocean thinking:

- Callaway Golf designed "Big Bertha," a golf club with a large head and expanded sweet spot that helped golfers frustrated by the difficulty of hitting a golf ball squarely.

- NetJets figured out how to offer private jet service to a larger group of customers through fractional ownership.

- Cirque du Soleil reinvented circus as a higher form of entertainment by eliminating high-cost elements such as animals and enhancing the theatrical experience instead.

Kim and Mauborgne propose four crucial questions for marketers to ask themselves in guiding blue-ocean thinking and creating value innovation:

1. Which of the factors that our industry takes for granted should we eliminate?

2. Which factors should we reduce well *below* the industry's standard?

3. Which factors should we raise well *above* the industry's standard?

4. Which factors should we create that the industry has never offered?

They maintain that the most successful blue-ocean thinkers took advantage of all three platforms on which value innovation can take place: *physical product*, *service* including maintenance, customer service, warranties, and training for distributors and retailers; and *delivery*, meaning channels and logistics.

Sources: W. Chan Kim and Renée Mauborgne, *Blue-Ocean Strategy: How to Create Uncontested Market Space and Make the Competition Irrelevant* (Cambridge, MA: Harvard Business School Press, 2005); W. Chan Kim and Renée Mauborgne, "Creating New Market Space," *Harvard Business Review*, January–February 1999; W. Chan Kim and Renée Mauborgne, "Value Innovation: The Strategic Logic of High Growth," *Harvard Business Review*, January–February 1997.

ANALYZING COMPETITORS Chapter 2 described how to conduct a SWOT analysis that includes a competitive analysis. A company needs to gather information about each competitor's real and perceived strengths and weaknesses. ⬜ Table 10.2 shows the results of a company survey that asked customers to rate its three competitors, A, B, and C, on five attributes. Competitor A turns out to be well known and respected for producing high-quality products sold by a good sales force, but poor at providing product availability and technical assistance. Competitor B is good across the board and excellent in product availability and sales force. Competitor C rates poor to fair on most attributes. This result suggests that in its positioning, the company could attack Competitor A on product availability and technical assistance and Competitor C on almost anything, but it should not attack B, which has no glaring weaknesses. As part of this competitive analysis for positioning, the firm should also ascertain the strategies and objectives of its primary competitors.[11]

Once a company has identified its main competitors and their strategies, it must ask: What is each competitor seeking in the marketplace? What drives each competitor's behavior? Many factors shape a competitor's objectives, including size, history, current management, and financial situation. If the competitor is a division of a larger company, it's important to know whether the parent company is running it for growth or for profits, or milking it.[12]

Finally, based on all this analysis, marketers must formally define the competitive frame of reference to guide positioning. In stable markets with little short-term change likely, it may be fairly easy to define one, two, or perhaps three key competitors. In dynamic categories where competition may exist or arise in a variety of different forms, multiple frames of reference may arise, as we discuss next.

TABLE 10.2 ⬜ Customers' Ratings of Competitors on Key Success Factors					
	Customer Awareness	**Product Quality**	**Product Availability**	**Technical Assistance**	**Selling Staff**
Competitor A	E	E	P	P	G
Competitor B	G	G	E	G	E
Competitor C	F	P	G	F	F

Note: E = excellent, G = good, F = fair, P = poor.

Identifying Optimal Points-of-Difference and Points-of-Parity

Once marketers have fixed the competitive frame of reference for positioning by defining the customer target market and the nature of the competition, they can define the appropriate points-of-difference and points-of-parity associations.[13]

POINTS-OF-DIFFERENCE **Points-of-difference (PODs)** are attributes or benefits that consumers strongly associate with a brand, positively evaluate, and believe they could not find to the same extent with a competitive brand. Associations that make up points-of-difference may be based on virtually any type of attribute or benefit. Strong brands may have multiple points-of-difference. Some examples are Apple (*design, ease-of-use,* and *irreverent attitude*), Nike (*performance, innovative technology,* and *winning*), and Southwest Airlines (*value, reliability,* and *fun personality*). Creating strong, favorable, and unique associations is a real challenge, but an essential one for competitive brand positioning.

Three criteria determine whether a brand association can truly function as a point-of-difference—desirability, deliverability, and differentiability. Some key considerations follow.

- *Desirable to consumer.* Consumers must see the brand association as personally relevant to them. The Westin Stamford hotel in Singapore advertised that it was the world's tallest hotel, but a hotel's height is not important to many tourists. Consumers must also be given a compelling reason to believe and an understandable rationale for why the brand can deliver the desired benefit. Mountain Dew may argue that it is more energizing than other soft drinks and support this claim by noting that it has a higher level of caffeine. Chanel No. 5 perfume may claim to be the quintessentially elegant French perfume and support this claim by noting the long association between Chanel and haute couture. Substantiators can also come in the form of patented, branded ingredients, such as NIVEA Wrinkle Control Crème with Q10 co-enzyme or Herbal Essences hair conditioner with Hawafena.
- *Deliverable by the company.* The company must have the internal resources and commitment to feasibly and profitably create and maintain the brand association in the minds of consumers. The product design and marketing offering must support the desired association. Does communicating the desired association require real changes to the product itself, or just perceptual shifts in the way the consumer thinks of the product or brand? Creating the latter is typically easier. General Motors has had to work to overcome public perceptions that Cadillac is not a youthful, modern brand and has done so through bold designs and contemporary images. The ideal brand association is preemptive, defensible, and difficult to attack. It is generally easier for market leaders such as ADM, Visa, and SAP to sustain their positioning, based as it is on demonstrable product or service performance, than it is for market leaders such as Fendi, Prada, and Hermès, whose positioning is based on fashion and is thus subject to the whims of a more fickle market.
- *Differentiating from competitors.* Finally, consumers must see the brand association as distinctive and superior to relevant competitors. Splenda sugar substitute overtook Equal and Sweet'N Low to become the leader in its category in 2003 by differentiating itself on its authenticity as a product derived from sugar, without any of the associated drawbacks.[14]

Any attribute or benefit associated with a product or service can function as a point-of-difference for a brand as long as it is sufficiently desirable, deliverable, and differentiating. The brand must demonstrate clear superiority on an attribute or benefit, however, for it to function as a true point-of-difference. Consumers must be convinced, for example, that Louis Vuitton has the most stylish handbags, Energizer is the longest-lasting battery, and Fidelity Investments offers the best financial advice and planning.

POINTS-OF-PARITY **Points-of-parity (POPs)**, on the other hand, are attribute or benefit associations that are not necessarily unique to the brand but may in fact be shared with other brands.[15] These types of associations come in two basic forms: category and competitive.

Category points-of-parity are attributes or benefits that consumers view as essential to a legitimate and credible offering within a certain product or service category. In other words, they represent necessary—but not sufficient—conditions for brand choice. Consumers might not consider a travel agency truly a travel agency unless it is able to make air and hotel reservations, provide advice about leisure packages, and offer various ticket payment and delivery options. Category points-of-parity may change over time due to technological advances, legal developments, or consumer trends, but to use a golfing analogy, they are the "greens fees" necessary to play the marketing game.

Competitive points-of-parity are associations designed to overcome perceived weaknesses of the brand. A competitive point-of-parity may be required to either (1) negate *competitors'* perceived points-of-difference or (2) negate a perceived vulnerability of the brand as a result of its own points-of-difference. The latter consideration, which we discuss in more detail later in this chapter, arises when consumers feel that if a brand is good at one thing (easy to use), it must not be good at something else (having advanced features).

One good way to uncover key competitive points-of-parity is to role-play competitors' positioning and infer their intended points-of-difference. Competitor's PODs will, in turn, suggest the brand's POPs. Consumer research into the trade-offs consumers make in their purchasing decisions can also be informative.

Regardless of the source of perceived weaknesses, if, in the eyes of consumers, a brand can "break even" in those areas where it appears to be at a disadvantage *and* achieve advantages in other areas, the brand should be in a strong—and perhaps unbeatable—competitive position.

Hyundai Cars

In recent years, Hyundai Motor Company has succeeded in boosting its presence in the world car market by setting up overseas production bases and engaging in aggressive marketing. As South Korea's largest and the world's number five automaker, Hyundai has driven its sales growth through improvements in quality and design. While its rivals are using reliability and fuel economy to build market share, Hyundai has taken the formula further with a focus on making its cars more attractive and often at lower prices. The brand's goal is to entice customers with the speed and appeal of luxury European models, but at non-premium prices. To win the hearts of car buyers, Hyundai engages credible and attractive spokespersons like Bollywood actor Shah Rukh Khan and German football celebrity Jürgen Klinsmann to help communicate its value proposition. To improve its overall brand perception, the company has a long-term commitment with FIFA to sponsor the FIFA World Cup until 2022.[16]

POINTS-OF-PARITY VERSUS POINTS-OF-DIFFERENCE For an offering to achieve a point-of-parity on a particular attribute or benefit, a sufficient number of consumers must believe the brand is "good enough" on that dimension. There is a zone or range of tolerance or acceptance with points-of-parity. The brand does not literally need to be seen as equal to competitors, but consumers must feel it does well enough on that particular attribute or benefit. If they do, they may be willing to base their evaluations and decisions on other factors potentially more favorable to the brand. A light beer presumably would never taste as good as a full-strength beer, but it would need to taste close enough to be able to effectively compete.

Often, the key to positioning is not so much achieving a point-of-difference as achieving points-of-parity!

Visa versus American Express

Visa's POD in the credit card category is that it is the most widely available card, which underscores the category's main benefit of convenience. American Express, on the other hand, has built the equity of its brand by highlighting the prestige associated with the use of its card. Having established their PODs, Visa and American Express now compete to create POPs by attempting to blunt each other's advantage. Visa offers gold and platinum cards to enhance the prestige of its brand and for years advertised, "It's Everywhere You Want to Be," showing desirable travel

Visa has established a strong point-of-difference versus American Express on the basis of acceptability.

and leisure locations that accepted only the Visa card, to reinforce both its exclusivity and its acceptability. American Express has substantially increased the number of merchants that accept its cards and created other value enhancements while also reinforcing its cachet through advertising that showcases celebrities such as Jerry Seinfeld, Robert De Niro, Tina Fey, Ellen DeGeneres, and Beyoncé.

MULTIPLE FRAMES OF REFERENCE It is not uncommon for a brand to identify more than one actual or potential competitive frame of reference, if competition widens or the firm plans to expand into new categories. For example, Starbucks could define very distinct sets of competitors, suggesting different possible POPs and PODs as a result:

1. *Quick-serve restaurants and convenience shops (McDonald's and Dunkin' Donuts).* Intended PODs might be quality, image, experience, and variety; intended POPs might be convenience and value.
2. *Supermarket brands for home consumption (Folgers and NESCAFÉ).* Intended PODs might be quality, image, experience, variety, and freshness; intended POPs might be convenience and value.
3. *Local cafés.* Intended PODs might be convenience and service quality; intended POPs might be quality, variety, price, and community.

Note that some potential POPs and PODs for Starbucks are shared across competitors; others are unique to a particular competitor.

Under such circumstances, marketers have to decide what to do. There are two main options with multiple frames of reference. One is to first develop the best possible positioning for each type or class of competitors and then see whether there is a way to create one combined positioning robust enough to effectively address them all. If competition is too diverse, however, it may be necessary to prioritize competitors and then choose the most important set of competitors to serve as the competitive frame. One crucial consideration is not to try to be all things to all people—that leads to lowest-common-denominator positioning, which is typically ineffective.

Starbucks has encountered some stiff competition in the coffee market in recent years from McDonald's and Dunkin' Donuts.

Finally, if there are many competitors in different categories or subcategories, it may be useful to either develop the positioning at the categorical level for all relevant categories ("quick-serve restaurants" or "supermarket take-home coffee" for Starbucks) or with an exemplar from each category (McDonald's or NESCAFÉ for Starbucks).

STRADDLE POSITIONING Occasionally, a company will be able to straddle two frames of reference with one set of points-of-difference and points-of-parity. In these cases, the points-of-difference for one category become points-of-parity for the other and vice versa. Subway restaurants are positioned as offering healthy, good-tasting sandwiches. This positioning allows the brand to create a POP on taste and a POD on health with respect to quick-serve restaurants such as McDonald's and Burger King and, at the same time, a POP on health and a POD on taste with respect to health food restaurants and cafés. Straddle positions allow brands to expand their market coverage and potential customer base. Another example of a straddle positioning is BMW.

BMW When BMW first made a strong competitive push into the U.S. market in the early 1980s, it positioned the brand as the only automobile that offered both luxury *and* performance. At that time, consumers saw U.S. luxury cars as lacking performance, and U.S. performance cars as lacking luxury. By relying on the design of its cars, its German heritage, and other aspects of a well-conceived marketing program, BMW was able to simultaneously achieve: (1) a point-of-difference on luxury and a point-of-parity on performance with respect to U.S. performance cars like the Chevy Corvette, and (2) a point-of-difference on performance and a point-of-parity on luxury with respect to U.S. luxury cars like Cadillac. The clever slogan "The Ultimate Driving Machine" effectively captured the newly created umbrella category—luxury performance cars.

Although a straddle positioning is often attractive as a means of reconciling potentially conflicting consumer goals and creating a "best of both worlds" solution, it also carries an extra burden. If the points-of-parity and points-of-difference with respect to both categories are not credible, the brand may not be viewed as a legitimate player in either category. Many early PDAs that unsuccessfully tried to straddle categories ranging from pagers to laptop computers provide a vivid illustration of this risk.

Choosing POPs and PODs

Marketers typically focus on brand benefits in choosing the points-of-parity and points-of-difference that make up their brand positioning. Brand attributes generally play more of a supporting role by providing "reasons to believe" or "proof points" as to why a brand can credibly claim it offers certain benefits. Marketers of Dove soap, for example, will talk about how its attribute of one-quarter cleansing cream uniquely creates the benefit of softer skin. Consumers are usually more interested in benefits and what exactly they will get from a product. Multiple attributes may support a certain benefit, and they may change over time.

For choosing specific benefits as POPs and PODs to position a brand, perceptual maps may be useful. *Perceptual maps* are visual representations of consumer perceptions and preferences. They provide quantitative portrayals of market situations and the way consumers view different products, services, and brands along various dimensions. By overlaying consumer preferences with brand perceptions, marketers can reveal "holes" or "openings" that suggest unmet consumer needs and marketing opportunities.

For example, △ Figure 10.1(a) shows a hypothetical perceptual map for a beverage category. The four brands—A, B, C, and D—vary in terms of how consumers view their taste profile (light versus strong) and personality and imagery (contemporary versus modern). Also displayed on the map are ideal point "configurations" for three market segments (1, 2, and 3). The ideal points represent each segment's most preferred ("ideal") combination of taste and imagery.

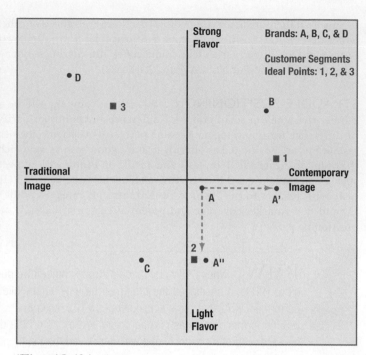

|Fig. 10.1a| ▲

(a) Hypothetical Beverage Perceptual Map: Current Perceptions

|Fig. 10.1b| ▲

(b) Hypothetical Beverage Perceptual Map: Possible Repositioning for Brand A

Consumers in Segment 3 prefer beverages with a strong taste and traditional imagery. Brand D is well-positioned for this segment as it is strongly associated in the marketplace with both these benefits. Given that none of the competitors is seen as anywhere close, we would expect Brand D to attract many of the Segment 3 customers.

Brand A, on the other hand, is seen as more balanced in terms of both taste and imagery. Unfortunately, no market segment seems to really desire this balance. Brands B and C are better positioned with respect to Segments 2 and 3, respectively.

- By making its image more contemporary, Brand A could move to A' to target consumers in Segment 1 and achieve a point-of-parity on imagery and maintain its point-of-difference on taste profile with respect to Brand B.
- By changing its taste profile to make it lighter, Brand A could move to A" to target consumers in Segment 2 and achieve a point-of-parity on taste profile and maintain its point-of-difference on imagery with respect to Brand C.

Deciding which repositioning is most promising, A' or A", would require detailed consumer and competitive analysis on a host of factors—including the resources, capabilities, and likely intentions of competing firms—to choose the markets where consumers can profitably be served.

Brand Mantras

To further focus the intent of the brand positioning and the way firms would like consumers to think about the brand, it is often useful to define a brand mantra.[17] A *brand mantra* is an articulation of the heart and soul of the brand and is closely related to other branding concepts like "brand essence" and "core brand promise." Brand mantras are short, three- to five-word phrases that capture the irrefutable essence or spirit of the brand positioning. Their purpose is to ensure that all employees within the organization and all external marketing partners understand what the brand is most fundamentally to represent with consumers so they can adjust their actions accordingly.

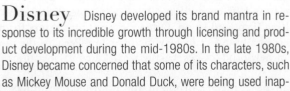

Nike's brand mantra of "authentic athletic performance" guides the types of products it makes and the athletes it hires as endorsers.

Brand mantras are powerful devices. They can provide guidance about what products to introduce under the brand, what ad campaigns to run, and where and how to sell the brand. Their influence, however, can extend beyond these tactical concerns. Brand mantras may even guide the most seemingly unrelated or mundane decisions, such as the look of a reception area and the way phones are answered. In effect, they create a mental filter to screen out brand-inappropriate marketing activities or actions of any type that may have a negative bearing on customers' impressions of a brand.

Brand mantras must economically communicate what the brand is and what it is *not*. What makes for a good brand mantra? McDonald's brand philosophy of "Food, Folks, and Fun" captures its brand essence and core brand promise. Two high-profile and successful examples—Nike and Disney—show the power and utility of a well-designed brand mantra.

Nike Nike has a rich set of associations with consumers, based on its innovative product designs, its sponsorships of top athletes, its award-winning advertising, its competitive drive, and its irreverent attitude. Internally, Nike marketers adopted the three-word brand mantra, "authentic athletic performance," to guide their marketing efforts. Thus, in Nike's eyes, its entire marketing program—its products and how they are sold—must reflect those key brand values. Over the years, Nike has expanded its brand meaning from "running shoes" to "athletic shoes" to "athletic shoes and apparel" to "all things associated with athletics (including equipment)." Each step of the way, however, it has been guided by its "authentic athletic performance" brand mantra. For example, as Nike rolled out its successful apparel line, one important hurdle for the products was that they could be made innovative enough through material, cut, or design to truly benefit top athletes. At the same time, the company has been careful to avoid using the Nike name to brand products that do not fit with the brand mantra (like casual "brown" shoes).

Disney's brand mantra of "fun family entertainment" provides guardrails so its marketing stays on track.

Disney Disney developed its brand mantra in response to its incredible growth through licensing and product development during the mid-1980s. In the late 1980s, Disney became concerned that some of its characters, such as Mickey Mouse and Donald Duck, were being used inappropriately and becoming overexposed. The characters were on so many products and marketed in so many ways that in some cases it was difficult to discern what could have been the rationale behind the deal to start with. Moreover, because of the broad exposure of the characters in the marketplace, many consumers had begun to feel Disney was exploiting its name. Disney moved quickly to ensure that a consistent image—reinforcing its key brand associations—was conveyed by all third-party products and services. To facilitate this supervision, Disney adopted an internal brand mantra of "fun family entertainment" to serve as a screen for proposed ventures. Opportunities that were not consistent with the brand mantra—no matter how appealing—were rejected.

DESIGNING A BRAND MANTRA Brand mantras are designed with internal purposes in mind. A brand slogan is an external translation that attempts to creatively engage consumers. Although Nike's internal mantra was "authentic athletic performance," its external slogan was "Just Do It." Here are the three key criteria for a brand mantra.

- *Communicate.* A good brand mantra should define the category (or categories) of business for the brand and set the brand boundaries. It should also clarify what is unique about the brand.
- *Simplify.* An effective brand mantra should be memorable. For that, it should be short, crisp, and vivid in meaning.
- *Inspire.* Ideally, the brand mantra should also stake out ground that is personally meaningful and relevant to as many employees as possible.

Brand mantras typically are designed to capture the brand's points-of-difference, that is, what is unique about the brand. Other aspects of the brand positioning—especially the brand's points-of-parity—may also be important and may need to be reinforced in other ways.

For brands facing rapid growth, it is helpful to define the product or benefit space in which the brand would like to compete, as Nike did with "athletic performance" and Disney with "family entertainment." Words that describe the nature of the product or service, or the type of experiences or benefits the brand provides, can be critical to identifying appropriate categories into which to extend. For brands in more stable categories where extensions into more distinct categories are less likely to occur, the brand mantra may focus more exclusively on points-of-difference.

Brand mantras derive their power and usefulness from their collective meaning. Other brands may be strong on one, or perhaps even a few, of the brand associations making up the brand mantra. But for the brand mantra to be effective, no other brand should singularly excel on all dimensions. Part of the key to both Nike's and Disney's success is that for years no competitor could really deliver on the combined promise suggested by their brand mantras.

Establishing Brand Positioning

Once they have determined the brand positioning strategy, marketers should communicate it to everyone in the organization so it guides their words and actions. One helpful schematic to do so is a brand-positioning bull's-eye. Constructing a bull's-eye for the brand ensures that no steps are skipped in its development. "Marketing Memo: Constructing a Brand Positioning Bull's-eye" outlines one way marketers can formally express brand positioning.

Establishing the brand positioning in the marketplace requires that consumers understand what the brand offers and what makes it a superior competitive choice. To do so, consumers need to understand in which category or categories it competes and its points-of-parity and points-of-difference with respect to those competitors.

Category membership may be obvious in some cases. Target customers are aware that Maybelline is a leading brand of cosmetics, Cheerios is a leading brand of cereal, Accenture is a leading consulting firm, and so on. Often, however, marketers for many other brands must inform consumers of a brand's category membership. Perhaps the most obvious situation is the introduction of new products, especially when category identification itself is not apparent.

Category membership can be a special problem for high-tech products. When GO Corporation created the first pen-based tablet computer in the early 1990s, analysts and the

marketing Memo

Constructing a Brand Positioning Bull's-eye

A brand bull's-eye provides content and context to improve everyone's understanding of the positioning of a brand in the organization. Here we describe the components of a brand bull's-eye, illustrating with a hypothetical Starbucks example.

In the inner two circles is the heart of the bull's-eye—key points-of-parity and points-of-difference, as well as the brand mantra. In the next circle out are the substantiators or reasons-to-believe (RTB)—attributes or benefits that provide factual or demonstrable support for the points-of-parity and points-of-difference. Finally, the outer circle contains two other useful branding concepts: (1) the brand values, personality, or character—intangible associations that help to establish the tone for the words and actions for the

brand; and (2) executional properties and visual identity—more tangible components of the brand that affect how it is seen.

Three boxes outside the bull's-eye provide useful context and interpretation. To the left, two boxes highlight some of the input to the positioning analysis: One includes the consumer target and a key insight about consumer attitudes or behavior that significantly influenced the actual positioning; the other box provides competitive information about the key consumer need the brand is attempting to satisfy and some competitive products or brands that need suggests. To the right of the bull's-eye, one box offers a "big picture" view of the output—the ideal consumer takeaway that would result if the brand positioning efforts were successful.

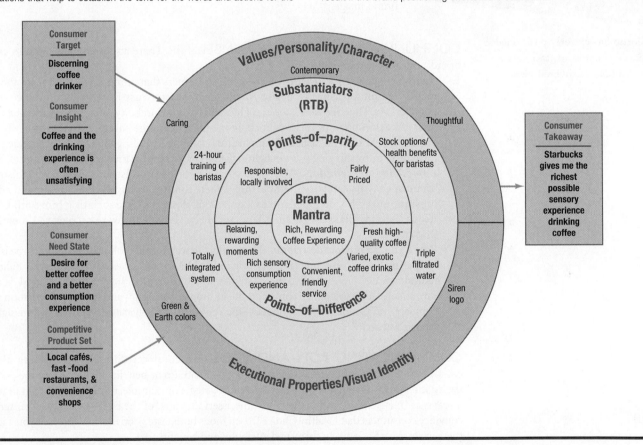

media responded enthusiastically to the concept, but consumer interest never materialized. GO was eventually purchased by AT&T for use in a pen computer venture that folded in 1994.[18]

There are also situations in which consumers know a brand's category membership but may not be convinced the brand is a valid member of the category. They may be aware that Hewlett-Packard produces digital cameras, but they may not be certain whether Hewlett-Packard cameras are in the same class as Sony, Olympus, Kodak, and Nikon. In this instance, HP might find it useful to reinforce category membership.

Brands are sometimes affiliated with categories in which they do *not* hold membership. This approach is one way to highlight a brand's point-of-difference, providing consumers know the

DiGiorno has cleverly positioned itself as a convenient, tasty alternative to home-delivered pizza.

brand's actual membership. DiGiorno's frozen pizza has adopted such a positioning strategy—instead of putting it in the frozen pizza category, the marketers have positioned it in the delivered pizza category with ads that claim, "It's Not Delivery, It's DiGiorno!"

With this approach, however, it's important not to be trapped between categories. Consumers should understand what the brand stands for, and not just what it's not. The Konica e-mini M digital camera and MP3 player was marketed as the "four-in-one entertainment solution," but it suffered from functional deficiencies in each of its product applications and languished in the marketplace as a result.[19]

The typical approach to positioning is to inform consumers of a brand's membership before stating its point-of-difference. Presumably, consumers need to know what a product is and what function it serves before deciding whether it is superior to the brands against which it competes. For new products, initial advertising often concentrates on creating brand awareness, and subsequent advertising attempts to create the brand image.

COMMUNICATING CATEGORY MEMBERSHIP There are three main ways to convey a brand's category membership:

1. *Announcing category benefits.* To reassure consumers that a brand will deliver on the fundamental reason for using a category, marketers frequently use benefits to announce category membership. Thus, industrial tools might claim to have durability, and antacids might announce their efficacy. A brownie mix might attain membership in the baked desserts category by claiming the benefit of great taste and support this claim by including high-quality ingredients (performance) or by showing users delighting in its consumption (imagery).

2. *Comparing to exemplars.* Well-known, noteworthy brands in a category can also help a brand specify its category membership. When Tommy Hilfiger was an unknown, advertising announced his membership as a great U.S. designer by associating him with Geoffrey Beene, Stanley Blacker, Calvin Klein, and Perry Ellis, who were recognized members of that category.

3. *Relying on the product descriptor.* The product descriptor that follows the brand name is often a concise means of conveying category origin. Ford Motor Co. invested more than $1 billion on a radical new 2004 model called the X-Trainer, which combined the attributes of an SUV, a minivan, and a station wagon. To communicate its unique position—and to avoid association with its Explorer and Country Squire models—the vehicle, eventually called Freestyle, was designated a "sports wagon."[20]

COMMUNICATING POPs AND PODs One common difficulty in creating a strong, competitive brand positioning is that many of the attributes or benefits that make up the points-of-parity and points-of-difference are negatively correlated. For example, it might be difficult to position a brand as "inexpensive" and at the same time assert that it is "of the highest quality." ConAgra must convince consumers that Healthy Choice frozen foods both taste good *and* are good for you. Consider these examples of negatively correlated attributes and benefits:

Low price vs. High quality	Powerful vs. Safe
Taste vs. Low calories	Strong vs. Refined
Nutritious vs. Good tasting	Ubiquitous vs. Exclusive
Efficacious vs. Mild	Varied vs. Simple

Moreover, individual attributes and benefits often have positive *and* negative aspects. For example, consider a long-lived brand such as La-Z-Boy recliners, Burberry outerwear, or the *New York Times*. The brand's heritage could suggest experience, wisdom, and expertise. On the other hand, it could also imply being old-fashioned and not up-to-date.[21]

Unfortunately, consumers typically want to maximize *both* of the negatively correlated attributes or benefits. Much of the art and science of marketing is dealing with trade-offs, and positioning is no different. The best approach clearly is to develop a product or service that performs well on both dimensions. GORE-TEX was able to overcome the seemingly conflicting product images of "breathable" and "waterproof" through technological advances. When in-depth and quantitative interviews and focus groups suggested that consumers wanted the benefits of technology without the hassles, Royal Philips launched its "Sense and Simplicity" advertising campaign for its Philips brand of electronics, using print, online, and television advertising.[22]

Some marketers have adopted other approaches to address attribute or benefit trade-offs: launching two different marketing campaigns, each one devoted to a different brand attribute or benefit; linking themselves to any kind of entity (person, place, or thing) that possesses the right kind of equity as a means to establish an attribute or benefit as a POP or POD; and even attempting to convince consumers that the negative relationship between attributes and benefits, if they consider it differently, is in fact positive.

Differentiation Strategies

To build a strong brand and avoid the commodity trap, marketers must start with the belief that you can differentiate anything. **Competitive advantage** is a company's ability to perform in one or more ways that competitors cannot or will not match. Michael Porter urged companies to build a sustainable competitive advantage.[23] But few competitive advantages are sustainable. At best, they may be leverageable. A *leverageable advantage* is one that a company can use as a springboard to new advantages, much as Microsoft has leveraged its operating system to Microsoft Office and then to networking applications. In general, a company that hopes to endure must be in the business of continuously inventing new advantages.[24]

For a brand to be effectively positioned, however, customers must see any competitive advantage as a *customer advantage*. For example, if a company claims its product works faster than its competitors, it won't be a customer advantage if customers don't value speed. Select Comfort has made a splash in the mattress industry with its Sleep Number beds, which allow consumers to adjust the support and fit of the mattress for optimal comfort with a simple numbering index.[25] Companies must also focus on building customer advantages.[26] Then they will deliver high customer value and satisfaction, which leads to high repeat purchases and ultimately to high company profitability.

Julius Baer
Julius Baer (also know as Julius Bär) is a leading Swiss private banking group focusing exclusively on servicing and advising private clients. It has more than 3,500 employees in 40 locations around the world. The competitive advantage of Julius Baer is its ability to provide excellent service to its clients.

Customization is of utmost importance for individual clients with varied needs. In November 2010, Julius Baer was named Best Swiss Bank by Fuchsbriefe publishers. This is an affirmation of the bank's ability to transform client needs into tailor-made sustainable solutions.

Performance is a key indicator for clients. Julius Baer was named Foreign Private Bank of the Year by *SPEAR'S Russia Wealth* magazine for demonstrating outstanding performance and service for Russian high net-worth individuals during 2009–2010. Julius Baer was named Best

Julius Baer has won numerous awards for its commitment to customer service and customization of services, including being named Best Swiss Bank by Fuchsbriefe publishers.

Private Bank in Switzerland and Best Private Bank Strategy for Growth by *Financial Times* publications for setting new best practices for the wealth management industry.

Excellent service comes from outstanding staff. During the Private Banker International's Annual Awards 2010, Julius Baer was presented with the Outstanding Wealth Manager—Customer Relationship Skills award and its CEO for Asia and the Middle East was named Outstanding Private Banker—Asia Pacific. These customer advantages have enabled the bank to continue thriving since 1890.[27]

MEANS OF DIFFERENTIATION The obvious means of differentiation, and often the ones most compelling to consumers, relate to aspects of the product and service (reviewed in Chapters 12 and 13). Swatch offers colorful, fashionable watches; GEICO offers reliable insurance at discount prices. In competitive markets, however, firms may need to go beyond these. Consider these other dimensions, among the many that a company can use to differentiate its market offerings:

- *Employee differentiation.* Companies can have better-trained employees who provide superior customer service. Singapore Airlines is well regarded in large part because of its flight attendants. The sales forces of such companies as General Electric, Cisco, Frito-Lay, Northwestern Mutual Life, and Pfizer enjoy an excellent reputation.[28]
- *Channel differentiation.* Companies can more effectively and efficiently design their distribution channels' coverage, expertise, and performance to make buying the product easier and more enjoyable and rewarding. Back in 1946, pet food was cheap, not too nutritious, and available exclusively in supermarkets and the occasional feed store. Dayton, Ohio–based Iams found success selling premium pet food through regional veterinarians, breeders, and pet stores.
- *Image differentiation.* Companies can craft powerful, compelling images that appeal to consumers' social and psychological needs. The primary explanation for Marlboro's extraordinary worldwide market share (around 30 percent) is that its "macho cowboy" image has struck a responsive chord with much of the cigarette-smoking public. Wine and liquor companies also work hard to develop distinctive images for their brands. Even a seller's physical space can be a powerful image generator. Hyatt Regency hotels developed a distinctive image through its atrium lobbies.
- *Services differentiation.* A service company can differentiate itself by designing a better and faster delivery system that provides more effective and efficient solutions to consumers. There are three levels of differentiation.[29] The first is *reliability:* Some suppliers are more reliable in their on-time delivery, order completeness, and order-cycle time. The second is *resilience:* Some suppliers are better at handling emergencies, product recalls, and inquiries. The third is *innovativeness:* Some suppliers create better information systems, introduce bar coding and mixed pallets, and in other ways help the customer.

EMOTIONAL BRANDING Many marketing experts believe a brand positioning should have both rational and emotional components. In other words, a good positioning should contain points-of-difference and points-of-parity that appeal both to the head and to the heart.

To do this, strong brands often seek to build on their performance advantages to strike an emotional chord with their customers. When research on scar-treatment product Mederma found that women were buying it not just for the physical treatment but also to increase their self-esteem, the marketers of the brand added emotional messaging to what had traditionally been a practical message that stressed physician recommendations: "What we have done is supplement the rational with the emotional."[30]

A person's emotional response to a brand and its marketing will depend on many factors. One increasingly important factor is a brand's authenticity.[31] Brands such as Hershey's, Kraft, Crayola, Kellogg's, and Johnson & Johnson that are seen as authentic and genuine can evoke trust, affection, and strong loyalty.[32] Guinness celebrated its heritage, quality, and authenticity with a 250th anniversary marketing campaign whose ads depict consumers all over the world toasting the brand.[33]

Brand consultant Marc Gobé believes emotional brands share three specific traits: (1) strong people-focused corporate culture, (2) a distinctive communication style and philosophy, and (3) a compelling emotional hook.[34] Saatchi & Saatchi CEO Kevin Roberts advocates that brands strive to become lovemarks. Brands that are *lovemarks*, according to Roberts, command both respect and love and result from a brand's ability to achieve mystery, sensuality, and intimacy:[35]

1. *Mystery* draws together stories, metaphors, dreams, and symbols. Mystery adds to the complexity of relationships and experiences because people are naturally drawn to what they don't know.
2. *Sensuality* keeps the five senses of sight, hearing, smell, touch, and taste on constant alert for new textures, intriguing scents and tastes, wonderful music, and other sensory stimuli.
3. *Intimacy* means empathy, commitment, and passion. The close connections that win intense loyalty as well as the small perfect gesture.

By successfully differentiating themselves, emotional brands can also provide financial payoffs. As part of its IPO, the UK mobile phone operator O2 was rebranded from British Telecom's struggling BT Cellnet, based on a powerful emotional campaign about freedom and enablement. When customer acquisition, loyalty, and average revenue soared, the business was acquired by Spanish multinational Telefonica after only five years for more than three times its IPO price.[36]

In general, the firm should monitor three variables when analyzing potential threats posed by competitors:

1. *Share of market*—The competitor's share of the target market.
2. *Share of mind*—The percentage of customers who named the competitor in responding to the statement, "Name the first company that comes to mind in this industry."
3. *Share of heart*—The percentage of customers who named the competitor in responding to the statement, "Name the company from which you would prefer to buy the product."

There's an interesting relationship among these three measures. 🔲 Table 10.3 shows them as recorded for three hypothetical competitors. Competitor A enjoys the highest market share but is slipping. Its mind share and heart share are also slipping, probably because it's not providing good product availability and technical assistance. Competitor B is steadily gaining market share, probably due to strategies that are increasing its mind share and heart share. Competitor C seems to be stuck at a low level of market, mind, and heart share, probably because of its poor product and marketing attributes. We could generalize as follows: *Companies that make steady gains in mind share and heart share will inevitably make gains in market share and profitability.* Firms such as CarMax, Timberland, Jordan's Furniture, Wegmans, and Toyota are all reaping the benefits of providing emotional, experiential, social, and financial value to satisfy customers and all their constituents.[37]

Alternative Approaches to Positioning

The competitive brand positioning model we've reviewed in this chapter is a structured way to approach positioning based on in-depth consumer, company, and competitive analysis. Some marketers have proposed other, less-structured approaches in recent years that offer provocative ideas on how to position a brand. We highlight a few of those here.

TABLE 10.3 🔲 Market Share, Mind Share, and Heart Share								
	Market Share			Mind Share			Heart Share		
	2011	2012	2013	2011	2012	2013	2011	2012	2013
Competitor A	50%	47%	44%	60%	58%	54%	45%	42%	39%
Competitor B	30	34	37	30	31	35	44	47	53
Competitor C	20	19	19	10	11	11	11	11	8

BRAND NARRATIVES AND STORYTELLING Rather than outlining specific attributes or benefits, some marketing experts describe positioning a brand as telling a narrative or story.[38]

Randall Ringer and Michael Thibodeau see *narrative branding* as based on deep metaphors that connect to people's memories, associations, and stories.[39] They identify five elements of narrative branding: (1) the brand story in terms of words and metaphors, (2) the consumer journey in terms of how consumers engage with the brand over time and touch points where they come into contact with it, (3) the visual language or expression for the brand, (4) the manner in which the narrative is expressed experientially in terms of how the brand engages the senses, and (5) the role/relationship the brand plays in the lives of consumers. Based on literary convention and brand experience, they also offer the following framework for a brand story:

- *Setting.* The time, place, and context
- *Cast.* The brand as a character, including its role in the life of the audience, its relationships and responsibilities, and its history or creation myth
- *Narrative arc.* The way the narrative logic unfolds over time, including actions, desired experiences, defining events, and the moment of epiphany
- *Language.* The authenticating voice, metaphors, symbols, themes, and leitmotifs

Patrick Hanlon developed the related concept of "primal branding" that views brands as complex belief systems. According to Hanlon, diverse brands such as Google, MINI Cooper, the U.S. Marine Corps, Starbucks, Apple, UPS, and Aveda all have a "primal code" or DNA that resonates with their customers and generates their passion and fervor. He outlines seven assets that make up this belief system or primal code: a creation story, creed, icon, rituals, sacred words, a way of dealing with nonbelievers, and a good leader.[40]

BRAND JOURNALISM When he was CMO at McDonald's, Larry Light advocated an approach to brand positioning that he called "brand journalism." Just as editors and writers for newspapers and magazines tell many facets of a story to capture the interests of diverse groups of people, Light believes marketers should communicate different messages to different market segments, as long as they at least broadly fit within the basic broad image of the brand.[41]

> Brand Journalism is a chronicle of the varied things that happen in our brand world, throughout our day, throughout the years. Our brand means different things to different people. It does not have one brand position. It is positioned differently in the minds of kids, teens, young adults, parents and seniors. It is positioned differently at breakfast, lunch, dinner, snack, weekday, weekend, with kids or on a business trip. Brand Journalism allows us to be a witness to the multi-faceted aspects of a brand story. No one communication alone tells the whole brand story. Each communication provides a different insight into our brand. It all adds up to a McDonald's journalistic brand chronicle.

CULTURAL BRANDING Oxford University's Douglas Holt believes for companies to build iconic, leadership brands, they must assemble cultural knowledge, strategize according to cultural branding principles, and hire and train cultural experts.[42] Even Procter & Gamble, a company that has long orchestrated how shoppers perceive its products, has started on what its chief executive, A.G. Lafley, calls "a learning journey" with the consumer. "Consumers are beginning in a very real sense to own our brands and participate in their creation," he said. "We need to learn to begin to let go."

The University of Wisconsin's Craig Thompson view brands as sociocultural templates, citing research investigating brands as cultural resources that shows how ESPN Zone restaurants tap into competitive masculinity; and how American Girl dolls tap into mother-daughter relationships and the cross-generational transfer of femininity.[43] Experts who see consumers actively cocreating brand meaning and positioning even refer to this as "Brand Wikification," given that wikis are written by contributors from all walks of life and all points of view.[44]

Positioning and Branding a Small Business

Building brands for a small business is a challenge because these firms have limited resources and budgets. Nevertheless, numerous success stories exist of entrepreneurs who have built their brands up essentially from scratch to become powerhouse brands.

vitaminwater In 1996, J. Darius Bickoff launched an electrolyte-enhanced line of bottled water called smartwater, followed by the introduction of vitaminwater, a vitamin-enhanced and flavored alternative to plain bottled water, two years later, and fruitwater two years after that. Clever marketing including endorsement deals with rapper 50 Cent, singer Kelly Clarkson, actress Jennifer Aniston, and football star Tom Brady helped to drive success. Less than 10 years after its launch, Bickoff's Energy Brands company, also known as Glacéau, was sold to the Coca-Cola company for $4.2 billion in cash.[45]

With a unique formulation and shrewd marketing, vitaminwater made a splash in the beverage market.

In general, with limited resources behind the brand, both focus and consistency in marketing programs are critically important. Creativity is also paramount—finding new ways to market new ideas about products to consumers. Some specific branding guidelines for small businesses are as follows.

- *Creatively conduct low-cost marketing research.* There are a variety of low-cost marketing research methods that help small businesses connect with customers and study competitors. One way is to set up course projects at local colleges and universities to access the expertise of both students and professors.
- *Focus on building one or two strong brands based on one or two key associations.* Small businesses often must rely on only one or two brands and key associations as points of difference for those brands. These associations must be consistently reinforced across the marketing program and over time. Rooted in the snowboarding and surfing cultures, Volcom has adopted a "Youth Against Establishment" credo that has resulted in steady sales of its music, athletic apparel, and jewelry.
- *Employ a well-integrated set of brand elements.* Tactically, it is important for small businesses to maximize the contribution of each of the three main sets of brand equity drivers. First, they should develop a distinctive, well-integrated set of brand elements that enhances both brand awareness and brand image. Brand elements should be memorable and meaningful, with as much creative potential as possible. Innovative packaging can substitute for ad campaigns by capturing attention at the point of purchase. SMARTFOOD introduced its first product without any advertising by means of both a unique package that served as a strong visual symbol on the shelf and an extensive sampling program that encouraged trial. Proper names or family names, which often characterize small businesses, may provide some distinctiveness but can suffer in terms of pronounceability, meaningfulness, memorability, or other branding considerations. If these deficiencies are too great, explore alternative brand elements.

Some hard-core fans of Mozilla Firefox carved out a massive logo for the brand in the fields outside Portland, Oregon.

- *Create buzz and a loyal brand community.* Because small businesses often must rely on word of mouth to establish their positioning, public relations, social networking, and low-cost promotions and sponsorship can be inexpensive alternatives. As discussed in Chapter 9, creating a vibrant brand community among current and prospective customers can also be a cost-effective way to reinforce loyalty and help spread the word to new prospects. Web browser Mozilla Firefox is able to compete with Microsoft's Internet Explorer in part because of its dedicated volunteer group

of 10,000 programmers who work on its open source coding. Twelve fans of the brand felt so strongly about it they used two-by-fours and rope to hollow out a 30,000-square-foot impression of the brand's logo in an oat field outside Salem, Oregon![46]

- **_Leverage as many secondary associations as possible._** Secondary associations—any persons, places, or things with potentially relevant associations—are often a cost-effective, shortcut means to build brand equity, especially those that help to signal quality or credibility. Cogent, makers of software that can identify people through fingerprints, draws 12 percent of its revenues and much brand equity from the fact that the Department of Homeland Security uses its products to police the U.S. border.[47]

Unlike major brands that often have more resources at their disposal, small businesses usually do not have the luxury to make mistakes and must design and implement marketing programs much more carefully.

Summary

1. To develop an effective positioning, a company must study competitors as well as actual and potential customers. Marketers need to identify competitors' strategies, objectives, strengths, and weaknesses.

2. Developing a positioning requires the determination of a frame of reference—by identifying the target market and the resulting nature of the competition—and the optimal points-of-parity and points-of-difference brand associations.

3. A company's closest competitors are those seeking to satisfy the same customers and needs and making similar offers. A company should also pay attention to latent competitors, who may offer new or other ways to satisfy the same needs. A company should identify competitors by using both industry- and market-based analyses.

4. Points-of-difference are those associations unique to the brand that are also strongly held and favorably evaluated by consumers. Points-of-parity are those associations not necessarily unique to the brand but perhaps shared with other brands. Category point-of-parity associations

are associations consumers view as being necessary to a legitimate and credible product offering within a certain category. Competitive point-of-parity associations are those associations designed to negate competitors' points-of-difference or overcome perceived weaknesses or vulnerabilities of the brand.

5. The key to competitive advantage is relevant brand differentiation—consumers must find something unique and meaningful about a market offering. These differences may be based directly on the product or service itself or on other considerations related to factors such as employees, channels, image, or services.

6. Emotional branding is becoming an important way to connect with customers and create differentiation from competitors.

7. Although small businesses should adhere to many of the branding and positioning principles larger companies use, they must place extra emphasis on their brand elements and secondary associations and must be more focused and create a buzz for their brand.

Applications

Marketing Debate
What Is the Best Way to Position?

Marketers have different views of how to position a brand. Some value structured approaches such as the competitive positioning model described in the chapter, which focuses on specific points-of-parity and points-of-difference. Others prefer unstructured approaches that rely more on stories, narratives, and other flowing depictions.

Take a position: The best way to position a brand is through a structured approach *versus* The best way to position a brand is through an unstructured approach.

Marketing Discussion
Attributes and Benefits

Identify other negatively correlated attributes and benefits *not* described in this chapter. What strategies do firms use to try to position themselves on the basis of pairs of attributes and benefits?

Marketing Excellence

>>Louis Vuitton

Louis Vuitton (LV) is one of the world's most legendary brands and is synonymous with images of luxury, wealth, and fashion. The company is known for its iconic handbags, leather goods, shoes, watches, jewelry, accessories, and sunglasses, and is the highest-ranked luxury brand in the world.

It was 1854 when Louis Vuitton opened his first store in Paris and sold handmade, high-quality trunks and luggage. In the late 19th century, Vuitton introduced his signature Damier and Monogram Canvas materials, featuring the famous design still used in most of the company's products today. Throughout the 20th century, the company that carries his name continued to grow internationally, expanding into the fashion world by the 1950s and reaching $10 million in sales by 1977. In 1987, Louis Vuitton merged with Moët et Chandon and Hennessy, leading manufacturers of champagne and cognac, and created LVMH, a luxury goods conglomerate.

Louis Vuitton's products are made with state-of-the-art materials, and its designers use a combination of art, precision, and craftsmanship to produce only the finest products. The legendary LV monogram appears on all the company's products and stands for the highest quality, premium status, and luxury travel. Over the years, however, counterfeiting has become a huge problem and one of Louis Vuitton's most difficult challenges. Louis Vuitton is one of the most counterfeited brands in the world, and the company takes the problem very seriously because it feels that counterfeits dilute its prestigious brand image. Louis Vuitton employs a full team of lawyers and fights counterfeiting in a variety of ways with special agencies and investigative teams.

Until the 1980s, Louis Vuitton products were available in a wide variety of department stores. However, to reduce the risk of counterfeiting, the company now maintains tighter control over its distribution channels. Today, it sells its products only through authentic Louis Vuitton boutiques located in upscale shopping areas and high-end department stores, all run independently with their own employees and managers. Louis Vuitton prices are never reduced, and only recently did the company start selling through louisvuitton.com in hopes of reaching new consumers and regions.

Over the years, a wide variety of high-profile celebrities and supermodels have used LV products, including Madonna, Audrey Hepburn, and Jennifer Lopez. In its marketing efforts, the company has used high-fashion celebrities, billboards, print ads, and its own international regatta—the Louis Vuitton Cup. Recently, LV broke tradition and featured nontraditional celebrities such as Steffi Graf, Mikhail Gorbachev, Buzz Aldrin, and Keith Richards in a campaign entitled "Core Values." LV also launched its first television commercial focused on luxury traveling rather than fashion and has formed new partnerships with international artists, museums, and cultural organizations in hopes of keeping the brand fresh. That said, Louis Vuitton still spends up to 60 hours making one piece of luggage by hand—the same way it did 150 years ago.

Today, Louis Vuitton holds a brand value of $26 billion according to *Forbes* and is ranked the 17th most powerful global brand according to Interbrand. The company is focused on expanding its luxury brand into growing markets such as China and India as well as continuing to grow in strong markets like Japan and Europe. It also continues to add new product lines to its portfolio.

Questions

1. How does an exclusive brand such as Louis Vuitton grow and stay fresh while retaining its cachet?

2. Is the counterfeiting of Louis Vuitton always a negative? Are there any circumstances where it can be seen as having some positive aspects?

Sources: Reena Jana, "Louis Vuitton's Life of Luxury," *BusinessWeek*, August 6, 2007; Eric Pfanner, "Luxury Firms Move to Make Web Work for Them," *New York Times*, November 17, 2009; www.louisvuitton.com.

Marketing Excellence

>>Philips

Royal Philips Electronics, established in 1891, is one of the world's largest electronics companies and one of the most respected brands. Anton and Gerard Philips started Philips & Co., in 1891 in Eindhoven, Netherlands, by manufacturing carbon filament lamps. Their firm eventually evolved into a global company and today employs a workforce of 116,000 around the world. A market leader in medical diagnostic imaging, patient monitoring systems, energy-efficient lighting solutions, and lifestyle solutions for personal well-being, Philips manufactures more than 50,000 products across 100 countries, in which it also operates sales and service outlets. In 2009, the firm reported sales of around $30.6 billion. It offers product content and support in 57 countries and in over 35 languages. With global outreach and products in many areas, Philips needs to develop a borderless style of brand management to solidify its reputation as a global brand. The company has experimented with many different ways of doing this.

The branding of Philips started when Anton Philips created a logo for the company by using the initial letters of Philips & Co. The word *Philips* also appeared on the glass of its metal filament lamps. In 1898, postcards showing a variety of Dutch national costumes were used as marketing tools, with the letters of the word *Philips* printed in a row of lightbulbs at the top of every card. In 1926, Philips introduced a symbol that featured waves and stars. The waves symbolized radio waves, and the stars represented the evening sky through which those radio waves travel. In 1930, the waves and stars were enclosed in a circle as part of the design. To avoid legal problems with owners of well-known circular emblems and to find a trademark that would be unique to Philips, the company eventually created a shield including the circle and word mark, which it has used consistently since the 1930s. However, marketing and advertising have varied across products. Between 1930 and 1995, all advertising and marketing campaigns were carried out at the product level, on a local market basis. The company thus found itself running many different marketing campaigns at once, and not allowing for a global representation of the company.

Between 1970 and 1995, Philips also faced tough competition from up-and-coming Japanese electronics companies, which cut into its market share. Because they had large automated plants, the Japanese companies were able to flood markets with inexpensive consumer electronics. This required Philips to close its less profitable factories and start creating larger and more effective units. The company also closed its business units in defense and home appliances, which were not directly related to its core business. To reduce costs, it began sharing its R&D expenses with other large corporations, including AT&T and Siemens AG.

Philips has always been known for its technological prowess and ability to innovate. It is credited with the introduction of innovative products including the radio, audio cassette, video cassette recorder (VCR), compact disc (CD), and digital video disc (DVD). However, simply being able to use technology in new and innovative ways was not enough for the company. It wanted to become a global brand and champion the idea that technology will improve people's lives.

For this purpose, Philips initiated a new branding campaign, "Let's make things better," which emphasized improving people's lives through technological solutions. The company rolled the campaign out globally in all markets and related the campaign to all its products. This also brought the whole company together, gave employees a sense of belonging and provided a unified company look for an external audience. Its primary objective was to help Philips connect with people, and in this endeavor it was successful. Nonetheless, the management team was concerned that the campaign did not convey the design excellence or technical superiority of its products.

To identify the perceptions consumers had, Philips undertook a market research study of more than 1,650 consumers and 180 companies who were customers of Philips around the world. It also undertook research among 26,000 respondents to measure the brand equity. Focus groups and questionnaires helped to (a) identify and test new routes for moving the Philips brand going forward, and (b) enable the company to better understand its current market position. The results showed that consumers believed they could "rely on Philips' products," and that the company did live up to its promise to "make things better." The company also discovered that its core target group consisted of well-educated and affluent decision makers between 35 and 55. This group typically disliked the unnecessary hassle often created by new technology and valued simplicity and efficiency in all fields. Its members wanted technology that could get the job done without drawing attention to itself and were put off by the need to read and understand complicated manuals before trying out their new purchases.

Philips acted on this information by rebranding itself again. The new campaign was called "sense and simplicity." The emphasis in sense and simplicity is on the benefits of technology without the hassle of understanding the technology and this strategy characterizes everything Philips does and reflects that the company is market-oriented, that is, everything is designed to meet customer needs and consumer insights. Catalogues and instruction manuals were prepared in 35 different languages and written in such a way that the consumers need not have to understand the technological aspects of the product while using them. Sense and simplicity was about promising customers a more comfortable and straightforward relationship with technology, and certainly with the company that delivered

it. "Sense and simplicity" was based on three premises. First, products are designed *around the consumer*; second, they are *easy to experience*; and third, they are *advanced*.

Philips continues to develop new products based on these three premises and communicates its brand position through advertisements that target the core group with relevant and interesting content. The new brand positioning has proved a success. In 2008, the company realized an 8 percent growth in total brand value in Interbrand's annual ranking, its fifth increase in as many years. In 2004, before the launch of the new campaign, the estimate of total brand value was $4.4 billion; by 2008, it had almost doubled to $8.3 billion.

Questions

1. Evaluate Philips' "sense and simplicity" strategy. What are the risks the company faces in using this tagline?

2. What strategies can Philips follow to ward off competition from Japanese manufacturers of consumer electronics?

Source: *Philips*, www.philips.com; "Philips—Strengthening a Global Brand," *BrandingAsia*.com, www.brandingasia.com/cases/philips.htm.

Chapter 11

In This Chapter, We Will Address the Following Questions

1. How can market leaders expand the total market and defend market share?

2. How should market challengers attack market leaders?

3. How can market followers or nichers compete effectively?

4. What marketing strategies are appropriate at each stage of the product life cycle?

5. How should marketers adjust their strategies and tactics for an economic downturn or recession?

Through innovative new products and aggressive advertising, Under Armour has played the role of a challenger brand to market leader Nike.

Competitive Dynamics

To be a long-term market leader is the goal of any marketer. Today's challenging marketing circumstances, however, often dictate that companies reformulate their marketing strategies and offerings several times. Economic conditions change, competitors launch new assaults, and buyer interest and requirements evolve. Different market positions can suggest different market strategies.

 Former University of Maryland football player Kevin Plank was dissatisfied in his playing days with cotton T-shirts that retained water and became heavy during practice. So with $500 and several yards of coat lining, he worked with a local tailor to create seven prototypes of snug-fitting T-shirts that absorbed perspiration and kept athletes dry. Under Armour was born and quickly became a favorite at high schools, colleges, and universities. Intense, in-your-face advertising featuring NFL player "Big E" Eric Ogbogu grunting and screaming, "We must protect this house," sent a loud message to target teens and young adult males that a new brand of athletic clothing and gear had arrived. With a focus on performance and authenticity, Under Armour later introduced football cleats to cover players literally from head to foot. The introduction of a full line of running shoes in 2009, however, put them squarely into competition with formidable opponents Nike and adidas. The launch also reflected an attempt to move away some from team sports to attract individual consumers and, in particular, reach a new demographic—women. An ad campaign themed "Athletes Run" introduced the technologically advanced, high-end Apparition and Revenant running shoes showing many accomplished athletes who were not well-known as runners running in the shoes. The next new product initiative under consideration—basketball shoes—would capitalize on one of their athletic endorsers, up-and-coming NBA player Brandon Jennings, but would also represent an even more full-on, direct assault of some of Nike's and adidas's market turf.[1]

This chapter examines the role competition plays and how marketers can best manage their brands depending on their market position and stage of the product life cycle. Competition grows more intense every year—from global competitors eager to grow sales in new markets, from online competitors seeking cost-efficient ways to expand distribution, from private-label and store brands providing low-price alternatives, and from brand extensions by mega-brands moving into new categories.[2] For these reasons and more, product and brand fortunes change over time, and marketers must respond accordingly.

Competitive Strategies for Market Leaders

Suppose a market is occupied by the firms shown in △ Figure 11.1. Forty percent is in the hands of a *market leader*; another 30 percent belongs to a *market challenger*; and 20 percent is claimed by a *market follower* willing to maintain its share and not rock the boat. *Market nichers,* serving small segments larger firms don't reach, hold the remaining 10 percent.

A market leader has the largest market share and usually leads in price changes, new-product introductions, distribution coverage, and promotional intensity. Some historical market leaders are Microsoft (computer software), Gatorade (sports drinks), Best Buy (retail electronics), McDonald's (fast food), Blue Cross Blue Shield (health insurance), and Visa (credit cards).

Although marketers assume well-known brands are distinctive in consumers' minds, unless a dominant firm enjoys a legal monopoly, it must maintain constant vigilance. A powerful product innovation may come along; a competitor might find a fresh marketing angle or commit to a major marketing investment; or the leader's cost structure might spiral upward. One well-known brand and market leader that has worked to stay on top is Xerox.

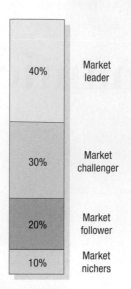

40%	Market leader
30%	Market challenger
20%	Market follower
10%	Market nichers

|Fig. 11.1| △

Hypothetical Market Structure

Xerox   Xerox has had to become more than just a copier company. Now the blue-chip icon with the name that became a verb sports the broadest array of imaging products in the world and dominates the market for high-end printing systems. And it's making a huge product line transition as it moves from the old light lens technology to digital systems. Xerox is preparing for a world in which most pages are printed in color (which, not incidentally, generates five times the revenue of black-and-white). Besides revamping its machines, Xerox is beefing up sales by providing annuity-like products and services that are ordered again and again: document management, ink, and toners. It has even introduced the managed print-services business to help companies actually eliminate desktop printers and let employees share multifunction devices that copy, print, and fax. Once slow to respond to the emergence of Canon and the small-copier market, Xerox is doing everything it can to stay ahead of the game.[3] ▭

In many industries, a discount competitor has undercut the leader's prices. "Marketing Insight: When Your Competitor Delivers More for Less" describes how leaders can respond to an aggressive competitive price discounter.

Marketing Insight

When Your Competitor Delivers More for Less

Companies offering the powerful combination of low prices and high quality are capturing the hearts and wallets of consumers all over the world. In the United States, more than half the population now shops weekly at mass merchants such as Walmart and Target. In the United Kingdom, premium retailers such as Boots and Sainsbury are scrambling to meet intensifying price—and quality—competition from ASDA and Tesco.

These and similar value players, such as Aldi, Dell, E*TRADE Financial, JetBlue Airways, Ryanair, and Southwest Airlines, are transforming the way consumers of nearly every age and income level purchase groceries, apparel, airline tickets, financial services, and computers. Traditional players are right to feel threatened. Upstart firms often rely on serving one or a few consumer segments, providing better delivery or just one additional benefit, and matching low prices with highly efficient operations to keep costs down. They

have changed consumer expectations about the trade-off between quality and price.

To compete, mainstream companies need to infuse their timeless strategies like cost control and product differentiation with greater intensity and focus, and then execute them flawlessly. Differentiation, for example, becomes less about the abstract goal of rising above competitive clutter and more about identifying openings left by the value players' business models. Effective pricing means waging a transaction-by-transaction perception battle for consumers predisposed to believe value-oriented competitors are always cheaper.

Competitive outcomes will be determined, as always, on the ground—in product aisles, merchandising displays, reconfigured processes, and pricing stickers. Traditional players can't afford to drop a stitch. The new competitive environment places a new premium on—and adds new twists to—the old imperatives of differentiation and execution.

Differentiation

Marketers need to protect areas where their business models give other companies room to maneuver. Instead of trying to compete with Walmart and other value retailers on price, for example, Walgreens emphasizes convenience. It has expanded rapidly to make its stores ubiquitous, mostly on corners with easy parking, and overhauled store layouts to speed consumers in and out, placing key categories such as convenience foods and one-hour photo services near the front. To simplify prescription orders, the company has installed a telephone and online ordering system and drive-through windows at most freestanding stores. These steps helped it increase its revenue from $15 billion in 1998 to over $59 billion in 2008, making it the largest U.S. drugstore chain.

Execution

Kmart's disastrous experience trying to compete head-on with Walmart on price highlights the difficulty of challenging value leaders on their own terms. To compete effectively, firms may instead need to downplay or even abandon some market segments. To compete with Ryanair and easyJet, British Airways has put more emphasis on its long-haul routes, where value-based players are not active, and less on the short-haul routes where they thrive.

Major airlines have also introduced their own low-cost carriers. But Continental's Lite, KLM's Buzz, SAS's Snowflake, and United's Shuttle have all been unsuccessful. One school of thought is that companies should set up low-cost operations only if: (1) their existing businesses will become more competitive as a result and (2) the new business will derive some advantages it would not have gained if independent. Low-cost operations set up by HSBC, ING, Merrill Lynch, and Royal Bank of Scotland—First Direct, ING Direct, ML Direct, and Direct Line Insurance, respectively—succeed in part thanks to synergies between the old and new lines of business. The low-cost operation must be designed and launched as a moneymaker in its own right, not just as a defensive play.

Sources: Adapted from Nirmalya Kumar, "Strategies to Fight Low-Cost Rivals," *Harvard Business Review* December 2006, pp. 104–12; Robert J. Frank, Jeffrey P. George, and Laxman Narasimhan, "When Your Competitor Delivers More for Less," *McKinsey Quarterly* (Winter 2004): 48–59. See also Jan-Benedict E. M. Steenkamp and Nirmalya Kumar, "Don't Be Undersold," *Harvard Business Review*, December 2009, pp. 90–95.

To stay number one, the firm must first find ways to expand total market demand. Second, it must protect its current share through good defensive and offensive actions. Third, it should increase market share, even if market size remains constant. Let's look at each strategy.

Expanding Total Market Demand

When the total market expands, the dominant firm usually gains the most. If Heinz can convince more people to use ketchup, or to use ketchup with more meals, or to use more ketchup on each occasion, the firm will benefit considerably because it already sells almost two-thirds of the country's ketchup. In general, the market leader should look for new customers or more usage from existing customers.

NEW CUSTOMERS Every product class has the potential to attract buyers who are unaware of the product or are resisting it because of price or lack of certain features. As Chapter 2 suggested, a company can search for new users among three groups: those who might use it but do not *(market-penetration strategy)*, those who have never used it *(new-market segment strategy)*, or those who live elsewhere *(geographical-expansion strategy)*.

Here is how Starbucks describes its multipronged approach to growth on its corporate Web site.[4]

> Starbucks purchases and roasts high-quality whole bean coffees and sells them along with fresh, rich-brewed, Italian style espresso beverages, a variety of pastries and confections, and coffee-related accessories and equipment—primarily through its company-operated retail stores. In addition to sales through our company-operated retail stores, Starbucks sells whole bean coffees through a specialty sales group and supermarkets. Additionally, Starbucks produces and sells bottled Frappuccino® coffee drinks and a line of premium ice creams through its joint venture partnerships and offers a line of innovative premium teas produced by its wholly owned subsidiary, Tazo Tea Company. The Company's objective is to establish Starbucks as the most recognized and respected brand in the world.

MORE USAGE Marketers can try to increase the amount, level, or frequency of consumption. They can sometimes boost the *amount* through packaging or product redesign. Larger package sizes increase the amount of product consumers use at one time.[5] Consumers use more of impulse products such as soft drinks and snacks when the product is made more available.

Frappuccino coffee drinks have been a new source of growth and revenues for Starbucks.

Increasing *frequency* of consumption, on the other hand, requires either (1) identifying additional opportunities to use the brand in the same basic way or (2) identifying completely new and different ways to use the brand.

Additional Opportunities to Use the Brand A marketing program can communicate the appropriateness and advantages of using the brand. Clorox ads stress the many benefits of its bleach, such as that it eliminates kitchen odors.

Another opportunity arises when consumers' perceptions of their usage differs from reality. Consumers may fail to replace a short-lived product when they should because they overestimate how long it stays fresh.[6] One strategy is to tie the act of replacing the product to a holiday, event, or time of year. Another might be to provide consumers with better information about when they first used the product or need to replace it, or (2) the current level of product performance. Gillette razor cartridges feature colored stripes that slowly fade with repeated use, signaling the user to move on to the next cartridge.

New Ways to Use the Brand The second approach to increasing frequency of consumption is to identify completely new and different applications. Food product companies have long advertised recipes that use their branded products in different ways. After discovering that some consumers used Arm & Hammer baking soda as a refrigerator deodorant, the company launched a heavy promotion campaign focusing on this use and succeeded in getting half the homes in the United States to adopt it. Next, the company expanded the brand into a variety of new product categories such as toothpaste, antiperspirant, and laundry detergent.

Protecting Market Share

While trying to expand total market size, the dominant firm must actively defend its current business: Boeing against Airbus, Staples against Office Depot, and Google against Yahoo! and Microsoft.[7] How can the leader do so? The most constructive response is *continuous innovation*. The front-runner should lead the industry in developing new products and customer services, distribution effectiveness, and cost cutting. Comprehensive solutions increase its competitive strength and value to customers.

PROACTIVE MARKETING In satisfying customer needs, we can draw a distinction between responsive marketing, anticipative marketing, and creative marketing. A *responsive* marketer finds a stated need and fills it. An *anticipative* marketer looks ahead to needs customers may have in the near future. A *creative* marketer discovers solutions customers did not ask for but to which they enthusiastically respond. Creative marketers are proactive *market-driving* firms, not just market-driven ones.[8]

Many companies assume their job is just to adapt to customer needs. They are reactive mostly because they are overly faithful to the customer-orientation paradigm and fall victim to the "tyranny of the served market." Successful companies instead proactively shape the market to their own interests. Instead of trying to be the best player, they change the rules of the game.[9]

A company needs two proactive skills: (1) *responsive anticipation* to see the writing on the wall, as when IBM changed from a hardware producer to a service business and (2) *creative anticipation* to devise innovative solutions, as when PepsiCo introduced H2OH! (a soft drink–bottled water hybrid). Note that *responsive anticipation* is performed before a given change, while *reactive response* happens after the change takes place.

Proactive companies create new offers to serve unmet—and maybe even unknown—consumer needs. In the late 1970s, Akio Morita, the Sony founder, was working on a pet project that would revolutionize the way people listened to music: a portable cassette player he called the Walkman. Engineers at the company insisted there was little demand for such a product, but Morita refused to part with his vision. By the 20th anniversary of the Walkman, Sony had sold over 250 million in nearly 100 different models.[10]

Proactive companies may redesign relationships within an industry, like Toyota and its relationship to its suppliers. Or they may educate customers, as Body Shop does in stimulating the choice of environmental-friendly products.

Companies need to practice "uncertainty management." Proactive firms:

- Are ready to take risks and make mistakes,
- Have a vision of the future and of investing in it,

Arm & Hammer has expanded its classic baking soda product line to encompass many new products and uses.

- Have the capabilities to innovate,
- Are flexible and nonbureaucratic, and
- Have many managers who think proactively.

Companies that are *too* risk-averse won't be winners.

DEFENSIVE MARKETING Even when it does not launch offensives, the market leader must not leave any major flanks exposed. The aim of defensive strategy is to reduce the probability of attack, divert attacks to less-threatened areas, and lessen their intensity. Speed of response can make an important difference to profit. A dominant firm can use the six defense strategies summarized in △ Figure 11.2.[11]

- *Position Defense.* Position defense means occupying the most desirable market space in consumers' minds, making the brand almost impregnable, as Procter & Gamble has done with Tide detergent for cleaning, Crest toothpaste for cavity prevention, and Pampers diapers for dryness.
- *Flank Defense.* The market leader should erect outposts to protect a weak front or support a possible counterattack. Procter & Gamble brands such as Gain and Cheer laundry detergent and Luvs diapers have played strategic offensive and defensive roles.
- *Preemptive Defense.* A more aggressive maneuver is to attack first, perhaps with guerrilla action across the market—hitting one competitor here, another there—and keeping everyone off balance. Another is to achieve broad market envelopment that signals competitors not to attack.[12] Bank of America's 18,500 ATMs and 6,100 retail branches nationwide provide steep competition to local and regional banks. Yet another preemptive defense is to introduce a stream of new products and announce them in advance.[13] Such "preannouncements" can signal competitors that they will need to fight to gain market share.[14] If Microsoft announces plans for a new-product development, smaller firms may choose to concentrate their development efforts in other directions to avoid head-to-head competition. Some high-tech firms have been accused of selling "vaporware"—announcing products that miss delivery dates or are never introduced.[15]
- *Counteroffensive Defense.* In a counteroffensive, the market leader can meet the attacker frontally and hit its flank, or launch a pincer movement so it will have to pull back to defend itself. After FedEx watched UPS successfully invade its airborne delivery system, it invested heavily in ground delivery through a series of acquisitions to challenge UPS on its home turf.[16] Another common form of counteroffensive is the exercise of economic or political clout. The leader may try to crush a competitor by subsidizing lower prices for the vulnerable product with revenue from its more profitable products, or it may prematurely announce a product upgrade to prevent customers from buying the competitor's product. Or the leader may lobby legislators to take political action to inhibit the competition.
- *Mobile Defense.* In mobile defense, the leader stretches its domain over new territories through market broadening and market diversification. *Market broadening* shifts the company's focus from the current product to the underlying generic need. Thus, "petroleum" companies such as BP sought to recast themselves as "energy" companies. This change required them to research the oil, coal, nuclear, hydroelectric, and chemical industries.

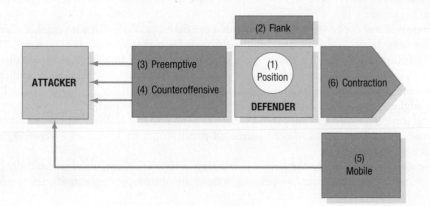

|Fig. 11.2| △

Six Types of Defense Strategies

By introducing ground delivery, FedEx challenged UPS on its home turf.

Market diversification shifts the company's focus into unrelated industries. When U.S. tobacco companies such as Reynolds and Philip Morris acknowledged the growing curbs on cigarette smoking, instead of defending their market position or looking for cigarette substitutes, they moved quickly into new industries such as beer, liquor, soft drinks, and frozen foods.

- **Contraction Defense.** Sometimes large companies can no longer defend all their territory. In *planned contraction* (also called *strategic withdrawal*), they give up weaker markets and reassign resources to stronger ones. Since 2006, Sara Lee has spun off products that accounted for a large percentage of its revenues—including its strong Hanes hosiery brand and global body care and European detergents businesses—to focus on its core food business.[17]

Increasing Market Share

No wonder competition has turned fierce in so many markets: one share point can be worth tens of millions of dollars. Gaining increased share does not automatically produce higher profits, however—especially for labor-intensive service companies that may not experience many economies of scale. Much depends on the company's strategy.[18]

Because the cost of buying higher market share through acquisition may far exceed its revenue value, a company should consider four factors first:

- **The possibility of provoking antitrust action.** Frustrated competitors are likely to cry "monopoly" and seek legal action if a dominant firm makes further inroads. Microsoft and Intel have had to fend off numerous lawsuits and legal challenges around the world as a result of what some feel are inappropriate or illegal business practices and abuse of market power.
- **Economic cost.** △ Figure 11.3 shows that profitability might *fall* with market share gains after some level. In the illustration, the firm's *optimal market share* is 50 percent. The cost of gaining further market share might exceed the value if holdout customers dislike the company, are loyal to competitors, have unique needs, or prefer dealing with smaller firms. And the costs of legal work, public relations, and lobbying rise with market share. Pushing for higher share is less justifiable when there are unattractive market segments, buyers who want multiple sources of supply, high exit barriers, and few scale or experience economies. Some market leaders have even increased profitability by selectively *decreasing* market share in weaker areas.[19]
- **The danger of pursuing the wrong marketing activities.** Companies successfully gaining share typically outperform competitors in three areas: new-product activity, relative product

|Fig. 11.3| △

The Concept of
Optimal Market Share

quality, and marketing expenditures.[20] Companies that attempt to increase market share by cutting prices more deeply than competitors typically don't achieve significant gains, because rivals meet the price cuts or offer other values so buyers don't switch.

- **The effect of increased market share on actual and perceived quality.**[21] Too many customers can put a strain on the firm's resources, hurting product value and service delivery. Charlotte-based FairPoint Communications struggled to integrate the 1.3 million customers it gained in buying Verizon Communications's New England franchise. A slow conversion and significant service problems led to customer dissatisfaction, regulator's anger, and eventually bankruptcy.[22]

Other Competitive Strategies

Firms that occupy second, third, and lower ranks in an industry are often called runner-up or trailing firms. Some, such as PepsiCo, Ford, and Avis, are quite large in their own right. These firms can adopt one of two postures. They can attack the leader and other competitors in an aggressive bid for further market share as *market challengers*, or they can choose to not "rock the boat" as *market followers*.

Market-Challenger Strategies

Many market challengers have gained ground or even overtaken the leader. Toyota today produces more cars than General Motors, Lowe's is putting pressure on Home Depot, and AMD has been chipping away at Intel's market share.[23] A successful challenger brand in the beverage business is SoBe.

SoBe   One of the most competitive aisles in any supermarket, grocery store, or convenience store is the beverage aisle. SoBe's successful launch in 1996 was a result of shrewd planning and creative execution. Positioning against the established Snapple and Arizona brands, founder John Bello wanted to create a smart fruit juice and iced tea alternative that was fun and innovative and offered added value. The first successful product was SoBe Black Tea 3G with ginseng, guarana, and ginkgo. The lizard character on the packaging, from an iconic South Beach hotel, became an integral part of SoBe's brand imagery. SoBe's explosive growth was based on a combination of functional benefits (the 3 Gs), colorful packaging, a powerful sales force establishing strong shelf presence in the store, and a steady stream of new products. The slogan "SoBe Yourself" captured the brand's challenger ethos and supported its nontraditional, guerilla marketing appeals. SoBe Love Buses created product sampling opportunities, and sponsorship of iconoclastic athletes like skier Bode Miller and golfer John Daly created buzz. SoBe was purchased by PepsiCo in January 2001 and now offers exotic teas, fruit juices and blends, elixirs, vitamin- and antioxidant-enhanced water (Lifewater), and sports drinks. Its name is also licensed for gum and chocolate.[24]

Challengers set high aspirations while market leaders can fall prey to running business as usual. Now let's examine the competitive attack strategies available to challengers.[25]

DEFINING THE STRATEGIC OBJECTIVE AND OPPONENT(S) A market challenger must first define its strategic objective, usually to increase market share. The challenger must decide whom to attack:

- **It can attack the market leader.** This is a high-risk but potentially high-payoff strategy and makes good sense if the leader is not serving the market well. Xerox wrested the copy market from 3M by developing a better copying process. Later, Canon grabbed a large chunk of Xerox's market by introducing desk copiers. This strategy often has the added benefit of distancing the firm from other challengers. When Miller Lite attacked Bud Light on product quality during the mid 2000s, Coors Light was left out of the conversation.

- *It can attack firms its own size that are not doing the job and are underfinanced.* These firms have aging products, are charging excessive prices, or are not satisfying customers in other ways.
- *It can attack small local and regional firms.* Several major banks grew to their present size by gobbling up smaller regional banks, or "guppies."

CHOOSING A GENERAL ATTACK STRATEGY Given clear opponents and objectives, what attack options are available? We can distinguish five: frontal, flank, encirclement, bypass, and guerilla attacks.

- *Frontal Attack.* In a pure *frontal attack,* the attacker matches its opponent's product, advertising, price, and distribution. The principle of force says the side with the greater resources will win. A modified frontal attack, such as cutting price, can work if the market leader doesn't retaliate, and if the competitor convinces the market its product is equal to the leader's. Helene Curtis is a master at convincing the market that its brands—such as Suave and Finesse—are equal in quality but a better value than higher-priced brands.
- *Flank Attack.* A *flanking* strategy is another name for identifying shifts that are causing gaps to develop, then rushing to fill the gaps. Flanking is particularly attractive to a challenger with fewer resources and can be more likely to succeed than frontal attacks. In a geographic attack, the challenger spots areas where the opponent is underperforming. Although the Internet has siphoned newspaper readers and advertisers away in many markets, Independent News & Media, a 102-year-old Irish media company, sells a majority of its 175 newspaper and magazine titles where the economy is strong but the Internet is still relatively weak—countries such as Ireland, South Africa, Australia, New Zealand, and India.[26] The other flanking strategy is to serve uncovered market needs. Ariat's cowboy boots have challenged long-time market leaders Justin Boots and Tony Lama by making boots that were every bit as ranch-ready, but ergonomically designed to feel as comfortable as a running shoe—a totally new benefit in the category.[27]
- *Encirclement Attack. Encirclement* attempts to capture a wide slice of territory by launching a grand offensive on several fronts. It makes sense when the challenger commands superior resources. In making a stand against archrival Microsoft, Sun Microsystems licensed its Java software to hundreds of companies and thousands of software developers for all sorts of consumer devices. As consumer electronics products began to go digital, Java started appearing in a wide range of gadgets.

Combining comfort with rugged wear, Ariat is taking on the market leaders in the cowboy boot market.

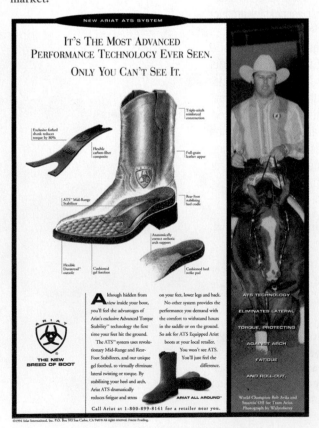

- *Bypass Attack. Bypassing* the enemy altogether to attack easier markets instead offers three lines of approach: diversifying into unrelated products, diversifying into new geographical markets, and leapfrogging into new technologies. Pepsi has used a bypass strategy against Coke by (1) rolling out Aquafina bottled water nationally in 1997 before Coke launched its Dasani brand; (2) purchasing orange juice giant Tropicana in 1998, when it owned almost twice the market share of Coca-Cola's Minute Maid; and (3) purchasing the Quaker Oats Company, owner of market leader Gatorade sports drink, for $14 billion in 2000.[28] In *technological leapfrogging,* the challenger patiently researches and develops the next technology, shifting the battleground to its own territory where it has an advantage. Google used technological leapfrogging to overtake Yahoo! and become the market leader in search.
- *Guerrilla Attacks.* Guerrilla attacks consist of small, intermittent attacks, conventional and unconventional, including selective price cuts, intense promotional blitzes, and occasional legal action, to harass the opponent and eventually secure permanent footholds. A guerrilla campaign can be expensive, although less so than a frontal, encirclement, or flank attack, but it typically must be backed by a stronger attack to beat the opponent.

CHOOSING A SPECIFIC ATTACK STRATEGY Any aspect of the marketing program can serve as the basis for attack, such as lower-priced or discounted products, new or improved products and services, a wider variety of offerings, and innovative distribution strategies. A challenger's success depends on combining several, more specific, strategies to improve its position over time.

Market-Follower Strategies

Theodore Levitt argues that a strategy of *product imitation* might be as profitable as a strategy of *product innovation*.[29] In "innovative imitation," as he calls it, the innovator bears the expense of developing the new product, getting it into distribution, and informing and educating the market. The reward for all this work and risk is normally market leadership. However, another firm can come along and copy or improve on the new product. Although it probably will not overtake the leader, the follower can achieve high profits because it did not bear any of the innovation expense.

Pepsi has used a bypass approach to battle Coke by finding new markets to enter.

S&S Cycle   S&S Cycle is the biggest supplier of complete engines and major motor parts to more than 15 companies that build several thousand Harley-like cruiser bikes each year. These cloners charge as much as $30,000 for their customized creations. S&S has built its name by improving on Harley-Davidson's handiwork. Its customers are often would-be Harley buyers frustrated by long waiting lines at the dealer. Others simply want S&S's incredibly powerful engines. S&S stays abreast of its evolving market by ordering a new Harley bike every year and taking apart the engine to see what it can improve upon.[30]

Many companies prefer to follow rather than challenge the market leader. Patterns of "conscious parallelism" are common in capital-intensive, homogeneous-product industries such as steel, fertilizers, and chemicals. The opportunities for product differentiation and image differentiation are low, service quality is comparable, and price sensitivity runs high. The mood in these industries is against short-run grabs for market share, because that only provokes retaliation. Instead, most firms present similar offers to buyers, usually by copying the leader. Market shares show high stability.

That's not to say market followers lack strategies. They must know how to hold current customers and win a fair share of new ones. Each follower tries to bring distinctive advantages to its target market—location, services, financing–while defensively keeping its manufacturing costs low and its product quality and services high. It must also enter new markets as they open up. The follower must define a growth path, but one that doesn't invite competitive retaliation. We distinguish four broad strategies:

1. *Counterfeiter*—The counterfeiter duplicates the leader's product and packages and sells it on the black market or through disreputable dealers. Music firms, Apple, and Rolex have been plagued by the counterfeiter problem, especially in Asia.
2. *Cloner*—The cloner emulates the leader's products, name, and packaging, with slight variations. For example, Ralcorp Holdings sells imitations of name-brand cereals in look-alike boxes. Its Tasteeos, Fruit Rings, and Corn Flakes sell for nearly $1 a box less than the leading name brands; the company's sales were up 28 percent in 2008.
3. *Imitator*—The imitator copies some things from the leader but differentiates on packaging, advertising, pricing, or location. The leader doesn't mind as long as the imitator doesn't attack aggressively. Fernandez Pujals grew up in Fort Lauderdale, Florida, and took Domino's home delivery idea to Spain, where he borrowed $80,000 to open his first store in Madrid. His Telepizza chain now operates almost 1,050 stores in Europe and Latin America.
4. *Adapter*—The adapter takes the leader's products and adapts or improves them. The adapter may choose to sell to different markets, but often it grows into a future challenger, as many Japanese firms have done after improving products developed elsewhere.

What does a follower earn? Normally, less than the leader. A study of food-processing companies showed the largest averaging a 16 percent return on investment, the number two firm, 6 percent, the number three firm, –1 percent, and the number four firm, –6 percent. No wonder Jack Welch, former CEO of GE, told his business units that each must reach the number one or two position in its market or else! Followership is often not a rewarding path.

Telepizza adapted Domino's pizza delivery concept to Spain with much success.

Market-Nicher Strategies

An alternative to being a follower in a large market is to be a leader in a small market, or niche, as we introduced in Chapter 8. Smaller firms normally avoid competing with larger firms by targeting small markets of little or no interest to the larger firms. But even large, profitable firms may choose to use niching strategies for some of their business units or companies.

ITW Illinois Tool Works (ITW) manufactures thousands of products, including nails, screws, plastic six-pack holders for soda cans, bicycle helmets, backpacks, plastic buckles for pet collars, resealable food packages, and more. Since the late 1980s, the company has made between 30 and 40 acquisitions each year that added new products to the product line. ITW has more than 875 highly autonomous and decentralized business units in 54 countries employing 65,000 people. When one division commercializes a new product, the company spins the product and people off into a new entity. Despite tough economic times, ITW experienced an increase in revenue in 2008.[31]

Firms with low shares of the total market can become highly profitable through smart niching. Such companies tend to offer high value, charge a premium price, achieve lower manufacturing costs, and shape a strong corporate culture and vision. Family-run Tire Rack sells 2 million specialty tires a year through the Internet, telephone, and mail from its South Bend, Indiana, location.[32] Houston-based VAALCO Energy decided that its odds of striking it rich were better in foreign territory than at home where it faced hundreds of wildcatters. Drilling in an oil field off the coast of Gabon in West Central Africa, it has met with a lot less competition and a lot more revenue.[33]

Return on investment for businesses in smaller markets exceeds that in larger markets on average.[34] Why is niching so profitable? The market nicher knows the target customers so well, it meets their needs better than other firms selling to them casually. As a result, the nicher can charge a substantial price over costs. The nicher achieves *high margin*, whereas the mass marketer achieves *high volume*.

Nichers have three tasks: creating niches, expanding niches, and protecting niches. The risk is that the niche might dry up or be attacked. The company is then stuck with highly specialized resources that may not have high-value alternative uses.

Zippo With smoking on a steady decline, Bradford, Pennsylvania–based Zippo Manufacturing is finding the market for its iconic metal cigarette lighter drying up. Its marketers need to diversify and broaden their focus to "selling flame." Although its goal of reducing reliance on tobacco-related products to 50 percent of revenue by 2010 was sidetracked by the recession, the company is determined to broaden its brand meaning to encompass "all flame-related products." It introduced a long, slender multipurpose lighter for candles, grills, and fireplaces in 2001; acquired W.R. Case & Sons Cutlery, a knife maker, and DDM Italia, known throughout Europe for its fine Italian leather goods; and plans to sell a line of outdoor products in outlets such as Dicks, REI, and True Value.[35]

Because niches can weaken, the firm must continually create new ones. "Marketing Memo: Niche Specialist Roles" outlines some options. The firm should "stick to its niching" but not necessarily to its niche. That is why *multiple niching* can be preferable to *single niching*. With strength in two or more niches, the company increases its chances for survival.

Firms entering a market should initially aim at a niche rather than the whole market. The cell phone industry has experienced phenomenal growth but is now facing fierce competition as the number of new potential users dwindles. An Irish upstart company, Digicel Group, has successfully tapped into one of the few remaining high-growth segments: poor people without cell phones.

Digicel Group In 2001, Digicel CEO Denis O'Brien heard that the government of Jamaica was opening its local phone market, long monopolized by British telecom giant Cable & Wireless. O'Brien spent nearly $50 million for a license, using money from the sale of his first telecom venture, Esat Telecom Group PLC. O'Brien took the plunge because he knew Jamaicans had to wait over two years for a landline, and only 4 percent of the population had cell phones. Within 100 days, Digicel had signed on 100,000 subscribers, luring them with inexpensive rates and phones and

Zippo has expanded its brand meaning to encompass "all flame-related products" to ensure its long-term growth prospects.

marketing Memo

Niche Specialist Roles

The key idea in successful nichemanship is specialization. Here are some possible niche roles:

- *End-user specialist.* The firm specializes in one type of end-use customer. For example, a *value-added reseller (VAR)* customizes computer hardware and software for specific customer segments and earns a price premium in the process.

- *Vertical-level specialist.* The firm specializes at some vertical level of the production-distribution value chain. A copper firm may concentrate on producing raw copper, copper components, or finished copper products.

- *Customer-size specialist.* The firm concentrates on either small, medium-sized, or large customers. Many nichers serve small customers neglected by the majors.

- *Specific-customer specialist.* The firm limits its selling to one or a few customers. Many firms sell their entire output to a single company, such as Walmart or General Motors.

- *Geographic specialist.* The firm sells only in a certain locality, region, or area of the world.

- *Product or product line specialist.* The firm carries or produces only one product line or product. A manufacturer may produce only lenses for microscopes. A retailer may carry only ties.

- *Product-feature specialist.* The firm specializes in producing a certain type of product or product feature. Zipcar's car-sharing services target people who live and work in seven major U.S. cities, frequently use public transportation, but still need a car a few times a month.

- *Job-shop specialist.* The firm customizes its products for individual customers.

- *Quality-price specialist.* The firm operates at the low- or high-quality ends of the market. Sharp AQUOS specializes in the high-quality, high-price LCD television and component screen market.

- *Service specialist.* The firm offers one or more services not available from other firms. A bank might take loan requests over the phone and hand-deliver the money to the customer.

- *Channel specialist.* The firm specializes in serving only one channel of distribution. For example, a soft drink company makes a very large-sized serving available only at gas stations.

Proudly sponsored by Digicel

Digicel, Proud Sponsor of Usain Bolt,
the World's Fastest Man, since 2004.

The fastest growing mobile operator
in the Caribbean.

Digicel
The Bigger, Better Network.

Digicel has captured a large
segment of the mobile market
in the Caribbean, using Jamaican
world-record sprinter Usain Bolt
as a spokesperson.

improved service. After eight years, Digicel has more than 8 million customers across its Caribbean and Central American markets, earning a reputation for competitive rates, comprehensive coverage, superior customer care, and a wide variety of products and services. Digicel has also moved into the Pacific in Fiji, Samoa, Papua New Guinea, and other markets. Back in Jamaica, it has become an active sponsor of sports and supporter of causes, befitting for its ascendance as a market leader in the region.[36] ▭

Product Life-Cycle Marketing Strategies

A company's positioning and differentiation strategy must change as the product, market, and competitors change over the *product life cycle* (PLC). To say a product has a life cycle is to assert four things:

1. Products have a limited life.
2. Product sales pass through distinct stages, each posing different challenges, opportunities, and problems to the seller.
3. Profits rise and fall at different stages of the product life cycle.
4. Products require different marketing, financial, manufacturing, purchasing, and human resource strategies in each life-cycle stage.

Product Life Cycles

Most product life-cycle curves are portrayed as bell-shaped (see ▲ Figure 11.4). This curve is typically divided into four stages: introduction, growth, maturity, and decline.[37]

1. *Introduction*—A period of slow sales growth as the product is introduced in the market. Profits are nonexistent because of the heavy expenses of product introduction.
2. *Growth*—A period of rapid market acceptance and substantial profit improvement.
3. *Maturity*—A slowdown in sales growth because the product has achieved acceptance by most potential buyers. Profits stabilize or decline because of increased competition.
4. *Decline*—Sales show a downward drift and profits erode.

We can use the PLC concept to analyze a product category (liquor), a product form (white liquor), a product (vodka), or a brand (Smirnoff). Not all products exhibit a bell-shaped PLC.[38] Three common alternate patterns are shown in ▲ Figure 11.5.

Figure 11.5(a) shows a *growth-slump-maturity pattern*, characteristic of small kitchen appliances, for example, such as handheld mixers and bread makers. Sales grow rapidly when the product is first introduced and then fall to a "petrified" level sustained by late adopters buying the product for the first time and early adopters replacing it.

|Fig. 11.4| ▲

Sales and Profit Life
Cycles

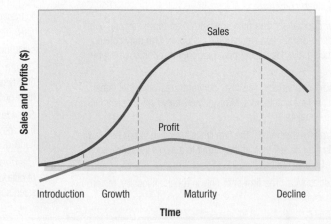

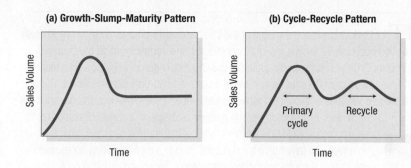

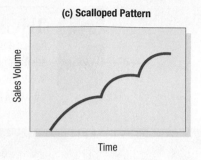

|Fig. 11.5| ▲

Common Product Life-Cycle Patterns

The *cycle-recycle pattern* in Figure 11.5(b) often describes the sales of new drugs. The pharmaceutical company aggressively promotes its new drug, producing the first cycle. Later, sales start declining, and another promotion push produces a second cycle (usually of smaller magnitude and duration).[39]

Another common pattern is the *scalloped PLC* in Figure 11.5(c). Here, sales pass through a succession of life cycles based on the discovery of new-product characteristics, uses, or users. Sales of nylon have shown a scalloped pattern because of the many new uses—parachutes, hosiery, shirts, carpeting, boat sails, automobile tires—discovered over time.[40]

Style, Fashion, and Fad Life Cycles

We need to distinguish three special categories of product life cycles—styles, fashions, and fads (▲ Figure 11.6). A *style* is a basic and distinctive mode of expression appearing in a field of human endeavor. Styles appear in homes (colonial, ranch, Cape Cod), clothing (formal, business casual, sporty), and art (realistic, surrealistic, abstract). A style can last for generations and go in and out of vogue. A *fashion* is a currently accepted or popular style in a given field. Fashions pass through four stages: distinctiveness, emulation, mass fashion, and decline.[41]

The length of a fashion cycle is hard to predict. One view is that fashions end because they represent a purchase compromise, and consumers soon start looking for the missing attributes.[42] For example, as automobiles become smaller, they become less comfortable, and then a growing number of buyers start wanting larger cars. Another explanation is that too many consumers adopt the fashion, thus turning others away. Still another is that the length of a particular fashion cycle depends on the extent to which the fashion meets a genuine need, is consistent with other trends in the society, satisfies societal norms and values, and keeps within technological limits as it develops.[43]

Fads are fashions that come quickly into public view, are adopted with great zeal, peak early, and decline very fast. Their acceptance cycle is short, and they tend to attract only a limited following who are searching for excitement or want to distinguish themselves from others. Fads fail to survive because they don't normally satisfy a strong need. The marketing winners are those who recognize fads early and leverage them into products with staying power. Here's a success story of a company that managed to take a fad and make it a long-term success story.

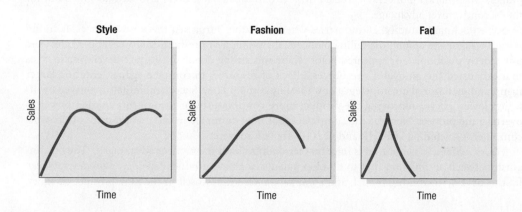

|Fig. 11.6| ▲

Style, Fashion, and Fad Life Cycles

Trivial Pursuit Since its debut at the International Toy Fair in 1982, Trivial Pursuit has sold 88 million copies in 17 languages in 26 countries, and it remains one of the best-selling adult games. Parker Brothers has kept it popular by making a new game with updated questions every year. It also keeps creating offshoots—travel packs, a children's version, Trivial Pursuit Genus IV, and themed versions tapping into niches tied to various sports, movies, and decades—23 different versions in all. The game is available in a variety of platforms: as an interactive CD-ROM from Virgin Entertainment Interactive, online at its own Web site (www.trivialpursuit.com), and in a mobile edition accessible via cell phone. If you're having trouble making dinner conversation on a date—no problem: NTN Entertainment Network has put Trivial Pursuit in about 3,000 restaurants.[44]

Through countless variations, Trivial Pursuit has proven to be more than a passing fad.

Marketing Strategies: Introduction Stage and the Pioneer Advantage

Because it takes time to roll out a new product, work out the technical problems, fill dealer pipelines, and gain consumer acceptance, sales growth tends to be slow in the introduction stage.[45] Profits are negative or low, and promotional expenditures are at their highest ratio to sales because of the need to (1) inform potential consumers, (2) induce product trial, and (3) secure distribution in retail outlets.[46] Firms focus on buyers who are the most ready to buy. Prices tend to be higher because costs are high.

Companies that plan to introduce a new product must decide when to enter the market. To be first can be rewarding, but risky and expensive. To come in later makes sense if the firm can bring superior technology, quality, or brand strength to create a market advantage.

Speeding up innovation time is essential in an age of shortening product life cycles. Being early has been shown to pay. One study found that products coming out six months late—but on budget—earned an average of 33 percent less profit in their first five years; products that came out on time but 50 percent over budget cut their profits by only 4 percent.[47]

Most studies indicate the market pioneer gains the greatest advantage.[48] Campbell, Coca-Cola, Hallmark, and Amazon.com developed sustained market dominance. Nineteen of twenty-five market leaders in 1923 were still the market leaders in 1983, 60 years later.[49] In a sample of industrial-goods businesses, 66 percent of pioneers survived at least 10 years, versus 48 percent of early followers.[50]

What are the sources of the pioneer's advantage?[51] Early users will recall the pioneer's brand name if the product satisfies them. The pioneer's brand also establishes the attributes the product class should possess.[52] It normally aims at the middle of the market and so captures more users. Customer inertia also plays a role; and there are producer advantages: economies of scale, technological leadership, patents, ownership of scarce assets, and other barriers to entry. Pioneers can spend marketing dollars more effectively and enjoy higher rates of repeat purchases. An alert pioneer can lead indefinitely by pursuing various strategies.[53]

But the advantage is not inevitable.[54] Bowmar (hand calculators), Apple's Newton (personal digital assistant), Netscape (Web browser), Reynolds (ballpoint pens), and Osborne (portable computers) were market pioneers overtaken by later entrants. First movers also have to watch out for the "second-mover advantage."

Steven Schnaars studied 28 industries where imitators surpassed the innovators.[55] He found several weaknesses among the failing pioneers, including new products that were too crude, were improperly positioned, or appeared before there was strong demand; product-development costs that exhausted the innovator's resources; a lack of resources to compete against entering larger firms; and managerial incompetence or unhealthy complacency. Successful imitators thrived by offering lower prices, improving the product more continuously, or using brute market power to overtake the pioneer. None of the companies that now dominate in the manufacture of personal computers—including Dell, HP, and Acer—were first movers.[56]

Peter Golder and Gerald Tellis raise further doubts about the pioneer advantage.[57] They distinguish between an *inventor*, first to develop patents in a new-product category, a *product pioneer*, first to develop a working model, and a *market pioneer*, first to sell in the new-product category.

They also include nonsurviving pioneers in their sample. They conclude that although pioneers may still have an advantage, a larger number of market pioneers fail than has been reported, and a larger number of early market leaders (though not pioneers) succeed. Later entrants overtaking market pioneers include IBM over Sperry in mainframe computers, Matsushita over Sony in VCRs, and GE over EMI in CAT scan equipment.

Tellis and Golder more recently identified five factors underpinning long-term market leadership: vision of a mass market, persistence, relentless innovation, financial commitment, and asset leverage.[58] Other research has highlighted the importance of the novelty of the product innovation.[59] When a pioneer starts a market with a really new product, like the Segway Human Transporter, surviving can be very challenging. In the case of incremental innovation, like MP3 players with video capabilities, survival rates are much higher.

The pioneer should visualize the product markets it could enter, knowing it cannot enter all of them at once. Suppose market-segmentation analysis reveals the product market segments shown in △ Figure 11.7. The pioneer should analyze the profit potential of each product market singly and in combination and decide on a market expansion path. Thus, the pioneer in Figure 11.7 plans first to enter product market P_1M_1, then move the product into a second market (P_1M_2), then surprise the competition by developing a second product for the second market (P_2M_2), then take the second product back into the first market (P_2M_1), then launch a third product for the first market (P_3M_1). If this game plan works, the pioneer firm will own a good part of the first two segments and serve them with two or three products.

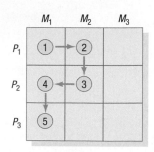

|Fig. 11.7| △

Long-Range Product Market Expansion Strategy (P_i = product i; M_j = market j)

Marketing Strategies: Growth Stage

The growth stage is marked by a rapid climb in sales. Early adopters like the product and additional consumers start buying it. New competitors enter, attracted by the opportunities. They introduce new product features and expand distribution.

Prices stabilize or fall slightly, depending on how fast demand increases. Companies maintain promotional expenditures or raise them slightly, to meet competition and continue to educate the market. Sales rise much faster than promotional expenditures, causing a welcome decline in the promotion–sales ratio. Profits increase as promotion costs are spread over a larger volume, and unit manufacturing costs fall faster than price declines, owing to the producer-learning effect. Firms must watch for a change to a decelerating rate of growth in order to prepare new strategies.

To sustain rapid market share growth now, the firm:

- improves product quality and adds new features and improved styling.
- adds new models and flanker products (of different sizes, flavors, and so forth) to protect the main product.
- enters new market segments.
- increases its distribution coverage and enters new distribution channels.
- shifts from awareness and trial communications to preference and loyalty communications.
- lowers prices to attract the next layer of price-sensitive buyers.

By spending money on product improvement, promotion, and distribution, the firm can capture a dominant position. It trades off maximum current profit for high market share and the hope of even greater profits in the next stage.

Marketing Strategies: Maturity Stage

At some point, the rate of sales growth will slow, and the product will enter a stage of relative maturity. Most products are in this stage of the life cycle, which normally lasts longer than the preceding ones.

The maturity stage divides into three phases: growth, stable, and decaying maturity. In the first, sales growth starts to slow. There are no new distribution channels to fill. New competitive forces emerge. In the second phase, sales per capita flatten because of market saturation. Most potential consumers have tried the product, and future sales depend on population growth and replacement demand. In the third phase, decaying maturity, the absolute level of sales starts to decline, and customers begin switching to other products.

This third phase poses the most challenges. The sales slowdown creates overcapacity in the industry, which intensifies competition. Weaker competitors withdraw. A few giants dominate—perhaps a quality leader, a service leader, and a cost leader—and profit mainly through high volume and lower costs. Surrounding them is a multitude of market nichers, including market specialists, product specialists, and customizing firms.

The question is whether to struggle to become one of the big three and achieve profits through high volume and low cost, or pursue a niching strategy and profit through low volume and high margins. Sometimes the market will divide into low- and high-end segments, and market shares of firms in the middle steadily erode. Here's how Swedish appliance manufacturer, Electrolux, has coped with this situation.

Electrolux AB

In 2002, Electrolux faced a rapidly polarizing appliance market. Low-cost Asian companies such as Haier, LG, and Samsung were applying downward price pressure, while premium competitors like Bosch, Sub-Zero, and Viking were growing at the expense of the middle-of-the-road brands. Electrolux's new CEO Hans Stråberg decided to escape the middle by rethinking Electrolux customers' wants and needs. He segmented the market according to the lifestyle and purchasing patterns of about 20 different types of consumers. Electrolux now successfully markets its steam ovens to health-oriented consumers, for example, and its compact dishwashers, originally for smaller kitchens, to a broader consumer segment that washes dishes more often. To companies stuck in the middle of a mature market, Stråberg offers this advice: "Start with consumers and understand what their latent needs are and what problems they experience . . . then put the puzzle together yourself to discover what people really want to have. Henry Ford is supposed to have said, 'If I had asked people what they really wanted, I would have made faster horses' or something like that. You need to figure out what people really want, although they can't express it."[60]

Electrolux uses an elaborate segmentation plan and an expansive product line to make sure its brand is not stuck in the middle of a shrinking market.

Some companies abandon weaker products to concentrate on new and more profitable ones. Yet they may be ignoring the high potential many mature markets and old products still have. Industries widely thought to be mature—autos, motorcycles, television, watches, cameras—were proved otherwise by the Japanese, who found ways to offer customers new value. Three ways to change the course for a brand are market, product, and marketing program modifications.

MARKET MODIFICATION A company might try to expand the market for its mature brand by working with the two factors that make up sales volume: Volume = number of brand users × usage rate per user, as in Table 11.1, but may also be matched by competitors.

PRODUCT MODIFICATION Managers also try to stimulate sales by improving quality, features, or style. *Quality improvement* increases functional performance by launching a "new and improved" product. *Feature improvement* adds size, weight, materials, supplements, and accessories that expand the product's performance, versatility, safety, or convenience. *Style improvement* increases the product's esthetic appeal. Any of these can attract consumer attention.

MARKETING PROGRAM MODIFICATION Finally, brand managers might also try to stimulate sales by modifying nonproduct elements—price, distribution, and communications in particular. They should assess the likely success of any changes in terms of effects on new and existing customers.

Marketing Strategies: Decline Stage

Sales decline for a number of reasons, including technological advances, shifts in consumer tastes, and increased domestic and foreign competition. All can lead to overcapacity, increased price

TABLE 11.1 ▭ Alternate Ways to Increase Sales Volume	
Expand the Number of Users	**Increase the Usage Rates Among Users**
• *Convert nonusers.* The key to the growth of air freight service was the constant search for new users to whom air carriers can demonstrate the benefits of using air freight rather than ground transportation.	• *Have consumers use the product on more occasions.* Serve Campbell's soup for a snack. Use Heinz vinegar to clean windows.
• *Enter new market segments.* When Goodyear decided to sell its tires via Walmart, Sears, and Discount Tire, it immediately boosted its market share.	• *Have consumers use more of the product on each occasion.* Drink a larger glass of orange juice.
• *Attract competitors' customers.* Marketers of Puffs facial tissues are always wooing Kleenex customers.	• *Have consumers use the product in new ways.* Use Tums antacid as a calcium supplement.

cutting, and profit erosion. The decline might be slow, as for sewing machines and newspapers, or rapid, as for 5.25 floppy disks and eight-track cartridges. Sales may plunge to zero or petrify at a low level. These structural changes are different from a short-term decline resulting from a marketing crisis of some sort. "Marketing Insight: Managing a Brand Crisis," describes strategies for a brand in temporary trouble.

As sales and profits decline over a long period of time, some firms withdraw. Those remaining may reduce the number of products they offer, withdrawing from smaller segments and weaker trade channels, cutting marketing budgets, and reducing prices further. Unless strong reasons for retention exist, carrying a weak product is often very costly.

Besides being unprofitable, weak products consume a disproportionate amount of management's time, require frequent price and inventory adjustments, incur expensive setup for short production runs, draw advertising and sales force attention better used to make healthy products more profitable, and cast a negative shadow on company image. Failing to eliminate them also delays the aggressive search for replacement products, creating a lopsided product mix long on yesterday's breadwinners and short on tomorrow's.

Unfortunately, most companies have not developed a policy for handling aging products. The first task is to establish a system for identifying them. Many companies appoint a product-review committee with representatives from marketing, R&D, manufacturing, and finance who, based on all available information, makes a recommendation for each product—leave it alone, modify its marketing strategy, or drop it.[61]

Some firms abandon declining markets earlier than others. Much depends on the height of exit barriers in the industry.[62] The lower the barriers, the easier for firms to leave the industry, and the more tempting for the remaining firms to stay and attract the withdrawing firms' customers. Procter & Gamble stayed in the declining liquid-soap business and improved its profits as others withdrew.

The appropriate strategy also depends on the industry's relative attractiveness and the company's competitive strength in it. A company in an unattractive industry that possesses competitive strength should consider shrinking selectively. A company in an attractive industry that has competitive strength should consider strengthening its investment. Companies that successfully restage or rejuvenate a mature product often do so by adding value to it.

Strategies for harvesting and divesting are quite different. *Harvesting* calls for gradually reducing a product or business's costs while trying to maintain sales. The first step is to cut R&D costs and plant and equipment investment. The company might also reduce product quality, sales force size, marginal services, and advertising expenditures, ideally without letting customers, competitors, and employees know what is happening. Harvesting is difficult to execute, yet many mature products warrant this strategy. It can substantially increase current cash flow.[63]

When a company decides to divest a product with strong distribution and residual goodwill, it can probably sell the product to another firm. Some firms specialize in acquiring and revitalizing

Marketing Insight

Managing a Brand Crisis

Marketing managers must assume a brand crisis will someday arise. Whole Foods, Taco Bell, JetBlue, and toy and pet food brands have all experienced potentially crippling brand crises, and AIG, Merrill Lynch, and Citi were rocked by investment lending scandals that eroded consumer trust. Widespread repercussions include (1) lost sales, (2) reduced effectiveness of marketing activities for the product, (3) increased sensitivity to rivals' marketing activities, and (4) reduced impact of the firm's marketing activities on competing brands.

In general, the stronger brand equity and corporate image are—especially credibility and trustworthiness—the more likely the firm can weather the storm. Careful preparation and a well-managed crisis management program, however, are also critical. As Johnson & Johnson's nearly flawless handling of the Tylenol product-tampering incident suggests, the key is that consumers see the firm's response as both *swift* and *sincere.* They must feel an immediate sense that the company truly cares. Listening is not enough.

The longer the firm takes to respond, the more likely consumers can form negative impressions from unfavorable media coverage or word of mouth. Perhaps worse, they may find they don't like the brand after all and permanently switch. Getting in front of a problem with PR, and perhaps ads, can help avoid those problems.

Consider Perrier. In 1994, Perrier was forced to halt production worldwide and recall all existing product when traces of benzene, a known carcinogen, were found in excessive quantities in its bottled water. Over the next weeks it offered several explanations, creating confusion and skepticism. Perhaps more damaging, the product was off shelves for over three months. Despite an expensive relaunch featuring ads and promotions, the brand struggled to regain lost market share, and a full year later sales were less than half what they had been. With its key "purity" association tarnished, Perrier had no other compelling points-of-difference. Consumers and retailers had found satisfactory substitutes, and the brand never recovered. Eventually it was taken over by Nestlé SA.

Second, the more sincere the firm's response—a public acknowledgment of the impact on consumers and willingness to take necessary steps—the less likely consumers will form negative attributions. When consumers reported finding shards of glass in some jars of its baby food, Gerber tried to reassure the public there were no problems in its manufacturing plants but adamantly refused to withdraw products from stores. After market share slumped from 66 percent to 52 percent within a couple of months, one company official admitted, "Not pulling our baby food off the shelf gave the appearance that we aren't a caring company."

Sources: Norman Klein and Stephen A. Greyser, "The Perrier Recall: A Source of Trouble," Harvard Business School Case #9-590-104 and "The Perrier Relaunch," Harvard Business School Case #9-590-130; Harald Van Heerde, Kristiaan Helsen, and Marnik G. Dekimpe, "The Impact of a Product-Harm Crisis on Marketing Effectiveness," *Marketing Science* 26 (March–April 2007), pp. 230–45; Michelle L. Roehm and Alice M. Tybout, "When Will a Brand Scandal Spill Over and How Should Competitors Respond?" *Journal of Marketing Research* 43 (August 2006), pp. 366–73; Michelle L. Roehm and Michael K. Brady, "Consumer Responses to Performance Failures by High Equity Brands," *Journal of Consumer Research*, 34 (December 2007), pp. 537–45; Alice M. Tybout and Michelle Roehm, "Let the Response Fit the Scandal," *Harvard Business Review*, December 2009, pp. 82–88; Andrew Pierce, "Managing Reputation to Rebuild Battered Brands, *Marketing News*, March 15, 2009, p. 19; Kevin O'Donnell, "In a Crisis Actions Matter," *Marketing News*, April 15, 2009, p. 22.

"orphan" or "ghost" brands that larger firms want to divest or that have encountered bankruptcy such as Linens n' Things, Folgers and Brim coffee, Nuprin pain reliever, and Salon Selective shampoos.[64] These firms attempt to capitalize on the residue of awareness in the market to develop a brand revitalization strategy. Reserve Brands bought Eagle Snacks in part because research showed 6 of 10 adults remembered the brand, leading Reserve's CEO to observe, "It would take $300 million to $500 million to recreate that brand awareness today."[65]

If the company can't find any buyers, it must decide whether to liquidate the brand quickly or slowly. It must also decide how much inventory and service to maintain for past customers.

Evidence for the Product Life-Cycle Concept

Table 11.2 summarizes the characteristics, marketing objectives, and marketing strategies of the four stages of the product life cycle. The PLC concept helps marketers interpret product and market dynamics, conduct planning and control, and do forecasting. One recent study of 30 product categories unearthed a number of interesting findings concerning the PLC:[66]

- New consumer durables show a distinct takeoff, after which sales increase by roughly 45 percent a year, but they also show a distinct slowdown, when sales decline by roughly 15 percent a year.
- Slowdown occurs at 34 percent penetration on average, well before most households own a new product.

- The growth stage lasts a little over eight years and does not seem to shorten over time.
- Informational cascades exist, meaning people are more likely to adopt over time if others already have, instead of by making careful product evaluations. One implication is that product categories with large sales increases at takeoff tend to have larger sales declines at slowdown.

Critique of the Product Life-Cycle Concept

PLC theory has its share of critics, who claim life-cycle patterns are too variable in shape and duration to be generalized, and that marketers can seldom tell what stage their product is in. A product may appear mature when it has actually reached a plateau prior to another upsurge. Critics also charge that, rather than an inevitable course, the PLC pattern is the self-fulfilling result of marketing strategies, and that skillful marketing can in fact lead to continued growth.[67]

Market Evolution

Because the PLC focuses on what's happening to a particular product or brand rather than the overall market, it yields a product-oriented rather than a market-oriented picture. Firms also need to visualize a *market's* evolutionary path as it is affected by new needs, competitors, technology, channels, and other developments and change product and brand positioning to keep pace.[68] Like products, markets evolve through four stages: emergence, growth, maturity, and decline. Consider the evolution of the paper towel market.

TABLE 11.2	Summary of Product Life-Cycle Characteristics, Objectives, and Strategies			
	Introduction	**Growth**	**Maturity**	**Decline**
Characteristics				
Sales	Low sales	Rapidly rising sales	Peak sales	Declining sales
Costs	High cost per customer	Average cost per customer	Low cost per customer	Low cost per customer
Profits	Negative	Rising profits	High profits	Declining profits
Customers	Innovators	Early adopters	Middle majority	Laggards
Competitors	Few	Growing number	Stable number beginning to decline	Declining number
Marketing Objectives				
	Create product awareness and trial	Maximize market share	Maximize profit while defending market share	Reduce expenditure and milk the brand
Strategies				
Product	Offer a basic product	Offer product extensions, service, warranty	Diversify brands and items models	Phase out weak products
Price	Charge cost-plus	Price to penetrate market	Price to match or best competitors'	Cut price
Distribution	Build selective distribution	Build intensive distribution	Build more intensive distribution	Go selective: phase out unprofitable outlets
Communications	Build product awareness and trial among early adopters and dealers	Build awareness and interest in the mass market	Stress brand differences and benefits and encourage brand switching	Reduce to minimal level needed to retain hard-core loyals

Sources: Chester R. Wasson, *Dynamic Competitive Strategy and Product Life Cycles* (Austin, TX: Austin Press, 1978); John A. Weber, "Planning Corporate Growth with Inverted Product Life Cycles," *Long Range Planning* (October 1976), pp. 12–29; Peter Doyle, "The Realities of the Product Life Cycle," *Quarterly Review of Marketing* (Summer 1976).

Paper Towels   Homemakers originally used cotton and linen dishcloths and towels in their kitchens. Then a paper company looking for new markets developed paper towels, crystallizing a latent market that other manufacturers entered. The number of brands grew and created market fragmentation. Industry overcapacity led manufacturers to search for new features. One manufacturer, hearing consumers complain that paper towels were not absorbent, introduced "absorbent" towels and increased its market share. Competitors produced their own versions of absorbent paper towels, and the market fragmented again. One manufacturer introduced a "superstrength" towel that was soon copied. Another introduced a "lint-free" towel, subsequently copied. The latest innovation is wipes containing a cleaning agent (like Clorox Disinfecting Wipes) that are often surface-specific (for wood, metal, stone). Thus, driven by innovation and competition, paper towels evolved from a single product to one with various absorbencies, strengths, and applications. ▭

Marketing in an Economic Downturn

Given economic cycles, there will always be tough times, such as 2008–2010 in many parts of the world. Despite reduced funding for marketing programs and intense pressure to justify them as cost effective, some marketers survived—or even thrived—in the recession. Here are five guidelines to improve the odds for success during an economic downturn.

Explore the Upside of Increasing Investment

Sainsbury's no-nonsense value appeal was just the right message to send to UK customers in the midst of a recession.

Does it pay to invest during a recession? Although the severity of the recent downturn took firms into uncharted territory, 40 years of evidence suggests those willing to invest during a recession have, on average, improved their fortunes when compared with those that cut back.[69]

The amount of investment isn't all that matters. Firms that received the most benefit from increasing marketing investments during a recession were often those best able to exploit a marketplace advantage such as an appealing new product, a weakened rival, or development of a neglected target market. With such strong evidence, marketers should consider the potential upside and positive payback of an increased investment that seizes market opportunities. Here are two companies that made such a decision.

- General Mills increased marketing expenditures for the 2009 fiscal year by 16 percent, increased revenues by 8 percent to $14.7 billion, and increased its operating profit by 4 percent. As CEO Ken Powell explained, "In an environment where you have consumers going to the grocery store more often and thinking more about meals at home, we think that is a great environment for brand building, to remind consumers about our products."[70]
- UK supermarket giant Sainsbury launched an advertising and in-store point-of-sale campaign called "Feed Your Family for a Fiver" that played off its corporate slogan, "Try Something New Today," to encourage shoppers to try new recipes that would feed families for only £5.

Get Closer to Customers

In tough times, consumers may change what they want and can afford, where and how they shop, even what they want to see and hear from a firm. A downturn is an opportunity for marketers to learn even more about what consumers are thinking, feeling, and doing, especially the loyal customer base that yields so much of a brand's profitability.[71]

Firms should characterize any changes as temporary adjustments versus permanent shifts.[72] In explaining why it is important to look forward during a recession, Eaton CEO Alex Cutler noted, "It is a time when businesses shouldn't be assuming that the future will be like the past. And I mean that in virtually every dimension whether it is economic growth, value propositions, or the level of government regulation and involvement."[73]

At the peak—the bottom—of the recession, a Booz & Company survey of 1,000 U.S. households found 43 percent were eating at home more and 25 percent were cutting spending on hobbies and sports activities. In both cases, respondents said they would likely do so even when the economy improved.[74] With consumer confidence at its lowest in decades, spending shifted in many ways. As one retail analyst commented, "Moms who used to buy every member of the family their own brand of shampoo are buying one big cheap one."[75]

The potential value and profitability of some target consumers may change. Marketers should evaluate this factor to fine-tune their marketing program and capitalize on new insights. After unsuccessfully chasing twenty-somethings with trendier clothing, Old Navy refocused its message to target a budget-conscious mom shopping for herself and the family.[76]

Review Budget Allocations

Budget allocations can be sticky and not change enough to reflect a fluid marketing environment. We've seen repeatedly that the vast penetration of the Internet, improved functionality of the cell phone, and increased importance of events, experiences, and emotions as marketing opportunities have dramatically changed the marketing communications and channels environment in just five years.

A recession provides an opportunity for marketers to closely review how much and in what ways they are spending their money. Budget reallocations can open up promising new options and eliminate sacred-cow approaches that no longer provide sufficient revenue benefits. Underperforming distributors can be weeded out and incentives provided to motivate the more effective product sellers.

Marketing communications allow much experimentation. In London, T-Mobile created spontaneous, large-scale, interactive "happenings" to convey its brand positioning that "Life's for Sharing" and generate massive publicity. Its "Dance" video, featuring 400 dancers getting the whole Liverpool tube station to dance, was viewed millions of times on YouTube.[77]

To reflect more challenging economic times, GE Profile changed its ad strategy to emphasize practicality.

Firms as diverse as Century 21 realtors and Red Robin gourmet burgers increased their Internet marketing activities during the recession.[78] The 120,000 U.S. dental practices were not immune to the economic downturn, as patients chose to postpone dental work and even skip routine cleanings. Many dentists turned to marketing and increased personal communications with patients via e-mail newsletters, calls to set up appointments, and even Twitter messages to share new product or service developments.[79]

Put Forth the Most Compelling Value Proposition

One mistake in a recession is to be overly focused on price reductions and discounts, which can harm long-term brand equity and price integrity. Marketers should increase—and clearly communicate—the value their brands offer, making sure consumers appreciate all the financial, logistical, and psychological benefits compared with the competition.[80] The more expensive the item, the more important this value framing becomes. In the recent recession, GE changed its ad messages for the $3,500 Profile washer-and-dryer set to emphasize its practicality—it optimizes the use of soap and water per load to reduce waste and saves customers money by being gentle on clothes, extending their life.[81]

Marketers should also review pricing to ensure it has not crept up over time and no longer reflects good value. Procter & Gamble adopted a "surgical" approach to reducing prices in specific categories in which its brands were perceived as costing too much compared with competitive products. At the same, it launched communications about the innovativeness and value of its many other brands to help

Why add detergent 365 times a year when you could just add it twice?

GE Profile's new frontload washer with the SmartDispense™ pedestal holds up to six months of detergent* and conveniently dispenses the right amount for each load. And now you can reduce wrinkles, refresh fabrics and improve cleaning with the addition of Steam technology to the washer and dryer. Just a few of the many features that will ensure your clothes are well taken care of. To learn more, visit geappliances.com/profilefrontload.

100 years of innovation. And we're just getting started.

GE *Profile*™

ensure consumers would continue to pay their premium prices. Ads for Bounty claimed it was more absorbent than a "bargain brand" of paper towels; headlines in print ads for Olay Professional Pro-X's Intensive Wrinkle Protocol proclaimed, "As Effective at Wrinkle Reduction as What the Doctor Prescribed. At Half the Price."[82]

Fine-tune Brand and Product Offerings

Marketers must ensure they have the right products to sell to the right consumers in the right places and times. They can review product portfolios and brand architecture to confirm that brands and sub-brands are clearly differentiated, targeted, and supported based on their prospects. Luxury brands can benefit from lower-priced brands or sub-brands in their portfolios. Take Armani as an example.

Armani   Armani differentiates its product line into three tiers distinct in style, luxury, customization, and price. In the most expensive, Tier I, it sells Giorgio Armani and Giorgio Armani Privé, custom-made couture products that sell for thousands of dollars. In Tier II, it offers Emporio Armani—young, modern, more affordable styles—and Armani jeans that convey technology and ecology. In lower-priced Tier III are more youthful and street-savvy translations of Armani style, AIX Armani Exchange, sold at retail locations in cities and suburban malls. The brand architecture has been carefully devised so each extension lives up to the core promise of the Armani brand without diluting the parent's image. But clear differentiation also exists, minimizing consumer confusion and brand cannibalization. In tough economic times, the lower end picks up the selling slack and helps maintain profitability. ▭

Because different brands or sub-brands appeal to different economic segments, those that target the lower end of the socioeconomic spectrum may be particularly important during a recession. Value-driven companies such as McDonald's, Walmart, Costco, Aldi, Dell, E*TRADE, Southwest Airlines, and IKEA are likely to benefit most. Spam, the oft-maligned gelatinous 12-ounce rectangle of spiced ham and pork, found its sales soaring during the recession. Affordably priced and requiring no refrigeration, Spam is, its maker Hormel claims, "like meat with a pause button."[83]

Bad times also are an opportunity to prune brands or products with diminished prospects. In the recession following the 9/11 tragedy, Procter & Gamble divested many stagnant brands such as Comet cleanser, Folgers coffee, Jif peanut butter, and Crisco oil and shortening, to concentrate on higher-growth opportunities with much success.

Summary

1. A market leader has the largest market share in the relevant product market. To remain dominant, the leader looks for ways to expand total market demand and attempts to protect and perhaps increase its current share.

2. A market challenger attacks the market leader and other competitors in an aggressive bid for more market share. There are five types of general attack; challengers must also choose specific attack strategies.

3. A market follower is a runner-up firm willing to maintain its market share and not rock the boat. It can play the role of counterfeiter, cloner, imitator, or adapter.

4. A market nicher serves small market segments not being served by larger firms. The key to nichemanship is specialization. Nichers develop offerings to fully meet a certain group of customers' needs, commanding a premium price in the process.

5. As important as a competitive orientation is in today's global markets, companies should not overdo the emphasis on competitors. They should maintain a good balance of consumer and competitor monitoring.

6. Because economic conditions change and competitive activity varies, companies normally must reformulate their marketing strategy several times during a product's life cycle. Technologies, product forms, and brands also exhibit life cycles with distinct stages. The life cycle stages are usually introduction, growth, maturity, and decline. Most products today are in the maturity stage.

7. Each product life cycle stage calls for different marketing strategies. The introduction is marked by slow growth and minimal profits. If successful, the product enters a growth stage marked by rapid sales growth and increasing profits. There follows a maturity stage in which sales

growth slows and profits stabilize. Finally, the product enters a decline stage. The company's task is to identify the truly weak products, develop a strategy for each, and phase them out in a way that minimizes impact on company profits, employees, and customers.

8. Like products, markets evolve through four stages: emergence, growth, maturity, and decline.

9. In a recession, marketers must explore the upside of possibly increasing investments, get closer to customers, review budget allocations, put forth the most compelling value proposition, and fine-tune brand and product offerings.

Applications

Marketing Debate
Do Brands Have Finite Lives?

Often, after a brand begins to slip in the marketplace or disappears altogether, commentators observe, "All brands have their day," implying brands have a finite life and cannot be expected to be leaders forever. Other experts contend brands *can* live forever, and that their long-term success depends on marketers' skill and insight.

Take a position: Brands cannot be expected to last forever *versus* There is no reason for a brand to ever become obsolete.

Marketing Discussion
Industry Roles

Pick an industry. Classify firms according to the four different roles they might play: leader, challenger, follower, and nicher. How would you characterize the nature of competition? Do the firms follow the principles described in this chapter?

Marketing Excellence

>>Samsung

Korean consumer electronics giant Samsung has made a remarkable transformation, from a provider of value-priced commodity products that original equipment manufacturers (OEMs) sold under their own brands, to a global marketer of premium-priced Samsung-branded consumer electronics such as flat-screen TVs, digital cameras, digital appliances, semiconductors, and cell phones. Samsung's high-end cell phones have been a growth engine for the company, which has also released a steady stream of innovations, popularizing the PDA phone, the first cell phone with an MP3 player, and the first Blu-ray disc player.

Samsung initially focused on volume and market domination rather than profitability. However, during the Asian financial crisis of the late 1990s, when other Korean *chaebols* collapsed beneath a mountain of debt, Samsung took a different approach. It cut costs and reemphasized product quality and manufacturing flexibility, which allowed its consumer electronics to go from project phase to store shelves within six months. Samsung invested heavily in innovation and focused intently on its memory-chip business, which established an important cash cow and rapidly made the company the largest chip maker in the world. The company continued to pour money into R&D during the 2000s, budgeting $40 billion for 2005–2010. Its focus on R&D and increasing digital convergence have let Samsung introduce a wide range of electronic products under its strong brand umbrella. The firm also partnered with longtime market leader Sony to create a $2 billion state-of-the-art LCD factory in South Korea and signed a milestone agreement to share 24,000 basic patents for components and production processes.

Samsung's success has been driven not only by successful product innovation, but also by aggressive brand building over the last decade. From 1998 to 2009, the company spent over $7 billion in marketing, sponsored six Olympics, and ran several global ad campaigns themed "Imagine," "Quietly Brilliant," and "YOU," all which included brand messages such as "technology," "design," and "sensation" (human). In 2005, Samsung surpassed Sony in the Interbrand brand ranking for the first time and continues to outperform Sony today.

The economic downturn during 2008 and 2009 significantly affected the semiconductor industry, overall consumer electronics sales, and Samsung's bottom line. To survive, Samsung slashed profit margins, decreased production, and cut inventories. As a result, the company emerged at the end of 2009 with record-high quarterly profits despite significantly smaller profit margins.

Today, Samsung is the global leader in flat-panel TVs and memory chips, and the number two player in mobile phones. It is focused on growing technologies such as smart phones and has partnered with both Microsoft's Windows Mobile and Google's Android software. In addition, Samsung has formed a green partnership with Microsoft to help create energy-efficient computers.

Unlike rival firms, Samsung has become a global leader by making both components for electronics products and the actual devices sold to consumers, and without acquiring major competitors. It has more than doubled its employees from a decade ago to over 164,000 around the world. With record sales of $110 billion in 2008, the company's CEO, Lee Yoon-woo, announced the firm hopes to hit $400 billion in revenue by the year 2020. To accomplish this aggressive goal, Samsung will explore areas like health care and home energy products.

Questions

1. What are some of Samsung's greatest competitive strengths?

2. Samsung's goal of $400 billion in sales by 2020 would bring it to the same level as Walmart. Is this feasible? Why or why not?

Sources: Moon Ihlwan, "Samsung Is Having a Sony Moment," *BusinessWeek*, July 30, 2007, p. 38; Martin Fackler, "Raising the Bar at Samsung," *New York Times*, April 25, 2006; "Brand New," *Economist*, January 15, 2005, pp. 10–11; Patricia O'Connell, "Samsung's Goal: Be Like BMW," *BusinessWeek*, August 1, 2005; Heidi Brown and Justin Doeble, "Samsung's Next Act," *Forbes*, July 26, 2004; John Quelch and Anna Harrington, "Samsung Electronics Company: Global Marketing Operations," *Harvard Business School*, January 16, 2008; Evan Ramstad, "Samsung's Swelling Size Brings New Challenges," *Wall Street Journal*, November 11, 2009; "Looking Good? LG v. Samsung," *Economist*, January 24, 2009.

Marketing Excellence

>>IBM

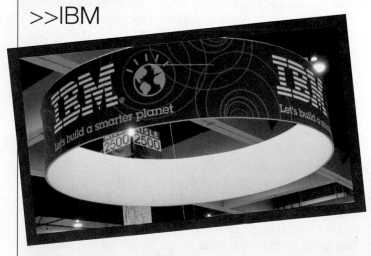

International Business Machines Corporation (IBM) manufactures and sells computer hardware and software, offers infrastructure services, and provides global consulting services. It dates to the 1880s but became known as IBM only in 1924, under the leadership of then-president Thomas J. Watson Sr. Watson led IBM for four decades and helped establish some of its most successful and continuing business tactics, such as exceptional customer service, a professional and knowledgeable sales force, and a focus on large-scale, custom-built solutions for businesses. Watson also created the company's first slogan, "THINK," which quickly became a corporate mantra.

From the 1910s to the 1940s, IBM's growth exploded, led primarily by sales of tabulating machines, which helped underpin the Social Security system in the 1930s, and of war-related technologies developed for the military during World War I and World War II.

IBM evolved in the 1950s when Watson's son, Thomas J. Watson Jr., took over as CEO. It was under his management that the company paved the way for innovations in computation. IBM worked with the government during the Cold War and built the air-defense SAGE computer system at the price of $30 million. In 1964, the firm launched a revolutionary large family of computers called the System/360, which used interchangeable software and peripheral equipment. For it to succeed, however, IBM had to cannibalize its own computer product lines and move its current systems to the new technology. Fortunately the risk paid off, and IBM architecture became the industry standard. By the 1960s, IBM was producing approximately 70 percent of all computers, beating out early competitors General Electric, RCA, and Honeywell.

The 1980s—the beginning of the personal computing era—were pivotal for IBM. In 1981, the firm launched the first personal computer, which offered 18KB of memory, floppy disk drives, and an optional color monitor. IBM also opened up new channels of distribution through companies like Sears and ComputerLand. However, its decision to outsource components of the PC to companies like Microsoft and Intel marked the end of IBM's monopoly in computing. During the 1980s, its market share and profits eroded as the PC revolution changed the way consumers viewed and bought technology. IBM's sales dropped from $5 billion in the early 1980s to $3 billion by 1989. The dip continued into the early 1990s when IBM felt pressure from Compaq and Dell and attempted to split the company into smaller business units to compete. The results were disastrous, and IBM posted net losses of $16 billion between 1991 and 1993.

Things turned around when a new CEO, Louis Gerstner, refocused the company in a new strategic direction. Gerstner reconnected the company's business units, shed its commodity products, and focused on high-margin businesses like consulting and middleware software. IBM then introduced the iconic ThinkPad, which helped regain lost share. To rebuild its brand image, the firm consolidated its marketing efforts from 70 advertising agencies to 1 and created a consistent, universal message. In 1997, IBM's chess-playing computer system, Deep Blue, also helped lift IBM's brand image by defeating the world's reigning chess champion in a historic event that captured the attention of millions.

At the turn of the 21st century, IBM's newest CEO, Samuel Palmisano, led IBM to new levels of success in the wake of the dot-com bust. He moved the company further away from hardware by selling its ThinkPad division to Lenovo and exiting disk drives. In addition, Palmisano embraced global consulting and data analytics by acquiring close to 100 firms, including PricewaterhouseCoopers.

IBM now focuses on solving the world's most challenging high-tech problems, such as better water management, lower traffic congestion, and collaborative health care solutions. Its most recent campaign, entitled "Smarter planet," highlights a few of the company's accomplishments to date and explores IBM's ideas for the future. Palmisano explained, "We are looking at huge problems that couldn't be solved before. We can solve congestion and pollution. We can make the grids more efficient. And quite honestly, it creates a big business opportunity."

Today, IBM is the largest and most profitable information technology company in the world, with over $103 billion in sales and 388,000 employees worldwide. It employs scientists, engineers, consultants, and sales professionals in over 170 countries and holds more patents than any other U.S.-based technology company. From 2000 to 2008, IBM spent over $50 billion on R&D; and approximately 30 percent of its annual R&D budget goes toward long-term research.

Questions

1. Few companies have had such a long history of ups and downs as IBM. What were some of the keys to its recent success? Can its plans to solve some of the world's most challenging problems succeed? Why or why not?

2. Who are IBM's biggest competitors today, and what risks do they face with their current strategy?

Sources: Steve Lohr, "IBM Showing That Giants Can Be Nimble," *New York Times,* July 18, 2007; Jeffrey M. O'Brien, "IBM's Grand Plan to Save the Planet," *Fortune,* April 21, 2009; "IBM Archives," *IBM,* www.ibm.com; Louis V. Gerstner Jr., Who Says Elephants Can't Dance? *Inside IBM's Historic Turnaround* (New York: Harper Business, 2002).

Chapter **12**

In This Chapter, We Will Address the Following Questions

1. What are the characteristics of products, and how do marketers classify products?

2. How can companies differentiate products?

3. Why is product design important and what factors affect a good design?

4. How can a company build and manage its product mix and product lines?

5. How can companies combine products to create strong co-brands or ingredient brands?

6. How can companies use packaging, labeling, warranties, and guarantees as marketing tools?

This trade show debut in Shanghai, China, in April 2009 was part of the global launch of the highly anticipated Ford Fiesta world car.

Setting Product Strategy

At the heart of a great brand is a great product. Product is a key element in the market offering. To achieve market leadership, firms must offer products and services of superior quality that provide unsurpassed customer value.

Ford Motor Company endured some tough times at the beginning of the 21st century. A safety controversy about its best-selling Ford Explorer and high gas prices that hurt sales of its trucks and SUVs put the company in deep financial straits. Perhaps the biggest concern was public perception that Ford products were not high quality. A new CEO, Alan Mulally, arrived in 2006 determined to set Ford on a different path. Rejecting government bailouts during the subsequent recession created some goodwill, but Mulally knew reliable, stylish, and affordable vehicles that performed well would make or break the company's fortunes. A redesigned high-mileage Ford Fusion with innovative Sync hands-free phone-and-entertainment system and an environmentally friendly hybrid option caught customers' attention, as did the hip, urban-looking seven-seat Ford Flex SUV with a center console mini-refrigerator.

Mulally felt it was critical to use Ford's vast infrastructure and scale to create vehicles that, with small adjustments, could easily be sold all over the world. The result of extensive global research, the Ford Fiesta hatchback was a striking example of this world-car concept. The rear of the car resembled a popular small sport-utility, its giant headlights were typical of more expensive cars, and dashboard instruments were modeled after a cell phone keypad. The company knew it had a winner when the Fiesta won a uniformly positive response in Chinese, European, and U.S. showrooms. Ford also relied on experiential and social media in marketing. Before its U.S. launch, 150 Fiestas toured the country for test drives and 100 were given to bloggers for six months to allow them to share their experiences. Ford's product and marketing innovations paid off. While the rest of the U.S. auto industry continued to tank, the Fiesta garnered thousands of preorders and Ford actually turned a profit in the first quarter of 2010.[1]

Marketing planning begins with formulating an offering to meet target customers' needs or wants. The customer will judge the offering by three basic elements: product features and quality, services mix and quality, and price (see △ Figure 12.1). In this chapter we examine product, in Chapter 13, services, and in Chapter 14, price. All three elements must be meshed into a competitively attractive offering.

Product Characteristics and Classifications

Many people think a product is tangible, but a **product** is anything that can be offered to a market to satisfy a want or need, including physical goods, services, experiences, events, persons, places, properties, organizations, information, and ideas.

Value-based prices

Attractiveness
of the market
offering

Product
features
and quality

Services
mix and
quality

|Fig. 12.1| △

Components of the Market Offering

Product Levels: The Customer-Value Hierarchy

In planning its market offering, the marketer needs to address five product levels (see △ Figure 12.2).[2] Each level adds more customer value, and the five constitute a **customer-value hierarchy**.

- The fundamental level is the **core benefit**: the service or benefit the customer is really buying. A hotel guest is buying rest and sleep. The purchaser of a drill is buying holes. Marketers must see themselves as benefit providers.
- At the second level, the marketer must turn the core benefit into a **basic product**. Thus a hotel room includes a bed, bathroom, towels, desk, dresser, and closet.
- At the third level, the marketer prepares an **expected product**, a set of attributes and conditions buyers normally expect when they purchase this product. Hotel guests minimally expect a clean bed, fresh towels, working lamps, and a relative degree of quiet.
- At the fourth level, the marketer prepares an **augmented product** that exceeds customer expectations. In developed countries, brand positioning and competition take place at this level. In developing and emerging markets such as India and Brazil, however, competition takes place mostly at the expected product level.
- At the fifth level stands the **potential product**, which encompasses all the possible augmentations and transformations the product or offering might undergo in the future. Here is where companies search for new ways to satisfy customers and distinguish their offering.

Differentiation arises and competition increasingly occurs on the basis of product augmentation, which also leads the marketer to look at the user's total **consumption system**: the way the user performs the tasks of getting and using products and related services.[3] Each augmentation adds cost, however, and augmented benefits soon become expected benefits and necessary points-of-parity in the category. If today's hotel guests expect satellite television, high-speed Internet access, and a fully equipped fitness center, competitors must search for still other features and benefits to differentiate themselves.

As some companies raise the price of their augmented product, others offer a stripped-down version for less. Thus, alongside the growth of fine hotels such as Four Seasons and Ritz-Carlton, we see lower-cost hotels and motels emerge such as Motel 6 and Comfort Inn, catering to clients who want simply the basic product. Striving to create an augmented product can be a key for success, as Jamestown Container has experienced.

Jamestown Container Companies What could be harder to differentiate than corrugated containers? Yet Jamestown Container Companies, a leading supplier of corrugated products for companies such as 3M, has formed strategic partnerships with area manufacturers to provide every part of the shipping system. It offers not only boxes

|Fig. 12.2| △

Five Product Levels

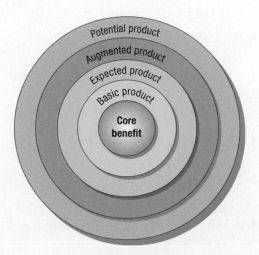

Potential product

Augmented product

Expected product

Basic product

Core benefit

but also tape, shrink-wrap, and everything else needed to display or ship a customer's final product. "It's a combination for survival," says the company's chief operating officer. "More customers want to call one place for everything. We have to keep reinventing ourselves and form these kinds of relationships to remain competitive."[4] ▭

Product Classifications

Marketers classify products on the basis of durability, tangibility, and use (consumer or industrial). Each type has an appropriate marketing-mix strategy.[5]

DURABILITY AND TANGIBILITY Products fall into three groups according to durability and tangibility:

1. **Nondurable goods** are tangible goods normally consumed in one or a few uses, such as beer and shampoo. Because these goods are purchased frequently, the appropriate strategy is to make them available in many locations, charge only a small markup, and advertise heavily to induce trial and build preference.
2. **Durable goods** are tangible goods that normally survive many uses: refrigerators, machine tools, and clothing. Durable products normally require more personal selling and service, command a higher margin, and require more seller guarantees.
3. **Services** are intangible, inseparable, variable, and perishable products that normally require more quality control, supplier credibility, and adaptability. Examples include haircuts, legal advice, and appliance repairs.

CONSUMER-GOODS CLASSIFICATION When we classify the vast array of consumer goods on the basis of shopping habits, we distinguish among convenience, shopping, specialty, and unsought goods.

The consumer usually purchases **convenience goods** frequently, immediately, and with minimal effort. Examples include soft drinks, soaps, and newspapers. *Staples* are convenience goods consumers purchase on a regular basis. A buyer might routinely purchase Heinz ketchup, Crest toothpaste, and Ritz crackers. *Impulse goods* are purchased without any planning or search effort, like candy bars and magazines. *Emergency goods* are purchased when a need is urgent—umbrellas during a rainstorm, boots and shovels during the first winter snow. Manufacturers of impulse and emergency goods will place them where consumers are likely to experience an urge or compelling need to purchase.

Shopping goods are those the consumer characteristically compares on such bases as suitability, quality, price, and style. Examples include furniture, clothing, and major appliances. *Homogeneous shopping goods* are similar in quality but different enough in price to justify shopping comparisons. *Heterogeneous shopping goods* differ in product features and services that may be more important than price. The seller of heterogeneous shopping goods carries a wide assortment to satisfy individual tastes and trains salespeople to inform and advise customers.

Specialty goods have unique characteristics or brand identification for which enough buyers are willing to make a special purchasing effort. Examples include cars, stereo components, and men's suits. A Mercedes is a specialty good because interested buyers will travel far to buy one. Specialty goods don't require comparisons; buyers invest time only to reach dealers carrying the wanted products. Dealers don't need convenient locations, although they must let prospective buyers know where to find them.

Unsought goods are those the consumer does not know about or normally think of buying, such as smoke detectors. Classic examples of known but unsought goods are life insurance, cemetery plots, and gravestones. Unsought goods require advertising and personal-selling support.

INDUSTRIAL-GOODS CLASSIFICATION We classify industrial goods in terms of their relative cost and how they enter the production process: materials and parts, capital items, and supplies and business services. **Materials and parts** are goods that enter the manufacturer's product completely. They fall into two classes: raw materials, and manufactured materials and parts. *Raw materials* fall into two major groups: *farm products* (wheat, cotton, livestock, fruits, and vegetables) and *natural products* (fish, lumber, crude petroleum, iron ore). Farm products are supplied by many producers, who turn them over to marketing intermediaries, who provide assembly, grading, storage, transportation, and selling services. Their perishable and seasonal

Jamestown Containers is offering additional packaging features to provide more value to customers.

nature gives rise to special marketing practices, whereas their commodity character results in relatively little advertising and promotional activity, with some exceptions. At times, commodity groups will launch campaigns to promote their product—potatoes, cheese, and beef. Some producers brand their products—Dole salads, Mott's apples, and Chiquita bananas.

Natural products are limited in supply. They usually have great bulk and low unit value and must be moved from producer to user. Fewer and larger producers often market them directly to industrial users. Because users depend on these materials, long-term supply contracts are common. The homogeneity of natural materials limits the amount of demand-creation activity. Price and delivery reliability are the major factors influencing the selection of suppliers.

Manufactured materials and parts fall into two categories: component materials (iron, yarn, cement, wires) and component parts (small motors, tires, castings). *Component materials* are usually fabricated further—pig iron is made into steel, and yarn is woven into cloth. The standardized nature of component materials usually makes price and supplier reliability key purchase factors. *Component parts* enter the finished product with no further change in form, as when small motors are put into vacuum cleaners, and tires are put on automobiles. Most manufactured materials and parts are sold directly to industrial users. Price and service are major marketing considerations, with branding and advertising less important.

Capital items are long-lasting goods that facilitate developing or managing the finished product. They include two groups: installations and equipment. *Installations* consist of buildings (factories, offices) and heavy equipment (generators, drill presses, mainframe computers, elevators). Installations are major purchases. They are usually bought directly from the producer, whose sales force includes technical personnel, and a long negotiation precedes the typical sale. Producers must be willing to design to specification and to supply postsale services. Advertising is much less important than personal selling.

Equipment includes portable factory equipment and tools (hand tools, lift trucks) and office equipment (personal computers, desks). These types of equipment don't become part of a finished product. They have a shorter life than installations but a longer life than operating supplies. Although some equipment manufacturers sell direct, more often they use intermediaries, because the market is geographically dispersed, buyers are numerous, and orders are small. Quality, features, price, and service are major considerations. The sales force tends to be more important than advertising, although advertising can be used effectively.

Supplies and business services are short-term goods and services that facilitate developing or managing the finished product. Supplies are of two kinds: *maintenance and repair items* (paint, nails, brooms) and *operating supplies* (lubricants, coal, writing paper, pencils). Together, they go under the name of MRO goods. Supplies are the equivalent of convenience goods; they are usually purchased with minimum effort on a straight-rebuy basis. They are normally marketed through intermediaries because of their low unit value and the great number and geographic dispersion of customers. Price and service are important considerations, because suppliers are standardized and brand preference is not high.

Business services include *maintenance and repair services* (window cleaning, copier repair) and *business advisory services* (legal, management consulting, advertising). Maintenance and repair services are usually supplied under contract by small producers or from the manufacturers of the original equipment. Business advisory services are usually purchased on the basis of the supplier's reputation and staff.

Product and Services Differentiation

To be branded, products must be differentiated. At one extreme are products that allow little variation: chicken, aspirin, and steel. Yet even here, some differentiation is possible: Perdue chickens, Bayer aspirin, and India's Tata Steel have carved out distinct identities in their categories. Procter & Gamble makes Tide, Cheer, and Gain laundry detergents, each with a separate brand identity. At the other extreme are products capable of high differentiation, such as automobiles, commercial buildings, and furniture. Here the seller faces an abundance of differentiation possibilities, including form, features, customization, performance quality, conformance quality, durability, reliability, repairability, and style.[6] Design has become an increasingly important means of differentiation and we will discuss it in a separate section later.

Product Differentiation

FORM Many products can be differentiated in **form**—the size, shape, or physical structure of a product. Consider the many possible forms of aspirin. Although essentially a commodity, it can be differentiated by dosage size, shape, color, coating, or action time.

FEATURES Most products can be offered with varying **features** that supplement their basic function. A company can identify and select appropriate new features by surveying recent buyers and then calculating *customer value* versus *company cost* for each potential feature. Marketers should consider how many people want each feature, how long it would take to introduce it, and whether competitors could easily copy it.[7]

To avoid "feature fatigue," the company must prioritize features and tell consumers how to use and benefit from them.[8] Companies must also think in terms of feature bundles or packages. Auto companies often manufacture cars at several "trim levels." This lowers manufacturing and inventory costs. Each company must decide whether to offer feature customization at a higher cost or a few standard packages at a lower cost.

CUSTOMIZATION Marketers can differentiate products by customizing them. As companies have grown proficient at gathering information about individual customers and business partners (suppliers, distributors, retailers), and as their factories are being designed more flexibly, they have increased their ability to individualize market offerings, messages, and media. **Mass customization** is the ability of a company to meet each customer's requirements—to prepare on a mass basis individually designed products, services, programs, and communications.[9]

Levi's and Lands' End were among the first to introduce custom jeans. Other firms have introduced mass customization into other markets. Online retailers such as Zazzle and CafePress allow users to upload images and create their own clothing and posters or buy merchandise created by other users. Customers must know how to express their personal product preferences, however, or be given assistance to best customize a product.[10]

PERFORMANCE QUALITY Most products occupy one of four performance levels: low, average, high, or superior. **Performance quality** is the level at which the product's primary characteristics operate. Quality is increasingly important for differentiation as companies adopt a value model and provide higher quality for less money. Firms should design a performance level appropriate to the target market and competition, however, not necessarily the highest level possible. They must also manage performance quality through time. Continuously improving the product can produce high returns and market share; failing to do so can have negative consequences.

When Mercedes-Benz's quality ratings took a dive, the automaker instituted a number of significant changes to bring them back up.

Mercedes-Benz From 2003 to 2006, Mercedes-Benz endured one of its most painful stretches in its 127-year history. Its stellar quality reputation took a beating in J.D. Power and other surveys, and BMW surpassed it in global sales. To recoup, a new management team reorganized the company around functional elements—motors, chassis, and electronic systems—instead of by model lines. Engineers begin testing electronic systems a year earlier and put each new model through 10,000 tests that ran 24 hours a day for three weeks. Mercedes tripled its number of prototypes for new designs, allowing engineers to drive them 3 million miles before production. With these and other changes, the number of flaws in the cars dropped 72 percent from their 2002 peak and warranty costs decreased by 25 percent. As a side effect, Mercedes-Benz dealers have had to contend with a sizable drop in their repair and service businesses![11]

CONFORMANCE QUALITY Buyers expect a high **conformance quality**, the degree to which all produced units are identical and meet promised specifications. Suppose a Porsche 911 is designed to accelerate to 60 miles per hour within 10 seconds. If every Porsche 911 coming off the assembly line does this, the model is said to have high conformance quality. A product with low conformance quality will disappoint some buyers.

DURABILITY **Durability**, a measure of the product's expected operating life under natural or stressful conditions, is a valued attribute for vehicles, kitchen appliances, and other durable goods. The extra price for durability must not be excessive, however, and the product must not be subject to rapid technological obsolescence, as personal computers, televisions, and cell phones have sometimes been.

RELIABILITY Buyers normally will pay a premium for more reliable products. **Reliability** is a measure of the probability that a product will not malfunction or fail within a specified time period. Maytag has an outstanding reputation for creating reliable home appliances. Its long-running "Lonely Repairman" ad campaign was designed to highlight that attribute.

REPAIRABILITY **Repairability** measures the ease of fixing a product when it malfunctions or fails. Ideal repairability would exist if users could fix the product themselves with little cost in money or time. Some products include a diagnostic feature that allows service people to correct a problem over the telephone or advise the user how to correct it. Many computer hardware and software companies offer technical support over the phone, by fax or e-mail, or via real-time chat online.

STYLE **Style** describes the product's look and feel to the buyer. It creates distinctiveness that is hard to copy. Car buyers pay a premium for Jaguars because of their extraordinary looks. Aesthetics play a key role in such brands as Apple computers, Montblanc pens, Godiva chocolate, and Harley-Davidson motorcycles.[12] Strong style does not always mean high performance, however. A car may look sensational but spend a lot of time in the repair shop.

Services Differentiation

When the physical product cannot easily be differentiated, the key to competitive success may lie in adding valued services and improving their quality. Rolls-Royce PLC has ensured its aircraft engines are in high demand by continuously monitoring their health for 45 airlines through live satellite feeds. Under its TotalCare program, airlines pay Rolls a fee for every hour an engine is in flight, and Rolls assumes the risks and costs of downtime and repairs.[13]

The main service differentiators are ordering ease, delivery, installation, customer training, customer consulting, and maintenance and repair.

Cemex guarantees cement delivery as fast as placing a pizza order.

ORDERING EASE **Ordering ease** refers to how easy it is for the customer to place an order with the company. Baxter Healthcare supplies hospitals with computer terminals through which they send orders directly to the firm. Many financial service institutions offer secure online sites to help customers get information and complete transactions more efficiently.

DELIVERY **Delivery** refers to how well the product or service is brought to the customer. It includes speed, accuracy, and care throughout the process. Today's customers have grown to expect speed: pizza delivered in one-half hour, eyeglasses made in one hour, cars lubricated in 15 minutes. Many firms have computerized *quick response systems* (QRS) that link the information systems of their suppliers, manufacturing plants, distribution centers, and retailing outlets. Cemex, a giant cement company based in Mexico, has transformed its business by promising to deliver concrete faster than pizza. It equips every truck with a *global positioning system* (GPS) so dispatchers know its real-time location. If your load is more than 10 minutes late, you get up to a 20 percent discount.[14]

INSTALLATION **Installation** refers to the work done to make a product operational in its planned location. Ease of installation is a true selling point for buyers of complex products like heavy equipment and for technology novices.

CUSTOMER TRAINING **Customer training** helps the customer's employees use the vendor's equipment properly and efficiently. General Electric not only sells and installs expensive X-ray equipment in hospitals, it also gives extensive training to users. McDonald's requires its new franchisees to attend Hamburger University in Oak Brook, Illinois, for two weeks, to learn how to manage the franchise properly.

CUSTOMER CONSULTING **Customer consulting** includes data, information systems, and advice services the seller offers to buyers. Technology firms such as IBM, Oracle, and others have learned that such consulting is an increasingly essential—and profitable—part of their business.

MAINTENANCE AND REPAIR **Maintenance and repair** programs help customers keep purchased products in good working order. Firms such as Hewlett-Packard offer online technical support, or "e-support," for customers, who can search an online database for fixes or seek online help from a technician. Even retailers are getting into the act.

Best Buy As consolidation and competitive pricing among electronics retailers continue, companies are increasingly looking for new ways to stand out in the crowd. That's why Best Buy contracted with the Geek Squad, a small residential computer services company, to revamp the chain's in-store computer repair services. Best Buy used to send PCs to regional repair facilities, a time-consuming process that contributed to a high degree of consumer dissatisfaction. Now about half of all repairs are made in Best Buy stores. But the real differentiator is the Geek Squad's ability to make house calls (at a higher fee) using its signature fleet of VW Beetles. Geek Squad employees even dress differently for house calls—they wear a distinctive "geek" look instead of the traditional Best Buy blue they wear at the in-store service centers.[15]

RETURNS A nuisance to customers, manufacturers, retailers, and distributors alike, product returns are also an unavoidable reality of doing business, especially with online purchases. Although the average return rate for online sales is roughly 5 percent, return and exchange policies are estimated to serve as a deterrent for one-third to one-half of online buyers. The cost of processing a return can be two to three times that of sending an outbound shipment, totaling an average of $30 to $35 for items bought online.

We can think of product returns in two ways:[16]

- *Controllable returns* result from problems or errors by the seller or customer and can mostly be eliminated with improved handling or storage, better packaging, and improved transportation and forward logistics by the seller or its supply chain partners.
- *Uncontrollable returns* result from the need for customers to actually see, try, or experience products in person to determine suitability and can't be eliminated by the company in the short run through any of these means.

One basic strategy is to eliminate the root causes of controllable returns while developing processes for handling uncontrollable returns. The goal is to have fewer products returned and put a higher percentage back into the distribution pipeline to be sold again.

Road Runner Sports   San Diego–based Road Runner Sports sells running shoes, clothing, and equipment through multiple channels. The firm trains its salespeople to be as knowledgeable as possible about recommending the right products. As a result, its return rate on running shoes is 12 percent, noticeably below the industry average of 15 percent to 20 percent. Road Runner also uses SmartLabels—prepaid, preaddressed, bar-coded return labels—to make returns quick and easy for those customers who need them.[17]

Design

As competition intensifies, design offers a potent way to differentiate and position a company's products and services.[18] **Design** is the totality of features that affect how a product looks, feels, and functions to a consumer. Design offers functional and aesthetic benefits and appeals to both our rational and emotional sides.[19]

The designer must figure out how much to invest in form, feature development, performance, conformance, durability, reliability, repairability, and style. To the company, a well-designed product is easy to manufacture and distribute. To the customer, a well-designed product is a pleasant to look at and easy to open, install, use, repair, and dispose of. The designer must take all these factors into account.[20]

As holistic marketers recognize the emotional power of design and the importance to consumers of how things look and feel as well as work, design is exerting a stronger influence in categories where it once played a smaller role. One factor fueling Hewlett-Packard's rise in the PC market is its strong emphasis on design, forcing Dell and others to become more style-conscious to compete. The rationale behind this shift is clear: in one survey consumers reported they would pay an average of $204 more for a high-end laptop that was well-designed.[21]

Certain companies and countries are winning on design.

Road Runner Sports goes to great lengths to minimize the number of product returns from customers.

Top Design Companies and Countries   Some countries have developed strong reputations for their design skills and accomplishments, such as Italy in apparel and furniture and Scandinavia in products designed for functionality, aesthetics, and environmental consciousness. Finland's Nokia was the first to introduce user-changeable covers for cell phones, the first to have elliptical-shaped, soft, and friendly forms, and the first with big screens, all contributing to its remarkable ascent. Braun, a German division of Gillette, has elevated design to a high art in its electric shavers, coffeemakers, hair dryers, and food processors. Kohler brought art and design to luxury kitchen and bath fixtures and faucets. The International Design and Excellence Awards (IDEA) are given each year based on benefit to the user, benefit to the client/business, benefit to society, ecological responsibility, appropriate aesthetics and appeal, and usability testing. In 2009, Samsung won eight awards, Apple seven, Dell Experience Design Group six, and GE Healthcare five. One of the more successful design companies is IDEO.[22]

In an increasingly visually oriented culture, transmitting brand meaning and positioning through design is critical. "In a crowded marketplace," writes Virginia Postrel in *The Substance of Style*, "aesthetics is often the only way to make a product stand out."[23] The GM design team for the new plug-in electric 2011 Chevy Volt wanted to make sure the car looked better than other electric car models. As the Volt design director said, "Most electric cars are like automotive Brussels sprouts. They're good for you, but you don't want to eat them."

Bang & Olufsen's timeless, stylish designs command a significant price premium in the market.

Design can shift consumer perceptions to make brand experiences more rewarding. Consider the lengths Boeing went to in making its 777 airplane seem roomier and more comfortable. Raised center bins, side luggage bins, divider panels, gently arched ceilings, and raised seats made the aircraft interior seem bigger. As one design engineer noted, "If we do our jobs, people don't realize what we have done. They just say they feel more comfortable."

A bad design can also ruin a product's prospects. Sony's eVilla Internet appliance was intended to give consumers Internet access from their kitchens. But at nearly 32 pounds and 16 inches, the mammoth product was so awkward and heavy that the owner's manual recommended customers bend their legs, not their back, to pick it up. The product was withdrawn after only three months.

Design should penetrate all aspects of the marketing program so that all design aspects work together. In search of a universal identity scheme for Coca-Cola, David Butler, vice-president of global design, established four core principles. Each design, whether of packaging, point of sale, equipment, or any other consumer touch point, should reflect (1) bold simplicity, (2) real authenticity, (3) the power of red, and (4) a "familiar yet surprising" nature.[24]

Given the creative nature of design, it's no surprise that there isn't one widely adopted approach. Some firms employ formal, structured processes. *Design thinking* is a very data-driven approach with three phases: observation, ideation, and implementation. Design thinking requires intensive ethnographic studies of consumers, creative brainstorming sessions, and collaborative teamwork to decide how to bring the design idea to reality. Whirlpool used design thinking to develop the Architect Series II kitchen appliances with a more harmonized look than had existed in the category.[25]

On the other hand, the Danish firm Bang & Olufsen (B&O)—which has received many kudos for the design of its stereos, TV equipment, and telephones—trusts the instincts of a handful of designers who rarely consult with consumers. B&O does not introduce many new products in a given year, so every new product is expected to be sold for years. Its BeoLab 8000 speakers sold for $3,000 a pair when introduced in 1992 and for $4,500 more than 15 years later. Their designer, David Lewis, has seen three of his most successful B&O product creations placed in the Museum of Modern Art's permanent collection in New York.[26]

Design is often an important aspect of luxury products. "Marketing Insight: Marketing Luxury Brands" describes some of the broader marketing issues luxury brands face.

Product and Brand Relationships

Each product can be related to other products to ensure that a firm is offering and marketing the optimal set of products.

Marketing Insight

Marketing Luxury Brands

Luxury products are perhaps one of the purest examples of branding, because the brand and its image are often key competitive advantages that create enormous value and wealth for organizations. Marketers for luxury brands such as Prada, Gucci, Cartier, and Louis Vuitton manage lucrative franchises that have endured for decades in what some believe is now a $270 billion industry.

Just like marketers in less expensive and more "down-to-earth" categories, however, those guiding the fortunes of luxury brands must do so in a constantly evolving—and sometimes rapidly changing—marketing environment. Globalization, new technologies, financial crises, shifting consumer cultures, and other forces necessitate that marketers of luxury brands be skillful and adept at their brand stewardship to succeed. Table 12.1 summarizes some key guidelines in marketing luxury brands.

Significantly higher priced than typical items in a category, luxury brands for years were about social status and who a customer was—or perhaps wanted to be. Times have changed, and especially in the face of a crippling recession, luxury has for many become more about personal pleasure and self-expression.

The common denominators of luxury brands are quality and uniqueness. A luxury shopper must feel that what he or she is getting is truly special. Enduring style and authenticity are often critical to justifying a sometimes highly extravagant price. Hermès, the French luxury leather-goods maker, sells its classic designs for hundreds or even thousands of dollars, "not because they are in fashion," as one writer put it, "but [because] they never go out of fashion." Look at how luxury brands have been created across a range of other categories:

- **Sub-Zero refrigerators.** Sub-Zero sells refrigerators that range from $1,600 for small, under-counter types to $12,000 for its specialty Pro 48 model with a stainless steel interior. The target is home owners with high standards of performance and design who cherish their home and what they buy to furnish it. Sub-Zero extensively surveys this group as well as the kitchen designers, architects, and retailers who plan for and sell their products.

- **Patrón tequila.** Cofounded by Paul Mitchell hair care founder John Paul DeJoria, Patrón came about after a 1989 trip to a distillery in the small Mexican state of Jalisco. Named Patrón to convey "the boss, the cool guy," the smooth agave tequila comes in an elegant hand-blown decanter and is sold in individually numbered bottles for $45 or more.

- **Hearts on Fire diamonds.** De Beers brought branding to diamonds decades ago, making them a symbol of love and commitment in part through its "Diamonds Are Forever" ad campaign in 1948. The marketers of Hearts of Fire diamonds have found a market niche as the "World's Most Perfectly Cut Diamond." Although diamonds have become increasingly commoditized on the basis of the four Cs that define quality—cut, clarity, color, and carat—Hearts on Fire have a unique "hearts and arrow" design. When viewed magnified from the bottom, eight perfect hearts appear; from the top, eight perfect fire bursts are seen. Sold through independent jewelers, Hearts on Fire commands a 15 percent to 20 percent premium over a comparable diamond from Tiffany & Co.

The recent economic recession challenged many luxury brands as they tried to justify their value proposition and avoid discounting their products. Those that have successfully extended their brands vertically across a range of price points are usually the most immune to economic downturns.

The Armani brand extended from high-end Giorgio Armani and Giorgio Armani Privé to mid-range luxury with Emporio Armani, to affordable luxury with Armani Jeans and Armani Exchange. Clear differentiation exists between these brands, minimizing the potential for consumer confusion and brand cannibalization. Each also lives up to the core promise of the parent brand, reducing chances of hurting the parent's image.

Horizontal extensions into new categories can also be tricky for luxury brands. Even the most loyal consumer might question a $7,300 Ferragamo watch or an $85 bottle of Roberto Cavalli vodka. Jewelry maker Bulgari has moved into hotels, fragrances, chocolate, and skin care, prompting some branding experts to deem the brand overstretched.

In the past, iconic fashion designers Pierre Cardin and Halston licensed their names to so many ordinary products that the brands were badly tarnished. Ralph Lauren, however, has successfully marketed an aspirational luxury brand with wholesome all-American lifestyle imagery across a wide range of products. Besides clothing and fragrances, Lauren boutiques sell linens, candles, beds, couches, dishware, photo albums, and jewelry. Calvin Klein has adopted a similarly successful expansive strategy, though with different lifestyle imagery.

In an increasingly wired world, some luxury marketers have struggled to find the appropriate online selling and communication strategies for their brand. Ultimately, success depends on getting the right balance of classic and contemporary imagery and continuity and change in marketing programs and activities. Luxury is also not viewed in the same way everywhere. In post-communist Russia for a time, the bigger and gaudier the logo the better. But in the end, luxury brand marketers have to remember they are often selling a dream, anchored in product quality, status, and prestige.

Sources: Beth Snyder Bulik, "Sub-Zero Keeps Its Cool in a Value-Obsessed Economy," *Advertising Age*, May 25, 2009, p. 14; David K. Randall, "Dandy Corn," *Forbes*, March 10, 2008, p. 70; Christopher Palmeri, "The Barroom Brawl over Patron," *BusinessWeek*, September 17, 2007, p. 72; Bethany McLean, "Classic Rock," *Fortune*, November 12, 2007, pp. 35–39; Dan Heath and Chip Heath, "The Inevitability of $300 Socks," *Fast Company*, September 2007, pp. 68–70; Stellene Volande, "The Secret to Hermès's Success," *Departures*, November–December 2009, pp. 110–12; Cathy Horyn, "Why So Stodgy, Prada.com?" *New York Times*, December 30, 2009; Christina Binkley, "Like Our Sunglasses? Try Our Vodka! Brand Extensions Get Weirder, Risking Customer Confusion," *Wall Street Journal*, November 8, 2007; Special Issue on Luxury Brands, *Fortune*, September 17, 2007.

TABLE 12.1 🖾	Guidelines for Marketing Luxury Brands

1. Maintaining a premium image for luxury brands is crucial; controlling that image is thus a priority.
2. Luxury branding typically includes the creation of many intangible brand associations and an aspirational image.
3. All aspects of the marketing program for luxury brands must be aligned to ensure quality products and services and pleasurable purchase and consumption experiences.
4. Brand elements besides brand names—logos, symbols, packaging, signage—can be important drivers of brand equity for luxury brands.
5. Secondary associations from linked personalities, events, countries, and other entities can be important drivers of brand equity for luxury brands.
6. Luxury brands must carefully control distribution via a selective channel strategy.
7. Luxury brands must employ a premium pricing strategy with strong quality cues and few discounts and markdowns.
8. Brand architecture for luxury brands must be managed very carefully.
9. Competition for luxury brands must be defined broadly as it often comes from other categories.
10. Luxury brands must legally protect all trademarks and aggressively combat counterfeits.

Source: Based on Kevin Lane Keller, "Managing the Growth Tradeoff: Challenges and Opportunities in Luxury Branding," *Journal of Brand Management* 16 (March–May 2009), pp. 290–301.

Sub-Zero targets its high-end refrigerators to homeowners looking for the best.

The Product Hierarchy

The product hierarchy stretches from basic needs to particular items that satisfy those needs. We can identify six levels of the product hierarchy, using life insurance as an example:

1. *Need family*—The core need that underlies the existence of a product family. Example: security.
2. *Product family*—All the product classes that can satisfy a core need with reasonable effectiveness. Example: savings and income.
3. *Product class*—A group of products within the product family recognized as having a certain functional coherence, also known as a product category. Example: financial instruments.
4. *Product line*—A group of products within a product class that are closely related because they perform a similar function, are sold to the same customer groups, are marketed through the same outlets or channels, or fall within given price ranges. A product line may consist of different brands, or a single family brand, or individual brand that has been line extended. Example: life insurance.
5. *Product type*—A group of items within a product line that share one of several possible forms of the product. Example: term life insurance.
6. *Item* (also called *stock-keeping unit* or *product variant*)—A distinct unit within a brand or product line distinguishable by size, price, appearance, or some other attribute. Example: Prudential renewable term life insurance.

Product Systems and Mixes

A **product system** is a group of diverse but related items that function in a compatible manner. For example, the extensive iPod product system includes headphones and headsets, cables and docks, armbands, cases, power and car accessories, and speakers. A **product mix** (also called a **product assortment**) is the set of all products and items a particular seller offers for sale.

A product mix consists of various product lines. NEC's (Japan) product mix consists of communication products and computer products. Michelin has three product lines: tires, maps, and restaurant-rating services. At Northwestern University, separate academic deans oversee the schools of medicine, law, business, engineering, music, speech, journalism, and liberal arts among others.

A company's product mix has a certain width, length, depth, and consistency. These concepts are illustrated in ▭ Table 12.2 for selected Procter & Gamble consumer products.

• The *width* of a product mix refers to how many different product lines the company carries. Table 12.2 shows a product mix width of five lines. (In fact, P&G produces many additional lines.)

Michelin has three distinct, but somewhat related, product lines.

TABLE 12.2	Product Mix Width and Product Line Length for Procter & Gamble Products (including dates of introduction)				
	Product Mix Width				
	Detergents	**Toothpaste**	**Bar Soap**	**Disposable Diapers**	**Paper Products**
Product Line Length	Ivory Snow (1930)	Gleem (1952)	Ivory (1879)	Pampers (1961)	Charmin (1928)
	Dreft (1933)	Crest (1955)	Camay (1926)	Luvs (1976)	Puffs (1960)
	Tide (1946)		Zest (1952)		Bounty (1965)
	Cheer (1950)		Safeguard (1963)		
	Dash (1954)		Oil of Olay (1993)		
	Bold (1965)				
	Gain (1966)				
	Era (1972)				

- The *length* of a product mix refers to the total number of items in the mix. In Table 12.2, it is 20. We can also talk about the average length of a line. We obtain this by dividing the total length (here 20) by the number of lines (here 5), for an average product line length of 4.
- The *depth* of a product mix refers to how many variants are offered of each product in the line. If Tide came in two scents (Mountain Spring and Regular), two formulations (liquid and powder), and two additives (with or without bleach), it would have a depth of eight because there are eight distinct variants.[27] We can calculate the average depth of P&G's product mix by averaging the number of variants within the brand groups.
- The *consistency* of the product mix describes how closely related the various product lines are in end use, production requirements, distribution channels, or some other way. P&G's product lines are consistent in that they are consumer goods that go through the same distribution channels. The lines are less consistent in the functions they perform for buyers.

These four product mix dimensions permit the company to expand its business in four ways. It can add new product lines, thus widening its product mix. It can lengthen each product line. It can add more product variants to each product and deepen its product mix. Finally, a company can pursue more product line consistency. To make these product and brand decisions, it is useful to conduct product line analysis.

Product Line Analysis

In offering a product line, companies normally develop a basic platform and modules that can be added to meet different customer requirements and lower production costs. Car manufacturers build cars around a basic platform. Homebuilders show a model home to which buyers can add additional features. Product line managers need to know the sales and profits of each item in their line to determine which items to build, maintain, harvest, or divest.[28] They also need to understand each product line's market profile.

SALES AND PROFITS △ Figure 12.3 shows a sales and profit report for a five-item product line. The first item accounts for 50 percent of total sales and 30 percent of total profits. The first two items account for 80 percent of total sales and 60 percent of total profits. If these two items were suddenly hurt by a competitor, the line's sales and profitability could collapse. These items must be carefully monitored and protected. At the other end, the last item delivers only 5 percent of the product line's sales and profits. The product line manager may consider dropping this item unless it has strong growth potential.

Every company's product portfolio contains products with different margins. Supermarkets make almost no margin on bread and milk, reasonable margins on canned and frozen foods, and better margins on flowers, ethnic food lines, and freshly baked goods. A telecommunication company makes different margins on its core telephone service than on added services such as call waiting, caller ID,

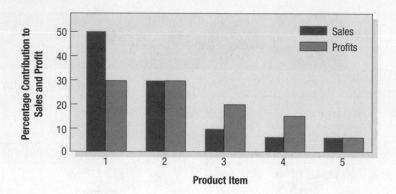

|Fig. 12.3| △

Product-Item Contributions to a Product Line's Total Sales and Profits

and voice mail. Companies should recognize that items can differ in their potential for being priced higher or advertised more as ways to increase their sales, their margins, or both.[29]

MARKET PROFILE The product line manager must review how the line is positioned against competitors' lines. Consider paper company X with a paperboard product line.[30] Two paperboard attributes are weight and finish quality. Paper is usually offered at standard levels of 90, 120, 150, and 180 weights. Finish quality is offered at low, medium, and high levels. △ Figure 12.4 shows the location of the various product line items of company X and four competitors, A, B, C, and D. Competitor A sells two product items in the extra-high weight class ranging from medium to low finish quality. Competitor B sells four items that vary in weight and finish quality. Competitor C sells three items in which the greater the weight, the greater the finish quality. Competitor D sells three items, all lightweight but varying in finish quality. Company X offers three items that vary in weight and finish quality.

The **product map** shows which competitors' items are competing against company X's items. For example, company X's low-weight, medium-quality paper competes against competitor D's and B's papers, but its high-weight, medium-quality paper has no direct competitor. The map also reveals possible locations for new items. No manufacturer offers a high-weight, low-quality paper. If company X estimates a strong unmet demand and can produce and price this paper at low cost, it could consider adding this item to its line.

Another benefit of product mapping is that it identifies market segments. Figure 12.4 shows the types of paper, by weight and quality, preferred by the general printing industry, the point-of-purchase display industry, and the office supply industry. The map shows that company X is well positioned to serve the needs of the general printing industry but less effective in serving the other two industries.

Product line analysis provides information for two key decision areas—product line length and product mix pricing.

|Fig. 12.4| △

Product Map for a Paper-Product Line

Source: Benson P. Shapiro, *Industrial Product Policy: Managing the Existing Product Line* (Cambridge, MA: Marketing Science Institute Report No. 77–110). Copyright © 2003. Reprinted by permission of Marketing Science Institute and Benson P. Shapiro.

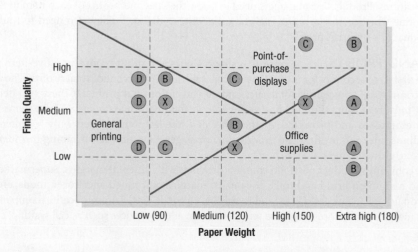

Product Line Length

Company objectives influence product line length. One objective is to create a product line to induce up-selling: Thus BMW would like to move customers up from a 3-series vehicle to a 5-series and eventually even a 7-series vehicle. A different objective is to create a product line that facilitates cross-selling: Hewlett-Packard sells printers as well as computers. Still another objective is to create a product line that protects against economic ups and downs: Electrolux offers white goods such as refrigerators, dishwashers, and vacuum cleaners under different brand names in the discount, middle-market, and premium segments, in part in case the economy moves up or down. Companies seeking high market share and market growth will generally carry longer product lines. Companies that emphasize high profitability will carry shorter lines consisting of carefully chosen items.

Product lines tend to lengthen over time. Excess manufacturing capacity puts pressure on the product line manager to develop new items. The sales force and distributors also pressure the company for a more complete product line to satisfy customers. But as items are added, costs rise for design and engineering, inventory carrying, manufacturing changeover, order processing, transportation, and new-item promotions. Eventually, top management may stop development because of insufficient funds or manufacturing capacity. A pattern of product line growth followed by massive pruning may repeat itself many times. Increasingly, consumers are growing weary of dense product lines, overextended brands, and feature-laden products (see "Marketing Insight: When Less Is More").

A company lengthens its product line in two ways: line stretching and line filling.

LINE STRETCHING Every company's product line covers a certain part of the total possible range. For example, Mercedes automobiles are located in the upper price range of the automobile

---

Marketing Insight

When Less Is More

With thousands of new products introduced each year, consumers find it ever harder to navigate store aisles. One study found the average shopper spent 40 seconds or more in the supermarket soda aisle, compared to 25 seconds six or seven years ago.

Although consumers may think greater product variety increases their likelihood of finding the right product for them, the reality is often different. One study showed that although consumers expressed greater interest in shopping with a larger assortment of 24 flavored jams than a smaller assortment of 6, they were 10 times more likely to actually make a selection with the smaller assortment.

Similarly, if the product quality in an assortment is high, consumers would actually prefer a smaller than a larger set of choices. Although consumers with well-defined preferences may benefit from more differentiated products that offer specific benefits to better suit their needs, too much product choice may be a source of frustration, confusion, and regret for other consumers. Product proliferation has another downside. Exposing the customer to constant product changes and introductions may nudge them into reconsidering their choices and perhaps switching to a competitor's product.

Smart marketers realize it's not just the product lines making consumer heads spin—many products themselves are too complicated for the average consumer. Royal Philips Electronics asked 100 of its top managers to take various Philips electronic products home one weekend and see whether they could make them work. The number of executives who returned frustrated and angry spoke volumes about the challenges the ordinary consumer faced.

Sources: Dimitri Kuksov and J. Miguel Villas-Boas, "When More Alternatives Lead to Less Choice," *Marketing Science*, 2010, in press; Kristin Diehl and Cait Poynor, "Great Expectations?! Assortment Size, Expectations, and Satisfaction," *Journal of Marketing Research* 46 (April 2009), pp. 312–22; Joseph P. Redden and Stephen J. Hoch, "The Presence of Variety Reduces Perceived Quantity," *Journal of Consumer Research* 36 (October 2009), pp. 406–17; Alexander Chernev and Ryan Hamilton, "Assortment Size and Option Attractiveness in Consumer Choice Among Retailers," *Journal of Marketing Research* 46 (June 2009), pp. 410–20; Richard A. Briesch, Pradeep K. Chintagunta, and Edward J. Fox, "How Does Assortment Affect Grocery Store Choice," *Journal of Marketing Research* 46 (April 2009), pp. 176–89; Aner Sela, Jonah Berger, and Wendy Liu, "Variety, Vice and Virtue: How Assortment Size Influences Option Choice," *Journal of Consumer Research* 35 (April 2009), pp. 941–51; Susan M. Broniarczyk, "Product Assortment," Curt P. Haugtvedt, Paul M. Herr, and Frank R. Kardes, eds., *Handbook of Consumer Psychology* (New York: Taylor & Francis, 2008), pp. 755–79; Cassie Mogilner, Tamar Rudnick, and Sheena S. Iyengar, "The Mere Categorization Effect: How the Presence of Categories Increases Choosers' Perceptions of Assortment Variety and Outcome Satisfaction," *Journal of Consumer Research* 35 (August 2008), pp. 202–15; Alexander Chernev, "The Role of Purchase Quantity in Assortment Choice: The Quantity Matching Heuristic," *Journal of Marketing Research* 45 (April 2008), pp. 171–81; John Gourville and Dilip Soman, "Overchoice and Assortment Type: When and Why Variety Backfires," *Marketing Science* 24 (Summer 2005), pp. 382–95; Barry Schwartz, *The Paradox of Choice: Why More Is Less* (New York: Harper Collins Ecco, 2004); Alexander Chernev, "When More Is Less and Less Is More: The Role of Ideal Point Availability and Assortment in Choice," *Journal of Consumer Research* 30 (September 2003), pp. 170–83; Sheena S. Iyengar and Mark R. Lepper, "When Choice Is Demotivating: Can One Desire Too Much of a Good Thing?" *Journal of Personality and Social Psychology* 79, no. 6 (December 2000), pp. 995–1006.

market. **Line stretching** occurs when a company lengthens its product line beyond its current range, whether down-market, up-market, or both ways.

Down-Market Stretch   A company positioned in the middle market may want to introduce a lower-priced line for any of three reasons:

1. The company may notice strong growth opportunities as mass retailers such as Walmart, Best Buy, and others attract a growing number of shoppers who want value-priced goods.
2. The company may wish to tie up lower-end competitors who might otherwise try to move up-market. If the company has been attacked by a low-end competitor, it often decides to counterattack by entering the low end of the market.
3. The company may find that the middle market is stagnating or declining.

A company faces a number of naming choices in deciding to move a brand down-market:

1. Use the parent brand name on all its offerings. Sony has used its name on products in a variety of price tiers.
2. Introduce lower-priced offerings using a sub-brand name, such as P&G's Charmin Basics and Bounty Basics.
3. Introduce the lower-priced offerings under a different name, such as the Gap's Old Navy brand. This strategy is expensive to implement and means brand equity will have to be built from scratch, but the equity of the parent brand name is protected.

Moving down-market carries risks. Kodak introduced Kodak Funtime Film to counter lower-priced brands, but it did not price it low enough to match the lower-priced film. It also found some of its regular customers buying Funtime, so it was cannibalizing its core brand. Kodak withdrew the product and may have also lost some of its quality image in the process.

On the other hand, Mercedes successfully introduced its C-Class cars at $30,000 without injuring its ability to sell other Mercedes cars for $100,000. John Deere introduced a lower-priced line of lawn tractors called Sabre from John Deere while still selling its more expensive tractors under the John Deere name. In these cases, consumers may have been better able to compartmentalize the different brand offerings and understand functional differences between offerings in higher and lower price tiers.

Up-Market Stretch   Companies may wish to enter the high end of the market to achieve more growth, realize higher margins, or simply position themselves as full-line manufacturers. Many markets have spawned surprising upscale segments: Starbucks in coffee, Häagen-Dazs in ice cream, and Evian in bottled water. The leading Japanese auto companies have each introduced an upscale automobile: Toyota's Lexus, Nissan's Infiniti, and Honda's Acura. They invented entirely new names, because consumers might not have given the brand "permission" to stretch upward when those lines were first introduced.

Other companies have included their own name in moving up-market. Gallo sells Gallo Family Vineyards (priced at $10 to $30 a bottle) with a hip, young image to compete in the premium wine segment. General Electric introduced the GE Profile brand for its large appliance offerings in the upscale market.[31] Some brands have used modifiers to signal a quality improvement, such as Ultra Dry Pampers, Extra Strength Tylenol, and Power Pro Dustbuster Plus.

Two-Way Stretch   Companies serving the middle market might stretch their line in both directions. Robert Mondavi Winery, now owned by Constellation Brands, sells $35 bottles of wines as the first premium "New World wine," but it also sells $125 bottles of Mondavi Reserve at high-end wineries, restaurants, and vineyards and through direct order, as well as $11 bottles of Woodbridge created during the grape oversupply of the mid-1990s. Purina Dog Food has stretched up and down to create a product line differentiated by benefits to dogs, breadth of varieties, ingredients, and price:

- Pro Plan ($34.89/18 lb. bag)—helps dogs live long and healthy lives with high-quality ingredients (real meat, fish, and poultry)
- Purina ONE ($29.79/18 lb. bag)—meets dogs' changing and unique nutritional needs and provides superpremium nutrition for good health
- Purina Dog Chow ($18.49/20 lb. bag)—provides dogs with complete nutrition to build, replenish, and repair at each life stage
- Alpo by Purina ($10.99/17.6 lb. bag)—offers beef, liver, and cheese flavor combinations and three meaty varieties

Intercontinental Hotels Group Intercontinental Hotels Group's Holiday Inn brand broke its domestic hotels into four separate chains to tap into different benefit segments—the upscale Crowne Plaza, the traditional Holiday Inn, the budget Holiday Inn Express, and the business-oriented Holiday Inn Select. Each chain received a different marketing program and emphasis. Holiday Inn Express launched the humorous "Stay Smart" advertising campaign, showing the brilliant feats ordinary people could attempt after staying at the chain. By developing the brands for distinct consumer targets with unique needs, Holiday Inn prevents overlap between them.[32]

LINE FILLING A firm can also lengthen its product line by adding more items within the present range. Motives for *line filling* include reaching for incremental profits satisfying dealers who complain about lost sales because of items missing from the line, utilizing excess capacity, trying to become the leading full-line company, and plugging holes to keep out competitors.

BMW AG In four years BMW has morphed from a one-brand, five-model carmaker into a powerhouse with 3 brands, 14 "Series," and roughly 30 distinct models. Not only has the carmaker expanded its product range downward with MINI Coopers and its compact 1-series models, but it has also built it upward with Rolls-Royce and filled the gaps in between with its X3, X5, and X6 sports activity vehicles, Z4 roadsters, and a 6-series coupe. The company has used line filling successfully to boost its appeal to the rich, the super-rich, and the wannabe-rich, all without departing from its pure premium positioning. The latest challenges? Launching the 5-series Gran Turismo, which combines the formality of a four-door sedan, the cargo capacity of a station wagon, and the high seating position and convenient hatchback of a crossover SUV. After that, BMW still has to decide what type of environmentally friendly "green" vehicles to introduce.[33]

Line filling is overdone if it results in self-cannibalization and customer confusion. The company needs to differentiate each item in the consumer's mind with a *just-noticeable difference.* According to Weber's law, customers are more attuned to relative than to absolute difference.[34] They will perceive the difference between boards 2 and 3 feet long and boards 20 and 30 feet long, but not between boards 29 and 30 feet long. The proposed item should also meet a market need and is not added simply to satisfy an internal need. The infamous Edsel automobile, on which Ford lost $350 million in the late 1950s, met Ford's internal positioning need for a car between its Ford and Lincoln lines, but not the market's needs.

LINE MODERNIZATION, FEATURING, AND PRUNING Product lines need to be modernized. The question is whether to overhaul the line piecemeal or all at once. A piecemeal approach allows the company to see how customers and dealers take to the new style. It is also less draining on the company's cash flow, but it lets competitors see changes and start redesigning their own lines.

In rapidly changing markets, modernization is continuous. Companies plan improvements to encourage customer migration to higher-valued, higher-priced items. Microprocessor companies such as Intel and AMD, and software companies such as Microsoft and Oracle continually introduce more-advanced versions of their products. It's important to time improvements so they do not appear too early (damaging sales of the current line) or too late (giving the competition time to establish a strong reputation).[35]

The product line manager typically selects one or a few items in the line to feature. Sears will announce a special low-priced washing machine to attract customers. At other times, managers will feature a high-end item to lend prestige to the product line. Sometimes a company finds one end of its line selling well and the other end selling poorly.

The company may try to boost demand for slower sellers, especially if a factory is idled by lack of demand, but it could be counterargued that the firm should promote items that sell well rather than prop up weak ones. Nike's Air Force 1 basketball shoe, introduced in the 1980s, is a billion-dollar brand that is still a consumer and retailer favorite and a moneymaker for the company due to collectable designs and tight supplies. Since their introduction, Air Force 1 shoes have been designed or inspired by many celebrities and athletes.[36]

Nike's classic Air Force 1 sneaker has been refreshed time and time again over the years, as these 25th-anniversary models show.

Using sales and cost analysis, product line managers must periodically review the line for deadwood that depresses profits.[37] One study found that for a big Dutch retailer, a major assortment reduction led to a short-term drop in category sales, caused mainly by fewer category purchases by former buyers, but it attracted new category buyers at the same time. These new buyers partially offset the sales losses among former buyers of the delisted items.[38]

In 1999, Unilever announced its "Path to Growth" program designed to get the most value from its brand portfolio by eliminating three-quarters of its 1,600 distinct brands by 2003.[39] More than 90 percent of its profits came from just 400 brands, prompting Unilever cochairman Niall FitzGerald to liken the brand reduction to weeding a garden, so "the light and air get in to the blooms which are likely to grow the best." The company retained global brands such as Lipton, as well as regional brands and "local jewels" like Persil, the leading detergent in the United Kingdom.

Multibrand companies all over the world try to optimize their brand portfolios. This often means focusing on core brand growth and concentrating resources on the biggest and most established brands. Hasbro has designated a set of core toy brands, including GI Joe, Transformers, and My Little Pony, to emphasize in its marketing. Procter & Gamble's "back to basics strategy" concentrated on brands with over $1 billion in revenue, such as Tide, Crest, Pampers, and Pringles. Every product in a product line must play a role, as must any brand in the brand portfolio.

Volkswagen Volkswagen has four different core brands of particular importance in its European portfolio. Initially, Audi and Seat had a sporty image and VW and Skoda had a family-car image. Audi and VW were in a higher price-quality tier than Skoda and Seat, which had spartan interiors and utilitarian engine performance. To reduce costs, streamline part/systems designs, and eliminate redundancies, Volkswagen upgraded the Seat and Skoda brands, which captured market share with splashy interiors, a full array of safety systems, and reliable power trains. The danger, of course, is that by borrowing from its upper-echelon Audi and Volkswagen products, Volkswagen could dilute their cachet. Frugal European consumers may convince themselves that a Seat or Skoda is almost identical to its VW sister, at several thousand euros less.[40]

Product Mix Pricing

Marketers must modify their price-setting logic when the product is part of a product mix. In **product mix pricing**, the firm searches for a set of prices that maximizes profits on the total mix. Pricing is difficult because the various products have demand and cost interrelationships and are subject to different degrees of competition. We can distinguish six situations calling for product-mix pricing: product line pricing, optional-feature pricing, captive-product pricing, two-part pricing, by-product pricing, and product-bundling pricing.

PRODUCT LINE PRICING Companies normally develop product lines rather than single products and introduce price steps. A men's clothing store might carry men's suits at three price levels: $300, $600, and $900, which customers associate with low-, average-, and high-quality. The seller's task is to establish perceived quality differences that justify the price differences.[41]

OPTIONAL-FEATURE PRICING Many companies offer optional products, features, and services with their main product. A buyer of the 2010 Subaru Outback 2.5i can order four-way power passenger seats, an All-Weather package, and a power moon roof as optional features.

Pricing options is a sticky problem, because companies must decide which to include in the standard price and which to offer separately. Many restaurants price their beverages high and their food low. The food revenue covers costs, and the beverages—especially liquor—produce the profit.

My Little Pony is one of Hasbro's core toy brands that receives special attention and support.

This explains why servers often press hard to get customers to order drinks. Other restaurants price their liquor low and food high to draw in a drinking crowd.

CAPTIVE-PRODUCT PRICING Some products require the use of ancillary or **captive products**. Manufacturers of razors and cameras often price them low and set high markups on razor blades and film.[42] AT&T may give a cellular phone free if the person commits to buying two years of phone service. If the captive product is priced too high in the aftermarket, however, counterfeiting and substitutions can erode sales. Consumers now can buy cartridge refills for their printers from discount suppliers and save 20 percent to 30 percent off the manufacturer's price.

Hewlett-Packard In 1996, Hewlett-Packard (HP) began drastically cutting prices on its printers, by as much as 60 percent in some cases. HP could afford to make these cuts because customers typically spend twice as much on replacement ink cartridges, toner, and specialty paper as on the printer over the life of the product, and inkjet supplies typically carry 45 percent to 60 percent profit margins. As the price of printers dropped, printer sales rose, and so did aftermarket sales. HP now owns about 46 percent of the worldwide printer business, a share that accounted for 32 percent of HP's $13.4 billion profit in 2008.[43]

TWO-PART PRICING Service firms engage in **two-part pricing**, consisting of a fixed fee plus a variable usage fee. Cell phone users pay a minimum monthly fee plus charges for calls that exceed their allotted minutes. Amusement parks charge an admission fee plus fees for rides over a certain minimum. The service firm faces a problem similar to captive-product pricing—namely, how much to charge for the basic service and how much for the variable usage. The fixed fee should be low enough to induce purchase; profit can then come from the usage fees.

BY-PRODUCT PRICING The production of certain goods—meats, petroleum products, and other chemicals—often results in by-products that should be priced on their value. Any income earned on the by-products will make it easier for the company to charge a lower price on its main product if competition forces it to do so. Formed in 1855, Australia's CSR was originally named Colonial Sugar Refinery and forged its early reputation as a sugar company. The company began to sell by-products of its sugar cane: waste sugar cane fiber was used to manufacture wallboard. Today, through product development and acquisition, the renamed CSR has become one of the top 10 companies in Australia selling building and construction materials.

PRODUCT-BUNDLING PRICING Sellers often bundle products and features. **Pure bundling** occurs when a firm offers its products only as a bundle. A talent agency might insist that a "hot" actor can be signed to a film only if the film company also accepts other talents the agency represented (directors, writers). This is a form of *tied-in sales*.

In **mixed bundling**, the seller offers goods both individually and in bundles, normally charging less for the bundle than if the items were purchased separately. An auto manufacturer might offer an option package at less than the cost of buying all the options separately. A theater will price a season subscription lower than the cost of buying all the performances separately. Customers may not have planned to buy all the components, so savings on the price bundle must be enough to induce them to buy it.[44]

Some customers want less than the whole bundle in exchange for a lower price.[45] These customers ask the seller to "unbundle" or "rebundle" its offer. If a supplier saves $100 by not supplying unwanted delivery and reduces the customer's price by $80, it has kept the customer happy while increasing its profit by $20. "Marketing Memo: Product-Bundle Pricing Considerations" offers a few tips.

Co-Branding and Ingredient Branding

CO-BRANDING Marketers often combine their products with products from other companies in various ways. In **co-branding**—also called dual branding or brand bundling—two or more well-known brands are combined into a joint product or marketed together in some fashion.[46] One form of co-branding is *same-company co-branding*, as when General Mills advertises Trix cereal and Yoplait yogurt. Another form is *joint-venture co-branding*, such as General Electric and Hitachi lightbulbs in Japan, and the Citibank AAdvantage credit card. There is *multiple-sponsor co-branding*, such as Taligent, a one-time technological alliance of Apple, IBM, and Motorola.[47] Finally, there is *retail co-branding* in which two retail establishments use the same location to optimize space and profits, such as jointly owned Pizza Hut, KFC, and Taco Bell restaurants.

marketing Memo

Product-Bundle Pricing Considerations

As promotional activity increases on individual items in the bundle, buyers perceive less savings on the bundle and are less apt to pay for it. Research suggests the following guidelines for implementing a bundling strategy:

- Don't promote individual products in a package as frequently and cheaply as the bundle. The bundle price should be much lower than the sum of individual products or the consumer will not perceive its attractiveness.

- Limit promotions to a single item in the mix if you still want to promote individual products. Another option: alternate promotions, one after another, to avoid running conflicting promotions.

- If you offer large rebates on individual products, make them the absolute exception and do it with discretion. Otherwise, the consumer uses the price of individual products as an external reference for the bundle, which then loses value.

- Consider how experienced and knowledgeable your customer is. More knowledgeable customers may be less likely to need or want bundled offerings and prefer the freedom to choose components individually.

- Remember costs play a role. If marginal costs for the products are low—such as for proprietary software components that can be easily copied and distributed—a bundling strategy can be preferable to a pure component strategy where each component is purchased separately.

- Firms with single-products bundling products together to compete against a multiproduct firm may not be successful if a price war ensues.

Sources: Amiya Basu and Padmal Vitharana, "Impact of Customer Knowledge Heterogeneity on Bundling Strategy," *Marketing Science* 28 (July–August 2009), pp. 792–801; Bikram Ghosh and Subramanian Balachnadar, "Competitive Bundling and Counterbundling with Generalist and Specialist Firms," *Management Science* 53 (January 2007), pp. 159–68; Loren M. Hitt and Pei-yu Chen, "Bundling with Customer Self-Selection: A Simple Approach to Bundling Low-Marginal-Cost Goods," *Management Science* 51 (October 2005), pp. 1481–93; George Wuebker, "Bundles Effectiveness Often Undermined," *Marketing News*, March 18, 2002, pp. 9–12; Stefan Stremersch and Gerard J. Tellis, "Strategic Bundling of Products and Prices," *Journal of Marketing* 66 (January 2002), pp. 55–72.

The main advantage of co-branding is that a product can be convincingly positioned by virtue of the multiple brands. Co-branding can generate greater sales from the existing market and open opportunities for new consumers and channels. It can also reduce the cost of product introduction, because it combines two well-known images and speeds adoption. And co-branding may be a valuable means to learn about consumers and how other companies approach them. Companies in the automotive industry have reaped all these benefits.

The potential disadvantages of co-branding are the risks and lack of control in becoming aligned with another brand in consumers' minds. Consumer expectations of co-brands are likely to be high, so unsatisfactory performance could have negative repercussions for both brands. If the other brand enters a number of co-branding arrangements, overexposure may dilute the transfer of any association. It may also result in a lack of focus on existing brands. Consumers may feel less sure of what they know about the brand.[48]

For co-branding to succeed, the two brands must separately have brand equity—adequate brand awareness and a sufficiently positive brand image. The most important requirement is a logical fit between the two brands, to maximize the advantages of each while minimizing disadvantages. Consumers are more apt to perceive co-brands favorably if they are complementary and offer unique quality, rather than overly similar and redundant.[49]

Managers must enter co-branding ventures carefully, looking for the right fit in values, capabilities, and goals and an appropriate balance of brand equity. There must be detailed plans to legalize contracts, make financial arrangements, and coordinate marketing programs. As one executive at Nabisco put it, "Giving away your brand is a lot like giving away your child—you want to make sure everything is perfect." Financial arrangements between brands vary; one common approach is for the brand more deeply invested in the production process to pay the other a licensing fee and royalty.

Brand alliances require a number of decisions.[50] What capabilities do you *not* have? What resource constraints do you face (people, time, money)? What are your growth goals or revenue needs? Ask whether the opportunity is a profitable business venture. How does it help maintain or strengthen brand equity? Is there any risk of diluting brand equity? Does the opportunity offer extrinsic advantages such as learning opportunities?

INGREDIENT BRANDING **Ingredient branding** is a special case of co-branding.[51] It creates brand equity for materials, components, or parts that are necessarily contained within other branded products. Successful ingredient brands include Dolby noise reduction technology, GORE-TEX water-resistant fibers, and Scotchgard fabrics. Some popular ingredient-branded products are Lunchables lunch combinations with Taco Bell tacos and Lay's potato chips made with KC Masterpiece barbecue sauce.

An interesting take on ingredient branding is "self-branded ingredients" that companies advertise and even trademark. Westin Hotels advertises its own "Heavenly Bed" and "Heavenly Shower." The Heavenly Bed has been so successful that Westin now sells the bed, pillows, sheets, and blankets via an online catalog, along with other "Heavenly" gifts, bath products, and even pet items. If it can be done well, using self-branded ingredients makes sense because firms have more control over them and can develop them to suit their purposes.[52]

Ingredient brands try to create enough awareness and preference for their product so consumers will not buy a "host" product that doesn't contain it.[53] DuPont has done so successfully.

DuPont's Stainmaster carpets have become a household name.

DuPont DuPont has introduced a number of innovative products, such as Corian® solid-surface material, for use in markets ranging from apparel to aerospace. Many, such as Tyvek® house wrap, Teflon® non-stick coating, and Kevlar® fiber, became household names as ingredient brands in consumer products manufactured by other companies. Since 2004, DuPont has introduced more than 5,000 new products and received over 2,400 new patents. One of its recent award winners, Sorona® is a renewably sourced or bio-based polymer for use in carpet and apparel markets.[54]

Many manufacturers make components or materials that enter final branded products but lose their individual identity. One of the few companies that avoided this fate is Intel. Intel's consumer-directed brand campaign convinced many personal computer buyers to buy only brands with "Intel Inside." As a result, major PC manufacturers—IBM, Dell, Compaq—purchase their chips from Intel at a premium price rather than buy equivalent chips from an unknown supplier.

What are the requirements for successful ingredient branding?[55]

1. Consumers must believe the ingredient matters to the performance and success of the end product. Ideally, this intrinsic value is easily seen or experienced.
2. Consumers must be convinced that not all ingredient brands are the same and that the ingredient is superior.
3. A distinctive symbol or logo must clearly signal that the host product contains the ingredient. Ideally, this symbol or logo functions like a "seal" and is simple and versatile, credibly communicating quality and confidence.
4. A coordinated "pull" and "push" program must help consumers understand the advantages of the branded ingredient. Channel members must offer full support such as consumer advertising and promotions and—sometimes in collaboration with manufacturers—retail merchandising and promotion programs.

Packaging, Labeling, Warranties, and Guarantees

Some product packages—such as the Coke bottle and Red Bull can—are world famous. Many marketers have called packaging a fifth P, along with price, product, place, and promotion. Most, however, treat packaging and labeling as an element of product strategy. Warranties and guarantees can also be an important part of the product strategy and often appear on the package.

Packaging

Packaging includes all the activities of designing and producing the container for a product. Packages might have up to three layers. Cool Water cologne comes in a bottle (*primary package*) in a cardboard box (*secondary package*) in a corrugated box (*shipping package*) containing six dozen bottles in cardboard boxes.

The package is the buyer's first encounter with the product. A good package draws the consumer in and encourages product choice. In effect, they can act as "five-second commercials" for the product. Packaging also affects consumers' later product experiences when they go to open the package and use the product at home. Some packages can even be attractively displayed at home. Distinctive packaging like that for Kiwi shoe polish, Altoids mints, and Absolut vodka is an important part of a brand's equity.[56]

Various factors contribute to the growing use of packaging as a marketing tool:

- *Self-service.* An increasing number of products are sold on a self-serve basis. In an average supermarket, which may stock 15,000 items, the typical shopper passes some 300 products per minute. Given that 50 percent to 70 percent of all purchases are made in the store, the effective package must perform many sales tasks: attract attention, describe the product's features, create consumer confidence, and make a favorable overall impression.
- *Consumer affluence.* Rising affluence means consumers are willing to pay a little more for the convenience, appearance, dependability, and prestige of better packages.
- *Company and brand image.* Packages contribute to instant recognition of the company or brand. In the store, they can create a billboard effect, such as Garnier Fructis with its bright green packaging in the hair care aisle.
- *Innovation opportunity.* Unique or innovative packaging such as resealable spouts can bring big benefits to consumers and profits to producers.

Packaging must achieve a number of objectives:[57]

1. Identify the brand.
2. Convey descriptive and persuasive information.
3. Facilitate product transportation and protection.
4. Assist at-home storage.
5. Aid product consumption.

To achieve these objectives and satisfy consumers' desires, marketers must choose the aesthetic and functional components of packaging correctly. Aesthetic considerations relate to a package's size and shape, material, color, text, and graphics. There are a number of factors and criteria in each area.

Color is a particularly important aspect of packaging and carries different meanings in different cultures and market segments. 📖 Table 12.3 summarizes the beliefs of some visual marketing experts about its role.

Kiwi's distinctive packaging, name, and logo are all brand assets.

TABLE 12.3 📖 The Color Wheel of Branding and Packaging
Red is a powerful color, symbolizing energy, passion or even danger. Red works best for action-oriented products or brands, products associated with speed or power, or dominant or iconic brands.
Orange often connotes adventure and fun. Like red, it's an attention-grabber and is thought to stimulate appetites, but it's less aggressive than red can be. Orange has been used to convey value and discounts, and recently has earned young, stylish associations thanks to the fashion industry.
Yellow is equated with sunny warmth and cheeriness. Its more vibrant shades elicit feelings of well-being and are said to stimulate mental activity, so yellow is often associated with wisdom and intellect. Yellow works well for products or brands tied to sports or social activities, or for products or content looking to garner attention.
Green connotes cleanliness, freshness and renewal—and, of course, environmental friendliness—but experts warn that green now is overused in the marketplace. It is one of the most predominant, naturally occurring colors, so it often is associated with wholesome attributes. It works well for organic or recycled products, or for brands associated with health and wellness.
Blue, another naturally predominant color, is regularly associated with security, efficiency, productivity and a clearness of mind. It has become a popular color in the corporate world and particularly in the high-tech industry. Blue also symbolizes cleanliness, openness and relaxation, and works well for everything from cleaning and personal care products to spas and vacation destinations.
Purple, for centuries, has symbolized nobility and wealth, and those associations hold true today. Purple is a powerful color for luxury brands and products, or for companies that want to lend an air of mystery or uniqueness to their wares. Purple is particularly popular with females of all ages.
Pink is a stereotypically girly color associated with frilliness and warmth, and is considered to have soft, peaceful, comforting qualities. Pink works well for personal care products and baby-related brands. Pink also is associated with sweetness and works well for food marketers touting sugary treats.
Brown is a strong, earthy color that connotes honesty and dependability. Brown often is cited as a favorite color among men. Its darker shades are rich and solid, while other shades work well as a foundational color. Brown often works best in conjunction with other colors
Black is classic and strong, and is a regular fixture in marketers' color schemes as either a primary component or an accent color for font or graphics. Black can convey power, luxury, sophistication and authority, and can be used to market everything from cars and electronics to high-end hotels and financial services.
White, the color of puffy clouds and fresh snow, logically connotes purity and cleanliness. It often is used as a background or accent color to brighten a color scheme, but also it can be used liberally to create clean associations for organic foods or personal care products. White also can symbolize innovation and modernity.

Source: Elisabeth Sullivan, "Color Me Profitable," *Marketing News*, October 15, 2008, p. 8. Reprinted with permission from *Marketing News*, published by the American Marketing Association.

Functionally, structural design is crucial. The packaging elements must harmonize with each other and with pricing, advertising, and other parts of the marketing program.

Packaging updates or redesigns can occur frequently to make the brand more contemporary, relevant, or practical. Although these can have immediate impact on sales, they also can have a downside, as PepsiCo learned for its Tropicana brand.

Tropicana PepsiCo experienced great success with its Tropicana brand, acquired in 1998. Then in 2009, the company launched a redesigned package to "refresh and modernize" the brand. The goal was to create an "emotional attachment by 'heroing' the juice and trumpeting the natural fruit goodness." Arnell Group led the extreme makeover that led to an entirely new look, downplaying the brand name, raising the prominence of the phrase "100 percent orange pure & natural," and replacing the "straw in an orange" graphic on the front of the package with a close-up of a glass of orange juice. Consumer response was swift and negative. The package looked "ugly" or "stupid," and some even confused it with a store brand. Sales dropped 20 percent. After only two months, PepsiCo management announced it would revert to the old packaging.[58]

After the company designs its packaging, it must test it. *Engineering tests* ensure that the package stands up under normal conditions; *visual tests,* that the script is legible and the colors harmonious; *dealer tests,* that dealers find the packages attractive and easy to handle; and *consumer tests,* that buyers will respond favorably. Eye tracking by hidden cameras can assess how much consumers notice and examine packages. For Comtrex cold medicine, tracking research was able to confirm that only 50 percent of consumers considered the old package on the shelf, versus 62 percent for a newly redesigned package.[59]

Although developing effective packaging may require several months and several hundred thousand dollars, companies must consider growing environmental and safety concerns about reducing packaging. Fortunately, many companies have gone "green" and are finding creative new ways to develop packaging. Frito-Lay's Sun Chips multigrain snacks, containing 30 percent less fat than potato chips, are positioned as a healthier, "good for you" snack option. Part of the firm's effort to also support a "healthier planet" was to unveil a fully compostable bag made from plant-based materials (although later withdrawn for some flavors when consumers complained of the noise the bags made) and to run its factory in Modesto on solar power.

Marketers must balance competing demands in their packaging; Sun Chips' environmentally friendly packaging was cut back shortly after its launch because many consumers complained about how noisy the bags were.

Labeling

The label can be a simple attached tag or an elaborately designed graphic that is part of the package. It might carry a great deal of information, or only the brand name. Even if the seller prefers a simple label, the law may require more.

A label performs several functions. First, it *identifies* the product or brand—for instance, the name Sunkist stamped on oranges. It might also *grade* the product; canned peaches are grade-labeled A, B, and C. The label might *describe* the product: who made it, where and when, what it contains, how it is to be used, and how to use it safely. Finally, the label might *promote* the product through attractive graphics. Advanced technology allows 360-degree shrink-wrapped labels to surround containers with bright graphics and accommodate more product information, replacing glued-on paper labels.[60]

Labels eventually need freshening up. The label on Ivory soap has been redone at least 18 times since the 1890s, with gradual changes in the size and design of the letters. As Tropicana found out, companies with labels that have become icons need to tread very carefully when initiating a redesign to preserve key branding elements.

A long history of legal concerns surrounds labels, as well as packaging. In 1914, the Federal Trade Commission Act held that false, misleading, or deceptive labels or packages constitute unfair competition. The Fair Packaging and Labeling Act, passed by Congress in 1967, set mandatory labeling requirements, encouraged voluntary industry packaging standards, and allowed federal agencies to set packaging regulations in specific industries.

The Food and Drug Administration (FDA) has required processed-food producers to include nutritional labeling that clearly states the amounts of protein, fat, carbohydrates, and calories contained in products, as well as vitamin and mineral content as a percentage of the recommended daily allowance.[61] The FDA has also taken action against potentially misleading uses of such descriptions as "light," "high fiber," and "low fat."

Warranties and Guarantees

All sellers are legally responsible for fulfilling a buyer's normal or reasonable expectations. **Warranties** are formal statements of expected product performance by the manufacturer. Products under warranty can be returned to the manufacturer or designated repair center for repair, replacement, or refund. Whether expressed or implied, warranties are legally enforceable.

Extended warranties and service contracts can be extremely lucrative for manufacturers and retailers. Analysts estimate that warranty sales have accounted for a large percentage of Best Buy's operating profits.[62] Despite evidence that extended warranties do not pay off, some consumers value the peace of mind.[63] These warranties still generate multibillion dollars in revenue for electronic goods in the United States, though the total has declined as consumers have become more comfortable seeking solutions to technical problems online or from friends.[64]

Many sellers offer either general or specific guarantees.[65] A company such as Procter & Gamble promises general or complete satisfaction without being more specific—"If you are not satisfied for any reason, return for replacement, exchange, or refund." A. T. Cross guarantees its Cross pens and pencils for life. The customer mails the pen to A. T. Cross (mailers are provided at stores), and the pen is repaired or replaced at no charge.

Guarantees reduce the buyer's perceived risk. They suggest that the product is of high quality and the company and its service performance are dependable. They can be especially helpful when the company or product is not well known or when the product's quality is superior to that of competitors. Hyundai's and Kia's highly successful 10-year or 100,000 mile power train warranty programs were designed in part to assure potential buyers of the quality of the products and the companies' stability.

Summary

1. Product is the first and most important element of the marketing mix. Product strategy calls for making coordinated decisions on product mixes, product lines, brands, and packaging and labeling.

2. In planning its market offering, the marketer needs to think through the five levels of the product: the core benefit, the basic product, the expected product, the augmented product, and the potential product, which encompasses all the augmentations and transformations the product might ultimately undergo.

3. Products can be nondurable goods, durable goods, or services. In the consumer-goods category are convenience goods (staples, impulse goods, emergency goods), shopping goods (homogeneous and heterogeneous), specialty goods, and unsought goods. The industrial-goods category has three subcategories: materials and parts (raw materials and manufactured materials and parts), capital items (installations and equipment), and supplies and business services (operating supplies, maintenance and repair items, maintenance and repair services, and business advisory services).

4. Brands can be differentiated on the basis of product form, features, performance, conformance, durability, reliability, repairability, style, and design, as well as such service dimensions as ordering ease, delivery, installation, customer training, customer consulting, and maintenance and repair.

5. Design is the totality of features that affect how a product looks, feels, and functions. A well-designed product offers

functional and aesthetic benefits to consumers and can be an important source of differentiation.

6. Most companies sell more than one product. A product mix can be classified according to width, length, depth, and consistency. These four dimensions are the tools for developing the company's marketing strategy and deciding which product lines to grow, maintain, harvest, and divest. To analyze a product line and decide how many resources to invest in it, product line managers need to look at sales and profits and market profile.

7. A company can change the product component of its marketing mix by lengthening its product via line stretching (down-market, up-market, or both) or line filling, by modernizing its products, by featuring certain products, and by pruning its products to eliminate the least profitable.

8. Brands are often sold or marketed jointly with other brands. Ingredient brands and co-brands can add value, assuming they have equity and are perceived as fitting appropriately.

9. Physical products must be packaged and labeled. Well-designed packages can create convenience value for customers and promotional value for producers. Warranties and guarantees can offer further assurance to consumers.

Applications

Marketing Debate
With Products, Is It Form or Function?

The "form versus function" debate applies in many arenas, including marketing. Some marketers believe product performance is the be-all and end-all. Other marketers maintain that the look, feel, and other design elements of products are what really make the difference.

Take a position: Product functionality is the key to brand success *versus* Product design is the key to brand success.

Marketing Discussion
Product & Service Differentiation

Consider the different means of differentiating products and services. Which ones have the most impact on your choices? Why? Can you think of certain brands that excel on a number of these different means of differentiation?

Marketing Excellence
>>Caterpillar

Caterpillar was founded in 1925 when two California-based tractor companies merged. The name "Caterpillar," however, dates back to the early 1900s when Benjamin Holt, one of the company's founders, designed a tractor crawler with wide, thick tracks instead of wheels. These tracks prevented the machine from sinking into California's deep, rich soil, which was impassable when wet. The new farm tractor crept along the farmland in such a way that one observer said it "crawled like a caterpillar."

Holt sold the tractor under the Caterpillar brand, and once the merger occurred, the newly formed company became Caterpillar Tractor Company. Since then, Caterpillar Inc., or CAT, has grown into the largest manufacturer of earth-moving equipment and engines in the world. With over 300 different machines for sale, Caterpillar offers product solutions for eight industries: residential, nonresidential, industrial, infrastructure, mining and quarrying, energy, waste, and forestry. Its distinctive yellow machines are found all over the globe and have helped make the brand a U.S. icon.

So how did a small tractor company grow to become one of the biggest companies in the world? The company grew steadily at first, hitting a few critical milestones including the use of Caterpillar's trademark farm treads on Army tanks in WWI and WWII. Huge postwar construction and strong overseas demand kept sales strong through the mid-21st century, as did innovations like the diesel tractor and rubber-tired tractors.

Things changed, however, when the recession of the early 1980s hit Caterpillar hard and international competitors gained market share, including Japan's Komatsu. Caterpillar's high prices and inflexible bureaucracy nearly sent the company into bankruptcy. In 1982 alone, the firm lost $6.5 billion, laid off thousands of employees, closed several factories, and suffered a long United Auto Workers strike.

In the 1990s, Caterpillar recognized that it desperately needed to change, and under new leadership it successfully pulled off one of the biggest turnarounds in corporate history. Several factors played a role.

- Caterpillar boldly fought the United Auto Workers and outlasted two strikes and seven years of disagreements.

- It decentralized and restructured into several business units, each responsible for its own P&L.

- It invested a significant amount of money (ultimately $1.8 billion) in a factory-modernizing program that automated and streamlined its manufacturing process with a combination of just-in-time inventory and flexible manufacturing. By automating its manufacturing system, the company became more efficient and competitive, although it also was forced to lay off more of its workforce.

- It made research and development one of its biggest priorities, investing hundreds of millions of dollars in new technologies, products, and machines. As a result, CAT construction trucks became more high-tech, competitive, and environmentally friendly.

Today, Caterpillar ranks number one or number two in every industry it serves. Its products are unmatched in quality and reliability and the company has maintained its strong focus on innovation. With a $2 billion annual research and development budget, new products are launched every year. Recent innovations include hybrid diesel-electric tractors—the first of their kind—and lower-emission engines with ACERT technology, a clean-diesel technology that also improves fuel efficiency.

Caterpillar's product range is immense. From a small 47 horsepower skid steer to an 850 horsepower tractor to a massive 3,370 horsepower mining truck, the firm develops products that serve each market and region's specific needs. In China, for example, a critical market to the future of Caterpillar, the company has divided its product strategy into three segments: World Class, Mid-Tier, and Low-End. Caterpillar is focused on innovating high-tech machinery for the growing World Class segment and leaving the Low-End segment to local competitors that will eventually be consolidated.

Another reason for Caterpillar's dominance in the market is its business model. Caterpillar sells it all: machines, services, and support for a wide range of industries. Fifty-three percent of its sales come from products and the rest from integrated services. Caterpillar accomplishes this feat through its extensive Global Dealer Network—specially trained independent CAT dealers who can provide services on a local basis, giving the global company a personal feel.

Feeling local is important considering that 56 percent of Caterpillar's business comes from overseas, making it one of the United States' biggest exporters. Caterpillar has been a leader in building roads, bridges, highways, and airports all over the world. In developing cities like Antamin, Peru, for example, which is abundant in copper, large mining companies spend hundreds of millions of dollars on CAT machinery and services each year. Up to 50 different kinds of CAT bulldozers, front loaders, excavators, and special mining trucks help clear roads, clean up spills, and dig for copper. These massive trucks are all manufactured in Decatur, Illinois, shipped in pieces, and assembled at the job site.

Caterpillar's sales hit $51 billion in 2008 and dropped to $32 billion in 2009 due to the recession. Japan's Komatsu remains a distant number two, with less than half the sales of Caterpillar. Caterpillar maintains 50 production facilities in the United States and 60 overseas, selling products in over 200 countries.

What's next for Caterpillar? As the company moves forward, it remains focused on reducing greenhouse gas emissions in its machinery, innovating more green technologies, maintaining its strong brand, and investing in the future of emerging countries like India and China. The company believes that in order to grow, it must be successful in emerging markets.

Questions

1. What were some of the key steps that led to Caterpillar's becoming the industry leader in earth-moving machinery?

2. Discuss Caterpillar's future. What should it do next with its product line? Where is the future growth for this company?

Sources: Green Rankings, The 2009 List," *Newsweek*, http://greenrankings.newsweek.com; Tim McKeough, "The Caterpillar Self-Driving Dump Truck," *Fast Company*, December 1, 2008; Alex Taylor III, "Caterpillar: Big Trucks, Big Sales, Big Attitude," *Fortune*, August 13, 2007; Tudor Van Hampton, "A New Heavyweight Among Hybrids," *New York Times*, January 21, 2010; Steven Pearlstein, "After Caterpillar's Turnaround, A Chance to Reinvent Globalization," *Washington Post*, April 19, 2006; Dale Buss, "CAT Is Back: An Icon That Once Seemed Headed for the Dustbin, Caterpillar Has Made an Impressive Turnaround. Here's How," *Chief Executive*, July 2005; Jessie Scanlon, "Caterpillar Rolls Out Its Hybrid D7E Tractor," *BusinessWeek*, July 20, 2009; Caterpillar, Inc. supporting materials at CLSA Asia USA Forum; www.cat.com.

Marketing Excellence

>>Toyota

In 1936, Toyota admitted following Chrysler's landmark Airflow and patterning its engine after a 1933 Chevrolet engine. But by 2000, when it introduced the first hybrid electric-gasoline car, the Prius, Toyota was the leader. In 2002, when the second-generation Prius hit showrooms, dealers received 10,000 orders before the car was even available. GM followed with an announcement that it would enter the hybrid market with models of its own.

Toyota offers a full line of cars for the U.S. market, from family sedans and sport utility vehicles to trucks and minivans. It has products for different price points, from lower-cost Scions to mid-priced Camrys to the luxury Lexus. Designing these different products means listening to different customers, building the cars they want, and then crafting marketing to reinforce each make's image.

After four years of carefully listening to teens, for instance, Toyota learned that the Scion's target age group of 16- to 21-year-olds wanted personalization. So it builds the car "mono-spec" at the factory, with just one well-equipped trim level, and lets customers choose from over 40 customization elements at dealerships, from stereo components to wheels and even floor mats. Toyota markets the Scion at music events and has showrooms where "young people feel comfortable hanging out and not a place where they just go stare at a car," said Scion Vice President Jim Letz.

In contrast, the tagline for the Lexus global strategy is "Passionate Pursuit of Perfection." Dealerships offer white-glove treatment, though Toyota understands that each country defines perfection differently. In the United States, perfection and luxury mean comfort, size, and dependability. In Europe, luxury means attention to detail and brand heritage. Thus, although Toyota maintains a consistent Lexus visual vocabulary, logo, font, and overall communication, the advertising varies by country.

Another big reason behind Toyota's success is its manufacturing. The firm is the master of lean manufacturing and continuous improvement. Its plants can make as many as eight different models at the same time, bringing huge increases in productivity and market responsiveness. And Toyota relentlessly innovates. A typical Toyota assembly line makes thousands of operational changes in the course of a single year. Toyota employees see their purpose as threefold: making cars, making cars better, and teaching everyone how to make cars better. The company encourages problem solving, always looking to improve the process by which it improves all other processes.

Toyota is integrating its assembly plants around the world into a single giant network. The plants will customize cars for local markets and shift production quickly to satisfy any surges in demand from markets worldwide. With a manufacturing network, Toyota can build a wide variety of models much more inexpensively. That means it will be able to fill market niches as they emerge without building whole new assembly operations. "If there's a market or market segment where they aren't present, they go there," said Tatsuo Yoshida, auto analyst at Deutsche Securities Ltd. And with consumers increasingly fickle about what they want in a car, such market agility gives Toyota a huge competitive edge.

In 2006, Toyota earned over $11 billion—more than all other major automakers *combined*. In 2007, it edged past General Motors to become the world's largest carmaker. And, in 2008, it manufactured 9.2 million vehicles, 1 million more than GM and almost 3 million more than Volkswagen.

Over the years, Toyota's automobiles have consistently ranked high in quality and reliability. That all changed in 2009 and 2010, however, when Toyota experienced a massive recall of over 8 million of its vehicles. A variety of problems ranging from sticking accelerator pedals to sudden acceleration to software glitches in the braking system affected many Toyota brands, including Lexus, Prius, Camry, Corolla, and Tundra.

Not only had these mechanical defects caused numerous crashes, they were linked to the deaths of over 50 people. Toyota's President Akio Toyoda testified before Congress and offered an explanation of what went wrong: "We pursued growth over the speed at which we were able to develop our people and our organization. I regret that this has resulted in the safety issues described in the recalls we face today, and I am deeply sorry for any accidents that Toyota drivers have experienced."

Analysts estimated the worldwide recall will cost Toyota $2 billion to $6 billion including repair costs, legal settlements, and lost sales. Market share dropped 4 percent in the first three months of the recall and was expected to drop even further as problems continued to unfold. Hoping to bring consumers back to the Toyota brand, the company offered incentives such as two years of free maintenance and zero-percent financing.

While Toyota rides the recall storm of 2010 and faces some challenging times, it can be comforted by the fact that it continues to lead the industry in a wide range of areas including lean manufacturing and environmentally friendly technologies.

Questions

1. Toyota has built a huge manufacturing company that can produce millions of cars each year for a wide variety of consumers. Why was it able to grow so much bigger than any other auto manufacturer?

2. Has Toyota done the right thing by manufacturing a car brand for everyone? Why or why not?

3. Did Toyota grow too quickly as Toyoda suggested? What should the company do over the next year, 5 years, and 10 years? How can growing companies avoid quality problems in the future?

Sources: Martin Zimmerman, "Toyota's First Quarter Global Sales Beat GM's Preliminary Numbers," *Los Angeles Times*, April 24, 2007; Charles Fishman, "No Satisfaction at Toyota," *Fast Company,* December 2006–January 2007, pp. 82–90; Stuart F. Brown, "Toyota's Global Body Shop," *Fortune*, February 9, 2004, p. 120; James B. Treece, "Ford Down; Toyota Aims for No. 1," *Automotive News*, February 2, 2004, p. 1; Brian Demner and Chester Dawson, "Can Anything Stop Toyota?" *BusinessWeek*, November 17, 2003, pp. 114–22; Tomoko A. Hosaka, "Toyota Counts Rising Costs of Recall Woes," *Associated Press,* March 16, 2010; "World Motor Vehicle Production by Manufacturer," *OICA*, July 2009; Chris Isidore, "Toyota Recall Costs: $2 billion," http://money.cnn.com, February 4, 2010; www.toyota.com.

Chapter 13

In This Chapter, We Will Address the Following Questions

1. How do we define and classify services, and how do they differ from goods?

2. What are the new services realities?

3. How can we achieve excellence in services marketing?

4. How can we improve service quality?

5. How can goods marketers improve customer-support services?

The unconventional Cirque du Soleil organization creates memorable experiences for its audiences through its creative redefinition of the circus concept.

Designing and Managing Services

As product companies find it harder and harder to differentiate their physical products, they turn to service differentiation. Many in fact find significant profitability in delivering superior service, whether that means on-time delivery, better and faster answering of inquiries, or quicker resolution of complaints. Top service providers know these advantages well and also how to create memorable customer experiences.[1]

 In its 25-year history, Cirque du Soleil (French for "circus of the sun") has continually broken loose from circus convention. It takes traditional ingredients such as trapeze artists, clowns, muscle men, and contortionists and places them in a nontraditional setting with lavish costumes, new age music, and spectacular stage designs. And it eliminates other commonly observed circus elements—there are no animals. Each production is loosely tied together with a theme such as "a tribute to the nomadic soul" (Varekai) or "a phantasmagoria of urban life" (Saltimbanco). The group has grown from its Quebec street-performance roots to become a half-billion-dollar global enterprise, with 3,000 employees on four continents entertaining audiences of millions annually.

Part of its success comes from a company culture that encourages artistic creativity and innovation and carefully safeguards the brand. One new production is created each year—always in-house— and is unique: There are no duplicate touring companies. In addition to Cirque's mix of media and local promotion, an extensive interactive e-mail program to its million-plus-member Cirque Club creates an online community of fans—20 percent to 30 percent of all ticket sales come from club members. Generating $800 million in revenue annually, the Cirque du Soleil brand has expanded to encompass a record label, a retail operation, and resident productions in Las Vegas (five in all), Orlando, Tokyo, and other cities.[2]

Because it is critical to understand the special nature of services and what that means to marketers, in this chapter we systematically analyze services and how to market them most effectively.

The Nature of Services

The Bureau of Labor Statistics reports that the service-producing sector will continue to be the dominant employment generator in the economy, adding about 14.6 million jobs through 2018, or 96 percent of the expected increase in total employment. By 2018, the goods-producing sector is expected to account for 12.9 percent of total jobs, down from 17.3 percent in 1998 and 14.2 percent in 2008. Manufacturing lost 4.1 million jobs from 1998 through 2008 and is expected to lose another 1.2 million jobs between 2008 and 2018.[3] These numbers and others have led to a growing interest in the special problems of marketing services.[4]

Service Industries Are Everywhere

The *government sector,* with its courts, employment services, hospitals, loan agencies, military services, police and fire departments, postal service, regulatory agencies, and schools, is in the service business. The *private nonprofit sector*—museums, charities, churches, colleges, foundations, and hospitals—is in the service business. A good part of the *business sector,* with its airlines, banks, hotels, insurance companies, law firms, management consulting firms, medical practices, motion picture companies, plumbing repair companies, and real estate firms, is in the service business. Many workers in the *manufacturing sector,* such as computer operators, accountants, and legal staff, are really service providers. In fact, they make up a "service factory" providing services to the "goods factory." And those in the *retail sector,* such as cashiers, clerks, salespeople, and customer service representatives, are also providing a service.

A **service** is any act or performance one party can offer to another that is essentially intangible and does not result in the ownership of anything. Its production may or may not be tied to a physical product. Increasingly, manufacturers, distributors, and retailers are providing value-added services, or simply excellent customer service, to differentiate themselves. Many pure service firms are now using the Internet to reach customers; some are purely online. Monster.com's Webby-award-winning site offers online career advice and employment recruiting. Done right, improvements or innovations in customer service can have a big payoff, as Zipcar found.

Zipcar   Car sharing started in Europe as a means to extend public transportation. In the United States the appeal of Zipcar, the market leader and pioneer, is both environmental and economic. With a $50 membership fee and rates that total less than $100 a day—which includes gas, insurance, and parking—a typical family could save $3,000 to $4,000 a year by substituting Zipcar use for car ownership. Zipcar's fleet includes all types of popular models—BMWs, Volvos, pickup trucks, and even MINI Coopers and the Toyota Prius hybrid—and the firm estimates that every car it adds keeps up to 20 private cars off the road. Consumers—and an increasing number of universities and businesses—book online and use a sophisticated reservation system to reserve a specific car in their neighborhood. There are a number of rules for car care (such as no smoking) and logistics (such as calling to extend a reservation if running late). As CEO Scott Griffith states, "Our business model depends on the kindness of others." To help increase awareness, Zipcar slaps its logo on the side of all but the high-end luxury models. Unusual marketing stunts such as a contest to guess how many Swedish meatballs had been stuffed into a MINI Cooper parked in an IKEA parking lot also help to spread the word. Targeting major cities and college towns, the company is growing about 30 percent a year.[5]

Zipcar offers its fast-growing customer base a practical, environmentally friendly alternative to car ownership.

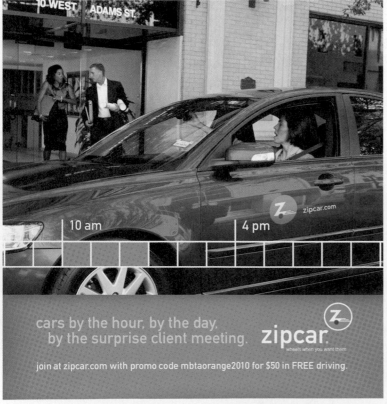

Categories of Service Mix

The service component can be a minor or a major part of the total offering. We distinguish five categories of offerings:

1. *Pure tangible good*—a tangible good such as soap, toothpaste, or salt with no accompanying services.
2. *Tangible good with accompanying services*—a tangible good, like a car, computer, or cell phone, accompanied by one or more services. Typically, the more technologically advanced the product, the greater the need for high-quality supporting services.
3. *Hybrid*—an offering, like a restaurant meal, of equal parts goods and services. People patronize restaurants for both the food and its preparation.

4. **Major service with accompanying minor goods and services**—a major service, like air travel, with additional services or supporting goods such as snacks and drinks. This offering requires a capital-intensive good—an airplane—for its realization, but the primary item is a service.
5. **Pure service**—primarily an intangible service, such as babysitting, psychotherapy, or massage.

The range of service offerings makes it difficult to generalize without a few further distinctions.

- Services vary as to whether they are *equipment based* (automated car washes, vending machines) or *people based* (window washing, accounting services). People-based services vary by whether unskilled, skilled, or professional workers provide them.
- Service companies can choose among different *processes* to deliver their service. Restaurants offer cafeteria-style, fast-food, buffet, and candlelight service formats.
- Some services need the *client's presence*. Brain surgery requires the client's presence, a car repair does not. If the client must be present, the service provider must be considerate of his or her needs. Thus beauty salon operators will invest in décor, play background music, and engage in light conversation with the client.
- Services may meet a *personal need* (personal services) or a *business need* (business services). Service providers typically develop different marketing programs for these markets.
- Service providers differ in their *objectives* (profit or nonprofit) and *ownership* (private or public). These two characteristics, when crossed, produce four quite different types of organizations. The marketing programs of a private investor hospital will differ from those of a private charity hospital or a Veterans Administration hospital.[6]

Customers typically cannot judge the technical quality of some services even after they have received them. △ Figure 13.1 shows various products and services according to difficulty of evaluation.[7] At the left are goods high in *search qualities*—that is, characteristics the buyer can evaluate before purchase. In the middle are goods and services high in *experience qualities*—characteristics the buyer can evaluate after purchase. At the right are goods and services high in *credence qualities*—characteristics the buyer normally finds hard to evaluate even after consumption.[8]

Because services are generally high in experience and credence qualities, there is more risk in their purchase, with several consequences. First, service consumers generally rely on word of mouth rather than advertising. Second, they rely heavily on price, provider, and physical cues to judge quality. Third, they are highly loyal to service providers who satisfy them. Fourth, because switching costs are high, consumer inertia can make it challenging to entice business away from a competitor.

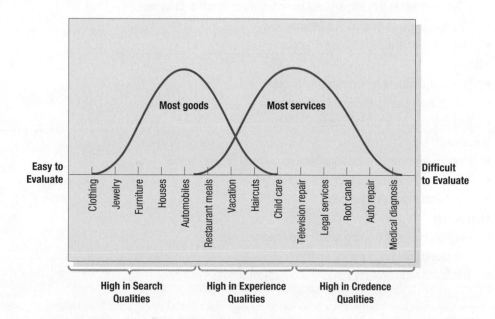

|Fig. 13.1| △

Continuum of Evaluation for Different Types of Products

Source: Valarie A. Zeithaml, "How Consumer Evaluation Processes Differ between Goods and Services," James H. Donnelly and William R. George, eds., *Marketing of Services* (Chicago: American Marketing Association, 1981). Reprinted with permission of the American Marketing Association.

Distinctive Characteristics of Services

Four distinctive service characteristics greatly affect the design of marketing programs: *intangibility, inseparability, variability,* and *perishability*.[9]

INTANGIBILITY Unlike physical products, services cannot be seen, tasted, felt, heard, or smelled before they are bought. A person getting cosmetic surgery cannot see the results before the purchase, and the patient in the psychiatrist's office cannot know the exact outcome of treatment. To reduce uncertainty, buyers will look for evidence of quality by drawing inferences from the place, people, equipment, communication material, symbols, and price. Therefore, the service provider's task is to "manage the evidence," to "tangibilize the intangible."[10]

Service companies can try to demonstrate their service quality through *physical evidence* and *presentation*.[11] Suppose a bank wants to position itself as the "fast" bank. It could make this positioning strategy tangible through any number of marketing tools:

1. *Place*—The exterior and interior should have clean lines. The layout of the desks and the traffic flow should be planned carefully. Waiting lines should not get overly long.
2. *People*—Employees should be busy, but there should be a sufficient number to manage the workload.
3. *Equipment*—Computers, copy machines, desks, and ATMs should look like, and be, state of the art.
4. *Communication material*—Printed materials—text and photos—should suggest efficiency and speed.
5. *Symbols*—The bank's name and symbol could suggest fast service.
6. *Price*—The bank could advertise that it will deposit $5 in the account of any customer who waits in line more than five minutes.

Service marketers must be able to transform intangible services into concrete benefits and a well-defined experience.[12] Disney is a master at "tangibilizing the intangible" and creating magical fantasies in its theme parks; so are companies such as Jamba Juice and Barnes & Noble in their respective retail stores.[13] 📖 Table 13.1 measures brand experiences in general along sensory, affective, behavioral, and intellectual dimensions. Applications to services are clear.

TABLE 13.1 📖 Dimensions of Brand Experience
Sensory
• This brand makes a strong impression on my visual sense or other senses.
• I find this brand interesting in a sensory way.
• This brand does not appeal to my senses.
Affective
• This brand induces feelings and sentiments.
• I do not have strong emotions for this brand.
• This brand is an emotional brand.
Behavioral
• I engage in physical actions and behaviors when I use this brand.
• This brand results in bodily experiences.
• This brand is not action-oriented.
Intellectual
• I engage in a lot of thinking when I encounter this brand.
• This brand does not make me think.
• This brand stimulates my curiosity and problem solving.

Source: Joško Brakus, Bernd H. Schmitt, and Lia Zarantonello, "Brand Experience: What Is It? How Is It Measured? Does It Affect Loyalty?" *Journal of Marketing* 73 (May 2009), pp. 52–68. Reprinted with permission from *Journal of Marketing*, published by the American Marketing Association.

Because there is no physical product, the service provider's facilities—its primary and secondary signage, environmental design and reception area, employee apparel, collateral material, and so on—are especially important. All aspects of the service delivery process can be branded, which is why Allied Van Lines is concerned about the appearance of its drivers and laborers, why UPS has developed such strong equity with its brown trucks, and why Hilton's Doubletree Hotels offers fresh-baked chocolate chip cookies to symbolize care and friendliness.[14]

Service providers often choose brand elements—logos, symbols, characters, and slogans—to make the service and its key benefits more tangible—for example, the "friendly skies" of United, the "good hands" of Allstate, and the "bullish" nature of Merrill Lynch.

INSEPARABILITY Whereas physical goods are manufactured, then inventoried, then distributed, and later consumed, services are typically produced and consumed simultaneously.[15] A haircut can't be stored—or produced without the barber. The provider is part of the service. Because the client is also often present, provider–client interaction is a special feature of services marketing. Buyers of entertainment and professional services are very interested in the specific provider. It's not the same concert if Taylor Swift is indisposed and replaced by Beyoncé, or if a corporate legal defense is supplied by an intern because antitrust expert David Boies is unavailable. When clients have strong provider preferences, the provider can raise its price to ration its limited time.

Several strategies exist for getting around the limitations of inseparability. The service provider can work with larger groups. Some psychotherapists have moved from one-on-one therapy to small-group therapy to groups of over 300 people in a large hotel ballroom. The service provider can work faster—the psychotherapist can spend 30 more efficient minutes with each patient instead of 50 less-structured minutes and thus see more patients. The service organization can train more service providers and build up client confidence, as H&R Block has done with its national network of trained tax consultants.

VARIABILITY Because the quality of services depends on who provides them, when and where, and to whom, services are highly variable. Some doctors have an excellent bedside manner; others are less empathic.

A different entertainer creates a different concert experience—a Beyoncé concert is not the same as a Taylor Swift concert.

Service buyers are aware of this variability and often talk to others before selecting a service provider. To reassure customers, some firms offer *service guarantees* that may reduce consumer perceptions of risk.[16] Here are three steps service firms can take to increase quality control.

1. ***Invest in good hiring and training procedures.*** Recruiting the right employees and providing them with excellent training is crucial, regardless of whether employees are highly skilled professionals or low-skilled workers. Better-trained personnel exhibit six characteristics: Competence, courtesy, credibility, reliability, responsiveness, and communication.[17] Given the diverse nature of its customer base in California, banking and mortgage giant Wells Fargo actively seeks and trains a diverse workforce. The average Wells Fargo customer uses 5.2 different bank products, roughly twice the industry average, thanks in part to the teamwork of its highly motivated staff.[18]

2. ***Standardize the service-performance process throughout the organization.*** A *service blueprint* can map out the service process, the points of customer contact, and the evidence of service from the customer's point of view.[19] △ Figure 13.2 shows a service blueprint for a guest spending a night at a hotel.[20] Behind the scenes, the hotel must skillfully help the guest move from one step to the next. Service blueprints can be helpful in developing new service, supporting a zero-defects culture, and devising service recovery strategies.

3. ***Monitor customer satisfaction.*** Employ suggestion and complaint systems, customer surveys, and comparison shopping. Customer needs may vary in different areas, allowing firms to develop region-specific customer satisfaction programs.[21] Firms can also develop customer information databases and systems for more personalized service, especially online.[22]

Because services are a subjective experience, service firms can also design marketing communication and information programs so consumers learn more about the brand than what they get from service encounters alone.

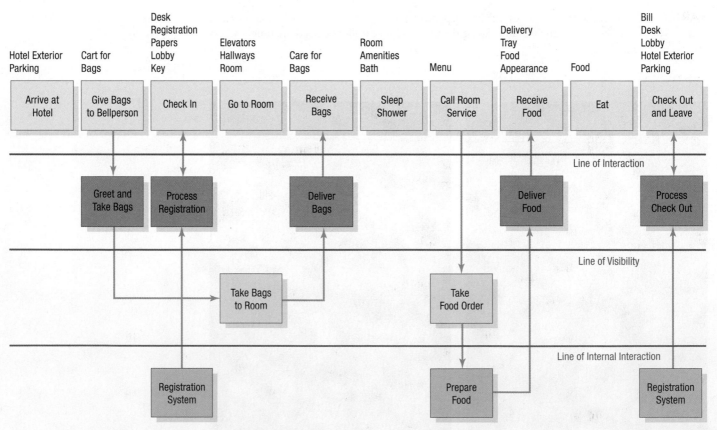

|Fig. 13.2| △

Blueprint for Overnight Hotel Stay

Source: Valarie Zeithaml, Mary Jo Bitner, and Dwayne D. Gremler, *Services Marketing: Integrating Customer Focus across the Firm*, 4th ed. (New York: McGraw-Hill, 2006).

PERISHABILITY Services cannot be stored, so their perishability can be a problem when demand fluctuates. Public transportation companies must own much more equipment because of rush-hour demand than if demand were even throughout the day. Some doctors charge patients for missed appointments because the service value (the doctor's availability) exists only at the time of the appointment.

Demand or yield management is critical—the right services must be available to the right customers at the right places at the right times and right prices to maximize profitability. Several strategies can produce a better match between service demand and supply.[23] On the demand side:

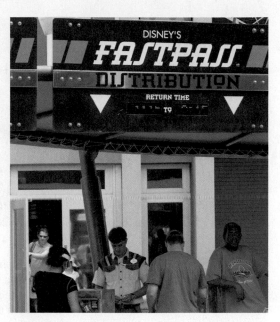

- *Differential pricing* will shift some demand from peak to off-peak periods. Examples include low matinee movie prices and weekend discounts for car rentals.[24]
- *Nonpeak demand* can be cultivated. McDonald's pushes breakfast service, and hotels promote minivacation weekends.
- *Complementary services* can provide alternatives to waiting customers, such as cocktail lounges in restaurants and automated teller machines in banks.
- *Reservation systems* are a way to manage the demand level. Airlines, hotels, and physicians employ them extensively.

On the supply side:

- *Part-time employees* can serve peak demand. Colleges add part-time teachers when enrollment goes up; stores hire extra clerks during holiday periods.
- *Peak-time efficiency* routines can allow employees to perform only essential tasks during peak periods. Paramedics assist physicians during busy periods.
- *Increased consumer participation* frees service providers' time. Consumers fill out their own medical records or bag their own groceries.
- *Shared services* can improve offerings. Several hospitals can share medical-equipment purchases.
- *Facilities for future expansion* can be a good investment. An amusement park buys surrounding land for later development.

Disney's innovative FASTPASS system helps to match supply and demand for its Disney World theme park rides.

Many airlines, hotels, and resorts e-mail short-term discounts and special promotions to self-selected customers. After 40 years of making people stand in line at its theme parks, Disney instituted FASTPASS, which allows visitors to reserve a spot in line and eliminate the wait. Polls revealed 95 percent like the change. Disney's vice president, Dale Stafford, told a reporter, "We have been teaching people how to stand in line since 1955, and now we are telling them they don't have to. Of all the things we can do and all the marvels we can create with the attractions, this is something that will have a profound effect on the entire industry."[25]

The New Services Realities

Service firms once lagged behind manufacturers in their use of marketing because they were small, or they were professional businesses that did not use marketing, or they faced large demand or little competition. This has certainly changed. Some of the most skilled marketers now are service firms. One that wins praise for its marketing success is Singapore Airlines.

Singapore Airlines (SIA) Singapore Airlines is consistently recognized as the world's "best" airline—it wins so many awards, it has to update its Web site monthly to keep up to date—in large part due to its stellar holistic marketing. Famous for pampering passengers, SIA continually strives to create a "wow effect" and surpass customers' expectations. It was the first to launch individual video screens at airplane seats. Thanks to the first-of-its-kind $1 million simulator SIA built to mimic the air pressure and humidity inside a plane, the carrier found that taste buds change in the air and that, among other things, it needed to cut back on spices in its food. SIA places a high value on training; its "Transforming Customer Service (TCS)" program includes staff in five key operational areas: cabin crew, engineering, ground services, flight operations, and sales support. The TCS culture is also embedded in all management training, company-wide. It

Singapore Airlines goes to extraordinary lengths to ensure that every aspect of the passenger experience exceeds expectations.

applies a 40-30-30 rule in its holistic approach to people, processes, and products: 40 percent of resources go to training and invigorating staff, 30 percent to reviewing process and procedures, and 30 percent to creating new product and service ideas. With its innovatively designed Boeing 777-300 ERS and Airbus A380 planes, SIA set new standards of comforts in all classes of service, from eight private minirooms in first class to wider seats, AC power supplies, and USB ports in coach.[26]

A Shifting Customer Relationship

Not all companies, however, have invested in providing superior service, at least not to all customers. In many service industries, such as airlines, banks, stores, and hotels, customer satisfaction in the United States has not significantly improved—or in some cases actually dropped—in recent years.[27] Customers complain about inaccurate information; unresponsive, rude, or poorly trained workers; and long wait times. Even worse, many find their complaints never actually reach a live human being because of slow or faulty phone or online reporting systems.

It doesn't have to be that way. Fifty-five operators handle 100,000 calls a year on Butterball Turkeys' 800 number—10,000 on Thanksgiving Day alone—about how to prepare, cook, and serve turkeys. Trained at Butterball University, the operators have all cooked turkeys dozens of different ways and can handle the myriad queries that come their way, including why customers shouldn't stash turkeys in snow banks or thaw them in bathtubs.[28]

Savvy services marketers are recognizing the new services realities, such as the importance of the newly empowered customer, customer coproduction, and the need to engage employees as well as customers.

Customer service dissatisfaction increasingly goes viral—Canadian singer Dave Carroll's musical frustration with United Airlines was downloaded by millions.

CUSTOMER EMPOWERMENT Customers are becoming more sophisticated about buying product-support services and are pressing for "unbundled services." They may desire separate prices for each service element and the right to select the elements they want. Customers also increasingly dislike having to deal with a multitude of service providers handling different types of equipment. Some third-party service organizations now service a greater range of equipment.

Most importantly, the Internet has empowered customers by letting them vent their rage about bad service—or reward good service—and send their comments around the world with a mouse click. Although a person who has a good customer experience is more likely to talk about it, someone who has a bad experience will talk to more people.[29] Ninety percent of angry customers reported sharing their story with a friend. Now, they can share their stories with strangers too. At PlanetFeedback.com, shoppers can send a complaint, compliment, suggestion, or question directly to a company, with the option to post comments publicly on the site as well.

United Breaks Guitars When Canadian singer Dave Carroll faced $1,200 in damages to his $3,000 Gibson guitar after a United flight, he put his creative energy to good use. He created a humorous video, *United Breaks Guitars*, and launched it on YouTube with this catchy refrain:

"United, you broke my Taylor guitar. United, some big help you are. You broke it, you should fix it. You're liable, just admit it. I should have flown with someone else or gone by car 'cuz United breaks guitars."

Viewed over 5 million times, his follow-up video focused on his frustrating efforts to get United to pay for the damage. United got the message. It donated a check for $1,200 to a charity Carroll designated and now uses the incident in training baggage handlers and customer-service representatives.[30]

Most companies respond quickly. Comcast allows contact 24/7 by phone and e-chat but also reaches out to customers and monitors blogs, Web sites, and social media. If employees see a customer report a problem on a blog, they get in touch and offer help. E-mail responses to customers must be implemented properly to be effective. One expert believes companies should (1) send an automated reply to tell customers when a more complete answer will arrive (ideally within 24 hours), (2) ensure the subject line always contains the company name, (3) make the message easy to scan for relevant information, and (4) give customers an easy way to respond with follow-up questions.[31]

More important than simply responding to a disgruntled customer, however, is preventing dissatisfaction from occurring in the future. That may mean simply taking the time to nurture customer relationships and give customers attention from a real person. Columbia Records spent $10 million to improve its call center, and customers who phone the company can now opt out to reach an operator at any point in their call. JetBlue took a service disaster and used it to improve its customer service approach.

JetBlue CEO David Neeleman set the bar high for responding to enraged customers after the company's drastic Valentine's Day failure of 2007. During storms in New York City, JetBlue left hundreds of passengers stranded aboard grounded aircraft—some for longer than 9 hours without amenities—and cancelled more than 1,000 flights. JetBlue had built its reputation on being a more responsive, humane airline in an era of minimal services and maximal delays. Neeleman knew he had to act fast to stem another kind of storm: a whirlwind of customer defections. Within 24 hours, he had placed full-page ads in newspapers nationwide in which he personally responded to JetBlue's debacle. "We are sorry and embarrassed," the ads declared, "But most of all we are deeply sorry." JetBlue gave concrete reparations to passengers. Neeleman announced a new "customer bill of rights" that promised passengers travel credits for excessive waits. For instance, passengers who are unable to disembark from an arriving flight for 3 hours or more would receive vouchers worth the full value of their round-trip ticket. JetBlue will also hand out vouchers for the full amount of passengers' round trips if a flight is cancelled within 12 hours of a scheduled departure. The apology, backed by concrete benefits for the angry and inconvenienced passengers, netted kudos for the company from both the business press and JetBlue's own true blue customers. Neeleman eventually stepped down as new management was brought in to address some of the growth challenges the airline faced.[32]

CUSTOMER COPRODUCTION The reality is that customers do not merely purchase and use a service; they play an active role in its delivery.[33] Their words and actions affect the quality of their service experiences and those of others, and the productivity of frontline employees.

Customers often feel they derive more value, and feel a stronger connection to the service provider, if they are actively involved in the service process. This coproduction can put stress on employees, however, and reduce their satisfaction, especially if they differ culturally or in other ways from customers.[34] Moreover, one study estimated that one-third of all service problems are caused by the customer.[35] The growing shift to self-service technologies will likely increase this percentage.

Preventing service failures is crucial, since recovery is always challenging. One of the biggest problems is attribution—customers often feel the firm is at fault or, even if not, that it is still responsible for righting any

JetBlue weathered a customer service disaster and continues to receive kudos from its passengers.

wrongs. Unfortunately, although many firms have well-designed and executed procedures to deal with their own failures, they find managing *customer* failures—when a service problem arises from a customer's lack of understanding or ineptitude—much more difficult. △ Figure 13.3 displays the four broad causes of customer failures. Solutions come in all forms, as these examples show:[36]

1. ***Redesign processes and redefine customer roles to simplify service encounters.*** One of the keys to Netflix's success is that it charges a flat fee and allows customers to return DVDs by mail at their leisure, giving customers greater control and flexibility.

2. ***Incorporate the right technology to aid employees and customers.*** Comcast, the largest cable operator by subscribers in the United States, introduced software to identify network glitches before they affected service and to better inform call-center operators about customer problems. Repeat service calls dropped 30 percent as a result.

3. ***Create high-performance customers by enhancing their role clarity, motivation, and ability.*** USAA reminds enlisted policyholders to suspend their car insurance when they are stationed overseas.

4. ***Encourage "customer citizenship" so customers help customers.*** At golf courses, players can not only follow the rules by playing and behaving appropriately, they can encourage others to do so.

SATISFYING EMPLOYEES AS WELL AS CUSTOMERS Excellent service companies know that positive employee attitudes will promote stronger customer loyalty.[37] Instilling a strong customer orientation in employees can also increase their job satisfaction and commitment, especially if they have high customer contact. Employees thrive in customer-contact positions when they have an internal drive to (1) pamper customers, (2) accurately read customer needs, (3) develop a personal relationship with customers, and (4) deliver quality service to solve customers' problems.[38]

Consistent with this reasoning, Sears found a high correlation between customer satisfaction, employee satisfaction, and store profitability. In companies such as Hallmark, John Deere, and Four Seasons Hotels, employees exhibit real company pride. The downside of not treating employees right is significant. A survey of 10,000 employees from the largest 1,000 companies found that 40 percent of workers cited "lack of recognition" as a key reason for leaving a job.[39]

Given the importance of positive employee attitudes to customer satisfaction, service companies must attract the best employees they can find. They need to market a career rather than just a job. They must design a sound training program and provide support and rewards for good performance. They can use the intranet, internal newsletters, daily reminders, and employee roundtables to reinforce customer-centered attitudes. Finally, they must audit employee job satisfaction regularly.

|Fig. 13.3| △

Root Causes of Customer Failure

Source: Stephen Tax, Mark Colgate, and David Bowen, *MIT Sloan Management Review* (Spring 2006): pp. 30–38. ©2006 by Massachusetts Institute of Technology. All rights reserved. Distributed by Tribune Media Services.

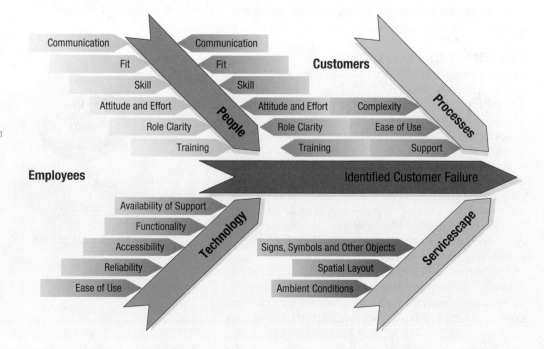

The Panda Express restaurant chain has management turnover that's half the industry average, due in part to a combination of ample bonuses and health benefits with a strong emphasis on worker self-improvement through meditation, education, and hobbies. Special wellness seminars and get-to-know-you events outside work help to create a caring, nurturing atmosphere.[40]

Achieving Excellence in Services Marketing

The increased importance of the service industry has sharpened the focus on what it takes to excel in the marketing of services.[41] Here are some guidelines.

Marketing Excellence

Marketing excellence with services requires excellence in three broad areas: external, internal, and interactive marketing (see △ Figure 13.4).[42]

- *External marketing* describes the normal work of preparing, pricing, distributing, and promoting the service to customers.
- *Internal marketing* describes training and motivating employees to serve customers well. The most important contribution the marketing department can make is arguably to be "exceptionally clever in getting everyone else in the organization to practice marketing."[43]
- *Interactive marketing* describes the employees' skill in serving the client. Clients judge service not only by its *technical quality* (Was the surgery successful?), but also by its *functional quality* (Did the surgeon show concern and inspire confidence?).[44]

A good example of a service company achieving marketing excellence is Charles Schwab.

Charles Schwab Charles Schwab, one of the nation's largest discount brokerage houses, uses the telephone, Internet, and wireless devices to create an innovative combination of high-tech and high-touch services. One of the first major brokerage houses to provide online trading, Schwab today services more than 8 million individual and institutional accounts. It offers account information and proprietary research from retail brokers, real-time quotes, an after-hours trading program, the Schwab learning center, live events, online chats with customer service representatives, a global investing service, and market updates delivered by e-mail. Besides the discount brokerage, the firm offers mutual funds, annuities, bond trading, and now mortgages through its Charles Schwab Bank. Schwab's success has been driven by its efforts to lead in three areas: superior service (online, via phone, and in local branch offices), innovative products, and low prices. Daily customer feedback reports are reviewed and acted on the next day. If customers have trouble filling out a form or experience an unexpected delay, a Schwab representative calls to ask about the source of the problem and how it can be solved.[45]

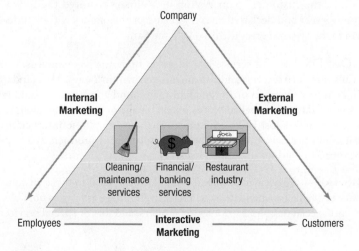

|Fig. 13.4| △

Three Types of Marketing in Service Industries

In interactive marketing, teamwork is often key, and delegating authority to frontline employees can allow for greater service flexibility and adaptability through better problem solving, closer employee cooperation, and more efficient knowledge transfer.[46]

Technology also has great power to make service workers more productive. When US Airways deployed handheld scanners to better track baggage in 2008, mishandled baggage decreased almost 50 percent from the year before. The new technology paid for itself in the first year and helped contribute to a 35 percent drop in complaints.[47]

Sometimes new technology has unanticipated benefits. When BMW introduced Wi-Fi to its dealerships to help customers pass the time more productively while their cars were being serviced, more customers chose to stay rather than use loaner cars, an expensive item for dealers to maintain.[48]

Companies must avoid pushing productivity so hard, however, that they reduce perceived quality. Some methods lead to too much standardization. Service providers must deliver "high touch" as well as "high tech." Amazon.com has some of the most amazing technological innovations in online retailing, but it also keeps customers extremely satisfied when a problem arises even if they don't actually talk to an Amazon.com employee.[49]

The Internet lets firms improve their service offerings and strengthen their relationships with customers by allowing for true interactivity, customer-specific and situational personalization, and real-time adjustments of the firm's offerings.[50] But as companies collect, store, and use more information about customers, they have also raised concerns about security and privacy.[51] Companies must incorporate the proper safeguards and reassure customers about their efforts.

Best Practices of Top Service Companies

In achieving marketing excellence with their customers, well-managed service companies share a strategic concept, a history of top-management commitment to quality, high standards, profit tiers, and systems for monitoring service performance and customer complaints.

STRATEGIC CONCEPT Top service companies are "customer obsessed." They have a clear sense of their target customers and their needs and have developed a distinctive strategy for satisfying these needs. At the Four Seasons luxury hotel chain, employees must pass four interviews before being hired. Each hotel also employs a "guest historian" to track guest preferences. With more branch offices in the United States than Starbucks has, Edward Jones brokerage stays close to customers by assigning a single financial advisor and one administrator to each office. Although costly, maintaining such small teams fosters personal relationships.[52]

TOP-MANAGEMENT COMMITMENT Companies such as Marriott, Disney, and USAA have a thorough commitment to service quality. Their managements look monthly not only at financial performance, but also at service performance. Ray Kroc of McDonald's insisted on continually measuring each McDonald's outlet on its conformance to QSCV: quality, service, cleanliness, and value. Some companies insert a reminder along with employees' paychecks: "Brought to you by the customer." Sam Walton of Walmart required the following employee pledge: "I solemnly swear and declare that every customer that comes within 10 feet of me, I will smile, look them in the eye, and greet them, so help me Sam."

HIGH STANDARDS The best service providers set high quality standards. Citibank aims to answer phone calls within 10 seconds and customer letters within 2 days. The standards must be set *appropriately* high. A 98 percent accuracy standard may sound good, but it would result in 64,000 lost FedEx packages a day; 6 misspelled words on each page of a book; 400,000 incorrectly filled prescriptions daily; 3 million lost USPS mail pieces each day; no phone/Internet/electricity 8 days per year or 29 minutes per day; 1,000 mislabeled or (mispriced) products at a supermarket; and 6 million people unaccounted for in a U.S. census.

PROFIT TIERS Firms have decided to raise fees and lower services to those customers who barely pay their way, and to coddle big spenders to retain their patronage as long as possible. Customers in high-profit tiers get special discounts, promotional offers, and lots of special service; customers in lower-profit tiers may get more fees, stripped-down service, and voice messages to process their inquiries.

When the recent recession hit, Zappos decided to stop offering complimentary overnight shipping to first-time buyers and offer it to repeat buyers only. The money saved was invested in a new VIP service for the company's most loyal customers.[53] Companies that provide differentiated levels of service must be careful about claiming superior service, however—customers who receive lesser treatment will bad-mouth the company and injure its reputation. Delivering services that maximize both customer satisfaction and company profitability can be challenging.

MONITORING SYSTEMS Top firms audit service performance, both their own and competitors', on a regular basis. They collect *voice of the customer (VOC) measurements* to probe customer satisfiers and dissatisfiers. They use comparison shopping, mystery or ghost shopping, customer surveys, suggestion and complaint forms, service-audit teams, and customers' letters to the president.

We can judge services on *customer importance* and *company performance. Importance-performance analysis* rates the various elements of the service bundle and identifies required actions. 🔲 Table 13.2 shows how customers rated 14 service elements or attributes of an automobile dealer's service department on importance and performance. For example, "Job done right the first time" (attribute 1) received a mean importance rating of 3.83 and a mean performance rating of 2.63, indicating that customers felt it was highly important but not performed well. The ratings of the 14 elements are divided into four sections in 🔺 Figure 13.5.

- Quadrant A in the figure shows important service elements that are not being performed at the desired levels; they include elements 1, 2, and 9. The dealer should concentrate on improving the service department's performance on these elements.

TABLE 13.2 🔲	Customer Importance and Performance Ratings for an Auto Dealership		
Number Attribute	Attribute Description	Mean Importance Rating[a]	Mean Performance Rating[b]
1	Job done right the first time	3.83	2.63
2	Fast action on complaints	3.63	2.73
3	Prompt warranty work	3.60	3.15
4	Able to do any job needed	3.56	3.00
5	Service available when needed	3.41	3.05
6	Courteous and friendly service	3.41	3.29
7	Car ready when promised	3.38	3.03
8	Perform only necessary work	3.37	3.11
9	Low prices on service	3.29	2.00
10	Clean up after service work	3.27	3.02
11	Convenient to home	2.52	2.25
12	Convenient to work	2.43	2.49
13	Courtesy buses and cars	2.37	2.35
14	Send out maintenance notices	2.05	3.33

[a] Ratings obtained from a four-point scale of "extremely important" (4), "important" (3), "slightly important" (2), and "not important" (1).

[b] Ratings obtained from a four-point scale of "excellent" (4), "good" (3), "fair" (2), and "poor" (1). A "no basis for judgment" category was also provided.

|Fig. 13.5| ▲

Importance-
Performance Analysis

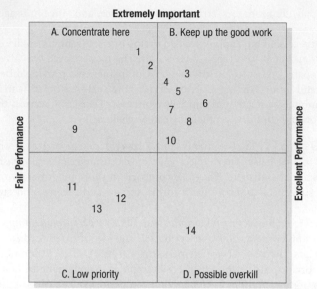

- Quadrant B shows important service elements that are being performed well; the company needs to maintain the high performance.
- Quadrant C shows minor service elements that are being delivered in a mediocre way but do not need any attention.
- Quadrant D shows that a minor service element, "Send out maintenance notices," is being performed in an excellent manner.

Perhaps the company should spend less on sending out maintenance notices and use the savings to improve performance on important elements. Management can enhance its analysis by checking on the competitors' performance levels on each element.[54]

SATISFYING CUSTOMER COMPLAINTS On average, 40 percent of customers who suffer through a bad service experience stop doing business with the company.[55] But if those customers are willing to complain first, they actually offer the company a gift if the complaint is handled well.

Companies that encourage disappointed customers to complain—and also empower employees to remedy the situation on the spot—have been shown to achieve higher revenues and greater profits than companies without a systematic approach for addressing service failures.[56] Pizza Hut prints its toll-free number on all pizza boxes. When a customer complains, Pizza Hut sends a voice mail to the store manager, who must call the customer within 48 hours and resolve the complaint.

Getting frontline employees to adopt *extra-role behaviors,* and to advocate the interests and image of the firm to consumers, as well as take initiative and engage in conscientious behavior in dealing with customers, can be a critical asset in handling complaints.[57] Customers evaluate complaint incidents in terms of the outcomes they receive, the procedures used to arrive at those outcomes, and the nature of interpersonal treatment during the process.[58]

Companies also are increasing the quality of their *call centers* and their *customer service representatives* (CSRs). "Marketing Insight: Improving Company Call Centers" illustrates what top companies are doing.

Differentiating Services

Finally, customers who view a service as fairly homogeneous care less about the provider than about the price. Marketing excellence requires service marketers to continually differentiate their brands so they are not seen as a commodity.

PRIMARY AND SECONDARY SERVICE OPTIONS Marketers can differentiate their service offerings in many ways, through people and processes that add value. What the customer

Marketing Insight

Improving Company Call Centers

Many firms have learned the hard way that demanding, empowered customers will no longer put up with poor service when contacting companies.

After Sprint and Nextel merged, they set out to run their call centers as cost centers, rather than a means to enhance customer loyalty. Employee rewards were based on keeping customer calls short, and when management started to monitor even bathroom trips, morale sank. With customer churn spinning out of control, Sprint Nextel began a service improvement plan at the end of 2007 to put more emphasis on service over efficiency. Among other changes that accompanied the appointment of the firm's first chief service officer, call center operators were rewarded for solving problems on a customer's first call, rather than for keeping their calls short. The average customer contacted customer service four times in 2008, a drop from eight times in 2007.

Some firms are getting smarter about the type of calls they send overseas to off-shore call centers. They are investing more in training as

well as returning more complex calls to highly trained domestic customer service reps. *Homeshoring* occurs when a customer service rep works from home with a broadband line and computer. These at-home reps often provide higher-quality service at less cost and with lower turnover.

Firms have to manage their number of customer service reps carefully. One study showed that cutting just four reps at a call center of three dozen sent the number of customers put on hold for four minutes or more from zero to eighty. Firms can also try to reasonably get more from each rep. USAA cross-trains its call center reps so that agents who answer investment queries can also respond to Insurance-related calls, reducing the number of transfers between agents and increasing productivity as a result. USAA and other firms such as KeyBank and Ace Hardware have also consolidated call center operations into fewer locations, allowing them to maintain their number of reps in the process.

Finally, keeping call center reps happy and motivated is obviously also a key to their ability to offer excellent customer service. American Express lets call center reps choose their own hours and swap shifts without a supervisor's approval.

Sources: Michael Sanserino and Cari Tuna, "Companies Strive Harder to Please Customers," *Wall Street Journal*, July 27, 2009, p. B4; Spencer E. Ante, "Sprint's Wake-Up Call," *BusinessWeek*, March 3, 2008, pp. 54–57; Jena McGregor, "Customer Service Champs," *BusinessWeek*, March 5, 2007; Jena McGregor, "When Service Means Survival," *BusinessWeek*, March 2, 2009, pp. 26–30.

---

expects is called the *primary service package*. Vanguard, the second-largest no-load mutual fund company, has a unique client ownership structure that lowers costs and permits better fund returns. Strongly differentiated from many competitors, the brand grew through word of mouth, PR, and viral marketing.[59]

The provider can add *secondary service features* to the package. In the hotel industry, various chains have introduced such secondary service features as merchandise for sale, free breakfast buffets, and loyalty programs.

The major challenge is that most service offerings and innovations are easily copied. Still, the company that regularly introduces innovations will gain a succession of temporary advantages over competitors. Schneider National keeps a step ahead of its competitors by never standing still.

Long-haul truckload freight carrier Schneider National goes to great lengths to satisfy its customers and build its brand.

Schneider National
Schneider National is the world's largest long-haul truckload freight carrier, with $3.7 billion in revenues and more than 54,000 bright orange tractors and trailers on the roads. Although its core benefit is to move freight from one location to another, Schneider sees itself in the *customer solutions* business. Its service guarantees are backed by monetary incentives for drivers who meet tight schedules; driver-training programs improve performance. Schneider was the first to introduce in-cab satellite technology and mobile technology to every driver. In 2009, it had its biggest award-winning year, garnering 43 awards for strong customer service, solutions, and commitment to the environment from shippers, government organizations, and industry media. To actively recruit the best drivers, Schneider advertises on television shows such as

Treatments: Price listed <u>or</u> your insurance co-pay

Strep Throat, Rapid Test	$48	Ringworm	$25
(with Overnight Culture add $14)		Athlete's Foot	$25
Seasonal Allergies (ages 6+)	$44	Ear Infections	$44
Bronchitis (ages 10-65)	$44	Swimmer's Ear	$44
Flu Treatment (ages 10-65)	$78	Deer Tick Bites	$25
Female Bladder Infections (ages 12-65)	$48	Cold Sores	$25
Poison Ivy (ages 3+)	$44	Sinus Infections	$44
Pink Eye & Styes	$44	Laryngitis	$44
Mono	$51	Allergy Testing	$99
Minor Skin Infections	$44		

Prescriptions written when clinically appropriate.

Vaccines: Price listed <u>or</u> your insurance co-pay

Td (Tetanus, Diphtheria)	$38	Pneumonia	$25
Hepatitis B (adult)	$60	Flu Fall 2005	
Hepatitis B (child)	$45		

Retail health clinics are reinventing patient care for minor illnesses and injuries.

Trick My Truck, on satellite radio, in newspapers, and online; employs Webinars and PR; and partners with AARP, local organizations, and veterans' groups. Even painting the trucks Omaha orange was part of a branding strategy to improve safety and create awareness.[60]

INNOVATION WITH SERVICES Innovation is as vital in services as in any industry. After years of losing customers to its Hilton and Marriott hotel competitors, Starwood decided to invest $1.7 billion in its Sheraton chain of 400 properties worldwide to give them fresher décor and brighter colors, as well as more enticing lobbies, restaurants, and cafés. In explaining the need for the makeover, one hospitality industry expert noted, "There was a time when Sheraton was one of the leading brands. But it lagged in introducing new design and service concepts and developed a level of inconsistency."[61]

On the other hand, consider how these relatively new service categories emerged and how, in some cases, organizations created creative solutions in existing categories.[62]

- **Online Travel.** Online travel agents such as Expedia and Travelocity offer customers the opportunity to conveniently book travel at discount prices. However, they make money only when visitors go to their Web sites and book travel. Kayak is a newer online travel agency that applies the Google business model of collecting money on a per-click basis. Kayak's marketing emphasis is on building a better search engine by offering more alternatives, flexibility, and airlines.

- **Retail Health Clinics.** One of the hardest areas in which to innovate is health care. But whereas the current health care system is designed to treat a small number of complex cases, retail health clinics address a large number of simple cases. Retail health clinics such as Quick Care, RediClinic, and MinuteClinic are often found in drugstores and other retail chain stores such as Target and Walmart. They typically use nurse practitioners to handle minor illnesses and injuries such as colds, flu, and ear infections, offer various health and wellness services such as physicals and exams for high school sports, and perform vaccinations. They seek to offer convenient, predictable service and transparent pricing, without an appointment, seven days a week. Most visits take no more than 15 minutes, and costs vary from $25 to $100.

- **Private Aviation.** Initially, private aviation was restricted to owning or chartering a private plane. Fractional ownership pioneered by NetJets allowed customers to pay a percentage of the cost of a private plane plus maintenance and a direct hourly cost. Marquis Jets further innovated with a simple idea of combining prepaid time on the world's largest, best-maintained fleet, offering the consistency and benefits of fractional ownership without the long-term commitment.

Many companies are using the Web to offer primary or secondary service features that were never possible before. Salesforce.com uses cloud computing—centralized computing services delivered over the Internet—to run customer-management databases for companies. Häagen-Dazs estimated it would have had to spend $65,000 for a custom-designed database to stay in contact with the company's retail franchises across the country. Instead, it spent only $20,000 to set up an account with Salesforce.com and pays $125 per month for 20 users to remotely monitor franchises via the Web.[63]

Managing Service Quality

The service quality of a firm is tested at each service encounter. If employees are bored, cannot answer simple questions, or are visiting each other while customers are waiting, customers will think twice about doing business there again. One business that understands how to treat customers right is USAA.

USAA From its beginnings, USAA focused on selling auto insurance, and later other insurance products, to those with military service. It increased its share of each customer's business by launching a consumer bank, issuing credit cards, opening a discount brokerage, and offering a selection of no-load mutual funds. Though it now conducts transactions for more than 150 products and services on the phone or online, USAA boasts one of the highest customer satisfaction ratings of any company in the United States. It was the first bank to allow iPhone deposits for its military customers, to routinely text balances to soldiers in the field, and to heavily discount customers' car insurance when they are deployed overseas. A leader in virtually every customer service award or survey, the company inspired one industry expert to comment: "There is nobody on this earth who understands their customer better than USAA."[64] ▭

LOWER YOUR RATES. NOT YOUR EXPECTATIONS.

Try **usaa**insurance.com

By relentlessly focusing on its military customers, USAA has created extraordinary levels of customer satisfaction.

Service outcome and customer loyalty are influenced by a host of variables. One study identified more than 800 critical behaviors that cause customers to switch services.[65] These behaviors fall into eight categories (see ▭ Table 13.3).

A more recent study honed in on the service dimensions customers would most like companies to measure. As ▭ Table 13.4 shows, knowledgeable frontline workers and the ability to achieve one-call-and-done rose to the top.[66]

Flawless service delivery is the ideal state for any service organization. "Marketing Memo: Recommendations for Improving Service Quality" offers a comprehensive set of guidelines to

TABLE 13.3 ▭	Factors Leading to Customer Switching Behavior

Pricing
- High price
- Price increases
- Unfair pricing
- Deceptive pricing

Inconvenience
- Location/hours
- Wait for appointment
- Wait for service

Core Service Failure
- Service mistakes
- Billing errors
- Service catastrophe

Service Encounter Failures
- Uncaring
- Impolite
- Unresponsive
- Unknowledgeable

Response to Service Failure
- Negative response
- No response
- Reluctant response

Competition
- Found better service

Ethical Problems
- Cheat
- Hard sell
- Unsafe
- Conflict of interest

Involuntary Switching
- Customer moved
- Provider closed

Source: Susan M. Keaveney, "Customer Switching Behavior in Service Industries: An Exploratory Study," *Journal of Marketing* (April 1995), pp. 71–82. Reprinted with permission from *Journal of Marketing*, published by the American Marketing Association.

TABLE 13.4	Dimensions of Service Customers Want Companies to Deliver

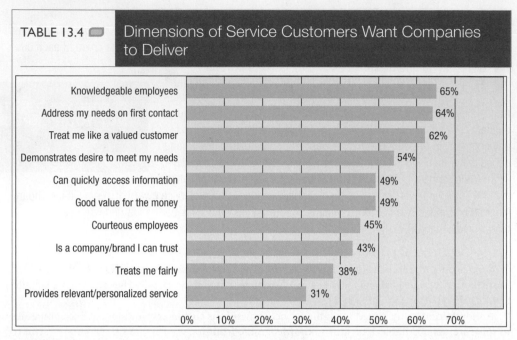

Source: Convergys 2008 U.S. Customer Scorecard

marketing Memo

Recommendations for Improving Service Quality

Pioneers in conducting academic service research, Berry, Parasuraman, and Zeithaml offer 10 lessons they maintain are essential for improving service quality across service industries.

1. *Listening*—Service providers should understand what customers really want through continuous learning about the expectations and perceptions of customers and noncustomers (for instance, by means of a service-quality information system).

2. *Reliability*—Reliability is the single most important dimension of service quality and must be a service priority.

3. *Basic service*—Service companies must deliver the basics and do what they are supposed to do—keep promises, use common sense, listen to customers, keep customers informed, and be determined to deliver value to customers.

4. *Service design*—Service providers should take a holistic view of the service while managing its many details.

5. *Recovery*—To satisfy customers who encounter a service problem, service companies should encourage customers to complain (and make it easy for them to do so), respond quickly and personally, and develop a problem-resolution system.

6. *Surprising customers*—Although reliability is the most important dimension in *meeting* customers' service expectations, process dimensions such as assurance, responsiveness, and empathy are most important in *exceeding* customer expectations, for example, by surprising them with uncommon swiftness, grace, courtesy, competence, commitment, and understanding.

7. *Fair play*—Service companies must make special efforts to *be* fair, and to *demonstrate* fairness, to customers and employees.

8. *Teamwork*—Teamwork is what enables large organizations to deliver service with care and attentiveness by improving employee motivation and capabilities.

9. *Employee research*—Marketers should conduct research with employees to reveal why service problems occur and what companies must do to solve problems.

10. *Servant leadership*—Quality service comes from inspired leadership throughout the organization; from excellent service-system design; from the effective use of information and technology; and from a slow-to-change, invisible, all-powerful, internal force called corporate culture.

Sources: Leonard L. Berry, A. Parasuraman, and Valarie A. Zeithaml, "Ten Lessons for Improving Service Quality," *MSI Reports Working Paper Series, No.03-001* (Cambridge, MA: Marketing Science Institute, 2003), pp. 61–82. See also, Leonard L. Berry's books, *On Great Service: A Framework for Action* (New York: Free Press, 2006) and *Discovering the Soul of Service* (New York: Free Press, 1999), as well as his articles; Leonard L. Berry, Venkatesh Shankar, Janet Parish, Susan Cadwallader, and Thomas Dotzel, "Creating New Markets through Service Innovation," *Sloan Management Review* (Winter 2006): 56–63; Leonard L. Berry, Stephan H. Haeckel, and Lewis P. Carbone, "How to Lead the Customer Experience," *Marketing Management* (January–February 2003), pp. 18–23; and Leonard L. Berry, Kathleen Seiders, and Dhruv Grewal, "Understanding Service Convenience," *Journal of Marketing* (July 2002), pp. 1–17.

which top service marketing organizations can adhere. Two important considerations in service delivery are managing customer expectations and incorporating self-service technologies.

Managing Customer Expectations

Customers form service expectations from many sources, such as past experiences, word of mouth, and advertising. In general, customers compare the *perceived service* with the *expected service*.[67] If the perceived service falls below the expected service, customers are disappointed. Successful companies add benefits to their offering that not only *satisfy* customers but surprise and *delight* them. Delighting customers is a matter of exceeding expectations.[68]

The service-quality model in △ Figure 13.6 highlights the main requirements for delivering high service quality.[69] It identifies five gaps that cause unsuccessful delivery:

1. *Gap between consumer expectation and management perception*—Management does not always correctly perceive what customers want. Hospital administrators may think patients want better food, but patients may be more concerned with nurse responsiveness.
2. *Gap between management perception and service-quality specification*—Management might correctly perceive customers' wants but not set a performance standard. Hospital administrators may tell the nurses to give "fast" service without specifying it in minutes.
3. *Gap between service-quality specifications and service delivery*—Employees might be poorly trained, or incapable of or unwilling to meet the standard; they may be held to conflicting standards, such as taking time to listen to customers and serving them fast.
4. *Gap between service delivery and external communications*—Consumer expectations are affected by statements made by company representatives and ads. If a hospital brochure shows a beautiful room but the patient finds it to be cheap and tacky looking, external communications have distorted the customer's expectations.

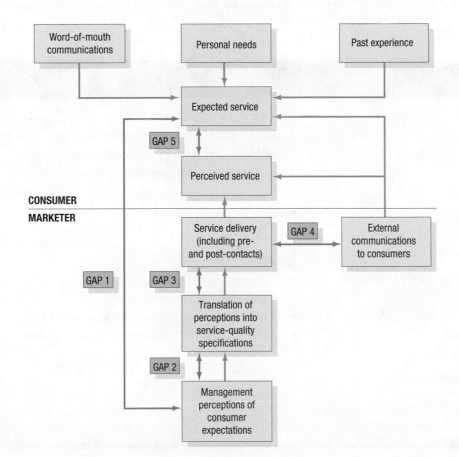

|Fig. 13.6| △

Service-Quality Model

Sources: A. Parasuraman, Valarie A. Zeithaml, and Leonard L. Berry, "A Conceptual Model of Service Quality and Its Implications for Future Research," *Journal of Marketing* (Fall 1985), p. 44. Reprinted with permission of the American Marketing Association. The model is more fully discussed or elaborated in Valarie Zeithaml, Mary Jo Bitner, and Dwayne D. Gremler, *Services Marketing: Integrating Customer Focus across the Firm*, 4th ed. (New York: McGraw-Hill, 2006).

5. *Gap between perceived service and expected service*—This gap occurs when the consumer misperceives the service quality. The physician may keep visiting the patient to show care, but the patient may interpret this as an indication that something really is wrong.

Based on this service-quality model, researchers identified five determinants of service quality, in this order of importance:[70]

1. *Reliability*—The ability to perform the promised service dependably and accurately.
2. *Responsiveness*—Willingness to help customers and provide prompt service.
3. *Assurance*—The knowledge and courtesy of employees and their ability to convey trust and confidence.
4. *Empathy*—The provision of caring, individualized attention to customers.
5. *Tangibles*—The appearance of physical facilities, equipment, personnel, and communication materials.

Based on these five factors, the researchers developed the 21-item SERVQUAL scale (see 🞏 Table 13.5).[71] They also note there is a *zone of tolerance,* or a range where a service dimension would be deemed satisfactory, anchored by the minimum level consumers are willing to accept and the level they believe can and should be delivered.

The service-quality model in Figure 13.6 highlights some of the gaps that cause unsuccessful service delivery. Subsequent research has extended the model. One *dynamic process model* of service quality was based on the premise that customer perceptions and expectations of service quality change over time, but at any one point they are a function of prior expectations about what *will* and what *should* happen during the service encounter, as well as the *actual* service delivered during the last contact.[72] Tests of the dynamic process model reveal that the two different types of expectations have opposite effects on perceptions of service quality.

1. *Increasing* customer expectations of what the firm *will* deliver can lead to improved perceptions of overall service quality.
2. *Decreasing* customer expectations of what the firm *should* deliver can also lead to improved perceptions of overall service quality.

TABLE 13.5 🞏 SERVQUAL Attributes

Reliability
- Providing service as promised
- Dependability in handling customers' service problems
- Performing services right the first time
- Providing services at the promised time
- Maintaining error-free records
- Employees who have the knowledge to answer customer questions

Empathy
- Giving customers individual attention
- Employees who deal with customers in a caring fashion
- Having the customer's best interests at heart
- Employees who understand the needs of their customers
- Convenient business hours

Responsiveness
- Keeping customer informed as to when services will be performed
- Prompt service to customers
- Willingness to help customers
- Readiness to respond to customers' requests

Tangibles
- Modern equipment
- Visually appealing facilities
- Employees who have a neat, professional appearance
- Visually appealing materials associated with the service

Assurance
- Employees who instill confidence in customers
- Making customers feel safe in their transactions
- Employees who are consistently courteous

Source: A. Parasuraman, Valarie A. Zeithaml, and Leonard L. Berry, "A Conceptual Model of Service Quality and Its Implications for Future Research," *Journal of Marketing* (Fall 1985), pp. 41–50. Reprinted by permission of the American Marketing Association.

Much work has validated the role of expectations in consumers' interpretations and evaluations of the service encounter and the relationship they adopt with a firm over time.[73] Consumers are often forward-looking with respect to their decision to keep or switch from a service relationship. Any marketing activity that affects current or expected future usage can help to solidify a service relationship.

With continuously provided services, such as public utilities, health care, financial and computing services, insurance, and other professional, membership, or subscription services, customers have been observed to mentally calculate their *payment equity*—the perceived economic benefits in relationship to the economic costs. In other words, customers ask themselves, "Am I using this service enough, given what I pay for it?"

Long-term service relationships can have a dark side. An ad agency client may feel that over time the agency is losing objectivity, becoming stale in its thinking, or beginning to take advantage of the relationship.[74]

Incorporating Self-Service Technologies (SSTs)

Consumers value convenience in services.[75] Many person-to-person service interactions are being replaced by self-service technologies (SSTs). To the traditional vending machines we can add automated teller machines (ATMs), self-pumping at gas stations, self-checkout at hotels, and a variety of activities on the Internet, such as ticket purchasing, investment trading, and customization of products.

Not all SSTs improve service quality, but they can make service transactions more accurate, convenient, and faster. Obviously, they can also reduce costs. One technology firm, Comverse, estimates the cost to answer a query through a call center at $7, but only 10 cents online. One of its clients was able to direct 200,000 calls a week through online self-service support, saving $52 million a year.[76] Every company needs to think about improving its service using SSTs.

Marketing academics and consultants Jeffrey Rayport and Bernie Jaworski define a *customer-service interface* as any place at which a company seeks to manage a relationship with a customer, whether through people, technology, or some combination of the two.[77] They feel that although many companies serve customers through a broad array of interfaces, from retail sales clerks to Web sites to voice-response telephone systems, the whole often does not add up to the sum of its parts, increasing complexity, costs, and customer dissatisfaction as a result. Successfully integrating technology into the workforce thus requires a comprehensive reengineering of the front office to identify what people do best, what machines do best, and how to deploy them separately and together.

Some companies have found that the biggest obstacle is not the technology itself, but convincing customers to use it, especially for the first time. Customers must have a clear sense of their roles in the SST process, must see a clear benefit, and must feel they can actually use it.[78] SST is not for everyone. Although some automated voices are actually popular with customers—the unfailingly polite and chipper voice of Amtrak's "Julie" consistently wins kudos from callers—many can incite frustration and even rage.

Managing Product-Support Services

No less important than service industries are product-based industries that must provide a service bundle. Manufacturers of equipment—small appliances, office machines, tractors, mainframes, airplanes—all must provide *product-support services.* Product-support service is becoming a major battleground for competitive advantage.

Chapter 12 described how products could be augmented with key service differentiators—ordering ease, delivery, installation, customer training, customer consulting, maintenance, and repair. Some equipment companies, such as Caterpillar Tractor and John Deere, make a significant percentage of their profits from these services.[79] In the global marketplace, companies that make a good product but provide poor local service support are seriously disadvantaged.

Many product companies have a stronger Web presence than they had before. They must ensure that they offer adequate—if not superior—service online as well. "Marketing Memo: Assessing E-Service Quality" reviews two models of online service quality.

Identifying and Satisfying Customer Needs

Traditionally, customers have had three specific worries about product service:[80]

- They worry about reliability and *failure frequency*. A farmer may tolerate a combine that will break down once a year, but not two or three times a year.
- They worry about *downtime*. The longer the downtime, the higher the cost. The customer counts on the seller's *service dependability*—the seller's ability to fix the machine quickly or at least provide a loaner.[81]
- They worry about *out-of-pocket costs*. How much does the customer have to spend on regular maintenance and repair costs?

A buyer takes all these factors into consideration and tries to estimate the **life-cycle cost**, which is the product's purchase cost plus the discounted cost of maintenance and repair less the discounted salvage value. A one-computer office will need higher product reliability and faster repair service than an office where other computers are available if one breaks down. An airline needs 100 percent reliability in the air. Where reliability is important, manufacturers or service providers can offer guarantees to promote sales.

---

marketing Memo

Assessing E-Service Quality

Academic researchers Zeithaml, Parasuraman, and Malhotra define online service quality as the extent to which a Web site facilitates efficient and effective shopping, purchasing, and delivery. They identified 11 dimensions of perceived e-service quality: access, ease of navigation, efficiency, flexibility, reliability, personalization, security/privacy, responsiveness, assurance/trust, site aesthetics, and price knowledge. Some of these service-quality dimensions were the same online as offline, but some specific underlying attributes were different. Different dimensions emerged with e-service quality too. Empathy didn't seem to be as important online, unless there were service problems. Core dimensions of regular service quality were efficiency, fulfillment, reliability, and privacy; core dimensions of service recovery were responsiveness, compensation, and real-time access to help.

Another set of academic researchers, Wolfinbarger and Gilly, developed a reduced scale of online service quality with four key dimensions: reliability/fulfillment, Web site design, security/privacy, and customer service. The researchers interpret their study findings to suggest that the most basic building blocks of a "compelling online experience" are reliability and functionality to provide time savings, easy transactions, good selection, in-depth information, and the "right" level of personalization. Their 14-item scale looks like this:

Reliability/Fulfillment

The product that came was represented accurately by the Web site.

You get what you ordered from this Web site.

The product is delivered by the time promised by the company.

Web Site Design

This Web site provides in-depth information.

The site doesn't waste my time.

It is quick and easy to complete a transaction at this Web site.

The level of personalization at this site is about right, not too much or too little.

This Web site has good selection.

Security/Privacy

I feel that my privacy is protected at this site.

I feel safe in my transactions with this Web site.

This Web site has adequate security transactions.

Customer Service

The company is willing and ready to respond to customer needs.

When you have a problem, the Web site shows a sincere interest in solving it.

Inquiries are answered promptly.

Sources: Mary Wolfinbarger and Mary C. Gilly, "E-TailQ: Dimensionalizing, Measuring, and Predicting E-Tail Quality," *Journal of Retailing* 79 (Fall 2003), pp. 183–98; Valarie A. Zeithaml, A. Parasuraman, and Arvind Malhotra, "A Conceptual Framework for Understanding E-Service Quality: Implications for Future Research and Managerial Practice," *Marketing Science Institute Working Paper*, Report No. 00-115, 2000.

To provide the best support, a manufacturer must identify the services customers value most and their relative importance. For expensive equipment, manufacturers offer *facilitating services* such as installation, staff training, maintenance and repair services, and financing. They may also add *value-augmenting services* that extend beyond the functioning and performance of the product itself. Johnson Controls reached beyond its climate control equipment and components business to manage integrated facilities by offering products and services that optimize energy use and improve comfort and security.

A manufacturer can offer, and charge for, product-support services in different ways. One specialty organic-chemical company provides a standard offering plus a basic level of services. If the customer wants additional services, it can pay extra or increase its annual purchases to a higher level, in which case additional services are included. Many companies offer *service contracts* (also called *extended warranties*), in which sellers agree to provide free maintenance and repair services for a specified period of time at a specified contract price.

Product companies must understand their strategic intent and competitive advantage in developing services. Are service units supposed to support or protect existing product businesses or to grow as an independent platform? Are the sources of competitive advantage based on economies of scale or economies of skill?[82] See △ Figure 13.7 strategies of different service companies.

Postsale Service Strategy

The quality of customer service departments varies greatly. At one extreme are departments that simply transfer customer calls to the appropriate person or department for action with little follow-up. At the other extreme are departments eager to receive customer requests, suggestions, and even complaints and handle them expeditiously. Some firms even proactively contact customers to provide service after the sale is complete.[83]

CUSTOMER-SERVICE EVOLUTION Manufacturers usually start by running their own parts-and-service departments. They want to stay close to the equipment and know its problems. They also find it expensive and time consuming to train others and discover they can make good money from parts and service if they are the only supplier and can charge a premium price. In fact, many equipment manufacturers price their equipment low and compensate by charging high prices for parts and service.

|Fig. 13.7| △

Service Strategies for Product Companies

		Strategic Intent	
		Protect or Enhance Product	**Expand Independent Service**
Source of Competitive Advantage	**Economies of scale**	• Apple's iPod music download and transaction management service (iTunes) • Otis Elevator's remote monitoring and diagnostics services • General Motors' OnStar auto remote diagnostics service • Symantec's virus protection and data security services	• Cardinal Healthcare's hospital inventory-management services • Cincinnati Bell's billing services (now part of Convergys) • IBM's data-center-outsourcing services • Johnson Controls' integrated facilities-management services
	Economies of skill	• Cisco's network integration and maintenance services • EMC's storage-management and maintenance services • SAP Systems' integration services • UTC's utilities field support services	• Cincinnati Bell's call-center-management services (now part of Convergys) • General Electric's aircraft-engine-maintenance services • GE Healthcare's hospital equipment—support and diagnostics services for hospital equipment • IBM's systems integration services

Over time, manufacturers switch more maintenance and repair service to authorized distributors and dealers. These intermediaries are closer to customers, operate in more locations, and can offer quicker service. Still later, independent service firms emerge and offer a lower price or faster service. A significant percentage of auto-service work is now done outside franchised automobile dealerships by independent garages and chains such as Midas Muffler, and Sears. Independent service organizations handle mainframes, telecommunications equipment, and a variety of other equipment lines.

THE CUSTOMER-SERVICE IMPERATIVE Customer-service choices are increasing rapidly, however, and equipment manufacturers increasingly must figure out how to make money on their equipment, independent of service contracts. Some new-car warranties now cover 100,000 miles before servicing. The increase in disposable or never-fail equipment makes customers less inclined to pay 2 percent to 10 percent of the purchase price every year for a service. A company with several hundred laptops, printers, and related equipment might find it cheaper to have its own service people on-site.

Summary

1. A service is any act or performance that one party can offer to another that is essentially intangible and does not result in the ownership of anything. It may or may not be tied to a physical product.

2. Services are intangible, inseparable, variable, and perishable. Each characteristic poses challenges and requires certain strategies. Marketers must find ways to give tangibility to intangibles, to increase the productivity of service providers, to increase and standardize the quality of the service provided, and to match the supply of services with market demand.

3. Marketing of services faces new realities in the 21st century due to customer empowerment, customer co-production, and the need to satisfy employees as well as customers.

4. In the past, service industries lagged behind manufacturing firms in adopting and using marketing concepts and tools, but this situation has changed. Achieving excellence in service marketing calls not only for external marketing but also for internal marketing to motivate employees, as well as interactive marketing to emphasize the importance of both "high tech" and "high touch."

5. Top service companies excel at the following practices: a strategic concept, a history of top-management commitment to quality, high standards, profit tiers, and systems for monitoring service performance and customer complaints. They also differentiate their brands through primary and secondary service features and continual innovation.

6. Superior service delivery requires managing customer expectations and incorporating self-service technologies. Customers' expectations play a critical role in their service experiences and evaluations. Companies must manage service quality by understanding the effects of each service encounter.

7. Even product-based companies must provide post-purchase service. To offer the best support, a manufacturer must identify the services customers value most and their relative importance. The service mix includes both presale services (facilitating and value-augmenting services) and postsale services (customer service departments, repair and maintenance services).

Applications

Marketing Debate
Is Service Marketing Different from Product Marketing?

Some service marketers maintain that service marketing is fundamentally different from product marketing and relies on different skills. Some traditional product marketers disagree, saying "good marketing is good marketing."

Take a position: Product and service marketing are fundamentally different *versus* Product and service marketing are highly related.

Marketing Discussion
Educational Institutions

Colleges, universities, and other educational institutions can be classified as service organizations. How can you apply the marketing principles developed in this chapter to your school? Do you have any advice as to how it could become a better service marketer?

Marketing Excellence

>>The Ritz-Carlton

Few brands attain such a high standard of customer service as the luxury hotel, The Ritz-Carlton. The Ritz-Carlton dates back to the early 20th century and the original Ritz-Carlton Boston, which revolutionized the way U.S. travelers viewed and experienced customer service and luxury in a hotel. The Ritz-Carlton Boston was the first of its kind to provide guests with a private bath in each guest room, fresh flowers throughout the hotel, and an entire staff dressed in formal white tie, black tie, or morning coat attire.

In 1983, hotelier Horst Schulze and a four-person development team acquired the rights to the Ritz-Carlton name and created the Ritz-Carlton concept as it is known today: a company-wide concentration on both the personal and the functional side of service. The five-star hotel provides impeccable facilities but also takes customer service extremely seriously. Its credo is, "We are Ladies and Gentlemen serving Ladies and Gentlemen." According to the company's Web site, The Ritz-Carlton "pledge(s) to provide the finest personal service and facilities for our guests who will always enjoy a warm, relaxed, yet refined ambience."

The Ritz-Carlton fulfills this promise by providing impeccable training for its employees and executing its Three Steps of Service and 12 Service Values. The Three Steps of Service state that employees must use a warm and sincere greeting always using the guest's name, anticipate and fulfill each guest's needs, and give a warm good-bye again using the guest's name. Every manager carries a laminated card with the 12 Service Values, which include bullets such as number 3: "I am empowered to create unique, memorable and personal experiences for our guests," and number 10: "I am proud of my professional appearance, language and behavior." Simon Cooper, the company president and chief operating officer, explained, "It's all about people. Nobody has an emotional experience with a thing. We're appealing to emotions." The Ritz-Carlton's 38,000 employees at 70 hotels in 24 countries go out of their way to create unique and memorable experiences for their guests.

While The Ritz-Carlton is known for training its employees on exceptional customer service, the hotel also reinforces its mission and values to its employees on a daily basis. Each day, managers gather their employees for a 15-minute "line up." During this time, managers touch base with their employees, resolve any impending problems, and spend the remaining time reading and discussing what The Ritz-Carlton calls "wow stories."

The same "wow story" of the day is read to every single employee around the world. These true stories recognize an individual employee for his or her outstanding customer service and also highlight one of the 12 Service Values. For example, one family staying at the Ritz-Carlton, Bali, needed a particular type of egg and milk for their son who suffered from food allergies. Employees could not find the appropriate items in town, but the executive chef at the hotel remembered a store in Singapore that sold them. He contacted his mother-in-law, who purchased the items and personally flew them over 1,000 miles to Bali for the family. This example showcased Service Value 6: "I own and immediately resolve guests' problems."

In another instance, a waiter overheard a man telling his wife, who used a wheelchair, that it was too bad he couldn't get her down to the beach. The waiter told the maintenance crew, and by the next day they had constructed a wooden walkway down to the beach and pitched a tent at the far end where the couple had dinner. According to Cooper, the daily wow story is "the best way to communicate what we expect from our ladies and gentlemen around the world. Every story reinforces the actions we are looking for and demonstrates how each and every person in our organization contributes to our service values." As part of company policy, each employee is entitled to spend up to $2,000 on a guest to help deliver an anticipated need or desire.

The hotel measures the success of its customer service efforts through Gallup phone interviews, which ask both functional and emotional questions. Functional questions ask "How was the meal? Was your bedroom clean?" while emotional questions uncover a sense of the customer's well-being. The Ritz-Carlton uses these findings as well as day-to-day experiences to continually enhance and improve the experience for its guests.

In less than three decades, The Ritz-Carlton has grown from 4 locations to over 70 and earned two Malcolm Baldrige Quality Awards—the only company ever to win the prestigious award twice.

Questions

1. How does The Ritz-Carlton match up to competitive hotels? What are the key differences?

2. Discuss the importance of the "wow stories" in customer service for a luxury hotel like The Ritz-Carlton.

Sources: Robert Reiss, "How Ritz-Carlton Stays at Top," *Forbes,* October 30, 2009; Carmine Gallo, "Employee Motivation the Ritz-Carlton Way," *BusinessWeek,* February 29, 2008; Carmine Gallo, "How Ritz-Carlton Maintains Its Mystique," *BusinessWeek,* February 13, 2007; Jennifer Robison, "How The Ritz-Carlton Manages the Mystique," *Gallup Management Journal,* December 11, 2008; *The Ritz Carlton,* www.RitzCarlton.com.

Marketing Excellence

>>>Parkway Group Hospitals

Parkway Group Healthcare, headquartered in Singapore, was founded by Dr. Lim Cheok Peng and others in 1987 and has grown internationally by annexing other hospitals. For example, Parkway's joint venture with Apollo Hospitals in India has facilitated its expansion into that market. Parkway's hospitals provide exceptional patient care and offer specialty clinics in areas including oncology, neurology, optometry, and fertility. Its radiology department serves hospitals regionally, its laboratories serve inpatients and outpatients in Singapore, and it runs a physical rehabilitation service. In 2010, the Medical Travel and Health Tourism Quality Alliance (MTQVA) ranked Singapore's Gleneagles Hospital, Parkway's flagship facility, as second-highest on its list for medical tourism in 2010. According to the MTQVA, Gleneagles provides top-quality medical

services in a top-quality location. This high acclaim is testament to Parkway Group's primary mission which is to make a difference in people's lives through a high level of patient care.

Parkway's focus on providing excellent service starts with its pre-admission procedure and continues through post-surgical care. To take patient needs fully into account, the company applies a different set of service standards at different hospitals. In all its hospitals, however, patients can just approach the reception counter and ask for assistance instead of making appointments beforehand. Doctors on duty make the preliminary recommendations; then hospital administrators bring in appropriate specialists to provide the necessary care.

Parkway operates 16 hospitals with over 3,400 beds in Singapore, Malaysia, Brunei, India, China, and the United Arab Emirates. Patients are treated like five-star hotel guests. At Danat Al Emarat Women & Children's Hospital in Abu Dhabi, patient rooms are fully equipped with high-speed Internet, video-on-demand, and video games for children. The Royal Suites at Danat Al Emarat have dedicated medical staff exclusive to each suite. But Parkway attends to more than just a patient's comforts. At Singapore's flagship Gleneagles Hospital, post-surgical care insurance provides coverage for treatment of post-surgical complications for all patients. Coverage begins from the moment initial surgery is completed and ends 24 hours after a patient has been discharged.

Parkway's Pantai Hospital in Penang, Malaysia, caters to patients at all socioeconomic levels. At the lowest price range, beds in the open ward, painted a cool lavender, begin at $7.00 (20 Malaysian ringgits (RM)). However, a Deluxe Room costing $120 (RM365) per night has the feel of a luxury chalet. It is fully air-conditioned and features a lounge area with a dining table and private bathroom. A refrigerator is provided as well: patients in Pantai Penang's Deluxe suites are meant to feel as much at home as possible.

Gleneagles Singapore has a novel way of attracting new patients. The hospital invites specialists to purchase or rent rooms on its premises. Then, because of proximity, these doctors tend to admit their patients to Gleneagles, where the admissions desk operates around the clock.

A patient is allowed to proceed to the admission desk at any time of day, without the need for a referral, and be guaranteed a bed. Gleneagles has a 68 percent share of accredited specialists, and 44 percent of private hospital admissions in all of Singapore.

Parkway understands that patients have the right to be treated with dignity, respect and to be kept fully apprised of the progress of their treatment, via a translator if needed. A patient in a Parkway hospital is also always entitled to request a second opinion from an accredited doctor; the company believes every patient must be allowed to participate in, and understand, their own health care needs. Parkway Patient Assistance (PPA), one of the Gleneagles Singapore's initiatives, provides a one-stop service for international patients looking for specialist expertise, personalized care, and cutting-edge technology. PPA staff also provide advice on estimated costs of treatments and procedures.

The CEO of Parkway Holdings, Dr. Tan See Leng, has noted that Asia is becoming a hub for patient treatment. He believes that the next 1–2 years will see great benefits for Asian health care providers, as long as high-quality service is provided. Parkway Group's biggest strength lies in its ability to capture the market for medical tourists in the Asian region, expected to be worth at least $4 billion by 2012. Low-cost, high-quality health care in Asia is estimated to attract over 1.3 million tourists a year. If Parkway Group continues to expand its reach and maintain the world-class quality of its medical establishments, then the sky is the limit for what it can achieve.

Questions

1   With many hospitals in Asia competing in the medical tourism market, how can Parkway position itself in order to attract more patients?

2.   Parkway hospitals do not employ many doctors but depend on the use of the hospital services by private specialists. What are the risks in this approach?

Sources: Moving Up the Value Chain," *Business Times*, November 10, 2009, www.biotechsingapore.com/Singlenews.aspx?DirID=111&rec_code=664739; "Patient Guide," *Parkway Health*, www.parkwayhealth.com/patients_and_visitors/patient_guide/rights; "Overview," *Pantai Holdings Berhad*, www.pantai.com.my/about_us_overview.php; "Sustainable Design," *Danat Al Emarat Women & Children's Hospital*, www.danatalemarat.ae/sustainable-design.html; "Gleneagles Hospital," *Parkway Health*, www.parkwayhealth.com/hospitals/gleneagles_hospital.

Chapter 14

In This Chapter, We Will Address the Following Questions

1. How do consumers process and evaluate prices?

2. How should a company set prices initially for products or services?

3. How should a company adapt prices to meet varying circumstances and opportunities?

4. When should a company initiate a price change?

5. How should a company respond to a competitor's price change?

As a high-end luxury goods provider, Tiffany & Co. knows the importance of preserving the integrity of its prices.

Developing Pricing Strategies and Programs

Price is the one element of the marketing mix that produces revenue; the other elements produce costs. Prices are perhaps the easiest element of the marketing program to adjust; product features, channels, and even communications take more time. Price also communicates to the market the company's intended value positioning of its product or brand. A well-designed and marketed product can command a price premium and reap big profits. But new economic realities have caused many consumers to pinch pennies, and many companies have had to carefully review their pricing strategies as a result.

 For its entire century-and-a-half history, Tiffany's name has connoted diamonds and luxury. Tiffany designed a pitcher for Abraham Lincoln's inaugural, made swords for the Civil War, introduced sterling silver to the United States, and designed the "E Pluribus Unum" insignia that adorns $1 bills as well as the Super Bowl and NASCAR trophies. A cultural icon—its Tiffany Blue color is even trademarked—Tiffany has survived the economy's numerous ups and downs through the years. With the emergence in the late 1990s of the notion of "affordable luxuries," Tiffany seized the moment by creating a line of cheaper silver jewelry. Its "Return to Tiffany" silver bracelet became a must-have item for teens of a certain set. Earnings skyrocketed for the next five years, but the affordable jewelry brought both an image and a pricing crisis for the company: What if all those teens who bought Tiffany charm bracelets grew up to think of Tiffany only as a place where they got the jewelry of their girlhood? Starting in 2002, the company began hiking prices again. At the same time, it launched higher-end collections, renovated stores to feature expensive items appealing to mature buyers, and expanded aggressively into new cities and shopping malls. When the recession began in 2008, the firm knew it had to be careful not to dilute its high-end appeal. Tiffany offset softer sales largely with cost-cutting and inventory management, and—very quietly—it lowered prices on its best-selling engagement rings only, by roughly 10 percent.[1]

Pricing decisions are clearly complex and difficult, and many marketers neglect their pricing strategies.[2] Holistic marketers must take into account many factors in making pricing decisions—the company, the customers, the competition, and the marketing environment. Pricing decisions must be consistent with the firm's marketing strategy and its target markets and brand positionings.

In this chapter, we provide concepts and tools to facilitate the setting of initial prices and adjusting prices over time and markets.

Understanding Pricing

Price is not just a number on a tag. It comes in many forms and performs many functions. Rent, tuition, fares, fees, rates, tolls, retainers, wages, and commissions are all the price you pay for some good or service. Price also has many components. If you buy a new car, the sticker price may be adjusted by rebates and dealer incentives. Some firms allow for payment through multiple forms, such as $150 plus 25,000 frequent flier miles for a flight.[3]

Throughout most of history, prices were set by negotiation between buyers and sellers. Bargaining is still a sport in some areas. Setting one price for all buyers is a relatively modern idea that arose with the development of large-scale retailing at the end of the nineteenth century. F. W. Woolworth, Tiffany & Co., John Wanamaker, and others advertised a "strictly one-price policy," because they carried so many items and supervised so many employees.

Traditionally, price has operated as a major determinant of buyer choice. Consumers and purchasing agents who have access to price information and price discounters put pressure on retailers to lower their prices. Retailers in turn put pressure on manufacturers to lower their prices. The result can be a marketplace characterized by heavy discounting and sales promotion.

A Changing Pricing Environment

Pricing practices have changed significantly. At the turn of the 21st century, consumers had easy access to credit, so by combining unique product formulations with enticing marketing campaigns, many firms successfully traded consumers up to more expensive products and services. The onset of the Great Recession—a recession more severe than previous recessions, which resulted in many jobs lost and many businesses and consumers unable to receive loans due to their poorly leveraged situations—changed things though.

A combination of environmentalism, renewed frugality, and concern about jobs and home values forced many U.S. consumers to rethink how they spent their money. They replaced luxury purchases with basics. They bought fewer accessories like jewelry, watches, and bags. They ate at home more often and purchased espresso machines to make lattes in their kitchens instead of buying them at expensive cafés. If they bought a new car at all, they downsized to smaller, more fuel-efficient models. They even cut back spending on hobbies and sports activities.[4]

Downward price pressure from a changing economic environment coincided with some longer-term trends in the technological environment. For some years now, the Internet has been changing how buyers and sellers interact. Here is a short list of how the Internet allows sellers to discriminate between buyers, and buyers to discriminate between sellers.[5]

Buyers can:

- ***Get instant price comparisons from thousands of vendors.*** Customers can compare the prices offered by multiple bookstores by just clicking mySimon.com. PriceSCAN.com lures thousands of visitors a day, most of them corporate buyers. Intelligent shopping agents ("bots") take price comparison a step further and seek out products, prices, and reviews from hundreds if not thousands of merchants.
- ***Name their price and have it met.*** On Priceline.com, the customer states the price he or she wants to pay for an airline ticket, hotel, or rental car, and Priceline looks for any seller willing to meet that price.[6] Volume-aggregating sites combine the orders of many customers and press the supplier for a deeper discount.
- ***Get products free.*** Open Source, the free software movement that started with Linux, will erode margins for just about any company creating software. The biggest challenge confronting Microsoft, Oracle, IBM, and virtually every other major software producer is: How do you compete with programs that can be had for free? "Marketing Insight: Giving It All Away" describes how different firms have been successful with essentially free offerings.

Marketing Insight

Giving It All Away

Giving away products for free via sampling has been a successful marketing tactic for years. Estée Lauder gave free samples of cosmetics to celebrities, and organizers at awards shows lavish winners with plentiful free items or gifts known as "swag." Other manufacturers, such as Gillette and HP, have built their business model around selling the host product essentially at cost and making money on the sale of necessary supplies, such as razor blades and printer ink.

With the advent of the Internet, software companies began to adopt similar practices. Adobe gave away its PDF Reader for free in 1994, as did Macromedia with its Shockwave player in 1995. Their software became the industry standard, but the firms really made their money selling their authoring software. More recently, Internet start-ups such as Blogger Weblog publishing tool, MySpace online community, and Skype Internet phone calls have all achieved some success with a "freemium" strategy—free online services with a premium component.

Chris Anderson, editor-in-chief of *Wired*, strongly believes that in a digital marketplace, companies can make money with "free" products. As evidence, he offers revenue models involving cross-subsidies (giving away a DVR to sell cable service) and freemiums (offering the Flickr online photo management and sharing application for free to everyone while selling the superior FlickrPro to more highly involved users).

Some online firms have successfully moved "from free to fee" and begun charging for services. Under a new participative pricing mechanism that lets consumers decide the price they feel is warranted, buyers often choose to pay more than zero and even enough that the seller's revenues increase over what a fixed price would have yielded.

Offline, profits for discount air carrier Ryanair have been sky-high thanks to its revolutionary business model. The secret? Founder Michael O'Leary thinks like a retailer, charging for almost everything but the seat itself:

1. A quarter of Ryanair's seats are free. O'Leary wants to double that within five years, with the ultimate goal of making all seats free. Passengers currently pay only taxes and fees of about $10 to $24, with an average one-way fare of roughly $52.

2. Passengers pay extra for everything else: for checked luggage ($9.50 per bag), snacks ($5.50 for a hot dog, $4.50 for chicken soup, $3.50 for water), and bus or train transportation into town from the far-flung airports Ryanair uses ($24).

3. Flight attendants sell a variety of merchandise, including digital cameras ($137.50) and iPocket MP3 players ($165). Onboard gambling and cell phone service are projected new revenue sources.

Other strategies cut costs or generate outside revenue:

4. Seats don't recline, window shades and seat-back pockets have been removed, and there is no entertainment. Seat-back trays now carry ads, and the exteriors of the planes are giant revenue-producing billboards for Vodafone Group, Jaguar, Hertz, and others.

5. More than 99 percent of tickets are sold online. The Web site also offers travel insurance, hotels, ski packages, and car rentals.

6. Only Boeing 737–800 jets are flown to reduce maintenance, and flight crews buy their own uniforms.

The formula works for Ryanair's customers; the airline flies 50 million of them to over 150 airports each year. All the extras add up to 20 percent of revenue. Ryanair enjoys net margins of 25 percent, more than three times Southwest's 7 percent. Some industry pundits even refer to Ryanair as "Walmart with wings!" European discount carrier easyJet has adopted many of the same practices.

Sources: Chris Anderson, *Free: The Future of a Radical Price* (New York: Hyperion, 2009); Peter J. Howe, "The Next Pinch: Fees to Check Bags," *Boston Globe,* March 8, 2007; Katherine Heires, "Why It Pays to Give Away the Store," *Business 2.0* (October 2006): 36–37; Kerry Capel, "'Wal-Mart with Wings,'" *BusinessWeek,* November 27, 2006, pp. 44–45; Matthew Maier, "A Radical Fix for Airlines: Make Flying Free," *Business 2.0* (April 2006): 32–34; Ju-Young Kim, Martin Natter, and Martin Spann, "Pay What You Want: A New Participative Pricing Mechanism," *Journal of Marketing* 73 (January 2009), pp. 44–58; Koen Pauwels and Allen Weiss, "Moving from Free to Fee: How Online Firms Market to Change Their Business Model Successfully," *Journal of Marketing* 72 (May 2008), pp. 14–31; Bruce Myerson, "Skype Takes Its Show on the Road," *BusinessWeek,* October 29, 2007, p. 38.

Sellers can:

- *Monitor customer behavior and tailor offers to individuals.* GE Lighting, which gets 55,000 pricing requests a year, has Web programs that evaluate 300 factors that go into a pricing quote, such as past sales data and discounts, so it can reduce processing time from up to 30 days to 6 hours.

Discount airline Ryanair's revolutionary business model is to charge next to nothing for a seat on a flight, but something for virtually everything else.

- *Give certain customers access to special prices.* Ruelala is a members-only Web site that sells upscale women's fashion, accessories, and footwear through limited-time sales, usually two-day events. Other business marketers are already using extranets to get a precise handle on inventory, costs, and demand at any given moment in order to adjust prices instantly.

Both buyers and sellers can:

- *Negotiate prices in online auctions and exchanges or even in person.* Want to sell hundreds of excess and slightly worn widgets? Post a sale on eBay. Want to purchase vintage baseball cards at a bargain price? Go to www.baseballplanet.com. With the advent of the recession, many consumers began to take the practice of haggling over price honed at car dealers and flea markets into other realms like real estate, jewelry, or virtually any retail durable purchase. Almost three-quarters of U.S. consumers reported negotiating for lower prices in recent years, up a third from the five years before the recession hit.[7]

How Companies Price

Companies do their pricing in a variety of ways. In small companies, the boss often sets prices. In large companies, division and product line managers do. Even here, top management sets general pricing objectives and policies and often approves lower management's proposals.

Where pricing is a key factor (aerospace, railroads, oil companies), companies often establish a pricing department to set or assist others in setting appropriate prices. This department reports to the marketing department, finance department, or top management. Others who influence pricing include sales managers, production managers, finance managers, and accountants.

Executives complain that pricing is a big headache—and getting worse by the day. Many companies do not handle pricing well and fall back on "strategies" such as: "We determine our costs and take our industry's traditional margins." Other common mistakes are not revising price often enough to capitalize on market changes; setting price independently of the rest of the marketing program rather than as an intrinsic element of market-positioning strategy; and not varying price enough for different product items, market segments, distribution channels, and purchase occasions.

For any organization, effectively designing and implementing pricing strategies requires a thorough understanding of consumer pricing psychology and a systematic approach to setting, adapting, and changing prices.

Consumer Psychology and Pricing

Many economists traditionally assumed that consumers were "price takers" and accepted prices at "face value" or as given. Marketers, however, recognize that consumers often actively process price information, interpreting it from the context of prior purchasing experience, formal communications (advertising, sales calls, and brochures), informal communications (friends, colleagues, or family members), point-of-purchase or online resources, and other factors.[8]

Purchase decisions are based on how consumers perceive prices and what they consider the current actual price to be—*not* on the marketer's stated price. Customers may have a lower price threshold below which prices signal inferior or unacceptable quality, as well as an upper price threshold above which prices are prohibitive and the product appears not worth the money. The following example helps illustrate the large part consumer psychology plays in determining three different prices for essentially the same item: a black T-shirt.

 A Black T-Shirt The black T-shirt for women looks pretty ordinary. In fact, it's not that different from the black T-shirt sold by Gap and by Swedish discount clothing chain H&M. Yet, the Armani T-shirt costs $275.00, whereas the Gap item costs $14.90 and the H&M one $7.90. Customers who purchase the Armani T-shirt are paying for a T-shirt made of 70 percent nylon, 25 percent polyester, and 5 percent elastane, whereas the Gap and H&M shirts are made mainly of cotton. True, the Armani T is a bit more stylishly cut than the other two and sports a "Made in Italy" label, but how does it command a $275.00 price tag? A luxury brand, Armani is primarily known for suits, handbags, and evening gowns that sell for thousands of dollars. In that context, it can sell its T-shirts for more. But because there aren't many takers for $275.00 T-shirts, Armani doesn't make many, thus further enhancing the appeal for status seekers who like the idea of having a "limited edition" T-shirt. "Value is not only quality, function, utility, channel of distribution," says Arnold Aronson, managing director of retail strategies for Kurt Salmon Associates and former CEO of Saks Fifth Avenue; it's also a customer's perception of a brand's luxury connotations.[9]

Consumer attitudes about pricing took a dramatic shift in the recent economic downturn as many found themselves unable to sustain their lifestyles.[10] Consumers began to buy more for need than desire and to trade down more frequently in price. They shunned conspicuous consumption, and sales of luxury goods suffered. Even purchases that had never been challenged before were scrutinized. Almost 1 million U.S. patients became "medical tourists" in 2010 and traveled overseas for medical procedures at lower costs, sometimes at the urging of U.S. health insurance companies.[11]

The perceived value of a product as simple as a black T-shirt depends in part on where it is sold.

Even in a recession, however, some companies can command a price premium if their offerings are unique and relevant enough to a large enough market segment. Pangea Organics expanded distribution of its pricey $8 soaps and $50 oils, thanks to environmentally friendly organic formulations and clever, seed-infused packaging.[12]

Understanding how consumers arrive at their perceptions of prices is an important marketing priority. Here we consider three key topics—reference prices, price–quality inferences, and price endings.

REFERENCE PRICES Although consumers may have fairly good knowledge of price ranges, surprisingly few can accurately recall specific prices.[13] When examining products, however, they often employ **reference prices**, comparing an observed price to an internal reference price they remember or an external frame of reference such as a posted "regular retail price."[14]

All types of reference prices are possible (see 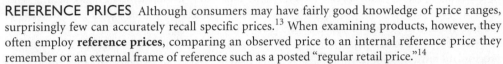 Table 14.1), and sellers often attempt to manipulate them. For example, a seller can situate its product among expensive competitors to imply that it belongs in the same class. Department stores will display women's apparel in separate departments differentiated by price; dresses in the more expensive department are assumed to be of better quality.[15] Marketers also encourage reference-price thinking by stating a high manufacturer's suggested price, indicating that the price was much higher originally, or pointing to a competitor's high price.[16]

When consumers evoke one or more of these frames of reference, their perceived price can vary from the stated price.[17] Research has found that unpleasant surprises—when perceived price is lower than the stated price—can have a greater impact on purchase likelihood than pleasant surprises.[18] Consumer expectations can also play a key role in price response. On Internet auction sites such as eBay, when consumers know similar goods will be available in future auctions, they will bid less in the current auction.[19]

TABLE 14.1 🔲 Possible Consumer Reference Prices
• "Fair Price" (what consumers feel the product should cost)
• Typical Price
• Last Price Paid
• Upper-Bound Price (reservation price or the maximum most consumers would pay)
• Lower-Bound Price (lower threshold price or the minimum most consumers would pay)
• Historical Competitor Prices
• Expected Future Price
• Usual Discounted Price

Source: Adapted from Russell S. Winer, *Pricing*, MSI Relevant Knowledge Series (Cambridge, MA: Marketing Science Institute, 2006).

Clever marketers try to frame the price to signal the best value possible. For example, a relatively expensive item can look less expensive if the price is broken into smaller units, such as a $500 annual membership for "under $50 a month," even if the totals are the same.[20]

PRICE-QUALITY INFERENCES Many consumers use price as an indicator of quality. Image pricing is especially effective with ego-sensitive products such as perfumes, expensive cars, and designer clothing. A $100 bottle of perfume might contain $10 worth of scent, but gift givers pay $100 to communicate their high regard for the receiver.

Price and quality perceptions of cars interact.[21] Higher-priced cars are perceived to possess high quality. Higher-quality cars are likewise perceived to be higher priced than they actually are. When information about true quality is available, price becomes a less significant indicator of quality. When this information is not available, price acts as a signal of quality.

Some brands adopt exclusivity and scarcity to signify uniqueness and justify premium pricing. Luxury-goods makers of watches, jewelry, perfume, and other products often emphasize exclusivity in their communication messages and channel strategies. For luxury-goods customers who desire uniqueness, demand may actually increase price, because they then believe fewer other customers can afford the product.[22]

PRICE ENDINGS Many sellers believe prices should end in an odd number. Customers see an item priced at $299 as being in the $200 rather than the $300 range; they tend to process prices "left-to-right" rather than by rounding.[23] Price encoding in this fashion is important if there is a mental price break at the higher, rounded price.

Another explanation for the popularity of "9" endings is that they suggest a discount or bargain, so if a company wants a high-price image, it should probably avoid the odd-ending tactic.[24] One study showed that demand actually increased one-third when the price of a dress *rose* from $34 to $39 but was unchanged when it rose from $34 to $44.[25]

Prices that end with 0 and 5 are also popular and are thought to be easier for consumers to process and retrieve from memory.[26] "Sale" signs next to prices spur demand, but only if not overused: Total category sales are highest when some, but not all, items in a category have sale signs; past a certain point, sale signs may cause total category sales to fall.[27]

Pricing cues such as sale signs and prices that end in 9 are more influential when consumers' price knowledge is poor, when they purchase the item infrequently or are new to the category, and when product designs vary over time, prices vary seasonally, or quality or sizes vary across stores.[28] They are less effective the more they are used. Limited availability (for example, "three days only") also can spur sales among consumers actively shopping for a product.[29]

A product priced at $2.99 can be perceived as distinctly less expensive than one priced at $3.00.

Setting the Price

A firm must set a price for the first time when it develops a new product, when it introduces its regular product into a new distribution channel or geographical area, and when it enters bids on new contract work. The firm must decide where to position its product on quality and price.

Most markets have three to five price points or tiers. Marriott Hotels is good at developing different brands or variations of brands for different price points: Marriott Vacation Club—Vacation Villas (highest price), Marriott Marquis (high price), Marriott (high-medium price), Renaissance (medium-high price), Courtyard (medium price), TownePlace Suites (medium-low price), and Fairfield Inn (low price). Firms devise their branding strategies to help convey the price-quality tiers of their products or services to consumers.[30]

The firm must consider many factors in setting its pricing policy.[31] 🔲 Table 14.2 summarizes the six steps in the process.

Marriott's hotel brands differ in price points and the levels of service they offer.

Step 1: Selecting the Pricing Objective

The company first decides where it wants to position its market offering. The clearer a firm's objectives, the easier it is to set price. Five major objectives are: survival, maximum current profit, maximum market share, maximum market skimming, and product-quality leadership.

SURVIVAL Companies pursue *survival* as their major objective if they are plagued with overcapacity, intense competition, or changing consumer wants. As long as prices cover variable costs and some fixed costs, the company stays in business. Survival is a short-run objective; in the long run, the firm must learn how to add value or face extinction.

MAXIMUM CURRENT PROFIT Many companies try to set a price that will *maximize current profits*. They estimate the demand and costs associated with alternative prices and choose the price that produces maximum current profit, cash flow, or rate of return on investment. This strategy assumes the firm knows its demand and cost functions; in reality, these are difficult to estimate. In emphasizing current performance, the company may sacrifice long-run performance by ignoring the effects of other marketing variables, competitors' reactions, and legal restraints on price.

MAXIMUM MARKET SHARE Some companies want to *maximize their market share*. They believe a higher sales volume will lead to lower unit costs and higher long-run profit. They set the lowest price, assuming the market is price sensitive. Texas Instruments (TI) famously practiced this **market-penetration pricing** for years. TI would build a large plant, set its price as low as possible, win a large market share, experience falling costs, and cut its price further as costs fell.

The following conditions favor adopting a market-penetration pricing strategy: (1) The market is highly price sensitive and a low price stimulates market growth; (2) production and distribution

TABLE 14.2 🔲 Steps in Setting a Pricing Policy	
1.	Selecting the Pricing Objective
2.	Determining Demand
3.	Estimating Costs
4.	Analyzing Competitors' Costs, Prices, and Offers
5.	Selecting a Pricing Method
6.	Selecting the Final Price

costs fall with accumulated production experience; and (3) a low price discourages actual and potential competition.

MAXIMUM MARKET SKIMMING Companies unveiling a new technology favor setting high prices to *maximize market skimming*. Sony is a frequent practitioner of **market-skimming pricing**, in which prices start high and slowly drop over time. When Sony introduced the world's first high-definition television (HDTV) to the Japanese market in 1990, it was priced at $43,000. So that Sony could "skim" the maximum amount of revenue from the various segments of the market, the price dropped steadily through the years—a 28-inch Sony HDTV cost just over $6,000 in 1993, but a 40-inch Sony HDTV cost only $600 in 2010.

This strategy can be fatal, however, if a worthy competitor decides to price low. When Philips, the Dutch electronics manufacturer, priced its videodisc players to make a profit on each, Japanese competitors priced low and rapidly built their market share, which in turn pushed down their costs substantially.

Moreover, consumers who buy early at the highest prices may be dissatisfied if they compare themselves to those who buy later at a lower price. When Apple dropped the iPhone's price from $600 to $400 only two months after its introduction, public outcry caused the firm to give initial buyers a $100 credit toward future Apple purchases.[32]

Market skimming makes sense under the following conditions: (1) A sufficient number of buyers have a high current demand; (2) the unit costs of producing a small volume are high enough to cancel the advantage of charging what the traffic will bear; (3) the high initial price does not attract more competitors to the market; (4) the high price communicates the image of a superior product.

Apple created an uproar among its early-adopter customers when it significantly lowered the price of its iPhone after only two months.

PRODUCT-QUALITY LEADERSHIP A company might aim to be the *product-quality leader* in the market. Many brands strive to be "affordable luxuries"—products or services characterized by high levels of perceived quality, taste, and status with a price just high enough not to be out of consumers' reach. Brands such as Starbucks, Aveda, Victoria's Secret, BMW, and Viking have positioned themselves as quality leaders in their categories, combining quality, luxury, and premium prices with an intensely loyal customer base.[33] Grey Goose and Absolut carved out a superpremium niche in the essentially odorless, colorless, and tasteless vodka category through clever on-premise and off-premise marketing that made the brands seem hip and exclusive.[34]

OTHER OBJECTIVES Nonprofit and public organizations may have other pricing objectives. A university aims for *partial cost recovery,* knowing that it must rely on private gifts and public grants to cover its remaining costs. A nonprofit hospital may aim for full cost recovery in its pricing. A nonprofit theater company may price its productions to fill the maximum number of seats. A social service agency may set a service price geared to client income.

Whatever the specific objective, businesses that use price as a strategic tool will profit more than those that simply let costs or the market determine their pricing. For art museums, which earn an average of only 5 percent of their revenues from admission charges, pricing can send a message that affects their public image and the amount of donations and sponsorships they receive.

Step 2: Determining Demand

Each price will lead to a different level of demand and have a different impact on a company's marketing objectives. The normally inverse relationship between price and demand is captured in a demand curve (see △ Figure 14.1): The higher the price, the lower the demand. For prestige goods, the demand curve sometimes slopes upward. One perfume company raised its price and sold more rather than less! Some consumers take the higher price to signify a better product. However, if the price is too high, demand may fall.

PRICE SENSITIVITY The demand curve shows the market's probable purchase quantity at alternative prices. It sums the reactions of many individuals with different price sensitivities. The first step in estimating demand is to understand what affects price sensitivity. Generally speaking, customers are less price sensitive to low-cost items or items they buy infrequently. They are also less price sensitive when (1) there are few or no substitutes or competitors; (2) they do not readily

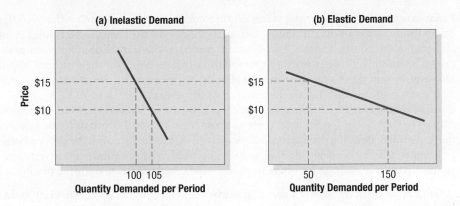

|Fig. 14.1| △

Inelastic and Elastic Demand

notice the higher price; (3) they are slow to change their buying habits; (4) they think the higher prices are justified; and (5) price is only a small part of the total cost of obtaining, operating, and servicing the product over its lifetime.

A seller can successfully charge a higher price than competitors if it can convince customers that it offers the lowest *total cost of ownership* (TCO). Marketers often treat the service elements in a product offering as sales incentives rather than as value-enhancing augmentations for which they can charge. In fact, pricing expert Tom Nagle believes the most common mistake manufacturers have made in recent years is to offer all sorts of services to differentiate their products without charging for them.[35]

Of course, companies prefer customers who are less price-sensitive. Table 14.3 lists some characteristics associated with decreased price sensitivity. On the other hand, the Internet has the potential to *increase* price sensitivity. In some established, fairly big-ticket categories, such as auto retailing and term insurance, consumers pay lower prices as a result of the Internet. Car buyers use the Internet to gather information and borrow the negotiating clout of an online buying service.[36] But customers may have to visit multiple sites to realize these savings, and they don't always do so. Targeting only price-sensitive consumers may in fact be "leaving money on the table."

ESTIMATING DEMAND CURVES Most companies attempt to measure their demand curves using several different methods.

- *Surveys* can explore how many units consumers would buy at different proposed prices. Although consumers might understate their purchase intentions at higher prices to discourage the company from pricing high, they also tend to actually exaggerate their willingness to pay for new products or services.[37]

TABLE 14.3 Factors Leading to Less Price Sensitivity
• The product is more distinctive.
• Buyers are less aware of substitutes.
• Buyers cannot easily compare the quality of substitutes.
• The expenditure is a smaller part of the buyer's total income.
• The expenditure is small compared to the total cost of the end product.
• Part of the cost is borne by another party.
• The product is used in conjunction with assets previously bought.
• The product is assumed to have more quality, prestige, or exclusiveness.
• Buyers cannot store the product.

Source: Based on information from Thomas T. Nagle, John E. Hogan, and Joseph Zale, *The Strategy and Tactics of Pricing,* 5th ed. (Upper Saddle River, NJ: Prentice Hall, 2011). Printed and electronically reproduced by permission of Pearson Education, Inc., Upper Saddle River, New Jersey.

- *Price experiments* can vary the prices of different products in a store or charge different prices for the same product in similar territories to see how the change affects sales. Another approach is to use the Internet. An e-business could test the impact of a 5 percent price increase by quoting a higher price to every 40th visitor, to compare the purchase response. However, it must do this carefully and not alienate customers or be seen as reducing competition in any way (and thus violate the Sherman Antitrust Act).[38]
- *Statistical analysis* of past prices, quantities sold, and other factors can reveal their relationships. The data can be longitudinal (over time) or cross-sectional (from different locations at the same time). Building the appropriate model and fitting the data with the proper statistical techniques calls for considerable skill, but sophisticated price optimization software and advances in database management have improved marketers' abilities to optimize pricing.

One large retail chain was selling a line of "good-better-best" power drills at $90, $120, and $130, respectively. Sales of the least and most expensive drills were fine, but sales of the midpriced drill lagged. Based on a price optimization analysis, the retailer dropped the price of the midpriced drill to $110. Sales of the low-priced drill dropped 4 percent because it seemed less of a bargain, but the sales of the midpriced drill increased by 11 percent. Profits rose as a result.[39]

In measuring the price-demand relationship, the market researcher must control for various factors that will influence demand.[40] The competitor's response will make a difference. Also, if the company changes other aspects of the marketing program besides price, the effect of the price change itself will be hard to isolate.

PRICE ELASTICITY OF DEMAND Marketers need to know how responsive, or elastic, demand is to a change in price. Consider the two demand curves in Figure 14.1. In demand curve (a), a price increase from $10 to $15 leads to a relatively small decline in demand from 105 to 100. In demand curve (b), the same price increase leads to a substantial drop in demand from 150 to 50. If demand hardly changes with a small change in price, we say the demand is *inelastic*. If demand changes considerably, demand is *elastic*.

The higher the elasticity, the greater the volume growth resulting from a 1 percent price reduction. If demand is elastic, sellers will consider lowering the price. A lower price will produce more total revenue. This makes sense as long as the costs of producing and selling more units do not increase disproportionately.[41]

Price elasticity depends on the magnitude and direction of the contemplated price change. It may be negligible with a small price change and substantial with a large price change. It may differ for a price cut versus a price increase, and there may be a *price indifference band* within which price changes have little or no effect.

Finally, long-run price elasticity may differ from short-run elasticity. Buyers may continue to buy from a current supplier after a price increase but eventually switch suppliers. Here demand is more elastic in the long run than in the short run, or the reverse may happen: Buyers may drop a supplier after a price increase but return later. The distinction between short-run and long-run elasticity means that sellers will not know the total effect of a price change until time passes.

One comprehensive study reviewing a 40-year period of academic research that investigated price elasticity yielded interesting findings:[42]

- The average price elasticity across all products, markets, and time periods studied was −2.62. In other words, a 1 percent decrease in prices led to a 2.62 percent increase in sales.
- Price elasticity magnitudes were higher for durable goods than for other goods, and higher for products in the introduction/growth stages of the product life cycle than in the mature/decline stages.
- Inflation led to substantially higher price elasticities, especially in the short run.
- Promotional price elasticities were higher than actual price elasticities in the short run (although the reverse was true in the long run).
- Price elasticities were higher at the individual item or SKU level than at the overall brand level.

Step 3: Estimating Costs

Demand sets a ceiling on the price the company can charge for its product. Costs set the floor. The company wants to charge a price that covers its cost of producing, distributing, and selling the product, including a fair return for its effort and risk. Yet when companies price products to cover their full costs, profitability isn't always the net result.

TYPES OF COSTS AND LEVELS OF PRODUCTION A company's costs take two forms, fixed and variable. **Fixed costs**, also known as **overhead**, are costs that do not vary with production level or sales revenue. A company must pay bills each month for rent, heat, interest, salaries, and so on regardless of output.

Variable costs vary directly with the level of production. For example, each hand calculator produced by Texas Instruments incurs the cost of plastic, microprocessor chips, and packaging. These costs tend to be constant per unit produced, but they're called *variable* because their total varies with the number of units produced.

Total costs consist of the sum of the fixed and variable costs for any given level of production. **Average cost** is the cost per unit at that level of production; it equals total costs divided by production. Management wants to charge a price that will at least cover the total production costs at a given level of production.

To price intelligently, management needs to know how its costs vary with different levels of production. Take the case in which a company such as TI has built a fixed-size plant to produce 1,000 hand calculators a day. The cost per unit is high if few units are produced per day. As production approaches 1,000 units per day, the average cost falls because the fixed costs are spread over more units. Short-run average cost *increases* after 1,000 units, however, because the plant becomes inefficient: Workers must line up for machines, getting in each other's way, and machines break down more often (see ▲ Figure 14.2(a)).

If TI believes it can sell 2,000 units per day, it should consider building a larger plant. The plant will use more efficient machinery and work arrangements, and the unit cost of producing 2,000 calculators per day will be lower than the unit cost of producing 1,000 per day. This is shown in the long-run average cost curve (LRAC) in Figure 14.2(b). In fact, a 3,000-capacity plant would be even more efficient according to Figure 14.2(b), but a 4,000-daily production plant would be less so because of increasing diseconomies of scale: There are too many workers to manage, and paperwork slows things down. Figure 14.2(b) indicates that a 3,000-daily production plant is the optimal size if demand is strong enough to support this level of production.

There are more costs than those associated with manufacturing. To estimate the real profitability of selling to different types of retailers or customers, the manufacturer needs to use activity-based cost (ABC) accounting instead of standard cost accounting, as described in Chapter 5.

ACCUMULATED PRODUCTION Suppose TI runs a plant that produces 3,000 hand calculators per day. As TI gains experience producing hand calculators, its methods improve. Workers learn shortcuts, materials flow more smoothly, and procurement costs fall. The result, as ▲ Figure 14.3 shows, is that average cost falls with accumulated production experience. Thus the average cost of producing the first 100,000 hand calculators is $10 per calculator. When the company has produced the first 200,000 calculators, the average cost has fallen to $9. After its accumulated production experience doubles again to 400,000, the average cost is $8. This decline in the average cost with accumulated production experience is called the **experience curve** or **learning curve**.

Now suppose three firms compete in this industry, TI, A, and B. TI is the lowest-cost producer at $8, having produced 400,000 units in the past. If all three firms sell the calculator for $10, TI

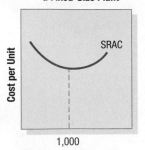

(a) Cost Behavior in a Fixed-Size Plant

SRAC

Cost per Unit

1,000

Quantity Produced per Day

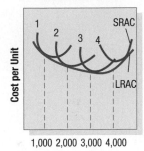

(b) Cost Behavior over Different-Size Plants

SRAC

LRAC

Cost per Unit

1,000 2,000 3,000 4,000

Quantity Produced per Day

|Fig. 14.2| ▲

Cost per Unit at Different Levels of Production per Period

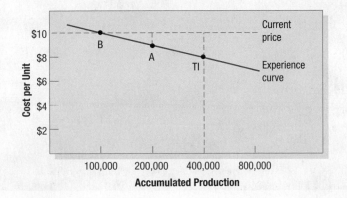

Accumulated Production

|Fig. 14.3| ▲

Cost per Unit as a Function of Accumulated Production: The Experience Curve makes $2 profit per unit, A makes $1 per unit, and B breaks even. The smart move for TI would be to lower its price to $9. This will drive B out of the market, and even A may consider leaving. TI will pick up the business that would have gone to B (and possibly A). Furthermore, price-sensitive customers will enter the market at the lower price. As production increases beyond 400,000 units, TI's costs will drop still further and faster and will more than restore its profits, even at a price of $9. TI has used this aggressive pricing strategy repeatedly to gain market share and drive others out of the industry.

Experience-curve pricing nevertheless carries major risks. Aggressive pricing might give the product a cheap image. It also assumes competitors are weak followers. The strategy leads the company to build more plants to meet demand, but a competitor may choose to innovate with a lower-cost technology. The market leader is now stuck with the old technology.

Most experience-curve pricing has focused on manufacturing costs, but all costs can be improved on, including marketing costs. If three firms are each investing a large sum of money in marketing, the firm that has used it longest might achieve the lowest costs. This firm can charge a little less for its product and still earn the same return, all other costs being equal.[43]

TARGET COSTING Costs change with production scale and experience. They can also change as a result of a concentrated effort by designers, engineers, and purchasing agents to reduce them through **target costing**.[44] Market research establishes a new product's desired functions and the price at which it will sell, given its appeal and competitors' prices. This price less desired profit margin leaves the target cost the marketer must achieve.

The firm must examine each cost element—design, engineering, manufacturing, sales—and bring down costs so the final cost projections are in the target range. When ConAgra Foods decided to increase the list prices of its Banquet frozen dinners to cover higher commodity costs, the average retail price of the meals increased from $1 to $1.25. When sales dropped significantly, management vowed to return to a $1 price, which necessitated cutting $250 million in other costs through a variety of methods, such as centralized purchasing and shipping, less expensive ingredients, and smaller portions.[45]

Companies can cut costs in many ways.[46] With General Mills, it was as simple as reducing the number of varieties of Hamburger Helper from 75 to 45 and the number of pasta shapes from 30 to 10. Dropping multicolored Yoplait lids saved $2 million a year. Some companies are applying what they learned from making affordable products with scarce resources in developing countries such as India to cutting costs in developed markets. Cisco blends teams of U.S. software engineers with Indian supervisors. Other companies such as Aldi take advantage of the global scope.

ConAgra learned the importance to its customers of keeping its Banquet frozen dinners priced at $1.

Aldi Germany's Aldi follows a simple formula globally. It stocks only about 1,000 of the most popular everyday grocery and household items, compared with more than 20,000 at a traditional grocer such as Royal Ahold's Albert Heijn. Almost all the products carry Aldi's own exclusive label. Because it sells so few items, Aldi can exert strong control over quality and price and simplify shipping and handling, leading to high margins. With more than 8,200 stores worldwide currently, Aldi brings in almost $60 billion in annual sales.[47]

Step 4: Analyzing Competitors' Costs, Prices, and Offers

Within the range of possible prices determined by market demand and company costs, the firm must take competitors' costs, prices, and possible price reactions into account. If the firm's offer contains features not offered by the nearest competitor, it should evaluate their worth to the customer and add that value to the competitor's price. If the competitor's offer contains some features not offered by the firm, the firm should subtract their value from its own price. Now the firm can decide whether it can charge more, the same, or less than the competitor.

The introduction or change of any price can provoke a response from customers, competitors, distributors, suppliers, and even government. Competitors are most likely to react when the number of firms is few, the product is homogeneous, and buyers are highly informed. Competitor reactions can be a special problem when these firms have a strong value proposition, as Green Works did.

Green Works Although the natural cleaner market was pioneered by Seventh Generation and method cleaning products, Clorox Green Works now commands 42 percent market share. The Green Works product line consists of 10 natural cleaners using biodegradable ingredients, packaged in recyclable materials, and not tested on animals. The first major new Clorox brand in more than 20 years, it doubled the size of the natural cleaning category with its strategy of "delivering a line of affordable products that are good for consumers, good for retailers, and good for the environment." The company charges only a 10 percent to 20 percent premium over conventional cleaners, versus the premium of 40 percent or more charged by other natural cleaners. Launch marketing efforts included the use of viral marketing and social media, prominent TV coverage in shows like *Ellen* and *Oprah*, collaborations with retail customers such as Safeway and Walmart in product development and in-store promotion, and an endorsement from and cause marketing program with the Sierra Club (resulting in a donation of $645,000 to the organization in 2009).[48]

How can a firm anticipate a competitor's reactions? One way is to assume the competitor reacts in the standard way to a price being set or changed. Another is to assume the competitor treats each price difference or change as a fresh challenge and reacts according to self-interest at the time. Now the company will need to research the competitor's current financial situation, recent sales, customer loyalty, and corporate objectives. If the competitor has a market share objective, it is likely to match price differences or changes.[49] If it has a profit-maximization objective, it may react by increasing its advertising budget or improving product quality.

The problem is complicated because the competitor can put different interpretations on lowered prices or a price cut: that the company is trying to steal the market, that it is doing poorly and trying to boost its sales, or that it wants the whole industry to reduce prices to stimulate total demand.

Step 5: Selecting a Pricing Method

Given the customers' demand schedule, the cost function, and competitors' prices, the company is now ready to select a price. △ Figure 14.4 summarizes the three major considerations in price setting: Costs set a floor to the price. Competitors' prices and the price of substitutes provide an orienting point. Customers' assessment of unique features establishes the price ceiling.

|Fig. 14.4| △

The Three Cs Model for Price Setting

Companies select a pricing method that includes one or more of these three considerations. We will examine six price-setting methods: markup pricing, target-return pricing, perceived-value pricing, value pricing, going-rate pricing, and auction-type pricing.

MARKUP PRICING The most elementary pricing method is to add a standard **markup** to the product's cost. Construction companies submit job bids by estimating the total project cost and adding a standard markup for profit. Lawyers and accountants typically price by adding a standard markup on their time and costs.

Variable cost per unit	$10
Fixed costs	$300,000
Expected unit sales	50,000

Suppose a toaster manufacturer has the following costs and sales expectations:
The manufacturer's unit cost is given by:

$$\text{Unit cost} = \text{variable cost} + \frac{\text{fixed cost}}{\text{unit sales}} = \$10 + \frac{\$300,00}{50,000} = \$16$$

Now assume the manufacturer wants to earn a 20 percent markup on sales. The manufacturer's markup price is given by:

$$\text{Markup price} = \frac{\text{unit cost}}{(1 - \text{desired return on sales})} = \frac{\$16}{1 - 0.2} = \$20$$

The manufacturer will charge dealers $20 per toaster and make a profit of $4 per unit. If dealers want to earn 50 percent on their selling price, they will mark up the toaster 100 percent to $40. Markups are generally higher on seasonal items (to cover the risk of not selling), specialty items, slower-moving items, items with high storage and handling costs, and demand-inelastic items, such as prescription drugs.

Does the use of standard markups make logical sense? Generally, no. Any pricing method that ignores current demand, perceived value, and competition is not likely to lead to the optimal price. Markup pricing works only if the marked-up price actually brings in the expected level of sales. Consider what happened at Parker Hannifin.

Parker Hannifin
When Donald Washkewicz took over as CEO of Parker Hannifin, maker of 800,000 industrial parts for the aerospace, transportation, and manufacturing industries, pricing was done one way: Calculate how much it costs to make and deliver a product and then add a flat percentage (usually 35 percent). Even though this method was historically well received, Washkewicz set out to get the company to think more like a retailer and charge what customers were willing to pay. Encountering initial resistance from some of the company's 115 different divisions, Washkewicz assembled a list of the 50 most commonly given reasons why the new pricing scheme would fail and announced he would listen only to arguments that were not on the list. The new pricing scheme put Parker Hannifin's products into one of four categories depending on how much competition existed. About one-third fell into niches where Parker offered unique value, there was little competition, and higher prices were appropriate. Each division now has a pricing guru or specialist who assists in strategic pricing. The division making industrial fittings reviewed 2,000 different items and concluded that 28 percent were priced too low, raising prices anywhere from 3 percent to 60 percent.[50]

Still, markup pricing remains popular. First, sellers can determine costs much more easily than they can estimate demand. By tying the price to cost, sellers simplify the pricing task. Second, where

Electro-Hydraulic Axes

aerospace
climate control
electromechanical
filtration
fluid & gas handling
hydraulics
pneumatics
process control
sealing & shielding

Parker

ENGINEERING **YOUR** SUCCESS.

With a stronger focus on customer value and competitive pressures, Parker Hannifin was able to simplify its approach to the pricing of its thousands of products.

all firms in the industry use this pricing method, prices tend to be similar and price competition is minimized. Third, many people feel that cost-plus pricing is fairer to both buyers and sellers. Sellers do not take advantage of buyers when the latter's demand becomes acute, and sellers earn a fair return on investment.

TARGET-RETURN PRICING In **target-return pricing**, the firm determines the price that yields its target rate of return on investment. Public utilities, which need to make a fair return on investment, often use this method.

Suppose the toaster manufacturer has invested $1 million in the business and wants to set a price to earn a 20 percent ROI, specifically $200,000. The target-return price is given by the following formula:

$$\text{Target-return price} = \text{unit cost} + \frac{\text{desired return} \times \text{invested capital}}{\text{unit sales}}$$

$$= \$16 + \frac{.20 \times \$1,000,000}{50,000} = \$20$$

|Fig. 14.5| △

Break-Even Chart for Determining Target-Return Price and Break-Even Volume

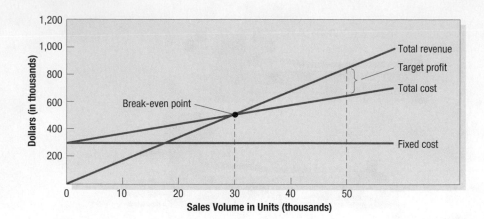

The manufacturer will realize this 20 percent ROI provided its costs and estimated sales turn out to be accurate. But what if sales don't reach 50,000 units? The manufacturer can prepare a break-even chart to learn what would happen at other sales levels (see △ Figure 14.5). Fixed costs are $300,000 regardless of sales volume. Variable costs, not shown in the figure, rise with volume. Total costs equal the sum of fixed and variable costs. The total revenue curve starts at zero and rises with each unit sold.

The total revenue and total cost curves cross at 30,000 units. This is the break-even volume. We can verify it by the following formula:

$$\text{Break-even volume} = \frac{\text{fixed cost}}{(\text{price} - \text{variable cost})} = \frac{\$300,000}{\$20 - \$10} = 30,000$$

The manufacturer, of course, is hoping the market will buy 50,000 units at $20, in which case it earns $200,000 on its $1 million investment, but much depends on price elasticity and competitors' prices. Unfortunately, target-return pricing tends to ignore these considerations. The manufacturer needs to consider different prices and estimate their probable impacts on sales volume and profits.

The manufacturer should also search for ways to lower its fixed or variable costs, because lower costs will decrease its required break-even volume. Acer has been gaining share in the netbook market through rock-bottom prices made possible because of its bare-bones cost strategy. Acer sells only via retailers and other outlets and outsources all manufacturing and assembly, reducing its overhead to 8 percent of sales versus 14 percent at Dell and 15 percent at HP.[51]

PERCEIVED-VALUE PRICING An increasing number of companies now base their price on the customer's **perceived value**. Perceived value is made up of a host of inputs, such as the buyer's image of the product performance, the channel deliverables, the warranty quality, customer support, and softer attributes such as the supplier's reputation, trustworthiness, and esteem. Companies must deliver the value promised by their value proposition, and the customer must perceive this value. Firms use the other marketing program elements, such as advertising, sales force, and the Internet, to communicate and enhance perceived value in buyers' minds.[52]

Caterpillar uses perceived value to set prices on its construction equipment. It might price its tractor at $100,000, although a similar competitor's tractor might be priced at $90,000. When a prospective customer asks a Caterpillar dealer why he should pay $10,000 more for the Caterpillar tractor, the dealer answers:

$90,000	is the tractor's price if it is only equivalent to the competitor's tractor
$7,000	is the price premium for Caterpillar's superior durability
$6,000	is the price premium for Caterpillar's superior reliability
$5,000	is the price premium for Caterpillar's superior service

$2,000	is the price premium for Caterpillar's longer warranty on parts
$110,000	is the normal price to cover Caterpillar's superior value
– $10,000	discount
$100,000	final price

The Caterpillar dealer is able to show that although the customer is asked to pay a $10,000 premium, he is actually getting $20,000 extra value! The customer chooses the Caterpillar tractor because he is convinced its lifetime operating costs will be lower.

Ensuring that customers appreciate the total value of a product or service offering is crucial. Consider the experience of PACCAR.

PACCAR

PACCAR Inc., maker of Kenworth and Peterbilt trucks, is able to command a 10 percent premium through its relentless focus on all aspects of the customer experience to maximize total value. Contract Freighters trucking company, a loyal PACCAR customer for 20 years, justified ordering another 700 new trucks, despite their higher price, because of their higher perceived quality—greater reliability, higher trade-in value, even the superior plush interiors that might attract better drivers. PACCAR bucks the commoditization trend by custom-building its trucks to individual specifications. The company invests heavily in technology and can prototype new parts in hours versus days and weeks, allowing more frequent upgrades. PACCAR was the first to roll out hybrid vehicles in the fuel-intensive commercial trucking industry (and sell at a premium). The company generated $1 billion of profit on $15 billion of revenue in 2008—its 70th consecutive year of profitability—bolstered by record European sales and $2.3 billion in sales of aftermarket parts.[53]

Because of its high standards for quality and continual innovation, PACCAR can charge a premium for its trucks.

Even when a company claims its offering delivers more total value, not all customers will respond positively. Some care only about price. But there is also typically a segment that cares about quality. The makers of Stag umbrellas in India—umbrellas are essential in the three months of near-non-stop monsoon rain in cities such as Mumbai—found themselves in a bitter price war with cheaper Chinese competitors. After realizing they were sacrificing quality too much, Stag's managers decided to increase quality with new colors, designs, and features such as built-in high-power flashlights and prerecorded music. Despite higher prices, sales of the improved Stag umbrellas actually increased.[54]

The key to perceived-value pricing is to deliver more unique value than the competitor and to demonstrate this to prospective buyers. Thus a company needs to fully understand the customer's decision-making process. For example, Goodyear found it hard to command a price premium for its more expensive new tires despite innovative new features to extend tread life. Because consumers had no reference price to compare tires, they tended to gravitate toward the lowest-priced offerings. Goodyear's solution was to price its models on expected miles of wear rather than their technical product features, making product comparisons easier.[55]

The company can try to determine the value of its offering in several ways: managerial judgments within the company, value of similar products, focus groups, surveys, experimentation, analysis of historical data, and conjoint analysis.[56] Table 14.4 contains six key considerations in developing value-based pricing.

VALUE PRICING In recent years, several companies have adopted **value pricing**: They win loyal customers by charging a fairly low price for a high-quality offering. Value pricing is thus not a

TABLE 14.4	A Framework of Questions for Practicing Value-Based Pricing
1.	What is the market strategy for the segment? (What does the supplier want to accomplish? What would the supplier like to have happen?)
2.	What is the differential value that is *transparent* to target customers? (*Transparent* means that target customers easily understand how the supplier calculates the differential value between its offering and the next best alternative, and that the differential value can be verified with the customer's own data.)
3.	What is the price of the next best alternative offering?
4.	What is the cost of the supplier's market offering?
5.	What pricing tactics will be used initially or eventually? ("Pricing tactics" are changes from a price that a supplier has set for its marketing offering—such as discounts—that motivate customers to take actions that benefit the supplier.)
6.	What is the customer's expectation of a "fair" price?

Source: James C. Anderson, Marc Wouters, and Wouter Van Rossum, "Why the Highest Price Isn't the Best Price," *MIT Sloan Management Review* (Winter 2010), pp. 69–76. © 2006 by Massachusetts Institute of Technology. All rights reserved. Distributed by Tribune Media Services.

matter of simply setting lower prices; it is a matter of reengineering the company's operations to become a low-cost producer without sacrificing quality, to attract a large number of value-conscious customers.

Among the best practitioners of value pricing are IKEA, Target, and Southwest Airlines. In the early 1990s, Procter & Gamble created quite a stir when it reduced prices on supermarket staples such as Pampers and Luvs diapers, liquid Tide detergent, and Folgers coffee to value price them. To do so, P&G redesigned the way it developed, manufactured, distributed, priced, marketed, and sold products to deliver better value at every point in the supply chain.[57] Its acquisition of Gillette in 2005 for $57 billion (a record five times its sales) brought another brand into its fold that has also traditionally adopted a value pricing strategy.

Gillette   In 2006, Gillette launched the "best shave on the planet" with the six-bladed Fusion—five blades in the front for regular shaving and one in the back for trimming—in both power and nonpower versions. Gillette conducts exhaustive consumer research in designing its new products and markets aggressively to spread the word. The company spent over $1.2 billion on research and development after the Fusion's predecessor, the Mach3, was introduced. About 9,000 men tested potential new products and preferred the new Fusion over the Mach3 by a two-to-one margin. To back the introduction, Procter & Gamble spent $200 million in the United States and over $1 billion worldwide. The payoff? Gillette enjoys enormous market leadership in the razor and blade categories, with 70 percent of the global market, and sizable price premiums. Refills for the Fusion Power cost $14 for a four-pack, compared to $5.29 for a five-pack of Sensor Excel. All this adds up to significant, sustained profitability for corporate owner P&G.[58]

Value pricing can change the manner by which a company sets prices too. One company that sold and maintained switch boxes in a variety of sizes for telephone lines found that the probability of failure—and thus maintenance costs—was proportional to the number of switches customers had in their boxes rather than to the dollar value of the installed boxes. The number of switches could vary in a box, though. Therefore, rather than charging customers based on the total spent on their installation, the company began charging based on the total number of switches needing servicing.[59]

An important type of value pricing is **everyday low pricing (EDLP)**. A retailer that holds to an EDLP pricing policy charges a constant low price with little or no price promotions and special sales. Constant prices eliminate week-to-week price uncertainty and the "high-low" pricing of promotion-oriented competitors. In **high-low pricing**, the retailer charges higher prices on an everyday basis but runs frequent promotions with prices temporarily lower than the EDLP level.[60] These two strategies have been shown to affect consumer price judgments—deep discounts (EDLP) can lead customers to perceive lower prices over time than frequent, shallow discounts (high-low), even if the actual averages are the same.[61]

In recent years, high-low pricing has given way to EDLP at such widely different venues as Toyota Scion car dealers and upscale department stores such as Nordstrom, but the king of EDLP is surely Walmart, which practically defined the term. Except for a few sale items every month, Walmart promises everyday low prices on major brands.

EDLP provides customer benefits of time and money. Toyota believes its Gen Y target dislikes haggling because it takes too long. These buyers collect a lot of information online anyway, so Toyota cut the time to sell Scions from the industry average of 4.5 hours to 45 minutes requiring fewer managers to approve negotiated prices and less advertising of sales.[62] Some retailers base their entire marketing strategy around *extreme* everyday low pricing.

Daiso   Daiso is the famous one-price Japanese livingware store that recently opened in Kuala Lumpur, Malaysia. Primarily based on the *extreme* EDLP (Every Day Low Pricing) strategy and modeled after Japanese 100 Yen shops, the chain has about 3,000 stores in almost 25 countries worldwide, including Australia, China, Japan, Korea, Kuwait, Saudi Arabia, Singapore, the United Kingdom, and the United States. Daiso is the ideal place for an enjoyable, fast, cheap, and easy shopping experience where everything sells at the same low fixed price; for example, in the Kuala Lumpur store, each item is 5 Malaysian ringgits, or approximately $1.60. Each store stocks a range of kitchenware, tableware, bathroom accessories, houseware items, storage units, and skin care products from Japan. Daiso stores in Kuala Lumpur also introduced imported Japanese products that were not available there before, such as sweet and savory Japanese crackers, confectioneries, and *furikake* or Japanese savory rice sprinkles. In fact, Daiso stores sell more than 9,000 products and introduce 1,000 new ones every month.[63]

Daiso, based on the *extreme* 'Every Day Low Pricing' concept, is known for its fast, cheap, and easy shopping experience where everything in one of its stores is sold at the same low fixed price.

The most important reason retailers adopt EDLP is that constant sales and promotions are costly and have eroded consumer confidence in everyday shelf prices. Consumers also have less time and patience for past traditions like watching for supermarket specials and clipping coupons. Yet, promotions do create excitement and draw shoppers, so EDLP does not guarantee success. As supermarkets face heightened competition from their counterparts and alternative channels, many find the key is a combination of high-low and everyday low pricing strategies, with increased advertising and promotions.

GOING-RATE PRICING
In **going-rate pricing**, the firm bases its price largely on competitors' prices. In oligopolistic industries that sell a commodity such as steel, paper, or fertilizer, all firms normally charge the same price. Smaller firms "follow the leader," changing their prices when the market leader's prices change rather than when their own demand or costs change. Some may charge a small premium or discount, but they preserve the difference. Thus minor gasoline retailers usually charge a few cents less per gallon than the major oil companies, without letting the difference increase or decrease.

Going-rate pricing is quite popular. Where costs are difficult to measure or competitive response is uncertain, firms feel the going price is a good solution because it is thought to reflect the industry's collective wisdom.

AUCTION-TYPE PRICING
Auction-type pricing is growing more popular, especially with scores of electronic marketplaces selling everything from pigs to used cars as firms dispose of excess

inventories or used goods. These are the three major types of auctions and their separate pricing procedures:

- **English auctions (ascending bids)** have one seller and many buyers. On sites such as eBay and Amazon.com, the seller puts up an item and bidders raise the offer price until the top price is reached. The highest bidder gets the item. English auctions are used today for selling antiques, cattle, real estate, and used equipment and vehicles. After watching eBay and other ticket brokers, scalpers, and middlemen reap millions by charging what the market would bear, Ticketmaster has overhauled the way it sells tickets to try to gain more of the multi-billion-dollar ticket resale industry. It now runs auctions for 30 percent of major music tours including popular artists such as Christina Aguilera and Madonna and allows some customers to resell their seats on its Web site.[64]

- **Dutch auctions (descending bids)** feature one seller and many buyers, or one buyer and many sellers. In the first kind, an auctioneer announces a high price for a product and then slowly decreases the price until a bidder accepts. In the other, the buyer announces something he or she wants to buy, and potential sellers compete to offer the lowest price. FreeMarkets.com—later acquired by Ariba—helped Royal Mail Group plc, the United Kingdom's public mail service company, save approximately £2.5 million (almost $4 million), in part via an auction where 25 airlines bid for its international freight business.[65]

- **Sealed-bid auctions** let would-be suppliers submit only one bid; they cannot know the other bids. The U.S. government often uses this method to procure supplies. A supplier will not bid below its cost but cannot bid too high for fear of losing the job. The net effect of these two pulls is the bid's *expected profit*.[66]

To buy equipment for its drug researchers, Pfizer uses reverse auctions in which suppliers submit online the lowest price they are willing to be paid. If the increased savings a firm obtains in an online auction translates into decreased margins for an incumbent supplier, however, the supplier may feel the firm is opportunistically squeezing out price concessions.[67] Online auctions with a large number of bidders, greater economic stakes, and less visibility in pricing result in greater overall satisfaction, more positive future expectations, and fewer perceptions of opportunism.

Step 6: Selecting the Final Price

Pricing methods narrow the range from which the company must select its final price. In selecting that price, the company must consider additional factors, including the impact of other marketing activities, company pricing policies, gain-and-risk-sharing pricing, and the impact of price on other parties.

IMPACT OF OTHER MARKETING ACTIVITIES The final price must take into account the brand's quality and advertising relative to the competition. In a classic study, Paul Farris and David Reibstein examined the relationships among relative price, relative quality, and relative advertising for 227 consumer businesses and found the following:[68]

- Brands with average relative quality but high relative advertising budgets could charge premium prices. Consumers were willing to pay higher prices for known rather than for unknown products.

- Brands with high relative quality and high relative advertising obtained the highest prices. Conversely, brands with low quality and low advertising charged the lowest prices.

- For market leaders, the positive relationship between high prices and high advertising held most strongly in the later stages of the product life cycle.

These findings suggest that price is not necessarily as important as quality and other benefits.

COMPANY PRICING POLICIES The price must be consistent with company pricing policies. Yet companies are not averse to establishing pricing penalties under certain circumstances.[69]

Airlines charge $150 to those who change their reservations on discount tickets. Banks charge fees for too many withdrawals in a month or early withdrawal of a certificate of deposit. Dentists, hotels, car rental companies, and other service providers charge penalties for no-shows who miss appointments or reservations. Although these policies are often justifiable, marketers must use them judiciously and not unnecessarily alienate customers. (See "Marketing Insight: Stealth Price Increases.")

Many companies set up a pricing department to develop policies and establish or approve decisions. The aim is to ensure that salespeople quote prices that are reasonable to customers and profitable to the company.

Marketing Insight

Stealth Price Increases

With consumers resisting higher prices, companies are trying to figure out how to increase revenue without really raising prices. They often resort to adding fees for once-free features. Although some consumers abhor "nickel-and-dime" pricing strategies, small additional charges can add up to a substantial source of revenue.

The numbers can be staggering. The telecommunications industry has been aggressive at adding fees for setup, change-of-service, service termination, directory assistance, regulatory assessment, number portability, and cable hookup and equipment, costing consumers billions of dollars. Fees for consumers who pay bills online, bounce checks, or use automated teller machines bring banks billions of dollars annually.

When credit card companies were faced with a set of reforms in 2009 to some of their most reviled practices—including abrupt interest rate changes and late payment fees—they responded with new ways to raise revenue, such as rate floors for variable rate cards, higher penalty fees for overdue payments at lower balance thresholds, and inactivity fees for not using cards.

This explosion of fees has a number of implications. Given that list prices stay fixed, they may understate inflation. They also make it harder for consumers to compare competitive offerings. Although various citizens' groups have tried to pressure companies to roll back some of these fees, they don't always get a sympathetic ear from state and local governments, which have been guilty of using their own array of fees, fines, and penalties to raise necessary revenue.

Companies justify the extra fees as the only fair and viable way to cover expenses without losing customers. Many argue that it makes sense to charge a premium for added services that cost more to provide, rather than charging all customers the same amount whether or not they use the extra service. Breaking out charges and fees according to the related services is a way to keep basic costs low. Companies also use fees as a means to weed out unprofitable customers or get them to change their behavior.

Ultimately, the viability of extra fees will be decided in the marketplace, and by the willingness of consumers to vote with their wallets and pay the fees, or vote with their feet and move on.

Sources: Alexis Leondis and Jeff Plungis, "The Latest Credit Card Tricks," *Bloomberg BusinessWeek*, December 28, 2009 & January 4, 2010, p. 95; Brian Burnsed, "A New Front in the Credit Card Wars," *BusinessWeek*, November 9, 2009, p. 60; Kathy Chu, "Credit Card Fees Can Suck You In," *USA Today*, December 15, 2006; Michael Arndt, "Fees! Fees! Fees!" *BusinessWeek*, September 29, 2003, pp. 99–104; "The Price Is Wrong," *Economist*, May 25, 2002, pp. 59–60.

GAIN-AND-RISK-SHARING PRICING Buyers may resist accepting a seller's proposal because of a high perceived level of risk. The seller has the option of offering to absorb part or all the risk if it does not deliver the full promised value. Some recent risk-sharing applications include big computer hardware purchases and health plans for big unions.

Baxter Healthcare, a leading medical products firm, was able to secure a contract for an information management system from Columbia/HCA, a leading health care provider, by guaranteeing the firm several million dollars in savings over an eight-year period. An increasing number of companies, especially business marketers who promise great savings with their equipment, may have to stand ready to guarantee the promised savings but also participate in the upside if the gains are much greater than expected.

IMPACT OF PRICE ON OTHER PARTIES How will distributors and dealers feel about the contemplated price?[70] If they don't make enough profit, they may choose not to bring the product to market. Will the sales force be willing to sell at that price? How will competitors react? Will suppliers raise their prices when they see the company's price? Will the government intervene and prevent this price from being charged?

U.S. legislation states that sellers must set prices without talking to competitors: Price-fixing is illegal. Many federal and state statutes protect consumers against deceptive pricing practices. For example, it is illegal for a company to set artificially high "regular" prices, then announce a "sale" at prices close to previous everyday prices.

Adapting the Price

Companies usually do not set a single price but rather develop a pricing structure that reflects variations in geographical demand and costs, market-segment requirements, purchase timing, order levels, delivery frequency, guarantees, service contracts, and other factors. As a result of discounts, allowances, and promotional support, a company rarely realizes the same profit from each unit of a product that it sells. Here we will examine several price-adaptation strategies: geographical pricing, price discounts and allowances, promotional pricing, and differentiated pricing.

Geographical Pricing (Cash, Countertrade, Barter)

In geographical pricing, the company decides how to price its products to different customers in different locations and countries. Should the company charge higher prices to distant customers to cover the higher shipping costs, or a lower price to win additional business? How should it account for exchange rates and the strength of different currencies?

Another question is how to get paid. This issue is critical when buyers lack sufficient hard currency to pay for their purchases. Many buyers want to offer other items in payment, a practice known as **countertrade**. U.S. companies are often forced to engage in countertrade if they want the business. Countertrade may account for 15 percent to 20 percent of world trade and takes several forms:[71]

- *Barter.* The buyer and seller directly exchange goods, with no money and no third party involved.
- *Compensation deal.* The seller receives some percentage of the payment in cash and the rest in products. A British aircraft manufacturer sold planes to Brazil for 70 percent cash and the rest in coffee.
- *Buyback arrangement.* The seller sells a plant, equipment, or technology to another country and agrees to accept as partial payment products manufactured with the supplied equipment. A U.S. chemical company built a plant for an Indian company and accepted partial payment in cash and the remainder in chemicals manufactured at the plant.
- *Offset.* The seller receives full payment in cash but agrees to spend a substantial amount of the money in that country within a stated time period. PepsiCo sold its cola syrup to Russia for rubles and agreed to buy Russian vodka at a certain rate for sale in the United States.

Price Discounts and Allowances

Most companies will adjust their list price and give discounts and allowances for early payment, volume purchases, and off-season buying (see Table 14.5).[72] Companies must do this carefully or find that their profits are much lower than planned.[73]

TABLE 14.5	Price Discounts and Allowances
Discount:	A price reduction to buyers who pay bills promptly. A typical example is "2/10, net 30," which means that payment is due within 30 days and that the buyer can deduct 2 percent by paying the bill within 10 days.
Quantity Discount:	A price reduction to those who buy large volumes. A typical example is "$10 per unit for fewer than 100 units; $9 per unit for 100 or more units." Quantity discounts must be offered equally to all customers and must not exceed the cost savings to the seller. They can be offered on each order placed or on the number of units ordered over a given period.
Functional Discount:	Discount (also called *trade discount*) offered by a manufacturer to trade-channel members if they will perform certain functions, such as selling, storing, and record keeping. Manufacturers must offer the same functional discounts within each channel.
Seasonal Discount:	A price reduction to those who buy merchandise or services out of season. Hotels, motels, and airlines offer seasonal discounts in slow selling periods.
Allowance:	An extra payment designed to gain reseller participation in special programs. *Trade-in allowances* are granted for turning in an old item when buying a new one. *Promotional allowances* reward dealers for participating in advertising and sales support programs.

Discount pricing has become the modus operandi of a surprising number of companies offering both products and services. Salespeople, in particular, are quick to give discounts in order to close a sale. But word can get around fast that the company's list price is "soft," and discounting becomes the norm, undermining the value perceptions of the offerings. Some product categories self-destruct by always being on sale.

Some companies with overcapacity are tempted to give discounts or even begin to supply a retailer with a store-brand version of their product at a deep discount. Because the store brand is priced lower, however, it may start making inroads on the manufacturer's brand. Manufacturers should consider the implications of supplying retailers at a discount, because they may end up losing long-run profits in an effort to meet short-run volume goals.

Only people with higher incomes and higher product involvement willingly pay more for features, customer service, quality, added convenience, and the brand name. So it can be a mistake for a strong, distinctive brand to plunge into price discounting to respond to low-price attacks. At the same time, discounting can be a useful tool if a company can gain concessions in return, such as the customer agreeing to sign a longer contract, order electronically, or buy in truckload quantities.

Sales management needs to monitor the proportion of customers receiving discounts, the average discount, and any salespeople over-relying on discounting. Higher levels of management should conduct a **net price analysis** to arrive at the "real price" of the offering. The real price is affected not only by discounts, but by other expenses that reduce the realized price (see "Promotional Pricing"). Suppose the company's list price is $3,000. The average discount is $300. The company's promotional spending averages $450 (15 percent of the list price). Retailers are given co-op advertising money of $150 to back the product. The company's net price is $2,100, not $3,000.

Promotional Pricing

Companies can use several pricing techniques to stimulate early purchase:

- *Loss-leader pricing.* Supermarkets and department stores often drop the price on well-known brands to stimulate additional store traffic. This pays if the revenue on the additional sales compensates for the lower margins on the loss-leader items. Manufacturers of loss-leader brands typically object because this practice can dilute the brand image and bring complaints from retailers who charge the list price. Manufacturers have tried to keep intermediaries from using loss-leader pricing through lobbying for retail-price-maintenance laws, but these laws have been revoked.

- *Special event pricing.* Sellers will establish special prices in certain seasons to draw in more customers. Every August, there are back-to-school sales.

- *Special customer pricing.* Sellers will offer special prices exclusively to certain customers. Road Runner Sports offers members of its Run America Club "exclusive" online offers with price discounts twice those for regular customers.[74]

- *Cash rebates.* Auto companies and other consumer-goods companies offer cash rebates to encourage purchase of the manufacturers' products within a specified time period. Rebates can help clear inventories without cutting the stated list price.

- *Low-interest financing.* Instead of cutting its price, the company can offer customers low-interest financing. Automakers have used no-interest financing to try to attract more customers.

- *Longer payment terms.* Sellers, especially mortgage banks and auto companies, stretch loans over longer periods and thus lower the monthly payments. Consumers often worry less about the cost (the interest rate) of a loan, and more about whether they can afford the monthly payment.

- *Warranties and service contracts.* Companies can promote sales by adding a free or low-cost warranty or service contract.

- *Psychological discounting.* This strategy sets an artificially high price and then offers the product at substantial savings; for example, "Was $359, now $299." Discounts from normal prices are a legitimate form of promotional pricing; the Federal Trade Commission and Better Business Bureaus fight illegal discount tactics.

Promotional-pricing strategies are often a zero-sum game. If they work, competitors copy them and they lose their effectiveness. If they don't work, they waste money that could have been put into other marketing tools, such as building up product quality and service or strengthening product image through advertising.

Differentiated Pricing

Companies often adjust their basic price to accommodate differences in customers, products, locations, and so on. Lands' End creates men's shirts in many different styles, weights, and levels of quality. As of January 2010, a men's white button-down shirt could cost as little as $14.99 or as much as $79.50.[75]

Price discrimination occurs when a company sells a product or service at two or more prices that do not reflect a proportional difference in costs. In first-degree price discrimination, the seller charges a separate price to each customer depending on the intensity of his or her demand.

In second-degree price discrimination, the seller charges less to buyers of larger volumes. With certain services such as cell phone service, however, tiered pricing results in consumers paying *more* with higher levels of usage. With the iPhone, 3 percent of users accounted for 40 percent of the traffic on AT&T's network, resulting in costly network upgrades.[76]

In third-degree price discrimination, the seller charges different amounts to different classes of buyers, as in the following cases:

- *Customer-segment pricing.* Different customer groups pay different prices for the same product or service. For example, museums often charge a lower admission fee to students and senior citizens.
- *Product-form pricing.* Different versions of the product are priced differently, but not proportionately to their costs. Evian prices a 48-ounce bottle of its mineral water at $2.00 and 1.7 ounces of the same water in a moisturizer spray at $6.00.
- *Image pricing.* Some companies price the same product at two different levels based on image differences. A perfume manufacturer can put the perfume in one bottle, give it a name and image, and price it at $10 an ounce. The same perfume in another bottle with a different name and image and price can sell for $30 an ounce.
- *Channel pricing.* Coca-Cola carries a different price depending on whether the consumer purchases it in a fine restaurant, a fast-food restaurant, or a vending machine.
- *Location pricing.* The same product is priced differently at different locations even though the cost of offering it at each location is the same. A theater varies its seat prices according to audience preferences for different locations.
- *Time pricing.* Prices are varied by season, day, or hour. Public utilities vary energy rates to commercial users by time of day and weekend versus weekday. Restaurants charge less to "early bird" customers, and some hotels charge less on weekends.

The airline and hospitality industries use yield management systems and **yield pricing**, by which they offer discounted but limited early purchases, higher-priced late purchases, and the lowest rates on unsold inventory just before it expires.[77] Airlines charge different fares to passengers on the same flight, depending on the seating class; the time of day (morning or night coach); the day of the week (workday or weekend); the season; the person's employer, past business, or status (youth, military, senior citizen); and so on.

That's why on a flight from New York City to Miami you might pay $200 and sit across from someone who paid $1,290. Continental Airlines launches 2,000 flights a day and each has between 10 and 20 prices. The carrier starts booking flights 330 days in advance, and every flying day is different from every other flying day. At any given moment the market has more than 7 million prices. And in a system that tracks the difference in prices and the price of competitors' offerings, airlines collectively charge 75,000 different prices a day! It's a system designed to punish procrastinators by charging them the highest possible prices.

The phenomenon of offering different pricing schedules to different consumers and dynamically adjusting prices is exploding.[78] Many companies are using software packages that provide real-time controlled tests of actual consumer response to different pricing schedules. Constant price variation can be tricky, however, where consumer relationships are concerned. Research shows it's most effective when there's no bond between the buyer and the seller. One way to make it work is to offer customers a unique bundle of products and services to meet their needs precisely, making it harder to make price comparisons.

The tactic most companies favor, however, is to use variable prices as a reward rather than a penalty. For instance, shipping company APL rewards customers who can better predict how much cargo space they'll need with cheaper rates for booking early. Customers are also getting savvier about how to avoid buyer's remorse from overpaying. They are changing their buying behavior to

The likelihood is extremely high that every passenger shown in this airport lobby is paying a different price, even if they are all on the same flight.

accommodate the new realities of dynamic pricing—where prices vary frequently by channels, products, customers, and time.

Most consumers are probably not even aware of the degree to which they are the targets of discriminatory pricing. For instance, catalog retailers such as Victoria's Secret routinely send out catalogs that sell identical goods at different prices. Consumers who live in a more free-spending zip code may see only the higher prices. Office product superstore Staples also sends out office supply catalogs with different prices.

Although some forms of price discrimination (in which sellers offer different price terms to different people within the same trade group) are illegal, price discrimination is legal if the seller can prove its costs are different when selling different volumes or different qualities of the same product to different retailers. Predatory pricing—selling below cost with the intention of destroying competition—is unlawful, though.[79]

For price discrimination to work, certain conditions must exist. First, the market must be segmentable and the segments must show different intensities of demand. Second, members in the lower-price segment must not be able to resell the product to the higher-price segment. Third, competitors must not be able to undersell the firm in the higher-price segment. Fourth, the cost of segmenting and policing the market must not exceed the extra revenue derived from price discrimination. Fifth, the practice must not breed customer resentment and ill will. Sixth, of course, the particular form of price discrimination must not be illegal.[80]

Initiating and Responding to Price Changes

Companies often need to cut or raise prices.

Initiating Price Cuts

Several circumstances might lead a firm to cut prices. One is *excess plant capacity*: The firm needs additional business and cannot generate it through increased sales effort, product improvement, or other measures. Companies sometimes initiate price cuts in a *drive to dominate the market through lower costs*. Either the company starts with lower costs than its competitors, or it initiates price cuts in the hope of gaining market share and lower costs.

Cutting prices to keep customers or beat competitors often encourages customers to demand price concessions, however, and trains salespeople to offer them.[81] A price-cutting strategy can lead to other possible traps:

- *Low-quality trap.* Consumers assume quality is low.
- *Fragile-market-share trap.* A low price buys market share but not market loyalty. The same customers will shift to any lower-priced firm that comes along.
- *Shallow-pockets trap.* Higher-priced competitors match the lower prices but have longer staying power because of deeper cash reserves.
- *Price-war trap.* Competitors respond by lowering their prices even more, triggering a price war.[82]

Customers often question the motivation behind price changes.[83] They may assume the item is about to be replaced by a new model; the item is faulty and is not selling well; the firm is in financial trouble; the price will come down even further; or the quality has been reduced. The firm must monitor these attributions carefully.

Initiating Price Increases

A successful price increase can raise profits considerably. If the company's profit margin is 3 percent of sales, a 1 percent price increase will increase profits by 33 percent if sales volume is unaffected. This situation is illustrated in ▭ Table 14.6. The assumption is that a company charged $10 and sold 100 units and had costs of $970, leaving a profit of $30, or 3 percent on sales. By raising its price by 10 cents (a 1 percent price increase), it boosted its profits by 33 percent, assuming the same sales volume.

A major circumstance provoking price increases is *cost inflation*. Rising costs unmatched by productivity gains squeeze profit margins and lead companies to regular rounds of price increases. Companies often raise their prices by more than the cost increase, in anticipation of further inflation or government price controls, in a practice called *anticipatory pricing*.

Another factor leading to price increases is *overdemand*. When a company cannot supply all its customers, it can raise its prices, ration supplies, or both. It can increase price in the following ways, each of which has a different impact on buyers.

- *Delayed quotation pricing.* The company does not set a final price until the product is finished or delivered. This pricing is prevalent in industries with long production lead times, such as industrial construction and heavy equipment.
- *Escalator clauses.* The company requires the customer to pay today's price and all or part of any inflation increase that takes place before delivery. An escalator clause bases price increases on some specified price index. Escalator clauses are found in contracts for major industrial projects, such as aircraft construction and bridge building.
- *Unbundling.* The company maintains its price but removes or prices separately one or more elements that were part of the former offer, such as free delivery or installation. Car companies sometimes add higher-end audio entertainment systems or GPS navigation systems as extras to their vehicles.
- *Reduction of discounts.* The company instructs its sales force not to offer its normal cash and quantity discounts.

TABLE 14.6 ▭ Profits Before and After a Price Increase			
	Before	**After**	
Price	$10	$10.10	(a 1% price increase)
Units sold	100	100	
Revenue	$1,000	$1,010	
Costs	−970	−970	
Profit	$30	$40	(a 33 1/3% profit increase)

Although there is always a chance a price increase can carry some positive meanings to customers—for example, that the item is "hot" and represents an unusually good value—consumers generally dislike higher prices. In passing price increases on to customers, the company must avoid looking like a price gouger.[84] Coca-Cola's proposed smart vending machines that would raise prices as temperatures rose and Amazon.com's dynamic pricing experiment that varied prices by purchase occasion both became front-page news. The more similar the products or offerings from a company, the more likely consumers are to interpret any pricing differences as unfair. Product customization and differentiation and communications that clarify differences are thus critical.[85]

Generally, consumers prefer small price increases on a regular basis to sudden, sharp increases. Their memories are long, and they can turn against companies they perceive as price gougers. Price hikes without corresponding investments in the value of the brand increase vulnerability to lower-priced competition. Consumers may be willing to "trade down" because they can no longer convince themselves the higher priced brand is worth it.

Several techniques help consumers avoid sticker shock and a hostile reaction when prices rise: One is maintaining a sense of fairness around any price increase, such as by giving customers advance notice so they can do forward buying or shop around. Sharp price increases need to be explained in understandable terms. Making low-visibility price moves first is also a good technique: Eliminating discounts, increasing minimum order sizes, and curtailing production of low-margin products are examples, and contracts or bids for long-term projects should contain escalator clauses based on such factors as increases in recognized national price indexes.[86]

Given strong consumer resistance, marketers go to great lengths to find alternate approaches that avoid increasing prices when they otherwise would have done so. Here are a few popular ones.

- Shrinking the amount of product instead of raising the price. (Hershey Foods maintained its candy bar price but trimmed its size. Nestlé maintained its size but raised the price.)
- Substituting less-expensive materials or ingredients. (Many candy bar companies substituted synthetic chocolate for real chocolate to fight cocoa price increases.)
- Reducing or removing product features. (Sears engineered down a number of its appliances so they could be priced competitively with those sold in discount stores.)
- Removing or reducing product services, such as installation or free delivery.
- Using less-expensive packaging material or larger package sizes.
- Reducing the number of sizes and models offered.
- Creating new economy brands. (Jewel food stores introduced 170 generic items selling at 10 percent to 30 percent less than national brands.)

Responding to Competitors' Price Changes

How should a firm respond to a competitor's price cut? In general, the best response varies with the situation. The company must consider the product's stage in the life cycle, its importance in the company's portfolio, the competitor's intentions and resources, the market's price and quality sensitivity, the behavior of costs with volume, and the company's alternative opportunities.

In markets characterized by high product homogeneity, the firm can search for ways to enhance its augmented product. If it cannot find any, it may need to meet the price reduction. If the competitor raises its price in a homogeneous product market, other firms might not match it if the increase will not benefit the industry as a whole. Then the leader will need to roll back the increase.

In nonhomogeneous product markets, a firm has more latitude. It needs to consider the following issues: (1) Why did the competitor change the price? To steal the market, to utilize excess capacity, to meet changing cost conditions, or to lead an industry-wide price change? (2) Does the competitor plan to make the price change temporary or permanent? (3) What will happen to the company's market share and profits if it does not respond? Are other companies going to respond? (4) What are the competitors' and other firms' responses likely to be to each possible reaction?

Market leaders often face aggressive price cutting by smaller firms trying to build market share. Using price, Fuji has attacked Kodak, Schick has attacked Gillette, and AMD has attacked Intel.

Brand leaders also face lower-priced store brands. Three possible responses to low-cost competitors are: (1) further differentiate the product or service, (2) introduce a low-cost venture, or (3) reinvent as a low-cost player.[87] The right strategy depends on the ability of the firm to generate more demand or cut costs.

An extended analysis of alternatives may not always be feasible when the attack occurs. The company may have to react decisively within hours or days, especially where prices change with some frequency and it is important to react quickly, such as the meatpacking, lumber, or oil industries. It would make better sense to anticipate possible competitors' price changes and prepare contingent responses.

Summary

1. Despite the increased role of nonprice factors in modern marketing, price remains a critical element of marketing. Price is the only element that produces revenue; the others produce costs. Pricing decisions have become more challenging, however, in a changing economic and technological environment.

2. In setting pricing policy, a company follows a six-step procedure. It selects its pricing objective. It estimates the demand curve, the probable quantities it will sell at each possible price. It estimates how its costs vary at different levels of output, at different levels of accumulated production experience, and for differentiated marketing offers. It examines competitors' costs, prices, and offers. It selects a pricing method, and it selects the final price.

3. Companies usually set not a single price, but rather a pricing structure that reflects variations in geographical demand and costs, market-segment requirements, purchase timing, order levels, and other factors. Several price-adaptation strategies are available: (1) geographical pricing, (2) price discounts and allowances, (3) promotional pricing, and (4) discriminatory pricing.

4. Firms often need to change their prices. A price decrease might be brought about by excess plant capacity, declining market share, a desire to dominate the market through lower costs, or economic recession. A price increase might be brought about by cost inflation or overdemand. Companies must carefully manage customer perceptions when raising prices.

5. Companies must anticipate competitor price changes and prepare contingent responses. A number of responses are possible in terms of maintaining or changing price or quality.

6. The firm facing a competitor's price change must try to understand the competitor's intent and the likely duration of the change. Strategy often depends on whether a firm is producing homogeneous or nonhomogeneous products. A market leader attacked by lower-priced competitors can seek to better differentiate itself, introduce its own low-cost competitor, or transform itself more completely.

Applications

Marketing Debate
Is the Right Price a Fair Price?

Prices are often set to satisfy demand or to reflect the premium that consumers are willing to pay for a product or service. Some critics shudder, however, at the thought of $2 bottles of water, $150 running shoes, and $500 concert tickets.

Take a position: Prices should reflect the value consumers are willing to pay *versus* Prices should reflect only the cost of making a product or delivering a service.

Marketing Discussion
Pricing Methods

Think about the pricing methods described in this chapter—markup pricing, target-return pricing, perceived-value pricing, value pricing, going-rate pricing, and auction-type pricing. As a consumer, which do you prefer to deal with? Why? If the average price were to stay the same, which would you prefer a firm to do: (1) set one price and not deviate or (2) employ slightly higher prices most of the year but offer slightly discounted prices or specials for certain occasions?

Marketing Excellence

>>eBay

In 1995, Pierre Omidayar, a French-Iranian immigrant, wrote the code for an auction Web site where everyone would have equal access to a single global marketplace. Omidayar couldn't believe it when a collector bought the first item, a broken laser pointer, for $14.83.* Soon the site grew into a broader auction site where consumers could auction collectibles such as baseball cards and Barbie dolls. The momentum continued when individuals and small businesses discovered that eBay was an efficient way to reach new consumers and other businesses. Large companies began using eBay as a means of selling their bulk lots of unsold inventory. Today, people can buy and sell virtually any product or service, on the world's largest online marketplace. From appliances and computers to cars and real estate, sellers can list anything as long as it is not illegal or violates eBay's rules and policies.

eBay's success truly created a pricing revolution by allowing buyers to determine what they would pay for an item; the result pleases both sides because customers gain control and receive the best possible price while sellers make good margins due to the site's efficiency and wide reach. For years, buyers and sellers used eBay as an informal guide to market value. Even a company with a new-product design that wanted to know the going price for anything from a copier to a new DVD player checked on eBay.

eBay has evolved to also offer a fixed-price "buy it now" option to those who don't want to wait for an auction and are willing to pay the seller's price. Sellers can also use the fixed price format with a "best offer" option that allows the seller to counteroffer, reject, or accept an offer.

The impact of eBay's global reach is significant. In 2009, over $60 billion worth of goods was sold on eBay—that's almost $2,000 worth every second. The site has 405 million registered and 90 million active users and receives 81 million unique visitors a month. More than 1 million members make their living from the site. Yet eBay itself doesn't buy any inventory or own the products on its site. It earns its money by collecting fees: an insertion fee for each listing plus a final-value fee based on the auction or fixed price. For example, if an item sells for $60.00, the seller pays 8.75 percent on the first $25.00 ($2.19) plus 3.5 percent on the remaining $35.00 ($1.23). Therefore, the final-value fee for the sale is $3.42. This pricing structure was developed to attract high-volume sellers and deter those who list only a few low-priced items. With eBay's expansion into a wide range of other categories—from boats and cars and travel and tickets to health and beauty and home and garden—collectibles now make up only a small percentage of eBay sales.

eBay's business model is based on connecting individuals who otherwise would not be connected. It was the first example of online social networking, years before Twitter and Facebook existed, and consumer trust is a key element of its success. While skeptics initially questioned whether consumers would buy products from strangers, Omidayar believed people are innately good, and eBay's originators did two things well: they worked hard to make their Web site a community, and they developed tools to help reinforce trust between strangers. The company tracks and publishes the reputations of both buyers and sellers on the basis of feedback from each transaction. eBay extended its feedback service in 2007 by adding four different seller categories: items as described, communication, shipping time, and shipping and handling rate. The ratings are anonymous but visible to other buyers. Sellers with the highest rankings appear at the top of search results.

eBay's millions of passionate users also have a voice in all major decisions the company makes through its Voice of the Customer program. Every few months, eBay brings in as many as a dozen sellers and buyers and asks them questions about how they work and what else eBay needs to do. At least twice a week the company holds hour-long teleconferences to poll users on almost every new feature or policy. The result is that users (eBay's customers) feel like owners, and they have taken the initiative to expand the company into ever-new territory.

eBay continues to expand its capabilities to build its community and connect people around the world by adding services, partnerships, and investments. The company acquired PayPal, an online payment service, in 2002 after eBay members made it clear that PayPal was the preferred method of payment. The acquisition lowered currency and language barriers and allowed merchants to easily sell products around the world. eBay also acquired Skype Internet voice and video

---

*Some falsely believe that eBay was created to help Omidayar's girlfriend find and collect Pez candy dispensers. That story, however, was created by an employee to help generate initial interest in the company.

communication service in 2005, which allowed buyers and sellers to communicate over voice or video free and generated additional ad revenue for eBay. However, in 2009 eBay sold a majority stake in Skype to focus more on its e-commerce and payments businesses, leading the company to acquire Shopping.com, StubHub, Bill Me Later, and others. eBay now has a presence in 39 markets around the world.

Although eBay was a darling in the dot-com boom and has achieved tremendous success since then, it is not without challenges. These include a worldwide recession, increased competition from Google, and difficulties as it expands globally into tough markets such as China. Its CEO, Meg Whitman, retired in 2008 after leading the company for 10 years and was replaced by John Donahue. Under its new leadership, the company continues to focus on one of its founding beliefs: a strong commitment to and investment in technologies that help people connect. Recent efforts to adopt mobile applications, integrate with iPhones, and become more green

have helped take the company to the top of such lists such as *Newsweek*'s Greenest Companies in America and *Fortune*s 100 Best Companies to Work For in back-to-back years.

Questions

1. Why has eBay succeeded as an online auction marketplace while so many others have failed?

2. Evaluate eBay's fee structure. Is it optimal or could it be improved? Why? How?

3. What's next for eBay? How does it continue to grow when it needs both buyers and sellers? Where will this growth come from?

Sources: Douglas MacMillan, "Can eBay Get Its Tech Savvy Back?" *BusinessWeek*, June 22, 2009, pp. 48–49; Cattherine Holahan, "eBay's New Tough Love CEO," *BusinessWeek*, February 4, 2008, pp. 58–59; Adam Lashinsky, "Building eBay 2.0," *Fortune*, October 16, 2006, pp. 161–64; Matthew Creamer, "A Million Marketers," *Advertising Age*, June 26, 2006, pp. 1, 71; Clive Thompson, "eBay Heads East," *Fast Company* (July–August 2006): 87–89; Glen L. Urban, "The Emerging Era of Customer Advocacy," *MIT Sloan Management Review* (Winter 2004): 77–82; www.ebay.com.

Marketing Excellence

>>Southwest Airlines

Southwest Airlines entered the airline industry in 1971 with little money but lots of personality. Marketing itself as the LUV airline, the company featured a bright red heart as its first logo and relied on outrageous antics to generate word of mouth and new business. Flight attendants in red-orange hot pants served Love Bites (peanuts) and Love Potions (drinks).

As Southwest grew, its advertising showcased its focus on low fares, frequent flights, on-time arrivals, top safety record, and how bags fly free. Throughout all its

communication efforts, Southwest uses humor to poke fun at itself and convey its warm, friendly personality. One TV spot showed a small bag of peanuts with the words, "This is what our meals look like at Southwest Airlines. . . . It's also what our fares look like." Its ongoing "Wanna Get Away?" campaign uses embarrassing situations to hit a funny bone with consumers. And its tagline: "Ding! You are now free to move around the country" is a self-parody of its in-flight announcements. This lighthearted attitude carries over to the entertaining on-board announcements, crews that burst into song in the terminal, and several personalized aircrafts, including three painted as flying killer whales, "Lone Star One" painted like the Texas flag, and "Slam Dunk One," symbolizing the airline's partnership with the NBA.

Southwest's business model is based on streamlining its operations, which results in low fares and satisfied consumers. The airline takes several steps to save money and passes the savings to customers through low fares. It flies over 3,100 short, "point-to-point" trips in a day—shuttling more passengers per plane than any other airline. Each aircraft makes an average of 6.25 flights a day, or almost 12 hours each day. Southwest can accomplish such a feat because it avoids the traditional hub-and-spoke system and has extremely fast turnaround service. In its early years, it turned planes around in less than 10 minutes. Today, its turnaround averages 20 to 30 minutes—still the best in the industry and half the industry average. Southwest's unique boarding process helps. Instead of assigned seating, passengers are assigned to one of three groups (A, B, C) and a number when they check in. The number refers to where they stand in line at the gate. Group A boards first, and once on board, passengers may sit anywhere they like.

Southwest grows by entering new markets other airlines overprice and underserve. The company believes it can bring fares down by one-third to one-half whenever it enters a new market, and it expands every market it serves by making flying affordable to people who could not afford it before. Southwest currently serves 68 cities in 35 states, usually secondary cities with smaller airports that have lower gate fees and less congestion—another factor that leads to faster turnaround and lower fares.

Another unique cost savings strategy is Southwest's decision to operate Boeing 737s for all its flights. This simplifies the training process for pilots, flight attendants, and mechanics, and management can substitute aircraft, reschedule flight crews, or transfer mechanics quickly.

Jet fuel is an airline's biggest expense. According to the industry's trade group, Air Transport Association, jet fuel now accounts for 40 percent of an airplane ticket versus 15 percent just eight years ago. Southwest's biggest cost savings technique and competitive advantage has long been its program to hedge fuel prices by purchasing options years in advance. Many of its long-term contracts allow the airline to purchase fuel at $51 per barrel, a significant savings especially during the oil shocks of the 2000s that drove oil past $100 per barrel. Analysts estimate that Southwest has saved more than $2 billion with fuel hedging.

Because lighter planes use less fuel, Southwest makes its planes lighter by, for instance, power-washing their jet engines to remove dirt each night. It carries less water for bathrooms and has replaced its seats with lighter models. Southwest consumes approximately 1.5 billion gallons of jet fuel each year so every minor change adds up. The airline estimates that these changes saved $1.6 million in fuel costs over just three months.

Southwest has pioneered services and programs such as same-day freight service, senior discounts, Fun Fares, and Ticketless Travel. It was the first airline with a Web site, the first to deliver live updates on ticket deals, and the first to post a blog. Despite its reputation for low fares and no-frills service, Southwest wins the hearts of customers. It consistently ranks at the top of lists of customer service for airlines and receives the lowest ratio of complaints per passenger.

Southwest has been ranked by *Fortune* magazine as the United States' most admired airline since 1997, the fifth-most admired corporation in 2007, and one of the top five best places to work. Its financial results also shine: the company has been profitable for 37 straight years. It has been the only airline to report profits every quarter since September 11, 2001, and one of the few with no layoffs amid a travel slump created by the slow economy and the threat of terrorism.

Although the hot pants are long gone, the LUVing spirit remains at the heart of Southwest. The company's stock symbol on the NYSE is LUV, and red hearts can be found across the company. These symbols embody the Southwest spirit of employees "caring about themselves, each other, and Southwest's customers." "Our fares can be matched; our airplanes and routes can be copied. But we pride ourselves on our customer service," said Sherry Phelps, director of corporate employment. That's why Southwest looks for and hires people who generate enthusiasm. In fact, having a sense of humor is a selection criterion it uses for hiring. As one employee explained, "We can train you to do any job, but we can't give you the right spirit." And the feeling is reciprocated. When Southwest needed to close reservation centers in three cities in 2004, it didn't fire a single employee but rather paid for relocation and commuting expenses.

Questions

1. Southwest has mastered the low-price model and has the financial results to prove it. Why don't the other airlines copy Southwest's model?

2. What risks does Southwest face? Can it continue to thrive as a low-cost airline when tough economic times hit?

Sources: Barney Gimbel, "Southwest's New Flight Plan," *Fortune*, May 16, 2005, pp. 93–98; Melanie Trottman, "Destination: Philadelphia," *Wall Street Journal*, May 4, 2004; Andy Serwer, "Southwest Airlines: The Hottest Thing in the Sky," *Fortune*, March 8, 2004; Colleen Barrett, "Fasten Your Seat Belts," *Adweek*, January 26, 2004, p. 17; Jeff Bailey, "Southwest Airlines Gains Advantage by Hedging on Long-Term Oil Contracts." *New York Times,* November 28, 2007; Michelle Maynard, "To Save Fuel, Airlines Find No Speck Too Small," *New York Times,* June 11, 2008; Daniel B. Honigan, "Fred Taylor Leads Southwest Airlines' Customers to New Heights of Customer Satisfaction," *Marketing News,* May 1, 2008, pp. 24–26; Matthew Malone, "In for a Landing," *Condé Nast Portfolio*, August 2008, pp. 91–93; www.southwest.com.

PART 6   Delivering Value

Chapter **15** | **Designing and Managing Integrated Marketing Channels**
Chapter **16** | Managing Retailing, Wholesaling, and Logistics

In This Chapter, We Will Address the
Following Questions

1. What is a marketing channel system and value network?

2. What work do marketing channels perform?

3. How should channels be designed?

4. What decisions do companies face in managing their channels?

5. How should companies integrate channels and manage channel conflict?

6. What are the key issues with e-commerce and m-commerce?

> With a novel pricing and distribution scheme for DVD rentals, Netflix founder Reid Hastings has found heaps of success.

Designing and Managing Integrated Marketing Channels

Successful value creation needs successful value delivery. Holistic marketers are increasingly taking a value network view of their businesses. Instead of limiting their focus to their immediate suppliers, distributors, and customers, they are examining the whole supply chain that links raw materials, components, and manufactured goods and shows how they move toward the final consumers. Companies are looking at their suppliers' suppliers upstream and at their distributors' customers downstream. They are looking at customer segments and considering a wide range of new and different means to sell, distribute, and service their offerings.

Convinced that DVDs were the home video medium of the future, Netflix founder Reed Hastings came up with a form of DVD rental distribution in 1997 different from the brick-and-mortar stores used by market leader Blockbuster. Netflix's strong customer loyalty and positive word of mouth is a result of the service's distinctive capabilities: modest subscription fees (as low as $9 a month), no late fees, (mostly) overnight mail delivery, a deep catalog of over 100,000 movie titles, and a growing library of over 12,000 movies and television episodes. The service also has proprietary software that allows customers to easily search for obscure films and discover new ones. To improve the quality of its searches, Netflix sponsored a million-dollar contest that drew thousands of entrants. The winning team consisted of seven members with diverse backgrounds and skills whose solution was estimated to make Netflix's recommendations twice as effective. With new competition from Redbox's thousands of DVD-rental kiosks in McDonald's and other locations, Netflix is putting more emphasis on streaming videos and instantaneous delivery mechanisms. But it still sees growth in DVD rentals from its over 11 million subscriber base. Netflix's success has also captured Hollywood's attention. Its online communities of customers who provide and read reviews and feedback can be an important source of fans for films.[1]

Companies today must build and manage a continuously evolving and increasingly complex channel system and value network. In this chapter, we consider strategic and tactical issues with integrating marketing channels and developing value networks. We will examine marketing channel issues from the perspective of retailers, wholesalers, and physical distribution agencies in Chapter 16.

Marketing Channels and Value Networks

Most producers do not sell their goods directly to the final users; between them stands a set of intermediaries performing a variety of functions. These intermediaries constitute a marketing channel (also called a trade channel or distribution channel). Formally, **marketing channels** are sets of interdependent organizations participating in the process of making a product or service available for use or consumption. They are the set of pathways a product or service follows after production, culminating in purchase and consumption by the final end user.[2]

Some intermediaries—such as wholesalers and retailers—buy, take title to, and resell the merchandise; they are called *merchants*. Others—brokers, manufacturers' representatives, sales agents—search for customers and may negotiate on the producer's behalf but do not take title to the goods; they are called *agents*. Still others—transportation companies, independent warehouses, banks, advertising agencies—assist in the distribution process but neither take title to goods nor negotiate purchases or sales; they are called *facilitators*.

Channels of all types play an important role in the success of a company and affect all other marketing decisions. Marketers should judge them in the context of the entire process by which their products are made, distributed, sold, and serviced. We consider all these issues in the following sections.

The Importance of Channels

A **marketing channel system** is the particular set of marketing channels a firm employs, and decisions about it are among the most critical ones management faces. In the United States, channel members collectively have earned margins that account for 30 percent to 50 percent of the ultimate selling price. In contrast, advertising typically has accounted for less than 5 percent to 7 percent of the final price.[3] Marketing channels also represent a substantial opportunity cost. One of their chief roles is to convert potential buyers into profitable customers. Marketing channels must not just *serve* markets, they must also *make* markets.[4]

The channels chosen affect all other marketing decisions. The company's pricing depends on whether it uses online discounters or high-quality boutiques. Its sales force and advertising decisions depend on how much training and motivation dealers need. In addition, channel decisions include relatively long-term commitments with other firms as well as a set of policies and procedures. When an automaker signs up independent dealers to sell its automobiles, it cannot buy them out the next day and replace them with company-owned outlets. But at the same time, channel choices themselves depend on the company's marketing strategy with respect to segmentation, targeting, and positioning. Holistic marketers ensure that marketing decisions in all these different areas are made to collectively maximize value.

In managing its intermediaries, the firm must decide how much effort to devote to push versus pull marketing. A **push strategy** uses the manufacturer's sales force, trade promotion money, or other means to induce intermediaries to carry, promote, and sell the product to end users. A push strategy is particularly appropriate when there is low brand loyalty in a category, brand choice is made in the store, the product is an impulse item, and product benefits are well understood. In a **pull strategy** the manufacturer uses advertising, promotion, and other forms of communication to persuade consumers to demand the product from intermediaries, thus inducing the intermediaries to order it. Pull strategy is particularly appropriate when there is high brand loyalty and high involvement in the category, when consumers are able to perceive differences between brands, and when they choose the brand before they go to the store.

Top marketing companies such as Coca-Cola, Intel, and Nike skillfully employ both push and pull strategies. A push strategy is more effective when accompanied by a well-designed and well-executed pull strategy that activates consumer demand. On the other hand, without at least some consumer interest, it can be very difficult to gain much channel acceptance and support, and vice versa for that matter.

Hybrid Channels and Multichannel Marketing

Today's successful companies typically employ hybrid channels and multichannel marketing, multiplying the number of "go-to-market" channels in any one market area. **Hybrid channels** or **multichannel marketing** occurs when a single firm uses two or more marketing channels to reach customer segments. HP has used its sales force to sell to large accounts, outbound telemarketing to sell to medium-sized accounts, direct mail with an inbound number to sell to small accounts, retailers to sell to still smaller accounts, and the Internet to sell specialty items. Philips also is a multichannel marketer.

Philips   Royal Philips Electronics of the Netherlands is one of the world's biggest electronics companies and Europe's largest, with sales of over $66 billion in 2009. Philips's electronics products are channeled toward the consumer primarily through local and international retailers. The company offers a broad range of products from high to low price/value quartiles, relying on a diverse distribution model that includes mass merchants, retail chains, independents, and small specialty stores. To work most effectively with these retail channels, Philips has created an organization designed around its retail customers, with dedicated global key account managers serving leading retailers such as Best Buy, Carrefour, Costco, Dixons, and Tesco. Like many modern firms, Philips also sells via the Web through its own online store as well as through a number of other online retailers.[5]

In multichannel marketing, each channel targets a different segment of buyers, or different need states for one buyer, and delivers the right products in the right places in the right way at the least cost. When this doesn't happen, there can be channel conflict, excessive cost, or insufficient demand. Launched in 1976, Dial-a-Mattress successfully grew for three decades by selling mattresses directly over the phone and, later, the Internet. A major expansion into 50 brick-and-mortar stores in major metro areas was a failure, however. Secondary locations, chosen because management considered prime locations too expensive, could not generate enough customer traffic. The company eventually declared bankruptcy.[6]

On the other hand, when a major catalog and Internet retailer invested significantly in brick-and-mortar stores, different results emerged. Customers near the store purchased through the catalog less frequently, but their Internet purchases were unchanged. As it turned out, customers who liked to spend time browsing were happy to either use a catalog or visit the store; those channels were interchangeable. Customers who used the Internet, on the other hand, were more transaction focused and interested in efficiency, so they were less affected by the introduction of stores. Returns and exchanges at the stores were found to increase because of ease and accessibility, but extra purchases made by customers returning or exchanging at the store offset any revenue deficit.

Companies that manage hybrid channels clearly must make sure their channels work well together and match each target customer's preferred ways of doing business. Customers expect *channel integration*, which allows them to:

- Order a product online and pick it up at a convenient retail location
- Return an online-ordered product to a nearby store of the retailer
- Receive discounts and promotional offers based on total online and offline purchases

Here's a company that has carefully managed its multiple channels. We discuss the topic of optimal channel integration in greater detail later.

REI   Outdoor supplier REI has been lauded by industry analysts for the seamless integration of its retail store, Web site, Internet kiosks, mail-order catalogs, value-priced outlets, and toll-free order number. If an item is out of stock in the store, all customers need to do is tap into the store's Internet kiosk to order it from REI's Web site. Less Internet-savvy customers can get clerks to place the order for them at the checkout counters. And REI not only generates store-to-Internet traffic, it also sends Internet shoppers into its stores. If a customer browses REI's site and stops to read an REI "Learn and Share" article on backpacking, the site might highlight an in-store promotion on hiking boots. Like many retailers, REI has found that dual-channel shoppers spend significantly more than single-channel shoppers, and tri-channel shoppers spend even more.[7]

Value Networks

A supply chain view of a firm sees markets as destination points and amounts to a linear view of the flow of ingredients and components through the production process to their ultimate sale to customers. The company should first think of the target market, however, and then design the supply chain backward from that point. This strategy has been called **demand chain planning**.[8]

A broader view sees a company at the center of a **value network**—a system of partnerships and alliances that a firm creates to source, augment, and deliver its offerings. A value network includes a firm's suppliers and its suppliers' suppliers, and its immediate

REI's in-store Internet kiosk gives customers a convenient way to order out-of-stock items.

customers and their end customers. The value network includes valued relationships with others such as university researchers and government approval agencies.

A company needs to orchestrate these parties in order to deliver superior value to the target market. Oracle relies on 5.2 million developers and 400,000 discussion forum threads to advance its products.[9] Apple's Developer Connection—where folks create iPhone apps and the like—has 50,000 members at different levels of membership.[10] Developers keep 70 percent of any revenue their products generate, and Apple gets 30 percent.

Demand chain planning yields several insights.[11] First, the company can estimate whether more money is made upstream or downstream, in case it can integrate backward or forward. Second, the company is more aware of disturbances anywhere in the supply chain that might change costs, prices, or supplies. Third, companies can go online with their business partners to speed communications, transactions, and payments; reduce costs; and increase accuracy. Ford not only manages numerous supply chains but also sponsors or operates on many B2B Web sites and exchanges.

Managing a value network means making increasing investments in information technology (IT) and software. Firms have introduced supply chain management (SCM) software and invited such software firms as SAP and Oracle to design comprehensive *enterprise resource planning* (ERP) systems to manage cash flow, manufacturing, human resources, purchasing, and other major functions within a unified framework. They hope to break up departmental silos—where each department only acts in its own self interest—and carry out core business processes more seamlessly. Most, however, are still a long way from truly comprehensive ERP systems.

Marketers, for their part, have traditionally focused on the side of the value network that looks toward the customer, adopting customer relationship management (CRM) software and practices. In the future, they will increasingly participate in and influence their companies' upstream activities and become network managers, not just product and customer managers.

The Role of Marketing Channels

Why would a producer delegate some of the selling job to intermediaries, relinquishing control over how and to whom products are sold? Through their contacts, experience, specialization, and scale of operation, intermediaries make goods widely available and accessible to target markets, usually offering the firm more effectiveness and efficiency than it can achieve on its own.[12]

Many producers lack the financial resources and expertise to sell directly on their own. The William Wrigley Jr. Company would not find it practical to establish small retail gum shops throughout the world or to sell gum by mail order. It is easier to work through the extensive network of privately owned distribution organizations. Even Ford would be hard-pressed to replace all the tasks done by its almost 12,000 dealer outlets worldwide.

Channel Functions and Flows

A marketing channel performs the work of moving goods from producers to consumers. It overcomes the time, place, and possession gaps that separate goods and services from those who need or want them. Members of the marketing channel perform a number of key functions (see ▭ Table 15.1).

Some of these functions (storage and movement, title, and communications) constitute a *forward flow* of activity from the company to the customer; other functions (ordering and payment) constitute a *backward flow* from customers to the company. Still others (information, negotiation, finance, and risk taking) occur in both directions. Five flows are illustrated in △ Figure 15.1 for the marketing of forklift trucks. If these flows were superimposed in one diagram, we would see the tremendous complexity of even simple marketing channels.

A manufacturer selling a physical product and services might require three channels: a *sales channel*, a *delivery channel*, and a *service channel*. To sell its Bowflex fitness equipment, the Nautilus Group historically has emphasized direct marketing via television infomercials and ads, inbound/outbound call centers, response mailings, and the Internet as sales channels; UPS ground service as the delivery channel; and local repair people as the service channel. Reflecting shifting consumer buying habits, Nautilus now also sells Bowflex through commercial, retail, and specialty retail channels.

TABLE 15.1 🖭	Channel Member Functions
• Gather information about potential and current customers, competitors, and other actors and forces in the marketing environment.	
• Develop and disseminate persuasive communications to stimulate purchasing.	
• Negotiate and reach agreements on price and other terms so that transfer of ownership or possession can be affected.	
• Place orders with manufacturers.	
• Acquire the funds to finance inventories at different levels in the marketing channel.	
• Assume risks connected with carrying out channel work.	
• Provide for the successive storage and movement of physical products.	
• Provide for buyers' payment of their bills through banks and other financial institutions.	
• Oversee actual transfer of ownership from one organization or person to another.	

The question for marketers is not *whether* various channel functions need to be performed—they must be—but rather, *who* is to perform them. All channel functions have three things in common: They use up scarce resources; they can often be performed better through specialization; and they can be shifted among channel members. Shifting some functions to intermediaries lowers the producer's costs and prices, but the intermediary must add a charge to cover its work. If the intermediaries are more efficient than the manufacturer, prices to consumers should be lower. If consumers perform some functions themselves, they should enjoy even lower prices. Changes in channel institutions thus largely reflect the discovery of more efficient ways to combine or separate the economic functions that provide assortments of goods to target customers.

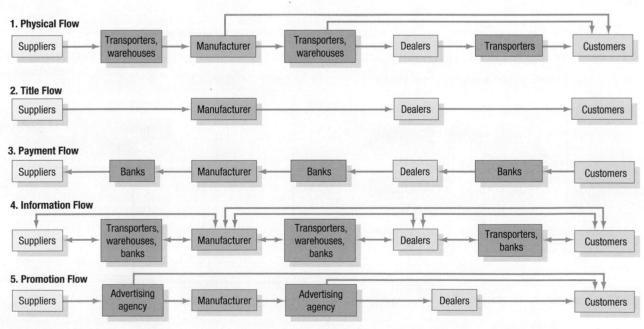

|Fig. 15.1| ◬

Five Marketing Flows in the Marketing Channel for Forklift Trucks

Bowflex fitness equipment is sold through a variety of channels.

Channel Levels

The producer and the final customer are part of every channel. We will use the number of intermediary levels to designate the length of a channel. ▲ Figure 15.2(a) illustrates several consumer-goods marketing channels of different lengths.

A **zero-level channel**, also called a **direct marketing channel**, consists of a manufacturer selling directly to the final customer. The major examples are door-to-door sales, home parties, mail order, telemarketing, TV selling, Internet selling, and manufacturer-owned stores. Traditionally, Avon sales representatives sell cosmetics door-to-door; Franklin Mint sells collectibles through mail order; Verizon uses the telephone to prospect for new customers or to sell enhanced services to existing customers; Time-Life sells music and video collections through TV commercials or

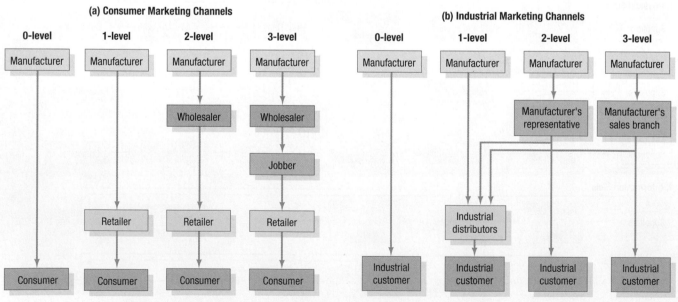

|Fig. 15.2| ▲

Consumer and Industrial Marketing Channels

longer "infomercials"; Red Envelope sells gifts online; and Apple sells computers and other consumer electronics through its own stores. Many of these firms now sell directly to customers in more ways than one, via online, catalogs, etc.

A *one-level channel* contains one selling intermediary, such as a retailer. A *two-level channel* contains two intermediaries. In consumer markets, these are typically a wholesaler and a retailer. A *three-level channel* contains three intermediaries. In the meatpacking industry, wholesalers sell to **jobbers**, essentially small-scale wholesalers, who sell to small retailers. In Japan, food distribution may include as many as six levels. Obtaining information about end users and exercising control becomes more difficult for the producer as the number of channel levels increases.

Figure 15.2(b) shows channels commonly used in B2B marketing. An industrial-goods manufacturer can use its sales force to sell directly to industrial customers; or it can sell to industrial distributors who sell to industrial customers; or it can sell through manufacturer's representatives or its own sales branches directly to industrial customers, or indirectly to industrial customers through industrial distributors. Zero-, one-, and two-level marketing channels are quite common.

Channels normally describe a forward movement of products from source to user, but *reverse-flow channels* are also important (1) to reuse products or containers (such as refillable chemical-carrying drums), (2) to refurbish products for resale (such as circuit boards or computers), (3) to recycle products (such as paper), and (4) to dispose of products and packaging. Reverse-flow intermediaries include manufacturers' redemption centers, community groups, trash-collection specialists, recycling centers, trash-recycling brokers, and central processing warehousing.[13] Many creative solutions have emerged in this area in recent years, such as Greenopolis.

RedEnvelope has built an online gift powerhouse.

Greenopolis is a novel recycling system that offers financial and environmental benefits to consumers and companies.

Greenopolis
Launched by Waste Management Corporation after it acquired the Code Blue Recycling company, Greenopolis is a new company with an entirely different recycling system that allows consumers and a consortium of consumer packaged goods (CPG) companies to "close the loop" in the recovery and reuse of postconsumer material. With its mantra, "Rethink. Recycle. Reward," Greenopolis consists of (1) an extensive set of interactive, on-street recycling kiosks in various retail settings, (2) a number of material reprocessing facilities, (3) a menu of consumer recycling rewards, and (4) a significant online community and social media network. Participating CPG companies use the Greenopolis symbol on their product packaging. The kiosk system is designed to collect those products, track and reward consumers who bring them, and put packaging into reuse or reprocessing. An important feature is that Greenopolis is fully accountable. Innovative kiosk technology allows consumers to follow their recycling contribution, as well as the rewards they earn from the partnering companies. CPG companies, in turn, are able to measure their share of recovery. By achieving sufficient scale and accessibility in the marketplace and making recycling fun, easy, and personally rewarding to consumers, Greenopolis aims to improve recycling rates and make an important environmental difference.[14]

Service Sector Channels

As Internet and other technologies advance, service industries such as banking, insurance, travel, and stock buying and selling are operating through new channels. Kodak offers its customers four ways to print their digital photos—minilabs in retail outlets, home printers, online services at its Ofoto Web site, and self-service kiosks. The world leader with 80,000 kiosks, Kodak makes money both by selling the units and by supplying the chemical and paper they use to make the prints.[15]

Marketing channels also keep changing in "person marketing." Besides live and programmed entertainment, entertainers, musicians, and other artists can reach prospective and existing fans online in many ways—their own Web sites, social community sites such as Facebook and Twitter, and third-party Web sites. Politicians also must choose a mix of channels—mass media, rallies, coffee hours, spot TV ads, direct mail, billboards, faxes, e-mail, blogs, podcasts, Web sites, and social networking sites—for delivering their messages to voters.

Nonprofit service organizations such as schools develop "educational-dissemination systems" and hospitals develop "health-delivery systems." These institutions must figure out agencies and locations for reaching a far-flung population.

Cleveland Clinic   One of the largest and most respected hospitals in the country, Cleveland Clinic, provides medical care in a variety of ways and settings. The main campus in Cleveland, whose 50 buildings occupy 166 acres, is the hub for patient care, research, and education. Cleveland Clinic also operates 15 family primary-care centers in the suburbs. Eight hospitals extend the clinic's reach in Northeast Ohio. Community outreach programs in all these areas provide education and free health screenings. Cleveland Clinic also offers major medical care in Florida, Toronto, and, as of 2012, Abu Dhabi. It has a suite of secure online health services for both patients and physicians and is developing partnerships with Google and Microsoft to further its Internet capabilities.[16]

Cleveland Clinic provides health care services in a variety of different locations and settings.

Channel-Design Decisions

To design a marketing channel system, marketers analyze customer needs and wants, establish channel objectives and constraints, and identify and evaluate major channel alternatives.

Analyzing Customer Needs and Wants

Consumers may choose the channels they prefer based on price, product assortment, and convenience, as well as their own shopping goals (economic, social, or experiential).[17] As with products, segmentation exists, and marketers must be aware that different consumers have different needs during the purchase process.

One study of 40 grocery and clothing retailers in France, Germany, and the United Kingdom found that they served three types of shoppers: (1) *service/quality customers* who cared most about the variety and performance of products and service, (2) *price/value customers* who were most concerned about spending wisely, and (3) *affinity customers* who primarily sought stores that suited people like themselves or groups they aspired to join. As ▲ Figure 15.3 shows, customer profiles differed across the three markets: In France, shoppers stressed service and quality, in the United Kingdom, affinity, and in Germany, price and value.[18]

Even the same consumer, though, may choose different channels for different functions in a purchase, browsing a catalog before visiting a store or test driving a car at a dealer before ordering online. Some consumers are willing to "trade up" to retailers offering higher-end goods such as TAG Heuer watches or Callaway golf clubs and "trade down" to discount retailers for private-label paper towels, detergent, or vitamins.[19]

Channels produce five service outputs:

1. *Lot size*—The number of units the channel permits a typical customer to purchase on one occasion. In buying cars for its fleet, Hertz prefers a channel from which it can buy a large lot size; a household wants a channel that permits a lot size of one.
2. *Waiting and delivery time*—The average time customers wait for receipt of goods. Customers increasingly prefer faster delivery channels.
3. *Spatial convenience*—The degree to which the marketing channel makes it easy for customers to purchase the product. Toyota offers greater spatial convenience than Lexus because there are

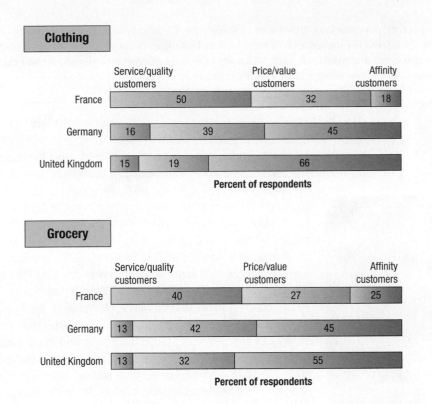

|Fig. 15.3| △

What Do European Consumers Value

Source: Peter N. Child, Suzanne Heywood, and Michael Kliger, "Do Retail Brands Travel?" *The McKinsley Quarterly*, 2002, Number 1, pp. 11–13. All rights reserved. Reprinted by permission of McKinsey & Company.

more Toyota dealers, helping customers save on transportation and search costs in buying and repairing an automobile.

4. **Product variety**—The assortment provided by the marketing channel. Normally, customers prefer a greater assortment because more choices increase the chance of finding what they need, although too many choices can sometimes create a negative effect.[20]

5. **Service backup**—Add-on services (credit, delivery, installation, repairs) provided by the channel. The greater the service backup, the greater the work provided by the channel.[21]

Providing greater service outputs also means increasing channel costs and raising prices. The success of discount stores such as Walmart and Target and extreme examples like Dollar General and Family Dollar indicates that many consumers are willing to accept smaller service outputs if they can save money.

Establishing Objectives and Constraints

Marketers should state their channel objectives in terms of service output levels and associated cost and support levels. Under competitive conditions, channel members should arrange their functional tasks to minimize costs and still provide desired levels of service.[22] Usually, planners can identify several market segments based on desired service and choose the best channels for each.

Channel objectives vary with product characteristics. Bulky products, such as building materials, require channels that minimize the shipping distance and the amount of handling. Nonstandard products such as custom-built machinery are sold directly by sales representatives. Products requiring installation or maintenance services, such as heating and cooling systems, are usually sold and maintained by the company or by franchised dealers. High-unit-value products such as generators and turbines are often sold through a company sales force rather than intermediaries.

Marketers must adapt their channel objectives to the larger environment. When economic conditions are depressed, producers want to move goods to market using shorter channels and without services that add to the final price. Legal regulations and restrictions also affect channel design. U.S. law looks unfavorably on channel arrangements that substantially lessen competition or create a monopoly.

In entering new markets, firms often closely observe what other firms are doing. France's Auchan considered the presence of its French rivals Leclerc and Casino in Poland as key to its decision to also enter that market.[23] Apple's channel objectives of creating a dynamic retail experience for consumers was not being met by existing channels, so it chose to open it own stores.[24]

Apple Stores   When Apple stores were launched in 2001, many questioned their prospects and *BusinessWeek* published an article titled, "Sorry Steve, Here's Why Apple Stores Won't Work." Fast-forward five years, and Apple was celebrating the launch of its spectacular new Manhattan showcase store. With almost 275 locations by the end of 2009, net revenue from stores totaled $6.6 billion and represented roughly 20 percent of total corporate revenue. Annual sales per square foot of an Apple store have been estimated at $4,700—the Fifth Avenue location is reported to do a staggering $35,000 of business per square foot—compared to Tiffany's $2,666, Best Buy's $930, and Saks's $362. Any way you look at it, Apple stores have been an unqualified success. Designed to fuel excitement for the brand, they let people see and touch Apple products—and experience what Apple can do for them—making it more likely they'll become Apple customers. They target tech-savvy customers with in-store product presentations and workshops; a full line of Apple products, software, and accessories; and a "Genius Bar" staffed by Apple specialists who provide technical support, often free of charge. Although the stores upset existing retailers, Apple has worked hard to smooth relationships, in part justifying the decision as a natural evolution of its existing online sales channel. ◉

Apple stores offer a unique brand experience to Apple enthusiasts and prospects.

Identifying Major Channel Alternatives

Each channel—from sales forces to agents, distributors, dealers, direct mail, telemarketing, and the Internet—has unique strengths and weaknesses. Sales forces can handle complex products and transactions, but they are expensive. The Internet is inexpensive but may not be as effective with complex products. Distributors can create sales, but the company loses direct contact with customers. Several clients can share the cost of manufacturers' reps, but the selling effort is less intense than company reps provide.

Channel alternatives differ in three ways: the types of intermediaries, the number needed, and the terms and responsibilities of each. Let's look at these factors.

TYPES OF INTERMEDIARIES   Consider the channel alternatives identified by a consumer electronics company that produces satellite radios. It could sell its players directly to automobile manufacturers to be installed as original equipment, auto dealers, rental car companies, or satellite radio specialist dealers through a direct sales force or through distributors. It could also sell its players through company stores, online retailers, mail-order catalogs, or mass merchandisers such as Best Buy.

As Netflix did, companies should search for innovative marketing channels. Columbia House has successfully merchandised music albums through the mail and Internet. Harry and David and Calyx & Corolla have creatively sold fruit and flowers, respectively, through direct delivery.

Sometimes a company chooses a new or unconventional channel because of the difficulty, cost, or ineffectiveness of working with the dominant channel. One advantage is often reduced competition, at least at first. Years ago, after trying to sell its inexpensive Timex watches through jewelry stores, the U.S. Time Company placed them instead in fast-growing mass-merchandise outlets. Frustrated with a printed catalog it saw as out-of-date and unprofessional, commercial lighting company Display Supply & Lighting developed an interactive online catalog that drove down costs, speeded the sales process, and increased revenue.[25]

NUMBER OF INTERMEDIARIES   Three strategies based on the number of intermediaries are exclusive distribution, selective distribution, and intensive distribution.

Exclusive distribution means severely limiting the number of intermediaries. It's appropriate when the producer wants to maintain control over the service level and outputs offered by the resellers, and it often includes *exclusive dealing* arrangements. By granting exclusive distribution, the producer hopes to obtain more dedicated and knowledgeable selling. It requires a closer partnership between seller and reseller and is used in the distribution of new automobiles, some major appliances, and some women's apparel brands.

Exclusive deals are becoming a mainstay for specialists looking for an edge in markets increasingly driven by price.[26] When the legendary Italian designer label Gucci found its image severely tarnished by overexposure from licensing and discount stores, it decided to end contracts with third-party suppliers, control its distribution, and open its own stores to bring back some of the luster.[27]

Selective distribution relies on only some of the intermediaries willing to carry a particular product. Whether established or new, the company does not need to worry about having too many outlets; it can gain adequate market coverage with more control and less cost than intensive distribution. STIHL is a good example of selective distribution.

STIHL's selective distribution strategy includes 8,000 independent dealers but does *not* include other, broader forms of distribution.

STIHL   STIHL manufactures handheld outdoor power equipment. All its products are branded under one name and it does not make private labels for other companies. Best known for chain saws, it has expanded into string trimmers, blowers, hedge trimmers, and cut-off machines. It sells exclusively to six independent U.S. distributors and six STIHL-owned marketing and distribution centers, which sell to a nationwide network of more than 8,000 servicing retail dealers. The company is also a worldwide exporter of U.S. manufactured STIHL products to 80 countries. STIHL is one of the few outdoor-power-equipment companies that do not sell through mass merchants, catalogs, or the Internet.[28] ▱

Intensive distribution places the goods or services in as many outlets as possible. This strategy serves well for snack foods, soft drinks, newspapers, candies, and gum—products consumers buy frequently or in a variety of locations. Convenience stores such as 7-Eleven, Circle K, and gas-station-linked stores such as ExxonMobil's On the Run have survived by selling items that provide just that—location and time convenience.

Manufacturers are constantly tempted to move from exclusive or selective distribution to more intensive distribution to increase coverage and sales. This strategy may help in the short term, but if not done properly, it can hurt long-term performance by encouraging retailers to compete aggressively. Price wars can then erode profitability, dampening retailer interest and harming brand equity. Some firms do not want to be sold everywhere. After Sears acquired discount chain Kmart, Nike pulled all its products from Sears to make sure Kmart could not carry the brand.[29]

TERMS AND RESPONSIBILITIES OF CHANNEL MEMBERS Each channel member must be treated respectfully and given the opportunity to be profitable. The main elements in the "trade-relations mix" are price policies, conditions of sale, territorial rights, and specific services to be performed by each party.

- *Price policy* calls for the producer to establish a price list and schedule of discounts and allowances that intermediaries see as equitable and sufficient.
- *Conditions of sale* refers to payment terms and producer guarantees. Most producers grant cash discounts to distributors for early payment. They might also offer a guarantee against defective merchandise or price declines, creating an incentive to buy larger quantities.
- *Distributors' territorial rights* define the distributors' territories and the terms under which the producer will enfranchise other distributors. Distributors normally expect to receive full credit for all sales in their territory, whether or not they did the selling.
- *Mutual services and responsibilities* must be carefully spelled out, especially in franchised and exclusive-agency channels. McDonald's provides franchisees with a building, promotional support, a record-keeping system, training, and general administrative and technical assistance. In turn, franchisees are expected to satisfy company standards for the physical facilities, cooperate with new promotional programs, furnish requested information, and buy supplies from specified vendors.

Evaluating Major Channel Alternatives

Each channel alternative needs to be evaluated against economic, control, and adaptive criteria.

ECONOMIC CRITERIA Each channel alternative will produce a different level of sales and costs. △ Figure 15.4 shows how six different sales channels stack up in terms of the value added per sale and the cost per transaction. For example, in the sale of industrial products costing between $2,000 and $5,000, the cost per transaction has been estimated at $500 (field sales), $200 (distributors), $50 (telesales), and $10 (Internet). A Booz Allen Hamilton study showed that the average transaction at a full-service branch costs the bank $4.07, a phone transaction costs $.54, and an ATM transaction costs $.27, but a typical Web-based transaction costs only $.01.[30]

Firms will try to align customers and channels to maximize demand at the lowest overall cost. Clearly, sellers try to replace high-cost channels with low-cost channels as long as the value added per sale is sufficient. Consider the following situation:

> A North Carolina furniture manufacturer wants to sell its line to retailers on the West Coast. One alternative is to hire 10 new sales representatives to operate out of a sales office in San Francisco and receive a base salary plus commissions. The other alternative is to use a San Francisco manufacturer's sales agency that has extensive contacts with retailers. Its 30 sales representatives would receive a commission based on their sales.

|Fig. 15.4| △

The Value-Adds versus Costs of Different Channels

Source: Oxford Associates, adapted from Dr. Rowland T. Moriarty. Cubex Corp.

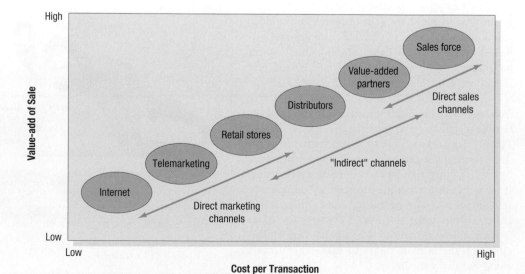

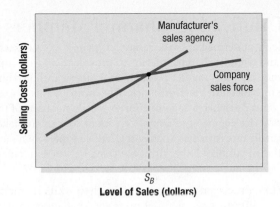

|Fig. 15.5| ◮

Break-Even Cost
Chart for the Choice
between a Company
Sales Force and
a Manufacturer's
Sales Agency

The first step is to estimate how many sales each alternative will likely generate. A company sales force will concentrate on the company's products, be better trained to sell them, be more aggressive because each rep's future depends on the company's success, and be more successful because many customers prefer to deal directly with the company. The sales agency however has 30 representatives, not just 10; it may be just as aggressive, depending on the commission level; customers may appreciate its independence; and it may have extensive contacts and market knowledge. The marketer needs to evaluate all these factors in formulating a demand function for the two different channels.

The next step is to estimate the costs of selling different volumes through each channel. The cost schedules are shown in ◮ Figure 15.5. Engaging a sales agency is less expensive than establishing a new company sales office, but costs rise faster through an agency because sales agents get larger commissions.

The final step is comparing sales and costs. As Figure 15.5 shows, there is one sales level (S_B) at which selling costs are the same for the two channels. The sales agency is thus the better channel for any sales volume below S_B, and the company sales branch is better at any volume above S_B. Given this information, it is not surprising that sales agents tend to be used by smaller firms, or by large firms in smaller territories where the volume is low.

CONTROL AND ADAPTIVE CRITERIA Using a sales agency can pose a control problem. Agents may concentrate on the customers who buy the most, not necessarily those who buy the manufacturer's goods. They might not master the technical details of the company's product or handle its promotion materials effectively.

To develop a channel, members must commit to each other for a specified period of time. Yet these commitments invariably reduce the producer's ability to respond to change and uncertainty. The producer needs channel structures and policies that provide high adaptability.

Channel-Management Decisions

After a company has chosen a channel system, it must select, train, motivate, and evaluate individual intermediaries for each channel. It must also modify channel design and arrangements over time. As the company grows, it can also consider channel expansion into international markets.

Selecting Channel Members

To customers, the channels are the company. Consider the negative impression customers would get of McDonald's, Shell Oil, or Mercedes-Benz if one or more of their outlets or dealers consistently appeared dirty, inefficient, or unpleasant.

To facilitate channel member selection, producers should determine what characteristics distinguish the better intermediaries—number of years in business, other lines carried, growth and profit record, financial strength, cooperativeness, and service reputation. If the intermediaries are sales agents, producers should evaluate the number and character of other lines carried and the size and quality of the sales force. If the intermediaries are department stores that want exclusive distribution, their locations, future growth potential, and type of clientele will matter.

Training and Motivating Channel Members

A company needs to view its intermediaries the same way it views its end users. It should determine their needs and wants and tailor its channel offering to provide them with superior value.

Carefully implemented training, market research, and other capability-building programs can motivate and improve intermediaries' performance. The company must constantly communicate that intermediaries are crucial partners in a joint effort to satisfy end users of the product. Microsoft requires its third-party service engineers to complete a set of courses and take certification exams. Those who pass are formally recognized as Microsoft Certified Professionals and can use this designation to promote their own business. Other firms use customer surveys rather than exams.

CHANNEL POWER Producers vary greatly in their skill in managing distributors. **Channel power** is the ability to alter channel members' behavior so they take actions they would not have taken otherwise.[31] Manufacturers can draw on the following types of power to elicit cooperation:

- *Coercive power.* A manufacturer threatens to withdraw a resource or terminate a relationship if intermediaries fail to cooperate. This power can be effective, but its exercise produces resentment and can lead the intermediaries to organize countervailing power.
- *Reward power.* The manufacturer offers intermediaries an extra benefit for performing specific acts or functions. Reward power typically produces better results than coercive power, but intermediaries may come to expect a reward every time the manufacturer wants a certain behavior to occur.
- *Legitimate power.* The manufacturer requests a behavior that is warranted under the contract. As long as the intermediaries view the manufacturer as a legitimate leader, legitimate power works.
- *Expert power.* The manufacturer has special knowledge the intermediaries value. Once the intermediaries acquire this expertise, however, expert power weakens. The manufacturer must continue to develop new expertise so intermediaries will want to continue cooperating.
- *Referent power.* The manufacturer is so highly respected that intermediaries are proud to be associated with it. Companies such as IBM, Caterpillar, and Hewlett-Packard have high referent power.[32]

Coercive and reward power are objectively observable; legitimate, expert, and referent power are more subjective and depend on the ability and willingness of parties to recognize them.

Most producers see gaining intermediaries' cooperation as a huge challenge. They often use positive motivators, such as higher margins, special deals, premiums, cooperative advertising allowances, display allowances, and sales contests. At times they will apply negative sanctions, such as threatening to reduce margins, slow down delivery, or terminate the relationship. The weakness of this approach is that the producer is using crude, stimulus-response thinking.

In many cases, retailers hold the power. Manufacturers offer the nation's supermarkets between 150 and 250 new items each week, of which store buyers reject over 70 percent. Manufacturers need to know the acceptance criteria buyers, buying committees, and store managers use. ACNielsen interviews found that store managers were most influenced by (in order of importance) strong evidence of consumer acceptance, a well-designed advertising and sales promotion plan, and generous financial incentives.

CHANNEL PARTNERSHIPS More sophisticated companies try to forge a long-term partnership with distributors.[33] The manufacturer clearly communicates what it wants from its distributors in the way of market coverage, inventory levels, marketing development, account solicitation, technical advice and services, and marketing information and may introduce a compensation plan for adhering to the policies.

To streamline the supply chain and cut costs, many manufacturers and retailers have adopted *efficient consumer response (ECR) practices* to organize their relationships in three areas: (1) *demand side management* or collaborative practices to stimulate consumer demand by promoting joint marketing and sales activities, (2) *supply side management* or collaborative practices to optimize supply (with a focus on joint logistics and supply chain activities), and (3) *enablers and integrators,* or collaborative information technology and process improvement tools to support joint activities that reduce operational problems, allow greater standardization, and so on.

Research has shown that although ECR has a positive impact on manufacturers' economic performance and capability development, manufacturers may also feel they are inequitably sharing the burdens of adopting it and not getting as much as they deserve from retailers.[34]

Evaluating Channel Members

Producers must periodically evaluate intermediaries' performance against such standards as sales-quota attainment, average inventory levels, customer delivery time, treatment of damaged and lost goods, and cooperation in promotional and training programs. A producer will occasionally discover it is overpaying particular intermediaries for what they are actually doing. One manufacturer compensating a distributor for holding inventories found the inventories were actually held in a public warehouse at its own expense. Producers should set up functional discounts in which they pay specified amounts for the trade channel's performance of each agreed upon service. Underperformers need to be counseled, retrained, motivated, or terminated.

Modifying Channel Design and Arrangements

No channel strategy remains effective over the whole product life cycle. In competitive markets with low entry barriers, the optimal channel structure will inevitably change over time. The change could mean adding or dropping individual market channels or channel members or developing a totally new way to sell goods.

CHANNEL EVOLUTION A new firm typically starts as a local operation selling in a fairly circumscribed market, using a few existing intermediaries. Identifying the best channels might not be a problem; the problem is often to convince the available intermediaries to handle the firm's line.

If the firm is successful, it might branch into new markets with different channels. In smaller markets, the firm might sell directly to retailers; in larger markets, through distributors. In rural areas, it might work with general-goods merchants; in urban areas, with limited-line merchants. It might grant exclusive franchises or sell through all willing outlets. In one country, it might use international sales agents; in another, it might partner with a local firm.

Early buyers might be willing to pay for high-value-added channels, but later buyers will switch to lower-cost channels. Small office copiers were first sold by manufacturers' direct sales forces, later through office equipment dealers, still later through mass merchandisers, and now by mail-order firms and Internet marketers.

In short, the channel system evolves as a function of local opportunities and conditions, emerging threats and opportunities, company resources and capabilities, and other factors. Consider some of the challenges Dell has encountered in recent years.[35]

Dell Dell revolutionized the personal computer category by selling directly to customers via the telephone and later the Internet. Customers could custom-design the exact PC they wanted, and rigorous cost cutting allowed for low everyday prices. Sound like a winning formula? It was for almost two decades. But by 2006, the company was encountering problems that led to a steep stock price decline. First, reinvigorated competitors such as HP narrowed the gap in productivity and price. Always focused more on the business market, Dell struggled to sell effectively to the consumer market. A shift in consumer preferences to buying in retail stores didn't help, but self-inflicted damage from an ultra-efficient supply chain model that squeezed costs—and quality—out of customer service was perhaps the most painful. Managers evaluated call center employees primarily on how quickly they finished each call—a recipe for disaster as scores of customers felt their problems were ignored or not properly handled. A drop in R&D spending that hindered new-product development and led to a lack of differentiation didn't help either. Clearly, Dell had entered a new chapter in its history. A fundamental rethinking of its channel strategy and its marketing approach as a whole would consume the company for the next five years.

Channel Modification Decisions

A producer must periodically review and modify its channel design and arrangements.[36] The distribution channel may not work as planned, consumer buying patterns change, the market expands, new competition arises, innovative distribution channels emerge, and the product moves into later stages in the product life cycle.[37]

Adding or dropping individual channel members requires an incremental analysis. Increasingly detailed customer databases and sophisticated analysis tools can provide guidance into those decisions.[38] A basic question is: What would the firm's sales and profits look like with and without this intermediary?

Perhaps the most difficult decision is whether to revise the overall channel strategy.[39] Avon's door-to-door system for selling cosmetics was modified as more women entered the workforce. Despite the convenience of automated teller machines, online banking, and telephone call centers, many bank customers still want "high touch" over "high tech," or at least they want the choice. Banks are thus opening more branches and developing cross-selling and up-selling practices to capitalize on the face-to-face contact that results.

Global Channel Considerations

International markets pose distinct challenges, including variations in customers' shopping habits, but opportunities at the same time.[40] In India, sales from "organized retail"—hypermarkets, supermarkets, and department stores—make up only 4 percent of the $322 billion market. Most shopping still takes place in millions of independent grocery shops or *kirana* stores, run by an owner and one or perhaps two other people.[41] Many top global retailers such as Germany's Aldi, the United Kingdom's Tesco, and Spain's Zara have tailored their image to local needs and wants when entering a new market.

Franchised companies such as Curves women's fitness centers and Subway sandwich shops have experienced double-digit growth overseas, especially in developing markets such as Brazil and Central and Eastern Europe. In some cases, *master franchisees* pay a significant fee to acquire a territory or country where they operate as a "mini-franchiser" in their own right. More knowledgeable about local laws, customs, and consumer needs than foreign companies, they sell and oversee franchises and collect royalties.[42]

Subway has franchise operators all over the world, including in the Doha City Center Shopping Mall in Qatar, shown here.

But many pitfalls exist in global expansion, and retailers must also be able to defend their home turf from the entry of foreign retailers. Selling everything from food to televisions, France's Carrefour, the world's second-biggest retailer, has encountered stiff competition in its home markets from smaller supermarkets for groceries and from specialist retailers such as IKEA or Fnac for other goods. Although strong in parts of Europe, Asia, and Latin America, Carrefour (which means "crossroads" in French) has been forced to cease operations in a number of countries, such as Japan, South Korea, Mexico, Czech Republic, Slovakia, Russia, Switzerland, and Portugal. Another of France's mega-retailers the Walmart-like Auchan, has been quite successful in entering emerging markets like China while unable to crack markets in the United States or Britain.[43]

The first step in global channel planning, as is often the case in marketing, is to get close to customers. To adapt its clothing lines to better suit European tastes, Philadelphia-based Urban Outfitters set up a separate design and merchandising unit in London before it opened its first store in Europe. Although they increased costs, the blended American and European looks helped the retailer stand out.[44] Crossing the Atlantic the other way, Tesco introduced its Fresh & Easy gourmet minisupermarkets into California after 20 years of research that included spending time with U.S. families and videotaping the contents of their refrigerators. The retailer had gone through similar steps before entering China.[45]

A good retail strategy that offers customers a positive shopping experience and unique value, if properly adapted, is likely to find success in more than one market. Take Topshop for instance.

Topshop   Founded by Sir Richard Green in the United Kingdom in 1994, clothing retailer Topshop is a chain of 310 UK stores and 116 international franchisees that commands intense loyalty from its trendy, style-obsessed customer base. Selling primarily party clothes, accessories, and daywear to women, Topshop blends English street fashion, reasonable prices, and fun services. A higher-end, quirkier version of fast-fashion chains H&M and Zara, Topshop allows middle-market consumers to dress upscale affordably. Partnering with style icons Kate Moss, Stella Vine, and Celia Birtwell to create the latest designs, Topshop offers style advisors, Topshop-to-Go (a Tupperware-type party that brings a style advisor to a customer's home with outfits for up to 10 people), and Topshop Express (an express delivery service via Vespa scooters for fashion "emergencies"). The 60,000 square foot store on Broadway in New York City is Topshop's second biggest and first flagship store outside the United Kingdom.[46]

Topshop's unique combination of fashion, value, and fun is finding success both inside and outside the United Kingdom.

Channel Integration and Systems

Distribution channels don't stand still. We'll look at the recent growth of vertical, horizontal, and multichannel marketing systems; the next section examines how these systems cooperate, conflict, and compete.

Vertical Marketing Systems

A **conventional marketing channel** consists of an independent producer, wholesaler(s), and retailer(s). Each is a separate business seeking to maximize its own profits, even if this goal reduces profit for the system as a whole. No channel member has complete or substantial control over other members.

A **vertical marketing system (VMS)**, by contrast, includes the producer, wholesaler(s), and retailer(s) acting as a unified system. One channel member, the *channel captain*, owns or franchises the others or has so much power that they all cooperate. "Marketing Insight: Channel Stewards Take Charge" provides some perspective on how *channel stewards*, a closely related concept, can work.

Channel Stewards Take Charge

Harvard's V. Kasturi Rangan believes companies should adopt a new approach to going to market—**channel stewardship**. Rangan defines channel stewardship as the ability of a given participant in a distribution channel—a steward—to create a go-to-market strategy that simultaneously addresses customers' best interests and drives profits for all channel partners. The channel steward accomplishes channel coordination without issuing commands or directives by persuading channel partners to act in the best interest of all.

A channel steward might be the maker of the product or service (Procter & Gamble or American Airlines), the maker of a key component (microchip maker Intel), the supplier or assembler (Dell or Arrow Electronics), or the distributor (W.W. Grainger) or retailer (Walmart). Within a company, stewardship might rest with the CEO, a top manager, or a team of senior managers.

Channel stewardship should appeal to any organization that wants to bring a disciplined approach to channel strategy. With the customer's point of view in mind, the steward advocates for change among all participants, transforming them into partners with a common purpose.

Channel stewardship has two important outcomes. First it expands value for the steward's customers, enlarging the market or existing customers' purchases through the channel. A second outcome is to create a more tightly woven and yet adaptable channel, in which valuable members are rewarded and the less valuable members are weeded out.

Rangan outlines three key disciplines of channel management:

1. *Mapping* at the industry level provides a comprehensive view of the key determinants of channel strategy and how they are evolving. It identifies current best practices and gaps, and it projects future requirements.

2. *Building and editing* assesses the producer's own channels to identify any deficits in meeting customers' needs and/or competitive best practices to put together a new and improved overall system.

3. *Aligning and influencing* closes the gaps and works out a compensation package in tune with effort and performance for channel members that add or could add value.

Channel stewardship works at the customer level, not at the level of channel institutions. Thus, channel managers can adapt their fulfillment of customer needs without having to change channel structure all at once. An evolutionary approach to channel change, stewardship requires constant monitoring, learning, and adaptation, but all in the best interests of customers, channel partners, and channel steward. A channel steward need not be a huge company or market leader; Rangan cites smaller players, such as Haworth and Atlas Copco, as well as distributors and retailers such as Walmart, Best Buy, and HEB (supermarkets).

Sources: V. Kasturi Rangan, *Transforming Your Go-to-Market Strategy: The Three Disciplines of Channel Management* (Boston: Harvard Business School Press, 2006); Kash Rangan, "Channel Stewardship: An Introductory Guide," www.channelstewardship.com; Partha Rose and Romit Dey, "Channel Stewardship: Driving Profitable Revenue Growth in High-Tech with Multi-Channel Management," *Infosys ViewPoint*, August 2007.

Vertical marketing systems (VMSs) arose from strong channel members' attempts to control channel behavior and eliminate conflict over independent members pursuing their own objectives. VMSs achieve economies through size, bargaining power, and elimination of duplicated services. Business buyers of complex products and systems value the extensive exchange of information they can obtain from a VMS,[47] and VMSs have become the dominant mode of distribution in the U.S. consumer marketplace, serving 70 percent to 80 percent of the market. There are three types: corporate, administered, and contractual.

CORPORATE VMS A *corporate VMS* combines successive stages of production and distribution under single ownership. Sears for years obtained over half the goods it sells from companies it partly or wholly owned. Sherwin-Williams makes paint but also owns and operates 3,300 retail outlets.

ADMINISTERED VMS An *administered VMS* coordinates successive stages of production and distribution through the size and power of one of the members. Manufacturers of dominant brands can secure strong trade cooperation and support from resellers. Thus Kodak, Gillette, and Campbell Soup command high levels of cooperation from their resellers in connection with displays, shelf space, promotions, and price policies. The most advanced supply-distributor arrangement for administered VMSs relies on **distribution programming**, which builds a planned, professionally managed, vertical marketing system that meets the needs of both manufacturer and distributors.

CONTRACTUAL VMS A *contractual VMS* consists of independent firms at different levels of production and distribution, integrating their programs on a contractual basis to obtain more economies or sales impact than they could achieve alone.[48] Sometimes thought of as "value-adding partnerships" (VAPs), contractual VMSs come in three types:

1. *Wholesaler-sponsored voluntary chains*—Wholesalers organize voluntary chains of independent retailers to help standardize their selling practices and achieve buying economies in competing with large chain organizations.

2. *Retailer cooperatives*—Retailers take the initiative and organize a new business entity to carry on wholesaling and possibly some production. Members concentrate their purchases through the retailer co-op and plan their advertising jointly. Profits pass back to members in proportion to their purchases. Nonmember retailers can also buy through the co-op but do not share in the profits.

3. *Franchise organizations*—A channel member called a *franchisor* might link several successive stages in the production-distribution process. Franchising has been the fastest-growing retailing development in recent years.

Although the basic idea is an old one, some forms of franchising are quite new. The traditional system is the *manufacturer-sponsored retailer franchise.* Ford licenses independent businesspeople to sell its cars who agree to meet specified conditions of sales and services. Another system is the *manufacturer-sponsored wholesaler franchise.* Coca-Cola licenses bottlers (wholesalers) in various markets that buy its syrup concentrate and then carbonate, bottle, and sell it to retailers in local markets. A newer system is the *service-firm-sponsored retailer franchise,* organized by a service firm to bring its service efficiently to consumers. We find examples in auto rental (Hertz and Avis), fast food (McDonald's and Burger King), and the motel business (Howard Johnson and Ramada Inn). In a dual distribution system, firms use both vertical integration (the franchisor actually owns and runs the units) and market governance (the franchisor licenses the units to other franchisees).[49]

THE NEW COMPETITION IN RETAILING Many independent retailers that have not joined VMSs have developed specialty stores serving special market segments. The result is a polarization in retailing between large vertical marketing organizations and independent specialty stores, which creates a problem for manufacturers. They are strongly tied to independent intermediaries but must eventually realign themselves with the high-growth vertical marketing systems on less attractive terms. Furthermore, vertical marketing systems constantly threaten to bypass large manufacturers and set up their own manufacturing. The new competition in retailing is no longer between independent business units but between whole systems of centrally programmed networks (corporate, administered, and contractual), competing against one another to achieve the best cost economies and customer response.

Horizontal Marketing Systems

Another channel development is the **horizontal marketing system**, in which two or more unrelated companies put together resources or programs to exploit an emerging marketing opportunity. Each company lacks the capital, know-how, production, or marketing resources to venture alone, or it is afraid of the risk. The companies might work together on a temporary or permanent basis or create a joint venture company.

For example, many supermarket chains have arrangements with local banks to offer in-store banking. Citizens Bank has over 523 branches in supermarkets, making up roughly 35 percent of its branch network. Citizens's staff members in these locations are more sales oriented, younger, and more likely to have some retail sales background than staff in the traditional brick-and-mortar branches.[50]

Integrating Multichannel Marketing Systems

Most companies today have adopted multichannel marketing. Disney sells its DVDs through five main channels: movie rental stores such as Blockbuster, Disney Stores (now owned and run by The Children's Place), retail stores such as Best Buy, online retailers such as Disney's own online stores and Amazon.com, and the Disney catalog and other catalog sellers. This variety affords Disney maximum market coverage and enables it to offer its videos at a number of price points.[51] Here are some of the channel options for leather goods maker Coach.

Coach   Coach markets a high-end line of luxury handbags, briefcases, luggage, and accessories. Roughly 84 percent of its sales are via the Internet, catalog, company retail stores in North America, Japan, Hong Kong, Macau and mainland China, and its North American outlet stores. Coach also has store-in-store offerings in Japan and China inside major department stores. Ten percent of sales are from 930 U.S. department store locations, such as Macy's (including Bloomingdale's), Dillard's, Nordstrom, Saks (including Carson's) and Lord & Taylor, as well as some of those retailer's Web sites. Five percent of sales are from international wholesalers in 20 countries, mostly department stores. Finally, Coach has licensing relationships with Movado (watches), Jimlar (footwear), and Marchon (eyewear). These licensed products are sometimes sold in other channels such as jewelry stores, high-end shoe stores, and optical retailers.[52]

Luxury goods maker Coach has a variety of carefully selected and managed channel options.

An **integrated marketing channel system** is one in which the strategies and tactics of selling through one channel reflect the strategies and tactics of selling through one or more other channels. Adding more channels gives companies three important benefits. The first is increased market coverage. Not only are more customers able to shop for the company's products in more places, but those who buy in more than one channel are often more profitable than single-channel customers.[53] The second benefit is lower channel cost—selling by phone is cheaper than personal selling to small customers. The third is more customized selling—such as by adding a technical sales force to sell complex equipment.

There is a trade-off, however. New channels typically introduce conflict and problems with control and cooperation. Two or more may end up competing for the same customers.

Clearly, companies need to think through their channel architecture and determine which channels should perform which functions. ▲ Figure 15.6 shows a simple grid to help make channel architecture decisions. The grid consists of major marketing channels (as rows) and the major channel tasks to be completed (as columns).[54]

The grid illustrates why using only one channel is not efficient. Consider a direct sales force. A salesperson would have to find leads, qualify them, presell, close the sale, provide service, and manage account growth. An integrated multichannel approach would be better. The company's marketing department could run a preselling campaign informing prospects about the company's products through advertising, direct mail, and telemarketing; generate leads through telemarketing, direct mail, advertising, and trade shows; and qualify leads into hot, warm, and cool. The salesperson enters when the prospect is ready to talk business and invests his or her costly time primarily in closing the sale. This multichannel architecture optimizes coverage, customization, and control while minimizing cost and conflict.

Companies should use different sales channels for different-sized business customers—a direct sales force for large customers, telemarketing for midsize customers, and distributors for small customers—but be alert for conflict over account ownership. For example, territory-based sales representatives may want credit for all sales in their territories, regardless of the marketing channel used.

Multichannel marketers also need to decide how much of their product to offer in each of the channels. Patagonia views the Web as the ideal channel for showing off its entire line of goods, given that its 20 stores and 5 outlets are limited by space to offering a selection only, and even its catalog promotes less than 70 percent of its total merchandise.[55] Other marketers prefer to limit their online offerings, theorizing that customers look to Web sites

		Demand-generation Tasks								
		Gather relevant information	Develop & disseminate communications	Reach price agreements	Place orders	Acquire funds for inventories	Assume risks	Facilitate product storage & movement	Facilitate payment	Oversee ownership transfer
	Internet									
	National account management									
	Direct sales									
VENDOR	Telemarketing									
	Direct mail									
	Retail stores									
	Distributors									
	Dealers and value-added resellers									

(Left axis label: Marketing Channels and Methods; Right axis label: CUSTOMER)

|Fig. 15.6| ▲

The Hybrid Grid

Source: Adapted from Rowland T. Moriarty and Ursula Moran, "Marketing Hybrid Marketing Systems," *Harvard Business Review*, November–December, 1990, p. 150.

and catalogs for a "best of" array of merchandise and don't want to have to click through dozens of pages.

Conflict, Cooperation, and Competition

No matter how well channels are designed and managed, there will be some conflict, if only because the interests of independent business entities do not always coincide. **Channel conflict** is generated when one channel member's actions prevent another channel from achieving its goal. Software giant Oracle Corp., plagued by channel conflict between its sales force and its vendor partners, decided to roll out new "All Partner Territories" where all deals except for specific strategic accounts would go through select Oracle partners.[56]

Channel coordination occurs when channel members are brought together to advance the goals of the channel, as opposed to their own potentially incompatible goals.[57] Here we examine three questions: What types of conflict arise in channels? What causes conflict? What can marketers do to resolve it?

Types of Conflict and Competition

Suppose a manufacturer sets up a vertical channel consisting of wholesalers and retailers hoping for channel cooperation and greater profits for each member. Yet horizontal, vertical, and multi-channel conflict can occur.

- *Horizontal channel conflict* occurs between channel members at the same level. Some Pizza Inn franchisees complained about others cheating on ingredients, providing poor service, and hurting the overall brand image.
- *Vertical channel conflict* occurs between different levels of the channel. When Estée Lauder set up a Web site to sell its Clinique and Bobbi Brown brands, the department

When Goodyear expanded its channels to include mass-market retailers, it angered its long-time independent dealers.

store Dayton Hudson reduced its space for Estée Lauder products.[58] Greater retailer consolidation—the 10 largest U.S. retailers account for over 80 percent of the average manufacturer's business—has led to increased price pressure and influence from retailers.[59] Walmart, for example, is the principal buyer for many manufacturers, including Disney, Procter & Gamble, and Revlon, and is able to command reduced prices or quantity discounts from these and other suppliers.[60]

- *Multichannel conflict* exists when the manufacturer has established two or more channels that sell to the same market.[61] It's likely to be especially intense when the members of one channel get a lower price (based on larger-volume purchases) or work with a lower margin. When Goodyear began selling its popular tire brands through Sears, Walmart, and Discount Tire, it angered its independent dealers and eventually placated them by offering exclusive tire models not sold in other retail outlets.

Causes of Channel Conflict

Some causes of channel conflict are easy to resolve, others are not. Conflict may arise from:

- *Goal incompatibility.* The manufacturer may want to achieve rapid market penetration through a low-price policy. Dealers, in contrast, may prefer to work with high margins and pursue short-run profitability.
- *Unclear roles and rights.* HP may sell personal computers to large accounts through its own sales force, but its licensed dealers may also be trying to sell to large accounts. Territory boundaries and credit for sales often produce conflict.
- *Differences in perception.* The manufacturer may be optimistic about the short-term economic outlook and want dealers to carry higher inventory. Dealers may be pessimistic. In the beverage category, it is not uncommon for disputes to arise between manufacturers and their distributors about the optimal advertising strategy.
- *Intermediaries' dependence on the manufacturer.* The fortunes of exclusive dealers, such as auto dealers, are profoundly affected by the manufacturer's product and pricing decisions. This situation creates a high potential for conflict.

Managing Channel Conflict

Some channel conflict can be constructive and lead to better adaptation to a changing environment, but too much is dysfunctional.[62] The challenge is not to eliminate all conflict, which is

TABLE 15.2   Strategies to Manage Channel Conflict
Strategic justification
Dual compensation
Superordinate goals
Employee exchange
Joint memberships
Co-optation
Diplomacy, mediation, or arbitration
Legal recourse

impossible, but to manage it better. There are a number of mechanisms for effective conflict management (see   Table 15.2).[63]

Strategic Justification In some cases, a convincing strategic justification that they serve distinctive segments and do not compete as much as they might think can reduce potential for conflict among channel members. Developing special versions of products for different channel members—branded variants as described in Chapter 9—is a clear way to demonstrate that distinctiveness.

Dual Compensation Dual compensation pays existing channels for sales made through new channels. When Allstate started selling insurance online, it agreed to pay agents a 2 percent commission for face-to-face service to customers who got their quotes on the Web. Although lower than the agents' typical 10 percent commission for offline transactions, it did reduce tensions.[64]

Superordinate Goals Channel members can come to an agreement on the fundamental or superordinate goal they are jointly seeking, whether it is survival, market share, high quality, or customer satisfaction. They usually do this when the channel faces an outside threat, such as a more efficient competing channel, an adverse piece of legislation, or a shift in consumer desires.

Employee Exchange A useful step is to exchange persons between two or more channel levels. GM's executives might agree to work for a short time in some dealerships, and some dealership owners might work in GM's dealer policy department. Thus participants can grow to appreciate each other's point of view.

Joint Memberships Similarly, marketers can encourage joint memberships in trade associations. Good cooperation between the Grocery Manufacturers of America and the Food Marketing Institute, which represents most of the food chains, led to the development of the universal product code (UPC). The associations can consider issues between food manufacturers and retailers and resolve them in an orderly way.

Co-option Co-optation is an effort by one organization to win the support of the leaders of another by including them in advisory councils, boards of directors, and the like. If the organization treats invited leaders seriously and listens to their opinions, co-optation can reduce conflict, but the initiator may need to compromise its policies and plans to win outsiders' support.

Diplomacy, Mediation, and Arbitration When conflict is chronic or acute, the parties may need to resort to stronger means. *Diplomacy* takes place when each side sends a person or group to meet with its counterpart to resolve the conflict. *Mediation* relies on a neutral third party skilled in conciliating the two parties' interests. In *arbitration* two parties agree to present their arguments to one or more arbitrators and accept their decision.

Legal Recourse If nothing else proves effective, a channel partner may choose to file a lawsuit. When Coca-Cola decided to distribute Powerade thirst quencher directly to Walmart's regional warehouses, 60 bottlers complained the practice would undermine their core direct-store-distribution (DSD) duties and filed a lawsuit. A settlement allowed for the mutual exploration of new service and distribution systems to supplement the DSD system.[65]

Dilution and Cannibalization

Marketers must be careful not to dilute their brands through inappropriate channels, particularly luxury brands whose images often rest on exclusivity and personalized service. Calvin Klein and Tommy Hilfiger took a hit when they sold too many of their products in discount channels.

To reach affluent shoppers who work long hours and have little time to shop, high-end fashion brands such as Dior, Louis Vuitton, and Fendi have unveiled e-commerce sites as a way for customers to research items before walking into a store, and a means to help combat fakes sold on the Internet. Given the lengths to which these brands go to pamper customers in their stores—doormen, glasses of champagne, extravagant surroundings—they have had to work hard to provide a high-quality experience online.[66]

Legal and Ethical Issues in Channel Relations

Companies are generally free to develop whatever channel arrangements suit them. In fact, the law seeks to prevent them from using exclusionary tactics that might keep competitors from using a channel. Here we briefly consider the legality of certain practices, including exclusive dealing, exclusive territories, tying agreements, and dealers' rights.

With *exclusive distribution*, only certain outlets are allowed to carry a seller's products. Requiring that these dealers not handle competitors' products is called *exclusive dealing*. Both parties benefit from exclusive arrangements: The seller obtains more loyal and dependable outlets, and the dealers obtain a steady supply of special products and stronger seller support. Exclusive arrangements are legal as long as they do not substantially lessen competition or tend to create a monopoly, and as long as both parties enter into them voluntarily.

Exclusive dealing often includes exclusive territorial agreements. The producer may agree not to sell to other dealers in a given area, or the buyer may agree to sell only in its own territory. The first practice increases dealer enthusiasm and commitment. It is also perfectly legal—a seller has no legal obligation to sell through more outlets than it wishes. The second practice, whereby the producer tries to keep a dealer from selling outside its territory, has become a major legal issue. One bitter lawsuit was brought by GT Bicycles of Santa Ana, California, against the giant PriceCostco chain, which sold 2,600 of its high-priced mountain bikes at a huge discount, upsetting GT's other U.S. dealers. GT alleges that it first sold the bikes to a dealer in Russia and that they were meant for sale only in Russia. The firm maintains that when discounters work with middlemen to get exclusive goods, it constitutes fraud.[67]

Producers of a strong brand sometimes sell it to dealers only if they will take some or all of the rest of the line. This practice is called *full-line forcing*. Such **tying agreements** are not necessarily illegal, but they do violate U.S. law if they tend to lessen competition substantially.

Producers are free to select their dealers, but their right to terminate dealers is somewhat restricted. In general, sellers can drop dealers "for cause," but they cannot drop dealers if, for example, they refuse to cooperate in a doubtful legal arrangement, such as exclusive dealing or tying agreements.

E-Commerce Marketing Practices

E-commerce uses a Web site to transact or facilitate the sale of products and services online. Online retail sales have exploded in recent years, and it is easy to see why. Online retailers can predictably provide convenient, informative, and personalized experiences for vastly different types of consumers and businesses. By saving the cost of retail floor space, staff, and inventory, online retailers can profitably sell low-volume products to niche markets. Online retailers compete in three key aspects of a transaction: (1) customer interaction with the Web site, (2) delivery, and (3) ability to address problems when they occur.[68]

We can distinguish between **pure-click** companies, those that have launched a Web site without any previous existence as a firm, and **brick-and-click** companies, existing companies that have added an online site for information or e-commerce.

Pure-Click Companies

There are several kinds of pure-click companies: search engines, Internet service providers (ISPs), commerce sites, transaction sites, content sites, and enabler sites. Commerce sites sell all types of products and services, notably books, music, toys, insurance, stocks, clothes, financial services, and so on. They use various strategies to compete: AutoNation is a leading metamediary of car buying and related services; Hotels.com is the information leader in hotel reservations; Buy.com leads on price; and Wine Spectator is a single-category specialist.

E-COMMERCE SUCCESS FACTORS Companies must set up and operate their e-commerce Web sites carefully. Customer service is critical. Online shoppers may select an item for purchase but fail to complete the transaction—one estimate of the conversion rate of Internet shoppers in March 2008 was only about 35 percent. Worse, only 2 percent to 3 percent of visits to online retailers lead to sales, compared with 5 percent of visits to department stores.[69] To improve conversion rates, firms should make the Web site fast, simple, and easy to use. Something as simple as enlarging product images on-screen can increase perusal time and the amount customers buy.[70]

Consumer surveys suggest that the most significant inhibitors of online shopping are the absence of pleasurable experiences, social interaction, and personal consultation with a company representative.[71] Firms are responding. Many now offer live online chat to give potential customers immediate advice about products and suggest purchasing additional items. When a representative is active in the sale, the average amount per order is typically higher. B2B marketers also need to put a human face on their e-commerce presence, and some are taking advantage of Web 2.0 technologies such as virtual environments, blogs, online videos, and click-to-chat.

To increase customer satisfaction and the entertainment and information value of Web-based shopping experiences, some firms are employing *avatars,* graphical representations of virtual, animated characters that act as company representatives, personal shopping assistants, Web site guides, or conversation partners. Avatars can enhance the effectiveness of a Web-based sales channel, especially if they are seen as expert or attractive.[72]

Ensuring security and privacy online remains important. Customers must find the Web site trustworthy, even if it represents an already highly credible offline firm. Investments in Web site design and processes can help reassure customers sensitive to online risk.[73] Online retailers are also trying new technologies such as blogs, social networks, and mobile marketing to attract new shoppers.

B2B E-COMMERCE Although business-to-consumer (B2C) Web sites have attracted much attention in the media, even more activity is being conducted on business-to-business (B2B) sites, which are changing the supplier–customer relationship in profound ways.

In the past, buyers exerted a lot of effort to gather information about worldwide suppliers. B2B sites make markets more efficient, giving buyers easy access to a great deal of information from (1) supplier Web sites; (2) *infomediaries,* third parties that add value by aggregating information about alternatives; (3) *market makers,* third parties that link buyers and sellers; and (4) *customer communities,* where buyers can swap stories about suppliers' products and services.[74] Firms are using B2B auction sites, spot exchanges, online product catalogs, barter sites, and other online resources to obtain better prices. Ironically, the largest of the B2B market makers is Alibaba, homegrown in China where businesses have faced decades of Communist antipathy to private enterprise.

Alibaba   The brainchild of Jack Ma, Alibaba began in 1999 and grew over the next decade to become the world's largest online B2B marketplace and Asia's most popular online auction site. Its numbers are staggering. The $9 billion company has 43 million registered users (35 million in China and 10.5 million internationally) and hosts more than 5.5 million shop fronts; at any moment, more than 4 million businesses are trading. At Alibaba's heart are two B2B Web sites: alibaba.com, a marketplace for companies around the globe to buy and sell in English, and china.alibaba, a domestic Chinese marketplace. The Chinese powerhouse has a nationalist agenda: to build markets for China's vast number of small and medium-sized businesses. Alibaba enables these businesses to trade with each other and link to global supply chains. To establish customer trust, the company set up TrustPass, in which users pay Alibaba a fee to hire a third party that verifies them. Users must have five people vouch for them and provide a list of all their certificates/business licenses. Anyone on Alibaba who has done business with a user is encouraged to comment on the firm, in the same way buyers comment on sellers in Amazon.com's or eBay's marketplace. Businesses are even starting to print "TrustPass" on their business cards, a true sign of Alibaba's B2B credibility. Global growth has become a priority. Home pages in Spanish, German, Italian, French, Portuguese, and Russian were launched in 2008 to complement Chinese and U.S. options. After its IPO of $1.7 billion in 2007 (second only to Google's among Internet firms), Alibaba, says Jack Ma, will "create the e-commerce platform for 10 million small enterprises creating 100 million jobs around the world and providing an online retail platform to supply the everyday needs of 1 billion people."[75]

Jack Ma has been the visionary force behind the highly successful Chinese online marketplace and auction site Alibaba.

The effect of these mechanisms is to make prices more transparent.[76] For undifferentiated products, price pressure will increase. For highly differentiated products, buyers will gain a better picture of the items' true value. Suppliers of superior products will be able to offset price transparency with value transparency; suppliers of undifferentiated products will need to drive down their costs in order to compete.

Brick-and-Click Companies

Although many brick-and-mortar companies may have initially debated whether to add an online e-commerce channel for fear of channel conflict with their offline retailers, agents, or their own stores, most eventually added the Internet as a distribution channel after seeing how much business was generated online.[77] Even Procter & Gamble, which used traditional physical channels of distribution exclusively for years, is selling some big brands such as Tide, Pampers, and Olay online, in part to be able to examine consumer shopping habits more closely.[78] Managing the online and offline channels has thus become a priority for many firms.[79]

Adding an e-commerce channel creates the possibility of a backlash from retailers, brokers, agents, and other intermediaries. The question is how to sell both through intermediaries and online. There are at least three strategies for trying to gain acceptance from intermediaries. One, offer different brands or products on the Internet. Two, offer offline partners higher commissions to cushion the negative impact on sales. Three, take orders on the Web site but have retailers deliver and collect payment. Harley-Davidson decided to tread carefully before going online.

Harley-Davidson   Given that Harley sells more than $860 million worth of parts and accessories to its loyal followers, an online venture was an obvious next step to generate even more revenue. Harley needed to be careful, however, to avoid the wrath of 850 dealers who benefited from the high margins on those sales. Its solution was to send customers seeking to buy accessories online to the company's Web site. Before they can buy anything, they are prompted to select a participating Harley-Davidson dealer. When the customer places the order, it is transmitted to the selected dealer for fulfillment, ensuring that the dealer still remains the focal point of the customer experience. Dealers, in turn, agreed to a number of standards, such as checking for orders twice a day and shipping promptly. The Web site now gets more than 1 million visitors a month.[80]

Many brick-and-click retailers are trying to give their customers more control over their shopping experiences by bringing Web technologies into the store. Food Lion has experimented with personal scanners so customers can keep track of their supermarket purchases. Barnes & Noble has kiosks that allow customers to search inventory, locate merchandise, and order out-of-stock items.[81]

M-Commerce Marketing Practices

The widespread penetration of cell phones and smart phones—there are currently more mobile phones than personal computers in the world—allows people to connect to the Internet and place online orders on the move. Many see a big future in what is now called *m-commerce* (*m* for *mobile*).[82] The existence of mobile channels and media can keep consumers connected and interacting with a brand throughout their day-to-day lives. GPS-type features can help identify shopping or purchase opportunities for consumers for their favorite brands.

Although in 2009 only one in five phones in the United States was a smart phone such as an iPhone or BlackBerry, sales of smart phones are forecast to exceed those of regular phones by 2011. As their penetration and adoption of 3G increases, and as easy payment options and various apps for mobile phones are developed, m-commerce will take off. By 2015, more people are expected to access the Internet with mobile phones than with PCs.[83]

In some countries, m-commerce already has a strong foothold. Millions of Japanese teenagers carry DOCOMO phones available from NTT (Nippon Telephone and Telegraph). They can also use their phones to order goods. Each month, the subscriber receives a bill from NTT listing the monthly subscriber fee, the usage fee, and the cost of all the transactions. Bills can be paid at the nearest 7-Eleven store.

In the United States, mobile marketing is becoming more prevalent and taking all forms.[84] Retailers such as Amazon.com, CVS, and Sears have launched m-commerce sites that allow consumers to buy books, medicine, and even lawn mowers from their smart phones. The travel industry has used m-commerce to target businesspeople who need to book air or hotel reservations while on the move.[85]

One Nordstrom salesperson increased the amount of merchandise he sold by 37 percent by sending text messages and e-mails of news and promotions to the cell phones of his customers.[86] Mobile marketing can have influence inside the store too. Consumers increasingly are using a cell phone to text a friend or relative about a product while shopping.

Here is how Dunkin' Donuts developed an m-commerce strategy to complement its broader marketing efforts.

Dunkin' Donuts Dunkin' Donuts targets busy people on the go, serving 2.7 million customers daily at approximately 8,800 stores in 31 countries, including roughly 6,400 U.S. locations. Portability remains an essential part of the value proposition, evidenced in the campaign theme, "America Runs on Dunkin.'" Knowing that many customers make a "Dunkin' Run" or visit, especially in the afternoon to bring back goodies for others, the company introduced new interactive Web tools and an iPhone application to create a social group ordering experience. The Dunkin' Run mobile campaign featured interactive alerts set to a customer's list of friends or coworkers, telling them when a trip to Dunkin' Donuts was planned, along with a personal message inviting them to place an order online. Invitees could view the menu to make an order or use a personalized list of favorites. All the orders were integrated onto a single screen that the runner could print out or display on a mobile and bring to the store. Dunkin' Run was not the company's first mobile marketing effort. An earlier two-month SMS promotional campaign in Italy increased sales almost 10 percent.[87]

Mobile marketing and the fact that a company can potentially pinpoint a customer or employee's location with GPS technology also raises privacy issues. What if an employer learns an employee is being treated for AIDS at a local clinic, or a wife finds her husband is out clubbing? Like so many new technologies, location-based services have potential for good or harm and ultimately will warrant public scrutiny and regulation.

Summary

1. Most producers do not sell their goods directly to final users. Between producers and final users stands one or more marketing channels, a host of marketing intermediaries performing a variety of functions.

2. Marketing channel decisions are among the most critical decisions facing management. The company's chosen channel(s) profoundly affect all other marketing decisions.

3. Companies use intermediaries when they lack the financial resources to carry out direct marketing, when direct marketing is not feasible, and when they can earn more by doing so. The most important functions performed by intermediaries are information, promotion, negotiation, ordering, financing, risk taking, physical possession, payment, and title.

4. Manufacturers have many alternatives for reaching a market. They can sell direct or use one-, two-, or three-level channels. Deciding which type(s) of channel to use calls for analyzing customer needs, establishing channel objectives, and identifying and evaluating the major alternatives, including the types and numbers of intermediaries involved in the channel.

5. Effective channel management calls for selecting intermediaries and training and motivating them. The goal is to build a long-term partnership that will be profitable for all channel members.

6. Marketing channels are characterized by continuous and sometimes dramatic change. Three of the most important trends are the growth of vertical marketing systems, horizontal marketing systems, and multichannel marketing systems.

7. All marketing channels have the potential for conflict and competition resulting from such sources as goal incompatibility, poorly defined roles and rights, perceptual differences, and interdependent relationships. There are a number of different approaches companies can take to try to manage conflict.

8. Channel arrangements are up to the company, but there are certain legal and ethical issues to be considered with regard to practices such as exclusive dealing or territories, tying agreements, and dealers' rights.

9. E-commerce has grown in importance as companies have adopted "brick-and-click" channel systems. Channel integration must recognize the distinctive strengths of online and offline selling and maximize their joint contributions.

10. An area of increasing importance is m-commerce and marketing through smart phones and PDAs.

Applications

Marketing Debate
Does It Matter Where You Sell?

Some marketers feel that the image of the particular channel in which they sell their products does not matter—all that matters is that the right customers shop there and the product is displayed in the right way. Others maintain that channel images—such as a retail store—can be critical and must be consistent with the image of the product.

Take a position: Channel images do not really affect the brand images of the products they sell that much *versus* Channel images must be consistent with the brand image.

Marketing Discussion
Channel Integrations

Think of your favorite retailers. How have they integrated their channel system? How would you like their channels to be integrated? Do you use multiple channels from them? Why?

Marketing Excellence

>>Amazon.com

Founded by Jeff Bezos, Amazon.com started as the "world's largest bookstore" in July 1995. A virtual bookstore that physically owned no books, Amazon.com promised to revolutionize retailing. Although some may debate whether it accomplished that, Bezos clearly blazed a trail of e-commerce innovations that many have studied and followed.

Amazon.com set out to create personalized storefronts for each customer by providing more useful information and more choices than could be found in your typical neighborhood bookstore. Readers can review books and evaluate them on a one- to five-star rating scale, and browsers can rate the reviews for helpfulness. Amazon.com's personal recommendation service aggregates data on buying patterns to infer who might like which book. The site offers peeks into books' contents, index, and beginning pages with a "search inside the book" feature that also lets customers search the entire text of 120,000 books—about as many titles as are in a Barnes & Noble bookstore. Amazon.com's one-click shopping lets buyers make purchases with one click.

Over the years, Amazon.com has diversified its product lines into DVDs, music CDs, computer software, video games, electronics, apparel, furniture, food, toys, and more. In addition, it has established separate Web sites in Canada, the United Kingdom, Germany, France, China, and Japan. Amazon.com continued to expand its product offerings with the 2007 launch of Amazon Video On Demand, allowing consumers to rent or purchase films and television shows on their computers or televisions. Later that year, Amazon.com introduced Amazon MP3, which competes directly with Apple's iTunes and has participation from all the major music labels. The company's most successful recent product launch was the Amazon-branded Kindle, an electronic book reader that can deliver hundreds of thousands of books, magazines, blogs, and newspapers wirelessly in a matter of seconds. As thin as a magazine and light as a paperback, the device was Amazon.com's number one selling product in 2009.

To overcome the lag between purchase and delivery of product, Amazon.com offers fast, inexpensive shipping. For a $79 annual fee, Amazon.com Prime provides unlimited free express shipping for most items. While free shipping and price cuts are sometimes unpopular with investors, Bezos believes it builds customer satisfaction, loyalty, and frequency of purchase orders.

Amazon.com has established itself as an electronic marketplace by enabling merchants of all kinds to sell items on the site. It powers and operates retail Web sites for Target, the NBA, Timex, and Marks & Spencer. Amazon.com derives about 40 percent of its sales from its million-plus affiliates called "Associates," independent sellers or businesses that receive commissions for referring customers who then make a purchase at the Amazon.com site. Associates can refer consumers to Amazon.com through a variety of ways, including direct links and banner ads as well as Amazon Widgets, mini-applications that feature Amazon.com's wide selection of products.

Amazon.com also launched an affiliate product called aStore, which gives Associates the ability to create an Amazon-operated online store easily and without any programming knowledge. Amazon.com then supports these merchants by providing new tools for their Web site, offering access to Amazon.com's catalog of products, and handling all payments and payment security through its Web Services. Amazon.com can also "pick, pack and ship the products to the merchant's customers anytime and to any place" through its Fulfillment by Amazon (FBA). This essentially creates a virtual store for the third-party merchants with low risk and no additional cost.

One key to Amazon.com's success in all these different ventures was a willingness to invest in the latest Internet technology to make shopping online faster, easier, and more personally rewarding for its customers and third-party merchants. The company continues to invest in technology, is focused on the long-term, and has successfully positioned itself as a technology company with its wide range of Amazon Web Services. This growing collection of infrastructure services meets the retailing needs of companies of virtually all sizes.

From the beginning, Bezos stated that even though he started as an online bookstore, he eventually wanted to sell everything through Amazon.com. Now, with more than 600 million annual visitors, the company continues to get closer to that goal with revolutionary products like the Kindle and cloud computing Web services.

Questions

1. Why has Amazon.com succeeded online when so many other companies have failed?

2. Will the Kindle revolutionize the book industry? Why or why not?

3. What's next for Amazon.com? Is cloud computing the right direction for the company? Where else can it grow?

Sources: "Click to Download," *Economist*, August 19, 2006, pp. 57–58; Robert D. Hof, "Jeff Bezos' Risky Bet," *BusinessWeek*, November 13, 2006; Erick Schonfeld, "The Great Giveaway," *Business 2.0*, April 2005, pp. 80–86; Elizabeth West, "Who's Next?" *Potentials*, February 2004, pp. 7–8; Robert D. Hof, "The Wizard of Web Retailing," *BusinessWeek*, December 20, 2004, p. 18; Chris Taylor, "Smart Library," *Time*, November 17, 2003, p. 68; Deborah Solomon, "Questions for Jeffrey P. Bezos," *New York Times*, December 2, 2009; Patrick Seitz, "Amazon.com Whiz Jeff Bezos Keeps Kindling Hot Concepts," *Investors' Daily Business*, December 31, 2009; Amazon.com, Amazon.com 2009 Annual Report.

Marketing Excellence

>>Tesco

Tesco's main purpose is to earn a customer's lifetime loyalty by creating value. To achieve this goal, the company has adopted the values of understanding customers, being the first to meet their needs, and acting responsibly for communities.

Tesco was founded in 1919 by Jack Kohen, who began to sell surplus groceries from a stall in London's East End. On his first day, Kohen had sales of roughly $6.40 and a profit of $1.60. In fiscal year 2009, Tesco Group had sales of $62.5 billion, with a profit before taxes of $4.96 billion and an enterprise value of $64.73 billion. The firm employs more than 472,000 people and occupies 94 million square feet of selling space in 14 countries.

Tesco's success comes from years of building customer loyalty through merchandising and pricing strategy. Over the years, the company has expanded its range of products and services from simple grocery items to almost everything, including PCs and peripherals, cameras, phones, home electrical appliances, televisions, AV equipment, furniture, kitchen appliances, and home furnishings, so customers can buy everything under one roof. Tesco also offers services that include petrol stations, opticians, and pharmacies.

Tesco started expanding overseas in 1995, starting with Hungary, and now has a presence in China, the Czech Republic, Hungary, India, Japan, Malaysia, Poland, Ireland, Slovakia, Thailand, and Turkey. In the United States, it operates under the name Fresh & Easy Neighborhood Market.

In trying to understand its customers based on their total spending, Tesco found that the top 100 customers were worth the same as the bottom 4,000. The bottom 25 percent of customers represented only 2 percent of sales, whereas the top 5 percent accounted for 20 percent. This showed the firm that all customers are not equal; as a result, it started to measure its more valuable customers by frequency of purchase and value of expenditure.

Tesco began its Customer Relationship Management Program in 1995 by introducing Clubcard, which offered loyal shoppers points on purchases and small rebates. Stores captured valuable information with every swipe of the card and built a powerful customer database that could show what products customers were and were not buying, and where they were spending their time in the store (measured by what they spent their money on). Clubcard customers received vouchers for items they specifically liked to buy, rather than general vouchers sent to all customers. Different lifestyle magazines were created for different customers. High-value shoppers received calls from store managers, valet parking when they came to shop, and other privileges so they would feel special and continue to be loyal to Tesco. Tesco now has more than 15 million cardholders and sends about 8 million unique coupon variations with each Clubcard mailing, to ensure that everybody who receives an offer receives an appropriate one. The Clubcard data provides Tesco with detailed information about customers' purchasing behavior. In addition to this data, the company polls around 12,000 customers in their annual Customer Question Time. They receive more direct feedback on products, price, quality, service, and the company's role within the community.

Stores are designed based on consumers' needs. The smallest floor plan, called 'Express', is less than 600 square feet and sells only grocery and food items; the largest 'Home Plus' stores are more than 50,000 square feet in size and sell only non-food items. In 1999, Tesco opened its online store and online banking initiatives. In 2000, it opened Tesco.com.

Tesco Direct, another online initiative, sells over 12,500 non-food products, guaranteeing next-day delivery for store pick-up. It is also experimenting with "drive-thru" supermarket service for customers who order through Tesco Direct and can pick up the items within a 2-hour block at designated parking spots without getting out of their cars.

In 2009, Tesco branched out to the iPhone by launching three different applications. The first allowed customers to scan their Clubcards using the iPhone's camera, so they don't even have to carry the card on a shopping trip. The second was a Storefinder, which allowed customers to find a nearby Tesco outlet. The third is a wine application that allows customers to take a photograph of a wine they like, so that they can read product information and place an order using the phone.

In 2010, Tesco created a new mobile Web site to facilitate easy shopping for non-food and household items using smart phones. This followed the launch of a grocery application that allows barcode scanning by the iPhone. Using the mobile Web site, customers can conveniently search and buy everything from televisions to tables to toys. This initiative is part of a commitment to make Tesco available to everyone, anywhere, at any time—whether through the catalog, in-store, online, or by phone.

Tesco also concentrates on providing efficient service. Under its "one-in-front" plan, for instance, if there is more than one customer at a single checkout counter, another counter will be opened. A number of self-service check-outs are also available in all stores. With improved CRM and service, Tesco has become the leading supermarket in the United Kingdom and is now expanding in other parts of the world.

Questions

1. As Tesco expands overseas, can it succeed by using the same strategies it has used in the United Kingdom? Why or why not? What factors should it take into account while formulating strategies in global markets?

2. What are the ways in which Tesco connects with its customers to provide more value for them?

Sources: "Tesco—The Brand Experience Is Everything," *BrandingAsia.com*, www.brandingasia.com/cases/tesco.htm; *Tesco*, www.tescoplc.com.

Chapter 16

In This Chapter, We Will Address the Following Questions

1. What major types of marketing intermediaries occupy this sector?

2. What marketing decisions do these marketing intermediaries make?

3. What are the major trends with marketing intermediaries?

4. What does the future hold for private label brands?

Cofounder Tony Hsieh has ensured that a strong customer-service culture is at the heart of operations at Zappos, the online footwear and accessories retailer.

Managing Retailing, Wholesaling, and Logistics

In the previous chapter, we examined marketing intermediaries from the viewpoint of manufacturers who wanted to build and manage marketing channels. In this chapter, we view these intermediaries—retailers, wholesalers, and logistical organizations—as requiring and forging their own marketing strategies in a rapidly changing world. Intermediaries also strive for marketing excellence and can reap the benefits like any other type of company.

Online footwear retailer Zappos was co-founded by Tony Hsieh in 1999 with superior customer service and an improved customer experience at the core of its corporate culture. With free shipping and returns, 24/7 customer service, and fast turnaround on a wide selection of 200,000 shoe styles from 1,200 makers, Zappos finds that three-fourths of purchases during any one day are by repeat customers. Unlike many other companies, Zappos has not outsourced its call centers; Hsieh sees that function as too important. In fact, Zappos empowers its customer service reps to solve problems. When a customer called to complain that a pair of boots was leaking after a year of use, the customer service rep sent out a new pair even though the company's policy is that only unworn shoes are returnable. Every employee has a chance each year to contribute a passage to the firm's Culture Book, about life at Zappos, and how each department implements superior customer service from selling to warehousing and delivery, to pricing and billing. Half the interview process for potential new hires is devoted to finding out whether they are sufficiently outgoing, open-minded, and creative to be a good cultural fit for the company. Bought by Amazon.com in 2009 for a reported $850 million but still run separately, the company now also sells clothing, handbags, and accessories. Thanks to its success, it even offers two-day, $4,000 seminars to business executives eager to learn about the secrets behind Zappos's unique corporate culture and approach to customer service.[1]

While innovative retailers such as Zappos, Sweden's H&M, Spain's Zara and Mango, and Britain's Topshop have thrived in recent years, others such as former U.S. stalwarts Gap, Home Depot, and Kmart have struggled. The more successful intermediaries use strategic planning, advanced information systems, and sophisticated marketing tools. They segment their markets, improve their market targeting and positioning, and aggressively pursue market expansion and diversification strategies. In this chapter, we consider marketing excellence in retailing, wholesaling, and logistics.

Retailing

Retailing includes all the activities in selling goods or services directly to final consumers for personal, nonbusiness use. A **retailer** or **retail store** is any business enterprise whose sales volume comes primarily from retailing.

Any organization selling to final consumers—whether it is a manufacturer, wholesaler, or retailer—is doing retailing. It doesn't matter *how* the goods or services are sold (in person, by mail, telephone, vending machine, or on the Internet) or *where* (in a store, on the street, or in the consumer's home).

After reviewing the different types of retailers and the new retail marketing environment, we examine the marketing decisions retailers make. The following are four examples of innovative retail organizations that have experienced market success in recent years.

Innovative Retail Organizations

Panera Bread. The $2.6 billion Panera Bread restaurant chain targets "food people who understand and respond to food or those on the verge of that" by selling fresh "real" food—and lots of warm bread—at full prices that customers are more than willing to pay. An unpretentious atmosphere—no table service, but no time limit—encourages customers to linger. The brand is seen as family-oriented but also sophisticated, offering an appealing combination of fresh, customizable, convenient, and affordable food.

GameStop. Video game and entertainment software retailer GameStop has over 6,000 locations in malls and shopping strips all over the United States, making it highly convenient for customers. Staffed by hard-core gamers who like to connect with customers, GameStop boasts a trade-in policy that gives customers credit for an old game traded in for a new one.

Lumber Liquidators. Lumber Liquidators buys excess wood directly from lumber mills at a discount and stocks almost 350 kinds of hardwood flooring, about the same as Lowe's and Home Depot. It sells at lower prices because it keeps operating costs down by cutting out the middlemen and locating stores in inexpensive locations. Lumber Liquidators also knows a lot about its customers, such as the fact that shoppers who request product samples have a 30 percent likelihood of buying within a month, and that most tend to renovate one room at a time, not the entire home at once.

Panera Bread appeals to food lovers of all kinds.

Net-a-Porter. London-based Net-a-Porter is an online luxury clothing and accessories retailer whose Web site combines the style of a fashion magazine with the thrill of shopping at a chic boutique. Seen by its loyal customers as an authoritative fashion voice, Net-a-Porter stocks over 300 international brands, such as Jimmy Choo, Alexander McQueen, Stella McCartney, Givenchy, Marc Jacobs, and others. The company ships to 170 countries and offers same-day delivery in London and Manhattan; the average order is $250.

Sources: Kate Rockwood, "Rising Dough, *Fast Company*, October 2009, pp. 69–71; Devin Leonard, "GameStop Racks Up the Points," *Fortune*, June 9, 2008, pp. 109–22; Helen Coster, "Hardwood Hero," *Forbes*, November 30, 2009, pp. 60–62; John Brodie, "The Amazon of Fashion," *Fortune*, September 14, 2009, pp. 86–95.

Types of Retailers

Consumers today can shop for goods and services at store retailers, nonstore retailers, and retail organizations.

STORE RETAILERS Perhaps the best-known type of store retailer is the department store. Japanese department stores such as Takashimaya and Mitsukoshi attract millions of shoppers each year and feature art galleries, restaurants, cooking classes, fitness clubs, and children's playgrounds. The most important types of major store retailers are summarized in Table 16.1.

Different formats of store retailers will have different competitive and price dynamics. Discount stores, for example, compete much more intensely with each other than other formats.[2] Retailers also meet widely different consumer preferences for service levels and specific services. Specifically, they position themselves as offering one of four levels of service:

1. *Self-service*—Self-service is the cornerstone of all discount operations. Many customers are willing to carry out their own "locate-compare-select" process to save money.
2. *Self-selection*—Customers find their own goods, although they can ask for assistance.
3. *Limited service*—These retailers carry more shopping goods and services such as credit and merchandise-return privileges. Customers need more information and assistance.
4. *Full service*—Salespeople are ready to assist in every phase of the "locate-compare-select" process. Customers who like to be waited on prefer this type of store. The high staffing cost, along with the higher proportion of specialty goods and slower-moving items and the many services, result in high-cost retailing.

TABLE 16.1 ▭ Major Types of Store Retailers
Specialty store: Narrow product line. The Limited, The Body Shop.
Department store: Several product lines. JCPenney, Bloomingdale's.
Supermarket: Large, low-cost, low-margin, high-volume, self-service store designed to meet total needs for food and household products. Kroger, Safeway.
Convenience store: Small store in residential area, often open 24/7, limited line of high-turnover convenience products plus takeout. 7-Eleven, Circle K.
Drug store: Prescription and pharmacies, health and beauty aids, other personal care, small durable, miscellaneous items. CVS, Walgreens.
Discount store: Standard or specialty merchandise; low-price, low-margin, high-volume stores. Walmart, Kmart.
Extreme value or hard-discount store: A more restricted merchandise mix than discount stores but at even lower prices. ALDI, Lidl, Dollar General, Family Dollar.
Off-price retailer: Leftover goods, overruns, irregular merchandise sold at less than retail. Factory outlets; independent off-price retailers such as TJ Maxx; warehouse clubs such as Costco.
Superstore: Huge selling space, routinely purchased food and household items, plus services (laundry, shoe repair, dry cleaning, check cashing). Category killer (deep assortment in one category) such as Staples; combination store such as Jewel-Osco; hypermarket (huge stores that combine supermarket, discount, and warehouse retailing) such as Carrefour in France and Meijer in the Netherlands.
Catalog showroom: Broad selection of high-markup, fast-moving, brand-name goods sold by catalog at a discount. Customers pick up merchandise at the store. Inside Edge Ski and Bike.

Source: Data from www.privatelabelmag.com.

NONSTORE RETAILING Although the overwhelming bulk of goods and services— 97 percent—is sold through stores, *nonstore retailing* has been growing much faster than store retailing. Nonstore retailing falls into four major categories: direct selling, direct marketing (which includes telemarketing and Internet selling), automatic vending, and buying services:

1. *Direct selling,* also called *multilevel selling* and *network marketing,* is a multibillion-dollar industry, with hundreds of companies selling door to door or at home sales parties. Well-known in one-to-one selling are Avon, Electrolux, and Southwestern Company of Nashville (Bibles). Tupperware and Mary Kay Cosmetics are sold one-to-many: A salesperson goes to the home of a host who has invited friends; the salesperson demonstrates the products and takes orders. Pioneered by Amway, the multilevel (network) marketing sales system works by recruiting independent businesspeople who act as distributors. The distributor's compensation includes a percentage of sales made by those he or she recruits, as well as earnings on direct sales to customers. These direct-selling firms, now finding fewer consumers at home, are developing multidistribution strategies.

2. *Direct marketing* has roots in direct-mail and catalog marketing (Lands' End, L.L.Bean); it includes *telemarketing* (1-800-FLOWERS), *television direct-response marketing* (HSN, QVC), and *electronic shopping* (Amazon.com, Autobytel.com). As people become more accustomed to shopping on the Internet, they are ordering a greater variety of goods and services from a wider range of Web sites. In the United States, online sales were estimated to be $210 billion in 2009, with travel being the biggest category ($80 billion).[3]

3. *Automatic vending* offers a variety of merchandise, including impulse goods such as soft drinks, coffee, candy, newspapers, magazines, and other products such as hosiery, cosmetics, hot food, and paperbacks. Vending machines are found in factories, offices, large retail stores, gasoline stations, hotels, restaurants, and many other places. They offer 24-hour selling, self-service, and merchandise that is stocked to be fresh. Japan has the most vending machines per person—Coca-Cola has over 1 million machines there and annual vending sales of $50 billion—twice its U.S. figures.

4. *Buying service* is a storeless retailer serving a specific clientele—usually employees of large organizations—who are entitled to buy from a list of retailers that have agreed to give discounts in return for membership.

TABLE 16.2	Major Types of Corporate Retail Organizations

Corporate chain store: Two or more outlets owned and controlled, employing central buying and merchandising, and selling similar lines of merchandise. Gap, Pottery Barn.

Voluntary chain: A wholesaler-sponsored group of independent retailers engaged in bulk buying and common merchandising. Independent Grocers Alliance (IGA).

Retailer cooperative: Independent retailers using a central buying organization and joint promotion efforts. Associated Grocers, ACE Hardware.

Consumer cooperative: A retail firm owned by its customers. Members contribute money to open their own store, vote on its policies, elect a group to manage it, and receive dividends. Local cooperative grocery stores can be found in many markets.

Franchise organization: Contractual association between a franchisor and franchisees, popular in a number of product and service areas. McDonald's, Subway, Pizza Hut, Jiffy Lube, 7-Eleven.

Merchandising conglomerate: A corporation that combines several diversified retailing lines and forms under central ownership, with some integration of distribution and management. Federated Department Stores renamed itself after one of its best-known retailers, Macy's, but also owns other retailers such as Bloomingdale's.

CORPORATE RETAILING AND FRANCHISING Although many retail stores are independently owned, an increasing number are part of a **corporate retailing** organization. These organizations achieve economies of scale, greater purchasing power, wider brand recognition, and better-trained employees than independent stores can usually gain alone. The major types of corporate retailing—corporate chain stores, voluntary chains, retailer and consumer cooperatives, franchises, and merchandising conglomerates—are described in Table 16.2.

Franchise businesses such as Subway, Jiffy-Lube, Holiday Inn, Supercuts, and 7-Eleven account for more than $1 trillion of annual U.S. sales and roughly 40 percent of all retail transactions. One of every 12 U.S. retail businesses is a franchise establishment; these firms employ 1 in every 16 workers in the country.[4]

In a franchising system, individual *franchisees* are a tightly knit group of enterprises whose systematic operations are planned, directed, and controlled by the operation's innovator, called a *franchisor*. Franchises are distinguished by three characteristics:

1. The franchisor owns a trade or service mark and licenses it to franchisees in return for royalty payments.
2. The franchisee pays for the right to be part of the system. Start-up costs include rental and lease equipment and fixtures, and usually a regular license fee. McDonald's franchisees may invest as much as $1.6 million in total start-up costs and fees. The franchisee then pays McDonald's a certain percentage of sales plus a monthly rent.
3. The franchisor provides its franchisees with a system for doing business. McDonald's requires franchisees to attend "Hamburger University" in Oak Brook, Illinois, for two weeks to learn how to manage the business. Franchisees must follow certain procedures in buying materials.

Franchising benefits both franchisor and franchisee. Franchisors gain the motivation and hard work of employees who are entrepreneurs rather than "hired hands," the franchisees' familiarity with local communities and conditions, and the enormous purchasing power of being a franchisor. Franchisees benefit from buying into a business with a well-known and accepted brand name. They find it easier to borrow money for their business from financial institutions, and they receive support in areas ranging from marketing and advertising to site selection and staffing.

Franchisees do walk a fine line between independence and loyalty to the franchisor. Some franchisors are giving their franchisees freedom to run their own operations, from personalizing store names to adjusting offerings and price. Beef 'O' Brady's sports pub franchisees are allowed to set prices to reflect their local markets. Great Harvest Bread believes in a "freedom franchise" approach that encourages its franchisee bakers to create new items for their store menus and to share with other franchisees if they are successful.[5]

As part of their franchise agreement, new McDonald's franchisors must attend the company's Hamburger University for two weeks to learn how to properly manage their restaurants.

The New Retail Environment

With the onset of the recession in 2008, many retailers had to fundamentally reassess virtually everything they did. Some adopted a cautious, defensive response, cutting stock levels, slowing expansion, and discounting deeply. Others were more creative about managing inventory, adjusting product lines, and carefully avoiding overpromoting. For example, JCPenney held back 60 percent of inventory for the fall 2009 holiday season, compared to its usual 20 percent, to avoid having empty shelves and stock-outs on one hand and overflowing shelves and heavy discounting on the other hand. Some firms, such as the Container Store and Saks, lowered average prices; others, such as Gilt.com and Neiman Marcus, introduced selective and very short-term deep discounts. Restoration Hardware chose to move its furniture product lines more upscale.[6]

Although many of these short-term adjustments were likely to remain longer-term, a number of other long-term trends are also evident in the retail marketing environment. Here are some that are changing the way consumers buy and manufacturers and retailers compete (see Table 16.3 for a summary).

- *New Retail Forms and Combinations.* To better satisfy customers' need for convenience, a variety of new retail forms have emerged. Bookstores feature coffee shops. Gas stations include food stores. Loblaw's Supermarkets have fitness clubs. Shopping malls and bus and train stations have peddlers' carts in their aisles. Retailers are also experimenting with limited-time "pop-up" stores that let them promote brands to seasonal shoppers for a few weeks

TABLE 16.3	Recent Retail Developments
• New Retail Forms and Combinations	
• Growth of Intertype Competition	
• Competition between Store-Based and Nonstore-Based Retailing	
• Growth of Giant Retailers	
• Decline of Middle-Market Retailers	
• Growing Investment in Technology	
• Global Profile of Major Retailers	
• Growth of Shopper Marketing	

in busy areas and create buzz. For the 2009 holiday season, Toys "R" Us set up 350 temporary stores and toy boutiques, in many cases taking over vacant retail space in shopping centers and malls.[7]

- **Growth of Intertype Competition.** Department stores can't worry just about other department stores—discount chains such as Walmart and Tesco are expanding into product areas such as clothing, health, beauty, and electrical appliances. Different types of stores—discount stores, catalog showrooms, department stores—all compete for the same consumers by carrying the same type of merchandise.

- **Competition between Store-Based and Nonstore-Based Retailing.** Consumers now receive sales offers through direct-mail letters and catalogs, television, cell phones, and the Internet. The nonstore-based retailers making these offers are taking business away from store-based retailers. Store-based retailers have responded by increasing their Web presence and finding different ways to sell online, including through their own Web sites, as well as creating more involving and engaging experiences in their stores. Store-based retailers want their stores to be destinations where consumers enjoy rich experiences that captivate all their senses. Sophisticated lighting, use of appropriate scents, and inviting, intimate designs are all being increasingly employed.[8]

- **Growth of Giant Retailers.** Through their superior information systems, logistical systems, and buying power, giant retailers such as Walmart are able to deliver good service and immense volumes of product to masses of consumers at appealing prices. They are crowding out smaller manufacturers that cannot deliver enough quantity and often dictate to the most powerful manufacturers what to make, how to price and promote, when and how to ship, and even how to improve production and management. Manufacturers need these accounts; otherwise they would lose 10 percent to 30 percent of the market. Some giant retailers are *category killers* that concentrate on one product category, such as pet food (PETCO), home improvement (Home Depot), or office supplies (Staples). Others are *supercenters* that combine grocery items with a huge selection of nonfood merchandise (Walmart).

- **Decline of Middle-Market Retailers.** We can characterize the retail market today as hourglass or dog-bone shaped: Growth seems to be centered at the top (with luxury offerings from retailers such as Nordstrom and Neiman Marcus) and at the bottom (with discount pricing from retailers such as Target and Walmart). As discount retailers improve their quality and image, consumers have been willing to trade down. Target offers Proenza Schouler designs and Kmart sells an extensive line of Joe Boxer underwear and sleepwear. At the other end of the spectrum, Coach recently converted 40 of its nearly 300 stores to a more upscale format that offers higher-priced bags and concierge services. Opportunities are scarcer in the middle where one-time successful retailers such as Sears, CompUSA, and Montgomery Ward have struggled or even gone out of business.[9]

  Kohl's has found some success going after middle-market consumers by bringing in trendy names such as Lauren Conrad, Vera Wang, Daisy Fuentes, and Tony Hawk. In addition to offering more up-market merchandise, Kohl's also adapted the stores themselves to make the shopping experience more convenient and pleasant.[10] Marks & Spencer in the United Kingdom features in-house brands and has built a strong retail brand image. Although these stores tend to have high operating costs, they command high margins if their in-house brands are both fashionable and popular.[11]

- **Growing Investment in Technology.** Almost all retailers now use technology to produce better forecasts, control inventory costs, and order electronically from suppliers. Technology is also affecting what happens inside the store. In-store programming on plasma TVs can run continual demonstrations or promotional messages. After encountering problems measuring store traffic up and down aisles—GPS on shopping carts didn't work because consumers tended to abandon their carts at times during trips and thermal imaging couldn't tell the difference between turkeys and babies during tests—bidirectional infrared sensors sitting on store shelves have been successfully introduced. Electronic shelf labeling allows retailers to change price levels instantaneously at any time of the day or week. Retailers are also introducing features to help customers as they shop. Some supermarkets are employing "smart" shopping carts or mobile phones that help customers locate items in the store, find out about sales and special offers, and pay for items more easily. As exciting as these new technologies are, their cost and unproven effectiveness in many cases can create significant drawbacks.[12]

- *Global Profile of Major Retailers.* Retailers with unique formats and strong brand positioning are increasingly appearing in other countries. U.S. retailers such as The Limited and the Gap have become globally prominent. Walmart operates over 3,600 stores abroad where it does 25 percent of its business. Dutch retailer Ahold and Belgian retailer Delhaize earn almost two-thirds and four-fifths of their sales, respectively, in nondomestic markets. Among foreign-based global retailers in the United States are Italy's Benetton, Sweden's IKEA home furnishings stores, and Japan's UNIQLO casual apparel retailer and Yaohan supermarkets.
- *Growth of Shopper Marketing.* Buoyed by research suggesting that as much as 70 percent to 80 percent of purchase decisions are made inside the retail store, firms are increasingly recognizing the importance of influencing consumers at the point of purchase.[13] Where and how a product is displayed and sold can have a significant effect on sales.[14] More communication options are available through in-store advertising such as Walmart TV.[15] Some employ goggle-like devices that record what test customers see by projecting an infrared beam onto the wearer's retina. One finding was that many shoppers ignored products at eye level—the optimum location was between waist and chest level.[16]

Marketing Decisions

With this new retail environment as a backdrop, we will examine retailers' marketing decisions in the areas of target market, channels, product assortment, procurement, prices, services and store atmosphere, store activities and experiences, communications, and location. We discuss the important topic of private labels for retailers in the next section.

TARGET MARKET Until it defines and profiles the target market, the retailer cannot make consistent decisions about product assortment, store decor, advertising messages and media, price, and service levels. Ann Taylor has used a panel of 3,000 customers to provide feedback on its merchandise and even its marketing campaign. The firm also solicits employees' input.[17] Whole Foods has found success by offering a unique shopping experience to a customer base interested in organic and natural foods.

High-tech shopping carts allow customers to keep track of their total expenditures, search for products, find out what is on sale, and even pay without waiting in line.

Whole Foods Market In 284 stores in North America and the United Kingdom, Whole Foods creates celebrations of food. The markets are bright and well staffed, and food displays are bountiful and seductive. Whole Foods is the largest organic and natural foods grocer in the country, offering more than 2,400 items in four lines of private-label products that add up to 11 percent of sales: the premium Whole Foods Market, Whole Kitchen, and Whole Market lines and the low-priced 365 Everyday Value line. Whole Foods also offers lots of information about its food. If you want to know, for instance, whether the chicken in the display case lived a happy, free-roaming life, you can get a 16-page booklet and an invitation to visit the farm in Pennsylvania where it was raised. If you can't find the information you need, you have only to ask a well-trained and knowledgeable employee. Whole Foods' approach is working, especially for consumers who view organic and artisanal food as an affordable luxury. From 1991–2009, sales grew at a 28 percent compounded annual growth rate (CAGR).[18]

Mistakes in choosing or switching target markets can be costly. When historically mass-market jeweler Zales decided to chase upscale customers, it replaced one-third of its merchandise, dropping inexpensive, low-quality diamond jewelry for high-margin, fashionable 14-karat gold and silver pieces and shifting its ad campaign in the process. The move was a disaster. Zales lost many of its traditional customers without winning over the new customers it had hoped to attract.[19]

To better hit their targets, retailers are slicing the market into ever-finer segments and introducing new lines of stores to exploit niche markets with more relevant offerings: Gymboree launched Janie and Jack, selling apparel and gifts for babies and toddlers; Hot Topic introduced Torrid, selling fashions for plus-sized teen girls; and Limited Brand's Tween Brands sells lower-priced fashion to tween girls.

Channels

Based on a target market analysis and other considerations we reviewed in Chapter 15, retailers must decide which channels to employ to reach their customers. Increasingly, the answer is multiple channels. Staples sells through its traditional retail channel, a direct-response Internet site, virtual malls, and thousands of links on affiliated sites.

As Chapter 15 explained, channels should be designed to work together effectively. Century-old department store chain JCPenney has ensured that its Internet, store, and catalog businesses are fully intertwined. It sells a vast variety of goods online; has made Internet access available at its 35,000 checkout registers; and allows online shoppers to pick up and return orders at stores and check which clothes are in stock there. These strategies—as well as the introduction of a.n.a., a stylish line of women's clothing—have helped give JCPenney a younger, more upscale image.[20]

Although some experts predicted otherwise, catalogs have actually grown in an Internet world as more firms use them as branding devices. Victoria's Secret's integrated multichannel approach of retail stores, catalog, and Internet has played a key role in its brand development.

Victoria's Secret   Limited Brands founder Leslie Wexner felt U.S. women would relish the opportunity to have a European-style lingerie shopping experience. "Women need underwear, but women want lingerie," he observed. Wexner's assumption proved correct: A little more than a decade after he bought the business in 1982, Victoria's Secret's average customer was buying 8 to 10 bras per year, compared with the national average of two. To enhance its upscale reputation and glamorous appeal, the brand is endorsed by high-profile supermodels in ads and fashion shows. To expand its accessibility and offer privacy, the company began to sell directly to consumers. Victoria's Secret used a comprehensive marketing strategy to connect its retail, catalog, and Web sales. Wexner sought to make it: "stand [out] as an integrated world-class brand. Across all channels—catalogue, stores, Internet—the same products are launched at the same time, in exactly the same way, with the same quality, and same positioning." Since 1985, Victoria's Secret has delivered 25 percent annual sales growth, selling through its 1,000-plus stores, catalogs, and company Web site, posting $5.6 billion in revenues in 2009. Victoria's Secret ships 400 million catalogs a year, or 1.33 for every U.S. citizen, and catalog and online orders account for nearly 28 percent of its overall revenue, growing at double the rate of sales from its stores.[21]

PRODUCT ASSORTMENT   The retailer's product assortment must match the target market's shopping expectations in *breadth* and *depth*. A restaurant can offer a narrow and shallow assortment (small lunch counters), a narrow and deep assortment (delicatessen), a broad and shallow assortment (cafeteria), or a broad and deep assortment (large restaurant).

Identifying the right product assortment can be especially challenging in fast-moving industries such as technology or fashion. Urban Outfitters ran into trouble when it strayed from its "hip, but not too hip" formula, moving to embrace new styles too quickly. Sales fell over 25 percent during 2006.[22] On the other hand, active and casual apparel retailer Aéropostale has found success by carefully matching its product assortment to its young teen target market's needs.

Aéropostale   Aéropostale has chosen to embrace a key reality of its target market: 11- to 18-year-olds, especially those on the young end, often want to look like other teens. So while Abercrombie and American Eagle might reduce the number of cargo pants on the sales floor, Aéropostale will keep an ample supply on hand at an affordable price. Staying on top of the right trends isn't easy, but Aéropostale is among the most diligent of teen retailers when it comes to consumer research. In addition to running high school focus groups and in-store product tests, the company launched an Internet-based program that seeks online shoppers' input in creating new styles. It targets 10,000 of its best customers and averages 3,500 participants in each of 20 tests a year. Aéropostale has gone from being a lackluster performer with only 100 stores to a powerhouse with 914 total stores in the United States, Puerto Rico, and Canada. Net sales were up 19 percent in 2008 to $1.9 billion, and net sales from e-commerce business increased 85 percent to $79 million.[23]

Aéropostale's "Teens for Jeans" cause marketing campaign encourages its customers to donate used jeans for homeless teens in North America.

The real challenge begins after defining the store's product assortment, and that is to develop a product-differentiation strategy. To better differentiate themselves and generate consumer interest, some luxury retailers are making their stores and merchandise more varied. Chanel has expanded its "ultralux" goods, including $26,000 alligator bags, while ensuring an ample supply of "must-haves" that are consistently strong sellers.[24] Here are some other possibilities:

- *Feature exclusive national brands that are not available at competing retailers.* Saks might get exclusive rights to carry the dresses of a well-known international designer.
- *Feature mostly private-label merchandise.* Benetton and Gap design most of the clothes carried in their stores. Many supermarket and drug chains carry private-label merchandise.
- *Feature blockbuster distinctive merchandise events.* Bloomingdale's ran a month-long celebration for the Barbie doll's 50th anniversary in March 2009.
- *Feature surprise or ever-changing merchandise.* Off-price apparel retailer TJ Maxx offers surprise assortments of distress merchandise (goods the owner must sell immediately because it needs cash), overstocks, and closeouts, totaling 10,000 new items each week at prices 20 percent to 60 percent below department and specialty store regular prices.
- *Feature the latest or newest merchandise first.* Zara excels in and profits from being first-to-market with appealing new looks and designs.
- *Offer merchandise-customizing services.* Harrods of London will make custom-tailored suits, shirts, and ties for customers, in addition to ready-made menswear.
- *Offer a highly targeted assortment.* Lane Bryant carries goods for the larger woman. Brookstone offers unusual tools and gadgets for the person who wants to shop in a "toy store for grown-ups."

Merchandise may vary by geographical market. Electronics superstore Best Buy reviewed each of its 25,000 SKUs to adjust its merchandise according to income level and buying habits of shoppers. It also puts different store formats and staffs in different areas—a location with computer sophisticates gets a different store treatment than one with less technically sophisticated shoppers.[25] Macy's and Ross Stores employ *micro-merchandising* and let managers select a significant percentage of store assortments.[26]

PROCUREMENT After deciding on the product-assortment strategy, the retailer must establish merchandise sources, policies, and practices. In the corporate headquarters of a supermarket chain, specialist buyers (sometimes called *merchandise managers*) are responsible for developing brand assortments and listening to salespersons' presentations.

Retailers are rapidly improving their skills in demand forecasting, merchandise selection, stock control, space allocation, and display. They use computers to track inventory, compute economic order quantities, order goods, and analyze dollars spent on vendors and products. Supermarket chains use scanner data to manage their merchandise mix on a store-by-store basis.

Some stores are experimenting with radio frequency identification (RFID) systems made up of "smart" tags—microchips attached to tiny radio antennas—and electronic readers. The smart tags can be embedded on products or stuck on labels, and when the tag is near a reader, it transmits a unique identifying number to its computer database. The use of RFIDs has been steadily increasing. Coca-Cola and Gillette use them to monitor inventory and track goods in real time as they move from factories to supermarkets to shopping baskets.[27]

When retailers do study the economics of buying and selling individual products, they typically find that a third of their square footage is tied up in products that don't make an economic profit for them (profit above the cost of capital). Another third is typically allocated to product categories that break even. The final third of the space creates the vast majority of the economic profit, yet many retailers are unaware which third of their products generate it.[28]

Stores are using **direct product profitability (DPP)** to measure a product's handling costs (receiving, moving to storage, paperwork, selecting, checking, loading, and space cost) from the time it reaches the warehouse until a customer buys it in the retail store. They learn to their surprise that the gross margin on a product often bears little relation to the direct product profit. Some high-volume products may have such high handling costs that they are less profitable and deserve less shelf space than low-volume products.

ALDI has differentiated itself on its innovative procurement strategy.

ALDI focuses on a very narrow product range with a high turnover to keep its prices low, but it does not allow this strategy to compromise quality.

ALDI   The ALDI success story started in 1913 with a single small food market in Germany. Today, ALDI has two divisions, ALDI North and ALDI South, and 9,000 stores in 18 countries. While other food retailers carry thousands of products, ALDI's product range is very narrow. With about 1,000 core products, dominated by ALDI-exclusive private labels, ALDI is very focused on products with high turnover, which it can source in high quantities at low prices. Logistics, weekly promotions, and store displays of products in transport boxes are designed to keep costs as low as possible in order to provide value. Customer perception of ALDI and its products has improved significantly over the years. High quality at low prices is the brand promise, and ALDI brands have reached top ratings in many independent product tests. To its suppliers, ALDI is known as a tough but reliable partner. Price negotiations are known to be very demanding. ALDI also expects suppliers to guarantee high standards of quality, and it constantly monitors quality throughout its whole supply chain.[29]

PRICES   Prices are a key positioning factor and must be set in relationship to the target market, product-and-service assortment mix, and competition.[30] All retailers would like high *turns × earns* (high volumes and high gross margins), but the two don't usually go together. Most retailers fall into the *high-markup, lower-volume* group (fine specialty stores) or the *low-markup, higher-volume* group (mass merchandisers and discount stores). Within each of these groups are further gradations. Bijan on Rodeo Drive in Beverly Hills prices suits starting at $1,000 and shoes at $400. At the other end, Target has skillfully combined a hip image with discount prices to offer customers a strong value proposition.

As part of its "cheap chic" retail strategy, Target sells products from famous designers, like Issac Mizrahi, whose Target line included accessories, house wears, and pet products in addition to clothing. Source: Bloomberg/Getty Images

Target   In the mid-1980s, Kmart was the dominant mass retailer, and Walmart was growing rapidly. Sensing a gap in the market for "cheap chic" retail, Target strove to set itself apart from the other big-box retailers by enhancing the design quality of its product selection, focusing on merchandise that was contemporary and unique. The company's team of merchandisers traveled the world looking for the next hot items and trends to bring to the shelves. Target also differentiated its merchandising layout, using low shelves, halogen and track lighting, and wider aisles and avoiding "visual clutter" in stores. With the slogan "Expect More, Pay Less," Target seeks to build an up-market cachet for its brand without losing price-conscious consumers. It introduced a line of products from world-renowned designers such as Michael Graves, Isaac Mizrahi, Mossimo Giannulli, and Liz Lange and has kept innovating with its merchandising model. In 2006, it introduced U.S. consumers to the concept of "fast fashion," already popular in Europe, to help keep the product selection fresh, which in turn led to more frequent shopper visits.[31]

Most retailers will put low prices on some items to serve as traffic builders or loss leaders or to signal their pricing policies.[32] They will run storewide sales. They will plan markdowns on slower-moving merchandise. Shoe retailers, for example, expect to sell 50 percent of their shoes at the normal markup, 25 percent at a 40 percent markup, and the remaining 25 percent at cost.

As Chapter 14 noted, some retailers such as Walmart have abandoned "sales pricing" in favor of everyday low pricing (EDLP). EDLP can lead to lower advertising costs, greater pricing stability, a stronger image of fairness and reliability, and higher retail profits. Supermarket chains practicing everyday low pricing can be more profitable than those practicing high–low sale pricing, but only in certain circumstances.[33]

SERVICES Retailers must decide on the *services mix* to offer customers:

- *Prepurchase services* include accepting telephone and mail orders, advertising, window and interior display, fitting rooms, shopping hours, fashion shows, and trade-ins.
- *Postpurchase services* include shipping and delivery, gift wrapping, adjustments and returns, alterations and tailoring, installations, and engraving.
- *Ancillary services* include general information, check cashing, parking, restaurants, repairs, interior decorating, credit, rest rooms, and baby-attendant service.

Another differentiator is unerringly reliable customer service, whether face-to-face, across phone lines, or via online chat. Barnes & Noble hires clean-cut people with a passion for customer service and a general love of books; Borders employees are more likely to be tattooed or have multiple body piercings. The company prides itself on the diversity of its employees and hires people who radiate excitement about particular books and music, rather than simply finding a book for a customer.[34]

Whatever retailers do to enhance customer service, they must keep women in mind. Approximately 85 percent of everything sold in the United States is bought or influenced by a woman, and women are fed up with the decline in customer service. They are finding every possible way to get around the system, from ordering online to resisting fake sales to just doing without.[35] And when they do shop, they want well-organized layouts, helpful staff, and speedy checkouts.[36]

STORE ATMOSPHERE *Atmosphere* is another element in the store arsenal. Every store has a look, and a physical layout that makes it hard or easy to move around (see "Marketing Memo: Helping Stores to Sell"). Kohl's floor plan is modeled after a racetrack loop and is designed to convey customers smoothly past all the merchandise in the store. It includes a middle aisle that hurried shoppers can use as a shortcut and yields higher spending levels than many competitors.[37]

Retailers must consider all the senses in shaping the customer's experience. Varying the tempo of music affects average time and dollars spent in the supermarket. Sony Style stores are seasoned with a subtle vanilla and mandarin orange fragrance, and every surface, from countertops to paneling, is designed to be touchable. Bloomingdale's uses different essences in different departments: baby powder in the baby store; suntan lotion in the bathing suit area; lilacs in lingerie; and cinnamon and pine scent during the holiday season.[38]

Bass Pro Shops sells its outdoor sports equipment in an experiential retail environment conducive to product demos and tests.

STORE ACTIVITIES AND EXPERIENCES The growth of e-commerce has forced traditional brick-and-mortar retailers to respond. In addition to their natural advantages, such as products that shoppers can actually see, touch, and test; real-life customer service; and no delivery lag time for most purchases, stores also provide a shopping experience as a strong differentiator.[39]

The store atmosphere should match shoppers' basic motivations — if customers are likely to be in a task-oriented and functional mind-set, then a simpler, more restrained in-store environment may be better.[40] On the other hand, some retailers of experiential products are creating in-store entertainment to attract customers who want fun and excitement.[41] REI, seller of outdoor gear and clothing products, allows consumers to test climbing equipment on 25-foot or even 65-foot walls in the store and to try GORE-TEX raincoats under a simulated rain shower. Bass Pro Shops, a retailer of outdoor sports equipment, features giant aquariums, waterfalls, trout ponds, archery and rifle ranges, fly-tying demonstrations and some with an outdoor pond to test equipment, indoor driving range and putting greens, and classes in everything from ice fishing to conservation—all free. Its first and largest showroom in Missouri is the number one tourist destination in the state.

marketing
Memo

Helping Stores to Sell

In pursuit of higher sales volume, retailers are studying their store environments for ways to improve the shopper experience. Paco Underhill is managing director of the retail consultant Envirosell, whose clients include McDonald's, Starbucks, Estée Lauder, Blockbuster, Citibank, Gap, Burger King, CVS, and Wells Fargo. Using a combination of in-store video recording and observation, Underhill and his colleagues study 50,000 people each year as they shop. He offers the following advice for fine-tuning retail space:

- *Attract shoppers and keep them in the store.* The amount of time shoppers spend in a store is perhaps the single most important factor in determining how much they buy. To increase shopping time, give shoppers a sense of community; recognize them in some way; give them ways to deal with their accessories, such as chairs in convenient locations for boyfriends, husbands, children, or bags; and make the environment both familiar and fresh each time they come in.

- *Honor the "transition zone."* On entering a store, people need to slow down and sort out the stimuli, which means they will likely be moving too fast to respond positively to signs, merchandise, or sales clerks in the zone they cross before making that transition. Make sure there are clear sight lines. Create a focal point for information within the store. Most right-handed people turn right upon entering a store.

- *Avoid overdesign.* Store fixtures, point-of-sales information, packaging, signage, and flat-screen televisions can combine to create a visual cacophony. Use crisp and clear signage—"Our Best Seller" or "Our Best Student Computer"—where people feel comfortable stopping and facing the right way. Window signs, displays, and mannequins communicate best when angled 10 to 15 degrees to face the direction that people are moving.

- *Don't make them hunt.* Put the most popular products up front to reward busy shoppers and encourage leisurely shoppers to look more. At Staples, ink cartridges are one of the first products shoppers encounter after entering.

- *Make merchandise available to the reach and touch.* It is hard to overemphasize the importance of customers' hands. A store can offer the finest, cheapest, sexiest goods, but if the shopper cannot reach or pick them up, much of their appeal can be lost.

- *Make kids welcome.* If kids feel welcome, parents will follow. Take a three-year-old's perspective and make sure there are engaging sights at eye level. A virtual hopscotch pattern or dinosaur on the floor can turn a boring shopping trip for a child into a friendly experience.

- *Note that men do not ask questions.* Men always move faster than women do through a store's aisles. In many settings, it is hard to get them to look at anything they had not intended to buy. Men also do not like asking where things are. If a man cannot find the section he is looking for, he will wheel about once or twice, then leave the store without ever asking for help.

- *Remember women need space.* A shopper, especially a woman, is far less likely to buy an item if her derriere is brushed, even lightly, by another customer when she is looking at a display. Keeping aisles wide and clear is crucial.

- *Make checkout easy.* Be sure to have the right high-margin goods near cash registers to satisfy impulse shoppers. People love to buy candy when they check out—so satisfy their sweet tooth.

Sources: Paco Underhill, *Call of the Mall: The Geography of Shopping* (New York: Simon & Schuster, 2004); Paco Underhill, *Why We Buy: The Science of Shopping* (New York: Simon & Schuster, 1999). See also, Kenneth Hein, "Shopping Guru Sees Death of Detergent Aisle," *Brandweek*, March 27, 2006, p. 11; Bob Parks, "5 Rules of Great Design," *Business 2.0* (March 2003): 47–49; Russell Boniface, "I Spy a Shopper!" *AIArchitect*, June 2006; Susan Berfield, "Getting the Most Out of Every Shopper, *BusinessWeek*, February 9, 2009, pp. 45–46; www.envirosell.com.

COMMUNICATIONS Retailers use a wide range of communication tools to generate traffic and purchases. They place ads, run special sales, issue money-saving coupons, and run frequent-shopper-reward programs, in-store food sampling, and coupons on shelves or at checkout points. They work with manufacturers to design point-of-sale materials that reflect both their images.[42] Upscale retailers place tasteful, full-page ads in magazines such as *Vogue, Vanity Fair,* or *Esquire* and carefully train salespeople to greet customers, interpret their needs, and handle complaints. Off-price retailers will arrange their merchandise to promote bargains and savings, while conserving on service and sales assistance. Retailers are also using interactive and social media to pass on information and create communities around their brands.[43] Casual dining chain Houlihan's created a social network site, HQ, to gain honest, immediate feedback from 10,500 invitation-only "Houlifan" customers in return for insider information.

LOCATION The three keys to retail success are often said to be "location, location, and location." Department store chains, oil companies, and fast-food franchisers exercise great care in selecting regions of the country in which to open outlets, then particular cities, and then particular sites. Retailers can place their stores in the following locations:

- **Central business districts.** The oldest and most heavily trafficked city areas, often known as "downtown"

- *Regional shopping centers.* Large suburban malls containing 40 to 200 stores, typically featuring one or two nationally known anchor stores, such as Macy's or Lord & Taylor or a combination of big-box stores such as PETCO, Payless Shoes, Borders, or Bed Bath & Beyond, and a great number of smaller stores, many under franchise operation[44]
- *Community shopping centers.* Smaller malls with one anchor store and 20 to 40 smaller stores
- *Shopping strips.* A cluster of stores, usually in one long building, serving a neighborhood's needs for groceries, hardware, laundry, shoe repair, and dry cleaning
- *A location within a larger store.* Certain well-known retailers—McDonald's, Starbucks, Nathan's, Dunkin' Donuts—locate new, smaller units as concession space within larger stores or operations, such as airports, schools, or department stores.
- *Stand-alone stores.* Some retailers such as Kohl's and JCPenney are avoiding malls and shopping centers to locate new stores in free-standing sites on streets, so they are not connected directly to other retail stores.

In view of the relationship between high traffic and high rents, retailers must decide on the most advantageous locations for their outlets, using traffic counts, surveys of consumer shopping habits, and analysis of competitive locations.

Private Labels

A **private label brand** (also called a reseller, store, house, or distributor brand) is a brand that retailers and wholesalers develop. Benetton, The Body Shop, and Marks & Spencer carry mostly own-brand merchandise. In grocery stores in Europe and Canada, store brands account for as much as 40 percent of the items sold. In Britain, the largest food chains, roughly half of what Sainsbury and Tesco sell is store-label goods.

For many manufacturers, retailers are both collaborators and competitors. According to the Private Label Manufacturers' Association, store brands now account for one of every four items sold in U.S. supermarkets, drug chains, and mass merchandisers, up from 19 percent in 1999. In one study, seven of ten shoppers believed the private label products they bought were as good as, if not better than, their national brand. Setting aside beverages, private labels account for roughly 30 percent of all food served in U.S. homes, and virtually every household purchases private label brands from time to time.[45]

Private labels are rapidly gaining ascendance in a way that has many manufacturers of name brands running scared. Some experts believe though that 50 percent is the natural limit for volume of private labels to carry because (1) consumers prefer certain national brands, and (2) many product categories are not feasible or attractive on a private-label basis.[46] 🗂 Table 16.4 displays the product categories that have the highest private-label sales.

TABLE 16.4 🗂	Top 10 Private Label Categories–2009 (billions of dollars)
• Milk ($8.1)	
• Bread & Baked Good ($4.2)	
• Cheese ($3.5)	
• Medications/Remedies/Vitamins ($3.4)	
• Paper Products ($2.6)	
• Eggs—Fresh ($1.9)	
• Fresh Produce ($1.5)	
• Packaged Meat ($1.5)	
• Pet Food ($1.5)	
• Unprepared Meat/Frozen Seafood ($1.4)	

Source: Data from www.privatelabelmag.com. December 9, 2010. Used with permission.

Role of Private Labels

Why do intermediaries sponsor their own brands?[47] First, these brands can be more profitable. Intermediaries search for manufacturers with excess capacity that will produce private label goods at low cost. Other costs, such as research and development, advertising, sales promotion, and physical distribution, are also much lower, so private labels can generate a higher profit margin. Retailers also develop exclusive store brands to differentiate themselves from competitors. Many price-sensitive consumers prefer store brands in certain categories. These preferences give retailers increased bargaining power with marketers of national brands.

Private label or store brands should be distinguished from generics. **Generics** are unbranded, plainly packaged, less expensive versions of common products such as spaghetti, paper towels, and canned peaches. They offer standard or lower quality at a price that may be as much as 20 percent to 40 percent lower than nationally advertised brands and 10 percent to 20 percent lower than the retailer's private-label brands. The lower price is made possible by lower-cost labeling and packaging and minimal advertising, and sometimes lower-quality ingredients. Generics can be found in a wide range of different products, even medicines.

Generic Drugs
Generic drugs have become big business. Branded drug sales actually declined for the first time in 2009. By making knockoffs faster and in larger quantities, Israel's Teva has become the world's biggest generic drugmaker, with revenue of $14 billion. Pharma giant Novartis is one of the world's top five makers of branded drugs, with such successes as Diovan for high blood pressure and Gleevec for cancer, but it has also become the world's second-largest maker of generic drugs following its acquisition of Sandoz, HEXAL, Eon Labs, and others. Other pharmaceutical companies such as Sanofi-Aventis and GlaxoSmithKline have entered the generic drug market not in the United States but in emerging markets in Eastern Europe, Latin America, and Asia, where some consumers cannot afford expensive brand-name drugs but worry about counterfeit or low-quality drugs. These consumers are willing to pay at least a small premium for a drug backed by a trusted company.[48]

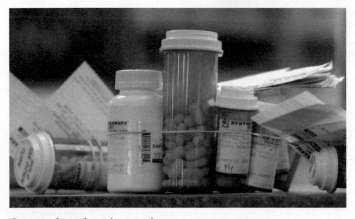

Generic drugs have become big business as a means to lower health care costs.

Private-Label Success Factors

In the confrontation between manufacturers' and private labels, retailers have many advantages and increasing market power.[49] Because shelf space is scarce, many supermarkets charge a *slotting fee* for accepting a new brand, to cover the cost of listing and stocking it. Retailers also charge for special display space and in-store advertising space. They typically give more prominent display to their own brands and make sure they are well stocked.

Retailers are building better quality into their store brands. Supermarket retailers are adding premium store-brand items like organics or creating new products without direct competition, such as three-minute microwaveable snack pizzas. They are also emphasizing attractive, innovative packaging. Some are even advertising aggressively: Safeway ran a $100 million integrated communication program that featured TV and print ads, touting the store brand's quality.[50]

Loblaw
Since 1984, when its President's Choice line of foods made its debut, the term *private label* has brought Loblaw instantly to mind. Toronto-based Loblaw's Decadent Chocolate Chip Cookie quickly became a Canadian leader and showed how innovative store brands could compete effectively with national brands by matching or even exceeding their quality. A finely tuned brand strategy for its premium President's Choice line and its no-frills, yellow-labeled No Name line (which the company relaunched with a vengeance during the recent recession) has helped differentiate its stores and built Loblaw into a powerhouse in Canada and the United States. The President's Choice line of products has become so successful that Loblaw is licensing it to noncompetitive retailers in other countries. In 2010, Loblaw introduced a new tier of low-priced store brands, priced slightly above the No Name line, to be made available at its chain of 175 No Frills "hard discount" grocery stores.[51]

Marketing Insight

Manufacturer's Response to the Private Label Threat

To maintain their marketplace power, leading brand marketers are investing significantly in R&D to bring out new brands, line extensions, features, and quality improvements to stay a step ahead of the store brands. They are also investing in strong "pull" advertising programs to maintain high consumer brand recognition and preference and overcome the in-store marketing advantage that private labels can enjoy. Top-brand marketers also are seeking to partner with major mass distributors in a joint search for logistical economies and competitive strategies that produce savings for both sides. Cutting all unnecessary costs allows national brands to command a price premium, although it can't exceed the value perceptions of consumers.

University of North Carolina's Jan-Benedict E. M. Steenkamp and London Business School's Nirmalya Kumar offer four strategic recommendations for manufacturers to compete against or collaborate with private labels.

- *Fight selectively* where manufacturers can win against private labels and add value for consumers, retailers, and shareholders. This is typically where the brand is one or two in the category or occupying a premium niche position. Procter & Gamble rationalized its

portfolio, selling off various brands such as Sunny Delight juice drink, Jif peanut butter, and Crisco shortening, in part so it could concentrate on strengthening its 20+ brands with more than $1 billion in sales.

- *Partner effectively* by seeking win-win relationships with retailers through strategies that complement the retailer's private labels. Estée Lauder created four brands (American Beauty, Flirt, Good Skin, and Grassroots) exclusively for Kohl's, to help the retailer generate volume and protect its more prestigious brands in the process. Manufacturers selling through hard discounters such as Lidl and ALDI have increased sales by finding new customers who have not previously bought the brand.

- *Innovate brilliantly* with new products to help beat private labels. Continuously launching incremental new products keeps the manufacturer brands looking fresh, but the firm must also periodically launch radical new products and protect the intellectual property of all brands. Kraft doubled its number of patent lawyers to make sure its innovations were legally protected as much as possible.

- *Create winning value propositions* by imbuing brands with symbolic imagery as well as functional quality that beats private labels. Too many manufacturer brands have let private labels equal and sometimes better them on functional quality. In addition, to have a winning value proposition, marketers need to monitor pricing and ensure that perceived benefits equal the price premium.

Sources: James A. Narus and James C. Anderson, "Contributing as a Distributor to Partnerships with Manufacturers," *Business Horizons* (September–October 1987); Nirmalya Kumar and Jan-Benedict E. M. Steenkamp, *Private Label Strategy: How to Meet the Store-Brand Challenge* (Boston: Harvard Business School Press, 2007); Nirmalya Kumar, "The Right Way to Fight for Shelf Domination," *Advertising Age*, January 22, 2007; Jan-Benedict E. M. Steenkamp and Nirmalya Kumar, "Don't Be Undersold, *Harvard Business Review*, December 2009, p. 91.

Although retailers get credit for the success of private labels, the growing power of store brands has also benefited from the weakening of national brands. Many consumers have become more price sensitive, a trend reinforced by the continuous barrage of coupons and price specials that has trained a generation to buy on price. Competing manufacturers and national retailers copy and duplicate the quality and features of the best brands in a category, reducing physical product differentiation. Moreover, by cutting marketing communication budgets, some firms have made it harder to create any intangible differences in brand image. A steady stream of brand extensions and line extensions has blurred brand identity at times and led to a confusing amount of product proliferation.

Bucking these trends, many manufacturers or national brands are fighting back. "Marketing Insight: Manufacturer's Respond to the Private Label Threat," describes the strategies and tactics being taken to compete more effectively with private labels.

Wholesaling

Wholesaling includes all the activities in selling goods or services to those who buy for resale or business use. It excludes manufacturers and farmers because they are engaged primarily in production, and it excludes retailers. The major types of wholesalers are described in ▭ Table 16.5.

Wholesalers (also called *distributors*) differ from retailers in a number of ways. First, wholesalers pay less attention to promotion, atmosphere, and location because they are dealing with business customers rather than final consumers. Second, wholesale transactions are usually larger than retail

TABLE 16.5	Major Wholesaler Types

Merchant wholesalers: Independently owned businesses that take title to the merchandise they handle. They are full-service and limited-service jobbers, distributors, and mill supply houses.

Full-service wholesalers: Carry stock, maintain a sales force, offer credit, make deliveries, provide management assistance. Wholesale merchants sell primarily to retailers: Some carry several merchandise lines, some carry one or two lines, others carry only part of a line. Industrial distributors sell to manufacturers and also provide services such as credit and delivery.

Limited-service wholesalers: *Cash and carry wholesalers* sell a limited line of fast-moving goods to small retailers for cash. *Truck wholesalers* sell and deliver a limited line of semiperishable goods to supermarkets, grocery stores, hospitals, restaurants, hotels. *Drop shippers* serve bulk industries such as coal, lumber, and heavy equipment. They assume title and risk from the time an order is accepted to its delivery. *Rack jobbers* serve grocery retailers in nonfood items. Delivery people set up displays, price goods, and keep inventory records; they retain title to goods and bill retailers only for goods sold to the end of the year. *Producers' cooperatives* assemble farm produce to sell in local markets. *Mail-order wholesalers* send catalogs to retail, industrial, and institutional customers; orders are filled and sent by mail, rail, plane, or truck.

Brokers and agents: Facilitate buying and selling, on commission of 2 percent to 6 percent of the selling price; limited functions; generally specialize by product line or customer type. *Brokers* bring buyers and sellers together and assist in negotiation; they are paid by the party hiring them—food brokers, real estate brokers, insurance brokers. *Agents* represent buyers or sellers on a more permanent basis. Most manufacturers' agents are small businesses with a few skilled salespeople: Selling agents have contractual authority to sell a manufacturer's entire output; purchasing agents make purchases for buyers and often receive, inspect, warehouse, and ship merchandise; commission merchants take physical possession of products and negotiate sales.

Manufacturers' and retailers' branches and offices: Wholesaling operations conducted by sellers or buyers themselves rather than through independent wholesalers. Separate branches and offices are dedicated to sales or purchasing. Many retailers set up purchasing offices in major market centers.

Specialized wholesalers: Agricultural assemblers (buy the agricultural output of many farms), petroleum bulk plants and terminals (consolidate the output of many wells), and auction companies (auction cars, equipment, etc., to dealers and other businesses).

transactions, and wholesalers usually cover a larger trade area than retailers. Third, the government deals with wholesalers and retailers differently in terms of legal regulations and taxes.

Why do manufacturers not sell directly to retailers or final consumers? Why are wholesalers used at all? In general, wholesalers are more efficient in performing one or more of the following functions:

- *Selling and promoting.* Wholesalers' sales forces help manufacturers reach many small business customers at a relatively low cost. They have more contacts, and buyers often trust them more than they trust a distant manufacturer.
- *Buying and assortment building.* Wholesalers are able to select items and build the assortments their customers need, saving them considerable work.
- *Bulk breaking.* Wholesalers achieve savings for their customers by buying large carload lots and breaking the bulk into smaller units.
- *Warehousing.* Wholesalers hold inventories, thereby reducing inventory costs and risks to suppliers and customers.
- *Transportation.* Wholesalers can often provide quicker delivery to buyers because they are closer to the buyers.
- *Financing.* Wholesalers finance customers by granting credit, and finance suppliers by ordering early and paying bills on time.
- *Risk bearing.* Wholesalers absorb some risk by taking title and bearing the cost of theft, damage, spoilage, and obsolescence.
- *Market information.* Wholesalers supply information to suppliers and customers regarding competitors' activities, new products, price developments, and so on.

- *Management services and counseling.* Wholesalers often help retailers improve their operations by training sales clerks, helping with store layouts and displays, and setting up accounting and inventory-control systems. They may help industrial customers by offering training and technical services.

Trends in Wholesaling

Wholesaler-distributors have faced mounting pressures in recent years from new sources of competition, demanding customers, new technologies, and more direct-buying programs by large industrial, institutional, and retail buyers. Manufacturers' major complaints against wholesalers are: They don't aggressively promote the manufacturer's product line and they act more like order takers; they don't carry enough inventory and therefore don't fill customers' orders fast enough; they don't supply the manufacturer with up to date market, customer, and competitive information; they don't attract high-caliber managers to bring down their own costs; and they charge too much for their services.

Savvy wholesalers have rallied to the challenge and adapted their services to meet their suppliers' and target customers' changing needs. They recognize that they must add value to the channel.

Arrow Electronics Arrow Electronics is a global provider of products, services, and solutions to the electronic component and computer product industries. It serves as a supply channel partner for more than 900 suppliers and 125,000 original equipment manufacturers, contract manufacturers, and commercial customers through a global network of 310 locations in 51 countries and territories. With huge contract manufacturers buying more parts directly from suppliers, distributors such as Arrow are being squeezed out. To better compete, Arrow has embraced services, providing financing, on-site inventory management, parts-tracking software, and chip programming. Services helped quadruple Arrow's share price in five years, and the company approached $15 billion in sales in 2009.[52]

Wholesalers have worked to increase asset productivity by managing inventories and receivables better. They're also reducing operating costs by investing in more advanced materials-handling technology, information systems, and the Internet. Finally, they're improving their strategic decisions about target markets, product assortment and services, price, communications, and distribution.

Narus and Anderson interviewed leading industrial distributors and identified four ways they strengthened their relationships with manufacturers:

1. They sought a clear agreement with their manufacturers about their expected functions in the marketing channel.
2. They gained insight into the manufacturers' requirements by visiting their plants and attending manufacturer association conventions and trade shows.
3. They fulfilled their commitments to the manufacturer by meeting the volume targets, paying bills promptly, and feeding back customer information to their manufacturers.
4. They identified and offered value-added services to help their suppliers.[53]

The wholesaling industry remains vulnerable to one of the most enduring trends—fierce resistance to price increases and the winnowing out of suppliers based on cost and quality. The trend toward vertical integration, in which manufacturers try to control or own their intermediaries, is still strong. One firm that succeeds in the wholesaling business is W.W. Grainger.

W.W. Grainger W.W. Grainger is the leading supplier of facilities maintenance products that help 1.8 million businesses and institutions stay up and running. Sales for 2008 were $6.9 billion. Grainger serves customers through a network of over 600 branches in North America and China, 18 distribution centers, numerous catalogs and direct-mail pieces, and four Web sites to guarantee product availability and quick service. Its 4,000-plus-page catalog features 138,000 products, such as motors, lighting, material handlers, fasteners, tools, and safety supplies, and customers can purchase over 300,000 products at Grainger.com. The distribution centers are linked by satellite network, which has reduced customer-response time and boosted sales. Helped by more than 3,000 suppliers, Grainger offers customers a total of more than 900,000 supplies and repair parts in all.[54] ▱

Market Logistics

Physical distribution starts at the factory. Managers choose a set of warehouses (stocking points) and transportation carriers that will deliver the goods to final destinations in the desired time or at the lowest total cost. Physical distribution has now been expanded into the broader concept of **supply chain management (SCM)**. Supply chain management starts before physical distribution and means strategically procuring the right inputs (raw materials, components, and capital equipment), converting them efficiently into finished products, and dispatching them to the final destinations. An even broader perspective looks at how the company's suppliers themselves obtain their inputs.

The supply chain perspective can help a company identify superior suppliers and distributors and help them improve productivity and reduce costs. Consumer goods manufacturers admired for their supply chain management include P&G, Kraft, General Mills, PepsiCo, and Nestlé; noteworthy retailers include Walmart, Target, Publix, Costco, Kroger, and Meijer.[55]

Firms are also striving to improve the environmental impact and sustainability of their supply chain by shrinking their carbon footprint and using recyclable packaging. Johnson & Johnson switched to Forest Stewardship Council (FSC)–certified paperboard for its BAND-AID brand boxes. As one executive noted, "Johnson & Johnson and its operating companies are positioned to make paper and packaging procurement decisions that could help influence responsible forest management."[56]

Market logistics includes planning the infrastructure to meet demand, then implementing and controlling the physical flows of materials and final goods from points of origin to points of use, to meet customer requirements at a profit. Market logistics planning has four steps:[57]

1. Deciding on the company's value proposition to its customers. (What on-time delivery standard should we offer? What levels should we attain in ordering and billing accuracy?)
2. Selecting the best channel design and network strategy for reaching the customers. (Should the company serve customers directly or through intermediaries? What products should we source from which manufacturing facilities? How many warehouses should we maintain and where should we locate them?)
3. Developing operational excellence in sales forecasting, warehouse management, transportation management, and materials management
4. Implementing the solution with the best information systems, equipment, policies, and procedures

Studying market logistics leads managers to find the most efficient way to deliver value. For example, a software company might traditionally produce and package software disks and manuals, ship them to wholesalers, which ship them to retailers, which sell them to customers, who bring them home to download onto their PCs. Market logistics offers two superior delivery systems. The first lets the customer download the software directly onto his or her computer. The second allows the computer manufacturer to download the software onto its products. Both solutions eliminate the need for printing, packaging, shipping, and stocking millions of disks and manuals.

Integrated Logistics Systems

The market logistics task calls for **integrated logistics systems (ILS),** which include materials management, material flow systems, and physical distribution, aided by information technology (IT). Information systems play a critical role in managing market logistics, especially via computers, point-of-sale terminals, uniform product bar codes, satellite tracking, electronic data interchange (EDI), and electronic funds transfer (EFT). These developments have shortened the order-cycle time, reduced clerical labor, reduced errors, and provided improved control of operations. They have enabled companies to promise "the product will be at dock 25 at 10:00 AM tomorrow," and deliver on that promise.

Market logistics encompass several activities. The first is sales forecasting, on the basis of which the company schedules distribution, production, and inventory levels. Production plans indicate the materials the purchasing department must order. These materials arrive through inbound transportation, enter the receiving area, and are stored in raw-material inventory. Raw materials are converted into finished goods. Finished-goods inventory is the link between customer orders and manufacturing activity. Customers' orders draw down the finished-goods inventory level, and manufacturing activity builds it up. Finished goods flow off the assembly line and pass through packaging, in-plant warehousing, shipping-room processing, outbound transportation, field warehousing, and customer delivery and servicing.

Management has become concerned about the total cost of market logistics, which can amount to as much as 30 percent to 40 percent of the product's cost. In the U.S. grocery business, waste or "shrink" affects 8 percent to 10 percent of perishable goods, costing $20 billion annually. To reduce shrink, grocery retailer Stop & Shop looked across its entire fresh-food supply chain and reduced everything from the size of suppliers' boxes to the number of products on display. With these changes, the supermarket chain cut shrink by almost a third, saving over $50 million and eliminating 36,000 pounds of rotten food, improving customer satisfaction at the same time.[58]

Many experts call market logistics "the last frontier for cost economies," and firms are determined to wring every unnecessary cost out of the system: In 1982, logistics represented 14.5 percent of U.S. GDP; by 2007, the share had dropped to about 10 percent.[59] Lower market-logistics costs will permit lower prices, yield higher profit margins, or both. Even though the cost of market logistics can be high, a well-planned program can be a potent tool in competitive marketing.

Many firms are embracing **lean manufacturing,** originally pioneered by Japanese firms such as Toyota, to produce goods with minimal waste of time, materials, and money. CONMED's disposable devices are used by a hospital somewhere in the world every 90 seconds to insert and remove fluid around joints during orthoscopic surgery,

---

ConMed To streamline production, medical manufacturer ConMed set out to link its operations as closely as possible to the ultimate buyer of its products. Rather than moving manufacturing to China, which might have lowered labor costs but could have also risked long lead times, inventory buildup, and unanticipated delays, the firm put new production processes into place to assemble its disposable products only after hospitals placed orders. Some 80 percent of orders were predictable enough that demand forecasts updated every few months could set hourly production targets. As proof of the firm's new efficiency, the assembly area for fluid-injection devices went from covering 3,300 square feet and stocking $93,000 worth of parts to 650 square feet and $6,000 worth of parts. Output per worker increased 21 percent.[60]

By redesigning its production assembly, medical manufacturer ConMed significantly increased productivity.

Lean manufacturing must be implemented thoughtfully and monitored closely. Toyota's recent crisis in product safety that resulted in extensive product recalls has been attributed in part to the fact that some aspects of the lean manufacturing approach—eliminating overlap by using common parts and designs across multiple product lines, and reducing the number of suppliers to procure parts in greater scale—can backfire when quality-control issues arise.[61]

Market-Logistics Objectives

Many companies state their market-logistics objective as "getting the right goods to the right places at the right time for the least cost." Unfortunately, this objective provides little practical guidance. No system can simultaneously maximize customer service and minimize distribution cost. Maximum customer service implies large inventories, premium transportation, and multiple warehouses, all of which raise market-logistics costs.

Nor can a company achieve market-logistics efficiency by asking each market-logistics manager to minimize his or her own logistics costs. Market-logistics costs interact and are often negatively related. For example:

- The traffic manager favors rail shipment over air shipment because rail costs less. However, because the railroads are slower, rail shipment ties up working capital longer, delays customer payment, and might cause customers to buy from competitors who offer faster service.
- The shipping department uses cheap containers to minimize shipping costs. Cheaper containers lead to a higher rate of damaged goods and customer ill will.
- The inventory manager favors low inventories. This increases stock-outs, back orders, paperwork, special production runs, and high-cost, fast-freight shipments.

Given that market-logistics activities require strong trade-offs, managers must make decisions on a total-system basis. The starting point is to study what customers require and what competitors are offering. Customers are interested in on-time delivery, supplier willingness to meet emergency needs, careful handling of merchandise, and supplier willingness to take back defective goods and resupply them quickly.

The company must then research the relative importance of these service outputs. For example, service-repair time is very important to buyers of copying equipment. Xerox developed a service delivery standard that "can put a disabled machine anywhere in the continental United States back into operation within three hours after receiving the service request." It then designed a service division of personnel, parts, and locations to deliver on this promise.

The company must also consider competitors' service standards. It will normally want to match or exceed the competitors' service level, but the objective is to maximize profits, not sales. Some companies offer less service and charge a lower price; other companies offer more service and charge a premium price.

The company ultimately must establish some promise it makes to the market. Coca-Cola wants to "put Coke within an arm's length of desire." Lands' End, the giant clothing retailer, aims to respond to every phone call within 20 seconds and to ship every order within 24 hours of receipt. Some companies define standards for each service factor. One appliance manufacturer has established the following service standards: to deliver at least 95 percent of the dealer's orders within seven days of order receipt, to fill them with 99 percent accuracy, to answer dealer inquiries on order status within three hours, and to ensure that merchandise damaged in transit does not exceed 1 percent.

Given the market-logistics objectives, the company must design a system that will minimize the cost of achieving these objectives. Each possible market-logistics system will lead to the following cost:

$$M = T + FW + VW + S$$

where M = total market-logistics cost of proposed system

T = total freight cost of proposed system

FW = total fixed warehouse cost of proposed system

VW = total variable warehouse costs (including inventory) of proposed system

S = total cost of lost sales due to average delivery delay under proposed system

Choosing a market-logistics system calls for examining the total cost (M) associated with different proposed systems and selecting the system that minimizes it. If it is hard to measure S, the company should aim to minimize $T + FW + VW$ for a target level of customer service.

Market-Logistics Decisions

The firm must make four major decisions about its market logistics: (1) How should we handle orders (order processing)? (2) Where should we locate our stock (warehousing)? (3) How much stock should we hold (inventory)? and (4) How should we ship goods (transportation)?

ORDER PROCESSING Most companies today are trying to shorten the *order-to-payment cycle*—that is, the elapsed time between an order's receipt, delivery, and payment. This cycle has many steps, including order transmission by the salesperson, order entry and customer credit check, inventory and production scheduling, order and invoice shipment, and receipt of payment. The longer this cycle takes, the lower the customer's satisfaction and the lower the company's profits.

WAREHOUSING Every company must store finished goods until they are sold, because production and consumption cycles rarely match. Consumer-packaged-goods companies have been reducing their number of stocking locations from 10 to 15 to about 5 to 7, and pharmaceutical and medical distributors have cut theirs from 90 to about 45. On the one hand, more stocking locations mean goods can be delivered to customers more quickly, but warehousing and inventory costs are higher. To reduce these costs, the company might centralize its inventory in one place and use fast transportation to fill orders.

Some inventory is kept at or near the plant, and the rest in warehouses in other locations. The company might own private warehouses and also rent space in public warehouses. *Storage warehouses* store goods for moderate to long periods of time. *Distribution warehouses* receive goods from various company plants and suppliers and move them out as soon as possible. *Automated warehouses* employ advanced materials-handling systems under the control of a central computer and are increasingly becoming the norm.

Some warehouses are now taking on activities formerly done in the plant. These include assembly, packaging, and constructing promotional displays. Postponing finalization of the offering to the warehouse can achieve savings in costs and finer matching of offerings to demand.

INVENTORY Salespeople would like their companies to carry enough stock to fill all customer orders immediately. However, this is not cost-effective. *Inventory cost increases at an accelerating rate as the customer-service level approaches 100 percent.* Management needs to know how much sales and profits would increase as a result of carrying larger inventories and promising faster order fulfillment times, and then make a decision.

As inventory draws down, management must know at what stock level to place a new order. This stock level is called the *order (or reorder) point.* An order point of 20 means reordering when the stock falls to 20 units. The order point should balance the risks of stock-out against the costs of overstock. The other decision is how much to order. The larger the quantity ordered, the less frequently an order needs to be placed. The company needs to balance order-processing costs and inventory-carrying costs. *Order-processing costs* for a manufacturer consist of *setup costs* and *running costs* (operating costs when production is running) for the item. If setup costs are low, the manufacturer can produce the item often, and the average cost per item is stable and equal to the running costs. If setup costs are high, however, the manufacturer can reduce the average cost per unit by producing a long run and carrying more inventory.

Order-processing costs must be compared with *inventory-carrying costs.* The larger the average stock carried, the higher the inventory-carrying costs. These carrying costs include storage charges, cost of capital, taxes and insurance, and depreciation and obsolescence. Carrying costs might run as high as 30 percent of inventory value. This means that marketing managers who want their companies to carry larger inventories need to show that the larger inventories would produce incremental gross profits to exceed incremental carrying costs.

We can determine the optimal order quantity by observing how order-processing costs and inventory-carrying costs sum up at different order levels. △ Figure 16.1 shows that the order-processing

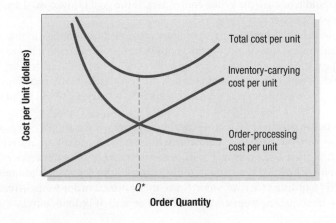

|Fig. 16.1| △

Determining Optimal Order Quantity

cost per unit decreases with the number of units ordered because the order costs are spread over more units. Inventory-carrying charges per unit increase with the number of units ordered, because each unit remains longer in inventory. We sum the two cost curves vertically into a total-cost curve and project the lowest point of the total-cost curve on the horizontal axis to find the optimal order quantity Q^*.[62]

Companies are reducing their inventory costs by treating inventory items differently, positioning them according to risk and opportunity. They distinguish between bottleneck items (high risk, low opportunity), critical items (high risk, high opportunity), commodities (low risk, high opportunity), and nuisance items (low risk, low opportunity).[63] They are also keeping slow-moving items in a central location and carrying fast-moving items in warehouses closer to customers. All these strategies give them more flexibility should anything go wrong, as it often does, be it a dock strike in California, a typhoon in Taiwan, a tsunami in Asia, or a hurricane in New Orleans.[64]

The ultimate answer to carrying *near-zero inventory* is to build for order, not for stock. Sony calls it SOMO, "Sell one, make one." Dell's inventory strategy for years has been to get the customer to order a computer and pay for it in advance. Then Dell uses the customer's money to pay suppliers to ship the necessary components. As long as customers do not need the item immediately, everyone can save money. Some retailers are unloading excess inventory on eBay where, by cutting out the traditional liquidator middleman, they can make 60 to 80 cents on the dollar as opposed to 10 cents.[65] And some suppliers are snapping up excess inventory to create opportunity.

Cameron Hughes

"If a winery has an eight-barrel lot, it may only use five barrels for its customers," says Cameron Hughes, a wine "négociant" who buys the excess juice from high-end wineries and wine brokers and combines it to make limited edition, premium blends that taste much more expensive than their price tags. Négociants have been around a long time, first as middlemen who sold or shipped wine as wholesalers, but the profession has expanded as opportunists such as Hughes became more involved in effectively making their own wines. Hughes doesn't own any grapes, bottling machines, or trucks. He outsources the bottling, and he sells directly to retailers such as Costco, Sam's Club, and Safeway, eliminating middlemen and multiple markups. Hughes never knows which or how many excess lots of wine he will have, but he's turned it to his advantage—he creates a new product with every batch. This rapid turnover is part of Costco's appeal for him. The discount store's customers love the idea of finding a rare bargain, and Hughes promotes his wines through in-store wine tastings and insider e-mails that alert Costco customers to upcoming numbered lots. Because lots sell out quickly, fans subscribe to Cameron's e-mail alerts at chwine.com that tell them when a new lot will be sold.[66]

Cameron Hughes has grown a thriving business by using excess lots of wine as input to his limited-edition premium wines.

TRANSPORTATION Transportation choices affect product pricing, on-time delivery performance, and the condition of the goods when they arrive, all of which affect customer satisfaction.

In shipping goods to its warehouses, dealers, and customers, the company can choose rail, air, truck, waterway, or pipeline. Shippers consider such criteria as speed, frequency, dependability, capability, availability, traceability, and cost. For speed, air, rail, and truck are the prime contenders. If the goal is low cost, then the choice is water or pipeline.

Shippers are increasingly combining two or more transportation modes, thanks to containerization. **Containerization** consists of putting the goods in boxes or trailers that are easy to transfer between two transportation modes. *Piggyback* describes the use of rail and trucks; *fishyback,* water and trucks; *trainship,* water and rail; and *airtruck,* air and trucks. Each coordinated mode offers specific advantages. For example, piggyback is cheaper than trucking alone yet provides flexibility and convenience.

Shippers can choose private, contract, or common carriers. If the shipper owns its own truck or air fleet, it becomes a *private carrier.* A *contract carrier* is an independent organization selling transportation services to others on a contract basis. A *common carrier* provides services between predetermined points on a scheduled basis and is available to all shippers at standard rates.

To reduce costly handing at arrival, some firms are putting items into shelf-ready packaging so they don't need to be unpacked from a box and placed on a shelf individually. In Europe, P&G uses a three-tier logistic system to schedule deliveries of fast- and slow-moving goods, bulky items, and small items in the most efficient way.[67] To reduce damage in shipping, the size, weight, and fragility of the item must be reflected in the crating technique used, the density of foam cushioning, etc.[68]

Organizational Lessons

Market-logistics strategies must be derived from business strategies, rather than solely from cost considerations. The logistics system must be information-intensive and establish electronic links among all the significant parties. Finally, the company should set its logistics goals to match or exceed competitors' service standards and should involve members of all relevant teams in the planning process.

Today's stronger demands for logistical support from large customers will increase suppliers' costs. Customers want more frequent deliveries so they don't have to carry as much inventory. They want shorter order-cycle times, which means suppliers must have high in-stock availability. Customers often want direct store delivery rather than shipments to distribution centers. They want mixed pallets rather than separate pallets. They want tighter promised delivery times. They may want custom packaging, price tagging, and display building.

Suppliers can't say "no" to many of these requests, but at least they can set up different logistical programs with different service levels and customer charges. Smart companies will adjust their offerings to each major customer's requirements. The company's trade group will set up *differentiated distribution* by offering different bundled service programs for different customers.

Summary

1. Retailing includes all the activities involved in selling goods or services directly to final consumers for personal, nonbusiness use. Retailers can be understood in terms of store retailing, nonstore retailing, and retail organizations.

2. Like products, retail-store types pass through stages of growth and decline. As existing stores offer more services to remain competitive, costs and prices go up, which opens the door to new retail forms that offer a mix of merchandise and services at lower prices. The major types of retail stores are specialty stores, department stores, supermarkets, convenience stores, discount stores, extreme value or hard-discount store, off-price retailers, superstores, and catalog showrooms.

3. Although most goods and services are sold through stores, nonstore retailing has been growing. The major types of nonstore retailing are direct selling (one-to-one selling, one-to-many party selling, and multilevel network marketing), direct marketing (which includes e-commerce and Internet retailing), automatic vending, and buying services.

4. Although many retail stores are independently owned, an increasing number are falling under some form of corporate retailing. Retail organizations achieve many economies of scale, greater purchasing power, wider brand recognition, and better-trained employees. The major types of corporate retailing are corporate chain stores, voluntary chains, retailer cooperatives, consumer cooperatives, franchise organizations, and merchandising conglomerates.

5. The retail environment has changed considerably in recent years; as new retail forms have emerged, intertype and store-based versus nonstore-based competition has increased, the rise of giant retailers has been matched by the decline of middle-market retailers, investment in technology and global expansion has grown, and shopper marketing inside stores has become a priority.

6. Like all marketers, retailers must prepare marketing plans that include decisions on target markets, channels, product assortment and procurement, prices, services, store atmosphere, store activities and experiences, communications, and location.

7. Wholesaling includes all the activities in selling goods or services to those who buy for resale or business use. Wholesalers can perform functions better and more cost-effectively than the manufacturer can. These functions include selling and promoting, buying and assortment building, bulk breaking, warehousing, transportation, financing, risk bearing, dissemination of market information, and provision of management services and consulting.

8. There are four types of wholesalers: merchant wholesalers; brokers and agents; manufacturers' and retailers' sales branches, sales offices, and purchasing offices; and miscellaneous wholesalers such as agricultural assemblers and auction companies.

9. Like retailers, wholesalers must decide on target markets, product assortment and services, price, promotion, and place. The most successful wholesalers are those who adapt their services to meet suppliers' and target customers' needs.

10. Producers of physical products and services must decide on market logistics—the best way to store and move goods and services to market destinations; to coordinate the activities of suppliers, purchasing agents, manufacturers, marketers, channel members, and customers. Major gains in logistical efficiency have come from advances in information technology.

Applications

Marketing Debate
Should National-Brand Manufacturers Also Supply Private-Label Brands?

Ralston-Purina, Borden, ConAgra, and Heinz have all admitted to supplying products—sometimes lower in quality—to be used for private labels. Other marketers, however, criticize this "if you can't beat them, join them" strategy, maintaining that these actions, if revealed, may create confusion or even reinforce a perception by consumers that all brands in a category are essentially the same.

Take a position: Manufacturers should feel free to sell private labels as a source of revenue *versus* National manufacturers should never get involved with private labels.

Marketing Discussion
Retail Customer Loyalty

Think of your favorite stores. What do they do that encourages your loyalty? What do you like about the in-store experience? What further improvements could they make?

Marketing Excellence

>>Zara

Spain's Zara has become Europe's leading apparel retailer, providing consumers with current, high fashion styles at reasonable prices. With over $8.7 billion in sales and more than 1,500 stores, the company's success has come from breaking virtually every traditional rule in the retailing industry.

The first Zara store opened in 1975. By the 1980s, Zara's founder, Amancio Ortega, was working with computer programmers to develop a new distribution model that would revolutionize the clothing industry. This new model takes several strategic steps to reduce the lead time from design to distribution to just two weeks—a significant difference from the industry average of six to nine months. As a result, the company makes approximately 20,000 different items a year, about triple what Gap or H&M make in a year. By reducing lead times to a fraction of its competitors, Zara has been able to provide "fast fashion" for its consumers at affordable prices. The company's success lies within four key strategic elements:

Design and Production. Zara employs hundreds of designers at its headquarters in Spain. Thus, new styles are constantly being created and put into production while others are tweaked with new colors or patterns. The firm enforces the speed at which it puts these designs into production by locating half its production facilities nearby in Spain, Portugal, and Morocco. Zara produces only a small quantity of each collection and is willing to experience occasional shortages to preserve an image of exclusivity. Clothes with a longer shelf life, like T-shirts, are outsourced to lower-cost suppliers in Asia and Turkey. With tight control on its manufacturing process, Zara can move more rapidly than any of its competitors and continues to deliver fresh styles to its stores every week.

Logistics. Zara distributes all its merchandise, regardless of origin, from Spain. Its distribution process is designed so that the time from receipt of an order to delivery in the store averages 24 hours in Europe and 48 hours in the United States and Asia. Having 50 percent of its production facilities nearby is key to the success of this model. All Zara stores receive new shipments twice a week, and the small quantities of each collection not only bring consumers back into Zara stores over and over but also entice them to make purchases more quickly. While an average shopper in Spain visits a high street (or main street) store three times a year, shoppers average 17 trips to Zara stores. Some Zara fans know exactly when new shipments arrive and show up early that day to be the first in line for the latest fashions. These practices keep sales strong throughout the year and help the company sell more products at full price—85 percent of its merchandise versus the industry average of 60 percent.

Customers. Everything revolves around Zara's customers. The retailer reacts to customers' changing needs, trends, and tastes with daily reports from Zara shop managers about which products and styles have sold and which haven't. With up to 70 percent of their salaries coming from commission, managers have a strong incentive to stay on top of things. Zara's designers don't have to predict what fashion trends will be in the future. They react to customer feedback—good and bad—and if something fails, the line is withdrawn immediately. Zara cuts its losses and the impact is minimal due to the low quantities of each style produced.

Stores. Zara has never run an advertising campaign. The stores, 90 percent of which it owns, are the key advertising element and are located in prestigious high-traffic locations around the world. Zara spends significant time and effort regularly changing store windows to help lure customers in. In comparison to other retailers, which spend 3 percent to 4 percent of revenues on big brand-building campaigns, Zara spends just 0.3 percent.

The company's success comes from having complete control over all the parts of its business—design, production, and distribution. Louis Vuitton's fashion director, Daniel Piette, described Zara as "possibly the most innovative and devastating retailer in the world." Now, as Zara continues to expand into new markets and countries, it risks losing some of its speed and will have to work hard to continue providing the same "newness"' all over the world that it does so well in Europe. It is also making a somewhat belated major push online that will need to work within its existing business model.

Questions

1. Would Zara's model work for other retailers? Why or why not?

2. How is Zara going to expand successfully all over the world with the same level of speed and instant fashion?

Sources: Rachel Tiplady, "Zara: Taking the Lead in Fast-Fashion." *BusinessWeek*, April 4, 2006; enotes.com, Inditex overview; "Zara: A Spanish Success Story." *CNN*, June 15, 2001; "Fashion Conquistador," *BusinessWeek*, September 4, 2006; Caroline Raux, "The Reign of Spain." *The Guardian*, October 28, 2002; Kerry Capell, "Zara Thrives by Breaking All the Rules," *BusinessWeek*, October 20, 2008, p. 66; Christopher Bjork, "Zara Is to Get Big Online Push," *Wall Street Journal*, September 17, 2009, p. B8.

Marketing Excellence

>>Best Buy

Best Buy is the world's largest consumer electronics retailer, with $34.2 billion in sales in fiscal 2009. Sales boomed in the 1980s as Best Buy expanded nationally and made some risky business decisions, like putting its sales staff on salary instead of commission pay. This decision created a more consumer-friendly, low-pressure shopping atmosphere and resulted in an instant spike in overall revenues. In the 1990s, Best Buy ramped up its computer product offerings and, by 1995, was the biggest seller of home PCs, a powerful position during the Internet boom.

At the turn of the century, Best Buy faced new competitors like Costco and Walmart, which started ramping up their electronics divisions and product offerings. Best Buy believed the best way to differentiate itself was to increase its focus on customer service by selling product warranties and offering personal services like installation and at-home delivery. Its purchase of Geek Squad, a

24-hour computer service company, proved extremely profitable and strategic as home and small office networks became more complex and the need for personal computing attention increased. By 2004, Best Buy had placed a Geek Squad station in each of its stores, providing consumers with personal computing services in the stores, online, on the phone, and at home.

Today, Best Buy has adopted a corporate strategy it calls Customer-Centricity. It has segmented its broad customer base into a handful of specific targets such as the affluent tech geek, the busy suburban mom, the young gadget enthusiast, and the price-conscious family dad. Next, it uses extensive research and analysis to determine which segments are the most abundant and lucrative in each market. Finally, it configures its stores and trains its employees to target those shoppers and encourage them to keep coming back again and again. For example, stores targeting affluent tech geeks have separate home theatre departments with knowledgeable salespeople who can spend time discussing all the different product options. Stores with a high volume of suburban mom shoppers offer personal shopping assistants to help mom get in and out as quickly as possible with the exact items she needs.

Sometimes a store will experience a new type of lucrative shopper. In the coastal town of Baytown, Texas, the local Best Buy observed frequent visits from Eastern European workers coming off cargo ships and oil tankers. These men and women were using their precious free time to race over to Best Buy and search the aisles for Apple's iPods and laptops, which are cheaper in the United States than in Europe. To cater to this unique consumer, the local Best Buy rearranged its store, moved iPods, MacBooks, and their accessories from the back of the store to the front, and added signage in simple English. The result: sales from these European workers increased 67 percent.

This local ingenuity paired with the ability to cater to each market and segment's needs have helped Best Buy survive the electronics storm while competitors like CompUSA and Circuit City have failed. The business is tough, with thin profit margins and continuously evolving products. However, with over 1,300 stores, including locations in Canada, Mexico, China, and Turkey, Best Buy has a 19 percent market share and a trusted, consumer-friendly brand.

Questions

1. What are the keys to Best Buy's success? What are the risks going forward?

2. How else can Best Buy compete against new competitors like Walmart and online companies?

PART 7 | **Communicating Value**

Chapter **17** | **Designing and Managing Integrated Marketing Communications**
Chapter **18** | Managing Mass Communications: Advertising, Sales Promotions, Events and Experiences, and Public Relations
Chapter **19** | Managing Personal Communications: Direct and Interactive Marketing, Word of Mouth, and Personal Selling

In This Chapter, We Will Address the Following Questions

1. What is the role of marketing communications?

2. How do marketing communications work?

3. What are the major steps in developing effective communications?

4. What is the communications mix, and how should it be set?

5. What is an integrated marketing communications program?

Ocean Spray has revitalized its brand through extensive new product development and a thoroughly integrated modern marketing communications program.

Designing and Managing Integrated Marketing Communications

Modern marketing calls for more than developing a good product, pricing it attractively, and making it accessible. Companies must also communicate with their present and potential stakeholders and the general public. For most marketers, therefore, the question is not *whether* to communicate but rather *what* to say, *how* and *when* to say it, to *whom*, and *how often*. Consumers can turn to hundreds of cable and satellite TV channels, thousands of magazines and newspapers, and millions of Internet pages. They are taking a more active role in deciding what communications they want to receive as well as how they want to communicate to others about the products and services they use. To effectively reach and influence target markets, holistic marketers are creatively employing multiple forms of communications. Ocean Spray—an agricultural cooperative of cranberry growers—has used a variety of communication vehicles to turn its sales fortunes around.

 *Facing stiff competition, a number of adverse consumer trends, and nearly a decade of declining sales, Ocean Spray COO Ken Romanzi and Arnold Worldwide decided to "reintroduce the cranberry to America" as the "surprisingly versatile little fruit that supplies modern-day benefits," through a true 360-degree campaign that used all facets of marketing communications to reach consumers in a variety of settings. The intent was to support the full range of products—cranberry sauce, fruit juices, and dried cranberries in different forms—and leverage the fact that the brand was born in the cranberry bogs and remained there still. The agency decided to tell an authentic, honest, and perhaps surprising story dubbed "Straight from the Bog." The campaign was designed to also reinforce two key brand benefits—that Ocean Spray products tasted good and were good for you. PR played a crucial role. Miniature bogs were brought to Manhattan and featured on an NBC Today morning segment. A "Bogs across America Tour" brought the experience to Los Angeles, Chicago, and even London. Television and print advertising featured two growers (depicted by actors) standing waist-deep in a bog and talking, often humorously, about what they did. The campaign also included a Web site, in-store displays, and events for consumers as well as for members of the growers' cooperative itself. Product innovation was crucial, too; new flavor blends were introduced, along with a line of 100 percent juice drinks, diet and light versions, and Craisins sweetened dried cranberries. The campaign hit the mark, lifting sales an average of 10 percent each year from 2005 to 2009 despite continued decline in the fruit juice category.[1]*

Done right, marketing communications can have a huge payoff. This chapter describes how communications work and what marketing communications can do for a company. It also addresses how holistic marketers combine and integrate marketing communications. Chapter 18 examines mass (nonpersonal) communications (advertising, sales promotion, events and experiences, and public relations and publicity); Chapter 19 examines personal communications (direct and interactive marketing, word-of-mouth marketing, and personal selling).

The Role of Marketing Communications

Marketing communications are the means by which firms attempt to inform, persuade, and remind consumers—directly or indirectly—about the products and brands they sell. In a sense, marketing communications represent the voice of the company and its brands; they are a means by which the firm can establish a dialogue and build relationships with consumers. By strengthening customer loyalty, marketing communications can contribute to customer equity.

Marketing communications also work for consumers when they show how and why a product is used, by whom, where, and when. Consumers can learn who makes the product and what the company and brand stand for, and they can get an incentive for trial or use. Marketing communications allow companies to link their brands to other people, places, events, brands, experiences, feelings, and things. They can contribute to brand equity—by establishing the brand in memory and creating a brand image—as well as drive sales and even affect shareholder value.[2]

The Changing Marketing Communications Environment

Technology and other factors have profoundly changed the way consumers process communications, and even whether they choose to process them at all. The rapid diffusion of multipurpose smart phones, broadband and wireless Internet connections, and ad-skipping digital video recorders (DVRs) have eroded the effectiveness of the mass media. In 1960, a company could reach 80 percent of U.S. women with one 30-second commercial aired simultaneously on three TV networks: ABC, CBS, and NBC. Today, the same ad would have to run on 100 channels or more to achieve this marketing feat. Consumers not only have more choices of media, they can also decide whether and how they want to receive commercial content. "Marketing Insight: Don't Touch That Remote" describes developments in television advertising.

Don't Touch That Remote

That consumers are more in charge in the marketplace is perhaps nowhere more evident than in television broadcasting, where DVRs allow consumers to skip past ads with a push of the fast-forward button. Estimates had DVRs in 34 percent of U.S. households at the end of 2009, and of viewers who use them, between 60 percent and 70 percent fast-forward through commercials (the others either like ads, don't mind them, or can't be bothered).

Is that all bad? Surprisingly, research shows that while focusing on an ad in order to fast-forward through it, consumers actually retain and recall a fair amount of information. The most successful ads in "fast-forward mode" were those consumers had already seen, that used familiar characters, and that didn't have lots of scenes. It also helped to have brand-related information in the center of the screen, where viewers' eyes focus while skipping through. Although consumers are still more likely to recall an ad the next day if they've watched it live, some brand recall occurs even after an ad was deliberately zapped.

Another challenge marketers have faced for a long time is viewers' tendency to switch channels during commercial breaks. Recently, however, Nielsen, which handles television program ratings, has begun to offer ratings for specific ads. Before, advertisers had to pay based on the rating of the program, even if as many as 5 percent to 15 percent of consumers temporarily tuned away. Now they can pay based on the actual commercial audience available when their ad is shown. To increase viewership during commercial breaks, the major broadcast and cable networks are shortening breaks and delaying them until viewers are more likely to be engaged in a program.

Sources: Andrew O'Connell, "Advertisers: Learn to Love the DVR," *Harvard Business Review*, April 2010, p. 22; Erik du Plesis, "Digital Video Recorders and Inadvertent Advertising Exposure," *Journal of Advertising Research* 49 (June 2009); S. Adam Brasel and James Gips, "Breaking Through Fast-Forwarding: Brand Information and Visual Attention," *Journal of Marketing* 72 (November 2008), pp. 31–48; "Watching the Watchers," *Economist*, November 15, 2008, p. 77; Stephanie Kang, "Why DVR Viewers Recall Some TV Spots," *Wall Street Journal*, February 26, 2008; Kenneth C. Wilbur, "How Digital Video Recorder Changes Traditional Television Advertising," *Journal of Advertising* 37 (Summer 2008), pp. 143–49; Burt Helm, "Cable Takes a Ratings Hit," *BusinessWeek*, September 24, 2007.

Ads are appearing everywhere—even on eggs for this popular CBS television show.

But as some marketers flee traditional media, they still encounter challenges. Commercial clutter is rampant. The average city dweller is exposed to an estimated 3,000 to 5,000 ad messages a day. Short-form video content and ads appear at gas stations, grocery stores, doctors' offices, and big-box retailers. Supermarket eggs have been stamped with the name of CBS programs; subway turnstiles carry GEICO's name; Chinese food cartons promote Continental Airlines; and US Airways has sold ads on its motion sickness bags. Dubai sold corporate branding rights to 23 of the 47 stops and two metro lines in its new mass transit rail system.[3]

Marketing communications in almost every medium and form have been on the rise, and some consumers feel they are increasingly invasive. Marketers must be creative in using technology but not intrude in consumers' lives. Consider what Motorola did to solve that problem.[4]

Motorola At Hong Kong International Airport, Motorola's special promotion enabled loved ones to "Say Goodbye" via photos and messages sent from their phones to digital billboards in the departure area. When they checked into the gate area, travelers saw photos of the friends and family who had just dropped them off as part of a digital billboard in the image of a giant Motorola mobile phone. The company also offered departing travelers special instructions for using their phones to send a Motorola-branded good-bye video to friends and families, featuring soccer star David Beckham and Asian pop star Jay Chou. ▬

Motorola's high-tech promotion creatively allowed passengers and those left behind to say one last good-bye with digital billboards.

Marketing Communications, Brand Equity, and Sales

In this new communication environment, although advertising is often a central element of a marketing communications program, it is usually not the only one—or even the most important one—for sales and building brand and customer equity. Like many other firms, over a five-year period from 2004 to 2008, Kimberly-Clark cut the percentage of its marketing budget spent on TV from 60 percent to a little over 40 percent as it invested more heavily in Internet and experiential marketing.[5] Consider Gap's effort in launching a new line of jeans.[6]

Gap By 2009, with sales slumping, Gap decided to celebrate the 40th anniversary of the opening of its first Gap store by introducing the "Born to Fit" 1969 Premium Jeans line. For its launch, Gap moved away from its typical media-intensive ad campaign, as exemplified by its popular 1998 "Khakis Swing" holiday ads. The campaign featured newer communications elements such as a Facebook page, video clips, a realistic online fashion show on a virtual catwalk, and a StyleMixer iPhone app. The app enabled users to mix and match clothes and organize outfits, get feedback from Facebook friends, and receive discounts when near a Gap store. Simultaneous in-store acoustic shows across 700 locations and temporary pop-up denim stores in major urban locations added to the buzz.

MARKETING COMMUNICATIONS MIX The **marketing communications mix** consists of eight major modes of communication:[7]

1. *Advertising*—Any paid form of nonpersonal presentation and promotion of ideas, goods, or services by an identified sponsor via print media (newspapers and magazines), broadcast media (radio and television), network media (telephone, cable, satellite, wireless), electronic media (audiotape, videotape, videodisk, CD-ROM, Web page), and display media (billboards, signs, posters).

2. *Sales promotion*—A variety of short-term incentives to encourage trial or purchase of a product or service including consumer promotions (such as samples, coupons, and premiums), trade promotions (such as advertising and display allowances), and business and sales force promotions (contests for sales reps).

3. *Events and experiences*—Company-sponsored activities and programs designed to create daily or special brand-related interactions with consumers, including sports, arts, entertainment, and cause events as well as less formal activities.

4. *Public relations and publicity*—A variety of programs directed internally to employees of the company or externally to consumers, other firms, the government, and media to promote or protect a company's image or its individual product communications.

5. *Direct marketing*—Use of mail, telephone, fax, e-mail, or Internet to communicate directly with or solicit response or dialogue from specific customers and prospects.

6. *Interactive marketing*—Online activities and programs designed to engage customers or prospects and directly or indirectly raise awareness, improve image, or elicit sales of products and services.

7. *Word-of-mouth marketing*—People-to-people oral, written, or electronic communications that relate to the merits or experiences of purchasing or using products or services.

8. *Personal selling*—Face-to-face interaction with one or more prospective purchasers for the purpose of making presentations, answering questions, and procuring orders.

Table 17.1 lists numerous communication platforms. Company communication goes beyond these. The product's styling and price, the shape and color of the package, the salesperson's manner and dress, the store décor, the company's stationery—all communicate something to buyers. Every *brand contact* delivers an impression that can strengthen or weaken a customer's view of a company.[8]

Marketing communication activities contribute to brand equity and drive sales in many ways: by creating brand awareness, forging brand image in consumers' memories, eliciting positive brand judgments or feelings, and strengthening consumer loyalty.

TABLE 17.1	Common Communication Platforms					
Advertising	**Sales Promotion**	**Events and Experiences**	**Public Relations and Publicity**	**Direct and Interactive Marketing**	**Word-of-Mouth Marketing**	**Personal Selling**
Print and broadcast ads	Contests, games, sweepstakes, lotteries	Sports	Press kits	Catalogs	Person-to-person	Sales presentations
Packaging–outer	Premiums and gifts	Entertainment	Speeches	Mailings	Chat rooms	Sales meetings
Packaging inserts	Sampling	Festivals	Seminars	Telemarketing	Blogs	Incentive programs
Cinema	Fairs and trade shows	Arts	Annual reports	Electronic shopping		Samples
Brochures and booklets	Exhibits	Causes	Charitable donations	TV shopping		Fairs and trade shows
Posters and leaflets	Demonstrations	Factory tours	Publications	Fax		
Directories	Coupons	Company museums	Community relations	E-mail		
Reprints of ads	Rebates	Street activities	Lobbying	Voice mail		
Billboards	Low-interest financing		Identity media	Company blogs		
Display signs	Trade-in allowances		Company magazine	Web sites		
Point-of-purchase displays	Continuity programs					
DVDs	Tie-ins					

MARKETING COMMUNICATION EFFECTS The way brand associations are formed does not matter. In other words, whether a consumer has an equally strong, favorable, and unique brand association of Subaru with the concepts "outdoors," "active," and "rugged" because of exposure to a TV ad that shows the car driving over rugged terrain at different times of the year, or because Subaru sponsors ski, kayak, and mountain bike events, the impact in terms of Subaru's brand equity should be identical.

But these marketing communications activities must be integrated to deliver a consistent message and achieve the strategic positioning. The starting point in planning marketing communications is a *communication audit* that profiles all interactions customers in the target market may have with the company and all its products and services. For example, someone interested in purchasing a new laptop computer might talk to others, see television ads, read articles, look for information on the Internet, and look at laptops in a store.

To implement the right communications programs and allocate dollars efficiently, marketers need to assess which experiences and impressions will have the most influence at each stage of the buying process. Armed with these insights, they can judge marketing communications according to their ability to affect experiences and impressions, build customer loyalty and brand equity, and drive sales. For example, how well does a proposed ad campaign contribute to awareness or to creating, maintaining, or strengthening brand associations? Does a sponsorship improve consumers' brand judgments and feelings? Does a promotion encourage consumers to buy more of a product? At what price premium?

In building brand equity, marketers should be "media neutral" and evaluate *all* communication options on effectiveness (how well does it work?) and efficiency (how much does it cost?). Personal financial Web site Mint challenged market leader Intuit—and was eventually acquired by the company—on a marketing budget a fraction of what companies typically spend. A well-read blog, a popular Facebook page, and other social media—combined with extensive PR—helped attract the younger crowd the Mint brand was after.[9] Philips also took another tack in launching a new product.[10]

Philips *Carousel* When Dutch electronics leader Philips wanted to demonstrate the quality of the "world's first cinema proportion" TV, it chose to create *Carousel*, an interactive, long-form Internet film. In this Cannes Grand Prix award-winning effort, online viewers could control the story of a botched robbery while seeing the benefits of the new $3,999 home cinema TV. The film showed an epic "frozen moment" cops and robbers shootout sequence that included clowns, explosions, a decimated hospital, and lots of broken glass, bullet casings, and money. By clicking hot spots in the video, viewers could toggle between the new set's 21:9 display proportion and a conventional flat screen's 16:9, as well as activate the set's signature Ambilight backlighting. The success of the campaign led Phillips to launch a "Parallel Lines" campaign with five short films from famed director Ridley Scott's shop, promoting its whole range of home cinema TVs. 🔲

The runaway success of the interactive, long-form Internet film *Carousel* for its new Home Cinema TV model led Philips to launch an even more extensive follow-up campaign.

The Communications Process Models

Marketers should understand the fundamental elements of effective communications. Two models are useful: a macromodel and a micromodel.

MACROMODEL OF THE COMMUNICATIONS PROCESS △ Figure 17.1 shows a macromodel with nine key factors in effective communication. Two represent the major parties—*sender* and *receiver*. Two represent the major tools—*message* and *media*. Four represent major communication functions—*encoding, decoding, response,* and *feedback.* The last element in the system is *noise,* random and competing messages that may interfere with the intended communication.[11]

Senders must know what audiences they want to reach and what responses they want to get. They must encode their messages so the target audience can decode them. They must transmit the message through media that reach the target audience and develop feedback channels to monitor the responses. The more the sender's field of experience overlaps that of the receiver, the more effective the message is likely to be. Note that selective attention, distortion, and retention processes—concepts first introduced in Chapter 6—may be operating during communication.

MICROMODEL OF CONSUMER RESPONSES Micromodels of marketing communications concentrate on consumers' specific responses to communications. △ Figure 17.2 summarizes four classic *response hierarchy models.*

All these models assume the buyer passes through cognitive, affective, and behavioral stages, in that order. This "learn-feel-do" sequence is appropriate when the audience has high involvement with a product category perceived to have high differentiation, such as an automobile or house. An alternative sequence, "do-feel-learn," is relevant when the audience has high involvement but perceives little or no differentiation within the product category, such as an airline ticket or personal

|Fig. 17.1| △

Elements in the
Communications
Process

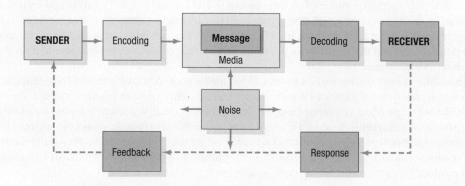

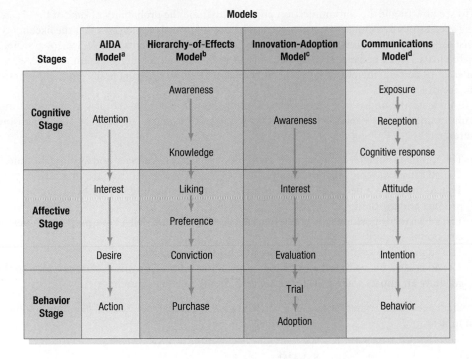

|Fig. 17.2| △

Response Hierarchy Models

Sources: [a]E. K. Strong, *The Psychology of Selling* (New York: McGraw-Hill, 1925), p. 9; [b]Robert J. Lavidge and Gary A. Steiner, "A Model for Predictive Measurements of Advertising Effectiveness," *Journal of Marketing* (October 1961), p. 61; [c]Everett M. Rogers, *Diffusion of Innovation* (New York: Free Press, 1962), pp. 79–86; [d]various sources.

computer. A third sequence, "learn-do-feel," is relevant when the audience has low involvement and perceives little differentiation, such as with salt or batteries. By choosing the right sequence, the marketer can do a better job of planning communications.[12]

Let's assume the buyer has high involvement with the product category and perceives high differentiation within it. We will illustrate the *hierarchy-of-effects model* (the second column of Figure 17.2) in the context of a marketing communications campaign for a small Iowa college named Pottsville:

- *Awareness.* If most of the target audience is unaware of the object, the communicator's task is to build awareness. Suppose Pottsville seeks applicants from Nebraska but has no name recognition there, although 30,000 Nebraska high school juniors and seniors could be interested in it. The college might set the objective of making 70 percent of these students aware of its name within one year.
- *Knowledge.* The target audience might have brand awareness but not know much more. Pottsville may want its target audience to know it is a private four-year college with excellent programs in English, foreign languages, and history. It needs to learn how many people in the target audience have little, some, or much knowledge about Pottsville. If knowledge is weak, Pottsville may select brand knowledge as its communications objective.
- *Liking.* Given target members know the brand, how do they feel about it? If the audience looks unfavorably on Pottsville College, the communicator needs to find out why. In the case of real problems, Pottsville will need to fix these and then communicate its renewed quality. Good public relations calls for "good deeds followed by good words."
- *Preference.* The target audience might like the product but not prefer it to others. The communicator must then try to build consumer preference by comparing quality, value, performance, and other features to those of likely competitors.
- *Conviction.* A target audience might prefer a particular product but not develop a conviction about buying it. The communicator's job is to build conviction and intent to apply among students interested in Pottsville College.
- *Purchase.* Finally, some members of the target audience might have conviction but not quite get around to making the purchase. The communicator must lead these consumers to take the final step, perhaps by offering the product at a low price, offering a premium, or letting them try it out. Pottsville might invite selected high school students to visit the campus and attend some classes, or it might offer partial scholarships to deserving students.

To see how fragile the communication process is, assume the probability of *each* of the six steps being successfully accomplished is 50 percent. The laws of probability suggest that the likelihood of *all* six steps occurring successfully, assuming they are independent events, is $.5 \times .5 \times .5 \times .5 \times .5 \times .5$, which equals 1.5625 percent. If the probability of each step's occurring were, on average, a more moderate 10 percent, then the joint probability of all six events occurring is .0001 percent—or only 1 chance in 1,000,000!

To increase the odds for a successful marketing communications campaign, marketers must attempt to increase the likelihood that *each* step occurs. For example, the ideal ad campaign would ensure that:

1. The right consumer is exposed to the right message at the right place and at the right time.
2. The ad causes the consumer to pay attention but does not distract from the intended message.
3. The ad properly reflects the consumer's level of understanding of and behaviors with the product and the brand.
4. The ad correctly positions the brand in terms of desirable and deliverable points-of-difference and points-of-parity.
5. The ad motivates consumers to consider purchase of the brand.
6. The ad creates strong brand associations with all these stored communications effects so they can have an impact when consumers are considering making a purchase.

The challenges in achieving success with communications necessitates careful planning, a topic we turn to next.

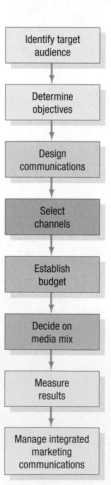

|Fig. 17.3| △

Steps in Developing Effective Communications

Developing Effective Communications

△ Figure 17.3 shows the eight steps in developing effective communications. We begin with the basics: identifying the target audience, determining the objectives, designing the communications, selecting the channels, and establishing the budget.

Identify the Target Audience

The process must start with a clear target audience in mind: potential buyers of the company's products, current users, deciders, or influencers, and individuals, groups, particular publics, or the general public. The target audience is a critical influence on the communicator's decisions about what to say, how, when, where, and to whom.

Though we can profile the target audience in terms of any of the market segments identified in Chapter 8, it's often useful to do so in terms of usage and loyalty. Is the target new to the category or a current user? Is the target loyal to the brand, loyal to a competitor, or someone who switches between brands? If a brand user, is he or she a heavy or light user? Communication strategy will differ depending on the answers. We can also conduct *image analysis* by profiling the target audience in terms of brand knowledge.

Determine the Communications Objectives

As we showed with Pottsville College, marketers can set communications objectives at any level of the hierarchy-of-effects model. John R. Rossiter and Larry Percy identify four possible objectives, as follows:[13]

1. *Category Need*—Establishing a product or service category as necessary to remove or satisfy a perceived discrepancy between a current motivational state and a desired motivational state. A new-to-the-world product such as electric cars will always begin with a communications objective of establishing category need.
2. *Brand Awareness*—Fostering the consumer's ability to recognize or recall the brand within the category, in sufficient detail to make a purchase. Recognition is easier to achieve than recall—consumers asked to think of a brand of frozen entrées are more likely to recognize Stouffer's distinctive orange packages than to recall the brand. Brand recall is important outside the store; brand recognition is important inside the store. Brand awareness provides a foundation for brand equity.

3. **Brand Attitude**—Helping consumers evaluate the brand's perceived ability to meet a currently relevant need. Relevant brand needs may be negatively oriented (problem removal, problem avoidance, incomplete satisfaction, normal depletion) or positively oriented (sensory gratification, intellectual stimulation, or social approval). Household cleaning products often use problem solution; food products, on the other hand, often use sensory-oriented ads emphasizing appetite appeal.

4. **Brand Purchase Intention**—Moving consumers to decide to purchase the brand or take purchase-related action. Promotional offers like coupons or two-for-one deals encourage consumers to make a mental commitment to buy. But many consumers do not have an expressed category need and may not be in the market when exposed to an ad, so they are unlikely to form buy intentions. In any given week, only about 20 percent of adults may be planning to buy detergent, only 2 percent to buy a carpet cleaner, and only 0.25 percent to buy a car.

The most effective communications can achieve multiple objectives. To promote its Smart Grid technology program, GE pushed a number of buttons.[14]

GE Smart Grid   The vision of GE's Smart Grid program is to fundamentally overhaul the United States' power grid, making it more efficient and sustainable and able also to deliver renewable-source energy such as wind and solar. An integrated campaign of print, TV, and online ads and an online augmented-reality demo was designed to increase understanding and support of the Smart Grid and GE's leadership in solving technological problems. GE and its agency partner BBDO chose to employ engaging creative and familiar cultural references to address the technical issues involved. In its 2009 Super Bowl launch TV spot, the famous scarecrow character from *The Wizard of Oz* was shown bouncing along the top of a transmission tower singing, "If I Only Had a Brain." A narrator voiced over the key communication message, "Smart Grid makes the way we distribute electricity more efficient simply by making it more intelligent." One online ad used a flock of birds on electrical wires chirping and flapping their wings in synchronized rhythm to Rossini's "Barber of Seville." Another showed power lines becoming banjo strings for electrical pylons to play "O Susannah." After drawing the audience in, the ads lay out the basic intent of the Smart Grid with links to more information. The augmented-reality GE microsite PlugIntoTheSmartGrid.com allowed users to create a digital hologram of Smart Grid technology using computer peripherals and 3D graphics. ▬

OUR SMART GRID TECHNOLOGY OFFERS A MORE

EFFICIENT WAY TO DISTRIBUTE ELECTRICITY

WHILE INCORPORATING RENEWABLE

ENERGY SOURCES. BEST OF ALL,

IT'S STARTING TO

COME ONLINE

NOW.

ecomagination.com

ge
imagination at work

GE's Smart Grid campaign has accomplished several different objectives for the GE brand, including strengthening the company's reputation as innovative.

Design the Communications

Formulating the communications to achieve the desired response requires solving three problems: what to say (message strategy), how to say it (creative strategy), and who should say it (message source).

MESSAGE STRATEGY In determining message strategy, management searches for appeals, themes, or ideas that will tie in to the brand positioning and help establish points-of-parity or points-of-difference. Some of these may be related directly to product or service performance (the quality, economy, or value of the brand), whereas others may relate to more extrinsic considerations (the brand as being contemporary, popular, or traditional).

Researcher John C. Maloney felt buyers expected one of four types of reward from a product: rational, sensory, social, or ego satisfaction.[15] Buyers might visualize these rewards from results-of-use experience, product-in-use experience, or incidental-to-use experience. Crossing the four types of rewards with the three types of experience generates 12 types of messages. For example, the appeal "gets clothes cleaner" is a rational-reward promise following results-of-use experience. The phrase "real beer taste in a great light beer" is a sensory-reward promise connected with product-in-use experience.

CREATIVE STRATEGY Communications effectiveness depends on how a message is being expressed, as well as on its content. If a communication is ineffective, it may mean the wrong message was used, or the right one was poorly expressed. *Creative strategies* are the way marketers translate their messages into a specific communication. We can broadly classify them as either **informational** or **transformational** appeals.[16]

Informational Appeals An *informational appeal* elaborates on product or service attributes or benefits. Examples in advertising are problem solution ads (Excedrin stops the toughest headache pain), product demonstration ads (Thompson Water Seal can withstand intense rain, snow, and heat), product comparison ads (DIRECTV offers better HD options than cable or other satellite operators), and testimonials from unknown or celebrity endorsers (NBA phenomenon LeBron James pitching Nike, Sprite, and McDonald's). Informational appeals assume strictly rational processing of the communication on the consumer's part. Logic and reason rule.

Carl Hovland's research at Yale has shed much light on informational appeals and their relationship to such issues as conclusion drawing, one-sided versus two-sided arguments, and order of argument presentation. Some early experiments supported stating conclusions for the audience. Subsequent research, however, indicates that the best ads ask questions and allow readers and viewers to form their own conclusions.[17] If Honda had hammered away that the Element was for young people, this strong definition might have blocked older drivers from buying it. Some stimulus ambiguity can lead to a broader market definition and more spontaneous purchases.

You might expect one-sided presentations that praise a product to be more effective than two-sided arguments that also mention shortcomings. Yet two-sided messages may be more appropriate, especially when negative associations must be overcome.[18] Two-sided messages are more effective with more educated audiences and those who are initially opposed.[19] Chapter 6 described how Domino's took the drastic step of admitting its pizza's taste problems to try to change the minds of consumers with negative perceptions.

Finally, the order in which arguments are presented is important.[20] In a one-sided message, presenting the strongest argument first arouses attention and interest, important in media where the audience often does not attend to the whole message. With a captive audience, a climactic presentation might be more effective. For a two-sided message, if the audience is initially opposed, the communicator might start with the other side's argument and conclude with his or her strongest argument.[21]

Transformational Appeals A *transformational appeal* elaborates on a nonproduct-related benefit or image. It might depict what kind of person uses a brand (VW advertised to active, youthful people with its famed "Drivers Wanted" campaign) or what kind of experience results from use (Pringles advertised "Once You Pop, the

Pringles capitalized on the popping sound that occurs when its package is opened to develop a highly successful ad campaign.

Fun Don't Stop" for years). Transformational appeals often attempt to stir up emotions that will motivate purchase.

Communicators use negative appeals such as fear, guilt, and shame to get people to do things (brush their teeth, have an annual health checkup) or stop doing things (smoking, abusing alcohol, overeating). Fear appeals work best when they are not too strong, when source credibility is high, and when the communication promises, in a believable and efficient way, to relieve the fear it arouses. Messages are most persuasive when moderately discrepant with audience beliefs. Stating only what the audience already believes at best just reinforces beliefs, and if the messages are too discrepant, audiences will counterargue and disbelieve them.[22]

Communicators also use positive emotional appeals such as humor, love, pride, and joy. Motivational or "borrowed interest" devices—such as the presence of cute babies, frisky puppies, popular music, or provocative sex appeals—are often employed to attract attention and raise involvement with an ad. These techniques are thought necessary in the tough new media environment characterized by low-involvement consumer processing and competing ad and programming clutter. Attention-getting tactics are often *too* effective. They may also detract from comprehension, wear out their welcome fast, and overshadow the product.[23] Thus, one challenge is figuring out how to "break through the clutter" *and* deliver the intended message.

Even highly entertaining and creative means of expression must still keep the appropriate consumer perspective. Toyota was sued in Los Angeles for a promotional campaign designed to create buzz for its youth-targeted Toyota Matrix. The online effort featured a series of e-mails to customers from a fictitious drunken British soccer hooligan, Sebastian Bowler. In his e-mails, he announced that he knew the recipient and was coming to stay with his pit bull, Trigger, to "avoid the cops." In her suit, the plaintiff said she was so convinced that "a disturbed and aggressive" stranger was headed to her house that she slept with a machete next to her in bed.[24]

The magic of advertising is to bring concepts on a piece of paper to life in the minds of the consumer target. In a print ad, the communicator must decide on headline, copy, illustration, and color.[25] For a radio message, the communicator must choose words, voice qualities, and vocalizations. The sound of an announcer promoting a used automobile should be different from one promoting a new Cadillac. If the message is to be carried on television or in person, all these elements plus body language must be planned. For the message to go online, layout, fonts, graphics, and other visual and verbal information must be laid out.

MESSAGE SOURCE Messages delivered by attractive or popular sources can achieve higher attention and recall, which is why advertisers often use celebrities as spokespeople.

Celebrities are likely to be effective when they are credible or personify a key product attribute. Statesman-like Dennis Haysbert for State Farm insurance, rugged Brett Favre for Wrangler jeans, and one-time television sweetheart Valerie Bertinelli for Jenny Craig weight loss program have all been praised by consumers as good fits. Celine Dion, however, failed to add glamour—or sales—to Chrysler, and even though she was locked into a three-year, $14 million deal, she was let go. Ozzy Osbourne would seem an odd choice to advertise "I Can't Believe It's Not Butter" given his seemingly perpetual confusion.

What *is* important is the spokesperson's credibility. The three most often identified sources of credibility are expertise, trustworthiness, and likability.[26] *Expertise* is the specialized knowledge the communicator possesses to back the claim. *Trustworthiness* describes how objective and honest the source is perceived to be. Friends are trusted more than strangers or salespeople, and people who are not paid to endorse a product are viewed as more trustworthy than people who are paid.[27] *Likability* describes the source's attractiveness. Qualities such as candor, humor, and naturalness make a source more likable.

The most highly credible source would score high on all three dimensions—expertise, trustworthiness, and likability. Pharmaceutical companies want doctors to testify about product benefits because doctors have high credibility. Charles Schwab became the centerpiece of ads for his $4 billion-plus discount brokerage firm via the "Talk to Chuck" corporate advertising campaign. Another credible pitchman was boxer George Foreman and his multimillion-selling Lean, Mean, Fat-Reducing Grilling Machine. "Marketing Insight: Celebrity Endorsements as a Strategy" focuses on the use of testimonials.

If a person has a positive attitude toward a source and a message, or a negative attitude toward both, a state of *congruity* is said to exist. But what happens if a consumer hears a likable celebrity praise a brand she dislikes? Charles Osgood and Percy Tannenbaum believe *attitude change will take*

Marketing Insight

Celebrity Endorsements as a Strategy

A well-chosen celebrity can draw attention to a product or brand—as Priceline found when it picked *Star Trek* icon William Shatner to star in campy ads to reinforce its low-price image. The quirky campaigns have run over a decade, and Shatner's decision to receive compensation in the form of stock options reportedly allowed him to net over $600 million for his work. The right celebrity can also lend his or her image to a brand. To reinforce its high status and prestige image, American Express has used movie legends Robert De Niro and Martin Scorsese in ads.

The choice of celebrity is critical. The person should have high recognition, high positive affect, and high appropriateness or "fit" with the product. Paris Hilton, Howard Stern, and Donald Trump have high recognition but negative affect among many groups. Johnny Depp has high recognition and high positive affect but might not seem relevant, for example, for advertising a new financial service. Tom Hanks and Oprah Winfrey could successfully advertise a large number of products because they have extremely high ratings for familiarity and likability (known as the Q factor in the entertainment industry).

Celebrities can play a more fundamentally strategic role for their brands, not only endorsing a product but also helping to design, position, and sell merchandise and services. Believing elite athletes have unique insights into sports performance, Nike often brings its athletic endorsers in on product design. Tiger Woods, Paul Casey, and Stewart Cink have helped to design, prototype, and test new golf clubs and balls at Nike Golf's Research & Development facility dubbed "The Oven."

Some celebrities lend their talents to brands without directly using their fame. A host of movie and TV stars—including Kiefer Sutherland (Bank of America), Alec Baldwin (Blockbuster), Patrick Dempsey (State Farm), Lauren Graham (Special K), and Regina King (Always)—do uncredited commercial voice-overs. Although advertisers assume some viewers will recognize the voices, the basic rationale for uncredited celebrity voice-overs is the incomparable voice talents and skills they bring from their acting careers.

Using celebrities poses certain risks. The celebrity might hold out for a larger fee at contract renewal or withdraw. And just like movies and album releases, celebrity campaigns can be expensive flops. The celebrity might lose popularity or, even worse, get caught in a scandal or embarrassing situation, as did Tiger Woods in a heavily publicized 2009 episode. Besides carefully checking endorsers' backgrounds, some marketers are choosing to use more than one to lessen their brand's exposure to any single person's flaws.

Another solution is for marketers to create their own brand celebrities. Dos Equis beer, imported from Mexico, grew U.S. sales by over 20 percent during the recent recession by riding on the popularity of its "Most Interesting Man in the World" ad campaign. Suave, debonair, with an exotic accent and a silver beard, the character has hundreds of thousands of Facebook friends despite being, of course, completely fictitious. Videos of his exploits log millions of views on YouTube. He even served as the basis of *The Most Interesting Show in the World* tour of the brand's 14 biggest urban markets, which featured one-of-a-kind circus-type performers such as a flaming bowling-ball-juggling stunt comedian, a robot-inspired break dancer, and a contortionist who shoots arrows with her feet. Through a combination of advertising and media coverage, almost 100 million media impressions were achieved on the tour.

Sources: Scott Huver, "Here's the Pitch!," *TV Guide*, May 23, 2010; Linda Massarella, "Shatner's Singing a Happy Tune," *Toronto Sun*, May 2, 2010; "Nike Golf Celebrates Achievements and Successes of Past Year," www.worldgolf.com, January 2, 2009; Piet Levy, "Keeping It Interesting," *Marketing News*, October 30, 2009, p. 8; Keith Naughton, "The Soft Sell," *Newsweek*, February 2, 2004, pp. 46–47; Irving Rein, Philip Kotler, and Martin Scoller, *The Making and Marketing of Professionals into Celebrities* (Chicago: NTC Business Books, 1997).

place in the direction of increasing the amount of congruity between the two evaluations.[28] The consumer will end up respecting the celebrity somewhat less or the brand somewhat more. If she encounters the same celebrity praising other disliked brands, she will eventually develop a negative view of the celebrity and maintain negative attitudes toward the brands. The **principle of congruity** implies that communicators can use their good image to reduce some negative feelings toward a brand but in the process might lose some esteem with the audience.

Select the Communications Channels

Selecting an efficient means to carry the message becomes more difficult as channels of communication become more fragmented and cluttered. Communications channels may be personal and nonpersonal. Within each are many subchannels.

PERSONAL COMMUNICATIONS CHANNELS **Personal communications channels** let two or more persons communicate face-to-face or person-to-audience through a phone, surface mail, or e-mail. They derive their effectiveness from individualized presentation and feedback and include direct and interactive marketing, word-of-mouth marketing, and personal selling.

We can draw a further distinction between advocate, expert, and social communications channels. *Advocate channels* consist of company salespeople contacting buyers in the target market. *Expert channels* consist of independent experts making statements to target buyers. *Social channels* consist of neighbors, friends, family members, and associates talking to target buyers.

A study by Burson-Marsteller and Roper Starch Worldwide found that one influential person's word of mouth tends to affect the buying attitudes of two other people, on average. That circle of influence, however, jumps to eight online. Word about good companies travels fast; word about bad companies travels even faster. Reaching the right people is key.

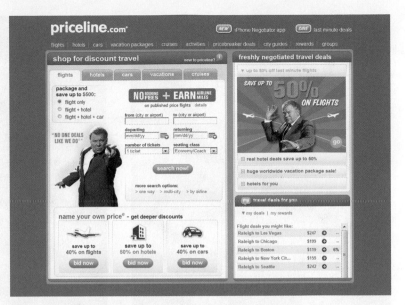

William Shatner has become the quirky but beloved spokesperson for Priceline in its advertising.

More advertisers now seek greater *earned media*—unsolicited professional commentary, personal blog entries, social network discussion—as a result of their paid media marketing efforts. Kimberly-Clark ran a 30-second TV spot prior to the Academy Awards in March 2010 for its Poise brand, which featured Whoopi Goldberg portraying famous women in history who may have suffered from incontinence. The goal was to get people talking, and talk they did! A social media avalanche followed, culminating in a *Saturday Night Live* spoof, which eventually added up to 200 million PR impressions in total.[29]

Personal influence carries especially great weight (1) when products are expensive, risky, or purchased infrequently, and (2) when products suggest something about the user's status or taste. People often ask others to recommend a doctor, plumber, hotel, lawyer, accountant, architect, insurance agent, interior decorator, or financial consultant. If we have confidence in the recommendation, we normally act on the referral. Service providers clearly have a strong interest in building referral sources.

Even business-to-business marketers can benefit from strong word of mouth. Here is how John Deere created anticipation and excitement when introducing its 764 High Speed Dozer, the category's first launch in 25 years.[30]

 John Deere Leading up to the unveiling of its high-speed dozer at the industry's largest CONEXPO trade show, John Deere created an extensive PR campaign. First, e-mail announcements were sent to all trade show registrants with images of the dozer covered in a tarp and teasing headlines, such as "Just a Few Years Ahead of the Competition" and "The Shape of Things to Come." Editors received an invitation to attend a closed-door press conference where they were given a VIP pass and admittance to a special viewing area at the CONEXPO show. Finally, editors were told they could also register for a special, invitation-only press conference with John Deere senior executives, including its CEO. Approximately 2,000 people attended the trade show for a rock-star unveiling of the dozer, with about 80 editors present. Customers at the event who declared their desire for the machine helped Deere staff secure more leads. Press reaction was also extremely positive, including several trade magazine cover stories on the dozer and three segments on CNBC. The integrated effort on behalf of John Deere, which included print ads in trade publications, took home the Grand CEBA Award in American Business Media's annual awards competition. ▭

NONPERSONAL (MASS) COMMUNICATIONS CHANNELS Nonpersonal channels are communications directed to more than one person and include advertising, sales promotions, events and experiences, and public relations. Much recent growth has taken place through events and experiences. Events marketers who once favored sports events are now using other venues such as art museums, zoos, and ice shows to entertain clients and employees. AT&T and IBM sponsor

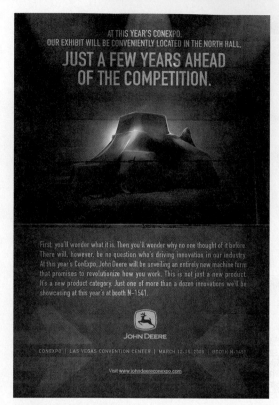

Through its print ad and trade show efforts, John Deere created buzz and much word of mouth in anticipation of the launch of its new high-speed dozer.

symphony performances and art exhibits, Visa is an active sponsor of the Olympics, and Harley-Davidson sponsors annual motorcycle rallies.

Companies are searching for better ways to quantify the benefits of sponsorship and demanding greater accountability from event owners and organizers. They are also creating events designed to surprise the public and create a buzz. Many efforts amount to guerrilla marketing tactics. As part of a $100 million global advertising and marketing campaign for its line of televisions, LG Electronics developed an elaborate promotion for a fake new TV series, *Scarlet*, including a heavily promoted Hollywood world premiere. Inside, attendees found a new series of actual LG TVs with a red back panel. Teaser TV and online commercials and extensive PR backed the effort.[31]

Events can create attention, although whether they have a lasting effect on brand awareness, knowledge, or preference will vary considerably depending on the quality of the product, the event itself, and its execution.

INTEGRATION OF COMMUNICATIONS CHANNELS Although personal communication is often more effective than mass communication, mass media might be the major means of stimulating personal communication. Mass communications affect personal attitudes and behavior through a two-step process. Ideas often flow from radio, television, and print to opinion leaders, and from these to less media-involved population groups.

This two-step flow has several implications. First, the influence of mass media on public opinion is not as direct, powerful, and automatic as marketers have supposed. It is mediated by opinion leaders, people whose opinions others seek or who carry their opinions to others. Second, the two-step flow challenges the notion that consumption styles are primarily influenced by a "trickle-down" or "trickle-up" effect from mass media. People interact primarily within their own social groups and acquire ideas from opinion leaders in their groups. Third, two-step communication suggests that mass communicators should direct messages specifically to opinion leaders and let them carry the message to others.

Establish the Total Marketing Communications Budget

One of the most difficult marketing decisions is determining how much to spend on marketing communications. John Wanamaker, the department store magnate, once said, "I know that half of my advertising is wasted, but I don't know which half."

Industries and companies vary considerably in how much they spend on marketing communications. Expenditures might be 40 percent to 45 percent of sales in the cosmetics industry, but only

5 percent to 10 percent in the industrial-equipment industry. Within a given industry, there are low- and high-spending companies.

How do companies decide on the communication budget? We will describe four common methods: the affordable method, the percentage-of-sales method, the competitive-parity method, and the objective-and-task method.

AFFORDABLE METHOD Some companies set the communication budget at what they think the company can afford. The affordable method completely ignores the role of promotion as an investment and the immediate impact of promotion on sales volume. It leads to an uncertain annual budget, which makes long-range planning difficult.

PERCENTAGE-OF-SALES METHOD Some companies set communication expenditures at a specified percentage of current or anticipated sales or of the sales price. Automobile companies typically budget a fixed percentage based on the planned car price. Oil companies appropriate a fraction of a cent for each gallon of gasoline sold under their own label.

Supporters of the percentage-of-sales method see a number of advantages. First, communication expenditures will vary with what the company can afford. This satisfies financial managers, who believe expenses should be closely related to the movement of corporate sales over the business cycle. Second, it encourages management to think of the relationship among communication cost, selling price, and profit per unit. Third, it encourages stability when competing firms spend approximately the same percentage of their sales on communications.

In spite of these advantages, the percentage-of-sales method has little to justify it. It views sales as the determiner of communications rather than as the result. It leads to a budget set by the availability of funds rather than by market opportunities. It discourages experimentation with countercyclical communication or aggressive spending. Dependence on year-to-year sales fluctuations interferes with long-range planning. There is no logical basis for choosing the specific percentage, except what has been done in the past or what competitors are doing. Finally, it does not encourage building the communication budget by determining what each product and territory deserves.

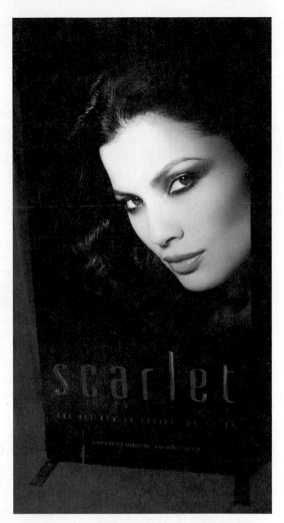

To promote its new line of televisions, LG pretended to launch a fake new TV series, even holding a heavily promoted premiere.

COMPETITIVE-PARITY METHOD Some companies set their communication budget to achieve share-of-voice parity with competitors. There are two supporting arguments: that competitors' expenditures represent the collective wisdom of the industry, and that maintaining competitive parity prevents communication wars. Neither argument is valid. There are no grounds for believing competitors know better. Company reputations, resources, opportunities, and objectives differ so much that communication budgets are hardly a guide. And there is no evidence that budgets based on competitive parity discourage communication wars.

OBJECTIVE-AND-TASK METHOD The objective-and-task method calls upon marketers to develop communication budgets by defining specific objectives, determining the tasks that must be performed to achieve these objectives, and estimating the costs of performing them. The sum of these costs is the proposed communication budget.

Suppose Dr. Pepper Snapple Group wants to introduce a new natural energy drink, called Sunburst, for the casual athlete.[32] Its objectives might be as follows:

1. ***Establish the market share goal.*** The company estimates 50 million potential users and sets a target of attracting 8 percent of the market—that is, 4 million users.
2. ***Determine the percentage of the market that should be reached by advertising.*** The advertiser hopes to reach 80 percent (40 million prospects) with its advertising message.
3. ***Determine the percentage of aware prospects that should be persuaded to try the brand.*** The advertiser would be pleased if 25 percent of aware prospects (10 million) tried Sunburst. It estimates that 40 percent of all triers, or 4 million people, will become loyal users. This is the market goal.

4. ***Determine the number of advertising impressions per 1 percent trial rate.*** The advertiser estimates that 40 advertising impressions (exposures) for every 1 percent of the population will bring about a 25 percent trial rate.

5. ***Determine the number of gross rating points that would have to be purchased.*** A gross rating point is one exposure to 1 percent of the target population. Because the company wants to achieve 40 exposures to 80 percent of the population, it will want to buy 3,200 gross rating points.

6. ***Determine the necessary advertising budget on the basis of the average cost of buying a gross rating point.*** To expose 1 percent of the target population to one impression costs an average of $3,277. Therefore, 3,200 gross rating points will cost $10,486,400 (= $3,277 × 3,200) in the introductory year.

The objective-and-task method has the advantage of requiring management to spell out its assumptions about the relationship among dollars spent, exposure levels, trial rates, and regular usage.

COMMUNICATION BUDGET TRADE-OFFS A major question is how much weight marketing communications should receive in relationship to alternatives such as product improvement, lower prices, or better service. The answer depends on where the company's products are in their life cycles, whether they are commodities or highly differentiable products, whether they are routinely needed or must be "sold," and other considerations. Marketing communications budgets tend to be higher when there is low channel support, much change in the marketing program over time, many hard-to-reach customers, more complex customer decision making, differentiated products and nonhomogeneous customer needs, and frequent product purchases in small quantities.[33]

In theory, marketers should establish the total communications budget so the marginal profit from the last communication dollar just equals the marginal profit from the last dollar in the best noncommunication use. Implementing this principle, however, is not easy.

Deciding on the Marketing Communications Mix

Companies must allocate the marketing communications budget over the eight major modes of communication—advertising, sales promotion, public relations and publicity, events and experiences, direct marketing, interactive marketing, word-of-mouth marketing, and the sales force. Within the same industry, companies can differ considerably in their media and channel choices. Avon concentrates its promotional funds on personal selling, whereas Revlon spends heavily on advertising. Electrolux spent heavily on a door-to-door sales force for years, whereas Hoover has relied more on advertising. ▭ Table 17.2 breaks down spending on some major forms of communication.

Companies are always searching for ways to gain efficiency by substituting one communications tool for others. Many are replacing some field sales activity with ads, direct mail, and telemarketing. One auto dealer dismissed his five salespeople and cut prices, and sales exploded. The substitutability among communications tools explains why marketing functions need to be coordinated.

Characteristics of the Marketing Communications Mix

Each communication tool has its own unique characteristics and costs. We briefly review them here and discuss them in more detail in Chapters 18 and 19.

ADVERTISING Advertising reaches geographically dispersed buyers. It can build up a long-term image for a product (Coca-Cola ads) or trigger quick sales (a Macy's ad for a weekend sale). Certain forms of advertising such as TV can require a large budget, whereas other forms such as newspaper do not. The mere presence of advertising might have an effect on sales: Consumers might believe a heavily advertised brand must offer "good value."[34] Because of the many forms and uses of advertising, it's difficult to make generalizations about it.[35] Yet a few observations are worthwhile:

1. *Pervasiveness*—Advertising permits the seller to repeat a message many times. It also allows the buyer to receive and compare the messages of various competitors. Large-scale advertising says something positive about the seller's size, power, and success.

TABLE 17.2 — Advertising and Digital Marketing Communications Forecast for 2010		
Global Advertising Spend Projections	**2009–2010 % Change**	**2010 $ (billions)**
Cinema	2.0%	2.23
Internet	12.0%	60.35
Magazines	−4.0%	43.10
Newspapers	−4.0%	97.85
Outdoor	2.0%	29.61
Radio	−2.0%	33.10
Television	2.0%	174.94
Total	0.9%	441.19
Source: ZenithOptimedia, December 2009.		
Digital Marketing Communications		
Display Advertising	7%	8.40
Email Marketing	8%	1.36
Mobile Marketing	44%	0.56
Search Marketing	15%	17.80
Social Media	31%	0.94
Total	13%	29.01
Source: Data from Figure 4 in *US Interactive Marketing Forecast 2009 to 2014*. Forester Reseach, Inc. July, 2009.		

Source: Table from Piet Levy, "The Oscar-Contending Drama: Finding the Right Marketing Mix," *Marketing News*, January 30, 2009, p. 15.

2. *Amplified expressiveness*—Advertising provides opportunities for dramatizing the company and its brands and products through the artful use of print, sound, and color.
3. *Control*—The advertiser can choose the aspects of the brand and product on which to focus communications.

SALES PROMOTION Companies use sales promotion tools—coupons, contests, premiums, and the like—to draw a stronger and quicker buyer response, including short-run effects such as highlighting product offers and boosting sagging sales. Sales promotion tools offer three distinctive benefits:

1. *Ability to be attention-getting*—They draw attention and may lead the consumer to the product.
2. *Incentive*—They incorporate some concession, inducement, or contribution that gives value to the consumer.
3. *Invitation*—They include a distinct invitation to engage in the transaction now.

PUBLIC RELATIONS AND PUBLICITY Marketers tend to underuse public relations, yet a well-thought-out program coordinated with the other communications-mix elements can be extremely effective, especially if a company needs to challenge consumers' misconceptions. The appeal of public relations and publicity is based on three distinctive qualities:

1. *High credibility*—News stories and features are more authentic and credible to readers than ads.
2. *Ability to reach hard-to-find buyers*—Public relations can reach prospects who prefer to avoid mass media and targeted promotions.
3. *Dramatization*—Public relations can tell the story behind a company, brand, or product.

EVENTS AND EXPERIENCES There are many advantages to events and experiences as long as they have the following characteristics:

1. *Relevant*—A well-chosen event or experience can be seen as highly relevant because the consumer is often personally invested in the outcome.
2. *Engaging*—Given their live, real-time quality, events and experiences are more actively engaging for consumers.
3. *Implicit*—Events are typically an indirect "soft sell."

DIRECT AND INTERACTIVE MARKETING Direct and interactive marketing messages take many forms—over the phone, online, or in person. They share three characteristics:

1. *Customized*—The message can be prepared to appeal to the addressed individual.
2. *Up-to-date*—A message can be prepared very quickly.
3. *Interactive*—The message can be changed depending on the person's response.

WORD-OF-MOUTH MARKETING Word of mouth also takes many forms both online or offline. Three noteworthy characteristics are:

1. *Influential*—Because people trust others they know and respect, word of mouth can be highly influential.
2. *Personal*—Word of mouth can be a very intimate dialogue that reflects personal facts, opinions, and experiences.
3. *Timely*—Word of mouth occurs when people want it to and are most interested, and it often follows noteworthy or meaningful events or experiences.

PERSONAL SELLING Personal selling is the most effective tool at later stages of the buying process, particularly in building up buyer preference, conviction, and action. Personal selling has three notable qualities:

1. *Personal interaction*—Personal selling creates an immediate and interactive episode between two or more persons. Each is able to observe the other's reactions.
2. *Cultivation*—Personal selling also permits all kinds of relationships to spring up, ranging from a matter-of-fact selling relationship to a deep personal friendship.
3. *Response*—The buyer is often given personal choices and encouraged to directly respond.

Factors in Setting the Marketing Communications Mix

Companies must consider several factors in developing their communications mix: type of product market, consumer readiness to make a purchase, and stage in the product life cycle.

TYPE OF PRODUCT MARKET Communications-mix allocations vary between consumer and business markets. Consumer marketers tend to spend comparatively more on sales promotion and advertising; business marketers tend to spend comparatively more on personal selling. In general, personal selling is used more with complex, expensive, and risky goods and in markets with fewer and larger sellers (hence, business markets).

Although marketers rely more on sales calls in business markets, advertising still plays a significant role:

- Advertising can provide an introduction to the company and its products.
- If the product has new features, advertising can explain them.
- Reminder advertising is more economical than sales calls.
- Advertisements offering brochures and carrying the company's phone number or Web address are an effective way to generate leads for sales representatives.
- Sales representatives can use copies of the company's ads to legitimize their company and products.
- Advertising can remind customers how to use the product and reassure them about their purchase.

Advertising combined with personal selling can increase sales over personal selling alone. Corporate advertising can improve a company's reputation and improve the sales force's chances of getting a favorable first hearing and early adoption of the product.[36] IBM's corporate marketing effort is a notable success in recent years.[37]

IBM Smarter Planet Working with long-time ad agency Ogilvy & Mather, IBM launched "Smarter Planet" in 2008 as a business strategy and multiplatform communications program to promote the way in which IBM technology and expertise helps industry, government, transportation, energy, education, health care, cities, and other businesses work better and "smarter." The point was that technology has evolved so far that many of the world's problems are now fixable. Emphasizing the United States, the United Kingdom, Germany, and China, the campaign began internally to inform and inspire IBM employees about how they could contribute to building a "Smarter Planet." An unconventional "Mandate for Change" series offered long-form, content-rich print ads in the business world's top newspapers outlining how IBM would address 25 key issues to make the world work better. Targeted TV ads and detailed online interactive ads provided more support and substance. A "Smarter Cities" tour hosted major events at which IBM and other experts discussed and debated challenges all cities face: transportation, energy, health care, education, and public safety. The success of the overall "Smarter Planet" campaign was evident in the significant improvements in IBM's image as a company "making the world better" and "known for solving its clients' most challenging problems." Despite a recession, significant increases occurred in new business opportunities and the number of companies interested in doing business with IBM. ▢

IBM's "Smarter Planet" corporate brand campaign, which has met with great success, sometimes breaks the rules, as with this text-heavy print ad.

On the flip side, personal selling can also make a strong contribution in consumer-goods marketing. Some consumer marketers use the sales force mainly to collect weekly orders from dealers and to see that sufficient stock is on the shelf. Yet an effectively trained company sales force can make four important contributions:

1. **Increase stock position.** Sales reps can persuade dealers to take more stock and devote more shelf space to the company's brand.
2. **Build enthusiasm.** Sales reps can build dealer enthusiasm by dramatizing planned advertising and communications support for the company's brand.
3. **Conduct missionary selling.** Sales reps can sign up more dealers.
4. **Manage key accounts.** Sales reps can take responsibility for growing business with the most important accounts.

BUYER-READINESS STAGE Communication tools vary in cost-effectiveness at different stages of buyer readiness. △ Figure 17.4 shows the relative cost-effectiveness of three communication tools. Advertising and publicity play the most important roles in the awareness-building stage. Customer comprehension is primarily affected by advertising and personal selling. Customer conviction is influenced mostly by personal selling. Closing the sale is influenced mostly by personal selling and sales promotion. Reordering is also affected mostly by personal selling and sales promotion, and somewhat by reminder advertising.

PRODUCT LIFE-CYCLE STAGE In the introduction stage of the product life cycle, advertising, events and experiences, and publicity have the highest cost-effectiveness, followed by personal selling to gain distribution coverage and sales promotion and direct marketing to induce trial. In the growth stage, demand has its own momentum through word of mouth and interactive marketing. Advertising, events and experiences, and personal selling all become more important in the maturity stage. In the decline stage, sales promotion continues strong, other communication tools are reduced, and salespeople give the product only minimal attention.

DESIGNING AND MANAGING INTEGRATED MARKE

|Fig. 17.4| ▲

Cost-Effectiveness of
Three Different
Communication Tools
at Different Buyer-
Readiness Stages

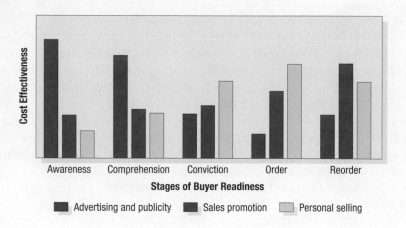

Measuring Communication Results

Senior managers want to know the *outcomes* and *revenues* resulting from their communications investments. Too often, however, their communications directors supply only *inputs* and *expenses:* press clipping counts, numbers of ads placed, media costs. In fairness, communications directors try to translate
inputs into intermediate outputs such as reach and frequency (the percentage of target market exposed
to a communication and the number of exposures), recall and recognition scores, persuasion changes,
and cost-per-thousand calculations. Ultimately, behavior-change measures capture the real payoff.

After implementing the communications plan, the communications director must measure its
impact. Members of the target audience are asked whether they recognize or recall the message,
how many times they saw it, what points they recall, how they felt about the message, and what are
their previous and current attitudes toward the product and the company. The communicator
should also collect behavioral measures of audience response, such as how many people bought the
product, liked it, and talked to others about it.

▲ Figure 17.5 provides an example of good feedback measurement. We find 80 percent of the
consumers in the total market are aware of brand A, 60 percent have tried it, and only 20 percent
who tried it are satisfied. This indicates that the communications program is effective in creating
awareness, but the product fails to meet consumer expectations. In contrast, 40 percent of the
consumers in the total market are aware of brand B and only 30 percent have tried it, but 80 percent
of them are satisfied. In this case, the communications program needs to be strengthened to take
advantage of the brand's potential power.

Managing the Integrated Marketing
Communications Process

Many companies still rely on only one or two communication tools. This practice persists in spite
of the fragmenting of mass markets into a multitude of minimarkets, each requiring its own approach; the proliferation of new types of media; and the growing sophistication of consumers. The

|Fig. 17.5| ▲

Current Consumer
States for Two Brands

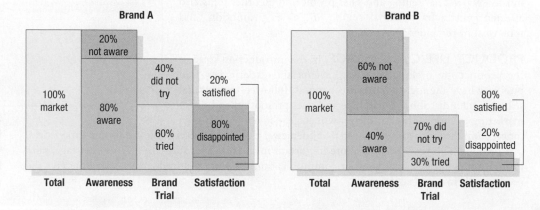

wide range of communication tools, messages, and audiences makes it imperative that companies move toward integrated marketing communications. Companies must adopt a "360-degree view" of consumers to fully understand all the different ways that communications can affect consumer behavior in their daily lives.[38]

The American Marketing Association defines **integrated marketing communications (IMC)** as "a planning process designed to assure that all brand contacts received by a customer or prospect for a product, service, or organization are relevant to that person and consistent over time." This planning process evaluates the strategic roles of a variety of communications disciplines—for example, general advertising, direct response, sales promotion, and public relations—and skillfully combines these disciplines to provide clarity, consistency, and maximum impact through the seamless integration of messages.

Media companies and ad agencies are expanding their capabilities to offer multiplatform deals for marketers. These expanded capabilities make it easier for marketers to assemble various media properties—as well as related marketing services—in an integrated communication program. Table 17.3 displays the different lines of businesses for marketing and advertising services giant WPP.

Coordinating Media

Media coordination can occur across and within media types, but marketers should combine personal and nonpersonal communications channels through *multiple-vehicle, multiple-stage campaigns* to achieve maximum impact and increase message reach and impact.

Promotions can be more effective when combined with advertising, for example.[39] The awareness and attitudes created by advertising campaigns can increase the success of more direct sales

TABLE 17.3 ▭	WPP's Lines of Businesses
Advertising	
Global, national and specialist advertising services from a range of top international and specialist agencies, amongst them Grey, JWT, Ogilvy & Mather, United Network and Y&R	
Media Investment Management	
Above- and below-the-line media planning and buying and specialist sponsorship and branded entertainment services from GroupM companies MediaCom, Mediaedge:cia, Mindshare, Maxus and others	
Consumer Insight	
WPP's Kantar companies, including TNS, Millward Brown, The Futures Company and many other specialists in brand, consumer, media and marketplace insight, work with clients to generate and apply great insights	
Public Relations & Public Affairs	
Corporate, consumer, financial and brand-building services from PR and lobbying firms Burson-Marsteller, Cohn & Wolfe, Hill & Knowlton, Ogilvy Public Relations Worldwide and others	
Branding & Identity	
Consumer, corporate and employee branding and design services, covering identity, packaging, literature, events, training and architecture from Addison, The Brand Union, Fitch, Lambie-Nairn, Landor Associates, The Partners and others	
Direct, Promotion & Relationship Marketing	
The full range of general and specialist customer, channel, direct, field, retail, promotional and point-of-sale services from Bridge Worldwide, G2, OgilvyOne, OgilvyAction, RTC Relationship Marketing, VML, Wunderman and others.	
Healthcare Communications	
CommonHealth, GCI Health, ghg, Ogilvy Healthworld, Sudler & Hennessey and others provide integrated healthcare marketing solutions from advertising to medical education and online marketing	
Specialist Communications	
A comprehensive range of specialist services, from custom media and multicultural marketing to event, sports, youth and entertainment marketing; corporate and business-to-business; media, technology and production services	
WPP Digital	
Through WPP Digital, WPP companies and their clients have access to a portfolio of digital experts including 24/7 Real Media, Schematic and BLUE	

Source: Adapted from WPP, "What We Do," www.wpp.com/wpp/about/whatwedo/ (as at 1 October 2010). Used with permission.

pitches. Advertising can convey the positioning of a brand and benefit from online display advertising or search engine marketing that offers a stronger call to action.[40]

Many companies are coordinating their online and offline communications activities. Web addresses in ads (especially print ads) and on packages allow people to more fully explore a company's products, find store locations, and get more product or service information. Even if consumers don't order online, marketers can use Web sites in ways that drive them into stores to buy.

Implementing IMC

In recent years, large ad agencies have substantially improved their integrated offerings. To facilitate one-stop shopping, these agencies have acquired promotion agencies, public relations firms, package-design consultancies, Web site developers, and direct-mail houses. They are redefining themselves as *communications companies* that assist clients to improve their overall communications effectiveness by offering strategic and practical advice on many forms of communication.[41] Many international clients such as IBM (Ogilvy), Colgate (Young & Rubicam), and GE (BBDO) have opted to put a substantial portion of their communications work through one full-service agency. The result is integrated and more effective marketing communications at a much lower total communications cost.

Integrated marketing communications can produce stronger message consistency and help build brand equity and create greater sales impact.[42] It forces management to think about every way the customer comes in contact with the company, how the company communicates its positioning, the relative importance of each vehicle, and timing issues. It gives someone the responsibility—where none existed before—to unify the company's brand images and messages as they come through thousands of company activities. IMC should improve the company's ability to reach the right customers with the right messages at the right time and in the right place.[43] "Marketing Memo: How Integrated Is Your IMC Program?" provides some guidelines.

marketing Memo

How Integrated Is Your IMC Program?

In assessing the collective impact of an IMC program, the marketer's over-riding goal is to create the most effective and efficient communications program possible. The following six criteria can help determine whether communications are truly integrated.

- *Coverage.* Coverage is the proportion of the audience reached by each communication option employed, as well as how much overlap exists among communication options. In other words, to what extent do different communication options reach the designated target market and the same or different consumers making up that market?

- *Contribution.* Contribution is the inherent ability of a marketing communication to create the desired response and communication effects from consumers in the absence of exposure to any other communication option. How much does a communication affect consumer processing and build awareness, enhance image, elicit responses, and induce sales?

- *Commonality.* Commonality is the extent to which *common* associations are reinforced across communication options; that is, the extent to which information conveyed by different communication options share meaning. The consistency and cohesiveness of the brand image is important because it determines how easily existing associations and responses can be recalled and how easily additional associations and responses can become linked to the brand in memory.

- *Complementarity.* Communication options are often more effective when used in tandem. Complementarity relates to the extent to which *different* associations and linkages are emphasized across communication options. Different brand associations may be most effectively established by capitalizing on those marketing communication options best suited to eliciting a particular consumer response or establishing a particular type of brand association. Many of the TV ads during the Super Bowl—America's biggest media event—are designed to create curiosity and interest so that consumers go online and engage in social media and word of mouth to experience and find more detailed information.[44] A 2010 Super Bowl spot for Snickers candy bar featuring legendary TV comedienne Betty White resulted in over 3.5 million visits to the brand's Web site after it was run.

- *Versatility.* In any integrated communication program, when consumers are exposed to a particular marketing communication, some will have already been exposed to other marketing communications for the brand, and some will not have had any prior exposure. Versatility refers to the extent to which a marketing communication option is robust and "works" for different groups of consumers. The ability of a marketing communication to work at two levels—effectively communicating to consumers who have or have *not* seen other communications—is critically important.

- *Cost.* Marketers must weigh evaluations of marketing communications on all these criteria against their cost to arrive at the most effective *and* efficient communications program.

Source: Adapted from Kevin Lane Keller, *Strategic Brand Management,* 3rd ed. (Upper Saddle River, NJ: Prentice Hall, 2008).

Summary

1. Modern marketing calls for more than developing a good product, pricing it attractively, and making it accessible to target customers. Companies must also communicate with present and potential stakeholders and with the general public.

2. The marketing communications mix consists of eight major modes of communication: advertising, sales promotion, public relations and publicity, events and experiences, direct marketing, interactive marketing, word-of-mouth marketing, and personal selling.

3. The communications process consists of nine elements: sender, receiver, message, media, encoding, decoding, response, feedback, and noise. To get their messages through, marketers must encode their messages in a way that takes into account how the target audience usually decodes messages. They must also transmit the message through efficient media that reach the target audience and develop feedback channels to monitor response to the message.

4. Developing effective communications requires eight steps: (1) Identify the target audience, (2) determine the communications objectives, (3) design the communications, (4) select the communications channels, (5) establish the total communications budget, (6) decide on the communications mix, (7) measure the communications results, and (8) manage the integrated marketing communications process.

5. In identifying the target audience, the marketer needs to close any gap that exists between current public perception and the image sought. Communications objectives can be to create category need, brand awareness, brand attitude, or brand purchase intention.

6. Designing the communication requires solving three problems: what to say (message strategy), how to say it (creative strategy), and who should say it (message source). Communications channels can be personal (advocate, expert, and social channels) or nonpersonal (media, atmospheres, and events).

7. Although other methods exist, the objective-and-task method of setting the communications budget, which calls upon marketers to develop their budgets by defining specific objectives, is typically most desirable.

8. In choosing the marketing communications mix, marketers must examine the distinct advantages and costs of each communication tool and the company's market rank. They must also consider the type of product market in which they are selling, how ready consumers are to make a purchase, and the product's stage in the company, brand, and product.

9. Measuring the effectiveness of the marketing communications mix requires asking members of the target audience whether they recognize or recall the communication, how many times they saw it, what points they recall, how they felt about the communication, and what are their previous and current attitudes toward the company, brand, and product.

10. Managing and coordinating the entire communications process calls for integrated marketing communications (IMC): marketing communications planning that recognizes the added value of a comprehensive plan to evaluate the strategic roles of a variety of communications disciplines, and that combines these disciplines to provide clarity, consistency, and maximum impact through the seamless integration of discrete messages.

Applications

Marketing Debate
Has TV Advertising Lost Its Power?

Long deemed the most successful marketing medium, television advertising is increasingly criticized for being too expensive and, even worse, no longer as effective as it once was. Critics maintain that consumers tune out too many ads by zipping and zapping and that it is difficult to make a strong impression. The future, claim some, is with online advertising. Supporters of TV advertising disagree, contending that the multisensory impact of TV is unsurpassed and that no other media option offers the same potential impact.

Take a position: TV advertising has faded in importance *versus* TV advertising is still the most powerful advertising medium.

Marketing Discussion
Communications Audit

Pick a brand and go to its Web site. Locate as many forms of communication as you can find. Conduct an informal communications audit. What do you notice? How consistent are the different communications?

Marketing Excellence

>>Red Bull

Red Bull's integrated marketing communications mix has been so successful that the company has created an entirely new drink category—functional energy drinks—and has become a multibillion-dollar brand among competition from beverage kings like Coca-Cola and Pepsi. In less than 20 years, Red Bull has become the energy drink market leader by skillfully connecting with the global youth. Dietrich Mateschitz founded Red Bull in Austria and introduced the energy drink into Hungary, its first foreign market, in 1992. Today, Red Bull sells 4 billion cans of energy drinks each year in over 160 countries.

So how does Red Bull do it? The answer: differently than others. For years, Red Bull offered just one product, Red Bull Energy Drink, in one size—a slick silver 250 ml. (8.3 oz.) can with a European look and feel. Red Bull's ingredients—amino acid taurine, B-complex vitamins, caffeine, and carbohydrates—mean it's highly caffeinated and energizing, so fans have called it "liquid cocaine" and "speed in a can." Over the last decade, Red Bull has introduced three additional products: Red Bull Sugarfree, Red Bull Energy Shots, and Red Bull Cola—each slight variations of the original energy drink.

Since its beginning, Red Bull has used little traditional advertising and no print, billboards, banner ads, or Super Bowl spots. While the company runs minimal television commercials, the animated spots and tagline "Red Bull Gives You Wiiings" are meant to amuse its young audience and connect in a nontraditional, nonpushy manner.

Red Bull builds buzz about the product through grassroots, viral marketing tactics, starting with its "seeding program" that microtargets trendy shops, clubs, bars, and stores. As one Red Bull executive explained, "We go to on-premise accounts first, because the product gets a lot of visibility and attention. It goes faster to deal with individual accounts, not big chains and their authorization process." Red Bull is easily accepted at clubs because "in clubs, people are open to new things."

Once Red Bull has gained some momentum in the bars, it next moves into convenience stores located near colleges, gyms, health-food stores, and supermarkets, prime locations for its target audience of men and women aged 16 to 29. Red Bull has also been known to target college students directly by providing them with free cases of Red Bull and encouraging them to throw a party. Eventually, Red Bull moves into restaurants and finally, into supermarkets.

Red Bull's marketing efforts strive to build its brand image of authenticity, originality, and community in several ways. First, Red Bull targets opinion leaders by sampling its product, a lot. Free Red Bull energy drinks are available at sports competitions, in limos before award shows, and at exclusive after-parties. Free samples are passed out on college campuses and city streets, given to those who look like they need a lift.

Next, Red Bull aligns itself with a wide variety of extreme sports, athletes, teams, events, and artists (in music, dance, and film). From motor sports to mountain biking, snowboarding to surfing, dancing to extreme sailing, there is no limit to the craziness of a Red Bull event or sponsorship. A few have become notorious for taking originality and extreme sporting to the limit, including the annual Flugtag. At Flugtag, contestants build homemade flying machines that must weigh less than 450 pounds, including the pilot. Teams then launch their contraptions off a specially designed Red Bull branded ramp, 30 feet above a body of water. Crowds of up to 300,000 young consumers cheer on as the contestants and their "planes" stay true to the brand's slogan: "Red Bull gives you wings!"

Another annual event, the Red Bull Air Race, tests the limits of sanity. Twelve of the world's top aerobatic stunt pilots compete in a 3.5 mile course through a low-level aerial racetrack made up of air-filled Red Bull branded pylons 33 feet apart and reaching 65 feet in height. In other words, pilots fly planes with a 26-foot wingspan through a gap of 33 feet at 230 mph. These Red Bull–branded planes crash occasionally, but to date no fatalities have ever occurred.

Red Bull's Web site provides consumers with information about how to find Red Bull events, videos of and interviews with Red Bull–sponsored athletes, and clips of amazing feats that will be tested next. For example, Bull Stratos is a mission one man is undertaking to free-fall from 120,000 feet, or 23 miles high. The jump will be attempted from the edge of space and, if successful, it will mark the first time a human being has reached supersonic speeds in a free fall.

Red Bull buys traditional advertising once the market is mature and the company needs to reinforce the brand to its consumers. As one Red Bull executive explained, "Media is not a tool that we use to establish the market. It is a critical part. It's just later in the development."

Red Bull's "anti-marketing" IMC strategy has been extremely successful connecting with its young consumers. It falls directly in line with the company's mission to be seen as unique, original, and rebellious—just as its Generation Y consumers want to be viewed.

Questions

1. What are Red Bull's greatest strengths and risks as more companies (like Coca-Cola, Pepsi, and Monster)

enter the energy drink category and gain market share?

2. Should Red Bull do more traditional advertising? Why or why not?

3. Discuss the effectiveness of Red Bull's sponsorships, for example, Bull Stratos. Is this a good use of Red Bull's marketing budget? Where should the company draw the line?

Sources: Kevin Lane Keller, "Red Bull: Managing a High-Growth Brand," *Best Practice Cases in Branding*, 3rd ed. (Upper Saddle River, NJ: Prentice Hall, 2008); Peter Ha, "Red Bull Stratos: Man Will Freefall from Earth's Stratosphere," *Timo*, January 22, 2010, Red Bull, www.redbull.com.

Marketing Excellence

>>Target

Like other discount retailers, Target sells a wide variety of products, including clothing, jewelry, sporting goods, household supplies, toys, electronics, and health and beauty products. However, since its founding in 1962, Target has focused on differentiating itself from the competition. This became evident in the mid-1980s when Kmart dominated the mass retail industry and Walmart was growing rapidly. Kmart and Walmart's marketing messages communicated their low price promise, but their merchandise was perceived as cheap and low-quality. Target sensed a gap in the market for "cheap chic" retail and set out to distinguish itself from the other big-box retailers.

Target planned to build an up-market cachet for its brand without losing its relevance for price-conscious consumers. It positioned itself as a high-fashion brand with trendy styles and quality merchandise at affordable low prices. To fulfill this brand promise, Target's teams of merchandisers travel the world looking for the next hot items. Next, Target brings these trends to the shelves faster than its competitors.

Many styles are sold exclusively at Target through partnerships with world-renowned designers, such as Mossimo Giannulli, Jean Paul Gaultier, and Liz Lange in clothes; Anya Hindmarch in handbags; Sigerson Morrison

in shoes; Michael Graves in home goods; and Pixi by Petra Strand in beauty. They are either staples in Target stores or part of the Go International line, a special design collection available for only a few months. In 2006, Target introduced U.S. consumers to the concept of "fast fashion," already popular in Europe, to help keep the product selection fresh, which in turn led to more frequent shopper visits.

Target's designer line collections are just one unique part of its entire integrated marketing communications mix. The company uses a variety of tactics to communicate its "cheap chic" positioning, beginning with its slogan, "Expect More, Pay Less." In its stores, Target uses strategically placed low shelves, halogen and track lighting, cleaner fixtures, and wider aisles to avoid visual clutter. Signage features contemporary imagery but is printed on less expensive materials. Target even catches the eye of consumers in the air by painting its signature red bull's eye on the roof of stores located near busy airports.

Target uses a wide range of traditional advertising such as television ads, direct mailers, print ads, radio, and circulars. Its messages feature hip young customers, a variety of strong name-brand products, and a lighthearted tone—all which have helped make Target's bull's eye logo well recognized. Target also aligns itself with a variety of events, sports, athletes, and museums through corporate sponsorships. From Target Field, the home of the Minnesota Twins in Minneapolis, to Target NASCAR and Indy racing teams and contemporary athletes like Olympic snowboarder Shaun White, sponsorships help Target pinpoint specific consumers, interests, attitudes, and demographics. Target also advertises on and sponsors major awards shows such as the Oscars, Emmys, Grammys, and the Golden Globes.

Target has a strong online presence and uses Target.com as a critical component in its retail and communications strategy. Target.com is able to gain insight into consumers' shopping preferences, which ultimately allows for more targeted direct marketing efforts. The site also features in-store items alongside Web-only items in hopes of driving traffic into the stores. On social Web sites such as Twitter and Facebook, Target builds loyalty and encourages young consumers to share their experiences, discounts, and great finds with each other.

Target reinforces its positive brand image by contributing significantly to surrounding communities. The company donates 5 percent of its annual income, or more than $3 million a week, to programs that focus on education, the arts, social service, and volunteerism. Target donated more than 16 million pounds of food in 2008 to Feed America, the nation's food bank network. Target also sponsors discounted or free days at art museums around the country, including the Museum of Modern Art in New York and the Museum of Contemporary Art in Chicago.

As a result of its integrated marketing plan, Target has attracted many shoppers who would not otherwise shop at a discount retailer. Its customers are younger, more affluent, and more educated than its competitors attract. The median age of Target shoppers is 41 and the median household income is $63,000. Three-quarters of Target consumers are female and 45 percent have children at home. In addition, 97 percent of U.S. consumers recognize the Target bull's eye logo.

While Target's marketing communication mix has effectively communicated its "cheap chic" message over the years, this strategy hurt sales during the recession in 2008–2009. During that time, consumers significantly cut their spending and shopped mostly for necessities at low-cost Walmart instead of for discretionary items, which make up about three-fifths of sales at Target.

As a result, Target tweaked its marketing message and merchandise profile. The company added perishables to its inventory—a necessity in slow economic times—and cut back on discretionary items such as clothing and home accessories. Target's marketing message remains focused on offering consumers high style and unique brand names but emphasizes value more, using phrases such as "fresh for less" and "new way to save."

Today, Target is the second-largest discount retailer in the United States, with $65.4 billion in sales in 2009, and ranks number 28 on the Fortune 500 list. Its successful integrated marketing mix has worked so well that consumers often jokingly pronounce the company's name as if it were an upscale boutique, "Tar-ZHAY."

Questions

1. What has Target done well over the years in terms of its integrated marketing communications strategy? What should it do going forward?

2. How does Target compete against mammoth Walmart? What are the distinct differences in their IMC strategies?

3. Did Target do the right thing by tweaking its message to focus more on value and less on trends? Why or why not?

Sources: "Value for Money Is Back—Target Does Marketing Right," *The Marketing Doctor*, October 2, 2006; Ben Steverman, "Target vs. Wal-Mart: The Next Phase," *BusinessWeek*, August 18, 2009; Ann Zimmerman, "Staying on Target," *Wall Street Journal*, May 7, 2007; Mya Frazier, "The Latest European Import: Fast Fashion," *Advertising Age*, January 9, 2006, p. 6; Julie Schlosser, "How Target Does It," *Fortune*, October 18, 2004, p. 100; Michelle Conlin, "Look Who's Stalking Wal-Mart," *BusinessWeek*, December 7, 2009, pp. 30–36; Wikinvest, www.wikinvest.com; Target, www.target.com.

In This Chapter, We Will Address the Following Questions

1. What steps are required in developing an advertising program?

2. How should sales promotion decisions be made?

3. What are the guidelines for effective brand-building events and experiences?

4. How can companies exploit the potential of public relations and publicity?

Old Spice has put more than a little swagger in its products—and in its advertising—to modernize the decades-old brand.

Managing Mass Communications: Advertising, Sales Promotions, Events and Experiences, and Public Relations

Although there has been an enormous increase in the use of personal communications by marketers in recent years, due to the rapid penetration of the Internet and other factors, the fact remains that mass media, if used correctly, is still an important component of a modern marketing communications program. The old days of "if you build a great ad, they will come," however, are long gone. To generate consumer interest and sales, mass media must often be supplemented and carefully integrated with other communications, as was the case with Procter & Gamble's Old Spice.[1]

Among the more successful of the 30-second ads estimated to cost over $2.5 million to run during the broadcast of the 2010 Super Bowl was one for Old Spice body wash. Turning a potential negative of being an old brand into a positive of being experienced, Old Spice has made a remarkable transformation in recent years from "your father's aftershave" to a contemporary men's fragrance brand. In a new strategic move, given their important role in the purchase process, the Super Bowl spot targeted women as well as men. The tongue-in-cheek ad featured rugged ex-NFL football player Isaiah Mustafa as "The Man Your Man Could Smell Like." In one seamless take, Mustafa confidently strikes a variety of romantic poses while passing from a shower in a bathroom to standing on a boat to riding a white horse. Uploaded onto YouTube and other social networking sites, the ad was viewed over 10 million additional times. Old Spice's Facebook page included a Web application called "My Perpetual Love," which featured Mustafa offering men the opportunity to be "more like him" by e-mailing and tweeting their sweethearts virtual love notes. For its efforts, the ad agency behind the campaign, Wieden+Kennedy, received a Grand Prix at the Cannes International Ad festival. A follow-up ad in June 2010 showed Mustafa in a new series of "perfect man" activities including baking birthday cakes, building a home with his own hands, swan-diving into a hot tub, and, yes, walking on water.

Although Old Spice clearly has found great success with its ad campaign, other marketers are trying to come to grips with how to best use mass media in the new—and still changing—communication environment.[2] In this chapter, we examine the nature and use of four mass-communication tools—advertising, sales promotion, events and experiences, and public relations and publicity.

Developing and Managing an Advertising Program

Advertising can be a cost-effective way to disseminate messages, whether to build a brand preference or to educate people. Even in today's challenging media environment, good ads can pay off. P&G has also enjoyed double-digit sales gains in recent years from ads touting the efficacy of Olay Definity antiaging skin products and Head & Shoulders Intensive Treatment shampoo.[3]

In developing an advertising program, marketing managers must always start by identifying the target market and buyer motives. Then they can make the five major decisions, known as "the five Ms": *Mission:* What are our advertising objectives? *Money:* How much can we spend and how do we allocate our spending across media types? *Message:* What message should we send? *Media:* What media should we use? *Measurement:* How should we evaluate the results? These decisions are summarized in △ Figure 18.1 and described in the following sections.

Setting the Objectives

The advertising objectives must flow from prior decisions on target market, brand positioning, and the marketing program.

An **advertising objective** (or goal) is a specific communications task and achievement level to be accomplished with a specific audience in a specific period of time:[4]

> *To increase among 30 million homemakers who own automatic washers the number who identify brand X as a low-sudsing detergent, and who are persuaded that it gets clothes cleaner, from 10 percent to 40 percent in one year.*

We can classify advertising objectives according to whether their aim is to inform, persuade, remind, or reinforce. These objectives correspond to different stages in the *hierarchy-of-effects* model discussed in Chapter 17.

- *Informative advertising* aims to create brand awareness and knowledge of new products or new features of existing products.[5] To promote its OnStar in-vehicle safety, security, and information service that uses wireless and GPS satellite technology, GM launched the "Real Stories" campaign in 2002. The award-winning TV, radio, and print ad campaign used actual subscriber stories in their own words and voices to share the importance and benefits of OnStar through life-changing experiences. By 2005, the OnStar brand had reached 100 percent awareness among consumers shopping for a new vehicle.[6]

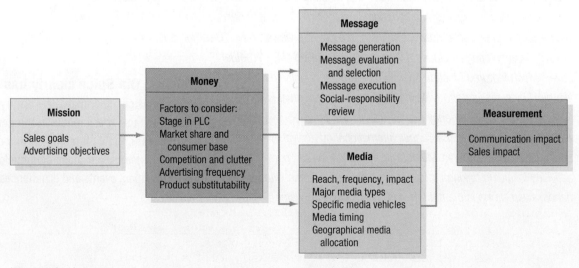

|Fig. 18.1| △

The Five Ms of Advertising

- *Persuasive advertising* aims to create liking, preference, conviction, and purchase of a product or service. Some persuasive advertising uses comparative advertising, which makes an explicit comparison of the attributes of two or more brands. Miller Lite took market share from Bud Lite by pointing out that Bud Lite had higher carbs. Comparative advertising works best when it elicits cognitive and affective motivations simultaneously, and when consumers are processing advertising in a detailed, analytical mode.[7]

- *Reminder advertising* aims to stimulate repeat purchase of products and services. Expensive, four-color Coca-Cola ads in magazines are intended to remind people to purchase Coca-Cola.

- *Reinforcement advertising* aims to convince current purchasers that they made the right choice. Automobile ads often depict satisfied customers enjoying special features of their new car.

The advertising objective should emerge from a thorough analysis of the current marketing situation. If the product class is mature, the company is the market leader, and brand usage is low, the objective is to stimulate more usage. If the product class is new, the company is not the market leader, but the brand is superior to the leader, then the objective is to convince the market of the brand's superiority.

Deciding on the Advertising Budget

How does a company know it's spending the right amount? Although advertising is treated as a current expense, part of it is really an investment in building brand equity and customer loyalty. When a company spends $5 million on capital equipment, it may treat the equipment as a five-year depreciable asset and write off only one-fifth of the cost in the first year. When it spends $5 million on advertising to launch a new product, it must write off the entire cost in the first year, reducing its reported profit, even if the effects will persist for many years to come.

FACTORS AFFECTING BUDGET DECISIONS Here are five specific factors to consider when setting the advertising budget:[8]

1. *Stage in the product life cycle*—New products typically merit large advertising budgets to build awareness and to gain consumer trial. Established brands usually are supported with lower advertising budgets, measured as a ratio to sales.

2. *Market share and consumer base*—High-market-share brands usually require less advertising expenditure as a percentage of sales to maintain share. To build share by increasing market size requires larger expenditures.

3. *Competition and clutter*—In a market with a large number of competitors and high advertising spending, a brand must advertise more heavily to be heard. Even simple clutter from advertisements not directly competitive to the brand creates a need for heavier advertising.

4. *Advertising frequency*—The number of repetitions needed to put the brand's message across to consumers has an obvious impact on the advertising budget.

5. *Product substitutability*—Brands in less-differentiated or commodity-like product classes (beer, soft drinks, banks, and airlines) require heavy advertising to establish a unique image.

ADVERTISING ELASTICITY The predominant response function for advertising is often concave but can be S-shaped. When consumer response is S-shaped, some positive amount of advertising is necessary to generate any sales impact, but sales increases eventually flatten out.[9]

One classic study found that increasing the TV advertising budget had a measurable effect on sales only half the time. The success rate was higher for new products or line extensions than for established brands, and when there were changes in copy or in media strategy (such as an expanded target market). When advertising increased sales, its impact lasted up to two years after peak spending. Moreover, the long-term incremental sales generated were approximately double the incremental sales observed in the first year of an advertising spending increase.[10]

Other studies reinforce these conclusions. In a 2004 IRI study of 23 brands, advertising often didn't increase sales for mature brands or categories in decline. A review of academic research found that advertising elasticities were estimated to be higher for new (.3) than for established products (.1).[11]

Developing the Advertising Campaign

In designing and evaluating an ad campaign, marketers employ both art and science to develop the *message strategy* or positioning of an ad—*what* the ad attempts to convey about the brand—and its *creative strategy*—*how* the ad expresses the brand claims. Advertisers go through three steps: message generation and evaluation, creative development and execution, and social-responsibility review.

MESSAGE GENERATION AND EVALUATION Many of today's automobile ads look similar—a car drives at high speed on a curved mountain road or across a desert. Advertisers are always seeking "the big idea" that connects with consumers rationally and emotionally, sharply distinguishes the brand from competitors, and is broad and flexible enough to translate to different media, markets, and time periods.[12] Fresh insights are important for avoiding using the same appeals and position as others.

Got Milk? After a 20-year decline in milk consumption among Californians, in 1993 milk processors from across the state formed the California Milk Processor Board (CMPB) with one goal in mind: to get people to drink more milk. The ad agency commissioned by the CMPB, Goodby, Silverstein & Partners, developed a novel approach to pitching milk's benefits. Research had shown that most consumers already believed milk was good for them. So the campaign would remind consumers of the inconvenience and annoyance of running out of milk when they went to eat certain foods, which became known as "milk deprivation." The "got milk?" tagline reminded consumers to make sure they had milk in their refrigerators. A year after the launch, sales volume had increased 1.07 percent. In 1995, the "got milk?" campaign was licensed to the National Dairy Board. In 1998, the National Fluid Milk Processor Education Program, which had been using the "milk mustache" campaign since 1994 to boost sales, bought the rights to the "got milk?" tagline. The "got milk?" campaign continues to pay strong dividends by halting the decline in sales of milk in California more than 13 years after its launch.[13] ▭

A good ad normally focuses on one or two core selling propositions. As part of refining the brand positioning, the advertiser should conduct market research to determine which appeal works best with its target audience and then prepare a *creative brief,* typically one or two pages. This is an elaboration of the *positioning statement* and includes considerations such as key message, target audience, communications objectives (to do, to know, to believe), key brand benefits, supports for the brand promise, and media.

How many alternative ad themes should the advertiser create before making a choice? The more ad themes explored, the higher the probability of finding an excellent one. Fortunately, an ad agency's creative department can inexpensively compose many alternative ads in a short time by drawing still and video images from computer files. Marketers can also cut the cost of creative dramatically by using consumers as their creative team, a strategy sometimes called "open source" or "crowdsourcing."[14]

The tagline for California Milk Processor Board's "Got milk?" campaign has also been used as part of the "milk mustache" print ad series, featuring numerous celebrities such as St. Louis Cardinals baseball slugger Albert Pujols.

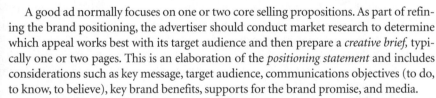

Consumer-Generated Advertising One of the first major marketers to feature consumer-generated ads was Converse, whose award-winning campaign, "Brand Democracy," used films created by consumers in a series of TV and Web ads. Some of the most popular ads during recent Super Bowl broadcasts have been homemade contest winners for Frito-Lay's Doritos tortilla chips. H. J. Heinz ran a "Top This TV Challenge" inviting the public to create the next commercial for its Heinz Ketchup brand and win $57,000. More than 6,000 submissions and more than 10 million online views resulted, and sales rose over 13 percent year over year. In addition to creating ads, consumers can help disseminate advertising. A UK "Life's for Sharing" ad for T-Mobile in which 400 people break into a choreographed dance routine in the Liverpool Street Station was shown exactly once on the *Celebrity Big Brother* television show, but it was watched more than 15 million times online when word about it spread via e-mail messages, blogs, and social networks. ▭

Although entrusting consumers with a brand's marketing effort can be pure genius, it can also be a regrettable failure. When Kraft sought a hip name for a new flavor variety of its iconic Vegemite

T-Mobile's highly entertaining "Life's for Sharing" subway dance became an online viral marketing sensation.

product in Australia, it labeled the first 3 million jars "Name Me" to enlist consumer support. From 48,000 entries, however, the marketer selected one that was thrown in as a joke—iSnack 2.0—and sales plummeted. The company had to pull iSnack jars from the shelves and start from scratch in a more conventional fashion, yielding the new name Cheesybite.[15]

CREATIVE DEVELOPMENT AND EXECUTION The ad's impact depends not only on what it says, but often more important, on *how* it says it. Execution can be decisive. Every advertising medium has advantages and disadvantages. Here, we briefly review television, print, and radio advertising media.

Television Ads Television is generally acknowledged as the most powerful advertising medium and reaches a broad spectrum of consumers at low cost per exposure. TV advertising has two particularly important strengths. First, it can vividly demonstrate product attributes and persuasively explain their corresponding consumer benefits. Second, it can dramatically portray user and usage imagery, brand personality, and other intangibles.

Because of the fleeting nature of the ad, however, and the distracting creative elements often found in it, product-related messages and the brand itself can be overlooked. Moreover, the high volume of nonprogramming material on television creates clutter that makes it easy for consumers to ignore or forget ads. Nevertheless, properly designed and executed TV ads can still be a powerful marketing tool and improve brand equity and affect sales and profits. In the highly competitive insurance category, advertising can help a brand to stand out.[16]

Aflac   Aflac, the largest supplier of supplemental insurance, was relatively unknown until a highly creative ad campaign made it one of the most recognized brands in recent history. (Aflac stands for American Family Life Assurance Company.) Created by the Kaplan Thaler ad agency, the lighthearted campaign features an irascible duck incessantly squawking the company's name, "Aflac!" while consumers or celebrities discuss its products. The duck's frustrated bid for attention appealed to consumers. Sales were up 28 percent in the first year the duck aired, and name recognition went from 13 percent to 91 percent. Aflac has stuck with the duck in its advertising, even incorporating it into its corporate logo in 2005. Social media have allowed marketers to further develop the personality of the duck—it has 170,000 Facebook fans and counting! The Aflac duck is not just a U.S. phenomenon. It also stars in Japanese TV ads—with a somewhat brighter disposition—where it has been credited with helping to drive sales in Aflac's biggest market.

Print Ads Print media offer a stark contrast to broadcast media. Because readers consume them at their own pace, magazines and newspapers can provide detailed product information and effectively

Aflac's iconic duck character has been the centerpiece of its brand-building advertising for years.

communicate user and usage imagery. At the same time, the static nature of the visual images in print media makes dynamic presentations or demonstrations difficult, and print media can be fairly passive.

The two main print media—magazines and newspapers—share many advantages and disadvantages. Although newspapers are timely and pervasive, magazines are typically more effective at building user and usage imagery. Newspapers are popular for local—especially retailer—advertising. On an average day, roughly one-half to three-quarters of U.S. adults read a newspaper, although increasingly that is an online version. Print newspaper circulation fell almost 9 percent in 2009.[17] Although advertisers have some flexibility in designing and placing newspaper ads, relatively poor reproduction quality and short shelf life can diminish the ads' impact.

Researchers studying print advertisements report that the *picture, headline,* and *copy* matter in that order. The picture must be strong enough to draw attention. The headline must reinforce the picture and lead the person to read the copy. The copy must be engaging and the brand's name sufficiently prominent. Even then, less than 50 percent of the exposed audience will notice even a really outstanding ad. About 30 percent might recall the headline's main point, about 25 percent register the advertiser's name, and fewer than 10 percent will read most of the body copy. Ordinary ads don't achieve even these results.

Given how consumers process print ads, some clear managerial implications emerge, as summarized in "Marketing Memo: Print Ad Evaluation Criteria." One print ad campaign that successfully carved out a brand image is Absolut vodka.[18]

Print Ad Evaluation Criteria

In judging the effectiveness of a print ad, in addition to considering the communication strategy (target market, communications objectives, and message and creative strategy), marketers should be able to answer yes to the following questions about the ad's execution:

1. Is the message clear at a glance? Can you quickly tell what the advertisement is all about?
2. Is the benefit in the headline?

3. Does the illustration support the headline?
4. Does the first line of the copy support or explain the headline and illustration?
5. Is the ad easy to read and follow?
6. Is the product easily identified?
7. Is the brand or sponsor clearly identified?

Source: Adapted from Scott C. Purvis and Philip Ward Burton, *Which Ad Pulled Best,* 9th ed. (Lincolnwood, IL: NTC Business Books, 2002).

Absolut Vodka   Vodka is generally viewed as a commodity product, yet the amount of brand preference and loyalty in the vodka market is astonishing and attributed mostly to brand image. When the Swedish brand Absolut entered the U.S. market in 1979, the company sold a disappointing 7,000 cases. By 1991, sales had soared to over 2 million cases. Absolut became the largest-selling imported vodka in the United States, with 65 percent of the market, thanks in large part to its marketing and advertising strategies aimed at sophisticated, upwardly mobile, affluent drinkers. The vodka comes in a distinctive clear bottle that served as the centerpiece of 15,000 ad executions over a 25-year period. The campaign cleverly juxtaposed a punning caption against a stylized image of the bottle—for example, "Absolut Texas" under an image of an oversized bottle, or "Absolut 19th" with a bottle made of a golf green. But feeling that consumers were beginning to tune out the message, in 2007 Absolut introduced a new global campaign that showed what things would be like "In an Absolut World." In this fantasy world, men get pregnant, soap bubbles flow from smokestacks, masterpiece paintings hang in Times Square, protesters and police fight with feather pillows, and perhaps most fantastically of all, the Cubs win the World Series. The revitalized campaign led to a 9 percent increase in case sales before the recession hit in 2008.

Radio Ads   Radio is a pervasive medium: Ninety-three percent of all U.S. citizens age 12 and older listen to the radio daily and for around 20 hours a week on average, numbers that have held steady in recent years. Much radio listening occurs in the car and out of home. As streaming Internet access gains ground, traditional AM/FM radio stations are feeling the pressure and account for less than half of all listening at home.[19]

Perhaps radio's main advantage is flexibility—stations are very targeted, ads are relatively inexpensive to produce and place, and short closings allow for quick response. Radio is a particularly effective medium in the morning; it can also let companies achieve a balance between broad and localized market coverage.

The obvious disadvantages of radio are its lack of visual images and the relatively passive nature of the consumer processing that results. Nevertheless, radio ads can be extremely creative. Some see the lack of visual images as a plus because they feel the clever use of music, sound, and other creative devices can tap into the listener's imagination to create powerfully relevant and liked images. Here is an example:

DFT   Faced with a high rate of motorcycle collisions with cars, the Department of Transport in the United Kingdom (DFT) conducted a research study. Its findings showed that many bike accidents resulted from "unintentional blindness," in which a car driver fails to see a motorcyclist. DFT wanted to increase drivers' awareness of motorcyclists by encouraging them to identify with riders and see them as real people. Radio was the only medium that allowed DFT to bring the campaign to life, with regional voices and copy, mentioning specific places and roads that listeners could identify with. It also allowed DFT to speak to listeners while they were driving. The aims of the advertising campaign were to increase awareness of motorcyclists from 51 percent to 58 percent, and to raise the number of motorists who checked their blind spots from 78 percent to 83 percent. DFT's advertisement won the award for the Best Use of Radio to Drive Awareness from the Radio Advertising Bureau in the United Kingdom.[20]

LEGAL AND SOCIAL ISSUES To break through clutter, some advertisers believe they have to be edgy and push the boundaries of what consumers are used to seeing in advertising. In doing so, marketers must be sure advertising does not overstep social and legal norms[21] or offend the general public, ethnic groups, racial minorities, or special-interest groups.

A substantial body of laws and regulations governs advertising. Under U.S. law, advertisers must not make false claims, such as stating that a product cures something when it does not. They must avoid false demonstrations, such as using sand-covered Plexiglas instead of sandpaper to demonstrate that a razor blade can shave sandpaper. It is illegal in the United States to create ads that have the capacity to deceive, even though no one may actually be deceived. A floor wax advertiser can't say the product gives six months' protection unless it does so under typical conditions, and the maker of a diet bread can't say it has fewer calories simply because its slices are thinner. The challenge is telling the difference between deception and "puffery"—simple exaggerations that are not meant to be believed and that *are* permitted by law.

Splenda versus Equal Splenda's tagline for its artificial sweetener was "Made from sugar, so it tastes like sugar," with "but it's not sugar" in small writing almost as an afterthought. McNeil Nutritionals, Splenda's manufacturer, does begin production of Splenda with pure cane sugar but burns it off in the manufacturing process. However, Merisant, maker of Equal, claimed that Splenda's advertising confuses consumers who are likely to conclude that a product "made from sugar" is healthier than one made from aspartame, Equal's main ingredient. A document used in court and taken from McNeil's own files notes that consumers' perception of Splenda as "not an artificial sweetener" was one of the biggest triumphs of the company's marketing campaign, which began in 2003. Splenda became the runaway leader in the sugar-substitute category with 60 percent of the market, leaving roughly 14 percent each to Equal (in the blue packets) and Sweet'N Low (pink packets). Although McNeil eventually agreed to settle the lawsuit and pay Merisant an undisclosed but "substantial" award (and change its advertising), it may have been too late for consumers to change their perception of Splenda as something sugary *and* sugar-free.[22]

Sellers in the United States are legally obligated to avoid bait-and-switch advertising that attracts buyers under false pretenses. Suppose a seller advertises a sewing machine at $149. When consumers try to buy the advertised machine, the seller cannot then refuse to sell it, downplay its features, show a faulty one, or promise unreasonable delivery dates in order to switch the buyer to a more expensive machine.[23]

Advertising can play a more positive broader social role. The Ad Council is a nonprofit organization that uses top-notch industry talent to produce and distribute public service announcements for nonprofits and government agencies. From its early origins with "Buy War Bonds" posters, the Ad Council has tackled innumerable pressing social issues through the years. One of its recent efforts featured beloved *Sesame Street* stars Elmo and Gordon exhorting children to wash their hands in the face of the H1N1 flu virus.[24]

Deciding on Media and Measuring Effectiveness

After choosing the message, the advertiser's next task is to choose media to carry it. The steps here are deciding on desired reach, frequency, and impact; choosing among major media types; selecting specific media vehicles; deciding on media timing; and deciding on geographical media allocation. Then the marketer evaluates the results of these decisions.

Deciding on Reach, Frequency, and Impact

Media selection is finding the most cost-effective media to deliver the desired number and type of exposures to the target audience. What do we mean by the desired number of exposures? The advertiser seeks a specified advertising objective and response from the target audience—for example, a target level of product trial. This level depends on, among other things, level of brand awareness. Suppose the rate of product trial increases at a diminishing rate with the level of audience awareness, as shown in △ Figure 18.2(a). If the advertiser seeks a product trial rate of T^*, it will be necessary to achieve a brand awareness level of A^*.

The next task is to find out how many exposures, E^*, will produce a level of audience awareness of A^*. The effect of exposures on audience awareness depends on the exposures' reach, frequency, and impact:

- **Reach (R).** The number of different persons or households exposed to a particular media schedule at least once during a specified time period
- **Frequency (F).** The number of times within the specified time period that an average person or household is exposed to the message
- **Impact (I).** The qualitative value of an exposure through a given medium (thus a food ad will have a higher impact in *Bon Appetit* than in *Fortune* magazine)

Figure 18.2(b) shows the relationship between audience awareness and reach. Audience awareness will be greater, the higher the exposures' reach, frequency, and impact. There are important trade-offs here. Suppose the planner has an advertising budget of $1,000,000 and the cost per thousand exposures of average quality is $5. This means 200,000,000 exposures ($1,000,000 ÷ [$5/1,000]). If the advertiser seeks an average exposure frequency of 10, it can reach 20,000,000 people (200,000,000 ÷ 10) with the given budget. But if the advertiser wants higher-quality media costing $10 per thousand exposures, it will be able to reach only 10,000,000 people unless it is willing to lower the desired exposure frequency.

The relationship between reach, frequency, and impact is captured in the following concepts:

- **Total number of exposures (E).** This is the reach times the average frequency; that is, $E = R \times F$, also called the *gross rating points* (GRP). If a given media schedule reaches 80 percent of homes with an average exposure frequency of 3, the media schedule has a GRP of 240 (80 × 3). If another media schedule has a GRP of 300, it has more weight, but we cannot tell how this weight breaks down into reach and frequency.
- **Weighted number of exposures (WE).** This is the reach times average frequency times average impact, that is $WE = R \times F \times I$.

Reach is most important when launching new products, flanker brands, extensions of well-known brands, or infrequently purchased brands; or when going after an undefined target market. Frequency is most important where there are strong competitors, a complex story to tell, high consumer resistance, or a frequent-purchase cycle.[25]

A key reason for repetition is forgetting. The higher the forgetting rate associated with a brand, product category, or message, the higher the warranted level of repetition. However, advertisers should not coast on a tired ad but insist on fresh executions by their ad agency.[26] GEICO has found advertising success by keeping both its campaigns and their executions fresh.

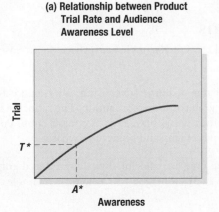

(a) Relationship between Product Trial Rate and Audience Awareness Level

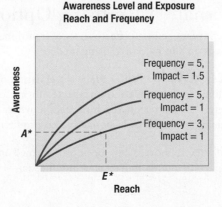

(b) Relationship between Audience Awareness Level and Exposure Reach and Frequency

|Fig. 18.2| △

Relationship Among Trial, Awareness, and the Exposure Function

GEICO   Have the hundreds of millions of dollars GEICO has spent on TV advertising been worth it? Warren Buffet, chairman and CEO of GEICO's parent company Berkshire Hathaway, sure thinks so. He told shareholders he would spend *millions* on GEICO advertising! GEICO has more than quadrupled its revenue over the last decade, from slightly under $3 billion in 1998 to more than $13 billion in 2009—making it the fastest-growing auto insurance company in the United States. The company eschews agents to sell directly to consumers with a basic message, "15 Minutes Could Save You 15% or More on Your Car Insurance." Partnering with The Martin Agency, GEICO has run different award-winning TV campaigns to emphasize different benefits of the brand. Popular TV spots advertising GEICO's claim that its Web site is "So Easy, a Caveman Can Use It" featured offended Neanderthals expressing indignation at the prejudice they face. TV ads featuring the Cockney-speaking Gecko lizard spokes-character reinforce GEICO's brand image as credible and accomplished. A third campaign, themed "Rhetorical Questions," uses cultural icons and touch points to make it seem obvious that GEICO saves customers money by asking self-evident questions such as, "Does Elmer Fudd have trouble with the letter R?" and "Did the Waltons take way too long to say goodnight?" The multiple campaigns complement each other and build on each other's success; the company dominates the TV airwaves with so many varied car insurance messages that any competitors' ads are lost.[27]

One of the most active advertisers around, GEICO employs multiple ad campaigns, including a series featuring the gecko lizard.

Choosing Among Major Media Types

The media planner must know the capacity of the major advertising media types to deliver reach, frequency, and impact. The major advertising media along with their costs, advantages, and limitations are profiled in ▭ Table 18.1. Media planners make their choices by considering factors such as target audience media habits, product characteristics, message requirements, and cost.

Alternate Advertising Options

In recent years, reduced effectiveness of traditional mass media has led advertisers to increase their emphasis on alternate advertising media.

PLACE ADVERTISING   Place advertising, or out-of-home advertising, is a broad category including many creative and unexpected forms to grab consumers' attention. The rationale is that marketers are better off reaching people where they work, play, and, of course, shop. Popular options include billboards, public spaces, product placement, and point of purchase.

Billboards   Billboards have been transformed and now use colorful, digitally produced graphics, backlighting, sounds, movement, and unusual—even 3D—images.[28] In New York, manhole covers

TABLE 18.1	Profiles of Major Media Types	
Medium	**Advantages**	**Limitations**
Newspapers	Flexibility; timeliness; good local market coverage; broad acceptance; high believability	Short life; poor reproduction quality; small "pass-along" audience
Television	Combines sight, sound, and motion; appealing to the senses; high attention; high reach	High absolute cost; high clutter; fleeting exposure; less audience selectivity
Direct mail	Audience selectivity; flexibility; no ad competition within the same medium; personalization	Relatively high cost; "junk mail" image
Radio	Mass use; high geographic and demographic selectivity; low cost	Audio presentation only; lower attention than television; nonstandardized rate structures; fleeting exposure
Magazines	High geographic and demographic selectivity; credibility and prestige; high-quality reproduction; long life; good pass-along readership	Long ad purchase lead time; some waste in circulation
Outdoor	Flexibility; high repeat exposure; low cost; low competition	Limited audience selectivity; creative limitations
Yellow Pages	Excellent local coverage; high believability; wide reach; low cost	High competition; long ad purchase lead time; creative limitations
Newsletters	Very high selectivity; full control; interactive opportunities; relative low costs	Costs could run away
Brochures	Flexibility; full control; can dramatize messages	Overproduction could lead to runaway costs
Telephone	Many users; opportunity to give a personal touch	Relative high cost; increasing consumer resistance
Internet	High selectivity; interactive possibilities; relatively low cost	Increasing clutter

have been reimagined as steaming cups of Folgers coffee; in Belgium, eBay posted "Moved to eBay" stickers on empty storefronts; and in Germany, imaginary workers toiling inside vending machines, ATMs, and photo booths were justification for a German job-hunting Web site to proclaim, "Life Is Too Short for the Wrong Job."[29]

New "Eyes On" measurement techniques allow marketers to better understand who actually has seen their outdoor ads.[30] The right billboard can make all the difference. Chang Soda in Bangkok had enough money in its budget for only one digital billboard. To maximize impact, it built a giant bubbling bottle onto the billboard to illustrate the product's carbonation. Subsequent word-of-mouth buzz quintupled bottle sales from 200,000 to 1 million.[31]

A strong creative message can also break through visual clutter. Snickers out-of-home program used billboards and taxi-top signs with puns combining the brand's benefits and key locations, such as "Satisflying" at the airport, "Transfer to the Ate Train" in the subway, and "Snackonomics" on cabs in Wall Street.[32]

Public Spaces Advertisers have been increasingly placing ads in unconventional places such as on movie screens, on airplanes, and in fitness clubs, as well as in classrooms, sports arenas, office and hotel elevators, and other public places.[33] Billboard-type poster ads are showing up everywhere. Transit ads on buses, subways, and commuter trains—around for years—have become a valuable way to reach working women. "Street furniture"—bus shelters, kiosks, and public areas—is another fast-growing option.

Advertisers can buy space in stadiums and arenas and on garbage cans, bicycle racks, parking meters, airport luggage carousels, elevators, gasoline pumps, the bottom of golf cups and swimming pools, airline snack packages, and supermarket produce in the form of tiny labels on apples and bananas. They can even buy space in toilet stalls and above urinals which, according to one

Snickers uses clever taxi-top signs
to increase its brand salience.

research study, office workers visit an average of three to four times a day for roughly four minutes per visit.[34]

Product Placement Marketers pay product placement fees of $100,000 to as much as $500,000 so their products will make cameo appearances in movies and on television.[35] Sometimes placements are the result of a larger network advertising deal, but other times they are the work of small product-placement shops that maintain ties with prop masters, set designers, and production executives. Some firms get product placement at no cost by supplying their product to the movie company (Nike does not pay to be in movies but often supplies shoes, jackets, bags, and so on). Increasingly, products and brands are being woven directly into the story.[36]

Staples and *The Office*   When Staples introduced a new $69.99 paper-shredding device called the MailMate in 2006, the company struck a two-episode deal with NBC's popular television program, *The Office*. In the first episode, the character Kevin Malone was given the responsibility of shredding paper with the MailMate; in the second, another character, Dwight Schrute, took a job at Staples. The writers and producers of the show tried to accommodate Staples' marketing objectives for the product as much as possible. To make sure the shredder looked small enough, it sat on Kevin's desk. To emphasize the shredder was sturdy, Kevin shredded not only paper but also his credit card. To emphasize that the shredder was available only at Staples, the episode closed with Kevin shredding lettuce and making it into a salad. When a colleague asked where he got the salad, he replied, "Staples."

Product placement is not immune to criticism as lawmakers increasingly criticize its stealth nature, threatening to force more explicit disclosure of participating advertisers.

Point of Purchase Chapter 16 discussed the importance of shopper marketing and in-store marketing efforts. The appeal of point-of-purchase advertising lies in the fact that in many product categories consumers make the bulk of their final brand decisions in the store, 74 percent according to one study.[37]

There are many ways to communicate with consumers at the **point of purchase** (**P-O-P**). In-store advertising includes ads on shopping carts, cart straps, aisles, and shelves, as well as promotion options such as in-store demonstrations, live sampling, and instant coupon machines.[38] Some supermarkets are selling floor space for company logos and experimenting with talking shelves. P-O-P radio provides FM-style programming and commercial messages to thousands of food stores and drugstores nationwide. Programming includes a store-selected music format, consumer tips, and commercials. Video screens in some stores allow for TV-type ads to be run.[39]

Walmart SMART Network   One of the in-store advertising pioneers, Walmart, replaced its original Walmart TV with its new SMART network in 2008. The new TV network allows Walmart to monitor and control more than 27,000 individual screens in some 2,700 stores nationwide, reaching 160 million viewers every four weeks. Its "triple play" feature permits ads to be shown on a large welcome screen at the entrance of the store, a category screen in departments, and endcap screens on each aisle. Those highly visible endcap viewings are not cheap. Advertisers pay $325,000 for 30-second spots per two-week cycle in the grocery section and $650,000 per four-week run in the health and beauty aid department. Five-second ads running every two minutes for two weeks on the welcome screens cost advertisers $80,000, and 10-second spots running twice every six minutes on the full network cost $50,000 per week. By linking the time when ads were shown and when product sales were made, Walmart can estimate how much ads increase sales by department (from 7 percent in Electronics to 28 percent in Health & Beauty) and by product type (mature items increase by 7 percent, seasonal items by 18 percent).

EVALUATING ALTERNATE MEDIA   Ads now can appear virtually anywhere consumers have a few spare minutes or even seconds to notice them. The main advantage of nontraditional media is that they can often reach a very precise and captive audience in a cost-effective manner. The message must be simple and direct. Outdoor advertising, for example, is often called the "15-second sell." It's more effective at enhancing brand awareness or brand image than creating new brand associations.

Unique ad placements designed to break through clutter may also be perceived as invasive and obtrusive, however. Consumer backlash often results when people see ads in traditionally ad-free spaces, such as in schools, on police cruisers, and in doctors' waiting rooms. Nevertheless, perhaps because of its sheer pervasiveness, some consumers seem to be less bothered by nontraditional media now than in the past.

The challenge for nontraditional media is demonstrating its reach and effectiveness through credible, independent research. Consumers must be favorably affected in some way to justify the marketing expenditures. But there will always be room for creative means of placing the brand in front of consumers, as occurred with McDonald's' alternate-reality game called "The Lost Ring."[40] "Marketing Insight: Playing Games with Brands" describes the role of gaming in marketing in general.

McDonald's and The Lost Ring   As an official sponsor of the 2008 Beijing Olympics, McDonald's created a multipronged marketing effort. Looking to engage young adults immune to traditional media ploys, McDonald's, its marketing agency AKQA, and game developer Jane McGonigal created a global, multilingual alternate-reality game (ARG) called The Lost Ring. The Web-based game centered around Ariadne, a fictional amnesiac female Olympic athlete from a parallel universe, and united players around the world in an online quest to recover ancient Olympic secrets. Discreetly sponsored by McDonald's, the game began with 50 gaming bloggers receiving enigmatic packages on February 29, 2008 (Leap Day). The packages included an Olympic-themed poster from 1920 and other teasers with a clue to TheLostRing.com. Almost 3 million people in more than 100 countries eventually played the game, which ended August 24, 2008, the last day of the Olympics. The game received the Grand Prize in *Adweek*'s 2008 Buzz Awards.

Marketing Insight

Playing Games with Brands

More than half of U.S. adults age 18 and older play video games, and about one in five play every day or almost every day. Virtually all teens (97 percent) play video games. As many as 40 percent of gamers are women. Women seem to prefer puzzles and collaborative games, whereas men seem more attracted to competitive or simulation games. Given this explosive popularity, many advertisers have decided, "if you can't beat them, join them."

A top-notch "advergame" can cost between $100,000 and $500,000 to develop. The game can be played on the sponsor's corporate homepage, on gaming portals, or even on public locations such as at restaurants. 7-Up, McDonald's, and Porsche have all been featured in games. Honda developed a game that allowed players to choose a Honda and zoom around city streets plastered with Honda logos. In the first three months, 78,000 people played for an average of eight minutes each. The game's cost per thousand (CPM) of $7 compared favorably to a prime-time TV commercial's CPM of $11.65. Marketers collect valuable customer data upon registration and often seek permission to send e-mail. Of game players sponsored by Ford Escape SUV, 54 percent signed up to receive e-mail.

Marketers are also playing starring roles in popular video games. In multiplayer Test Drive Unlimited, players can take a break from the races to go shopping, where they can encounter at least 10 real-world brands such as Lexus and Hawaiian Airlines. Tomb Raider's Lara Craft tools around in a Jeep Commander. Mainstream marketers such as Apple, Procter & Gamble, Toyota, and Visa are all jumping on board. Overall, research suggests that gamers are fine with ads and the way they affect the game experience. One study showed that 70 percent of gamers felt dynamic in-game ads "contributed to realism," "fit the games" in which they served, and looked "cool."

Sources: "In-Game Advertising Research Proves Effectiveness for Brands across Categories and Game Titles," www.microsoft.com, June 3, 2008; Amanda Lenhart, "Video Games: Adults Are Players Too," Pew Internet & American Life Project, www.pewresearch.org, December 7, 2008; "Erika Brown, "Game On!" Forbes, July 24, 2006, pp. 84–86; David Radd, "Advergaming: You Got It," BusinessWeek, October 11, 2006; Stuart Elliott, "Madison Avenue's Full-Court Pitch to Video Gamers," New York Times, October 16, 2005.

Selecting Specific Media Vehicles

The media planner must search for the most cost-effective vehicles within each chosen media type. The advertiser who decides to buy 30 seconds of advertising on network television can pay around $100,000 for a new show, over $300,000 for a popular prime-time show such as *Sunday Night Football, American Idol, Grey's Anatomy,* or *Desperate Housewives,* or over $2.5 million for an event such as the Super Bowl.[41] These choices are critical: The average cost to produce a national 30-second television commercial in 2007 was about $342,000.[42] It can cost as much to run an ad once on network TV as to create and produce the ad to start with!

In making choices, the planner must rely on measurement services that estimate audience size, composition, and media cost. Media planners then calculate the cost per thousand persons reached by a vehicle. A full-page, four-color ad in *Sports Illustrated* cost approximately $350,000 in 2010. If *Sports Illustrated*'s estimated readership was 3.15 million people, the cost of exposing the ad to 1,000 persons is approximately $11.20. The same ad in *Time* cost approximately $500,000, but reached 4.25 million people—at a higher cost-per-thousand of $11.90.

The media planner ranks each magazine by cost per thousand and favors magazines with the lowest cost per thousand for reaching target consumers. The magazines themselves often put together a "reader profile" for their advertisers, describing average readers with respect to age, income, residence, marital status, and leisure activities.

Marketers need to apply several adjustments to the cost-per-thousand measure. First, they should adjust for *audience quality.* For a baby lotion ad, a magazine read by 1 million young mothers has an exposure value of 1 million; if read by 1 million teenagers, it has an exposure value of almost zero. Second, adjust the exposure value for the *audience-attention probability.* Readers of *Vogue* may pay more attention to ads than do readers of *Newsweek.*[43] Third, adjust for the medium's *editorial quality* (prestige and believability). People are more likely to believe a TV or radio ad and to become more positively disposed toward the brand when the ad is placed within a program they like.[44] Fourth, consider *ad placement policies and extra services* (such as regional or occupational editions and lead-time requirements for magazines).

Media planners are using more sophisticated measures of effectiveness and employing them in mathematical models to arrive at the best media mix. Many advertising agencies use software programs to select the initial media and make improvements based on subjective factors.[45]

Deciding on Media Timing and Allocation

In choosing media, the advertiser has both a macroscheduling and a microscheduling decision. The *macroscheduling decision* relates to seasons and the business cycle. Suppose 70 percent of a product's sales occur between June and September. The firm can vary its advertising expenditures to follow the seasonal pattern, to oppose the seasonal pattern, or to be constant throughout the year.

The *microscheduling decision* calls for allocating advertising expenditures within a short period to obtain maximum impact. Suppose the firm decides to buy 30 radio spots in the month of September. Figure 18.3 shows several possible patterns. The left side shows that advertising messages for the month can be concentrated ("burst" advertising), dispersed continuously throughout the month, or dispersed intermittently. The top side shows that the advertising messages can be beamed with a level, rising, falling, or alternating frequency.

The chosen pattern should meet the communications objectives set in relationship to the nature of the product, target customers, distribution channels, and other marketing factors. The timing pattern should consider three factors. *Buyer turnover* expresses the rate at which new buyers enter the market; the higher this rate, the more continuous the advertising should be. *Purchase frequency* is the number of times the average buyer buys the product during the period; the higher the purchase frequency, the more continuous the advertising should be. The *forgetting rate* is the rate at which the buyer forgets the brand; the higher the forgetting rate, the more continuous the advertising should be.

In launching a new product, the advertiser must choose among continuity, concentration, flighting, and pulsing.

- *Continuity* means exposures appear evenly throughout a given period. Generally, advertisers use continuous advertising in expanding market situations, with frequently purchased items, and in tightly defined buyer categories.
- *Concentration* calls for spending all the advertising dollars in a single period. This makes sense for products with one selling season or related holiday.
- *Flighting* calls for advertising during a period, followed by a period with no advertising, followed by a second period of advertising activity. It is useful when funding is limited, the purchase cycle is relatively infrequent, or items are seasonal.
- *Pulsing* is continuous advertising at low-weight levels, reinforced periodically by waves of heavier activity. It draws on the strength of continuous advertising and flights to create a compromise scheduling strategy.[46] Those who favor pulsing believe the audience will learn the message more thoroughly, and at a lower cost to the firm.

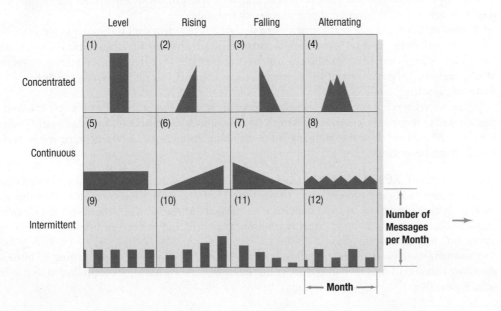

|Fig. 18.3|

Classification of Advertising Timing Patterns

TABLE 18.2	Advertising Pretest Research Techniques

For Print Ads

Starch and Gallup & Robinson Inc. are two widely used print pretesting services. Test ads are placed in magazines, which are then circulated to consumers. These consumers are contacted later and interviewed. Recall and recognition tests are used to determine advertising effectiveness.

For Broadcast Ads

In-home tests: A video is taken or downloaded into the homes of target consumers, who then view the commercials.

Trailer tests: In a trailer in a shopping center, shoppers are shown the products and given an opportunity to select a series of brands. They then view commercials and are given coupons to be used in the shopping center. Redemption rates indicate commercials' influence on purchase behavior.

Theater tests: Consumers are invited to a theater to view a potential new television series along with some commercials. Before the show begins, consumers indicate preferred brands in different categories; after the viewing, consumers again choose preferred brands. Preference changes measure the commercials' persuasive power.

On-air tests: Respondents are recruited to watch a program on a regular TV channel during the test commercial or are selected based on their having viewed the program. They are asked questions about commercial recall.

A company must decide how to allocate its advertising budget over space as well as over time. The company makes "national buys" when it places ads on national TV networks or in nationally circulated magazines. It makes "spot buys" when it buys TV time in just a few markets or in regional editions of magazines. These markets are called *areas of dominant influence* (ADIs) or *designated marketing areas* (DMAs). The company makes "local buys" when it advertises in local newspapers, radio, or outdoor sites.

Evaluating Advertising Effectiveness

Most advertisers try to measure the communication effect of an ad—that is, its potential impact on awareness, knowledge, or preference. They would also like to measure the ad's sales effect.

COMMUNICATION-EFFECT RESEARCH **Communication-effect research**, called *copy testing*, seeks to determine whether an ad is communicating effectively. Marketers should perform this test both before an ad is put into media and after it is printed or broadcast. Table 18.2 describes some specific advertising pretest research techniques.

Pretest critics maintain that agencies can design ads that test well but may not necessarily perform well in the marketplace. Proponents maintain that useful diagnostic information can emerge and that pretests should not be used as the sole decision criterion anyway. Widely acknowledged as one of the best advertisers around, Nike is notorious for doing very little ad pretesting.

Many advertisers use posttests to assess the overall impact of a completed campaign. If a company hoped to increase brand awareness from 20 percent to 50 percent and succeeded in increasing it to only 30 percent, then the company is not spending enough, its ads are poor, or it has overlooked some other factor.

SALES-EFFECT RESEARCH What sales are generated by an ad that increases brand awareness by 20 percent and brand preference by 10 percent? The fewer or more controllable other factors such as features and price are, the easier it is to measure advertising's effect on sales. The sales impact is easiest to measure in direct marketing situations and hardest in brand or corporate image-building advertising.

Companies are generally interested in finding out whether they are overspending or underspending on advertising. One way to answer this question is to work with the formulation shown in Figure 18.4.

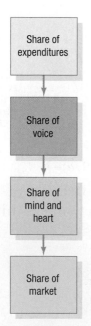

|Fig. 18.4|

Formula for Measuring Different Stages in the Sales Impact of Advertising

A company's *share of advertising expenditures* produces a *share of voice* (proportion of company advertising of that product to all advertising of that product) that earns a *share of consumers' minds and hearts* and, ultimately, a *share of market*.

Researchers try to measure the sales impact by analyzing historical or experimental data. The *historical approach* correlates past sales to past advertising expenditures using advanced statistical techniques.[47] Other researchers use an *experimental design* to measure advertising's sales impact.

A growing number of researchers are striving to measure the sales effect of advertising expenditures instead of settling for communication-effect measures.[48] Millward Brown International has conducted tracking studies for years to help advertisers decide whether their advertising is benefiting their brand.[49]

Sales Promotion

Sales promotion, a key ingredient in marketing campaigns, consists of a collection of incentive tools, mostly short term, designed to stimulate quicker or greater purchase of particular products or services by consumers or the trade.[50]

Whereas advertising offers a *reason* to buy, sales promotion offers an *incentive*. Sales promotion includes tools for *consumer promotion* (samples, coupons, cash refund offers, prices off, premiums, prizes, patronage rewards, free trials, warranties, tie-in promotions, cross-promotions, point-of-purchase displays, and demonstrations), *trade promotion* (prices off, advertising and display allowances, and free goods), and *business* and *sales force promotion* (trade shows and conventions, contests for sales reps, and specialty advertising).

Objectives

Sales promotion tools vary in their specific objectives. A free sample stimulates consumer trial, whereas a free management-advisory service aims at cementing a long-term relationship with a retailer.

Sellers use incentive-type promotions to attract new triers, to reward loyal customers, and to increase the repurchase rates of occasional users. Sales promotions often attract brand switchers, who are primarily looking for low price, good value, or premiums. If some of them would not have otherwise tried the brand, promotion can yield long-term increases in market share.[51]

Sales promotions in markets of high brand similarity can produce a high sales response in the short run but little permanent gain in brand preference over the longer term. In markets of high brand dissimilarity, they may be able to alter market shares permanently. In addition to brand switching, consumers may engage in stockpiling—purchasing earlier than usual (purchase acceleration) or purchasing extra quantities. But sales may then hit a postpromotion dip.[52]

Advertising versus Promotion

Sales promotion expenditures increased as a percentage of budget expenditure for a number of years, although its growth has recently slowed. Several factors contributed to this growth, particularly in consumer markets. Promotion became more accepted by top management as an effective sales tool, the number of brands increased, competitors used promotions frequently, many brands were seen as similar, consumers became more price-oriented, the trade demanded more deals from manufacturers, and advertising efficiency declined.

But the rapid growth of sales promotion created clutter. Consumers began to tune out promotions: Coupon redemption peaked in 1992 at 7.9 billion coupons redeemed but dropped to 2.6 billion by 2008. Incessant price reductions, coupons, deals, and premiums can also devalue the product in buyers' minds. There is a risk in putting a well-known brand on promotion over 30 percent of the time. Having turned to 0 percent financing, hefty cash rebates, and special lease programs to ignite sales in the soft post-9/11 economy, auto manufacturers have found it difficult to wean consumers from discounts ever since.[53]

Loyal brand buyers tend not to change their buying patterns as a result of competitive promotions. Advertising appears to be more effective at deepening brand loyalty, although we can distinguish added-value promotions from price promotions.[54] Gain's "Love at First Sniff" campaign used direct mail and in-store scented tear-pads and ShelfVision TV to entice consumers to smell the product, resulting in an almost 500 percent increase in shipments over the goal.[55]

Price promotions may not build permanent total-category volume. One study of more than 1,000 promotions concluded that only 16 percent paid off.[56] Small-share competitors may find it advantageous to use sales promotion, because they cannot afford to match the market leaders' large advertising budgets, nor can they obtain shelf space without offering trade allowances or stimulate consumer trial without offering incentives. Dominant brands offer deals less frequently, because most deals subsidize only current users.

The upshot is that many consumer-packaged-goods companies feel forced to use more sales promotion than they wish. They blame heavy use of sales promotion for decreased brand loyalty, increased price sensitivity, brand-quality image dilution, and a focus on short-run marketing planning. One review of promotion effectiveness concluded, "When the strategic disadvantages of promotions are included, that is, losing control to the trade and training consumers to buy only on deal, the case is compelling for a reevaluation of current practices and the incentive systems responsible for this trend."[57]

Major Decisions

In using sales promotion, a company must establish its objectives, select the tools, develop the program, pretest the program, implement and control it, and evaluate the results.

ESTABLISHING OBJECTIVES Sales promotion objectives derive from broader communication objectives, which derive from more basic marketing objectives for the product. For consumers, objectives include encouraging purchase of larger-sized units, building trial among nonusers, and attracting switchers away from competitors' brands. Ideally, promotions with consumers would have short-run sales impact as well as long-run brand equity effects.[58] For retailers, objectives include persuading retailers to carry new items and higher levels of inventory, encouraging off-season buying, encouraging stocking of related items, offsetting competitive promotions, building brand loyalty, and gaining entry into new retail outlets. For the sales force, objectives include encouraging support of a new product or model, encouraging more prospecting, and stimulating off-season sales.[59]

SELECTING CONSUMER PROMOTION TOOLS The promotion planner should take into account the type of market, sales promotion objectives, competitive conditions, and each tool's cost-effectiveness. The main consumer promotion tools are summarized in ▭ Table 18.3. *Manufacturer promotions* are, for instance in the auto industry, rebates, gifts to motivate test-drives and purchases, and high-value trade-in credit. *Retailer promotions* include price cuts, feature advertising, retailer coupons, and retailer contests or premiums.[60]

We can also distinguish between sales promotion tools that are *consumer franchise building* and those that are not. The former impart a selling message along with the deal, such as free samples, frequency awards, coupons when they include a selling message, and premiums when they are related to the product. Sales promotion tools that typically are *not* brand building include price-off packs, consumer premiums not related to a product, contests and sweepstakes, consumer refund offers, and trade allowances.

Consumer franchise-building promotions offer the best of both worlds—they build brand equity while moving product. Sampling has gained popularity in recent years—companies such as McDonald's, Dunkin' Donuts, and Starbucks have given away millions of samples of their new products—because consumers like them and they often lead to higher long-term sales for quality products.[61]

Digital coupons eliminate printing costs, reduce paper waste, are easily updatable, and have higher redemption rates. Coupons.com receives almost 5 million unique visitors a month for money-saving deals. Almost 2 million consumers visit CoolSavings.com each month for money-saving coupons and offers from name brands, as well as helpful tips and articles, newsletters, free recipes, sweepstakes, free trials, free samples, and more. Electronic coupons can arrive by cell phone, Twitter, e-mail, or Facebook.[62]

SELECTING TRADE PROMOTION TOOLS Manufacturers use a number of trade promotion tools (see ▭ Table 18.4).[63] Manufacturers award money to the trade (1) to persuade the retailer or wholesaler to carry the brand; (2) to persuade the retailer or wholesaler to carry more units than the normal amount; (3) to induce retailers to promote the brand by featuring, display, and price reductions; and (4) to stimulate retailers and their sales clerks to push the product.

The growing power of large retailers has increased their ability to demand trade promotion at the expense of consumer promotion and advertising.[64] The company's sales force and its brand

TABLE 18.3   Major Consumer Promotion Tools
Samples: Offer of a free amount of a product or service delivered door-to-door, sent in the mail, picked up in a store, attached to another product, or featured in an advertising offer.
Coupons: Certificates entitling the bearer to a stated saving on the purchase of a specific product: mailed, enclosed in other products or attached to them, or inserted in magazine and newspaper ads.
Cash Refund Offers (rebates): Provide a price reduction after purchase rather than at the retail shop: Consumer sends a specified "proof of purchase" to the manufacturer who "refunds" part of the purchase price by mail.
Price Packs (cents-off deals): Offers to consumers of savings off the regular price of a product, flagged on the label or package. A *reduced-price pack* is a single package sold at a reduced price (such as two for the price of one). A *banded pack* is two related products banded together (such as a toothbrush and toothpaste).
Premiums (gifts): Merchandise offered at a relatively low cost or free as an incentive to purchase a particular product. A *with-pack premium* accompanies the product inside or on the package. A *free in-the-mail premium* is mailed to consumers who send in a proof of purchase, such as a box top or UPC code. A *self-liquidating premium* is sold below its normal retail price to consumers who request it.
Frequency Programs: Programs providing rewards related to the consumer's frequency and intensity in purchasing the company's products or services.
Prizes (contests, sweepstakes, games): *Prizes* are offers of the chance to win cash, trips, or merchandise as a result of purchasing something. A *contest* calls for consumers to submit an entry to be examined by a panel of judges who will select the best entries. A *sweepstakes* asks consumers to submit their names in a drawing. A *game* presents consumers with something every time they buy—bingo numbers, missing letters—which might help them win a prize.
Patronage Awards: Values in cash or in other forms that are proportional to patronage of a certain vendor or group of vendors.
Free Trials: Inviting prospective purchasers to try the product without cost in the hope that they will buy.
Product Warranties: Explicit or implicit promises by sellers that the product will perform as specified or that the seller will fix it or refund the customer's money during a specified period.
Tie-in Promotions: Two or more brands or companies team up on coupons, refunds, and contests to increase pulling power.
Cross-Promotions: Using one brand to advertise another noncompeting brand.
Point-of-Purchase (P-O-P) Displays and Demonstrations: P-O-P displays and demonstrations take place at the point of purchase or sale.

TABLE 18.4   Major Trade Promotion Tools
Price-Off (off-invoice or off-list): A straight discount off the list price on each case purchased during a stated time period.
Allowance: An amount offered in return for the retailer's agreeing to feature the manufacturer's products in some way. An *advertising allowance* compensates retailers for advertising the manufacturer's product. A *display allowance* compensates them for carrying a special product display.
Free Goods: Offers of extra cases of merchandise to intermediaries who buy a certain quantity or who feature a certain flavor or size.

Reflecting changes in consumer behavior, digital coupons such as these, available at Coupons.com, have grown in importance.

managers are often at odds over trade promotion. The sales force says local retailers will not keep the company's products on the shelf unless they receive more trade promotion money, whereas brand managers want to spend their limited funds on consumer promotion and advertising.

Manufacturers face several challenges in managing trade promotions. First, they often find it difficult to police retailers to make sure they are doing what they agreed to do. Manufacturers increasingly insist on proof of performance before paying any allowances. Second, some retailers are doing *forward buying*—that is, buying a greater quantity during the deal period than they can immediately sell. Retailers might respond to a 10 percent-off-case allowance by buying a 12-week or longer supply. The manufacturer must then schedule more production than planned and bear the costs of extra work shifts and overtime. Third, some retailers are *diverting*, buying more cases than needed in a region where the manufacturer offers a deal and shipping the surplus to their stores in nondeal regions. Manufacturers handle forward buying and diverting by limiting the amount they will sell at a discount, or by producing and delivering less than the full order in an effort to smooth production.[65]

Ultimately, many manufacturers feel trade promotion has become a nightmare. It contains layers of deals, is complex to administer, and often leads to lost revenues.

SELECTING BUSINESS AND SALES FORCE PROMOTION TOOLS Companies spend billions of dollars on business and sales force promotion tools (see ▢ Table 18.5) to gather leads, impress and reward customers, and motivate the sales force.[66] They typically develop budgets for tools that remain fairly constant from year to year. For many new businesses that want to make a splash to a targeted audience, especially in the B2B world, trade shows are an important tool, but the cost per contact is the highest of all communication options.

DEVELOPING THE PROGRAM In planning sales promotion programs, marketers are increasingly blending several media into a total campaign concept, such as the following award-winning promotion.[67]

Oreo Double Stuf Promotion Winner of the Promotional Marketing Association's Super Reggie award for best integrated marketing program of 2008, Kraft's Oreo Double Stuf Racing League promotion cleverly capitalized on the images of professional athlete siblings. In its teaser launch ad, NFL star quarterback brothers Peyton and Eli

TABLE 18.5 ▭ Major Business and Sales Force Promotion Tools
Trade Shows and Conventions: Industry associations organize annual trade shows and conventions. Trade shows are an $11.5 billion business, and business marketers may spend as much as 35 percent of their annual promotion budget on trade shows. Trade show attendance can range from a few thousand people to over 70,000 for large shows held by the restaurant or hotel-motel industries. The International Consumer Electronics Show is one of the largest trade shows in the world with more than 200,000 attendees in 2009. Participating vendors expect several benefits, including generating new sales leads, maintaining customer contacts, introducing new products, meeting new customers, selling more to present customers, and educating customers with publications, videos, and other audiovisual materials.
Sales Contests: A sales contest aims at inducing the sales force or dealers to increase their sales results over a stated period, with prizes (money, trips, gifts, or points) going to those who succeed.
Specialty Advertising: Specialty advertising consists of useful, low-cost items bearing the company's name and address, and sometimes an advertising message that salespeople give to prospects and customers. Common items are ballpoint pens, calendars, key chains, flashlights, tote bags, and memo pads.

Manning announced they were officially becoming two-sport competitors. A follow-up ad with the brothers revealed that the classic "split and lick" ritual with Oreo cookies was becoming a professional sport. The Mannings encouraged the public to join the league and to enter a sweepstakes that would award 10 winners a three-day trip to New Orleans to take part in a Double Stuf Lick Race (DSLR) competition and compete for a $10,000 prize. Kraft promoted the DSLR sweepstakes by placing the image of the Mannings on 15 million Oreo packages and setting up in-store and point-of-purchase displays. An instant-win game on the Web site gave visitors a chance to earn one of 2,000 DSLR "training kits," including a cooler, two glasses, and a branded jersey. Professional tennis star sisters Serena and Venus Williams later appeared in a second round of ads, challenging the Mannings to cookie-licking supremacy in what was billed as the "ultimate sibling rivalry." ▭

In deciding to use a particular incentive, marketers must first determine its *size*. A certain minimum is necessary if the promotion is to succeed. Second, the marketing manager must establish *conditions* for participation. Incentives might be offered to everyone or to select groups. Third, the marketer must decide on the *duration* of the promotion. Fourth, the marketer must choose a *distribution vehicle*. A 15-cents-off coupon can be distributed in the product package, in stores, by mail, online, or in advertising. Fifth, the marketing manager must establish the *timing* of promotion, and finally, the *total sales promotion budget*. The cost of a particular promotion consists of the administrative cost (printing, mailing, and promoting the deal) and the incentive cost (cost of premium or cents-off, including redemption costs), multiplied by the expected number of units sold. The cost of a coupon deal would recognize that only a fraction of consumers will redeem the coupons.

IMPLEMENTING AND EVALUATING THE PROGRAM Marketing managers must prepare implementation and control plans that cover lead time and sell-in time for each individual promotion. *Lead time* is the time necessary to prepare the program prior to launching it.[68] *Sell-in time* begins with the promotional launch and ends when approximately 95 percent of the deal merchandise is in the hands of consumers.

Manufacturers can evaluate the program using sales data, consumer surveys, and experiments. Sales (scanner) data helps analyze the types of people who took advantage of the promotion, what they bought before the promotion, and how they behaved later toward the brand and other brands. Sales promotions work best when they attract competitors' customers who then switch. *Consumer surveys* can uncover how many consumers recall the promotion, what they thought of it, how many took advantage of it, and how the promotion affected subsequent brand-choice behavior.[69] *Experiments* vary such attributes as incentive value, duration, and distribution media. For example, coupons can be sent to half the households in a consumer panel. Scanner data can track whether the coupons led more people to buy the product and when.

Additional costs beyond the cost of specific promotions include the risk that promotions might decrease long-run brand loyalty. Second, promotions can be more expensive than they appear. Some are inevitably distributed to the wrong consumers. Third are the costs of special production runs, extra sales force effort, and handling requirements. Finally, certain promotions irritate retailers, who may demand extra trade allowances or refuse to cooperate.

Events and Experiences

The IEG Sponsorship Report projected that $17.1 billion would be spent on sponsorships in North America during 2010, with 68 percent going to sports; another 10 percent to entertainment tours and attractions; 5 percent to festivals, fairs, and annual events; 5 percent to the arts; 3 percent to associations and membership organizations; and 9 percent to cause marketing.[70] Becoming part of a personally relevant moment in consumers' lives through events and experiences can broaden and deepen a company or brand's relationship with the target market.

Daily encounters with brands may also affect consumers' brand attitudes and beliefs. *Atmospheres* are "packaged environments" that create or reinforce leanings toward product purchase. Law offices decorated with Oriental rugs and oak furniture communicate "stability" and "success."[71] A five-star hotel will use elegant chandeliers, marble columns, and other tangible signs of luxury. Many firms are creating on-site and off-site product and brand experiences. There is Everything Coca-Cola in Las Vegas and M&M World in Times Square in New York.[72]

Many firms are creating their own events and experiences to create consumer and media interest and involvement. To showcase its international reach and upgrades in seating, food, and beverage, Delta Airlines created a temporary SKY360 pop-up retail lounge on West 57th Street in Manhattan. The lounge featured samples of wine and food items from chef Todd English to eat and drink, comfortable leather seats found in coach to sit in, and the seat-back entertainment system to listen to.[73] Given its central business location for the media industry, Manhattan is the site of many events and experiences.[74]

 GE Profile To promote its new GE Profile Frontload Washer and Dryer with SmartDispense Technology—designed to optimize the amount of detergent used in any one wash—GE used traditional online and mass media. To create even more buzz, the firm hung 800 feet of jeans and shirts on a massive clothesline in Times Square to represent the six months' worth of washing the new machines could typically handle before needing more detergent. On one of the traffic islands were 20-foot-high inflatable versions of the new washer/dryer. A live celebrity auction to benefit the nonprofit Clothes Off Our Back Foundation was hosted by television mom Alison Sweeney. A small army of 20 representatives handing out product-related goodies (such as bottles of water and coloring books shaped like the appliance's door) added to the spectacle. GE also ran an online promotion. All these efforts combined to attract 150,000 entrants to a washer/dryer giveaway contest.

A major Times Square event to support the launch of a new line of GE Profile washers and dryers was part of an extensive integrated marketing communications program.

Events Objectives

Marketers report a number of reasons to sponsor events:

1. *To identify with a particular target market or lifestyle*—Customers can be targeted geographically, demographically, psychographically, or behaviorally according to events. Old Spice sponsors college sports and motor sports—including a 10-year deal with driver Tony Stewart's entries in the Nextel Cup and Busch Series—to highlight product relevance and sample among its target audience of 16- to 24-year-old males.[75]

2. *To increase salience of company or product name*—Sponsorship often offers sustained exposure to a brand, a necessary condition to reinforce brand salience. Top-of-mind awareness for World Cup soccer sponsors such as Emirates, Hyundai, Kia, and Sony benefited from the repeated brand and ad exposure over the one month–long tournament.

3. **To create or reinforce perceptions of key brand image associations**—Events themselves have associations that help to create or reinforce brand associations.[76] To toughen its image and appeal to America's heartland, Toyota Tundra elected to sponsor B.A.S.S. fishing tournaments and a Brooks & Dunn country music tour.

4. **To enhance corporate image**—Sponsorship can improve perceptions that the company is likable and prestigious. Although Visa views its long-standing Olympic sponsorship as a means of enhancing international brand awareness and increasing usage and volume, it also engenders patriotic goodwill and taps into the emotional Olympic spirit.[77]

5. **To create experiences and evoke feelings**—The feelings engendered by an exciting or rewarding event may indirectly link to the brand. Audi models featured prominently in the 2010 blockbuster *Iron Man 2*, including main character Tony Stark's personal R8 Spyder, the A8, Q5 and Q7 SUVs, and A3 hatchback. Backed by a month-long marketing blitz, surveys revealed that positive word of mouth doubled for the brand.[78]

6. **To express commitment to the community or on social issues**—Cause-related marketing sponsors nonprofit organizations and charities. Firms such as Timberland, Stonyfield Farms, Home Depot, Starbucks, American Express, and Tom's of Maine have made cause-related marketing an important cornerstone of their marketing programs.

7. **To entertain key clients or reward key employees**—Many events include lavish hospitality tents and other special services or activities only for sponsors and their guests. These perks engender goodwill and establish valuable business contacts. From an employee perspective, events can also build participation and morale or serve as an incentive. BB&T Corp., a major banking and financial services player in the South and Southeast United States, used its NASCAR Busch Series sponsorship to entertain business customers and its minor league baseball sponsorship to generate excitement among employees.[79]

8. **To permit merchandising or promotional opportunities**—Many marketers tie contests or sweepstakes, in-store merchandising, direct response, or other marketing activities with an event. Ford, Coca-Cola, and AT&T Mobility have all used their sponsorship of the hit TV show *American Idol* in this way.

Despite these potential advantages, the result of an event can still be unpredictable and beyond the sponsor's control. Although many consumers will credit sponsors for providing the financial assistance to make an event possible, some may resent the commercialization of events.

Major Sponsorship Decisions

Making sponsorships successful requires choosing the appropriate events, designing the optimal sponsorship program, and measuring the effects of sponsorship.[80]

CHOOSING EVENTS Because of the number of opportunities and their huge cost, many marketers are becoming more selective about choosing sponsorship events.

The event must meet the marketing objectives and communication strategy defined for the brand. The audience must match the target market. The event must have sufficient awareness, possess the desired image, and be capable of creating the desired effects. Consumers must make favorable attributions for the sponsor's engagement. An ideal event is also unique but not encumbered with many sponsors, lends itself to ancillary marketing activities, and reflects or enhances the sponsor's brand or corporate image.[81]

DESIGNING SPONSORSHIP PROGRAMS Many marketers believe the marketing program accompanying an event sponsorship ultimately determines its success. At least two to three times the amount of the sponsorship expenditure should be spent on related marketing activities.

Event creation is a particularly important skill in publicizing fund-raising drives for nonprofit organizations. Fund-raisers have developed a large repertoire of special events, including anniversary celebrations, art exhibits, auctions, benefit evenings, book sales, cake sales, contests, dances, dinners, fairs, fashion shows, phonathons, rummage sales, tours, and walkathons.

More firms are now using their names to sponsor arenas, stadiums, and other venues that hold events. Billions of dollars have been spent over the past decade for naming rights to major North American sports facilities. But as with any sponsorship, the most important consideration is the additional marketing activities.[82]

MEASURING SPONSORSHIP ACTIVITIES It's a challenge to measure the success of events. The *supply-side* measurement method focuses on potential exposure to the brand by assessing the extent of media coverage, and the *demand-side* method focuses on exposure reported by consumers. "Marketing Memo: Measuring High Performance Sponsorship Programs" offers some guidelines critical to issues of sponsorship measurement from industry experts IEG.

Supply-side methods approximate the amount of time or space devoted to media coverage of an event, for example, the number of seconds the brand is clearly visible on a television screen or the column inches of press clippings that mention it. These potential "impressions" translate into a value equivalent to the dollar cost of actually advertising in the particular media vehicle. Some industry consultants have estimated that 30 seconds of TV logo exposure during a televised event can be worth 6 percent, 10 percent, or as much as 25 percent of a 30-second TV ad spot.

Although supply-side exposure methods provide quantifiable measures, equating media coverage with advertising exposure ignores the content of the respective communications. The advertiser uses media space and time to communicate a strategically designed message. Media coverage and telecasts only expose the brand and don't necessarily embellish its meaning in any direct way. Although some public relations professionals maintain that positive editorial coverage can be worth 5 to 10 times the equivalent advertising value, sponsorship rarely provides such favorable treatment.[83]

The **demand-side method** identifies the effect sponsorship has on consumers' brand knowledge. Marketers can survey event spectators to measure recall of the event as well as resulting attitudes and intentions toward the sponsor.

Creating Experiences

A large part of local, grassroots marketing is experiential marketing, which not only communicates features and benefits but also connects a product or service with unique and interesting experiences. "The idea is not to sell something, but to demonstrate how a brand can enrich a customer's life."[84]

---

marketing Memo
Measuring High Performance Sponsorship Programs

1. *Measure outcomes, not outputs.* Focus on what a sponsorship actually produced rather than what a sponsor got or did—rather than focus on 5,000 people sampled at an event, how many of those people would be classified as members of the target market and what is the likely conversion rate between their trial and future behaviors?

2. *Define and benchmark objectives on the front end.* Specific objectives help to identify what measures should be tracked. An objective of motivating the sales force and distributors suggests different measures than one of building brand image and key brand benefits. Contrast measures in terms of sponsorship effects and what might have happened if the sponsorship had not occurred.

3. *Measure return for each objective against prorated share of rights and activation fees.* Rank and rate objectives by importance and allocate the total sponsorship budget against each of those objectives.

4. *Measure behavior.* Conduct a thorough sales analysis to identify shifts in marketplace behavior as a result of the sponsorship.

5. *Apply the assumptions and ratios used by other departments within the company.* Applying statistical methods used by other departments makes it easier to gain acceptance for any sponsorship analysis.

6. *Research the emotional identities of customers and measure the results of emotional connections.* In what ways does a sponsorship psychologically affect consumers and facilitate and deepen long-term loyalty relationships?

7. *Identify group norms.* How strong of a community exists around the sponsored event or participants? Are their formal groups that share interests that will be impacted by the sponsorship?

8. *Include cost savings in ROI calculations.* Contrast expenses that a firm has typically incurred in the past achieving a particular objective from those expenses allocated to achieve the objective as part of the sponsorship.

9. *Slice the data.* Sponsorship affects market segments differently. Breaking down a target market into smaller segments can better identify sponsorship effects.

10. *Capture normative data.* Develop a core set of evaluation criteria that can be applied across all different sponsorship programs.

Source: "Measuring High Performance Sponsorship Programs," IEG Executive Brief, IEG Sponsorship Consulting, www.sponsorship.com, 2009.

Consumers seem to appreciate that. In one survey, four of five respondents found participating in a live event was more engaging than all other forms of communication. The vast majority also felt experiential marketing gave them more information than other forms of communication and would make them more likely to tell others about participating in the event and to be receptive to other marketing for the brand.[85]

Companies can even create a strong image by inviting prospects and customers to visit their headquarters and factories. Ben & Jerry's, Boeing, Crayola, and Hershey's all sponsor excellent company tours that draw millions of visitors a year. Companies such as Hallmark, Kohler, and Beiersdorf (makers of NIVEA) have built corporate museums at or near their headquarters that display their history and the drama of producing and marketing their products.

Public Relations

Not only must the company relate constructively to customers, suppliers, and dealers, it must also relate to a large number of interested publics. A **public** is any group that has an actual or potential interest in or impact on a company's ability to achieve its objectives. **Public relations (PR)** includes a variety of programs to promote or protect a company's image or individual products.

The wise company takes concrete steps to manage successful relationships with its key publics. Most companies have a public relations department that monitors the attitudes of the organization's publics and distributes information and communications to build goodwill. The best PR departments counsel top management to adopt positive programs and eliminate questionable practices so negative publicity doesn't arise in the first place. They perform the following five functions:

Crayola brings colorful fun to its company tours and visits.

1. *Press relations*—Presenting news and information about the organization in the most positive light
2. *Product publicity*—Sponsoring efforts to publicize specific products
3. *Corporate communications*—Promoting understanding of the organization through internal and external communications
4. *Lobbying*—Dealing with legislators and government officials to promote or defeat legislation and regulation
5. *Counseling*—Advising management about public issues, and company positions and image during good times and bad

Marketing Public Relations

Many companies are turning to **marketing public relations (MPR)** to support corporate or product promotion and image making. MPR, like financial PR and community PR, serves a special constituency, the marketing department.

The old name for MPR was **publicity**, the task of securing editorial space—as opposed to paid space—in print and broadcast media to promote or "hype" a product, service, idea, place, person, or organization. MPR goes beyond simple publicity and plays an important role in the following tasks:

- *Launching new products.* The amazing commercial success of toys such as LeapFrog, Beanie Babies, and even the latest kids' craze, Silly Bandz, owes a great deal to strong publicity.
- *Repositioning a mature product.* In a classic PR case study, New York City had extremely bad press in the 1970s until the "I Love New York" campaign.
- *Building interest in a product category.* Companies and trade associations have used MPR to rebuild interest in declining commodities such as eggs, milk, beef, and potatoes and to expand consumption of such products as tea, pork, and orange juice.
- *Influencing specific target groups.* McDonald's sponsors special neighborhood events in Latino and African American communities to build goodwill.

- *Defending products that have encountered public problems.* PR professionals must be adept at managing crises, such as those weathered by such well-established brands as Tylenol, Toyota, and BP in 2010.
- *Building the corporate image in a way that reflects favorably on its products.* Steve Jobs's heavily anticipated Macworld keynote speeches have helped to create an innovative, iconoclastic image for Apple Corporation.

As the power of mass advertising weakens, marketing managers are turning to MPR to build awareness and brand knowledge for both new and established products. MPR is also effective in blanketing local communities and reaching specific groups and can be more cost-effective than advertising. Nevertheless, it must be planned jointly with advertising.[86]

Clearly, creative public relations can affect public awareness at a fraction of the cost of advertising. The company doesn't pay for media space or time but only for a staff to develop and circulate the stories and manage certain events. An interesting story picked up by the media can be worth millions of dollars in equivalent advertising. Some experts say consumers are five times more likely to be influenced by editorial copy than by advertising. The following is an example of an award-winning PR campaign.[87]

Man Lives in IKEA
IKEA showed that a highly successful marketing campaign does not have to cost a lot of money if PR is properly employed. With its PR firm Ketchum, the company created the clever "Man Lives in IKEA" PR campaign. Using a budget of only $13,500, IKEA allowed comedian Mark Malkoff to live in an apartment in the Paramus, New Jersey, store from January 7 to 12, 2007, during which time he was allowed 24-hour access to film anything and everything. The campaign's goals included increasing sales, boosting traffic to IKEA-USA.com, and promoting two key brand messages: "IKEA has everything you need to live and make a home" and "Home is the most important place in the world." Ketchum and IKEA secured interviews with store executives and planned the week's schedule, which included a goodbye party featuring singer Lisa Loeb. Malkoff's team documented his interactions, including with security guards and customers relaxing in his "home," and posted 25 videos during the week. MarkLivesInIKEA.com received more than 15 million hits, and home-related IKEA blog coverage rose 356 percent from January 2007 to January 2008. IKEA calculated that the effort generated more than 382 million positive media impressions. Coverage highlights included the AP, *Today*, *Good Morning America*, and CNN. Sales at the Paramus store were up 5.5 percent compared to January 2007, while traffic to the IKEA Web site was up 6.8 percent.

In a clever PR campaign to reinforce its "everything for the home" brand message, a man lived in an IKEA store for almost a week, which many people heard about through the film crew following him for a short documentary on his Web site: http://www.marklivesinikea.com.

Major Decisions in Marketing PR

In considering when and how to use MPR, management must establish the marketing objectives, choose the PR messages and vehicles, implement the plan carefully, and evaluate the results. The main tools of MPR are described in Table 18.6.

ESTABLISHING OBJECTIVES MPR can build *awareness* by placing stories in the media to bring attention to a product, service, person, organization, or idea. It can build *credibility* by communicating the message in an editorial context. It can help boost sales force and dealer *enthusiasm* with stories about a new product before it is launched. It can hold down *promotion cost* because MPR costs less than direct-mail and media advertising.

Whereas PR practitioners reach their target publics through the mass media, MPR is increasingly borrowing the techniques and technology of direct-response marketing to reach target audience members one-on-one.

CHOOSING MESSAGES AND VEHICLES Suppose a relatively unknown college wants more visibility. The MPR practitioner will search for stories. Are any faculty members working on unusual projects? Are any new and unusual courses being taught? Are any interesting events taking place on campus? If there are no interesting stories, the MPR practitioner should propose newsworthy events the college could sponsor. Here the challenge is to create meaningful news.

TABLE 18.6 Major Tools in Marketing PR
Publications: Companies rely extensively on published materials to reach and influence their target markets. These include annual reports, brochures, articles, company newsletters and magazines, and audiovisual materials.
Events: Companies can draw attention to new products or other company activities by arranging and publicizing special events such as news conferences, seminars, outings, trade shows, exhibits, contests and competitions, and anniversaries that will reach the target publics.
Sponsorships: Companies can promote their brands and corporate name by sponsoring and publicizing sports and cultural events and highly regarded causes.
News: One of the major tasks of PR professionals is to find or create favorable news about the company, its products, and its people and to get the media to accept press releases and attend press conferences.
Speeches: Increasingly, company executives must field questions from the media or give talks at trade associations or sales meetings, and these appearances can build the company's image.
Public Service Activities: Companies can build goodwill by contributing money and time to good causes.
Identity Media: Companies need a visual identity that the public immediately recognizes. The visual identity is carried by company logos, stationery, brochures, signs, business forms, business cards, buildings, uniforms, and dress codes.

PR ideas include hosting major academic conventions, inviting expert or celebrity speakers, and developing news conferences.

Each event and activity is an opportunity to develop a multitude of stories directed at different audiences. A good PR campaign will engage the public from a variety of angles, as did this award-winning Dreyer's Ice Cream campaign.[88]

Dreyer's Ice Cream In *PRWeek*'s Campaign of the Year in 2010, Dreyer's Ice Cream teamed up with PR firm Ketchum to launch a campaign to turn the tough economic environment into a positive. Taking advantage of the 80th anniversary of its introduction of the Rocky Road flavor—designed to cheer people up during the Great Depression—Dreyer's launched a celebratory limited edition "Red, White & No More Blues!" flavor. The ice cream combined rich, creamy vanilla ice cream with swirls of real strawberry and blueberry. The ensuing "A Taste of Recovery" campaign was designed to reinforce the feel-good aspects of the brand. A Monster.com-posted contest asked contestants to submit videos explaining a personal dream they would fulfill if they earned $100,000 for scooping ice cream. The contest drew over 85,000 online visits and more than 14,000 entries. A media blitz greeting the winner helped to contribute to the 46 million media impressions the campaign enjoyed. Despite tough economic times, sales of Dreyer's Slow Churned Limited Editions ice cream increased over 25 percent from the previous year.

A brand anniversary is a great opportunity to celebrate what is good about a brand, as Dreyer's did via its special-edition ice cream.

IMPLEMENTING THE PLAN AND EVALUATING RESULTS MPR's contribution to the bottom line is difficult to measure, because it is used along with other promotional tools.

The easiest measure of MPR effectiveness is the number of *exposures* carried by the media. Publicists supply the client with a clippings book showing all the media that carried news about the product and a summary statement such as the following:

Media coverage included 3,500 column inches of news and photographs in 350 publications with a combined circulation of 79.4 million; 2,500 minutes of air time on

*290 radio stations and an estimated audience of 65 million; and 660 minutes of air time on
160 television stations with an estimated audience of 91 million. If this time and space had
been purchased at advertising rates, it would have amounted to $1,047,000.*[89]

This measure is not very satisfying because it contains no indication of how many people actually
read, heard, or recalled the message and what they thought afterward; nor does it contain information about the net audience reached, because publications overlap in readership. It also ignores the
effects of electronic media. Publicity's goal is reach, not frequency, so it would be more useful to
know the number of unduplicated exposures across all media types.

A better measure is the *change in product awareness, comprehension, or attitude* resulting from
the MPR campaign (after allowing for the effect of other promotional tools). For example, how
many people recall hearing the news item? How many told others about it (a measure of word of
mouth)? How many changed their minds after hearing it?

Summary

1. Advertising is any paid form of nonpersonal presentation and promotion of ideas, goods, or services by an identi-fied sponsor. Advertisers include not only business firms but also charitable, nonprofit, and government agencies.

2. Developing an advertising program is a five-step process: (1) Set advertising objectives, (2) establish a budget, (3) choose the advertising message and cre-ative strategy, (4) decide on the media, and (5) evaluate communication and sales effects.

3. Sales promotion consists of mostly short-term incentive tools, designed to stimulate quicker or greater purchase of particular products or services by consumers or the trade.

4. In using sales promotion, a company must establish its objectives, select the tools, develop the program, pretest the program, implement and control it, and eval-uate the results.

5. Events and experiences are a means to become part of special and more personally relevant moments in con-sumers' lives. Events can broaden and deepen the sponsor's relationship with its target market, but only if managed properly.

6. Public relations (PR) includes a variety of programs de-signed to promote or protect a company's image or its individual products. Marketing public relations (MPR), to support the marketing department in corporate or product promotion and image making, can affect public awareness at a fraction of the cost of advertising and is often much more credible. The main tools of PR are publications, events, news, community affairs, identifi-cation media, lobbying, and social responsibility.

Applications

Marketing Debate
Should Marketers Test Advertising?

Advertising creatives have long lamented ad pretesting. They believe it inhibits their creative process and results in too much sameness in commercials. Marketers, on the other hand, believe pretesting provides necessary checks and balances to ensure the ad campaign will connect with consumers and be well received in the marketplace.

Take a position: Ad pretesting in often an unnecessary waste of marketing dollars *versus* Ad pretesting pro-vides an important diagnostic for marketers as to the likely success of an ad campaign.

Marketing Discussion
Television Advertising

What are some of your favorite TV ads? Why? How effective are the message and creative strategies? How are they creating consumer preference and loyalty and building brand equity?

Marketing Excellence

>>Coca-Cola

When it comes to mass marketing, perhaps no one does it better than Coca-Cola. Coke is the most popular and best-selling soft drink in history. With an annual marketing budget of nearly $3 billion and annual sales exceeding $30 billion, the brand tops the Interbrand ranking year after year. Today, Coca-Cola holds a current brand value of $68 billion and reaches consumers in over 200 countries, making it the best-known product in the world. In fact, Coca-Cola is such a global phenomenon that its name is the second-most understood word in the world (after *okay*).

The history of Coke's success is astonishing. The drink was invented in 1886 by Dr. John S. Pemberton, who mixed a syrup of his own invention with carbonated water to cure headaches. The company's first president later turned the product into a pop culture phenomenon by introducing it to pharmacists and consumers around the world and handing out clocks, posters, and other paraphernalia with the Coca-Cola logo.

Coca-Cola believed early on that to gain worldwide acceptance, the brand needed to connect emotionally and socially with the masses, and the product needed to be "within arm's-length of desire." So the company focused on gaining extensive distribution and worked hard at making the product loved by all. In World War II, it declared that "every man in uniform gets a bottle of Coca-Cola for 5 cents, wherever he is, and whatever it costs the company." This strategy helped introduce the soft drink to people around the world as well as connect with them positively in a time of turmoil.

Why is Coca-Cola so much bigger than any other competitor? What Coke does better than everyone else is create highly current, uplifting global campaigns that translate well into different countries, languages, and cultures. Coke's advertising over the years has primarily focused on the product's ability to quench thirst and the brand's magical ability to connect people no matter who they are or how they live. Andy Warhol said it best, "A Coke is a Coke and no amount of money can get you a better Coke than the one the bum on the corner is drinking."

One of Coca-Cola's most memorable and successful commercials was called "Hilltop" and featured the song, "I'd like to buy the world a Coke." Launched in 1971, the ad featured young adults from all over the world sharing a happy, harmonious moment and common bond (drinking a Coke) on a hillside in Italy. The commercial touched so many consumers emotionally and so effectively showed the worldwide appeal of Coke that the song became a top ten hit single later that year.

Coca-Cola's television commercials still touch upon the message of universal connection over a Coke, often in a lighthearted tone to appeal to a young audience. In one spot, a group of young adults sit around a campfire, playing the guitar, laughing, smiling, and passing around a bottle of Coke. The bottle reaches a slimy, one-eyed alien who joins in on the fun, takes a sip from the bottle, and passes it along. When the next drinker wipes off the slime in disgust, the music stops suddenly and the group stares at him in disappointment. The man hesitantly hands the bottle back to the alien to get re-slimed and then drinks from it, and the music and the party continue in perfect harmony.

Coca-Cola's mass communications strategy has evolved over the years and today mixes a wide range of media including television, radio, print, online, in-store, digital, billboard, public relations, events, paraphernalia, and even its own museum. The company's target audience and reach are so massive that choosing the right media and marketing message is critical. Coca-Cola uses big events to hit huge audiences; it has sponsored the Olympics since 1928 and advertises during the Super Bowl. Red Coke cups are placed front and center during top-rated television shows like *American Idol*, and the company spends over $1 billion a year on sports sponsorships such as NASCAR and the World Cup. Coca-Cola's global campaigns must also be relevant on a local scale. In China, for example, Coca-Cola has given its regional managers control over its advertising so they can include appropriate cultural messages.

The delicate balance between Coca-Cola's local and global marketing is crucial because, as one Coca-Cola executive explained, "Creating effective marketing at a local level in the absence of global scale can lead to huge inefficiencies." In 2006, for example, Coca-Cola ran two campaigns during the FIFA World Cup as well as several local campaigns. In 2010, the company ran a single campaign during the same event in over 100 markets. Executives at Coca-Cola estimated that the latter, more global strategy saved the company over $45 million in efficiencies.

Despite its unprecedented success over the years, Coke is not perfect. In 1985, in perhaps the worst product launch ever, Coca-Cola introduced New Coke—a sweeter concoction of the original secret formula. Consumers instantly rejected it and sales plummeted. Three months later, Coca-Cola retracted New Coke and relaunched the original formula under the name Coca-Cola Classic, to the delight of customers everywhere. Then-CEO Roberto Goizueta stated, "The simple fact is that all the time and money and skill poured into consumer research on the new Coca-Cola could not measure or reveal the deep and abiding emotional attachment to original Coca-Cola felt by so many people."

Coca-Cola's success at marketing a product on such a global, massive scale is unique. No other product is so universally available, universally accepted, and universally loved. As the company continues to grow, it seeks out new ways to better connect with even more individuals.

Referring to itself as a "Happiness Factory," it is optimistic that it will succeed.

Questions

1. What does Coca-Cola stand for? Is it the same for everyone? Explain.

2. Coca-Cola has successfully marketed to billions of people around the world. Why is it so successful?

3. Can Pepsi or any other company ever surpass Coca-Cola? Why or why not? What are Coca-Cola's greatest risks?

Sources: Natalie Zmuda, "Coca-Cola Lays Out Its Vision for the Future at 2010 Meeting." *Advertising Age,* November 22, 2009; Natalie Zmuda, "Coke's 'Open Happiness' Keeps It Simple for Global Audience," *Advertising Age,* January 21, 2009; John Greenwald, "Will Teens Buy It?" *Time,* June 24, 2001; "Coca-Cola Still Viewed as Most Valuable Brand." *USA Today,* September 18, 2009; Edward Rothstein, "Ingredients: Carbonated Water, High-Fructose Corniness . . ." *New York Times,* July 30, 2007; Brad Cook, "Coca-Cola: A Classic," *Brandchannel,* December 2, 2002; Coca-Cola, *Annual Report.*

Marketing Excellence

>>Gillette

Gillette knows men. Not only does the company understand what products men desire for their grooming needs, it also knows how to market to men all around the world. Since the invention of the safety razor by King C. Gillette in 1901, Gillette has had a number of breakthrough product innovations. These include the first twin-blade shaving system in 1971 named the Trac II, a razor with a pivoting head in 1977 called the Atra, and the first razor with spring-mounted twin blades in 1989 dubbed the Sensor. In 1998, Gillette introduced the first triple-blade system, Mach3, which became a billion-dollar brand surpassed only by the 2006 launch of the "best shave on the planet"—the six-bladed Fusion, with five blades in the front for regular shaving and one in the back for trimming.

Today, Gillette holds a commanding lead in the shaving and razor business with a 70 percent global market share and $7.5 billion in annual sales. Six hundred million men use a Gillette product every day, and the Fusion razor accounts for 45 percent of the men's razors sold in the United States. Gillette's mass appeal is a result of several factors, including extensive consumer research, quality product innovations, and successful mass communications.

While Gillette's product launches have improved male grooming, it's the company's impressive marketing knowledge and campaigns that have helped it reach this international level of success. Traditionally, Gillette uses one global marketing message rather than individual targeted messages for each country or region. This message is backed by a wide spectrum of advertising support, including athletic sponsorships, television campaigns, in-store promotions, print ads, online advertising, and direct marketing.

Gillette's most recent global marketing effort, "The Moment," launched in 2009, is an extension of its well-recognized campaign, "The Best a Man Can Get." The campaign features everyday men as well as the Gillette Champions—baseball star Derek Jeter, tennis champion Roger Federer, and soccer great Thierry Henry—experiencing moments of doubt and Gillette's grooming products helping them gain confidence. The campaign was designed to help Gillette expand beyond razors and shaving and increase sales of its entire line of grooming products. The massive marketing effort launched around the globe and included television, print, online, and point-of-sale advertising.

Another crucial element in Gillette's marketing strategy is sports marketing. Gillette's natural fit with baseball and tradition has helped the company connect emotionally with its core audience, and its sponsorship with Major League Baseball dates to 1939. Tim Brosnan, EVP for Major League Baseball, explained, "Gillette is a sports marketing pioneer that paved the way for modern day sports sponsorship and endorsements." Gillette ads have featured baseball heroes such as Hank Aaron, Mickey Mantle, and Honus Wagner from as early as 1910.

Gillette also has ties to football. The company sponsors Gillette Stadium, home of the New England Patriots, and is a corporate sponsor of the NFL, making four of its products, Gillette, Old Spice, Head & Shoulders, and Febreze, "Official Locker Room Products of the NFL." Gillette's partnership includes sweepstakes to win NFL game tickets, Web site promotions, and ties to the NFL, such as the presence of some NFL players in its commercials. Gillette also sponsors several NASCAR races and drivers and the UK Tri-Nations rugby tournament. It even created a Zamboni at the Boston Bruins game that looked like a huge Fusion razor shaving the ice.

While sports marketing is a critical element of Gillette's marketing strategy, the brand aims to reach all men and therefore aligns itself with musicians, video games, and movies—in one James Bond film, *Goldfinger*, a Gillette razor contained a homing device.

When Procter & Gamble acquired Gillette in 2005 for $57 billion (a record five times sales), it aimed for more than sales and profit. P&G, an expert on marketing to women, wanted to learn about marketing to men on a global scale, and no one tops Gillette.

Questions

1. Gillette has successfully convinced the world that "more is better" in terms of number of blades and other razor features. Why has that worked in the past? What's next?

2. Some of Gillette's spokespeople such as Tiger Woods have run into controversy after becoming endorsers for the brand. Does this hurt Gillette's brand equity or marketing message? Explain.

3. Can Gillette ever become as successful at marketing to women? Why or why not?

Sources: Gillette press release, "Gillette Launches New Global Brand Marketing Campaign," July 1, 2009; Major League Baseball press release, "Major League Baseball Announces Extension of Historic Sponsorship with Gillette Dating Back to 1939," April 16, 2009; Gillette, *2009 Annual Report*; Jeremy Mullman and Rich Thomaselli, "Why Tiger Is Still the Best Gillette Can Get," *Advertising Age,* December 7, 2009; Louise Story, "Procter and Gillette Learn from Each Other's Marketing Ways," *New York Times,* April 12, 2007; Dan Beucke, "A Blade Too Far," *BusinessWeek,* August 14, 2006; Jenn Abelson, "And Then There Were Five," *Boston Globe*, September 15, 2005; Jack Neff, "Six-Blade Blitz," *Advertising Age*, September 19, 2005, pp. 3, 53; Editorial, "Gillette Spends Smart on Fusion," *Advertising Age*, September 26, 2005, p. 24.

In This Chapter, We Will Address the Following **Questions**

1. How can companies conduct direct marketing for competitive advantage?

2. How can companies carry out effective interactive marketing?

3. How does word of mouth affect marketing success?

4. What decisions do companies face in designing and managing a sales force?

5. How can salespeople improve their selling, negotiating, and relationship marketing skills?

Reflecting new consumer sensibilities that focus on the good that companies do, Pepsi used the Super Bowl to launch a major new cause marketing initiative instead of its typical splashy ad campaigns.

Chapter 19

WHAT DO YOU CARE ABOUT?

health   arts & culture   food & shelter   the planet   neighborhoods   education

This year, the Pepsi Refresh Project™ is giving millions of dollars to fund ideas, across six different categories, that will refresh the world. Maybe it's green spaces. Or educational comic books. Maybe it's teaching kids to rock out. So submit your idea and vote for what you care about most at refresh**everything**.com

The Pepsi Refresh Project
Thousands of ideas. Millions in grants.™

every pepsi refreshes the world™

PEPSI, DIET PEPSI, PEPSI MAX, the Pepsi Globe, PEPSI REFRESH PROJECT, THOUSANDS OF IDEAS. MILLIONS IN GRANTS., and EVERY PEPSI REFRESHES THE WORLD are trademarks

Managing Personal Communications: Direct and Interactive Marketing, Word of Mouth, and Personal Selling

In the face of the Internet revolution, marketing communications today increasingly occur as a kind of personal dialogue between the company and its customers. Companies must ask not only "How should we reach our customers?" but also "How should our customers reach us?" and "How can our customers reach each other?" New technologies have encouraged companies to move from mass communication to more targeted, two-way communications. Consumers now play a much more participatory role in the marketing process. Consider how Pepsi has engaged the consumer in its marketing communications.[1]

 For the first time in 23 years, PepsiCo chose not to advertise any of its soft drink brands during the biggest U.S. media event, the Super Bowl. Instead, it launched its ambitious Pepsi Refresh Project. With a tagline "Every Pepsi Refreshes the World," Pepsi earmarked $20 million for the program to fund ideas from anyone, anywhere, anytime to make a difference in six areas: health, arts and culture, food and shelter, the planet, neighborhoods, and education. Ideas are submitted at refresheverything.com and voted online by the general public. A significant presence on Facebook, Twitter, and other social networks is a key aspect to the program. The first grant recipients received funding for a variety of different projects, including building a community playground, providing care packages and comfort items for troops in the field or recovering from wounds at home, and conducting financial literacy sessions for teens. Pepsi also allocated an additional $1.3 million in the summer of 2010 to support communities in the Gulf of Mexico region affected by the catastrophic oil spill.

Marketers are trying to figure out the right way to be part of the consumer conversation. Personalizing communications and creating dialogues by saying and doing the right thing to the right person at the right time is critical for marketing effectiveness. In this chapter, we consider how companies personalize their marketing communications to have more impact. We begin by evaluating direct and interactive marketing, then move to word-of-mouth marketing, and finish by considering personal selling and the sales force.

Direct Marketing

Today, many marketers build long-term relationships with customers.[2] They send birthday cards, information materials, or small premiums. Airlines, hotels, and other businesses adopt frequency reward programs and club programs.[3] **Direct marketing** is the use of consumer-direct (CD) channels to reach and deliver goods and services to customers without using marketing middlemen.

Direct marketers can use a number of channels to reach individual prospects and customers: direct mail, catalog marketing, telemarketing, interactive TV, kiosks, Web sites, and mobile devices. They often seek a measurable response, typically a customer order, through **direct-order marketing**. Direct marketing has been a fast-growing avenue for serving customers, partly in response to the high and increasing costs of reaching business markets through a sales force. Sales produced through traditional direct marketing channels (catalogs, direct mail, and telemarketing) have been growing rapidly, along with direct-mail sales, which include sales to the consumer market, B2B, and fund-raising by charitable institutions.

Direct marketing has been outpacing U.S. retail sales. It accounted for almost 53 percent of total advertising spending in 2009, and companies spent more than $149 billion on direct marketing per year, accounting for 8.3 percent of GDP.[4]

The Benefits of Direct Marketing

Market demassification has resulted in an ever-increasing number of market niches. Consumers short of time and tired of traffic and parking headaches appreciate toll-free phone numbers, always-open Web sites, next-day delivery, and direct marketers' commitment to customer service. In addition, many chain stores have dropped slower-moving specialty items, creating an opportunity for direct marketers to promote these to interested buyers instead.

Sellers benefit from demassification as well. Direct marketers can buy a mailing list containing the names of almost any group: left-handed people, overweight people, millionaires. They can customize and personalize messages and build a continuous relationship with each customer. New parents will receive periodic mailings describing new clothes, toys, and other goods as their child grows.

Direct marketing can reach prospects at the moment they want a solicitation and therefore be noticed by more highly interested prospects. It lets marketers test alternative media and messages to find the most cost-effective approach. Direct marketing also makes the direct marketer's offer and strategy less visible to competitors. Finally, direct marketers can measure responses to their campaigns to decide which have been the most profitable. One successful direct marketer is L.L.Bean.[5]

L.L.Bean   L.L.Bean's founder Leon Leonwood (L.L.) Bean returned from a Maine hunting trip in 1911 with cold, damp feet and a revolutionary idea. His Maine Hunting Shoe stitched leather uppers to workmen's rubber boots to create a comfortable, functional boot. To a mailing list of hunters, Bean sent a three-page flyer describing the benefits of the new product and backing it with a complete guarantee. The shoe, however, did not meet with initial success. Of his first 100 orders, 90 were returned when the tops and bottoms separated. True to his word, Bean refunded the purchase price and the problem was fixed. L.L.Bean quickly became known as a trusted source for reliable outdoor equipment and expert advice. The L.L.Bean guarantee of 100 percent satisfaction is still at the core of the company's business, as is the original L.L. Bean's Golden Rule, "Sell good merchandise at a reasonable profit, treat your customers like human beings, and they will always come back for more." Today, L.L.Bean is a $1.4 billion company. In 2009, it produced 49 different catalogs and received 11 million customer contacts. The company's Web site is among the top-rated e-commerce sites, and its growing number of retail stores and outlets retain the company's legendary customer service.

Direct marketing must be integrated with other communications and channel activities.[6] Direct marketing companies such as Eddie Bauer, Lands' End, and the Franklin Mint made fortunes building their brands in the direct marketing mail-order and phone-order business and then opened retail stores. They cross-promote their stores, catalogs, and Web sites, for example, by putting their Web addresses on their shopping bags.

Successful direct marketers view a customer interaction as an opportunity to up-sell, cross-sell, or just deepen a relationship. These marketers make sure they know enough about each customer to customize and personalize offers and messages and develop a plan for lifetime marketing to each valuable customer, based on their knowledge of life events and transitions. They also carefully

orchestrate each element of their campaigns. Here is an example of an award-winning campaign that did just that.[7]

New Zealand Yellow Pages
One of the Direct Marketing Association's top ECHO award winners in 2009 was New Zealand's Yellow Pages Group. With a theme of "Job Done," the group recruited a young woman to be the focus of the campaign and gave her the task of building a restaurant 40 feet above the ground in a redwood tree, using only help found via the Yellow Pages. A TV ad, billboard, and online media launched the campaign, and a Web site provided updates. Access to the striking pod-shaped structure Treehouse was provided by an elevated treetop walkway. The restaurant actually operated from December 2008 to February 2009 as part of the campaign. Highly popular, the campaign was credited with increasing the use of Yellow Pages by 11 percent to record levels.

We next consider some of the key issues that characterize different direct marketing channels.

To dramatically demonstrate the utility of its product, the New Zealand Yellow Pages engaged a designer to build a tree-top restaurant using only help hired through the Yellow Pages.

Direct Mail

Direct-mail marketing means sending an offer, announcement, reminder, or other item to an individual consumer. Using highly selective mailing lists, direct marketers send out millions of mail pieces each year—letters, flyers, foldouts, and other "salespeople with wings." Some direct marketers mail multimedia DVDs to prospects and customers.

Direct mail is a popular medium because it permits target market selectivity, can be personalized, is flexible, and allows early testing and response measurement. Although the cost per thousand is higher than for mass media, the people reached are much better prospects. The success of direct mail, however, has also become its liability—so many marketers are sending out direct-mail pieces that mailboxes are becoming stuffed, leading some consumers to disregard the blizzard of solicitations they receive.

In constructing an effective direct-mail campaign, direct marketers must choose their objectives, target markets and prospects, offer elements, means of testing the campaign, and measures of campaign success.

OBJECTIVES Most direct marketers aim to receive an order from prospects and judge a campaign's success by the response rate. An order-response rate of 2 percent to 4 percent is normally considered good, although this number varies with product category, price, and the nature of the offering.[8] Direct mail can also produce prospect leads, strengthen customer relationships, inform and educate customers, remind customers of offers, and reinforce recent customer purchase decisions.

TARGET MARKETS AND PROSPECTS Most direct marketers apply the RFM (*recency, frequency, monetary amount*) formula to select customers according to how much time has passed since their last purchase, how many times they have purchased, and how much they have spent since becoming a customer. Suppose the company is offering a leather jacket. It might make this offer to the most attractive customers—those who made their last purchase between 30 and 60 days ago, who make three to six purchases a year, and who have spent at least $100 since becoming customers. Points are established for varying RFM levels; the more points, the more attractive the customer.[9]

Marketers also identify prospects on the basis of age, sex, income, education, previous mail-order purchases, and occasion. College freshmen will buy laptop computers, backpacks, and compact refrigerators; newlyweds look for housing, furniture, appliances, and bank loans. Another useful variable is consumer lifestyle or "passions" such as electronics, cooking, and the outdoors.

Dun & Bradstreet provides a wealth of data for B2B direct marketing. Here the prospect is often not an individual but a group or committee of both decision makers and decision influencers. Each member needs to be treated differently, and the timing, frequency, nature, and format of contact must reflect the member's status and role.

The company's best prospects are customers who have bought its products in the past. The direct marketer can also buy lists of names from list brokers, but these lists often have problems, including name duplication, incomplete data, and obsolete addresses. Better lists include overlays of demographic and psychographic information. Direct marketers typically buy and test a sample before buying more names from the same list. They can build their own lists by advertising a promotional offer and collecting responses.

OFFER ELEMENTS The offer strategy has five elements—the *product*, the *offer*, the *medium*, the *distribution method*, and the *creative strategy*.[10] Fortunately, all can be tested. The direct-mail marketer also must choose five components of the mailing itself: the outside envelope, sales letter, circular, reply form, and reply envelope. A common direct marketing strategy is to follow up direct mail with an e-mail.

TESTING ELEMENTS One of the great advantages of direct marketing is the ability to test, under real marketplace conditions, different elements of an offer strategy, such as products, product features, copy platform, mailer type, envelope, prices, or mailing lists.

Response rates typically understate a campaign's long-term impact. Suppose only 2 percent of the recipients who receive a direct-mail piece advertising Samsonite luggage place an order. A much larger percentage became aware of the product (direct mail has high readership), and some percentage may have formed an intention to buy at a later date (either by mail or at a retail outlet). Some may mention Samsonite luggage to others as a result of the direct-mail piece. To better estimate a promotion's impact, some companies measure the impact of direct marketing on awareness, intention to buy, and word of mouth.

MEASURING CAMPAIGN SUCCESS: LIFETIME VALUE By adding up the planned campaign costs, the direct marketer can determine the needed break even response rate. This rate must be net of returned merchandise and bad debts. A specific campaign may fail to break even in the short run but can still be profitable in the long run if customer lifetime value is factored in (see Chapter 5) by calculating the average customer longevity, average customer annual expenditure, and average gross margin, minus the average cost of customer acquisition and maintenance (discounted for the opportunity cost of money).[11]

Catalog Marketing

In catalog marketing, companies may send full-line merchandise catalogs, specialty consumer catalogs, and business catalogs, usually in print form but also as DVDs or online. In 2009, three of the top B-to-C catalog sellers were Dell ($51 billion), Staples ($8.9 billion), and CDW ($8.1 billion). Three top B-to-B catalog sellers were Thermo Scientific lab and research supplies ($10.5 billion), Henry Schien dental, medical, and vet supplies ($6.4 billion), and WESCO International electrical and industry maintenance supplies ($6.1 billion). Thousands of small businesses also issue specialty catalogs.[12] Many direct marketers find combining catalogs and Web sites an effective way to sell.

Catalogs are a huge business—the Internet and catalog retailing industry includes 16,000 companies with combined annual revenue of $235 billion.[13] The success of a catalog business depends on managing customer lists carefully to avoid duplication or bad debts, controlling inventory, offering good-quality merchandise so returns are low, and projecting a distinctive image. Some companies add literary or information features, send swatches of materials, operate a special online or telephone hotline to answer questions, send gifts to their best customers, and donate a percentage of profits to good causes. Putting their entire catalog online also provides business marketers with better access to global consumers than ever before, saving printing and mailing costs.

Telemarketing

Telemarketing is the use of the telephone and call centers to attract prospects, sell to existing customers, and provide service by taking orders and answering questions. It helps companies increase revenue, reduce selling costs, and improve customer satisfaction. Companies use call centers for *inbound telemarketing*—receiving calls from customers—and *outbound telemarketing*—initiating calls to prospects and customers.

Although outbound telemarketing historically has been a major direct marketing tool, its potentially intrusive nature led the Federal Trade Commission to establish a National Do Not Call Registry in 2003. About 191 million consumers who did not want telemarketing calls at home were registered by 2009. Because only political organizations, charities, telephone surveyors, or companies with existing relationships with consumers are exempt, consumer telemarketing has lost much of its effectiveness.[14]

Business-to-business telemarketing is increasing, however. Raleigh Bicycles used telemarketing to reduce the personal selling costs of contacting its dealers. In the first year, sales force travel costs dropped 50 percent and sales in a single quarter went up 34 percent. As it improves with the use of videophones, telemarketing will increasingly replace, though never eliminate, more expensive field sales calls.

Other Media for Direct-Response Marketing

Direct marketers use all the major media. Newspapers and magazines carry ads offering books, clothing, appliances, vacations, and other goods and services that individuals can order via toll-free numbers. Radio ads present offers 24 hours a day. Some companies prepare 30- and 60-minute *infomercials* to combine the sell of television commercials with the draw of information and entertainment. Infomercials promote products that are complicated or technologically advanced, or that require a great deal of explanation (Carnival Cruises, Mercedes, Universal Studios, and even Monster.com). At-home shopping channels are dedicated to selling goods and services on a toll-free number or via the Web for delivery within 48 hours.

Public and Ethical Issues in Direct Marketing

Direct marketers and their customers usually enjoy mutually rewarding relationships. Occasionally, however, a darker side emerges:

* *Irritation.* Many people don't like hard-sell, direct marketing solicitations.
* *Unfairness.* Some direct marketers take advantage of impulsive or less sophisticated buyers or prey on the vulnerable, especially the elderly.[15]
* *Deception and fraud.* Some direct marketers design mailers and write copy intended to mislead or exaggerate product size, performance claims, or the "retail price." The Federal Trade Commission receives thousands of complaints each year about fraudulent investment scams and phony charities.
* *Invasion of privacy.* It seems that almost every time consumers order products by mail or telephone, apply for a credit card, or take out a magazine subscription, their names, addresses, and purchasing behavior may be added to several company databases. Critics worry that marketers may know too much about consumers' lives, and that they may use this knowledge to take unfair advantage.

People in the direct marketing industry know that, left unattended, such problems will lead to increasingly negative consumer attitudes, lower response rates, and calls for greater state and federal regulation. Most direct marketers want the same thing consumers want: honest and well-designed marketing offers targeted only to those who appreciate hearing about them.

Interactive Marketing

The newest and fastest-growing channels for communicating and selling directly to customers are electronic.[16] The Internet provides marketers and consumers with opportunities for much greater *interaction* and *individualization*. Soon few marketing programs will be considered complete without a meaningful online component.

Advantages and Disadvantages of Interactive Marketing

The variety of online communication options means companies can send tailored messages that engage consumers by reflecting their special interests and behavior. The Internet is also highly accountable and its effects can be easily traced by noting how many unique visitors or "UVs" click on a page or ad, how long they spend with it, and where they go afterward.[17]

Marketers can build or tap into online communities, inviting participation from consumers and creating a long-term marketing asset in the process. The Web offers the advantage of *contextual placement,* buying ads on sites related to the marketer's offerings. Marketers can also place advertising based on keywords from search engines, to reach people when they've actually started the buying process.

Using the Web also has disadvantages. Consumers can effectively screen out most messages. Marketers may think their ads are more effective than they are if bogus clicks are generated by software-powered Web sites.[18] Advertisers also lose some control over their online messages, which can be hacked or vandalized.

But many feel the pros outweigh the cons, and the Web is attracting marketers of all kinds. Beauty pioneer Estée Lauder, who said she relied on three means of communication to build her multimillion-dollar cosmetics business—"telephone, telegraph, and tell a woman"—would now have to add the Web, where the company's official site describes new and old products, announces special offers and promotions, and helps customers locate stores where they can buy Estée Lauder products.[19]

Marketers must go where the customers are, and increasingly that's online. U.S. consumers go to the Web over 25 percent of the time they spend with all media (see ▲ Figure 19.1). Customers

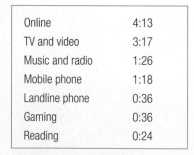

Online	4:13
TV and video	3:17
Music and radio	1:26
Mobile phone	1:18
Landline phone	0:36
Gaming	0:36
Reading	0:24

|Fig. 19.1| ▲

Average Time Spent per Day with Select Media According to US Consumers, 2009 (hrs:mins)

define the rules of engagement, however, and insulate themselves with the help of agents and intermediaries if they so choose. Customers define what information they need, what offerings they're interested in, and what they're willing to pay.[20]

Online advertising continues to gain on traditional media. Total Internet ad spending is estimated to have grown to $26 billion in 2009 from $24 billion in 2008; TV advertising was estimated to have dropped to $41 billion in 2009 from $52 billion in 2008. Helping fuel online growth is the emergence of rich media ads that combine animation, video, and sound with interactive features.[21] Consider what Burger King has done online.

Burger King

"If you have a global brand promise, 'Have It Your Way,'" said Russ Klein, Burger King's former president for global marketing, strategy, and innovation, "it's about putting the customer In charge," even If they say "bad things" about the brand. In competing against McDonald's, with its family-friendly image, "it's more important for us to be provocative than pleasant," added Klein, especially when appealing to a market of mainly teenage boys. Burger King's brash ad campaigns—featuring its creepy bobble-head king and talking chicken—have appeared on YouTube and MySpace, so the company can take advantage of "social connectivity" as consumers react to the ads. Burger King encourages customers to build online communities around their favorite company icons and products. To celebrate the 50th anniversary of its popular Whopper hamburger, the company took over a Burger King restaurant in Las Vegas for a day and told people the Whopper had been permanently removed from the menu. Customers' outraged reactions were filmed as part of an award-winning campaign dubbed "Whopper Freakout," which served as the basis of TV ads and online videos. Over 5 million consumers watched an 8-minute streaming video, another 14 million watched it or the TV spots on YouTube, and millions more heard or read about it via PR or word of mouth.[22]

Interactive Marketing Communication Options

A company chooses which forms of interactive marketing will be most cost-effective in achieving communication and sales objectives.[23] Some of the main categories, discussed next, are: (1) Web sites, (2) search ads, (3) display ads, and (4) e-mails. After summarizing some developments in mobile marketing, we'll describe social media and word-of-mouth effects.

WEB SITES Companies must design Web sites that embody or express their purpose, history, products, and vision and that are attractive on first viewing and interesting enough to encourage repeat visits.[24] Jeffrey Rayport and Bernard Jaworski propose that effective sites feature seven design

Vividly demonstrating its customers' loyalty, Burger King's online "Whopper Freakout" videos became a viral hit.

|Fig. 19.2| ▲

Seven Key Design Elements of an Effective Web Site

Source: Jeffrey F. Rayport and Bernard J. Jaworski, *e-commerce* (New York: McGraw-Hill, 2001), p. 116.

- *Context.* Layout and design
- *Content.* Text, pictures, sound, and video the site contains
- *Community.* How the site enables user-to-user communication
- *Customization.* Site's ability to tailor itself to different users or to allow users to personalize the site
- *Communication.* How the site enables site-to-user, user-to-site, or two-way communication
- *Connection.* Degree that the site is linked to other sites
- *Commerce.* Site's capabilities to enable commercial transactions

elements they call the 7Cs (see ▲ Figure 19.2):[25] To encourage repeat visits, companies must pay special attention to context and content factors and embrace another "C"—constant change.[26]

Visitors will judge a site's performance on ease of use and physical attractiveness.[27] *Ease of use* means: (1) The site downloads quickly, (2) the first page is easy to understand, and (3) it is easy to navigate to other pages that open quickly. *Physical attractiveness* is assured when: (1) Individual pages are clean and not crammed with content, (2) typefaces and font sizes are very readable, and (3) the site makes good use of color (and sound).

Firms such as comScore and Nielsen Online track where consumers go online through page views, unique visitors, length of visit, and so on.[28] Companies must also be sensitive to online security and privacy-protection issues.[29]

Besides their Web sites, companies may employ **microsites,** individual Web pages or clusters of pages that function as supplements to a primary site. They're particularly relevant for companies selling low-interest products. People rarely visit an insurance company's Web site, but the company can create a microsite on used-car sites that offers advice for buyers of used cars and at the same time a good insurance deal.

SEARCH ADS   A hot growth area in interactive marketing is **paid search** or **pay-per-click ads**, which now account for roughly half of all online ad spending.[30] Thirty-five percent of all searches are reportedly for products or services.

In paid search, marketers bid in a continuous auction on search terms that serve as a proxy for the consumer's product or consumption interests. When a consumer searches for any of the words with Google, Yahoo!, or Bing, the marketer's ad may appear above or next to the results, depending on the amount the company bids and an algorithm the search engines use to determine an ad's relevance to a particular search.[31]

Advertisers pay only if people click on the links, but marketers believe consumers who have already expressed interest by engaging in search are prime prospects. Average click-through is about 2 percent, much more than for comparable online ads. The cost per click depends on how high the link is ranked and the popularity of the keyword. The ever-increasing popularity of paid search has increased competition among keyword bidders, significantly raising search prices and putting a premium on choosing the best possible keywords, bidding on them strategically, and monitoring the results for effectiveness and efficiency.

Search engine optimization has become a crucial part of marketing given the large amount of money being spent by marketers on search. A number of guidelines have been suggested for more effective search ads.[32] Broader search terms are useful for general brand building; more specific ones—for example, specifying a particular product model or service—are useful for generating and converting sales leads. Search terms need to be spotlighted on the appropriate pages so search engines can easily identify them. Multiple keywords are usually needed for any one product, but each keyword must be bid for according to its likely return on revenue. It also helps to have popular sites link back to the site. Data can be collected to track the effects of paid search.

DISPLAY ADS   **Display ads** or **banner ads** are small, rectangular boxes containing text and perhaps a picture that companies pay to place on relevant Web sites.[33] The larger the audience, the higher the cost. Some banners are accepted on a barter basis. In the early days of the Internet, viewers clicked on 2 percent to 3 percent of the banner ads they saw, but that percentage quickly plummeted to as little as 0.25 percent and advertisers began to explore other forms of communication.

Given that Internet users spend only 5 percent of their time online actually searching for information, display ads still hold great promise compared to popular search ads. But ads need to be more attention-getting and influential, better targeted, and more closely tracked.[34]

Interstitials are advertisements, often with video or animation, which pop up between changes on a Web site. For example, ads for Johnson & Johnson's Tylenol headache reliever would pop up on brokers' Web sites whenever the stock market fell by 100 points or more. Because consumers find pop-up ads intrusive and distracting, many use software to block them.

A popular vehicle for advertising is *podcasts*, digital media files created for playback on portable MP3 players, laptops, or PCs. Sponsors pay roughly $25 per thousand listeners to run a 15- or 30-second audio ad at the beginning of the podcast. Although these rates are higher than for popular radio shows, podcasts are able to reach very specific market segments, and their popularity has grown.[35]

E-MAIL E-mail allows marketers to inform and communicate with customers at a fraction of the cost of a "d-mail," or direct mail, campaign. Consumers are besieged by e-mails, though, and many employ spam filters. Some firms are asking consumers to say whether and when they would like to receive emails. FTD, the flower retailer, allows customers to choose whether to receive e-mail reminders to send flowers for virtually any holiday as well as specific birthdays and anniversaries.[36]

E-mails must be timely, targeted, and relevant. For example, the United Way of Massachusetts Bay and Merrimack Valley used video-embedded e-mails to increase sign-ups for their events and to cut costs. Videos were made one minute in length when testing revealed that two minutes was too long but 30 seconds was too short.[37] "Marketing Memo: How to Maximize the Marketing Value of E-mails" provides some important guidelines for productive e-mail campaigns.

MOBILE MARKETING With cell phones' ubiquitous nature and marketers' ability to personalize messages based on demographics and other consumer behavior characteristics (see Chapter 15), the appeal of mobile marketing as a communication tool is obvious.[38]

With over 4.1 billion mobile subscribers in the world in 2009—there are more than twice as many mobile phones in the world as personal computers—cell phones represent a major opportunity for advertisers to reach consumers on the "third screen" (TV and the computer are first and second). Some firms are moving fast into m-space. One mobile pioneer in the banking industry is Bank of America.[39]

---

marketing Memo

How to Maximize the Marketing Value of E-mails

- *Give the customer a reason to respond.* Offer powerful incentives for reading e-mail pitches and online ads, such as trivia games, scavenger hunts, and instant-win sweepstakes.

- *Personalize the content of your e-mails.* Customers who agree to receive IBM's weekly iSource newsletter select "the news they choose" from topics on an interest profile.

- *Offer something the customer can't get via direct mail.* Because e-mail campaigns can be carried out quickly, they can offer time-sensitive information. Travelocity sends frequent e-mails pitching last-minute cheap airfares, and Club Med pitches unsold vacation packages at a discount.

- *Make it easy for customers to "unsubscribe."* Online customers demand a positive exit experience. Dissatisfied customers leaving on a sour note are more likely to spread the displeasure to others.

- *Combine with other communications such as social media.* Southwest Airlines found the highest number of reservations occur after an e-mail campaign followed by a social media campaign. Papa John's was able to add 45,000 fans to its Facebook page through an e-mail campaign inviting customers to participate in a "March Madness" NCAA basketball tournament contest.

To increase the effectiveness of e-mails, some researchers are employing "heat mapping," by which they can measure what people read on a computer screen by using cameras attached to a computer that track eye movements. One study showed that clickable graphic icons and buttons that linked to more details of a marketing offer increased click-through rates by 60 percent over links that used just an Internet address.

Sources: Richard Westlund, "Success Stories in eMail Marketing," *Adweek Special Advertising Section to Adweek, Brandweek, and Mediaweek*, February 16, 2010; Suzanne Vranica, "Marketers Give E-mail Another Look," *Wall Street Journal*, July 17, 2006; Seth Godin, *Permission Marketing: Turning Strangers into Friends and Friends into Customers* (New York: Simon & Schuster, 1999).

Bank of America   Bank of America is using mobile as a communication channel and a means to provide banking solutions for the many ways its customers lead their lives. More than 2 million of its 59 million customers use mobile banking applications, which the bank credits as a significant drawing card given that 8 percent to 10 percent of these mobile users are new customers. Initially targeting a younger group of users between 18 and 30 years old—with special emphasis on college students—the bank's mobile banking services increasingly appeal to other groups such as older, higher-income users. Its smart-phone apps and traditional browser-based solutions have been praised for clean navigation, ease of use, and reach. The branch and ATM locator, for instance, is used by one in eight mobile customers. Mobile marketing is integrated all through the bank's marketing efforts: The Web site provides demos and tours of its mobile services; the TV campaigns stress the benefits of its mobile banking. With one click on a mobile banner ad, smart-phone users can download the free Bank of America app or just learn more about its mobile banking services.

- *Mobile marketing options.* Mobile ad spending was almost $1 billion worldwide in 2009, most of which went into SMS text messages and simple display ads. With the increased capabilities of smart phones, however, mobile ads can be more than just a display medium using static "mini-billboards."[40]

  Much recent interest has been generated in mobile apps—"bite-sized" software programs that can be loaded on to smart phones. In a short period of time, thousands were introduced by companies large and small. VW chose to launch its GTI in the United States with an iPhone app, receiving 2 million downloads in three weeks. In Europe, it launched the VW Tiguan with a mobile app as well as text messages and an interstitial Web site.[41]

  Smart phones also allow loyalty programs with which customers can track their visits and purchases at a merchant and receive rewards.[42] By tracking the location of receptive customers who opt in to receive communications, retailers can send them location-specific promotions when they are in proximity to shops or outlets. Sonic Corp. used GPS data and proximity to cell towers in Atlanta to identify when those customers who had signed up for company communications were near one of roughly 50 Sonic restaurants in the area. When that was the case, Sonic sent customers a text message with a discount offer or an ad to entice them to visit the restaurant.[43]

  With traditional coupon redemption rates declining for years, the ability of cell phones to permit more relevant and timely offers to consumers at or near the point of purchase has piqued the interest of many marketers. These new coupons can take all forms; digital in-store signs can now dispense them to smart phones.[44]

- *Developing mobile marketing programs.* Even with newer generation smart phones, the Web experience can be very different for users given smaller screen sizes, longer downloads, and the lack of some software capabilities (such as Adobe Flash Player on iPhones). Marketers would be wise to design simple, clear, and "clean" sites, paying even greater attention than usual to user experience and navigation.[45]

VW launched its GTI model in the United States with an iPhone app for its Real Racing game.

U.S. marketers can learn much about mobile marketing by looking overseas. In developed Asian markets such as Hong Kong, Japan, Singapore, and South Korea, mobile marketing is fast becoming a central component of customer experiences.[46] In developing markets, high cell phone penetration also makes mobile marketing attractive. A pioneer in China, Coca-Cola created a national campaign asking Beijing residents to send text messages guessing the high temperature in the city every day for just over a month, for a chance to win a one-year supply of Coke products. The campaign attracted more than 4 million messages over the course of 35 days.[47]

Although a growing population segment uses mobile phones for everything from entertainment to banking, different people have different attitudes and experiences with mobile technology. "Marketing Memo: Segmenting Tech Users" profiles the role of mobile Internet access in several groups' digital lifestyles.

marketing
Memo

Segmenting Tech Users

Group Name	% of Adults	What You Need to Know About Them	Key Demographic Facts
Motivated by Mobility (39%)			
Digital Collaborators	8%	With the most tech assets, Digital Collaborators use them to work with and share their creations with others. They are enthusiastic about how ICTs help them connect with others and confident in how to manage digital devices and information.	Mostly male (56%), late 30s, well-educated, and well-off.
Ambivalent Networkers	7%	Ambivalent Networkers have folded mobile devices into how they run their social lives, whether through texting or social networking tools online. They also rely on ICTs for entertainment. But they also express worries about connectivity; some find that mobile devices are intrusive and many think it is good to take a break from online use.	Primarily male (60%), they are young (late 20s) and ethnically diverse.
Media Movers	7%	Media Movers have a wide range of online and mobile habits, and they are bound to find or create an information nugget, such as a digital photo, and pass it on. These social exchanges are central to this group's use of ICTs. Cyberspace, as a path to personal productivity or an outlet for creativity, is less important.	Males (56%) in their mid-30s, many with children and in middle income range.
Roving Nodes	9%	Roving Nodes are active managers of their social and work lives using their mobile device. They get the most out of basic applications with their assets such as e-mail or texting and find them great for arranging the logistics of their lives and enhancing personal productivity.	Mostly women (56%), in their late 30s, well educated and well-off.
Mobile Newbies	8%	This group rates low on tech assets, but its members really like their cell phones. Mobile Newbies, many of whom acquired a cell in the past year, like how the device helps them be more available to others. They would be hard pressed to give up the cell phone.	Mainly women (55%), about age 50, lower educational and income levels.
Stationary Media Majority (61%)			
Desktop Veterans	13%	This group of older, veteran online users is content to use a high-speed connection and a desktop computer to explore the Internet and stay in touch with friends, placing their cell phone and mobile applications in the background.	Mainly men (55%), in their mid 40s, well-educated and well-off economically.
Drifting Surfers	14%	Many have the requisite tech assets, such as broadband or a cell phone, but Drifting Surfers are infrequent online users. When they use technology, it is for basic information gathering. It wouldn't bother the typical Drifting Surfer to give up the Internet or a cell phone.	Majority women (56%), in their early 40s, middle income, and average education levels.
Information Encumbered	10%	Most people in this group suffer from information overload and think taking time off from the Internet is a good thing. The Information Encumbered are firmly rooted in old media to get information.	Two-thirds men, in their early 50s, average education, lower-middle income.
Tech Indifferent	10%	Members of this group are not heavy Internet users and although most have cell phones, they don't like their intrusiveness. The Indifferent could easily do without modern gadgets and services.	Mainly women (55%), in their late 50s, low-income and education levels.
Off the Network	14%	Members of this group have neither cell phones nor online access, and tend to be older and low-income. But a few have experience with ICTs; some used to have online access and as many as one in five used to have a cell phone.	Low-income senior women, high share of African Americans.

Source: "The Mobile Difference—Tech User Types," Pew Internet & American Life Project, March 31, 2009, www.pewinternet.org/Infographics/The-Mobile-Difference—Tech-User-Types.aspx.

Word of Mouth

Consumers use *word of mouth* to talk about dozens of brands each day, from media and entertainment products such as movies, TV shows, and publications to food products, travel services, and retail stores.[48]

Companies are acutely aware of the power of word of mouth. Hush Puppies shoes, Krispy Kreme doughnuts, the blockbuster movie *The Passion of the Christ*, and, more recently, Crocs shoes have been built through strong word of mouth, as were companies such as The Body Shop, Palm, Red Bull, Starbucks, and Amazon.com.

Positive word of mouth sometimes happens organically with little advertising, but it can also be managed and facilitated.[49] It is particularly effective for smaller businesses, with whom customers may feel a more personal relationship. Many small businesses are investing in various forms of social media at the expense of newspapers, radio, and Yellow Pages to get the word out. Southern Jewelz, started by a recent college grad, found sales doubling over six months after it began to actively use Facebook, Twitter, and e-commerce software.[50]

With the growth of social media, as Chapter 17 noted, marketers sometimes distinguish paid media from earned or free media. Although different points of view prevail, *paid media* results from press coverage of company-generated advertising, publicity, or other promotional efforts. *Earned media*—sometimes called *free media*—is all the PR benefits a firm receives without having directly paid for anything—all the news stories, blogs, social network conversations that deal with a brand. Earned media isn't literally free—the company has to invest in products, services, and their marketing to some degree to get people to pay attention and write and talk about them, but the expenses are not devoted to eliciting a media response.

We first consider how social media promotes the flow of word of mouth before delving into more detail on how word of mouth is formed and travels. To start our discussion, consider some of the different ways Intuit uses social media.[51]

Intuit Always a marketing pioneer in the software industry, Intuit has received much recognition for its extensive social media programs. Intuit adopted a narrowcasting approach with its QuickBooks Live Community, which serves the small business market: It is available only to customers who buy QuickBooks 2009 on a PC or a Mac and is a place where customers can trade tips and ask questions, 70 percent of which are answered by other QuickBooks customers. One accountant has posted 5,600 answers on the site. The community also provides Intuit with useful product feedback. Intuit has run TurboTax contests to encourage product placement in Facebook, MySpace, and Twitter. Users with the most "original and unique" status updates related to TurboTax receive prizes. Intuit's "Love a Local Business" program awards $1,000 grants to local businesses based on the community's online votes. A variety of other social networking events help Intuit interact with small businesses. As one social media expert at the company said: "Social media is one of the key trends driving our business . . . It's about fast connections with customers and building an on-going relationship."

Social Media

Social media are a means for consumers to share text, images, audio, and video information with each other and with companies and vice versa. Social media allow marketers to establish a public voice and presence on the Web and reinforce other communication activities. Because of their day-to-day immediacy, they can also encourage companies to stay innovative and relevant.

There are three main platforms for social media: (1) online communities and forums, (2) bloggers (individuals and networks such as Sugar and Gawker), and (3) social networks (like Facebook, Twitter, and YouTube).

ONLINE COMMUNITIES AND FORUMS Online communities and forums come in all shapes and sizes. Many are created by consumers or groups of consumers with no commercial interests or company affiliations. Others are sponsored by companies whose members communicate with the company and with each other through postings, instant messaging, and chat discussions about special interests related to the company's products and brands. These online communities and forums can be a valuable resource for companies and provide multiple functions by both collecting and conveying key information.

A technology marketing pioneer, Intuit created a strong online brand community for its QuickBooks software product.

A key for success of online communities is to create individual and group activities that help form bonds among community members. The Idea Center at Kodak Gallery is an online community for exchanging ideas about how to use Kodak products to create personalized gifts and other creative products using digital photos. Kodak has found that peer-to-peer recommendations within the community led to more frequent, larger purchases.[52] Apple hosts a large number of discussion groups organized by product lines and also by consumer versus professional use. These groups are customers' primary source of product information after warranties expire.

Information flow in online communities and forums is two-way and can provide companies with useful, hard-to-get customer information and insights. When GlaxoSmithKline prepared to launch its first weight-loss drug, Alli, it sponsored a weight-loss community. The firm felt the feedback it gained was more valuable than what it could have received from traditional focus groups. Research has shown, however, that firms should avoid too much democratization of innovation. Groundbreaking ideas can be replaced by lowest-common-denominator solutions.[53]

BLOGS *Blogs*, regularly updated online journals or diaries, have become an important outlet for word of mouth. There are millions in existence and they vary widely, some personal for close friends and families, others designed to reach and influence a vast audience. One obvious appeal of blogs is bringing together people with common interests. Blog networks such as Gawker Media offer marketers a portfolio of choices. Online celebrity gossip blog PopSugar has spawned a family of breezy blogs on fashion (FabSugar), beauty (BellaSugar), and romance and culture (TrèsSugar), attracting women aged 18 to 49.[54]

Corporations are creating their own blogs and carefully monitoring those of others.[55] Blog search engines provide up-to-the-minute analysis of millions of blogs to find out what's on people's minds.[56] Popular blogs are creating influential opinion leaders. At the TreeHugger site, a team of bloggers tracks green consumer products for 3.5 million unique visitors per month, offering video and reference guides and an average of 35 daily posts.[57]

Because many consumers examine product information and reviews contained in blogs, the Federal Trade Commission has also taken steps to require bloggers to disclose their relationship with marketers whose products they endorse. At the other extreme, some consumers use blogs and videos as a means of retribution and revenge on companies for bad service and faulty products. Dell's customer-service shortcomings were splashed all over the Internet through a series of "Dell Hell" postings. AOL took some heat when a frustrated customer recorded and broadcast online a service representative's emphatic resistance to canceling his service. Comcast was embarrassed when a video surfaced of one of its technicians sleeping on a customer's couch.[58]

The TreeHugger Web site tracks blogs and Internet activity with respect to green products.

SOCIAL NETWORKS Social networks have become an important force in both business-to-consumer and business-to-business marketing.[59] Major ones include Facebook, which is the world's biggest; MySpace, which concentrates on music and entertainment; LinkedIn, which targets career-minded professionals; and Twitter, which allows members to network via 140-character messages or "tweets." Different networks offer different benefits to firms. For example, Twitter can be an early warning system that permits rapid response, whereas Facebook allows deeper dives to engage consumers in more meaningful ways.[60]

Marketers are still learning how to best tap into social networks and their huge, well-defined audiences. Given networks' noncommercial nature—users are generally there looking to connect with others—attracting attention and persuading are more challenging. Also, given that users generate their own content, ads may find themselves appearing beside inappropriate or even offensive content.[61]

Advertising is only one avenue, however. Like any individual, companies can also join the social groups and actively participate. Having a Facebook page has become a virtual prerequisite for many companies. Twitter can benefit even the smallest firm. To create interest in its products and the events it hosted, small San Francisco bakery Mission Pie began to send tweet alerts, quickly gaining 1,000 followers and a sizable up-tick in business. "Follow Me on Twitter" signs are appearing on doors and windows of more small shops.[62]

And although major social networks offer the most exposure, niche networks provide a more targeted market that may be more likely to spread the brand message, as with CafeMom.[63]

CafeMom Started in 2006 by parent company CMI Marketing, CafeMom has 6.7 million unique visitors per month on Cafemom.com and 18 million on boutique ad network CafeMom plus. Visitors participate in dozens of different forums for moms. When the site started a forum for discussing developmentally appropriate play activities, toymaker Playskool sent toy kits to over 5,000 members and encouraged them to share their experiences with each other, resulting in 11,600 posts at Playskool Preschool Playgroup. "The great thing is you get direct feedback from actual moms," says the director of media at Hasbro, Playskool's parent company. This kind of feedback can be invaluable in the product-development process as well. The site's sweet spot is young, middle-class women with kids who love the opportunity to make friends and seek support, spending an average of 44 minutes a day on the site.

USING SOCIAL MEDIA Social media allow consumers to become engaged with a brand at perhaps a deeper and broader level than ever before. Marketers should do everything they can to encourage willing consumers to engage productively. But as useful as they may be, social media can never become the sole source of marketing communications.

Embracing social media, harnessing word of mouth, and creating buzz requires companies to take the good with the bad. Look what happened to the marketers of Motrin at Johnson & Johnson.[64]

Motrin When marketers at J&J decided to run a slightly tongue-in-cheek online Web video for Motrin implying that young mothers carrying their babies everywhere in slings and chest packs as a means of bonding—or perhaps just to be trendy—were inadvertently risking back pain, they had no idea the pain they would in fact experience. After the ad ran online for several weeks without notice, a few vocal mothers took offense on Twitter on a Friday night, creating a weekend firestorm that stretched all over the Web. On the following Monday, marketers for Motrin quickly took to e-mail to personally apologize and replaced the video with a broader message of apology. Then they were criticized for caving in to pressure and overreacting.

The negative online response to Motrin's new ad posed a significant social media challenge to the brand.

The Motrin example shows the power and speed of social media, but also the challenges they pose to companies. The reality, however, is that whether a company chooses to engage in social media or not, the Internet will always permit scrutiny, criticism, and even "cheap shots" from consumers and organizations. By using social media and the Web in a constructive, thoughtful way, firms at least have a means to create a strong online presence and better offer credible alternative points of view if such events occur.[65]

Buzz and Viral Marketing

Some marketers highlight two particular forms of word of mouth—buzz and viral marketing.[66] *Buzz marketing* generates excitement, creates publicity, and conveys new relevant brand-related information through unexpected or even outrageous means.[67] *Viral marketing* is another form of word of mouth, or "word of mouse," that encourages consumers to pass along company-developed products and services or audio, video, or written information to others online.[68]

With user-generated content sites such as YouTube, MySpace Video, and Google Video, consumers and advertisers can upload ads and videos to be shared virally by millions of people. Online videos can be cost-effective—costing $50,000 to $200,000—and marketers can take more freedoms with them.

Blendtec Utah-based Blendtec used to be known primarily for its commercial blenders and food mills. The company wasn't really familiar to the general public until it launched a hilarious series of "Will It Blend?" online videos to promote some of its commercial products for home use. The videos feature founder and CEO Tom Dickson wearing a white lab coat and pulverizing objects ranging from golf balls and pens to beer bottles, all in a genial but deadpan manner. The genius of the videos (www.willitblend.com) is that they tie into current events. As soon as the iPhone was launched with huge media fanfare, Blendtec aired a video in which Dickson smiled and said, "I love my iPhone. It does everything. But will it blend?" After the blender crushed the iPhone to bits, Dickson lifted the lid on the small pile of black dust and said simply, "iSmoke." The clip drew more than 3.5 million downloads on YouTube. Dickson has appeared on the *Today* and other network television shows and has had a cameo in a Weezer video. One of the few items *not* to blend: A crowbar![69]

Blendtec's classic "Will It Blend?" online videos created significant brand equity for a brand that was previously fairly unknown.

Outrageousness is a two-edged sword. The Blendtec Web site clearly puts its comic videos in the "*Don't* try this at home" category and another set showing how to grind up vegetables for soup, for instance, in the "*Do* try this at home" category.

Contrary to popular opinion, products don't have to be outrageous or edgy to generate buzz. Companies can help to create buzz; and media or advertising are not always necessary for buzz to occur.[70] Some agencies have been created solely to help clients create buzz. P&G has 225,000 teens enlisted in Tremor and 600,000 mothers enrolled in Vocalpoint. Both groups are built on the premise that certain individuals want to learn about products, receive samples and coupons, share their opinions with companies, and, of course, talk up their experiences with others. P&G chooses well-connected people—the Vocalpoint moms have big social networks and generally speak to 25 to 30 other women during the day, compared to an average of 5 for other moms—and their messages carry a strong reason to share product information with a friend.[71] BzzAgent is another buzz-building firm.[72]

BzzAgent Boston-based BzzAgent has assembled an international word-of-mouth media network powered by 600,000 demographically diverse—but essentially ordinary—people who volunteer to talk up any of the clients' products they deem worth promoting. The company pairs consumers with products, information, and digital tools to activate widespread opinion-sharing throughout its own social media site, called BzzScapes, and within each member's personal social circles. BzzAgent believes this unique combination of people and platform accelerates measurable word of mouth and fosters sustained brand advocacy. BzzAgent participants have spread their own personal views and opinions to nearly 100 million friends and family. Each time an agent completes an activity, he or she is expected to file a report describing the nature of the buzz and its effectiveness. The company claims the buzz is honest because the process requires just enough work that few agents enroll solely for freebies, and agents don't talk up products they don't like. Agents are also supposed to disclose they're connected to BzzAgent. The company has completed hundreds of projects, working with clients such as Levi's Dockers, Anheuser-Busch, Cadbury-Schweppes, V Guide, Bacardi, Dunkin' Donuts, Silk, Tropicana Pure, Mrs. Dash, and the publishers of *Freakonomics* and *Eats, Shoots and Leaves*, both bestsellers.

Buzz and viral marketing both try to create a splash in the marketplace to showcase a brand and its noteworthy features. Some believe these influences are driven more by the rules of entertainment than the rules of selling. Consider these examples: Quicksilver puts out surfing videos and surf-culture books for teens, Johnson & Johnson and Pampers both have popular Web sites with parenting advice for babies; Walmart places videos with money-saving tips on YouTube; Grey Goose vodka has an entire entertainment division; Mountain Dew has a record label; and Hasbro is joining forces with Discovery to create a TV channel.[73] Ultimately, however, the success of any viral or buzz campaign depends on the willingness of consumers to talk to other consumers.[74]

Opinion Leaders

Communication researchers propose a social-structure view of interpersonal communication.[75] They see society as consisting of *cliques*, small groups whose members interact frequently. Clique members are similar, and their closeness facilitates effective communication but also insulates the clique from new ideas. The challenge is to create more openness so cliques exchange information with others in society. This openness is helped along by people who function as liaisons and connect two or more cliques without belonging to either, and by *bridges*, people who belong to one clique and are linked to a person in another.

Best-selling author Malcolm Gladwell claims three factors work to ignite public interest in an idea.[76] According to the first, "The Law of the Few," three types of people help to spread an idea like an epidemic. First are *Mavens*, people knowledgeable about big and small things. Second are *Connectors*, people who know and communicate with a great number of other people. Third are *Salesmen*, who possess natural persuasive power. Any idea that catches the interest of Mavens, Connectors, and Salesmen is likely to be broadcast far and wide. The second factor is "Stickiness." An idea must be expressed so that it motivates people to act. Otherwise, "The Law of the Few" will not lead to a self-sustaining epidemic. Finally, the third factor, "The Power of Context," controls whether those spreading an idea are able to organize groups and communities around it.

Not everyone agrees with Gladwell's ideas.[77] One team of viral marketing experts caution that although influencers or "alphas" start trends, they are often too introspective and socially alienated to spread them. They advise marketers to cultivate "bees," hyperdevoted customers who are not just satisfied knowing about the next trend but live to spread the word.[78] More firms are in fact finding ways to actively engage their passionate brand evangelists. LEGO's Ambassador Program targets its most enthusiastic followers for brainstorming and feedback.[79]

Companies can stimulate personal influence channels to work on their behalf. "Marketing Memo: How to Start a Buzz Fire" describes some techniques. Companies can also trace online activity to identify more influential users who may function as opinion leaders.[80]

Consumers can resent personal communications if unsolicited. Some word-of-mouth tactics walk a fine line between acceptable and unethical. One controversial tactic, sometimes called *shill marketing* or *stealth marketing*, pays people to anonymously promote a product or service in public places without disclosing their financial relationship to the sponsoring firm. To launch its T681 mobile camera phone, Sony Ericsson hired actors dressed as tourists to approach people at tourist locations and ask to have their photo taken. Handing over the mobile phone created an opportunity to discuss its merits, but many found the deception distasteful.[81] Heineken took another tack and turned an admittedly deceptive stunt into a huge PR win.[82]

marketing
Memo

How to Start a Buzz Fire

Although many word-of-mouth effects are beyond marketers' control, certain steps improve the likelihood of starting a positive buzz.

- *Identify influential individuals and companies and devote extra effort to them.* In technology, influencers might be large corporate customers, industry analysts and journalists, selected policy makers, and a sampling of early adopters.

- *Supply key people with product samples.* When two pediatricians launched MD Moms to market baby skin care products, they liberally sampled the product to physicians and mothers hoping for mentions on Internet message boards and parenting Web sites. The strategy worked—the company hit year one distribution goals by the end of the first month.

- *Work through community influentials such as local disk jockeys, class presidents, and presidents of women's organizations.* Ford's prelaunch "Fiesta Movement" campaign invited 100 handpicked young adults or "millennials" to live with the Fiesta car for six months. People were chosen based on their online experience with blogging and social friends and a video they submitted about their desire for adventure. After six months, the campaign had 4.3 million YouTube views, over 500,000 Flickr views, over 3 million Twitter impressions, and 50,000 potential customers, 97 percent of whom didn't already own a Ford.[83]

- *Develop word-of-mouth referral channels to build business.* Professionals will often encourage clients to recommend their services.

Weight Watchers found that word-of-mouth referrals from someone in the program had a huge impact on business.

- *Provide compelling information that customers want to pass along.* Companies shouldn't communicate with customers in terms better suited for a press release. Make it easy and desirable for a customer to borrow elements from an e-mail message or blog. Information should be original and useful. Originality increases the amount of word of mouth, but usefulness determines whether it will be positive or negative.

Ford Fiesta used 100 young adult consumers to provide an online, real-life preview of its new car.

Sources: Matthew Dolan, "Ford Takes Online Gamble with New Fiesta," *Wall Street Journal*, April 8, 2009; Sarit Moldovan, Jacob Goldenberg, and Amitava Chattopadhyay, "What Drives Word of Mouth? The Roles of Product Originality and Usefulness," *MSI Report No. 06-111* (Cambridge, MA: Marketing Science Institute, 2006); Karen J. Bannan, "Online Chat Is a Grapevine That Yields Precious Fruit," *New York Times*, December 25, 2006; John Batelle, "The Net of Influence," *Business 2.0* (March 2004): 70; Ann Meyer, "Word-of-Mouth Marketing Speaks Well for Small Business," *Chicago Tribune*, July 28, 2003; Malcolm Macalister Hall, "Selling by Stealth," *Business Life* (November 2001), pp. 51–55.

Heineken   Nothing may be more important to young European adult males than soccer—which they call football. Heineken took advantage of that fact to stage a fake classical musical concert at the same time as a crucial Real Madrid versus AC Milan match, enlisting girlfriends, bosses, and professors as accomplices in the hoax. Over 1,000 passionate AC Milan fans reluctantly showed up at the theater with their companions for the performance. As the string quarter began to play and the soccer fans squirmed, words on a screen behind the musicians slowly revealed clues about the nature of the prank and then showed the game in all its big-screen glory. Over 1.5 million people watched the audience reactions on live SkySport TV, and the Heineken site devoted to the event received 5 million visitors. Subsequent PR and word of mouth made it a worldwide phenomenon. ▭

Measuring the Effects of Word of Mouth[84]

Research and consulting firm Keller Fay notes that although 80 percent of word of mouth occurs offline, many marketers concentrate on online effects given the ease of tracking them through advertising, PR, or digital agencies.[85] Gatorade created a "Mission Control Center"—set up like a broadcast television control room—to monitor the brand on social networks around the clock.

Through demographic information or proxies and cookies, firms can monitor when customers blog, comment, post, share, link, upload, friend, stream, write on a wall, or update a profile. With these tracking tools it is possible, for example, to sell movie advertisers "1 million American women between the ages of 14 and 24 who had uploaded, blogged, rated, shared, or commented on entertainment in the previous 24 hours."[86]

DuPont employs measures of online word of mouth such as campaign scale (how far it reached), speed (how fast it spread), share of voice in that space, share of voice in that speed, whether it achieved positive lift in sentiment, whether the message was understood, whether it was relevant, whether it had sustainability (and was not a one-shot deal), and how far it moved from its source.

Other researchers focus more on characterizing the source of word of mouth. For example, one group is looking to evaluate blogs according to three dimensions: relevance, sentiment, and authority.[87]

Designing the Sales Force

The original and oldest form of direct marketing is the field sales call. To locate prospects, develop them into customers, and grow the business, most industrial companies rely heavily on a professional sales force or hire manufacturers' representatives and agents. Many consumer companies such as Allstate, Amway, Avon, Mary Kay, Merrill Lynch, and Tupperware use a direct-selling force.

U.S. firms spend over a trillion dollars annually on sales forces and sales force materials—more than on any other promotional method. Over 10 percent of the total workforce work full time in sales occupations, both nonprofit and for profit.[88] Hospitals and museums, for example, use fund-raisers to contact donors and solicit donations. For many firms, sales force performance is critical.[89]

 SoBe   John Bello, founder of SoBe nutritionally enhanced teas and juices, has given much credit to his sales force for the brand's successful ascent. Bello claims that the superior quality and consistent sales effort from the 150 salespeople the company had at its peak was directed toward one simple goal: "SoBe won in the street because our salespeople were there more often and in greater numbers than the competition, and they were more motivated by far." SoBe's sales force operated at every level of the distribution chain: At the distributor level, steady communication gave SoBe disproportionate focus relative to the other brands; at the trade level, with companies such as 7-Eleven, Costco, and Safeway, most senior salespeople had strong personal relationships; and at the individual store level, the SoBe team was always at work setting and restocking shelves, cutting in product, and putting up point-of-sale displays. According to Bello, bottom-line success in any entrepreneurial endeavor depends on sales execution.

An essential ingredient to SoBe's initial beverage market success was a highly motivated and skilled sales force.

Although no one debates the importance of the sales force in marketing programs, companies are sensitive to the high and rising costs of maintaining one, including salaries, commissions, bonuses, travel expenses, and benefits. Not surprisingly, companies are trying to increase sales force productivity through better selection, training, supervision, motivation, and compensation.[90]

The term *sales representative* covers six positions, ranging from the least to the most creative types of selling:[91]

1. *Deliverer*—A salesperson whose major task is the delivery of a product (water, fuel, oil).
2. *Order taker*—An inside order taker (standing behind the counter) or outside order taker (calling on the supermarket manager).
3. *Missionary*—A salesperson not permitted to take an order but expected rather to build goodwill or educate the actual or potential user (the medical "detailer" representing an ethical pharmaceutical house).
4. *Technician*—A salesperson with a high level of technical knowledge (the engineering salesperson who is primarily a consultant to client companies).
5. *Demand creator*—A salesperson who relies on creative methods for selling tangible products (vacuum cleaners, cleaning brushes, household products) or intangibles (insurance, advertising services, or education).
6. *Solution vendor*—A salesperson whose expertise is solving a customer's problem, often with a system of the company's products and services (for example, computer and communications systems).

|Fig. 19.3| △

Designing a Sales
Force

|Fig. 19.4| △

A Hypothetical
(Dysfunctional) Sales
Marketing Exchange

Source: Based on a talk by Scott Sanderude and Jeff Standish, "Work Together, Win Together: Resolving Misconceptions between Sales and Marketing," talk given at Marketing Science Institute's *Marketing, Sales, and Customers* conference, December 7, 2005.

Salespeople are the company's personal link to its customers. In designing the sales force, the company must develop sales force objectives, strategy, structure, size, and compensation (see △ Figure 19.3).

Sales Force Objectives and Strategy

The days when all the sales force did was "sell, sell, and sell" are long gone. Sales reps need to know how to diagnose a customer's problem and propose a solution that can help improve the customer's profitability.

Companies need to define specific sales force objectives. For example, a company might want its sales representatives to spend 80 percent of their time with current customers and 20 percent with prospects, and 85 percent of their time on established products and 15 percent on new products. Regardless of the selling context, salespeople perform one or more specific tasks:

- *Prospecting.* Searching for prospects or leads
- *Targeting.* Deciding how to allocate their time among prospects and customers
- *Communicating.* Communicating information about the company's products and services
- *Selling.* Approaching, presenting, answering questions, overcoming objections, and closing sales
- *Servicing.* Providing various services to the customers—consulting on problems, rendering technical assistance, arranging financing, expediting delivery
- *Information gathering.* Conducting market research and doing intelligence work
- *Allocating.* Deciding which customers will get scarce products during product shortages

To manage costs, most companies are choosing a *leveraged sales force* that focuses reps on selling the company's more complex and customized products to large accounts and uses inside salespeople and Web ordering for low-end selling. Salespeople handle fewer accounts and are rewarded for key account growth; lead generation, proposal writing, order fulfillment, and postsale support are turned over to others. This is far different from expecting salespeople to sell to every possible account, the common weakness of geographically based sales forces.[92]

Companies must deploy sales forces strategically so they call on the right customers at the right time in the right way, acting as "account managers" who arrange fruitful contact between people in the buying and selling organizations. Selling increasingly calls for teamwork and the support of others, such as *top management,* especially when national accounts or major sales are at stake; *technical people,* who supply information and service before, during, and after product purchase; *customer service representatives,* who provide installation, maintenance, and other services; and *office staff,* consisting of sales analysts, order expediters, and assistants.[93]

To maintain a market focus, salespeople should know how to analyze sales data, measure market potential, gather market intelligence, and develop marketing strategies and plans. Especially at the higher levels of sales management, they need analytical marketing skills. Marketers believe sales forces are more effective in the long run if they understand and appreciate marketing as well as selling. Too often marketing and sales are in conflict: the sales force complains marketing isn't generating enough leads and marketers complain the sales force isn't converting them (see △ Figure 19.4). Improved collaboration and communication between these two can increase revenues and profits.[94]

Sales: I need leads, but marketing never sends me any good leads. How am I supposed to get new business with no good leads?

Marketing: We deliver tons of leads and they just sit in the system. Why won't sales call on any of them?

Sales: I have nothing new to sell. What is marketing doing? Why can't they figure out what customers want before they give it to us? Why don't they give me anything that's easy to sell?

Marketing: Why won't sales get out and sell my new programs? How do they expect customers to place orders without sales contacts?

Sales: My people spend too much time on administration and paperwork. I need them out selling.

Marketing: We need information to get new ideas. How long does it take to type in a few words? Don't they know their own customers?

Sales: How am I going to hit my number? Marketing is a waste of time. I'd rather have more sales reps.

Marketing: How am I going to hit my number? Sales won't help and I don't have enough people to do it myself.

Once the company chooses its strategy, it can use a direct or a contractual sales force. A **direct (company) sales force** consists of full- or part-time paid employees who work exclusively for the company. Inside sales personnel conduct business from the office using the telephone and receive visits from prospective buyers, and field sales personnel travel and visit customers. A **contractual sales force** consists of manufacturers' reps, sales agents, and brokers, who earn a commission based on sales.

Sales Force Structure

The sales force strategy also has implications for its structure. A company that sells one product line to one end-using industry with customers in many locations would use a territorial structure. A company that sells many products to many types of customers might need a product or market structure. Some companies need a more complex structure. Motorola, for example, manages four types of sales forces: (1) a strategic market sales force composed of technical, applications, and quality engineers and service personnel assigned to major accounts; (2) a geographic sales force calling on thousands of customers in different territories; (3) a distributor sales force calling on and coaching Motorola distributors; and (4) an inside sales force doing telemarketing and taking orders via phone and fax.

Established companies need to revise their sales force structures as market and economic conditions change. SAS, seller of business intelligence software, reorganized its sales force into industry-specific groups such as banks, brokerages, and insurers and saw revenue soar by 14 percent.[95] "Marketing Insight: Major Account Management" discusses a specialized form of sales force structure.

Major Account Management

Marketers typically single out for attention major accounts (also called key accounts, national accounts, global accounts, or house accounts). These are important customers with multiple divisions in many locations who use uniform pricing and coordinated service for all divisions. A major account manager (MAM) usually reports to the national sales manager and supervises field reps calling on customer plants within their territories. The average company manages about 75 key accounts. If a company has several such accounts, it's likely to organize a major account management division, in which the average MAM handles nine accounts.

Large accounts are often handled by a strategic account management team with cross-functional members who integrate new-product development, technical support, supply chain, marketing activities, and multiple communication channels to cover all aspects of the relationship. Procter & Gamble has a strategic account management team of 300 staffers to work with Walmart in its Bentonville, Arkansas, headquarters, with more stationed at Walmart headquarters in Europe, Asia, and Latin America. P&G has credited this relationship with saving the company billions of dollars.

Major account management is growing. As buyer concentration increases through mergers and acquisitions, fewer buyers are accounting for a larger share of sales. Many are centralizing their purchases of certain items, gaining more bargaining power. And as products become more complex, more groups in the buyer's organization participate in the purchase process. The typical salesperson might not have the skill, authority, or coverage to sell effectively to the large buyer.

In selecting major accounts, companies look for those that purchase a high volume (especially of more profitable products), purchase centrally, require a high level of service in several geographic locations, may be price sensitive, and want a long-term partnership. Major account managers act as the single point of contact, develop and grow customer business, understand customer decision processes, identify added-value opportunities, provide competitive intelligence, negotiate sales, and orchestrate customer service.

Many major accounts look for added value more than a price advantage. They appreciate having a single point of dedicated contact; single billing; special warranties; EDI links; priority shipping; early information releases; customized products; and efficient maintenance, repair, and upgraded service. And there's the value of goodwill. Personal relationships with people who value the major account's business and have a vested interest in its success are compelling reasons for remaining a loyal customer.

Sources: Noel Capon, Dave Potter, and Fred Schindler, *Managing Global Accounts: Nine Critical Factors for a World-Class Program*, 2nd ed. (Bronxville, NY: Wessex Press, 2008); Peter Cheverton, *Global Account Management: A Complete Action Kit of Tools and Techniques for Managing Key Global Customers* (London, UK: Kogan Page, 2008); Malcolm McDonald and Diana Woodburn, *Key Account Management: The Definitive Guide*, 2nd ed. (Oxford, UK: Butterworth-Heinemann, 2007); Jack Neff, "Bentonville or Bust," *Advertising Age*, February 24, 2003. More information can be obtained from SAMA (Strategic Account Management Association) and the *Journal of Selling and Major Account Management*.

Sales Force Size

Sales representatives are one of the company's most productive and expensive assets. Increasing their number increases both sales and costs. Once the company establishes the number of customers it wants to reach, it can use a *workload approach* to establish sales force size. This method has five steps:

1. Group customers into size classes according to annual sales volume.
2. Establish desirable call frequencies (number of calls on an account per year) for each customer class.
3. Multiply the number of accounts in each size class by the corresponding call frequency to arrive at the total workload for the country, in sales calls per year.
4. Determine the average number of calls a sales representative can make per year.
5. Divide the total annual calls required by the average annual calls made by a sales representative, to arrive at the number of sales representatives needed.

Suppose the company estimates it has 1,000 A accounts and 2,000 B accounts. A accounts require 36 calls a year, and B accounts require 12, so the company needs a sales force that can make 60,000 sales calls (36,000 + 24,000) a year. If the average full-time rep can make 1,000 calls a year, the company needs 60.

Sales Force Compensation

To attract top-quality reps, the company must develop an attractive compensation package. Sales reps want income regularity, extra reward for above-average performance, and fair pay for experience and longevity. Management wants control, economy, and simplicity. Some of these objectives will conflict. No wonder compensation plans exhibit a tremendous variety from industry to industry and even within the same industry.

The company must quantify four components of sales force compensation. The *fixed amount,* a salary, satisfies the need for income stability. The *variable amount,* whether commissions, bonus, or profit sharing, serves to stimulate and reward effort. *Expense allowances* enable sales reps to meet the expenses of travel and entertaining. *Benefits,* such as paid vacations, sickness or accident benefits, pensions, and life insurance, provide security and job satisfaction.

Fixed compensation is common in jobs with a high ratio of nonselling to selling duties, and jobs where the selling task is technically complex and requires teamwork. Variable compensation works best where sales are cyclical or depend on individual initiative. Fixed and variable compensation give rise to three basic types of compensation plans—straight salary, straight commission, and combination salary and commission. One survey revealed that over half of sales reps receive 40 percent or more of their compensation in variable pay.[96]

Straight-salary plans provide a secure income, encourage reps to complete nonselling activities, and reduce incentive to overstock customers. For the firm, these plans represent administrative simplicity and lower turnover. Straight-commission plans attract higher performers, provide more motivation, require less supervision, and control selling costs. On the negative side, they emphasize getting the sale over building the relationship. Combination plans feature the benefits of both plans while limiting their disadvantages.

Plans that combine fixed and variable pay link the variable portion to a wide variety of strategic goals. One current trend deemphasizes sales volume in favor of gross profitability, customer satisfaction, and customer retention. Other companies reward reps partly on sales team or even company-wide performance, motivating them to work together for the common good.

Managing the Sales Force

Various policies and procedures guide the firm in recruiting, selecting, training, supervising, motivating, and evaluating sales representatives to manage its sales force (see △ Figure 19.5).

Recruiting and Selecting Representatives

At the heart of any successful sales force is a means of selecting effective representatives. One survey revealed that the top 25 percent of the sales force brought in over 52 percent of the sales. It's a great

|Fig. 19.5| △

Managing the Sales Force

waste to hire the wrong people. The average annual turnover rate of sales reps for all industries is almost 20 percent. Sales force turnover leads to lost sales, the expense of finding and training replacements, and often pressure on existing salespeople to pick up the slack.[97]

After management develops its selection criteria, it must recruit. The human resources department solicits names from current sales representatives, uses employment agencies, places job ads, and contacts college students. Selection procedures can vary from a single informal interview to prolonged testing and interviewing.

Studies have shown little relationship between sales performance on one hand, and background and experience variables, current status, lifestyle, attitude, personality, and skills on the other. More effective predictors have been composite tests and assessment centers that simulate the working environment so applicants are assessed in an environment similar to the one in which they would work.[98] Although scores from formal tests are only one element in a set that includes personal characteristics, references, past employment history, and interviewer reactions, they have been weighted quite heavily by companies such as IBM, Prudential, and Procter & Gamble. Gillette claims tests have reduced turnover and scores correlated well with the progress of new reps.

Training and Supervising Sales Representatives

Today's customers expect salespeople to have deep product knowledge, add ideas to improve operations, and be efficient and reliable. These demands have required companies to make a much greater investment in sales training.

New reps may spend a few weeks to several months in training. The median training period is 28 weeks in industrial-products companies, 12 in service companies, and 4 in consumer-products companies. Training time varies with the complexity of the selling task and the type of recruit. For all sales, new hire "ramp up" to full effectiveness is taking longer than ever, with 27 percent taking 3 to 6 months, 38 percent taking 6 to 12 months, and 28 percent needing 12 months or more.

New methods of training are continually emerging, such as the use of audio- and videotapes, CDs and CD-ROMs, programmed learning, distance learning, and films. Some firms use role playing and sensitivity or empathy training to help reps identify with customers' situations and motives.

Reps paid mostly on commission generally receive less supervision. Those who are salaried and must cover definite accounts are likely to receive substantial supervision. With multilevel selling, such as Avon, Sara Lee, Virgin, and others use, independent distributors are also in charge of their own sales force selling company products. These independent contractors or reps are paid a commission not only on their own sales but also on the sales of people they recruit and train.[99]

Sales Rep Productivity

How many calls should a company make on a particular account each year? Some research suggests today's sales reps spend too much time selling to smaller, less profitable accounts instead of focusing on larger, more profitable accounts.[100]

NORMS FOR PROSPECT CALLS Left to their own devices, many reps will spend most of their time with current customers, who are known quantities. Reps can depend on them for some business, whereas a prospect might never deliver any. Companies therefore often specify how much time reps should spend prospecting for new accounts. Spector Freight wants its sales representatives to spend 25 percent of their time prospecting and stop after three unsuccessful calls. Some companies rely on a missionary sales force to open new accounts.

USING SALES TIME EFFICIENTLY The best sales reps manage their time efficiently. *Time-and-duty analysis* helps reps understand how they spend their time and how they might increase their productivity. In the course of a day, sales reps spend time planning, traveling, waiting, selling, and doing administrative tasks (report writing and billing; attending sales meetings; and talking to others in the company about production, delivery, billing, and sales performance). It's no wonder face-to-face selling accounts for as little as 29 percent of total working time![101]

Companies constantly try to improve sales force productivity.[102] To cut costs, reduce time demands on their outside sales force, and leverage computer and telecommunications innovations, many have increased the size and responsibilities of their inside sales force.

Inside salespeople are of three types: *Technical support people* provide technical information and answers to customers' questions. *Sales assistants* provide clerical backup for outside salespersons, call ahead to confirm appointments, run credit checks, follow up on deliveries, and answer customers' business-related questions. *Telemarketers* use the phone to find new leads, qualify them, and sell to them. Telemarketers can call up to 50 customers a day, compared to 4 for an outside salesperson.

The inside sales force frees outside reps to spend more time selling to major accounts, identifying and converting new major prospects, placing electronic ordering systems in customers' facilities, and obtaining more blanket orders and systems contracts. Inside salespeople spend more time checking inventory, following up orders, and phoning smaller accounts. Outside sales reps are paid largely on an incentive-compensation basis, and inside reps on a salary or salary-plus-bonus pay.

SALES TECHNOLOGY The salesperson today has truly gone electronic. Not only is sales and inventory information transferred much faster, but specific computer-based decision support systems have been created for sales managers and sales representatives. Using laptop computers, salespeople can access valuable product and customer information. With a few keystrokes, salespeople can prime themselves on backgrounds of clients; call up prewritten sales letters; transmit orders and resolve customer-service issues on the spot; and send samples, pamphlets, brochures, and other materials to clients.

One of the most valuable electronic tools for the sales rep is the company Web site, and one of its most useful applications is as a prospecting tool. Company Web sites can help define the firm's relationships with individual accounts and identify those whose business warrants a personal sales call. They provide an introduction to self-identified potential customers and might even receive the initial order. For more complex transactions, the site provides a way for the buyer to contact the seller. Selling over the Internet supports relationship marketing by solving problems that do not require live intervention and thus allows more time for issues best addressed face-to-face.

Motivating Sales Representatives

The majority of sales representatives require encouragement and special incentives, especially those in the field who encounter daily challenges.[103] Most marketers believe that the higher the salesperson's motivation, the greater the effort and the resulting performance, rewards, and satisfaction—all of which in turn further increase motivation.

INTRINSIC VERSUS EXTRINSIC REWARDS Marketers reinforce intrinsic and extrinsic rewards of all types. One research study found the reward with the highest value was pay, followed by promotion, personal growth, and sense of accomplishment.[104] Least valued were liking and respect, security, and recognition. In other words, salespeople are highly motivated by pay and the chance to get ahead and satisfy their intrinsic needs, and may be less motivated by compliments and security. Some firms use sales contests to increase sales effort.[105]

SALES QUOTAS Many companies set annual sales quotas, developed from the annual marketing plan, on dollar sales, unit volume, margin, selling effort or activity, or product type. Compensation is often tied to degree of quota fulfillment. The company first prepares a sales forecast that becomes the basis for planning production, workforce size, and financial requirements. Management then establishes quotas for regions and territories, which typically add up to more than the sales forecast to encourage managers and salespeople to perform at their best. Even if they fail to make their quotas, the company nevertheless may reach its sales forecast.

Each area sales manager divides the area's quota among its reps. Sometimes a rep's quotas are set high, to spur extra effort, or more modestly, to build confidence. One general view is that a salesperson's quota should be at least equal to last year's sales, plus some fraction of the difference between territory sales potential and last year's sales. The more favorably the salesperson reacts to pressure, the higher the fraction should be.

Conventional wisdom is that profits are maximized by sales reps focusing on the more important products and more profitable products. Reps are unlikely to achieve their quotas for established products when the company is launching several new products at the same time. The company will need to expand its sales force for new-product launches.

Setting sales quotas can create problems. If the company underestimates and the sales reps easily achieve their quotas, it has overpaid them. If it overestimates sales potential, the salespeople will find it very hard to reach their quotas and be frustrated or quit. Another downside is that quotas can drive reps to get as much business as possible—often ignoring the service side of the business. The company gains short-term results at the cost of long-term customer satisfaction. For these reasons, some companies are dropping quotas. Even hard-driving Oracle has changed its approach to sales compensation.

Oracle Finding sales flagging and customers griping, Oracle, the second-largest software company in the world, decided to overhaul its sales department and practices. Its rapidly expanding capabilities, with diverse applications such as human resources, supply chain, and CRM, meant one rep could no longer be responsible for selling all Oracle products to certain customers. Reorganization let reps specialize in a few particular products. To tone down the sales force's reputation as overly aggressive, Oracle changed the commission structure from a range of 2 percent to 12 percent to a flat 4 percent to 6 percent and adopted guidelines on how to "play nice" with channels, independent software vendors (ISVs), resellers, integrators, and value-added resellers (VARs). The six principles instructed sales staff to identify and work with partners in accounts and respect their positions and the value they add, in order to address partner feedback that Oracle should be more predictable and reliable.[106]

Evaluating Sales Representatives

We have been describing the *feed-forward* aspects of sales supervision—how management communicates what the sales reps should be doing and motivates them to do it. But good feed-forward requires good *feedback,* which means getting regular information from reps to evaluate performance.

SOURCES OF INFORMATION The most important source of information about reps is sales reports. Additional information comes through personal observation, salesperson self-reports, customer letters and complaints, customer surveys, and conversations with other reps.

Sales reports are divided between *activity plans* and *write-ups of activity results.* The best example of the former is the salesperson's work plan, which reps submit a week or month in advance to describe intended calls and routing. This report forces sales reps to plan and schedule their activities and inform management of their whereabouts. It provides a basis for comparing their plans and accomplishments or their ability to "plan their work and work their plan."

Many companies require representatives to develop an annual territory-marketing plan in which they outline their program for developing new accounts and increasing business from existing accounts. Sales managers study these plans, make suggestions, and use them to develop sales quotas. Sales reps write up completed activities on *call reports.* Sales representatives also submit expense reports, new-business reports, lost-business reports, and reports on local business and economic conditions.

These reports provide raw data from which sales managers can extract key indicators of sales performance: (1) average number of sales calls per salesperson per day, (2) average sales call time per contact, (3) average revenue per sales call, (4) average cost per sales call, (5) entertainment cost per sales call, (6) percentage of orders per hundred sales calls, (7) number of new customers per period, (8) number of lost customers per period, and (9) sales force cost as a percentage of total sales.

FORMAL EVALUATION The sales force's reports along with other observations supply the raw materials for evaluation. One type of evaluation compares current to past performance. An example is shown in Table 19.1.

The sales manager can learn many things about a rep from this table. Total sales increased every year (line 3). This does not necessarily mean he is doing a better job. The product breakdown shows he has been able to push the sales of product B further than the sales of product A (lines 1 and 2). According to his quotas for the two products (lines 4 and 5), his increasing product B sales could be at the expense of product A sales. According to gross profits (lines 6 and 7), the company earns more selling A than B. The rep might be pushing the higher-volume, lower-margin product at the expense of the more profitable product. Although the rep increased total sales by $1,100 between 2009 and 2010 (line 3), gross profits on total sales actually decreased by $580 (line 8).

Sales expense (line 9) shows a steady increase, although total expense as a percentage of total sales seems to be under control (line 10). The upward trend in total dollar expense does not seem to be explained by any increase in the number of calls (line 11), although it might be related to success in

TABLE 19.1 ☐ Form for Evaluating Sales Representative's Performance				
Territory: Midland Sales Representative: John Smith	**2007**	**2008**	**2009**	**2010**
1. Net sales product A	$251,300	$253,200	$270,000	$263,100
2. Net sales product B	423,200	439,200	553,900	561,900
3. Net sales total	674,500	692,400	823,900	825,000
4. Percent of quota product A	95.6	92.0	88.0	84.7
5. Percent of quota product B	120.4	122.3	134.9	130.8
6. Gross profits product A	$50,260	$50,640	$54,000	$52,620
7. Gross profits product B	42,320	43,920	55,390	56,190
8. Gross profits total	92,580	94,560	109,390	108,810
9. Sales expense	$10,200	$11,100	$11,600	$13,200
10. Sales expense to total sales (%)	1.5	1.6	1.4	1.6
11. Number of calls	1,675	1,700	1,680	1,660
12. Cost per call	$6.09	$6.53	$6.90	$7.95
13. Average number of customers	320	24	328	334
14. Number of new customers	13	14	15	20
15. Number of lost customers	8	10	11	14
16. Average sales per customer	$2,108	$2,137	$2,512	$2,470
17. Average gross profit per customer	$289	$292	$334	$326

acquiring new customers (line 14). Perhaps in prospecting for new customers, this rep is neglecting present customers, as indicated by an upward trend in the annual number of lost accounts (line 15).

The last two lines show the level and trend in sales and gross profits per customer. These figures become more meaningful when compared with overall company averages. If this rep's average gross profit per customer is lower than the company's average, he could be concentrating on the wrong customers or not spending enough time with each customer. A review of annual number of calls (line 11) shows he might be making fewer annual calls than the average salesperson. If distances in the territory are similar to those in other territories, the rep might not be putting in a full workday, is poor at sales planning and routing, or is spending too much time with certain accounts.

Even if effective in producing sales, the rep may not rate high with customers. Success may come because competitors' salespeople are inferior, the rep's product is better, or new customers are always found to replace those who dislike the rep. Managers can glean customer opinions of the salesperson, product, and service by mail questionnaires or telephone calls. Sales reps can analyze the success or failure of a sales call and how they would improve the odds on subsequent calls. Their performance could be related to internal factors (effort, ability, and strategy) and/or external factors (task and luck).[107]

Principles of Personal Selling

Personal selling is an ancient art. Effective salespeople today have more than instinct, however. Companies now spend hundreds of millions of dollars each year to train them in methods of analysis and customer management and to transform them from passive order takers into active order getters. Reps are taught the SPIN method to build long-term relationships, with questions such as:[108]

1. *Situation questions*—These ask about facts or explore the buyer's present situation. For example, "What system are you using to invoice your customers?"
2. *Problem questions*—These deal with problems, difficulties, and dissatisfactions the buyer is experiencing. For example, "What parts of the system create errors?"
3. *Implication questions*—These ask about the consequences or effects of a buyer's problems, difficulties, or dissatisfactions. For example, "How does this problem affect your people's productivity?"
4. *Need-payoff questions*—These ask about the value or usefulness of a proposed solution. For example, "How much would you save if our company could help reduce errors by 80 percent?"

Most sales training programs agree on the major steps in any effective sales process. We show these steps in △ Figure 19.6 and discuss their application to industrial selling next.[109]

The Six Steps

PROSPECTING AND QUALIFYING The first step in selling is to identify and qualify prospects. More companies are taking responsibility for finding and qualifying leads so salespeople can use their expensive time doing what they can do best: selling. Companies qualify the leads by contacting them by mail or phone to assess their level of interest and financial capacity. "Hot" prospects are turned over to the field sales force and "warm" prospects to the telemarketing unit for follow-up. Even then, it takes about four calls on a prospect to consummate a business transaction.

PREAPPROACH The salesperson needs to learn as much as possible about the prospect company (what it needs, who takes part in the purchase decision) and its buyers (personal characteristics and buying styles). How is the purchasing process conducted at the company? How is purchasing structured? Many purchasing departments in larger companies have been elevated into strategic supply departments with more professional practices. Centralized purchasing may put a premium on having larger suppliers able to meet all the company's needs. At the same time, some companies are also decentralizing purchasing for smaller items such as coffeemakers, office supplies, and other inexpensive necessities.

The sales rep must thoroughly understand the purchasing process in terms of "who, when, where, how, and why" in order to set call objectives: to qualify the prospect, gather information, or make an immediate sale. Another task is to choose the best contact approach—a personal visit, a phone call, or a letter. The right approach is crucial given that it has become harder and harder for sales reps to get into the offices of purchasing agents, physicians, and other possible time-starved and Internet-enabled customers. Finally, the salesperson should plan an overall sales strategy for the account.

PRESENTATION AND DEMONSTRATION The salesperson tells the product "story" to the buyer, using a *features, advantages, benefits,* and *value* (FABV) approach. Features describe physical characteristics of a market offering, such as chip processing speeds or memory capacity. Advantages describe why the features provide an advantage to the customer. Benefits describe the economic, technical, service, and social pluses delivered by the offering. Value describes the offering's worth (often in monetary terms). Salespeople often spend too much time on product features (a product orientation) and not enough time stressing benefits and value (a customer orientation). The pitch to a prospective client must be highly relevant, engaging, and compelling—there is always another company waiting to take that business.[110]

OVERCOMING OBJECTIONS Customers typically pose objections. *Psychological resistance* includes resistance to interference, preference for established supply sources or brands, apathy, reluctance to give up something, unpleasant associations created by the sales rep, predetermined ideas, dislike of making decisions, and neurotic attitude toward money. *Logical resistance* might be objections to the price, delivery schedule, or product or company characteristics.

To handle these objections, the salesperson maintains a positive approach, asks the buyer to clarify the objection, questions in such a way that the buyer answers his own objection, denies the validity of the objection, or turns it into a reason for buying. Although price is the most frequently negotiated issue—especially in an economic recession—others include contract completion time; quality of goods and services offered; purchase volume; responsibility for financing, risk taking, promotion, and title; and product safety.

Salespeople sometimes give in too easily when customers demand a discount. One company recognized this problem when sales revenues went up 25 percent but profit remained flat. The company decided to retrain its salespeople to "sell the price," rather than "sell through price." Salespeople were given richer information about each customer's sales history and behavior. They received training to recognize value-adding opportunities rather than price-cutting opportunities. As a result, the company's sales revenues climbed and so did its margins.[111]

CLOSING Closing signs from the buyer include physical actions, statements or comments, and questions. Reps can ask for the order, recapitulate the points of agreement, offer to help write up the order, ask whether the buyer wants A or B, get the buyer to make minor choices such as color or size, or indicate what the buyer will lose by not placing the order now. The salesperson might offer specific inducements to close, such as an additional service, an extra quantity, or a token gift.

|Fig. 19.6| △

Major Steps in Effective Selling

If the client still isn't budging, perhaps the salesperson is not interacting with the right executive—a more senior person may have the necessary authority. The salesperson also may need to find other ways to reinforce the value of the offering and how it alleviates financial or other pressures the client faces.[112]

FOLLOW-UP AND MAINTENANCE Follow-up and maintenance are necessary to ensure customer satisfaction and repeat business. Immediately after closing, the salesperson should cement any necessary details about delivery time, purchase terms, and other matters important to the customer. The salesperson should schedule a follow-up call after delivery to ensure proper installation, instruction, and servicing and to detect any problems, assure the buyer of the salesperson's interest, and reduce any cognitive dissonance. The salesperson should develop a maintenance and growth plan for the account.

Relationship Marketing

The principles of personal selling and negotiation are largely transaction-oriented because their purpose is to close a specific sale. But in many cases the company seeks not an immediate sale but rather a long-term supplier–customer relationship. Today's customers prefer suppliers who can sell and deliver a coordinated set of products and services to many locations, who can quickly solve problems in different locations, and who can work closely with customer teams to improve products and processes.

Salespeople working with key customers must do more than call only when they think customers might be ready to place orders. They should call or visit at other times and make useful suggestions about the business. They should monitor key accounts, know customers' problems, and be ready to serve them in a number of ways, adapting and responding to different customer needs or situations.[113]

Relationship marketing is not effective in all situations. But when it is the right strategy and is properly implemented, the organization will focus as much on managing its customers as on managing its products.

Summary

1. Direct marketing is an interactive marketing system that uses one or more media to effect a measurable response or transaction at any location. Direct marketing, especially electronic marketing, is showing explosive growth.

2. Direct marketers plan campaigns by deciding on objectives, target markets and prospects, offers, and prices. Next, they test and establish measures to determine the campaign's success.

3. Major channels for direct marketing include face-to-face selling, direct mail, catalog marketing, telemarketing, interactive TV, kiosks, Web sites, and mobile devices.

4. Interactive marketing provides marketers with opportunities for much greater interaction and individualization through well-designed and executed Web sites, search ads, display ads, and e-mails. Mobile marketing is another growing form of interactive marketing that relies on text messages, software apps, and ads.

5. Word-of-mouth marketing finds ways to engage customers so they choose to talk with others about products, services, and brands. Increasingly, word of mouth is being driven by social media in the form of online communities and forums, blogs, and social networks such as Facebook, Twitter, and YouTube.

6. Two notable forms of word-of-mouth marketing are buzz marketing, which seeks to get people talking about a brand by ensuring that a product or service or how it is marketed is out of the ordinary, and viral marketing, which encourages people to exchange online information related to a product or service.

7. Salespeople serve as a company's link to its customers. The sales rep *is* the company to many of its customers, and it is the rep who brings back to the company much-needed information about the customer.

8. Designing the sales force requires choosing objectives, strategy, structure, size, and compensation. Objectives may include prospecting, targeting, communicating, selling, servicing, information gathering, and allocating. Determining strategy requires choosing the most effective mix of selling approaches. Choosing the sales force structure entails dividing territories by geography, product, or market (or some combination of these). To estimate how large the sales force needs to be, the firm estimates the total workload and how many sales hours (and hence salespeople) will be needed. Compensating the sales force entails determining what types of salaries, commissions, bonuses, expense accounts, and benefits to give, and how much weight customer satisfaction should have in determining total compensation.

9. There are five steps in managing the sales force: (1) recruiting and selecting sales representatives; (2) training the representatives in sales techniques and in the company's products, policies, and customer-satisfaction orientation; (3) supervising the sales force and helping

reps to use their time efficiently; (4) motivating the sales force and balancing quotas, monetary rewards, and supplementary motivators; (5) evaluating individual and group sales performance.

10. Effective salespeople are trained in the methods of analysis and customer management, as well as the art of sales

professionalism. No single approach works best in all circumstances, but most trainers agree that selling is a six-step process: prospecting and qualifying customers, preapproach, presentation and demonstration, overcoming objections, closing, and follow-up and maintenance.

Applications

Marketing Debate
Are Great Salespeople Born or Made?

One debate in sales is about the impact of training versus selection in developing an effective sales force. Some observers maintain the best salespeople are born that way and are effective due to their personalities and interpersonal skills developed over a lifetime. Others contend that application of leading-edge sales techniques can make virtually anyone a sales star.

Take a position: The key to developing an effective sales force is selection *versus* The key to developing an effective sales force is training.

Marketing Discussion
Corporate Web Sites

Pick a company and go to its corporate Web site. How would you evaluate the Web site? How well does it score on the 7Cs of design elements: context, content, community, customization, communication, connection, and commerce?

Marketing Excellence

>>Facebook

Facebook has brought a whole new level of personal marketing to the world of business. The social networking Web site fulfills people's desire to communicate and interact with each other and uses that power to help other companies target very specific audiences with personalized messages.

Facebook was founded in 2004 by Mark Zuckerberg, who was a student at Harvard University at the time and created the first version of the Web site in his dorm room. Zuckerberg recalled, "I just thought that being able to have access to different people's profiles would be interesting. Obviously, there's no way you can get access to that stuff

unless people are throwing up profiles, so I wanted to make an application that would allow people to do that, to share as much information as they wanted while having control over what they put up." From the beginning, Facebook has kept its profiles and navigation tools relatively simple in order to unify the look and feel for each individual. Within the first 24 hours the Facebook Web site was up, between 1,200 and 1,500 Harvard students had registered and become part of the Facebook community. Within the first month, half the campus had registered.

Initially, Facebook's Web site could only be viewed and used by Harvard students. The early momentum was tremendous, though, and Facebook soon expanded to include students throughout the Ivy League and other colleges. The initial decision to keep Facebook exclusive to college students was critical to its early success. It gave the social Web site a sense of privacy, unity, and exclusivity that social media competitors like MySpace did not offer. Eventually, in 2006, Facebook opened up to everyone.

Today, Facebook is the most popular social networking Web site in the world, with over 500 million active users. The site allows users to create personal profiles with information such as their hometowns, work, educational background, favorite things, and religious affiliation. It encourages them to extend their network by adding other users as friends, and many people try to see how many "friends" they can accumulate. To interact with Facebook friends, users can send messages; "poke" each other; upload and view albums, photos, games, and videos; and "tag" or label people in their photos. They can post comments on friends' "walls" and create status updates viewable to everyone. In summary, Facebook is fulfilling its mission to "give people the power to share and make the world more open and connected."

Facebook has become a critical marketing component for just about any brand for several reasons. First, companies, sports teams, musicians, and politicians can create Facebook pages—a place to communicate to and with their fans. Facebook pages offer groups and brands a way to personally interact, build awareness, communicate, and offer information to anyone who takes an interest. Companies use Facebook to introduce new products, launch videos and promotions, upload images, communicate to consumers, listen to feedback, and create an overall personal look and feel. Even politicians from around the world—from the United States to the Philippines—use Facebook to push their campaigns and communicate with supporters on a local, personalized basis.

Facebook also offers targeted advertising opportunities. Banner ads—the company's major source of income—can target individuals by demographic or keywords based on the specific information they have placed in their profiles. adidas, for example, uses Facebook to promote specific labels within the company, target consumers regionally, and give the brand a personal touch. The head of adidas's digital marketing group explained, "Wherever our fans are, we're going to use Facebook to speak to them and we're going to try to speak to them in a locally relevant way."

Facebook's growth and influence have been incredible. In one survey, college students named Facebook the second most popular thing in their undergraduate world, tied only with beer. And Facebook is not used only by undergrads. Of the 150+ million users in the United States, 29 percent are aged 35 to 54, while 25 percent are aged 18 to 24. Overall, women represent the fast-growing segment. Facebook also tends to have a more upscale, educated, desirable demographic than competitive social networks, and therefore it charges more for its advertising ads.

In 2010, Facebook surpassed Google as the top Web site in the world based on unique visitors per month and also ranked number one for number of pages viewed per month. Facebook has become an important part of consumers' everyday lives and therefore a critical component in personal marketing strategies.

Questions

1. Why is Facebook unique in the world of personal marketing?

2. Is Facebook just a passing fad or is it here to stay? What are the company's greatest strengths and risks?

3. Discuss the recent privacy issues that challenged Facebook. Will privacy restrictions limit its ability to offer personal marketing opportunities?

Sources: John Cassidy, "Me Media," *New Yorker,* May 15, 2006; "Survey: College Kids Like iPods Better Than Beer," *Associated Press,* June 8, 2006; Peter Corbett, "Facebook Demographics and Statistics Report 2010," I Strategy Labs, www.istrategylabs.com; Brian Womack, "Facebook Sees Fourfold Jump in Number of Advertisers Since 2009," *BusinessWeek,* June 2, 2010; Kermit Pattison, "How to Market Your Business with Facebook," *New York Times,* November 11, 2009; Facebook, www.facebook.com.

Marketing Excellence

>>Oxford University

In the past, universities had to mail out bulky printed prospectuses to prospective students who had expressed an interest in their courses. Universities around the world are now using Web-based marketing communications to enable interaction with their prospective and current students and to provide information for their local, national, and international communities.

According to the Times Higher Education World University rankings 2010, Oxford University is ranked sixth among the world's top 200 universities. With its 800-year history, iconic buildings, and famous alumni from around the world, Oxford University enjoys an international reputation for excellence in teaching and research. Sir Tim Berners-Lee, inventor of the World Wide Web, is a former student of the University.

The university's Web site has a distinctive blue background to reflect its logo and corporate color. A single photograph showing an image of university life appears at the top of the page and is changed regularly to reflect current news. The homepage has a clear, uncluttered structure, and it is divided into eight sections with drop-down menus targeted at specific audiences. The university attracts students from 138 countries, so the admissions section provides links to information about undergraduate and postgraduate courses and additional information for international students. Prospectuses are available online or can be downloaded in PDF format. An admissions icon provides a link to direct contact details for visitors who want further information to meet their personal requirements

Prospective students can access information about the university using a variety of media. A link to the *Wall of 100 Faces* feature uses video technology to show short films of current students discussing their experiences of studying at Oxford. Users can customize the video wall feature by clicking the *Only Show Me* option; for example, the films featuring interviews only with international students can be specifically selected for viewing.

The Web site also hosts links to other media such as podcasts, video-sharing Web sites, and social networking. Through *i-Tunes U*, the university makes available to a wide range of audiences material including podcasts about the university's applications process and lectures on subjects such as the works of William Shakespeare,

tropical medicine, and philosophy. Oxford University has its own education channel on YouTube, which provides access to filmed lectures and admissions information. Potential, present, and past students can also access short, instant updates on the latest news by following the university on Twitter, and Oxford also has a Facebook page.

Web-based marketing communications enable Oxford University to provide direct information for a range of audiences, to establish a dialogue with interested parties, and to build long-term relationships. In the increasingly competitive world of higher education, the ability to communicate directly with worldwide audiences is an important part of a university's marketing strategy.

Questions

1. With reference to the 7Cs model, discuss why the Oxford University Web site is an example of effective design.

2. What are the advantages and disadvantages of using social networking as part of a university marketing strategy?

3. How can Web-based communications help universities build long-term relationships with their students?

Sources: *Oxford University*, www.ox.ac.uk; *Times Higher Education*, www.timeshighereducation.co.uk; *YouTube*, www.youtube.com.

PART 8 | Creating Successful Long-term Growth

Chapter 20

In This Chapter, We Will Address the Following Questions

With a unique approach to video game playing, Nintendo's highly interactive and engaging Wii became a huge hit.

1. What challenges does a company face in developing new products and services?

2. What organizational structures and processes do managers use to oversee new-product development?

3. What are the main stages in developing new products and services?

4. What is the best way to manage the new-product development process?

5. What factors affect the rate of diffusion and consumer adoption of newly launched products and services?

Introducing New Market Offerings

New-product development shapes the company's future. Improved or replacement products and services can maintain or build sales; new-to-the-world products and services can transform industries and companies and change lives. But the low success rate of new products and services points to the many challenges they face. Companies are doing more than just talking about innovation. They are challenging industry norms and past conventions to develop new products and services that delight and engage consumers. Nintendo's Wii is a prime example.[1]

 Although Nintendo helped create the $30 billion global video game business, its U.S. sales had shrunk in half by 2006. CEO Satoru Iwata and game designer Shigeru Miyamoto decided to address two troubling trends in the industry: As players got older and acquired families and careers, they played less often, and as video game consoles got more powerful, they grew more expensive. Nintendo's solution? Redesign the game controllers and the way they interacted with the consoles. Bucking industry trends, Nintendo chose a cheaper, lower-power chip with fewer graphics capabilities, creating a totally different style of play based on physical gestures. A sleek white design and a new motion-sensitive wireless controller made it much more engaging and interactive. Nintendo's decision to embrace outside software developers meant a number of titles quickly became available. Thus Wii was born. Its collaborative nature made it a hit with nongamers drawn by its capabilities and hard-core players seeking to master its many intriguing games.

Marketers play a key role in new-product development by identifying and evaluating ideas and working with R&D and other areas in every stage of development. This chapter provides a detailed analysis of the new-product development process. Much of the discussion is equally relevant to new products, services, or business models. Chapter 21 considers how marketers can tap into global markets as another source of long-term growth.

New-Product Options

There are a variety of types of new products and ways to create them.[2]

Make or Buy

A company can add new products through acquisition or development. When acquiring, the company can buy other companies, patents from other companies, or a license or franchise from another company. Swiss food giant Nestlé has increased its presence in North America by acquiring such diverse brands as Carnation, Hills Brothers, Stouffer's, Ralston Purina, Dreyer's Ice Cream, Chef America, Jenny Craig, and Gerber.

But firms can successfully make only so many acquisitions. At some point, they need *organic growth*— the development of new products from within. Praxair, worldwide provider of industrial gases, achieved an ambitious goal of $200 million per year of double-digit new annual sales growth only through a healthy dose of organic growth and a large number of smaller but significant $5 million projects.[3]

For product development, the company can create new products in its own laboratories, or it can contract with independent researchers or new-product development firms to develop specific new products or provide new technology.[4] Firms such as Samsung, GE, Diageo, Hershey, and USB have engaged new-product consulting boutiques to provide fresh insights and points of view.

Types of New Products

New products range from new-to-the-world products that create an entirely new market to minor improvements or revisions of existing products. Most new-product activity is devoted to improving existing products. Some of the most successful recent new consumer products have been brand extensions: Tide Total Care, Gillette Venus Embrace, Bounce Extra Soft, Always Infinity, and Secret Flawless deodorant.[5] At Sony, modifications of established products account for over 80 percent of new-product activity.

It is increasingly difficult to identify blockbuster products that will transform a market, but continuous innovation can force competitors to play catch-up and also broaden the brand meaning.[6] Once a running-shoe manufacturer, Nike now competes with makers of all types of athletic shoes, clothing, and equipment. Armstrong World Industries moved from selling floor coverings to ceilings to total interior surface decoration.

Fewer than 10 percent of all new products are truly innovative and new to the world.[7] These products incur the greatest cost and risk. Although radical innovations can hurt the company's bottom line in the short run, if they succeed they can create a greater sustainable competitive advantage than ordinary products and produce significant financial rewards as a result.[8]

Companies typically must create a strong R&D and marketing partnership to pull off a radical innovation.[9] The right corporate culture is another crucial determinant; the firm must prepare to cannibalize existing products, tolerate risk, and maintain a future market orientation.[10] Few reliable techniques exist for estimating demand for radical innovations.[11] Focus groups can provide perspective on customer interest and need, but marketers may need a probe-and-learn approach based on observation and feedback of early users' experiences and other means such as online chats or product-focused blogs.

High-tech firms in telecommunications, computers, consumer electronics, biotech, and software in particular seek radical innovation.[12] They face a number of product-launch challenges: high technological uncertainty, high market uncertainty, fierce competition, high investment costs, short product life cycles, and scarce funding sources for risky projects.[13] Successes abound, however.[14] BMW is spending more than $1 billion to develop a small car for urban drivers, including an electric-powered version. Blackboard e-learning software brings new technology into the classroom to help professors manage their classes and course materials. Even consumer packaged goods makers can benefit from a healthy dose of technology. Danone uses sophisticated R&D techniques to study bacteria, coming up with billion-dollar sellers such as Activia yogurt, sold as an aid for regularity.

Challenges in New-Product Development

New-product introductions have accelerated, and in retailing, consumer goods, electronics, autos, and other industries, the time to bring a product to market has been cut in half.[15] Luxury leather-goods maker Louis Vuitton implemented a new factory format dubbed Pégase so it could ship fresh collections to its boutiques every six weeks—more than twice as frequently as in the past—giving customers more new looks to choose from.[16]

The Innovation Imperative

In an economy of rapid change, continuous innovation is a necessity. Highly innovative firms are able to identify and quickly seize new market opportunities. They create a positive attitude toward innovation and risk taking, routinize the innovation process, practice teamwork, and allow their people to experiment and even fail. One such firm is W. L. Gore.

W. L. Gore   Best known for its GORE-TEX high-performance fabrics, W. L. Gore has introduced breakthrough products as diverse as guitar strings, dental floss, medical devices, and fuel cells—while constantly reinventing the uses of the polymer polytetrafluoroethylene (PTFE). Several principles guide its new-product development. First, it works with potential customers. Its thoracic graft, designed to combat heart disease, was developed in close collaboration with physicians. Second, it lets employees choose projects and appoints few product leaders and teams. Gore likes to nurture "passionate champions" who convince others a project is worth their time and commitment. Thus leaders have positions of authority because they have followers. The development of the fuel cell rallied more than 100 of Gore's 9,000 research associates. Third, Gore gives employees "dabble" time. All research associates spend 10 percent of their work hours developing their own ideas. Promising ideas are pushed forward and judged according to a "Real, Win, Worth" exercise: Is the opportunity real? Can we win? Can we make money? Fourth, Gore knows when to let go, though dead ends in one area can spark innovation in another: Elixir acoustic guitar strings were the result of a failed venture into bike cables. Even successful ventures may need to move on. Glide shred-resistant dental floss was sold to Procter & Gamble because GORE-TEX knew retailers want to deal with a company selling a whole family of health care products.[17]

If it doesn't say
GORE-TEX® Footwear,
it's not!

W. L. Gore's thoughtful new-product development strategy has led to many successful innovations over the years, starting with its waterproof, breathable GORE-TEX fabric.

Companies that fail to develop new products leave their existing offerings vulnerable to changing customer needs and tastes, new technologies, shortened product life cycles, increased domestic and foreign competition, and especially new technologies. Kodak, long-time leader in the vanishing traditional film market, has worked hard to develop a new business model and product-development processes for a digital-photography world. Its new goal is to do for photos what Apple does for music by helping people organize and manage their personal libraries of images.

Innovation is about "creating new choices" the competition doesn't have access to, says IDEO's CEO Tim Brown. It isn't about brilliant people spontaneously generating new ideas, he argues, but about finding hidden assumptions and ignored processes that can change the way a company does business.[18]

New-Product Success

Most established companies focus on *incremental innovation*, entering new markets by tweaking products for new customers, using variations on a core product to stay one step ahead of the market, and creating interim solutions for industry-wide problems.

When Scott Paper couldn't compete with Fort Howard Paper Co. on price for the lucrative institutional toilet tissue market, it borrowed a solution from European companies: a dispenser that held bigger rolls. Scott made the larger rolls of paper and provided institutional customers with free dispensers, later doing the same thing with paper towels. Scott not only won over customers in a new market; it became less vulnerable to competitors, such as Fort Howard, which could lower prices but weren't offering the larger rolls or tailor-made dispensers.

Newer companies create *disruptive technologies* that are cheaper and more likely to alter the competitive space. Established companies can be slow to react or invest in these disruptive technologies because they threaten their investment. Then they suddenly find themselves facing formidable new competitors, and many fail.[19] To avoid this trap, incumbent firms must carefully monitor the preferences of both customers and noncustomers and uncover evolving, difficult-to-articulate customer needs.[20]

What else can a company do? In a study of industrial products, new-product specialists Cooper and Kleinschmidt found that the number one success factor is a unique, superior product. Such products succeed 98 percent of the time, compared to products with a moderate advantage (58 percent success) or minimal advantage (18 percent success). Another key factor is a well-defined product concept. The company carefully defines and assesses the target market, product requirements, and benefits before proceeding. Other success factors are technological and marketing synergy, quality of execution in all stages, and market attractiveness.[21]

Cooper and Kleinschmidt also found that products designed solely for domestic markets tend to show a high failure rate, low market share, and low growth. Those designed for the world market—or at least neighboring countries—achieve significantly more profits at home and abroad. Yet only 17 percent of the products in their study were designed with an international orientation.[22] The implication is that companies should consider adopting an international perspective in designing and developing new products, even if only to sell in their home market.

New-Product Failure

New products continue to fail at estimated rates as high as 50 percent or even 95 percent in the United States and 90 percent in Europe.[23] They fail for many reasons: ignored or misinterpreted market research; overestimates of market size; high development costs; poor design or ineffectual performance; incorrect positioning, advertising, or price; insufficient distribution support; competitors who fight back hard; and inadequate ROI or payback. Some additional drawbacks are:[24]

- *Shortage of important ideas in certain areas.* There may be few ways left to improve some basic products (such as steel or detergent).
- *Fragmented markets.* Companies must aim their new products at smaller market segments, which can mean lower sales and profits for each product.
- *Social, economic, and governmental constraints.* New products must satisfy consumer safety and environmental concerns. They must also be resilient if economic times are tough.
- *Cost of development.* A company typically must generate many ideas to find just one worthy of development and thus often faces high R&D, manufacturing, and marketing costs.
- *Capital shortages.* Some companies with good ideas cannot raise the funds to research and launch them.
- *Shorter required development time.* Companies must learn to compress development time with new techniques, strategic partners, early concept tests, and advanced marketing planning.
- *Poor launch timing.* New products are sometimes launched after the category has already taken off or when there is still insufficient interest.
- *Shorter product life cycles.* Rivals are quick to copy success. Sony used to enjoy a three-year lead on its new products. Now Matsushita can copy them within six months, barely leaving Sony time to recoup its investment.
- *Organizational support.* The new product may not mesh with the corporate culture or receive the financial or other support it needs.

But failure comes with the territory, and truly innovative firms accept it as part of what's needed to be successful. Silicon Valley marketing expert Seth Godin maintains: "It is not just OK to fail; it's imperative to fail."[25] Many Web companies are the result of failed earlier ventures and experience numerous failures as their services evolve. Dogster.com, a social network site for dog lovers, emerged after the spectacular demise of Pets.com.[26]

Initial failure is not always the end of the road for an idea. Recognizing that 90 percent of experimental drugs are unsuccessful, Eli Lilly looks at failure as an inevitable part of discovery. Its scientists are encouraged to find new uses for compounds that fail at any stage in a human clinical trial. Evista, a failed contraceptive, became a $1 billion-a-year drug for osteoporosis. Strattera was unsuccessful as an antidepressant, but became a top seller for attention deficit/hyperactivity disorder. One promising cardiovascular drug in development started as an asthma project.[27]

Organizational Arrangements

Many companies use *customer-driven engineering* to develop new products, incorporating customer preferences in the final design. Some rely on internal changes to develop more successful new products. Consider Johnson & Johnson.

Johnson & Johnson To improve the odds for new-product success in its growing medical device business, Johnson & Johnson has made a number of changes. First, it is trying to replicate the dynamic venture-capital world within the company by creating internal start-ups that seek financing from other J&J units. J&J is also pushing for greater input from doctors and insurers to provide stronger assurance that any devices it introduces will be highly desirable, feasible, and cost-effective. The Ethicon-Endo unit designed new surgical clips based on discussions with physicians about the need to make surgery less invasive. J&J also put one of its most successful scientists in the newly created position of chief science and technology officer, to encourage collaboration between J&J's different businesses and overcome barriers in its decentralized structure. One notable success: the $2.6 billion CYPHER drug-coated stent.[28]

New-product development requires senior management to define business domains, product categories, and specific criteria. One company established the following acceptance criteria:

- The product can be introduced within five years.
- The product has a market potential of at least $50 million and a 15 percent growth rate.
- The product can provide at least 30 percent return on sales and 40 percent on investment.
- The product can achieve technical or market leadership.

Budgeting for New-Product Development

R&D outcomes are so uncertain that it is difficult to use normal investment criteria when budgeting for new-product development. Some companies simply finance as many projects as possible, hoping to achieve a few winners. Other companies apply a conventional percentage-of-sales figure or spend what the competition spends. Still others decide how many successful new products they need and work backward to estimate the required investment.

Table 20.1 shows how a company might calculate the cost of new-product development. The new-products manager at a large consumer packaged-goods company reviewed 64 ideas. Sixteen passed the screening stage and cost $1,000 each to review at this point. Half those, or eight, survived the concept-testing stage, at a cost of $20,000 each. Half of these, or four, survived the product-development stage, at a cost of $200,000 each. Two did well in the test market, costing $500,000 each. When they were launched, at a cost of $5 million each, one was highly successful. Thus, this one successful idea cost the company $5,721,000 to develop, while 63 others fell by the wayside for a total development cost of $13,984,000. Unless the company can improve its pass ratios and reduce costs at each stage, it will need to budget nearly $14 million for each successful new idea it hopes to find.

Hit rates vary. Inventor Sir James Dyson claims he made 5,127 prototypes of his bagless, transparent vacuum cleaner over a 14-year period before getting it right, resulting in the best-selling vacuum cleaner by revenue in the United States with over 20 million sold and annual revenue of $1 billion. He doesn't lament his failures, though: "If you want to discover something that other people haven't, you

TABLE 20.1 Finding One Successful New Product (Starting with 64 New Ideas)				
Stage	Number of Ideas	Pass Ratio	Cost per Product Idea	Total Cost
1. Idea screening	64	1:4	$ 1,000	$ 64,000
2. Concept testing	16	1:2	20,000	320,000
3. Product development	8	1:2	200,000	1,600,000
4. Test marketing	4	1:2	500,000	2,000,000
5. National launch	2	1:2	5,000,000	10,000,000
			$5,721,000	$13,984,000

need to do things the wrong way…watching why that fails can take you on a completely different path." His latest successes: the Airblade, an energy-efficient hand drier for public restrooms, and the Air Multiplier, a bladeless table fan.[29]

Organizing New-Product Development

Companies handle the organizational aspect of new-product development in several ways.[30] Many assign responsibility to *product managers.* But product managers are often busy managing existing lines and may lack the skills and knowledge to develop and critique new products.

Kraft and Johnson & Johnson employ *new-product managers* who report to category managers. Westinghouse has *growth leaders*—a full-time job for its most creative and successful managers.[31] Some companies have a *high-level management committee* charged with reviewing and approving proposals. Large companies often establish a *new-product department* headed by a manager with substantial authority and access to top management whose responsibilities include generating and screening new ideas, working with the R&D department, and carrying out field testing and commercialization.

Inventor Sir James Dyson is willing to endure many failed prototypes as long as he comes up with a winner, like the Air Multiplier bladeless table fan.

Adobe Systems Inc.   Adobe Systems, a developer of graphic design and publishing software, established a task force to identify the obstacles its employees faced in trying to develop new products. The team discovered that ideas needing a new sales channel, new business model, or even new packaging failed due to the corporate hierarchy. In addition, Adobe had grown so large that ideas originating in branch offices were not getting a fair shake. As a result, Adobe established a New Business Initiatives Group that mimics the venture capital model, backing entrepreneurial people and putting employees in front of their ideas. The Group holds quarterly Idea Champion Showcases where approximately 20 product managers and other employees (except top executives who are barred from the proceedings) watch as potential employee-entrepreneurs give brief presentations and Q&A sessions. The ideas are vetted by Adobe Entrepreneurs-in-Residence and the best ideas are given a first round of funding. But even ideas that are nixed can still get a hearing on the company's brainstorming site. The event has become extremely popular within Adobe—an *American Idol*–style way for good ideas to come to the fore.[32]

CROSS-FUNCTIONAL TEAMS   3M, Dow, and General Mills have assigned new-product development to **venture teams**, cross-functional groups charged with developing a specific product or business. These "intrapreneurs" are relieved of other duties and given a budget, time frame, and "skunkworks" setting. *Skunkworks* are informal workplaces, sometimes garages, where intrapreneurial teams attempt to develop new products.

Cross-functional teams can collaborate and use concurrent new-product development to push new products to market.[33] Concurrent product development resembles a rugby match, with team members passing the new product back and forth as they head toward the goal. Using this system, Allen-Bradley Corporation (a maker of industrial controls) was able to develop a new device in just two years, down from six under its old system. Cross-functional teams help ensure that engineers are not driven to create a "better mousetrap" when potential customers don't need or want one.

STAGE-GATE SYSTEMS   Many top companies use the *stage-gate system* to divide the innovation process into stages, with a gate or checkpoint at the end of each.[34] The project leader, working with a cross-functional team, must bring a set of known deliverables to each gate before the project can pass to the next stage. To move from the business plan stage into product development requires a convincing market research study of consumer needs and interest, a competitive analysis, and a technical appraisal. Senior managers review the criteria at each gate to make one of four decisions: *go, kill, hold,* or *recycle.* Stage-gate systems make the innovation process visible to all and clarify the project leader's and team's responsibilities at each stage.[35] The gates or controls should not be so rigid, however, that they inhibit learning and the development of novel products.[36]

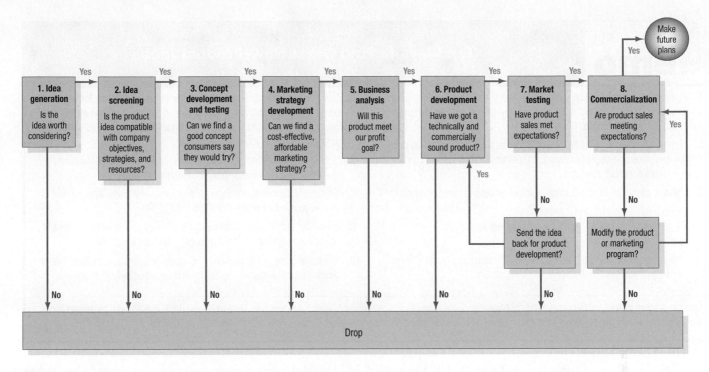

|Fig. 20.1| △

The New-Product Development Decision Process

The stages in the new-product development process are shown in △ Figure 20.1. Many firms have parallel sets of projects working through the process, each at a different stage.[37] Think of the process as a *funnel:* A large number of initial new-product ideas and concepts are winnowed down to a few high-potential products that are ultimately launched. But the process is not always linear. Many firms use a *spiral development process* that recognizes the value of returning to an earlier stage to make improvements before moving forward.[38]

Ansell Healthcare, the world's largest manufacturer of protective gloves and clothing, adopted a stage-gate process and found the contribution of new products to overall sales jumped from 4.5 percent to 13 percent in a little over two years. Hydro Quebec, one of the world's largest hydro-electricity utilities, implemented a stage-gate system that focused resources on the most valuable projects and reaped over $1 billion in benefits.[39]

Managing the Development Process: Ideas

Generating Ideas

The new-product development process starts with the search for ideas. Some marketing experts believe the greatest opportunities and highest leverage with new products are found by uncovering the best possible set of unmet customer needs or technological innovation.[40] New-product ideas can come from interacting with various groups and using creativity-generating techniques.[41] (See "Marketing Memo: Ten Ways to Find Great New-Product Ideas.")

Erich Joachimsthaler believes some of the best new-product opportunities are right in front of marketers' eyes. The mistake too many make, he says, is to view the world from the perspective of their own products and services and search for customers for them. His demand-first innovation and growth (DIG) framework is designed to provide companies with an unbiased view and an outside-in perspective of demand opportunities. It has three parts:[42]

1. *The demand landscape*—Use observational, anthropological, and ethnographic methods or consumer self-reports to map consumer needs, wants, and even beyond.
2. *The opportunity space*—Use conceptual lens and structured innovative-thinking tools to achieve market perspectives from different angles.
3. *The strategic blueprint*—Think about how the new product can fit into customers lives and how it can be distinguished from competitors.

As one DIG-type application, Joachimsthaler notes how Intel famously abandoned its highly competitive memory business to pursue more fertile opportunities with microprocessors.

INTERACTING WITH OTHERS Encouraged by the *open innovation* movement, many firms are going outside their bounds to tap external sources of new ideas, including customers, employees, scientists, engineers, channel members, marketing agencies, top management, and even competitors.[43] "Marketing Insight: P&G's New Connect-and-Develop Approach to Innovation" describes how P&G has made new-product development more externally focused.

Marketing Insight

P&G'S New Connect + Develop Approach to Innovation

In the first decade of the 21st century, one of the fastest-growing major corporations in revenue and profit was Procter & Gamble. Fueling that growth were successful new products such as Swiffer, Mr. Clean Magic Eraser, and Actonel (a prescription medication for osteoporosis). Many of these new products reflected innovation in what ex-CEO A.G. Lafley calls "the core"—core markets, categories, brands, technologies, and capabilities.

To more effectively develop its core, P&G adopted a "Connect + Develop" model that emphasizes the pursuit of outside innovation. The firm collaborates with organizations and individuals around the world, searching for proven technologies, packages, and products it can improve, scale up, and market on its own or in partnership with other companies. It has strong relationships with external designers, distributing product development around the world to increase what it calls "consumer sensing."

P&G identifies the top 10 customer needs, closely related products that could leverage or benefit from existing brand equity, and "game boards" that map the adoption of technology across different product categories. It may consult government and private labs as well as academic and other research institutions, VC firms, individual entrepreneurs, and suppliers, retailers, competitors, and development and trade partners, using online networks to reach thousands of experts worldwide.

P&G's three core requirements for a successful Connect + Develop strategy are:

1. *Never assume that "ready to go" ideas found outside are truly ready to go.* There will always be development work to do, including risky scale-up.

2. *Don't underestimate the internal resources required.* You'll need a full-time, senior executive to run any connect-and-develop initiative.

3. *Never launch without a mandate from the CEO.* Connect and develop cannot succeed if it's cordoned off in R&D. It must be a top-down, company-wide strategy.

Through Connect + Develop—and improvements in product cost, design, and marketing—P&G increased R&D productivity by nearly 60 percent during the decade. The innovation success rate more than doubled, and cost has fallen.

Sources: www.pgconnectdevelop.com A.G. Lafley and Ram Charan, *The Game Changer: How You Can Drive Revenue and Profit Growth Through Innovation* (New York: Crown Business, 2009); Robert Berner, "How P&G Pampers New Thinking," *BusinessWeek*, April 14, 2008, pp. 73–74; Steve Hamm, "Speed Demons," *BusinessWeek*, March 27, 2006, pp. 69–76; Larry Huston and Nabil Sakkab, "Connect and Develop: Inside Procter & Gamble's New Model for Innovation," *Harvard Business Review*, March 2006, pp. 58–66; Geoff Colvin, "Lafley and Immelt: In Search of Billions," *Fortune*, December 11, 2006, pp. 70–72; Rajat Gupta and Jim Wendler, "Leading Change: An Interview with the CEO of P&G," *McKinsey Quarterly* (July 2005).

Customer needs and wants are the logical place to start the search.[44] Griffin and Hauser suggest that conducting 10 to 20 in-depth experiential interviews per market segment often uncovers the vast majority of customer needs.[45] But other approaches can be profitable (see "Marketing Memo: Seven Ways to Draw New Ideas from Your Customers"). One marketer-sponsored café in Tokyo tests products of all kinds with affluent, influential young Japanese women.[46]

The traditional company-centric approach to product innovation is giving way to a world in which companies cocreate products with consumers.[47] Companies are increasingly turning to "crowdsourcing" to generate new ideas or, as we saw in the preceding chapter, to create consumer-generated marketing campaigns. *Crowdsourcing* means inviting the Internet community to help create content or software, often with prize money or a moment of glory as an incentive.[48]

This strategy has helped create new products and companies such as Wikipedia, YouTube (which was eventually purchased by Google), and iStockphoto, a "microstock" company. One recent convert to crowdsourcing is Cisco.[49]

P&G's Connect + Develop approach to innovation enabled Swiffer Dusters to make the leap to global market success.

Cisco   Cisco's I-Prize, an external innovation competition, gives a team outside the company the chance to join Cisco in heading an emerging technology business while receiving a $250,000 signing bonus and up to $10 million in funding for the first two years. Cisco's rationale for the contest—which drew 1,200 entrants from 104 countries—was simple: "In many parts of the world, you have incredibly smart people with incredibly great ideas who have absolutely no access to capital to take a great idea and turn it into a business." Judges applied five main criteria: (1) Does it address a real pain point? (2) Will it appeal to a big enough market? (3) Is the timing right? (4) If we pursue the idea, will we be good at it? and (5) Can we exploit the opportunity for the long term? The public judged the entries online, where Cisco found the detailed comments even more useful than the actual votes. The winning entry in the first competition was a plan for a sensor-enabled smart-electricity grid.

Besides producing new and better ideas, cocreation can help customers to feel closer to and more favorably toward the company and to create favorable word of mouth.[50] Getting the right customers engaged in the right way, however, is critical.[51]

Lead users can be a good source of input, even when they innovate products without the consent or knowledge of the companies that produce them. Mountain bikes developed as a result of youngsters taking their bikes to the top of a mountain and riding down. When the bikes broke, the

marketing Memo

Seven Ways to Draw New Ideas from Your Customers

1. **Observe how customers are using your product.** Medtronic, a medical device company, has salespeople and market researchers regularly observe spine surgeons who use their products and competitive products, to learn how theirs can be improved. After living with lower-middle-class families in Mexico City, Procter & Gamble researchers devised Downy Single Rinse, a fabric softener that removed an arduous step from the partly manual laundry process there.

2. **Ask customers about their problems with your products.** Komatsu Heavy Equipment sent a group of engineers and designers to the United States for six months to ride with equipment drivers and learn how to make products better. Procter & Gamble, recognizing consumers were frustrated that potato chips break and are difficult to save after opening the bag, designed Pringles to be uniform in size and encased in a protective tennis-ball-type can.

3. **Ask customers about their dream products.** Ask your customers what they want your product to do, even if the ideal sounds impossible. One 70-year-old camera user told Minolta he would like the camera to make his subjects look better and not show their wrinkles and aging. In response, Minolta produced a camera with two lenses, one for rendering softer images of the subjects.

4. **Use a customer advisory board to comment on your company's ideas.** Levi Strauss uses youth panels to discuss lifestyles, habits, values, and brand engagements; Cisco runs Customer Forums to improve its offerings; and Harley-Davidson solicits product ideas from its one million H.O.G. (Harley Owners Group) members.

5. **Use Web sites for new ideas.** Companies can use specialized search engines such as Technorati and Daypop to find blogs and postings relevant to their businesses. P&G's site has *We're Listening* and *Share Your Thoughts* sections and Advisory Feedback sessions to gain advice and feedback from customers.

6. **Form a brand community of enthusiasts who discuss your product.** Harley-Davidson and Apple have strong brand enthusiasts and advocates; Sony engaged in collaborative dialogues with consumers to codevelop Sony's PlayStation 2. LEGO draws on kids and influential adult enthusiasts for feedback on new-product concepts in early stages of development.

7. **Encourage or challenge your customers to change or improve your product.** Salesforce.com wants its users to develop and share new software applications using simple programming tools. International Flavors & Fragrances gives a toolkit to its customers to modify specific flavors, which IFF then manufactures; LSI Logic Corporation also provides customers with do-it-yourself toolkits so customers can design their own specialized chips; and BMW posted a toolkit on its Web site to let customers develop ideas using telematics and in-car online services.

Source: From an unpublished paper, Philip Kotler, "Drawing New Ideas from Your Customers," 2007.

Some of the best new-product ideas come from highly involved consumers or lead users, as was the case in the birth of the mountain bike.

youngsters began building more durable bikes and adding motorcycle brakes, improved suspension, and accessories. They, not the companies, developed these innovations.

Some companies, particularly those that want to appeal to hip young consumers, bring their lead users into their product-design process. Technical companies can learn a great deal by studying customers who make the most advanced use of the company's products and who recognize the need for improvements before other customers do.[52] In a business-to-business market, collecting information from distributors and retailers who are not in close contact can provide more diverse insights and information.[53]

Not everyone believes a customer focus helps to create better new products. As Henry Ford famously said, "If I'd asked people what they wanted, they would have said a faster horse." And some still caution that being overly focused on consumers who may not really know what they want, or what could be possible, can result in shortsighted product development and miss real potential breakthroughs.[54]

INTERACTING WITH EMPLOYEES Employees can be a source of ideas for improving production, products, and services.[55] Toyota claims its employees submit 2 million ideas annually (about 35 suggestions per employee), over 85 percent of which are implemented. Kodak, Milliken, and other firms give monetary, holiday, or recognition awards to employees who submit the best ideas. Nokia inducts engineers who file for at least 10 patents into its "Club 10," recognizing them each year in a formal awards ceremony hosted by the company's CEO.[56] A company can motivate its employees to submit new ideas to an *idea manager* whose name and contact information are widely circulated.

Top management can be another major source of ideas. Some company leaders, such as former CEO Andy Grove of Intel, take personal responsibility for technological innovation in the firm. New-product ideas can come from inventors, patent attorneys, university and commercial laboratories, industrial consultants, advertising agencies, marketing research firms, and industrial publications. However, their chances of receiving serious attention often depend on someone in the organization taking the role of product champion.

STUDYING COMPETITORS Companies can find good ideas by researching the products and services of competitors and other companies. They can find out what customers like and dislike about competitors' products. They can buy their competitors' products, take them apart, and build better ones. Company sales representatives and intermediaries are a particularly good source of ideas. These groups have firsthand exposure to customers and are often the first to learn about competitive developments. Electronic retailer Best Buy actually checks with venture capitalists to find out what start-ups are working on.

ADOPTING CREATIVITY TECHNIQUES Internal brainstorming sessions also can be quite effective—if conducted correctly. "Marketing Memo: How to Run a Successful Brainstorming Session" provides some brainstorming guidelines.

The following list is a sampling of techniques for stimulating creativity in individuals and groups.[57]

- *Attribute listing.* List the attributes of an object, such as a screwdriver. Then modify each attribute, such as replacing the wooden handle with plastic, providing torque power, adding different screw heads, and so on.
- *Forced relationships.* List several ideas and consider each in relationship to each of the others. In designing new office furniture, for example, consider a desk, bookcase, and filing cabinet as separate ideas. Then imagine a desk with a built-in bookcase or a desk with built-in files or a bookcase with built-in files.
- *Morphological analysis.* Start with a problem, such as "getting something from one place to another via a powered vehicle." Now think of dimensions, such as the type of platform (cart, chair, sling, bed), the medium (air, water, oil, rails), and the power source (compressed air, electric motor, magnetic fields). By listing every possible combination, you can generate many new solutions.
- *Reverse assumption analysis.* List all the normal assumptions about an entity and then reverse them. Instead of assuming that a restaurant has menus, charges for food, and serves food, reverse each assumption. The new restaurant may decide to serve only what the chef bought that morning and cooked; may provide some food and charge only for how long the person sits at the table; and may design an exotic atmosphere and rent out the space to people who bring their own food and beverages.

---

marketing Memo

How to Run a Successful Brainstorming Session

If done correctly, group brainstorming sessions can create insights, ideas, and solutions that would have been impossible without everyone's participation. If done incorrectly, they are a painful waste of time that can frustrate and antagonize participants. To ensure success, experts recommend the following guidelines:

1. A trained facilitator should guide the session.
2. Participants must feel they can express themselves freely.
3. Participants must see themselves as collaborators working toward a common goal.
4. Rules need to be set up and followed, so conversations don't get off track.
5. Participants must be given proper background preparation and materials so they can get into the task quickly.
6. Individual sessions before and after the brainstorming can be useful for thinking and learning about the topic ahead of time and for reflecting afterward on what happened.
7. Brainstorming sessions must lead to a clear plan of action and implementation, so the ideas that materialize can provide tangible value.
8. Brainstorming sessions can do more than just generate ideas—they can help build teams and leave participants better informed and energized.

Sources: Linda Tischler, "Be Creative: You Have 30 Seconds," *Fast Company,* May 2007, pp. 47–50; Michael Myser, "When Brainstorming Goes Bad," *Business 2.0*, October 2006, p. 76; Robert I. Sutton, "Eight Rules to Brilliant Brainstorming," *BusinessWeek IN Inside Innovation,* September 2006, pp. 17–21.

An example of lateral marketing, Kinder Surprise combines two product concepts—candy and toy—into one product offering.

- **New contexts.** Take familiar processes, such as people-helping services, and put them into a new context. Imagine helping dogs and cats instead of people with day care service, stress reduction, psychotherapy, funerals, and so on. As another example, instead of sending hotel guests to the front desk to check in, greet them at curbside and use a wireless device to register them.
- **Mind mapping.** Start with a thought, such as a car, write it on a piece of paper, then think of the next thought that comes up (say Mercedes), link it to car, then think of the next association (Germany), and do this with all associations that come up with each new word. Perhaps a whole new idea will materialize.

Increasingly, new-product ideas arise from *lateral marketing* that combines two product concepts or ideas to create a new offering.[58] Here are some successful examples:

- Gas station stores = gas stations + food
- Cybercafés = cafeteria + Internet
- Cereal bars = cereal + snacking
- Kinder Surprise = candy + toy
- Sony Walkman = audio + portable

Using Idea Screening

In screening ideas, the company must avoid two types of errors. A *DROP-error* occurs when the company dismisses a good idea. It is extremely easy to find fault with other people's ideas (⬛ Figure 20.2). Some companies shudder when they look back at ideas they dismissed or breathe sighs of relief when they realize how close they came to dropping what eventually became a huge success. Consider the hit television show *Friends*.

Friends   The NBC situation comedy *Friends* enjoyed a 10-year run from 1994 to 2004 as a perennial ratings powerhouse. But the show almost didn't see the light of the day. According to an internal NBC research report, the pilot episode was described as "not very entertaining, clever, or original" and was given a failing grade, scoring 41 out of 100. Ironically, the pilot for an earlier hit sitcom, *Seinfeld,* was also rated "weak," although the pilot for the medical drama *ER* scored a healthy 91. Courtney Cox's Monica was the *Friends* character who scored best with test audiences, but characters portrayed by Lisa Kudrow and Matthew Perry were deemed to have marginal appeal, and the Rachel, Ross, and Joey characters scored even lower. Adults 35 and over in the sample found the characters as a whole "smug, superficial, and self-absorbed."[59] ⬛

The purpose of screening is to drop poor ideas as early as possible. The rationale is that product-development costs rise substantially with each successive development stage. Most companies require new-product ideas to be described on a standard form for a new-product committee's review. The description states the product idea, the target market, and the competition and roughly estimates market size, product price, development time and costs, manufacturing costs, and rate of return.

The executive committee then reviews each idea against a set of criteria. Does the product meet a need? Would it offer superior value? Can it be distinctively advertised? Does the company have the necessary know-how and capital? Will the new product deliver the expected sales volume, sales growth, and profit? Consumer input may be necessary to tap into marketplace realities.[60]

Management can rate the surviving ideas using a weighted-index method like that in ⬛ Table 20.2. The first column lists factors required for successful product launches, and the second column assigns importance weights. The third column scores the product idea on a scale from 0 to 1.0, with 1.0 the highest score. The final step multiplies each factor's importance by the product score to obtain an overall rating. In this example, the product idea scores 0.69, which places it in the "good idea" level. The purpose of this basic rating device is to promote systematic evaluation and discussion. It is not supposed to make the decision for management.

TABLE 20.2 ⬭ Product–Idea Rating Device			
Product Success Requirements	**Relative Weight (a)**	**Product Score (b)**	**Product Rating (c = a × b)**
Unique or superior product	.40	.8	.32
High performance-to-cost ratio	.30	.6	.18
High marketing dollar support	.20	.7	.14
Lack of strong competition	.10	.5	.05
Total	1.00		.69[a]

[a] Rating scale: .00–.30 poor; .31–.60 fair; .61–.80 good. Minimum acceptance rate: .61

As the idea moves through development, the company will need to constantly revise its estimate of the product's overall probability of success, using the following formula:

$$\text{Overall probability of success} = \text{Probability of technical completion} \times \text{Probability of commercialization given technical completion} \times \text{Probability of economic success given commercialization}$$

For example, if the three probabilities are estimated at 0.50, 0.65, and 0.74, respectively, the overall probability of success is 0.24. The company then must judge whether this probability is high enough to warrant continued development.

Managing the Development Process: Concept to Strategy

Attractive ideas must be refined into testable product concepts. A *product idea* is a possible product the company might offer to the market. A *product concept* is an elaborated version of the idea expressed in consumer terms.

Concept Development and Testing

Concept development is a necessary but not sufficient step for new product success. Marketers must also distinguish winning concepts from losers.

CONCEPT DEVELOPMENT Let us illustrate concept development with the following situation: A large food-processing company gets the idea of producing a powder to add to milk to increase its nutritional value and taste. This is a product *idea*, but consumers don't buy product ideas; they buy product *concepts*.

A product idea can be turned into several concepts. The first question is: Who will use this product? It can be aimed at infants, children, teenagers, young or middle-aged adults, or older adults. Second, what primary benefit should this product provide: Taste, nutrition, refreshment, or energy? Third, when will people consume this drink: Breakfast, midmorning, lunch, midafternoon, dinner, late evening? By answering these questions, a company can form several concepts:

- *Concept 1.* An instant drink for adults who want a quick nutritious breakfast without preparation.
- *Concept 2.* A tasty snack for children to drink as a midday refreshment.
- *Concept 3.* A health supplement for older adults to drink in the late evening before they go to bed.

Each concept represents a *category concept* that defines the product's competition. An instant breakfast drink would compete against bacon and eggs, breakfast cereals, coffee and pastry, and other breakfast alternatives. A snack drink would compete against soft drinks, fruit juices, sports drinks, and other thirst quenchers.

"I've got a great idea!"

"It won't work here."

"We've tried it before."

"This isn't the right time."

"It can't be done."

"It's not the way we do things."

"We've done all right without it."

"It will cost too much."

"Let's discuss it at our next meeting."

|Fig. 20.2| △

Forces Fighting New Ideas

Source: With permission of Jerold Panas, Young & Partners Inc.

(a) Product-positioning Map (Breakfast Market)

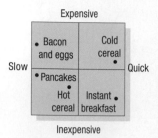

(b) Brand-positioning Map (Instant Breakfast Market)

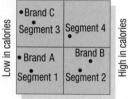

|Fig. 20.3| △

Product and Brand Positioning

Suppose the instant-breakfast-drink concept looks best. The next task is to show where this powdered product would stand in relationship to other breakfast products via perceptual mapping. △ Figure 20.3(a) uses the two dimensions of cost and preparation time to create a *product-positioning map* for the breakfast drink. An instant breakfast drink offers low cost and quick preparation. Its nearest competitor is cold cereal or breakfast bars; its most distant is bacon and eggs. These contrasts can help communicate and promote the concept to the market.

Next, the product concept becomes a *brand concept*. Figure 20.3(b) is a *brand-positioning map*, a perceptual map showing the current positions of three existing brands of instant breakfast drinks (A–C), as seen by consumers. It can also be useful to overlay consumer preferences on to the map in terms of their current or desired preferences. Figure 20.3(b) also shows four segments of consumers (1–4) whose preferences are clustered around the points on the map.

The brand-positioning map helps the company to decide how much to charge and how calorific to make its drink. Three segments (1–3) are well served by existing brands (A–C). The company would not want to position itself next to one of those existing brands, unless that brand is weak or inferior or market demand was high enough to be shared. As it turns out, the new brand would be distinctive in the medium-price, medium-calorie market or in the high-price, high-calorie market. There is also a segment of consumers (4) clustered fairly near the medium-price, medium-calorie market, suggesting that this may offer the greatest opportunity.

CONCEPT TESTING Concept testing means presenting the product concept to target consumers, physically or symbolically, and getting their reactions. The more the tested concepts resemble the final product or experience, the more dependable concept testing is. Concept testing of prototypes can help avoid costly mistakes, but it may be especially challenging with radically different, new-to-the-world products.[61] Visualization techniques can help respondents match their mental state with what might occur when they are actually evaluating or choosing the new product.[62]

In the past, creating physical prototypes was costly and time consuming, but today firms can use *rapid prototyping* to design products on a computer and then produce rough models to show potential consumers for their reactions. In response to a short-term oversupply of wine in the marketplace, the makers of Kendall-Jackson developed two new brands by using rapid prototyping to quickly bring its ideas to life, selling 100,000 cases, 10 times more than expected, for each brand in the process.[63]

Companies are also using *virtual reality* to test product concepts. Virtual reality programs use computers and sensory devices (such as gloves or goggles) to simulate reality. Supercomputers also allow for elaborate product testing to assess changes in performance and supplement consumer input. Kenworth trucks used to test new truck designs with clay models and wind tunnels. Using supercomputer analysis, it can now make more accurate estimates of how much drag and fuel use it can eliminate with new trimmed and tapered mud flaps (answer: $400 of a typical truck's annual gas bill).[64]

Concept testing presents consumers with an elaborated version of the concept. Here is the elaboration of concept 1 in our milk example:

> Our product is a powdered mixture added to milk to make an instant breakfast that gives all the day's needed nutrition along with good taste and high convenience. The product comes in three flavors (chocolate, vanilla, and strawberry) and individual packets, six to a box, at $2.49 a box.

After receiving this information, researchers measure product dimensions by having consumers respond to questions like these:

1. *Communicability and believability*—"Are the benefits clear to you and believable?" If the scores are low, the concept must be refined or revised.
2. *Need level*—"Do you see this product solving a problem or filling a need for you?" The stronger the need, the higher the expected consumer interest.
3. *Gap level*—"Do other products currently meet this need and satisfy you?" The greater the gap, the higher the expected consumer interest. Marketers can multiply the need level by the gap level to produce a *need-gap score*. A high score means the consumer sees the product as filling a strong need not satisfied by available alternatives.
4. *Perceived value*—"Is the price reasonable in relationship to value?" The higher the perceived value, the higher is expected consumer interest.

Conjoint analysis was instrumental in the design of Courtyard by Marriott.

5. **Purchase intention**—"Would you (definitely, probably, probably not, definitely not) buy the product?" Consumers who answered the first three questions positively should answer "Definitely" here.

6. **User targets, purchase occasions, purchasing frequency**—"Who would use this product, when, and how often?"

Respondents' answers indicate whether the concept has a broad and strong consumer appeal, what products it competes against, and which consumers are the best targets. The need-gap levels and purchase-intention levels can be checked against norms for the product category to see whether the concept appears to be a winner, a long shot, or a loser. One food manufacturer rejects any concept that draws a definitely-would-buy score lower than 40 percent.

CONJOINT ANALYSIS Consumer preferences for alternative product concepts can be measured with **conjoint analysis**, a method for deriving the utility values that consumers attach to varying levels of a product's attributes.[65] Conjoint analysis has become one of the most popular concept-development and testing tools. For example, Marriott used it to design its Courtyard hotel concept.[66]

With conjoint analysis, respondents see different hypothetical offers formed by combining varying levels of the attributes, then rank the various offers. Management can identify the most appealing offer and its estimated market share and profit. In a classic illustration, academic research pioneers Green and Wind used this approach in connection with developing a new spot-removing, carpet-cleaning agent for home use.[67] Suppose the new-product marketer is considering five design elements:

- Three package designs (A, B, C—see △ Figure 20.4)
- Three brand names (K2R, Glory, Bissell)
- Three prices ($1.19, $1.39, $1.59)
- A possible Good Housekeeping seal (yes, no)
- A possible money-back guarantee (yes, no)

Although the researcher can form 108 possible product concepts ($3 \times 3 \times 3 \times 2 \times 2$), it would be too much to ask consumers to rank them all from most to least preferred. A sample of, say, 18 contrasting product concepts is feasible.

The marketer now uses a statistical program to derive the consumer's utility functions for each of the five attributes (see △ Figure 20.5). Utility ranges between zero and one; the higher the utility, the stronger the consumer's preference for that level of the attribute. Looking at packaging, package B is the most favored, followed by C and then A (A hardly has any utility). The preferred names are Bissell, K2R, and Glory, in that order. The consumer's utility varies inversely with price.

|Fig. 20.4| △

Samples for Conjoint Analysis

|Fig. 20.5| △

Utility Functions
Based on Conjoint
Analysis

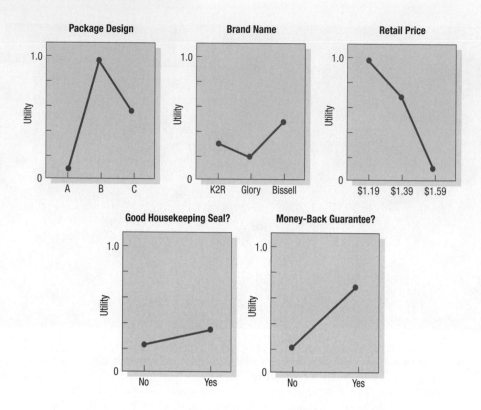

A Good Housekeeping seal is preferred, but it does not add that much utility and may not be worth the effort to obtain it. A money-back guarantee is strongly preferred.

The consumer's most desired offer is package design B, brand name Bissell, priced at $1.19, with a Good Housekeeping seal and a money-back guarantee. We can also determine the relative importance of each attribute to this consumer—the difference between the highest and lowest utility level for that attribute. The greater the difference, the more important the attribute. Clearly, this consumer sees price and package design as the most important attributes, followed by money-back guarantee, brand name, and a Good Housekeeping seal.

Preference data from a sufficient sample of target consumers helps to estimate the market share any specific offer is likely to achieve, given any assumptions about competitive response. Still, the company may not launch the market offer that promises to gain the greatest market share, because of cost considerations. The most customer-appealing offer is not always the most profitable offer to make.

Under some conditions, researchers will collect the data not with a full-profile description of each offer, but by presenting two factors at a time. For example, respondents may see a table with three price levels and three package types and indicate which of the nine combinations they would like most, second-best, and so on. A further table consists of trade-offs between two other variables. The trade-off approach may be easier to use when there are many variables and possible offers. However, it is less realistic in that respondents are focusing on only two variables at a time. Adaptive conjoint analysis (ACA) is a "hybrid" data collection technique that combines self-explicated importance ratings with pair-wise trade-off tasks.

Marketing Strategy Development

Following a successful concept test, the new-product manager will develop a preliminary three-part strategy plan for introducing the new product into the market. The first part describes the target market's size, structure, and behavior; the planned product positioning; and the sales, market share, and profit goals sought in the first few years:

> The target market for the instant breakfast drink is families with children who are receptive to a new, convenient, nutritious, and inexpensive form of breakfast. The company's brand will be positioned at the higher-price, higher-quality end of the instant-breakfast-drink category. The company will aim initially to sell 500,000 cases or 10 percent of the market,

with a loss in the first year not exceeding $1.3 million. The second year will aim for 700,000 cases or 14 percent of the market, with a planned profit of $2.2 million.

The second part outlines the planned price, distribution strategy, and marketing budget for the first year:

The product will be offered in chocolate, vanilla, and strawberry, in individual packets of six to a box, at a retail price of $2.49 a box. There will be 48 boxes per case, and the case price to distributors will be $24. For the first two months, dealers will be offered one case free for every four cases bought, plus cooperative-advertising allowances. Free samples will be distributed door-to-door. Coupons for 50 cents off will appear in newspapers. The total sales promotional budget will be $2.9 million. An advertising budget of $6 million will be split 50:50 between national and local. Two-thirds will go into television and one-third into online. Advertising copy will emphasize the benefit concepts of nutrition and convenience. The advertising-execution concept will revolve around a small boy who drinks instant breakfast and grows strong. During the first year, $100,000 will be spent on marketing research to buy store audits and consumer-panel information to monitor market reaction and buying rates.

The third part of the marketing strategy plan describes the long-run sales and profit goals and marketing-mix strategy over time:

The company intends to win a 25 percent market share and realize an after-tax return on investment of 12 percent. To achieve this return, product quality will start high and be improved over time through technical research. Price will initially be set at a high level and lowered gradually to expand the market and meet competition. The total promotion budget will be boosted each year about 20 percent, with the initial advertising–sales promotion split of 65:35 evolving eventually to 50:50. Marketing research will be reduced to $60,000 per year after the first year.

Business Analysis

After management develops the product concept and marketing strategy, it can evaluate the proposal's business attractiveness. Management needs to prepare sales, cost, and profit projections to determine whether they satisfy company objectives. If they do, the concept can move to the development stage. As new information comes in, the business analysis will undergo revision and expansion.

ESTIMATING TOTAL SALES Total estimated sales are the sum of estimated first-time sales, replacement sales, and repeat sales. Sales-estimation methods depend on whether the product is purchased once (such as an engagement ring or retirement home), infrequently, or often. For one-time products, sales rise at the beginning, peak, and approach zero as the number of potential buyers is exhausted [see △ Figure 20.6(a)]. If new buyers keep entering the market, the curve will not go down to zero.

Infrequently purchased products—such as automobiles, toasters, and industrial equipment—exhibit replacement cycles dictated by physical wear or obsolescence associated with changing styles, features, and performance. Sales forecasting for this product category calls for estimating first-time sales and replacement sales separately [see Figure 20.6(b)].

Frequently purchased products, such as consumer and industrial nondurables, have product life-cycle sales resembling Figure 20.6(c). The number of first-time buyers initially increases and then decreases as fewer buyers are left (assuming a fixed population). Repeat purchases occur soon, providing the product satisfies some buyers. The sales curve eventually falls to a plateau representing a level of steady repeat-purchase volume; by this time, the product is no longer a new product.

In estimating sales, the manager's first task is to estimate first-time purchases of the new product in each period. To estimate replacement sales, management researches the product's *survival-age distribution*—that is, the number of units that fail in year one, two, three, and so on. The low end of the distribution indicates when the first replacement sales will take place. Because replacement sales are difficult to estimate before the product is in use, some manufacturers base the decision to launch a new product solely on their estimate of first-time sales.

For a frequently purchased new product, the seller estimates repeat sales as well as first-time sales. A high rate of repeat purchasing means customers are satisfied; sales are likely to stay high

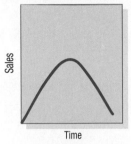

(a) One-time Purchased Product

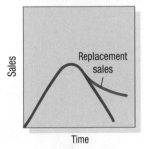

(b) Infrequently Purchased Product

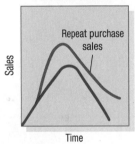

(c) Frequently Purchased Product

|Fig. 20.6|

Product Life-Cycle Sales for Three Types of Products

even after all first-time purchases take place. Some products and brands are bought a few times and dropped. Colgate's Wisp disposable toothbrush received much trial but repeat sales slowed considerably after that.[68]

ESTIMATING COSTS AND PROFITS Costs are estimated by the R&D, manufacturing, marketing, and finance departments. ▣ Table 20.3 illustrates a five-year projection of sales, costs, and profits for the instant breakfast drink.

Row 1 shows projected sales revenue over the five-year period. The company expects to sell $11,889,000 (approximately 500,000 cases at $24 per case) in the first year. Behind this projection is a set of assumptions about the rate of market growth, the company's market share, and the factory-realized price. *Row 2* shows the cost of goods sold, which hovers around 33 percent of sales revenue. We find this cost by estimating the average cost of labor, ingredients, and packaging per case. *Row 3* shows the expected gross margin, the difference between sales revenue and cost of goods sold.

Row 4 shows anticipated development costs of $3.5 million, including product-development cost, marketing research costs, and manufacturing development costs. *Row 5* shows the estimated marketing costs over the five-year period to cover advertising, sales promotion, and marketing research and an amount allocated for sales force coverage and marketing administration. *Row 6* shows the allocated overhead to this new product to cover its share of the cost of executive salaries, heat, light, and so on.

Row 7, the gross contribution, is gross margin minus the preceding three costs. *Row 8,* supplementary contribution, lists any change in income to other company products caused by the new-product introduction. *Dragalong income* is additional income to them, and *cannibalized income* is reduced income.[69] Table 20.3 assumes no supplementary contributions. *Row 9* shows net contribution, which in this case is the same as gross contribution. *Row 10* shows discounted contribution—that is, the present value of each future contribution discounted at 15 percent per annum. For example, the company will not receive $4,716,000 until the fifth year. This amount is worth only $2,346,000 today if the company can earn 15 percent on its money through other investments.[70]

Finally, *row 11* shows the cumulative discounted cash flow, the accumulation of the annual contributions in row 10. Two points are of central interest. First is the maximum investment exposure, the highest loss the project can create. The company will be in a maximum loss position of $4,613,000 in year 1. The second is the payback period, the time when the company recovers all its investment, including the built-in return of 15 percent. The payback period here is about three and a half years. Management must decide whether to risk a maximum investment loss of $4.6 million and a possible payback period of three and a half years. As part of their financial analysis, firms may conduct a breakeven or risk analysis.

TABLE 20.3 ▣ Projected Five-Year Cash Flow Statement (in thousands of dollars)

	Year 0	Year 1	Year 2	Year 3	Year 4	Year 5
1. Sales revenue	$ 0	$11,889	$15,381	$19,654	$28,253	$32,491
2. Cost of goods sold	0	3,981	5,150	6,581	9,461	10,880
3. Gross margin	0	7,908	10,231	13,073	18,792	21,611
4. Development costs	−3,500	0	0	0	0	0
5. Marketing costs	0	8,000	6,460	8,255	11,866	13,646
6. Allocated overhead	0	1,189	1,538	1,965	2,825	3,249
7. Gross contribution	−3,500	−1,281	2,233	2,853	4,101	4,716
8. Supplementary contribution	0	0	0	0	0	0
9. Net contribution	−3,500	−1,281	2,233	2,853	4,101	4,716
10. Discounted contribution (15%)	−3,500	−1,113	1,691	1,877	2,343	2,346
11. Cumulative discounted cash flow	−3,500	−4,613	−2,922	−1,045	1,298	3,644

Managing the Development Process: Development to Commercialization

Up to now, the product has existed only as a word description, a drawing, or a prototype. The next step represents a jump in investment that dwarfs the costs incurred so far. The company will determine whether the product idea can translate into a technically and commercially feasible product. If not, the accumulated project cost will be lost, except for any useful information gained in the process.

Product Development

The job of translating target customer requirements into a working prototype is helped by a set of methods known as *quality function deployment* (QFD). The methodology takes the list of desired *customer attributes* (CAs) generated by market research and turns them into a list of *engineering attributes* (EAs) that engineers can use. For example, customers of a proposed truck may want a certain acceleration rate (CA). Engineers can turn this into the required horsepower and other engineering equivalents (EAs). A major contribution of QFD is improved communication between marketers, engineers, and manufacturing people.[71]

PHYSICAL PROTOTYPES The goal of the R&D department is to find a prototype that embodies the key attributes in the product-concept statement, performs safely under normal use and conditions, and can be produced within budgeted manufacturing costs. In the past, developing and manufacturing a successful prototype could take weeks or even years. Sophisticated virtual reality technology and the Web now permit more rapid prototyping and more flexible development processes. Simulations, for example, give companies the flexibility to respond to new information and resolve uncertainties by quickly exploring alternatives.

R&D must also decide how consumers will react to different colors, sizes, and weights. Historically, a yellow mouthwash supported an "antiseptic" claim (Listerine), red a "refreshing" claim (Lavoris), and green or blue a "cool" claim (Scope). Marketers need to supply R&D with information about what attributes consumers seek and how they judge whether these are present.

CUSTOMER TESTS When the prototypes are ready, they must be put through rigorous functional and customer tests before they enter the marketplace. *Alpha testing* tests the product within the firm to see how it performs in different applications. After refining the prototype further, the company moves to *beta testing* with customers.[72]

Consumer testing can bring consumers into a laboratory or give them samples to use at home. Procter & Gamble has on-site labs such as a diaper-testing center where dozens of mothers bring their babies to be studied. To develop its Cover Girl Outlast all-day lip color, P&G invited 500 women to come to its labs each morning to apply the lipstick, record their activities, and return eight hours later so it could measure remaining lip color, resulting in a product that came with a tube of glossy moisturizer that women could apply on top of their color without looking at a mirror. In-home placement tests are common for products from ice cream flavors to new appliances.

Market Testing

After management is satisfied with functional and psychological performance, the product is ready to be branded with a name, logo, and packaging and go into a market test.

Not all companies undertake market testing. A company officer at Revlon stated: "In our field—primarily higher-priced cosmetics not geared for mass distribution—it would be unnecessary for us to market test. When we develop a new product, say an improved liquid makeup, we know it's going to sell because we're familiar with the field. And we've got 1,500 demonstrators in department stores to promote it." Many companies, however, believe market testing can yield valuable information about buyers, dealers, marketing program effectiveness, and market potential. The main issues are: How much market testing should be done, and what kind(s)?

The amount is influenced by the investment cost and risk on the one hand, and the time pressure and research cost on the other. High-investment–high-risk products, whose chance of failure

Consumer tests are typically an integral step in the new-product development process.

is high, must be market tested; the cost will be an insignificant percentage of total project cost. High-risk products that create new-product categories (first instant breakfast drink) or have novel features (first gum-strengthening toothpaste) warrant more market testing than modified products (another toothpaste brand).

CONSUMER-GOODS MARKET TESTING Consumer-products tests seek to estimate four variables: *trial*, *first repeat*, *adoption*, and *purchase frequency*. Many consumers may try the product but not rebuy it, or it might achieve high permanent adoption but low purchase frequency (like gourmet frozen foods).

Here are four major methods of consumer-goods market testing, from least to most costly.

Sales-Wave Research Consumers who initially try the product at no cost are reoffered it, or a competitor's product, at slightly reduced prices. The offer may be made as many as five times (sales waves), while the company notes how many customers select it again and their reported level of satisfaction.

Sales-wave research can be implemented quickly, conducted with a fair amount of security, and carried out without final packaging and advertising. However, because customers are preselected, it does not indicate trial rates the product would achieve with different sales incentives, nor does it indicate the brand's power to gain distribution and favorable shelf position.

Simulated Test Marketing Thirty to 40 qualified shoppers are asked about brand familiarity and preferences in a specific product category and attend a brief screening of both well-known and new TV commercials or print ads. One ad advertises the new product but is not singled out for attention. Consumers receive a small amount of money and are invited into a store where they may buy any items. The company notes how many consumers buy the new brand and competing brands. This provides a measure of the ad's relative effectiveness against competing ads in stimulating trial. Consumers are asked the reasons for their purchases or nonpurchases. Those who did not buy the new brand are given a free sample. Some weeks later, they are interviewed by phone to determine product attitudes, usage, satisfaction, and repurchase intention and are offered an opportunity to repurchase any products.

This method can give some surprisingly accurate results on advertising effectiveness and trial rates (and repeat rates if extended) in a much shorter time and at a fraction of the cost of using real test markets.[73] As media and channels grow more fragmented, however, it will become harder to truly simulate market conditions with only traditional approaches.

Controlled Test Marketing The company with the new product specifies the number of stores and geographic locations it wants to test. A research firm delivers the product to a panel of participating stores and controls shelf position, pricing, and number of facings, displays, and point-of-purchase promotions. Electronic scanners measure sales at checkout. The company can also evaluate the impact of local advertising and promotions and interview a sample of customers later to get their impressions of the product. It does not have to use its own sales force, give trade allowances, or "buy" distribution. However, controlled test marketing provides no information about how to sell the trade on carrying the new product. It also exposes the product and its features to competitors' scrutiny.

Test Markets The ultimate way to test a new consumer product is to put it into full-blown test markets. The company chooses a few representative cities and puts on a full marketing communications campaign, and the sales force tries to sell the trade on carrying the product and giving it good shelf exposure. Test marketing also measures the impact of alternative marketing plans by implementing them in different cities. A full-scale test can cost over $1 million, depending on the number of test cities, the test duration, and the amount of data the company wants to collect.

Management faces several decisions:

1. *How many test cities?* Most tests use two to six cities. The greater the possible loss, the number of contending marketing strategies, the regional differences, and the chance of test-market interference by competitors, the more cities management should test.
2. *Which cities?* Selection criteria include good media coverage, cooperative chain stores, and average competitive activity. How representative the city is of other markets must also be considered.
3. *Length of test?* Market tests last a few months to a year. The longer the average repurchase period, the longer the test period.
4. *What information to collect?* Warehouse shipment data will show gross inventory buying but will not indicate weekly sales at the retail level. Store audits will show retail sales and competitors' market shares but will not reveal buyer characteristics. Consumer panels will indicate which people are buying which brands and their loyalty and switching rates. Buyer surveys will yield in-depth information about consumer attitudes, usage, and satisfaction.
5. *What action to take?* If the test markets show high trial and repurchase rates, the marketer should launch the product nationally; if a high trial rate and low repurchase rate, redesign or drop the product; if a low trial rate and high repurchase rate, develop marketing communications to convince more people to try it. If trial and repurchase rates are both low, abandon the product. Many managers find it difficult to kill a project that created much effort and attention even if they should, resulting in an unfortunate (and typically unsuccessful) escalation of commitment.[74]

Despite its benefits, many companies today skip test marketing and rely on faster and more economical testing methods. General Mills prefers to launch new products in 25 percent of the country, an area too large for rivals to disrupt. Managers review retail scanner data, which tell them within days how the product is doing and what corrective fine-tuning to do. Colgate-Palmolive often launches a new product in a set of small "lead countries" and keeps rolling it out if it proves successful.

BUSINESS-GOODS MARKET TESTING Business goods can also benefit from market testing. Expensive industrial goods and new technologies will normally undergo alpha and beta testing. During beta testing, the company's technical people observe how customers use the product, a practice that often exposes unanticipated problems of safety and servicing and alerts the company to customer training and servicing requirements. The company can also observe how much value the equipment adds to the customer's operation as a clue to subsequent pricing.

Companies must interpret beta test results carefully, because only a small number of test customers are used, they are not randomly drawn, and tests are somewhat customized to each site. Another risk is that testers unimpressed with the product may leak unfavorable reports about it.

At trade shows the company can observe how much interest buyers show in the new product, how they react to various features and terms, and how many express purchase intentions or place orders. In distributor and dealer display rooms, products may stand next to the manufacturer's other products and possibly competitors' products, yielding preference and pricing information in the product's normal selling atmosphere. However, customers who come in might not represent the target market, or they might want to place early orders that cannot be filled.

Companies such as General Mills may avoid test markets to use limited-scope product launches instead.

Industrial manufacturers come close to using full test marketing when they give a limited supply of the product to the sales force to sell in a limited number of areas that receive promotion support and printed catalog sheets.

Commercialization

Commercialization incurs the company's highest costs to date.[75] The firm will need to contract for manufacture or build or rent a full-scale manufacturing facility. To introduce a major new consumer packaged good into the national market can cost $25 million to $100 million in advertising, promotion, and other communications in the first year. For new food products, marketing expenditures typically represent 57 percent of first-year sales. Most new-product campaigns rely on a sequenced mix of market communication tools.

WHEN (TIMING) Suppose a company has almost completed the development work on its new product and learns a competitor is nearing the end of its development work. The company faces three choices:

1. *First entry*—The first firm entering a market usually enjoys the "first mover advantages" of locking up key distributors and customers and gaining leadership. But if rushed to market before it has been thoroughly debugged, the first entry can backfire.
2. *Parallel entry*—The firm might time its entry to coincide with the competitor's entry. The market may pay more attention when two companies are advertising the new product.[76]
3. *Late entry*—The firm might delay its launch until after the competitor has borne the cost of educating the market, and its product may reveal flaws the late entrant can avoid. The late entrant can also learn the size of the market.

If a new product replaces an older product, the company might delay until the old product's stock is drawn down. If the product is seasonal, it might wait until the season arrives; often a product waits for a "killer application" to occur. Many companies are now encountering competitive "design-arounds"—rivals are making their own versions just different enough to avoid patent infringement and royalties.[77]

WHERE (GEOGRAPHIC STRATEGY) Most companies will develop a planned market rollout over time. In choosing rollout markets, the major criteria are market potential, the company's local reputation, the cost of filling the pipeline, the cost of communication media, the influence of the area on other areas, and competitive penetration. Small companies select an attractive city and put on a blitz campaign, entering other cities one at a time. Large companies introduce their product into a whole region and then move to the next. Companies with national distribution networks, such as auto companies, launch new models nationally.

With the Web connecting far-flung parts of the globe, competition is more likely to cross national borders. Companies are increasingly rolling out new products simultaneously across the globe. However, masterminding a global launch poses challenges, and a sequential rollout across countries may still be the best option.[78]

TO WHOM (TARGET-MARKET PROSPECTS) Within the rollout markets, the company must target initial distribution and promotion to the best prospect groups. Ideally they should be early adopters, heavy users, and opinion leaders it can reach at low cost.[79] Few groups include all these, so the company should rate prospects and target the best group. The aim is to generate strong sales as soon as possible to attract further prospects.

HOW (INTRODUCTORY MARKET STRATEGY) Because new-product launches often take longer and cost more than expected, many potentially successful offerings suffer from underfunding. It's important to allocate sufficient time and resources—yet not overspend—as the new product gains traction in the marketplace.[80]

To coordinate the many tasks in launching a new product, management can use network-planning techniques such as **critical path scheduling (CPS)**, which develops a master chart showing the simultaneous and sequential activities that must take place. By estimating how much time each activity takes, planners estimate completion time for the entire project. Any delay in any activity on the critical path—the shortest route to completion—will delay the project. If the launch must be completed sooner, the planner searches for ways to reduce time along the critical path.[81]

The Consumer-Adoption Process

Adoption is an individual's decision to become a regular user of a product and is followed by the *consumer-loyalty process*. New-product marketers typically aim at early adopters and use the theory of innovation diffusion and consumer adoption to identify them.

Stages in the Adoption Process

An **innovation** is any good, service, or idea that someone *perceives* as new, no matter how long its history. Everett Rogers defines the **innovation diffusion process** as "the spread of a new idea from its source of invention or creation to its ultimate users or adopters."[82] The *consumer-adoption process* is the mental steps through which an individual passes from first hearing about an innovation to final adoption.[83] They are:

1. *Awareness*—The consumer becomes aware of the innovation but lacks information about it.
2. *Interest*—The consumer is stimulated to seek information about the innovation.
3. *Evaluation*—The consumer considers whether to try the innovation.
4. *Trial*—The consumer tries the innovation to improve his or her estimate of its value.
5. *Adoption*—The consumer decides to make full and regular use of the innovation.

The new-product marketer should facilitate movement through these stages. A water filtration system manufacturer might discover that many consumers are stuck in the interest stage; they do not buy because of their uncertainty and the large investment cost.[84] But these same consumers would be willing to use a water filtration system at home on a trial basis for a small monthly fee. The manufacturer should consider offering a trial-use plan with option to buy.

Factors Influencing the Adoption Process

Marketers recognize the following characteristics of the adoption process: differences in individual readiness to try new products, the effect of personal influence, differing rates of adoption, and differences in organizations' readiness to try new products. Some researchers are focusing on use-diffusion processes as a complement to adoption process models, to see how consumers actually use new products.[85]

READINESS TO TRY NEW PRODUCTS AND PERSONAL INFLUENCE Everett Rogers defines a person's level of innovativeness as "the degree to which an individual is relatively earlier in adopting new ideas than the other members of his social system." Some people are the first to adopt new clothing fashions or new appliances; some doctors are the first to prescribe new medicines.[86] See the adopter categories in △ Figure 20.7. After a slow start, an increasing number of people adopt the innovation, the number reaches a peak, and then it diminishes as fewer nonadopters remain. The five adopter groups differ in their value orientations and their motives for adopting or resisting the new product.[87]

Many innovators and early adopters were thrilled when Apple CEO Steve Jobs announced the launch of the iPad in January 2010.

- *Innovators* are technology enthusiasts; they are venturesome and enjoy tinkering with new products and mastering their intricacies. In return for low prices, they are happy to conduct alpha and beta testing and report on early weaknesses.
- *Early adopters* are opinion leaders who carefully search for new technologies that might give them a dramatic competitive advantage. They are less price sensitive and willing to adopt the product if given personalized solutions and good service support.
- *Early majority* are deliberate pragmatists who adopt the new technology when its benefits are proven and a lot of adoption has already taken place. They make up the mainstream market.
- *Late majority* are skeptical conservatives who are risk averse, technology shy, and price sensitive.
- *Laggards* are tradition-bound and resist the innovation until the status quo is no longer defensible.

Each group requires a different type of marketing if the firm wants to move its innovation through the full product life cycle.[88]

|Fig. 20.7| ▲

Adopter Categorization on the Basis of Relative Time of Adoption of Innovations

Source: Tungsten, http://en.wikipedia.ord/wiki/ Everett_Rogers. Based on Rogers, E. (1962) *Diffusion of Innovations.* Free Press, London, NY, USA.

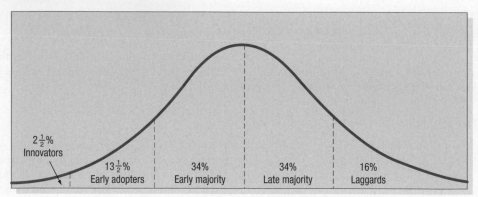

Time of Adoption of Innovations

Personal influence, the effect one person has on another's attitude or purchase probability, has greater significance in some situations and for some individuals than others, and it is more important in evaluation than the other stages. It has more power over late than early adopters and in risky situations.

Companies often target innovators and early adopters with product rollouts. When Nike entered the skateboarding market, it recognized an antiestablishment, big-company bias from the target market could present a sizable challenge. To gain "street cred" with teen skaters, it sold exclusively to independent shops, advertised nowhere but skate magazines, and gained sponsorships from well-admired pro riders by engaging them in product design.[89]

CHARACTERISTICS OF THE INNOVATION
Some products catch on immediately (roller blades), whereas others take a long time to gain acceptance (diesel engine autos). Five characteristics influence an innovation's rate of adoption. We consider them for digital video recorders (DVRs) for home use, as exemplified by TiVo.[90]

The first characteristic is *relative advantage*—the degree to which the innovation appears superior to existing products. The greater the perceived relative advantage of using a DVR, say, for easily recording favorite shows, pausing live TV, or skipping commercials, the more quickly it will be adopted. The second is *compatibility*—the degree to which the innovation matches the values and experiences of the individuals. DVRs are highly compatible with the preferences of avid television watchers. Third is *complexity*—the degree to which the innovation is difficult to understand or use. DVRs are somewhat complex and will therefore take a slightly longer time to penetrate into home use. Fourth is *divisibility*—the degree to which the innovation can be tried on a limited basis. This provides a sizable challenge for DVRs—sampling can occur only in a retail store or perhaps a friend's house. Fifth is *communicability*—the degree to which the benefits of use are observable or describable to others. The fact that DVRs have some clear advantages can help create interest and curiosity.

Other characteristics that influence the rate of adoption are cost, risk and uncertainty, scientific credibility, and social approval. The new-product marketer must research all these factors and give the key ones maximum attention in designing the product and marketing program.[91]

ORGANIZATIONS' READINESS TO ADOPT INNOVATIONS
The creator of a new teaching method would want to identify innovative schools. The producer of a new piece of medical equipment would want to identify innovative hospitals. Adoption is associated with variables in the organization's environment (community progressiveness, community income), the organization itself (size, profits, pressure to change), and the administrators (education level, age, sophistication). Other forces come into play in trying to get a product adopted into organizations that receive the bulk of their funding from the government, such as public schools. A controversial or innovative product can be squelched by negative public opinion.

Summary

1. Once a company has segmented the market, chosen its target customer groups and identified their needs, and determined its desired market positioning, it is ready to develop and launch appropriate new products and services. Marketing should participate with other departments in every stage of new-product development.

2. Successful new-product development requires the company to establish an effective organization for managing the development process. Companies can choose to use product managers, new-product managers, new-product committees, new-product departments, or new-product venture teams. Increasingly, companies are adopting cross-functional teams, connecting to individuals and organizations outside the company, and developing multiple product concepts.

3. Eight stages take place in the new-product development process: idea generation, screening, concept development and testing, marketing strategy development, business analysis, product development, market testing, and commercialization. At each stage, the company must determine whether the idea should be dropped or moved to the next stage.

4. The consumer-adoption process is the process by which customers learn about new products, try them, and adopt or reject them. Today many marketers are targeting heavy users and early adopters of new products, because both groups can be reached by specific media and tend to be opinion leaders. The consumer-adoption process is influenced by many factors beyond the marketer's control, including consumers' and organizations' willingness to try new products, personal influences, and the characteristics of the new product or innovation.

Applications

Marketing Debate
Whom Should You Target with New Products?

Some new-products experts maintain that getting close to customers through intensive research is the only way to develop successful new products. Other experts disagree and maintain that customers can't possibly provide useful feedback on what they don't know and can't provide insights that will lead to breakthrough products.

Take a position: Consumer research is critical to new-product development *versus* Consumer research may not be all that helpful in new-product development.

Marketing Discussion
Product Innovativeness

Think about the last new product you bought. How do you think its success will be affected by the five characteristics of an innovation: relative advantage, compatibility, complexity, divisibility, and communicability?

Marketing Excellence

>>Apple

Over the past decade, Apple has become a world leader in innovative new product launches. The company has truly transformed the way people listen to music, play video games, talk on the phone, and even read books. Apple's evolutionary product innovations include the iPod, iMac, iPhone, and iPad and are the reason the company topped *Fortune* magazine's World's Most Admired Companies list three years in a row, from 2008 to 2010.

One of Apple's most important innovations over the past decade was the iPod MP3 player. Not only has the iPod become a cultural phenomenon; it introduced many consumers to Apple and initiated a series of monumental product innovations. The iPod exemplified Apple's innovative design skills and looked, felt, and operated like no other device. With the launch of the iTunes Music Store, a dynamic duo of legally downloadable music and cutting-edge portable music player caused iPod sales to skyrocket. To the delight of Apple (and the chagrin of competitor Sony), the iPod has become "the Walkman of the 21st century."

Beyond spurring sales, the iPod has been central in changing the way people listen to and use music. According to musician John Mayer, "People feel they're walking through musicology" when they use their iPods, leading them to listen to more music, and with more passion. The iPod has gone through a series of generations, and along the way Apple has added features like photo, video, and radio capabilities.

Apple reached its impressive market domination through a combination of shrewd product innovation and clever marketing. It defined a broad access point for its target market—music lovers who wanted *their* music, whenever and wherever. The marketing effort was designed to appeal to Mac fans as well as people who had not used Apple products in the past. This broader access required a shift in Apple's channel strategies. As a result, Apple added "mass electronic" retailers such as Best Buy and (now defunct) Circuit City to its existing channels, quadrupling its number of outlets.

Besides this enhanced "push" effort, Apple also developed memorable, creative "pull" advertising that helped drive the popularity of the iPod. The Silhouettes campaign, featuring people in silhouette listening to iPods and dancing, appeared all over the world with a message simple enough to work across cultures, portraying the iPod as cool but not beyond the reach of anyone who enjoyed music.

As the iPod's popularity grew, a halo effect helped increase Apple's market share in its other products. In fact, in 2007 Apple officially changed its name from Apple Computer Inc. to Apple Inc. to help communicate the company's focus in noncomputer products. By 2009, iPod sales had topped $8 billion, and by 2010 more than 250 million had been sold worldwide.

Apple's next-largest product launch after the iPod was the iPhone, its 2007 entry to the cell phone industry. With its touch-screen pad, virtual keyboard, and Internet and e-mail capabilities, the iPhone launched to huge consumer excitement; people lined up for hours to be among the first to buy one. But investment analysts feared Apple's two-year contract with AT&T and high initial price would hinder the iPhone's success. Seventy-four days after the product's debut, however, Apple had sold its one millionth iPhone. It had taken the iPod two years to reach the cumulative sales ($1.1 million) the iPhone had reached after its first quarter. In fact, half the iPods' buyers switched to AT&T from a different wireless carrier, incurring fees to break their contracts, just to have a chance to own an iPhone.

Over the next three years, Apple dropped the price of the iPhone significantly and added impressive picture and video capabilities, video game features, a faster processor, and hundreds of thousands of additional applications. By then, the iPhone had become a game-changing technological invention. Apple took in $13 billion in iPhone sales worldwide in 2009, and when the iPhone 4 launched in 2010, showcasing Face Time video calling, Steve Jobs declared it "the most successful product launch in Apple's history."

Also in 2010, a media frenzy helped Apple launch the iPad, a multitouch device that combines the look and feel of the iPhone with the power of a MacBook. The slick handheld device gives consumers access to music, books, movies, pictures, and work documents at the touch of a finger without mouse or keyboard. Apple's marketing campaign emphasized its appeal: "What is iPad? iPad is thin. iPad is beautiful. iPad goes anywhere and lasts all day. There is no right way or wrong way. It's crazy powerful. It's magical. You already know how to use it. It's 200,000 apps and counting. . . It's already a revolution and it's only just begun."

With $42 billion in annual revenue, Apple continues to increase its annual R&D budget each year, spending $1.3 billion in 2009 alone. The company takes creating, producing, and launching new products very seriously. With creative marketing support behind them, these products are the reason consumers and analysts alike stay on their toes awaiting Apple's latest product news.

Questions

1. Apple's product launches over the past decade have been monumental. What makes the company so good at innovation? Is anyone comparable to Apple in this respect?

2. How important was the iPod to Apple's current success? Discuss the significance of the iPhone and iPad launches to Apple's new product development strategy.

3. What's next for Apple? Should it continue to move away from computers and toward more new handheld devices?

Sources: "World's Most Admired Companies," *Fortune,* 2010; "iPhone4: The 'Most Successful Product Launch' in Apple's History," *Independent,* June 28, 2010; Joseph De Avila, "Why Some Apple Fans Won't Buy the iPhone," *Wall Street Journal,* September 12, 2007, D.3; Nick Wingfield, "Apple Businesses Fuel Each Other; Net Jumps as Mac Sales Top PC-Industry Growth Rate; iPhones, iPods Also Thrive," *Wall Street Journal,* October 23, 2007; Terril Yue Jones, "How Long Can the iPod Stay on Top?" *Los Angeles Times,* March 5, 2006; Beth Snyder Bulik, "Grab an Apple and a Bag of Chips," *Advertising Age,* May 23, 2005; Jay Parsons, "A Is for Apple on iPod," *Dallas Morning News,* October 6, 2005; Peter Burrows, "Rock On, iPod," *BusinessWeek,* June 7, 2004, pp. 130–31; Jay Lyman, "Mini iPod Moving Quickly, Apple Says," *TechNewsWorld,* February 26, 2004; Steven Levy, "iPod Nation," *Newsweek,* July 25, 2004; "Apple Computer: iPod Silhouettes," New York Marketing Association; Steven Levy, "iPod Nation," *Newsweek,* July 25, 2004; Apple, www.apple.com; Effie Worldwide, www.effie.org.

Marketing Excellence

>>Research In Motion

Research in Motion (RIM) is the company behind BlackBerry, the best-selling smart-phone brand in the United States. RIM went public in 1997 and introduced the first BlackBerry two years later—a bulky corporate paging device that ran off an AA battery to read e-mail. Today, the company is credited with launching the handheld smart-phone craze and the obsession with 24/7/365 access to e-mail and the Internet. BlackBerry eventually earned the

appropriate nickname, "CrackBerry," as consumers became addicted to their latest technological gadget.

The obsession started with RIM founder Mike Lazaridis, who used to collect business cards from bankers on Wall Street and send college kids to their offices to set them up with the first BlackBerry devices. "It was a puppy dog sale," Lazaridis says. "'Take a puppy dog home, and if you don't like it, bring it back.' They never come back." Within a few years the BlackBerry had become a Wall Street staple, and after September 11, 2001, it gained nationwide attention as a critical security and communications device for the government.

RIM continued to launch new generations of BlackBerry products that focused on high-security capabilities and essential business features, including an organizer, calendar, pager, longer-lasting battery, and improved wireless Internet access. The firm focused its push strategy on building the BlackBerry brand as the most secure, reliable, and efficient data device solution on the market.

It took five years, but in 2003 RIM sold its one millionth BlackBerry. Only one year later it sold its two millionth device, and the BlackBerry's growth exploded. In 2005, *PCWorld* named the BlackBerry 850 the 14th greatest gadget of the past 50 years, and between 2006 and 2008, *Fortune* dubbed RIM the fastest-growing company in the world.

Several factors led to RIM's explosive growth during the mid-2000s. First, it was the innovation leader at the time. The BlackBerry changed the way people communicated, worked, and lived. And unlike competitors, RIM offered an end-to-end solution; it developed and produced the hardware as well as the software and services that made BlackBerry work.

As RIM expanded, it made the strategic decision to partner with numerous carriers around the globe instead of just one. This conferred two advantages. First, consumers could easily purchase a BlackBerry device no matter what their carrier or geographical location was and not worry about breaking an existing carrier contract. Secondly, RIM started producing unique products for its different carriers and their audiences. It also licensed its architecture to third-party devices, making BlackBerry wireless solutions available to other companies. All these decisions increased revenue and subscribers around the world.

In terms of marketing, RIM successfully targeted its initial efforts at the business community, branding the BlackBerry smart phone a workforce "must have" and focusing its product and software innovations on meeting the needs of businesses. It continues to serve this market today, with solutions like its BlackBerry Enterprise Server for small and medium-sized businesses.

Finally, BlackBerry rode the coattails of the iPhone launch in 2007. Apple's iPhone sparked interest in many consumers—telling them smart phones were not just for the business community—and as a result, many consumers tried out a BlackBerry for the first time. In 2008, RIM launched its first mass advertising campaign targeting consumers, and new subscriber sales skyrocketed. Perhaps BlackBerry's biggest salesperson was President Obama, who could be seen carrying and checking his BlackBerry throughout the election year. Instantly, the BlackBerry became "cool" in the eyes of younger consumers.

Today, BlackBerry continues to compete in the smartphone category, adding more consumers than business customers each year. Recent product launches have added video, photo, and music capabilities, touch-screen pads, and instant messaging—features that attract tweens and young adults. RIM had $15 billion in sales during fiscal 2010, sold 37 million smart phones in 2010 alone, and now has over 41 million users in 175 countries. While competition has increased tremendously and remains stiff, the company's focus on generating new products and solutions is clear. Lazaridis explained, "There is great depth and breadth to what we do. It's more than just the BlackBerry. We develop silicon, operating systems, industrial design; we manufacture. We run our own network. RIM is an industry unto itself."

Questions

1. Evaluate Research In Motion's keys to success. What did the company do well and, in hindsight, what should it have done differently during its decade of extreme growth?

2. Is Research In Motion still a leader in innovation? Why or why not? What's next for the company?

Sources: Jessi Hempel, "Smartphone Wars—BlackBerry's Plan to Win," *Fortune,* August 17, 2009; Saul Hansell and Ian Austen, "BlackBerry, Upgraded, Aims to Suit Every User," *New York Times,* October 13, 2009; Michael Comeau, "Can Research In Motion's BlackBerry Regain Market Share?" *Minyanville,* July 12, 2010; "The World Masters of Innovation," *BusinessWeek*; Research In Motion, Annual Reports; RIM, www.rim.com.

Chapter 21

In This Chapter, We Will Address the Following Questions

1. What factors should a company review before deciding to go abroad?

2. How can companies evaluate and select specific foreign markets to enter?

3. What are the differences between marketing in a developing and a developed market?

4. What are the major ways of entering a foreign market?

5. To what extent must the company adapt its products and marketing program to each foreign country?

6. How do marketers influence country-of-origin effects?

7. How should the company manage and organize its international activities?

India's Tata Group has a wide range of global businesses, including one that produces the remarkably priced $2,500 Tata Nano or the "People's Car."

Tapping into Global Markets

With ever faster communication, transportation, and financial flows, the world is rapidly shrinking. Countries are increasingly multicultural, and products and services developed in one country are finding enthusiastic acceptance in others. A German businessman may wear an Italian suit to meet an English friend at a Japanese restaurant, who later returns home to drink Russian vodka and watch a U.S. movie on a Korean TV. Emerging markets that embrace capitalism and consumerism are especially attractive targets. They are also creating marketing powerhouses all their own.[1]

 Tata Group, India's biggest conglomerate, operates successful businesses that range from software, cars, and steel to phone service, tea bags, and wristwatches. Its business dealings stretch far and wide and have included purchases of South Korea's Daewoo Motors truck unit, Dutch-British steel giant Corus Group, and UK-based Tetley Tea. The proprietor of the Taj luxury hotels, Tata also owns or manages the rebranded Ritz-Carlton in Boston, the Pierre in New York City, and Camden Place in San Francisco. Tata Consultancy Services, India's largest tech-services company, collects roughly half its revenues in North America. Tata is also India's largest commercial vehicle maker and created a stir with the recent launch of its $2,500 Tata Nano, dubbed the "People's Car." Although impossibly low-priced by Western standards, at one Indian lakh the Nano's price is three times higher than India's annual per capita income. Looking somewhat like an egg on wheels, the Nano comfortably seats five while running a 33-horsepower engine that gets nearly 50 miles per gallon. Aiming to sell 250,000 units annually, Tata is targeting the 7 million Indians who buy scooters and motorcycles every year, in part because they cannot afford a car. The market potential is huge—there are just seven automobiles per 1,000 people in India. Tata is also targeting other "bottom of the pyramid" markets such as Africa and Southeast Asia and perhaps even parts of Eastern Europe and Latin America.

Companies need to be able to cross boundaries within and outside their country. Although opportunities to enter and compete in international markets are significant, the risks can also be high. Companies selling in global industries, however, have no choice but to internationalize their operations. In this chapter, we review the major decisions in expanding into global markets.

Competing on a Global Basis

Many companies have been global marketers for decades—firms like Shell, Bayer, and Toshiba have sold goods around the world for years. In luxury goods such as jewelry, watches, and handbags, where the addressable market is relatively small, a global profile is essential for firms like Prada, Gucci, and Louis Vuitton to profitably grow. But global competition is intensifying in more product categories as new firms make their mark on the international stage.[2]

The automotive market is becoming a worldwide free-for-all. In Chile, with no domestic auto manufacturers, imports are coming from all over the world, including 14 different brands of Chinese cars, trucks, and commercial vehicles.[3] In China's fast-moving mobile-phone market, Motorola found its market share cut in half over a two-year period from inroads by Nokia and Asian competitors.

Competition from developing-market firms is also heating up. Mahindra Motors' four-door, diesel-powered short-bed trucks from India are tackling Europe, Asia, and the United States, promising superior fuel economy.[4] Founded in Guatemala, Pollo Campero (Spanish for "country

Latin America's fried chicken favorite, Pollo Campero, has entered the U.S. market in part by targeting areas populated by Hispanic immigrants.

chicken') has used Latin American immigrants to launch over 50 U.S. stores, blending old favorites such as fried plantains and milky *horchata* drinks with traditional U.S. fare such as grilled chicken and mashed potatoes.[5]

Although some U.S. businesses may want to eliminate foreign competition through protective legislation, the better way to compete is to continuously improve products at home and expand into foreign markets. In a **global industry**, competitors' strategic positions in major geographic or national markets are affected by their overall global positions.[6] A **global firm** operates in more than one country and captures R&D, production, logistical, marketing, and financial advantages not available to purely domestic competitors.

Global firms plan, operate, and coordinate their activities on a worldwide basis. Otis Elevator uses door systems from France, small geared parts from Spain, electronics from Germany, and motor drives from Japan; systems integration happens in the United States. Consider the international success of Hyundai.[7]

Hyundai   Once synonymous with cheap and unreliable cars, Hyundai Motor Company has experienced a massive global transformation. In 1999, its new chairman, Mong-Koo Chung, declared that Hyundai would no longer focus on volume and market share but on quality instead. A number of changes were instituted: Hyundai began to benchmark industry leader Toyota, adopted Six Sigma processes, organized product development cross-functionally, partnered more closely with suppliers, and increased quality oversight meetings. From a place near the bottom of J.D. Power's study of U.S. new vehicle quality in 2001—32nd out of 37 brands—Hyundai zoomed to number four by 2009, surpassed only by luxury brands Lexus, Porsche, and Cadillac. Hyundai also transformed its marketing. Its "Assurance" campaign, backed by a pricey Super Bowl ad, allowed new buyers to return their cars risk-free if they lost their jobs. Other programs guaranteed customers low gas prices for a year and tax credits in advance of the government's "Cash for Clunkers" program. The U.S. market was not the only one receiving attention from Hyundai and its younger, more affordably priced brand sibling, Kia. Hyundai is the second-largest car-maker in India, it is supplying Europe with a new €1 billion factory in the Czech Republic, and a joint venture with Beijing Automotive is targeting China.

Many successful global U.S. brands have tapped into universal consumer values and needs—such as Nike with athletic performance, MTV with youth culture, and Coca-Cola with youthful optimism. These firms hire thousands of employees abroad and make sure their products and marketing activities are consistent with local sensibilities.

Global marketing extends beyond products. Services represent the fastest-growing sector of the global economy and account for two-thirds of global output, one-third of global employment, and nearly 20 percent of global trade. Although some countries have erected entry barriers or regulations, the World Trade Organization, consisting of 150 countries, continues to press for more free trade in international services and other areas.[8]

For a company of any size or any type to go global, it must make a series of decisions (see △ Figure 21.1). We'll examine each of these decisions here.[9]

Deciding Whether to Go Abroad

Most companies would prefer to remain domestic if their domestic market were large enough. Managers would not need to learn other languages and laws, deal with volatile currencies, face political and legal uncertainties, or redesign their products to suit different customer needs and expectations. Business would be easier and safer. Yet several factors can draw companies into the international arena:

- Some international markets present better profit opportunities than the domestic market.
- The company needs a larger customer base to achieve economies of scale.
- The company wants to reduce its dependence on any one market.
- The company decides to counterattack global competitors in their home markets.
- Customers are going abroad and require international service.

Reflecting the power of these forces, exports accounted for roughly 13 percent of U.S. GDP in 2008, almost double the figure 40 years ago.[10] Before making a decision to go abroad, the company must also weigh several risks:

- The company might not understand foreign preferences and could fail to offer a competitively attractive product.
- The company might not understand the foreign country's business culture.
- The company might underestimate foreign regulations and incur unexpected costs.
- The company might lack managers with international experience.
- The foreign country might change its commercial laws, devalue its currency, or undergo a political revolution and expropriate foreign property.

Some companies don't act until events thrust them into the international arena. The *internationalization process* typically has four stages:[11]

1. No regular export activities
2. Export via independent representatives (agents)
3. Establishment of one or more sales subsidiaries
4. Establishment of production facilities abroad

The first task is to move from stage 1 to stage 2. Most firms work with an independent agent and enter a nearby or similar country. Later, the firm establishes an export department to manage its agent relationships. Still later, it replaces agents with its own sales subsidiaries in its larger export markets. This increases investment and risk, but also earning potential. Next, to manage subsidiaries, the company replaces the export department with an international department or division. If markets are large and stable, or the host country requires local production, the company will locate production facilities there.

By this time, it's operating as a multinational and optimizing its sourcing, financing, manufacturing, and marketing as a global organization. According to some researchers, top management begins to focus on global opportunities when more than 15 percent of revenue comes from international markets.[12]

Deciding Which Markets to Enter

In deciding to go abroad, the company needs to define its marketing objectives and policies. What proportion of international to total sales will it seek? Most companies start small when they venture abroad. Some plan to stay small; others have bigger plans.

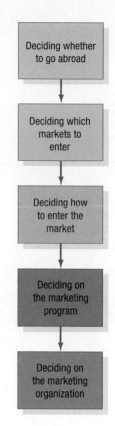

|Fig. 21.1| △

Major Decisions in International Marketing

How Many Markets to Enter

The company must decide how many countries to enter and how fast to expand. Typical entry strategies are the *waterfall* approach, gradually entering countries in sequence, and the *sprinkler* approach, entering many countries simultaneously. Increasingly, firms—especially technology-intensive firms—are *born global* and market to the entire world from the outset.[13]

Matsushita, BMW, General Electric, Benetton, and The Body Shop followed the waterfall approach. It allows firms to carefully plan expansion and is less likely to strain human and financial resources. When first-mover advantage is crucial and a high degree of competitive intensity prevails, the sprinkler approach is better. Microsoft sold over 150 million copies of Windows 7 in 100 countries in fall 2009 with only minor tweaks in its marketing. The main risk is the substantial resources needed and the difficulty of planning entry strategies for many diverse markets.[14]

The company must also choose the countries to consider based on the product and on geography, income and population, and political climate.

Developed versus Developing Markets

One of the sharpest distinctions in global marketing is between developed and developing or emerging markets such as Brazil, Russia, India, and China (often called "BRIC" for short: Brazil, Russia, India, and China).[15] Two other developing markets with much economic and marketing significance are Indonesia and South Africa. The unmet needs of the developing world represent huge potential markets for food, clothing, shelter, consumer electronics, appliances, and many other goods. Market leaders rely on developing markets to fuel their growth. Consider the following:

- Coca-Cola, Unilever, Colgate-Palmolive, Groupe Danone, and PepsiCo earn 5 percent to 15 percent of their total revenues from the three largest emerging markets in Asia—China, India, and Indonesia.[16]
- Developing markets make up over 25 percent of Kraft's total business, almost 40 percent of Cadbury's, and over 50 percent of Tupperware's sales.[17]
- Nestlé estimates about 1 billion consumers in emerging markets will increase their incomes enough to afford its products within the next decade. The world's largest food company gets about a third of its revenue from emerging economies and aims to lift that to 45 percent within a decade.[18]

Developed nations account for about 20 percent of the world's population. Can marketers serve the other 80 percent, which has much less purchasing power and living conditions ranging from mild deprivation to severe deficiency? This imbalance is likely to get worse, as more than 90 percent of future population growth is projected to occur in the less developed countries.[19]

Successfully entering developing markets requires a special set of skills and plans. Consider how these companies pioneered ways to serve "invisible" consumers:[20]

Microsoft launched Windows 7 with a massive global campaign.

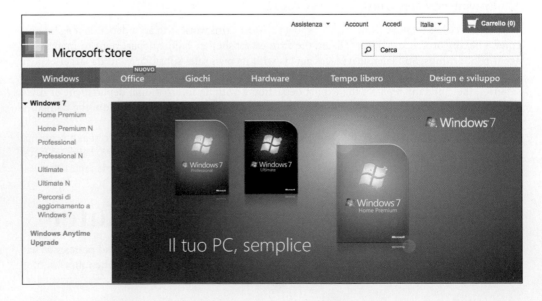

- Grameenphone marketed cell phones to 35,000 villages in Bangladesh by hiring village women as agents who leased phone time to other villagers, one call at a time.
- Colgate-Palmolive rolled into Indian villages with video vans that showed the benefits of toothbrushing.
- Corporación GEO builds low-income housing in Mexico. The two-bedroom homes are modular and expandable.

These marketers capitalized on the potential of developing markets by changing their conventional marketing practices.[21] Selling in developing areas can't be "business as usual." Economic and cultural differences abound, a marketing infrastructure may barely exist, and local competition can be surprisingly stiff.[22]

Local Dynamos   An extensive study by the Boston Consulting Group identifies 50 firms in 10 emerging economies as "local dynamos." According to BCG, a local dynamo is (1) prospering in its home market, (2) fending off multinational rivals, and (3) not focused on expanding abroad. India's Amul farmers' cooperative sells dairy products through a network of 2.8 million members supported by one of the longest-running and best-loved ad campaigns in India. Its ice-cream and chocolate milk businesses have survived the entry of Unilever and Nestlé, respectively. Brazilian budget airline Gol has targeted thrifty Brazilian consumers willing to sacrifice convenience for price; planes often depart at odd hours and make multiple stops. In Mexico, retailer Grupo Elektra [a Mexican financial and retail corporation owned by Grupo Salinas that is listed on the New York Stock Exchange (EKT), the Bolsa Mexicana de Valores (ELEKTRA), and the Spanish Stock Market Latibex (XEKT)] is selling washing machines, refrigerators, televisions, and other items on credit to people making less than $10 a day. The company's many stores double as bank branches where people can withdraw, deposit, and transmit cash, as well as get loans. According to BCG, local dynamos often combine in-depth understanding of consumer tastes with cost-effective production techniques to create a locally laser-focused business model.[23]

Grupo Elektra's retail stores in Mexico and Latin America sell appliances and offer financial services to low-income consumers.

Getting the marketing equation right in developing markets can pay big dividends:

- Smaller packaging and lower sales prices are often critical when incomes and housing spaces are limited. Unilever's 4-cent sachets of detergent and shampoo were a big hit in rural India, where 70 percent of the population still lives.[24]
- Eighty percent of consumers in emerging markets buy their products from tiny bodegas, stalls, kiosks, and mom-and-pop stores not much bigger than a closet, which Procter & Gamble calls "high-frequency stores." In India, 98 percent of food is still purchased from the 12 million neighborhood mom-and-pop outfits called kirana stores.[25]
- Nokia sends marketing, sales, and engineering staff from its entry-level phone group to spend a week in people's homes in rural China, Thailand, and Kenya to observe how they use phones. By developing rock-bottom-priced phones with just the right functionality, Nokia has become the market-share leader in Africa and Asia.[26]
- A Western image can be helpful. Coca-Cola's success against local cola brand Jianlibao in China was partly due to its symbolic values of modernity and affluence.[27]

Competition is also growing from companies based in developing markets. China has been exporting cars to Africa, Southeast Asia, and the Middle East. Tata of India, Cemex of Mexico, and Petronas of Malaysia have emerged from developing markets to become strong multinationals selling in many countries.[28]

Many firms are using lessons gleaned from marketing in developing markets to better compete in their developed markets (recall the "bottom of the pyramid" discussion from Chapter 3). John Deere's research facility in Pune, India, developed four no-frills tractors whose affordability and maneuverability also found a market in the United States and elsewhere. About half the tractors Deere makes in India are sold overseas.[29]

Product innovation has become a two-way street between developing and developed markets. The challenge is to think creatively about how marketing can fulfill the dreams of most of the world's population for a better standard of living.[30] Many companies are betting they can do that. "Marketing Insight: Spotlight on Key Developing Markets" highlights some important developments in the BRIC countries plus South Africa and Indonesia.

Marketing Insight

Spotlight on Key Developing Markets

Brazil

According to the World Bank, 25 percent of Latin Americans live on less than $2 a day; millions more earn only a few hundred dollars a month. In Brazil, the region's biggest market, low-income groups make up 87 percent of the population but earn only 53 percent of the income. Marketers are finding innovative ways to sell products and services to these poor and low-income residents. Nestlé Brazil boosted sales of Bono cookies 40 percent after shrinking the package from 200 to 140 grams and lowering the price. With illiteracy widespread, Unilever launched a brand of soap in northeast Brazil with the simple name, "Ala."

Brazil experienced some "go-go" growth years in the 1960s and 1970s, when it was the world's second-fastest-growing large economy. As a result, it now boasts large and well-developed agricultural, mining, manufacturing, and service sectors. Brazilian firms that have succeeded internationally include aircraft manufacturer Embraer, sandal maker Havaianas, and brewer and beverage producer AmBev, which merged with Interbrew to form InBev. It also differs from other emerging markets in being a full-blown democracy, unlike Russia and China, and it has no serious disputes with neighbors, unlike India.

A number of obstacles exist, however, that are popularly called custo Brasil ("the cost of Brazil"). The cost of transporting products eats up nearly 13 percent of Brazil's GDP, five percentage points more than in the United States. Unloading a container is twice as expensive as in India and takes three times longer than in China. Most observers see Brazil's economic, social, and political transformation as a work in process, although it emerged from the recent economic recession relatively unscathed.

Russia

The 1991 splintering of the Soviet Union transformed Russia's isolated, centrally planned economy to a globally integrated, market-based economy. Russia is the largest exporter of natural gas, the second-largest exporter of oil, and the third-largest exporter of steel and primary aluminum. Reliance on commodities has its downside, however. Russia's economy was hammered in the recent recession by plunging commodity prices and the credit crunch.

Dutch brewer Heineken, Swedish retailer IKEA, U.S. banker Citibank, and more than a dozen carmakers recently ramped up operations in Russia to target its growing middle class, now one-quarter to one-third of the population with fast-rising salaries and access to consumer credit. But the average Russian still earns only $700 a month, a fraction of the U.S. average, and many feel left behind. The economic crisis also saw a significant reduction in foreign investment in the country.

Russia has a dwindling workforce and poor infrastructure. The Organization for Economic Cooperation & Development (OECD) cautions that economic reforms have stagnated and ranks Russia as one of the most corrupt countries in the world. Many feel Vladimir Putin's government has been unpredictable and difficult to work with.

Still, companies remain optimistic. In 2006, more than 167,000 Motorola handsets were seized on arrival at Moscow airport. The interior ministry supposedly destroyed around 50,000 as smuggled or counterfeit, though some were later reported found on the black market. Eventually most were returned, but more telling was Motorola's reaction. With Russia as its third-biggest handset market in the world at the time, an unshaken Motorola stayed the course.

India

Reforms in the early 1990s that lowered trade barriers and liberalized capital markets have brought India booming investment and consumption. But it's not all about demand. With many low-cost, high-IQ, English-speaking employees, India is gaining programming and call center jobs once held by U.S. workers. Its growth has been driven largely by the manufacturing and service sectors where most of its workers reside.

India's ascent opens a larger market for U.S. and Western goods. Almost two-thirds of the population is under 35, and about 16 million, or 3 percent, are high-earning targets of youth lifestyle brands connoting status and affluence. Luxury cars and shiny motorbikes are the most sought-after status symbols, followed by clothing, food, entertainment, consumer durables, and travel.

India still struggles with poor infrastructure and public services—education, health, and water supply—and restrictive labor laws. Its 28 separate states each have their own policies and tax rules. But global firms such as Mittal, Reliance, Tata, Wipro, and Infosys all have achieved international success, and many outside firms are setting their sights there.

China

China's 1.3 billion people have marketers scrambling to gain a foothold, and competition has heated up between domestic and international firms. Its 2001 entry into the World Trade Organization eased China's manufacturing and investment rules and modernized retail and logistics industries. Greater competition in pricing, products, and channels resulted, but publishing, telecommunications, oil exploration, marketing, pharmaceuticals, banking, and insurance remained fiercely protected or off-limits to foreigners altogether. Foreign businesses complain about subsidized competition, restricted access, conflicting regulations, lack of protection for intellectual property, and opaque and seemingly arbitrary bureaucracy.

Selling in China means going beyond the big cities to the 700 million potential consumers who live in small communities in the rural interior. About half of potential PC buyers live outside major cities; only one-third of overall retail revenues come from China's 24 largest cities. Rural consumers can be challenging; they have lower incomes, are less sophisticated, and often cling to local habits. PC maker Lenovo, mobile-phone provider TCL, and appliance manufacturer Haier have thrived despite strong foreign competition. Besides their sharp grasp of Chinese tastes, they have vast distribution networks, especially in rural areas.

China's emerging urban middle class is active and discerning, demanding higher-quality products and variety. Although they number four times the U.S. population, Chinese consumers spend a fraction of what U.S. consumers spend. Luxury cars are the fastest-growing auto segment thanks to China's swelling ranks of millionaires.

Indonesia

Indonesia's reputation as a country historically struggling with natural disasters, terrorism, and economic uncertainty is quickly being replaced by a country characterized by political stability and economic growth. The fourth largest country in the world and the largest Muslim country, given all its progress, it is perhaps no surprise that Morgan Stanley suggested adding Indonesia to the four BRIC countries to make it the BRICI countries.

Indonesia has become the third fastest-growing economy in the region—behind India and China—largely on the basis of its 240 million consumers. Foreign direct investments account for only 25 percent of gross domestic product. Although half the population live on less than $2 a day, their spending and those of an active younger population is driving economic growth.

Some foreign firms are taking advantage of opportunities there. Indonesia is one of Reach In Motion's (RIM's) hottest markets, and the BlackBerry has achieved iconic status in the country. RIM has taken advantage of a mobile-friendly environment (broadband service is patchy and expensive) and has also customized its offerings with dozens of applications designed specifically for the Indonesian market. Its success is not without some downside though—it has inspired scores of knockoffs from China dubbed "Chinaberries" by locals.

Indonesia presents other challenges. An archipelago with more than 14,000 islands in a hot and humid climate, effective, efficient distribution is critical. Large importers have established extensive distribution networks which allow them to extend beyond the one-third of the population that lives in the six or seven largest cities. Like many developing countries, infrastructure can be lacking.

But the progress of Indonesia in recent years is noteworthy. As further proof, with over 20 percent of the Indonesian Internet users having a Twitter account, Indonesia is the sixth most active country on the micro-blogging site.

South Africa

Although South Africa is a developed market, it is included here in its role as an access point to the African region as well as an important market in its own right. According to the World Bank, of the 35 least business-friendly countries, 27 are in sub-Saharan Africa; 42 percent of the region's economy is informal. Bad roads, unreliable electricity, and volatile currency fluctuations add logistical and financial challenges. War, famine, AIDS, and disaster are even more significant human difficulties. Most Africans live in poverty; 60 percent still engage in agriculture for their primary income.

But a recent period of relative stability has coincided with improvements in health, education, and social services. The 2010 World Cup offered a chance to reexamine economic progress in South Africa and other African countries. Many international companies are using South Africa as a launch pad.

- Mobile phone operator Celtel invested in rural services by introducing the Me2U service, by which callers could send airtime credit to other mobile phones. Because most Africans don't have bank accounts, it became a convenient and cheap way to transfer money, even substituting for cash in some villages.

- South Africa's MTN, the region's largest mobile phone company, built its own microwave transmission backbone and power supplies in Nigeria, and the first solar pay phone in Lake Victoria, Uganda.

- South Africa's Net1 has built a customer base of 3.6 million accounts by issuing free smart cards to indigent people who lack bank accounts or credit cards, taking tiny percentages of their transactions for revenue.

The payoff for companies willing to do business in Africa is often large margins and minimal competition. SABMiller, the world's second-largest brewer, enjoys its best operating margins in Africa. Finding a local partner can add expertise and contacts. SABMiller's African operations are joint ventures with locals, some of them government. The Boston Consulting Group has dubbed eight of Africa's strongest economies the "African Lions": Algeria, Botswana, Egypt, Libya, Mauritius, Morocco, South Africa, and Tunisia.

Sources: *Brazil:* Antonio Regalado, "Marketers Pursue the Shallow Pocketed," *Wall Street Journal,* January 26, 2007; "Land of Promise," *Economist,* April 12, 2007; Melissa Campanelli, "Marketing to Latin America? Think Brazil," *DMNews,* June 20, 2006. *Russia:* Jason Bush, "Russia Economy Turns Swiftly Siberian," *BusinessWeek,* December 15, 2008, p.68; "Risk and Reward in Russia," *BusinessWeek Emerging Market Report,* October 20, 2008; "Dancing with the Bear," *Economist,* February 3, 2007, pp. 63–64; Jason Bush, "Russia: How Long Can the Fun Last?" *BusinessWeek,* December 18, 2006, pp. 50–51; Steven Lee Myers, "Business as Usual, Russian-Style," *International Herald Tribune,* June 13, 2006. *India:* Nandan Nilekani, *Imagining India: The Idea of a Renewed Nation* (New York: Penguin Press, 2009); Anil K. Gupta and Haiyan Wang, "Five Myths about India," *Economic Times,* December 29, 2009; "India on Fire," *Economist,* February 3, 2007, pp. 69–71; "16m. Young High-Earning Consumers Are Targets of High-End Lifestyle Products," *News India Times,* August 4, 2006, p. 16. *China:* Edward Wong, "China's Export Economy Begins Turning Inward," *New York Times,* June 24, 2010; Arthur Kroeber, "Five Myths about the Chinese Economy, *Washington Post,* April 11, 2010; "Impenetrable: Selling Foreign Goods in China," *Economist,* October 17, 2009;

Dexter Roberts, "Cadillac Floors It in China," *BusinessWeek*, June 4, 2007, p. 52; Bruce Einhorn, "Grudge Match in China," *BusinessWeek*, April 2, 2007, pp. 42–43; Russell Flannery, "Watch Your Back," *Forbes*, April 23, 2007, pp. 104–5; Dexter Roberts, "Cautious Consumers," *BusinessWeek*, April 30, 2007, pp. 32–34; Seung Ho Park and Wilfried R. Vanhonacker, "The Challenge for Multinational Corporations in China: Think Local, Act Global," *MIT Sloan Management Review* (May 31, 2007); Dexter Roberts, "Scrambling to Bring Crest to the Masses," *BusinessWeek*, June 25, 2007, pp. 72–73. *Indonesia*: Louise Lavabre, "Talking with Our Thumbs: Twitter in Indonesia," *Jakarta Post*, September 22, 2010; Alexandra A. Seno, "Gung-ho

Attitude Delivers Success in Indonesia," *Globe and Mail*, March 25, 2010; Mark MacKinnon, "RIM's Indonesian Bonanza," *Globe and Mail*, March 24, 2010; Peter Geiling, "Will Indonesia Make It BRICI?" *GlobalPost*, July 7, 2009; Margie Bauer, Indonesia—An Economic Success Story," www.fas.usda.gov, October 14, 2004. *South Africa*: "The Price of Freedom: A Special Report on South Africa," *Economist*, June 5, 2010; "Africa's Dynamo," *BusinessWeek Emerging Market Report*, December 15, 2008; Frank Aquilla, "Africa's Biggest Score: A Thriving Economy," *BusinessWeek*, June 28, 2010; Helen Coster, "Great Expectations," *Forbes*, February 12, 2007, pp. 56–58; *All*: *CIA World Factbook*, www.cia.gov.

Regional economic integration—the creation of trading agreements between blocs of countries—has intensified in recent years. This means companies are more likely to enter entire regions at the same time. Certain countries have formed free trade zones or economic communities—groups of nations organized to work toward common goals in the regulation of international trade (see Table 21.1).

Evaluating Potential Markets

However much nations and regions integrate their trading policies and standards, each still has unique features. Its readiness for different products and services, and its attractiveness as a market, depend on its demographic, economic, sociocultural, natural, technological, and political-legal environments.

How does a company choose among potential markets to enter? Many prefer to sell to neighboring countries because they understand them better and can control their entry costs more effectively. It's not surprising that the two largest U.S. export markets are Canada and Mexico, or that Swedish companies first sold to their Scandinavian neighbors.

At other times, *psychic proximity* determines choices. Given more familiar language, laws, and culture, many U.S. firms prefer to sell in Canada, England, and Australia rather than in larger markets such as Germany and France. Companies should be careful, however, in choosing markets according to cultural distance. Besides overlooking potentially better markets, they may only superficially analyze real differences that put them at a disadvantage.[31]

TABLE 21.1 💬 Regional Trade Areas and Agreements
The European Union Formed in 1957, the European Union set out to create a single European market by reducing barriers to the free flow of products, services, finances, and labor among member countries, and by developing trade policies with nonmember nations. Today, it's one of the world's largest single markets, with 27 member countries, a common currency—the euro—and more than 495 million consumers, accounting for 37 percent of the world's exports. Still, companies marketing in Europe face 23 different languages, 2,000 years of historical and cultural differences, and a daunting mass of local rules.
NAFTA In January 1994, the North American Free Trade Agreement (NAFTA) unified the United States, Mexico, and Canada in a single market of 440 million people who produce and consume $16 trillion worth of goods and services annually. Implemented over a 15-year period, NAFTA eliminates all trade barriers and investment restrictions among the three countries. Before NAFTA, tariffs on U.S. products entering Mexico averaged 13 percent, whereas U.S. tariffs on Mexican goods averaged 6 percent.
MERCOSUR MERCOSUR (or MERCOSUL) links Brazil, Argentina, Paraguay, Uruguay, and (soon) Venezuela to promote free trade and the fluid movement of goods, people, and currency. These five countries have 270 million citizens and collective GDP of $2.4 trillion. Bolivia, Chile, Columbia, Ecuador, and Peru are associate members and do not enjoy full voting rights or access to all the same markets. NAFTA will likely eventually merge with this and other arrangements to form an all-Americas free trade zone.
APEC Twenty-one countries, as well as the NAFTA members and Japan and China, are working to create a pan-Pacific free trade area under the auspices of the Asian Pacific Economic Cooperation (APEC) forum. These countries account for approximately 40.5 percent of the world's population, approximately 54.2 percent of world GDP, and about 43.7 percent of world trade. Heads of government of APEC members meet at an annual summit to discuss regional economy, cooperation, trade, and investment.
ASEAN Ten countries make up the Association of Southeast Asian Nations: Brunei Darussalam, Cambodia, Indonesia, Lao PDR, Malaysia, Myanmar, Philippines, Singapore, Thailand, and Viet Nam. The region is an attractive market of over 590 million people with $1.2 trillion in GDP. Member countries aim to enhance the area as a major production and export center.

Sources: www.europa.eu; "World Trade Report 2009," www.wto.org; www.naftanow.org; Council on Foreign Relations, "Mercosur: South America's Fractious Trade Bloc," www.cfr.org; www.apec.org; www.asean.org.

Busy ports, such as in Buenos Aires, Argentina, are fueling the demand for greater trade cooperation.

It often makes sense to operate in fewer countries, with a deeper commitment and penetration in each. In general, a company prefers to enter countries that have high market attractiveness and low market risk, and in which it possesses a competitive advantage. Consider how these firms have assessed market opportunities:

- Coke and Suntory are looking for energy-drink distribution opportunities outside saturated North America where Red Bull and Monster rule, focusing on less competitive markets in Western Europe and Asia. Both companies are considering using their extensive distribution networks to sell brands whose rights they have acquired, Monster and V, respectively.[32]
- Jamaica-based Digicel has conquered politically unstable developing countries such as Papua New Guinea, Haiti, and Tonga with products appealing to poor and typically overlooked consumers, whose fierce loyalty helps protect Digicel from aggressive government interventions.[33]
- Bechtel Corporation, the construction giant, does a cost-benefit analysis of overseas markets, factoring in the position of competitors, infrastructure, regulatory and trade barriers, and corporate and individual taxes. It looks for untapped needs for its products or services, a skilled labor pool, and a welcoming environment (governmental and physical).[34]

Deciding How to Enter the Market

Once a company decides to target a particular country, it must determine the best mode of entry. Its broad choices are *indirect exporting, direct exporting, licensing, joint ventures,* and *direct investment,* shown in △ Figure 21.2. Each succeeding strategy entails more commitment, risk, control, and profit potential.

Indirect and Direct Export

Companies typically start with export, specifically *indirect exporting*—that is, they work through independent intermediaries. *Domestic-based export merchants* buy the manufacturer's products and then sell them abroad. *Domestic-based export agents,* including trading companies, seek and negotiate foreign purchases for a commission. *Cooperative organizations* conduct exporting activities for several producers—often of primary products such as fruits or nuts—and are partly under their administrative control. *Export-management companies* agree to manage a company's export activities for a fee.

Indirect export has two advantages. First, there is less investment: The firm doesn't have to develop an export department, an overseas sales force, or a set of international contacts. Second, there's less risk: Because international marketing intermediaries bring know-how and services to the relationship, the seller will make fewer mistakes.

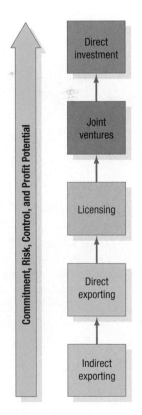

|Fig. 21.2| △

Five Modes of Entry into Foreign Markets

Companies may eventually decide to handle their own exports.[35] The investment and risk are somewhat greater, but so is the potential return. Direct exporting happens in several ways:

- **Domestic-based export department or division.** A purely service function may evolve into a self-contained export department operating as its own profit center.
- **Overseas sales branch or subsidiary.** The sales branch handles sales and distribution and perhaps warehousing and promotion as well. It often serves as a display and customer-service center.
- **Traveling export sales representatives.** Home-based sales representatives travel abroad to find business.
- **Foreign-based distributors or agents.** These third parties can hold limited or exclusive rights to represent the company in that country.

Many companies use direct or indirect exporting to "test the waters" before building a plant and manufacturing their product overseas. A company does not necessarily have to attend international trade shows if it can effectively use the Internet to attract new customers overseas, support existing customers who live abroad, source from international suppliers, and build global brand awareness.

Successful companies adapt their Web sites to provide country-specific content and services to their highest-potential international markets, ideally in the local language. Finding free information about trade and exporting has never been easier. Here are some places to start a search:

www.trade.gov	U.S. Department of Commerce's International Trade Administration
www.exim.gov	Export-Import Bank of the United States
www.sba.gov	U.S. Small Business Administration
www.bis.doc.gov	Bureau of Industry and Security, a branch of the Commerce Department

Many states' export-promotion offices also have online resources and allow businesses to link to their sites.

Licensing

Licensing is a simple way to engage in international marketing. The licensor issues a license to a foreign company to use a manufacturing process, trademark, patent, trade secret, or other item of value for a fee or royalty. The licensor gains entry at little risk; the licensee gains production expertise or a well-known product or brand name.

The licensor, however, has less control over the licensee than over its own production and sales facilities. If the licensee is very successful, the firm has given up profits, and if and when the contract ends, it might find it has created a competitor. To prevent this, the licensor usually supplies some proprietary product ingredients or components (as Coca-Cola does). But the best strategy is to lead in innovation so the licensee will continue to depend on the licensor.

Licensing arrangements vary. Companies such as Hyatt and Marriott sell *management contracts* to owners of foreign hotels to manage these businesses for a fee. The management firm may have the option to purchase some share in the managed company within a stated period.

In *contract manufacturing,* the firm hires local manufacturers to produce the product. When Sears opened department stores in Mexico and Spain, it found qualified local manufacturers to produce many of its products. Contract manufacturing reduces the company's control over the process and risks loss of potential profits. However, it offers a chance to start faster, with the opportunity to partner with or buy out the local manufacturer later.

Finally, a company can enter a foreign market through *franchising,* a more complete form of licensing. The franchisor offers a complete brand concept and operating system. In return, the franchisee invests in and pays certain fees to the franchisor. McDonald's, Ramada, and Avis have entered scores of countries by franchising their retail concepts and making their marketing culturally relevant.[36]

KFC Corporation   KFC is the world's largest fast-food chicken chain, serving more than 12 million customers at more than 5,200 restaurants in the United States and more than 15,000 units in 109 countries and territories around the world. KFC is world famous for its Original Recipe fried chicken—made with the same secret blend of

11 herbs and spices Colonel Harland Sanders perfected more than a half-century ago. Its success in Asia is instructive:

- When KFC entered the Japanese market in 1970, the Japanese saw fast food as artificial, made by mechanical means, and unhealthy. To build trust in the brand, advertising depicted Colonel Sanders's beginnings in Kentucky to convey Southern hospitality, old U.S. tradition, and authentic home cooking. The campaign was hugely successful. KFC now offers sesame and soy sauce–flavored chicken and a panko-fried salmon sandwich.

- In China, KFC is the largest, oldest, most popular, and fastest-growing quick-service restaurant chain, with over 3,400 locations in 650 towns or cities and healthy margins of 20 percent per store. Using its own supply and distribution system, it has expanded quickly into ever-smaller cities. The company has also tailored its menu to local tastes with items such as the Dragon Twister, a sandwich stuffed with chicken strips, Peking duck sauce, cucumbers, and scallions. KFC even has a Chinese mascot—a kid-friendly character named Chicky, which the company boasts has become "the Ronald McDonald of China."

By adapting its marketing to different regions of the world, KFC has met with much global success, such as with its many restaurants in Tokyo, Japan.

Joint Ventures

Historically, foreign investors have often joined local investors in a **joint venture** company in which they share ownership and control. To reach more geographic and technological markets and to diversify its investments and risk, GE Money—GE's retail lending arm—views joint ventures as one of its "most powerful strategic tools." It has formed joint ventures with financial institutions in South Korea, Spain, Turkey, and elsewhere.[37] Emerging markets, especially large, complex countries such as China and India, see much joint venture action.

A joint venture may be necessary or desirable for economic or political reasons. The foreign firm might lack the financial, physical, or managerial resources to undertake the venture alone, or the foreign government might require joint ownership as a condition for entry. Joint ownership has drawbacks. The partners might disagree over investment, marketing, or other policies. One might want to reinvest earnings for growth, the other to declare more dividends. Joint ownership can also prevent a multinational company from carrying out specific manufacturing and marketing policies on a worldwide basis.

The value of a partnership can extend far beyond increased sales or access to distribution. Good partners share "brand values" that help maintain brand consistency across markets. For example, McDonald's fierce commitment to product and service standardization is one reason its retail outlets are so similar around the world. McDonald's handpicks its global partners one by one to find "compulsive achievers" who will put forth the desired effort.

Direct Investment

The ultimate form of foreign involvement is direct ownership: the foreign company can buy part or full interest in a local company or build its own manufacturing or service facilities. Cisco had no presence in India before 2005 but opened a second headquarters in Bangalore to take advantage of opportunities in India and other locations such as Dubai.[38]

If the market is large enough, direct investment offers distinct advantages. First, the firm secures cost economies through cheaper labor or raw materials, government incentives, and freight savings. Second, the firm strengthens its image in the host country because it creates jobs. Third, the firm deepens its relationship with government, customers, local suppliers, and distributors, enabling it to better adapt its products to the local environment. Fourth, the firm retains full control over its investment and therefore can develop manufacturing and marketing policies that serve its long-term international objectives. Fifth, the firm assures itself of access to the market in case the host country insists locally purchased goods have domestic content.

The main disadvantage of direct investment is that the firm exposes a large investment to risks such as blocked or devalued currencies, worsening markets, or expropriation. If the host country requires substantial severance for employees, reducing or closing operations can be expensive.

TABLE 21.2 🗔 Globally Standardized Marketing Pros and Cons
Advantages
Economies of scale in production and distribution
Lower marketing costs
Power and scope
Consistency in brand image
Ability to leverage good ideas quickly and efficiently
Uniformity of marketing practices
Disadvantages
Ignores differences in consumer needs, wants, and usage patterns for products
Ignores differences in consumer response to marketing programs and activities
Ignores differences in brand and product development and the competitive environment
Ignores differences in the legal environment
Ignores differences in marketing institutions
Ignores differences in administrative procedures

Deciding on the Marketing Program

International companies must decide how much to adapt their marketing strategy to local conditions.[39] At one extreme is a *standardized marketing program* worldwide, which promises the lowest costs; 🗔 Table 21.2 summarizes some pros and cons. At the other extreme is an *adapted marketing program* in which the company, consistent with the marketing concept, believes consumer needs vary and tailors marketing to each target group.

Global Similarities and Differences

The development of the Web, the spread of cable and satellite TV, and the global linking of telecommunications networks have led to a convergence of lifestyles. Increasingly common needs and wants have created global markets for more standardized products, particularly among the young middle class. Once the butt of jokes, after being acquired by VW, the Czech carmaker Skoda used its investments to upgrade its quality and image and offer an affordable option to lower-income consumers worldwide.[40]

At the same time, consumers still vary across markets in significant ways.[41] The median age is about 25 in India and China, and around 43 in Japan, Germany, and Italy. When asked if they are more concerned with getting a specific brand than the best price, roughly two-thirds of U.S. consumers agreed, compared to around 80 percent in Russia and India.[42] Consider the following beverage facts.[43]

As this Prague waiter demonstrates, many Czech people like to drink beer!

- U.S. per capita consumption of soft drinks is 760 eight-ounce servings, the highest in the world. Mexicans drink 674 servings per year, Brazilians 315, Russians 149, and the Chinese 39.
- When it comes to beer, the Czech Republic leads the pack in Europe with 81.9 liters per capita; Norway is among the lowest at 40.3 liters.
- With wine, Portugal tops Europe with 33.1 liters per capita, while Finland is among the lowest at 9.9 liters.

Consumer behavior may reflect cultural differences that can be pronounced across countries.[44] Hofstede identifies four cultural dimensions that differentiate countries:[45]

1. ***Individualism versus collectivism***—In collectivist societies, the self-worth of an individual is rooted more in the social system than in individual achievement (high collectivism: Japan; low: United States).
2. ***High versus low power distance***—High power distance cultures tend to be less egalitarian (high: Russia; low: Nordic countries).
3. ***Masculine versus feminine***—This dimension measures how much the culture is dominated by assertive males versus nurturing females (highly masculine: Japan; low: Nordic countries).
4. ***Weak versus strong uncertainty avoidance***—Uncertainty avoidance indicates how risk-aversive people are (high avoidance: Greece; low: Jamaica).

Consumer behavior differences as well as historical market factors lead marketers to position brands differently in different markets.[46]

- Heineken beer is a high-end super-premium offering in the United States but middle-of-the-road in its Dutch home market.
- Honda automobiles denote speed, youth, and energy in Japan and quality and reliability in the United States.
- The Toyota Camry is the quintessential middle-class car in the United States but is at the high end in China, though in the two markets the cars differ only in cosmetic ways.

Marketing Adaptation

Because of all these differences, most products require at least some adaptation. Even Coca-Cola is sweeter or less carbonated in certain countries. Rather than assuming it can introduce its domestic product "as is" in another country, the company should review the following elements and determine which add more revenue than cost if adapted:

- Product features
- Labeling
- Colors
- Materials
- Sales promotion
- Advertising media
- Brand name
- Packaging
- Advertising execution
- Prices
- Advertising themes

The best global brands are consistent in theme but reflect significant differences in consumer behavior, brand development, competitive forces, and the legal or political environment.[47] Oft-heard—and sometime modified—advice to marketers of global brands is to: "Think Global, Act Local." In that spirit, HSBC is even explicitly positioned as "The World's Local Bank." Take McDonald's for example.[48]

McDonald's McDonald's allows countries and regions to customize its basic layout and menu staples. In China, corn replaces fries in Happy Meals, some U.S. stores blend fruit smoothies, and Australia and France have Starbucks-like lounges. In India, the mutton-based Maharaja Mac replaces the beefy Big Mac, and cottage cheese wraps and potato patties are offered for vegetarians. In cities plagued by traffic tie-ups like Manila, Taipei, Jakarta, and Cairo, McDonald's delivers via fleets of motor scooters.

Companies must make sure their brands are relevant to consumers in every market they enter. (See "Marketing Memo: The Ten Commandments of Global Branding.")

We next consider some specific issues in developing global product, communications, pricing, and distribution strategies.

McDonald's customizes its menu offerings and even its service delivery to suit the markets to which it sells—in busy cities, it may deliver meals via scooters.

marketing Memo

The Ten Commandments of Global Branding

These guidelines can help a company retain the advantages of global branding while minimizing potential disadvantages:

1. *Understand the global branding landscape.* One international market is rarely identical to or completely different from another in brand development, consumer behavior, competitive activity, or legal restrictions.

2. *Avoid shortcuts in brand building.* Build from the bottom up, creating awareness before brand image (strategy) and developing the right sources of brand equity (tactics).

3. *Establish a marketing infrastructure.* Build marketing infrastructure from scratch or adapt to and modify existing infrastructure in other countries.

4. *Embrace integrated marketing communications.* Many forms of communication work in overseas markets, not just advertising.

5. *Establish brand partnerships.* Most global brands carefully choose marketing partners that help improve distribution, profitability, and added value.

6. *Balance standardization and customization.* Packaging and brand name can often be standardized, while distribution channels and communications typically require greater customization.

7. *Balance global and local control.* Companies must balance global and local control within the organization and distribute decision making between global and local managers.

8. *Establish operable guidelines.* Brand definition and guidelines let marketers everywhere know what to do and not do. The goal is to communicate and enforce rules for positioning and marketing the brand.

9. *Implement a global brand-equity measurement system.* Information from a global brand-equity system lets marketers make the best short-run tactical and long-run strategic decisions in each market.

10. *Leverage brand elements.* Proper design and implementation of brand name and trademarked identifiers can be an invaluable source of brand equity worldwide.

Source: Adapted from Kevin Lane Keller and Sanjay Sood, "The Ten Commandments of Global Branding," *Asian Journal of Marketing* 8, no. 2 (2001), pp. 97–108.

Global Product Strategies

Developing global product strategies requires knowing what types of products or services are easily standardized and appropriate adaptation strategies.

PRODUCT STANDARDIZATION Some products cross borders without adaptation better than others. While mature products have separate histories or positions in different markets, consumer knowledge about new products is generally the same everywhere because perceptions have yet to be formed. Many leading Internet brands—Google, eBay, Amazon.com—made quick progress in overseas markets.

High-end products also benefit from standardization, because quality and prestige often can be marketed similarly across countries. Food and beverage marketers find it more challenging to standardize given widely varying tastes and cultural habits. Culture and wealth factors influence how quickly a new product takes off in a country, although adoption and diffusion rates are becoming more alike across countries over time.[49]

A company may emphasize its products differently across markets. IBM takes a two-track approach for its services business: because U.S. clients often are economizing, it focuses on helping them cut costs; for developing-market clients seeking to modernize and catch up with other countries, IBM helps develop their technology infrastructure. In its medical-equipment business, Philips reserves higher-end, premium products for developed markets and emphasizes products with basic functionality and affordability in developing markets.[50]

PRODUCT ADAPTATION STRATEGIES Warren Keegan has distinguished five product and communications adaptation strategies (see △ Figure 21.3).[51] We review the product strategies here and the communication strategies in the next section.

Straight extension introduces the product in the foreign market without any change. Tempting because it requires no additional R&D expense, manufacturing retooling, or promotional modification, it's been successful for cameras, consumer electronics, and many machine tools. In other cases, it has been a disaster. Campbell Soup Company lost an estimated $30 million introducing condensed soups in England; consumers saw expensive small-sized cans and didn't realize water needed to be added.

Product adaptation alters the product to meet local conditions or preferences. Flexible manufacturing makes it easier to do so on several levels.

|Fig. 21.3| △

Five International Product and Communication Strategies

		Product		
		Do Not Change Product	Adapt Product	Develop New Product
Communications	Do Not Change Communications	Straight extension	Product adaptation	Product invention
	Adapt Communications	Communication adaptation	Dual adaptation	

- A company can produce a *regional version* of its product, such as a Western European version. Finnish cellular phone superstar Nokia customized its 6100 series phone for every major market. Developers built in rudimentary voice recognition for Asia, where keyboards are a problem, and raised the ring volume to make it audible on crowded Asian streets.
- A company can produce a *country version*. Kraft blends different coffees for the British (who drink coffee with milk), the French (who drink it black), and Latin Americans (who want a chicory taste).
- A company can produce a *city version*—for instance, a beer to meet Munich's or Tokyo's tastes.
- A company can produce different *retailer versions*, such as one coffee brew for the Migros chain store and another for the Cooperative chain store, both in Switzerland.

Some companies have learned adaptation the hard way. The Euro Disney theme park, launched outside Paris in 1992, was harshly criticized as an example of U.S. cultural imperialism that ignored French customs and values, such as serving wine with meals. As one Euro Disney executive noted, "When we first launched, there was the belief that it was enough to be Disney. Now we realize our guests need to be welcomed on the basis of their own culture and travel habits." Renamed Disneyland Paris, the theme park eventually became Europe's biggest tourist attraction—even more popular than the Eiffel Tower—by implementing a number of changes and more local touches.[52]

Product invention creates something new. It can take two forms:

- **Backward invention** reintroduces earlier product forms well adapted to a foreign country's needs. The National Cash Register Company reintroduced its crank-operated cash register at half the price of a modern model and sold substantial numbers in Latin America and Africa.
- **Forward invention** creates a new product to meet a need in another country. Less-developed countries need low-cost, high-protein foods. Companies such as Quaker Oats, Swift, and Monsanto have researched their nutrition requirements, formulated new foods, and developed advertising to gain product trial and acceptance.

BRAND ELEMENT ADAPTATION When they launch products and services globally, marketers may need to change certain brand elements.[53] Even a brand name may require a choice between phonetic and semantic translations.[54] When Clairol introduced the "Mist Stick," a curling iron, in Germany, it found that *mist* is slang for *manure*. Brand slogans or ad taglines sometimes need to be changed too:[55]

- When Coors put its brand slogan "Turn it loose" into Spanish, some read it as "suffer from diarrhea."
- A laundry soap ad claiming to wash "really dirty parts" was translated in French-speaking Quebec to read "a soap for washing private parts."
- Perdue's slogan—"It takes a tough man to make a tender chicken"—was rendered into Spanish as "It takes a sexually excited man to make a chick affectionate."
- Electrolux's British ad line for its vacuum cleaners—"Nothing sucks like an Electrolux"—would certainly not lure customers in the United States!

Table 21.3 lists some other famous marketing mistakes in this area.

Disneyland Paris found greater success when it adapted more closely to the local culture and traditions in France.

là où les rêves deviennent réalité

TABLE 21.3	Classic Blunders in Global Marketing

- Hallmark cards failed in France, where consumers dislike syrupy sentiment and prefer writing their own cards.

- Philips became profitable in Japan only after reducing the size of its coffeemakers to fit smaller kitchens and its shavers to fit smaller hands.

- Coca-Cola withdrew its big two-liter bottle in Spain after discovering that few Spaniards owned refrigerators that could accommodate it.

- General Foods' Tang initially failed in France when positioned as a substitute for orange juice at breakfast. The French drink little orange juice and almost never at breakfast.

- Kellogg's Pop-Tarts failed in Britain because fewer homes have toasters than in the United States, and the product was too sweet for British tastes.

- The U.S. campaign for Procter & Gamble's Crest toothpaste initially failed in Mexico. Mexicans did not care as much about the decay-prevention benefit, nor did scientifically oriented advertising appeal.

- General Foods squandered millions trying to introduce packaged cake mixes to Japan, where only 3 percent of homes at the time were equipped with ovens.

- S.C. Johnson's wax floor polish initially failed in Japan. It made floors too slippery for a culture where people do not wear shoes at home.

Global Communication Strategies

Changing marketing communications for each local market is a process called **communication adaptation**. If it adapts both the product and the communications, the company engages in **dual adaptation**.

Consider the message. The company can use one message everywhere, varying only the language, name, and perhaps colors to avoid taboos in some countries.[56] Purple is associated with death in Burma and some Latin American nations, white is a mourning color in India, and in Malaysia green connotes disease.[57]

The second possibility is to use the same message and creative theme globally but adapt the execution. GE's global "Ecomagination" ad campaign substitutes creative content in Asia and the Middle East to reflect the cultural interest there. Even in the high-tech space, local adaptations may be necessary.[58]

Apple Apple Computer's highly successful "Mac vs. PC" ad campaign featured two actors bantering. One is hip (Apple), the other nerdy (PC). Apple dubbed the ads for Spain, France, Germany, and Italy but chose to reshoot and rescript for the United Kingdom and Japan—two important markets with unique advertising and comedy cultures. The UK ads followed a similar formula but used two well-known actors in character and tweaked the jokes to reflect British humor; the Japanese ads avoided direct comparisons and were more subtle in tone. Played by comedians from a local troupe called the Rahmens, the two characters were more alike and represented work (PC) vs. home (Mac).

The third approach, which Coca-Cola and Goodyear have used, consists of developing a global pool of ads from which each country selects the most appropriate. Finally, some companies allow their country managers to create country-specific ads—within guidelines, of course. The challenge is to make the message as compelling and effective as in the home market.

GLOBAL ADAPTATIONS Companies that adapt their communications wrestle with a number of challenges. They first must ensure their communications are legally and culturally acceptable. Beer, wine, and spirits cannot be advertised or sold in many Muslim countries. Tobacco products are subject to strict regulation in many places. U.S. toy makers were surprised to learn that in many countries (Norway and Sweden, for example) no TV ads may be directed at children under 12. To play it safe, McDonald's advertises itself as a family restaurant in Sweden.

Firms next must check their creative strategies and communication approaches for appropriateness. Comparative ads, although acceptable and even common in the United States and Canada, are less frequent in the United Kingdom, unacceptable in Japan, and illegal in India and Brazil. The EU seems to have a very low tolerance for comparative advertising and prohibits bashing rivals in ads.

Companies also must be prepared to vary their messages' appeal.[59] In advertising its hair care products, Helene Curtis observed that middle-class British women wash their hair frequently, Spanish women less so. Japanese women avoid overwashing for fear of removing protective oils. Language can vary too, whether the local language, another such as English, or some combination.[60]

Many messages need adjustment because the brand is at an earlier stage of development in its new market. Consumer education about the product itself may then need to accompany brand development efforts.

- In certain developing markets in Asia, consumers loved the Coca-Cola brand but had never tasted it. They needed to be advised to drink it cold.[61]
- When launching Chik shampoo in rural areas of South India, where hair is washed with soap, CavinKare showed people how to use the product through live "touch and feel" demonstrations and free sachets at fairs.[62]

Personal selling tactics may need to change too. The direct, no-nonsense approach favored in the United States ("let's get down to business" and "what's in it for me") may not work as well in Europe or Asia as an indirect, subtle approach.[63]

Global Pricing Strategies

Multinationals selling abroad must contend with price escalation and transfer prices (and dumping charges). Two particularly thorny pricing problems are gray markets and counterfeits.

PRICE ESCALATION A Gucci handbag may sell for $120 in Italy and $240 in the United States. Why? Gucci must add the cost of transportation, tariffs, importer margin, wholesaler margin, and retailer margin to its factory price. **Price escalation** from these added costs and currency-fluctuation risk might make the price two to five times as much in another country to earn the same profit for the manufacturer.

Companies have three choices for setting prices in different countries:

1. *Set a uniform price everywhere.* PepsiCo might want to charge 75 cents for Pepsi everywhere in the world, but then it would earn quite different profit rates in different countries. Also, this strategy would make the price too high in poor countries and not high enough in rich countries.
2. *Set a market-based price in each country.* PepsiCo would charge what each country could afford, but this strategy ignores differences in the actual cost from country to country. It could also motivate intermediaries in low-price countries to reship their Pepsi to high-price countries.[64]
3. *Set a cost-based price in each country.* Here PepsiCo would use a standard markup of its costs everywhere, but this strategy might price it out of markets where its costs are high.

When companies sell their wares over the Internet, price becomes transparent and price differentiation between countries declines. Consider an online training course. Whereas the price of a classroom-delivered day of training can vary significantly from the United States to France to Thailand, the price of an online-delivered day would be similar everywhere.

In another new global pricing challenge, countries with overcapacity, cheap currencies, and the need to export aggressively have pushed prices down and devalued their currencies. Sluggish demand and reluctance to pay higher prices make selling in these markets difficult. Here is what IKEA did to compete in China's challenging pricing market.[65]

IKEA IKEA has used market-penetration pricing to get a lock on China's surging market for home furnishings. When the Swedish home furnishings giant opened its first store in Beijing in 2002, shops were selling copies of its designs at a fraction of IKEA's prices. The only way to lure China's frugal customers was to drastically slash prices. Western brands in China usually price products such as makeup and running shoes 20 percent to 30 percent higher than in their other markets, both to make up for China's high import taxes and to give their products added cachet. By stocking its Chinese stores with Chinese-made products, IKEA has been able to slash prices as low as 70 percent below their level outside China. Although it still contends with persistent knockoffs, IKEA maintains sizable stores in Beijing, Shanghai, Guangzhou, Chengdu, and Tianjin, opening one or two new locations each year.

TRANSFER PRICES A different problem arises when one unit charges another unit in the same company a **transfer price** for goods it ships to its foreign subsidiaries. If the company charges a subsidiary too *high* a price, it may end up paying higher tariff duties, although it may pay lower income taxes in the foreign country. If the company charges its subsidiary too *low* a price, it can be accused of **dumping**, charging either less than its costs or less than it charges at home in order to enter or win a market. Various governments are watching for abuses and often force companies to charge the **arm's-length price**—the price charged by other competitors for the same or a similar product.

When the U.S. Department of Commerce finds evidence of dumping, it can levy a dumping tariff on the guilty company. After finding that exporters and producers from China were selling off-road tires in the United States at 11 percent to 210 percent below fair market value, the U.S. Department of Commerce imposed a duty of 11 percent to 52 percent on four Chinese tire manufactures and an average duty of 25 percent on 23 other tire makers there.[66]

GRAY MARKETS Many multinationals are plagued by the **gray market**, which diverts branded products from authorized distribution channels either in-country or across international borders. Dealers in the low-price country find ways to sell some of their products in higher-price countries, thus earning more. Often a company finds some enterprising distributors buying more than they can sell in their own country and reshipping the goods to another country to take advantage of price differences.

Research suggests that gray market activity accounts for billions of dollars in revenue each year and makes up about 8 percent of total global IT sales of $725 billion. Information technology manufacturers lose about $10 billion in profits to the gray market each year.[67]

Gray markets create a free-rider problem, making legitimate distributors' investments in supporting a manufacturer's product less productive and selective distribution systems more intensive. They harm distributor relations, tarnish the manufacturer's brand equity, and undermine the integrity of the distribution channel. They can even pose risks to consumers if the seemingly brand-new product they think they are buying is damaged, remarked, obsolete, without warranty or support, or just counterfeit.

Multinationals try to prevent gray markets by policing the distributors, raising their prices to lower-cost distributors, or altering product characteristics or service warranties for different countries.[68] 3Com successfully sued several companies in Canada (for a total of $10 million) that provided written and oral misrepresentations to get deep discounts on 3Com networking equipment. The equipment, worth millions of dollars, was to be sold to a U.S. educational software company and sent to China and Australia but instead ended up back in the United States.

One research study found that gray market activity was most effectively deterred when penalties were severe, manufacturers were able to detect violations or mete out punishments in a timely fashion, or both.[69]

Counterfeit products are a major headache for luxury-goods makers.

COUNTERFEIT PRODUCTS Name a popular brand, and chances are a counterfeit version of it exists somewhere in the world.[70] Counterfeiting is estimated to cost over a trillion dollars a year. U.S. Customs and Border Protection seized $260 million worth of goods in 2009; the chief culprits were China (81 percent) and Hong Kong (10 percent), and the chief product was footwear (38 percent).[71]

Fakes take a big bite of the profits of luxury brands such as Hermès, LVMH Moët Hennessy Louis Vuitton, and Tiffany, but faulty counterfeits can literally kill people. Cell phones with counterfeit batteries, fake brake pads made of compressed grass trimmings, and counterfeit airline parts pose safety risks to consumers. Virtually every product is vulnerable. As one anticounterfeit consultant observed, "If you can make it, they can fake it." Defending against counterfeiters is a never-ending struggle; some observers estimate that a new security system can be just months old before counterfeiters start nibbling at sales again.[72]

The Web has been especially problematic. After surveying thousands of items, LVMH estimated 90 percent of Louis Vuitton and Christian Dior pieces listed on eBay were fakes, prompting the firm to sue. Manufacturers are fighting back online with Web-crawling software that detects fraud and automatically warns apparent violators without the need for any human intervention. Acushnet, maker of Titleist golf clubs and balls, shut down 75 auctions of knockoff gear in one day with just one mouse click.[73]

Web-crawling technology searches for counterfeit storefronts and sales by detecting domain names similar to legitimate brands and unauthorized Web sites that plaster brand trademarks and logos on their homepages. It also checks for keywords such as *cheap, discount, authentic,* and *factory variants,* as well as colors that products were never made in and prices that are far too low.

Global Distribution Strategies

Too many U.S. manufacturers think their job is done once the product leaves the factory. They should instead note how the product moves within the foreign country and take a whole-channel view of distributing products to final users.

CHANNEL ENTRY △ Figure 21.4 shows three links between the seller and the final buyer. In the first, *seller's international marketing headquarters,* the export department or international division makes decisions about channels and other marketing activities. The second link, *channels between nations,* gets the products to the borders of the foreign nation. Decisions made in this link include the types of intermediaries (agents, trading companies), type of transportation (air, sea), and financing and risk management. The third link, *channels within foreign nations,* gets products from their entry point to final buyers and users.

When multinationals first enter a country, they prefer to work with local distributors with good local knowledge, but friction often arises later.[74] The multinational complains that the local distributor doesn't invest in business growth, doesn't follow company policy, and doesn't share enough information. The local distributor complains of insufficient corporate support, impossible goals, and confusing policies. The multinational must choose the right distributors, invest in them, and set up performance goals to which they can agree.[75]

CHANNEL DIFFERENCES Distribution channels across countries vary considerably. To sell consumer products in Japan, companies must work through one of the most complicated distribution systems in the world. They sell to a general wholesaler, who sells to a product wholesaler, who sells to a product-specialty wholesaler, who sells to a regional wholesaler, who sells to a local wholesaler, who finally sells to retailers. All these distribution levels can make the consumer's price double or triple the importer's price. Taking these same consumer products to tropical Africa, the company might sell to an import wholesaler, who sells to several jobbers, who sell to petty traders (mostly women) working in local markets.

Another difference is the size and character of retail units abroad. Large-scale retail chains dominate the U.S. scene, but much foreign retailing is in the hands of small, independent retailers. Millions of Indian retailers operate tiny shops or sell in open markets. Markups are high, but the real price comes down through haggling. Incomes are low, most homes lack storage and refrigeration, and people shop daily for whatever they can carry home on foot or bicycle. In India, people often buy one cigarette at a time. Breaking bulk remains an important function of intermediaries and helps perpetuate long channels of distribution, a major obstacle to the expansion of large-scale retailing in developing countries.

Sometimes companies mistakenly adapt infrastructure strategies that were critical success factors, only to discover that these changes eroded the brand's competitive advantage. Dell Computer initially abandoned its direct distribution strategy in Europe for a traditional retailer network of existing channels, with poor results. Ignoring critics who claimed the direct distribution model would never work in Europe, Dell then revamped its direct approach, relaunching its personal computer line with a new management team to execute the direct model it had pioneered in the United States, finding greater success as a result.

Increasingly, retailers are moving into new global markets, offering firms the opportunity to sell across more countries and creating a challenge to local distributors and retailers.[76] France's Carrefour, Germany's Metro, and United Kingdom's Tesco have all established global positions. But some of the world's most successful retailers have had mixed success abroad. Despite concerted efforts and earlier success in Latin America and China, Walmart had to withdraw from both the German and South Korean markets.

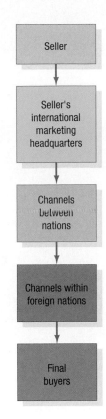

|Fig. 21.4| △

Whole-Channel Concept for International Marketing

Country-of-Origin Effects

Country-of-origin perceptions are the mental associations and beliefs triggered by a country. Government officials want to strengthen their country's image to help domestic marketers who export, and to attract foreign firms and investors. Marketers want to use positive country-of-origin perceptions to sell their products and services.

Building Country Images

Governments now recognize that the images of their cities and countries affect more than tourism and have important value in commerce. Attracting foreign business can boost the local economy, provide jobs, and improve infrastructure. Image can also help sell products. For its first global ad campaign for Infiniti luxury cars, Nissan chose to tap into its Japanese roots and association with Japanese-driven art and engineering.[77]

Countries are being marketed like any other brand.[78] New Zealand developed concerted marketing programs both to sell its products outside the country, via its New Zealand Way program, and to attract tourists by showing the dramatic landscapes featured in *The Lord of the Rings* film trilogy. Both efforts reinforce the image of New Zealand as fresh and pure.[79]

Another film affected the image of a country in an entirely different way. Although Kazakhstan has a positive story to tell given its huge size, rich natural resources, and rapid modernization, British comedian Sacha Baron Cohen's mock documentary *Borat* portrayed the country in a sometimes crude and vulgar light. As one government official noted, "the only fact of the movie is the geographic location of Kazakhstan." Fortunately, the tongue-in-cheek film also created awareness and interest in the country and what has been called the "Borat Bounce," an unanticipated surge in tourism.[80]

Attitudes toward countries can change over time. Before World War II, Japan had a poor image, which the success of Sony with its Trinitron TV sets and of Japanese automakers Honda and Toyota helped change. A strong company that emerges as a global player can do wonders for a country's image. Relying partly on the global success of Nokia, Finland campaigned to enhance its image as a center of high-tech innovation.[81]

Current events can also shape the image of a country. With public unrest and violent protests surrounding the austerity program to address Greece's debt crisis, tourist bookings there dropped as much as 30 percent.[82]

Although the film *Borat* poked fun at Kazakhstan, it also created much public awareness of and interest in the country.

Consumer Perceptions of Country of Origin

Global marketers know that buyers hold distinct attitudes and beliefs about brands or products from different countries.[83] These perceptions can be an attribute in decision making or influence other attributes in the process ("if it's French, it must be stylish"). The mere fact that a brand is perceived as successful on a global stage—whether it sends a quality signal, taps into cultural myths, or reinforces a sense of social responsibility—may lend credibility and respect.[84] Several studies have found the following:[85]

- People are often ethnocentric and favorably predisposed to their own country's products, unless they come from a less developed country.
- The more favorable a country's image, the more prominently the "Made in..." label should be displayed.
- The impact of country of origin varies with the type of product. Consumers want to know where a car was made, but not the lubricating oil.
- Certain countries enjoy a reputation for certain goods: Japan for automobiles and consumer electronics; the United States for high-tech innovations, soft drinks, toys, cigarettes, and jeans; France for wine, perfume, and luxury goods.
- Sometimes country-of-origin perception can encompass an entire country's products. In one study, Chinese consumers in Hong Kong perceived U.S. products as prestigious, Japanese products as innovative, and Chinese products as cheap.

Marketers must look at country-of-origin perceptions from both a domestic and a foreign perspective. In the domestic market, these perceptions may stir consumers' patriotic notions or remind them of their past. As international trade grows, consumers may view certain brands as symbolically important in their own cultural heritage and identity.

Patriotic appeals underlie marketing strategies all over the world, but they can lack uniqueness and even be overused, especially in economic or political crises. Many small businesses tap into community pride to emphasize their local roots. To be successful, these need to be clearly local and offer appealing product and service offerings.[86]

Sometimes consumers don't know where brands come from. In surveys, they routinely guess that Heineken is German and Nokia is Japanese (they are Dutch and Finnish, respectively). Few consumers know Häagen-Dazs and Estée Lauder originated in the United States.

With outsourcing and foreign manufacturing, it's hard to know what the country of origin really is anyway. Only 65 percent of the content of a Ford Mustang comes from the United States or Canada, whereas the Toyota Sienna is assembled in Indiana with 90 percent local components. Foreign automakers are pouring money into North America, investing in plants, suppliers, and dealerships as well as design, testing, and research centers. But what makes a product more "American"—having a higher percentage of North American components or creating more jobs in North America? The two measures may not lead to the same conclusion.[87]

Many brands have gone to great lengths to weave themselves into the cultural fabric of their foreign markets. One Coca-Cola executive tells of a young child visiting the United States from Japan who commented to her parents on seeing a Coca-Cola vending machine—"Look, they have Coca-Cola too!" As far as she was concerned, Coca-Cola was a Japanese brand.

Even when the United States has not been that popular, its brands typically have been. One recent study found that 70 percent of consumers in developing countries, ranging from Argentina to the United Arab Emirates, felt local products weren't as good as international brands.[88] In Saudi Arabia, Kraft packaged cheese, Lay's potato chips, and McDonald's restaurants were all viewed as top brands in their categories. As one marketer said of the study, "Regardless of all the problems we have as a country, we are still looked to as the consumer capital of the world."[89]

Companies can target niches to establish a footing in new markets. China's leading maker of refrigerators, washing machines, and air conditioners, Haier, is building a beachhead among U.S. college students who loyally buy its mini-fridges at Walmart and elsewhere. Haier's long-term plans are to introduce innovative products in other areas, such as flat-screen TV sets and wine-cooling cabinets.[90]

China's Haier has ambitious plans to sell its many different appliances in the United States and other markets.

Deciding on the Marketing Organization

Companies manage their international marketing activities in three ways: through export departments, international divisions, or a global organization.

Export Department

A firm normally gets into international marketing by simply shipping out its goods. If its international sales expand, it organizes an export department consisting of a sales manager and a few assistants. As sales increase, the export department expands to include various marketing services so the company can go after business more aggressively. If the firm moves into joint ventures or direct investment, the export department will no longer be adequate to manage international operations.

International Division

Sooner or later, companies that engage in several international markets and ventures create an international division to handle all this activity. The unit is headed by a division president who sets goals and budgets and is responsible for the company's international growth.

The international division's corporate staff consists of functional specialists who provide services to various operating units. Operating units can be *geographical organizations.* Reporting to the international-division president might be regional vice presidents for North America, Latin America, Europe, Africa, the Middle East, and the Far East. Reporting to the regional vice presidents are country managers responsible for a sales force, sales branches, distributors, and licensees in the respective countries. Or the operating units may be *world product groups,* each with an international vice president responsible for worldwide sales of each product group. The vice presidents may draw on corporate-staff area specialists for expertise on different geographical areas. Finally, operating units may be *international subsidiaries,* each headed by a president who reports to the president of the international division.

Global Organization

Several firms have become truly global organizations. Their top corporate management and staff plan worldwide manufacturing facilities, marketing policies, financial flows, and logistical systems. The global operating units report directly to the chief executive or executive committee, not to the head of an international division. The firm trains its executives in worldwide operations, recruits management from many countries, purchases components and supplies where it can obtain them at least cost, and makes investments where anticipated returns are greatest.

These companies face several organizational complexities. For example, when the firm is pricing a company's mainframe computers for a large banking system in Germany, how much influence should the headquarters product manager have? And the company's market manager for the banking sector? And the company's German country manager?

When forces for "global integration" (capital-intensive production, homogeneous demand) are strong and forces for "national responsiveness" (local standards and barriers, strong local preferences) are weak, a global strategy that treats the world as a single market can make sense (for example, with consumer electronics). When the reverse is true, a multinational strategy that treats the world as a portfolio of national opportunities can be more appropriate (such as for food or cleaning products).[91]

Korea's globally integrated LG decided to hire a number of top executives from Western firms to help transform it from "an engineering powerhouse that excelled at manufacturing and selling in different parts of the world" to a "globally efficient, trend-setting organization." The new executives were charged with standardizing the hodgepodge of processes and systems LG had developed in different markets in purchasing, the supply chain, marketing, and other areas. A single agency (London's Bartle Bogle Hegarty) was given global responsibility to sell an increasing number of higher-end products.[92]

When both forces prevail to some extent, a "glocal" strategy that standardizes certain elements and localizes others can be the way to go (for instance, with telecommunications). Many firms seek a blend of centralized global control from corporate headquarters with input from local and regional marketers. As one top marketer for global brand icon Jack Daniels described the challenges of managing the world's biggest-selling whiskey brand across 135 countries: "'Not invented' here is a good thing; 'invented here' is also a good thing; 'not invented but improved here' is the best!"[93]

Finding the balance can be tricky, though. Coca-Cola adopted a "think local, act local" philosophy, decentralizing power and responsibility for designing marketing programs and activities. Execution faltered because many local managers lacked the skills or discipline to do the job. Decidedly un-Coke-like ads appeared—such as skinny-dippers streaking down a beach in Italy—and sales stalled. The pendulum swung back, and Coke executives in Atlanta resumed a strong strategic role.[94]

Effectively transferring successful marketing ideas from one region to another is a key priority for many firms. Rather than developing global products for jointly owned Renault and Nissan, CEO Carlos Ghosn has mandated that companies design for local tastes and have the flexibility to export the design to other regions to tap into similar consumer trends. The no-frills Logan was developed by Renault for Eastern Europe and Latin America but found another home in France. When products cross a region, ideas and a way of thinking may also transfer in the process. Ghosn teamed Nissan and Renault with Bajaj Auto to sell a $3,000 car in the Indian market, in part to infuse those companies with India's low-cost design thinking: "They understand frugal engineering, which is something we aren't as good at in Europe or Japan."[95]

Summary

1. Despite shifting borders, unstable governments, foreign-exchange problems, corruption, and technological pirating, companies selling in global industries need to internationalize their operations.

2. Upon deciding to go abroad, a company needs to define its international marketing objectives and policies. It must determine whether to market in a few or many countries and rate candidate countries on three criteria: market attractiveness, risk, and competitive advantage.

3. Developing countries offer a unique set of opportunities and risks. The "BRIC" countries—Brazil, Russia, India, and China—plus other significant markets such as Indonesia and South Africa are a top priority for many firms.

4. Modes of entry are indirect exporting, direct exporting, licensing, joint ventures, and direct investment. Each succeeding strategy entails more commitment, risk, control, and profit potential.

5. In deciding how much to adapt their marketing programs at the product level, firms can pursue a strategy of straight extension, product adaptation, or product invention. At the communication level, they may choose communication adaptation or dual adaptation. At the price level, firms may encounter price escalation, dumping, gray markets, and discounted counterfeit products. At the distribution level, firms need to take a whole-channel view of distributing products to the final users. Firms must always consider the cultural, social, political, technological, environmental, and legal limitations they face in other countries.

6. Country-of-origin perceptions can affect consumers and businesses alike. Managing those perceptions to best advantage is a marketing priority.

7. Depending on their level of international involvement, companies manage international marketing activity in three ways: through export departments, international divisions, or a global organization.

Applications

Marketing Debate
Is the World Coming Closer Together?

Many social commentators maintain that youth and teens are becoming more alike across countries over time. Others, although not disputing the fact, point out that differences between cultures at even younger ages by far exceed the similarities.

Take a position: People are becoming more and more similar *versus* The differences between people of different cultures far outweigh their similarities.

Marketing Discussion
Country of Origin

Think of some of your favorite brands. Do you know where they come from? Where and how are they made or provided? Do you think knowing these answers would affect your perceptions of quality or satisfaction?

Marketing Excellence

>>Nokia

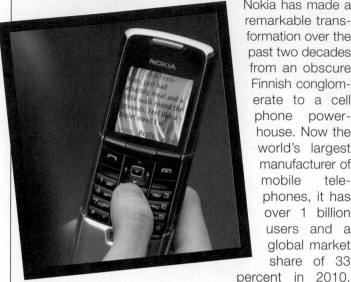

Nokia has made a remarkable transformation over the past two decades from an obscure Finnish conglomerate to a cell phone powerhouse. Now the world's largest manufacturer of mobile telephones, it has over 1 billion users and a global market share of 33 percent in 2010. The company sells approximately 11 cell phones every second and is the standout leader in Asia, Eastern Europe, and Africa.

Nokia's transformation started in the early 1990s with its strategic decision to divest its product portfolio and focus entirely on telecommunications. Business soon exploded, in part due to Nokia's mastery in innovating telecommunications technologies. Nokia was a key developer of new mobile technologies like GSM (Global System for Mobile Communications) that allow consumers to roam internationally and use new data services like text messaging. Although the firm has struggled in North America—in part because many networks there use a different wireless standard (CDMA) than in Europe (GSM)—its global footprint is still impressive.

Nokia's success also derives from its broad strategic view of how to build a global brand and international consumer base. The company sells a wide range of products and services in all price ranges to different types of consumers all over the world. In short, its approach is "All price points, all markets." Nokia has a practical understanding of what consumers need, value, and can afford depending on their geographical location and demographics. By providing the right products, features, and price, the firm has successfully built long-term brand value all over the world.

With the bulk of industry growth coming from developing markets, Nokia has made sure its cheapest handsets are appealing—and profitable—in markets such as China, India, and Latin America. On the flip side, to sustain its market leadership and compete in challenging markets like Europe and the United States, it has launched a range of high-end handsets with advanced features and applications. This consumer base is so critical to Nokia's growth that it has created a business division focused entirely on creating software and services for it, including music, video, games, maps, messaging, and media. Today, Nokia's products range from $30 basic models to $600 smart phones that include video editing, voice-guided navigation, and thousands of applications. Nokia's future also lies in its growing line of mobile computers, devices with the advanced capabilities of a computer that fit into the palm of your hand.

Nokia takes a broad perspective on competition as well, viewing Apple, Sony, and Canon as threats as much as traditional rivals Motorola and Samsung. Competitors' products like the iPhone, BlackBerry, and Android smart phones have all gained significant market share. Although 84 percent of its sales consist of cell phones, Nokia is focused on making its smart phones durable, reliable, and affordable to consumers in emerging markets, as it did with cell phones.

As a global leader, Nokia understands how critical it is to have a finger on the pulse of countries and cultures all over the world. With 16 different R&D factories, manufacturing plants in 10 countries, Web sites in 7 countries, and 650,000 points-of-sale—the widest distribution network in the world—Nokia strives to be a global leader but locally relevant. It forms relationships with local business partners, gets involved in the community, and works to earn consumers' trust on a local level.

In India, for example, the company has increased its local involvement by including in the Nokia Music Store a significant percentage of songs by local and regional artists, adding thousands of local customer care services, and supporting a local environmental initiative called "Planet Ke Rakwale" that encourages consumers to recycle their old phones and batteries. Nokia even added the tagline, "Made in India for India."

Today, with a value of nearly $35 billion, Nokia is the fifth most valuable global brand in the Interbrand/*BusinessWeek* ranking, surpassing Google, Samsung, Apple, and BlackBerry. The brand continues to rank well in consumers' minds as high quality, robust, easy to use, and trustworthy—a perfect combination for succeeding in both emerging and mature countries.

Questions

1. What have been the keys to Nokia's global strength?

2. What can Nokia do to gain market share in the United States and Europe where its presence is not as strong?

3. In the ever-changing world of mobile technology, what are the greatest threats to Nokia's global presence?

Sources: Jack Ewing, "Nokia: Lesson Learned, Reward Reaped," *BusinessWeek*, July 30, 2007; "Face Value," *Economist*, May 27, 2006; Oli Pekka Kalasvuo, "Brand Identity: A Delicate Balance between Image and Authenticity," *Economic Times*, August 31, 2010; Kevin J. O'Brien, "Nokia Seeks to Reconnect with the U.S. Market," *New York Times*, August 15, 2010; "Best Global Brands 2009," *Interbrand/BusinessWeek*; Nokia Capital Markets Day presentation, 2009; Nokia, www.nokia.com.

Marketing Excellence

>>L'Oréal

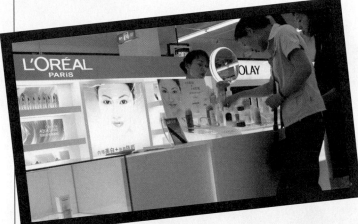

When it comes to globalizing beauty, no one does it better than L'Oréal. The company was founded in Paris over 100 years ago by a young chemist, Eugene Schueller, who sold his patented hair dyes to local hairdressers and salons. By the 1930s, Schueller had invented beauty products like suntan oil and the first mass-marketed shampoo. Today, the company has evolved into the world's largest beauty and cosmetics company, with distribution in 130 countries, 23 global brands, and over €17.5 billion in sales.

Much of the company's international expansion and success is credited to Sir Lindsay Owen-Jones, who transformed L'Oréal from a small French business to an international cosmetics phenomenon with strategic vision and precise brand management. During his almost 20 years as CEO and chairman, Owen-Jones divested weak brands, invested heavily in product innovation, acquired ethnically diverse brands, and expanded into markets no one had dreamed of, including China, South America, and the former Soviet Union. His quest: to achieve diversity, "meet the needs of men and women around the globe, and make beauty products available to as many people as possible."

Today, L'Oréal focuses on its five areas of expertise: skin care, hair care, makeup, hair coloring, and perfume. Its brands fall into four different groups: (1) Consumer Products (52 percent of L'Oréal's portfolio, including mass-marketed Maybelline and high-technology products sold at competitive prices through mass-market retailing chains), (2) Luxury Products (prestigious brands like Ralph Lauren perfume offered only in premium stores, department stores, or specialty stores), (3) Professional Products (brands such as Redken designed specifically for professional hair salons), and (4) Active (dermo-cosmetic products sold at pharmacies).

L'Oréal believes precise target marketing—hitting the right audience with the right product at the right place—is crucial to its global success. Owen-Jones explained,

"Each brand is positioned on a very precise [market] segment, which overlaps as little as possible with the others."

The company has built its portfolio primarily by purchasing local beauty companies all over the world, revamping them with strategic direction, and expanding the brand into new areas through its powerful marketing arm. For example, L'Oréal instantly became a player (with 20 percent market share) in the growing ethnic hair care industry when it purchased and merged the U.S. companies Soft Sheen Products in 1998 and Carson Products in 2000. L'Oréal believed the competition had overlooked this category because it was previously fragmented and misunderstood. SoftSheen-Carson now derives approximately 30 percent of its annual revenues from South Africa.

L'Oréal also invests money and time in innovating at 14 research centers around the world, spending 3 percent of annual sales on R&D, more than one percentage point above the industry average. Understanding the unique beauty routines and needs of different cultures, countries, and consumers is critical to L'Oréal's global success. Hair and skin greatly differ from one part of the world to another, so L'Oréal scientists study consumers in laboratory bathrooms and in their own homes, sometimes achieving scientific beauty milestones. In Japan, for example, L'Oréal developed Wondercurl mascara specially formulated to curl Asian women's eyelashes, which are usually short and straight. The result: within three months it had become Japan's number-one selling mascara, and girls excitedly lined up in front of stores to buy it. L'Oréal continued to research the market and developed nail polish, blush, and other cosmetics aimed at this new generation of Asian girls.

Well known for its 1973 advertising tagline—"Because I'm Worth It"—L'Oréal is now a leader in beauty products around the world. As Gilles Weil, L'Oréal's head of luxury products, explained, "You have to be local and as strong as the best locals, but backed by an international image and strategy."

Questions

1. Review L'Oréal's brand portfolio. What role have target marketing, smart acquisitions, and R&D played in growing those brands?

2. Who are L'Oréal's greatest competitors? Local, global, or both? Why?

3. What has been the key to successful local product launches such as Maybelline's Wondercurl in Japan?

4. What's next for L'Oréal on a global level? If you were CEO, how would you sustain the company's global leadership?

Sources: Andrew Roberts, "L'Oréal Quarterly Sales Rise Most Since 2007 on Luxury Perfume," *Bloomberg BusinessWeek*, April 22, 2010; Richard Tomlinson, "L'Oréal's Global Makeover," *Fortune,* September 30, 2002; Doreen Carvajal, "International Business; Primping for the Cameras in the Name of Research," *New York Times*, February 7, 2006; Richard C. Morais, "The Color of Beauty," *Forbes*, November 27, 2000; L'Oréal, www.loreal.com.

In This Chapter, We Will Address the Following Questions

1. What are important trends in marketing practices?

2. What are the keys to effective internal marketing?

3. How can companies be responsible social marketers?

4. How can a company improve its marketing skills?

5. What tools are available to help companies monitor and improve their marketing activities?

Timberland's passion for the outdoors and the environment influences its choice of products to sell and the way it makes and sells those products.

Managing a Holistic Marketing Organization for the Long Run

Healthy long-term growth for a brand requires that the marketing organization be managed properly. Holistic marketers must engage in a host of carefully planned, interconnected marketing activities and satisfy an increasingly broader set of constituents and objectives. They must also consider a wider range of effects of their actions. Corporate social responsibility and sustainability have become a priority as organizations grapple with the short-term and long-term effects of their marketing. Some firms have embraced this new vision of corporate enlightenment and made it the very core of what they do. Consider Timberland.[1]

 Timberland, the maker of rugged boots, shoes, clothing, and gear, has a passion for the great outdoors. The company targets individuals who live, work, and play outdoors, so it only makes sense that it wants to do whatever it takes to protect the environment. Over the past two decades, Timberland's commitment and actions have blazed trails for green companies around the world. Its revolutionary initiatives include giving its shoes a "nutrition label" that measures their "greenness"—how much energy was used in making them, what transportation and labor costs were incurred, and what portion is renewable. Timberland also introduced a new line of shoes called Earthkeepers, made of organic cotton, recycled PET, and recycled tires (for the soles). The shoes are designed to be taken apart and over 50 percent of the parts can be recycled. Timberland has attracted an online community for Earthkeepers by offering tips and information about events focused on preserving the environment. Its business accomplishments prove that socially and environmentally responsible companies can be successful. Sales topped $1.2 billion in 2009, and Timberland has won numerous awards from a steady spot on Fortune's 100 Best Companies to Work For to the Ron Brown Award for Corporate Leadership, the only Presidential Award recognizing companies for outstanding employee and community relations.

Many other brands such as Ben & Jerry's, Odwalla, Patagonia, Stonyfield Farm, Whole Foods, and Seventh Generation have embraced similar philosophies and practices. Successful holistic marketing requires effective relationship marketing, integrated marketing, internal marketing, and performance marketing. Preceding chapters addressed the first two topics and the strategy and tactics of marketing. In this chapter, we consider the latter two topics and how to conduct marketing responsibly. We look at how firms organize, implement, evaluate, and control marketing activities in a context heightened by social responsibility. We begin by examining changes in the way companies conduct marketing today.

Trends in Marketing Practices

Chapters 1 and Chapter 3 described important changes in the marketing macroenvironment, such as globalization, deregulation, market fragmentation, consumer empowerment, and environmental concerns.[2] With these and all the remarkable developments in computers, software, the Internet, and cell phones, the world has unquestionably become a very different place for marketers. In earlier chapters, we detailed the many shifts in marketing that dominated the first decade of the 21st century.[3] Table 22.1 summarizes some important ones and we briefly review a few next.

TABLE 22.1	Important Shifts in Marketing and Business Practices
• **Reengineering.** Appointing teams to manage customer-value-building processes and break down walls between departments
• **Outsourcing.** Buying more goods and services from outside domestic or foreign vendors
• **Benchmarking.** Studying "best practice companies" to improve performance
• **Supplier partnering.** Partnering with fewer but better value-adding suppliers
• **Customer partnering.** Working more closely with customers to add value to their operations
• **Merging.** Acquiring or merging with firms in the same or complementary industries to gain economies of scale and scope
• **Globalizing.** Increasing efforts to "think global" and "act local"
• **Flattening.** Reducing the number of organizational levels to get closer to the customer
• **Focusing.** Determining the most profitable businesses and customers and focusing on them
• **Justifying.** Becoming more accountable by measuring, analyzing, and documenting the effects of marketing actions
• **Accelerating.** Designing the organization and setting up processes to respond more quickly to changes in the environment
• **Empowering.** Encouraging and empowering personnel to produce more ideas and take more initiative
• **Broadening.** Factoring the interests of customers, employees, shareholders, and other stakeholders into the activities of the enterprise
• **Monitoring.** Tracking what is said online and elsewhere and studying customers, competitors, and others to improve business practices

Recently, marketers have had to operate in a slow-growth economic environment characterized by discriminating consumers, aggressive competition, and a turbulent marketplace. An era of conspicuous consumption has come to an end as many consumers cope with reduced incomes and less wealth.[4] A debt-laden consumer base penalizes companies still promoting a "buy now, pay later" sales philosophy, and consumers and companies alike are increasingly considering the environmental and social consequences of their actions.

As consumers become more disciplined in their spending and adopt a "less is more" attitude, it is incumbent on marketers to create and communicate the true value of their products and services.[5] Marketing can and should play a key role in improving standards of living and quality of life, especially in tough times. Marketers must continually seek to improve what they do.[6]

In today's highly competitive, ever-changing marketing environment, firms such as Blockbuster that do not adapt fast enough may encounter financial setbacks or even failure.

Companies can't win by standing still. Recent business problems and failures by firms such as Blockbuster, Barnes & Noble, and Kodak reflect an inability to adjust to a dramatically different marketing environment. Firms must invest instead in improving their offerings and finding big new ideas. Sometimes, like IBM, Microsoft, and Intel, they may have to fundamentally change their business models. Marketers must collaborate closely and early with product development and R&D, and later with the sales force, to develop and sell products and services that fully satisfy customer needs and wants. They must also work with finance, manufacturing, and logistics to establish a value-creation mind-set in the organization.

Emerging markets such as India and China offer enormous new sources of demand—but often only for certain types of products and at certain price points. Across all markets, marketing plans and programs will grow more localized and culturally sensitive, while strong brands that are well differentiated and continually improved will remain fundamental to marketing success. Businesses will continue to use social media more and traditional media less. The Web allows unprecedented depth and breadth in communications and distribution, and its transparency requires companies to be honest and authentic.

Marketers also face ethical dilemmas and perplexing trade-offs. Consumers may value convenience, but how to justify disposable products or elaborate packaging in a world trying to minimize waste? Increasing material aspirations can defy the need for sustainability. Given increasing consumer sensitivity and government regulation, smart companies are creatively designing with energy efficiency, carbon footprints, toxicity, and disposability in mind. Some are choosing local suppliers over distant ones. Auto companies and airlines must be particularly conscious of releasing CO_2 in the atmosphere.

Toyota Prius   Some auto experts scoffed when Toyota predicted sales of 300,000 cars within five years of launching its gas-and-electric Prius hybrid sedan in 2001. But by 2004, the Prius had a six-month waiting list. Toyota's winning formula consists of a powerful electric motor and the ability to quickly switch power sources—resulting in 55 miles per gallon for city and highway driving—with the roominess and power of a family sedan and an eco-friendly design and look, for a little over $20,000. The lesson? Functionally successful products that consumers see as good for the environment can offer enticing options. Toyota is now rolling out hybrids throughout its auto lineup, and U.S. automakers have followed suit.[7]

Now more than ever, marketers must think holistically and use creative win-win solutions to balance conflicting demands. They must develop fully integrated marketing programs and meaningful relationships with a range of constituents.[8] They must do all the right things inside their company and consider the broader consequences in the marketplace, topics we turn to next.

Internal Marketing

Traditionally, marketers played the role of middleman, charged with understanding customers' needs and transmitting their voice to various functional areas.[9] But in a networked enterprise, *every* functional area can interact directly with customers. Marketing no longer has sole ownership of customer interactions; rather, it now must integrate all the customer-facing processes so customers see a single face and hear a single voice when they interact with the firm.[10]

Internal marketing requires that everyone in the organization accept the concepts and goals of marketing and engage in choosing, providing, and communicating customer value. Only when *all* employees realize their job is to create, serve, and satisfy customers does the company become an effective marketer.[11] "Marketing Memo: Characteristics of Company Departments That Are Truly Customer Driven" presents a tool that evaluates which company departments are truly customer driven.

Let's look at how marketing departments are being organized, how they can work effectively with other departments, and how firms can foster a creative marketing culture across the organization.[12]

Organizing the Marketing Department

Modern marketing departments can be organized in a number of different, sometimes overlapping ways: functionally, geographically, by product or brand, by market, or in a matrix.

FUNCTIONAL ORGANIZATION   In the most common form of marketing organization, functional specialists report to a marketing vice president who coordinates their activities. △ Figure 22.1 shows five specialists. Others might include a customer service manager,

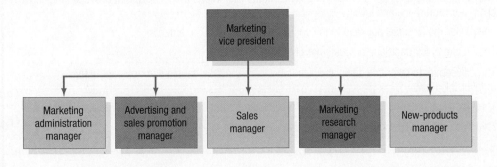

|Fig. 22.1| △

Functional
Organization

marketing
Memo

Characteristics of Company Departments That Are Truly Customer Driven

R&D	___	They spend time meeting customers and listening to their problems.
	___	They welcome the involvement of marketing, manufacturing, and other departments on each new project.
	___	They benchmark competitors' products and seek "best of class" solutions.
	___	They solicit customer reactions and suggestions as the project progresses.
	___	They continuously improve and refine the product on the basis of market feedback.
Purchasing	___	They proactively search for the best suppliers rather than choose only from those who solicit their business.
	___	They build long-term relationships with fewer but more reliable high-quality suppliers.
	___	They do not compromise quality for price savings.
Manufacturing	___	They invite customers to visit and tour their plants.
	___	They visit customer factories to see how customers use the company's products.
	___	They willingly work overtime when it is important to meet promised delivery schedules.
	___	They continuously search for ways to produce goods faster and/or at lower costs.
	___	They continuously improve product quality, aiming for zero defects.
	___	They meet customer requirements for "customization" where this can be done profitably.
Marketing	___	They study customer needs and wants in well-defined market segments.
	___	They allocate marketing effort in relationship to the long-run profit potential of the targeted segments.
	___	They develop winning offerings for each target segment.
	___	They measure company image and customer satisfaction on a continuous basis.
	___	They continuously gather and evaluate ideas for new products, product improvements, and services to meet customers' needs.
	___	They influence all company departments and employees to be customer-centered in their thinking and practice.
Sales	___	They acquire specialized knowledge of the customer's industry.
	___	They strive to give the customer "the best solution" but make only promises they can keep.
	___	They feed customers' needs and ideas back to those in charge of product development.
	___	They serve the same customers for a long period of time.
Logistics	___	They set a high standard for service delivery time and meet it consistently.
	___	They operate a knowledgeable and friendly customer service department that can answer questions, handle complaints, and resolve problems in a satisfactory and timely manner.
Accounting	___	They prepare periodic profitability reports by product, market segment, sales territory, order size, and individual customers.
	___	They prepare invoices tailored to customer needs and answer customer queries courteously and quickly.
Finance	___	They understand and support marketing investments (like image advertising) that produce long-term customer preference and loyalty.
	___	They tailor the financial package to the customers' financial requirements.
	___	They make quick decisions on customer creditworthiness.
Public Relations	___	They disseminate favorable news about the company and they handle damage control for unfavorable news.
	___	They act as an internal customer and public advocate for better company policies and practices.
Other Customer-Contact Personnel	___	They are competent, courteous, cheerful, credible, reliable, and responsive.

Some companies employ market specialists who focus on very specific regions of the country, for example, Miami-Dade County in Florida.

a marketing planning manager, a market logistics manager, a direct marketing manager, and a digital marketing manager.

The main advantage of a functional marketing organization is its administrative simplicity. It can be quite a challenge for the department to develop smooth working relationships, however. This form also can result in inadequate planning as the number of products and markets increases and each functional group vies for budget and status. The marketing vice president constantly weighs competing claims and faces a difficult coordination problem.

GEOGRAPHIC ORGANIZATION A company selling in a national market often organizes its sales force (and sometimes marketing) along geographic lines.[13] The national sales manager may supervise 4 regional sales managers, who each supervise 6 zone managers, who in turn supervise 8 district sales managers, who each supervise 10 salespeople.

Some companies are adding *area market specialists* (regional or local marketing managers) to support sales efforts in high-volume markets. One such market might be Miami-Dade County, Florida, where almost two-thirds of the households are Hispanic.[14] The Miami specialist would know Miami's customer and trade makeup, help marketing managers at headquarters adjust their marketing mix for Miami, and prepare local annual and long-range plans for selling all the company's products there. Some companies must develop different marketing programs in different parts of the country because geography alters their brand development so much.

PRODUCT- OR BRAND-MANAGEMENT ORGANIZATION Companies producing a variety of products and brands often establish a product- (or brand-) management organization. This does not replace the functional organization but serves as another layer of management. A group product manager supervises product category managers, who in turn supervise specific product and brand managers.

A product-management organization makes sense if the company's products are quite different or there are more than a functional organization can handle. This form is sometimes characterized as a **hub-and-spoke system**. The brand or product manager is figuratively at the center, with spokes leading to various departments representing working relationships (see △ Figure 22.2). The manager may:

- Develop a long-range and competitive strategy for the product.
- Prepare an annual marketing plan and sales forecast.
- Work with advertising and merchandising agencies to develop copy, programs, and campaigns.
- Increase support of the product among the sales force and distributors.
- Gather continuous intelligence about the product's performance, customer and dealer attitudes, and new problems and opportunities.
- Initiate product improvements to meet changing market needs.

The product-management organization lets the product manager concentrate on developing a cost-effective marketing program and react more quickly to new products in the

|Fig. 22.2| ◬

The Product Manager's Interactions

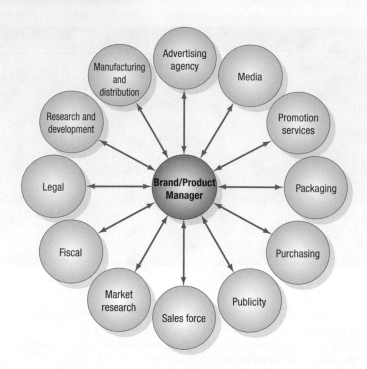

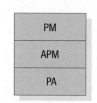

(a) Vertical Product Team

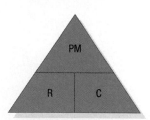

(b) Triangular Product Team

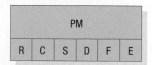

(c) Horizontal Product Team

PM = product manager
APM = associate product manager
PA = product assistant
R   = market researcher
C   = communication specialist
S   = sales manager
D   = distribution specialist
F   = finance/accounting specialist
E   = engineer

|Fig. 22.3| ◬

Three Types of Product Teams

marketplace; it also gives the company's smaller brands a product advocate. However, it has disadvantages too:

- Product and brand managers may lack authority to carry out their responsibilities.
- They become experts in their product area but rarely achieve functional expertise.
- The system often proves costly. One person is appointed to manage each major product or brand, and soon more are appointed to manage even minor products and brands.
- Brand managers normally manage a brand for only a short time. Short-term involvement leads to short-term planning and fails to build long-term strengths.
- The fragmentation of markets makes it harder to develop a national strategy. Brand managers must please regional and local sales groups, transferring power from marketing to sales.
- Product and brand managers focus the company on building market share rather than customer relationships.

A second alternative in a product-management organization is *product teams*. There are three types: vertical, triangular, and horizontal (see ◬ Figure 22.3). The triangular and horizontal product-team approaches let each major brand be run by a **brand-asset management team (BAMT)** consisting of key representatives from functions that affect the brand's performance. The company consists of several BAMTs that periodically report to a BAMT directors committee, which itself reports to a chief branding officer. This is quite different from the way brands have traditionally been handled.

A third alternative is to eliminate product manager positions for minor products and assign two or more products to each remaining manager. This is feasible where two or more products appeal to a similar set of needs. A cosmetics company doesn't need product managers for each product because cosmetics serve one major need—beauty. A toiletries company needs different managers for headache remedies, toothpaste, soap, and shampoo because these products differ in use and appeal.

In a fourth alternative, *category management*, a company focuses on product categories to manage its brands. Procter & Gamble, a pioneer of the brand-management system, and other top packaged-goods firms have made a major shift to category management, as have firms outside the grocery channel.[15] P&G cites a number of advantages. By fostering internal competition among brand managers, the traditional brand-management system created strong incentives to excel, but also internal competition for resources and a lack of coordination. The new scheme was designed to ensure adequate resources for all categories.

Another rationale is the increasing power of the retail trade, which has thought of profitability in terms of product categories. P&G felt it only made sense to deal along similar lines. Retailers and regional grocery chains such as Walmart and Dominick's embrace category management as a means to define a particular product category's strategic role within the store and address logistics, the role of private-label products, and the trade-offs between product variety and inefficient duplication.[16]

In fact, in some packaged-goods firms, category management has evolved into aisle management and encompasses multiple related categories typically found in the same sections of supermarkets and grocery stores. General Mills' Yoplait Yogurt has served as category advisor to the dairy aisle for 24 major retailers, boosting the yogurt base footprint four to eight feet at a time and increasing sales of yogurt by 9 percent and category sales in dairy by 13 percent nationwide.[17]

Marketers of General Mills' Yoplait Yogurt used category management to help major retailers gain more profit by reorganizing their yogurt shelves.

MARKET-MANAGEMENT ORGANIZATION Canon sells fax machines to consumer, business, and government markets. Nippon Steel sells to the railroad, construction, and public utility industries. When customers fall into different user groups with distinct buying preferences and practices, a **market-management organization** is desirable. Market managers supervise several market-development managers, market specialists, or industry specialists and draw on functional services as needed. Market managers of important markets might even have functional specialists reporting to them.

Market managers are staff (not line) people, with duties like those of product managers. They develop long-range and annual plans for their markets and are judged by their market's growth and profitability. Because this system organizes marketing activity to meet the needs of distinct customer groups, it shares many advantages and disadvantages of product-management systems. Many companies are reorganizing along market lines and becoming **market-centered organizations**. Xerox converted from geographic selling to selling by industry, as did IBM and Hewlett-Packard.

When a close relationship is advantageous, such as when customers have diverse and complex requirements and buy an integrated bundle of products and services, a **customer-management organization**, which deals with individual customers rather than the mass market or even market segments, should prevail.[18] One study showed that companies organized by customer groups reported much higher accountability for the overall quality of relationships and employees' freedom to take actions to satisfy individual customers.[19]

MATRIX-MANAGEMENT ORGANIZATION Companies that produce many products for many markets may adopt a matrix organization employing both product and market managers. The rub is that it's costly and often creates conflicts. There's the cost of supporting all the managers, and questions about where authority and responsibility for marketing activities should reside—at headquarters or in the division?[20] Some corporate marketing groups assist top management with overall opportunity evaluation, provide divisions with consulting assistance on request, help divisions that have little or no marketing, and promote the marketing concept throughout the company.

Relationships with Other Departments

Under the marketing concept, all departments need to "think customer" and work together to satisfy customer needs and expectations. Yet departments define company problems and goals from their viewpoint, so conflicts of interest and communications problems are unavoidable. The marketing vice president, or the CMO, must usually work through persuasion rather than through authority to (1) coordinate the company's internal marketing activities and (2) coordinate marketing with finance, operations, and other company functions to serve the customer.[21] To help marketing and other functions jointly determine what is in the company's best interests, firms can provide joint seminars, joint committees and liaison employees, employee exchange programs, and analytical methods to determine the most profitable course of action.[22]

Many companies now focus on key processes rather than departments, because departmental organization can be a barrier to smooth performance. They appoint process leaders, who manage cross-disciplinary teams that include marketing and sales people. Marketers thus may have a solid-line responsibility to their teams and a dotted-line responsibility to the marketing department.

Building a Creative Marketing Organization

Many companies realize they're not yet really market and customer driven—they are product and sales driven. Transforming into a true market-driven company requires:

1.   Developing a company-wide passion for customers
2.   Organizing around customer segments instead of products
3.   Understanding customers through qualitative and quantitative research

The task is not easy, but the payoffs can be considerable. It won't happen as a result of the CEO making speeches and urging every employee to "think customer." See "Marketing Insight: The Marketing CEO" for concrete actions a CEO can take to improve marketing capabilities.

Although it's *necessary* to be customer oriented, it's not *enough*. The organization must also be creative.[23] Companies today copy each others' advantages and strategies with increasing speed, making differentiation harder to achieve and lowering margins as firms become more alike. The only answer is to build a capability in strategic innovation and imagination. This capability comes from assembling tools, processes, skills, and measures that let the firm generate more and better new ideas than its competitors.[24]

Companies must watch trends and be ready to capitalize on them. Motorola was 18 months late in moving from analog to digital cellular phones, giving Nokia and Ericsson a big lead. Nestlé was

Marketing Insight

The Marketing CEO

What steps can a CEO take to create a market- and customer-focused company?

1.   ***Convince senior management of the need to become customer focused.*** The CEO personally exemplifies strong customer commitment and rewards those in the organization who do likewise. Former CEOs Jack Welch of GE and Lou Gerstner of IBM were said to have each spent 100 days a year visiting customers in spite of their many strategic, financial, and administrative burdens.

2.   ***Appoint a senior marketing officer and marketing task force.*** The marketing task force should include the CEO, the vice presidents of sales, R&D, purchasing, manufacturing, finance, and human resources, and other key individuals.

3.   ***Get outside help and guidance.*** Consulting firms have considerable experience helping companies adopt a marketing orientation.

4.   ***Change the company's reward measurement and system.*** As long as purchasing and manufacturing are rewarded for keeping costs low, they will resist accepting some costs required to serve customers better. As long as finance focuses on short-term profit, it will oppose major investments designed to build satisfied, loyal customers.

5.   ***Hire strong marketing talent.*** The company needs a strong marketing vice president who not only manages the marketing

department but also gains respect from and influence with the other vice presidents. A multidivisional company will benefit from establishing a strong corporate marketing department.

6.   ***Develop strong in-house marketing training programs.*** The company should design well-crafted marketing training programs for corporate management, divisional general managers, marketing and sales personnel, manufacturing personnel, R&D personnel, and others. GE, Motorola, and Accenture run such programs.

7.   ***Install a modern marketing planning system.*** The planning format will require managers to think about the marketing environment, opportunities, competitive trends, and other forces. These managers then prepare strategies and sales-and-profit forecasts for specific products and segments and are accountable for performance.

8.   ***Establish an annual marketing excellence recognition program.*** Business units that believe they've developed exemplary marketing plans should submit a description of their plans and results. Winning teams should be rewarded at a special ceremony and the plans disseminated to the other business units as "models of marketing thinking." Becton, Dickinson and Company; Procter & Gamble; and SABMiller follow this strategy.

9.   ***Shift from a department focus to a process-outcome focus.*** After defining the fundamental business processes that determine its success, the company should appoint process leaders and cross-disciplinary teams to reengineer and implement these processes.

10. ***Empower the employees.*** Progressive companies encourage and reward their employees for coming up with new ideas and empower them to settle customer complaints to save the customer's business. IBM lets frontline employees spend up to $5,000 to solve a customer problem on the spot.

late seeing the trend toward coffeehouses such as Starbucks. Coca-Cola was slow to pick up beverage trends toward fruit-flavored drinks such as Snapple, energy drinks such as Gatorade, and designer water brands. Market leaders can miss trends when they are risk averse, obsessed about protecting their existing markets and physical resources, and more interested in efficiency than innovation.[25]

Socially Responsible Marketing

Effective internal marketing must be matched by a strong sense of ethics, values, and social responsibility.[26] A number of forces are driving companies to practice a higher level of corporate social responsibility, such as rising customer expectations, evolving employee goals and ambitions, tighter government legislation and pressure, investor interest in social criteria, media scrutiny, and changing business procurement practices.[27]

Virtually all firms have decided to take a more active, strategic role in corporate social responsibility, carefully scrutinizing what they believe in and how they should treat their customers, employees, competitors, community, and the environment. Taking this broader stakeholder view is believed to also benefit another important constituency—shareholders. Look at how Walmart is addressing corporate social responsibility.[28]

Walmart In 2005, Walmart ex-CEO Lee Scott said, "We thought we could sit in Bentonville [Arkansas], take care of customers, take care of associates—and the world would leave us alone. It doesn't work that way anymore." Determined to become more environmentally friendly, Scott vowed that the company would invest $500 million in sustainability projects, such as doubling the efficiency of its vehicle fleet over the next ten years, eliminating 30 percent of the energy used in stores, and reducing solid waste from U.S. stores by 25 percent in three years. Little decisions can make big differences for the retail giant. By eliminating excess packaging on its Kid Connection private-label toys, the company saved 3,800 trees and 1 million barrels of oil, along with an estimated $2.4 million a year in shipping costs. It redirected more than 57 percent of the waste generated by stores and Sam's Club facilities to recycling centers instead of landfills, and it enlisted long-time environmentalist and Patagonia founder Yvon Chouinard to provide insight and advice. Major environmental groups have been pleased, but Walmart still faces criticism from union leaders and liberal activists about its wage rates, employee health care, gender discrimination, and treatment of local competition. The company has responded by citing progress in each area, such as the fact that it created approximately 63,000 jobs around the world in 2008, including more than 33,000 in the United States.

Businesses have not always believed in the value of social responsibility. In 1776, Adam Smith proclaimed, "I have never known much good done by those who profess to trade for the public good." Legendary economist Milton Friedman famously declared social initiatives "fundamentally subversive" because he felt they undermined the profit-seeking purpose of public companies and wasted shareholders' money. Some critics worry that important business investment in areas such as R&D could suffer as a result of a focus on social responsibility.[29]

But these critics are in a tiny minority. Many now believe that satisfying customers, employees, and other stakeholders and achieving business success are closely tied to the adoption and implementation of high standards of business and marketing conduct. A further benefit of being seen as socially responsible is the ability to attract employees, especially younger people who want to work for companies they feel good about.

The most admired—and most successful—companies in the world abide by a code of serving people's interests, not only their own. Procter & Gamble's new CEO Bob McDonald has made "brand purpose" a key component of the company's marketing strategies, noting: "Consumers have a higher expectation of brands and want to know what they are doing for the world. But it has to be authentic with a genuine desire to do it." Downy fabric softener's "Touch of Comfort" cause program, for example, donates 5 cents from purchases to Quilts for Kids, an organization that works with volunteer quilters to make and distribute custom-sewn quilts to children in hospitals.[30] P&G is not alone, as the following demonstrates.

Downy fabric softener's "Touch of Comfort" cause marketing program donated thousand of blankets to hospitalized children.

Firms of Endearment

Firms of Endearment

Researchers Raj Sisodia, David Wolfe, and Jag Sheth believe humanistic companies make great companies. They see "Firms of Endearment" as those with a culture of caring that serve the interests of their stakeholders, defined by the acronym SPICE: Society, Partners, Investors, Customers, and Employees. Sisodia et al. believe Firms of Endearment create a love affair with stakeholders. Their senior managers run an open-door policy, are passionate about customers, and earn modest compensation. They pay more to their employees, relate more closely to a smaller group of excellent suppliers, and give back to the communities in which they work. The researchers assert that Firms of Endearment actually spend less on marketing as a percentage of sales yet earn greater profits, because customers who love the company do most of the marketing. The authors see the 21st-century marketing paradigm as creating value for all stakeholders and becoming a beloved firm. Table 22.2 lists firms receiving top marks as Firms of Endearment from a sample of thousands of customers, employees, and suppliers.[31]

Corporate Social Responsibility

Raising the level of socially responsible marketing calls for making a three-pronged attack that relies on proper legal, ethical, and social responsibility behavior. One company that puts social responsible marketing squarely at the center of all it does is Stonyfield Farm.[32]

Stonyfield Farm

Stonyfield Farm

As Chapter 1 described, social responsibility is at the foundation of Stonyfield Farm. The company was cofounded in 1983 by long-time "CE-Yo" Gary Hirshberg on the belief that there was a business opportunity in selling organic dairy products while "restoring the environment." The global market leader in organic yogurt, Stonyfield works

TABLE 22.2	Top Firms of Endearment		
Best Buy	BMW	CarMax	Caterpillar
Commerce Bank	Container Store	Costco	eBay
Google	Harley-Davidson	Honda	IDEO
IKEA	JetBlue	Johnson & Johnson	Jordan's Furniture
L.L.Bean	New Balance	Patagonia	Progressive Insurance
REI	Southwest	Starbucks	Timberland
Toyota	Trader Joe's	UPS	Wegmans
Whole Foods			

Source: Raj Sisodia, David B. Wolfe, and Jag Sheth, *Firms of Endearment: How World-Class Companies Profit from Passion and Purpose* (Upper Saddle River, NJ: Wharton School Publishing, 2007), p. 16, © 2007. Printed and electronically reproduced by permission of Pearson Education, Inc., Upper Saddle River, New Jersey.

with socially responsible suppliers, adopts environmentally friendly manufacturing practices, and uses packaging to promote its views on environmental and health issues. Stonyfield donates 10 percent of profits "to efforts that help protect and restore the Earth" and has launched a nonprofit foundation called "Climate Counts." Progressive business practices have not hurt its financial performance. Stonyfield is the number three yogurt brand in the United States, and it now also sells smoothies, milk, frozen yogurt, and ice cream.

LEGAL BEHAVIOR Organizations must ensure every employee knows and observes relevant laws.[33] For example, it's illegal for salespeople to lie to consumers or mislead them about the advantages of buying a product. Salespeople may not offer bribes to purchasing agents or others influencing a B2B sale. Their statements must match advertising claims, and they may not obtain or use competitors' technical or trade secrets through bribery or industrial espionage. Finally, they must not disparage competitors or their products by suggesting things that are not true. Managers must make sure every sales representative knows the law and acts accordingly.

ETHICAL BEHAVIOR Business practices come under attack because business situations routinely pose ethical dilemmas: It's not easy to draw a clear line between normal marketing practice and unethical behavior. Some issues sharply divide critics. Though Kraft chose to stop advertising some of its less healthy products such as Oreos and Chips Ahoy! on television programs targeted to children ages 6 to 11, some watch groups felt that was not enough.[34]

Of course certain business practices are clearly unethical or illegal. These include bribery, theft of trade secrets, false and deceptive advertising, exclusive dealing and tying agreements, quality or safety defects, false warranties, inaccurate labeling, price-fixing or undue discrimination, and barriers to entry and predatory competition.

Companies must adopt and disseminate a written code of ethics, build a company tradition of ethical behavior, and hold their people fully responsible for observing ethical and legal guidelines.[35] In the past, a disgruntled customer might bad-mouth an unethical or poorly performing firm to 12 other people; today, via the Internet, he or she can reach thousands. Microsoft, for example, has attracted scores of anti-Microsoft sites, including www.msboycott.com and www.ihatemicrosoft.com. The general distrust of companies among U.S. consumers is evident in research showing the percentage who view corporations unfavorably has reached 26 percent.[36]

SOCIAL RESPONSIBILITY BEHAVIOR Individual marketers must exercise their social conscience in specific dealings with customers and stakeholders. Some top-rated companies for corporate social responsibility are Microsoft, Johnson & Johnson, 3M, Google, Coca-Cola, General Mills, UPS, Sony, and Procter & Gamble.[37]

Increasingly, people want information about a company's record on social and environmental responsibility to help them decide which companies to buy from, invest in, and work for.[38] H. J. Heinz received awards for its 108-page 2009 Corporate Social Responsibility report, which reflects the company's commitment to "achieving sustainable growth that benefits our shareholders, consumers, customers, employees and communities, guided by the principles of integrity, transparency and social responsibility." Table 22.3 contains the opening words of that report.

Communicating corporate social responsibility can be a challenge. Once a firm touts an environmental initiative, it can become a target for criticism. Many well-intentioned product or marketing initiatives can have unforeseen or unavoidable negative consequences.[39]

Nestlé Palm oil was hailed as a renewable fuel for food companies looking to find a solution to a trans-fat ban, until its use was linked to the destruction of tropical rain forests and the extinction of the orangutan and the sun bear. When Greenpeace released a report criticizing Nestlé for purchasing palm oil for its KitKat candy bars from an Indonesian firm linked to rain forest destruction there, a social media war ensued. Protestors posted a negative video on YouTube, bombarded Twitter and Nestlé's Facebook page, and took to the

TABLE 22.3 Excerpt from the H. J. Heinz 2009 Corporate Social Responsibility Report

Message from Chairman, President and CEO

Making a Difference for People and the Planet

The H. J. Heinz Company has been a good corporate citizen for 140 years. Throughout the Company's history, it has made a positive social and economic impact in the community and pursuing sustainable business practices. . . .

In Fiscal Years 2008 and 2009, Heinz delivered record sales, higher earnings per share and dividend growth for our shareholders while staying true to the principles that have guided our Company since 1869—Quality, Integrity, Innovation and Food Safety.

At the same time, we expanded our strong commitment to environmental responsibility by launching a global initiative across six continents that aims to achieve a 20% reduction in our greenhouse gas emissions, water and energy consumption, and solid waste by 2015.

Our Company has been working to achieve transparency and sustainability ever since Henry John Heinz started selling horseradish, his first product, in clear glass bottles so consumers could see its wholesome purity. . . .

Heinz has a strong and independent Board of Directors and a Global Code of Conduct, Global Operating Principles and Supplier Guiding Principles that set high ethical standards for our employees and suppliers.

Most importantly, Heinz is a global company that values people, their dignity and their rights, in the workplace and in the community. We empower our diverse workforce of approximately 33,000 men and women to make a sustainable difference on the job and in their communities and we foster a workplace culture where competitive wages, safety, fairness and respect are the pillars of our success.

Finally, as one of the world's premier food companies, Heinz is dedicated to enhancing the health and wellness of men, women and children around the world. . . .

The Heinz Micronutrient Campaign is combating the global problem of iron-deficiency anemia and malnutrition among infants and children. The campaign has provided nutritional supplements to almost three million children in 15 developing nations and it is expanding to other countries to help many more children in the years to come.

Our Company has invested millions in the Heinz Micronutrient Campaign to ensure a sustainable future for people and our planet.

I invite you to learn more about Heinz, our performance and our progress by visiting the Social, Environment and Economic sections of this interactive Web-based report, where you will find comprehensive facts and data, videos and photos, and links to other informative Heinz documents.

Thank you for your interest in Heinz.

Sincerely,

William R. Johnson
Chairman, President and Chief Executive Officer

Source: Excerpt from the H. J. Heinz 2009 Corporate Social Responsibility Report.

In Indonesia, Greenpeace activists' dramatic protests drew attention to the environmental effects of Nestlé's manufacturing of products such as KitKat candy bars.

streets outside Nestlé's Jakarta offices. Nestlé cut ties with the firm and took other steps to address the controversy but continued to receive criticism.

Often, the more committed a company is to sustainability and environmental protection, the more dilemmas that can arise. Vermont-based Green Mountain Coffee Roasters prides itself on sustainability efforts that have, in part, helped the firm become one of the fastest-selling coffee brands around. Then its 2006 purchase of Kuerig and its popular single-cup brewing system posed a quandary: The K-Cups used with the Kuerig brewing system were made of totally nonrecyclable plastic and foil. Given its environmental heritage and beliefs, Green Mountain Coffee saw only one course of action, and it has been engaged in extensive R&D to find a more environmentally sound solution.[40]

Corporate philanthropy also can pose dilemmas. Merck, DuPont, Walmart, and Bank of America have each donated $100 million or more to charities in a year. Yet good deeds can be overlooked—even resented—if the company is seen as exploitive or fails to live up to a "good guys" image. Philip Morris Company's $250 million ad campaign touting its charitable activities was met with skepticism because of its negative image as a tobacco company. Some critics worry that cause marketing or "consumption philanthropy" may replace virtuous actions with less-thoughtful buying, reduce emphasis on real solutions, or deflect attention from the fact that markets may create many social problems to begin with.[41]

SUSTAINABILITY *Sustainability*—the ability to meet humanity's needs without harming future generations—now tops many corporate agendas. Major corporations outline in great detail how they are trying to improve the long-term impact of their actions on communities and the environment. As one sustainability consultant put it, "There is a triple bottom line—people, planet, and profit—and the people part of the equation must come first. Sustainability means more than being eco-friendly, it also means you are in it for the long haul."[42]

Sustainability ratings exist, but there is no consistent agreement about what metrics are appropriate.[43] One comprehensive study used 11 factors to evaluate and assemble a list of the Top 100 Sustainable Corporations in the World: energy, water, CO_2, and waste productivity; leadership diversity; CEO-to-average-worker pay; taxes paid; sustainability leadership; sustainability pay link; innovation capacity; and transparency. The top 5 firms were GE, PG&E, TNT, H&M, and Nokia.[44]

Some feel companies that score well on sustainability typically exhibit high-quality management in that "they tend to be more strategically nimble and better equipped to compete in the complex, high-velocity, global environment."[45] Consumer interest is also creating market opportunities. Clorox's line of naturally derived Green Works laundry and home cleaners—aided by restrained price premiums and a Sierra Club endorsement—has experienced early success.[46] Another good example is organic products (see "Marketing Insight: The Rise of Organic").

Heightened interest in sustainability has also unfortunately resulted in *greenwashing,* which gives products the appearance of being environmentally friendly without living up to that promise. One study revealed that half the labels on allegedly green products focus on an eco-friendly benefit (such as recycled content) while omitting information about significant environmental drawbacks (such as manufacturing intensity or transportation costs).[47]

Because of insincere firms jumping on the green bandwagon, consumers bring a healthy skepticism to environmental claims, but they are also unwilling to sacrifice product performance and quality.[48] Many firms are rising to the challenge and are using the need for sustainability to fuel

Marketing Insight

The Rise of Organic

Organic products have become a strong presence in many food and beverage categories. Caster & Pollux's success with organic and natural pet foods led to its distribution in major specialty retail chains such as Petco. All-organic Honest Tea grew 50 percent a year after its founding in 1998; the firm sold 40 percent of the business to Coca-Cola in 2008.

Organic and natural are at the core of some brands' positioning. Chipotle Mexican Grill's mission statement, "Food with Integrity," reflects its focus on good food with a socially responsible message. One

of the first fast-casual restaurant chains, Chipotle uses natural and organic ingredients and serves more naturally raised meat than any other restaurant. Making each burrito by hand takes time, but the quality of the food and the message behind it are a satisfying payoff for many customers.

Many companies beyond the food industry are embracing organic offerings that avoid chemicals and pesticides to stress ecological preservation. Apparel and other nonfood items make up the second-fastest growth category of the $3.5 billion organic product industry. Organic nonfood grew 9.1 percent in 2009 to $1.8 billion—now 7 percent of the $26.6 billion organic products industry. Organic cotton grown by farmers who fight boll weevils with ladybugs, weed crops by hand, and use manure for fertilizer has become a hot product at retail.

Sources: "Industry Statistics and Projected Growth," Organic Trade Association, June 2010; Jessica Shambora, "The Honest Tea Guys Look Back," *Fortune,* July 26, 2010; Arianne Cohen, "Ode to a Burrito," *Fast Company,* April 2008, pp. 54–56; Kenneth Hein, "The World on a Platter," *Brandweek,* April 23, 2007, pp. 27–28; Megan Johnston, "Hard Sell for a Soft Fabric," *Forbes,* October 30, 2006, pp. 73–80.

innovation. Sales of products emphasizing sustainability remained strong through the recent economic recession.[49]

Socially Responsible Business Models

The future holds a wealth of opportunities, yet forces in the socioeconomic, cultural, and natural environments will impose new limits on marketing and business practices. Companies that innovate solutions and values in a socially responsible way are most likely to succeed.[50]

Companies such as The Body Shop, Working Assets, and Smith & Hawken are giving social responsibility a more prominent role. Late actor Paul Newman's homemade salad dressing has grown to a huge business. Newman's Own brand also includes pasta sauce, salsa, popcorn, and lemonade sold in 15 countries. The company has given away all its profits and royalties after tax—almost $300 million so far—to educational and charitable programs such as the Hole in the Wall Gang camps Newman created for children with serious illnesses.[51]

Corporate philanthropy as a whole is on the rise: After years of steady growth, with $14.1 billion in cash and in-kind support given in 2009, it held fairly steady even during a recession.[52] In addition to these contributions, more firms are coming to believe corporate social responsibility in the form of cause marketing and employee volunteerism programs are not just the "right thing" but also the "smart thing to do."[53]

Cause-Related Marketing

Many firms blend corporate social responsibility initiatives with marketing activities.[54] **Cause-related marketing** links the firm's contributions to a designated cause to customers' engaging directly or indirectly in revenue-producing transactions with the firm.[55] Cause marketing is part of *corporate societal marketing (CSM)*, which Minette Drumwright and Patrick Murphy define as marketing efforts "that have at least one noneconomic objective related to social welfare and use the resources of the company and/or its partners."[56] Drumwright and Murphy also include traditional and strategic philanthropy and volunteerism in CSM.

Table 22.4 summarizes three award-winning and highly successful cause marketing programs. We next review pros and cons of such programs and some important guidelines.

TABLE 22.4   Three Classic Cause Marketing Programs

Tesco

Tesco, a leading UK retailer, has created a "Tesco for Schools and Clubs" program that dovetails well with its overall corporate brand positioning of "Every Little Bit Helps." Customers receive one voucher for every £10 spent, which they can donate to a school of their choice or any registered amateur club for children under 18. In 2009, the company gave away 540,000 items worth £13.4 million. It also offers vouchers for recycled inkjet cartridges and donated working phones.

Dawn

Procter & Gamble's Dawn, the top dishwashing liquid in the United States, has long highlighted its unusual side benefit—it can clean birds caught in oil spills. A report by the U.S. Fish and Wildlife Service called Dawn "the only bird-cleaning agent that is recommended because it removes oil from feathers; is non-toxic; and does not leave a residue." A Web site launched in 2006, www.DawnSavesWildlife.com, drew 130,000 people who formed virtual groups to encourage friends and others to stop gas and oil leaks from their cars. After the catastrophic BP oil spill in 2010, P&G donated thousands of bottles as well as placing a code on bottles and donating $1 to Gulf wildlife causes for each code customers activated, eventually totaling $500,000. The brand also drew massive publicity and visits to its Facebook site, which outlined the environmental cleanup and relief effort.

British Airways

British Airways developed a cause-marketing campaign called "Change for Good" to encourage its passengers to help by donating the foreign currency left over from their travels to UNICEF. The airline advertised its program during an in-flight video, on the backs of seat cards, and with in-flight announcements. It also developed a television ad that featured a child thanking British Airways for its contribution to UNICEF. Because Change for Good directly targeted passengers, it did not require extensive advertising or promotion and was highly cost-efficient. It produced immediate results, and over a 15-year period from 1994 to 2009, it distributed almost $45 million around the world.

Sources: www.tescoforschoolsandclubs.co.uk; www.dawnsaveswildlife.com; www.britishairways.com; Jack Neff and Stephanie Thompson, "Eco-Marketing Has Staying Power This Time Around," *Advertising Age*, April 30, 2007, p. 55.

CAUSE-MARKETING BENEFITS AND COSTS A successful cause-marketing program can improve social welfare, create differentiated brand positioning, build strong consumer bonds, enhance the company's public image, create a reservoir of goodwill, boost internal morale and galvanize employees, drive sales, and increase the firm's market value.[57] Consumers may develop a strong, unique bond with the firm that transcends normal marketplace transactions.

Specifically, from a branding point of view, cause marketing can (1) build brand awareness, (2) enhance brand image, (3) establish brand credibility, (4) evoke brand feelings, (5) create a sense of brand community, and (6) elicit brand engagement.[58] It has a particularly interested audience in civic-minded 18- to 24-year-old Millennial consumers (see ▢ Table 22.5).

Cause-related marketing could backfire, however, if consumers question the link between the product and the cause or see the firm as self-serving and exploitive.[59] Problems can also arise if consumers do not think a company is consistent and sufficiently responsible in all its behavior, as happened to KFC.[60]

The double meaning in British Airways "Change for Good" cause marketing program cleverly highlighted how the program worked and the benefits it created.

KFC KFC's "Buckets for the Cure" program was to donate 50 cents for every $5 "pink" bucket of fried chicken purchased over a one-month period to the famed Susan G. Komen for the Cure Foundation. It was slotted to be the single biggest corporate donation ever to fund breast cancer research—over $8.5 million. One problem: At virtually the same time, KFC also launched its Double Down sandwich with two pieces of fried chicken, bacon, and cheese. Critics immediately pointed out that KFC was selling a food item with excessively high calories, fat, and sodium that contributed to obesity, a significant risk factor for breast cancer. On the Susan G. Komen site itself, being overweight was flagged for increasing the risk of breast cancer by 30 percent to 60 percent in postmenopausal women, also leaving the foundation open to criticism over the partnership. ▢

To avoid backlash, some firms take a soft-sell approach to their cause efforts. Nike's alliance with the Lance Armstrong Foundation for cancer research sold over 80 million yellow LIVESTRONG bracelets for $1 from 2004 to 2010, but intentionally the famed Nike swoosh was nowhere to be seen.[61] One interesting recent cause program is the PRODUCT(RED) campaign.[62]

TABLE 22.5 ▢	Millennial Data Points: 18- to 24-Year-Olds' Attitudes about Causes
85% are likely to switch from one brand to another brand that is about the same in price and quality, if the other brand is associated with a good cause.	
86% consider a company's social or environmental commitments when deciding which products and services to recommend to others.	
84% consider a company's social or environmental commitments when deciding what to buy or where to shop.	
87% consider a company's social or environmental commitments when deciding where to work.	
86% say when a product or company supports a cause (a social or environmental issue) they care about, they have a more positive image of that product or company.	

Source: 2010 Cone Cause Evolution Study; for additional content, see www.coneinc.com/2010-cone-cause-evolution-study.

Nike deliberately downplays its role in cause marketing programs, such as Lance Armstrong Foundation's LIVESTRONG bracelets.

PRODUCT(RED) The highly publicized launch of PRODUCT (RED) in 2006, championed by U2 singer and activist Bono and Bobby Shriver, chairman of DATA, raised awareness and money for The Global Fund by teaming with some of the world's most iconic branded products—American Express cards, Motorola phones, Converse sneakers, Gap T-shirts, Apple iPods, and Emporio Armani sunglasses—to produce (RED)-branded products. Up to 50 percent of the profits from sales of these products go to The Global Fund to help women and children affected by HIV/AIDS in Africa. Each company that becomes PRODUCT(RED) places its logo in the "embrace" signified by the parentheses and is "elevated to the power of red." Although some critics felt the PRODUCT(RED) project was overmarketed, in its first 18 months its contribution to The Global Fund surpassed $36 million, more than seven times what businesses had contributed since the fund's founding in 2002. Many well-known brands have joined the cause since then, such as Dell computers, Hallmark cards, and Starbucks coffee. ▬

The knowledge, skills, and resources of a top firm may be even more important to a nonprofit or community group than funding. Nonprofits must be clear about what their goals are, communicate clearly what they hope to accomplish, and devise an organizational structure to work with different firms. Developing a long-term relationship with a firm can take time. As one consultant noted, "What's often a problem between corporations and nonprofits is different expectations and different understanding about the amount of time everything will take."[63]

Firms must make a number of decisions in designing and implementing a cause-marketing program, such as how many and which cause(s) to choose and how to brand the cause program.

DESIGNING A CAUSE PROGRAM Some experts believe the positive impact of cause-related marketing is reduced by sporadic involvement with numerous causes. Cathy Chizauskas, Gillette's director of civic affairs, states: "When you're spreading out your giving in fifty-dollar to one-thousand-dollar increments, no one knows what you are doing. . . . It doesn't make much of a splash."[64]

Many companies focus on one or a few main causes to simplify execution and maximize impact. McDonald's Ronald McDonald Houses in 30-plus countries offer more than 7,200 rooms each night to families needing support while their child is in the hospital, saving them a total of $257 million annually in hotel costs. The program has provided a "home away from home" for nearly 10 million family members since 1974.[65]

Limiting support to a single cause, however, may limit the pool of consumers or other stakeholders who can transfer positive feelings from the cause to the firm. Many popular causes also already have numerous corporate sponsors. Over 300 companies, including Avon, Ford, Estée Lauder, Revlon, Lee Jeans, Polo Ralph Lauren, Yoplait, Saks, BMW, and American Express, have associated themselves with breast cancer as a cause.[66] Thus a brand may find itself overlooked in a sea of symbolic pink ribbons.

Opportunities may be greater with "orphan causes"— diseases that afflict fewer than 200,000 people.[67] Another option is overlooked diseases; pancreatic cancer is the fourth-deadliest form of cancer behind skin, lung, and breast yet has received little or no corporate support. Even major killers such as prostate cancer for men and heart disease for women have been relatively neglected compared to breast cancer, but some firms have begun to fill the void. Gillette and Grolsch beer have joined longtime supporters Safeway and Major League Baseball in the fight against prostate cancer. The American Heart Association launched a "Go Red for Women" program with a red dress symbol to heighten awareness and attract interest from corporations and others to a disease that kills roughly 12 times more women than breast cancer each year.[68]

Most firms choose causes that fit their corporate or brand image and matter to their employees and shareholders. LensCrafters' Give the Gift of Sight program—now rebranded as OneSight after the company was purchased by the Italian firm Luxottica—is a family of charitable vision-care programs providing free vision screenings, eye exams, and glasses to more than 6 million needy people

Making a Difference: Top 10 Tips for Cause Branding

Cone, a Boston-based strategic communications agency specializing in cause branding and corporate responsibility, offers these tips for developing authentic and substantive programs:

1. *Select a focus area that aligns with your mission, goals and organization.*

2. *Evaluate your institutional "will" and resources.* If you, your employees and other allies don't believe or invest in your organization's cause, neither will your audience.

3. *Analyze your competitors' cause positioning.* There are few remaining wide, open spaces, but this may help you locate a legitimate societal need or an untapped element within a more crowded space that you can own.

4. *Choose your partners carefully.* Look for alignment in values, mission and will. Carefully outline roles and responsibilities. Set your sights on a multi-year sustainable relationship, with annual measurement of accomplishments for both partners.

5. *Don't underestimate the name of your program—it's key to the identity of your campaign.* Develop a few words that say exactly what you do and create a visual identity that is simple, yet memorable. The Avon Breast Cancer Crusade, American Heart Association's Go Red for Women and Target Take Charge of Education are good examples.

6. *To create a sustainable and effective program, start by developing a cross-functional strategy team.* Include representatives from the office of the CEO, public affairs, human resources, marketing, public and community relations, research/measurement, volunteer and program management, among others. If you're in silos, you will spend too much valuable time building bridges to other departments to get the real work done.

7. *Leverage both your assets and those of your partner(s) to bring the program to life.* Assets may include volunteers, cash and in-kind donations, special events, in store presence, partner resources and marketing/advertising support. And remember, emotion is one of your greatest assets. It can help you to connect with your audience and differentiate your organization in a crowded marketplace.

8. *Communicate through every possible channel.* Craft compelling words *and* visuals because stirring images can penetrate the heart. Then, take your messages beyond traditional media outlets and become multi-dimensional! Think special events, Web sites, workshops, PSAs, expert spokespersons and even celebrity endorsements.

9. *Go local.* National programs reach the "grass tops," but true transformation begins at the grassroots. Engage citizens/volunteers through hands-on activities at local events, cause promotions and fundraisers.

10. *Innovate.* True cause leaders constantly evolve their programs to add energy, new engagement opportunities and content to remain relevant and to build sustainability.

Sources: Cone, "Top 10 Tips for Cause Branding," www.coneinc.com/10-tips-cause-branding; See also, Carol L. Cone, Mark A. Feldman, and Alison T. DaSilva, "Cause and Effects," *Harvard Business Review* (July 2003): 95–101.

in North America and developing countries around the world. All stores are empowered to deliver free glasses in their communities, and two traveling Vision Vans target children in North America and make monthly two-week optical missions overseas. Luxottica pays most of the overhead, so 92 percent of all donations go directly to fund programming.[69]

Another good cause fit is Barnum's Animal Crackers, which launched a campaign to raise awareness of endangered species and help protect the Asian tiger. "Marketing Memo: Making a Difference" provides some tips from a top cause-marketing firm. Here is an example of a new firm using cause marketing to successfully build a new business.[70]

TOMS Shoes Although Blake Mycoskie did not win the around-the-world reality show *Amazing Race* as a contestant, his return trip to Argentina in 2006 sparked a desire to start a business to help the scores of kids he saw who suffered for one simple reason—they lacked shoes. Shoeless children incur a health risk but are also disadvantaged in that they often are not permitted to go to school. Thus was born TOMS shoes, its name chosen to convey "a better tomorrow," with a pledge to donate a pair of shoes to needy children for each pair of shoes sold. Picked up by stores like Whole Foods, Nordstrom, and Neiman Marcus and also sold online, TOMS shoes are based on the classic *alpargata* footwear of Argentina. As a result of the company's One for One program, the lightweight shoes can also be found on the feet of more than 1 million kids in developing countries such as Argentina and Ethiopia. Using money that would have been used to fund promotional efforts to instead pay for donated shoes has been good marketing too: The firm has garnered heaps of

These two Argentinean children are wearing shoes donated by TOMS as the result of customer purchases of two pairs of its classic *alpargata* footwear.

publicity—AT&T even featured Mycoskie in a commercial—and sales revenue for the first five years of the firm's existence has been estimated at $50 million.

Social Marketing

Cause-related marketing supports a cause. **Social marketing** by nonprofit or government organizations *furthers* a cause, such as "say no to drugs" or "exercise more and eat better."[71]

Social marketing goes back many years. In the 1950s, India started family planning campaigns. In the 1970s, Sweden introduced social marketing campaigns to turn itself into a nation of nonsmokers and nondrinkers, the Australian government ran "Wear Your Seat Belt" campaigns, and the Canadian government launched campaigns to "Say No to Drugs," "Stop Smoking," and "Exercise for Health." In the 1980s, the World Bank, World Health Organization, and Centers for Disease Control and Prevention started to use the term *social marketing* and promote interest in it. Some notable global social marketing successes are:

- Oral rehydration therapy in Honduras significantly decreased deaths from diarrhea in children under five.
- Social marketers created booths in marketplaces where Ugandan midwives sold contraceptives at affordable prices.
- Population Communication Services created and promoted two extremely popular songs in Latin America, "Stop" and "When We Are Together," to help young women "say no."
- The National Heart, Lung, and Blood Institute successfully raised awareness about cholesterol and high blood pressure, which helped significantly reduce deaths.

Different types of organizations conduct social marketing in the United States. Government agencies include the Centers for Disease Control and Prevention, Departments of Health, Social, and Human Services, Department of Transportation, and the U.S. Environmental Protection Agency. The literally hundreds of nonprofit organizations that conduct social marketing include the American Red Cross, the United Way, and the American Cancer Society.

Choosing the right goal or objective for a social marketing program is critical. Should a family-planning campaign focus on abstinence or birth control? Should a campaign to fight air pollution focus on ride-sharing or mass transit? Social marketing campaigns may try to change people's cognitions, values, actions, or behaviors. The following examples illustrate the range of possible objectives.

Cognitive campaigns

- Explain the nutritional values of different foods.
- Demonstrate the importance of conservation.

Action campaigns

- Attract people for mass immunization.
- Motivate people to vote "yes" on a certain issue.
- Inspire people to donate blood.
- Motivate women to take a pap test.

Behavioral campaigns

- Demotivate cigarette smoking.
- Demotivate use of hard drugs.
- Demotivate excessive alcohol consumption.

Value campaigns

- Alter ideas about abortion.
- Change attitudes of bigoted people.

TABLE 22.6	The Social Marketing Planning Process

Where Are We?
- Determine program focus.
- Identify campaign purpose.
- Conduct an analysis of strengths, weaknesses, opportunities, and threats (SWOT).
- Review past and similar efforts.

Where Do We Want to Go?
- Select target audiences.
- Set objectives and goals.
- Analyze target audiences and the competition.

How Will We Get There?
- Product: Design the market offering.
- Price: Manage costs of behavior change.
- Distribution: Make the product available.
- Communications: Create messages and choose media.

How Will We Stay on Course?
- Develop a plan for evaluation and monitoring.
- Establish budgets and find funding sources.
- Complete an implementation plan.

While social marketing uses a number of different tactics to achieve its goals, the planning process follows many of the same steps as for traditional products and services (see ⬜ Table 22.6).[72] Some key success factors for changing behavior include:[73]

- Choose target markets that are most ready to respond.
- Promote a single, doable behavior in clear, simple terms.
- Explain the benefits in compelling terms.
- Make it easy to adopt the behavior.
- Develop attention-grabbing messages and media.
- Consider an education-entertainment approach.

One organization that has accomplished most of these goals through the application of modern marketing practices is the World Wildlife Foundation.

World Wildlife Foundation The World Wildlife Foundation (WWF) consists of 30 independent World Wildlife organizations around the globe that once operated separately. Its early achievements include helping to form the Forest Stewardship Council in 1993 and cofounding the Marine Stewardship Council with Unilever in 1996. In the United States, its annual budget does not allow for lavish marketing expenditures, so the WWF relies primarily on extensive, creative direct marketing campaigns to bring its message to the public and solicit contributions. One recent mailing offered recipients a chance to win one of several trips, including an African safari and an Alaskan cruise, in a sweepstakes. WWF has an award-winning Web site, and it also earns revenue through different types of corporate partnerships with top firms such as Goldman Sachs, Tiffany's, IKEA, Nike, Johnson & Johnson, Cargill, Dole, adidas, Walmart, IBM, and Tyco. Since 1985, the WWF Network has invested over $1.165 billion in more than 11,000 projects in 130 countries. ⬜

Protecting the Future of Nature

The Amazon is the largest rain forest and is among the last places on earth where the jaguar, one of the most powerful cats can be found. Unfortunately, the rain forest is being destroyed by development and logging. WWF is a leader in the conservation of over 56 million acres of the Amazon. We are creating a system of protected areas that animals, local communities and companies can benefit from. We can protect the needs of animals while respecting the needs of local communities.

Be Part of Our Work   worldwildlife.org

The World Wildlife Fund uses modern marketing communications and programs to actively support its cause.

662 PART 8 CREATING SUCCESSFUL LONG-TERM GROWTH

Social marketing programs are complex; they take time and may require phased programs or actions. You may recall the many steps in discouraging smoking: release of cancer reports, labeling of cigarettes as harmful, bans on cigarette advertising, education about secondary smoke effects, bans on smoking in restaurants and planes, increased taxes on cigarettes to pay for antismoking campaigns, and states' suits against tobacco companies.

Social marketing organizations should evaluate program success in terms of their objectives. Criteria might include incidence of adoption, speed of adoption, continuance of adoption, low cost per unit of adoption, and absence of counterproductive consequences.

Marketing Implementation and Control

Table 22.7 summarizes the characteristics of a great marketing company, great not for what it is but for what it does. Great marketing companies know the best marketers thoughtfully and creatively devise marketing plans and then bring them to life. Marketing implementation and control are critical to making sure marketing plans have their intended results year after year.

Marketing Implementation

Marketing implementation is the process that turns marketing plans into action assignments and ensures they accomplish the plan's stated objectives.[74] A brilliant strategic marketing plan counts for little if not implemented properly. Strategy addresses the *what* and *why* of marketing activities; implementation addresses the *who*, *where*, *when*, and *how*. They are closely related: One layer of strategy implies certain tactical implementation assignments at a lower level. For example, top management's strategic decision to "harvest" a product must be translated into specific actions and assignments.

Companies today are striving to make their marketing operations more efficient and their return on marketing investment more measurable (see Chapter 4). Marketing costs can amount to as much as a quarter of a company's total operating budget. Marketers need better templates for marketing processes, better management of marketing assets, and better allocation of marketing resources.

Marketing resource management (MRM) software provides a set of Web-based applications that automate and integrate project management, campaign management, budget management, asset management, brand management, customer relationship management, and knowledge

TABLE 22.7   Characteristics of a Great Marketing Company
• The company selects target markets in which it enjoys superior advantages and exits or avoids markets where it is intrinsically weak.
• Virtually all the company's employees and departments are customer- and market-minded.
• There is a good working relationship between marketing, R&D, and manufacturing.
• There is a good working relationship between marketing, sales, and customer service.
• The company has installed incentives designed to lead to the right behaviors.
• The company continuously builds and tracks customer satisfaction and loyalty.
• The company manages a value delivery system in partnership with strong suppliers and distributors.
• The company is skilled in building its brand name(s) and image.
• The company is flexible in meeting customers' varying requirements.

TABLE 22.8	Types of Marketing Control		
Type of Control	**Prime Responsibility**	**Purpose of Control**	**Approaches**
I. Annual-plan control	Top management Middle management	To examine whether the planned results are being achieved	• Sales analysis • Market share analysis • Sales-to-expense ratios • Financial analysis • Market-based scorecard analysis
II. Profitability control	Marketing controller	To examine where the company is making and losing money	Profitability by: • product • territory • customer • segment • trade channel • order size
III. Efficiency control	Line and staff management Marketing controller	To evaluate and improve the spending efficiency and impact of marketing expenditures	Efficiency of: • sales force • advertising • sales promotion • distribution
IV. Strategic control	Top management Marketing auditor	To examine whether the company is pursuing its best opportunities with respect to markets, products, and channels	• Marketing effectiveness rating instrument • Marketing audit • Marketing excellence review • Company ethical and social responsibility review

management. The knowledge management component consists of process templates, how-to wizards, and best practices. Software packages can provide what some have called *desktop marketing,* giving marketers information and decision structures on computer dashboards. MRM software lets marketers improve spending and investment decisions, bring new products to market more quickly, and reduce decision time and costs.

Marketing Control

Marketing control is the process by which firms assess the effects of their marketing activities and programs and make necessary changes and adjustments. Table 22.8 lists four types of needed marketing control: annual-plan control, profitability control, efficiency control, and strategic control.

Annual-Plan Control

Annual-plan control ensures the company achieves the sales, profits, and other goals established in its annual plan. At its heart is management by objectives (see △ Figure 22.4). First, management sets monthly or quarterly goals. Second, it monitors performance in the marketplace. Third, management determines the causes of serious performance deviations. Fourth, it takes corrective action to close gaps between goals and performance.

This control model applies to all levels of the organization. Top management sets annual sales and profit goals; each product manager, regional district manager, sales manager, and sales rep is committed to attaining specified levels of sales and costs. Each period, top management reviews and

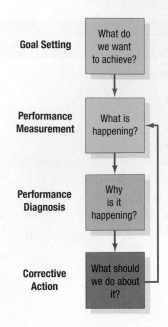

Goal Setting — What do we want to achieve?

Performance Measurement — What is happening?

Performance Diagnosis — Why is it happening?

Corrective Action — What should we do about it?

|Fig. 22.4| △

The Control Process

interprets the results. Marketers today have better marketing metrics for measuring the performance of marketing plans (see 🖰 Table 22.9 for some samples).[75] Four tools for the purpose are sales analysis, market share analysis, marketing expense-to-sales analysis, and financial analysis. The chapter appendix outlines them in detail.

Profitability Control

Companies should measure the profitability of their products, territories, customer groups, segments, trade channels, and order sizes to help determine whether to expand, reduce, or eliminate any products or marketing activities. The chapter appendix shows how to conduct and interpret a marketing profitability analysis.

Efficiency Control

Suppose a profitability analysis reveals the company is earning poor profits in certain products, territories, or markets. Are there more efficient ways to manage the sales force, advertising, sales promotion, and distribution?

Some companies have established a *marketing controller* position to work out of the controller's office but specialize in improving marketing efficiency. General Foods, DuPont, and Johnson & Johnson perform a sophisticated financial analysis of marketing expenditures and results. Their marketing controllers examine adherence to profit plans, help prepare brand managers' budgets, measure the efficiency of promotions, analyze media production costs, evaluate customer and geographic profitability, and educate marketing staff on the financial implications of marketing decisions.[76]

TABLE 22.9 🖰	Marketing Metrics

Sales Metrics
- Sales growth
- Market share
- Sales from new products

Customer Readiness to Buy Metrics
- Awareness
- Preference
- Purchase intention
- Trial rate
- Repurchase rate

Customer Metrics
- Customer complaints
- Customer satisfaction
- Ratio of promoters to detractors
- Customer acquisition costs
- New-customer gains
- Customer losses
- Customer churn
- Retention rate
- Customer lifetime value
- Customer equity
- Customer profitability
- Return on customer

Distribution Metrics
- Number of outlets
- Share in shops handling
- Weighted distribution
- Distribution gains
- Average stock volume (value)
- Stock cover in days
- Out of stock frequency
- Share of shelf
- Average sales per point of sale

Communication Metrics
- Spontaneous (unaided) brand awareness
- Top of mind brand awareness
- Prompted (aided) brand awareness
- Spontaneous (unaided) advertising awareness
- Prompted (aided) advertising awareness
- Effective reach
- Effective frequency
- Gross rating points (GRP)
- Response rate

Strategic Control

Each company should periodically reassess its strategic approach to the marketplace with a good marketing audit. Companies can also perform marketing excellence reviews and ethical/social responsibility reviews.

THE MARKETING AUDIT The average U.S. corporation loses half its customers in five years, half its employees in four years, and half its investors in less than one year. Clearly, this points to some weaknesses. Companies that discover weaknesses should undertake a thorough study known as a marketing audit.[77]

A **marketing audit** is a comprehensive, systematic, independent, and periodic examination of a company's or business unit's marketing environment, objectives, strategies, and activities, with a view to determining problem areas and opportunities and recommending a plan of action to improve the company's marketing performance.

Let's examine the marketing audit's four characteristics:

1. *Comprehensive*—The marketing audit covers all the major marketing activities of a business, not just a few trouble spots as in a functional audit. Although functional audits are useful, they sometimes mislead management. Excessive sales force turnover, for example, could be a symptom not of poor sales-force training or compensation but of weak company products and promotion. A comprehensive marketing audit usually is more effective in locating the real source of problems.

2. *Systematic*—The marketing audit is an orderly examination of the organization's macro- and micromarketing environments, marketing objectives and strategies, marketing systems, and specific activities. It identifies the most-needed improvements and incorporates them into a corrective-action plan with short- and long-run steps.

3. *Independent*— Self-audits, in which managers rate their own operations, lack objectivity and independence.[78] The 3M Company has made good use of a corporate auditing office, which provides marketing audit services to divisions on request.[79] Usually, however, outside consultants bring the necessary objectivity, broad experience in a number of industries, familiarity with the industry being audited, and undivided time and attention.

4. *Periodic*—Firms typically initiate marketing audits only after failing to review their marketing operations during good times, with resulting problems. A periodic marketing audit can benefit companies in good health as well as those in trouble.

A marketing audit starts with agreement between the company officer(s) and the marketing auditor(s) on the audit's objectives and time frame, and a detailed plan of who is to be asked what questions. The cardinal rule for marketing auditors is: Don't rely solely on company managers for data and opinions. Ask customers, dealers, and other outside groups. Many companies don't really know how their customers and dealers see them, nor do they fully understand customer needs.

The marketing audit examines six major components of the company's marketing situation. ▢ Table 22.10 lists the major questions.

THE MARKETING EXCELLENCE REVIEW The three columns in ▢ Table 22.11 distinguish among poor, good, and excellent business and marketing practices. The profile management creates from indicating where it thinks the business stands on each line can highlight where changes could help the firm become a truly outstanding player in the marketplace.

The Future of Marketing

Top management recognizes that marketing requires more accountability than in the past. "Marketing Memo: Major Marketing Weaknesses" summarizes companies' major deficiencies in marketing, and how to find and correct them.

To succeed in the future, marketing must be more holistic and less departmental. Marketers must achieve larger influence in the company, continuously create new ideas, and strive for customer insight by treating customers differently but appropriately. They must build their brands more through

Johnson & Johnson, maker of a famous baby powder, conducts careful analysis of its marketing expenditures and results.

TABLE 22.10 Components of a Marketing Audit

Part I. Marketing Environment Audit

Macroenvironment

A. Demographic	What major demographic developments and trends pose opportunities or threats to this company? What actions have the company taken in response to these developments and trends?
B. Economic	What major developments in income, prices, savings, and credit will affect the company? What actions have the company been taking in response to these developments and trends?
C. Environmental	What is the outlook for the cost and availability of natural resources and energy needed by the company? What concerns have been expressed about the company's role in pollution and conservation, and what steps have the company taken?
D. Technological	What major changes are occurring in product and process technology? What is the company's position in these technologies? What major generic substitutes might replace this product?
E. Political	What changes in laws and regulations might affect marketing strategy and tactics? What is happening in the areas of pollution control, equal employment opportunity, product safety, advertising, price control, and so forth that affects marketing strategy?
F. Cultural	What is the public's attitude toward business and toward the company's products? What changes in customer lifestyles and values might affect the company?

Task Environment

A. Markets	What is happening to market size, growth, geographical distribution, and profits? What are the major market segments?
B. Customers	What are the customers' needs and buying processes? How do customers and prospects rate the company and its competitors on reputation, product quality, service, sales force, and price? How do different customer segments make their buying decisions?
C. Competitors	Who are the major competitors? What are their objectives, strategies, strengths, weaknesses, sizes, and market shares? What trends will affect future competition and substitutes for the company's products?
D. Distribution and Dealers	What are the main trade channels for bringing products to customers? What are the efficiency levels and growth potentials of the different trade channels?
E. Suppliers	What is the outlook for the availability of key resources used in production? What trends are occurring among suppliers?
F. Facilitators and Marketing Firms	What is the cost and availability outlook for transportation services, warehousing facilities, and financial resources? How effective are the company's advertising agencies and marketing research firms?
G. Publics	Which publics represent particular opportunities or problems for the company? What steps has the company taken to deal effectively with each public?

Part II. Marketing Strategy Audit

A. Business Mission	Is the business mission clearly stated in market-oriented terms? Is it feasible?
B. Marketing Objectives and Goals	Are the company and marketing objectives and goals stated clearly enough to guide marketing planning and performance measurement? Are the marketing objectives appropriate, given the company's competitive position, resources, and opportunities?
C. Strategy	Has the management articulated a clear marketing strategy for achieving its marketing objectives? Is the strategy convincing? Is the strategy appropriate to the stage of the product life cycle, competitors' strategies, and the state of the economy? Is the company using the best basis for market segmentation? Does it have clear criteria for rating the segments and choosing the best ones? Has it developed accurate profiles of each target segment? Has the company developed an effective positioning and marketing mix for each target segment? Are marketing resources allocated optimally to the major elements of the marketing mix? Are enough resources or too many resources budgeted to accomplish the marketing objectives?

Part III. Marketing Organization Audit

A. Formal Structure	Does the marketing vice president or CMO have adequate authority and responsibility for company activities that affect customers' satisfaction? Are the marketing activities optimally structured along functional, product, segment, end user, and geographical lines?

TABLE 22.10 (Continued)	
B. Functional Efficiency	Are there good communication and working relations between marketing and sales? Is the product-management system working effectively? Are product managers able to plan profits or only sales volume? Are there any groups in marketing that need more training, motivation, supervision, or evaluation?
C. Interface Efficiency	Are there any problems between marketing and manufacturing, R&D, purchasing, finance, accounting, and/or legal that need attention?
Part IV. Marketing Systems Audit	
A. Marketing Information System	Is the marketing information system producing accurate, sufficient, and timely information about marketplace developments with respect to customers, prospects, distributors and dealers, competitors, suppliers, and various publics? Are company decision makers asking for enough marketing research, and are they using the results? Is the company employing the best methods for market measurement and sales forecasting?
B. Marketing Planning System	Is the marketing planning system well conceived and effectively used? Do marketers have decision support systems available? Does the planning system result in acceptable sales targets and quotas?
C. Marketing Control System	Are the control procedures adequate to ensure that the annual-plan objectives are being achieved? Does management periodically analyze the profitability of products, markets, territories, and channels of distribution? Are marketing costs and productivity periodically examined?
D. New-Product Development System	Is the company well organized to gather, generate, and screen new-product ideas? Does the company do adequate concept research and business analysis before investing in new ideas? Does the company carry out adequate product and market testing before launching new products?
Part V. Marketing Proaductivity Audit	
A. Profitability Analysis	What is the profitability of the company's different products, markets, territories, and channels of distribution? Should the company enter, expand, contract, or withdraw from any business segments?
B. Cost-Effectiveness Analysis	Do any marketing activities seem to have excessive costs? Can cost-reducing steps be taken?
Part VI. Marketing Function Audits	
A. Products	What are the company's product line objectives? Are they sound? Is the current product line meeting the objectives? Should the product line be stretched or contracted upward, downward, or both ways? Which products should be phased out? Which products should be added? What are the buyers' knowledge and attitudes toward the company's and competitors' product quality, features, styling, brand names, and so on? What areas of product and brand strategy need improvement?
B. Price	What are the company's pricing objectives, policies, strategies, and procedures? To what extent are prices set on cost, demand, and competitive criteria? Do the customers see the company's prices as being in line with the value of its offer? What does management know about the price elasticity of demand, experience-curve effects, and competitors' prices and pricing policies? To what extent are price policies compatible with the needs of distributors and dealers, suppliers, and government regulation?
C. Distribution	What are the company's distribution objectives and strategies? Is there adequate market coverage and service? How effective are distributors, dealers, manufacturers' representatives, brokers, agents, and others? Should the company consider changing its distribution channels?
D. Marketing Communications	What are the organization's advertising objectives? Are they sound? Is the right amount being spent on advertising? Are the ad themes and copy effective? What do customers and the public think about the advertising? Are the advertising media well chosen? Is the internal advertising staff adequate? Is the sales promotion budget adequate? Is there effective and sufficient use of sales promotion tools such as samples, coupons, displays, and sales contests? Is the public relations staff competent and creative? Is the company making enough use of direct, online, and database marketing?
E. Sales Force	What are the sales force's objectives? Is the sales force large enough to accomplish the company's objectives? Is the sales force organized along the proper principles of specialization (territory, market, product)? Are there enough (or too many) sales managers to guide the field sales representatives? Do the sales compensation level and structure provide adequate incentive and reward? Does the sales force show high morale, ability, and effort? Are the procedures adequate for setting quotas and evaluating performance? How does the company's sales force compare to competitors' sales forces?

TABLE 22.11	The Marketing Excellence Review: Best Practices	
Poor	**Good**	**Excellent**
Product driven	Market driven	Market driving
Mass-market oriented	Segment-oriented	Niche-oriented and customer-oriented
Product offer	Augmented product offer	Customer solutions offer
Average product quality	Better than average	Legendary
Average service quality	Better than average	Legendary
End-product oriented	Core-product oriented	Core-competency oriented
Function oriented	Process oriented	Outcome oriented
Reacting to competitors	Benchmarking competitors	Leapfrogging competitors
Supplier exploitation	Supplier preference	Supplier partnership
Dealer exploitation	Dealer support	Dealer partnership
Price driven	Quality driven	Value driven
Average speed	Better than average	Legendary
Hierarchy	Network	Teamwork
Vertically integrated	Flattened organization	Strategic alliances
Stockholder driven	Stakeholder driven	Societally driven

performance than promotion. They must go electronic and win through building superior information and communication systems.

The coming years will see:

- The demise of the marketing department and the rise of holistic marketing
- The demise of free-spending marketing and the rise of ROI marketing
- The demise of marketing intuition and the rise of marketing science
- The demise of manual marketing and the rise of both automated *and* creative marketing
- The demise of mass marketing and the rise of precision marketing

To accomplish these changes and become truly holistic, marketers need a new set of skills and competencies in:

- Customer relationship management (CRM)
- Partner relationship management (PRM)
- Database marketing and data mining
- Contact center management and telemarketing
- Public relations marketing (including event and sponsorship marketing)
- Brand-building and brand-asset management
- Experiential marketing
- Integrated marketing communications
- Profitability analysis by segment, customer, and channel

The benefits of successful 21st-century marketing are many, but they will come only with hard work, insight, and inspiration. New rules and practices are emerging, and it is an exciting time. The words of 19th-century U.S. author Ralph Waldo Emerson may never have been more true: "This time like all times is a good one, if we but know what to do with it."

marketing Memo

Major Marketing Weaknesses

A number of "deadly sins" signal that the marketing program is in trouble. Here are 10 deadly sins, the signs, and some solutions.

Deadly Sin: The company is not sufficiently market focused and customer driven.

Signs: There is evidence of poor identification of market segments, poor prioritization of market segments, no market segment managers, employees who think it is the job of marketing and sales to serve customers, no training program to create a customer culture, and no incentives to treat the customer especially well.

Solutions: Use more advanced segmentation techniques, prioritize segments, specialize the sales force, develop a clear hierarchy of company values, foster more "customer consciousness" in employees and company agents, and make it easy for customers to reach the company and respond quickly to any communication.

Deadly Sin: The company does not fully understand its target customers.

Signs: The latest study of customers is three years old; customers are not buying your product like they once did; competitors' products are selling better; and there is a high level of customer returns and complaints.

Solutions: Do more sophisticated consumer research, use more analytical techniques, establish customer and dealer panels, use customer relationship software, and do data mining.

Deadly Sin: The company needs to better define and monitor its competitors.

Signs: The company focuses on near competitors, misses distant competitors and disruptive technologies, and has no system for gathering and distributing competitive intelligence.

Solutions: Establish an office for competitive intelligence, hire competitors' people, watch for technology that might affect the company, and prepare offerings like those of competitors.

Deadly Sin: The company does not properly manage relationships with stakeholders.

Signs: Employees, dealers, and investors are not happy; and good suppliers do not come.

Solutions: Move from zero-sum thinking to positive-sum thinking; and do a better job of managing employees, supplier relations, distributors, dealers, and investors.

Deadly Sin: The company is not good at finding new opportunities.

Signs: The company has not identified any exciting new opportunities for years, and the new ideas the company has launched have largely failed.

Solutions: Set up a system for stimulating the flow of new ideas.

Deadly Sin: The company's marketing planning process is deficient.

Signs: The marketing plan format does not have the right components, there is no way to estimate the financial implications of different strategies, and there is no contingency planning.

Solutions: Establish a standard format including situational analysis, SWOT, major issues, objectives, strategy, tactics, budgets, and controls; ask marketers what changes they would make if they were given 20 percent more or less budget; and run an annual marketing awards program with prizes for best plans and performance.

Deadly Sin: Product and service policies need tightening.

Signs: There are too many products and many are losing money; the company is giving away too many services; and the company is poor at cross-selling products and services.

Solutions: Establish a system to track weak products and fix or drop them; offer and price services at different levels; and improve processes for cross-selling and up-selling.

Deadly Sin: The company's brand-building and communications skills are weak.

Signs: The target market does not know much about the company; the brand is not seen as distinctive; the company allocates its budget to the same marketing tools in about the same proportion each year; and there is little evaluation of the ROI impact of promotions.

Solutions: Improve brand-building strategies and measurement of results; shift money into effective marketing instruments; and require marketers to estimate the ROI impact in advance of funding requests.

Deadly Sin: The company is not organized for effective and efficient marketing.

Signs: Staff lacks 21st-century marketing skills, and there are bad vibes between marketing/sales and other departments.

Solutions: Appoint a strong leader and build new skills in the marketing department, and improve relationships between marketing and other departments.

Deadly Sin: The company has not made maximum use of technology.

Signs: There is evidence of minimal use of the Internet, an outdated sales automation system, no market automation, no decision-support models, and no marketing dashboards.

Solutions: Use the Internet more, improve the sales automation system, apply market automation to routine decisions, and develop formal marketing decision models and marketing dashboards.

Source: Philip Kotler, *Ten Deadly Marketing Sins: Signs and Solutions* (Hoboken, NJ: Wiley, 2004). © Philip Kotler.

Summary

1. The modern marketing department has evolved through the years from a simple sales department to an organizational structure where marketers work mainly on cross-disciplinary teams.

2. Some companies are organized by functional specialization; others focus on geography and regionalization, product and brand management, or market-segment management. Some companies establish a matrix organization consisting of both product and market managers.

3. Effective modern marketing organizations are marked by customer focus within and strong cooperation among marketing, R&D, engineering, purchasing, manufacturing, operations, finance, accounting, and credit.

4. Companies must practice social responsibility through their legal, ethical, and social words and actions. Cause marketing can be a means for companies to productively link social responsibility to consumer marketing programs. Social marketing is done by a nonprofit or government organization to directly address a social problem or cause.

5. A brilliant strategic marketing plan counts for little unless implemented properly, including recognizing and diagnosing a problem, assessing where the problem exists, and evaluating results.

6. The marketing department must monitor and control marketing activities continuously. Marketing plan control ensures the company achieves the sales, profits, and other goals in its annual plan. The main tools are sales analysis, market share analysis, marketing expense-to-sales analysis, and financial analysis of the marketing plan. Profitability control measures and controls the profitability of products, territories, customer groups, trade channels, and order sizes. Efficiency control finds ways to increase the efficiency of the sales force, advertising, sales promotion, and distribution. Strategic control periodically reassesses the company's strategic approach to the marketplace using marketing effectiveness and marketing excellence reviews, as well as marketing audits.

7. Achieving marketing excellence in the future will require a new set of skills and competencies.

Applications

Marketing Debate
Is Marketing Management an Art or a Science?

Some observers maintain that good marketing is mostly an art and does not lend itself to rigorous analysis and deliberation. Others contend it is a highly disciplined enterprise that shares much with other business disciplines.

Take a position: Marketing management is largely an artistic exercise and therefore highly subjective *versus* Marketing management is largely a scientific exercise with well-established guidelines and criteria.

Marketing Discussion
Cause Marketing

How does cause or corporate societal marketing affect your personal consumer behavior? Do you ever buy or not buy any products or services from a company because of its environmental policies or programs? Why or why not?

Marketing Excellence

>>Starbucks

Starbucks opened in Seattle in 1971 at a time when coffee consumption in the United States had been declining for a decade and rival brands used cheaper coffee beans to compete on price. Starbucks's founders decided to experiment with a new concept: a store that would sell only the finest imported coffee beans and coffee-brewing equipment. (The original store didn't sell coffee by the cup, only beans.)

Howard Schultz came to Starbucks in 1982. While in Milan on business, he had walked into an Italian coffee bar and had an epiphany: "There was nothing like this in America. It was an extension of people's front porch. It was an emotional experience." To bring this concept to the United States, Schultz set about creating an environment for Starbucks coffeehouses that would reflect Italian elegance melded with U.S. informality. He envisioned Starbucks as a "personal treat" for its customers, a "Third Place"—a comfortable, sociable gathering spot bridging the workplace and home.

Starbucks's expansion throughout the United States was carefully planned. All stores were company-owned and operated, ensuring complete control over an unparalleled image of quality. In a "hub" strategy, coffeehouses entered a

donated 5 cents from every sale of its Ethos bottled water to improving the quality of water in poor countries, part of a five-year, $10 million pledge.

Ethical Sourcing: Starbucks has partnered with Conservation International to ensure that coffee it purchases is not only of the highest quality but also "responsibly grown and ethically traded." Starbucks is the world's biggest buyer of fair-trade coffee and pays an average of 23 percent above market price for 40 million pounds a year. It works continuously with farmers on responsible methods such as planting trees along rivers and using shade-growing techniques to help preserve forests.

The Environment: It took Starbucks 10 years of development to create the world's first recycled beverage cup made of 10 percent postconsumer fiber, conserving 5 million pounds of paper or approximately 78,000 trees a year. Now the team is working to ensure that customers recycle. Jim Hanna, Starbucks's director of environmental impact, explained, "[Starbucks] defines a recyclable cup not by what the cup is made out of but by our customers actually having access to recycling services." Starbucks's goal: make 100 percent of its cups recycled or reused by 2015. The firm also emphasizes energy and water conservation and building green, LEED-certified buildings around the world.

new market in a clustered group. Although this deliberate saturation often cannibalized 30 percent of one store's sales by introducing a store nearby, any drop in revenue was offset by efficiencies in marketing and distribution costs, and the enhanced image of convenience. A typical customer would stop by Starbucks 18 times a month. No U.S. retailer has had a higher frequency of customer visits.

Part of Starbucks's success undoubtedly lies in its products and services, and its relentless commitment to providing the richest possible sensory experiences. But another key is its enlightened sense of responsibility, manifested in a number of different ways. Schultz believed that to exceed customers' expectations it is first necessary to exceed employees'. Since 1990, Starbucks has provided comprehensive health care to all employees, including part-timers. Health insurance now costs the company more each year than coffee. A stock option plan called Bean Stock allows employees also to participate in its financial success.

Schultz also believed Starbucks's operations should run in a respectful, ethical manner, making decisions with a positive impact on communities and the planet.

Community: The Starbucks Foundation, created in 1997 with proceeds from the sale of Schultz's book, aims to "create hope, discovery, and opportunity in communities where Starbucks partners [employees] live and work." Its primary focus is supporting literacy programs for children and families in the United States and Canada; expanded, it has now donated millions of dollars to charities and communities worldwide.

Starbucks's employees volunteer community service hours for causes big and small—such as rebuilding New Orleans after Hurricane Katrina—and wants to have employees and customers volunteering over 1 million community service hours each year by the end of 2015. As described in the chapter, Starbucks is also a partner in PRODUCT(RED), an initiative to help fight and stop the spread of HIV in Africa, and so far has donated enough money to purchase 14 million days of medicine. It has also

Howard Schultz stepped down as CEO in 2000 but returned as CEO, president, and chairman in 2008 to help restore growth and excitement to the powerhouse chain. Today, Starbucks has over 16,700 stores worldwide, approximately 142,000 employees, $9.8 billion in revenue, and plans to expand worldwide. To achieve its international growth goals, Schultz believes Starbucks must retain a passion for coffee and a sense of humanity, to remain small even as it gets big, and to be a responsible company.

Questions

1. Starbucks has worked hard to act ethically and responsibly. Has it done a good job communicating its efforts to consumers? Do consumers believe Starbucks is a responsible company? Why or why not?

2. Where does a company like Starbucks draw the line on supporting socially responsible programs? For example, how much of its annual budget should go toward these programs? How much time should employees focus on them? Which programs should it support?

3. How do you measure the results of Starbucks's socially responsible programs?

Sources: Howard Schultz, "Dare to Be a Social Entrepreneur," *Business 2.0*, December 2006, p. 87; Edward Iwata, "Owner of Small Coffee Shop Takes on Java Titan Starbucks," *USA Today*, December 20, 2006; "Staying Pure: Howard Schultz's Formula for Starbucks," *Economist*, February 25, 2006, p. 72; Diane Anderson, "Evolution of the Eco Cup," *Business 2.0*, June 2006, p. 50; Bruce Horovitz, "Starbucks Nation," *USA Today*, May 19, 2006; Theresa Howard, "Starbucks Takes Up Cause for Safe Drinking Water," *USA Today*, August 2, 2005; Howard Schultz and Dori Jones Yang, *Pour Your Heart into It: How Starbucks Built a Company One Cup at a Time* (New York: Hyperion, 1997); "At MIT-Starbucks Symposium, Focus on Holistic Approach to Recycling," *MIT*, www.mit.edu, May 12, 2010; Starbucks.

Marketing Excellence

>>Virgin Group

Virgin roared onto the British stage in the 1970s with the innovative Virgin Records, brainchild of Richard Branson, who signed unknown artists and began a marathon of publicity that continues to this day. The flamboyant Branson sold Virgin Records (to Thorn-EMI for nearly $1 billion in 1992) but went on to create over 200 companies worldwide whose combined revenues exceeded €11.5 billion (about $16.2 billion) in 2009.

The Virgin name—the third most respected brand in Britain—and the Branson personality help to sell such diverse products and services as planes, trains, finance, soft drinks, music, mobile phones, cars, wine, publishing, and even bridal wear. Branson can create interest in almost any business he wants by simply attaching the "Virgin" name to it. He supplies the brand and a small initial investment and takes a majority control, and big-name partners come up with the cash.

The Virgin Group looks for new opportunities in markets with underserved, overcharged customers and complacent competition. Branson explained, "Wherever we find them, there is a clear opportunity area for Virgin to do a much better job than the competition. We introduce trust, innovation, and customer friendliness where they don't exist."

Some marketing and financial critics point out that Branson is diluting the brand, that it covers too many businesses. There have been some fumbles: Virgin Cola, Virgin Cosmetics, and Virgin Vodka have all but disappeared. But despite the diversity, all the lines connote value for money, quality, innovation, fun, and a sense of competitive challenge. And then Virgin's vaunted marketing expertise kicks in.

A master of the strategic publicity stunt, Branson knew photographers have a job to do and they'd turn up at his events if he gave them a good reason. He took on stodgy, overpriced British Airways by wearing World War I–era flying gear to announce the formation of Virgin Atlantic in 1984. The first Virgin flight took off laden with celebrities and media and equipped with a brass band, waiters from Maxim's in white tie and tails, and free-flowing champagne. The airborne party enjoyed international press coverage and millions of dollars' worth of free publicity.

When Branson launched Virgin Cola in the United States in 1998, he steered an army tank down Fifth Avenue in New York, garnering interviews on each of the network morning TV shows. In 2002, he plunged into Times Square from a crane to announce his mobile phone business. In 2004, introducing a line of hip techie gadgets called Virgin Pulse, Branson again took center stage, appearing at a New York City nightclub wearing a pair of flesh-colored tights and a strategically placed portable CD player.

Although he eschews traditional market research for a "screw it, let's do it" attitude, Branson stays in touch through constant customer contact. When he first set up Virgin Atlantic, he called 50 customers every month to chat and get their feedback. He appeared in airports to rub elbows with customers, and if a plane was delayed, he handed out gift certificates to a Virgin Megastore or discounts on future travel.

A nonprofit foundation called Virgin Unite has started to tackle global, social, and environmental problems with an entrepreneurial approach. A team of scientists, entrepreneurs, and environmental enthusiasts consult with Virgin about what it needs to do on a grassroots and global level. The goal is to change the way "businesses and the social sector work together—driving business as a force for good."

Clearly, Branson cares about Virgin's customers and the impact his companies have on people and the planet. That's why he recently made corporate responsibility and sustainable development (CR/SD) a key priority for every one of his companies. Each must act socially responsible and lower its carbon footprint. Branson stated, "I believe that in the future, we will be able to enjoy healthy and fulfilling lifestyles whilst minimizing the negative impact we have on the world."

Virgin categorizes its businesses into eight socially responsible and sustainable groups: Flying high, We're all going on a summer holiday, Staying in touch, Watching the pennies, Getting from A to B, My body is a temple, Out of this world, and Just get out and relax. Each is to do exceptionally good things in its industry as well as help to alleviate the bad things that come with the category. Virgin Wines strives to purchase only from small farms and pay fair prices while promoting responsible drinking. Virgin

Games, an online gambling Web site, promotes responsible gambling and helps identify and alleviate gambling addiction. Virgin Money focuses on fair lending, and the list goes on.

Virgin Aviation is perhaps the toughest challenge; it represents 7 million of the 8 million tons of CO_2 Virgin emits each year. Branson, however, has turned the problem into an opportunity. In 2006, he announced that all dividends from Virgin's rail and airline businesses "will be invested into renewable energy initiatives . . . to tackle emissions related to global warming." That effort has evolved into the Virgin Green Fund, which invests in renewable energy opportunities from solar energy to water purification and is estimated to reach $3 billion in value by 2016.

But Branson hasn't stopped there. In 2007, he established the Earth Challenge to award $25 million to any person or group who develops a safe, long-term, commercially viable way to remove greenhouse gases from the atmosphere. Submitted inventions are now being reviewed by a team of scientists, professors, and environment professionals.

Once known as the "hippie capitalist" and now knighted by the Queen of England, Sir Richard never does anything small and quiet. Whether looking for a new business, generating publicity in his characteristic style, or encouraging research to help the planet, Branson does it with a bang.

Questions

1. How is Virgin unique in its quest to be a socially responsible and sustainable company?

2. Discuss the pros and cons of Virgin's "green" message. How do you feel about the company's having such a negative environmental impact on the world (via air and rail) and the message it communicates through efforts like the Earth Challenge?

3. If you were Richard Branson, what would you do with Virgin's holistic marketing strategy?

Sources: Peter Elkind, "Branson Gets Grounded," *Fortune*, February 5, 2007, pp. 13–14; Alan Deutschman, "The Enlightenment of Richard Branson," *Fast Company*, September 2006, p. 49; Andy Serwer, "Do Branson's Profits Equal His *Joie de Vivre*?" *Fortune*, October 17, 2005, p. 57; Kerry Capell with Wendy Zellner, "Richard Branson's Next Big Adventure," *BusinessWeek,* March 8, 2004, pp. 44–45; Melanie Wells, "Red Baron," *Forbes,* July 3, 2000, pp. 151–60; Sam Hill and Glenn Rifkin, *Radical Marketing* (New York: HarperBusiness, 1999); "Branson Pledges Three Billion Dollars to Develop Cleaner Energy," *Terra Daily,* September 21, 2006; Virgin, www.virgin.com.

APPENDIX

Tools for Marketing Control

In this appendix, we provided detailed guidelines and insights about how to best conduct several marketing control procedures.

Annual Plan Control

Four sets of analyses can be useful for annual plan control.

Sales Analysis **Sales analysis** measures and evaluates actual sales in relationship to goals. Two specific tools make it work.

Sales-variance analysis measures the relative contribution of different factors to a gap in sales performance. Suppose the annual plan called for selling 4,000 widgets in the first quarter at $1 per widget, for total revenue of $4,000. At quarter's end, only 3,000 widgets were sold at $.80 per widget, for total revenue of $2,400. How much of the sales performance gap is due to the price decline, and how much to the volume decline? This calculation answers the question:

Variance due to price decline: ($1.00–$.80) (3,000)	=	$ 600	37.5%
Variance due to volume decline: ($1.00) (4,000–3,000)	=	$1,000	62.5%
		$1,600	100.0%

Almost two-thirds of the variance is due to failure to achieve the volume target. The company should look closely at why it failed to achieve expected sales volume.

Microsales analysis looks at specific products, territories, and so forth that failed to produce expected sales. Suppose the company sells in three territories, and expected sales were 1,500 units, 500 units, and 2,000 units, respectively. Actual volumes were 1,400 units, 525 units, and 1,075 units, respectively. Thus territory 1 showed a 7 percent shortfall in terms of expected sales; territory 2, a 5 percent improvement over expectations; and territory 3, a 46 percent shortfall! Territory 3 is causing most of the trouble. Maybe the sales rep in territory 3 is underperforming, a major competitor has entered this territory, or business is in a recession there.

Market Share Analysis Company sales don't reveal how well the company is performing relative to competitors. For this, management needs to track its market share in one of three ways.

Overall market share expresses the company's sales as a percentage of total market sales. **Served market share** is sales as a percentage of the total sales to the market. The **served market** is all the buyers able and willing to buy the product, and served market share is always larger than overall market share. A company could capture 100 percent of its served market and yet have a relatively small share of the total market. **Relative market share** is market share in relationship to the largest competitor. A relative market share of exactly 100 percent means the company is tied for the lead; over 100 percent indicates a market leader. A rise in relative market share means a company is gaining on its leading competitor.

Conclusions from market share analysis, however, are subject to qualifications:

- *The assumption that outside forces affect all companies in the same way is often not true.* The U.S. Surgeon General's report on the harmful consequences of smoking depressed total cigarette sales, but not equally for all companies.
- *The assumption that a company's performance should be judged against the average performance of all companies is not always valid.* A company's performance is best judged against that of its closest competitors.
- *If a new firm enters the industry, every existing firm's market share might fall.* A decline in market share might not mean the company is performing any worse than other companies. Share loss depends on the degree to which the new firm hits the company's specific markets.
- *Sometimes a market share decline is deliberately engineered to improve profits.* For example, management might drop unprofitable customers or products.

- *Market share can fluctuate for many minor reasons.* For example, it can be affected by whether a large sale occurs on the last day of the month or at the beginning of the next month. Not all shifts in market share have marketing significance.[80]

A useful way to analyze market share movements is in terms of four components:

$$\begin{array}{c} \text{Overall} \\ \text{market} \\ \text{share} \end{array} = \begin{array}{c} \text{Customer} \\ \text{penetration} \end{array} \times \begin{array}{c} \text{Customer} \\ \text{loyalty} \end{array} \times \begin{array}{c} \text{Customer} \\ \text{selectivity} \end{array} \times \begin{array}{c} \text{Price} \\ \text{selectivity} \end{array}$$

where:

Customer penetration	Percentage of all customers who buy from the company
Customer loyalty	Purchases from the company by its customers as a percentage of their total purchases from all suppliers of the same products
Customer selectivity	Size of the average customer purchase from the company as a percentage of the size of the average customer purchase from an average company
Price selectivity	Average price charged by the company as a percentage of the average price charged by all companies

Now suppose the company's dollar market share falls during the period. The overall market share equation provides four possible explanations: The company lost some customers (lower customer penetration); existing customers are buying less from the company (lower customer loyalty); the company's remaining customers are smaller in size (lower customer selectivity); or the company's price has slipped relative to competition (lower price selectivity).

Marketing Expense-to-Sales Analysis Annual-plan control requires making sure the company isn't overspending to achieve sales goals. The key ratio to watch is *marketing expense-to-sales*. In one company, this ratio was 30 percent and consisted of five component expense-to-sales ratios: sales force-to-sales (15 percent), advertising-to-sales (5 percent), sales promotion-to-sales (6 percent), marketing research-to-sales (1 percent), and sales administration-to-sales (3 percent).

Fluctuations outside the normal range are cause for concern. Management needs to monitor period-to-period fluctuations in each ratio on a *control chart* (see △ Figure 22.5). This chart shows the advertising expense-to-sales ratio normally fluctuates between 8 percent and 12 percent, say 99 of 100 times. In the 15th period, however, the ratio exceeded the upper control limit. Either (1) the company still has good expense control and this situation represents a rare chance event, or (2) the company has lost control over this expense and should find the cause. If there is no investigation, the risk is that some real change might have occurred, and the company will fall behind.

Managers should make successive observations even within the upper and lower control limits. Note in Figure 22.5 that the level of the expense-to-sales ratio rose steadily from the 8th period onward. The probability of encountering six successive increases in what should be independent events is only 1 in 64.[81] This unusual pattern should have led to an investigation sometime before the 15th observation.

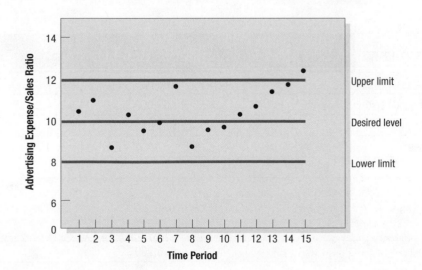

|Fig. 22.5| △

The Control-Chart Model

|Fig. 22.6| △

Financial Model of Return on Net Worth

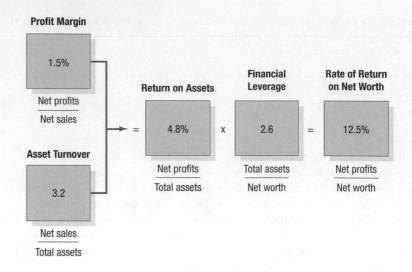

Financial Analysis Marketers should analyze the expense-to-sales ratios in an overall financial framework to determine how and where the company is making its money. They can, and are increasingly, using financial analysis to find profitable strategies beyond building sales.

Management uses financial analysis to identify factors that affect the company's *rate of return on net worth*.[82] The main factors are shown in △ Figure 22.6, along with illustrative numbers for a large chain-store retailer. The retailer is earning a 12.5 percent return on net worth. The return on net worth is the product of two ratios, the company's *return on assets* and its *financial leverage*. To improve its return on net worth, the company must increase its ratio of net profits to assets, or increase the ratio of assets to net worth. The company should analyze the composition of its assets (cash, accounts receivable, inventory, and plant and equipment) and see whether it can improve its asset management.

The return on assets is the product of two ratios, the *profit margin* and the *asset turnover*. The profit margin in Figure 22.6 seems low, whereas the asset turnover is more normal for retailing. The marketing executive can seek to improve performance in two ways: (1) Increase the profit margin by increasing sales or cutting costs, and (2) increase the asset turnover by increasing sales or reducing assets (inventory, receivables) held against a given level of sales.[83]

Profitability Control

Marketing Profitability Analysis We will illustrate the steps in marketing profitability analysis with the following example: The marketing vice president of a lawn mower company wants to determine the profitability of selling through three types of retail channels: hardware stores, garden supply shops, and department stores. The company's profit-and-loss statement is shown in ▭ Table 22.12.

TABLE 22.12 ▭ A Simplified Profit-and-Loss Statement		
Sales		$60,000
Cost of goods sold		39,000
Gross margin		$21,000
Expenses		
Salaries	$9,300	
Rent	3,000	
Supplies	3,500	
		15,800
Net profit		$ 5,200

Step 1: Identifying Functional Expenses Assume the expenses listed in Table 22.12 are incurred to sell the product, advertise it, pack and deliver it, and bill and collect for it. The first task is to measure how much of each expense was incurred in each activity.

Suppose most of the salary expense went to sales representatives and the rest to an advertising manager, packing and delivery help, and an office accountant. Let the breakdown of the $9,300 be $5,100, $1,200, $1,400, and $1,600, respectively. ⬜ Table 22.13 shows the allocation of the salary expense to these four activities.

TABLE 22.13 ⬜	Mapping Natural Expenses into Functional Expenses				
Natural Accounts	**Total**	**Selling**	**Advertising**	**Packing and Delivery**	**Billing and Collecting**
Salaries	$ 9,300	$5,100	$1,200	$1,400	$1,600
Rent	3,000	—	400	2,000	600
Supplies	3,500	400	1,500	1,400	200
	$15,800	$5,500	$3,100	$4,800	$2,400

Table 22.13 also shows the rent account of $3,000 allocated to the four activities. Because the sales reps work away from the office, none of the building's rent expense is assigned to selling. Most of the expenses for floor space and rented equipment are for packing and delivery. The supplies account covers promotional materials, packing materials, fuel purchases for delivery, and home office stationery. The $3,500 in this account is reassigned to functional uses of the supplies.

Step 2: Assigning Functional Expenses to Marketing Entities The next task is to measure how much functional expense was associated with selling through each type of channel. Consider the selling effort, indicated by the number of sales in each channel. This number is in the selling column of ⬜ Table 22.14. Altogether, 275 sales calls were made during the period. Because the total selling expense amounted to $5,500 (see Table 22.14), the selling expense averaged $20 per call.

TABLE 22.14 ⬜	Bases for Allocating Functional Expenses to Channels			
Channel Type	**Selling**	**Advertising**	**Packing and Delivery**	**Billing and Collecting**
Hardware	200	50	50	50
Garden supply	65	20	21	21
Department stores	10	30	9	9
	275	**100**	**80**	**80**
Functional expense ÷ No. of Units	$5,500	$3,100	$4,800	$2,400
	275	100	80	80
Equals	$ 20	$ 31	$ 60	$ 30

We can allocate advertising expense according to the number of ads addressed to different channels. Because there were 100 ads altogether, the average ad cost $31.

The packing and delivery expense is allocated according to the number of orders placed by each type of channel. This same basis was used for allocating billing and collection expense.

Step 3: Preparing a Profit-and-Loss Statement for Each Marketing Entity We can now prepare a profit-and-loss statement for each type of channel (see ⬜ Table 22.15). Because hardware stores accounted for half of total sales ($30,000 out of $60,000), charge this channel

TABLE 22.15	Profit-and-Loss Statements for Channels			
	Hardware	Garden Supply	Dept. Stores	Whole Company
Sales	$30,000	$10,000	$20,000	$60,000
Cost of goods sold	19,500	6,500	13,000	39,000
Gross margin	$10,500	$ 3,500	$ 7,000	$21,000
Expenses				
Selling ($20 per call)	$ 4,000	$ 1,300	$ 200	$ 5,500
Advertising ($31 per advertisement)	1,550	620	930	3,100
Packing and delivery ($60 per order)	3,000	1,260	540	4,800
Billing ($30 per order)	1,500	630	270	2,400
Total expenses	$10,050	$ 3,810	$ 1,940	$15,800
Net profit or loss	$ 450	$ (310)	$ 5,060	$ 5,200

with half the cost of goods sold ($19,500 out of $39,000). This leaves a gross margin from hardware stores of $10,500. From this we deduct the proportions of functional expenses hardware stores consumed.

According to Table 22.14, hardware stores received 200 of 275 total sales calls. At an imputed value of $20 a call, hardware stores must bear a $4,000 selling expense. Table 22.14 also shows hardware stores were the target of 50 ads. At $31 an ad, the hardware stores are charged with $1,550 of advertising. The same reasoning applies in computing the share of the other functional expenses. The result is that hardware stores gave rise to $10,050 of the total expenses. Subtracting this from gross margin, we find the profit of selling through hardware stores is only $450.

Repeat this analysis for the other channels. The company is losing money in selling through garden supply shops and makes virtually all its profits through department stores. Notice that gross sales is not a reliable indicator of the net profits for each channel.

Determining Corrective Action It would be naive to conclude the company should drop garden supply and hardware stores to concentrate on department stores. We need to answer the following questions first:

- To what extent do buyers buy on the basis of type of retail outlet versus brand?
- What trends affect the relative importance of these three channels?
- How good are the company's marketing strategies for the three channels?

Using the answers, marketing management can evaluate five alternatives:

1. Establish a special charge for handling smaller orders.
2. Give more promotional aid to garden supply shops and hardware stores.
3. Reduce sales calls and advertising to garden supply shops and hardware stores.
4. Ignore the weakest retail units in each channel.
5. Do nothing.

Marketing profitability analysis indicates the relative profitability of different channels, products, territories, or other marketing entities. It does not prove the best course of action is to drop unprofitable marketing entities or capture the likely profit improvement of doing so.

Direct versus Full Costing Like all information tools, marketing profitability analysis can lead or mislead, depending on how well marketers understand its methods and limitations. The lawn mower company chose bases somewhat arbitrarily for allocating the functional expenses to its marketing entities. It used "number of sales calls" to allocate selling expenses, generating less record keeping and computation, when in principle "number of sales working hours" is a more accurate indicator of cost.

A far more serious decision is whether to allocate full costs or only direct and traceable costs in evaluating a marketing entity's performance. The lawn mower company sidestepped this problem by assuming only simple costs that fit with marketing activities, but we cannot avoid the question in real-world analyses of profitability. We distinguish three types of costs:

1. *Direct costs*—We can assign direct costs directly to the proper marketing entities. Sales commissions are a direct cost in a profitability analysis of sales territories, sales representatives, or customers. Advertising expenditures are a direct cost in a profitability analysis of products to the extent that each advertisement promotes only one product. Other direct costs for specific purposes are sales force salaries and traveling expenses.

2. *Traceable common costs*—We can assign traceable common costs only indirectly, but on a plausible basis, to the marketing entities. In the example, we analyzed rent this way.

3. *Nontraceable common costs*—Common costs whose allocation to the marketing entities is highly arbitrary are nontraceable common costs. To allocate "corporate image" expenditures equally to all products would be arbitrary, because all products don't benefit equally. To allocate them proportionately to the sales of the various products would be arbitrary, because relative product sales reflect many factors besides corporate image making. Other examples are top management salaries, taxes, interest, and other overhead.

No one disputes the inclusion of direct costs in marketing cost analysis. There is some controversy about including traceable common costs, which lump together costs that would and would not change with the scale of marketing activity. If the lawn mower company drops garden supply shops, it would probably continue to pay the same rent. Its profits would not rise immediately by the amount of the present loss in selling to garden supply shops ($310).

The major controversy is about whether to allocate the nontraceable common costs to the marketing entities. Such allocation is called the *full-cost approach*, and its advocates argue that all costs must ultimately be imputed in order to determine true profitability. However, this argument confuses the use of accounting for financial reporting with its use for managerial decision making. Full costing has three major weaknesses:

1. The relative profitability of different marketing entities can shift radically when we replace one arbitrary way to allocate nontraceable common costs by another.

2. The arbitrariness demoralizes managers, who feel their performance is judged adversely.

3. The inclusion of nontraceable common costs could weaken efforts at real cost control.

Operating management is most effective in controlling direct costs and traceable common costs. Arbitrary assignments of nontraceable common costs can lead managers to spend their time fighting cost allocations instead of managing controllable costs well.

Companies show growing interest in using marketing profitability analysis, or its broader version, activity-based cost accounting (ABC), to quantify the true profitability of different activities.[84] Managers can then reduce the resources required to perform various activities, make the resources more productive, acquire them at lower cost, or raise prices on products that consume heavy amounts of support resources. The contribution of ABC is to refocus management's attention away from using only labor or material standard costs to allocate full cost, and toward capturing the actual costs of supporting individual products, customers, and other entities.

Appendix

The Marketing Plan: An Introduction

As a marketer, you'll need a good marketing plan to provide direction and focus for your brand, product, or company. With a detailed plan, any business will be better prepared to launch an innovative new product or increase sales to current customers. Nonprofit organizations also use marketing plans to guide their fund-raising and outreach efforts. Even government agencies put together marketing plans for initiatives such as building public awareness of proper nutrition and stimulating area tourism.

The Purpose and Content of a Marketing Plan

A marketing plan has a more limited scope than a business plan, which offers a broad overview of the entire organization's mission, objectives, strategy, and resource allocation. The marketing plan documents how the organization's strategic objectives will be achieved through specific marketing strategies and tactics, with the customer as the starting point. It is also linked to the plans of other organizational departments. Suppose a marketing plan calls for selling 200,000 units annually. The production department must gear up to make that many units, finance must arrange funding to cover the expenses, human resources must be ready to hire and train staff, and so on. Without the appropriate level of organizational support and resources, no marketing plan can succeed.

Although the exact length and layout varies from company to company, a marketing plan usually contains the sections described in Chapter 2. Smaller businesses may create shorter or less formal marketing plans, whereas corporations generally require highly structured marketing plans. To guide implementation effectively, every part of the plan must be described in considerable detail. Sometimes a company will post its marketing plan on an internal Web site so managers and employees in different locations can consult specific sections and collaborate on additions or changes.

The Role of Research

To develop innovative products, successful strategies, and action programs, marketers need up-to-date information about the environment, the competition, and the selected market segments. Often, analysis of internal data is the starting point for assessing the current marketing situation, supplemented by marketing intelligence and research investigating the overall market, the competition, key issues, threats, and opportunities. As the plan is put into effect, marketers use research to measure progress toward objectives and to identify areas for improvement if results fall short of projections.

Finally, marketing research helps marketers learn more about their customers' requirements, expectations, perceptions, satisfaction, and loyalty. This deeper understanding provides a foundation for building competitive advantage through well-informed segmenting, targeting, and positioning decisions. Thus, the marketing plan should outline what marketing research will be conducted and when, as well as how, the findings will be applied.

The Role of Relationships

Although the marketing plan shows how the company will establish and maintain profitable customer relationships, it also affects both internal and external relationships. First, it influences how marketing personnel work with each other and with other departments to deliver value and satisfy customers. Second, it affects how the company works with suppliers, distributors, and partners to achieve the plan's objectives. Third, it influences the company's dealings with other stakeholders, including government regulators, the media, and the community at large. All these relationships are important to the organization's success and must be considered when developing a marketing plan.

From Marketing Plan to Marketing Action

Most companies create yearly marketing plans, although some plans cover a longer period. Marketers start planning well in advance of the implementation date to allow time for marketing research, analysis, management review, and coordination between departments. Then, after each action program begins, marketers monitor ongoing results, investigate any deviation from the projected outcome, and take corrective steps as needed. Some marketers also prepare contingency plans for implementation if certain conditions emerge. Because of inevitable and sometimes unpredictable environmental changes, marketers must be ready to update and adapt marketing plans at any time.

For effective implementation and control, the marketing plan should define how progress toward objectives will be measured. Managers typically use budgets, schedules, and marketing metrics for monitoring and evaluating results. With budgets, they can compare planned expenditures with actual expenditures for a given period. Schedules allow management to see when tasks were supposed to be completed and when they were actually completed. Marketing metrics track the actual outcomes of marketing programs to see whether the company is moving forward toward its objectives.

Sample Marketing Plan for Sonic

This section takes you inside the sample marketing plan for Sonic, a hypothetical start-up company. The company's first product is the Sonic 1000, a state-of-the-art, fully loaded multimedia smart phone. Sonic will be competing with Apple, BlackBerry, Motorola, Nokia, Samsung, and other well-established rivals in a crowded, fast-changing marketplace where smart phones have many communication and entertainment capabilities. The annotations explain more about what each section of the plan should contain.

1.0 Executive Summary

This section summarizes market opportunities, marketing strategy, and marketing and financial objectives for senior managers who will read and approve the marketing plan.

Sonic is preparing to launch a major new state-of-the-art multimedia smart phone, the Sonic 1000, in a mature market. We can effectively compete with many types of smart phones because our product offers a unique combination of advanced features and functionality at a very competitive value-added price. We are targeting specific segments in the consumer and business markets, taking advantage of the growing interest in a single powerful but affordable device with extensive communication, organization, and entertainment benefits.

The primary marketing objective is to achieve first-year U.S. market share of 1 percent with unit sales of 800,000. The primary financial objectives are to achieve first-year sales revenues of $200 million, keep first-year losses to less than $40 million, and break even early in the second year.

2.0 Situation Analysis

The situation analysis describes the market, the company's capability to serve targeted segments, and the competition.

Sonic, founded 18 months ago by two well-known entrepreneurs with telecommunications experience, is about to enter the highly competitive smart phone market. Multifunction cell phones are increasingly popular for both personal and professional use, with more than 320 million smart phones sold worldwide in 2010. Competition is increasingly intense even as technology evolves, industry consolidation continues, and pricing pressures squeeze profitability. Palm, a PDA pioneer, is one of several key players having difficulty adapting to the smart phone challenge. To gain market share in this dynamic environment, Sonic must carefully target specific segments with valued features and plan for a next-generation product to keep brand momentum going.

Market summary includes size, needs, growth, and trends. Describing the targeted segments in detail provides context for marketing strategies and programs discussed later in the plan.

2.1 Market Summary Sonic's market consists of consumers and business users who prefer to use a powerful but affordable single device for fully functional communication, information storage and exchange, organization, and entertainment on the go. Specific segments being targeted during the first year include professionals, corporations, students, entrepreneurs, and medical users. △ Exhibit A.1 shows how the Sonic 1000 addresses some of the most basic needs of targeted consumer and business segments in a cost-effective manner. The additional communication and entertainment benefits of the product just enhance its appeal to those segments.

Smart phone purchasers can choose between models based on several different operating systems. The biggest selling smart phone operating system is Symbian OS. Symbian's smaller rivals

Targeted Segment	Customer Need	Corresponding Feature/Benefit
Professionals (consumer market)	■ Stay in touch while on the go	■ Wireless e-mail to conveniently send and receive messages from anywhere; cell phone capability for voice communication from anywhere
	■ Record information while on the go	■ Voice recognition for no-hands recording
Students (consumer market)	■ Perform many functions without carrying multiple gadgets	■ Compatible with numerous applications and peripherals for convenient, cost-effective functionality
	■ Express style and individuality	■ Case wardrobe of different colors and patterns allows users to make a fashion statement
Corporate users (business market)	■ Input and access critical data on the go	■ Compatible with widely available software
	■ Use for proprietary tasks	■ Customizable to fit diverse corporate tasks and networks
Entrepreneurs (business market)	■ Organize and access contacts, schedule details	■ No-hands, wireless access to calendar and address book to easily check appointments and connect with contacts
Medical users (business market)	■ Update, access, and exchange medical records	■ No-hands, wireless recording and exchange of information to reduce paperwork and increase productivity

|Exh. A.1| △

Needs and Corresponding Features/Benefits of Sonic Smart Phone

include Android, BlackBerry OS, iOS, and the Windows Phone OS. Several mobile operating systems including Android and iOS are based on Linux and Unix. Sonic licenses a Linux-based system because it is somewhat less vulnerable to attack by hackers and viruses. Storage capacity (hard drive or flash drive) is an expected feature, so Sonic is equipping its first product with an ultra-fast 64-gigabyte drive that can be supplemented by extra storage. Technology costs are decreasing even as capabilities are increasing, which makes value-priced models more appealing to consumers and to business users with older smart phones who want to trade up to new, high-end multifunction units.

2.2 Strengths, Weaknesses, Opportunities, and Threat Analysis Sonic has several powerful strengths on which to build, but our major weakness is <u>lack of brand awareness and image</u>. The major opportunity is demand for multifunction communication, organization, and entertainment devices that deliver a number of valued benefits at a <u>lower cost.</u> We also face the threat of ever-higher competition and downward pricing pressure.

Strengths Sonic can build on three important strengths:

1. *Innovative product*—The Sonic 1000 offers a combination of features that are hard to find in single devices, with extensive telecommunications capabilities and highest quality digital video/music/TV program storage/playback.
2. *Security*—Our smart phone uses a Linux-based operating system that is less vulnerable to hackers and other security threats that can result in stolen or corrupted data.
3. *Pricing*—Our product is priced lower than competing smart phones—none of which offer the same bundle of features—which gives us an edge with price-conscious customers.

Weaknesses By waiting to enter the smart phone market until considerable consolidation of competitors has occurred, Sonic has learned from the successes and mistakes of others. Nonetheless, we have two main weaknesses:

1. *Lack of brand awareness*—Sonic has no established brand or image, whereas Samsung, Apple, Motorola, and others have strong brand recognition. We will address this issue with aggressive promotion.
2. *Heavier and thicker unit*—The Sonic 1000 is slightly heavier and thicker than most competing models because it incorporates so many telecommunication and multimedia features. To counteract this weakness, we will emphasize our product's benefits and value-added pricing, two compelling competitive strengths.

Strengths are internal capabilities that can help the company reach its objectives.

Weaknesses are internal elements that may interfere with the company's ability to achieve its objectives.

Opportunities Sonic can take advantage of two major market opportunities:

1. *Increasing demand for state-of-the-art multimedia devices with a full array of communication functions*—The market for cutting-edge multimedia, multifunction devices is growing much rapidly. Smart phones are already commonplace in public, work, and educational settings; in fact, users who bought entry-level models are now trading up.
2. *Lower technology costs*—Better technology is now available at a lower cost than ever before. Thus, Sonic can incorporate advanced features at a value-added price that allows for reasonable profits.

Threats We face three main threats at the introduction of the Sonic 1000:

1. *Increased competition*—More companies are offering devices with some but not all of the features and benefits provided by the Sonic 1000. Therefore, Sonic's marketing communications must stress our clear differentiation and value-added pricing.
2. *Downward pressure on pricing*—Increased competition and market share strategies are pushing smart phone prices down. Still, our objective of breaking even with second-year sales of the original model is realistic, given the lower margins in the smart phone market.
3. *Compressed product life cycle*—Smart phones are reaching the maturity stage of their life cycle more quickly than earlier technology products. Because of this compressed life cycle, we plan to introduce an even greater enhanced media-oriented second product during the year following the Sonic 1000's launch.

2.3 Competition The emergence of well-designed multifunction smart phones, including the Apple iPhone, has increased competitive pressure. Competitors are continually adding features and sharpening price points. Key competitors:

- *Motorola.* Motorola has a long tradition of successful cell phones—it sold millions and millions of its RAZR clamshell phones worldwide. It has struggled in recent years, however, to keep up with competition.
- *Apple.* The initial iPhone, a smart phone with a 3.5-inch color screen, was designed with entertainment enthusiasts in mind. It's well equipped for music, video, and Web access, plus calendar and contact management functions. Apple initially partnered only with the AT&T network and cut the product's price to $399 two months after introduction to speed market penetration.
- *RIM.* Research In Motion makes the lightweight BlackBerry wireless phone/PDA products that are popular among corporate users. RIM's continuous innovation and solid customer service support strengthen its competitive standing as it introduces more smart phones and PDAs.
- *Samsung.* Value, style, function: Samsung is a powerful competitor, offering a variety of smart phones and Ultra-Mobile PCs for consumer and business segments. Some of its smart phones are available for specific telecommunications carriers and some are "unlocked," ready for any compatible telecommunications network.
- *Nokia.* With a presence in virtually every possible cell phone market, Nokia is always an experienced, formidable opponent. Having launched one of the early smart phones, it will be expected to aggressively compete in the smart phone market.

Despite strong competition, Sonic can carve out a definite image and gain recognition among targeted segments. Our appealing combination of state-of-the-art features and low price is a critical point of differentiation for competitive advantage. Our second product will be even more media-oriented to appeal to segments where we will have strong brand recognition. ◢ Exhibit A.2 shows a sample of competitive products and prices.

2.4 Product Offerings The Sonic 1000 offers the following standard features:

- Voice recognition for hands-free operation
- Full array of apps
- Complete organization functions, including linked calendar, address book, synchronization
- Digital music/video/television recording, wireless downloading, and instant playback
- Wireless Web and e-mail, text messaging, instant messaging
- Four-inch high-quality color touch screen

	Samsung Galaxy S – Captivate	Apple iPhone 4	Motorola Droid Pro	Nokia N900	BlackBerry Storm 2 9550
Storage	32 GB memory card	32 GB flash drive	Supports up to 32 GB micro SD	Up to 32 GB Internal 16 GB mirco SD (sold separately)	2GB eMMC 16MB media card included
Display	WVGA 4" touch screen	Retina display 3.5" (diagonal) widescreen multi-touch screen	HGVA 3.1" touch screen	WVGA 3.5" touch screen	3.25" touch screen
Camera	Auto focus 5.0 MP 4× digital zoom Video MPEG4, AAC, AAC+ H.263 H.264 Video streaming	Tap to focus 5.0 MP VGA quality photos LED flash Video recording Geotagging	Auto focus 5 MP Digital zoom LED flash Image editing tools	Auto focus with two-stage capture key 5 MP Dual LED flash Image editing tools Geotagging	Auto focus 3.2 MP 2x digital zoom Flash Auto focus Image stabilization Video recording
Price	$449-$599	$723 $199 16 GB $299 32 GB	$449-$489	$349	$349

|Exh. A.2| ▲

Selected Smart Phone Products and Pricing

- Ultra-fast 64-gigabyte drive and expansion slots
- Integrated 12 megapixel camera with flash and photo editing/sharing tools

First-year sales revenues are projected to be $200 million, based on sales of 800,000 of the Sonic 1000 model at a wholesale price of $250 each. Our second-year product will be the Sonic All Media 2000, stressing enhanced multimedia communication, networking, and entertainment functions. The Sonic All Media 2000 will include Sonic 1000 features plus additional features such as:

- Built-in media beaming to share music, video, and television files with other devices
- Webcam for instant video capture and uploading to popular video Web sites
- Voice-command access to popular social networking Web sites

2.5 Distribution Sonic-branded products will be distributed through a network of retailers in the top 50 U.S. markets. Among the most important channel partners being contacted are:

Distribution explains each channel for the company's products and mentions new developments and trends.

- *Office supply superstores.* Office Max, Office Depot, and Staples will all carry Sonic products in stores, in catalogs, and online.
- *Computer stores.* CompUSA and independent computer retailers will carry Sonic products.
- *Electronics specialty stores.* Best Buy will feature Sonic smart phones in its stores, online, and in its media advertising.
- *Online retailers.* Amazon.com will carry Sonic smart phones and, for a promotional fee, will give Sonic prominent placement on its homepage during the introduction.

Distribution will initially be restricted to the United States, with appropriate sales promotion support. Later, we plan to expand into Canada and beyond.

3.0 Marketing Strategy

3.1 Objectives We have set aggressive but achievable objectives for the first and second years of market entry.

Objectives should be defined in specific terms so management can measure progress and take corrective action to stay on track.

- *First-Year Objectives.* We are aiming for a 1 percent share of the U.S. smart phone market through unit sales volume of 800,000.
- *Second-Year Objectives.* Our second-year objective is to achieve break-even on the Sonic 1000 and launch our second model.

3.2 Target Markets Sonic's strategy is based on a positioning of product differentiation. Our primary consumer target for the Sonic 1000 is middle- to upper-income professionals who need one fully loaded device to coordinate their busy schedules, stay in touch with family and colleagues, and be entertained on the go. Our secondary consumer target is high school, college, and graduate students who want a multimedia, dual-mode device. This segment can be described demographically by age (16–30) and education status. Our Sonic All Media 2000 will be aimed at teens and twentysomethings who want a device with features to support social networking and heavier, more extensive entertainment media consumption.

The primary business target for the Sonic 1000 is mid- to large-sized corporations that want to help their managers and employees stay in touch and input or access critical data when out of the office. This segment consists of companies with more than $25 million in annual sales and more than 100 employees. A secondary target is entrepreneurs and small business owners. Also we will target medical users who want to update or access patients' medical records.

Each of the marketing-mix strategies conveys Sonic's differentiation to these target market segments.

3.3 Positioning Using product differentiation, we are positioning the Sonic smart phone as the most versatile, convenient, value-added model for personal and professional use. Our marketing will focus on the value-priced multiple communication, entertainment, and information capabilities differentiating the Sonic 1000.

3.4 Strategies

Product The Sonic 1000, including all the features described in the earlier Product Review section and more, will be sold with a one-year warranty. We will introduce the Sonic All Media 2000 during the following year, after we have established our Sonic brand. The brand and logo (Sonic's distinctive yellow thunderbolt) will be displayed on our products and packaging as well as in all marketing campaigns.

Pricing The Sonic 1000 will be introduced at a $250 wholesale price and a $300 estimated retail price per unit. We expect to lower the price of this model when we expand the product line by launching the Sonic All Media 2000, to be priced at $350 wholesale per unit. These prices reflect a strategy of (1) attracting desirable channel partners and (2) taking share from established competitors.

Distribution Our channel strategy is to use selective distribution, marketing Sonic smart phones through well-known stores and online retailers. During the first year, we will add channel partners until we have coverage in all major U.S. markets and the product is included in the major electronics catalogs and Web sites. We will also investigate distribution through cell-phone outlets maintained by major carriers such as Verizon Wireless. In support of channel partners, we will provide demonstration products, detailed specification handouts, and full-color photos and displays featuring the product. Finally, we plan to arrange special payment terms for retailers that place volume orders.

Marketing Communications By integrating all messages in all media, we will reinforce the brand name and the main points of product differentiation. Research about media consumption patterns will help our advertising agency choose appropriate media and timing to reach prospects before and during product introduction. Thereafter, advertising will appear on a pulsing basis to maintain brand awareness and communicate various differentiation messages. The agency will also coordinate public relations efforts to build the Sonic brand and support the differentiation message. To generate buzz, we will host a user-generated video contest on our Web site. To attract, retain, and motivate channel partners for a push strategy, we will use trade sales promotions and personal selling. Until the Sonic brand has been established, our communications will encourage purchases through channel partners rather than from our Web site.

3.5 Marketing Mix The Sonic 1000 will be introduced in February. Here are summaries of action programs we will use during the first six months to achieve our stated objectives.

- *January.* We will launch a $200,000 trade sales promotion campaign and participate in major industry trade shows to educate dealers and generate channel support for the product launch

---

All marketing strategies start with segmentation, targeting, and positioning.

Positioning identifies the brand, benefits, points of difference, and parity for the product or line.

Product strategy includes decisions about product mix and lines, brands, packaging and labeling, and warranties.

Pricing strategy covers decisions about setting initial prices and adapting prices in response to opportunities and competitive challenges.

Distribution strategy includes selection and management of channel relationships to deliver value to customers.

Marketing communications strategy covers all efforts to communicate to target audiences and channel members.

The marketing mix includes tactics and programs that support product, pricing, distribution, and marketing communications strategy.

in February. Also, we will create buzz by providing samples to selected product reviewers, opinion leaders, influential bloggers, and celebrities. Our training staff will work with retail sales personnel at major chains to explain the Sonic 1000's features, benefits, and advantages.

- *February.* We will start an integrated print/radio/Internet campaign targeting professionals and consumers. The campaign will show how many functions the Sonic smart phone can perform and emphasize the convenience of a single, powerful handheld device. This multimedia campaign will be supported by point-of-sale signage as well as online-only ads and video tours.
- *March.* As the multimedia advertising campaign continues, we will add consumer sales promotions such as a contest in which consumers post videos to our Web site, showing how they use the Sonic in creative and unusual ways. We will also distribute new point-of-purchase displays to support our retailers.
- *April* We will hold a trade sales contest offering prizes for the salesperson and retail organization that sells the most Sonic smart phones during the four-week period.
- *May.* We plan to roll out a new national advertising campaign this month. The radio ads will feature celebrity voices telling their Sonic smart phones to perform functions such as initiating a phone call, sending an e-mail, playing a song or video, and so on. The stylized print and online ads will feature avatars of these celebrities holding their Sonic smart phones. We plan to repeat this theme for next year's product launch.
- *June.* Our radio campaign will add a new voice-over tagline promoting the Sonic 1000 as a graduation gift. We will exhibit at the semiannual electronics trade show and provide retailers with new competitive comparison handouts as a sales aid. In addition, we will analyze the results of customer satisfaction research for use in future campaigns and product development efforts.

Programs should coordinate with the resources and activities of other departments that contribute to customer value for each product.

3.6 Marketing Research Using research, we will identify specific features and benefits our target market segments value. Feedback from market tests, surveys, and focus groups will help us develop and fine-tune the Sonic All Media 2000. We are also measuring and analyzing customers' attitudes toward competing brands and products. Brand awareness research will help us determine the effectiveness and efficiency of our messages and media. Finally, we will use customer satisfaction studies to gauge market reaction.

This section shows how marketing research will support the development, implementation, and evaluation of marketing strategies and programs.

4.0 Financials

Total first-year sales revenue for the Sonic 1000 is projected at $200 million, with an average wholesale price of $250 per unit and variable cost per unit of $150 for unit sales volume of 800,000. We anticipate a first-year loss of up to $40 million. Break-even calculations indicate that the Sonic 1000 will become profitable after the sales volume exceeds 267,500 during the product's second year. Our break-even analysis assumes per-unit wholesale revenue of $250 per unit, variable cost of $150 per unit, and estimated first-year fixed costs of $26,750,000. With these assumptions, the break-even calculation is:

$$\frac{26,750,000}{\$250 - \$150} = 267,500 \text{ units}$$

Financials include budgets and forecasts to plan for marketing expenditures, scheduling, and operations.

5.0 Controls

Controls are being established to cover implementation and the organization of our marketing activities.

Controls help management measure results and identify any problems or performance variations that need corrective action.

5.1 Implementation We are planning tight control measures to closely monitor quality and customer service satisfaction. This will enable us to react very quickly in correcting any problems that may occur. Other early warning signals that will be monitored for signs of deviation from the plan include monthly sales (by segment and channel) and monthly expenses.

5.2 Marketing Organization Sonic's chief marketing officer, Jane Melody, holds overall responsibility for all of the company's marketing activities. ◭ Exhibit A.3 shows the structure

The marketing department may be organized by function, as in this sample, or by geography, product, customer, or some combination of these.

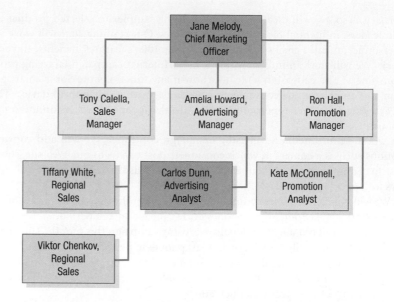

of the eight-person marketing organization. Sonic has hired Worldwide Marketing to handle national sales campaigns, trade and consumer sales promotions, and public relations efforts.

Sonic Marketing Plan Chapter Assignments[1]

Chapter 2

As an assistant to Jane Melody, Sonic's chief marketing officer, you've been assigned to draft a mission statement for top management's review. This should cover the competitive spheres within which the firm will operate and your recommendation of an appropriate generic competitive strategy. Using your knowledge of marketing, the information you have about Sonic, and library or Internet resources, answer the following questions.

- What should Sonic's mission be?
- In what competitive spheres (industry, products and applications, competence, market-segment, vertical, and geographic) should Sonic operate?
- Which of Porter's generic competitive strategies would you recommend Sonic follow in formulating overall strategy?

As your instructor directs, enter your answers and supporting information in a written marketing plan or use *Marketing Plan Pro* software to document your ideas.

Chapter 3

Jane Melody asks you to scan Sonic's external environment for early warning signals of new opportunities and emerging threats that could affect the success of the Sonic 1000 smart phone. Using Internet or library sources (or both), locate information to answer three questions about key areas of the macroenvironment.

- What demographic changes are likely to affect Sonic's targeted segments?
- What economic trends might influence buyer behavior in Sonic's targeted segments?
- How might the rapid pace of technological change/alter Sonic's competitive situation?

Enter your answers about Sonic's environment in the appropriate sections of a written marketing plan or use the *Marketing Plan Pro* software to record your comments.

Chapter 4

Your next task is to consider how marketing research can help Sonic support its marketing strategy. Jane Melody also asks you how Sonic can measure results after the marketing plan is implemented. She wants you to answer the following three questions.

- What surveys, focus groups, observation, behavioral data, or experiments will Sonic need to support its marketing strategy? Be specific about the questions or issues that Sonic needs to resolve using marketing research.
- Where can you find suitable secondary data about total demand for smart phones over the next two years? Identify at least two sources (online or offline), describe what you plan to draw from each source, and indicate how the data would be useful for Sonic's marketing planning.
- Recommend three specific marketing metrics for Sonic to apply in determining marketing effectiveness and efficiency.

Enter this information in the marketing plan you've been writing or use the *Marketing Plan Pro* software to document your responses.

Chapter 5

Sonic has decided to focus on total customer satisfaction as a way of encouraging brand loyalty in a highly competitive marketplace. With this in mind, you've been assigned to analyze three specific issues as you continue working on Sonic's marketing plan.

- How (and how often) should Sonic monitor customer satisfaction?
- Would you recommend that Sonic use the Net Promoter method? Explain your reasoning.
- Which customer touch points should Sonic pay particularly close attention to, and why?

Consider your answers in the context of Sonic's current situation and the objectives it has set. Then enter your latest decisions in the written marketing plan or using *Marketing Plan Pro* software.

Chapter 6

You're responsible for researching and analyzing the consumer market for Sonic's smart phone product. Look again at the data you've already entered about the company's current situation and macroenvironment, especially the market being targeted. Now answer these questions about the market and buyer behavior.

- What cultural, social, and personal factors are likely to most influence consumer purchasing of smart phones? What research tools would help you better understand the effect on buyer attitudes and behavior?
- Which aspects of consumer behavior should Sonic's marketing plan emphasize and why?
- What marketing activities should Sonic plan to coincide with each stage of the consumer buying process?

After you've analyzed these aspects of consumer behavior, consider the implications for Sonic's marketing efforts to support the launch of its smart phone. Finally, document your findings and conclusions in a written marketing plan or with *Marketing Plan Pro*.

Chapter 7

You've been learning more about the business market for Sonic's smart phone. Jane Melody has defined this market as mid- to large-sized corporations that want their employees to stay in touch and be able to input or access data from any location. Respond to the following three questions based on your knowledge of Sonic's current situation and business-to-business marketing.

- What types of businesses appear to fit Melody's market definition? How can you research the number of employees and find other data about these types of businesses?
- What type of purchase would a Sonic smart phone represent for these businesses? Who would participate in and influence this type of purchase?
- Would demand for smart phones among corporate buyers tend to be inelastic? What are the implications for Sonic's marketing plan?

Your answers to these questions will affect how Sonic plans marketing activities for the business segments to be targeted. Take a few minutes to note your ideas in a written marketing plan or using *Marketing Plan Pro*.

Chapter 8

Identifying suitable market segments and selecting targets are critical to the success of any marketing plan. As Jane Melody's assistant, you're responsible for market segmentation and targeting. Look back at the market information, buyer behavior data, and competitive details you previously gathered as you answer the following questions.

- Which variables should Sonic use to segment its consumer and business markets?
- How can Sonic evaluate the attractiveness of each identified segment? Should Sonic market to one consumer segment and one business segment or target more than one in each market? Why?
- Should Sonic pursue full market coverage, market specialization, product specialization, selective specialization, or single-segment concentration? Why?

Next, consider how your decisions about segmentation and targeting will affect Sonic's marketing efforts. Depending on your instructor's directions, summarize your conclusions in a written marketing plan or use *Marketing Plan Pro*.

Chapter 9

Sonic is a new brand with no prior brand associations, which presents a number of marketing opportunities and challenges. Jane Melody has given you responsibility for making recommendations about three brand equity issues that are important to Sonic's marketing plan.

- What brand elements would be most useful for differentiating the Sonic brand from competing brands?
- How can Sonic sum up its brand promise for the new smart phone?
- Should Sonic add a brand for its second product or retain the Sonic name?

Be sure your brand ideas are appropriate in light of what you've learned about your targeted segments and the competition. Then add this information to your written marketing plan or the plan you've been developing with *Marketing Plan Pro* software.

Chapter 10

As before, you're working with Jane Melody on Sonic's marketing plan for launching a new smart phone. Now you're focusing on Sonic's positioning and product life-cycle strategies by answering three specific questions.

- In a sentence or two, what is an appropriate positioning for the Sonic 1000 smart phone?
- Knowing the stage of Sonic's smart phone in the product life cycle, what are the implications for pricing, promotion, and distribution?
- In which stage of its evolution does the smart phone market appear to be? What does this mean for Sonic's marketing plans?

Document your ideas in a written marketing plan or in *Marketing Plan Pro*. Note any additional research you may need to determine how to proceed after the Sonic 1000 has been launched.

Chapter 11

Sonic is a new entrant in an established industry characterized by competitors with relatively high brand identity and strong market positions. Use research and your knowledge of how to deal with competitors to consider three issues that will affect the company's ability to successfully introduce its first product:

- What factors will you use to determine Sonic's strategic group?
- Should Sonic select a class of competitor to attack on the basis of strength versus weakness, closeness versus distance, or good versus bad? Why is this appropriate in the smart phone market?

- As a start-up company, what competitive strategy would be most effective as Sonic introduces its first product?

Take time to analyze how Sonic's competitive strategy will affect its marketing strategy and tactics. Now summarize your ideas in a written marketing plan or using *Marketing Plan Pro* software.

Chapter 12

Introducing a new product entails a variety of decisions about product strategy, including differentiation, ingredient branding, packaging, labeling, warranty, and guarantee. Your next task is to answer the following questions about Sonic's product strategy.

- Which aspect of product differentiation would be most valuable in setting Sonic apart from its competitors, and why?
- Should Sonic use ingredient branding to tout the Linux-based operating system that it says makes its smart phone more secure than smart phones based on some other operating systems?
- How can Sonic use packaging and labeling to support its brand image and help its channel partners sell the smart phone product more effectively?

Once you've answered these questions, incorporate your ideas into the marketing plan you've been writing or document them using the *Marketing Plan Pro* software.

Chapter 13

You're planning customer support services for Sonic's new smart phone product. Review what you know about your target market and its needs; also think about what Sonic's competitors are offering. Then respond to these three questions about designing and managing services.

- What support services are buyers of smart phone products likely to want and need?
- How can Sonic manage gaps between perceived service and expected service to satisfy customers?
- What postsale service arrangements must Sonic make and how would you expect these to affect customer satisfaction?

Consider how your service strategy will support Sonic's overall marketing efforts. Summarize your recommendations in a written marketing plan or use *Marketing Plan Pro* to document your ideas.

Chapter 14

You're in charge of pricing Sonic's product for its launch early next year. Review the SWOT analysis you previously prepared as well as Sonic's competitive environment, targeting strategy, and product positioning. Now continue working on your marketing plan by responding to the following questions.

- What should Sonic's primary pricing objective be? Explain your reasoning.
- Are smart phone customers likely to be price sensitive? What are the implications for your pricing decisions?
- What price adaptations (such as discounts, allowances, and promotional pricing) should Sonic include in its marketing plan?

Make notes about your answers to these questions and then document the information in a written marketing plan or use *Marketing Plan Pro* software, depending on your instructor's directions.

Chapter 15

At Sonic, you have been asked to develop a marketing channel system for the new Sonic 1000 smart phone. Based on what you know about designing and managing integrated marketing channels, answer the three questions that follow.

- Do you agree with Jane Melody's decision to use a push strategy for the new product? Explain your reasoning.
- How many channel levels are appropriate for Sonic's targeted consumer and business segments?
- In determining the number of channel members, should you use exclusive, selective, or intensive distribution? Why?

Be sure your marketing channel ideas support the product positioning and are consistent with the goals that have been set. Record your recommendations in a written marketing plan or use *Marketing Plan Pro*.

Chapter 16

At this point, you need to make more specific decisions about managing the marketing intermediaries for Sonic's first product. Formulate your ideas by answering the following questions.

- What types of retailers would be most appropriate for distributing Sonic's smart phone? What are the advantages and disadvantages of selling through these types of retailers?
- What role should wholesalers play in Sonic's distribution strategy? Why?
- What market-logistics issues must Sonic consider for the launch of its first smart phone?

Summarize your decisions about retailing, wholesaling, and logistics in the marketing plan you've been writing or in the *Marketing Plan Pro* software.

Chapter 17

Jane Melody has assigned you to plan integrated marketing communications for Sonic's new product introduction. Review the data, decisions, and strategies you previously documented in your marketing plan before you answer the next three questions.

- What communications objectives are appropriate for Sonic's initial campaign?
- How can Sonic use personal communications channels to influence its target audience?
- Which communication tools would you recommend using after Sonic's initial product has been in the market for six months? Why?

Confirm that your marketing communications plans make sense in light of Sonic's overall marketing efforts. Now, as your instructor directs, summarize your thoughts in a written marketing plan or in the *Marketing Plan Pro* software.

Chapter 18

Mass communications will play a key role in Sonic's product introduction. After reviewing your earlier decisions and thinking about the current situation (especially your competitive circumstances), respond to the following questions to continue planning Sonic's marketing communications strategy.

- Once Sonic begins to use consumer advertising, what goals would be appropriate?
- Should Sonic continue consumer and trade sales promotion after the new product has been in the market for six months? Explain your reasoning.
- Jane Melody wants you to recommend an event sponsorship possibility that would be appropriate for the new product campaign. What type of event would you suggest and what objectives would you set for the sponsorship?

Record your ideas about mass communications in the marketing plan you've been writing or use *Marketing Plan Pro*.

Chapter 19

Sonic needs a strategy for managing personal communications during its new product launch. This is the time to look at interactive marketing, word of mouth, and personal selling. Answer these three questions as you consider Sonic's personal communications strategy.

- Which forms of interactive marketing are appropriate for Sonic, given its objectives, mass communications arrangements, and channel decisions?
- How should Sonic use word of mouth to generate brand awareness and encourage potential buyers to visit retailers to see the new smart phone in person?
- Does Sonic need a direct sales force or can it sell through agents and other outside representatives?

Look back at earlier decisions and ideas before you document your comments about personal communications in your written marketing plan or using *Marketing Plan Pro* software.

Chapter 20

Knowing that the smart phone market is likely to remain highly competitive, Jane Melody wants you to look ahead at how Sonic can develop new products outside the smart phone market. Review the competitive situation and the market situation before you continue working on the Sonic marketing plan.

- List three new-product ideas that build on Sonic's strengths and the needs of its various target segments. What criteria should Sonic use to screen these ideas?
- Develop the most promising idea into a product concept and explain how Sonic can test this concept. What particular dimensions must be tested?
- Assume that the most promising idea tests well. Now develop a marketing strategy for introducing it, including a description of the target market; the product positioning; the estimated sales, profit, and market share goals for the first year; your channel strategy; and the marketing budget you will recommend for this new product introduction. If possible, estimate Sonic's costs and conduct a break-even analysis.

Document all the details of your new-product development ideas in the written marketing plan or use *Marketing Plan Pro* software.

Chapter 21

As Jane Melody's assistant, you're researching how to market the Sonic 1000 smart phone product outside the United States within a year. You've been asked to answer the following questions about Sonic's use of global marketing.

- As a start-up company, should Sonic use indirect or direct exporting, licensing, joint ventures, or direct investment to enter the Canadian market next year? To enter other markets? Explain your answers.
- If Sonic starts marketing its smart phone in other countries, which of the international product strategies is most appropriate? Why?
- Although some components are made in Asia, Sonic's smart phones will be assembled in Mexico through a contractual arrangement with a local factory. How are country-of-origin perceptions likely to affect your marketing recommendations?

Think about how these global marketing issues fit into Sonic's overall marketing strategy. Now document your ideas in the marketing plan you've been writing or using *Marketing Plan Pro*.

Chapter 22

With the rest of the marketing plan in place, you're ready to make recommendations about how to manage Sonic's marketing activities. Here are some specific questions Jane Melody wants you to consider.

- How can Sonic drive customer-focused marketing and strategic innovation throughout the organization?
- What role should social responsibility play in Sonic's marketing?
- How can Sonic evaluate its marketing? Suggest several specific steps the company should take.

To complete your marketing plan, enter your answers to these questions in the written marketing plan or in *Marketing Plan Pro* software. Finally, draft the executive summary of the plan's highlights.

Endnotes

Chapter 1

1. Michael Learmonth, "Social Media Paves Way to White House," *Advertising Age*, March 30, 2009, p. 16; Noreen O'Leary, "GMBB," *AdweekMedia*, June 15, 2009, p. 2; John Quelch, "The Marketing of a President," *Harvard Business School Working Knowledge*, November 12, 2008.

2. Philip Kotler, "Marketing: The Underappreciated Workhorse," *Market Leader* Quarter 2 (2009), pp. 8–10.

3. Peter C. Verhoef and Peter S. H. Leeflang, "Understanding the Marketing Department's Influence within the Firm," *Journal of Marketing 73* (March 2009), pp. 14–37.

4. Eric Newman, "To Boost the Bottom Line, Strengthen the Front Line," *Brandweek*, June 9, 2008, p. 10.

5. Stephanie Clifford, "A Video Prank at Domino's Taints Brand," *New York Times*, April 15, 2009; Thom Forbes, "Domino's Takes Cautious Approach to 'Prank' Video," *Ad Age*, April 15, 2009.

6. Jon Fine, "Marketing's Drift Away From Media," *BusinessWeek*, August 17, 2009, p. 64.

7. American Marketing Association, "Definition of Marketing," www.marketingpower.com/AboutAMA/Pages/DefinitionofMarketing.aspx, 2007; Lisa Keefe, "Marketing Defined," *Marketing News*, January 15, 2008, pp. 28–29.

8. Peter Drucker, *Management: Tasks, Responsibilities, Practices* (New York: Harper and Row, 1973), pp. 64–65.

9. B. Joseph Pine II and James Gilmore, *The Experience Economy* (Boston: Harvard Business School Press, 1999); Bernd Schmitt, *Experience Marketing* (New York: Free Press, 1999); Philip Kotler, "Dream Vacations: The Booming Market for Designed Experiences," *The Futurist*, October 1984, pp. 7–13.

10. Irving J. Rein, Philip Kotler, Michael Hamlin, and Martin Stoller, *High Visibility*, 3rd ed. (New York: McGraw-Hill, 2006).

11. Philip Kotler, Christer Asplund, Irving Rein, and Donald H. Haider, *Marketing Places in Europe: Attracting Investments, Industries, Residents, and Visitors to European Cities, Communities, Regions, and Nations* (London: Financial Times Prentice Hall, 1999); Philip Kotler, Irving J. Rein, and Donald Haider, *Marketing Places: Attracting Investment, Industry, and Tourism to Cities, States, and Nations* (New York: Free Press, 1993).

12. Michael McCarthy, "Vegas Goes Back to Naughty Roots," *USA Today*, April 11, 2005; Julie Dunn, "Vegas Hopes for Payoff with Denverites," *Denver Post*, June 16, 2005; John M. Broder, "The Pied Piper of Las Vegas Seems to Have Perfect Pitch," *New York Times*, June 4, 2004; Chris Jones, "Las Vegas Tourism: Fewer Visitors, Don't Blame Fuel," *Las Vegas Review-Journal*, July 15, 2006; Richard Velotta, "Report: Las Vegas Tourism Tumbles 11.9 percent in January," *Las Vegas Sun*, March 10, 2009.

13. Carl Shapiro and Hal R. Varian, "Versioning: The Smart Way to Sell Information," *Harvard Business Review*, November–December 1998, pp. 106–14.

14. John R. Brandt, "Dare to Be Different," *Chief Executive*, May 2003, pp. 34–38.

15. Jena McGregor, Matthew Boyle, and Peter Burrows, "Your New Customer: The State," *BusinessWeek*, March 23 and 30, 2009, p. 66.

16. Jeffrey Rayport and John Sviokla, "Exploring the Virtual Value Chain," *Harvard Business Review*, November–December 1995, pp. 75–85; Jeffrey Rayport and John Sviokla, "Managing in the Marketspace," *Harvard Business Review*, November–December 1994, pp. 141–150.

17. Mohan Sawhney, *Seven Steps to Nirvana* (New York: McGraw-Hill, 2001).

18. Nikolaus Franke, Peter Keinz, and Christoph J. Steger, "Testing the Value of Customization: When Do Customers Really Prefer Products Tailored to Their Preferences?" *Journal of Marketing 73* (September 2009), pp. 103–21.

19. Tom Szaky, "Revolution in a Bottle," *Portfolio Trade*, 2009; Linda M. Castellito, "TerraCycle Founder's Journey Started with Worm Poop," *USA Today*, September 25, 2009, p. 5B.

20. "Food Site Finds Recipe For Mixing in Sponsors, On the Hot Seat," *Boston Globe*, September 6, 2009, p. G3; "Allrecipes.com Stirs Up Success," press release, www.allrecipes.com, July 21, 2009; Eric Engelman, "Questions for Lisa Sharples, President of Allrecipes.com," *Puget Sound Business Journal*, October 10, 2008.

21. Adam Lashinsky, "Shoutout in Gadget Land," *Fortune*, November 10, 2003, pp. 77–86; "Computer Industry Trends: Top 100 Companies," www.netvalley.com; Tim Conneally, "Gartner: Acer Gains Big Worldwide, Apple Gains in US," *Betanews*, October 15, 2008.

22. "Dick's Sporting Goods, Inc. (DKS.N) (New York Stock Exchange)," *Reuters,* www.reuters.com.

23. Anya Kamenetz, "The Network Unbound," *Fast Company*, June 2006, pp. 69–73.

24. David Kiley, "Advertisers, Start Your Engines," *BusinessWeek*, March 6, 2006, p. 26; Cameron Wykes, "Making Sense Out of Social Nets," *AdweekMedia*, July 6, 2009, p. 2.

25. "2005 Marketing Receptivity Survey," *Yankelovich Partners Inc.*, April 18, 2005.

26. Kate Brumbeck, "Alabama Flea Market Owner Turns Into YouTube Phenomenon," *Associated Press*, June 30, 2007.

27. Martin Bosworth, "Loyalty Cards: Rewards or Threats?" *ConsumerAffairs.com*, July 11, 2005.

28. Antonio Gonsalves, "Dell Makes $3 Million from Twitter-Related Sales," *InformationWeek*, June 12, 2009.

29. Linda Tischler, "What's The Buzz?" *Fast Company*, May 2004, p. 76.

30. Valerie Alderson, "Measuring the Value of a Managed WOM Program in Test & Control Markets," *BzzAgent Inc.*, 2007.

31. Suzanne Vranica, "Marketers Aim New Ads at Video iPod Users," *Wall Street Journal*, January 31, 2006; Kevin Redmond, "GPS + Mobile Marketing = Goodness," *Barbarian Blog*, February 21, 2009.

32. Bruce Horovitz, "In Trend Toward Vanity Food, It's Getting Personal," *USA Today*, August 9, 2006.

33. Josh Catone, "15 Companies That Really Get Corporate Blogging," www.sitepoint.com.

34. "Intranet Case Study: GM's mySocrates," www.communitelligence.com.

35. Gail McGovern and John A. Quelch, "The Fall and Rise of the CMO," *Strategy + Business*, Winter 2004.

36. Richard Rawlinson, "Beyond Brand Management," *Strategy + Business*, Summer 2006.

37. Jennifer Rooney, "As If You Didn't Know by Now, It's About the Bottom Line for CMOs," *Advertising Age*, May 5, 2008, pp. 3–57.

38. Elisabeth Sullivan, "Solving the CMO Puzzle," *Marketing News*, March 30, 2009, p. 12.

39. Constantine von Hoffman, "Armed with Intelligence," *Brandweek*, May 29, 2006, pp. 17–20.

40. "China's Second Biggest PC Maker to Push Windows," www.digitalworldtokyo.com, April 15, 2006.

41. Robert J. Keith, "The Marketing Revolution," *Journal of Marketing* 24 (January 1960), pp. 35–38; John B. McKitterick, "What Is the Marketing Management Concept?" Frank M. Bass, ed., *The Frontiers of Marketing Thought and Action* (Chicago: American Marketing Association, 1957), pp. 71–82; Fred J. Borch, "The Marketing Philosophy as a Way of Business Life," *The Marketing Concept: Its Meaning to Management* (Marketing series, no. 99; New York: American Management Association, 1957), pp. 3–5.

42. Theodore Levitt, "Marketing Myopia," *Harvard Business Review*, July–August 1960, p. 50.

43. Rohit Deshpande and John U. Farley, "Measuring Market Orientation: Generalization and Synthesis," *Journal of Market-Focused Management* 2 (1998), pp. 213–32; Ajay K. Kohli and Bernard J. Jaworski, "Market Orientation: The Construct, Research Propositions, and Managerial Implications," *Journal of Marketing* 54 (April 1990), pp. 1–18; John C. Narver and Stanley F. Slater, "The Effect of a Market Orientation on Business Profitability," *Journal of Marketing* 54 (October 1990), pp. 20–35.

44. Evert Gummesson, *Total Relationship Marketing* (Boston: Butterworth-Heinemann, 1999); Regis McKenna, *Relationship Marketing* (Reading, MA: Addison-Wesley, 1991); Martin Christopher, Adrian Payne, and David Ballantyne, *Relationship Marketing: Bringing Quality, Customer Service, and Marketing Together* (Oxford, UK: Butterworth-Heinemann, 1991).

45. James C. Anderson, Hakan Hakansson, and Jan Johanson, "Dyadic Business Relationships within a Business Network Context," *Journal of Marketing* 58 (October 15, 1994), pp. 1–15.

46. Larry Selden and Yoko S. Selden, "Profitable Customer: The Key to Great Brands," *Advertising Age*, July 10, 2006, p. S7; Larry Selden and Geoffrey Colvin, *Angel Customers and Demon Customers* (New York, NY: Portfolio, 2003).

47. Allison Fass, "Theirspace.com," *Forbes*, May 8, 2006, pp. 122–24.

48. Paula Andruss, "Employee Ambassadors, *Marketing News*, December 15, 2008, pp. 26–27; www.snowshoemtn.com.

49. Christian Homburg, John P. Workman Jr., and Harley Krohmen, "Marketing's Influence within the Firm," *Journal of Marketing* 63 (January 1999), pp. 1–15.

50. Robert Shaw and David Merrick, *Marketing Payback: Is Your Marketing Profitable?* (London, UK: Pearson Education, 2005).

51. Rajendra Sisodia, David Wolfe, and Jagdish Sheth, *Firms of Endearment: How World-Class Companies Profit from Passion* (Upper Saddle River, NJ: Wharton School Publishing, 2007).

52. If choosing to develop a strategic corporate social responsibility program, see Michael E. Porter and Mark R. Kramer, "Strategy and Society: The Link between Competitive Advantage and Corporate Social Responsibility," *Harvard Business Review*, December 2006, pp. 78–92.

53. Jeffrey Hollender and Stephen Fenichell, *What Matters Most* (New York: Basic Books, 2004), p. 168.

54. Tara Weiss, "Special Report: Going Green," *Forbes.com*, July 3, 2007; Matthew Grimm, "Progressive Business," *Brandweek*, November 28, 2005, pp. 16–26.

55. E. Jerome McCarthy and William D. Perreault, *Basic Marketing: A Global-Managerial Approach*, 14th ed. (Homewood, IL: McGraw-Hill/Irwin, 2002).

56. Joann Muller, "Ford: Why It's Worse Than You Think," *BusinessWeek*, June 25, 2001; Ford 1999 Annual Report; Greg Keenan, "Six Degrees of Perfection," *Globe and Mail*, December 20, 2000.

Chapter 2

1. Catherine Holahan, "Yahoo!'s Bid to Think Small," *BusinessWeek*, February 26, 2007, p. 94; Ben Elgin, "Yahoo!'s Boulevard of Broken Dreams," *BusinessWeek*, March 13, 2006, pp. 76–77; Justin Hibbard, "How Yahoo! Gave Itself a Face-Lift," *BusinessWeek*, October 9, 2006, pp. 74–77; Kevin J. Delaney, "As Yahoo! Falters, Executive's Memo Calls for Overhaul," *Wall Street Journal*, November 18, 2006; "Yahoo!'s Personality Crisis," *Economist*, August 13, 2005, pp. 49–50; Fred Vogelstein, "Yahoo!'s Brilliant Solution," *Fortune*, August 8, 2005, pp. 42–55.

2. Nirmalya Kumar, *Marketing as Strategy: The CEO's Agenda for Driving Growth and Innovation* (Boston: Harvard Business School Press, 2004); Frederick E. Webster Jr., "The Future Role of Marketing in the Organization," Donald R. Lehmann and Katherine

Jocz, eds., *Reflections on the Futures of Marketing* (Cambridge, MA: Marketing Science Institute, 1997), pp. 39–66.

3. Michael E. Porter, *Competitive Advantage: Creating and Sustaining Superior Performance* (New York: Free Press, 1985).

4. For an academic treatment of benchmarking, see Douglas W. Vorhies and Neil A. Morgan, "Benchmarking Marketing Capabilities for Sustained Competitive Advantage," *Journal of Marketing* 69 (January 2005), pp. 80–94.

5. Michael Hammer and James Champy, *Reengineering the Corporation: A Manifesto for Business Revolution* (New York: Harper Business, 1993).

6. Ibid.; Jon R. Katzenbach and Douglas K. Smith, *The Wisdom of Teams: Creating the High-Performance Organization* (Boston: Harvard Business School Press, 1993).

7. Sachi Izumi, "Sony to Halve Suppliers," *Reuters*, May 21, 2009.

8. C. K. Prahalad and Gary Hamel, "The Core Competence of the Corporation," *Harvard Business Review,* May–June 1990, pp. 79–91.

9. George S. Day, "The Capabilities of Market-Driven Organizations," *Journal of Marketing* 58 (October 1994), p. 38.

10. George S. Day and Paul J. H. Schoemaker, *Peripheral Vision: Detecting the Weak Signals That Will Make or Break Your Company* (Cambridge, MA: Harvard Business School Press, 2006); Paul J. H. Schoemaker and George S. Day, "How to Make Sense of Weak Signals," *MIT Sloan Management Review* (Spring 2009), pp. 81–89.

11. "Kodak Plans to Cut Up to 5,000 More Jobs," *Bloomberg News,* February 8, 2007; Leon Lazaroff, "Kodak's Big Picture Focusing on Image Change," *Chicago Tribune*, January 29, 2006.

12. *Pew Internet and American Life Project Survey,* November–December 2000.

13. Peter Drucker, *Management: Tasks, Responsibilities and Practices* (New York: Harper and Row, 1973), chapter 7.

14. Kawasaki also humorously suggests checking out comic strip character Dilbert's mission statement generator first if one has to be developed by the organization: *Dilbert.com.*

15. *The Economist: Business Miscellany* (London: Profile Books Ltd, 2005), pp. 32–33.

16. Peter Freedman, "The Age of the Hollow Company," *TimesOnline,* April 25, 2004; *Pew Internet and American Life Project Survey,* November–December 2000.

17. Jeffrey F. Rayport and Bernard J. Jaworski, *e-commerce* (New York: McGraw-Hill, 2001), p. 116.

18. Tilman Kemmler, Monika Kubicová, Robert Musslewhite, and Rodney Prezeau, "E-Performance II—The Good, the Bad, and the Merely Average," an exclusive to *mckinseyquarterly.com,* 2001.

19. Bruce Horovitz, "Campbell's 10-Year Goal to Clean Up a Soupy Mess," *USA Today,* January 26, 2009, p. 1B.

20. *Dubai Tourism*, www.dubaitourism.ae, 2010; *Euromoney*, www.euromoney.com, December 2010; *Dubai World*, www.dubaiworld.ae/2010; *Arabian Business*, www.arabianbusiness.com, August 11, 2010; "Dubai World Faces Restructuring, Debt Standstill," *Reuters Dubai*, 25, November, 2009; "IMF Sees Dubai Growth in 2010, Debt Woes Ease," *Reuters Dubai*, 25, October 2010; "Dubai World Gets Full Support for Restructuring," *Reuters Dubai*, 27, October, 2010.

21. This section is based on Robert M. Grant, *Contemporary Strategy Analysis*, 7th ed. (New York: John Wiley & Sons, 2009), chapter 17.

22. *Nespresso*, www.nespresso.com/mediacenter/?pays= ch&lang=en, accessed December 7, 2010.

23. Jesse Eisinger, "The Marriage from Hell," *Condé Nast Portfolio*, February 2008, pp. 84–88, 132.

24. Tim Goodman, "NBC Everywhere?" *San Francisco Chronicle,* September 4, 2003.

25. Jon Fortt, "Mark Hurd, Superstar," *Fortune*, June 9, 2008, pp. 35–40.

26. Jena McGregor, "The World's Most Innovative Companies," *BusinessWeek*, April 24, 2006, pp. 63–74.

27. E. Jerome McCarthy, *Basic Marketing: A Managerial Approach,* 12th ed. (Homewood, IL: Irwin, 1996).

28. Paul J. H. Shoemaker, "Scenario Planning: A Tool for Strategic Thinking," *Sloan Management Review* (Winter 1995), pp. 25–40.

29. Ronald Grover, "Hollywood Ponders a Post-DVD Future, *BusinessWeek*, March 2, 2009, p. 56; Brooks Barnes, "Movie Studios See a Threat in Growth of Redbox," *New York Times*, September 7, 2009.

30. Philip Kotler, *Kotler on Marketing* (New York: Free Press, 1999).

31. Ibid.

32. Phaedra Hise, "Was It Time to Go Downmarket?" *Inc.*, September 2006, p. 47; Patrick J. Sauer, "Returning to Its Roots," *Inc.*, November 2007; www.loanbright.com.

33. Dominic Dodd and Ken Favaro, "Managing the Right Tension," *Harvard Business Review,* December 2006, pp. 62–74.

34. Michael E. Porter, *Competitive Strategy: Techniques for Analyzing Industries and Competitors* (New York: Free Press, 1980), chapter 2.

35. Michael E. Porter, "What Is Strategy?" *Harvard Business Review,* November–December 1996, pp. 61–78.

36. For some readings on strategic alliances, see John R. Harbison and Peter Pekar, *Smart Alliances: A Practical Guide to Repeatable Success* (San Francisco, CA: Jossey-Bass, 1998); Peter Lorange and Johan Roos, *Strategic Alliances: Formation, Implementation and Evolution* (Cambridge, MA: Blackwell, 1992); Jordan D. Lewis, *Partnerships for Profit: Structuring and Managing Strategic Alliances* (New York: Free Press, 1990).

37. Bharat Book Bureau, *Strategic Alliances in World Pharma and Biotech Markets*, May 2008.

38. Kerry Capell, "Vodafone: Embracing Open Source with Open Arms," *BusinessWeek*, April 20, 2009,

pp. 52–53; "Call the Carabiniere," *The Economist*, May 16, 2009, p. 75.

39. Robin Cooper and Robert S. Kalpan, "Profit Priorities from Activity-Based Costing," *Harvard Business Review*, May–June 1991, pp. 130–135.

40. See Robert S. Kaplan and David P. Norton, *The Balanced Scorecard: Translating Strategy into Action* (Boston: Harvard Business School Press, 1996) as a tool for monitoring stakeholder satisfaction.

41. Thomas J. Peters and Robert H. Waterman Jr., *In Search of Excellence: Lessons from America's Best-Run Companies* (New York: Harper and Row, 1982), pp. 9–12.

42. John P. Kotter and James L. Heskett, *Corporate Culture and Performance* (New York: Free Press, 1992); Stanley M. Davis, *Managing Corporate Culture* (Cambridge, MA: Ballinger, 1984); Terrence E. Deal and Allan A. Kennedy, *Corporate Cultures: The Rites and Rituals of Corporate Life* (Reading, MA: Addison-Wesley, 1982); "Corporate Culture," *BusinessWeek*, October 27, 1980, pp. 148–160.

43. Marian Burk Wood, *The Marketing Plan: A Handbook* (Upper Saddle River, NJ: Prentice Hall, 2003).

44. Donald R. Lehmann and Russell S. Winer, *Product Management*, 3rd ed. (Boston: McGraw-Hill/Irwin, 2001).

45. David B. Hertz, "Risk Analysis in Capital Investment," *Harvard Business Review*, January–February 1964, pp. 96–106.

Chapter 3

1. Susan Warren, "Pillow Talk: Stackers Outnumber Plumpers; Don't Mention Drool," *Wall Street Journal*, January 8, 1998.

2. Ronald D. Michman, Edward M. Mazze, and Alan J. Greco, *Lifestyle Marketing: Reaching the New American Consumer* (Westport: Praeger, 2008).

3. "Insights," *Nielsen*, www.claritas.com/target-marketing/resources/case-study/michigan-economic-development-corp.jsp.

4. "Mobile Access to Inventory Data Reduces Back Orders by 80 Percent," www.microsoft.com/casestudies; "Smarter Supply Chain Utilization for the Retailer," www.microsoft.com/casestudies; "Ten Ways to Reduce Inventory While Maintaining or Improving Service," www.microsoft.com/casestudies.

5. "Vendor-Managed Inventory in Consumer Electronics and Durables," *The Supply Chain Company*, www.i2.com/industries/consumer_industries/vmi/vmi_case_study.cfm.

6. William Holstein, "The Dot Com within Ford," *BusinessWeek*, January 30, 2000.

7. Mara Der Hovanesian, "Wells Fargo," *BusinessWeek*, November 24, 2004, p. 96.

8. Jeff Zabin, "The Importance of Being Analytical," *Brandweek*, July 24, 2006, p. 21; Stephen Baker, "Math Will Rock Your World," *BusinessWeek*, January 23, 2006, pp. 54–62; Michelle Kessler and Byron Acohido, "Data Miners Dig a Little Deeper," *USA Today*, July 11, 2006.

9. Leonard M. Fuld, "Staying a Step Ahead of the Rest," *Chief Executive* 218 (June 2006), p. 32.

10. "Spies, Lies & KPMG," *BusinessWeek*, February 26, 2007.

11. Jennifer Esty, "Those Wacky Customers!" *Fast Company*, January 2004, p. 40.

12. Helen Coster, "Shopping Cart Psychology," *Forbes*, September 7, 2009, pp. 64–65.

13. Sara Steindorf, "Shoppers Spy on Those Who Serve," *Christian Science Monitor*, May 28, 2002; Edward F. McQuarrie, *Customer Visits: Building a Better Market Focus*, 2nd ed. (Newbury Park, CA: Sage Press, 1998).

14. Shirely S. Wang, "Heath Care Taps 'Mystery Shoppers,'" *Wall Street Journal*, August 10, 2006.

15. Heather Green, "It Takes a Web Village," *Business Week*, September 4, 2006, p. 66.

16. Amy Merrick, "Counting on the Census," *Wall Street Journal*, February 14, 2001.

17. Kim Girard, "Strategies to Turn Stealth into Wealth," *Business 2.0*, May 2003, p. 66.

18. "The Blogs in the Corporate Machine," *The Economist*, February 11, 2006, pp. 55–56; also adapted from Robin T. Peterson and Zhilin Yang, "Web Product Reviews Help Strategy," *Marketing News*, April 7, 2004, p. 18.

19. American Productivity & Quality Center, "User-Driven Competitive Intelligence: Crafting the Value Proposition," December 3–4, 2002.

20. Alex Wright, "Mining the Web for Feelings, Not Facts," *New York Times*, August 24, 2009; Sarah E. Needleman, "For Companies, a Tweet in Time Can Avert PR Mess, *Wall Street Journal*, August 3, 2009, p. B6.

21. See *BadFads Museum*, www.badfads.com, for examples of fads and collectibles through the years.

22. Katy McLaunghlin, "Macaroni Grill's Order: Cut Calories, Keep Customers," *Wall Street Journal*, September 16, 2009, p. B6.

23. John Naisbitt and Patricia Aburdene, *Megatrends 2000* (New York: Avon Books, 1990).

24. Indata, *IN* (June 2006), p. 27.

25. World POPClock, U.S. Census Bureau, www.census.gov, 2009.

26. See Donella H. Meadows, Dennis L. Meadows, and Jorgen Randers, *Beyond Limits* (White River Junction, VT: Chelsea Green, 1993) for some commentary; http://geography.about.com/od/obtainpopulationdata/a/worldvillage.htm.

27. "World Development Indicators Database," *World Bank*, http://site resources.worldbank.org/DATASTATISTICS/Resources/POP.pdf, September 15, 2009; "World Population Growth," www.worldbank. org/depweb/english/beyond/beyondco/beg_03.pdf.

28. Andrew Zolli, "Demographics: The Population Hourglass," *Fast Company*, www.fastcompany.com/magazine/103/open_essay-demographics.html, December 19, 2007.

29. Brian Grow, "Hispanic Nation," *BusinessWeek*, March 15, 2004, pp. 58–70.

30. Queena Sook Kim, "Fisher-Price Reaches for Hispanics," *Wall Street Journal,* November 1, 2004.

31. For descriptions on the buying habits and marketing approaches to African Americans and Hispanics, see M. Isabel Valdes, *Marketing to American Latinos: A Guide to the In-Culture Approach, Part II* (Ithaca, NY: Paramount Market Publishing, 2002); Alfred L. Schreiber, *Multicultural Marketing* (Lincolnwood, IL: NTC Business Books, 2001).

32. Jacquelyn Lynn, "Tapping the Riches of Bilingual Markets," *Management Review,* March 1995, pp. 56–61; Mark R. Forehand and Rohit Deshpandé, "What We See Makes Us Who We Are: Priming Ethnic Self-Awareness and Advertising Response," *Journal of Marketing Research* 38 (August 2001), pp. 336–48.

33. Tennille M. Robinson, "Tapping into Black Buying Power," *Black Enterprise* 36 (January 2006), p. 64.

34. *The Central Intelligence Agency's World Factbook,* www.cia.gov/library/publications/the-world-factbook, December 9, 2010.

35. "Projections of the Number of Households and Families in the United States: 1995–2010, P25–1129," *U.S. Department of Commerce, Bureau of the Census,* www.census.gov/prod/1/pop/p25-1129.pdf, December 9, 2010.

36. Michelle Conlin, "Unmarried America," *BusinessWeek,* October 20, 2003, pp. 106–116; James Morrow, "A Place for One," *American Demographics,* November 2003, pp. 25–30.

37. Rebecca Gardyn, "A Market Kept in the Closet," *American Demographics,* November 2001, pp. 37–43.

38. Nanette Byrnes, "Secrets of the Male Shopper," *BusinessWeek,* September 4, 2006, p. 44.

39. Elisabeth Sullivan, "The Age of Prudence," *Marketing News,* April 15, 2009, pp. 8–11; Steve Hamm, "The New Age of Frugality," *BusinessWeek*, October 20, 2008, pp. 55–60; Jessica Deckler, "Never Pay Retail Again," *CNNMoney.com,* May 30, 2008.

40. David Welch, "The Incredible Shrinking Boomer Economy," *BusinessWeek,* August 3, 2009, pp. 27–30.

41. Julie Schlosser, "Infosys U.," *Fortune,* March 20, 2006, pp. 41–42.

42. Pamela Paul, "Corporate Responsibility," *American Demographics,* May 2002, pp. 24–25.

43. Stephen Baker, "Wiser about the Web," *BusinessWeek,* March 27, 2006, pp. 53–57.

44. "Clearing House Suit Chronology," *Associated Press,* January 26, 2001; Paul Wenske, "You Too Could Lose $19,000!" *Kansas City Star,* October 31, 1999.

45. Laura Zinn, "Teens: Here Comes the Biggest Wave Yet," *BusinessWeek,* April 11, 2004, pp. 76–86.

46. Chris Taylor (ed.), "Go Green. Get Rich." *Business 2.0*, January/February 2007, pp. 68–79.

47. Subhabrata Bobby Banerjee, Easwar S. Iyer, and Rajiv K Kashyap, "Corporate Enviromentalism: Antecedents and Influence of Industry Type," *Journal of Marketing* 67 (April 2003), pp. 106–22.

48. Chris Taylor, ed., "Go Green. Get Rich." *Business 2.0*, January/February 2007, pp. 68–79.

49. See Dorothy Cohen, *Legal Issues on Marketing Decision Making* (Cincinnati: South-Western, 1995).

50. Rebecca Gardyn, "Swap Meet," *American Demographics,* July 2001, pp. 51–55.

51. Pamela Paul, "Mixed Signals," *American Demographics,* July 2001, pp. 45–49.

52. Conference Summary, "Excelling in Today's Multimedia World," Economist Conferences' Fourth Annual Marketing Roundtable, Landor, March 2006.

53. For a good discussion and illustration, see Roger J. Best, *Market-Based Management,* 4th ed. (Upper Saddle River, NJ: Prentice Hall, 2005).

54. For further discussion, see Gary L. Lilien, Philip Kotler, and K. Sridhar Moorthy, *Marketing Models* (Upper Saddle River, NJ: Prentice Hall, 1992).

55. www.naics.com; www.census.gov/epcd/naics02, December 9, 2010.

56. Stanley F. Slater and Eric M. Olson, "Mix and Match," *Marketing Management,* July–August 2006, pp. 32–37; Brian Sternthal and Alice M. Tybout, "Segmentation and Targeting," Dawn Iacobucci, ed., *Kellogg on Marketing* (New York: John Wiley & Sons, 2001), pp. 3–30.

57. Stephanie Clifford, "Measuring the Results of an Ad Right Down to the City Block," *New York Times*, August 5, 2009.

58. For an excellent overview of market forecasting, see Scott Armstrong, ed., *Principles of Forecasting: A Handbook for Researchers and Practitioners* (Norwell, MA: Kluwer Academic Publishers, 2001) and his Web site: www.forecastingprinciples.com; Also see Roger J. Best, "An Experiment in Delphi Estimation in Marketing Decision Making," *Journal of Marketing Research* 11 (November 1974), pp. 447–52; Norman Dalkey and Olaf Helmer, "An Experimental Application of the Delphi Method to the Use of Experts," *Management Science*, April 1963, pp. 458–67.

Chapter 4

1. Jia Lynn Yang, "The Bottom Line," *Fortune*, September 1, 2008, pp. 107–12 Jack Neff, "From Mucus to Maxi Pads: Marketing's Dirtiest Jobs," *Advertising Age*, February 16, 2009, p. 9.

2. See Robert Schieffer, *Ten Key Customer Insights: Unlocking the Mind of the Market* (Mason, OH: Thomson, 2005) for a comprehensive, in-depth discussion of how to generate customer insights to drive business results.

3. Jenn Abelson, "Gillette Sharpens Its Focus on Women," *Boston Globe*, January 4, 2009; A.G. Lafley, interview, "It Was a No-Brainer," *Fortune*, February 21, 2005, p. 96; Naomi Aoki, "Gillette Hopes to Create a Buzz with Vibrating Women's Razor," *Boston Globe*, December 17, 2004; Chris Reidy, "The Unveiling of a New Venus," *Boston Globe*, November 3, 2000.

4. Natalie Zmuda, "Tropicana Line's Sales Plunge 20% Post-Rebranding," *Advertising Age*, April 2, 2009.

5. "2009 Global Market Research Report," *Esomar,* www.esomar.org.

6. Melanie Haiken, "Tuning In to Crowdcasting," *Business 2.0,* November 2006, pp. 66–68.

7. Michael Fielding, "Special Delivery: UPS Conducts Surveys to Help Customers Export to China," *Marketing News*, February 1, 2007, pp. 13–14.

8. "Would You Fly in Chattering Class?" *The Economist,* September 9, 2006, p. 63.

9. For some background information on in-flight Internet service, see "Boeing In-Flight Internet Plan Goes Airborne," *Associated Press,* April 18, 2004; John Blau, "In-Flight Internet Service Ready for Takeoff," *IDG News Service,* June 14, 2002; "In-Flight Dogfight," *Business2.com,* January 9, 2001, pp. 84–91.

10. For a discussion of the decision-theory approach to the value of research, see Donald R. Lehmann, Sunil Gupta, and Joel Steckel, *Market Research* (Reading, MA: Addison-Wesley, 1997).

11. Gregory Solman, "Finding Car Buyers at Their Home (sites)," *Adweek,* August 21–28, 2006, p. 8.

12. Linda Tischler, "Every Move You Make," *Fast Company*, April 2004, pp. 73–75; Allison Stein Wellner, "Look Who's Watching," *Continental*, April 2003, pp. 39–41.

13. For a detailed review of some relevant academic work, see Eric J. Arnould and Amber Epp, "Deep Engagement with Consumer Experience," Rajiv Grover and Marco Vriens, eds., *Handbook of Marketing Research* (Thousand Oaks, CA: Sage Publications, 2006); For a range of academic discussion, see the following special issue, "Can Ethnography Uncover Richer Consumer Insights?" *Journal of Advertising Research* 46 (September 2006); For some practical tips, see Richard Durante and Michael Feehan, "Leverage Ethnography to Improve Strategic Decision Making," *Marketing Research* (Winter 2005).

14. Eric J. Arnould and Linda L. Price, "Market-Oriented Ethnography Revisited," *Journal of Advertising Research* 46 (September 2006), pp. 251–62; Eric J. Arnould and Melanie Wallendorf, "Market-Oriented Ethnography: Interpretation Building and Marketing Strategy Formulation," *Journal of Marketing Research* 31 (November 1994), pp. 484–504.

15. "Case Study: Bank of America," Inside Innovation, *BusinessWeek,* June 19, 2006; Spencer E. Ante, "Inprogress," *IN,* June 2006, pp. 28–29; *Bank of America,* www.bankofamerica.com.

16. Helen Coster, "Shopping Cart Psychology," *Forbes,* September 7, 2009, pp. 64–65.

17. Andrew Kaplan, "Mass Appeal," *Beverage World,* February 2007, pp. 48–49.

18. Michael Fielding, "Shift the Focus," *Marketing News,* September 1, 2006, pp. 18–20.

19. Piet Levy, "In with the Old, in Spite of the New," *Marketing News*, May 30, 2009, p. 19.

20. Eric Schellhorn, "A Tsunami of Surveys Washes over Consumers," *Christian Science Monitor,* October 2, 2006, p. 13.

21. Catherine Marshall and Gretchen B. Rossman, *Designing Qualitative Research,* 4th ed. (Thousand Oaks, CA: Sage Publications, 2006); Bruce L. Berg, *Qualitative Research Methods for the Social Sciences,* 6th ed. (Boston: Allyn & Bacon, 2006); Norman K. Denzin and Yvonna S. Lincoln, eds., *The Sage Handbook of Qualitative Research,* 3rd ed. (Thousand Oaks, CA: Sage Publications, 2005); Linda Tischler, "Every Move You Make," *Fast Company*, April 2004, pp. 73–75.

22. Paula Andruss, "Keeping Both Eyes on Quality," *Marketing News*, September 15, 2008, pp. 22–23.

23. Louise Witt, "Inside Intent," *American Demographics*, March 2004, pp. 34–39; Andy Raskin, "A Face Any Business Can Trust," *Business 2.0,* December 2003, pp. 58–60; Gerald Zaltman, "Rethinking Market Research: Putting People Back In," *Journal of Marketing Research* 34 (November 1997), pp. 424–37; Wally Wood, "The Race to Replace Memory," *Marketing and Media Decisions*, July 1986, pp. 166–67; Roger D. Blackwell, James S. Hensel, Michael B. Phillips, and Brian Sternthal, *Laboratory Equipment for Marketing Research* (Dubuque, IA: Kendall/Hunt, 1970); Laurie Burkitt, "Battle for the Brain," *Forbes*, November 16, 2009, pp. 76–77.

24. Stephen Baker, "Wiser about the Web," *BusinessWeek,* March 27, 2006, pp. 54–62.

25. Michael Fielding, "Shift the Focus," *Marketing News,* September 1, 2006, pp. 18–20; Aaron Ukodie, "Worldwide Mobile Phones Reach Four Billion 2008," *allAfrica.com,* http://allafrica.com/stories/200810070774.html, October 6, 2008.

26. Kelly K. Spors, "The Customer Knows Best," *Wall Street Journal,* July 13, 2009, p. R5; Susan Kristoff, "Local Motors Breaking Design Rules in Engineering," www.suite.com, October 22, 2009; Emily Sweeney, "Machine Dream," *Boston Globe*, February 1, 2009.

27. Bradley Johnson, "Forget Phone and Mail: Online's the Best Place to Administer Surveys," *Advertising Age,* July 17, 2006, p. 23.

28. Emily Steel, "The New Focus Groups: Online Networks Proprietary Panels Help Consumer Companies Shape Products, Ads," *Wall Street Journal*, January 14, 2008.

29. Elisabeth A. Sullivan, "Delve Deeper," *Marketing News*, April 15, 2008, p. 24.

30. Kate Maddox, "The ROI of Research," *BtoB,* pp. 25, 28.

31. Bradley Johnson, "Online Methods Upend Consumer Survey Business," Advertising Age, July 17, 2006.

32. "Survey: Internet Should Remain Open to All," *ConsumerAffairs.com,* www.consumeraffairs.com/news04/2006/01/internet_survey.html, January 25, 2006; "Highlights from the National Consumers League's Survey on Consumers and Communications Technologies: Current and Future Use," www.nclnet.org/research/utilities/telecom_highlights.htm, July 21, 2005; Catherine Arnold, "Not Done Net; New Opportunities Still Exist in Online Research," *Marketing News,* April 1, 2004, p. 17; Louella Miles, "Online, on Tap," *Marketing,* June 16, 2004, pp. 39–40; Suzy Bashford, "The Opinion Formers," *Revolution,* May 2004, pp. 42–46; Nima M. Ray and Sharon W.

Tabor, "Contributing Factors; Several Issues Affect e-Research Validity," *Marketing News,* September 15, 2003, p. 50; Bob Lamons, "Eureka! Future of B-to-B Research Is Online," *Marketing News,* September 24, 2001, pp. 9–10; Burt Helm, "Online Polls: How Good Are They?" *BusinessWeek,* June 16, 2008, pp. 86–87.

33. *The Nielsen Company,* www.nielsen.com.

34. Elisabeth Sullivan, "Qual Research by the Numb3rs," *Marketing News*, September 1, 2008.

35. Deborah L. Vence, "In an Instant: More Researchers Use IM for Fast, Reliable Results," *Marketing News,* March 1, 2006, pp. 53–55.

36. Catherine Arnold, "Global Perspective: Synovate Exec Discusses Future of International Research," *Marketing News,* May 15, 2004, p. 43; Michael Erard, "For Technology, No Small World after All," *New York Times,* May 6, 2004; Deborah L. Vence, "Global Consistency: Leave It to the Experts," *Marketing News,* April 28, 2003, p. 37.

37. Jim Stachura and Meg Murphy, "Multicultural Marketing: Why One Size Doesn't Fit All," *MarketingProfs.com*, October 25, 2005.

38. Michael Fielding, "Global Insights: Synovate's Chedore Discusses MR Trends," *Marketing News,* May 15, 2006, pp. 41–42.

39. Kevin J. Clancy and Peter C. Krieg, *Counterintuitive Marketing: How Great Results Come from Uncommon Sense* (New York: Free Press, 2000).

40. See "Special Issue on Managerial Decision Making," *Marketing Science* 18 (1999) for some contemporary perspectives; See also John D. C. Little, "Decision Support Systems for Marketing Managers," *Journal of Marketing* 43 (Summer 1979), p. 11.

41. *Marketing News* can be found at www.marketingpower.com.

42. Rajiv Grover and Marco Vriens, "Trusted Advisor: How It Helps Lay the Foundation for Insight," *Handbook of Marketing Research* (Thousand Oaks, CA: Sage Publications, 2006), pp. 3–17; Christine Moorman, Gerald Zaltman, and Rohit Deshpandé, "Relationships between Providers and Users of Market Research: The Dynamics of Trust within and between Organizations," *Journal of Marketing Research* 29 (August 1992), pp. 314–28.

43. *The Advertising Research Foundation,* www.thearf.org/assets/ogilvy-09.

44. Adapted from Arthur Shapiro, "Let's Redefine Market Research," *Brandweek,* June 21, 2004, p. 20; Kevin Ohannessian, "Star Wars: Thirty Years of Success," *Fast Company*, May 29, 2007.

45. Karen V. Beaman, Gregory R. Guy, and Donald E. Sexton, "Managing and Measuring Return on Marketing Investment," The Conference Board Research Report R-1435-08-RR, 2008.

46. "Report: Marketers Place Priority on Nurturing Existing Customers," http://directmag.com/roi/0301-customer-satisfaction-retention.

47. Factor TG, www.factortg.com/ideas/CMO_MPM_Audit__cmo.pdf.

48. Paul Farris, Neil T. Bendle, Phillip E. Pfeifer, and David J. Reibstein, *Marketing Metrics: 50+ Metrics Every Executive Should Master* (Upper Saddle River, NJ: Pearson Education, 2006); John Davis, *Magic Numbers for Consumer Marketing: Key Measures to Evaluate Marketing Success* (Singapore: John Wiley & Sons, 2005).

49. Elisabeth Sullivan, "Measure Up," *Marketing News*, May 30, 2009, pp. 8–11.

50. Michael Krauss, "Which Metrics Matter Most?" *Marketing News*, February 28, 2009, p. 20.

51. Tim Ambler, *Marketing and the Bottom Line: The New Methods of Corporate Wealth,* 2nd ed. (London: Pearson Education, 2003).

52. Kusum L. Ailawadi, Donald R. Lehmann, and Scott A. Neslin, "Revenue Premium as an Outcome Measure of Brand Equity," *Journal of Marketing* 67 (October 2003), pp. 1–17.

53. Tim Ambler, *Marketing and the Bottom Line: The New Methods of Corporate Wealth,* 2nd ed. (London: Pearson Education, 2003).

54. Josh Bernoff, "Measure What Matters," *Marketing News*, December 15, 2008, p. 22; and information from Servus Credit Union, May 2010.

55. Gerard J. Tellis, "Modeling Marketing Mix," Rajiv Grover and Marco Vriens, eds., *Handbook of Marketing Research* (Thousand Oaks, CA: Sage Publications, 2006).

56. Jack Neff, "P&G, Clorox Rediscover Modeling," *Advertising Age,* March 29, 2004, p. 10.

57. Laura Q. Hughes, "Econometrics Take Root," *Advertising Age,* August 5, 2002, p. S-4.

58. David J. Reibstein, "Connect the Dots," *CMO Magazine*, May 2005.

59. Jeff Zabin, "Marketing Dashboards: The Visual Display of Marketing Data," *Chief Marketer*, June 26, 2006.

60. Robert S. Kaplan and David P. Norton, *The Balanced Scorecard* (Boston: Harvard Business School Press, 1996).

61. Spencer Ante, "Giving the Boss the Big Picture," *BusinessWeek,* February 13, 2006, pp. 48–50.

Chapter 5

1. Louis Columbus, "Lessons Learned in Las Vegas: Loyalty Programs Pay," *CRM Buyer,* July 29, 2005; Oskar Garcia, "Harrah's Broadens Customer Loyalty Program; Monitors Customer Behavior," *Associated Press*, September 27, 2008; Dan Butcher, "Harrah's Casino Chain Runs Mobile Coupon Pilot," *Mobile Marketer*, November 19, 2008; Michael Bush, "Why Harrah's Loyalty Effort Is Industry's Gold Standard," *Advertising Age*, October 5, 2009, p. 8.

2. Robert Schieffer, *Ten Key Consumer Insights* (Mason, OH: Thomson, 2005).

3. Don Peppers and Martha Rogers, "Customers Don't Grow on Trees," *Fast Company,* July 2005, pp. 25–26.

4. For discussion of some of the issues involved, see Glen Urban, *Don't Just Relate—Advocate* (Upper Saddle River, NJ: Pearson Education Wharton School Publishing, 2005).

5. See Glen L. Urban and John R. Hauser, "'Listening In' to Find and Explore New Combinations of Customer Needs," *Journal of Marketing* 68 (April 2004), pp. 72–87.

6. "Customer reviews drive 196% increase in paid search revenue for Office Depot," *Bazaarvoice,* www.bazaarvoice.com/cs_rr_adresults_ officedepot.html, 2008.

7. Glen L. Urban, "The Emerging Era of Customer Advocacy," *Sloan Management Review* 45 (2004), pp. 77–82.

8. Steven Burke, "Dell's vs. HP's Value," *CRN,* May 15, 2006, p. 46; David Kirkpatrick, "Dell in the Penalty Box," *Fortune*, September 18, 2006, p. 70.

9. Michael Bush, "Consumers Rate Brands that Give Best Bang for Buck," *Advertising Age*, November 3, 2008, p. 8.

10. Irwin P. Levin and Richard D. Johnson, "Estimating Price–Quality Tradeoffs Using Comparative Judgments," *Journal of Consumer Research* 11 (June 1984), pp. 593–600. Customer-perceived value can be measured as a difference or as a ratio. If total customer value is $20,000 and total customer cost is $16,000, then the customer-perceived value is $4,000 (measured as a difference) or 1.25 (measured as a ratio). Ratios that are used to compare offers are often called *value–price ratios.*

11. Alex Taylor, "Caterpillar: Big Trucks, Big Sales, Big Attitude," *Fortune*, August 20, 2007, pp. 48–53; Tim Kelly, "Squash the Caterpillar," *Forbes*, April 21, 2008, pp. 136–41; Jeff Borden, "Eat My Dust," *Marketing News*, February 1, 2008, pp. 20–22.

12. For more on customer-perceived value, see David C. Swaddling and Charles Miller, *Customer Power* (Dublin, OH: Wellington Press, 2001).

13. Gary Hamel, "Strategy as Revolution," *Harvard Business Review,* July–August 1996, pp. 69–82.

14. "2010 Brand Keys Customer Loyalty Engagement Index," *Brand Keys, Inc.*

15. Michael J. Lanning, *Delivering Profitable Value* (Oxford, UK: Capstone, 1998).

16. Vikas Mittal, Eugene W. Anderson, Akin Sayrak, and Pandu Tadilamalla, "Dual Emphasis and the Long-Term Financial Impact of Customer Satisfaction," *Marketing Science* 24 (Fall 2005), pp. 544–55.

17. Michael Tsiros, Vikas Mittal, and William T. Ross Jr., "The Role of Attributions in Customer Satisfaction: A Reexamination," *Journal of Consumer Research* 31 (September 2004), pp. 476–83; for a succinct review, see Richard L. Oliver, "Customer Satisfaction Research," Rajiv Grover and Marco Vriens, eds., *Handbook of Marketing Research* (Thousand Oaks, CA: Sage Publications, 2006), pp. 569–87.

18. For some provocative analysis and discussion, see Praveen K. Kopalle and Donald R. Lehmann, "Setting Quality Expectations when Entering a Market: What Should the Promise Be?" *Marketing Science* 25 (January–February 2006), pp. 8–24; Susan Fournier and David Glenmick, "Rediscovering Satisfaction," *Journal of Marketing* 63 (October 1999), pp. 5–23.

19. Jennifer Aaker, Susan Fournier, and S. Adam Brasel, "When Good Brands Do Bad," *Journal of Consumer Research* 31 (June 2004), pp. 1–16; Pankaj Aggrawal, "The Effects of Brand Relationship Norms on Consumer Attitudes and Behavior," *Journal of Consumer Research* 31 (June 2004), pp. 87–101.

20. For in-depth discussion, see Michael D. Johnson and Anders Gustafsson, *Improving Customer Satisfaction, Loyalty, and Profit* (San Francisco: Jossey-Bass, 2000).

21. For an interesting analysis of the effects of different types of expectations, see William Boulding, Ajay Kalra, and Richard Staelin, "The Quality Double Whammy," *Marketing Science* 18 (April 1999), pp. 463–84.

22. Neil A. Morgan, Eugene W. Anderson, and Vikas Mittal, "Understanding Firms' Customer Satisfaction Information Usage," *Journal of Marketing* 69 (July 2005), pp. 131–51.

23. Although for moderating factors, see Kathleen Seiders, Glenn B. Voss, Dhruv Grewal, and Andrea L. Godfrey, "Do Satisfied Customers Buy More? Examining Moderating Influences in a Retailing Context," *Journal of Marketing* 69 (October 2005), pp. 26–43.

24. See, for example, Christian Homburg, Nicole Koschate, and Wayne D. Hoyer, "Do Satisfied Customers Really Pay More? A Study of the Relationship between Customer Satisfaction and Willingness to Pay," *Journal of Marketing* 69 (April 2005), pp. 84–96.

25. Claes Fornell, Sunil Mithas, Forrest V. Morgeson III, and M. S. Krishnan, "Customer Satisfaction and Stock Prices: High Returns, Low Risk," *Journal of Marketing* 70 (January 2006), pp. 3–14. See also, Thomas S. Gruca and Lopo L. Rego, "Customer Satisfaction, Cash Flow, and Shareholder Value," *Journal of Marketing* 69 (July 2005), pp. 115–30; Eugene W. Anderson, Claes Fornell, and Sanal K. Mazvancheryl, "Customer Satisfaction and Shareholder Value," *Journal of Marketing* 68 (October 2004), pp. 172–85.

26. Thomas O. Jones and W. Earl Sasser Jr., "Why Satisfied Customers Defect," *Harvard Business Review,* November–December 1995, pp. 88–99.

27. Companies should also note that managers and salespeople can manipulate customer satisfaction ratings. They can be especially nice to customers just before the survey. They can also try to exclude unhappy customers. Another danger is that if customers know the company will go out of its way to please them, some may express high dissatisfaction in order to receive more concessions.

28. Jennifer Rooney, "Winning Hearts and Minds," *Advertising Age,* July 10, 2006, pp. S10–13.

29. For an empirical comparison of different methods to measure customer satisfaction, see Neil A. Morgan and Lopo Leotto Rego, "The Value of Different Customer Satisfaction and Loyalty Metrics in Predicting Business Performance," *Marketing Science* 25 (September–October 2006), pp. 426–39.

30. Frederick K. Reichheld, "The One Number You Need to Grow," *Harvard Business Review,* December 2003, pp. 46–54.

31. James C. Ward and Amy L. Ostrom, "Complaining to the Masses: The Role of Protest Framing in Customer-Created Complaint Sites," *Journal of Consumer Research* 33 (September 2006), pp. 220–30; Kim Hart, "Angry Customers Use Web to Shame Firms," *Washington Post,* July 5, 2006.

32. Eugene W. Anderson and Claes Fornell, "Foundations of the American Customer Satisfaction Index," *Total Quality Management* 11 (September 2000), pp. S869–82; Claes Fornell, Michael D. Johnson, Eugene W. Anderson, Jaaesung Cha, and Barbara Everitt Bryant, "The American Customer Satisfaction Index: Nature, Purpose, and Findings," *Journal of Marketing* 60 (October 1996), pp. 7–18.

33. Technical Assistance Research Programs (Tarp), *U.S. Office of Consumer Affairs Study on Complaint Handling in America,* 1986.

34. Stephen S. Tax and Stephen W. Brown, "Recovering and Learning from Service Failure," *Sloan Management Review* 40 (Fall 1998), pp. 75–88; Ruth Bolton and Tina M. Bronkhorst, "The Relationship between Customer Complaints to the Firm and Subsequent Exit Behavior," *Advances in Consumer Research,* vol. 22 (Provo, UT: Association for Consumer Research, 1995), pp. 94–100; Roland T. Rust, Bala Subramanian, and Mark Wells, "Making Complaints a Management Tool," *Marketing Management* 1 (March 1992), pp. 40–45; Karl Albrecht and Ron Zemke, *Service America!* (Homewood, IL: Dow Jones–Irwin, 1985), pp. 6–7.

35. Christian Homburg and Andreas Fürst, "How Organizational Complaint Handling Drives Customer Loyalty: An Analysis of the Mechanistic and the Organic Approach," *Journal of Marketing* 69 (July 2005), pp. 95–114.

36. Philip Kotler, *Kotler on Marketing* (New York: Free Press, 1999), pp. 21–22.

37. "Basic Concepts," *ASQ,* www.asq.org/glossary/q.html, January 16, 2010.

38. Robert D. Buzzell and Bradley T. Gale, "Quality Is King," *The PIMS Principles: Linking Strategy to Performance* (New York: Free Press, 1987), pp. 103–34. (PIMS stands for Profit Impact of Market Strategy.)

39. Brian Hindo, "Satisfaction Not Guaranteed," *BusinessWeek,* June 19, 2006, pp. 32–36.

40. "Flying into a Storm: British Airways (1996–2000)," INSEAD, France, 2002, www.srnleads.org/events/institutes/09-connected/docs/rao_british_airways.pdf, December 15, 2010; "Business Traveler Awards 2009," *Business Traveler,* www.businesstraveller.com/awards2009.

41. Lerzan Aksoy, Timothy L. Keiningham, and Terry G. Vavra, "Nearly Everything You Know about Loyalty Is Wrong," *Marketing News,* October 1, 2005, pp. 20–21; Timothy L. Keiningham, Terry G. Vavra, Lerzan Aksoy, and Henri Wallard, *Loyalty Myths* (Hoboken, NJ: John Wiley & Sons, 2005).

42. Werner J. Reinartz and V. Kumar, "The Impact of Customer Relationship Characteristics on Profitable Lifetime Duration," *Journal of Marketing* 67 (January 2003), pp. 77–99; Werner J. Reinartz and V. Kumar, "On the Profitability of Long-Life Customers in a Noncontractual Setting: An Empirical Investigation and Implications for Marketing," *Journal of Marketing* 64 (October 2000), pp. 17–35.

43. Rakesh Niraj, Mahendra Gupta, and Chakravarthi Narasimhan, "Customer Profitability in a Supply Chain," *Journal of Marketing* 65 (July 2001), pp. 1–16.

44. Thomas M. Petro, "Profitability: The Fifth 'P' of Marketing," *Bank Marketing,* September 1990, pp. 48–52; "Who Are Your Best Customers?" *Bank Marketing,* October 1990, pp. 48–52.

45. "Easier Than ABC," *Economist,* October 25, 2003, p. 56; Robert S. Kaplan and Steven R. Anderson, *Time-Driven Activity Based Costing* (Boston MA: Harvard Business School Press, 2007); "Activity-Based Accounting" *Economist,* June 29, 2009.

46. V. Kumar, "Customer Lifetime Value," Rajiv Grover and Marco Vriens, eds., *Handbook of Marketing Research* (Thousand Oaks, CA: Sage Publications, 2006), pp. 602–27; Sunil Gupta, Donald R. Lehmann, and Jennifer Ames Stuart, "Valuing Customers," *Journal of Marketing Research* 61 (February 2004), pp. 7–18; Rajkumar Venkatesan and V. Kumar, "A Customer Lifetime Value Framework for Customer Selection and Resource Allocation Strategy," *Journal of Marketing* 68 (October 2004), pp. 106–25.

47. V. Kumar, "Profitable Relationships," *Marketing Research* 18 (Fall 2006), pp. 41–46.

48. For some recent analysis and discussion, see Michael Haenlein, Andreas M. Kaplan, and Detlef Schoder, "Valuing the Real Option of Abandoning Unprofitable Customers when Calculating Customer Lifetime Value," *Journal of Marketing* 70 (July 2006), pp. 5–20; Teck-Hua Ho, Young-Hoon Park, and Yong-Pin Zhou, "Incorporating Satisfaction into Customer Value Analysis: Optimal Investment in Lifetime Value," *Marketing Science* 25 (May–June 2006), pp. 260–77; and Peter S. Fader, Bruce G. S. Hardie, and Ka Lok Lee, "RFM and CLV: Using Iso-Value Curves for Customer Base Analysis," *Journal of Marketing Research* 62 (November 2005), pp. 415–30; V. Kumar, Rajkumar Venkatesan, Tim Bohling, and Denise Beckmann, "The Power of CLV: Managing Customer Lifetime Value at IBM," *Marketing Science* 27 (2008), pp. 585–99.

49. Nicole E. Coviello, Roderick J. Brodie, Peter J. Danaher, and Wesley J. Johnston, "How Firms Relate to Their Markets: An Empirical Examination of Contemporary Marketing Practices," *Journal of*

Marketing 66 (July 2002), pp. 33–46. For a comprehensive set of articles from a variety of perspectives on brand relationships, see Deborah J. MacInnis, C. Whan Park, and Joseph R. Preister, eds., *Handbook of Brand Relationships* (Armonk, NY: M. E. Sharpe, 2009).

50. For an up-to-date view of academic perspectives, see the articles contained in the Special Section on Customer Relationship Management, *Journal of Marketing* 69 (October 2005). For a study of the processes involved, see Werner Reinartz, Manfred Kraft, and Wayne D. Hoyer, "The Customer Relationship Management Process: Its Measurement and Impact on Performance," *Journal of Marketing Research* 61 (August 2004), pp. 293–305.

51. Nora A. Aufreiter, David Elzinga, and Jonathan W. Gordon, "Better Branding," *The McKinsey Quarterly* 4 (2003), pp. 29–39.

52. Michael J. Lanning, *Delivering Profitable Value* (New York: Basic Books, 1998).

53. Kenneth Hein, "Satisfying a Publicity Jones with Hemp, Love Potions," *Brandweek,* March 13, 2006, p. 14; Corporate Design Foundation, "Keep Up with the Jones, Dude!" *BusinessWeek,* October 26, 2005; Ryan Underwood, "Jones Soda Secret," *Fast Company,* March 2005, p. 74; Maggie Overfelt, "Cult Brand Jones Soda Fights for Survival," *CNNMoney.com,* October 10, 2008.

54. Susan Stellin, "For Many Online Companies, Customer Service Is Hardly a Priority," *New York Times,* February 19, 2001; Michelle Johnson, "Getting Ready for the Onslaught," *Boston Globe,* November 4, 1999.

55. Julie Jargon, "Domino's IT Staff Delivers Slick Site, Ordering System," *Wall Street Journal,* November 24, 2009; Bruce Horovitz, "Where's Your Domino's Pizza? Track It Online," *USA Today,* January 30, 2008; Domino's Pizza, www.dominosbiz.com, January 16, 2010.

56. James H. Donnelly Jr., Leonard L. Berry, and Thomas W. Thompson, *Marketing Financial Services — A Strategic Vision* (Homewood, IL: Dow Jones–Irwin, 1985), p. 113.

57. Seth Godin, *Permission Marketing: Turning Strangers into Friends, and Friends into Customers* (New York: Simon & Schuster, 1999). See also Susan Fournier, Susan Dobscha, and David Mick, "Preventing the Premature Death of Relationship Marketing," *Harvard Business Review,* January–February 1998, pp. 42–51.

58. Don Peppers and Martha Rogers, *One-to-One B2B: Customer Development Strategies for the Business-to-Business World* (New York: Doubleday, 2001); Peppers and Rogers, *The One-to-One Future: Building Relationships One Customer at a Time* (London: Piatkus Books, 1996); Don Peppers and Martha Rogers, *The One-to-One Manager: Real-World Lessons in Customer Relationship Management* (New York: Doubleday, 1999); Don Peppers, Martha Rogers, and Bob Dorf, *The One-to-One Fieldbook: The Complete Toolkit for Implementing a One-to-One Marketing Program* (New York: Bantam, 1999); Don Peppers and Martha Rogers, *Enterprise One to One: Tools for Competing in the Interactive Age* (New York: Currency, 1997).

59. Mark Rechtin, "Aston Martin Woos Customers One by One," *Automotive News,* March 28, 2005.

60. Stuart Elliott, "Letting Consumers Control Marketing: Priceless," *New York Times,* October 9, 2006; Todd Wasserman and Jim Edwards, "Marketers' New World Order," *Brandweek,* October 9, 2006, pp. 4–6; Heather Green and Robert D. Hof, "Your Attention Please," *BusinessWeek,* July 24, 2006, pp. 48–53; Brian Sternberg, "The Marketing Maze," *Wall Street Journal,* July 10, 2006.

61. Rob Walker, "Amateur Hour, Web Style," *Fast Company,* October 2007, p. 87.

62. Ben McConnell and Jackie Huba, "Learning to Leverage the Lunatic Fringe," *Point,* July–August 2006, pp. 14–15; Michael Krauss, "Work to Convert Customers into Evangelists," *Marketing News,* December 15, 2006, p. 6; Ben McConnell and Jackie Huba, *Creating Customer Evangelists: How Loyal Customers Become a Loyal Sales Force* (New York: Kaplan Business, 2003).

63. Jonah Bloom, "The New Realities of a Low Trust Marketing World," *Advertising Age,* February 13, 2006.

64. Mylene Mangalindan, "New Marketing Style: Clicks and Mortar," *Wall Street Journal,* December 21, 2007, p. B5.

65. Nick Wingfield, "High Scores Matter to Game Makers, Too," *Wall Street Journal,* September 20, 2007, p. B1.

66. Candice Choi, "Bloggers Serve Up Opinions," *Associated Press,* March 23, 2008.

67. Elisabeth Sullivan, "Consider Your Source," *Marketing News,* February 15, 2008, pp. 16–19; Mylene Mangalindan, "Web Stores Tap Product Reviews," *Wall Street Journal,* September 11, 2007.

68. Erick Schonfeld, "Rethinking the Recommendation Engine," *Business 2.0,* July 2007, pp. 40–43.

69. Michael Lewis, "Customer Acquisition Promotions and Customer Asset Value," *Journal of Marketing Research* 63 (May 2006), pp. 195–203.

70. Hamish Pringle and Peter Field, "Why Customer Loyalty Isn't as Valuable as You Think," *Advertising Age,* March 23, 2009, p. 22.

71. Werner Reinartz, Jacquelyn S. Thomas, and V. Kumar, "Balancing Acquisition and Retention Resources to Maximize Customer Profitability," *Journal of Marketing* 69 (January 2005), pp. 63–79.

72. "Service Invention to Increase Retention," *CMO Council,* August 3, 2009, www.cmocouncil.org.

73. Frederick F. Reichheld, "Learning from Customer Defections," *Harvard Business Review,* March–April 1996, pp. 56–69.

74. Frederick F. Reichheld, *Loyalty Rules* (Boston: Harvard Business School Press, 2001); Frederick F. Reichheld, *The Loyalty Effect* (Boston: Harvard Business School Press, 1996).

75. Michael D. Johnson, and Fred Selnes, "Diversifying Your Customer Portfolio," *MIT Sloan Management Review* 46 (Spring 2005), pp. 11–14.

76. Tom Ostenon, *Customer Share Marketing* (Upper Saddle River, NJ: Prentice Hall, 2002); Alan W. H. Grant and Leonard A. Schlesinger, "Realize Your Customer's Full Profit Potential," *Harvard Business Review*, September–October 1995, pp. 59–72.

77. Gail McGovern and Youngme Moon, "Companies and the Customers Who Hate Them," *Harvard Business Review*, June 2007, pp. 78–84.

78. Elisabeth A. Sullivan, "Just Say No," *Marketing News*, April 15, 2008, p. 17.

79. Sunil Gupta and Carl F. Mela, "What Is a Free Customer Worth," *Harvard Business Review*, November 2008, pp. 102–9.

80. Leonard L. Berry and A. Parasuraman, *Marketing Services: Computing through Quality* (New York: Free Press, 1991), pp. 136–42. For an academic examination in a business-to-business context, see Robert W. Palmatier, Srinath Gopalakrishna, and Mark B. Houston, "Returns on Business-to-Business Relationship Marketing Investments: Strategies for Leveraging Profits," *Marketing Science* 25 (September–October 2006), pp. 477–93.

81. Frederick F. Reichheld, "Learning from Customer Defections," *Harvard Business Review,* March 3, 2009, pp. 56–69.

82. Mike White and Teresa Siles, email message, July 14, 2008.

83. Ben McConnell and Jackie Huba, "Learning to Leverage the Lunatic Fringe," *Point,* July–August 2006, pp. 14–15; Michael Krauss, "Work to Convert Customers into Evangelists," *Marketing News*, December 15, 2006, p. 6; Ben McConnell and Jackie Huba, *Creating Customer Evangelists: How Loyal Customers Become a Loyal Sales Force* (New York: Kaplan Business, 2003).

84. Utpal M. Dholakia, "How Consumer Self-Determination Influences Relational Marketing Outcomes: Evidence from Longitudinal Field Studies," *Journal of Marketing Research* 43 (February 2006), pp.109–20.

85. Allison Enright, "Serve Them Right," *Marketing News,* May 1, 2006, pp. 21–22.

86. For a review, see Grahame R. Dowling and Mark Uncles, "Do Customer Loyalty Programs Really Work?" *Sloan Management Review* 38 (Summer 1997), pp. 71–82.

87. Thomas Lee, "Retailers Look for a Hook," *St. Louis Post-Dispatch,* December 4, 2004.

88. Joseph C. Nunes and Xavier Drèze, "Feeling Superior: The Impact of Loyalty Program Structure on Consumers' Perception of Status," *Journal of Consumer Research* 35 (April 2009), pp. 890–905; Joseph C. Nunes and Xavier Drèze, "Your Loyalty Program Is Betraying You," *Harvard Business Review*, April 2006, pp. 124–31.

89. Adam Lashinsky, "The Decade of Steve Jobs," *Fortune*, November 23, 2009, pp. 93–100; *Apple,* www.apple.com, January 16, 2010; Peter Burrows, "Apple vs. Google," *BusinessWeek*, January 25, 2010, pp. 28–34.

90. Jacquelyn S. Thomas, Robert C. Blattberg, and Edward J. Fox, "Recapturing Lost Customers," *Journal of Marketing Research* 61 (February 2004), pp. 31–45.

91. Werner Reinartz and V. Kumar, "The Impact of Customer Relationship Characteristics on Profitable Lifetime Duration," *Journal of Marketing* 67 (January 2003), pp. 77–99; Werner Reinartz and V. Kumar, "The Mismanagement of Customer Loyalty," *Harvard Business Review,* July 2002, pp. 86–97.

92. V. Kumar, Rajkumar Venkatesan, and Werner Reinartz, "Knowing What to Sell, When, and to Whom," *Harvard Business Review,* March 2006, pp. 131–37.

93. Jeff Zabin, "The Importance of Being Analytical," *Brandweek*, July 24, 2006, p. 21. Stephen Baker, "Math Will Rock Your World," *BusinessWeek*, January 23, 2006, pp. 54–62. Michelle Kessler and Byron Acohido, "Data Miners Dig a Little Deeper," *USA Today*, July 11, 2006.

94. Burt Heim, "Getting Inside the Customer's Mind," *BusinessWeek*, September 22, 2008, p. 88; Mike Duff, "Dunnhumby Complicates Outlook for Tesco, Kroger, Wal-Mart," *bnet.com*, January 13, 2009; Sarah Mahoney, "Macy's Readies New Marketing Strategy, Hires Dunnhumby," *Marketing Daily*, August 14, 2008.

95. Christopher R. Stephens and R. Sukumar, "An Introduction to Data Mining," Rajiv Grover and Marco Vriens, eds., *Handbook of Marketing Research* (Thousand Oaks, CA: Sage Publications, 2006), pp. 455–86; Pang-Ning Tan, Michael Steinbach, and Vipin Kumar, *Introduction to Data Mining* (Upper Saddle River, NJ: Addison Wesley, 2005); Michael J. A. Berry and Gordon S. Linoff, *Data Mining Techniques: For Marketing, Sales, and Customer Relationship Management,* 2nd ed. (Hoboken, NJ: Wiley Computer, 2004); James Lattin, Doug Carroll, and Paul Green, *Analyzing Multivariate Data* (Florence, KY: Thomson Brooks/Cole, 2003).

96. George S. Day, "Creating a Superior Customer-Relating Capability," *Sloan Management Review* 44 (Spring 2003), pp. 77–82.

97. Ibid; George S. Day, "Creating a Superior Customer-Relating Capability," *MSI Report No. 03–101* (Cambridge, MA: Marketing Science Institute, 2003); "Why Some Companies Succeed at CRM (and Many Fail)," *Knowledge at Wharton,* http://knowledge. wharton.upenn. edu, January 15, 2003.

98. Werner Reinartz and V. Kumar, "The Mismanagement of Customer Loyalty," *Harvard Business Review*, July 2002, pp. 86–94; Susan M. Fournier, Susan Dobscha, and David Glen Mick, "Preventing the Premature Death of Relationship Marketing," *Harvard Business Review,* January–February 1998, pp. 42–51.

99. Jon Swartz, "Ebay Faithful Expect Loyalty in Return," *USA Today,* July 1, 2002.

Chapter 6

1. "Lego's Turnaround: Picking Up the Pieces," *The Economist,* October 28, 2006, p. 76; Paul Grimaldi, "Consumers Design Products Their Way," *Knight Ridder Tribune Business News,* November 25, 2006; Michael A. Prospero, *Fast Company*, September 2005, p. 35; David Robertson and Per Hjuler, "Innovating a Turnaround at LEGO," *Harvard Business Review*, September 2009, pp. 20–21; Kim Hjelmgaard, "Lego, Refocusing on Bricks, Builds on Image," *Wall Street Journal*, December 24, 2009.

2. Michael R. Solomon, *Consumer Behavior: Buying, Having, and Being,* 9th ed. (Upper Saddle River, NJ: Prentice Hall, 2011).

3. Leon G. Schiffman and Leslie Lazar Kanuk, *Consumer Behavior,* 10th ed. (Upper Saddle River, NJ: Prentice Hall, 2010).

4. For some classic perspectives, see Richard P. Coleman, "The Continuing Significance of Social Class to Marketing," *Journal of Consumer Research* 10 (December 1983), pp. 265–80; Richard P. Coleman and Lee P. Rainwater, *Social Standing in America: New Dimension of Class* (New York: Basic Books, 1978).

5. Leon G. Schiffman and Leslie Lazar Kanuk, *Consumer Behavior,* 10th ed. (Upper Saddle River, NJ: Prentice Hall, 2010).

6. Kimberly L. Allers, "Retail's Rebel Yell," *Fortune,* November 10, 2003, p. 137; Kate Rockwood, "Rock Solid," *Fast Company*, September 2009, pp. 44–48.

7. Elizabeth S. Moore, William L. Wilkie, and Richard J. Lutz, "Passing the Torch: Intergenerational Influences as a Source of Brand Equity," *Journal of Marketing* 66 (April 2002), pp. 17–37; Robert Boutilier, "Pulling the Family's Strings," *American Demographics,* August 1993, pp. 44–48; David J. Burns, "Husband-Wife Innovative Consumer Decision Making: Exploring the Effect of Family Power," *Psychology & Marketing* (May–June 1992), pp. 175–89; Rosann L. Spiro, "Persuasion in Family Decision Making," *Journal of Consumer Research* 9 (March 1983), pp. 393–402. For cross-cultural comparisons of husband–wife buying roles, see John B. Ford, Michael S. LaTour, and Tony L. Henthorne, "Perception of Marital Roles in Purchase-Decision Processes: A Cross-Cultural Study," *Journal of the Academy of Marketing Science* 23 (Spring 1995), pp. 120–31.

8. Kay M. Palan and Robert E. Wilkes, "Adolescent-Parent Interaction in Family Decision Making," *Journal of Consumer Research* 24 (March 1997), pp. 159–69; Sharon E. Beatty and Salil Talpade, "Adolescent Influence in Family Decision Making: A Replication with Extension," *Journal of Consumer Research* 21 (September 1994), pp. 332–41.

9. Chenting Su, Edward F. Fern, and Keying Ye, "A Temporal Dynamic Model of Spousal Family Purchase-Decision Behavior," *Journal of Marketing Research* 40 (August 2003), pp. 268–81.

10. Hillary Chura, "Failing to Connect: Marketing Messages for Women Fall Short," *Advertising Age,* September 23, 2002, pp. 13–14.

11. Valentyna Melnyk, Stijn M. J. van Osselaer, and Tammo H. A. Bijmolt, "Are Women More Loyal Customers Than Men? Gender Differences in Loyalty to Firms and Individual Service Providers," *Journal of Marketing* 73 (July 2009), pp. 82–96.

12. Michele Miller, *The Soccer Mom Myth* (Austin, TX: Wizard Academy Press, 2008).

13. "YouthPulse: The Definitive Study of Today's Youth Generation," *Harris Interactive*, www.harrisinteractive.com, January 29, 2010.

14. Dana Markow, "Today's Youth: Understanding Their Importance and Influence," *Trends & Tudes* 7, no. 1, www.harrisinteractive.com, February 2008.

15. Deborah Roedder John, "Consumer Socialization of Children: A Retrospective Look at Twenty-Five Years of Research," *Journal of Consumer Research* 26 (December 1999), pp. 183–213; Lan Nguyen Chaplin and Deborah Roedder John, "The Development of Self-Brand Connections in Children and Adolescents," *Journal of Consumer Research* 32 (June 2005), pp. 119–29; Lan Nguyen Chaplin and Deborah Roedder John, "Growing Up in a Material World: Age Differences in Materialism in Children and Adolescents," *Journal of Consumer Research* 34 (December 2007), pp. 480–93.

16. "Families and Living Arrangements," *U.S. Census Bureau*, www.census.gov/population/www/socdemo/hh-fam.html, January 29, 2010.

17. Rex Y. Du and Wagner A. Kamakura, "Household Life Cycles and Lifestyles in the United States," *Journal of Marketing Research* 48 (February 2006), pp. 121–32; Lawrence Lepisto, "A Life Span Perspective of Consumer Behavior," Elizabeth Hirshman and Morris Holbrook, eds., *Advances in Consumer Research,* vol. 12 (Provo, UT: Association for Consumer Research, 1985), p. 47; Also see Gail Sheehy, *New Passages: Mapping Your Life across Time* (New York: Random House, 1995).

18. Brooks Barnes and Monica M. Clark, "Tapping into the Wedding Industry to Sell Broadway Seats," *Wall Street Journal,* July 3, 2006; "Columbus, Ga.–Based Bank Targets Newlyweds for Online Banking," *Knight Ridder/Tribune Business News*, March 2, 2000.

19. Nicole Perlroth, "Survival of the Fittest," *Forbes*, January 12, 2009, pp. 54–55; "Snap Fitness Opens 1000th Club," *Club Solutions*, December 17, 2009; Becky Ebenkamp, "Snap Fitness Offers Leaner Gym Experience," *Brandweek*, January 24, 2009; Aim Jefferson, "A Snap of a Grand Opening: Snap Fitness, West Milford, *NorthJersey.com*, www.northjersey.com, January 8, 2010.

20. Harold H. Kassarjian and Mary Jane Sheffet, "Personality and Consumer Behavior: An Update," Harold H. Kassarjian and Thomas S. Robertson, eds.,

Perspectives in Consumer Behavior (Glenview, IL: Scott Foresman, 1981), pp. 160–80.

21. Jennifer Aaker, "Dimensions of Measuring Brand Personality," *Journal of Marketing Research* 34 (August 1997), pp. 347–56.

22. Jennifer L. Aaker, Veronica Benet-Martinez, and Jordi Garolera, "Consumption Symbols as Carriers of Culture: A Study of Japanese and Spanish Brand Personality Constructs," *Journal of Personality and Social Psychology* 81 (March 2001), pp. 492–508.

23. Yongjun Sung and Spencer F. Tinkham, "Brand Personality Structures in the United States and Korea: Common and Culture-Specific Factors," *Journal of Consumer Psychology* 15 (December 2005), pp. 334–50.

24. M. Joseph Sirgy, "Self Concept in Consumer Behavior: A Critical Review," *Journal of Consumer Research* 9 (December 1982), pp. 287–300.

25. Timothy R. Graeff, "Consumption Situations and the Effects of Brand Image on Consumers' Brand Evaluations," *Psychology & Marketing* 14 (January 1997), pp. 49–70; Timothy R. Graeff, "Image Congruence Effects on Product Evaluations: The Role of Self-Monitoring and Public/Private Consumption," *Psychology & Marketing* 13 (August 1996), pp. 481–99.

26. Jennifer L. Aaker, "The Malleable Self: The Role of Self-Expression in Persuasion," *Journal of Marketing Research* 36 (February 1999), pp. 45–57.

27. Neal Templin, "Boutique-Hotel Group Thrives on Quirks," *Wall Street Journal,* March 18, 1999; Chip Conley, *The Rebel Rules* (New York: Fireside, 2001); Tom Osborne, "What Is Your Band Personality," *Viget Inspire,* www.viget.com, February 2, 2009; Alice Z. Cuneo, "Magazines as Muses: Hotelier Finds Inspiration in Titles such as *Wired*," *Advertising Age,* November 6, 2006, p. 10.

28. "LOHAS Forum Attracts Fortune 500 Companies," *Environmental Leader*, June 22, 2009.

29. Toby Weber, "All Three? Gee," *Wireless Review,* May 2003, pp. 12–14.

30. Noel C. Paul, "Meal Kits in Home," *Christian Science Monitor,* June 9, 2003, p. 13; Anne D'Innocenzio, "Frugal Times: Hamburger Helper, Kool-Aid in Advertising Limelight," *Associated Press, Seattle Times*, April 29, 2009.

31. For a review of academic research on consumer behavior, see Barbara Loken, "Consumer Psychology: Categorization, Inferences, Affect, and Persuasion," *Annual Review of Psychology* 57 (2006), pp. 453–95. To learn more about how consumer behavior theory can be applied to policy decisions, see "Special Issue on Helping Consumers Help Themselves: Improving the Quality of Judgments and Choices," *Journal of Public Policy & Marketing* 25 (Spring 2006).

32. Thomas J. Reynolds and Jonathan Gutman, "Laddering Theory, Method, Analysis, and Interpretation," *Journal of Advertising Research* (February–March 1988), pp. 11–34; Thomas J. Reynolds and Jerry C. Olson, *Understanding Consumer Decision-Making: The Means-Ends Approach to Marketing and Advertising* (Mahwah, NJ: Lawrence Erlbaum, 2001); Brian Wansink, "Using Laddering to Understand and Leverage a Brand's Equity," *Qualitative Market Research* 6 (2003).

33. Ernest Dichter, *Handbook of Consumer Motivations* (New York: McGraw-Hill, 1964).

34. Jan Callebaut et al., *The Naked Consumer: The Secret of Motivational Research in Global Marketing* (Antwerp, Belgium: Censydiam Institute, 1994).

35. Melanie Wells, "Mind Games," *Forbes,* September 1, 2003, p. 70.

36. Clotaire Rapaille, "Marketing to the Reptilian Brain," *Forbes,* July 3, 2006; Clotaire Rapaille, *The Culture Code* (New York: Broadway Books, 2007).

37. Abraham Maslow, *Motivation and Personality* (New York: Harper & Row, 1954), pp. 80–106. For an interesting business application, see Chip Conley, *Peak: How Great Companies Get Their Mojo from Maslow* (San Francisco: Jossey Bass 2007).

38. See Frederick Herzberg, *Work and the Nature of Man* (Cleveland: William Collins, 1966); Thierry and Koopman-Iwema, "Motivation and Satisfaction," P. J. D. Drenth, H. Thierry, P. J. Willems, and C. J. de Wolff, eds., *A Handbook of Work and Organizational Psychology* (East Sussex, UK: Psychology Press, 1984), pp. 141–42.

39. Bernard Berelson and Gary A. Steiner, *Human Behavior: An Inventory of Scientific Findings* (New York: Harcourt Brace Jovanovich, 1964), p. 88.

40. J. Edward Russo, Margaret G. Meloy, and Victoria Husted Medvec, "The Distortion of Product Information during Brand Choice," *Journal of Marketing Research* 35 (November 1998), pp. 438–52.

41. Leslie de Chernatony and Simon Knox, "How an Appreciation of Consumer Behavior Can Help in Product Testing," *Journal of Market Research Society* (July 1990), p. 333. See also, Chris Janiszewski and Stiju M. J. Osselar, "A Connectionist Model of Brand–Quality Association," *Journal of Marketing Research* 37 (August 2000), pp. 331–51.

42. Florida's Chris Janiszewski has conducted fascinating research looking at preconscious processing effects. See Chris Janiszewski, "Preattentive Mere Exposure Effects," *Journal of Consumer Research* 20 (December 1993), pp. 376–92, as well as some of his earlier and subsequent research. For more perspectives, see also John A. Bargh and Tanya L. Chartrand, "The Unbearable Automaticity of Being," *American Psychologist* 54 (1999), pp. 462–79 and the research programs of both authors. For lively academic debate, see the "Research Dialogue" section of the July 2005 issue of the *Journal of Consumer Psychology.*

43. See Timothy E. Moore, "Subliminal Advertising: What You See Is What You Get," *Journal of Marketing* 46 (Spring 1982), pp. 38–47 for an early classic

discussion; and Andrew B. Aylesworth, Ronald C. Goodstein, and Ajay Kalra, "Effect of Archetypal Embeds on Feelings: An Indirect Route to Affecting Attitudes?" *Journal of Advertising* 28 (Fall 1999), pp. 73–81 for additional discussion.

44. Patricia Winters Lauro, "An Emotional Connection between Sleeper and Mattress," *New York Times*, July 5, 2007.

45. Ellen Byron, "Tide, Woolite Tout Their Fashion Sense," *Wall Street Journal*, March 11, 2009.

46. Robert S. Wyer Jr. and Thomas K. Srull, "Person Memory and Judgment," *Psychological Review* 96 (January 1989), pp. 58–83; John R. Anderson, *The Architecture of Cognition* (Cambridge, MA: Harvard University Press, 1983).

47. For additional discussion, see John G. Lynch Jr. and Thomas K. Srull, "Memory and Attentional Factors in Consumer Choice: Concepts and Research Methods," *Journal of Consumer Research* 9 (June 1982), pp. 18–36; and Joseph W. Alba, J. Wesley Hutchinson, and John G. Lynch Jr., "Memory and Decision Making," Harold H. Kassarjian and Thomas S. Robertson, eds., *Handbook of Consumer Theory and Research* (Englewood Cliffs, NJ: Prentice Hall, 1992), pp. 1–49.

48. Robert S. Lockhart, Fergus I. M. Craik, and Larry Jacoby, "Depth of Processing, Recognition, and Recall," John Brown, ed., *Recall and Recognition* (New York: John Wiley & Sons, 1976); Fergus I. M. Craik and Endel Tulving, "Depth of Processing and the Retention of Words in Episodic Memory," *Journal of Experimental Psychology* 104 (September 1975), pp. 268–94; Fergus I. M. Craik and Robert S. Lockhart, "Levels of Processing: A Framework for Memory Research," *Journal of Verbal Learning and Verbal Behavior* 11 (1972), pp. 671–84.

49. Leonard M. Lodish, Magid Abraham, Stuart Kalmenson, Jeanne Livelsberger, Beth Lubetkin, Bruce Richardson, and Mary Ellen Stevens, "How T.V. Advertising Works: A Meta-Analysis of 389 Real World Split Cable T.V. Advertising Experiments," *Journal of Marketing Research* 32 (May 1995), pp. 125–39.

50. Elizabeth F. Loftus and Gregory R. Loftus, "On the Permanence of Stored Information in the Human Brain," *American Psychologist* 35 (May 1980), pp. 409–20.

51. For a comprehensive review of the academic literature on decision making, see J. Edward Russo and Kurt A. Carlson, "Individual Decision Making," Bart Weitz and Robin Wensley, eds., *Handbook of Marketing* (London: Sage Publications, 2002), pp. 372–408.

52. Benson Shapiro, V. Kasturi Rangan, and John Sviokla, "Staple Yourself to an Order," *Harvard Business Review,* July–August 1992, pp. 113–22. See also, Carrie M. Heilman, Douglas Bowman, and Gordon P. Wright, "The Evolution of Brand Preferences and Choice Behaviors of Consumers New to a Market," *Journal of Marketing Research* 37 (May 2000), pp. 139–55.

53. Marketing scholars have developed several models of the consumer buying process through the years. See Mary Frances Luce, James R. Bettman, and John W. Payne, *Emotional Decisions: Tradeoff Difficulty and Coping in Consumer Choice* (Chicago: University of Chicago Press, 2001); James F. Engel, Roger D. Blackwell, and Paul W. Miniard, *Consumer Behavior,* 8th ed. (Fort Worth, TX: Dryden, 1994); John A. Howard and Jagdish N. Sheth, *The Theory of Buyer Behavior* (New York: John Wiley & Sons, 1969).

54. William P. Putsis Jr. and Narasimhan Srinivasan, "Buying or Just Browsing? The Duration of Purchase Deliberation," *Journal of Marketing Research* 31 (August 1994), pp. 393–402.

55. Chem L. Narayana and Rom J. Markin, "Consumer Behavior and Product Performance: An Alternative Conceptualization," *Journal of Marketing* 39 (October 1975), pp. 1–6. See also, Lee G. Cooper and Akihiro Inoue, "Building Market Structures from Consumer Preferences," *Journal of Marketing Research* 33 (August 1996), pp. 293–306; Wayne S. DeSarbo and Kamel Jedidi, "The Spatial Representation of Heterogeneous Consideration Sets," *Marketing Science* 14 (Summer 1995), pp. 326–42.

56. For a market-structure study of the hierarchy of attributes in the coffee market, see Dipak Jain, Frank M. Bass, and Yu-Min Chen, "Estimation of Latent Class Models with Heterogeneous Choice Probabilities: An Application to Market Structuring," *Journal of Marketing Research* 27 (February 1990), pp. 94–101. For an application of means-end chain analysis to global markets, see Frenkel Ter Hofstede, Jan-Benedict E. M. Steenkamp, and Michel Wedel, "International Market Segmentation Based on Consumer–Product Relations," *Journal of Marketing Research* 36 (February 1999), pp. 1–17.

57. Virginia Postrel, "The Lessons of the Grocery Shelf Also Have Something to Say about Affirmative Action," *New York Times,* January 30, 2003.

58. David Krech, Richard S. Crutchfield, and Egerton L. Ballachey, *Individual in Society* (New York: McGraw-Hill, 1962), chapter 2.

59. Seth Stevenson, "Like Cardboard," *Slate*, January 11, 2010; Ashley M. Heher, "Domino's Comes Clean with New Pizza Ads," *Associated Press*, January 11, 2010; Bob Garfield, "Domino's Does Itself a Disservice by Coming Clean about Its Pizza," *Advertising Age*, January 11, 2010; *Domino's Pizza,* www.pizzaturnaround.com.

60. See Leigh McAlister, "Choosing Multiple Items from a Product Class," *Journal of Consumer Research* 6 (December 1979), pp. 213–24; Paul E. Green and Yoram Wind, *Multiattribute Decisions in Marketing: A Measurement Approach* (Hinsdale, IL: Dryden, 1973), chapter 2; Richard J. Lutz, "The Role of Attitude Theory in Marketing," H. Kassarjian and T. Robertson, eds., *Perspectives in Consumer Behavior* (Lebanon, IN: Scott Foresman, 1981), pp. 317–39.

61. This expectancy-value model was originally developed by Martin Fishbein, "Attitudes and Prediction of Behavior," Martin Fishbein, ed., *Readings in Attitude*

Theory and Measurement (New York: John Wiley & Sons, 1967), pp. 477–92; For a critical review, see Paul W. Miniard and Joel B. Cohen, "An Examination of the Fishbein-Ajzen Behavioral-Intentions Model's Concepts and Measures," Journal of Experimental Social Psychology (May 1981), pp. 309–39.

62. Michael R. Solomon, Consumer Behavior: Buying, Having, and Being, 9th ed. (Upper Saddle River, NJ: Prentice Hall, 2011).

63. James R. Bettman, Eric J. Johnson, and John W. Payne, "Consumer Decision Making," Kassarjian and Robertson, eds., Handbook of Consumer Theory and Research (Upper Saddle River, NJ: Pearson Prentice Hall, 1991), pp. 50–84.

64. Jagdish N. Sheth, "An Investigation of Relationships among Evaluative Beliefs, Affect, Behavioral Intention, and Behavior," John U. Farley, John A. Howard, and L. Winston Ring, eds., Consumer Behavior: Theory and Application (Boston: Allyn & Bacon, 1974), pp. 89–114.

65. Martin Fishbein, "Attitudes and Prediction of Behavior," M. Fishbein, ed., Readings in Attitude Theory and Measurement (New York: John Wiley & Sons, 1967), pp. 477–492.

66. Andrew Hampp, "How 'Paranormal Activity,' Hit It Big," Advertising Age, October 12, 2009.

67. Margaret C. Campbell and Ronald C. Goodstein, "The Moderating Effect of Perceived Risk on Consumers' Evaluations of Product Incongruity: Preference for the Norm," Journal of Consumer Research 28 (December 2001), pp. 439–49; Grahame R. Dowling, "Perceived Risk," Peter E. Earl and Simon Kemp, eds., The Elgar Companion to Consumer Research and Economic Psychology (Cheltenham, UK: Edward Elgar, 1999), pp. 419–24; Grahame R. Dowling, "Perceived Risk: The Concept and Its Measurement," Psychology and Marketing 3 (Fall 1986), pp. 193–210; James R. Bettman, "Perceived Risk and Its Components: A Model and Empirical Test," Journal of Marketing Research 10 (May 1973), pp. 184–90; Raymond A. Bauer, "Consumer Behavior as Risk Taking," Donald F. Cox, ed., Risk Taking and Information Handling in Consumer Behavior (Boston: Division of Research, Harvard Business School, 1967).

68. Richard L. Oliver, "Customer Satisfaction Research," Rajiv Grover and Marco Vriens, eds., Handbook of Marketing Research (Thousand Oaks, CA: Sage Publications, 2006), pp. 569–87.

69. Ralph L. Day, "Modeling Choices among Alternative Responses to Dissatisfaction," Advances in Consumer Research 11 (1984), pp. 496–99. Also see Philip Kotler and Murali K. Mantrala, "Flawed Products: Consumer Responses and Marketer Strategies," Journal of Consumer Marketing (Summer 1985), pp. 27–36.

70. Albert O. Hirschman, Exit, Voice, and Loyalty (Cambridge, MA: Harvard University Press, 1970).

71. John D. Cripps, "Heuristics and Biases in Timing the Replacement of Durable Products," Journal of Consumer Research 21 (September 1994), pp. 304–18.

72. Ben Paytner, "From Trash to Cash," Fast Company, February 2009, p. 44.

73. Richard E. Petty, Communication and Persuasion: Central and Peripheral Routes to Attitude Change (New York: Springer-Verlag, 1986); Richard E. Petty and John T. Cacioppo, Attitudes and Persuasion: Classic and Contemporary Approaches (New York: McGraw-Hill, 1981).

74. For an overview of some issues involved, see James R. Bettman, Mary Frances Luce, and John W. Payne, "Constructive Consumer Choice Processes," Journal of Consumer Research 25 (December 1998), pp. 187–217; and Itamar Simonson, "Getting Closer to Your Customers by Understanding How They Make Choices," California Management Review 35 (Summer 1993), pp. 68–84. For examples of classic studies in this area, see some of the following: Dan Ariely and Ziv Carmon, "Gestalt Characteristics of Experiences: The Defining Features of Summarized Events," Journal of Behavioral Decision Making 13 (April 2000), pp. 191–201; Ravi Dhar and Klaus Wertenbroch, "Consumer Choice between Hedonic and Utilitarian Goods," Journal of Marketing Research 37 (February 2000), pp. 60–71; Itamar Simonson and Amos Tversky, "Choice in Context: Tradeoff Contrast and Extremeness Aversion," Journal of Marketing Research 29 (August 1992), pp. 281–95; Itamar Simonson, "The Effects of Purchase Quantity and Timing on Variety-Seeking Behavior," Journal of Marketing Research 27 (May 1990), pp. 150–62.

75. Leon Schiffman and Leslie Kanuk, Consumer Behavior, 10th ed. (Upper Saddle River, NJ: Prentice Hall, 2010); Wayne D. Hoyer and Deborah J. MacInnis, Consumer Behavior, 5th ed. (Cincinnati, OH: South-Western College Publishing, 2009).

76. For a detailed review of the practical significance of consumer decision making, see Itamar Simonson, "Get Close to Your Customers by Understanding How They Make Their Choices," California Management Review 35 (Summer 1993), pp. 78–79.

77. Richard H. Thaler and Cass R. Sunstein, Nudge: Improving Decisions about Health, Wealth, and Happiness (New York: Penguin, 2009); Michael Krauss, "A Nudge in the Right Direction," Marketing News, March 30, 2009, p. 20.

78. See Richard H. Thaler, "Mental Accounting and Consumer Choice," Marketing Science 4 (Summer 1985), pp. 199–214 for a seminal piece; and Richard Thaler, "Mental Accounting Matters," Journal of Behavioral Decision Making 12 (September 1999), pp. 183–206 for additional perspectives.

79. Gary L. Gastineau and Mark P. Kritzman, Dictionary of Financial Risk Management, 3rd ed. (New York: John Wiley & Sons, 1999).

80. Example adapted from Daniel Kahneman and Amos Tversky, "Prospect Theory: An Analysis of Decision under Risk," Econometrica 47 (March 1979), pp. 263–91.

Chapter 7

1. Adam Lashinsky, "The Enforcer," *Fortune*, September 28, 2009, pp. 117–24; Steve Hamm, "Oracle Faces Its Toughest Deal Yet," *BusinessWeek*, May 4, 2009, p. 24; Steve Hamm and Aaron Ricadela, "Oracle Has Customers Over a Barrel," *BusinessWeek*, September 21, 2009, pp. 52–55.

2. For a comprehensive review of the topic, see James C. Anderson and James A. Narus, *Business Market Management: Understanding, Creating, and Delivering Value,* 3rd ed. (Upper Saddle River, NJ: Prentice Hall, 2009).

3. Frederick E. Webster Jr. and Yoram Wind, *Organizational Buying Behavior* (Upper Saddle River, NJ: Prentice Hall, 1972), p. 2; For a review of some academic literature on the topic, see Håkan Håkansson and Ivan Snehota, "Marketing in Business Markets," Bart Weitz and Robin Wensley, eds., *Handbook of Marketing* (London: Sage Publications, 2002), pp. 513–26; Mark Glynn and Arch Woodside, eds., *Business-to-Business Brand Management: Theory, Research, and Executive Case Study Exercises in Advances in Business Marketing & Purchasing* series, Volume 15 (Bingley, UK: Emerald Group Publishing, 2009).

4. John Low and Keith Blois, "The Evolution of Generic Brands in Industrial Markets: The Challenges to Owners of Brand Equity," *Industrial Marketing Management* 31 (2002), pp. 385–92; Philip Kotler and Waldemar Pfoertsch, *B2B Brand Management* (Berlin, Germany: Springer, 2006).

5. Stuart Elliott, "A Film on the Trucking Life Also Promotes a Big Rig," *New York Times*, August 13, 2008; Nikki Hopewell, "Be Brave B-to-B Marketers," *Marketing News*, November 15, 2008, pp. 18–21.

6. "B-to-B Marketing Trends 2010," *Institute for the Study of Business Markets*, http://isbm.smeal.psu.edu.

7. Susan Avery, *Purchasing* 135 (November 2, 2006), p. 36; "PPG Honors Six Excellent Suppliers," www.ppg.com, June 16, 2009.

8. Michael Collins, "Breaking into the Big Leagues," *American Demographics,* January 1996, p. 24.

9. Patrick J. Robinson, Charles W. Faris, and Yoram Wind, *Industrial Buying and Creative Marketing* (Boston: Allyn & Bacon, 1967).

10. Michele D. Bunn, "Taxonomy of Buying Decision Approaches," *Journal of Marketing* 57 (January 1993), pp. 38–56; Daniel H. McQuiston, "Novelty, Complexity, and Importance as Causal Determinants of Industrial Buyer Behavior," *Journal of Marketing* 53 (April 1989), pp. 66–79; Peter Doyle, Arch G. Woodside, and Paul Mitchell, "Organizational Buying in New Task and Rebuy Situations," *Industrial Marketing Management* (February 1979), pp. 7–11.

11. Urban B. Ozanne and Gilbert A. Churchill Jr., "Five Dimensions of the Industrial Adoption Process," *Journal of Marketing Research* 8 (August 1971), pp. 322–28.

12. To learn more about how business-to-business firms can improve their branding, see Philip Kotler and Waldemar Pfoertsch, *B2B Brand Management* (Berlin, Germany: Springer, 2006).

13. Steve Hamm, "The Fine Art of Tech Mergers," *BusinessWeek,* July 10, 2006, pp. 70–71.

14. Elisabeth Sullivan, "Building a Better Brand," *Marketing News*, September 15, 2009, pp. 14–17.

15. Britt Dionne, "Behind the Scenes with NetApp," *The Hub*, July/August 2009; "Close-up with Jay Kidd, CMO, NetApp," *BtoB Magazine*, January 20, 2010; Piet Levy, "It's Alive! Alive!" *Marketing News*, April 30, 2009, p. 8.

16. Jeffrey E. Lewin and Naveen Donthu, "The Influence of Purchase Situation on Buying Center Structure and Involvement: A Select Meta-Analysis of Organizational Buying Behavior Research," *Journal of Business Research* 58 (October 2005), pp. 1381–90; R. Venkatesh and Ajay K. Kohli, "Influence Strategies in Buying Centers," *Journal of Marketing* 59 (October 1995), pp. 71–82; Donald W. Jackson Jr., Janet E. Keith, and Richard K. Burdick, "Purchasing Agents' Perceptions of Industrial Buying Center Influence: A Situational Approach," *Journal of Marketing* 48 (Fall 1984), pp. 75–83.

17. Frederic E. Webster and Yoram Wind, *Organizational Buying Behavior* (Saddle River, NJ: Prentice Hall, 1972), p. 6.

18. James C. Anderson and James A. Narus, *Business Market Management: Understanding, Creating, and Delivering Value,* 3rd ed. (Upper Saddle River, NJ: Prentice Hall, 2009); Frederick E. Webster Jr. and Yoram Wind, "A General Model for Understanding Organizational Buying Behavior," *Journal of Marketing* 36 (April 1972), pp. 12–19; Frederic E. Webster and Yoram Wind, *Organizational Buying Behavior* (Saddle River, NJ: Prentice Hall, 1972).

19. Allison Enright, "It Takes a Committee to Buy into B-to-B," *Marketing News,* February 15, 2006, pp. 12–13.

20. Frederick E. Webster Jr. and Kevin Lane Keller, "A Roadmap for Branding in Industrial Markets," *Journal of Brand Management* 11 (May 2004), pp. 388–402.

21. Scott Ward and Frederick E. Webster Jr., "Organizational Buying Behavior," Tom Robertson and Hal Kassarjian, eds., *Handbook of Consumer Behavior* (Upper Saddle River, NJ: Prentice Hall, 1991), chapter 12, pp. 419–58.

22. Bob Donath, "Emotions Play Key Role in Biz Brand Appeal," *Marketing News,* June 1, 2006, p. 7.

23. Michael Krauss, "Warriors of the Heart," *Marketing News,* February 1, 2006, p. 7; Brian Hindo, "Emerson Electric's Innovation Metrics," *BusinessWeek*, June 5, 2008.

24. Bob Lamons, "Branding, B-to-B Style," *Sales and Marketing Management* 157 (September 2005), pp. 46–50; David A. Kaplan, "No. 1 SAS," in "The 100 Best Companies to Work For," *Fortune*, February 8, 2010, pp. 56–64.

25. Piet Levy, "Reeling in the Hungry Fish," *Marketing News*, May 30, 2009, p. 6; Stephen Baker, Timken Plots a Rust Belt Resurgence," *BusinessWeek*, October 15, 2009; Matt McClellan, "Rolling Along," *Smart Business Akron/Canton*, October 2008.

26. Richard J. Harrington and Anthony K. Tjan, "Transforming Strategy One Customer at a Time," *Harvard Business Review*, March 2008, pp. 62–72; Stanley Reed, "The Rise of a Financial Data Powerhouse," *BusinessWeek*, May 15, 2007; Stanley Reed, "Media Giant or Media Muddle?" *BusinessWeek*, May 1, 2008.

27. Frederic E. Webster and Yoram Wind, *Organizational Buying Behavior* (Saddle River, NJ: Prentice Hall, 1972), p. 6.

28. James C. Anderson, James A. Narus, and Wouter van Rossum, "Customer Value Proposition in Business Markets," *Harvard Business Review,* March 2006, pp. 2–10; James C. Anderson, "From Understanding to Managing Customer Value in Business Markets," H. Håkansson, D. Harrison, and A. Waluszewski, eds., *Rethinking Marketing: New Marketing Tools* (London: John Wiley & Sons, 2004), pp. 137–59.

29. Susan Caminiti, "Drivers of the Economy," *Fortune*, April 17, 2006, p. C1; "Pfizer Turns Around Its Diversity & Inclusion Initiatives," *Diversity/Careers in Engineering and Information Technology*, December 2009/January 2010; Barbara Frankel, "Pfizer's Newest CDO Represents Transferable Talent," *Diversity Inc.*, November/December 2009; "From One Small Business to Another: Enhancing Community Through Commerce," *Pfizer,* www.pfizersupplierdiversity.com, February 6, 2010.

30. "Case Studies: Rio Tinto," *Quadrem,* www.quadrem.com, February 6, 2010.

31. "Case Study 2003: Mitsui & Co. Cuts the Cost of Trade Transactions by 50% by Using Trade Card," *Mitsui & Co., LTD.*, www.tradecard.com.

32. "Best Practices of the Best-Run Sales Organizations: Sales Opportunity Blueprinting," *SAP,* http://download.sap.com, February 6, 2010.

33. Patrick J. Robinson, Charles W. Faris, and Yoram Wind, *Industrial Buying and Creative Marketing* (Boston, MA: Allyn & Bacon, 1967).

34. *Institute Of Scrap Recycling Institute,* www.isri.org.

35. Geri Smith, "Hard Times Ease for a Cement King," *BusinessWeek*, November 9, 2009, p. 28.

36. Rajdeep Grewal, James M. Comer, and Raj Mehta, "An Investigation into the Antecedents of Organizational Participation in Business-to-Business Electronic Markets," *Journal of Marketing* 65 (July 2001), pp. 17–33.

37. "Open Sesame? Or Could the Doors Slam Shut for Alibaba.com?" *Knowledge@Wharton,* July 27, 2005; Julia Angwin, "Top Online Chemical Exchange Is Unlikely Success Story," *Wall Street Journal,* January 8, 2004; Olga Kharif, "B2B, Take 2," *BusinessWeek,* November 25, 2003; George S. Day, Adam J. Fein, and Gregg Ruppersberger, "Shakeouts in Digital Markets: Lessons from B2B Exchanges," *California Management Review* 45 (Winter 2003), pp. 131–51.

38. *Ritchie Bros Auctioneers,* www.rbauction.com.

39. Brian J. Carroll, *Lead Generation for the Complex Sale* (New York: McGraw-Hill, 2006).

40. "2009–10 B2B Marketing Benchmark Report," *Marketing Sherpa,* www.sherpastore.com, February 6, 2010.

41. Allison Enright, "It Takes a Committee to Buy into B-to-B," *Marketing News,* February 15, 2006, pp. 12–13.

42. Robert Hiebeler, Thomas B. Kelly, and Charles Ketteman, *Best Practices: Building Your Business with Customer-Focused Solutions* (New York: Arthur Andersen/Simon & Schuster, 1998), pp. 122–24.

43. Daniel J. Flint, Robert B. Woodruff, and Sarah Fisher Gardial, "Exploring the Phenomenon of Customers' Desired Value Change in a Business-to-Business Context," *Journal of Marketing* 66 (October 2002), pp. 102–17.

44. Ruth N. Bolton and Matthew B. Myers, "Price-Based Global Market Segmentation for Services," *Journal of Marketing* 67 (July 2003), pp. 108–28.

45. Wolfgang Ulaga and Andreas Eggert, "Value-Based Differentiation in Business Relationships: Gaining and Sustaining Key Supplier Status," *Journal of Marketing* 70 (January 2006), pp. 119–36.

46. Christopher Palmeri, "Serving Two (Station) Masters," *BusinessWeek,* July 24, 2006, p. 46.

47. David Kiley, "Small Print Jobs for Peanuts," *BusinessWeek,* July 17, 2006, p. 58.

48. Nirmalya Kumar, *Marketing as Strategy: Understanding the CEO's Agenda for Driving Growth and Innovation* (Boston: Harvard Business School Press, 2004).

49. Ibid.

50. See William Atkinson, "Now That's Value Added," *Purchasing,* December 11, 2003, p. 26; James A. Narus and James C. Anderson, "Turn Your Industrial Distributors into Partners," *Harvard Business Review,* March–April 1986, pp. 66–71; www.lincolnelectric.com/knowledge/custsolutions/gcr.asp.

51. "Case Study: Automotive Vendor Managed Inventory, Plexco (Australia)," www.marciajedd.com.

52. For foundational material, see Lloyd M. Rinehart, James A. Eckert, Robert B. Handfield, Thomas J. Page Jr., and Thomas Atkin, "An Assessment of Buyer–Seller Relationships," *Journal of Business Logistics* 25 (2004), pp. 25–62; F. Robert Dwyer, Paul Schurr, and Sejo Oh, "Developing Buyer–Supplier Relationships," *Journal of Marketing* 51 (April 1987), pp. 11–28; and Barbara Bund Jackson, *Winning & Keeping Industrial Customers: The Dynamics of Customer Relations* (Lexington, MA: D. C. Heath, 1985).

53. Arnt Buvik and George John, "When Does Vertical Coordination Improve Industrial Purchasing Relationships?" *Journal of Marketing* 64 (October 2000), pp. 52–64.

54. Piet Levy, "Ringing Up a New Approach," *Marketing News*, March 15, 2009, p. 8; "The Inspiration Behind Tellabs' 'New Life' Campaign," *Business Marketing Association,* www.bmachicago.org, February 6, 2010;

Kate Maddox, "Marketers Look to Social Media for Interaction," *BtoB Magazine*, January 15, 2007; Chelsea Ely, "Tellabs Aims to "Outsmart, Not Outspend Large Competitors," *BtoB Magazine*, January 9, 2009.

55. Das Narayandas and V. Kasturi Rangan, "Building and Sustaining Buyer–Seller Relationships in Mature Industrial Markets," *Journal of Marketing* 68 (July 2004), pp. 63–77.

56. Robert W. Palmatier, Rajiv P. Dant, Dhruv Grewal, and Kenneth R. Evans, "Factors Influencing the Effectiveness of Relationship Marketing: A Meta-Analysis," *Journal of Marketing* 70 (October 2006), pp. 136–53; Jean L. Johnson, Ravipreet S. Sohli, and Rajdeep Grewal, "The Role of Relational Knowledge Stores in Interfirm Partnering," *Journal of Marketing* 68 (July 2004), pp. 21–36; Fred Selnes and James Sallis, "Promoting Relationship Learning," *Journal of Marketing* 67 (July 2003), pp. 80–95; Patricia M. Doney and Joseph P. Cannon, "An Examination of the Nature of Trust in Buyer–Seller Relationships," *Journal of Marketing* 61 (April 1997), pp. 35–51; Shankar Ganesan, "Determinants of Long-Term Orientation in Buyer–Seller Relationships," *Journal of Marketing* 58 (April 1994), pp. 1–19.

57. William W. Keep, Stanley C. Hollander, and Roger Dickinson, "Forces Impinging on Long-Term Business-to-Business Relationships in the United States: An Historical Perspective," *Journal of Marketing* 62 (April 1998), pp. 31–45.

58. Joseph P. Cannon and William D. Perreault Jr., "Buyer–Seller Relationships in Business Markets," *Journal of Marketing Research* 36 (November 1999), pp. 439–60.

59. Jan B. Heide and Kenneth H. Wahne, "Friends, Businesspeople, and Relationship Roles: A Conceptual Framework and Research Agenda," *Journal of Marketing* 70 (July 2006), pp. 90–103.

60. Joseph P. Cannon and William D. Perreault Jr., "Buyer–Seller Relationships in Business Markets," *Journal of Marketing Research* 36 (November 1999), pp. 439–60.

61. Thomas G. Noordewier, George John, and John R. Nevin, "Performance Outcomes of Purchasing Arrangements in Industrial Buyer–Vendor Arrangements," *Journal of Marketing* 54 (October 1990), pp. 80–93; Arnt Buvik and George John, "When Does Vertical Coordination Improve Industrial Purchasing Relationships?" *Journal of Marketing* 64 (October 2000), pp. 52–64.

62. Akesel I. Rokkan, Jan B. Heide, and Kenneth H. Wathne, "Specific Investment in Marketing Relationships: Expropriation and Bonding Effects," *Journal of Marketing Research* 40 (May 2003), pp. 210–24.

63. Kenneth H. Wathne and Jan B. Heide, "Relationship Governance in a Supply Chain Network," *Journal of Marketing* 68 (January 2004), pp. 73–89; Douglas Bowman and Das Narayandas, "Linking Customer Management Effort to Customer Profitability in Business Markets," *Journal of Marketing Research* 61 (November 2004), pp. 433–47; Mrinal Ghosh and George John, "Governance Value Analysis and Marketing Strategy," *Journal of Marketing* 63 (Special Issue, 1999), pp. 131–45.

64. Sandy Jap, "Pie Expansion Effects: Collaboration Processes in Buyer–Seller Relationships," *Journal of Marketing Research* 36 (November 1999), pp. 461–75.

65. Buvik and John, "When Does Vertical Coordination Improve Industrial Purchasing Relationships?" pp. 52–64.

66. Kenneth H. Wathne and Jan B. Heide, "Opportunism in Interfirm Relationships: Forms, Outcomes, and Solutions," *Journal of Marketing* 64 (October 2000), pp. 36–51.

67. Mary Walton, "When Your Partner Fails You," *Fortune,* May 26, 1997, pp. 151–54.

68. Mark B. Houston and Shane A. Johnson, "Buyer–Supplier Contracts versus Joint Ventures: Determinants and Consequences of Transaction Structure," *Journal of Marketing Research* 37 (February 2000), pp. 1–15.

69. Aksel I. Rokkan, Jan B. Heide, and Kenneth H. Wathne, "Specific Investment in Marketing Relationships: Expropriation and Bonding Effects," *Journal of Marketing Research* 40 (May 2003), pp. 210–24.

70. Elisabeth Sullivan, "A Worthwhile Investment," *Marketing News,* December 30, 2009, p. 10.

71. Shar VanBoskirk, "B2B Email Marketing Best Practices: Hewlett Packard," *Forrester,* www.forrester.com, February 21, 2006.

72. Josh Bernoff, "Why B-to-B Ought to Love Social Media," *Marketing News,* April 15, 2009, p. 20; Elisabeth Sullivan, "A Long Slog," *Marketing News,* February 28, 2009, pp. 15–18.

73. Elisabeth Sullivan, "One to One," *Marketing News,* May 15, 2009, pp. 10–12.

74. Elisabeth Sullivan, "Cognos Inc.," *Marketing News,* April 1, 2008, p. 10.

75. Paul King, "Purchasing: Keener Competition Requires Thinking Outside the Box," *Nation's Restaurant News,* August 18, 2003, p. 87.

76. Bill Gormley, "The U.S. Government Can Be Your Lifelong Customer," *Washington Business Journal,* January 23, 2009; Chris Warren, "How to Sell to Uncle Sam," *BNET Crash Course,* www.bnet.com, February 6, 2010.

77. Matthew Swibel and Janet Novack, "The Scariest Customer," *Forbes,* November 10, 2003, pp. 96–97.

78. Laura M. Litvan, "Selling to Uncle Sam: New, Easier Rules," *Nation's Business* (March 1995), pp. 46–48.

79. Ellen Messmer, "Feds Do E-Commerce the Hard Way," *Network World,* April 13, 1998, pp. 31–32.

80. Bill Gormley, "The U.S. Government Can Be Your Lifelong Customer," *Washington Business Journal,* January 23, 2009.

Chapter 8

1. Jonathan Schneider, "Club Med—Sex, Sand, and Surf," *Club Med*, www.clubmed.us, January 26, 2010; *Brand Channel*, www.brandchannel.com, July 2, 2001; Christina White, "It's Raining Hard on Club Med," *BusinessWeek*, February 4, 2002; Susan Spano, "Club Med, Swinging into the Future," *Morning Call*, January 15, 2006; Cherisse Beh, "Club Med Unveils Global Branding Push," *Marketing Interactive.com,* www.marketing-interactive.com, March 31, 2008.

2. Dale Buss, "Brands in the 'Hood," *Point,* December 2005, pp. 19–24.

3. Nanette Byrnes, "What's Beyond for Bed Bath & Beyond?" *BusinessWeek,* January 19, 2004, pp. 45–50; Andrea Lillo, "Bed Bath Sees More Room for Growth," *Home Textiles Today,* July 7, 2003, p. 2.

4. By visiting the company's sponsored site, MyBestSegments.com, you can enter in a zip code and discover the top five clusters for that area. Note that another leading supplier of geodemographic data is ClusterPlus (Strategic Mapping).

5. Becky Ebenkamp, "Urban America Redefined," *Brandweek,* October 6, 2003, pp. 12–13.

6. Mike Freeman, "Clusters of Customers," *San Diego Union-Tribune*, December 19, 2004.

7. Michael J. Weiss, "To Be About to Be," *American Demographics,* September 2003, pp. 29–36.

8. "YouthPulse: The Definitive Study of Today's Youth Generation," *Harris Interactive*, 2009, www.harrisinteractive.com.

9. Gina Chon, "Car Makers Talk 'Bout G-G-Generations," *Wall Street Journal,* May 9, 2006.

10. For some practical implications, see Marti Barletta, *Marketing to Women: How to Increase Share of the World's Largest Market*, 2nd ed. (New York: Kaplan Business, 2006); Bridget Brennan, *Why She Buys: The New Strategy for Reaching the World's Most Powerful Consumers* (New York: Crown Business, 2009).

11. For more consumer behavior perspectives on gender, see Jane Cunningham and Philippa Roberts, "What Woman Want," *Brand Strategy,* December 2006–January 2007, pp. 40–41; Robert J. Fisher and Laurette Dube, "Gender Differences in Responses to Emotional Advertising: A Social Desirability Perspective," *Journal of Consumer Research* 31 (March 2005), pp. 850–58; Joan Meyers-Levy and Durairaj Maheswaran, "Exploring Males' and Females' Processing Strategies: When and Why Do Differences Occur in Consumers' Processing of Ad Claims," *Journal of Consumer Research* 18 (June 1991), pp. 63–70; Joan Meyers-Levy and Brian Sternthal, "Gender Differences in the Use of Message Cues and Judgments," *Journal of Marketing Research* 28 (February 1991), pp. 84–96.

12. Dawn Klingensmith, "Marketing Gurus Try to Read Women's Minds," *Chicago Tribune,* April 19, 2006; Elisabeth Sullivan, "The Mother Lode," *Marketing News*, July 15, 2008, p. 28; Claire Cain Miller, "Advertising Woman to Woman, Online," *New York Times*, August 13, 2008; Eric Newman, "The Mook Industrial Complex," *Brandweek*, January 14, 2008, pp. 21–24.

13. Marti Barletta, "Who's Really Buying That Car? Ask Her," *Brandweek,* September 4, 2006, p. 20; Robert Craven, Kiki Maurey, and John Davis, "What Women Really Want," *Critical Eye* 15 (July 2006), pp. 50–53; Michael J. Silverstein and Kate Sayre, "The Female Economy," *Harvard Business Review*, September 2009, pp. 46–53.

14. Aixa Pascual, "Lowe's Is Sprucing Up Its House," *BusinessWeek,* June 3, 2002, pp. 56–57; Pamela Sebastian Ridge, "Tool Sellers Tap Their Feminine Side," *Wall Street Journal,* June 16, 2002.

15. Michael J. Silverstein and Neil Fiske, *Trading Up: The New American Luxury* (New York: Portfolio, 2003); Dylan Machan, "Sharing Victoria's Secret," *Forbes,* June 5, 1995, p. 132; www.limitedbrands.com.

16. Ian Zack, "Out of the Tube," *Forbes,* November 26, 2001, p. 200.

17. Gregory L. White and Shirley Leung, "Middle Market Shrinks as Americans Migrate toward the Higher End," *Wall Street Journal,* March 29, 2002.

18. Burt Helm, "PNC Lures Gen Y with Its 'Virtual Wallet' Account," *BusinessWeek*, November 26, 2008; *Virtual Wallet by PNC Leading the Way,* www.pncvirtualwallet.com, January 26, 2010.

19. Charles D. Schewe and Geoffrey Meredith, "Segmenting Global Markets by Generational Cohort: Determining Motivations by Age," *Journal of Consumer Behavior* 4 (October 2004), pp. 51–63; Geoffrey E. Meredith and Charles D. Schewe, *Managing by Defining Moments: America's 7 Generational Cohorts, Their Workplace Values, and Why Managers Should Care* (New York: Hungry Minds, 2002); Geoffrey E. Meredith, Charles D. Schewe, and Janice Karlovich, *Defining Markets Defining Moments* (New York: Hungry Minds, 2001).

20. Piet Levy, "The Quest for Cool," *Marketing News*, February 28, 2009, p. 6; Michelle Conlin, "Youth Quake*," BusinessWeek*, January 21, 2008, pp. 32–36.

21. Karen E. Klein, "The ABCs of Selling to Generation X," *BusinessWeek*, April 15, 2004; M. J. Stephey, "Gen-X: the Ignored Generation?" *Time*, April 16, 2008; Tamara Erickson, "Don't Treat Them Like Baby Boomers," *BusinessWeek*, August 25, 2008, p. 64.

22. Louise Lee, "Love Those Boomers," *BusinessWeek,* October 24, 2005, p. 94; Bob Moos, "Last of Boomers Turn 40," *Dallas Morning News,* January 1, 2005; Linda Tischler, "Where the Bucks Are," *Fast Company*, March 2004, pp. 71–77; Alycia de Mesa, "Don't Ignore the Boomer Consumer," *brandchannel,* www.brandchannel.com, June 25, 2007; Judann Pollack, "Boomers Don't Want Your Pity, but They Do Demand Your Respect," *Advertising Age*, October 8, 2007, p. 24.

23. Mark Dolliver, "Marketing to Today's 65-plus Consumers," *Adweek*, July 27, 2009.

24. Stuart Elliott, "The Older Audience Is Looking Better Than Ever," *New York Times*, April 19, 2009.

25. Marissa Miley, "Don't Bypass African-Americans," *Advertising Age*, February 2, 2009.

26. Elisabeth Sullivan, "Choose Your Words Wisely," *Marketing News*, February 15, 2008, p. 22; Emily Bryson York, "Brands Prepare for a More Diverse 'General Market,'" *Advertising Age*, November 30, 2009, p. 6.

27. Emily Bryson York, "Brands Prepare for a More Diverse 'General Market,'" *Advertising Age*, November 30, 2009, p. 6.

28. Daniel B. Honigman, "10 Minutes with . . . Caralene Robinson," *Marketing News*, February 15, 2008, pp. 24–28; Sonya A. Grier, Anne Brumbaugh, and Corliss G. Thornton, "Crossover Dreams: Consumer Responses to Ethnic-Oriented Products," *Journal of Marketing* 70 (April 2006), pp. 35–51.

29. "Hispanics Will Top All U.S. Minority Groups for Purchasing Power by 2007," *Selig Center of Economic Growth, Terry College of Business, University of Georgia,*/www.selig.uga.edu, September 1, 2006; Jeffrey M. Humphreys, "The Multicultural Economy 2008," *Selig Center of Economic Growth, Terry College of Business, University of Georgia,* 2008.

30. Andrew Pierce, "Multiculti Markets Demand Multilayered Markets," *Marketing News*, May 1, 2008, p. 21.

31. Barbara De Lollis, "At Goya, It's All in La Familia," *USA Today*, March 24, 2008, pp. 1B–2B.

32. Ronald Grover, "The Payoff from Targeting Hispanics," *BusinessWeek*, April 20, 2009, p. 76; Della de Lafuente, "The New Weave," *Adweek Media*, March 3, 2008, pp. 26–28.

33. Piet Levy, "La Musica to Their Ears," *Marketing News*, May 15, 2009, pp. 14–16; Ronald Grover, "The Payoff from Targeting Hispanics," *BusinessWeek*, April 20, 2009, p. 76.

34. Elaine Wong, "Why Bounty Is a Hit with U.S. Hispanics," *Brandweek*, August 17, 2009, p. 6.

35. Samar Farah, "Latino Marketing Goes Mainstream," *Boston Globe*, July 9, 2006; Dianne Solis, "Latino Buying Power Still Surging," *Dallas Morning News*, September 1, 2006; Joseph Tarnowski, "Assimilate or Perish," *Progressive Grocer*, February 1, 2006.

36. Kevin Lane Keller, "got milk?: Branding a Commodity," *Best Practice Cases in Branding*, 3rd ed. (Upper Saddle River, NJ: Prentice Hall, 2008); *got milk?* www.gotmilk.com; Jeff Manning, *got milk?: The book* (Roseville, CA: Prima Lifestyles 1999).

37. Elisabeth A. Sullivan, "Speak Our Language," *Marketing News*, March 15, 2008, pp. 20–22.

38. Rita Chang, "Mobile Marketers Target Receptive Hispanic Audience," *Advertising Age*, January 26, 2009, p. 18.

39. Adele Lassere, "The Marketing Corner: Marketing to African-American Consumers," *Epoch Times*, November 27, 2009.

40. Lisa Sanders, "How to Target Blacks? First You Gotta Spend," *Advertising Age*, July 3, 2006, p. 19; Pepper Miller and Herb Kemp, *What's Black about It? Insights to Increase Your Share of a Changing African-American Market* (Ithaca, NY: Paramount Market Publishing, 2005).

41. Marissa Fabris, "Special Report on Multicultural Marketing: Market Power," *Target Marketing*, www.targetmarketingmag.com, May 2008.

42. Sonya A. Grier and Shiriki K. Kumanyika, "The Context for Choice: Health Implications of Targeted Food and Beverage Marketing to African-Americans," *American Journal of Public Health* 98 (September 2008), pp. 1616–29.

43. "The 'Invisible' Market," *Brandweek*, January 30, 2006.

44. Andrew Pierce, "Multiculti Markets Demand Multilayered Markets," *Marketing News*, May 1, 2008, p. 21.

45. "The 'Invisible' Market," *Brandweek*, January 30, 2006; Bill Imada, "Four Myths about the Asian-American Market," *Advertising Age*, October 31, 2007; "Kraft Targets Asian American Moms," *Brandweek*, September 1, 2005.

46. "Marketing to Asian-Americans," Special Supplement to *Brandweek*, May 26, 2008.

47. Kate Rockwood, "Partnering with Pride," *Fast Company*, November 2009, pp. 21–28.

48. *Prime Access, Inc,* www.primeaccess.net.

49. *Strategic Business Insights,* www.strategicbusiness insights.com.

50. Andrew Kaplan, "A Fruitful Mix," *Beverage World,* May 2006, pp. 28–36.

51. This classification was adapted from George H. Brown, "Brand Loyalty: Fact or Fiction?" *Advertising Age,* June 1952–January 1953, a series. See also, Peter E. Rossi, Robert E. McCulloch, and Greg M. Allenby, "The Value of Purchase History Data in Target Marketing," *Marketing Science* 15 (Fall 1996), pp. 321–40.

52. James C. Anderson and James A. Narus, "Capturing the Value of Supplementary Services," *Harvard Business Review,* January–February 1995, pp. 75–83.

53. For a review of many of the methodological issues in developing segmentation schemes, see William R. Dillon and Soumen Mukherjee, "A Guide to the Design and Execution of Segmentation Studies," Rajiv Grover and Marco Vriens, eds., *Handbook of Marketing Research* (Thousand Oaks, CA: Sage, 2006); and Michael Wedel and Wagner A. Kamakura, *Market Segmentation: Conceptual and Methodological Foundations* (Boston: Kluwer, 1997).

54. Michael E. Porter, *Competitive Strategy* (New York: Free Press, 1980), pp. 22–23.

55. *Estee Lauder,* www.esteelauder.com.

56. *Burberry,* www.burberryplc.com/bbry/corporateprofile/ overview/, accessed December 2010.

57. Jerry Harkavy, "Colgate Buying Control of Tom's of Maine for $100 Million," *Associated Press, Boston.com*, March 21, 2006.

58. Robert Blattberg and John Deighton, "Interactive Marketing: Exploiting the Age of Addressability," *Sloan Management Review* 33 (Fall 1991), pp. 5–14.

59. Don Peppers and Martha Rogers, *One-to-One B2B: Customer Development Strategies for the Business-To-Business World* (New York: Doubleday, 2001); Jerry Wind and Arvind Rangaswamy, "Customerization: The Next Revolution in Mass Customization," *Journal of Interactive Marketing* 15 (Winter 2001), pp. 13–32.

60. James C. Anderson and James A. Narus, "Capturing the Value of Supplementary Services," *Harvard Business Review,* January–February 1995, pp. 75–83.

61. Itamar Simonson, "Determinants of Customers' Responses to Customized Offers: Conceptual Framework and Research Propositions," *Journal of Marketing* 69 (January 2005), pp. 32–45.

62. Joann Muller, "Kmart con Salsa: Will It Be Enough?" *BusinessWeek,* September 9, 2002.

63. Bart Macchiette and Roy Abhijit, "Sensitive Groups and Social Issues," *Journal of Consumer Marketing* 11 (Fall 1994), pp. 55–64.

64. Roger O. Crockett, "They're Lining Up for Flicks in the 'Hood,'" *BusinessWeek,* June 8, 1998, pp. 75–76.

65. Caroline E. Mayer, "Nurturing Brand Loyalty; with Preschool Supplies, Firms Woo Future Customers—and Current Parents," *Washington Post,* October 12, 2003.

Chapter 9

1. Alli McConnon, "Lululemon's Next Workout," *BusinessWeek*, June 9, 2008, pp. 43–44; Danielle Sacks, "Lululemon's Cult of Selling," *Fast Company*, March 2009; Bryant Urstadt, "Lust for Lulu," *New York Magazine*, July 26, 2009.

2. For foundational work on branding, see Jean-Noel Kapferer, *The New Strategic Brand Management,* 4th ed. (New York: Kogan Page, 2008); David A. Aaker and Erich Joachimsthaler, *Brand Leadership* (New York: Free Press, 2000); David A. Aaker, *Building Strong Brands* (New York: Free Press, 1996); David A. Aaker, *Managing Brand Equity* (New York: Free Press, 1991).

3. Interbrand Group, *World's Greatest Brands: An International Review* (New York: John Wiley & Sons, 1992). See also Karl Moore and Susan Reid, "The Birth of Brand," *Business History* 50 (2008), pp. 419–32.

4. Rajneesh Suri and Kent B. Monroe, "The Effects of Time Pressure on Consumers' Judgments of Prices and Products," *Journal of Consumer Research* 30 (June 2003), pp. 92–104.

5. Rita Clifton and John Simmons, eds., *The Economist on Branding* (New York: Bloomberg Press, 2004); Rik Riezebos, *Brand Management: A Theoretical and Practical Approach* (Essex, England: Pearson Education, 2003); and Paul Temporal, *Advanced Brand Management: From Vision to Valuation* (Singapore: John Wiley & Sons, 2002).

6. Constance E. Bagley, *Managers and the Legal Environment: Strategies for the 21st Century,* 3rd ed. (Cincinnati, OH: South-Western College/West Publishing, 2005); For a marketing academic point of view of some important legal issues, see Judith Zaichkowsky, *The Psychology behind Trademark Infringement and Counterfeiting* (Mahwah, NJ: LEA Publishing, 2006) and Maureen Morrin and Jacob Jacoby, "Trademark Dilution: Empirical Measures for an Elusive Concept," *Journal of Public Policy & Marketing* 19 (May 2000), pp. 265–76; Maureen Morrin, Jonathan Lee, and Greg M. Allenby, "Determinants of Trademark Dilution," *Journal of Consumer Research* 33 (September 2006), pp. 248–57.

7. Tulin Erdem, "Brand Equity as a Signaling Phenomenon," *Journal of Consumer Psychology* 7 (1998), pp. 131–57; Joffre Swait and Tulin Erdem, "Brand Effects on Choice and Choice Set Formation Under Uncertainty," *Marketing Science* 26 (September–October 2007), pp. 679–97; Tulin Erdem, Joffre Swait, and Ana Valenzuela, "Brands as Signals: A Cross-Country Validation Study," *Journal of Marketing* 70 (January 2006), pp. 34–49.

8. Scott Davis, *Brand Asset Management: Driving Profitable Growth through Your Brands* (San Francisco: Jossey-Bass, 2000); Mary W. Sullivan, "How Brand Names Affect the Demand for Twin Automobiles," *Journal of Marketing Research* 35 (May 1998), pp. 154–65; D. C. Bello and M. B. Holbrook, "Does an Absence of Brand Equity Generalize across Product Classes?" *Journal of Business Research* 34 (October 1996), pp. 125–31; Adrian J. Slywotzky and Benson P. Shapiro, "Leveraging to Beat the Odds: The New Marketing Mindset," *Harvard Business Review,* September–October 1993, pp. 97–107.

9. The power of branding is not without its critics, however, some of whom reject the commercialism associated with branding activities. See Naomi Klein, *No Logo: Taking Aim at the Brand Bullies* (New York: Picador, 2000).

10. "Study: Food in McDonald's Wrapper Tastes Better to Kids," *Associated Press*, August 6, 2007.

11. Natalie Mizik and Robert Jacobson, "Talk about Brand Strategy," *Harvard Business Review,* October 2005, p. 1; Baruch Lev, *Intangibles: Management, Measurement, and Reporting* (Washington, DC: Brookings Institute, 2001).

12. For an academic discussion of how consumers become so strongly attached to people as brands, see Matthew Thomson, "Human Brands: Investigating Antecedents to Consumers' Stronger Attachments to Celebrities," *Journal of Marketing* 70 (July 2006), pp. 104–19; For some practical branding tips from the world of rock and roll, see Roger Blackwell and Tina Stephan, *Brands That Rock* (Hoboken, NJ: John Wiley & Sons, 2004); and from the world of sports, see Irving

Rein, Philip Kotler, and Ben Shields, *The Elusive Fan: Reinventing Sports in a Crowded Marketplace* (New York: McGraw-Hill, 2006).

13. *NBA,* www.nba.com, "Yao Ming," *Facts and Details,* factsanddetails.com/china.php? itemid=276&catid=12&subcatid=78, assessed December 7, 2010; Tom Lowry and Dexter Roberts, "Wow! Yao!," *BusinessWeek,* October 25, 2004, www.businessweek.com.

14. Kevin Lane Keller, *Strategic Brand Management,* 3rd ed. (Upper Saddle River, NJ: Prentice Hall, 2008); David A. Aaker and Erich Joachimsthaler, *Brand Leadership* (New York: Free Press 2000); David A. Aaker, *Building Strong Brands* (New York: Free Press, 1996); David A. Aaker, *Managing Brand Equity* (New York: Free Press, 1991).

15. Other approaches are based on economic principles of signaling, for example, Tulin Erdem, "Brand Equity as a Signaling Phenomenon," *Journal of Consumer Psychology* 7 (1998), pp. 131–57; or more of a sociological, anthropological, or biological perspective (e.g., Grant McCracken, *Culture and Consumption II: Markets, Meaning, and Brand Management* (Bloomington: Indiana University Press, 2005); Susan Fournier, "Consumers and Their Brands: Developing Relationship Theory in Consumer Research," *Journal of Consumer Research* 24 (September 1998), pp. 343–73; Craig J. Thompson, Aric Rindfleisch, and Zeynep Arsel, "Emotional Branding and the Strategic Value of the Doppelganger Brand Image," *Journal of Marketing* 70 (January 2006), pp. 50–64.

16. Jennifer L. Aaker, "Dimensions of Brand Personality," *Journal of Marketing Research* 34 (August 1997), pp. 347–56; Jean-Noel Kapferer, *Strategic Brand Management: New Approaches to Creating and Evaluating Brand Equity* (London: Kogan Page, 1992), p. 38; Scott Davis, *Brand Asset Management: Driving Profitable Growth through Your Brands* (San Francisco: Jossey-Bass, 2000). For an overview of academic research on branding, see Kevin Lane Keller, "Branding and Brand Equity," Bart Weitz and Robin Wensley, eds., *Handbook of Marketing* (London: Sage Publications, 2002), pp. 151–78; Kevin Lane Keller and Don Lehmann, "Brands and Branding: Research Findings and Future Priorities," *Marketing Science* 25 (November–December 2006), pp. 740–59.

17. Kevin Lane Keller, *Strategic Brand Management,* 3rd ed. (Upper Saddle River, NJ: Prentice Hall, 2008).

18. Theodore Levitt, "Marketing Success through Differentiation—of Anything," *Harvard Business Review,* January–February 1980, pp. 83–91.

19. Kusum Ailawadi, Donald R. Lehmann, and Scott Neslin, "Revenue Premium as an Outcome Measure of Brand Equity," *Journal of Marketing* 67 (October 2003), pp. 1–17.

20. Jon Miller and David Muir, *The Business of Brands* (West Sussex, England: John Wiley & Sons, 2004).

21. Michael Bush, "Virgin America," *Advertising Age,* November 16, 2009, p. 12.

22. Kevin Lane Keller, "Building Customer-Based Brand Equity: A Blueprint for Creating Strong Brands," *Marketing Management* 10 (July–August 2001), pp. 15–19.

23. For some academic insights, see Matthew Thomson, Deborah J. MacInnis, and C. W. Park, "The Ties That Bind: Measuring the Strength of Consumers' Emotional Attachments to Brands," *Journal of Consumer Psychology* 15 (2005), pp. 77–91; Alexander Fedorikhin, C. Whan Park, and Matthew Thomson, "Beyond Fit and Attitude: The Effect of Emotional Attachment on Consumer Responses to Brand Extensions," *Journal of Consumer Psychology* 18 (2008), pp. 281–91; Jennifer Edson Escalas, "Narrative Processing: Building Consumer Connections to Brands," *Journal of Consumer Psychology* 14 (1996), pp. 168–79. For some managerial guidelines, see Kevin Roberts, *Lovemarks: The Future beyond Brands* (New York: Powerhouse Books, 2004); and Douglas Atkins, *The Culting of Brands* (New York: Penguin Books, 2004).

24. Paul Rittenberg and Maura Clancey, "Testing the Value of Media Engagement for Advertising Effectiveness," www.knowledgenetworks.com, Spring–Summer 2006, pp. 35–42.

25. M. Berk Ataman, Carl F. Mela, and Harald J. van Heerde, "Building Brands," *Marketing Science* 27 (November–December 2008), pp. 1036–54.

26. Walter Mossberg, "Is Bing the Thing?" *Wall Street Journal,* June 2, 2009, p. R4; Burt Heim, "The Dubbing of 'Bing,'" *BusinessWeek,* June 15, 2009, p. 23; Todd Wasserman, "Why Microsoft Chose the Name 'Bing,'" *Brandweek,* June 1, 2009, p. 33.

27. Rachel Dodes, "From Tracksuits to Fast Track," *Wall Street Journal,* September 13, 2006.

28. "42 Below," www.betterbydesign.org.nz, September 14, 2007.

29. Amanda Baltazar, "Silly Brand Names Get Serious Attention," *Brandweek,* December 3, 2007, p. 4.

30. Alina Wheeler, *Designing Brand Identity* (Hoboken, NJ: John Wiley & Sons, 2003).

31. Pat Fallon and Fred Senn, *Juicing the Orange: How to Turn Creativity into a Powerful Business Advantage* (Cambridge, MA: Harvard Business School Press, 2006); Eric A. Yorkston and Geeta Menon, "A Sound Idea: Phonetic Effects of Brand Names on Consumer Judgments," *Journal of Consumer Research* 31 (June), pp. 43–51; Tina M. Lowery and L. J. Shrum, "Phonetic Symbolism and Brand Name Preference," *Journal of Consumer Research* 34 (October 2007), pp. 406–14.

32. For some interesting theoretical perspectives, see Claudiu V. Dimofte and Richard F. Yalch, "Consumer Response to Polysemous Brand Slogans," *Journal of Consumer Research* 33 (March 2007), pp. 515–22.

33. John R. Doyle and Paul A. Bottomly, "Dressed for the Occasion: Font-Product Congruity in the Perception of Logotype," *Journal of Consumer Psychology* 16 (2006), pp. 112–23; Kevin Lane Keller, Susan Heckler, and Michael J. Houston, "The Effects of Brand Name

Suggestiveness on Advertising Recall," *Journal of Marketing* 62 (January 1998), pp. 48–57; For an in-depth examination of how brand names get developed, see Alex Frankel, *Wordcraft: The Art of Turning Little Words into Big Business* (New York: Crown Publishers, 2004).

34. Don Schultz and Heidi Schultz, *IMC: The Next Generation* (New York: McGraw-Hill, 2003); Don E. Schultz, Stanley I. Tannenbaum, and Robert F. Lauterborn, *Integrated Marketing Communications* (Lincolnwood, IL: NTC Business Books, 1993).

35. Mohanbir Sawhney, "Don't Harmonize, Synchronize," *Harvard Business Review,* July–August 2001, pp. 101–8.

36. David C. Court, John E. Forsyth, Greg C. Kelly, and Mark A. Loch, "The New Rules of Branding: Building Strong Brands Faster," *McKinsey White Paper Fall 1999*; Scott Bedbury, *A New Brand World* (New York: Viking Press, 2002).

37. Sonia Reyes, "Cheerios: The Ride," *Brandweek,* September 23, 2002, pp. 14–16.

38. Dawn Iacobucci and Bobby Calder, eds., *Kellogg on Integrated Marketing* (New York: John Wiley & Sons, 2003).

39. Drew Madsen, "Olive Garden: Creating Value through an Integrated Brand Experience," presentation at Marketing Science Institute Conference, *Brand Orchestration,* Orlando, Florida, December 4, 2003.

40. Michael Dunn and Scott Davis, "Building Brands from the Inside," *Marketing Management* (May–June 2003), pp. 32–37; Scott Davis and Michael Dunn, *Building the Brand-Driven Business* (New York: John Wiley & Sons, 2002).

41. Stan Maklan and Simon Knox, *Competing on Value* (Upper Saddle River, NJ: Financial Times, Prentice Hall, 2000).

42. Coeli Carr, "Seeking to Attract Top Prospects, Employers Brush Up on Brands," *New York Times,* September 10, 2006.

43. The principles and examples from this passage are based on Colin Mitchell, "Selling the Brand Inside," *Harvard Business Review,* January 2002, pp. 99–105. For an in-depth discussion of how two organizations, QuikTrip and Wawa, have developed stellar internal branding programs, see Neeli Bendapudi and Venkat Bendapudi, "Creating the Living Brand," *Harvard Business Review,* May 2005, pp. 124–32.

44. James H. McAlexander, John W. Schouten and Harold F. Koenig, "Building Brand Community," *Journal of Marketing* 66 (January 2002), pp. 38–54. For some notable examinations of brand communities, see René Algesheimer, Uptal M. Dholakia, and Andreas Herrmann, "The Social Influence of Brand Community: Evidence from European Car Clubs," *Journal of Marketing* 69 (July 2005), pp. 19–34; Albert M. Muniz Jr. and Hope Jensen Schau, "Religiosity in the Abandoned Apple Newton Brand Community," *Journal of Consumer Research* 31 (2005), pp. 412–32; Robert Kozinets, "Utopian Enterprise: Articulating the Meanings of *Star Trek*'s Culture of Consumption,"

Journal of Consumer Research 28 (June 2001), pp. 67–87; John W. Schouten and James H. McAlexander, "Subcultures of Consumption: An Ethnography of New Bikers," *Journal of Consumer Research* 22 (June 1995), pp. 43–61.

45. Albert M. Muniz Jr. and Thomas C. O'Guinn, "Brand Community," *Journal of Consumer Research* 27 (March 2001), pp. 412–32.

46. Susan Fournier and Lara Lee, "The Seven Deadly Sins of Brand Community 'Management,'" Marketing Science Institute Special Report 08-208, 2008.

47. Harley-Davidson USA, www.hog.com; Joseph Weber, "Harley Just Keeps on Cruisin'," *BusinessWeek,* November 6, 2006, pp. 71–72.

48. Scott A. Thompson and Rajiv K. Sinha, "Brand Communities and New Product Adoption: The Influence and Limits of Oppositional Loyalty," *Journal of Marketing* 72 (November 2008), pp. 65–80.

49. Deborah Roeddder John, Barbara Loken, Kyeong-Heui Kim, and Alokparna Basu Monga, "Brand Concept Maps: A Methodology for Identifying Brand Association Networks," *Journal of Marketing Research* 43 (November 2006), pp. 549–63.

50. In terms of related empirical insights, see Manoj K. Agrawal and Vithala Rao "An Empirical Comparison of Consumer-Based Measures of Brand Equity," *Marketing Letters* 7 (July 1996), pp. 237–47; and Walfried Lassar, Banwari Mittal, and Arun Sharma, "Measuring Customer-Based Brand Equity," *Journal of Consumer Marketing* 12 (1995), pp. 11–19.

51. "The Best Global Brands," *BusinessWeek,* June 19, 2009; The article ranks and critiques the 100 best global brands using the valuation method developed by Interbrand. For more discussion on some brand winners and losers, see Matt Haig, *Brand Royalty: How the Top 100 Brands Thrive and Survive* (London: Kogan Page, 2004); Matt Haig, *Brand Failures: The Truth about the 100 Biggest Branding Mistakes of All Time* (London: Kogan Page, 2003); For an academic discussion of valuing brand equity, see V. Srinivasan, Chan Su Park, and Dae Ryun Chang, "An Approach to the Measurement, Analysis, and Prediction of Brand Equity and Its Sources," *Management Science* 51 (September 2005), pp. 1433–48.

52. Mark Sherrington, *Added Value: The Alchemy of Brand-Led Growth* (Hampshire, UK: Palgrave Macmillan, 2003).

53. For some discussion of what factors determine long-term branding success, see Allen P. Adamson, *Brand Simple* (New York: Palgrave Macmillan, 2006).

54. Nikhil Bahdur and John Jullens, "New Life for Tired Brands," *Strategy+Business* 50 (Spring 2008).

55. David Lieberman, "Discovery Chief Takes a Network on a Wild Ride," *USA Today,* September 2, 2009, pp. 1B–2B; Discovery Communications, www.corporate.discovery.com; Kenneth Hein, "Consumers Clinging to Old Favorite Brands," *Brandweek,* January 20, 2009; Linda Moss and Linda Haugsted, "Discovery Times New Branding Campaign to

'Deadliest Catch' Debut," *Multichannel News*, March 31, 2008.

56. Natalie Mizik and Robert Jacobson, "Trading Off between Value Creation and Value Appropriation: The Financial Implications of Shifts in Strategic Emphasis," *Journal of Marketing* 67 (January 2003), pp. 63–76.

57. Larry Light and Joan Kiddon, *Six Rules for Brand Revitalization: Learn How Companies Like McDonald's Can Re-Energize Their Brands* (Wharton School Publishing, 2009).

58. *Eu Yan Sang*, www.euyansang.com; Joyce Hooi, "A 130 Year Old TCM Heritage – Eu Yan Sang," *The Business Times*, August 8, 2009, www.asiaone.com.

59. Evan West, "Smells Like a Billion Bucks," *Fast Company*, May 2009, pp. 44–46; Patricia Winters Lauro, "Old Spice Begins a Revival as a Body-Care Line for College-Age Men, with Towelettes," *New York Times*, April 29, 2002.

60. Rebecca J. Slotegraaf and Koen Pauwels, "The Impact of Brand Equity and Innovation on the Long-Term Effectiveness of Promotions," *Journal of Marketing Research* 45 (June 2008), pp. 293–306.

61. Keith Naughton, "Fixing Cadillac," *Newsweek,* May 28, 2001, pp. 36–37.

62. Elizabeth Woyke, "Paul Stuart Tries to Unstuff the Shirts," *BusinessWeek*, October 8, 2007, p. 86.

63. Peter Farquhar, "Managing Brand Equity," *Marketing Research* 1 (September 1989), pp. 24–33.

64. Steven M. Shugan, "Branded Variants," 1989 AMA Educators' Proceedings (Chicago: American Marketing Association, 1989), pp. 33–38; M. Bergen, S. Dutta, and S. M. Shugan, "Branded Variants: A Retail Perspective," *Journal of Marketing Research* 33 (February 1996), pp. 9–21.

65. Adam Bass, "Licensed Extension—Stretching to Communicate," *Journal of Brand Management* 12 (September 2004), pp. 31–38; also see David A. Aaker, *Building Strong Brands* (New York: Free Press, 1996).

66. Jean Halliday, "Troubled Automakers' Golden Goose," *AutoWeek,* August 14, 2006; Becky Ebenkamp, "The Creative License," *Brandweek,* June 9, 2003, pp. 36–40; "Top 100 Global Licensors," *License! Global*, April 1, 2009.

67. For comprehensive corporate branding guidelines, see James R. Gregory, *The Best of Branding: Best Practices in Corporate Branding* (New York: McGraw-Hill, 2004). For some international perspectives, see Majken Schultz, Mary Jo Hatch, and Mogens Holten Larsen, eds., *The Expressive Organization: Linking Identity, Reputation, and Corporate Brand* (Oxford, UK: Oxford University Press, 2000); and Majken Schultz, Yun Mi Antorini, and Fabian F. Csaba, eds., *Corporate Branding: Purpose, People, and Process* (Denmark: Copenhagen Business School Press, 2005).

68. Guido Berens, Cees B. M. van Riel, and Gerrit H. van Bruggen, "Corporate Associations and Consumer Product Responses: The Moderating Role of Corporate Brand Dominance," *Journal of Marketing* 69 (July 2005), pp. 35–48; Zeynep Gürhan-Canli and Rajeev Batra, "When Corporate Image Affects Product Evaluations: The Moderating Role of Perceived Risk," *Journal of Marketing Research* 41 (May 2004), pp. 197–205; Kevin Lane Keller and David A. Aaker, "Corporate-Level Marketing: The Impact of Credibility on a Company's Brand Extensions," *Corporate Reputation Review* 1 (August 1998), pp. 356–78; Thomas J. Brown and Peter Dacin, "The Company and the Product: Corporate Associations and Consumer Product Responses," *Journal of Marketing* 61 (January 1997), pp. 68–84; Gabriel J. Biehal and Daniel A. Sheinin, "The Influence of Corporate Messages on the Product Portfolio," *Journal of Marketing* 71 (April 2007), pp. 12–25.

69. Vithala R. Rao, Manoj K. Agarwal, and Denise Dalhoff, "How Is Manifest Branding Strategy Related to the Intangible Value of a Corporation?" *Journal of Marketing* 68 (October 2004), pp. 126–41. For an examination of the financial impact of brand portfolio decisions, see Neil A. Morgan and Lopo L. Rego, "Brand Portfolio Strategy and Firm Performance," *Journal of Marketing* 73 (January 2009), pp. 59–74; S. Cem Bahadir, Sundar G. Bharadwaj, and Rajendra K. Srivastava, "Financial Value of Brands in Mergers and Acquisitions: Is Value in the Eye of the Beholder?" *Journal of Marketing* 72 (November 2008), pp. 49–64.

70. William J. Holstein, "The Incalculable Value of Building Brands," *Chief Executive,* April–May 2006, pp. 52–56.

71. David A. Aaker, *Brand Portfolio Strategy: Creating Relevance, Differentiation, Energy, Leverage, and Clarity* (New York: Free Press, 2004).

72. Christopher Hosford, "A Transformative Experience," *Sales & Marketing Management* 158 (June 2006), pp. 32–36; Mike Beirne and Javier Benito, "Starwood Uses Personnel to Personalize Marketing," *Brandweek*, April 24, 2006, p. 9.

73. Jack Trout, *Differentiate or Die: Survival in Our Era of Killer Competition* (New York: John Wiley & Sons, 2000); Kamalini Ramdas and Mohanbir Sawhney, "A Cross-Functional Approach to Evaluating Multiple Line Extensions for Assembled Products," *Management Science* 47 (January 2001), pp. 22–36.

74. Nirmalya Kumar, "Kill a Brand, Keep a Customer," *Harvard Business Review,* December 2003, pp. 87–95.

75. For a methodological approach for assessing the extent and nature of cannibalization, see Charlotte H. Mason and George R. Milne, "An Approach for Identifying Cannibalization within Product Line Extensions and Multibrand Strategies," *Journal of Business Research* 31 (October–November 1994), pp. 163–70.

76. Mark Ritson, "Should You Launch a Fighter Brand?" *Harvard Business Review*, October 2009, pp. 87–94.

77. Paul W. Farris, "The Chevrolet Corvette," Case UVA-M-320, The Darden Graduate Business School Foundation, University of Virginia, Charlottesville, 1988.

78. Byung-Do Kim and Mary W. Sullivan, "The Effect of Parent Brand Experience on Line Extension Trial and Repeat Purchase," *Marketing Letters* 9 (April 1998), pp. 181–93.

79. John Milewicz and Paul Herbig, "Evaluating the Brand Extension Decision Using a Model of Reputation Building," *Journal of Product & Brand Management* 3 (January 1994), pp. 39–47; Kevin Lane Keller and David A. Aaker, "The Effects of Sequential Introduction of Brand Extensions," *Journal of Marketing Research* 29 (February 1992), pp. 35–50.

80. Valarie A. Taylor and William O. Bearden, "Ad Spending on Brand Extensions: Does Similarity Matter?" *Journal of Brand Management* 11 (September 2003), pp. 63–74; Sheri Bridges, Kevin Lane Keller, and Sanjay Sood, "Communication Strategies for Brand Extensions: Enhancing Perceived Fit by Establishing Explanatory Links," *Journal of Advertising* 29 (Winter 2000), pp. 1–11; Daniel C. Smith, "Brand Extension and Advertising Efficiency: What Can and Cannot Be Expected," *Journal of Advertising Research* (November–December 1992), pp. 11–20; Daniel C. Smith and C. Whan Park, "The Effects of Brand Extensions on Market Share and Advertising Efficiency," *Journal of Marketing Research* 29 (August 1992), pp. 296–313.

81. Ralf van der Lans, Rik Pieters, and Michel Wedel, "Competitive Brand Salience," *Marketing Science* 27 (September–October 2008), pp. 922–31.

82. Subramanian Balachander and Sanjoy Ghose, "Reciprocal Spillover Effects: A Strategic Benefit of Brand Extensions," *Journal of Marketing* 67 (January 2003), pp. 4–13.

83. Bharat N. Anand and Ron Shachar, "Brands as Beacons: A New Source of Loyalty to Multiproduct Firms," *Journal of Marketing Research* 41 (May 2004), pp. 135–50.

84. Kevin Lane Keller and David A. Aaker, "The Effects of Sequential Introduction of Brand Extensions," *Journal of Marketing Research* 29 (February 1992), pp. 35–50. For consumer processing implications, see Huifung Mao and H. Shanker Krishnan, "Effects of Prototype and Exemplar Fit on Brand Extension Evaluations: A Two-Process Contingency Model," *Journal of Consumer Research* 33 (June 2006), pp. 41–49; Byung Chul Shine, Jongwon Park, and Robert S. Wyer Jr., "Brand Synergy Effects in Multiple Brand Extensions," *Journal of Marketing Research* 44 (November 2007), pp. 663–70.

85. Maureen Morrin, "The Impact of Brand Extensions on Parent Brand Memory Structures and Retrieval Processes," *Journal of Marketing Research* 36 (November 1999), pp. 517–25; John A. Quelch and David Kenny, "Extend Profits, Not Product Lines," *Harvard Business Review,* September–October 1994, pp. 153–60; Perspectives from the Editors, "The Logic of Product-Line Extensions," *Harvard Business Review,* November–December 1994, pp. 53–62.

86. Al Ries and Jack Trout, *Positioning: The Battle for Your Mind, 20th Anniversary Edition* (New York: McGraw-Hill, 2000).

87. David A. Aaker, *Brand Portfolio Strategy: Creating Relevance, Differentiation, Energy, Leverage, and Clarity* (New York: Free Press, 2004).

88. Mary W. Sullivan, "Measuring Image Spillovers in Umbrella-Branded Products," *Journal of Business* 63 (July 1990), pp. 309–29.

89. Deborah Roedder John, Barbara Loken, and Christopher Joiner, "The Negative Impact of Extensions: Can Flagship Products Be Diluted," *Journal of Marketing* 62 (January 1998), pp. 19–32; Susan M. Broniarcyzk and Joseph W. Alba, "The Importance of the Brand in Brand Extension," *Journal of Marketing Research* 31 (May 1994), pp. 214–28 (this entire issue of *JMR* is devoted to brands and brand equity); Barbara Loken and Deborah Roedder John, "Diluting Brand Beliefs: When Do Brand Extensions Have a Negative Impact?" *Journal of Marketing* 57 (July 1993), pp. 71–84. See also, Chris Pullig, Carolyn Simmons, and Richard G. Netemeyer, "Brand Dilution: When Do New Brands Hurt Existing Brands?" *Journal of Marketing* 70 (April 2006), pp. 52–66; R. Ahluwalia and Z. Gürhan-Canli, "The Effects of Extensions on the Family Brand Name: An Accessibility-Diagnosticity Perspective," *Journal of Consumer Research* 27 (December 2000), pp. 371–81; Z. Gürhan-Canli and M. Durairaj, "The Effects of Extensions on Brand Name Dilution and Enhancement," *Journal of Marketing Research* 35 (November 1998), pp. 464–73; S. J. Milberg, C. W. Park, and M. S. McCarthy, "Managing Negative Feedback Effects Associated with Brand Extensions: The Impact of Alternative Branding Strategies," *Journal of Consumer Psychology* 6 (1997), pp. 119–40.

90. See also, Franziska Völckner and Henrik Sattler, "Drivers of Brand Extension Success," *Journal of Marketing* 70 (April 2006), pp. 1–17.

91. For recent research on extension evaluations, see Alokparna Basu Monga and Deborah Roedder John, "Cultural Differences in Brand Extension Evaluation: The Influence of Analytical versus Holistic Thinking," *Journal of Marketing Research* 33 (March 2007), pp. 529–36; James L. Oakley, Adam Duhachek, Subramanian Balachander, and S. Sriram, "Order of Entry and the Moderating Role of Comparison Brands in Extension Evaluations," *Journal of Consumer Research* 34 (February 2008), pp. 706–12; Junsang Yeo and Jongwon Park, "Effects of Parent-Extension Similarity and Self Regulatory Focus on Evaluations of Brand Extensions," *Journal of Consumer Psychology* 16 (2006), pp. 272–82; Catherine W. M. Yeung and Robert S. Wyer, "Does Loving a Brand Mean Loving Its Products? The Role of Brand-Elicited Affect in Brand Extension Evaluations," *Journal of Marketing Research* 43 (November 2005), pp. 495–506; Huifang Mao and H. Shankar Krishnan, "Effects of Prototype and Exemplar Fit on Brand Extension Evaluations: A Two-Process Contingency Model," *Journal of Consumer Research* 33 (June 2006), pp. 41–49; Rohini Ahluwalia, "How Far Can a Brand Stretch? Understanding the Role of Self-Construal," *Journal of Marketing Research* 45 (June 2008), pp. 337–50.

92. Pierre Berthon, Morris B. Holbrook, James M. Hulbert, and Leyland F. Pitt, "Viewing Brands in Multiple

Dimensions," *MIT Sloan Management Review* (Winter 2007), pp. 37–43.

93. Andrea Rothman, "France's Bic Bets U.S. Consumers Will Go for Perfume on the Cheap," *Wall Street Journal,* January 12, 1989.

94. Roland T. Rust, Valerie A. Zeithaml, and Katherine A. Lemon, "Measuring Customer Equity and Calculating Marketing ROI," Rajiv Grover and Marco Vriens, eds., *Handbook of Marketing Research* (Thousand Oaks, CA: Sage Publications, 2006), pp. 588–601; Roland T. Rust, Valerie A. Zeithaml, and Katherine A. Lemon, *Driving Customer Equity* (New York: Free Press, 2000).

95. Robert C. Blattberg and John Deighton, "Manage Marketing by the Customer Equity Test," *Harvard Business Review,* July–August 1996, pp. 136–44.

96. Robert C. Blattberg and Jacquelyn S. Thomas, "Valuing, Analyzing, and Managing the Marketing Function Using Customer Equity Principles," Dawn Iacobucci, ed., *Kellogg on Marketing* (New York: John Wiley & Sons, 2002); Robert C. Blattberg, Gary Getz, and Jacquelyn S. Thomas, *Customer Equity: Building and Managing Relationships as Valuable Assets* (Boston: Harvard Business School Press, 2001).

97. Much of this section is based on: Robert Leone, Vithala Rao, Kevin Lane Keller, Man Luo, Leigh McAlister, and Rajendra Srivatstava, "Linking Brand Equity to Customer Equity," *Journal of Service Research* 9 (November 2006), pp. 125–38. This special issue is devoted to customer equity and has a number of thought-provoking articles.

98. Niraj Dawar, "What Are Brands Good For?" *MIT Sloan Management Review* (Fall 2004), pp. 31–37.

Chapter 10

1. Ilana DeBare, "Cleaning Up without Dot-coms," *San Francisco Chronicle,* October 8, 2006; "Marketers of the Next Generation," *Brandweek,* April 17, 2006, p. 30.

2. Al Ries and Jack Trout, *Positioning: The Battle for Your Mind, 20th Anniversary Edition* (New York: McGraw-Hill, 2000).

3. Nat Ives, "Donaton: EW Is Not a Celebrity Magazine," *Advertising Age*, June 23, 2008, p. 12.

4. Michael J. Lanning and Lynn W. Phillips, "Building Market-Focused Organizations," Gemini Consulting White Paper, 1991.

5. Kevin Maney, "Hello, Ma Google," *Condé Nast Portfolio*, October 2007, pp. 49–50.

6. David A. Aaker, "The Relevance of Brand Relevance," *Strategy+Business* 35 (Summer 2004), pp. 1–10; David A. Aaker, *Brand Portfolio Strategy: Creating Relevance, Differentiation, Energy, Leverage, and Clarity* (New York: Free Press, 2004).

7. Elaine Wong, "Unilever Marketer Reveals Bertolli's Secret Sauce," *Brandweek*, August 28, 2009.

8. Allan D. Shocker, "Determining the Structure of Product-Markets: Practices, Issues, and Suggestions," Barton A. Weitz and Robin Wensley, eds., *Handbook of Marketing*

(London: Sage, 2002), pp. 106–25. See also, Bruce H. Clark and David B. Montgomery, "Managerial Identification of Competitors," *Journal of Marketing* 63 (July 1999), pp. 67–83.

9. "What Business Are You In? Classic Advice from Theodore Levitt," *Harvard Business Review,* October 2006, pp. 127–37. See also Theodore Levitt's seminal article, "Marketing Myopia," *Harvard Business Review,* July–August 1960, pp. 45–56.

10. Jeffrey F. Rayport and Bernard J. Jaworski, *e-Commerce* (New York: McGraw-Hill, 2001), p. 53.

11. Richard A. D'Aveni, "Competitive Pressure Systems: Mapping and Managing Multimarket Contact," *MIT Sloan Management Review* (Fall 2002), pp. 39–49.

12. For discussion of some of the long-term implications of marketing activities, see Koen Pauwels, "How Dynamic Consumer Response, Competitor Response, Company Support, and Company Inertia Shape Long-Term Marketing Effectiveness," *Marketing Science* 23 (Fall 2004), pp. 596–610; Koen Pauwels, Dominique M. Hanssens, and S. Siddarth, "The Long-term Effects of Price Promotions on Category Incidence, Brand Choice, and Purchase Quantity," *Journal of Marketing Research* 34 (November 2002), pp. 421–39; and Marnik Dekimpe and Dominique Hanssens, "Sustained Spending and Persistent Response: A New Look at Long-term Marketing Profitability," *Journal of Marketing Research* 36 (November 1999), pp. 397–412.

13. Kevin Lane Keller, Brian Sternthal, and Alice Tybout, "Three Questions You Need to Ask about Your Brand," *Harvard Business Review,* September 2002, pp. 80–89.

14. Michael Applebaum, "Comfy to Cool: A Brand Swivel," *Brandweek,* May 2, 2005, pp. 18–19.

15. Thomas A. Brunner and Michaela Wänke, "The Reduced and Enhanced Impact of Shared Features on Individual Brand Evaluations," *Journal of Consumer Psychology* 16 (April 2006), pp. 101–11.

16. *Hyundai*, http://worldwide.hyundai.com/.

17. Scott Bedbury, *A New Brand World* (New York: Viking Press, 2002).

18. Patrick Tickle, Kevin Lane Keller, and Keith Richey, "Branding in High-Technology Markets," *Market Leader* 22 (Autumn 2003), pp. 21–26.

19. Jim Hopkins, "When the Devil Is in the Design," *USA Today,* December 31, 2001.

20. Keith Naughton, "Ford's 'Perfect Storm,'" *Newsweek,* September 17, 2001, pp. 48–50.

21. Susan M. Broniarczyk and Andrew D. Gershoff, "The Reciprocal Effects of Brand Equity and Trivial Attributes," *Journal of Marketing Research* 40 (May 2003), pp. 161–75; Gregory S. Carpenter, Rashi Glazer, and Kent Nakamoto, "Meaningful Brands from Meaningless Differentiation: The Dependence on Irrelevant Attributes," *Journal of Marketing Research* 31 (August 1994), pp. 339–50.

22. Kerry Capell, "Thinking Simple at Philips," *BusinessWeek*, December 11, 2006, p. 50; Philips, www.philips.com.

23. Michael E. Porter, *Competitive Strategy: Techniques for Analyzing Industries and Competitors* (New York: Free Press, 1980).

24. Francis J. Kelly III and Barry Silverstein, *The Breakaway Brand* (New York: McGraw-Hill, 2005).

25. Willow Duttge, "Counting Sleep," *Advertising Age*, June 5, 2006, pp. 4, 50.

26. Patrick Barwise, *Simply Better: Winning and Keeping Customers by Delivering What Matters Most* (Cambridge, MA: Harvard Business School Press, 2004).

27. *Julius Baer*, www.juliusbaer.com/htm/302/en/ Homepage.htm, accessed December 14, 2010.

28. "The 25 Best Sales Forces," *Sales & Marketing Management* (July 1998), pp. 32–50.

29. William C. Copacino, *Supply Chain Management* (Boca Raton, FL: St. Lucie Press, 1997).

30. Piet Levy, "Express Yourself, *Marketing News*, June 15, 2009, p. 6.

31. James H. Gilmore and B. Joseph Pine II, *Authenticity: What Consumers Really Want* (Cambridge, MA: Harvard Business School Press, 2007); Lynn B. Upshaw, *Truth: The New Rules for Marketing in a Skeptical World* (New York: AMACOM, 2007).

32. Owen Jenkins, "Gimme Some Lovin'," *Marketing News*, May 15, 2009, p. 19.

33. Heather Landi, "Raise a Glass," *Beverage World*, October 2009, pp. 16–19.

34. Marc Gobé, *Emotional Branding: The New Paradigm for Connecting Brands to People* (New York: Allworth Press, 2001).

35. Kevin Roberts, *Lovemarks: The Future Beyond Brands*, expanded edition (New York: Powerhouse Books, 2005); Kevin Roberts, *The Lovemarks Effect: Winning in the Consumer Revolution* (New York: Powerhouse Books, 2005); "The Lovemarks Heart Beat: January 2010," *Lovemarks*, www.lovemarks.com.

36. Hamish Pringle and Peter Field, "Why Emotional Messages Beat Rational Ones," *Advertising Age*, March 2, 2009, p. 13; Hamish Pringle and Peter Field, *Brand Immortality: How Brands Can Live Long and Prosper* (Philadelphia: Kogan Page, 2009).

37. Rajendra S. Sisodia, David B. Wolfe, and Jagdish N. Sheth, *Firms of Endearment: How World-Class Companies Benefit Profit from Passion & Purpose* (Upper Saddle River, NJ: Wharton School Publishing, 2007).

38. Ronald Grover, "Selling by Storytelling," *BusinessWeek*, May 25, 2009.

39. Randall Ringer and Michael Thibodeau, "A Breakthrough Approach to Brand Creation," *Verse, The Narrative Branding Company*, www.versegroup.com.

40. Patrick Hanlon, *Primal Branding: Create Zealots for Your Brand, Your Company, and Your Future* (New York: Free Press, 2006); ThinkTopia, www.thinktopia.com.

41. Hillary Chura, "McD's Mass Marketing Loses Luster," *Crain's Chicago Business*, June 16, 2004.

42. Douglas Holt, *How Brands Become Icons: The Principle of Cultural Branding* (Cambridge, MA: Harvard Business School Press, 2004); Douglas Holt, "Branding as Cultural Activism," www.zibs.com; Douglas Holt, "What Becomes an Icon Most," *Harvard Business Review*, March 2003, pp. 43–49; See also, Grant McKracken, *Culture and Consumption II: Markets, Meaning, and Brand Management* (Bloomington, IN: Indiana University Press, 2005).

43. Craig Thompson, "Brands as Culturally Embedded Resources," 43rd AMA Sheth Foundation Doctoral Consortium, University of Missouri, June 6, 2008. See also research by John Sherry and Robert Kozinets, including John F. Sherry Jr., Robert V. Kozinets, Adam Duhachek, Benét DeBerry-Spence, Krittinee Nuttavuthisit and Diana Storm, "Gendered Behavior in a Male Preserve: Role Playing at ESPN Zone Chicago," *Journal of Consumer Psychology* 14, nos. 1 & 2 (2004), pp. 151–58; Stephen Brown, Robert V. Kozinets, and John F. Sherry Jr., "Teaching Old Brands New Tricks: Retro Branding and the Revival of Brand Meaning," *Journal of Marketing* 67 (July 2003), pp. 19–33.

44. Nick Wreden, *Fusion Branding: How to Forge Your Brand for the Future* (Atlanta: Accountability Press, 2002); Fusion Branding, www.fusionbranding.com.

45. Andrew Ross Sorkin and Andrew Martin, "Coca-Cola Agrees to Buy Vitaminwater," *New York Times*, May 26, 2007.

46. Jeffrey Gangemi, "Small Company, Big Brand," *BusinessWeek*, August 28, 2006.

47. Kurt Badenhausen and Christina Settimi, "What's New," *Forbes*, October 27, 2008, p. 133.

Chapter 11

1. Luke Mullins, "Muscling Up in Sports Gear," *U.S. News & World Report*, December 10, 2007, pp. 57–58; Jeremy Mullman, "Protecting This Brand While Running Ahead," *Advertising Age*, January 12, 2009, p. 16; Elaine Wong, "Under Armour Makes a Long-Run Calculation," *Brandweek*, January 19, 2009, p. 28; Stephanie N. Mehta, "Under Armour Reboots," *Fortune*, February 2, 2009, pp. 29–33.

2. For a detailed academic treatment of a number of issues on competition, see the Special Issue on Competitive Responsiveness, *Marketing Science* 24 (Winter 2005).

3. Sandra Ward, "Warming Up the Copier," *Barron's*, May 1, 2006, pp. 19, 21; William M. Bulkeley, "Xerox Tries to Go Beyond Copiers," *Wall Street Journal*, February 24, 2009, p. B5; Nanette Byrnes and Roger O. Crockett, "An Historic Succession at Xerox," *BusinessWeek*, June 8, 2009, pp. 18–22.

4. Starbucks, www.starbucks.com/aboutus/overview.asp, December 1, 2009.

5. Brian Wansink, "Can Package Size Accelerate Usage Volume?" *Journal of Marketing* 60 (July 1996), pp. 1–14; See also, Priya Raghubir and Eric A. Greenleaf, "Ratios in Proportion: What Should the Shape of the Package Be?" *Journal of Marketing* 70 (April 2006), pp. 95–107; and Valerie Folkes and Shashi Matta, "The Effect of Package Shape on Consumers' Judgments of Product Volume: Attention as a Mental Contaminant," *Journal of Consumer Research* 31 (September 2004), pp. 390–401.

6. John D. Cripps, "Heuristics and Biases in Timing the Replacement of Durable Products," *Journal of Consumer Research* 21 (September 1994), pp. 304–18.

7. George Stalk Jr. and Rob Lachanauer, "Hardball: Five Killer Strategies for Trouncing the Competition," *Harvard Business Review,* April 2004, pp. 62–71; Richard D'Aveni, "The Empire Strikes Back: Counterrevolutionary Strategies for Industry Leaders," *Harvard Business Review*, November 2002, pp. 66–74.

8. Nirmalya Kumar, Lisa Sheer, and Philip Kotler, "From Market Driven to Market Driving," *European Management Journal* 18 (April 2000), pp. 129–42.

9. Much of the remaining section on proactive marketing is based on a provocative book by Leonardo Araujo and Rogerio Gava, *The Proactive Enterprise: How to Anticipate Market Changes* (In Press).

10. Jonathan Glancey, "The Private World of the Walkman," *Guardian,* October 11, 1999.

11. These six defense strategies, as well as the five attack strategies, are taken from Philip Kotler and Ravi Singh, "Marketing Warfare in the 1980s," *Journal of Business Strategy* (Winter 1981), pp. 30–41.

12. Michael E. Porter, "Market Signals, *Competitive Strategy: Techniques for Analyzing Industries and Competitors* (New York: Free Press, 1998), pp. 75–87; Jaideep Prabhu and David W. Stewart, "Signaling Strategies in Competitive Interaction: Building Reputations and Hiding the Truth," *Journal of Marketing Research* 38 (February 2001), pp. 62–72.

13. Roger J. Calantone and Kim E. Schatzel, "Strategic Foretelling: Communication-Based Antecedents of a Firm's Propensity to Preannounce," *Journal of Marketing* 64 (January 2000), pp. 17–30; Jehoshua Eliashberg and Thomas S. Robertson, "New Product Preannouncing Behavior: A Market Signaling Study," *Journal of Marketing Research* 25 (August 1988), pp. 282–92.

14. Thomas S. Robertson, Jehoshua Eliashberg, and Talia Rymon, "New-Product Announcement Signals and Incumbent Reactions," *Journal of Marketing* 59 (July 1995), pp. 1–15.

15. Yuhong Wu, Sridhar Balasubramanian, and Vijay Mahajan, "When Is a Preannounced New Product Likely to Be Delayed?" *Journal of Marketing* 68 (April 2004), pp. 101–13; Barry L. Bayus, Sanjay Jain, and Ambar G. Rao, "Truth or Consequences: An Analysis of Vaporware and New-Product Announcements," *Journal of Marketing Research* 38 (February 2001), pp. 3–13.

16. Kevin Kelleher, "Why FedEx Is Gaining Ground," *Business 2.0,* October 2003, pp. 56–57; Charles Haddad, "FedEx: Gaining on Ground," *BusinessWeek,* December 16, 2002, pp. 126–28.

17. "Sara Lee Cleans Out Its Cupboards," *Fortune,* March 7, 2005, p. 38; Jane Sassen, "How Sara Lee Left Hanes in Its Skivvies," *BusinessWeek,* September 18, 2006, p. 40.

18. J. Scott Armstrong and Kesten C. Green, "Competitor-Oriented Objectives: The Myth of Market Share," *International Journal of Business* 12 (Winter 2007), pp. 115–34; Stuart E. Jackson, *Where Value Hides: A New Way to Uncover Profitable Growth for Your Business* (New York: John Wiley & Sons, 2006).

19. Nirmalya Kumar, *Marketing as Strategy* (Cambridge, MA: Harvard Business School Press, 2004); Philip Kotler and Paul N. Bloom, "Strategies for High-Market-Share Companies," *Harvard Business Review,* November–December 1975, pp. 63–72.

20. Robert D. Buzzell and Frederick D. Wiersema, "Successful Share-Building Strategies," *Harvard Business Review,* January–February 1981, pp. 135–44.

21. Linda Hellofs and Robert Jacobson, "Market Share and Customer's Perceptions of Quality: When Can Firms Grow Their Way to Higher versus Lower Quality?" *Journal of Marketing* 63 (January 1999), pp. 16–25.

22. John Downey, "FairPoint Struggles with Merger, Declining Stock," *Charlotte Business Journal*, March 19, 2009; John Downey, FairPoint Faces Enduring Debt, Service Headaches," *Charlotte Business Journal*, September 15, 2009.

23. Jon Birger, "Second-Mover Advantage," *Fortune,* March 20, 2006, pp. 20–21.

24. This paragraph is based on a talk by John Bello at the Tuck School of Business at Dartmouth College on November 18, 2010.

25. Venkatesh Shankar, Gregory Carpenter, and Lakshman Krishnamurthi, "Late-Mover Advantage: How Innovative Late Entrants Outsell Pioneers," *Journal of Marketing Research* 35 (February 1998), pp. 54–70; Gregory S. Carpenter and Kent Nakamoto, "The Impact of Consumer Preference Formation on Marketing Objectives and Competitive Second-Mover Strategies," *Journal of Consumer Psychology* 5 (1996), pp. 325–58; Gregory S. Carpenter and Kent Nakamoto, "Competitive Strategies for Late Entry into a Market with a Dominant Brand," *Management Science* (October 1990), pp. 1268–78.

26. Megan Johnston, "The Ketchup Strategy," *Forbes,* November 13, 2006, p. 185.

27. Michael V. Copeland, "These Boots Really Were Made for Walking," *Business 2.0,* October 2004, pp. 72–74.

28. Katrina Booker, "The Pepsi Machine," *Fortune,* February 6, 2006, pp. 68–72.

29. Theodore Levitt, "Innovative Imitation," *Harvard Business Review,* September–October 1966, p. 63. Also see, Steven P. Schnaars, *Managing Imitation Strategies: How Later Entrants Seize Markets from Pioneers* (New York: Free Press, 1994).

30. Stuart F. Brown, "The Company That Out-Harleys Harley," *Fortune,* September 28, 1998, pp. 56–57; S&S Cycle, www.sscycle.com.

31. Melita Marie Garza, "Illinois Tool Works Stock Continues to Suffer Since Acquisition of Firm," *Chicago Tribune,* November 16, 2000; ITW, www.itw.com.

32. Jayne O'Donnell, "Family Rolling to Success on Tire Rack," *USA Today,* December 8, 2003.

33. Mark Morrison, "This Wildcatter Feels Right at Home in Gabon," *BusinessWeek,* June 5, 2006, p. 63.

34. Reported in E. R. Linneman and L. J. Stanton, *Making Niche Marketing Work* (New York: McGraw-Hill, 1991).

35. Thomas A. Fogarty, "Keeping Zippo's Flame Eternal," *USA Today,* June 24, 2003; Michael Learmonth, "Zippo Reignites Brand with Social Media, New Products, *Advertising Age*, August 10, 2009, p. 12; Zippo, www.zippo.com.

36. Kathleen Kingsbury, "The Cell Islands," *Time,* November 20, 2006, p. G20; "Traveling Made Easy with the New BlackBerry Curve 8520," *Digicel-News,* http://digicel-jamaica-news-procomm.blogspot.com, January 12, 2010.

37. Some authors distinguished additional stages. Wasson suggested a stage of competitive turbulence between growth and maturity. See Chester R. Wasson, *Dynamic Competitive Strategy and Product Life Cycles* (Austin, TX: Austin Press, 1978). Maturity describes a stage of sales growth slowdown and saturation, a stage of flat sales after sales have peaked.

38. John E. Swan and David R. Rink, "Fitting Market Strategy to Varying Product Life Cycles," *Business Horizons,* January–February 1982, pp. 72–76; Gerald J. Tellis and C. Merle Crawford, "An Evolutionary Approach to Product Growth Theory," *Journal of Marketing* 45 (Fall 1981), pp. 125–34.

39. William E. Cox Jr., "Product Life Cycles as Marketing Models," *Journal of Business* (October 1967), pp. 375–84.

40. Jordan P. Yale, "The Strategy of Nylon's Growth," *Modern Textiles Magazine,* February 1964, p. 32. Also see Theodore Levitt, "Exploit the Product Life Cycle," *Harvard Business Review,* November–December 1965, pp. 81–94.

41. Chester R. Wasson, "How Predictable Are Fashion and Other Product Life Cycles?" *Journal of Marketing* 32 (July 1968), pp. 36–43.

42. Ibid.

43. William H. Reynolds, "Cars and Clothing: Understanding Fashion Trends," *Journal of Marketing* 32 (July 1968), pp. 44–49.

44. Bryan Curtis, "Trivial Pursuit," *Slate.com,* April 13, 2005; Patrick Butters, "What Biggest-Selling Adult Game Still Cranks Out Vexing Questions?" *Insight on the News,* January 26, 1998, p. 39.

45. Robert D. Buzzell, "Competitive Behavior and Product Life Cycles," John S. Wright and Jack Goldstucker, eds., *New Ideas for Successful Marketing* (Chicago: American Marketing Association, 1956), p. 51.

46. Rajesh J. Chandy, Gerard J. Tellis, Deborah J. MacInnis, and Pattana Thaivanich, "What to Say When: Advertising Appeals in Evolving Markets," *Journal of Marketing Research* 38 (November 2001), pp. 399–414.

47. As reported in Joseph T. Vesey, "The New Competitors: They Think in Terms of Speed to Market," *Academy of Management Executive* 5 (May 1991), pp. 23–33; and Brian Dumaine, "How Managers Can Succeed through Speed," *Fortune,* February 13, 1989, pp. 54–59.

48. Glen L. Urban et al., "Market Share Rewards to Pioneering Brands: An Empirical Analysis and Strategic Implications," *Management Science* (June 1986), pp. 645–59; William T. Robinson and Claes Fornell, "Sources of Market Pioneer Advantages in Consumer Goods Industries," *Journal of Marketing Research* 22 (August 1985), pp. 305–17.

49. Gregory S. Carpenter and Kent Nakamoto, "Consumer Preference Formation and Pioneering Advantage," *Journal of Marketing Research* 26 (August 1989), pp. 285–98.

50. William T. Robinson and Sungwook Min, "Is the First to Market the First to Fail? Empirical Evidence for Industrial Goods Businesses," *Journal of Marketing Research* 39 (February 2002), pp. 120–28.

51. Frank R. Kardes, Gurumurthy Kalyanaram, Murali Chankdrashekaran, and Ronald J. Dornoff, "Brand Retrieval, Consideration Set Composition, Consumer Choice, and the Pioneering Advantage," *Journal of Consumer Research* 20 (June 1993), pp. 62–75. See also, Frank H. Alpert and Michael A. Kamins, "Pioneer Brand Advantage and Consumer Behavior: A Conceptual Framework and Propositional Inventory," *Journal of the Academy of Marketing Science* 22 (June 1994), pp. 244–53.

52. Kurt A. Carlson, Margaret G. Meloy, and J. Edward Russo, "Leader-Driven Primacy: Using Attribute Order to Affect Consumer Choice," *Journal of Consumer Research* 32 (March 2006), pp. 513–18.

53. Thomas S. Robertson and Hubert Gatignon, "How Innovators Thwart New Entrants into Their Market," *Planning Review,* September–October 1991, pp. 4–11, 48; Douglas Bowman and Hubert Gatignon, "Order of Entry as a Moderator of the Effect of Marketing Mix on Market Share," *Marketing Science* 15 (Summer 1996), pp. 222–42.

54. Venkatesh Shankar, Gregory S. Carpenter, and Lakshman Krishnamurthi, "Late Mover Advantage: How Innovative Late Entrants Outsell Pioneers," *Journal of Marketing Research* 35 (February 1998), pp. 54–70.

55. Steven P. Schnaars, *Managing Imitation Strategies* (New York: Free Press, 1994). See also, Jin K. Han, Namwoon Kim, and Hony-Bom Kin, "Entry Barriers: A Dull-, One-, or Two-Edged Sword for Incumbents? Unraveling the

Paradox from a Contingency Perspective," *Journal of Marketing* 65 (January 2001), pp. 1–14.

56. Victor Kegan, "Second Sight: Second Movers Take All," *The Guardian,* October 10, 2002.

57. Peter N. Golder, "Historical Method in Marketing Research with New Evidence on Long-term Market Share Stability," *Journal of Marketing Research* 37 (May 2000), pp. 156–72; Peter N. Golder and Gerald J. Tellis, "Pioneer Advantage: Marketing Logic or Marketing Legend?" *Journal of Marketing Research* 30 (May 1993), pp. 34–46. See also, Shi Zhang and Arthur B. Markman, "Overcoming the Early Advantage: The Role of Alignable and Nonalignable Differences," *Journal of Marketing Research* 35 (November 1998), pp. 1–15.

58. Gerald Tellis and Peter Golder, *Will and Vision: How Latecomers Can Grow to Dominate Markets* (New York: McGraw-Hill, 2001); Rajesh K. Chandy and Gerald J. Tellis, "The Incumbent's Curse? Incumbency, Size, and Radical Product Innovation," *Journal of Marketing Research* 64 (July 2000), pp. 1–17.

59. Sungwook Min, Manohar U. Kalwani, and William T. Robinson, "Market Pioneer and Early Follower Survival Risks: A Contingency Analysis of Really New Versus Incrementally New Product-Markets," *Journal of Marketing* 70 (January 2006), pp. 15–35. See also Raji Srinivasan, Gary L. Lilien, and Arvind Rangaswamy, "First In, First Out? The Effects of Network Externalities on Pioneer Survival," *Journal of Marketing* 68 (January 2004), pp. 41–58.

60. Trond Riiber Knudsen, "Escaping the Middle-Market Trap: An Interview with CEO of Electrolux," *McKinsey Quarterly* (December 2006), pp. 72–79.

61. Rajan Varadarajan, Mark P. DeFanti, and Paul S. Busch, "Brand Portfolio, Corporate Image, and Reputation: Managing Brand Deletions," *Journal of the Academy of Marketing Science* 34 (Spring 2006), pp. 195–205; Stephen J. Carlotti Jr., Mary Ellen Coe, and Jesko Perrey, "Making Brand Portfolios Work," *McKinsey Quarterly* 4 (2004), pp. 24–36; Nirmalya Kumar, "Kill a Brand, Keep a Customer," *Harvard Business Review,* December 2003, pp. 86–95; George J. Avlonitis, "Product Elimination Decision Making: Does Formality Matter?" *Journal of Marketing* 49 (Winter 1985), pp. 41–52; Philip Kotler, "Phasing Out Weak Products," *Harvard Business Review,* March–April 1965, pp. 107–18.

62. Kathryn Rudie Harrigan, "The Effect of Exit Barriers upon Strategic Flexibility," *Strategic Management Journal* 1 (February 1980), pp. 165–76.

63. Laurence P. Feldman and Albert L. Page, "Harvesting: The Misunderstood Market Exit Strategy," *Journal of Business Strategy* (Spring 1985), pp. 79–85; Philip Kotler, "Harvesting Strategies for Weak Products," *Business Horizons*, August 1978, pp. 15–22.

64. Rob Walker, "Can Ghost Brands . . .," *International Herald Tribune*, May 17–18, 2008, pp. 17–18; Peter Carbona, "The Rush to Grab Orphan Brands," *BusinessWeek*, August 3, 2009, pp. 47–48.

65. Stuart Elliott, "Those Shelved Brands Start to Look Tempting," *New York Times*, August 21, 2008.

66. Peter N. Golder and Gerard J. Tellis, "Growing, Growing, Gone: Cascades, Diffusion, and Turning Points in the Product Life Cycle," *Marketing Science* 23 (Spring 2004), pp. 207–18.

67. Youngme Moon, "Break Free from the Product Life Cycle," *Harvard Business Review,* May 2005, pp. 87–94.

68. Hubert Gatignon and David Soberman, "Competitive Response and Market Evolution," Barton A. Weitz and Robin Wensley, eds., *Handbook of Marketing* (London, UK: Sage Publications, 2002), pp. 126–47; Robert D. Buzzell, "Market Functions and Market Evolution," *Journal of Marketing* 63 (Special Issue 1999), pp. 61–63.

69. Raji Srinivasan, Arvind Rangaswamy, and Gary L. Lilien, "Turning Adversity into Advantage: Does Proactive Marketing During Recession Pay Off?" *International Journal of Research in Marketing* 22 (June 2005), pp. 109–25.

70. Jon Fine, "Why General Mills Marketing Pays Off," *BusinessWeek*, July 27, 2009, pp. 67–68; Matthew Boyle, "Snap, Crackle, Pop at the Food Giants," *BusinessWeek*, October 6, 2008, p. 48.

71. Philip Lay, Todd Hewlin, and Geoffrey Moore, "In a Downturn, Provoke Your Customers," *Harvard Business Review*, March 2009, pp. 48–56.

72. John A. Quelch and Katherine E. Jocz, "How to Market in a Downturn," *Harvard Business Review*, April 2009, pp. 52–62.

73. Maria Bartiromo, "Facetime: Inside a Company Resetting for Recovery," *BusinessWeek*, July 13 and 20, 2009, pp. 15–17.

74. Steve Hamm, "The New Age of Frugality," *BusinessWeek*, October 20, 2008, pp. 55–58.

75. Jane Porter and Burt Heim, "Doing Whatever Gets Them in the Door," *BusinessWeek*, June 30, 2008, p. 60.

76. Ibid.

77. David Taylor, David Nichols, Diego Kerner, and Anne Charbonneau, "Leading Brands Out of the Recession," *Brandgym Research Paper 2,* www.brandgym.com, September 2009.

78. Todd Wasserman, "Maverick CMOs Try Going without TV," *Brandweek*, January 24, 2009.

79. Maureen Scarpelli, "Dentists Step Up Marketing Efforts as Patients Scrimp by Skipping Visits, *Wall Street Journal*, August 11, 2009.

80. Peter J. Williamson and Ming Zeng, "Value for Money Strategies for Recessionary Times," *Harvard Business Review*, March 2009, pp. 66–74.

81. Burt Heim, "How to Sell Luxury to Penny-Pinchers," *BusinessWeek*, November 10, 2008, p. 60.

82. Stuart Elliott, "Trying to Pitch Products to the Savers," *New York Times*, June 3, 2009.

83. Andrew Martin, "In Tough Times, Spam Is Suddenly Appealing," *Boston Globe*, November 16, 2008.

Chapter 12

1. John Frank, "Beep! Beep! Coming Through," *Marketing News*, September 30, 2009, pp. 12-14; David Kiley, "Ford's Savior?" *BusinessWeek*, March 16, 2009, pp. 31–34; Alex Taylor III, "Fixing Up Ford," *Fortune*, May 25, 2009, pp. 45–50; David Kiley, "One Ford for the Whole Wide World," *BusinessWeek*, June 15, 2009, pp. 58–59; "Ford's European Arm Lends a Hand," *Economist*, March 8, 2008, pp. 72–73.

2. This discussion is adapted from a classic article: Theodore Levitt, "Marketing Success through Differentiation: Of Anything," *Harvard Business Review*, January–February 1980, pp. 83–91. The first level, core benefit, has been added to Levitt's discussion.

3. Harper W. Boyd Jr. and Sidney Levy, "New Dimensions in Consumer Analysis," *Harvard Business Review*, November–December 1963, pp. 129–40.

4. Jim Curley, "Niagara Sheet Feeder in Full Production," *The White Sheet: Board Converting News*, August 25, 2008; Jackie Schultz, "A Sheet Plant's Lean Journey," *Corrugated Today*, January–February 2005, pp. 42–47; Joe Iannarelli, "Jamestown Container Thinks Outside the Box," *Business First,* October 3, 2003, p. 4.

5. For some definitions, see Peter D. Bennett, ed., *Dictionary of Marketing Terms* (Chicago: American Marketing Association, 1995). Also see, Patrick E. Murphy and Ben M. Enis, "Classifying Products Strategically," *Journal of Marketing* 50 (July 1986), pp. 24–42.

6. Some of these bases are discussed in David A. Garvin, "Competing on the Eight Dimensions of Quality," *Harvard Business Review,* November–December 1987, pp. 101–9.

7. Marco Bertini, Elie Ofek, and Dan Ariely, "The Impact of Add-On Features on Product Evaluations," *Journal of Consumer Research* 36 (June 2009), pp. 17–28; Tripat Gill, "Convergent Products: What Functionalities Add More Value to the Base," *Journal of Marketing* 72 (March 2008), pp. 46–62; Robert J. Meyer, Sheghui Zhao, and Jin K. Han, "Biases in Valuation vs. Usage of Innovative Product Features," *Marketing Science* 27 (November–December 2008), pp. 1083–96.

8. Paul Kedrosky, "Simple Minds," *Business 2.0,* April 2006, p. 38; Debora Viana Thompson, Rebecca W. Hamilton, and Roland Rust, "Feature Fatigue: When Product Capabilities Become Too Much of a Good Thing," *Journal of Marketing Research* 42 (November 2005), pp. 431–42.

9. James H. Gilmore and B. Joseph Pine, *Markets of One: Creating Customer-Unique Value through Mass Customization,* (Boston: Harvard Business School Press, 2000).

10. Nikolaus Franke, Peter Keinz, Christoph J. Steger, "Testing the Value of Customization: When Do Customers Really Prefer Products Tailored to Their Preferences," *Journal of Marketing* 73 (September 2009), pp. 103–21.

11. Gail Edmondson, "Mercedes Gets Back up to Speed," *BusinessWeek,* November 13, 2006, pp. 46–47; Peter Gumble, "How Dr. Z Plans to Fix Mercedes," *CNNMoney.com.* http://money.cnn.com, July 13, 2009; Chris Shunk, "Paradox: As Quality Improves, Mercedes-Benz Dealership Profits Decline," *Automotive News*, January 27, 2009.

12. Bernd Schmitt and Alex Simonson, *Marketing Aesthetics: The Strategic Management of Brand, Identity, and Image* (New York: Free Press, 1997).

13. Stanley Reed, "Rolls-Royce at Your Service," *BusinessWeek*, November 15, 2005, pp. 92–93; *Rolls-Royce*, www.rolls-royce.com/civil/services/totalcare; "Rolls-Royce Secures USD 4.1 Billion Worth Orders During Paris Air Show," *India Defence*, www.india-defence.com, June 20, 2009; "Rolls-Royce Engine Support," *Aviation Today*, June 1, 2006.

14. For a comprehensive discussion of Cemex, see Adrian J. Slywotzky and David J. Morrison, "Digital Innovator: Cemex," *How Digital Is Your Business* (New York: Crown Business, 2000), pp. 78–100; see also Mohanbir Sawhney, Robert C. Wolcott, and Inigo Arroniz, "The 12 Different Ways for Companies to Innovate," *MIT Sloan Management Review* (April 1, 2006).

15. Cliff Edwards, "Why Tech Bows to Best Buy," *BusinessWeek*, December 10, 2009; Jena McGregor, "At Best Buy, Marketing Goes Micro," *BusinessWeek*, May 15, 2008; Matthew Boyle, "Best Buy's Giant Gamble," *Fortune,* April 3, 2006, pp. 69–75; Geoffrey Colvin, "Talking Shop," *Fortune,* August 21, 2006, pp. 73–80; "Best Buy Turns on the Geek Appeal," *DSN Retailing Today,* February 24, 2003, p. 22.

16. This section is based on a comprehensive treatment of product returns: James Stock, Thomas Speh, and Herbert Shear, "Managing Product Returns for Competitive Advantage," *MIT Sloan Management Review* (Fall 2006), pp. 57–62. See also, J. Andrew Petersen and V. Kumar, "Can Product Returns Make You Money?" *MIT Sloan Management Review* (Spring 2010), pp. 85–89.

17. Dave Blanchard, "Moving Forward in Reverse," *Logistics Today*, July 12, 2005; Kelly Shermach, "Taming CRM in the Retail Sector," *CRM Buyer*, October 12, 2006; www.epinions.com, June 28, 2010.

18. Bruce Nussbaum, "The Power of Design," *BusinessWeek,* May 17, 2004, pp. 88–94; "Masters of Design," *Fast Company*, June 2004, pp. 61–75; Also see, Philip Kotler, "Design: A Powerful but Neglected Strategic Tool," *Journal of Business Strategy* (Fall 1984), pp. 16–21.

19. Ravindra Chitturi, Rajagopal Raghunathan and Vijay Mahajan, "Delight by Design: The Role of Hedonic Versus Utilitarian Benefits," *Journal of Marketing* 72 (May 2008), pp. 48–63.

20. Ulrich R. Orth and Keven Malkewitz, "Holistic Package Design and Consumer Brand Impressions," *Journal of Marketing* 72 (May 2008), pp. 64–81; Mark Borden, "Less Hulk, More Bruce Lee," *Fast Company*, April 2007, pp. 86–91.

21. Steve Hamm and Jay Greene, "That Computer Is So You," *BusinessWeek*, January 14, 2008, pp. 24–26; Damon Darlin, "Design Helps H.P. Profit More on PCs," *New York Times*, May 17, 2007.

22. "IDEA Design Gallery," www.isda.org, May 14, 2010; "Design Winners: The List," *BusinessWeek*, July 22, 2009; David Carnoy, "The 20 Most Innovative Products of the Decade," *CNET Reviews*, December 10, 2009; Emily Lambert, "Splash," *Forbes*, July 23, 2007, pp. 66–68.

23. Virginia Postrel, *The Substance of Style: How the Rise of Aesthetic Value Is Remaking Commerce, Culture, and Consciousness* (New York: HarperCollins, 2003).

24. Linda Tischler, "Pop Artist David Butler," *Fast Company*, October 2009, pp. 91–97; Jessie Scanlon, "Coca-Cola's New Design Direction," *BusinessWeek*, August 25, 2008.

25. Todd Wasserman, "Thinking by Design," *Brandweek*, November 3, 2008, pp. 18–21.

26. Jay Green, "Where Designers Rule," *BusinessWeek*, November 5, 2007, pp. 46–51; Deborah Steinborn, "Talking About Design," *Wall Street Journal*, June 23, 2008, p. R6.

27. In reality, Tide's product line is actually deeper and more complex. There are 9 powder products, 16 liquid products, 1 Stain Release product, 1 Tide to Go product, 1 Tide Washing Machine Cleaner, and 9 Tide accessories.

28. A Yesim Orhun, "Optimal Product Line Design When Consumers Exhibit Choice Set-Dependent Preferences," *Marketing Science* 28 (September–October 2009), pp. 868–86; Robert Bordley, "Determining the Appropriate Depth and Breadth of a Firm's Product Portfolio," *Journal of Marketing Research* 40 (February 2003), pp. 39–53; Peter Boatwright and Joseph C. Nunes, "Reducing Assortment: An Attribute-Based Approach," *Journal of Marketing* 65 (July 2001), pp. 50–63.

29. Adapted from a Hamilton Consultants White Paper, December 1, 2000.

30. This illustration is found in Benson P. Shapiro, *Industrial Product Policy: Managing the Existing Product Line* (Cambridge, MA: Marketing Science Institute, 1977), pp. 3–5, 98–101.

31. Amna Kirmani, Sanjay Sood, and Sheri Bridges, "The Ownership Effect in Consumer Responses to Brand-Line Stretches," *Journal of Marketing* 63 (January 1999), pp. 88–101; T. Randall, K. Ulrich, and D. Reibstein, "Brand Equity and Vertical Product-Line Extent," *Marketing Science* 17 (Fall 1998), pp. 356–79; David A. Aaker, "Should You Take Your Brand to Where the Action Is?" *Harvard Business Review*, September–October 1997, pp. 135–43.

32. Michael Carolan, "InterContinental Hotels Sales Up After 18 Months of Falls," *Wall Street Journal*, May 11, 2010; Barbara De Lollis, "Holiday Inn Chain Upgrades With Style," *USA TODAY*, June 24, 2008; Bob Garfield, "What Makes This Commercial Great? The Bacon Bit Says It All," *Advertising Age*, February 25, 2008.

33. Alex Taylor III, "Bavaria's Next Top Model," *Fortune*, March 30, 2009, pp. 100–3; Neal E. Boudette, "BMW's Push to Broaden Line Hits Some Bumps in the Road," *Wall Street Journal*, January 25, 2005; Alex Taylor III, "The Ultimate Fairly Inexpensive Driving Machine," *Fortune*, November 1, 2004, pp. 130–40.

34. Steuart Henderson Britt, "How Weber's Law Can Be Applied to Marketing," *Business Horizons*, February 1975, pp. 21–29.

35. Brett R. Gordon, "A Dynamic Model of Consumer Replacement Cycles in the PC Processor Industry," *Marketing Science* 28 (September–October 2009), pp. 846–67; Raghunath Singh Rao, Om Narasimhan, and George John, "Understanding the Role of Trade-Ins in Durable Goods Markets: Theory and Evidence," *Marketing Science* 28 (September–October 2009), pp. 950–67.

36. Stanley Holmes, "All the Rage Since Reagan," *BusinessWeek*, July 25, 2005, p. 68.

37. Nirmalya Kumar, "Kill a Brand, Keep a Customer," *Harvard Business Review*, December 2003, pp. 86–95; Brad Stone, "Back to Basics," *Newsweek*, August 4, 2003, pp. 42–44; Sarah Skidmore, "Designers, Makers Tune In to Collectors for New Trends," *Associated Press*, January 21, 2007.

38. Laurens M. Sloot, Dennis Fok, and Peter Verhoef, "The Short- and Long-Term Impact of an Assortment Reduction on Category Sales," *Journal of Marketing Research* 43 (November 2006), pp. 536–48.

39. Patricia O'Connell, "A Chat with Unilever's Niall FitzGerald," *BusinessWeek*, www.businessweek.com, August 2, 2001; John Willman, "Leaner, Cleaner, and Healthier Is the Stated Aim," *Financial Times*, February 23, 2000; "Unilever's Goal: 'Power Brands'," *Advertising Age*, January 3, 2000.

40. "Volkswagen Brand Turnaround Drives Q1 Group Profits," *Reuters*, April 29, 2010; Andreas Cremer, "VW in 'Last Attempt' to Save Seat Amid Spanish Crisis," *Bloomberg BusinessWeek*, www.businessweek.com, May 14, 2010; George Rädler, Jan Kubes, and Bohdan Wojnar, "Skoda Auto: From 'No-Class' to World-Class in One Decade," *Critical EYE* 15 (July 2006); Scott D. Upham, "Beneath the Brand," *Automotive Manufacturing & Production*, June 2001.

41. Eric T. Anderson and Duncan I. Simester, "Does Demand Fall When Customers Perceive That Prices Are Unfair? The Case of Premium Pricing for Large Sizes," *Marketing Science* 27 (May–June 2008), pp. 492–500.

42. Ricard Gil and Wesley R. Hartmann, "Empirical Analysis of Metering Price Discrimination: Evidence from Concession Sales at Movie Theaters," *Marketing Science* 28 (November–December 2009), pp. 1046–62.

43. Connie Guglielmo, "Hewlett-Packard Says Printer Business is 'Healthy,'" *Bloomberg News*, December 22, 2009; "HP Annual Report 2008," HP, www.hp.com/hpinfo/investor/; Ben Elgin, "Can HP's Printer Biz Keep Printing Money?" *BusinessWeek*, July 14, 2003, pp. 68–70; Simon Avery, "H-P Sees

Room for Growth in Printer Market," *Wall Street Journal,* June 28, 2001.

44. Dilip Soman and John T. Gourville, "Transaction Decoupling: How Price Bundling Affects the Decision to Consume," *Journal of Marketing Research* 38 (February 2001), pp. 30–44; Ramanathan Subramaniam and R. Venkatesh, "Optimal Bundling Strategies in Multiobject Auctions of Complements or Substitutes," *Marketing Science* 28 (March–April 2009), pp. 264–73.

45. Anita Elberse, Bye-Bye Bundles: The Unbundling of Music in Digital Channels," *Journal of Marketing* 74 (May 2010), pp. 107–23.

46. Akshay R. Rao, Lu Qu, and Robert W. Ruekert, "Signaling Unobservable Quality through a Brand Ally," *Journal of Marketing Research* 36 (May 1999), pp. 258–68; Akshay R. Rao and Robert W. Ruekert, "Brand Alliances as Signals of Product Quality," *Sloan Management Review* (Fall 1994), pp. 87–97.

47. Bernard L. Simonin and Julie A. Ruth, "Is a Company Known by the Company It Keeps? Assessing the Spillover Effects of Brand Alliances on Consumer Brand Attitudes," *Journal of Marketing Research* 35 (February 1998), pp. 30–42; see also, C. W. Park, S. Y. Jun, and A. D. Shocker, "Composite Branding Alliances: An Investigation of Extension and Feedback Effects," *Journal of Marketing Research* 33 (November 1996), pp. 453–66.

48. Tansev Geylani, J. Jeffrey Inman, and Frenkel Ter Hofstede, "Image Reinforcement or Impairment: The Effects of Co-Branding on Attribute Uncertainty," *Marketing Science* 27 (July–August 2008), pp. 730–44; Ed Lebar, Phil Buehler, Kevin Lane Keller, Monika Sawicka, Zeynep Aksehirli, and Keith Richey, "Brand Equity Implications of Joint Branding Programs," *Journal of Advertising Research* 45 (December 2005).

49. C. W. Park, S. Y. Jun, and A. D. Shocker, "Composite Branding Alliances: An Investigation of Extension and Feedback Effects," *Journal of Marketing Research* 33 (November 1996), pp. 453–66.; Lance Leuthesser, Chiranjier Kohli, and Rajneesh Suri, "2 + 2 = 5? A Framework for Using Co-Branding to Leverage a Brand," *Journal of Brand Management* 2 (September 2003), pp. 35–47.

50. Based in part on a talk by Nancy Bailey, "Using Licensing to Build the Brand," Brand Masters Conference, December 7, 2000.

51. Philip Kotler and Waldermar Pfoertsch, *Ingredient Branding: Making the Invisible Visible*, (Heidelberg, Germany: Springer-Verlag, 2011).

52. Kalpesh Kaushik Desai and Kevin Lane Keller, "The Effects of Brand Expansions and Ingredient Branding Strategies on Host Brand Extendibility," *Journal of Marketing* 66 (January 2002), pp. 73–93; D. C. Denison, "Ingredient Branding Puts Big Names in the Mix," *Boston Globe,* May 26, 2002.

53. Joe Tradii, "Ingredient Branding: Time to Check That Recipe Again," *Brandweek,* March 29, 2010, p. 44; Piet Levy, "B-to-B-to-C," *Marketing News,* September 30, 2009, pp. 15–20.

54. "DuPont Receives Corporate Innovation Award," DuPont, www.dupont.com, November 13, 2009.

55. Kevin Lane Keller, *Strategic Brand Management,* 3rd ed. (Upper Saddle River, NJ: Prentice Hall, 2008); Philip Kotler and Waldemar Pfoertsch, *B2B Brand Management* (New York: Springer, 2006); Paul F. Nunes, Stephen F. Dull, and Patrick D. Lynch, "When Two Brands Are Better Than One," *Outlook,* January 2003, pp. 14–23.

56. Fred Richards, "Memo to CMOs: It's The Packaging, Stupid," *Brandweek*, August 17, 2009, p. 22.

57. Susan B. Bassin, "Value-Added Packaging Cuts through Store Clutter," *Marketing News,* September 26, 1988, p. 21. Reprinted with permission from *Marketing News*, published by the American Marketing Association.

58. Stuart Elliott, "Tropicana Discovers Some Buyers Are Passionate About Packaging," *New York Times*, February 23, 2009; Linda Tischler, "Never Mind! Pepsi Pulls Much-Loathed Tropicana Packaging," *Fast Company*, February 23, 2009; Natalie Zmuda, "Tropicana Line's Sales Plunge 20% Post-Rebranding," *Advertising Age*, April 2, 2009; Kenneth Hein, "Tropicana Squeezes Out Fresh Design with a Peel," *Brandweek*, January 19, 2009, p. 30.

59. Mya Frazier, "How Can Your Package Stand Out? Eye Tracking Looks Hard for Answers," *Advertising Age,* October 16, 2006, p. 14.

60. Kate Fitzgerald, "Packaging Is the Capper," *Advertising Age,* May 5, 2003, p. 22.

61. John C. Kozup, Elizabeth H. Creyer, and Scot Burton, "Making Healthful Food Choices: The Influence of Health Claims and Nutrition Information on Consumers' Evaluations of Packaged Food Products and Restaurant Menu Items," *Journal of Marketing* 67 (April 2003), pp. 19–34; Siva K. Balasubramanian and Catherine Cole, "Consumers' Search and Use of Nutrition Information: The Challenge and Promise of the Nutrition Labeling and Education Act," *Journal of Marketing* 66 (July 2002), pp. 112–27.

62. Robert Berner, "Watch Out, Best Buy and Circuit City," *BusinessWeek,* November 21, 2005, pp. 46–48.

63. Tao Chen, Ajay Kalra, and Baohung Sun, "Why Do Consumers Buy Extended Service Contracts," *Journal of Consumer Research* 36 (December 2009), pp. 611–23.

64. Chris Serres, "More Electronics Buyers Skip Extended Warranties," *Minneapolis Star Tribune*, July 14, 2007. For an empirical study, see Junhong Chu and Pradeep K. Chintagunta, "Quantifying the Economic Value of Warranties in the U.S. Server Market, *Marketing Science* 28 (January–February 2009), pp. 99–121.

65. Barbara Ettore, "Phenomenal Promises Mean Business," *Management Review* (March 1994), pp. 18–23; "More Firms Pledge Guaranteed Service," *Wall Street Journal,* July 17, 1991; also see, Sridhar Moorthy and Kannan Srinivasan, "Signaling Quality with a Money-Back Guarantee: The Role of Transaction Costs," *Marketing Science* 14 (Fall 1995), pp. 442–46; Christopher W. L. Hart, *Extraordinary Guarantees* (New York: AMACOM, 1993).

Chapter 13

1. Leonard L. Berry, *On Great Service: A Framework for Action* (New York: Free Press, 2006); Leonard L. Berry, *Discovering the Soul of Service: The Nine Drivers of Sustainable Business Success* (New York: Free Press, 1999); Fred Wiersema, ed., *Customer Service: Extraordinary Results at Southwest Airlines, Charles Schwab, Lands' End, American Express, Staples, and USAA* (New York: HarperBusiness, 1998).

2. Matt Krantz, "Tinseltown Gets Glitzy New Star," *USA TODAY*, August 24, 2009; Linda Tischler, "Join the Circus," *Fast Company,* July 2005, 53–58; "Cirque du Soleil," *America's Greatest Brands* 3 (2004); Geoff Keighley, "The Factory," *Business 2.0,* February 2004, p. 102; Robin D. Rusch, "Cirque du Soleil Phantasmagoria Contorts," *Brandchannel.com*, (December 1, 2003).

3. *United States Department of Labor, Bureau of Labor Statistics*. www.bls.gov/emp/home.htm.

4. Benjamin Scheider and David E. Bowen, *Winning the Service Game* (Boston: Harvard Business School Press, 1995); Leonard L. Berry, "Services Marketing Is Different," *Business,* May–June 1980, pp. 24–30. For a thorough review of academic research into services, see Roland T. Rust and Tuck Siong Chung, "Marketing Models of Service and Relationships," *Marketing Science* 25 (November–December 2006), pp. 560–80.

5. Paul Keegan, "The Best New Idea in Business," *Fortune*, September 14, 2009, pp. 42–52; Adam Ashton, "Growth Galore but Profits Are Zip," *BusinessWeek*, September 8, 2008, p. 62; Alex Frankel, "Zipcar Makes the Leap," *Fast Company*, March 2008, pp. 48–50; Mike Beirne, "Temporary Plates," *Brandweek*, July 9, 2007, pp. 30–34.

6. Further classifications of services are described in Christopher H. Lovelock, *Services Marketing*, 3rd ed. (Upper Saddle River, NJ: Prentice Hall, 1996). Also see John E. Bateson, *Managing Services Marketing: Text and Readings,* 3rd ed. (Hinsdale, IL: Dryden, 1995).

7. Valarie A. Zeithaml, "How Consumer Evaluation Processes Differ between Goods and Services," J. Donnelly and W. R. George, eds., *Marketing of Services* (Chicago: American Marketing Association, 1981), pp. 186–90.

8. Amy Ostrom and Dawn Iacobucci, "Consumer Trade-Offs and the Evaluation of Services," *Journal of Marketing* 59 (January 1995), pp. 17–28.

9. For discussion of how the blurring of the line distinguishing products and services changes the meaning of this taxonomy, see Christopher Lovelock and Evert Gummesson, "Whither Services Marketing? In Search of a New Paradigm and Fresh Perspectives," *Journal of Service Research* 7 (August 2004), pp. 20–41; and Stephen L. Vargo and Robert F. Lusch, "Evolving to a New Dominant Logic for Marketing," *Journal of Marketing* 68 (January 2004), pp. 1–17.

10. Theodore Levitt, "Marketing Intangible Products and Product Intangibles," *Harvard Business Review,* May–June 1981, pp. 94–102; Leonard L. Berry, "Services Marketing Is Different," *Business*, May–June, 1980, pp. 24–29.

11. B. H. Booms and M. J. Bitner, "Marketing Strategies and Organizational Structures for Service Firms," J. Donnelly and W. R. George, eds., *Marketing of Services* (Chicago: American Marketing Association, 1981), pp. 47–51.

12. Lewis P. Carbone and Stephan H. Haeckel, "Engineering Customer Experiences," *Marketing Management* 3 (Winter 1994), p. 17.

13. Bernd H. Schmitt, *Customer Experience Management* (New York: John Wiley & Sons, 2003); Bernd H. Schmitt, David L. Rogers, and Karen Vrotsos (2003), *There's No Business That's Not Show Business: Marketing in an Experience Culture* (Upper Saddle River, NJ: Prentice Hall Financial Times, 2004).

14. Chip Heath and Dan Heath, "Give 'Em Something to Talk About," *Fast Company,* June 2007, pp. 58–59.

15. For some emerging research results on the effects of creating time and place service separation, see Hean Tat Keh and Jun Pang, "Customer Reaction to Service Separation," *Journal of Marketing* 74 (March 2010), pp. 55–70.

16. Gila E. Fruchter and Eitan Gerstner, "Selling with 'Satisfaction Guaranteed,'" *Journal of Service Research* 1 (May 1999), pp. 313–23. See also, Rebecca J. Slotegraaf and J. Jeffrey Inman, "Longitudinal Shifts in the Drivers of Satisfaction with Product Quality: The Role of Attribute Resolvability," *Journal of Marketing Research* 41 (August 2004), pp. 269–80.

17. For a similar list, see Leonard L. Berry and A. Parasuraman, *Marketing Services: Competing through Quality* (New York: Free Press, 1991), p. 16.

18. G. Pascal Zachary and Dick Kovacevich, "Bank Different," *Business 2.0,* June 2006, pp. 101–3; Greg Farrell, "Banking on Success as a One-Stop Shop," *USA Today,* March 26, 2007.

19. The material in this paragraph is based in part on Valarie Zeithaml, Mary Jo Bitner, and Dwayne D. Gremler, "Service Development and Design," *Services Marketing: Integrating Customer Focus across the Firm,* 4th ed. (New York: McGraw-Hill, 2006), Chapter 9.

20. G. Lynn Shostack, "Service Positioning through Structural Change," *Journal of Marketing* 51 (January 1987), pp. 34–43.

21. Vikas Mittal, Wagner A. Kamakura, and Rahul Govind, "Geographical Patterns in Customer Service and Satisfaction: An Empirical Investigation," *Journal of Marketing* 68 (July 2004), pp. 48–62.

22. Jeffrey F. Rayport, Bernard J. Jaworski, and Ellie J. Kyung, "Best Face Forward: Improving Companies' Service Interface with Customers," *Journal of Interactive Marketing* 19 (Autumn 2005), pp. 67–80; Asim Ansari and Carl F. Mela, "E-Customization," *Journal of Marketing Research* 40 (May 2003), pp. 131–45.

23. W. Earl Sasser, "Match Supply and Demand in Service Industries," *Harvard Business Review,* November–December 1976, pp. 133–40.

24. Steven M. Shugan and Jinhong Xie, "Advance Selling for Services," *California Management Review* 46 (Spring 2004), pp. 37–54; Eyal Biyalogorsky and Eitan Gerstner, "Contingent Pricing to Reduce Price Risks," *Marketing Science* 23 (Winter 2004), pp. 146–55; Steven M. Shugan and Jinhong Xie, "Advance Pricing of Services and Other Implications of Separating Purchase and Consumption," *Journal of Service Research* 2 (February 2000), pp. 227–39.

25. Seth Godin, "If It's Broke, Fix It," *Fast Company,* October 2003, p. 131.

26. James Wallace, "Singapore Airlines Raises the Bar for Luxury Flying, *Seattle Post Intelligencer,* January 18, 2007; Justin Doebele, "The Engineer," *Forbes,* January 9, 2006, pp. 122–24; Stanley Holmes, "Creature Comforts at 30,000 Feet," *BusinessWeek,* December 18, 2006, p. 138; Anonymous, "What Makes Singapore a Service Champion?" *Strategic Direction,* April 2003, pp. 26–28; www.singaporeaire.com.

27. Diane Brady, "Why Service Stinks," *BusinessWeek,* October 23, 2000, pp. 119–28.

28. Mary Clingman, "Turkey Talker," *Fortune,* November 27, 2006, p. 70.

29. Elisabeth Sullivan, "Happy Endings Lead to Happy Returns," *Marketing News*, October 30, 2009, p. 20.

30. Dan Reed, "United Makeover Aims to Refresh and Renew," *USA Today*, September 17, 2009, pp. 1B–2B; Elisabeth Sullivan, "Happy Endings Lead to Happy Returns," *Marketing News*, October 30, 2009, p. 20.

31. Nikki Hopewell, "Moyer Is Committed to Delivering a Comcastic Experience," *Marketing News*, October 15, 2008, pp. 28–30; Hannah Clark, "Customer Service Hell," *Forbes,* March 30, 2006.

32. David Lazarus, "JetBlue Response Praised," *San Francisco Chronicle,* February 25, 2007, B1; Marc Gunther, "Nothing Blue About This Airline," *Fortune*, September 14, 2009, pp. 114–18.

33. Stephen S. Tax, Mark Colgate, and David Bowen, "How to Prevent Your Customers from Failing," *MIT Sloan Management Review* (Spring 2006), pp. 30–38; Mei Xue and Patrick T. Harker, "Customer Efficiency: Concept and Its Impact on E-Business Management," *Journal of Service Research* 4 (May 2002), pp. 253–67; Matthew L. Meuter, Amy L. Ostrom, Robert I. Roundtree, and Mary Jo Bitner, "Self-Service Technologies: Understanding Customer Satisfaction with Technology-Based Service Encounters," *Journal of Marketing* 64 (July 2000), pp. 50–64.

34. Kimmy Wa Chan, Chi Kin (Bennett) Yim, and Simon S. K. Lam, "Is Customer Participation in Value Creation a Double-Edged Sword? Evidence from Professional Financial Services Across Cultures," *Journal of Marketing* 74 (May 2010), pp. 48–64.

35. Valarie Zeithaml, Mary Jo Bitner, and Dwayne D. Gremler, *Services Marketing: Integrating Customer Focus across the Firm*, 4th ed. (New York: McGraw-Hill, 2006).

36. Stephen S. Tax, Mark Colgate, and David Bowen, "How to Prevent Your Customers from Failing," *MIT Sloan Management Review* (Spring 2006), pp. 30–38; Michael Sanserino and Cari Tuna, "Companies Strive Harder to Please Customers," *Wall Street Journal*, July 27, 2009, p. B4.

37. James L. Heskett, W, Earl Sasser Jr., and Joe Wheeler, *Ownership Quotient: Putting the Service Profit Chain to Work for Unbeatable Competitive Advantage* (Boston, MA: Harvard Business School Press, 2008).

38. D. Todd Donovan, Tom J. Brown, and John C. Mowen, "Internal Benefits of Service Worker Customer Orientation: Job Satisfaction, Commitment, and Organizational Citizenship Behaviors," *Journal of Marketing* 68 (January 2004), pp. 128–46.

39. Dan Heath and Chip Heath, "I Love You. Now What?" *Fast Company*, October 2008, pp. 95–96.

40. Evan Hessel, "Kung Pao Chicken for the Soul," *Forbes*, April 21, 2008, pp. 106–107.

41. Frances X. Frei, "The Four Things a Service Business Must Get Right," *Harvard Business Review*, April 2008, pp. 70–80.

42. Christian Gronroos, "A Service-Quality Model and Its Marketing Implications," *European Journal of Marketing* 18 (1984), pp. 36–44.

43. Leonard Berry, "Big Ideas in Services Marketing," *Journal of Consumer Marketing* (Spring 1986), pp. 47–51. See also, Jagdip Singh, "Performance Productivity and Quality of Frontline Employees in Service Organizations," *Journal of Marketing* 64 (April 2000), pp. 15–34; Detelina Marinova, Jun Ye, and Jagdip Singh, "Do Frontline Mechanisms Matter? Impact of Quality and Productivity Orientations on Unit Revenue, Efficiency, and Customer Satisfaction," *Journal of Marketing* 72 (March 2008), pp. 28–45; John R. Hauser, Duncan I. Simester, and Birger Wernerfelt, "Internal Customers and Internal Suppliers," *Journal of Marketing Research* 33 (August 1996), pp. 268–80; Walter E. Greene, Gary D. Walls, and Larry J. Schrest, "Internal Marketing: The Key to External Marketing Success," *Journal of Services Marketing* 8 (1994), pp. 5–13.

44. Christian Gronroos, "A Service-Quality Model and Its Marketing Implications," *European Journal of Marketing* 18 (1984), pp. 36–44; Michael D. Hartline, James G. Maxham III, and Daryl O. McKee, "Corridors of Influence in the Dissemination of Customer-Oriented Strategy to Customer-Contact Service Employees," *Journal of Marketing* 64 (April 2000), pp. 35–50.

45. John Batelle, "Charles Schwab, Back from the Brink," *Business 2.0,* March 2006; "Q&A with Becky Saeger, CMO, Charles Schwab," *ANA Marketing Musings*, September 11, 2006; Betsy Morris, "Charles Schwab's

Big Challenge," *Fortune*, May 30, 2005; Rob Markey, Fred Reichheld, and Andreas Dullweber, "Closing the Customer Feedback Loop," *Harvard Business Review*, December 2009, pp. 43–47.

46. Ad de Jong, Ko de Ruyter, and Jos Lemmink, "Antecedents and Consequences of the Service Climate in Boundary-Spanning Self-Managing Service Teams," *Journal of Marketing* 68 (April 2004), pp. 18–35; Michael D. Hartline and O. C. Ferrell, "The Management of Customer-Contact Service Employees: An Empirical Investigation," *Journal of Marketing* 60 (October 1996), pp. 52–70; Christian Homburg, Jan Wieseke, and Torsten Bornemann, "Implementing the Marketing Concept at the Employee-Customer Interface: The Role of Customer Need Knowledge," *Journal of Marketing* 73 (July 2009), pp. 64–81; Chi Kin (Bennett) Yim, David K. Tse, and Kimmy Wa Chan, "Strengthening Customer Loyalty through Intimacy and Passion: Roles of Customer-Firm Affection and Customer-Staff Relationships, *Journal of Marketing Research* 45 (December 2008), pp. 741–56.

47. Michael Sanserino and Cari Tuna, "Companies Strive Harder to Please Customers," *Wall Street Journal*, July 27, 2009, p. B4.

48. Jena McGregor, "When Service Means Survival," *BusinessWeek*, March 2, 2009, pp. 26–30.

49. Heather Green, "How Amazon Aims to Keep You Clicking," *BusinessWeek*, March 2, 2009, pp. 34–40.

50. Roland T. Rust and Katherine N. Lemon, "E-Service and the Consumer," *International Journal of Electronic Commerce* 5 (Spring 2001), pp. 83–99. See also, Balaji Padmanabhan and Alexander Tuzhilin, "On the Use of Optimization for Data Mining: Theoretical Interactions and ECRM opportunities," *Management Science* 49 (October 2003), pp. 1327–43; B. P. S. Murthi and Sumit Sarkar, "The Role of the Management Sciences in Research on Personalization," *Management Science* 49 (October 2003), pp. 1344–62.

51. Roland T. Rust, P. K. Kannan, and Na Peng, "The Customer Economics of Internet Privacy," *Journal of the Academy of Marketing Science* 30 (2002), pp. 455–64.

52. Jena McGregor, "Customer Service Champs," *BusinessWeek*, March 5, 2007, pp. 52–64.

53. Jena McGregor, "When Service Means Survival," *BusinessWeek*, March 2, 2009, pp. 26–30.

54. John A. Martilla and John C. James, "Importance-Performance Analysis," *Journal of Marketing* 41 (January 1977), pp. 77–79.

55. Dave Dougherty and Ajay Murthy, "What Service Customers Really Want," *Harvard Business Review*, September 2009, p. 22; for a contrarian point of view, see Edward Kasabov, "The Compliant Customer," *MIT Sloan Management Review* (Spring 2010), pp. 18–19.

56. Jeffrey G. Blodgett and Ronald D. Anderson, "A Bayesian Network Model of the Customer Complaint Process," *Journal of Service Research* 2 (May 2000), pp. 321–38; Stephen S. Tax and Stephen

W. Brown, "Recovering and Learning from Service Failures," *Sloan Management Review* (Fall 1998), pp. 75–88; Claes Fornell and Birger Wernerfelt, "A Model for Customer Complaint Management," *Marketing Science* 7 (Summer 1988), pp. 271–86.

57. James G. Maxham III and Richard G. Netemeyer, "Firms Reap What They Sow: The Effects of Shared Values and Perceived Organizational Justice on Customers' Evaluations of Complaint Handling," *Journal of Marketing* 67 (January 2003), pp. 46–62; Jagdip Singh, "Performance Productivity and Quality of Frontline Employees in Service Organizations," *Journal of Marketing* 64 (April 2000), pp. 15–34; Barry J. Rabin and James S. Boles, "Employee Behavior in a Service Environment: A Model and Test of Potential Differences between Men and Women," *Journal of Marketing* 62 (April 1998), pp. 77–91.

58. Stephen S. Tax, Stephen W. Brown and Murali Chandrashekaran, "Customer Evaluations of Service Complaint Experiences: Implications for Relationship Marketing," *Journal of Marketing* 62 (April 1998), pp. 60–76; Stephen S. Tax and Stephen W. Brown, "Recovering and Learning from Service Failures," *Sloan Management Review* (Fall 1998), pp. 75–88.

59. Amy Barrett, "Vanguard Gets Personal," *BusinessWeek*, October 3, 2005, pp. 115–18; Carolyn Marconi and Donna MacFarland, "Growth by Marketing under the Radar," Presentation made at Marketing Science Institute Board of Trustees Meeting: Pathways to Growth, Tucson, AZ, November 7, 2002.

60. www.schneider.com; www.informs.org; Todd Raphael, "Facing 'Fierce Competition,' Schneider National Struggles to Fill Trucking Jobs," *Inside Recruiting*, May 31, 2006.

61. Roger Yu, "Sheraton Has Designs on Fresh Look," *USA TODAY*, August 26, 2008, p. 4B.

62. Robert Levine, "Globe Trotter," *Fast Company*, September 2008, pp. 73–74; Andrew McMains, "Q&A: Kayak's Robert Birge," *Adweek.com*, June 2, 2009; Peter West, "Retail Medical Clinics Offer Quality Care: Study," *HealthDay*, August 31, 2009; "More Medical Clinics Opening in Retail Stores," *Associated Press*, February 2, 2006; Ellen McGirt, "Fast Food Medicine," *Fast Company*, September 2007, pp. 37–38; "Kenny Dichter: A Big Idea Takes Off," Special Advertising Supplement, CIT Behind the Business, *Condé Nast Portfolio*, September 2007.

63. Jessi Hempel, "Salesforce Hits Its Stride," *Fortune*, March 2, 2009, pp. 29–32.

64. Jena McGregor, "USAA's Battle Plan," *Bloomberg BusinessWeek*, March 1, 2010, pp. 40–43; Jena McGregor, "When Service Means Survival," *BusinessWeek*, March 2, 2009, pp. 26–30; "Customer Service Champs," *BusinessWeek*, March 5, 2007; "USAA Receives Chairman's Award," *San Antonio Business Journal,* June 20, 2002.

65. Susan M. Keaveney, "Customer Switching Behavior in Service Industries: An Exploratory Study," *Journal of Marketing* 59 (April 1995), pp. 71–82. See also,

Jaishankar Ganesh, Mark J. Arnold, and Kristy E. Reynolds, "Understanding the Customer Base of Service Providers: An Examination of the Differences between Switchers and Stayers," *Journal of Marketing* 64 (July 2000), pp. 65–87; Michael D. Hartline and O. C. Ferrell, "The Management of Customer-Contact Service Employees: An Empirical Investigation," *Journal of Marketing* 60 (October 1996), pp. 52–70; Linda L. Price, Eric J. Arnould, and Patrick Tierney, "Going to Extremes: Managing Service Encounters and Assessing Provider Performance," *Journal of Marketing* 59 (April 1995), pp. 83–97; Lois A. Mohr, Mary Jo Bitner, and Bernard H. Booms, "Critical Service Encounters: The Employee's Viewpoint," *Journal of Marketing* 58 (October 1994), pp. 95–106.

66. Dave Dougherty and Ajay Murthy, "What Service Customers Really Want," *Harvard Business Review*, September 2009, p. 22.

67. Glenn B. Voss, A. Parasuraman, and Dhruv Grewal, "The Role of Price, Performance, and Expectations in Determining Satisfaction in Service Exchanges," *Journal of Marketing* 62 (October 1998), pp. 46–61.

68. Roland T. Rust and Richard L. Oliver, "Should We Delight the Customer?" *Journal of the Academy of Marketing Science* 28 (December 2000), pp. 86–94.

69. A. Parasuraman, Valarie A. Zeithaml, and Leonard L. Berry, "A Conceptual Model of Service Quality and Its Implications for Future Research," *Journal of Marketing* 49 (Fall 1985), pp. 41–50. See also, Michael K. Brady and J. Joseph Cronin Jr., "Some New Thoughts on Conceptualizing Perceived Service Quality," *Journal of Marketing* 65 (July 2001), pp. 34–49; Susan J. Devlin and H. K. Dong, "Service Quality from the Customers' Perspective," *Marketing Research* (Winter 1994), pp. 4–13.

70. Leonard L. Berry and A. Parasuraman, *Marketing Services: Competing through Quality* (New York: Free Press, 1991), p. 16.

71. A. Parasuraman, Valarie A. Zeithaml, and Leonard L. Berry, "A Conceptual Model of Service Quality and Its Implications for Future Research," *Journal of Marketing* 49 (Fall 1985), pp. 41–50.

72. William Boulding, Ajay Kalra, Richard Staelin, and Valarie A. Zeithaml, "A Dynamic Model of Service Quality: From Expectations to Behavioral Intentions," *Journal of Marketing Research* 30 (February 1993), pp. 7–27.

73. Roland T. Rust and Tuck Siong Chung, "Marketing Models of Service and Relationships," *Marketing Science* 25 (November–December 2006), pp. 560–80; Katherine N. Lemon, Tiffany Barnett White, and Russell S. Winer, "Dynamic Customer Relationship Management: Incorporating Future Considerations into the Service Retention Decision," *Journal of Marketing* 66 (January 2002), pp. 1–14; Ruth N. Bolton and Katherine N. Lemon, "A Dynamic Model of Customers' Usage of Services: Usage as an Antecedent and Consequence of Satisfaction," *Journal of Marketing Research* 36 (May 1999), pp. 171–86.

74. Kent Grayson and Tim Ambler, "The Dark Side of Long-Term Relationships in Marketing Services," *Journal of Marketing Research* 36 (February 1999), pp. 132–41.

75. Leonard L. Berry, Kathleen Seiders, and Dhruv Grewal, "Understanding Service Convenience," *Journal of Marketing* 66 (July 2002), pp. 1–17.

76. "Help Yourself," *Economist*, July 2, 2009, pp. 62–63.

77. Jeffrey F. Rayport and Bernard J. Jaworski, *Best Face Forward* (Boston: Harvard Business School Press, 2005); Jeffrey F. Rayport, Bernard J. Jaworski, and Ellie J. Kyung, "Best Face Forward," *Journal of Interactive Marketing* 19 (Autumn 2005), pp. 67–80; Jeffrey F. Rayport and Bernard J. Jaworski, "Best Face Forward," *Harvard Business Review*, December 2004, pp. 47–58.

78. Matthew L. Meuter, Mary Jo Bitner, Amy L. Ostrom, and Stephen W. Brown, "Choosing among Alternative Service Delivery Modes: An Investigation of Customer Trial of Self-Service Technologies," *Journal of Marketing* 69 (April 2005), pp. 61–83.

79. Eric Fang, Robert W. Palmatier, and Jan-Benedict E. M. Steenkamp, "Effect of Service Transition Strategies on Firm Value," *Journal of Marketing* 72 (September 2008), pp. 1–14.

80. Mark Vandenbosch and Niraj Dawar, "Beyond Better Products: Capturing Value in Customer Interactions," *MIT Sloan Management Review* 43 (Summer 2002), pp. 35–42; Milind M. Lele and Uday S. Karmarkar, "Good Product Support Is Smart Marketing," *Harvard Business Review*, November–December 1983, pp. 124–32.

81. For research on the effects of delays in service on service evaluations, see Michael K. Hui and David K. Tse, "What to Tell Consumers in Waits of Different Lengths: An Integrative Model of Service Evaluation," *Journal of Marketing* 60 (April 1996), pp. 81–90; Shirley Taylor, "Waiting for Service: The Relationship between Delays and Evaluations of Service," *Journal of Marketing* 58 (April 1994), pp. 56–69.

82. Byron G. Auguste, Eric P. Harmon, and Vivek Pandit, "The Right Service Strategies for Product Companies," *McKinsey Quarterly* 1 (2006), pp. 41–51.

83. Goutam Challagalla, R. Venkatesh, and Ajay K. Kohli, "Proactive Postsales Service: When and Why Does it Pay Off?" *Journal of Marketing* 73 (March 2009), pp. 70–87.

Chapter 14

1. Brian Burnsed, "Where Discounting Can Be Dangerous," *BusinessWeek*, August 3, 2009, p. 49; "Tiffany's Profit Tops Expectations," *Associated Press*, November 26, 2009; Cintra Wilson, "If Bling Had a Hall of Fame," *New York Times*, July 30, 2009; Ellen Byron, "Fashion Victim: To Refurbish Its Image, Tiffany Risks Profits," *Wall Street Journal*, January 10, 2007, p. A1.

2. "The Price Is Wrong," *Economist*, May 25, 2002.

3. Xavier Dreze and Joseph C. Nunes, "Using Combined-Currency Prices to Lower Consumers' Perceived Cost," *Journal of Marketing Research* 41 (February 2004), pp. 59–72; Raghuram Iyengar, Kamel Jedidi, and Rajeev Kohli, "A Conjoint Approach to Multipart Pricing," *Journal of Marketing Research* 45 (April 2008), pp. 195–201; Marco Bertini and Luc Wathieu, "Attention Arousal Through Price Partitioning," *Marketing Science* 27 (March/April 2008), pp. 236–46.

4. Rick Newman, "The Great Retail Revolution," *U.S. News & World Report*, March 2010, pp. 19–20; Philip Moeller, "Tough Times Are Molding Tough Consumers," *U.S. News & World Report*, March 2010, pp. 22–25; Steve Hamm, "The New Age of Frugality," *BusinessWeek*, October 20, 2008, pp. 55–60; Timothy W. Martin, "Frugal Shoppers Drive Grocers Back to Basics," *Wall Street Journal*, June 24, 2009, p. B1; Daniel Gross, "The Latte Era Grinds Down," *Newsweek*, October 22, 2007, pp. 46–47.

5. Paul Markillie, "A Perfect Market: A Survey of E-Commerce," *Economist,* May 15, 2004, pp. 3–20; David Kirpatrick, "How the Open-Source World Plans to Smack Down Microsoft, and Oracle, and . . . ," *Fortune,* February 23, 2004, pp. 92–100; Faith Keenan, "The Price Is Really Right," *BusinessWeek,* March 31, 2003, pp. 61–67; Michael Menduno, "Priced to Perfection," *Business 2.0,* March 6, 2001, pp. 40–42; Amy E. Cortese, "Good-Bye to Fixed Pricing?" *BusinessWeek,* May 4, 1998, pp. 71–84. For a discussion of some of the basic academic issues involved, see Florian Zettelmeyer, "Expanding to the Internet: Pricing and Communication Strategies when Firms Compete on Multiple Channels," *Journal of Marketing Research* 37 (August 2000), pp. 292–308; John G. Lynch Jr. and Dan Ariely, "Wine Online: Search Costs Affect Competition on Price, Quality, and Distribution," *Marketing Science* 19 (Winter 2000), pp. 83–103; Rajiv Lal and Miklos Sarvary, "When and How Is the Internet Likely to Decrease Price Competition?" *Marketing Science* 18 (Fall 1999), pp. 485–503.

6. Daniel Fisher, "Cheap Seats," *Forbes*, August 24, 2009, pp. 102–3.

7. Bernard Condon, "The Haggle Economy," *Forbes*, June 8, 2009, pp. 26–27.

8. For a thorough review of pricing research, see Chezy Ofir and Russell S. Winer, "Pricing: Economic and Behavioral Models," Bart Weitz and Robin Wensley, eds., *Handbook of Marketing* (London: Sage Publications, 2002).

9. Based on Pia Sarkar, "Which Shirt Costs $275?—Brand Loyalty, Bargain Hunting, and Unbridled Luxury All Play a Part in the Price You'll Pay for a T-Shirt," *Final Edition,* March 15, 2007, p. C1. Reprinted by permission.

10. Bruce Horovitz, "Sale, Sale, Sale: Today Everyone Wants a Deal," *USA Today*, April 21, 2010, pp. 1A–2A.

11. Sbriya Rice, "'I Can't Afford Surgery in the U.S.,' Says Bargain Shopper," *CNN,* www.cnn.com, April 26, 2010.

12. Jay Greene, "Selling $8 Soap in an Era of Frugality," *BusinessWeek*, November 30, 2009, p. 66.

13. Peter R. Dickson and Alan G. Sawyer, "The Price Knowledge and Search of Supermarket Shoppers," *Journal of Marketing* 54 (July 1990), pp. 42–53. For a methodological qualification, however, see Hooman Estalami, Alfred Holden, and Donald R. Lehmann, "Macro-Economic Determinants of Consumer Price Knowledge: A Meta-Analysis of Four Decades of Research," *International Journal of Research in Marketing* 18 (December 2001), pp. 341–55.

14. For a comprehensive review, see Tridib Mazumdar, S. P. Raj, and Indrajit Sinha, "Reference Price Research: Review and Propositions," *Journal of Marketing* 69 (October 2005), pp. 84–102. For a different point of view, see Chris Janiszewski and Donald R. Lichtenstein, "A Range Theory Account of Price Perception," *Journal of Consumer Research* 25 (March 1999), pp. 353–68.

15. For a discussion of how "incidental" prices outside the category can serve as contextual reference prices, see Joseph C. Nunes and Peter Boatwright, "Incidental Prices and Their Effect on Willingness to Pay," *Journal of Marketing Research* 41 (November 2004), pp. 457–66.

16. K. N. Rajendran and Gerard J. Tellis, "Contextual and Temporal Components of Reference Price," *Journal of Marketing* 58 (January 1994), pp. 22–34; Gurumurthy Kalyanaram and Russell S. Winer, "Empirical Generalizations from Reference-Price Research," *Marketing Science* 14 (Summer 1995), pp. G161–69. See also, Ritesh Saini, Raghunath Singh Rao, and Ashwani Monga, "Is the Deal Worth My Time? The Interactive Effect of Relative and Referent Thinking on Willingness to Seek a Bargain," *Journal of Marketing* 74 (January 2010), pp. 34–48.

17. Gurumurthy Kalyanaram and Russell S. Winer, "Empirical Generalizations from Reference-Price Research," *Marketing Science* 14 (Summer 1995), pp. 161–69.

18. Glenn E. Mayhew and Russell S. Winer, "An Empirical Analysis of Internal and External Reference-Price Effects Using Scanner Data," *Journal of Consumer Research* 19 (June 1992), pp. 62–70.

19. Robert Ziethammer, "Forward-Looking Buying in Online Auctions," *Journal of Marketing Research* 43 (August 2006), pp. 462–76.

20. John T. Gourville, "Pennies-a-Day: The Effect of Temporal Reframing on Transaction Evaluation," *Journal of Consumer Research* 24 (March 1998), pp. 395–408.

21. Gary M. Erickson and Johny K. Johansson, "The Role of Price in Multi-Attribute Product-Evaluations," *Journal of Consumer Research* 12 (September 1985), pp. 195–99.

22. Wilfred Amaldoss and Sanjay Jain, "Pricing of Conspicuous Goods: A Competitive Analysis of Social Effects," *Journal of Marketing Research* 42 (February 2005); Angela Chao and Juliet B. Schor, "Empirical Tests of Status Consumption: Evidence from Women's

Cosmetics," *Journal of Economic Psychology* 19 (January 1998), pp. 107–31.

23. Mark Stiving and Russell S. Winer, "An Empirical Analysis of Price Endings with Scanner Data," *Journal of Consumer Research* 24 (June 1997), pp. 57–68.

24. Eric T. Anderson and Duncan Simester, "Effects of $9 Price Endings on Retail Sales: Evidence from Field Experiments," *Quantitative Marketing and Economics* 1 (March 2003), pp. 93–110.

25. Eric Anderson and Duncan Simester, "Mind Your Pricing Cues," *Harvard Business Review,* September 2003, pp. 96–103.

26. Robert M. Schindler and Patrick N. Kirby, "Patterns of Rightmost Digits Used in Advertised Prices: Implications for Nine-Ending Effects," *Journal of Consumer Research* 24 (September 1997), pp. 192–201.

27. Anderson and Simester, "Mind Your Pricing Cues," *Harvard Business Review*, September 2003, pp. 96–103.

28. Ibid.

29. Daniel J. Howard and Roger A. Kerin, "Broadening the Scope of Reference-Price Advertising Research: A Field Study of Consumer Shopping Involvement," *Journal of Marketing* 70 (October 2006), pp. 185–204.

30. Robert C. Blattberg and Kenneth Wisniewski, "Price-Induced Patterns of Competition," *Marketing Science* 8 (Fall 1989), pp. 291–309; Katherine N. Lemon and Stephen M. Nowlis, "Developing Synergies between Promotions and Brands in Different Price-Quality Tiers," *Journal of Marketing Research* 39 (May 2002), pp. 171–85; but see also, Serdar Sayman, Stephen J. Hoch, and Jagmohan S. Raju, "Positioning of Store Brands," *Marketing Science* 21 (Fall 2002), pp. 378–97.

31. Shantanu Dutta, Mark J. Zbaracki, and Mark Bergen, "Pricing Process as a Capability: A Resource-Based Perspective," *Strategic Management Journal* 24 (July 2003), pp. 615–30.

32. "To All iPhone Customers," *Apple Inc.*, www.apple.com/hotnews/openiphoneletter; Gary F. Gebhardt, "Price Skimming's Unintended Consequences," *Marketing Science Institute Working Paper Series*, MSI Report No. 09-109.

33. Michael Silverstein and Neil Fiske, *Trading Up: The New American Luxury* (New York: Portfolio, 2003).

34. Christopher Lawton, "A Liquor Maverick Shakes Up Industry with Pricey Brands," *Wall Street Journal,* May 21, 2003.

35. Timothy Aeppel, "Seeking Perfect Prices, CEO Tears Up the Rules," *Wall Street Journal,* March 27, 2007.

36. Florian Zettelmeyer, Fiona Scott Morton, and Jorge Silva-Risso, "How the Internet Lowers Prices: Evidence from Matched Survey and Automobile Transaction Data," *Journal of Marketing Research* 43 (May 2006), pp. 168–81; Jeffrey R. Brown and Austan Goolsbee, "Does the Internet Make Markets More Competitive? Evidence from the Life Insurance Industry," *Journal*

of *Political Economy* 110 (October 2002), pp. 481–507.

37. Joo Heon Park and Douglas L. MacLachlan, "Estimating Willingness to Pay with Exaggeration Bias-Corrected Contingent Valuation Method," *Marketing Science* 27 (July–August 2008), pp. 691–98.

38. Walter Baker, Mike Marn, and Craig Zawada, "Price Smarter on the Net," *Harvard Business Review*, February 2001, pp. 122–27.

39. Brian Bergstein, "The Price Is Right," *Associated Press*, April 29, 2007.

40. Thomas T. Nagle and Reed K. Holden, *The Strategy and Tactics of Pricing,* 3rd ed. (Upper Saddle River, NJ: Prentice Hall, 2002).

41. For a summary of elasticity studies, see Dominique M. Hanssens, Leonard J. Parsons, and Randall L. Schultz, *Market Response Models: Econometric and Time Series Analysis* (Boston: Kluwer, 1990), pp. 187–91.

42. Tammo H. A. Bijmolt, Harald J. Van Heerde, and Rik G. M. Pieters, "New Empirical Generalizations on the Determinants of Price Elasticity," *Journal of Marketing Research* 42 (May 2005), pp. 141–56.

43. William W. Alberts, "The Experience Curve Doctrine Reconsidered," *Journal of Marketing* 53 (July 1989), pp. 36–49.

44. Michael Sivy, "Japan's Smart Secret Weapon," *Fortune,* August 12, 1991, p. 75.

45. Joseph Weber, "Over a Buck for Dinner? Outrageous," *BusinessWeek*, March 9, 2009, p. 57.

46. Reena Jane, "From India, the Latest Management Fad," *Bloomberg BusinessWeek*, December 14, 2009, p. 57; Julie Jargon, "General Mills Takes Several Steps to Combat High Commodity Costs," *Wall Street Journal*, September 20, 2007; Mina Kimes, "Cereal Cost Cutters," *Fortune*, November 10, 2008, p. 24.

47. Jack Ewing, "The Next Wal-Mart?" *BusinessWeek,* April 26, 2004, pp. 60–62; "German Discounter Aldi Aims to Profit from Belt-Tightening in US," *DW World.de,* www.dw-world.de, January 15, 2009; Aldi, www.aldi.com.

48. "Green Works Natural Cleaners and Sierra Club Celebrate Two Year Anniversary; Doubling of Natural Cleaning Category," *Green Works,* www.greenworkscleaners.com, June 28, 2010; "This or That? Clorox Greenworks Cleaning Up in the Market Tip of the Day," *Green Daily*, www.greendaily.com, January 24, 2009; "Annual GMA Award Recognizes Clorox and Kettle Foods for Innovation and Creativity," *GMA,* www. gmaonline.org/awardssurvey/cpg.cfm, August 5, 2008.

49. Kusum L. Ailawadi, Donald R. Lehmann, and Scott A. Neslin, "Market Response to a Major Policy Change in the Marketing Mix: Learning from Procter & Gamble's Value Pricing Strategy," *Journal of Marketing* 65 (January 2001), pp. 44–61.

50. Timothy Aeppel, "Seeking Perfect Prices, CEO Tears Up the Rules," *Wall Street Journal,* March 27, 2007;

Todd Shryock, "Parker Hannifin: Perpetual Motion," *Smart Business Cleveland*, October 1, 2005; Tom Brennan, "High-Tech Parker Hannifin?" *CNBC*, www.cnbc.com, April 29, 2008.

51. Bruce Einhorn, "Acer's Game-Changing PC Offensive," *BusinessWeek*, April 20, 2009, p. 65; Bruce Einhorn and Tim Culpan, "With Dell in the Dust, Acer Chases HP," *Bloomberg BusinessWeek*, March 8, 2010, pp. 58–59.

52. Tung-Zong Chang and Albert R. Wildt, "Price, Product Information, and Purchase Intention: An Empirical Study," *Journal of the Academy of Marketing Science* 22 (Winter 1994), pp. 16–27. See also, G. Dean Kortge and Patrick A. Okonkwo, "Perceived Value Approach to Pricing," *Industrial Marketing Management* 22 (May 1993), pp. 133–40.

53. Michael Arndt, "PACCAR: Built for the Long-Haul," *BusinessWeek*, January 30, 2006; Jay Thompson, "The 2010 U.S. Diesel Engine Landscape—Paccar's Approach Will Be Most Changed Without Cat," *Gerson Lehrman Group,* www.glgroup.com; Angel Gonzales, "Paccar's Fuel-Saving Hybrid Truck Aimed at Nation's Distribution," *Seattle Times*, July 29, 2008; Paccar, www.paccar.com.

54. Anupam Mukerj, "Monsoon Marketing," *Fast Company*, April 2007, p. 22.

55. Marco Bertini and Luc Wathieu, "How to Stop Customers from Fixating on Price," *Harvard Business Review*, May 2010, pp. 85–91.

56. James C. Anderson, Dipak C. Jain, and Pradeep K. Chintagunta, "Customer Value Assessment in Business Markets: A State-of-Practice Study," *Journal of Business-to-Business Marketing* 1 (Spring 1993), pp. 3–29.

57. Bill Saporito, "Behind the Tumult at P&G," *Fortune,* March 7, 1994, pp. 74–82. For empirical analysis of its effects, see Kusim L. Ailawadi, Donald R. Lehmann, and Scott A. Neslin, "Market Response to a Major Policy Change in the Marketing Mix: Learning from Procter & Gamble's Value Pricing Strategy," *Journal of Marketing* 65 (January 2001), pp. 44–61.

58. Laurie Burkitt, "Take It All Off," *Forbes*, March 29, 2010, p. 59; Dan Beucke, "A Blade Too Far," *BusinessWeek*, August 14, 2006; Jenn Abelson, "And Then There Were Five," *Boston Globe,* September 15, 2005; Jack Neff, "Six-Blade Blitz," *Advertising Age,* September 19, 2005, pp. 3, 53; Editorial, "Gillette Spends Smart on Fusion," *Advertising Age,* September 26, 2005, p. 24.

59. Elisabeth Sullivan, "Value Pricing," *Marketing News*, January 15, 2008, p. 08.

60. Stephen J. Hoch, Xavier Dreze, and Mary J. Purk, "EDLP, Hi-Lo, and Margin Arithmetic," *Journal of Marketing* 58 (October 1994), pp. 16–27; Rajiv Lal and R. Rao, "Supermarket Competition: The Case of Everyday Low Pricing," *Marketing Science* 16 (Winter 1997), pp. 60–80; Michael Tsiros and David M. Hardesty, "Ending a Price Promotion: Retracting It in One Step or Phasing It Out Gradually," *Journal of Marketing* 74 (January 2010), pp. 49–64.

61. Joseph W. Alba, Carl F. Mela, Terence A. Shimp, and Joel E. Urbany, "The Effect of Discount Frequency and Depth on Consumer Price Judgments," *Journal of Consumer Research* 26 (September 1999), pp. 99–114; Paul B. Ellickson and Sanjog Misra, "Supermarket Pricing Strategies," *Marketing Science*, 27 (September–October 2008), pp. 811–28.

62. David Welch, "Haggling Starts to Go the Way of the Tail Fin," *BusinessWeek*, October 29, 2007, pp. 71–72.

63. "Pink Elle Reviews," reviews.pinkelle.com/2009/02/06/review-and-comparison-of-daiso-singapore-and-daiso-malaysia; "Smart Shopping at Daiso, The Curve Mutiara Damansara," *My Smart Money Tips*, mysmartmoneytips.com/2009/01/05/smart-shopping-at-daiso-the-curve-mutiara-damansara; "Daiso Japan is Now in the Curve," *Herbs & Spices*, January 11, 2009, http://herbdonald.wordpress.com/.

64. Ethan Smith and Sara Silver, "To Protect Its Box-Office Turf, Ticketmaster Plays Rivals' Tune," *Wall Street Journal,* September 12, 2006.

65. "Royal Mail Drives Major Cost Savings through Free Markets," Free Markets press release, December 15, 2003.

66. Using expected profit for setting price makes sense for the seller that makes many bids. The seller who bids only occasionally or who needs a particular contract badly will not find it advantageous to use expected profit. This criterion does not distinguish between a $1,000 profit with a 0.10 probability and a $125 profit with a 0.80 probability. Yet the firm that wants to keep production going would prefer the second contract to the first.

67. Bernard Condon, "The Haggle Economy," *Forbes*, June 8, 2009, pp. 26–27; Sandy D. Jap, "The Impact of Online Reverse Auction Design on Buyer-Supplier Relationships," *Journal of Marketing* 71 (January 2007), pp. 146–59; Sandy D. Jap, "An Exploratory Study of the Introduction of Online Reverse Auctions," *Journal of Marketing* 67 (July 2003), pp. 96–107.

68. Paul W. Farris and David J. Reibstein, "How Prices, Expenditures, and Profits Are Linked," *Harvard Business Review,* November–December 1979, pp. 173–84. See also, Makoto Abe, "Price and Advertising Strategy of a National Brand against Its Private-Label Clone: A Signaling Game Approach," *Journal of Business Research* 33 (July 1995), pp. 241–50.

69. Eugene H. Fram and Michael S. McCarthy, "The True Price of Penalties," *Marketing Management*, October 1999, pp. 49–56.

70. Joel E. Urbany, "Justifying Profitable Pricing," *Journal of Product and Brand Management* 10 (2001), pp. 141–57; Charles Fishman, "The Wal-Mart You Don't Know," *Fast Company,* December 2003, pp. 68–80.

71. P. N. Agarwala, *Countertrade: A Global Perspective* (New Delhi: Vikas, 1991); Michael Rowe, *Countertrade* (London: Euromoney Books, 1989); Christopher M. Korth, ed., *International Countertrade* (New York: Quorum Books, 1987).

72. For an interesting discussion of a quantity surcharge, see David E. Sprott, Kenneth C. Manning, and Anthony Miyazaki, "Grocery Price Settings and Quantity Surcharges," *Journal of Marketing* 67 (July 2003), pp. 34–46.

73. Michael V. Marn and Robert L. Rosiello, "Managing Price, Gaining Profit," *Harvard Business Review,* September–October 1992, pp. 84–94. See also, Kusum L. Ailawadi, Scott A. Neslin, and Karen Gedenk, "Pursuing the Value-Conscious Consumer: Store Brands versus National-Brand Promotions," *Journal of Marketing* 65 (January 2001), pp. 71–89; Gerard J. Tellis, "Tackling the Retailer Decision Maze: Which Brands to Discount, How Much, When, and Why?" *Marketing Science* 14 (Summer 1995), pp. 271–99.

74. Michael J. Barone and Tirthankar Roy, "Does Exclusivity Always Pay Off? Exclusive Price Promotions and Consumer Response," *Journal of Marketing* 74 (March 2010), pp. 121–32.

75. Jay E. Klompmaker, William H. Rogers, and Anthony E. Nygren, "Value, Not Volume," *Marketing Management* (May–June 2003), pp. 45–48; Lands' End, www.landsend.com, June 23, 2010.

76. Peter Burrows and Olga Kharif, "Can AT&T Tame the iHogs," *Bloomberg BusinessWeek*, December 28, 2009 and January 4, 2010, pp. 21–22.

77. Ramarao Deesiraju and Steven M. Shugan, "Strategic Service Pricing and Yield Management," *Journal of Marketing* 63 (January 1999), pp. 44–56; Robert E. Weigand, "Yield Management: Filling Buckets, Papering the House," *Business Horizons* 42 (September–October 1999), pp. 55–64.

78. Charles Fishman, "Which Price Is Right?" *Fast Company,* March 2003, pp. 92–102; Bob Tedeschi, "E-Commerce Report," *New York Times,* September 2, 2002; Faith Keenan, "The Price Is Really Right," *BusinessWeek,* March 31, 2003, pp. 62–67; Peter Coy, "The Power of Smart Pricing," *BusinessWeek,* April 10, 2000, pp. 160–64. For a review of some seminal work linking pricing decisions with operational insights, see Moritz Fleischmann, Joseph M. Hall, and David F. Pyke, "Research Brief: Smart Pricing," *MIT Sloan Management Review* (Winter 2004), pp. 9–13.

79. Mike France, "Does Predatory Pricing Make Microsoft a Predator?" *BusinessWeek,* November 23, 1998, pp. 130–32. Also see Joseph P. Guiltinan and Gregory T. Gundlack, "Aggressive and Predatory Pricing: A Framework for Analysis," *Journal of Advertising* 60 (July 1996), pp. 87–102.

80. For more information on specific types of price discrimination that are illegal, see Henry Cheeseman, *Business Law,* 6th ed. (Upper Saddle River, NJ: Prentice Hall, 2007).

81. Bob Donath, "Dispel Major Myths about Pricing," *Marketing News,* February 3, 2003, p. 10. For an interesting historical account, see Meghan R. Busse, Duncan I. Simester, Florian Zettelmeyer, "'The Best Price You'll Ever Get': The 2005 Employee Discount Pricing Promotions, in the U.S. Automobile Industry," *Marketing Science* 29 (March–April 2010), pp. 268–90.

82. Harald J. Van Heerde, Els Gijsbrechts, and Koen Pauwels, "Winners and Losers in a Major Price War," *Journal of Marketing Research* 45 (October 2008), pp. 499–518.

83. For a classic review, see Kent B. Monroe, "Buyers' Subjective Perceptions of Price," *Journal of Marketing Research* 10 (February 1973), pp. 70–80. See also, Z. John Zhang, Fred Feinberg, and Aradhna Krishna, "Do We Care What Others Get? A Behaviorist Approach to Targeted Promotions," *Journal of Marketing Research* 39 (August 2002), pp. 277–91.

84. Margaret C. Campbell, "Perceptions of Pricing Unfairness: Antecedents and Consequences," *Journal of Marketing Research* 36 (May 1999), pp. 187–99.

85. Lan Xia, Kent B. Monroe, and Jennifer L. Cox, "The Price Is Unfair! A Conceptual Framework of Price Fairness Perceptions," *Journal of Marketing* 68 (October 2004), pp. 1–15; Eric T. Anderson and Duncan Simester, "Does Demand Fall when Customers Perceive That Prices Are Unfair? The Case of Premium Pricing for Larger Sizes," *Marketing Science* 27 (May–June 2008), pp. 492–500.

86. Eric Mitchell, "How Not to Raise Prices," *Small Business Reports,* November 1990, pp. 64–67.

87. Nirmalya Kumar, "Strategies to Fight Low-Cost Rivals," *Harvard Business Review* (December 2006): 104–12. See also Michael F. Porter, *Competitive Strategy: Techniques for Analyzing Industries and Competitors* (New York: Free Press, 1980); Adrian Ryans, *Beating Low Cost Competition: How Premium Brands Can Respond to Cut-Price Rivals* (West Sussex, England: John Wiley & Sons, 2008); Jack Neff, "How the Discounters Hurt Themslevs," *Advertising Age*, December 10, 2007, p. 12.

Chapter 15

1. Gloria Goodale, "Netflix: From Movies in the Mall to Movies on Demand?" *Christian Science Monitor*, September 1, 2006, p. 11; Timothy J. Mullaney, "The Mail Order House That Clobbered Blockbuster," *BusinessWeek*, June 5, 2006, pp. 56–57; Jefferson Graham, "Netflix Is Still Renting Strong," *USA Today*, July 1, 2009, p. 2B; Ronald Grover, Adam Satariano, and Ari Levy, "Honest, Hollywood, Netflix Is Your Friend," *Bloomberg BusinessWeek*, January 11, 2010, pp. 54–55; Michael V. Copeland, "Tapping Tech's Beautiful Minds," *Fortune*, October 12, 2009, pp. 35–36; Clive Thompson, "If You Liked This, Sure to Love That," *New York Times*, November 21, 2008; Jessica Mintz, "Redbox Machines Take on Netflix's Red Envelope," *USA Today*, June 22, 2009; Michael Kraus, "How Redbox Is Changing Retail," *Marketing News*, November 15, 2009, p. 23.

2. Anne T. Coughlan, Erin Anderson, Louis W. Stern, and Adel I. El-Ansary, *Marketing Channels,* 7th ed. (Upper Saddle River, NJ: Prentice Hall, 2007).

3. Louis W. Stern and Barton A. Weitz, "The Revolution in Distribution: Challenges and Opportunities," *Long Range Planning* 30 (December 1997), pp. 823–29.

4. For an insightful summary of academic research, see Erin Anderson and Anne T. Coughlan, "Channel Management: Structure, Governance, and Relationship Management," Bart Weitz and Robin Wensley, eds., *Handbook of Marketing* (London: Sage, 2001), pp. 223–47. See also, Gary L. Frazier, "Organizing and Managing Channels of Distribution," *Journal of the Academy of Marketing Sciences* 27 (Spring 1999), pp. 226–40.

5. Kerry Capell, "Thinking Simple at Philips," *BusinessWeek,* December 11, 2006, p. 50; Royal Philips Electronics Annual Report, 2009; "Philips—Unfulfilled," *Brandchannel.com*, June 20, 2005; Jennifer L. Schenker, "Fine-Tuning a Fuzzy Image," *TIMEeurope.com,* Spring 2002.

6. Sarah E. Needleman, "Dial-a-Mattress Retailer Blames Troubles on Stores, Executive Team," *Wall Street Journal*, July 14, 2009, p. B1.

7. Martin Wildberger, "Multichannel Business Basics for Successful E-Commerce," *Electronic Commerce News,* September 16, 2002, p. 1; Matthew Haeberle, "REI Overhauls Its E-Commerce," *Chain Store Age,* January 2003, p. 64.

8. Chekitan S. Dev and Don E. Schultz, "In the Mix: A Customer-Focused Approach Can Bring the Current Marketing Mix into the 21st Century," *Marketing Management* 14 (January–February 2005).

9. www.oracle.com, December 09, 2010.

10. www.apple.com, December 09, 2010.

11. Robert Shaw and Philip Kotler, "Rethinking the Chain," *Marketing Management* (July/August 2009), pp. 18–23.

12. Anne T. Coughlan, "Channel Management: Structure, Governance, and Relationship Management," Bart Weitz and Robin Wensley, eds., *Handbook of Marketing* (London: Sage, 2001), pp. 223–47.

13. For additional information on backward channels, see Marianne Jahre, "Household Waste Collection as a Reverse Channel: A Theoretical Perspective," *International Journal of Physical Distribution and Logistics* 25 (1995), pp. 39–55; Terrance L. Pohlen and M. Theodore Farris II, "Reverse Logistics in Plastics Recycling," *International Journal of Physical Distribution and Logistics* 22 (1992), pp. 35–37.

14. Greenopolis, www.greenopolis.com, December 09, 2010.

15. William M. Bulkeley, "Kodak Revamps Wal-Mart Kiosks," *Wall Street Journal*, September 6, 2006, p. B2; Faith Keenan, "Big Yellow's Digital Dilemma," *BusinessWeek,* March 24, 2003, pp. 80–81.

16. www.clevelandclinic.org, December 09, 2010; Geoff Colvin, "The Cleveland Clinic's Delos Cosgrove," *Fortune*, March 1, 2010, pp. 38–45.

17. Asim Ansari, Carl F. Mela, and Scott A. Neslin, "Customer Channel Migration," *Journal of Marketing Research* 45 (February 2008), pp. 60–76; Jacquelyn S. Thomas and Ursula Y. Sullivan, "Managing Marketing Communications," *Journal of Marketing* 69 (October 2005), pp. 239–51; Sridhar Balasubramanian, Rajagopal Raghunathan, and Vijay Mahajan, "Consumers in a Multichannel Environment: Product Utility, Process Utility, and Channel Choice," *Journal of Interactive Marketing* 19 (Spring 2005), pp. 12–30; Edward J. Fox, Alan L. Montgomery, and Leonard M. Lodish, "Consumer Shopping and Spending across Retail Formats," *Journal of Business* 77 (April 2004), pp. S25–S60.

18. Peter Child, Suzanne Heywood, and Michael Kilger, "Do Retail Brands Travel?" *McKinsey Quarterly* (January 2002), pp. 11–13. For another taxonomy of shoppers, see also Paul F. Nunes and Frank V. Cespedes, "The Customer Has Escaped," *Harvard Business Review,* November 2003, pp. 96–105.

19. John Helyar, "The Only Company Wal-Mart Fears," *Fortune,* November 24, 2003, pp. 158–66. See also, Michael Silverstein and Neil Fiske, *Trading Up: The New American Luxury* (New York: Portfolio, 2003).

20. Susan Broniarczyk, "Product Assortment," Curtis Haugtvedt, Paul Herr, and Frank Kardes, eds., *Handbook of Consumer Psychology*, (New York: Lawrence Erlbaum Associates, 2008), pp. 755–79; Alexander Chernev and Ryan Hamilton, "Assortment Size and Option Attractiveness in Consumer Choice Among Retailers," *Journal of Marketing Research* 46 (June 2009), pp. 410–20; Richard A. Briesch, Pradeep K. Chintagunta, and Edward J. Fox, "How Does Assortment Affect Grocery Store Choice," *Journal of Marketing Research* 46 (April 2009), pp. 176–89.

21. Anne T. Coughlan, Erin Anderson, Louis W. Stern, and Adel I. El-Ansary, *Marketing Channels,* 7th ed. (Upper Saddle River, NJ: Prentice Hall, 2007).

22. Louis P. Bucklin, *A Theory of Distribution Channel Structure* (Berkeley: Institute of Business and Economic Research, University of California, 1966).

23. Katrijn Gielens and Marnik G. Dekimpe, "The Entry Strategies Retail Firms into Transition Economies," *Journal of Marketing* 71 (April 2007), pp. 196–212.

24. Alex Frankel, "Magic Shop," *Fast Company*, November 2007, pp. 45–49; "Apple Reports Fourth Quarter Results," www.apple.com, October 19, 2009; Jerry Useem, "Simply Irresistible," *Fortune,* March 19, 2007, pp. 107–12; Nick Wingfield, "How Apple's Store Strategy Beat the Odds," *Wall Street Journal,* May 17, 2006; Alice Z. Cuneo, "Apple Transcends as Lifestyle Brand," *Advertising Age,* June 15, 2003, pp. S2, S6; Tobi Elkin, "Apple Gambles with Retail Plan," *Advertising Age,* June 24, 2001.

25. Allison Enright, "Shed New Light," *Marketing News,* May 1, 2006, pp. 9–10.

26. "Exclusives Becoming a Common Practice," *DSN Retailing Today,* February 9, 2004, pp. 38, 44.

27. "Trouser Suit," *Economist,* November 24, 2001, p. 56.

28. www.stihlusa.com/corporate/corporate_facts.html.

29. "Nike Says No to Blue-Light Specials," *Fortune,* May 4, 2005.

30. Robert K. Heady, "Online Bank Offers Best Rates," *South Florida Sun-Sentinel,* November 22, 2004.

31. Anderson and Coughlan, "Channel Management: Structure, Governance, and Relationship Management," *Handbook of Marketing* (London: Sage Publications, 2002), pp. 223–47; Michaela Draganska, Daniel Klapper, and Sofia B. Villa-Boas, "A Larger Slice or a Larger Pie? An Empirical Investigation of Bargaining Power in the Distribution Channel," *Marketing Science* 29 (January–February 2010), pp. 57–74.

32. These bases of power were identified in John R. P. French and Bertram Raven, "The Bases of Social Power," Dorwin Cartwright, ed., *Studies in Social Power* (Ann Arbor: University of Michigan Press, 1959), pp. 150–67.

33. Joydeep Srivastava and Dipankar Chakravarti, "Channel Negotiations with Information Asymmetries: Contingent Influences of Communication and Trustworthiness Reputations," *Journal of Marketing Research* 46 (August 2009), pp. 557–72.

34. Daniel Corsten and Nirmalya Kumar, "Do Suppliers Benefit from Collaborative Relationships with Large Retailers? An Empirical Investigation of Efficient Consumer Response Adoption," *Journal of Marketing* 69 (July 2005), pp. 80–94; for some related research, see Ashwin W. Joshi, "Continuous Supplier Performance Improvement: Effects of Collaborative Communication and Control," *Journal of Marketing* 73 (January 2009), pp. 133–50.

35. Russ Mitchell, "Can Dell Save Dell?" *Condé Nast Portfolio*, July 2008, pp. 84–90; Cliff Edwards, "Dell's Do-Over," *BusinessWeek*, October 26, 2009, pp. 37–40; Christopher Helman, "The Second Coming," *Forbes*, December 10, 2007, pp. 79–86; David Whitford, "Uh . . . Maybe I Should Drive," *Fortune,* April 30, 2007, pp. 125–28; Louise Lee, "It's Dell vs. the Dell Way," *BusinessWeek,* March 6, 2006, pp. 61–62; David Kirkpatrick, "Dell in the Penalty Box," *Fortune,* September 18, 2006, pp. 70–78; Nanette Byrnes, Peter Burrows, and Louise Lee, "Dark Days at Dell," *BusinessWeek,* September 4, 2006, pp. 27–30; Elizabeth Corcoran, "A Bad Spell for Dell," *Forbes,* June 19, 2006, pp. 44–46.

36. For a detailed case study example, see Jennifer Shang, Tuba Pinar Yildrim, Pandu Tadikamalla, Vikas Mittal, and Lawrence Brown, "Distribution Network Redesign for Marketing Competitiveness," *Journal of Marketing* 73 (March 2009), pp. 146–63.

37. Xinlei Chen, George John, and Om Narasimhan, "Assessing the Consequences of a Channel Switch," *Marketing Science* 27 (May–June 2008), pp. 398–416.

38. Thomas H. Davenport and Jeanne G. Harris, *Competing on Analytics: The New Science of Winning* (Boston: Harvard Business School Press, 2007).

39. Junhong Chu, Pradeep K. Chintagunta, and Naufel J. Vilcassim, "Assessing the Economic Value of Distribution Channels: An Application to the Personal Computer Industry," *Journal of Marketing Research* 44 (February 2007), pp. 29–41.

40. Bruce Einhorn, "China: Where Retail Dinosaurs Are Thriving," *Bloomberg BusinessWeek*, February 1 and 8, 2010, p. 64.

41. "Unshackling the Chain Stores," *Economist*, May 31, 2008, pp. 69–70.

42. Richard Gibson, "U.S. Franchises Find Opportunities to Grow Abroad," *Wall Street Journal*, August 11, 2009, p. B5.

43. "Crossroads," *Economist*, March 17, 2007, pp. 71–72; "Shopped Around," *Economist*, October 18, 2008, p. 74; Carol Matlack, "A French Wal-Mart's Global Blitz," *BusinessWeek*, December 21, 2009, pp. 64–65.

44. Michael Arndt, "Urban Outfitters Grow-Slow Strategy," *Bloomberg BusinessWeek*, March 1, 2010, p. 56; Michael Arndt, "How to Play It: Apparel Makers," *Bloomberg BusinessWeek*, March 1, 2010, p. 61.

45. Matthew Boyle and Michael V. Copeland, "Tesco Reinvents the 7-Eleven," *Fortune*, November 26, 2007, p. 34.

46. Jenifer Reingold, "The British (Retail) Invasion," *Fortune*, July 7, 2008, pp. 132–38; Ruth La Ferla, "But Will It Play in Manhattan," *New York Times*, June 21, 2006; Damien Reece, "Topshop's Injection of True Brit Stirs Up the Big Apple," *Daily Telegraph*, April 2, 2009.

47. Stefan Wuyts, Stefan Stremersch, Christophe Van Den Bulte, and Philip Hans Franses, "Vertical Marketing Systems for Complex Products: A Triadic Perspective," *Journal of Marketing Research* 41 (November 2004), pp. 479–87.

48. Russell Johnston and Paul R. Lawrence, "Beyond Vertical Integration: The Rise of the Value-Adding Partnership," *Harvard Business Review,* July–August 1988, pp. 94–101. See also, Arnt Bovik and George John, "When Does Vertical Coordination Improve Industrial Purchasing Relationships," *Journal of Marketing* 64 (October 2000), pp. 52–64; Judy A. Siguaw, Penny M. Simpson, and Thomas L. Baker, "Effects of Supplier Market Orientation on Distributor Market Orientation and the Channel Relationship: The Distribution Perspective," *Journal of Marketing* 62 (July 1998), pp. 99–111; Narakesari Narayandas and Manohar U. Kalwani, "Long-Term Manufacturer– Supplier Relationships: Do They Pay Off for Supplier Firms?" *Journal of Marketing* 59 (January 1995), pp. 1–16.

49. Raji Srinivasan, "Dual Distribution and Intangible Firm Value: Franchising in Restaurant Chains," *Journal of Marketing* 70 (July 2006), pp. 120–35.

50. www.citizensbank.com, December 09, 2010.

51. www.disney.com, December 09, 2010; Joyceann Cooney, "Mooney's Kingdom," *License*, October 1, 2006.

52. Coach Inc. Form 10-K filed with SEC on August 19, 2009.

53. Rajkumar Venkatesan, V. Kumar, and Nalini Ravishanker, "Multichannel Shopping: Causes and

Consequences," *Journal of Marketing* 71 (April 2007), pp. 114–32.

54. Based on Rowland T. Moriarty and Ursula Moran, "Marketing Hybrid Marketing Systems," *Harvard Business Review,* November–December 1990, pp. 146–55.

55. Susan Casey, "Eminence Green," *Fortune,* April 2, 2007, pp. 64–70.

56. Barbara Darow, "Oracle's New Partner Path," *CRN,* August 21, 2006, p. 4.

57. Anne Coughlan and Louis Stern, "Marketing Channel Design and Management," Dawn Iacobucci, ed., *Kellogg on Marketing* (New York: John Wiley & Sons, 2001), pp. 247–69.

58. Nirmalya Kumar, "Some Tips on Channel Management," *rediff.com,* July 1, 2005.

59. Matthew Boyle, "Brand Killers," *Fortune,* August 11, 2003, pp. 51–56; for an opposing view, see Anthony J. Dukes, Esther Gal-Or, and Kannan Srinivasan, "Channel Bargaining with Retailer Asymmetry," *Journal of Marketing Research* 43 (February 2006), pp. 84–97.

60. Jerry Useem, Julie Schlosser, and Helen Kim, "One Nation under Wal-Mart," *Fortune* (Europe), March 3, 2003.

61. Sreekumar R. Bhaskaran and Stephen M. Gilbert, "Implications of Channel Structure for Leasing or Selling Durable Goods," *Marketing Science* 28 (September–October 2009), pp. 918–34.

62. For an example of when conflict can be viewed as helpful, see Anil Arya and Brian Mittendorf, "Benefits of Channel Discord in the Sale of Durable Goods," *Marketing Science* 25 (January–February 2006), pp. 91–96; and Nirmalya Kumar, "Living with Channel Conflict," *CMO Magazine,* October 2004.

63. This section draws on Coughlan, Anderson, Stern, and El-Ansary, *Marketing Channels,* Chapter 9. See also, Jonathan D. Hibbard, Nirmalya Kumar, and Louis W. Stern, "Examining the Impact of Destructive Acts in Marketing Channel Relationships," *Journal of Marketing Research* 38 (February 2001), pp. 45–61; Kersi D. Antia and Gary L. Frazier, "The Severity of Contract Enforcement in Interfirm Channel Relationships," *Journal of Marketing* 65 (October 2001), pp. 67–81; James R. Brown, Chekitan S. Dev, and Dong-Jin Lee, "Managing Marketing Channel Opportunism: The Efficiency of Alternative Governance Mechanisms," *Journal of Marketing* 64 (April 2000), pp. 51–65; Alberto Sa Vinhas and Erin Anderson, "How Potential Conflict Drives Channel Structure: Concurrent (Direct and Indirect) Channels," *Journal of Marketing Research* 42 (November 2005), pp. 507–15.

64. Nirmalya Kumar, "Living with Channel Conflict," *CMO Magazine,* October 2004.

65. Andrew Kaplan, "All Together Now?" *Beverage World,* March 2007, pp. 14–16.

66. Christina Passriello, "Fashionably Late? Designer Brands Are Starting to Embrace E-Commerce," *Wall Street Journal,* May 19, 2006.

67. Greg Johnson, "Gray Wail: Southern California Companies Are among the Many Upscale Manufacturers Voicing Their Displeasure about Middlemen Delivering Their Goods into the Hands of Unauthorized Discount Retailers," *Los Angeles Times,* March 30, 1997. Also see Paul R. Messinger and Chakravarthi Narasimhan, "Has Power Shifted in the Grocery Channel?" *Marketing Science* 14 (Spring 1995), pp. 189–223.

68. Joel C. Collier and Carol C. Bienstock, "How Do Customers Judge Quality in an E-tailer," *MIT Sloan Management Review* (Fall 2006), pp. 35–40.

69. *Coremetrics Benchmark December US Retail,* www.coremetrics.com/ downloads/coremetrics-benchmark-industry-report-2008-12-us.pdf.

70. Jeff Borden, "The Right Tools," *Marketing News,* April 15, 2008, pp. 19–21.

71. Alexis K. J. Barlow, Noreen Q. Siddiqui, and Mike Mannion, "Development in Information and Communication Technologies for Retail Marketing Channels," *International Journal of Retail and Distribution Management* 32 (March 2004), pp. 157–63; G&J Electronic Media Services, *7th Wave of the GfK-Online-Monitor* (Hamburg: GfK Press, 2001).

72. Martin Holzwarth, Chris Janiszewski, and Marcus M. Newmann, "The Influence of Avatars on Online Consumer Shopping Behavior," *Journal of Marketing* 70 (October 2006), pp. 19–36.

73. Ann E. Schlosser, Tiffany Barnett White, and Susan M. Lloyd, "Converting Web Site Visitors into Buyers: How Web Site Investment Increases Consumer Trusting Beliefs and Online Purchase Intentions," *Journal of Marketing* 70 (April 2006), pp. 133–48.

74. Ronald Abler, John S. Adams, and Peter Gould, *Spatial Organizations: The Geographer's View of the World* (Upper Saddle River, NJ: Prentice Hall, 1971), pp. 531–32.

75. "China's Pied Piper," *Economist,* September 23, 2006, p. 80; Alibaba.com, www.alibaba.com, December 09, 2010; Garry Barker, "The Treasure Keeps Coming for Alibaba," *The Age,* October 27, 2009; Jessica E. Vascellaro, "Alibaba.com Plans U.S Push," *Wall Street Journal,* August 7, 2009; Bruce Einhorn, "At Alibaba, Investors Come Last," *BusinessWeek,* August 17, 2009, p. 50.

76. For an in-depth academic examination, see John G. Lynch Jr. and Dan Ariely, "Wine Online: Search Costs and Competition on Price, Quality, and Distribution," *Marketing Science* 19 (Winter 2000), pp. 83–103.

77. Andrea Chang, "Retailers Fuse Stores with E-Commerce," *Los Angeles Times,* June 27, 2010.

78. Anjali Cordeiro, "Procter & Gamble Sees Aisle Expansion on the Web," *Wall Street Journal,* September 2, 2009, p. B6A; Anjali Cordeiro and Ellen Byron, "Procter & Gamble to Test Online Store to Study Buying Habits," *Wall Street Journal,* January 15, 2010.

79. Xubing Zhang, "Retailer's Multichannel and Price Advertising Strategies," *Marketing Science* 28 (November–December 2009), pp. 1080–94.

80. Susan Fournier and Lara Lee, "Getting Brand Communities Right," *Harvard Business Review,* April 2009, pp. 105–11; "New Harley Davidson Accessory and Clothing Store," *PRLog,* July 21, 2009; Bob Tedeshi, "How Harley Revved Online Sales," *Business 2.0,* December 2002–January 2003, pp. 44; John W. Schouten, and James H. McAlexander, "Market Impact of a Consumption Subculture: The Harley-Davidson Mystique," Gary J. Bamossy and W. Fred van Raaij, eds., *European Advances in Consumer Research* (Provo, UT: Association for Consumer Research, 1993), pp. 389–93.

81. Nanette Byrnes, "More Clicks at the Bricks," *BusinessWeek,* December 17, 2007, pp. 50–51.

82. Douglas Lamont, *Conquering the Wireless World: The Age of M-Commerce* (New York: John Wiley & Sons, 2001); Herbjørn Nysveen, Per E. Pedersen, Helge Thorbjørnsen, and Pierre Berthon, "Mobilizing the Brand: The Effects of Mobile Services on Brand Relationships and Main Channel Use," *Journal of Service Research* 7 (2005), pp. 257–76; Venkatesh Shankar and Sridhar Balasubramanian, "Mobile Marketing: A Synthesis and Prognosis," *Journal of Interactive Marketing* 23 (2009), pp. 118–29; Venkatesh Shankar, Alladi Venkatesh, Charles Hofacker, and Prasad Naik, "Mobile Marketing in the Retailing Environment: Current Insights and Future Research Avenues," special issue, *Journal of Interactive Marketing,* co-editors Venkatesh Shankar and Manjit Yadav, forthcoming.

83. "The Mobile Internet Report," *Morgan Stanley,* www.morganstanley.com, May 7, 2010.

84. Adam Cahill, Lars Albright, and Carl Howe, "Mobile Advertising and Branding," session as part of the Britt Technology Impact Series, Tuck School of Business, Dartmouth College, March 31, 2010; Alexandre Mars, "Importing Mobile Marketing Tools," *Brandweek,* February 15, 2010, p. 17.

85. Reena Jana, "Retailers Are Learning to Love Smartphones," *BusinessWeek,* October 26, 2009.

86. Nanette Byrnes, "More Clicks at the Bricks," *BusinessWeek,* December 17, 2007, pp. 50–51.

87. Dan Butcher, "Dunkin' Donuts Sweetens Dunkin' Run Campaign with Mobile," *Mobile Marketer,* June 23, 2009; "Dunkin' Donuts Unveils 'Dunkin' Run' Technology to make Group Orders Faster, Easier and More Fun," *Dunkin' Donuts,* press release, June 22, 2009, www.dunkindonuts.com; Rich Mathieson, "Mobile Marketing: Dunkin' Donuts Serves SMS," *Chief Marketer,* July 19, 2006.

Chapter 16

1. Helen Coster, "A Step Ahead," *Forbes,* June 2, 2008, pp. 78–80; Paula Andruss, "Delivering Wow Through Service," *Marketing News,* October 15, 2008, p. 10; Jeffrey M. O'Brien, "Zappos Knows How to Kick It," *Fortune,* February 2, 2009, pp. 55–60; Brian Morrissey, "Amazon to Buy Zappos," *Adweek,* July 22, 2009; Christopher Palmeri, "Now For Sale, the Zappos Culture," *Bloomberg BusinessWeek,* January 11, 2010, p. 57.

2. Karsten Hansen and Vishal Singh, "Market Structure Across Retail Formats," *Marketing Science* 28 (July–August 2009), pp. 656–73.

3. "US Retail E-Commerce Down 3% in Q4, Up Just 6% in 2008," *Retailer Daily,* February 12, 2009.

4. Richard Gibson, "Even 'Copycat' Businesses Require Creativity and Flexibility," *Wall Street Journal Online,* March 2004; *Entrepreneur,* www.entrepreneur.com, December 09, 2010.

5. Raymund Flandez, "New Franchise Idea: Fewer Rules, More Difference," *Wall Street Journal,* September 18, 2007, p. B4.

6. Jena McGregor, "The Hard Sell," *BusinessWeek,* October 26, 2009, pp. 43–45.

7. Joseph Pereira and Ann Zimmerman, "For Toys "R" Us, Holidays Are Open and Shut," *Wall Street Journal,* September 15, 2009, p. B8.

8. Eric Newman, "Retail Design for 2008: Thinking Outside the Box," *Brandweek,* December 17, 2007, p. 26.

9. Scott Cendrowski, "Extreme Retailing," *Fortune,* March 31, 2008, p. 14.

10. Cheryl Lu-Lien Tan, "Hot Kohl's," *Wall Street Journal,* April 16, 2007.

11. "Reinventing the Store—the Future of Retailing," *Economist,* November 22, 2003, pp. 65–68.

12. Matthew Boyle, "IBM Goes Shopping," *Fortune,* November 27, 2006, pp. 77–78; Todd Wasserman, "The Store of the Future," *Brandweek,* December 17, 2007, pp. 23–25; Emma Ritch, "Supermarkets Go Digital," *San Jose Business Journal,* April 11, 2008; Tim Dickey, "Electronic Shelf Labels," *Retail Technology Trends,* February 26, 2010.

13. Michael C. Bellas, "Shopper Marketing's Instant Impact," *Beverage World,* November 2007, p. 18; Richard Westlund, "Bringing Brands to Life: The Power of In-Store Marketing," Special Advertising Supplement to *Adweek,* January 2010.

14. Pierre Chandon, J. Wesley Hutchinson, Eric T. Bradlow, and Scott H. Young, "Does In-Store Marketing Work? Effects of the Number and Position of Shelf Facings on Brand Attention and Evaluation at the Point of Purchase," *Journal of Marketing Research* 73 (November 2009), pp. 1–17.

15. Anthony Dukes and Yunchuan Liu, "In-Store Media and Distribution Channel Coordination," *Marketing Science,* 29 (January–February 2010), pp. 94–107.

16. Michael Freedman, "The Eyes Have It," *Forbes,* September 4, 2006, p. 70.

17. Amy Merrick, "Asking 'What Would Ann Do?'" *Wall Street Journal,* September 15, 2006.

18. Charles Fishman, "The Anarchist's Cookbook," *Fast Company,* July 2004, pp. 70–78; "Whole Foods Market 2009 Annual Report," *Whole Foods Market,* www.wholefoodsmarket.com/company/pdfs/ar09.pdf.

19. Ann Zimmerman and Kris Hudson, "Chasing Upscale Customers Tarnishes Mass-Market Jeweler," *Wall Street Journal*, June 26, 2006; Kris Hudson, "Signet Sparkles with Jewelry Strategy," *Wall Street Journal*, June 26, 2006.

20. "JCPenney Transforms Catalog Strategy to Better Serve Customer Preferences," *BusinessWire*, November 18, 2009; Robert Berner, "JCPenney Gets the Net," *BusinessWeek*, May 7, 2007, p. 70; Robert Berner, "Penney: Back in Fashion," *BusinessWeek*, January 9, 2006, pp. 82–84.

21. Louise Lee, "Catalogs, Catalogs, Everywhere," *BusinessWeek,* December 4, 2006, pp. 32–34; Michael J. Silverstein and Neil Fiske, *Trading Up: The New American Luxury* (New York: Portfolio, 2003); "Victoria's Secret," Case #6-0014, Center for Digital Strategies, Tuck School of Business, Dartmouth College, 2002; www.biz.yahoo.com, December 09, 2010.

22. Jessi Hempel, "Urban Outfitters, Fashion Victim," *BusinessWeek*, July 17, 2006, p. 60.

23. Robert Berner, "To Lure Teenager Mall Rats, You Need the Right Cheese," *BusinessWeek,* June 7, 2004, pp. 96–101; Aeropostale, www.aeropostale.com, December 09, 2010; Jeanine Poggi, "Best in Class: Price Is Right at Aeropostale," TheStreet, www.thestreet.com/story/10514026/best-in-class-price-is-right-at-aeropostale.html, June 16, 2009; "Aeropostale, Inc. Seeks New Faces for Fall Ad Campaign with 'Real Teens 2010' Contest," *PR Newswire*, March 15, 2010.

24. Robert Berner, "Chanel's American in Paris," *BusinessWeek*, January 29, 2007, pp. 70–71.

25. Mark Tatge, "Fun & Games," *Forbes,* January 12, 2004, pp. 138–44.

26. Vanessa O'Connell, "Reversing Field, Macy's Goes Local," *Wall Street Journal*, April 21, 2008.

27. Diane Anderson, "RFID Technology Getting Static in New Hampshire," *Brandweek*, January 23, 2006, p. 13; Mary Catherine O'Conner, "Gillette Fuses RFID with Product Launch," *RFID Journal*, March 27, 2006; "The End of Privacy?" *Consumer Reports,* June 2006, pp. 33–40; Erick Schonfeld, "Tagged for Growth," *Business 2.0,* December 2006, pp. 58–61; "Radio Silence," *Economist*, June 9, 2007, pp. 20–21; Todd Lewan, "The Chipping of America," *Associated Press,* July 29, 2007.

28. Uta Werner, John McDermott, and Greg Rotz, "Retailers at the Crossroads: How to Develop Profitable New Growth Strategies," *Journal of Business Strategy* 25 (2004), pp. 10–17.

29. *ALDI South*, www.aldi-sued.de; *ALDI North*, www.aldi-nord.de.

30. Venkatesh Shankar and Ruth N. Bolton, "An Empirical Analysis of Determinants of Retailer Pricing Strategy," *Marketing Science* 23 (Winter 2004), pp. 28–49.

31. www.target.com, December 09, 2010; Ann Zimmerman, "Staying on Target," *Wall Street Journal*, May 7, 2007; Mya Frazier, "The Latest European Import: Fast Fashion," *Advertising Age*, January 9, 2006, p. 6; Julie Schlosser, "How Target Does It," *Fortune*, October 18, 2004, p. 100; Michelle Conlin, "Look Who's Stalking Walmart," *BusinessWeek*, December 7, 2009, pp. 30–36.

32. Duncan Simester, "Signaling Price Image Using Advertised Prices," *Marketing Science* 14 (Summer 1995), pp. 166–88; see also, Jiwoong Shin, "The Role of Selling Costs in Signaling Price Image," *Journal of Marketing Research* 42 (August 2005), pp. 305–12.

33. Frank Feather, *The Future Consumer* (Toronto: Warwick Publishing, 1994), p. 171. Also see David R. Bell and James M. Lattin, "Shopping Behavior and Consumer Preference for Retail Price Format: Why 'Large Basket' Shoppers Prefer EDLP," *Marketing Science* 17 (Spring 1998), pp. 66–68; Stephen J. Hoch, Xavier Dreeze, and Mary E. Purk, "EDLP, Hi-Lo, and Margin Arithmetic," *Journal of Marketing* 58 (October 1994), pp. 1–15.

34. Sarah Fister Gale, "The Bookstore Battle," *Workforce Management* (January 2004), pp. 51–53.

35. Constance L. Hays, "Retailers Seeking to Lure Customers with Service," *New York Times,* December 1, 2003.

36. Amy Gillentine, "Marketing Groups Ignore Women at Their Own Peril," *Colorado Springs Business Journal*, January 20, 2006; Mary Lou Quinlan, "Women Aren't Buying It," *Brandweek,* June 2, 2003, pp. 20–22.

37. Cecile B. Corral, "Profits Pinched, Kohl's Eyes Market Share," *Home Textiles Today*, February 27, 2009; Ilaina Jones, "Kohl's Looking at Spots in Manhattan," *Reuters*, August 19, 2009; Cametta Coleman, "Kohl's Retail Racetrack," *Wall Street Journal,* March 1, 2000.

38. Mindy Fetterman and Jayne O'Donnell, "Just Browsing at the Mall? That's What *You* Think," *USA Today*, September 1, 2006.

39. "Reinventing the Store," *Economist,* November 22, 2003, pp. 65–68; Moira Cotlier, "Census Releases First E-Commerce Report," *Catalog Age,* May 1, 2001; Associated Press, "Online Sales Boomed at End of 2000," *Star-Tribune of Twin Cities*, February 17, 2001; Kenneth T. Rosen and Amanda L. Howard, "E-Tail: Gold Rush or Fool's Gold?" *California Management Review*, April 1, 2000, pp. 72–100.

40. Velitchka D. Kaltcheva and Barton Weitz, "When Should a Retailer Create an Exciting Store Environment?" *Journal of Marketing* 70 (January 2006), pp. 107–18.

41. For more discussion, see Philip Kotler, "Atmospherics as a Marketing Tool," *Journal of Retailing* (Winter 1973–1974), pp. 48–64. Also see B. Joseph Pine II and James H. Gilmore, *The Experience Economy* (Boston: Harvard Business School Press, 1999).

42. Jeff Cioletti, "Super Marketing," *Beverage World* (November 2006), pp. 60–61.

43. Ben Paynter, "Happy Hour," *Fast Company*, March 2010, p. 34; Jessi Hempel, "Social Media Meets Retailing," *Fortune*, March 22, 2010, p. 30.

44. Carol Tice, "Anchors Away: Department Stores Lose Role at Malls," *Puget Sound Business Journal,* February 13, 2004, p. 1.

45. www.plma.com, April 3, 2010; Emily Bryson York, "Don't Blame Private Label Gains on the Recession," *Advertising Age*, April 21, 2009.

46. Kusum Ailawadi and Bari Harlam, "An Empirical Analysis of the Determinants of Retail Margins: The Role of Store-Brand Share," *Journal of Marketing* 68 (January 2004), pp. 147–65.

47. For a detailed analysis of contemporary research on private labels, see Michael R. Hyman, Dennis A. Kopf, and Dongdae Lee, "Review of Literature—Future Research Suggestions: Private Label Brands: Benefits, Success Factors, and Future Research, *Journal of Brand Management* 17 (March 2010), pp. 368–89. See also, Kusum Ailawadi, Bari Harlam, Jacques Cesar, and David Trounce, "Retailer Promotion Profitability: The Role of Promotion, Brand, Category, and Market Characteristics," *Journal of Marketing Research* 43 (November 2006), pp. 518–35; Kusum Ailawadi, Koen Pauwels, and Jan-Benedict E. M. Steenkamp, "Private Label Use and Store Loyalty," *Journal of Marketing* 72 (November 2008), pp. 19–30.

48. Natasha Singer, "Drug Firms Apply Brand to Generics," *New York Times*, February 16, 2010; Casey Feldman, "Generic Drug Superstars," *Fortune*, August 5, 2009; Mina Kimes, "Teva: The King of Generic Drugs," *Fortune*, August 5, 2009; Jeanne Whalen, "Betting $10 Billion on Generics, Novartis Seeks to Inject Growth," *Wall Street Journal*, May 4, 2006.

49. Michael Felding, "No Longer Plain, Simple," *Marketing News*, May 15, 2006, pp. 11–13; Rob Walker, "Shelf Improvement," *New York Times*, May 7, 2006.

50. Sonia Reyes, "Saving Private Labels," *Brandweek*, May 8, 2006, pp. 30–34; Andrew Martin, "Store Brands Lift Grocers in Troubled Times," *New York Times*, December 13, 2008.

51. Jim Chrizan, "Loblaw's Reverses Private Label Trend," *Packaging World*, January 22, 2010; "Loblaw Launches a New Line of Discount Store Brands," *Store Brand Decisions*, February 16, 2010; John J. Pierce, "Private Label Stimulus," *Private Label,* March/April 2009.

52. Brett Nelson, "Stuck in the Middle," *Forbes*, August 15, 2005, p. 88; "Arrow Investor Fact Sheet 2009," *Arrow*, www.arrow.com.

53. James A. Narus and James C. Anderson, "Contributing as a Distributor to Partnerships with Manufacturers," *Business Horizons* (September– October 1987). Also see Hlavecek and McCuistion, "Industrial Distributors—When, Who, and How," pp. 96–101.

54. www.grainger.com/Grainger/wwg/start.shtml, May 8, 2010; Sean Callahan, "Close-up with Deb Oler, VP-Grainger Industrial Supply Brand, W.W. Grainger," *BtoB*, March 3, 2010; Ian Heller, "The Secret of Being Grainger," www.ezinearticles.com, April 30, 2010.

55. "Who Has The Top Consumer Goods Industry Supply Chains for 2008?" *Supply Chain News*, December 17, 2008; "Who Has The Top Retail Industry Supply Chains for 2008?" *Supply Chain News*, January 5, 2009.

56. Johnson & Johnson 2007 Sustainability Report; talk by panelist Chris Hacker, "Production Innovation and Supply Chains: Creating Value for the Next Generation," *Business and Society Conference*, Tuck School of Business at Dartmouth College, January 15, 2009.

57. William C. Copacino, *Supply Chain Management* (Boca Raton, FL: St. Lucie Press, 1997); Robert Shaw and Philip Kotler, "Rethinking the Chain: Making Marketing Leaner, Faster, and Better," *Marketing Management* (July/August 2009), pp. 18–23.

58. "Shrink Rapped," *Economist*, May 17, 2008, p. 80.

59. "U.S. Logistics Cost 10% of GDP," *Logistics Today*, June 26, 2008.

60. Pete Engardio, "Lean and Mean Gets Extreme," *BusinessWeek*, March 23 and 30, 2009, pp. 60–62; Traci Gregory, "ConMed Takes Lean Approach," *Central New York Business Journal*, May 22, 2009.

61. Daisuke Wakabayashi, "How Lean Manufacturing Can Backfire," *Wall Street Journal*, January 30, 2010; for some additional discussion of the downside of lean manufacturing, see Brian Hindo, "At 3M, A Struggle between Efficiency and Creativity," *BusinessWeek*, June 11, 2007.

62. The optimal order quantity is given by the formula $Q^* = 2DS/IC$, where D = annual demand, S = cost to place one order, and I = annual carrying cost per unit. Known as the economic-order quantity formula, it assumes a constant ordering cost, a constant cost of carrying an additional unit in inventory, a known demand, and no quantity discounts. For further reading on this subject, see Richard J. Tersine, *Principles of Inventory and Materials Management,* 4th ed. (Upper Saddle River, NJ: Prentice Hall, 1994).

63. William C. Copacino, *Supply Chain Management* (Boca Raton, FL: St. Lucie Press, 1997), pp. 122–23.

64. "Shining Examples," *Economist: A Survey of Logistics*, June 17, 2006, pp. 4–6.

65. Renee DeGross, "Retailers Try eBay Overstocks, Returns for Sale Online," *Atlanta Journal-Constitution*, April 10, 2004.

66. Chuck Salter, "Savvy, with Hints of Guile and Resourcefulness," *Fast Company*, February 2007, p. 50; Heather Mcpherson, "Lots to Like about This Concept: As a Wine Négociant, Cameron Hughes Can Offer Premium Wines at Affordable Prices," *Knight Ridder Tribune Business News*, February 21, 2007, p. 1; Phaedrea Hise and Joanne Chen, "Sleeping with the Boss," *Forbes Small Business*, February 2008, pp. 68–78; Maureen Farrell, "Wine Workout," *Forbes*, March 30, 2009, pp. 64–65.

67. "Manufacturing Complexity," *Economist: A Survey of Logistics*, June 17, 2006, pp. 6–9.

68. Perry A. Trunick, "Nailing a Niche in Logistics," *Logistics Today*, March 4, 2008.

Chapter 17

1. Ken Romanzi, "Reintroducing the Cranberry to America!" Talk at the Tuck School of Business at Dartmouth," January 7, 2010; "Breakaway Brands: Ocean Spray Tells It Straight from the Bog," *MediaPost*, October 9, 2006; Francis J. Kelly III and Barry Silverstein, *The Breakaway Brand* (New York: McGraw-Hill, 2005).

2. Xueming Luo and Naveen Donthu, "Marketing's Credibility: A Longitudinal Investigation of Marketing Communication Productivity and Shareholder Value," *Journal of Marketing* 70 (October 2006), pp. 70–91.

3. Margaret Coker, "Dubai Pulls Out the Stops—for Naming Metro Stations, Lines Offered as Vehicles," *Wall Street Journal*, August 8, 2008; Linda Childers, "Can't-Escape TV," *Fast Company*, July/August 2008, p. 46; Louise Story, "Anywhere the Eye Can See, It's Likely to See an Ad," *New York Times*, January 15, 2007; Laura Petrecca, "Product Placement—You Can't Escape It," *USA Today*, October 11, 2006.

4. Burt Helm, "Attention-Deficit Advertising," *BusinessWeek*, May 5, 2008, p. 50; "Motorola's 'Say Goodbye' Campaign at Hong Kong Airport," *MobiAD News*, February 20, 2008.

5. Vanessa L. Facenda, "Kimberly-Clark's Paper Trail Leads to Creative Marketing," *Brandweek*, January 14, 2008, p. 11.

6. Stuart Elliott, "Covering Many Bases for a Brand of Blue Jeans," *New York Times*, August 13, 2009; Giselle Tsirulnik, "Gap Finds Right Fit with Mobile for New Jeans Campaign," *Mobile Marketer*, October 5, 2009; "Gap Introduces America's Best-Fitting Premium Jeans," *PRNewswire*, August 13, 2009; Jean-Claude Larreche, "Gap Lacked Momentum, So Rightly Cut TV," *Advertising Age*, June 23, 2008, p. 26.

7. Some of these definitions are adapted from Peter D. Bennett, ed., *Dictionary of Marketing Terms* (Chicago: American Marketing Association, 1995).

8. Tom Duncan and Sandra Moriarty, "How Integrated Marketing Communication's 'Touch Points' Can Operationalize the Service-Dominant Logic," Robert F. Lusch and Stephen L. Vargo, eds., *The Service-Dominant Logic of Marketing: Dialog, Debate, and Directions* (Armonk, NY: M.E. Sharpe, 2006); Tom Duncan, *Principles of Advertising and IMC,* 2nd ed. (New York: McGraw-Hill/Irwin, 2005).

9. Noreen O'Leary, "Mint's Fresh Approach: Marketing on $700 a Year," *Brandweek*, October 12, 2009, p. 4; Coloribus Global Advertising Archive, www.coloribus.com, December 09, 2010.

10. Theresa Howard, "Multiplatform Ads Clean Up at Cannes," *USA Today*, June 29, 2009, p. 3B; Kate Nettleton, "Tribal DDB Amsterdam's 'Carousel' for Philips Scoops Cannes Lions 2009 Film Grand Prix," *Campaign*, June 29, 2009; Daniel Farey-Jones, "Philips Promotes Home Cinema Range with Online Film Premiere," *Campaign*, February 18, 2010.

11. For an alternate communications model developed specifically for advertising communications, see Barbara B. Stern, "A Revised Communication Model for Advertising: Multiple Dimensions of the Source, the Message, and the Recipient," *Journal of Advertising* (June 1994), pp. 5–15. For some additional perspectives, see Tom Duncan and Sandra E. Morarity, "A Communication-Based Marketing Model for Managing Relationships," *Journal of Marketing* 62 (April 1998), pp. 1–13.

12. Demetrios Vakratsas and Tim Ambler, "How Advertising Works: What Do We Really Know?" *Journal of Marketing* 63 (January 1999), pp. 26–43.

13. This section is based on the excellent text, John R. Rossiter and Larry Percy, *Advertising and Promotion Management,* 2nd ed. (New York: McGraw-Hill, 1997).

14. "GE Gets Smart with Energy Awareness," *Special Advertising Section to Adweek and Brandweek*, October 14, 2009; "GE Plucks an Online Winner with Smart Grid," *Special Advertising Section to Adweek and Brandweek*, October 14, 2009; "Smart Grid," *GE*, http://ge.ecomagination.com/smartgrid; "Augmented Reality: Real Meets Virtual," *BizTechTalk*, February 25, 2009.

15. James F. Engel, Roger D. Blackwell, and Paul W. Minard, *Consumer Behavior,* 9th ed. (Fort Worth, TX: Dryden, 2001).

16. John R. Rossiter and Larry Percy, *Advertising and Promotion Management,* 2nd ed. (New York: McGraw-Hill, 1997).

17. James F. Engel, Roger D. Blackwell, and Paul W. Minard, *Consumer Behavior,* 9th ed. (Fort Worth, TX: Dryden, 2001).

18. Ayn E. Crowley and Wayne D. Hoyer, "An Integrative Framework for Understanding Two-Sided Persuasion," *Journal of Consumer Research* 20 (March 1994), pp. 561–74.

19. C. I. Hovland, A. A. Lumsdaine, and F. D. Sheffield, *Experiments on Mass Communication,* vol. 3 (Princeton, NJ: Princeton University Press, 1949); Crowley and Hoyer, "An Integrative Framework for Understanding Two-Sided Persuasion." For an alternative viewpoint, see George E. Belch, "The Effects of Message Modality on One- and Two-Sided Advertising Messages," Richard P. Bagozzi and Alice M. Tybout, eds., *Advances in Consumer Research* (Ann Arbor, MI: Association for Consumer Research, 1983), pp. 21–26.

20. Curtis P. Haugtvedt and Duane T. Wegener, "Message Order Effects in Persuasion: An Attitude Strength Perspective," *Journal of Consumer Research* 21 (June 1994), pp. 205–18; H. Rao Unnava, Robert E. Burnkrant, and Sunil Erevelles, "Effects of Presentation Order and Communication Modality on Recall and Attitude," *Journal of Consumer Research* 21 (December 1994), pp. 481–90.

21. Sternthal and Craig, *Consumer Behavior,* pp. 282–84. Sternthal and Craig, *Consumer Behavior: An Information Processing Perspective* (Englewood Cliffs, NJ: Prentice-Hall, 1982), pp. 282–84.

22. Michael R. Solomon, *Consumer Behavior,* 7th ed. (Upper Saddle River, NJ: Prentice Hall, 2007).

23. Some recent research on humor in advertising, for example, includes: Haseeb Shabbir and Des Thwaites, "The Use of Humor to Mask Deceptive Advertising: It's No Laughing Matter," *Journal of Advertising* 36 (Summer 2007), pp. 75–85; Thomas W. Cline and James J. Kellaris, "The Influence of Humor Strength and Humor Message Relatedness on Ad Memorability: A Dual Process Model," *Journal of Advertising* 36 (Spring 2007), pp. 55–67; H. Shanker Krishnan and Dipankar Chakravarti, "A Process Analysis of the Effects of Humorous Advertising Executions on Brand Claims Memory," *Journal of Consumer Psychology* 13 (2003), pp. 230–45.

24. "Follies," *Advertising Age*, December 14, 2009, p. 20.

25. Rik Pieters and Michel Wedel, "Attention Capture and Transfer in Advertising: Brand, Pictorial, and Text-Size Effects," *Journal of Marketing* 68 (April 2004), pp. 36–50.

26. Herbert C. Kelman and Carl I. Hovland, "Reinstatement of the Communication in Delayed Measurement of Opinion Change," *Journal of Abnormal and Social Psychology* 48 (July 1953), pp. 327–35.

27. David J. Moore, John C. Mowen, and Richard Reardon, "Multiple Sources in Advertising Appeals: When Product Endorsers Are Paid by the Advertising Sponsor," *Journal of the Academy of Marketing Science* 13 (Summer 1994), pp. 234–43.

28. C. E. Osgood and P. H. Tannenbaum, "The Principles of Congruity in the Prediction of Attitude Change," *Psychological Review* 62 (January 1955), pp. 42–55.

29. Brian Morrissey, "Traditional Ads Yield Social Traction," *Adweek*, May 16, 2010.

30. "Face-to-Face Report," American Business Media, January 2010; "John Deere Face-to-Face Campaign Races Past Competition," *Special Advertising Section to Adweek and Brandweek*, October 14, 2009; Gyro HSR, www.gyrohsr.com.

31. Suzanne Vranca, "New to the TV Lineup: A Flat-Panel Teaser LG Uses Ruse of Show to Market Its Screen," *Wall Street Journal*, April 29, 2008.

32. Adapted from G. Maxwell Ule, "A Media Plan for 'Sputnik' Cigarettes," *How to Plan Media Strategy* (American Association of Advertising Agencies, 1957 Regional Convention), pp. 41–52.

33. Thomas C. Kinnear, Kenneth L. Bernhardt, and Kathleen A. Krentler, *Principles of Marketing,* 6th ed. (New York: HarperCollins, 1995).

34. K. Sridhar Moorthy and Scott A. Hawkins, "Advertising Repetition and Quality Perceptions," *Journal of Business Research* 58 (March 2005), pp. 354–60; Amna Kirmani and Akshay R. Rao, "No Pain, No Gain: A Critical Review of the Literature on Signaling Unobservable Product Quality," *Journal of Marketing* 64 (April 2000), pp. 66–79; Amna Kirmani, "The Effect of Perceived Advertising Costs on Brand Perceptions," *Journal of Consumer Research* 17 (September 17, 1990), pp. 160–71; Amna Kirmani and Peter Wright, "Money Talks: Perceived Advertising Expense and Expected Product Quality," *Journal of Consumer Research* 16 (December 1989), pp. 344–53.

35. Demetrios Vakratsas and Tim Ambler, "How Advertising Works: What Do We Really Know?" *Journal of Marketing* 63 (January 1999), pp. 26–43.

36. Levitt, *Industrial Purchasing Behavior: A Study in Communication Effects* (Boston, MA: Harvard University Division of Research, 1965).

37. "Let's Build a Smarter Planet," *Effie Worldwide*, www.effie.org/winners/showcase/2010/; "IBM Smarter Planet Campaign from Ogilvy & Mather Wins Global Effie," *PRNewswire*, June 9, 2010; Jeffrey M. O'Brien, "IBM's Grand Plan to Save the Planet," *Fortune*, April 21, 2009.

38. Prasad A. Naik and Kalyan Raman, "Understanding the Impact of Synergy in Multimedia Communications," *Journal of Marketing Research* 40 (November 2003), pp. 375–88. See also, Prasad A. Naik, Kalyan Raman, and Russell S. Winer, "Planning Marketing-Mix Strategies in the Presence of Interaction Effects," *Marketing Science* 24 (January 2005), pp. 25–34.

39. Scott Neslin, *Sales Promotion*, MSI Relevant Knowledge Series (Cambridge, MA: Marketing Science Institute, 2002).

40. Markus Pfeiffer and Markus Zinnbauer, "Can Old Media Enhance New Media?" *Journal of Advertising Research* (March 2010), pp. 42–49.

41. Ellen Neuborne, "Ads That Actually Sell Stuff," *Business 2.0,* June 2004, p. 78.

42. Sreedhar Madhavaram, Vishag Badrinarayanan, and Robert E. McDonald, "Integrated Marketing Communication (IMC) and Brand Identity as Critical Components of Brand Equity Strategy," *Journal of Advertising* 34 (Winter 2005), pp. 69–80; Mike Reid, Sandra Luxton, and Felix Mavondo, "The Relationship between Integrated Marketing Communication, Market Orientation, and Brand Orientation," *Journal of Advertising* 34 (Winter 2005), pp. 11–23.

43. Don E. Schultz and Heidi Schultz, *IMC, The Next Generation: Five Steps for Delivering Value and Measuring Financial Returns* (New York: McGraw-Hill, 2003); Don E. Shultz, Stanley I. Tannenbaum, and Robert F. Lauterborn, *Integrated Marketing Communications: Putting It Together and Making It Work* (Lincolnwood, IL: NTC Business Books, 1992).

44. Bruce Horovitz, "Super Bowl Marketers Go All Out to Create Hype, Online Buzz," *USA Today*, February 8, 2010.

Chapter 18

1. Dan Sewall, "Old Spice Rolls Out New Ads," *Associated Press*, July 1, 2010; Adam Tschorn, "Old Spice Ad Connects Women to Male Brand with a Wink," *Los Angeles Times*, March 6, 2010; Mary Elizabeth Williams, "Take That, Super Bowl," *Salon.com*, www.salon.com, February 22, 2010.

2. Paul F. Nunes and Jeffrey Merrihue, "The Continuing Power of Mass Advertising," *Sloan Management Review* (Winter 2007), pp. 63–69.

3. Jack Neff, "'Broken' Ad Model Holds Big Advantages for P&G," *Advertising Age*, March 5, 2007.

4. Russell H. Colley, *Defining Advertising Goals for Measured Advertising Results* (New York: Association of National Advertisers, 1961).

5. Wilfred Amaldoss and Chuan He, "Product Variety, Informative Advertising, and Price Competition," *Journal of Marketing Research* 47 (February 2010), pp. 146–56.

6. Dale Buss, "OnStar First Aid," *Brandchannel*, www.brandchannel.com, February 15, 2010; "OnStar Expands TV Campaign Ads Based on Real-Life Stories," *Road & Travel Magazine*, November 5, 2003.

7. "Responses to Comparative Advertising," *Journal of Consumer Research* 32 (March 2006), pp. 530–40; Dhruv Grewal, Sukumar Kavanoor, and James Barnes, "Comparative versus Noncomparative Advertising: A Meta-Analysis," *Journal of Marketing* 61 (October 1997), pp. 1–15; Randall L. Rose, Paul W. Miniard, Michael J. Barone, Kenneth C. Manning, and Brian D. Till, "When Persuasion Goes Undetected: The Case of Comparative Advertising," *Journal of Marketing Research* 30 (August 1993), pp. 315–30.

8. Rajesh Chandy, Gerard J. Tellis, Debbie MacInnis, and Pattana Thaivanich, "What to Say When: Advertising Appeals in Evolving Markets," *Journal of Marketing Research* 38 (November 2001); Gerard J. Tellis, Rajesh Chandy, and Pattana Thaivanich, "Decomposing the Effects of Direct Advertising: Which Brand Works, When, Where, and How Long?" *Journal of Marketing Research* 37 (February 2000), pp. 32–46; Peter J. Danaher, André Bonfrer, and Sanjay Dhar, "The Effect of Competitive Advertising," *Journal of Marketing Research* 45 (April 2008), pp. 211–25; Donald E. Schultz, Dennis Martin, and William P. Brown, *Strategic Advertising Campaigns* (Chicago: Crain Books, 1984), pp. 192–97.

9. Demetrios Vakratsas, Fred M. Feinberg, Frank M. Bass, and Gurumurthy Kalyanaram, "The Shape of Advertising Response Functions Revisited: A Model of Dynamic Probabilistic Thresholds," *Marketing Science* 23 (Winter 2004), pp. 109–19; for an excellent review, see Greg Allenby and Dominique Hanssens, "Advertising Response," Marketing Science Institute, *Special Report*, No. 05-200, 2005.

10. Leonard M. Lodish, Magid Abraham, Stuart Kalmenson, Jeanne Livelsberger, Beth Lubetkin, Bruce Richardson, and Mary Ellen Stevens, "How T.V. Advertising Works: A Meta-Analysis of 389 Real-World Split Cable T.V. Advertising Experiments," *Journal of Marketing Research* 32 (May 1995), pp. 125–39.

11. Greg Allenby and Dominique Hanssens, "Advertising Response," Marketing Science Institute, *Special Report*, No. 05-200, 2005; Jack Neff, "TV Doesn't Sell Package Goods," *Advertising Age*, May 24, 2004, pp. 1, 30.

12. Cleve Langton, "Searching for the Holy Global Ad Grail," *Brandweek*, June 5, 2006, p. 16.

13. Jeff Manning, "Got Milk?" *Associations Now*, July 1, 2006, pp. 56–61; Jeff Manning and Kevin Lane Keller, "Making Advertising Work: How Got Milk? Marketing Stopped a 20-Year Sales Decline," *Marketing Management* (January–February 2003); Jeff Manning, *Got Milk? The Book* (New York: Prima Lifestyles, 1999).

14. Eric Pfanner, "When Consumers Help, Ads Are Free," *New York Times*, June 22, 2009, p. B6; Elisabeth Sullivan, "H. J. Heinz: Consumers Sit in the Director's Chair for Viral Effort," *Marketing News*, February 10, 2008, p. 10; Louise Story, "The High Price of Creating Free Ads," *New York Times*, May 26, 2007; Laura Petrecca, "Madison Avenue Wants You! (or at Least Your Videos)," *USA Today*, June 21, 2007; Eric Pfanner, "Leave It to the Professionals? Hey, Let Consumers Make Their Own Ads," *New York Times*, August 4, 2006.

15. Ruth Lamperd, "Vegemite Product Renamed Vegemite Cheesybite after iSnack 2.0 was Dumped," *Herald Sun*, October 7, 2009; "Follies," *Advertising Age*, December 14, 2009, p. 20.

16. Daniel P. Amos, "How I Did It: Aflac's CEO Explains How He Fell for the Duck," *Harvard Business Review*, January–February 2010; Stuart Elliott, "Not Daffy or Donald, But Still Aflac's Rising Star," *New York Times*, April 22, 2009; Kathleen Sampey, "Q&A: Aflac CMO Herbert," *Adweek*, October 16, 2006; Ron Insana, "Insurance Business Just Ducky for AFLAC," *USA Today*, July 5, 2005; Chad Bray, "If It Quacks, It May Be an Insurance Ad," *Wall Street Journal*, April 2, 2003; Stuart Elliott, "Why a Duck? Because It Sells Insurance," *New York Times*, June 24, 2002.

17. "Scarborough Writes a Refreshing Headline for the Newspaper Industry: Three-Quarters of Adults Are Reading Newspapers, in Print or Online," *Scarborough Research*, www.scarborough.com; Joseph Plambeck, "Newspaper Circulation Falls Nearly 9%," *New York Times*, April 26, 2010.

18. Jeremy Mullman, "Breaking with Bottle Fires Up Absolut Sales," *Advertising Age*, February 18, 2008; Andrew McMains, "'Absolut World' Debuts," *Adweek*, April 27, 2007; Stuart Elliott, "In an 'Absolut World,' a Vodka Could Use the Same Ads for More than 25 Years," *New York Times*, April 27, 2007; Theresa Howard, "Absolut Gets into Spirit of Name Play with New Ads," *USA Today*, January 16, 2006.

19. "The Infinite Dial 2009," *Arbitron*, April 2009.

20. *Department for Transport*, www.dft.gov.uk; *Radio Advertising Awards*, www.radioadvertisingawards.co.uk.

21. Kim Bartel Sheehan, *Controversies in Contemporary Advertising* (Thousand Oaks, CA: Sage, 2003).

22. Sarah Hills, "McNeil and Sugar Association Settle Splenda Dispute," *Food Navigator-usa.com*, www.foodnavigator-usa.com, November 18, 2008; James P. Miller, "Bitter Sweets Fight Ended," *Chicago*

Tribune, May 12, 2007; Avery Johnson, "How Sweet It Isn't: Maker of Equal Says Ads for J&J's Splenda Misled; Chemistry Lesson for Jurors," *Wall Street Journal*, April 6, 2007. For a discussion of the possible role of corrective advertising, see Peter Darke, Laurence Ashworth, and Robin J. B. Ritchie, "Damage from Corrective Advertising: Causes and Cures," *Journal of Marketing* 72 (November 2008), pp. 81–97.

23. For further reading, see Dorothy Cohen, *Legal Issues in Marketing Decision Making* (Cincinnati, OH: South-Western, 1995).

24. Jim Kavanagh, "Ad Council Gets Creative to Get Your Attention," *CNN*, www.cnn.com, September 2, 2009.

25. Schultz et al., *Strategic Advertising Campaigns* (Chicago: NTC/Contemporary Publishing Company, September 1994), p. 340.

26. Prashant Malaviya, "The Moderating Influence of Advertising Context on Ad Repetition Effects: The Role of Amount and Type of Elaboration," *Journal of Consumer Research* 34 (June 2007), pp. 32–40.

27. Elena Malykhina, "GEICO Poses 'Rhetorical Questions,'" *Brandweek*, December 28, 2009; Adam Armbruster, "GEICO Takes Varied Roads to Consumers," *Television Week*, March 12, 2007, p. 10; Rob Walker, "Pop-Culture Evolution," *New York Times Magazine*, April 15, 2007; *Yahoo Finance*, http://biz.yahoo.com/ic/10/10616.html.

28. Sam Jaffe, "Easy Riders," *American Demographics*, March 2004, pp. 20–23.

29. Max Chafkin, "Ads and Atmospherics," *Inc.*, February 2007.

30. Stephanie Clifford, "Billboards That Look Back," *New York Times*, May 31, 2008.

31. Abbey Klaassen and Andrew Hampp, "Inside Outdoor's Digital Makeover," *Advertising Age: Creativity*, June 14, 2010, p. 5.

32. Abbey Klaassen and Andrew Hampp, "Inside Outdoor's Digital Makeover," *Advertising Age: Creativity*, June 14, 2010, p. 5.

33. Jon Fine, "Where Are Advertisers? At the Movies," *BusinessWeek*, May 25, 2009, pp. 65–66; "Advertisers Go Outside to Play," *AdweekMedia*, March 9, 2009, p. 1; Zack O'Malley Greenburg, "Take Your Brand for a Ride," *Forbes*, March 2, 2009, p. 67.

34. Jeff Pelline, "New Commercial Twist in Corporate Restrooms," *San Francisco Chronicle*, October 6, 1986.

35. Brian Steinberg and Suzanne Vranica, "Prime-Time TV's New Guest Stars: Products," *Wall Street Journal*, January 13, 2004; Michael A. Wiles and Anna Danielova, "The Worth of Product Placement in Successful Films: An Event Study Analysis," *Journal of Marketing* 73 (July 2009), pp. 44–63; Siva K. Balasubramanian, James Karrh, and Hemant Patwardhan, "Audience Response to Product Placements: An Integrative Framework and Future Research Agenda," *Journal of Advertising* 35 (2006),

pp. 115–41; Cristel A. Russell and Barbara Stern, "Consumers, Characters, and Products: A Balance Model of Sitcom Product Placement Effects," *Journal of Advertising* 35 (2006), pp. 7–18; Cristel A. Russell and Michael Belch, "A Managerial Investigation into the Product Placement Industry," *Journal of Advertising Research* 45 (2005), pp. 73–92.

36. Stephanie Clifford, "Product Placements Acquire a Life of Their Own on Shows," *New York Times*, July 14, 2008; "FCC Opens Inquiry into Stealthy TV Product Placement," *Associated Press*, June 26, 2008; Chris Reidy, "Staples Gets an Office Encore," *Boston Globe*, November 4, 2006; James L. Johnston, "Branded Entertainment: The Old Is New Again and More Complicated Than Ever," *Journal of Sponsorship* 2 (February 2009), pp. 170–75.

37. Popai, www.popai.com, accessed August 22, 2010.

38. Ram Bezawada, S. Balachander, P. K. Kannan, and Venkatesh Shankar, "Cross-Category Effects of Aisle and Display Placements: A Spatial Modeling Approach and Insights," *Journal of Marketing* 73 (May 2009), pp. 99–117; Pierre Chandon, J. Wesley Hutchinson, Eric T. Bradlow, and Scott H. Young, "Does In-Store Marketing Work? Effects of the Number and Position of Shelf Facings on Brand Attention and Evaluation at the Point of Purchase," *Journal of Marketing* 73 (November 2009), pp. 1–17.

39. Bill Yackey, "Walmart Reveals 18-Month Results for SMART Network," *Digital Signage Today*, February 23, 2010; Mark Friedman, "Walmart's New In-Store Ads Turning Heads," *Arkansas Business*, September 22, 2008; Laura Petrecca, "Wal-Mart TV Sells Marketers Flexibility," *USA Today*, March 29, 2007.

40. Daniel Terdiman, "McDonald's Is Lead Sponsor of Olympics-Themed ARG, 'The Lost Ring,'" *CNET News*, March 6, 2008; Stephanie Clifford, "An Online Game So Mysterious Its Famous Sponsor Is Hidden," *New York Times*, April 1, 2008; Ben Arnoldy, "Wisdom of the Crowd Triumphs in Alternate Reality Games," *Christian Science Monitor*, March 26, 2008.

41. Brian Steinberg, "'Sunday Night Football' Remains Costliest TV Show," *Advertising Age*, October 26, 2009.

42. "4A's Television Production Cost Survey," *4A's*, www.aaaa.org, December 15, 2009.

43. For more on other media context effects, see Michael A. Kamins, Lawrence J. Marks, and Deborah Skinner, "Television Commercial Evaluation in the Context of Program-Induced Mood: Congruency versus Consistency Effects," *Journal of Advertising*, June 1991, pp. 1–14; see also, Jing Wang and Bobby J. Calder, "Media Transportation and Advertising," *Journal of Consumer Research* 33 (September 2006), pp. 151–62.

44. Kenneth R. Lord, Myung-Soo Lee, and Paul L. Sauer, "Program Context Antecedents of Attitude toward Radio Commercials," *Journal of the Academy of Marketing Science* 13 (Winter 1994), pp. 3–15; Kenneth R. Lord and Robert E. Burnkrant, "Attention

versus Distraction: The Interactive Effect of Program Involvement and Attentional Devices on Commercial Processing," *Journal of Advertising* (March 1993), pp. 47–60.

45. Roland T. Rust, *Advertising Media Models: A Practical Guide* (Lexington, MA: Lexington Books, 1986).

46. Hani I. Mesak, "An Aggregate Advertising Pulsing Model with Wearout Effects," *Marketing Science* 11 (Summer 1992), pp. 310–26; Fred M. Feinberg, "Pulsing Policies for Aggregate Advertising Models," *Marketing Science* 11 (Summer 1992), pp. 221–34.

47. David B. Montgomery and Alvin J. Silk, "Estimating Dynamic Effects of Market Communications Expenditures," *Management Science* (June 1972), pp. 485–501; Kristian S. Palda, *The Measurement of Cumulative Advertising Effect* (Upper Saddle River, NJ: Prentice Hall, 1964), p. 87.

48. Gerard J. Tellis, Rajesh K. Chandy, and Pattana Thaivanich, "Which Ad Works, When, Where, and How Often? Modeling the Effects of Direct Television Advertising," *Journal of Marketing Research* 37 (February 2000), pp. 32–46; Ajay Kalra and Ronald C. Goodstein, "The Impact of Advertising Positioning Strategies on Consumer Price Sensitivity," *Journal of Marketing Research* (May 1998), pp. 210–24; Anil Kaul and Dick R. Wittink, "Empirical Generalizations about the Impact of Advertising on Price Sensitivity and Price," *Marketing Science* 14 (Summer 1995), pp. G151–60; David Walker and Tony M. Dubitsky, "Why Liking Matters," *Journal of Advertising Research,* May–June 1994, pp. 9–18; Abhilasha Mehta, "How Advertising Response Modeling (ARM) Can Increase Ad Effectiveness," *Journal of Advertising Research* (May–June 1994), pp. 62–74; John Deighton, Caroline Henderson, and Scott Neslin, "The Effects of Advertising on Brand Switching and Repeat Purchasing," *Journal of Marketing Research* 31 (February 1994), pp. 28–43; Karin Holstius, "Sales Response to Advertising," *International Journal of Advertising* 9 (September 1990), pp. 38–56.

49. Nigel Hollis, "The Future of Tracking Studies," *Admap*, October 2004, pp. 151–53.

50. From Robert C. Blattberg and Scott A. Neslin, *Sales Promotion: Concepts, Methods, and Strategies* (Upper Saddle River, NJ: Prentice Hall, 1990). This text provides a detailed, analytical treatment of sales promotion. An comprehensive review of academic work on sales promotions can be found in Scott Neslin, "Sales Promotion," Bart Weitz and Robin Wensley, eds., *Handbook of Marketing* (London: Sage, 2002), pp. 310–38.

51. Kusum Ailawadi, Karen Gedenk, and Scott A. Neslin, "Heterogeneity and Purchase Event Feedback in Choice Models: An Empirical Analysis with Implications for Model Building," *International Journal of Research in Marketing* 16 (September 1999), pp. 177–98. See also, Kusum L. Ailawadi, Karen Gedenk, Christian Lutzky, and Scott A. Neslin, "Decomposition of the Sales Impact of Promotion-Induced Stockpiling,"

Journal of Marketing Research 44 (August 2007); Eric T. Anderson and Duncan Simester, "The Long-Run Effects of Promotion Depth on New versus Established Customers: Three Field Studies," *Marketing Science* 23 (Winter 2004), pp. 4–20; Luc Wathieu, A. V. Muthukrishnan, and Bart J. Bronnenberg. "The Asymmetric Effect of Discount Retraction on Subsequent Choice," *Journal of Consumer Research* 31 (December 2004), pp. 652–65; Praveen Kopalle, Carl F. Mela, and Lawrence Marsh, "The Dynamic Effect of Discounting on Sales: Empirical Analysis and Normative Pricing Implications," *Marketing Science* 18 (Summer 1999), pp. 317–32.

52. Harald J. Van Heerde, Sachin Gupta, and Dick Wittink, "Is 75% of the Sales Promotion Bump Due to Brand Switching? No, Only 33% Is," *Journal of Marketing Research* 40 (November 2003), pp. 481–91; Harald J. Van Heerde, Peter S. H. Leeflang, and Dick R. Wittink, "The Estimation of Pre- and Postpromotion Dips with Store-Level Scanner Data," *Journal of Marketing Research* 37 (August 2000), pp. 383–95.

53. For a good summary of the research on whether promotion erodes the consumer franchise of leading brands, see Blattberg and Neslin, "Sales Promotion: The Long and Short of It,"*Marketing Letters* 1 (December 2004); See also, "Stephanie Rosenbloom, "In Recession, Even the Holdouts Use Coupons," *New York Times*, September 24, 2009. For a related topic, see Michael J. Barone and Tirthankar Roy, "Does Exclusivity Pay Off? Exclusive Price Promotions and Consumer Response," *Journal of Marketing* 74 (March 2010), pp. 121–32.

54. Robert George Brown, "Sales Response to Promotions and Advertising," *Journal of Advertising Research* (August 1974), pp. 36–37. Also see Kamel Jedidi, Carl F. Mela, and Sunil Gupta, "Managing Advertising and Promotion for Long-Run Profitability," *Marketing Science* 18 (Winter 1999), pp. 1–22; Carl F. Mela, Sunil Gupta, and Donald R. Lehmann, "The Long-Term Impact of Promotion and Advertising on Consumer Brand Choice," *Journal of Marketing Research* 34 (May 1997), pp. 248–61; Purushottam Papatla and Lakshman Krishnamurti, "Measuring the Dynamic Effects of Promotions on Brand Choice," *Journal of Marketing Research* 33 (February 1996), pp. 20–35.

55. "2010 REGGIE Awards Shopper Marketing: P&G Gain—Project Gainiac," *Promotion Marketing Association*, www.pmalink.org.

56. Magid M. Abraham and Leonard M. Lodish, "Getting the Most out of Advertising and Promotion," *Harvard Business Review,* May–June 1990, pp. 50–60. See also, Shuba Srinivasan, Koen Pauwels, Dominique Hanssens, and Marnik Dekimpe, "Do Promotions Benefit Manufacturers, Retailers, or Both?" *Management Science* 50 (May 2004), pp. 617–29.

57. Leonard M. Lodish, Magid Abraham, Stuart Kalmenson, Jeanne Livelsberger, Beth Lubetkin, Bruce Richardson, and Mary Ellen Stevens, "How T.V.

Advertising Works: A Meta-Analysis of 389 Real World Split Cable T.V. Advertising Experiments," *Journal of Marketing Research* 32 (May 1995), pp. 125–39.

58. Rebecca J. Slotegraaf and Koen Pauwels, "The Impact of Brand Equity Innovation on the Long-Term Effectiveness of Promotions," *Journal of Marketing Research* 45 (June 2008), pp. 293–306.

59. For a model for setting sales promotions objectives, see David B. Jones, "Setting Promotional Goals: A Communications Relationship Model," *Journal of Consumer Marketing* 11 (1994), pp. 38–49.

60. Kusum L. Ailawadi, Bari A. Harlam, Jacques Cesar, and David Trounce, "Promotion Profitability for a Retailer: The Role of Promotion, Brand, Category, and Store Characteristics," *Journal of Marketing Research* 43 (November 2006), pp. 518–36.

61. Emily Bryson York and Natalie Zmuda, "Sampling: The New Mass Media," *Advertising Age*, May 12, 2008, pp. 3, 56.

62. Sarah Skidmore, "Coupons Evolve for the Digital Age," *Associated Press*, August 30, 2009; "20 Most Popular Comparison Shopping Websites," *eBizMBA*, www.ebizmba.com, June 2010.

63. Miguel Gomez, Vithala Rao, and Edward McLaughlin, "Empirical Analysis of Budget and Allocation of Trade Promotions in the U.S. Supermarket Industry," *Journal of Marketing Research* 44 (August 2007); Norris Bruce, Preyas S. Desai, and Richard Staelin, "The Better They Are, the More They Give: Trade Promotions of Consumer Durables," *Journal of Marketing Research* 42 (February 2005), pp. 54–66.

64. Kusum L. Ailawadi and Bari Harlam, "An Empirical Analysis of the Determinants of Retail Margins: The Role of Store Brand Share," *Journal of Marketing* 68 (January 2004), pp. 147–66; Kusum L. Ailawadi, "The Retail Power-Performance Conundrum: What Have We Learned?" *Journal of Retailing* 77 (Fall 2001), pp. 299–318; Paul W. Farris and Kusum L. Ailawadi, "Retail Power: Monster or Mouse?" *Journal of Retailing* (Winter 1992), pp. 351–69; Koen Pauwels, "How Retailer and Competitor Decisions Drive the Long-Term Effectiveness of Manufacturer Promotions," *Journal of Retailing* 83 (2007), pp. 364–90.

65. James Bandler, "The Shadowy Business of Diversion," *Fortune*, August 17, 2009, p. 65; Rajiv Lal, John Little, and J. M. Vilas-Boas, "A Theory of Forward Buying, Merchandising, and Trade Deals," *Marketing Science* 15 (Winter 1996), pp. 21–37.

66. IBIS World USA, www.ibisworld.com; Noah Lim, Michael J. Ahearne, and Sung H. Ham, "Designing Sales Contests: Does the Prize Structure Matter?" *Journal of Marketing Research* 46 (June 2009), pp. 356–71.

67. "Kraft's Oreo Takes Super Reggie," *Promo*, March 12, 2009; Elaine Wong, "How Kraft's Double Stuf Oreo Launch Trumped Expectations," *Brandweek*, August 31, 2009; "Oreo Double Stuf Racing League (DSRL)," *Promotion Marketing Association*, www.pmalink.org.

68. Kurt H. Schaffir and H. George Trenten, *Marketing Information Systems* (New York: AMACOM, 1973), p. 81.

69. Joe A. Dodson, Alice M. Tybout, and Brian Sternthal, "Impact of Deals and Deal Retraction on Brand Switching," *Journal of Marketing Research* 15 (February 1978), pp. 72–81.

70. *IEG Sponsorship Report*, as quoted in "Sponsorship Spending Revised, Growth Cut in Half: IEG," *Promo*, June 18, 2009.

71. Philip Kotler, "Atmospherics as a Marketing Tool," *Journal of Retailing* (Winter 1973–1974), pp. 48–64.

72. Kathleen Kerwin, "When the Factory Is a Theme Park," *BusinessWeek,* May 3, 2004, p. 94; Vanessa O'Connell, "'You-Are-There' Advertising," *Wall Street Journal,* August 5, 2002.

73. Jeff Borden, "Tornado: Experiential Marketing Takes the Industry by Storm in 2008," *Marketing News,* January 15, 2008, pp. 23–26.

74. Michael Schmelling, "Creative Mischief," *Fast Company*, November 2008, pp. 134–38; "GE Profile Inflatable Product Replicas Hit Times Square," *Landmark Creations,* www.landmarkcreations.com; Laurie Sullivan, "GE Ads Show How to Lighten the Laundry Load," *Marketing Daily*, August 27, 2008.

75. "Personal Care Marketers: Who Does What," *IEG Sponsorship Report*, April 16, 2007, p. 4.

76. Bettina Cornwell, Michael S. Humphreys, Angela M. Maguire, Clinton S. Weeks, and Cassandra Tellegen, "Sponsorship-Linked Marketing: The Role of Articulation in Memory," *Journal of Consumer Research* 33 (December 2006), pp. 312–21.

77. Hilary Cassidy, "So You Want to Be an Olympic Sponsor?" *Brandweek*, November 7, 2005, pp. 24–28.

78. "Brands Suit Up for 'Iron Man 2,'" *Adweek*, May 14, 2010.

79. "BB&T Continues Sponsorship with Clint Bowyer, Richard Childress Racing," *SceneDaily*, January 14, 2010; "BB&T Puts Name on New Winston-Salem Ballpark," *Winston-Salem Journal*, February 24, 2010; "Bank's New Department, Deals Reflect Elevated Sponsorship Status," *IEG Sponsorship Report*, April 16, 2007, pp. 1, 8.

80. The Association of National Advertisers has a useful source: *Event Marketing: A Management Guide,* which is available at www.ana.net/bookstore.

81. T. Bettina Cornwell, Clinton S. Weeks, and Donald P. Roy, "Sponsorship-Linked Marketing: Opening the Black Box," *Journal of Advertising* 34 (Summer 2005).

82. Constantine von Hoffman, "Buying Up the Bleachers," *Brandweek*, February 19, 2007, pp. 18–21.

83. William L. Shankin and John Kuzma, "Buying That Sporting Image," *Marketing Management* (Spring 1992), pp. 65.

84. B. Joseph Pine and James H. Gilmore, *The Experience Economy: Work Is Theatre and Every Business a Stage* (Cambridge, MA: Harvard University Press, 1999).

85. "2006 Experiential Marketing Study," *Jack Morton*, www.jackmorton.com.

86. "Do We Have a Story for You!" *Economist*, January 21, 2006, pp. 57–58; Al Ries and Laura Ries, *The Fall of Advertising and the Rise of PR* (New York: HarperCollins, 2002).

87. "*PRWeek* Campaign of the Year," *PRWeek*, March 5, 2009; "Man Lives in IKEA," *Ketchum*, www.ketchum.com; "Man Lives in NYC IKEA Store," *Associated Press*, January 8, 2008.

88. "Ketchum and Dreyer's Win *PRWeek* Campaign of the Year Award," *PRNewswire*, March 12, 2010; "Dreyer's Slow Churned Dishes Out a Taste of Recovery with the Debut of 'Red, White and No More Blues' Flavor," *PRNewswire*, June 23, 2009; "Beat the Blues with a Taste of Recovery," *CLIO 2010*, www.clioawards.com.

89. Arthur M. Merims, "Marketing's Stepchild: Product Publicity," *Harvard Business Review*, November–December 1972, pp. 111–12. Also see Katherine D. Paine, "There Is a Method for Measuring PR," *Marketing News*, November 6, 1987, p. 5.

Chapter 19

1. Elaine Wong, "Pepsi's Refresh Project Drives Social Buzz," *Brandweek*, June 9, 2010; Stuart Elliott, "Pepsi Invites the Public to Do Good," *New York Times*, February 1, 2010; Suzanne Vranica, "Pepsi Benches Its Drinks," *Wall Street Journal*, December 17, 2009.

2. The terms *direct-order marketing* and *direct-relationship marketing* were suggested as subsets of direct marketing by Stan Rapp and Tom Collins in *The Great Marketing Turnaround* (Upper Saddle River, NJ: Prentice Hall, 1990).

3. Ran Kivetz and Itamar Simonson, "The Idiosyncratic Fit Heuristic: Effort Advantage as a Determinant of Consumer Response to Loyalty Programs," *Journal of Marketing Research* 40 (November 2003), pp. 454–67; Ran Kivetz and Itamar Simonson, "Earning the Right to Indulge: Effort as a Determinant of Customer Preferences toward Frequency Program Rewards," *Journal of Marketing Research* 39 (May 2002), pp. 155–70.

4. www.the-dma.org homepage

5. L.L. Bean, www.llbean.com.

6. Stan Rapp and Thomas L. Collins, *Maximarketing* (New York: McGraw-Hill, 1987).

7. www.dma-echo.org; www.yellowtreehouse.co.nz; www.ameawards.com.

8. "DMA Releases 2010 Response Rate Trend Report," *Direct Marketing Association*, www.the-dma.org, June 15, 2010.

9. Bob Stone and Ron Jacobs, *Successful Direct Marketing Methods*, 8th ed. (New York: McGraw-Hill, 2007).

10. Edward L. Nash, *Direct Marketing: Strategy, Planning, Execution*, 4th ed. (New York: McGraw-Hill, 2000).

11. The *average customer longevity* (N) is related to the *customer retention rate* (CR). Suppose the company retains 80 percent of its customers each year. Then the average customer longevity is given by: $N = 1/(1 - CR) = 1/.2 = 5$ years.

12. "MCM 100," *Multi Channel Merchant*, www.multichannelmerchant.com, July 2009.

13. "Industry Overview: Internet and Catalog Retailers," *Hoovers*, www.hoovers.com, accessed August 22, 2010.

14. "Biennial Report to Congress: Pursuant to the Do Not Call Registry Fee Extension Act of 2007," *Federal Trade Commission*, www.ftc.gov, December 2009.

15. Charles Duhigg, "Telemarketing Thieves Sharpen Their Focus on the Elderly," *New York Times*, May 20, 2007.

16. Tony Case, "Growing Up," *Interactive Quarterly*, April 19, 2004, pp. 32–34.

17. For example, see André Bonfrer and Xavier Drèze, "Real-Time Evaluation of E-mail Campaign Performance," *Marketing Science* 28 (March–April 2009), pp. 251–63.

18. Kenneth C. Wilbur and Yi Zhu, "Click Fraud," *Marketing Science* 28 (March–April 2009), pp. 293–308.

19. Ellen Byron, "Estée Lauder Tests Web-Ad Waters," *Wall Street Journal*, September 19, 2006.

20. Asim Ansari and Carl F. Mela, "E-Customization," *Journal of Marketing Research* 40 (May 2003), pp. 131–45.

21. Daniel Michaels and J. Lynn Lunsford, "Ad-Sales Woes Likely to Continue," *Wall Street Journal*, December 4, 2006; Jack Neff, "Axe Cuts Past Competitors, Claims Market Lead," *Advertising Age*, May 14, 2006; Byron Acohido, "Rich Media Enriching PC Ads," *USA Today*, February 25, 2004.

22. Stuart Elliott, "Letting Consumers Control Marketing: Priceless," *New York Times*, October 9, 2006; Elizabeth Holmes, "On MySpace, Millions of Users Make 'Friends' with Ads," *Wall Street Journal*, August 7, 2006; "2009 Gold Effie Winner: 'Whopper Freakout,'" *Effie Awards*, *Effie Worldwide*, www.effie.org.

23. Allen P. Adamson, *Brand Digital* (New York: Palgrave Macmillan, 2008).

24. John R. Hauser, Glen L. Urban, Guilherme Liberali, and Michael Braun, "Website Morphing," *Marketing Science* 28 (March–April 2009), pp. 202–23; Peter J. Danaher, Guy W. Mullarkey, and Skander Essegaier, "Factors Affecting Web Site Visit Duration: A Cross-Domain Analysis," *Journal of Marketing Research* 43 (May 2006), pp. 182–94; Philip Kotler, *According to Kotler* (New York: American Management Association, 2005).

25. Jeffrey F. Rayport and Bernard J. Jaworski, *e-commerce* (New York: McGraw-Hill, 2001), p. 116.

26. Bob Tedeschi, "E-Commerce Report," *New York Times*, June 24, 2002.

27. Jan-Benedict E. M. Steenkamp and Inge Geyskens, "How Country Characteristics Affect the Perceived Value of Web Sites," *Journal of Marketing* 70 (July 2006), pp. 136–50.

28. Jessi Hempel, "The Online Numbers Game," *Fortune*, September 3, 2007, p. 18.

29. Julia Angwin and Tom McGinty, "Sites Feed Personal Details to New Tracking Industry," *Wall Street Journal*, July 31, 2010.

30. *eMarketer,* www.emarketer.com, May 2010.

31. Emily Steel, "Marketers Take Search Ads Beyond Search Engines," *Wall Street Journal*, January 19, 2009.

32. Paula Andruss, "How to Win the Bidding Wars," *Marketing News*, April 1, 2008, p. 28; "Jefferson Graham, "To Drive Traffic to Your Site, You Need to Give Good Directions," *USA Today*, June 23, 2008.

33. Peter J. Danaher, Janghyuk Lee, and Laoucine Kerbache, "Optimal Internet Media Selection," *Marketing Science* 29 (March–April 2010), pp. 336–47; Puneet Manchanda, Jean-Pierre Dubé, Khim Yong Ooh, and Pradeep K. Chintagunta, "The Effects of Banner Advertising on Internet Purchasing," *Journal of Marketing Research* 43 (February 2006), pp. 98–108.

34. Brian Morrissey, "Big Money Bet on Display Ad Tech," *Adweek*, August 1, 2010; Brian Morrissey, "Beefing Up Banner Ads," *Adweek NEXT*, February 15, 2010, pp. 10–11; Robert D. Hof, "The Squeeze on Online Ads," *BusinessWeek*, March 2, 2009, pp. 48–49; Emily Steel, "Web Sites Debate Best Values for Advertising Dollars," *Wall Street Journal*, August 13, 2009, p. B7.

35. Elisabeth Lewin, "Podcast Audience Growing Faster Than Podcast Advertising," *Podcasting News*, www.podcastingnews.com, May 13, 2009.

36. Natalie Zmuda, "How E-mail Became a Direct-Marketing Rock Star in Recession," *Advertising Age*, May 11, 2009, p. 27.

37. Piet Levy, "An E-motional Call to Action," *Marketing News*, April 30, 2010, p. 8.

38. Roger Cheng, "Mobile Ads Make Gains, But Pace Slows Sharply," *Wall Street Journal*, April 7, 2009; Mark Walsh, "Gartner: Mobile Advertising to Grow 74 percent In 2009," *MediaPost*, August 31, 2009; Amol Sharma, "Companies Vie for Ad Dollars on Mobile Web," *Wall Street Journal*, January 17, 2007; "Mobile Advertising: The Next Big Thing," *Economist*, October 7, 2007, pp. 73–74.

39. Giselle Tsirulnik, "Bank of America Uses Mobile Banners to Drive App Downloads," *Mobile Marketer*, September 4, 2009; Rita Chang, "Consumer Control Brings Brand Loyalty," *Advertising Age*, March 30, 2009, p. 26; Dan Butcher, "Bank of America Campaign Targets Students for Mobile Banking," *Mobile Marketer*, August 28, 2008; Mickey Alam Khan, "Bank of America Surpasses 1M Mobile Banking Customers," *Mobile Marketer*, June 13, 2008.

40. Brian Morrissey, "2009 Really Isn't the Year of Mobile. Here's Why," *Brandweek*, November 16, 2009, p. 6; Douglas MacMillan, Peter Burrows, and Spencer E. Ante, "The App Economy," *BusinessWeek*, November 2, 2009, pp. 44–49.

41. "VW Set for Launch in 8 Months," *WorldCarFans.com*, www.worldcarfans.com, March 20, 2007; Eleftheria Parpis, "Volkswagen's Public Polling Pays Off," *Adweek*, May 19, 2008; Andrew Grill, "Volkswagen Tiguan Mobile Advertising Case Study," *London Calling,* www.londoncalling.mobi, May 20, 2009.

42. Peter DaSilva, "Cellphone in New Role: Loyalty Card," *New York Times*, May 31, 2010.

43. Diana Ransom, "When the Customer Is in the Neighborhood," *Wall Street Journal*, May 17, 2010.

44. Don Clark and Nick Wingfield, "Intel, Microsoft Offer Smart Sign Technology," *Wall Street Journal*, January 12, 2010; Andrew Lavallee, "Unilever to Test Mobile Coupons in Trial at Supermarket, Cellphones Will Be the Medium for Discount Offers," *Wall Street Journal*, May 29, 2009; Bob Tedeschi, "Phone Smart Cents-Off Coupons and Other Special Deals, via Your Cellphone," *New York Times*, December 17, 2008.

45. Piet Levy, "Set Your Sites on Mobile," *Marketing News*, April 30, 2010, p.6; Tom Lowry, "Pandora: Unleashing Mobile-Phone Ads," *BusinessWeek*, June 1, 2009, pp. 52–53.

46. Elisabeth Sullivan, "The Tao of Mobile Marketing," *Marketing News*, April 30, 2010, pp. 16–20.

47. Loretta Chao, "Cell Phone Ads Are Easier Pitch in China Interactive Campaigns," *Wall Street Journal*, January 4, 2007.

48. Louise Story, "What We Talk About When We Talk About Brands," *New York Times*, November 24, 2006.

49. Robert V. Kozinets, Kristine de Valck, Andrea C. Wojnicki, and Sarah J. S. Wilner, "Networked Narratives: Understanding Word-of-Mouth Marketing in Online Communities," *Journal of Marketing* 74 (March 2010), pp. 71–89; David Godes and Dina Mayzlin, "Firm-Created Word-of-Mouth Communication: Evidence from a Field Test," *Marketing Science* 28 (July–August 2009), pp. 721–39.

50. Jon Swartz, "Small Firms Dive Into Social Media," *USA Today*, July 22, 2010, p. 3B.

51. Reena Jane, "How Intuit Makes a Social Network Pay," *Bloomberg BusinessWeek*, July 2, 2009; Justin Smith, "Intuit's 'Super Status Contest' Aims for Product Placement in Facebook Status Updates," *Inside Facebook*, www.insidefacebook.com, January 29, 2009; Christen Wegner, "How Intuit Stays Relevant Using Social Media," *KyleLacey.com*, www.kylelacy.com, March 3, 2010; Jon Swartz, "More Marketers Sign on to Social Media," *USA Today*, August 28, 2009, p. 1B.

52. *Effie Awards*, www.effie.org/downloads/2009_winners_list.pdf.

53. Heather Green, "It Takes a Web Village," *BusinessWeek*, September 4, 2006, p. 66; Paul Dwyer, *Measuring the Value of Word of Mouth and Its Impact in Consumer Communities*, MSI Report No. 06-118, *Marketing Science Institute*, Cambridge, MA.; Kelly K. Spors, "The Customer Knows Best," *Wall Street Journal*, July 13, 2009, p. R5.

54. Claire Cain Miller, "The Sweet Spot," *Forbes*, April 23, 2007, p. 41.

55. For an academic discussion of chat rooms, recommendation sites, and customer review sections

online, see Dina Mayzlin, "Promotional Chat on the Internet," *Marketing Science* 25 (March–April 2006), pp. 155–63; and Judith Chevalier and Dina Mayzlin, "The Effect of Word of Mouth on Sales: Online Book Reviews," *Journal of Marketing Research* 43 (August 2006), pp. 345–54.

56. Stephen Baker, "Looking for a Blog in a Haystack," *BusinessWeek*, July 25, 2006, p. 38.

57. Heather Green, "The Big Shots of Blogdom," *BusinessWeek*, May 7, 2007; TreeHugger, www.treehugger.com/about.

58. Kim Hart, "Angry Customers Use Web to Shame Firms," *Washington Post*, July 5, 2006.

59. For a thorough review of relevant academic literature, see Christophe Van Den Bulte and Stefan Wuyts, *Social Networks and Marketing* (Marketing Science Institute Relevant Knowledge Series, Cambridge, MA, 2007), and for some practical considerations, see "A World of Connections: A Special Report on Social Networking," *Economist*, January 30, 2010.

60. Allen Adamson, "No Contest: Twitter and Facebook Can Both Play a Role in Branding," www.forbes.com, May 6, 2009.

61. "Profiting From Friendship," *Economist*, January 30, 2010, pp. 9–12.

62. "A Peach of Opportunity," *Economist*, January 30, 2010, pp. 9–12.

63. Claire Cain Miller, "The New Back Fence," *Forbes*, April 7, 2008; CafeMom, www.cafemom.com/about.

64. Michael Learmonth and Rupal Parekh, "How Influential Are Angry Bloggers? Ask Johnson & Johnson," *Financial Week*, November 19, 2008; Seth Godin, "We Feel Your Pain," *Seth's Blog*, November 17, 2008; Jim Edwards, "J&J Triggers Mommy War With Motrin 'Anti-Baby Sling' Ad," www.bnet.com, November 17, 2008.

65. Stephen Baker, "Beware Social Media Snake Oil," *Bloomberg BusinessWeek*, December 14, 2009, pp. 48–51.

66. Ralf van der Lans, Gerrit van Bruggen, Jehoshua Eliashberg, Berend Wierenga, "A Viral Branching Model for Predicting the Spread of Electronic Word of Mouth," *Marketing Science* 29 (March–April 2010), pp. 348–65; Dave Balter and John Butman, "Clutter Cutter," *Marketing Management* (July–August 2006), pp. 49–50.

67. Emanuel Rosen, *The Anatomy of Buzz* (New York: Currency, 2000).

68. George Silverman, *The Secrets of Word-of-Mouth Marketing* (New York: AMACOM, 2001); Emanuel Rosen, *The Anatomy of Buzz* (New York: Currency, 2000), chapter 12; "Viral Marketing," *Sales & Marketing Automation* (November 1999), pp. 12–14.

69. *Will It Blend?* www.willitblend.com; Blendtec, www.blendtec.com; Piet Levy, "I Tube, YouTube," *Marketing News*, March 30, 2009, p. 8; Phyllis Berman, "Food Fight," *Forbes*, October 13, 2008, p. 110; Rob Walker, "Mixing It Up," *New York Times*, August 24, 2008; Jon Fine, "Ready to Get Weird, Advertisers?" *BusinessWeek*, January 8, 2007, p. 24.

70. Renée Dye, "The Buzz on Buzz," *Harvard Business Review* (November–December 2000), p. 139.

71. Robert Berner, "I Sold It through the Grapevine," *BusinessWeek*, May 29, 2006, pp. 32–34.

72. Barbara Kiviat, "Word on the Street," *Time*, April 12, 2007; Dave Balter, "Rules of the Game," *Advertising Age Point*, December 2005, pp. 22–23; Scott Kirsner, "How Much Can You Trust Buzz?" *Boston Globe*, November 14, 2005; Linda Tischler, "What's the Buzz?" *Fast Company*, May 2004, pp. 76–77.

73. Matthew Creamer and Rupal Parekh, "Ideas of the Decade," *Advertising Age*, December 14, 2009.

74. Amar Cheema and Andrew M. Kaikati, "The Effect of Need for Uniqueness on Word of Mouth," *Journal of Marketing Research* 47 (June 2010), pp. 553–63.

75. Jacqueline Johnson Brown, Peter M. Reingen, and Everett M. Rogers, *Diffusion of Innovations,* 4th ed. (New York: Free Press, 1995); J. Johnson Brown and Peter Reingen, "Social Ties and Word-of-Mouth Referral Behavior," *Journal of Consumer Research* 14 (December 1987), pp. 350–62; Peter H. Riengen and Jerome B. Kernan, "Analysis of Referral Networks in Marketing: Methods and Illustration," *Journal of Marketing Research* 23 (November 1986), pp. 37–78.

76. Malcolm Gladwell, *The Tipping Point: How Little Things Can Make a Big Difference* (Boston: Little, Brown & Company, 2000).

77. Terry McDermott, "Criticism of Gladwell Reaches Tipping Point," *Columbia Journalism Review*, November 17, 2009; Clive Thompson, "Is the Tipping Point Toast?" *Fast Company*, February 1, 2008; Duncan Watts, *Six Degrees: The Science of a Connected Age* (New York: W.W. Norton, 2003).

78. Douglas Atkin, *The Culting of Brands: When Customers Become True Believers* (New York: Penguin, 2004); Marian Salzman, Ira Matathia, and Ann O'Reilly, *Buzz: Harness the Power of Influence and Create Demand* (New York: Wiley, 2003).

79. Bob Greenberg, "A Platform for Life," *Adweek NEXT*, September 14, 2009, p. 38.

80. Michael Trusov, Anand V. Bodapati, and Randolph E. Bucklin, "Determining Influential Users in Internet Social Networks," *Journal of Marketing Research* 47 (August 2010), pp. 643–58.

81. Dave Balter and John Butman, "Clutter Cutter," *Marketing Management* (July–August 2006), pp. 49–50; "Is There a Reliable Way to Measure Word-of-Mouth Marketing?" *Marketing NPV* 3 (2006), pp. 3–9.

82. Digital Buzz, www.digitalbuzzblog.com; Mashable, www.mashable.com; Atomic Ideas, www. atomicideas.com, all accessed August 22, 2010.

83. Keith Barry, "Fiesta Stars in Night of the Living Social Media Campaign," *Wired*, May 21, 2010; Matthew Dolan, "Ford Takes Online Gamble with New Fiesta," *Wall Street Journal*, April 8, 2009.

84. This section is based in part on an excellent summary, "Is There a Reliable Way to Measure Word-of-Mouth

Marketing?" *Marketing NPV* 3 (2006), pp. 3–9, available at www.marketingnpv.com.

85. Suzanne Vranica, "Social Media Draws a Crowd," *Wall Street Journal*, July 19, 2010; Jessi Hempel, "He Measures the Web," *Fortune*, November 9, 2009, pp. 94–98.

86. Adam L. Penenberg, "How Much Are You Worth to Facebook?" *Fast Company*, October 1, 2009.

87. Rick Lawrence, Prem Melville, Claudia Perlich, Vikas Sindhwani, Steve Meliksetian, Pei-Yun Hsueh, and Yan Liu, "Social Media Analytics," *OR/MS Today*, February 2010, pp. 26–30.

88. "Employment by major occupational group, 2008 and projected 2018," http://www.bls.gov/emp/ep_table_101.pdf.

89. John Bello, "Sell Like Your Outfit Is at Stake. It Is," *BusinessWeek Online,* February 5, 2004; John Bello, "The Importance of Sales for Entrepreneurs," *USA Today*, February 11, 2004; Jeanine Prezioso, "Lizard King's Story," *Fairfield County Business Journal*, December 10, 2001.

90. Shrihari Sridhar, Murali K. Mantrala, and Sönke Albers, "Personal Selling Elasticities: A Meta-Analysis," *Journal of Marketing Research* 47 (October 2010).

91. Adapted from Robert N. McMurry, "The Mystique of Super-Salesmanship," *Harvard Business Review*, March–April 1961, p. 114. Also see William C. Moncrief III, "Selling Activity and Sales Position Taxonomies for Industrial Sales Forces," *Journal of Marketing Research* 23 (August 1986), pp. 261–70.

92. Lawrence G. Friedman and Timothy R. Furey, *The Channel Advantage: Going to Marketing with Multiple Sales Channels* (Oxford, UK: Butterworth-Heinemann, 1999).

93. Michael Ahearne, Scott B. MacKenzie, Philip M. Podsakoff, John E. Mathieu, and Son K. Lam, "The Role of Consensus in Sales Team Performance," *Journal of Marketing Research* 47 (June 2010), pp. 458–69.

94. Ashwin W. Joshi, "Salesperson Influence on Product Development: Insights from a Study of Small Manufacturing Organizations," *Journal of Marketing* 74 (January 2010), pp. 94–107; Philip Kotler, Neil Rackham, and Suj Krishnaswamy, "Ending the War between Sales & Marketing," *Harvard Business Review*, July–August 2006, pp. 68–78; Timothy M. Smith, Srinath Gopalakrishna, and Rubikar Chaterjee, "A Three-Stage Model of Integrated Marketing Communications at the Marketing-Sales Interface," *Journal of Marketing Research* 43 (November 2006), pp. 546–79.

95. Michael Copeland, "Hits and Misses," *Business 2.0,* April 2004, p. 142.

96. "Sales Performance Benchmarks," *Go-to-Market Strategies*, June 5, 2007. For international tax implications in compensation, see Dominique Rouziès, Anne T. Coughlan, Erin Anderson, and Dawn Iacobucci, "Determinants of Pay Levels and Structures in Sales Organizations," *Journal of Marketing* 73 (November 2009), pp. 92–104.

97. Tony Ritigliano and Benson Smith, *Discover Your Sales Strengths* (New York: Random House Business Books, 2004).

98. Sonke Albers, "Sales-Force Management—Compensation, Motivation, Selection, and Training," Bart Weitz and Robin Wensley, eds., *Handbook of Marketing* (London: Sage, 2002), pp. 248–66.

99. Nanette Byrnes, "Avon Calling—Lots of New Reps," *BusinessWeek,* June 2, 2003, pp. 53–54.

100. Michael R. W. Bommer, Brian F. O'Neil, and Beheruz N. Sethna, "A Methodology for Optimizing Selling Time of Salespersons," *Journal of Marketing Theory and Practice* (Spring 1994), pp. 61–75. See also, Lissan Joseph, "On the Optimality of Delegating Pricing Authority to the Sales Force," *Journal of Marketing* 65 (January 2001), pp. 62–70.

101. Dartnell Corporation, *30th Sales-Force Compensation Survey* (Chicago: Dartnell Corp., 1999). Other breakdowns show that 12.7 percent is spent in service calls, 16 percent in administrative tasks, 25.1 percent in telephone selling, and 17.4 percent in waiting/traveling. For analysis of this database, see Sanjog Misra, Anne T. Coughlan, and Chakravarthi Narasimhan, "Salesforce Compensation: An Analytical and Empirical Examination of the Agency Theoretic Approach, *Quantitative Marketing and Economics* 3 (March 2005), pp. 5–39.

102. Michael Ahearne, Son K. Lam, John E. Mathieu, and Willy Bolander, "Why Are Some Salespeople Better at Adapting to Organizational Change?" *Journal of Marketing* 74 (May 2010), pp. 65–79.

103. Willem Verbeke and Richard P. Bagozzi, "Sales-Call Anxiety: Exploring What It Means When Fear Rules a Sales Encounter," *Journal of Marketing* 64 (July 2000), pp. 88–101. See also, Douglas E. Hughes and Michael Ahearne, "Energizing the Reseller's Sales Force: The Power of Brand Identification," *Journal of Marketing* 74 (July 2010), pp. 81–96.

104. Gilbert A. Churchill Jr., Neil M. Ford, Orville C. Walker Jr., Mark W. Johnston, and Greg W. Marshall, *Sales-Force Management,* 9th ed. (New York: McGraw-Hill/Irwin, 2009). See also, Eric G. Harris, John C. Mowen, and Tom J. Brown, "Reexamining Salesperson Goal Orientations: Personality Influencers, Customer Orientation, and Work Satisfaction," *Journal of the Academy of Marketing Science* 33 (Winter 2005), pp. 19–35; Manfred Krafft, "An Empirical Investigation of the Antecedents of Sales-Force Control Systems," *Journal of Marketing* 63 (July 1999), pp. 120–34; Wujin Chu, Eitan Gerstner, and James D. Hess, "Costs and Benefits of Hard Sell," *Journal of Marketing Research* 32 (February 1995), pp. 97–102.

105. Noah Lim, Michael J. Ahearne, and Sung H. Ham, "Designing Sales Contests: Does the Prize Structure Matter?" *Journal of Marketing Research* 46 (June 2009), pp. 356–71.

106. Lisa Vaas, "Oracle Teaches Its Sales Force to Play Nice," *eWeek*, July 28, 2004; Lisa Vaas, "Oracle's Sales Force Reorg Finally Bears Fruit," *eWeek,*

December 17, 2003; Ian Mount, "Out of Control," *Business 2.0,* August 2002, pp. 38–44.

107. Philip M. Posdakoff and Scott B. MacKenzie, "Organizational Citizenship Behaviors and Sales-Unit Effectiveness," *Journal of Marketing Research* 31 (August 1994), pp. 351–63. See also, Andrea L. Dixon, Rosann L. Spiro, and Magbul Jamil, "Successful and Unsuccessful Sales Calls: Measuring Salesperson Attributions and Behavioral Intentions," *Journal of Marketing* 65 (July 2001), pp. 64–78; Willem Verbeke and Richard P. Bagozzi, "Sales-Call Anxiety: Exploring What It Means When Fear Rules a Sales Encounter," *Journal of Marketing* 64 (July 2000), pp. 88–101.

108. Neil Rackham, *SPIN Selling* (New York: McGraw-Hill, 1988). Also see his *The SPIN Selling Fieldbook* (New York: McGraw-Hill, 1996); James Lardner, "Selling Salesmanship," *Business 2.0*, December 2002–January 2003, p. 66; Sharon Drew Morgen, *Selling with Integrity: Reinventing Sales through Collaboration, Respect, and Serving* (New York: Berkeley Books, 1999); Neil Rackham and John De Vincentis, *Rethinking the Sales Force* (New York: McGraw-Hill, 1996).

109. Some of the following discussion is based on a classic analysis in W. J. E. Crissy, William H. Cunningham, and Isabella C. M. Cunningham, *Selling: The Personal Force in Marketing* (New York: Wiley, 1977), pp. 119–29. For some contemporary perspective and tips, see Jia Lynn Yang, "How to Sell in a Lousy Economy," *Fortune*, September 29, 2008, pp. 101–6 and Jessi Hempel, "IBM's All-Star Salesman," *Fortune*, September 29, 2008, pp. 110–19.

110. Stephanie Clifford, "Putting the Performance in Sales Performance," *Inc.*, February 2007, pp. 87–95.

111. Joel E. Urbany, "Justifying Profitable Pricing," *Journal of Product & Brand Management* 10 (2001), pp.141–59.

112. Jia Lynn Yang, "How Can I Keep My Sales Team Productive in a Recession?" *Fortune*, March 2, 2009, p. 22.

113. V. Kumar, Rajkumar Venkatesan, and Werner Reinartz, "Performance Implications of Adopting a Customer-Focused Sales Campaign," *Journal of Marketing* 72 (September 2008), pp. 50–68; George R. Franke and Jeong-Eun Park, "Salesperson Adaptive Selling Behavior and Customer Orientation: A Meta-Analysis," *Journal of Marketing Research* 43 (November 2006), pp. 693–702; Richard G. McFarland, Goutam N. Challagalla, and Tasadduq A. Shervani, "Influence Tactics for Effective Adaptive Selling," *Journal of Marketing* 70 (October 2006), pp. 103–17.

Chapter 20

1. Brad Stone, "Nintendo Wii to Add Netflix Service for Streaming Video," *New York Times*, January 13, 2010; Eric A. Taub, "Will Nothing Slow Wii?" *New York Times Bits Blog*, October 17, 2008; John Gaudiosi, "How the Wii Is Creaming the Competition," *Business 2.0*, April 25, 2007; Martin Fackler, "Putting the We Back in Wii," *New York Times*, June 8, 2007.

2. For some scholarly reviews, see Ely Dahan and John R. Hauser, "Product Development: Managing a Dispersed Process," Bart Weitz and Robin Wensley, eds., *Handbook of Marketing* (London: Sage, 2002), pp. 179–222; Dipak Jain, "Managing New-Product Development for Strategic Competitive Advantage," Dawn Iacobucci, ed., *Kellogg on Marketing*, (New York: Wiley, 2001), pp. 130–48; Jerry Wind and Vijay Mahajan, "Issues and Opportunities in New-Product Development: An Introduction to the Special Issue," *Journal of Marketing Research* 34 (February 1997), pp. 1–12. For an overview of different industry approaches, see Frank T. Rothaermel and Andrew M. Hess, "Innovation Strategies Combined," *MIT Sloan Management Review* (Spring 2010), pp. 13–15.

3. Scott Sanderude, "Growth from Harvesting the Sky: The $200 Million Challenge," talk at Marketing Science Institute Conference: New Frontiers for Growth, Boston, MA, April 2005.

4. Stephen J. Carson, "When to Give Up Control of Outsourced New-Product Development," *Journal of Marketing* 71 (January 2007), pp. 49–66.

5. Elaine Wong, "P&G's '09 Success Hinged on Value, Affordable Luxury," *Brandweek*, March 22, 2010, p. 8.

6. For some academic discussion of the effects of new-product introductions on markets, see Harald J. Van Heerde, Carl F. Mela, and Puneet Manchanda, "The Dynamic Effect of Innovation on Market Structure," *Journal of Marketing Research* 41 (May 2004), pp. 166–83; and for a contrast with radically different new products, see Khaled Aboulnasr, Om Narasimhan, Edward Blair, and Rajesh Chandy, "Competitive Response to Radical Product Innovations," *Journal of Marketing* 72 (May 2008), pp. 94–110.

7. "Enabling Multifaceted Innovation," *IBM Global Business Services,* www-935.ibm.com/services/us/gbs/bus/pdf/g510-6310-executive-brief-enabling-multifaceted.pdf, 2006.

8. Shuba Srinivasan, Koen Pauwels, Jorge Silva-Risso, and Dominique M. Hanssens, "Product Innovations, Advertising and Stock Returns," *Journal of Marketing* 73 (January 2009), pp. 24–43; Alina B. Sorescu and Jelena Spanjol, "Innovation's Effect on Firm Value and Risk: Insights from Consumer Packaged Goods," *Journal of Marketing* 72 (March 2008), pp. 114–32; Sungwook Min, Manohar U. Kalwani, and William T. Robinson, "Market Pioneer and Early Follower Survival Risks: A Contingency Analysis of Really New versus Incrementally New Product-Markets," *Journal of Marketing* 70 (January 2006), pp. 15–33; C. Page Moreau, Arthur B. Markman, and Donald R. Lehmann, "'What Is It?' Category Flexibility and Consumers' Response to Really New Products," *Journal of Consumer Research* 27 (March 2001), pp. 489–98.

9. Stefan Wuyts, Shantanu Dutta, and Stefan Stremersch, "Portfolios of Interfirm Agreements in Technology-Intensive Markets: Consequences for Innovation and Profitability," *Journal of Marketing* 68 (April 2004), pp. 88–100; Aric Rindfleisch and Christine Moorman, "The Acquisition and Utilization of Information in New-Product Alliance: A Strength-of-Ties Perspective," *Journal of Marketing* 65 (April 2001), pp. 1–18. See also, Raghunath Singh Rao, Rajesh K. Chandy, and Jaideep C. Prabhu, "The Fruits of Legitimacy: Why Some New Ventures Gain More from Innovation Than Others," *Journal of Marketing* 72 (July 2008), pp. 58–75.

10. Gerard J. Tellis, Jaideep C. Prabhu, and Rajesh K. Chandy, "Radical Innovation across Nations: The Preeminence of Corporate Culture," *Journal of Marketing* 73 (January 2009), pp. 3–23.

11. Steve Hoeffler, "Measuring Preferences for Really New Products," *Journal of Marketing Research* 40 (November 2003), pp. 406–20; Glen Urban, Bruce Weinberg, and John R. Hauser, "Premarket Forecasting of Really New Products," *Journal of Marketing* 60 (January 1996), pp. 47–60.

12. Andy Grove, "Think Disruptive," *Condé Nast Portfolio*, December 2007, pp. 170–75; Ashish Sood and Gerard J. Tellis, "Technological Evolution and Radical Innovation," *Journal of Marketing* 69 (July 2005), pp. 152–68.

13. For more discussion, see Jakki Mohr, *Marketing of High-Technology Products and Innovations*, 2nd ed. (Upper Saddle River, NJ: Prentice Hall, 2005).

14. Carol Matlack, "How Danone Turns Bacteria into Bucks," *BusinessWeek*, November 15, 2007, pp. 76–77; Jack Ewing, "The Bimmer, Plugged In," *BusinessWeek*, March 23 and 30, 2009, p. 78; Beth Kowitt, "Blackboard Rules the Schools," *Fortune*, November 9, 2009, p. 28.

15. Steve Hamm, "Speed Demons," *BusinessWeek*, March 27, 2006, pp. 69–76.

16. Christina Passariello, "Brand New Bag: Louis Vuitton Tries Modern Methods on Factory Lines," *Wall Street Journal*, October 9, 2006.

17. Gary Hamel, "W. L. Gore: Lessons from a Management Revolutionary," *Wall Street Journal*, March 18, 2010; "The World's Most Innovative Companies," *Fast Company*, March 2009; Brad Weiners, "Gore-Tex Tackles the Great Indoors," *Business 2.0*, April 2004, p. 32; Ann Harrington, "Who's Afraid of a New Product," *Fortune*, November 10, 2003, pp. 189–92.

18. Tim Brown, *Change by Design: How Design Thinking Transforms Organizations and Inspires Innovation* (New York: HarperCollins, 2009).

19. Clayton M. Christensen, *Disrupting Class: How Disruptive Innovation Will Change the Way the World Learns* (New York: McGraw-Hill, 2008); Clayton M. Christensen, *The Innovator's Solution: Creating and Sustaining Successful Growth* (Boston: Harvard University Press, 2003); Clayton M. Christensen, *The Innovator's Dilemma: When New Technologies Cause Great Firms to Fail* (Boston: Harvard University Press, 1997).

20. Ely Dahan and John R. Hauser, "Product Development: Managing a Dispersed Process," Bart Weitz and Robin Wensley, eds., *Handbook of Marketing* (London: Sage, 2002), pp. 179–222.

21. Robert G. Cooper and Elko J. Kleinschmidt, *New Products: The Key Factors in Success* (Chicago: American Marketing Association, 1990).

22. Ibid., pp. 35–38.

23. Susumu Ogama and Frank T. Piller, "Reducing the Risks of New-Product Development," *MIT Sloan Management Review* 47 (Winter 2006), pp. 65–71; A.C. Nielsen, "New-Product Introduction—Successful Innovation/Failure: Fragile Boundary," A.C. Nielsen BASES and Ernst & Young Global Client Consulting, June 24, 1999; Deloitte and Touche, "Vision in Manufacturing Study," Deloitte Consulting and Kenan-Flagler Business School, March 6, 1998.

24. For more discussion, see Dipak Jain, "Managing New-Product Development for Strategic Competitive Advantage," Dawn Iacobucci, ed., *Kellogg on Marketing* (New York: Wiley, 2001).

25. Steve Hamm, "Speed Demons," *BusinessWeek*, March 27, 2006, pp. 69–76.

26. Tom McNichol, "A Start-Up's Best Friend? Failure," *Business 2.0*, March 2007, pp. 39–41.

27. Thomas N. Burton, "By Learning from Failures Lilly Keeps Drug Pipelines Full," *Wall Street Journal*, April 21, 2004.

28. Amy Barrett, "J&J: Reinventing How It Invents," *BusinessWeek*, April 17, 2006, pp. 60–61.

29. Virginia Gardiner, "Dyson Airblade," *Dwell*, March 10, 2010; Reena Jana, "Dyson's Air Multiplier: Flaw as Function," *Bloomberg BusinessWeek*, October 12, 2009; Chuck Salter, "Failure Doesn't Suck," *Fast Company*, May 2007, p. 44.

30. Vijay Govindrajan and Chris Trimble, "Stop the Innovation Wars," *Harvard Business Review*, July–August 2010, pp. 76–83; Doug Ayers, Robert Dahlstrom, and Steven J. Skinner, "An Exploratory Investigation of Organizational Antecedents to New-Product Success," *Journal of Marketing Research* 34 (February 1997), pp. 107–16; David S. Hopkins, *Options in New-Product Organization* (New York: Conference Board, 1974).

31. Brian Hindo, "Rewiring Westinghouse," *BusinessWeek*, May 19, 2008, pp. 48–49.

32. Danielle Sacks, Chuck Salter, Alan Deutschman, and Scott Kirsner, "Innovation Scouts," *Fast Company*, May 2007, p. 90; "Ongoing Innovation: Tom Malloy on Sustaining the Relevance and Impact of Adobe's Advanced Technology Labs," *Knowledge@Wharton*, March 21, 2007; Shantanu Narayen, "Connecting the Dots Isn't Enough," *New York Times*, July 18, 2009.

33. Lisa C. Troy, Tanat Hirunyawipada, and Audhesh K. Paswan, "Cross-Functional Integration and New Product Success: An Empirical Investigation of the Findings," *Journal of Marketing* 72 (September 2008), pp. 132–46; Rajesh Sethi, Daniel C. Smith, and C.

Whan Park, "Cross-Functional Product Development Teams, Creativity, and the Innovativeness of New Consumer Products," *Journal of Marketing Research* 38 (February 2001), pp. 73–85.

34. Robert G. Cooper, *Winning at New Products: Accelerating the Process from Idea to Launch* (New York: Perseus Publishing, 2001); See also, Robert G. Cooper, "Stage-Gate Systems: A New Tool for Managing New Products," *Business Horizons,* May–June 1990, pp. 44–54; Robert G. Cooper, "The NewProd System: The Industry Experience," *Journal of Product Innovation Management* 9 (June 1992), pp. 113–27.

35. Robert G. Cooper, *Product Leadership: Creating and Launching Superior New Products* (New York: Perseus Books, 1998).

36. Rajesh Sethi and Zafar Iqbal, "Stage-Gate Controls, Learning Failure, and Adverse Effect on Novel New Products," *Journal of Marketing* 72 (January 2008), pp. 118–34.

37. Ely Dahan and John R. Hauser, "Product Development: Managing a Dispersed Process," Bart Weitz and Robin Wensley, eds., *Handbook of Marketing* (London: Sage, 2002), pp. 179–222.

38. Another alternative approach to the funnel process advocates "rocketing." See, David Nichols, *Return on Ideas* (West Sussex, England: Wiley, 2007).

39. Michael Zedalis, "Deploying Stage-Gate on a Global Scale—Critical Elements That Drive Performance" and Charles Gagnon, "Driving Value Creation with the Right Portfolio Mix," talks given at Stage-Gate Leadership Summit 2007.

40. John Hauser, Gerard J. Tellis, and Abbie Griffin, "Research on Innovation: A Review and Agenda for Marketing Science," *Marketing Science* 25 (November–December 2006), pp. 687–717.

41. Byron Acohido, "Microsoft Cultures Creativity in Unique Lab," *USA Today*, July 11, 2007; Erich Joachimsthaler, *Hidden in Plain Sight: How to Find and Execute Your Company's Next Big Growth Strategy* (Boston: Harvard Business School Press, 2007); Subin Im and John P. Workman Jr., "Market Orientation, Creativity, and New-Product Performance in High-Technology Firms," *Journal of Marketing* 68 (April 2004), pp. 114–32.

42. Erich Joachimsthaler, *Hidden in Plain Sight: How to Find and Execute Your Company's Next Big Growth Strategy* (Boston: Harvard Business School Publishing, 2007).

43. Henry Chesbrough, *Open Business Models: How to Thrive in the New-Innovation Landscape* (Boston: Harvard University Press, 2006); Eric Von Hippel, *Democratizing Innovation* (Cambridge, MA: MIT Press, 2005); Burt Helm, "Inside a White-Hot Idea Factory," *BusinessWeek*, January 15, 2005, pp. 72–73; C.K. Prahalad and Venkat Ramaswamy, *The Future of Competition: Cocreating Unique Value with Customers* (Boston: Harvard University Press, 2004); Henry Chesbrough, *Open Innovation: The New Imperative for Creating and Profiting from Technology* (Boston: Harvard University Press, 2003).

44. Bruce Horovitz, "Marketers Zooming in on Your Daily Routines," *USA Today*, April 30, 2007; Ashwin W. Joshi and Sanjay Sharma, "Customer Knowledge Development: Antecedents and Impact on New-Product Performance," *Journal of Marketing* 68 (October 2004), pp. 47–59.

45. Abbie J. Griffin and John Hauser, "The Voice of the Customer," *Marketing Science* 12 (Winter 1993), pp. 1–27.

46. Miho Inada, "Tokyo Café Targets Trend Makers," *Wall Street Journal*, August 24, 2008.

47. Peter C. Honebein and Roy F. Cammarano, "Customers at Work," *Marketing Management* 15 (January–February 2006), pp. 26–31; Peter C. Honebein and Roy F. Cammarano, *Creating Do-It-Yourself Customers: How Great Customer Experiences Build Great Companies* (Mason, OH: Texere Southwestern Educational Publishing, 2005).

48. Jeff Howe, *Crowdsourcing: Why the Power of the Crowd Is Driving the Future of Business* (New York, Crown Business, 2008).

49. Guido Jouret, "Inside Cisco's Search for the Next Big Idea," *Harvard Business Review*, September 2009, pp. 43–45; Anya Kamentz, "The Power of the Prize," *Fast Company*, May 2008, pp. 43–45; Cisco, www.cisco.com/web/solutions/iprize/index.html.

50. Patricia Seybold, *Outside Innovation: How Your Customers Will Codesign Your Company's Future* (New York: Collins, 2006).

51. Helena Yli-Renko and Ramkumar Janakiraman, "How Customer Portfolio Affects New Product Development in Technology-Based Firms, *Journal of Marketing* 72 (September 2008), pp. 131–48; Donna L. Hoffman, Praveen K. Kopalle, and Thomas P. Novak, "The 'Right' Consumers for Better Concepts: Identifying and Using Consumers High in Emergent Nature to Further Develop New Product Concepts," *Journal of Marketing Research* 47 (October 2010), in press.

52. Pioneering work in this area is represented by Eric von Hippel, "Lead Users: A Source of Novel Product Concepts," *Management Science* 32 (July 1986), pp. 791–805. Also see Eric von Hippel, *The Sources of Innovation* (New York: Oxford University Press, 1988); Eric von Hippel, *Democratizing Innovation* (Cambridge, MA: MIT Press, 2005); and Pamela D. Morrison, John H. Roberts and David F. Midgley, "The Nature of Lead Users and Measurement of Leading Edge Status," *Research Policy* 33 (2004), pp. 351–62.

53. John W. Heinke Jr. and Chun Zhang, "Increasing Supplier-Driven Innovation," *MIT Sloan Management Review* (Winter 2010), pp. 41–46; Eric (Er) Fang, "Customer Participation and the Trade-Off Between New Product Innovativeness and Speed to Market," *Journal of Marketing* 72 (July 2008), pp. 90–104. Note that this research also shows that customer involvement can also slow the development process if a high level of interaction and coordination is required across stages.

54. Kevin Zheng Zhou, Chi Kin (Bennett) Yim, and David K. Tse, "The Effects of Strategic Orientations on Technology- and Market-Based Breakthrough

Innovations," *Journal of Marketing* 69 (April 2005), pp. 42–60; Michael Treacy, "Ignore the Consumer," *Advertising Age Point* (September 2005), pp. 15–19.

55. Sharon Machlis, "Innovation and the 20% Solution," *Computerworld*, February 2, 2009.

56. "The World's Fifty Most Innovative Companies," Special Report, *BusinessWeek*, May 9, 2007.

57. Darren W. Dahl and Page Moreau, "The Influence and Value of Analogical Thinking during New-Product Ideation," *Journal of Marketing Research* 39 (February 2002), pp. 47–60; Michael Michalko, *Cracking Creativity: The Secrets of Creative Genius* (Berkeley, CA: Ten Speed Press, 1998); James M. Higgins, *101 Creative Problem-Solving Techniques* (New York: New Management, 1994).

58. Philip Kotler and Fernando Trias de Bes, *Lateral Marketing: New Techniques for Finding Breakthrough Ideas* (New York: Wiley, 2003).

59. NBC Research, "Friends," *Program Test Report,* May 27, 1994; and NBC's Failing Grade for "Friends," *The Smoking Gun.* May 10, 2004, www.smokinggun.com.

60. Olivier Toubia and Laurent Florès, "Adaptive Idea Screening Using Consumers," *Marketing Science* 26 (May–June 2007), pp. 342–60; Melanie Wells, "Have It Your Way," *Forbes*, February 14, 2005.

61. David L. Alexander, John G. Lynch Jr., and Qing Wang, "As Time Goes By: Do Cold Feet Follow Warm Intentions for Really New Versus Incrementally New Products," *Journal of Marketing Research* 45 (June 2008), pp. 307–19; Steve Hoeffler, "Measuring Preferences for Really New Products," *Journal of Marketing Research* 40 (November 2003), pp. 406–20.

62. Min Zhao, Steve Hoeffler, and Darren W. Dahl, "The Role of Imagination-Focused Visualization on New Product Evaluation," *Journal of Marketing Research* 46 (February 2009), pp. 46–55; Raquel Castano, Mita Sujan, Manish Kacker, Harish Sujan, "Managing Customer Uncertainty in the Adoption of New Products: Temporal Distance and Mental Stimulation," *Journal of Marketing Research* 45 (June 2008), pp. 320–36; Dahl and Moreau, "The Influence and Value of Analogical Thinking during New-Product Ideation," *Journal of Marketing Research* 39; Michelle L. Roehm and Brian Sternthal, "The Moderating Effect of Knowledge and Resources on the Persuasive Impact of Analogies," *Journal of Consumer Research* 28 (September 2001), pp. 257–72; Darren W. Dahl, Amitava Chattopadhyay, and Gerald J. Gorn, "The Use of Visual Mental Imagery in New-Product Design," *Journal of Marketing Research* 36 (February 1999), pp. 18–28.

63. Steve Hamm, "Speed Demons," *BusinessWeek*, March 27, 2006, pp. 69–76.

64. Jon Fortt, "Heavy Duty Computing," *Fortune*, March 2, 2009, pp. 34–36.

65. For additional information, also see David Bakken and Curtis L. Frazier, "Conjoint Analysis: Understanding Consumer Decision Making," Rajiv Grover and Marco Vriens, eds., *The Handbook of Marketing Research* (Thousand Oaks, CA: Sage, 2006); Vithala R. Rao and John R. Hauser, "Conjoint Analysis, Related Modeling, and Application," Yoram Wind and Paul E. Green, eds., *Market Research and Modeling: Progress and Prospects: A Tribute to Paul Green* (New York: Springer, 2004), pp. 141–68; Jordan J. Louviere, David A. Hensher, and Joffre D. Swait, *Stated Choice Models: Analysis and Applications* (New York: Cambridge University Press, 2000); Paul E. Green and V. Srinivasan, "Conjoint Analysis in Marketing: New Developments with Implications for Research and Practice," *Journal of Marketing* 54 (October 1990), pp. 3–19; *Sawtooth Software*. For another approach, see Young-Hoon Park, Min Ding and Vithala R. Rao, "Eliciting Preference for Complex Products: A Web-Based Upgrading Method," *Journal of Marketing Research* 45 (October 2008), pp. 562–74.

66. Jerry Wind, Paul Green, Douglas Shifflet, and Marsha Scarbrough, "Courtyard by Marriott: Designing a Hotel Facility with Consumer-Based Marketing Models," *Interfaces* 19 (January–February 1989), pp. 25–47; For another interesting application, see Paul E. Green, Abba M. Krieger, and Terry Vavra, "Evaluating EZ-Pass: Using Conjoint Analysis to Assess Consumer Response to a New Tollway Technology," *Marketing Research* (Summer 1999), pp. 5–16.

67. The full-profile example was taken from Paul E. Green and Yoram Wind, "New Ways to Measure Consumers' Judgments," *Harvard Business Review,* July–August 1975, pp. 107–17.

68. Peter N. Golder and Gerald J. Tellis, "Will It Ever Fly? Modeling the Takeoff of Really New Consumer Durables," *Marketing Science* 16 (Summer 1997), pp. 256–70; Glen L. Urban, Bruce D. Weinberg, and John R. Hauser, "Premarket Forecasting of Really New Products," *Journal of Marketing* 60 (January 1996), pp. 47–60; Robert Blattberg and John Golany, "Tracker: An Early Test-Market Forecasting and Diagnostic Model for New-Product Planning," *Journal of Marketing Research* 15 (May 1978), pp. 192–202.

69. Roger A. Kerin, Michael G. Harvey, and James T. Rothe, "Cannibalism and New-Product Development," *Business Horizons*, October 1978, pp. 25–31.

70. The present value (V) of a future sum (I) to be received t years from today and discounted at the interest rate (r) is given by $V = I_t/(1 + r)t$. Thus $\$4,716,000/(1.15)^5 = \$2,345,000$.

71. John Hauser, "House of Quality," *Harvard Business Review,* May–June 1988, pp. 63–73; Customer-driven engineering is also called "quality function deployment." See also, Lawrence R. Guinta and Nancy C. Praizler, *The QFD Book: The Team Approach to Solving Problems and Satisfying Customers through Quality Function Deployment* (New York: AMACOM, 1993); and V. Srinivasan, William S. Lovejoy, and David Beach, "Integrated Product Design for Marketability and Manufacturing," *Journal of Marketing Research* 34 (February 1997), pp. 154–63.

72. Tom Peters, *The Circle of Innovation* (New York: Vintage, 1999), p. 96. For more general discussion, see

also, Sethi, "New Product Quality and Product Development Teams," *Journal of Marketing* 64 (April 2000), pp. 1–14; Moorman and Miner, "The Convergence of Planning and Execution Improvisation in New-Product Development," pp. 1–20; MacChavan and Graver, "From Embedded Knowledge to Embodied Knowledge," pp. 1–12.

73. Kevin J. Clancy, Peter C. Krieg, and Marianne McGarry Wolf, *Marketing New Products Successfully: Using Simulated Test Marketing Methodology* (New York: Lexington Books, 2005); Glen L. Urban, John R. Hauser, and Roberta A. Chicos, "Information Acceleration: Validation and Lessons from the Field," *Journal of Marketing Research* 34 (February 1997), pp. 143–53; V. Mahajan and Jerry Wind, "New Product Models: Practice, Shortcomings, and Desired Improvements," *Journal of Product Innovation Management* 9 (June 1992), pp. 129–39.

74. Eyal Biyalogorsky, William Boulding, and Richard Staelin, "Stuck in the Past: Why Managers Persist with New-Product Failures," *Journal of Marketing* 70 (April 2006), pp. 108–21.

75. Rajesh Chandy, Brigette Hopstaken, Om Narasimhan, and Jaideep Prabhu, "From Invention to Innovation: Conversion Ability in Product Development," *Journal of Marketing Research* 43 (August 2006), pp. 494–508.

76. Remco Prins and Peter C. Verhoef, "Marketing Communication Drivers of Adoption Timing of a New E-Service among Existing Customers," *Journal of Marketing* 71 (April 2007), pp. 169–83.

77. For further discussion, see Feryal Erhun, Paulo Conçalves, and Jay Hopman, "The Art of Managing New Product Transitions," *MIT Sloan Management Review* 48 (Spring 2007), pp. 73–80; Yuhong Wu, Sridhar Balasubramanian, and Vijay Mahajan, "When Is a Preannounced New Product Likely to Be Delayed?" *Journal of Marketing* 68 (April 2004), pp. 101–13; Raji Srinivasan, Gary L. Lilien, and Arvind Rangaswamy, "First in First out? The Effects of Network Externalities on Pioneer Survival," *Journal of Marketing* 68 (January 2004), pp. 41–58; Barry L. Bayus, Sanjay Jain, and Ambar Rao, "Truth or Consequences: An Analysis of Truth or Vaporware and New-Product Announcements," *Journal of Marketing Research* 38 (February 2001), pp. 3–13; Thomas S. Robertson, Jehoshua Eliashberg, and Talia Rymon, "New-Product Announcement Signals and Incumbent Reactions," *Journal of Marketing* 59 (July 1995), pp. 1–15; Frank H. Alpert and Michael A. Kamins, "Pioneer Brand Advantages and Consumer Behavior: A Conceptual Framework and Propositional Inventory," *Journal of the Academy of Marketing Science* 22 (Summer 1994), pp. 244–336; Robert J. Thomas, "Timing: The Key to Market Entry," *Journal of Consumer Marketing* 2 (Summer 1985), pp. 77–87.

78. Yvonne van Everdingen, Dennis Folk, and Stefan Stremersch, "Modeling Global Spillover in New Product Takeoff," *Journal of Marketing Research* 46 (October 2009), pp. 637–52; Katrijn Gielens and Jan-Benedict E. M. Steenkamp, "Drivers of Consumer Acceptance of New Packaged Goods: An Investigation across Products and Countries," *International Journal of Research in Marketing* 24 (June 2007), pp. 97–111; Marc Fischer, Venkatesh Shankar, and Michael Clement, "Can a Late Mover Use International Market Entry Strategy to Challenge the Pioneer?" Marketing Science Institute Working Paper 05-118, Cambridge, MA; Venkatesh Shankar, Gregory S. Carpenter, and Lakshman Krishnamukthi, "Late Mover Advantages: How Innovative Late Entrants Outsell Pioneers," *Journal of Marketing Research* 35 (February 1998), pp. 54–70.

79. Philip Kotler and Gerald Zaltman, "Targeting Prospects for a New Product," *Journal of Advertising Research* (February 1976), pp. 7–20.

80. Mark Leslie and Charles A. Holloway, "The Sales Learning Curve," *Harvard Business Review,* July–August 2006, pp. 114–23.

81. For details, see Keith G. Lockyer, *Critical Path Analysis and Other Project Network Techniques* (London: Pitman, 1984); see also; Arvind Rangaswamy and Gary L. Lilien, "Software Tools for New-Product Development," *Journal of Marketing Research* 34 (February 1997), pp. 177–84.

82. The following discussion leans heavily on Everett M. Rogers, *Diffusion of Innovations* (New York: Free Press, 1962). Also see his third edition, published in 1983.

83. C. Page Moreau, Donald R. Lehmann, and Arthur B. Markman, "Entrenched Knowledge Structures and Consumer Response to New Products," *Journal of Marketing Research* 38 (February 2001), pp. 14–29.

84. John T. Gourville, "Eager Sellers & Stony Buyers," *Harvard Business Review,* June 2006, pp. 99–106.

85. Chuan-Fong Shih and Alladi Venkatesh, "Beyond Adoption: Development and Application of a Use-Diffusion Model," *Journal of Marketing* 68 (January 2004), pp. 59–72.

86. Michal Herzenstein, Steven S. Posavac, and J. Joško Brakuz, "Adoption of New and Really New Products: The Effects of Self-Regulation Systems and Risk Salience," *Journal of Marketing Research* 44 (May 2007), pp. 251–60; Christophe Van den Bulte and Yogesh V. Joshi, "New-Product Diffusion with Influentials and Imitators," *Marketing Science* 26 (May–June 2007), pp 400–21; Steve Hoeffler, "Measuring Preferences for Really New Products," *Journal of Marketing Research* 40 (November 2003), pp. 406–20.

87. Everett M. Rogers, *Diffusion of Innovations* (New York: Free Press, 1962), p. 192; Geoffrey A. Moore, *Crossing the Chasm: Marketing and Selling High-Tech Products to Mainstream Customers* (New York: HarperBusiness, 1999); For an interesting application with services, see Barak Libai, Eitan Muller, and Renana Peres, "The Diffusion of Services," *Journal of Marketing Research* 46 (April 2009), pp. 163–75.

88. A. Parasuraman and Charles L. Colby, *Techno-Ready Marketing* (New York: Free Press, 2001); Jakki Mohr, *Marketing of High-Technology Products and Innovations* (Upper Saddle River, NJ: Prentice Hall, 2001).

89. Jordan Robertson, "How Nike Got Street Cred," *Business 2.0,* May 2004, pp. 43–46.

90. Cliff Edwards, "Will Souping Up TiVo Save It?" *BusinessWeek,* May 17, 2004, pp. 63–64; Cliff Edwards, "Is TiVo's Signal Still Fading?" *BusinessWeek,* September 10, 2001, pp. 72–74.

91. Fareena Sultan, John U. Farley, and Donald R. Lehman, "Reflection on 'A Meta-Analysis of Applications of Diffusion Models,'" *Journal of Marketing Research* 33 (May 1996), pp. 247–49; Vijay Mahajan, Eitan Muller, and Frank M. Bass, "Diffusion of New Products: Empirical Generalizations and Managerial Uses," *Marketing Science* 14 (Summer 1995), pp. G79–G89; Minhi Hahn, Sehoon Park, and Andris A. Zoltners, "Analysis of New-Product Diffusion Using a Four-Segment Trial-Repeat Model," *Marketing Science* 13 (Summer 1994), pp. 224–47; Hubert Gatignon and Thomas S. Robertson, "A Propositional Inventory for New Diffusion Research," *Journal of Consumer Research* 11 (March 1985), pp. 849–67.

Chapter 21

1. Mehul Srivastava, "What the Nano Means to India," *BusinessWeek,* May 11, 2009, pp. 60–61; Steve Hamm, "IBM vs. Tata: Which Is More American?" *BusinessWeek,* May 5, 2008, p. 28; Manjeet Kirpalani, "Tata: The Master of The Gentle Approach," *BusinessWeek,* February 25, 2008, pp. 64–66; Kevin Maney, "Model T(ata)," *Condé Nast Portfolio,* February 2008, pp. 35–36; David Welch and Nandini Lakshman, "My Other Car Is a Tata," *BusinessWeek,* January 14, 2008, pp. 33–34; Robyn Meredith, "The Next People's Car," *Forbes,* April 16, 2007, pp. 70–74; Pete Engardo, "The Last Rajah," *BusinessWeek,* August 13, 2007, pp. 46–51.

2. Michael Elliott, "The New Global Opportunity, *Fortune,* July 5, 2010, pp. 96–102.

3. Alex Taylor III, "The New Motor City," *Fortune,* October 27, 2008, pp. 166–172.

4. David Kiley, "Baseball, Apple Pie . . . and Mihindra?" *BusinessWeek,* November 5, 2007, pp. 61–63.

5. Michael Arndt, "Invasion of the Guatemalan Chicken," *Bloomberg BusinessWeek,* March 22 and 29, 2010, pp. 72–73.

6. Michael E. Porter, *Competitive Strategy* (New York: Free Press, 1980), p. 275.

7. Alex Taylor III, "Hyundai Smokes the Competition," *Fortune,* January 18, 2010, pp. 62–71; Moon Ihlwan and David Kiley, "Hyundai Gains with Marketing Blitz, *BusinessWeek,* September 17, 2009; Moon Ihlwan and David Kiley," "Hyundai Floors It in the U.S.," *BusinessWeek,* February 27, 2009, pp. 30–31.

8. Charles P. Wallace, "Charge!" *Fortune,* September 28, 1998, pp. 189–96; World Trade Organization, www.wto.org.

9. For a comprehensive treatment, see Philip R. Cateora, Mary C. Gilly, and John L. Graham, *International Marketing* (New York: McGraw-Hill/Irwin, 2009).

10. "US Export Fact Sheet," *International Trade Administration,* http:// trade.gov/press/press_releases/ 2009/export-factsheet_021109.pdf.

11. Jan Johanson and Finn Wiedersheim-Paul, "The Internationalization of the Firm," *Journal of Management Studies* 12 (October 1975), pp. 305–22.

12. Michael R. Czinkota and Ilkka A. Ronkainen, *International Marketing,* 9th ed. (Cincinnati, OH: South-Western Cengage Learning, 2010).

13. For a thorough review of academic research on global marketing, see Johny K. Johansson, "Global Marketing: Research on Foreign Entry, Local Marketing, Global Management," Bart Weitz and Robin Wensley, eds., *Handbook of Marketing* (London: Sage, 2002), pp. 457–83. Also see Johny K. Johansson, *Global Marketing,* 5th ed. (New York: McGraw-Hill, 2009). For some global marketing research issues, see C. Samuel Craig and Susan P. Douglas, *International Marketing Research,* 3rd ed. (Chichester, UK: John Wiley & Sons, 2005).

14. Marc Gunther, "The World's New Economic Landscape," *Fortune,* July 26, 2010, pp. 105–106.

15. According to the *CIA World Factbook* (www.cia.gov/library/publications/the-world-factbook/ index.html), there are 34 developed countries: Andorra, Australia, Austria, Belgium, Bermuda, Canada, Denmark, Faroe Islands, Finland, France, Germany, Greece, Holy See, Iceland, Ireland, Israel, Italy, Japan, Liechtenstein, Luxembourg, Malta, Monaco, Netherlands, New Zealand, Norway, Portugal, San Marino, South Africa, Spain, Sweden, Switzerland, Turkey, United Kingdom, and United States. They note that DCs are similar to the new International Monetary Fund (IMF) term "*advanced economies*" that adds Hong Kong, South Korea, Singapore, and Taiwan but drops Malta, Mexico, South Africa, and Turkey.

16. Satish Shankar, Charles Ormiston, Nicolas Bloch, Robert Schaus, and Vijay Vishwanath, "How to Win in Emerging Markets," *MIT Sloan Management Review* (April 2008).

17. "Kraft Revamps Developing Markets after Cadbury," *Reuters,* June 30, 2010; Ned Douthat, "Tupperware Seals Up Growth in Emerging Markets," *Forbes,* www.forbes.com, April 21, 2010.

18. Tom Mulier and Shin Pei, "Nestle's $28.1 Billion Payday Gives Google-Size Cash," *Bloomberg BusinessWeek,* June 30, 2010.

19. "World Population to Exceed 9 Billion by 2050," press release, *United Nations,* www.un.org, March 11, 2009; "2008 World Population Data Sheet," *Population Reference Bureau,* www.pbr.org.

20. Adapted from Vijay Mahajan, Marcos V. Pratini De Moraes, and Jerry Wind, "The Invisible Global Market," *Marketing Management* (Winter 2000), pp. 31–35. See also, Joseph Johnson and Gerard J. Tellis, "Drivers of Success for Market Entry into China and India," *Journal of Marketing* 72 (May 2008), pp. 1–13; Tarun Khanna and Krishna G. Palepu, "Emerging Giants: Building

World-Class Companies in Developing Countries," *Harvard Business Review,* October 2006, pp. 60–69.

21. C. K. Prahalad, *The Fortune at the Bottom of the Pyramid: Eradicating Poverty through Profits* (Upper Saddle River, NJ: Wharton School Publishing, 2005); Niraj Dawar and Amitava Chattopadhyay, "Rethinking Marketing Programs for Emerging Markets," *Long Range Planning* 35 (October 2002).

22. Bart J. Bronnenberg, Jean-Pierre Dubé, and Sanjay Dhar, "Consumer Packaged Goods in the United States: National Brands, Local Branding," *Journal of Marketing Research* 44 (February 2007), pp. 4–13; Bart J. Bronnenberg, Jean-Pierre Dubé, and Sanjay Dhar, "National Brands, Local Branding: Conclusions and Future Research Opportunities," *Journal of Marketing Research* 44 (February 2007), pp. 26–28; Bart J. Bronnenberg, Sanjay K. Dhar, and Jean-Pierre Dubé, "Brand History, Geography, and the Persistence of CPG Brand Shares," *Journal of Political Economy* 117 (February 2009), pp. 87–115.

23. David Michael and Arindam Bhattacharya, "The BCG 50 Local Dynamos: How Dynamic RDE-Based Companies Are Mastering Their Home Markets—and What MNCs Need to Learn from Them," Boston Consulting Group, *BCG Report*, March 2008; "The Stay-at-Home Giants," *Economist*, March 15, 2008, p. 78; "In Emerging Markets 'Local Dynamos' Are Challenging Big Multinationals," *Manufacturing & Technology News*, April 17, 2008.

24. Manjeet Kripalani, "Finally, Coke Gets It Right," *BusinessWeek,* February 10, 2003, p. 47; Manjeet Kripalani, "Battling for Pennies in India's Villages," *BusinessWeek,* June 10, 2002, p. 22.

25. Carlos Niezen and Julio Rodriguez, "Distribution Lessons from Mom and Pop," *Harvard Business Review*, April 2008; "Sweet Surrender: Can Kraft's Cadbury Acquisition Help It Tap the Indian Market?" *Knowledge@Wharton,* February 25, 2010.

26. Clayton M. Christensen, Stephen Wunker, and Hari Nair, "Innovation vs. Poverty," *Forbes*, October 13, 2008.

27. Ellen Byron, "P&G's Global Target: Shelves of Tiny Stores," *Wall Street Journal*, July 16, 2007; "Not So Fizzy," *Economist,* February 23, 2002, pp. 66–67; Rajeev Batra, Venkatram Ramaswamy, Dana L. Alden, Jan-Benedict E. M. Steenkamp, and S. Ramachander, "Effects of Brand Local and Nonlocal Origin on Consumer Attitudes in Developing Countries," *Journal of Consumer Psychology* 9 (2000), pp. 83–95.

28. Bruce Einhorn, "Grudge Match in China," *BusinessWeek*, April 2, 2007, pp. 42–43; Russell Flannery, "Watch Your Back," *Forbes*, April 23, 2007, pp. 104–5; Steve Hamm and Dexter Roberts, "China's First Global Capitalist," *BusinessWeek*, December 11, 2006, pp. 52–57; "The Fast and the Furious," *Economist*, November 25, 2006, pp. 63–64.

29. Jenny Mero, "John Deere's Farm Team," *Fortune*, April 14, 2008, pp. 119–24.

30. Peter J. Williamson and Ming Zeng, "Value for Money Strategies for Recessionary Times," *Harvard Business Review*, March 2009, pp. 66–74; Vikram Skula, "Business Basics at the Base of the Pyramid," *Harvard Business Review*, June 2008, pp. 53–57.

31. Johny K. Johansson, "Global Marketing: Research on Foreign Entry, Local Marketing, Global Management," Bart Weitz and Robin Wensley, eds., *Handbook of Marketing* (London: Sage, 2002), pp. 457–83.

32. Jennifer Cirillo, "Western Europe Is Buzzing," *Beverage World*, June 2010, pp. 22–24.

33. Bernard Condon, "Babble Rouser," *Forbes*, August 11, 2008, pp. 72–77.

34. Bechtel, www.bechtel.com/overview.html; Jack Ewing, "Bechtel Drives a Highway through the Heart of Transylvania," *BusinessWeek*, January 7, 2008.

35. For an academic review, see Leonidas C. Leonidou, Constantine S. Katsikeas, and Nigel F. Piercy, "Identifying Managerial Influences on Exporting: Past Research and Future Directions," *Journal of International Marketing* 6 (Summer 1998), pp. 74–102.

36. Karen Cho, "KFC China's Recipe for Success," *Forbes India*, October 28, 2009; "Brands annual report 2009," *Yum!* www.yum.com/annualreport/pdf/2009AnnualReport. pdf; Michael Arndt and Dexter Roberts, "A Finger-Lickin' Good Time in China," *BusinessWeek*, October 30, 2006, p. 50; "Cola down Mexico Way," *Economist,* October 11, 2003, pp. 69–70.

37. Claudia H. Deutsch, "The Venturesome Giant," *New York Times*, October 5, 2007.

38. Vikram Mahidhar, Craig Giffi, and Ajit Kambil with Ryan Alvanos, "Rethinking Emerging Market Strategies," *Deloitte Review*, Issue 4, 2009.

39. "Burgers and Fries a la Francaise," *Economist,* April 17, 2004, pp. 60–61; Johny K. Johansson, "Global Marketing: Research on Foreign Entry, Local Marketing, Global Management," Bart Weitz and Robin Wensley, eds., *Handbook of Marketing* (London: Sage, 2002), pp. 457–83; Shaoming Zou and S. Tamer Cavusgil, "The GMS: A Broad Conceptualization of Global Marketing Strategy and Its Effect on Firm Performance," *Journal of Marketing* 66 (October 2002), pp. 40–56; "What Makes a Company Great?" *Fortune,* October 26, 1998, pp. 218–26; Bernard Wysocki Jr., "The Global Mall: In Developing Nations, Many Youths Splurge, Mainly on U.S. Goods," *Wall Street Journal,* June 26,1997; David M. Szymanski, Sundar G. Bharadwaj, and P. Rajan Varadarajan, "Standardization versus Adaptation of International Marketing Strategy: An Empirical Investigation," *Journal of Marketing* 57 (October 1993), pp.1–17; Theodore Levitt, "The Globalization of Markets," *Harvard Business Review,* May–June 1983, pp. 92–102.

40. Gail Edmondson, "Skoda Means Quality. Really," *BusinessWeek*, October 1, 2007, p. 46. Some of the more popular jokes from the past: "How do you double the value of a Škoda? Fill up the gas tank." "What do you call a Skoda with a sunroof? A dumpster." and "Why do you need a rear-window defroster on a Skoda? To keep your hands warm when pushing it."

41. For some research method issues in adapting surveys to different cultures, see Martijn G. de Jong, Jan-Benedict E. M. Steenkamp, and Bernard P. Veldkamp, "A Model for the Construction of Country-Specific Yet Internationally Comparable Short-Form Marketing Scales," *Marketing Science* 28 (July–August 2009), pp. 674–89.

42. Nigel Hollis, *The Global Brand* (New York: Palgrave Macmillan, 2008); Nigel Hollis, "Going Global? Better Think Local Instead," *Brandweek*, December 1, 2008, p. 14.

43. "U.S. Soft Drink Consumption on the Decline," *Reuters,* August 24, 2009; *The Economist: Pocket World in Figures* (Profile Books: London, 2009).

44. For some recent examples, see Ana Valenzuela, Barbara Mellers, and Judi Stebel, "Pleasurable Surprises: A Cross-Cultural Study of Consumer Responses to Unexpected Incentives," *Journal of Consumer Research* 36 (February 2010), pp. 792–805; Tuba Üstüner and Douglas B. Holt, "Toward a Theory of Status Consumption in Less Industrialized Countries," *Journal of Consumer Research* 37 (June 2010), pp. 37–56; Praveen K. Kopalle, Donald R. Lehmann, and John U. Farley, "Consumer Expectations and Culture: The Effect of Belief in Karma in India," *Journal of Consumer Research* 37 (August 2010), pp. 251–63.

45. Geert Hofstede, *Culture's Consequences* (Beverley Hills, CA: Sage, 1980).

46. D. A. Aaker and Erich Joachimsthaler, "The Lure of Global Branding," *Harvard Business Review*, 37 (November 1999), pp. 137–44.

47. For some in-depth treatments of branding in Asia in particular, see S. Ramesh Kumar, *Marketing & Branding: The Indian Scenario* (Delhi: Pearson Education, 2007); Martin Roll, *Asian Brand Strategy: How Asia Builds Strong Brands* (New York: Palgrave MacMillan, 2006); Paul Temporal, *Branding in Asia: The Creation, Development, and Management of Asian Brands for the Global Market* (Singapore: John Wiley & Sons, 2001).

48. Michael Arnt, "Knock Knock, It's Your Big Mac," *BusinessWeek*, July 23, 2007, p. 36; Lulu Raghavan, "Lessons from the Maharaja Mac: Five Rules for Entering the Indian Market," *Landor Associates*, www.landor.com, December 2007.

49. Deepa Chandrasekaran and Gerard J. Tellis, "Global Takeoff of New Products: Culture, Wealth, or Vanishing Differences?" *Marketing Science* 27 (September–October 2008), pp. 844–60.

50. Leila Abboud, "Philips Widens Marketing Push in India," *Wall Street Journal*, March 20, 2009.

51. Walter J. Keegan and Mark C. Green, *Global Marketing*, 4th ed. (Upper Saddle River, NJ: Prentice Hall, 2005); Warren J. Keegan, *Global Marketing Management,* 7th ed. (Upper Saddle River, NJ: Prentice Hall, 2002).

52. Paulo Prada and Bruce Orwall, "A Certain 'Je Ne Sais Quoi' at Disney's New Park," *Wall Street Journal,* March 12, 2003.

53. Ralf van der Lans, Joseph A. Cote, Catherine A. Cole, Siew Meng Leong, Ale Smidts, Pamela W. Henderson, Christian Bluemelhuber, Paul A. Bottomley, John R. Doyle, Alexander Fedorikhin, Janakiraman Moorthy, B. Ramaseshan, and Bernd H. Schmitt," Cross-National Logo Evaluation Analysis: An Individual-Level Approach," *Marketing Science* 28 (September–October 2009), pp. 968–85.

54. F. C. (Frank) Hong, Anthony Pecotich, and Clifford J. Shultz II, "Language Constraints, Product Attributes, and Consumer Perceptions in East and Southeast Asia," *Journal of International Marketing* 10 (June 2002), pp. 29–45.

55. Mark Lasswell, "Lost in Translation," *Business 2.0,* August 2004, pp. 68–70; Richard P. Carpenter and the *Globe* Staff, "What They Meant to Say Was . . .," *Boston Globe,* August 2, 1998.

56. For an interesting distinction based on the concept of global consumer culture positioning, see Dana L. Alden, Jan-Benedict E. M. Steenkamp, and Rajeev Batra, "Brand Positioning through Advertising in Asia, North America, and Europe: The Role of Global Consumer Culture," *Journal of Marketing* 63 (January 1999), pp. 75–87.

57. Thomas J. Madden, Kelly Hewett, and Martin S. Roth, "Managing Images in Different Cultures: A Cross-National Study of Color Meanings and Preferences," *Journal of International Marketing* 8 (Winter 2000), pp. 90–107; Zeynep Gürhan-Canli and Durairaj Maheswaran, "Cultural Variations in Country-of-Origin Effects," *Journal of Marketing Research* 37 (August 2000), pp. 309–17.

58. Geoffrey Fowler, Brian Steinberg, and Aaron O. Patrick, "Globalizing Apple's Ads," *Wall Street Journal*, March 1, 2007; Joan Voight, "Best Campaign of the Year: Apple "Mac vs. PC," *Adweek*, July 17, 2007.

59. See, for example, Haksin Chan, Lisa C. Wan, and Leo Y. M. Shin, "The Contrasting Effects of Culture on Consumer Tolerance: Interpersonal Face and Impersonal Fate," *Journal of Consumer Research* 36 (August 2009), pp. 292–304.

60. Aradhna Krishna and Rohini Ahluwalia, "Language Choice in Advertising to Bilinguals: Asymmetric Effects for Multinationals versus Local Firms," *Journal of Consumer Research* 35 (December 2008), pp. 692–705.

61. Normandy Madden, "Crossing Borders by Building Relationships," *Advertising Age*, October 13, 2008, p. 32.

62. Preeti Khicha, "Building Brands in Rural India," *Brandchannel,* www.brandchannel.com, October 8, 2007.

63. John L. Graham, Alma T. Mintu, and Waymond Rogers, "Explorations of Negotiations Behaviors in Ten Foreign Cultures Using a Model Developed in the United States," *Management Science* 40 (January 1994), pp. 72–95.

64. Price perceptions may differ too, see Lisa E. Bolton, Hean Tat Keh, and Joseph W. Alba, "How Do Price Fairness Perceptions Differ Across Culture?" *Journal of Marketing Research* 47 (June 2010), pp. 564–76.

65. David Pierson, "Beijing Loves IKEA—But Not for Shopping," *Los Angeles Times*, August 25, 2009; Mei Fong, "IKEA Hits Home in China: The Swedish Design Giant, Unlike Other Retailers, Slashes Prices for the Chinese," *Wall Street Journal,* March 3, 2006, p. B1.

66. Companies often fight back, however, and legally contest the imposition of any duties. After several years, the Chinese government was eventually able to overturn the duties slapped on the off-road tire makers. See "Commerce Finds Unfair Dumping of Off-Road Tires from China," *International Trade Association*, February 6, 2008; "Ministry: China Pleased U.S. Overturned Duties on its Off-Road Tires," *People's Daily*, August 17, 2010.

67. AGMA, "KPMG/AGMA Survey Projects Global 'Global Market' of $58 Billion for Information Technology Manufacturers," *KPMG,* www.kpmg.com, December 11, 2008.

68. David Blanchard, "Just in Time—How to Fix a Leaky Supply Chain," *IndustryWeek,* May 1, 2007.

69. Kersi D. Antia, Mark E. Bergen, Shantanu Dutta, and Robert J. Fisher, "How Does Enforcement Deter Gray Market Incidence?" *Journal of Marketing* 70 (January 2006), pp. 92–106; Matthew B. Myers and David A. Griffith, "Strategies for Combating Gray Market Activity," *Business Horizons* 42 (November–December 1999), pp. 2–8.

70. Brian Grow, Chi-Chu Tschang, Cliff Edwards, and Brian Burnsed, "Dangerous Fakes," *BusinessWeek*, October 8, 2008; Brian Burnsed, "The Most Counterfeited Products," *Businessweek,* www.businessweek. com, October 8, 2008.

71. "IPR Seizure Statistics," *US Department of Homeland Security,* www.cbp.gov/xp/cgov/trade/priority_trade/ipr/pubs/seizure/, December 9, 2010.

72. Eric Shine, "Faking Out the Fakers," *BusinessWeek,* June 4, 2007, pp. 76–80.

73. Deborah Kong, "Smart Tech Fights Fakes," *Business 2.0*, March 2007, p. 30.

74. David Arnold, "Seven Rules of International Distribution," *Harvard Business Review,* November–December 2000, pp. 131–37.

75. Ibid.

76. Katrijn Gielens, Linda M. Van De Gucht, Jan-Benedict E.M. Steenkamp, and Marnik G. Dekimpe, "Dancing with a Giant: The Effect of Wal-Mart's Entry into the United Kingdom on the Performance of European Retailers," *Journal of Marketing Research* 45 (October 2008), pp. 519–34.

77. Noreen O'Leary, "Infiniti Plays Up Japanese Heritage in Global Campaign," *Brandweek*, February 15, 2010, p. 5.

78. "The Shock of Old," *Economist,* July 13, 2002, p. 49.

79. "From Fantasy Worlds to Food," *Economist*, November 11, 2006, p. 73; "A New Sort of Beauty Contest," *Economist*, November 11, 2006, p. 68.

80. Flora Bagenal and John Harlow, "Borat Make Benefit Kazakh Tourist Boom," *Sunday Times*, December 3, 2006; Lisa Minot, "Borat Causes Tourism Boom," *The Sun*, March 5, 2007; "Borat 'Boosted Kazakh Tourism,'" *ABC News*, www.abc.net.au, November 13, 2008.

81. Jim Rendon, "When Nations Need a Little Marketing," *New York Times,* November 23, 2003.

82. Joanna Kakissis, "Vacationers Rethink Greece Amid Debt Crisis," *National Public Radio*, www.npr.org, June 22, 2010; Elena Becatoros, "Greece's Tourism Industry Under Threat," *MSNBC*, www.msnbc.com, June 15, 2010.

83. Zeynep Gurhan-Canli and Durairaj Maheswaran, "Cultural Variations in Country-of-Origin Effects," *Journal of Marketing Research* 37 (August 2000), pp. 309–17. For some different related issues, see also Lily Dong and Kelly Tian, "The Use of Western Brands in Asserting Chinese National Identity," *Journal of Consumer Research* 36 (October 2009), pp. 504–23; Yinlong Zhang and Adwait Khare, "The Impact of Accessible Identities on the Evaluation of Global versus Local Products," *Journal of Consumer Research* 36 (October 2009), pp. 524–37; Rohit Varman and Russell W. Belk, "Nationalism and Ideology in an Anticonsumption Movement," *Journal of Consumer Research* 36 (December 2009), pp. 686–700.

84. Douglas B. Holt, John A. Quelch, and Earl L. Taylor, "How Global Brands Compete," *Harvard Business Review* 82, September 2004, pp. 68–75; Jan-Benedict E. M. Steenkamp, Rajeev Batra, and Dana L. Alden, "How Perceived Brand Globalness Creates Brand Value," *Journal of International Business Studies* 34 (January 2003), pp. 53–65.

85. Gürhan-Canli and Maheswaran "Cultural Variations in Country-of-Origin Effects"; Johny K. Johansson, "Global Marketing: Research on Foreign Entry, Local Marketing, Global Management," Barton A. Weitz and Robin Wensley, eds., *Handbook of Marketing* (London: Sage, 2002), pp. 457–83; "Old Wine in New Bottles," *Economist,* February 21, 1998, p. 45; Johny K. Johansson, "Determinants and Effects of the Use of 'Made in' Labels," *International Marketing Review (UK)* 6 (January 1989), pp. 47–58; Warren J. Bilkey and Erik Nes, "Country-of-Origin Effects on Product Evaluations," *Journal of International Business Studies* 13 (Spring–Summer 1982), pp. 89–99.

86. Kimberly Weisul, "Why More Are Buying into 'Buy Local,'" *Bloomberg BusinessWeek*, March 1, 2010, pp. 57–60.

87. Jathon Sapsford and Norihiko Shirouzo, "Mom, Apple Pie and . . . Toyota?" *Wall Street Journal*, May 11, 2006.

88. Kenneth Hein, "Emerging Markets Still Like U.S. Brands," *Brandweek,* April 16, 2007, p. 4.

89. For additional discussion, see "Strengthening Brand America," *The Burghard Group*, www.strengtheningbrandamerica.com, December 9, 2010.

90. Joel Backaler, "Haier: A Chinese Company That Innovates," *China Tracker*, www.forbes.com, June 17, 2010; Zhang Ruimin, "Voices from China," *Forbes*, September 28, 2009.

91. Rajdeep Grewal, Murali Chandrashekaran, and F. Robert Dwyer, "Navigating Local Environments with

Global Strategies: A Contingency Model of Multinational Subsidiary Performance," *Marketing Science* 27 (September–October 2008), pp. 886–902. Christopher A. Bartlett and Sumantra Ghoshal, *Managing across Borders* (Cambridge, MA: Harvard Business School Press, 1989).

92. Moon Ihlwan, "The Foreigners at the Top of LG," *BusinessWeek*, December 22, 2008, pp. 56–57.

93. Jim Murphy, "The Jack's Eye-View on Marketing a Global Brand Locally," talk given at *The Beverage Forum*, New York, NY, May 20, 2009.

94. Betsy McKay, "Coke Hunts for Talent to Re-Establish Its Marketing Might," *Wall Street Journal,* March 6, 2002.

95. David Kiley, "Ghosn Hits the Accelerator," *BusinessWeek*, May 1, 2008.

Chapter 22

1. Mark Borden and Anya Kamentz, "The Prophet CEO," *Fast Company*, September 2008, pp. 126–29; Tara Weiss, "Special Report: Going Green," *Forbes.com.* Forbes.com, July 3, 2007; Matthew Grimm, "Progressive Business," *Brandweek*, November 28, 2005, pp. 16–26; Kate Galbraith, "Timberland's New Footprint: Recycled Tires," *New York Times,* April 3, 2009; Aman Singh, "Timberland's Smoking Ban: Good Corporate Citizenship or Overkill?" *Forbes,* June 3, 2010; Amy Cortese, "Products; Friend of Nature? Let's See Those Shoes," *New York Times,* March 6, 2007; Timberland, www.timberland.com.

2. Christopher Vollmer, *Always On: Advertising, Marketing, and Media in an Era of Consumer Control* (New York: McGraw-Hill, 2008).

3. For additional analysis and discussion, see Philip Kotler, Hermawan Karatajaya, and Iwan Setiawan, *Marketing 3.0: From Products to Consumers to the Human Spirit* (Hoboken, NJ: Wiley, 2010).

4. Devin Leonard, "The New Abnormal," *Bloomberg BusinessWeek*, August 2–August 10, 2010, pp. 50–55; Noreen O'Leary, "CMOs Face New Reality," *Adweek*, August 11, 2010.

5. John Gerzema and Michael D'Antonio, *Spend Shift: How the Post-Crisis Values Revolution Is Changing the Way We Buy, Sell, and Live* (San Francisco: Jossey-Bass, 2010).

6. John A. Quelch and Katherine E. Jocz, *Greater Good: How Good Marketing Makes for Better Democracy* (Boston, MA: Harvard Business School Press, 2007).

7. Clay Chandler, "Full Speed Ahead," *Fortune,* February 7, 2005, pp. 78–84; "What You Can Learn from Toyota," *Business 2.0,* January–February 2005, pp. 67–72; Keith Naughton, "Red, White, and Bold," *Newsweek,* April 25, 2005, pp. 34–36.

8. For some thoughtful academic perspectives on marketing strategy and tactics, see *Kellogg on Integrated Marketing,* Dawn Iacobucci and Bobby Calder, eds. (New York: Wiley, 2003); and *Kellogg on Marketing,* Dawn Iacobucci, ed. (New York: Wiley, 2001).

9. For a broad historical treatment of marketing thought, see D. G. Brian Jones and Eric H. Shaw, "A History of Marketing Thought," Barton A. Weitz and Robin Wensley, eds., *Handbook of Marketing* (London: Sage, 2002), pp. 39–65; for more specific issues related to the interface between marketing and sales, see Christian Homburg, Ove Jensen, and Harley Krohmer, "Configurations of Marketing and Sales: A Taxonomy," *Journal of Marketing* 72 (March 2008), pp. 133–54.

10. Frederick E. Webster Jr., "Expanding Your Network," *Marketing Management* (Fall 2010), pp. 16–23; Frederick E. Webster Jr., Alan J. Malter, and Shankar Ganesan, "Can Marketing Regain Its Seat at the Table?" *Marketing Science Institute Report No. 03-113* (Cambridge, MA: Marketing Science Institute, 2003); Frederick E. Webster Jr., "The Role of Marketing and the Firm," Barton A. Weitz and Robin Wensley, eds., *Handbook of Marketing* (London: Sage, 2002), pp. 39–65.

11. Jan Wieseke, Michael Ahearne, Son K. Lam, and Rolf van Dick, "The Role of Leaders in Internal Marketing," *Journal of Marketing* 73 (March 2009), pp. 123–45; Hamish Pringle and William Gordon, *Beyond Manners: How to Create the Self-Confident Organisation to Live the Brand* (West Sussex, England: John Wiley & Sons, 2001); John P. Workman Jr., Christian Homburg, and Kjell Gruner, "Marketing Organization: An Integrative Framework of Dimensions and Determinants," *Journal of Marketing* 62 (July 1998), pp. 21–41.

12. Grant McKracken, *Chief Culture Officer: How to Create a Living Breathing Corporation* (New York: Basic Books, 2009).

13. Todd Guild, "Think Regionally, Act Locally: Four Steps to Reaching the Asian Consumer," *McKinsey Quarterly* 4 (September 2009), pp. 22–30.

14. "State and Country Quick Facts," *U.S. Census Bureau*, http://quickfacts.census.gov/qfd/states/12/12086.html.

15. "Category Management Goes beyond Grocery," *Cannondale Associates White Paper,* www.cannondaleassoc.com, February 13, 2007; Laurie Freeman, "P&G Widens Power Base: Adds Category Managers," *Advertising Age*; Michael J. Zenor, "The Profit Benefits of Category Management," *Journal of Marketing Research* 31 (May 1994), pp. 202–13; Gerry Khermouch, "Brands Overboard," *Brandweek,* August 22, 1994, pp. 25–39; Zachary Schiller, "The Marketing Revolution at Procter & Gamble," *BusinessWeek,* July 25, 1988, pp. 72–76.

16. For some further reading on the origins of category management, see Robert Dewar and Don Shultz, "The Product Manager, an Idea Whose Time Has Gone," *Marketing Communications* (May 1998), pp. 28–35; George S. Low and Ronald A. Fullerton, "Brands, Brand Management, and the Brand Manager System: A Critical Historical Evaluation," *Journal of Marketing Research* 31 (May 1994), pp. 173–90; Michael J. Zanor, "The Profit Benefits of Category Management," *Journal of Marketing Research* 31 (May 1994), pp. 202–13.

17. D. Gail Fleenor, "The Next Space Optimizer," *Progressive Grocer*, March 2009.

18. Larry Selden and Geoffrey Colvin, *Angel Customers & Demon Customers* (New York: Portfolio [Penguin], 2003).

19. For an in-depth discussion of issues around implementing a customer-based organization on which much of this paragraph is based, see George S. Day, "Aligning the Organization with the Market," *MIT Sloan Management Review* 48 (Fall 2006), pp. 41–49.

20. Frederick E. Webster Jr., "The Role of Marketing and the Firm," Barton A. Weitz and Robin Wensley, eds., *Handbook of Marketing* (London: Sage, 2002), pp. 39–65.

21. For research on the prevalence of CMOs, see Pravin Nath and Vijay Mahajan, "Chief Marketing Officers: A Study of Their Presence in Firms' Top Management Teams," *Journal of Marketing* 72 (January 2008), pp. 65–81. For more discussion on the importance of CMOs, see David A. Aaker, *Spanning Silos: The New CMO Imperative* (Boston: Harvard Business School Press, 2008).

22. For some classic perspectives, see Benson P. Shapiro, "Can Marketing and Manufacturing Coexist?" *Harvard Business Review*, September– October 1977, pp. 104–14. Also see Robert W. Ruekert and Orville C. Walker Jr., "Marketing's Interaction with Other Functional Units: A Conceptual Framework with Other Empirical Evidence," *Journal of Marketing* 51 (January 1987), pp. 1–19.

23. For more on creativity, see Pat Fallon and Fred Senn, *Juicing the Orange: How to Turn Creativity into a Powerful Business Advantage* (Boston: Harvard Business School Press, 2006); Bob Schmetterer, *Leap: A Revolution in Creative Business Strategy* (Hoboken, NJ: Wiley, 2003); Jean-Marie Dru, *Beyond Disruption: Changing the Rules in the Marketplace* (Hoboken, NJ: Wiley, 2002); Michael Michalko, *Cracking Creativity: The Secrets of Creative Genius* (Berkeley, CA: Ten Speed Press, 1998); James M. Higgins, *101 Creative Problem-Solving Techniques* (New York: New Management Publishing, 1994); and all the books by Edward DeBono.

24. Gary Hamel, *Leading the Revolution* (Boston: Harvard Business School Press, 2000).

25. Jagdish N. Sheth, *The Self-Destructive Habits of Good Companies . . . And How to Break Them* (Upper Saddle River, NJ: Wharton School Publishing, 2007).

26. William L. Wilkie and Elizabeth S. Moore, "Marketing's Relationship to Society," Barton A. Weitz and Robin Wensley, eds., *Handbook of Marketing* (London: Sage, 2002), pp. 1–38.

27. "Special Report: Corporate Social Responsibility," *Economist,* January 17, 2008. For a broader academic perspective, see Michael E. Porter and Mark R. Kramer, "Strategy & Society," *Harvard Business Review* (December 2006): 78–82; Clayton M. Christensen, Heiner Baumann, Rudy Ruggles, and Thomas M. Stadtler, "Disruption Innovation for Social Change," *Harvard Business Review* (December 2006): 94–101.

28. Walmart, http://walmartstores.com/Sustainability/7951.aspx; Monte Burke, "Mr. Green Jeans," *Forbes,* May 24, 2010; Brian Grow, "The Debate over Doing Good," *BusinessWeek*, August 15, 2005, pp. 76–78.

29. Brian Grow, "The Debate over Doing Good," *BusinessWeek,* August 15, 2005.

30. MaryLou Costa, "P&G Marketing Boss Urges Brands to Move Beyond Traditional Advertising," *Marketing Week,* June 24, 2010; Elaine Wong, "P&G Shows Its Softer Side with Downy Cause Effort," *Brandweek*, February 1, 2010, p. 6; Elaine Wang, "P&G Throws Values into Value Equation," *Brandweek*, March 9, 2009, p. 5.

31. Raj Sisodia, David B. Wolfe, and Jag Sheth, *Firms of Endearment: How World-Class Companies Profit from Passion and Purpose* (Upper Saddle River, NJ: Wharton School Publishing, 2007).

32. Gary Hirshberg, *Stirring It Up: How to Make Money and Save the World* (New York: Hyperion, 2008); Marc Gunther, "Stonyfield Stirs Up the Yogurt Market, *Fortune.* www.cnnmoney.com, January 4, 2008; Melanie D. G. Kaplan, "Stonyfield Farm CEO: How an Organic Yogurt Business Can Scale," *SmartPlanet*, www.smartplanet.com, May 17, 2010.

33. Elisabeth Sullivan, "Play by the New Rules," *Marketing News*, November 30, 2009, pp. 5–9; For further reading, see Dorothy Cohen, *Legal Issues in Marketing Decision Making* (Cincinnati, OH: South-Western College Publishing, 1995).

34. Sarah Ellison, "Kraft Limits on Kids' Ads May Cheese Off Rivals," *Wall Street Journal*, January 13, 2005.

35. Shelby D. Hunt and Scott Vitell, "The General Theory of Marketing Ethics: A Retrospective and Revision," John Quelch and Craig Smith, eds., *Ethics in Marketing* (Chicago: Irwin, 1992).

36. "Distrust, Discontent, Anger and Partisan Rancor," *The Pew Research for the People & the Press*, April 18, 2010.

37. Ronald Alsop, "How a Boss's Deeds Buff a Firm's Reputation," *Wall Street Journal,* January 31, 2007.

38. Mary Jo Hatch and Majken Schultz, *Taking Brand Initiative: How Companies Can Align Strategy, Culture, and Identity through Corporate Branding* (San Francisco: Jossey-Bass, 2008); Majken Schultz, Yun Mi Antorini, and Fabian F. Csaba, *Corporate Branding: Purpose, People, and Process* (Køge, Denmark: Copenhagen Business School Press, 2005); Ronald J. Alsop, *The 18 Immutable Laws of Corporate Reputation: Creating, Protecting, and Repairing Your Most Valuable Asset* (New York: Free Press, 2004); Marc Gunther, "Tree Huggers, Soy Lovers, and Profits," *Fortune,* June 23, 2003, pp. 98–104; Ronald J. Alsop, "Perils of Corporate Philanthropy," *Wall Street Journal,* January 16, 2002.

39. Emily Steel, "Nestlé Takes a Beating on Social-Media Sites," *Wall Street Journal*, March 29, 2010, p. B5; Mya Frazier, "Going Green? Plant Deep Roots," *Advertising Age*, April 30, 2007, pp. 1, 54–55.

40. Scott Kirsner, "An Environmental Quandary Percolates at Green Mountain Coffee Roasters," *Boston Globe,* January 3, 2010; Natalie Zmuda, "Green Mountain

Takes on Coffee Giants Cup by Cup," *Advertising Age*, June 1, 2009, p. 38.

41. Angela M. Eikenberry, "The Hidden Cost of Cause Marketing," *Stanford Social Innovation Review* (Summer 2009); Aneel Karnani, "The Case Against Corporate Social Responsibility," *Wall Street Journal*, August 23, 2010.

42. Sandra O'Loughlin, "The Wearin' o' the Green," *Brandweek*, April 23, 2007, pp. 26–27. For a critical response, see also, John R. Ehrenfield, "Feeding the Beast," *Fast Company*, December 2006–January 2007, pp. 42–43.

43. Pete Engardio, "Beyond the Green Corporation," *BusinessWeek*, January 29, 2007, pp. 50–64.

44. Global 100, www.global100.org.

45. Pete Engardio, "Beyond the Green Corporation," *BusinessWeek*, January 29, 2007, pp. 50–64.

46. Noreen O' Leary, "Marketer of the Year: Jessica Buttimer," *Next*, September 14, 2009, p. 32; Jack Neff, "Marketing 50: Green Works (Jessica Buttimer), *Advertising Age*, November 17, 2008, p. S-2; Elaine Wong, "CPGs Watch as Clorox Crashes the Green Party," *Brandweek*, April 21, 2008, p. 13; Anya Kamenetz, "Cleaning Solution," *Fast Company*, September 2008, pp. 121–25.

47. David Roberts, "Another Inconvenient Truth," *Fast Company*, March 2008, p. 70; Melanie Warner, "P&G's Chemistry Test," *Fast Company*, July/August 2008, pp. 71–74.

48. Mark Dolliver, "Thumbs Down on Corporate Green Efforts," *Adweek*, August 31, 2010; Betsy Cummings, "A Green Backlash Gains Momentum," *Brandweek*, March 3, 2008, p. 6; Michael Hopkins, "What the 'Green' Consumer Wants," *MIT Sloan Management Review* (Summer 2009), pp. 87–89. For some related consumer research, see Julie R. Irwin and Rebecca Walker Naylor, "Ethical Decisions and Response Mode Compatibility: Weighting of Ethical Attributes in Consideration Sets Formed by Excluding versus Including Product Alternatives," *Journal of Marketing Research* 46 (April 2009), pp. 234–46.

49. Jack Neff, "Green-Marketing Revolution Defies Economic Downturn," *Advertising Age*, April 20, 2009, pp. 1, 23; Ram Nidumolu, C. K. Prahalad, and M. R. Rangaswami, "Why Sustainability Is Now the Key Driver of Innovation," *Harvard Business Review*, September 2009, p. 57.

50. John A. Quelch and Nathalie Laidler-Kylander, *The New Global Brands: Managing Non-Government Organizations in the 21st Century* (Mason, OH: South-Western, 2006); Philip Kotler and Nancy Lee, *Corporate Social Responsibility: Doing the Most Good for Your Company and Your Cause* (New York: Wiley, 2005); Lynn Upshaw, *Truth: The New Rules for Marketing in a Skeptical World* (New York: AMACOM, 2007).

51. Newman's Own Foundation, www.newmansown foundation.org; Paul Newman and A. E. Hotchner, *Shameless Exploitation in Pursuit of the Common*

Good: The Madcap Business Adventure by the Truly Oddest Couple (Waterville, ME: Thorndike Press, 2003).

52. "U.S. Charitable Giving Falls 3.6 Percent in 2009 to $303.75 Billion," *Giving USA 2010 Report,* June 9, 2010.

53. Robert Berner, "Smarter Corporate Giving," *BusinessWeek*, November 28, 2005, pp. 68–76; Craig N. Smith, "Corporate Social Responsibility: Whether or How?" *California Management Review* 45 (Summer 2003), pp. 52–76.

54. Larry Chiagouris and Ipshita Ray, "Saving the World with Cause-Related Marketing," *Marketing Management* 16 (July–August 2007), pp. 48–51; Hamish Pringle and Marjorie Thompson, *Brand Spirit: How Cause-Related Marketing Builds Brands* (New York: Wiley, 1999); Sue Adkins, *Cause-Related Marketing: Who Cares Wins* (Oxford, England: Butterworth-Heinemann, 1999); "Marketing, Corporate Social Initiatives, and the Bottom Line," Marketing Science Institute Conference Summary, *MSI Report No. 01-106, 2001.*

55. Rajan Varadarajan and Anil Menon, "Cause-Related Marketing: A Co-Alignment of Marketing Strategy and Corporate Philanthropy," *Journal of Marketing* 52 (July 1988), pp. 58–74.

56. Minette Drumwright and Patrick E. Murphy, "Corporate Societal Marketing," Paul N. Bloom and Gregory T. Gundlach, eds., *Handbook of Marketing and Society* (Thousand Oaks, CA: Sage, 2001), pp. 162–83. See also, Minette Drumwright, "Company Advertising with a Social Dimension: The Role of Noneconomic Criteria," *Journal of Marketing* 60 (October 1996), pp. 71–87.

57. C. B. Bhattacharya, Sankar Sen and Daniel Korschun, "Using Corporate Social Responsibility to Win the War for Talent," *MIT Sloan Management Review* 49 (January 2008), pp. 37–44; Xueming Luo and C. B. Bhattacharya, "Corporate Social Responsibility, Customer Satisfaction, and Market Value," *Journal of Marketing* 70 (October 2006), pp. 1–18; Pat Auger, Paul Burke, Timothy Devinney, and Jordan J. Louviere, "What Will Consumers Pay for Social Product Features?" *Journal of Business Ethics* 42 (February 2003), pp. 281–304; Dennis B. Arnett, Steve D. German, and Shelby D. Hunt, "The Identity Salience Model of Relationship Marketing Success: The Case of Nonprofit Marketing," *Journal of Marketing* 67 (April 2003), pp. 89–105; C. B. Bhattacharya and Sankar Sen, "Consumer-Company Identification: A Framework for Understanding Consumers' Relationships with Companies," *Journal of Marketing* 67 (April 2003), pp. 76–88; Sankar Sen and C. B. Bhattacharya, "Does Doing Good Always Lead to Doing Better? Consumer Reactions to Corporate Social Responsibility," *Journal of Marketing Research* 38 (May 2001), pp. 225–44.

58. Paul N. Bloom, Steve Hoeffler, Kevin Lane Keller, and Carlos E. Basurto, "How Social-Cause Marketing Affects Consumer Perceptions," *MIT Sloan Management Review* (Winter 2006), pp. 49–55; Carolyn J. Simmons and Karen L. Becker-Olsen, "Achieving Marketing

Objectives through Social Sponsorships," *Journal of Marketing* 70 (October 2006), pp. 154–69; Guido Berens, Cees B. M. van Riel, and Gerrit H. van Bruggen, "Corporate Associations and Consumer Product Responses: The Moderating Role of Corporate Brand Dominance," *Journal of Marketing* 69 (July 2005), pp. 35–48; Donald R. Lichtenstein, Minette E. Drumwright, and Bridgette M. Braig, "The Effect of Social Responsibility on Customer Donations to Corporate-Supported Nonprofits," *Journal of Marketing* 68 (October 2004), pp. 16–32; Stephen Hoeffler and Kevin Lane Keller, "Building Brand Equity through Corporate Societal Marketing," *Journal of Public Policy and Marketing* 21 (Spring 2002), pp. 78–89. See also, Special Issue: Corporate Responsibility, *Journal of Brand Management* 10, nos. 4–5 (May 2003).

59. Mark R. Forehand and Sonya Grier, "When Is Honesty the Best Policy? The Effect of Stated Company Intent on Consumer Skepticism," *Journal of Consumer Psychology* 13 (2003), pp. 349–56; Dwane Hal Dean, "Associating the Corporation with a Charitable Event through Sponsorship: Measuring the Effects on Corporate Community Relations," *Journal of Advertising* 31 (Winter 2002), pp. 77–87.

60. Susan Perry, "KFC-Komen 'Buckets for the Cure' Campaign Raises Questions," *MinnPost.com.* www.minnpost.com, April 20, 2010; Chuck English, "Cause Splash vs. Cause Marketing," *Doing Good for Business*, www.doinggoodforbusiness.wordpress.com, May 17, 2010; Nancy Schwartz, "Busted Nonprofit Brand: Anatomy of a Corporate Sponsorship Meltdown (Case Study)," *Getting Attention!* www.gettingattention. org, April 28, 2010.

61. "Nike Announces Global Expansion of LIVESTRONG Product Collection as Lance Armstrong Rides for Hope," *Nike.* www.nike.com, June 30, 2010; Reena Jana, "Nike Goes Green. Very Quietly," *BusinessWeek*, June 22, 2009, p. 56.

62. Mya Frazier, "Costly Red Campaign Reaps Meager $18 Million," *Advertising Age*, March 5, 2007; Viewpoint: Bobby Shriver, "CEO: Red's Raised Lots of Green," *Advertising Age*, March 12, 2007; Michelle Conlin, "Shop (in the Name of Love)," *BusinessWeek*, October 2, 2006, p. 9.

63. Todd Cohen, "Corporations Aim for Strategic Engagement," *Philanthropy Journal*, September 20, 2006; John A. Quelch and Nathalie Laidler-Kylander, *The New Global Brands: Managing Non-Governmental Organizations in the 21st Century* (Cincinnati, OH: South-Western, 2005).

64. Ronald J. Alsop, *The 18 Immutable Laws of Corporate Reputation: Creating, Protecting, and Repairing Your Most Valuable Asset* (New York: Free Press, 2004), p. 125.

65. Ronald McDonald House Charities, www.rmhc.org.

66. Susan Orenstein, "The Selling of Breast Cancer," *Business 2.0*, February 2003, pp. 88–94; H. Meyer, "When the Cause Is Just," *Journal of Business Strategy* 20 (November–December 1999), pp. 27–31.

67. Christine Bittar, "Seeking Cause and Effect," *Brandweek,* November 11, 2002, pp. 18–24.

68. Paula Andruss, "'Think Pink' Awareness Much Higher Than Threat," *Marketing News*, February 15, 2006, pp. 14–16; Jessi Hempel, "Selling a Cause, Better Make It Pop," *BusinessWeek*, February 13, 2006, p. 75; Elizabeth Woyke, "Prostate Cancer's Higher Profile," *BusinessWeek*, October 9, 2006, p. 14.

69. One Sight, www.onesight.org.

70. Christina Binkley, "Charity Gives Shoe Brand Extra Shine," *Wall Street Journal*, April 1, 2010; "How I Got Started . . . Blake Mycoskie, Founder of TOMS Shoes," *Fortune*, March 22, 2010, p. 72; Dan Heath and Chip Heath, "An Arms Race of Goodness," *Fast Company*, October 2009, pp. 82–83; Toms, www.toms.com/movement-one-for-one.

71. Philip Kotler and Nancy Lee, *Social Marketing: Influencing Behaviors for Good* (Thousand Oaks, CA: Sage, 2008); Alan Andreasen, *Social Marketing in the 21st Century* (Thousand Oaks, CA: Sage, 2006); Michael L. Rothschild, "Carrots, Sticks, and Promises: A Conceptual Framework for the Management of Public Health and Social Issue Behaviors," *Journal of Marketing* 63 (October 1999), pp. 24–37.

72. See Michael L. Rothschild, "Carrots, Sticks, and Promises: A Conceptual Framework for the Management of Public Health and Social Issue Behaviors," *Journal of Marketing* 63 (October 1999), pp. 24–37. For an application, see Sekar Raju, Priyali Rajagopal, and Timothy J. Gilbride, "Marketing Healthful Eating to Children: The Effectiveness of Incentives, Pledges, and Competitions," *Journal of Marketing* 74 (May 2010), pp. 93–106.

73. For some relevant recent academic research on developing social marketing programs, see Deborah A. Small and Nicole M. Verrochi, "The Face of Need: Facial Emotion Expression on Charity Advertisements," *Journal of Marketing Research* 46 (December 2009), pp. 777–87; Katherine White and John Peloza, "Self-Benefit versus Other-Benefit Marketing Appeals: Their Effectiveness in Generating Charitable Support," *Journal of Marketing* 73 (July 2009), pp. 109–24; Merel Van Diepen, Bas Donkers and Philip Hans Franses, "Dynamic and Competitive Effects of Direct Mailings: A Charitable Giving Application," *Journal of Marketing Research* 46 (February 2009), pp. 120–33; Jen Shang, Americus Reed II, and Rachel Croson, "Identity Congruency Effects on Donations," *Journal of Marketing Research* 45 (June 2008), pp. 351–61.

74. For more on developing and implementing marketing plans, see H. W. Goetsch, *Developing, Implementing, and Managing an Effective Marketing Plan* (Chicago: NTC Business Books, 1993). See also, Thomas V. Bonoma, *The Marketing Edge: Making Strategies Work* (New York: Free Press, 1985). Much of this section is based on Bonoma's work.

75. For other examples, see Paul W. Farris, Neil T. Bendle, Phillip E. Pfeifer, and David J. Reibstein, *Marketing*

Metrics: 50+ Metrics Every Executive Should Master (Upper Saddle River, NJ: Wharton School Publishing, 2006); John Davis, *Measuring Marketing: 103 Key Metrics Every Marketer Needs* (Hoboken, NJ: Wiley, 2006).

76. Sam R. Goodman, *Increasing Corporate Profitability* (New York: Ronald Press, 1982), chapter 1. See also, Bernard J. Jaworski, Vlasis Stathakopoulos, and H. Shanker Krishnan, "Control Combinations in Marketing: Conceptual Framework and Empirical Evidence," *Journal of Marketing* 57 (January 1993), pp. 57–69.

77. Philip Kotler, William Gregor, and William Rodgers, "The Marketing Audit Comes of Age," *Sloan Management Review* 30 (Winter 1989), pp. 49–62; Frederick Reichheld, *The Loyalty Effect* (Boston: Harvard Business School Press, 1996) discusses attrition of the figures.

78. Useful checklists for a marketing self-audit can be found in Aubrey Wilson, *Aubrey Wilson's Marketing Audit Checklists* (London: McGraw-Hill, 1982); Mike Wilson, *The Management of Marketing* (Westmead, England: Gower Publishing, 1980). A marketing audit software program is described in Ben M. Enis and Stephen J. Garfein, "The Computer-Driven Marketing Audit," *Journal of Management Inquiry* 1 (December 1992), pp. 306–18.

79. Philip Kotler, William Gregor, and William Rodgers, "The Marketing Audit Comes of Age," *Sloan Management Review* 30 (Winter 1989), pp. 49–62.

80. Alfred R. Oxenfeldt, "How to Use Market-Share Measurement," *Harvard Business Review*, January–February 1969, pp. 59–68.

81. There is a one-half chance that a successive observation will be higher or lower. Therefore, the probability of finding six successively higher values is given by 1/2 to the sixth, or 1/64.

82. Alternatively, companies need to focus on factors affecting shareholder value. The goal of marketing planning is to increase shareholder value, which is the present value of the future income stream created by the company's present actions. Rate-of-return analysis usually focuses on only one year's results. See, Alfred Rapport, *Creating Shareholder Value*, rev. ed. (New York: Free Press, 1997).

83. For additional reading on financial analysis, see Peter L. Mullins, *Measuring Customer and Product-Line Profitability* (Washington, DC: Distribution Research and Education Foundation, 1984).

84. Robin Cooper and Robert S. Kaplan, "Profit Priorities from Activity-Based Costing," *Harvard Business Review*, May–June 1991, pp. 130–35; for a recent application to shipping, see Tom Kelley, "What Is the *Real* Cost: How to Use Lifecycle Cost Analysis for an Accurate Comparison," *Beverage World*, January 2010, pp. 50–51.

Appendix

1. Background information and market data adapted from "Gartner Says Worldwide Mobile Phones Sales Grew 35 Percent in Third Quarter 2010; Smartphone Sales Increased 96 Percent," press release, November 18, 2010, www.gartner.com; Joseph Palenchar, "Smartphone Sales Rise as Selection Grows," *TWICE*, June 21, 2010; Sascha Segan, "Motorola RAZR2: The RAZR2 Cuts Four Ways," *PC Magazine,* October 2, 2007, pp. 32–33; Walter S. Mossberg, "Apple's iPod Touch Is a Beauty of a Player Short on Battery Life," *Wall Street Journal,* September 20, 2007, p. B1; "Roam If You Want To," *PC World,* September 2007, p. 134; Sascha Segam, "Exclusive: One RAZR2, Four Ways to Cut It," *PC Magazine Online,* August 13, 2007, www.pcmag.com; "Apple Unlikely to Budge Anytime Soon on iPhone Pricing," *InformationWeek,* July 26, 2007; "Smartphones Get Smarter, Thanks in Part to the iPhone," *InformationWeek,* July 21, 2007; "Nine Alternatives to Apple's iPhone,"*InformationWeek,* June 28, 2007; "Hospital Uses PDA App for Patient Transport," *Health Data Management,* June 2007, p. 14; Jessica E. Vascellaro and Pui-Wing Tam, "RIM's New Gear Fuels Profit Surge; Palm Sputters," *Wall Street Journal,* June 29, 2007, p. B4; "Smart Phones Force Dell from Handhelds," *MicroScope,* April 23, 2007; "2005 PDA Shipments Set Record," *Business Communications Review,* April 2006, p. 6; "Smartphone Market Grows Fast Despite Challenges," *Appliance,* March 2006, p. 16.

Glossary

A

activity-based cost (ABC) accounting procedures that can quantify the true profitability of different activities by identifying their actual costs.

adoption an individual's decision to become a regular user of a product.

advertising any paid form of nonpersonal presentation and promotion of ideas, goods, or services by an identified sponsor.

advertising objective a specific communications task and achievement level to be accomplished with a specific audience in a specific period of time.

anchoring and adjustment heuristic when consumers arrive at an initial judgment and then make adjustments of their first impressions based on additional information.

arm's-length price the price charged by other competitors for the same or a similar product.

aspirational groups groups a person hopes or would like to join.

associative network memory model a conceptual representation that views memory as consisting of a set of nodes and interconnecting links where nodes represent stored information or concepts and links represent the strength of association between this information or concepts.

attitude a person's enduring favorable or unfavorable evaluation, emotional feeling, and action tendencies toward some object or idea.

augmented product a product that includes features that go beyond consumer expectations and differentiate the product from competitors.

available market the set of consumers who have interest, income, and access to a particular offer.

availability heuristic when consumers base their predictions on the quickness and ease with which a particular example of an outcome comes to mind.

average cost the cost per unit at a given level of production; it is equal to total costs divided by production.

B

backward invention reintroducing earlier product forms that can be well adapted to a foreign country's needs.

banner ads (Internet) small, rectangular boxes containing text and perhaps a picture to support a brand.

basic product what specifically the actual product is.

belief a descriptive thought that a person holds about something.

brand a name, term, sign, symbol, or design, or a combination of them, intended to identify the goods or services of one seller or group of sellers and to differentiate them from those of competitors.

brand architecture *see* branding strategy.

brand-asset management team (BAMT) key representatives from functions that affect the brand's performance.

brand associations all brand-related thoughts, feelings, perceptions, images, experiences, beliefs, attitudes, and so on that become linked to the brand node.

brand audit a consumer-focused exercise that involves a series of procedures to assess the health of the brand, uncover its sources of brand equity, and suggest ways to improve and leverage its equity.

brand awareness consumers' ability to identify the brand under different conditions, as reflected by their brand recognition or recall performance.

brand community a specialized community of consumers and employees whose identification and activities focus around the brand.

brand contact any information-bearing experience a customer or prospect has with the brand, the product category, or the market that relates to the marketer's product or service.

brand development index (BDI) the index of brand sales to category sales.

brand dilution when consumers no longer associate a brand with a specific product or highly similar products or start thinking less favorably about the brand.

brand elements those trademarkable devices that serve to identify and differentiate the brand such as a brand name, logo, or character.

brand equity the added value endowed to products and services.

brand extension a company's use of an established brand to introduce a new product.

brand image the perceptions and beliefs held by consumers, as reflected in the associations held in consumer memory.

brand knowledge all the thoughts, feelings, images, experiences, beliefs, and so on that become associated with the brand.

brand line all products, original as well as line and category extensions, sold under a particular brand name.

brand mix the set of all brand lines that a particular seller makes available to buyers.

brand personality the specific mix of human traits that may be attributed to a particular brand.

brand portfolio the set of all brands and brand lines a particular firm offers for sale to buyers in a particular category.

brand promise the marketer's vision of what the brand must be and do for consumers.

brand-tracking studies collect quantitative data from consumers over time to provide consistent, baseline information about how brands and marketing program are performing.

brand valuation an estimate of the total financial value of the brand.

brand value chain a structured approach to assessing the sources and outcomes of brand equity and the manner in which marketing activities create brand value.

branded entertainment using sports, music, arts, or other entertainment activities to build brand equity.

branded variants specific brand lines uniquely supplied to different retailers or distribution channels.

branding endowing products and services with the power of a brand.

branding strategy the number and nature of common and distinctive brand elements applied to the different products sold by the firm.

breakeven analysis a means by which management estimates how many units of the product the company would have to sell to break even with the given price and cost structure.

brick-and-click existing companies that have added an online site for information and/or e-commerce.

business database complete information about business customers' past purchases; past volumes, prices, and profits.

business market all the organizations that acquire goods and services used in the production of other products or services that are sold, rented, or supplied to others.

C

capital items long-lasting goods that facilitate developing or managing the finished product.

captive products products that are necessary to the use of other products, such as razor blades or film.

category extension using the parent brand to brand a new product outside the product category currently served by the parent brand.

category membership the products or sets of products with which a brand competes and which function as close substitutes.

cause-related marketing marketing that links a firm's contributions to a designated cause to customers' engaging directly or indirectly in revenue-producing transactions with the firm.

channel conflict when one channel member's actions prevent the channel from achieving its goal.

channel coordination when channel members are brought together to advance the goals of the channel, as opposed to their own potentially incompatible goals.

channel power the ability to alter channel members' behavior so that they take actions they would not have taken otherwise.

club membership programs programs open to everyone who purchases a product or service, or limited to an affinity group of those willing to pay a small fee.

co-branding (also dual branding or brand bundling) two or more well-known brands are combined into a joint product or marketed together in some fashion.

cohorts groups of individuals born during the same time period who travel through life together.

communication adaptation changing marketing communications programs for each local market.

communication-effect research determining whether an ad is communicating effectively.

company demand the company's estimated share of market demand at alternative levels of company marketing effort in a given time period.

company sales forecast the expected level of company sales based on a chosen marketing plan and an assumed marketing environment.

competitive advantage a company's ability to perform in one or more ways that competitors cannot or will not match.

company sales potential the sales limit approached by company demand as company marketing effort increases relative to that of competitors.

conformance quality the degree to which all the produced units are identical and meet the promised specifications.

conjoint analysis a method for deriving the utility values that consumers attach to varying levels of a product's attributes.

conjunctive heuristic the consumer sets a minimum acceptable cutoff level for each attribute and chooses the first alternative that meets the minimum standard for all attributes.

consumer behavior the study of how individuals, groups, and organizations elect, buy, use, and dispose of goods, services, ideas, or experiences to satisfy their needs and wants.

consumer involvement the level of engagement and active processing undertaken by the consumer in responding to a marketing stimulus.

consumerist movement an organized movement of citizens and government to strengthen the rights and powers of buyers in relation to sellers.

consumption system the way the user performs the tasks of getting and using products and related services.

containerization putting the goods in boxes or trailers that are easy to transfer between two transportation modes.

contractual sales force manufacturers' reps, sales agents, and brokers, who are paid a commission based on sales.

convenience goods goods the consumer purchases frequently, immediately, and with a minimum of effort.

conventional marketing channel an independent producer, wholesaler(s), and retailer(s).

core benefit the service or benefit the customer is really buying.

core competency attribute that (1) is a source of competitive advantage in that it makes a significant contribution to perceived customer benefits, (2) has applications in a wide variety of markets, (3) is difficult for competitors to imitate.

core values the belief systems that underlie consumer attitudes and behavior, and that determine people's choices and desires over the long term.

corporate culture the shared experiences, stories, beliefs, and norms that characterize an organization.

corporate retailing corporately owned retailing outlets that achieve economies of scale, greater purchasing power, wider brand recognition, and better-trained employees.

countertrade offering other items in payment for purchases.

critical path scheduling (PS) network planning techniques to coordinate the many tasks in launching a new product.

cues stimuli that determine when, where, and how a person responds.

culture the fundamental determinant of a person's wants and behavior.

customer-based brand equity the differential effect that brand knowledge has on a consumer response to the marketing of that brand.

customer churn high customer defection.

customer consulting data, information systems, and advice services that the seller offers to buyers.

customer database an organized collection of comprehensive information about individual customers or prospects that is current, accessible, and actionable for marketing purposes.

customer equity the sum of lifetime values of all customers.

customer lifetime value (CLV) the net present value of the stream of future profits expected over the customer's lifetime purchases.

customer mailing list a set of names, addresses, and telephone numbers.

customer-management organization deals with individual customers rather than the mass market or even market segments.

customer perceived value (CPV) the difference between the prospective customer's evaluation of all the benefits and all the costs of an offering and the perceived alternatives.

customer-performance scorecard how well the company is doing year after year on particular customer-based measures.

customer profitability analysis (CPA) a means of assessing and ranking customer profitability through accounting techniques such as activity-based costing (ABC).

customer relationship management (CRM) the process of carefully managing detailed information about individual customers and all customer "touch points" to maximize loyalty.

customer training training the customer's employees to use the vendor's equipment properly and efficiently.

customer value analysis report of the company's strengths and weaknesses relative to various competitors.

customer-value hierarchy five product levels that must be addressed by marketers in planning a market offering.

customerization combination of operationally driven mass customization with customized marketing in a way that empowers consumers to design the product and service offering of their choice.

D

data mining the extracting of useful information about individuals, trends, and segments from the mass of data.

data warehouse a collection of current data captured, organized, and stored in a company's contact center.

database marketing the process of building, maintaining, and using customer databases and other databases for the purpose of contacting, transacting, and building customer relationships.

declining demand consumers begin to buy the product less frequently or not at all.

deep metaphors basic frames or orientations that consumers have toward the world around them.

delivery how well the product or service is delivered to the customer.

demand chain planning the process of designing the supply chain based on adopting a target market perspective and working backward.

demand-side method identifying the effect sponsorship has on consumers' brand knowledge.

design the totality of features that affect how a product looks, feels, and functions to a consumer.

direct (company) sales force full- or part-time paid employees who work exclusively for the company.

direct marketing the use of consumer-direct (CD) channels to reach and deliver goods and services to customers without using marketing middlemen.

direct-order marketing marketing in which direct marketers seek a measurable response, typically a customer order.

direct product profitability (DDP) a way of measuring a product's handling costs from the time it reaches the warehouse until a customer buys it in the retail store.

discrimination the process of recognizing differences in sets of similar stimuli and adjusting responses accordingly.

display ads small, rectangular boxes containing text and perhaps a picture to support a brand.

dissociative groups those groups whose values or behavior an individual rejects.

distribution programming building a planned, professionally managed, vertical marketing system that meets the needs of both manufacturer and distributors.

drive a strong internal stimulus impelling action.

dual adaptation adapting both the product and the communications to the local market.

dumping situation in which a company charges either less than its costs or less than it charges in its home market, in order to enter or win a market.

durability a measure of a product's expected operating life under natural or stressful conditions.

E

e-business the use of electronic means and platforms to conduct a company's business.

e-commerce a company or site offers to transact or facilitate the selling of products and services online.

elimination-by-aspects heuristic situation in which the consumer compares brands on an attribute selected probabilistically, and brands are eliminated if they do not meet minimum acceptable cutoff levels.

environmental threat a challenge posed by an unfavorable trend or development that would lead to lower sales or profit.

ethnographic research a particular observational research approach that uses concepts and tools from anthropology and other social science disciplines to provide deep cultural understanding of how people live and work.

everyday low pricing (EDLP) in retailing, a constant low price with few or no price promotions and special sales.

exchange the process of obtaining a desired product from someone by offering something in return.

exclusive distribution severely limiting the number of intermediaries, in order to maintain control over the service level and outputs offered by resellers.

expectancy-value model consumers evaluate products and services by combining their brand beliefs—positive and negative—according to their weighted importance.

expected product a set of attributes and conditions buyers normally expect when they purchase this product.

experience curve (learning curve) a decline in the average cost with accumulated production experience.

experimental research the most scientifically valid research designed to capture cause-and-effect relationships by eliminating competing explanations of the observed findings.

F

fad a craze that is unpredictable, short-lived, and without social, economic, and political significance.

family brand situation in which the parent brand is already associated with multiple products through brand extensions.

family of orientation parents and siblings.

family of procreation spouse and children.

features things that enhance the basic function of a product.

fixed costs (overhead) costs that do not vary with production or sales revenue.

flexible market offering (1) a naked solution containing the product and service elements that all segment members value, and (2) discretionary options that some segment members value.

focus group a gathering of six to ten people who are carefully selected based on certain demographic, psychographic, or other considerations and brought together to discuss various topics of interest.

forecasting the art of anticipating what buyers are likely to do under a given set of conditions.

form the size, shape, or physical structure of a product.

forward invention creating a new product to meet a need in another country.

frequency programs (FPs) designed to provide rewards to customers who buy frequently and in substantial amounts.

full demand consumers are adequately buying all products put into the marketplace.

G

generics unbranded, plainly packaged, less expensive versions of common products such as spaghetti, paper towels, and canned peaches.

global firm a firm that operates in more than one country and captures R&D, production, logistical, marketing, and financial advantages in its costs and reputation that are not available to purely domestic competitors.

global industry an industry in which the strategic positions of competitors in major geographic or national markets are fundamentally affected by their overall global positions.

goal formulation the process of developing specific goals for the planning period.

going-rate pricing price based largely on competitors' prices.

gray market branded products diverted from normal or authorized distribution channels in the country of product origin or across international borders.

H

hedonic bias when people have a general tendency to attribute success to themselves and failure to external causes.

heuristics rules of thumb or mental shortcuts in the decision process.

high-low pricing charging higher prices on an everyday basis but then running frequent promotions and special sales.

holistic marketing concept a concept based on the development, design, and implementation of marketing programs, processes, and activities that recognizes their breadth and interdependencies.

horizontal marketing system two or more unrelated companies put together resources or programs to exploit an emerging market opportunity.

hub-and-spoke system product-management organization where brand or product manager is figuratively at the center, with spokes leading to various departments representing working relationships.

hybrid channels use of multiple channels of distribution to reach customers in a defined market.

I

image the set of beliefs, ideas, and impressions a person holds regarding an object.

industry a group of firms that offer a product or class of products that are close substitutes for one another.

informational appeal elaborates on product or service attributes or benefits.

ingredient branding a special case of co-branding that involves creating brand equity for materials, components, or parts that are necessarily contained within other branded products.

innovation any good, service, or idea that is perceived by someone as new.

innovation diffusion process the spread of a new idea from its source of invention or creation to its ultimate users or adopters.

installation the work done to make a product operational in its planned location.

institutional market schools, hospitals, nursing homes, prisons, and other institutions that must provide goods and services to people in their care.

integrated logistics systems (ILS) materials management, material flow systems, and physical distribution, abetted by information technology (IT).

integrated marketing mixing and matching marketing activities to maximize their individual and collective efforts.

integrated marketing channel system the strategies and tactics of selling through one channel reflect the strategies and tactics of selling through one or more other channels.

integrated marketing communications (IMC) a concept of marketing communications planning that recognizes the added value of a comprehensive plan.

intensive distribution the manufacturer placing the goods or services in as many outlets as possible.

internal branding activities and processes that help to inform and inspire employees.

internal marketing an element of holistic marketing, is the task of hiring, training, and motivating able employees who want to serve customers well.

interstitials advertisements, often with video or animation, that pop up between changes on a Web site.

irregular demand consumer purchases vary on a seasonal, monthly, weekly, daily, or even hourly basis.

J

jobbers small-scale wholesalers who sell to small retailers.

joint venture a company in which multiple investors share ownership and control.

L

latent demand consumers may share a strong need that cannot be satisfied by an existing product.

lean manufacturing producing goods with minimal waste of time, materials, and money.

learning changes in an individual's behavior arising from experience.

lexicographic heuristic a consumer choosing the best brand on the basis of its perceived most important attribute.

licensed product one whose brand name has been licensed to other manufacturers who actually make the product.

life-cycle cost the product's purchase cost plus the discounted cost of maintenance and repair less the discounted salvage value.

life stage a person's major concern, such as going through a divorce, going into a second marriage, taking care of an older parent, deciding to cohabit with another person, deciding to buy a new home, and so on.

lifestyle a person's pattern of living in the world as expressed in activities, interests, and opinions.

line extension the parent brand is used to brand a new product that targets a new market segment within a product category currently served by the parent brand.

line stretching a company lengthens its product line beyond its current range.

long-term memory (LTM) a permanent repository of information.

loyalty a commitment to rebuy or repatronize a preferred product or service.

M

maintenance and repair the service program for helping customers keep purchased products in good working order.

market various groups of customers.

market-buildup method identifying all the potential buyers in each market and estimating their potential purchases.

market-centered organizations companies that are organized along market lines.

market demand the total volume of a product that would be bought by a defined customer group in a defined geographical area in a defined time period in a defined marketing environment under a defined marketing program.

market forecast the market demand corresponding to the level of industry marketing expenditure.

market logistics planning the infrastructure to meet demand, then implementing and controlling the physical flows or materials and final goods from points of origin to points of use, to meet customer requirements at a profit.

market-management organization a market manager supervising several market-development managers, market specialists, or industry specialists and draw on functional services as needed.

market opportunity analysis (MOA) system used to determine the attractiveness and probability of success.

market partitioning the process of investigating the hierarchy of attributes consumers examine in choosing a brand if they use phased decision strategies.

market penetration index a comparison of the current level of market demand to the potential demand level.

market-penetration pricing pricing strategy where prices start low to drive higher sales volume from price-sensitive customers and produce productivity gains.

market potential the limit approached by market demand as industry marketing expenditures approach infinity for a given marketing environment.

market share a higher level of selective demand for a product.

market-skimming pricing pricing strategy where prices start high and are slowly lowered over time to maximize profits from less price-sensitive customers.

marketer someone who seeks a response (attention, a purchase, a vote, a donation) from another party, called the prospect.

marketing the activity, set of institutions, and processes for creating, communicating, delivering, and exchanging offerings that have value for customers, clients, partners, and society at large.

marketing audit a comprehensive, systematic, independent, and periodic examination of a company's or business unit's marketing environment, objectives, strategies, and activities.

marketing channel system the particular set of marketing channels employed by a firm.

marketing channels sets of interdependent organizations involved in the process of making a product or service available for use or consumption.

marketing communications the means by which firms attempt to inform, persuade, and remind consumers—directly or indirectly—about products and brands that they sell.

marketing communications mix advertising, sales promotion, events and experiences, public relations and publicity, direct marketing, and personal selling.

marketing concept is to find not the right customers for your products, but the right products for your customers

marketing decision support system (MDSS) a coordinated collection of data, systems, tools, and techniques with supporting software and hardware by which an organization gathers and interprets relevant information from business and the environment and turns it into a basis for marketing action.

marketing funnel identifies the percentage of the potential target market at each stage in the decision process, from merely aware to highly loyal.

marketing implementation the process that turns marketing plans into action assignments and ensures that such assignments are executed in a manner that accomplishes the plan's stated objectives.

marketing information system (MIS) people, equipment, and procedures to gather, sort, analyze, evaluate, and distribute information to marketing decision makers.

marketing insights diagnostic information about how and why we observe certain effects in the marketplace, and what that means to marketers.

marketing intelligence system a set of procedures and sources managers use to obtain everyday information about developments in the marketing environment.

marketing management the art and science of choosing target markets and getting, keeping, and growing customers through creating, delivering, and communicating superior customer value.

marketing metrics the set of measures that helps firms to quantify, compare, and interpret their marketing performance.

marketing network the company and its supporting stakeholders, with whom it has built mutually profitable business relationships.

marketing opportunity an area of buyer need and interest in which there is a high probability that a company can profitably satisfy that need.

marketing plan written document that summarizes what the marketer has learned about the marketplace, indicates how the firm plans to reach its marketing objectives, and helps direct and coordinate the marketing effort.

marketing public relations (MPR) publicity and other activities that build corporate or product image to facilitate marketing goals.

marketing research the systematic design, collection, analysis, and reporting of data and findings relevant to a specific marketing situation facing the company.

markup pricing an item by adding a standard increase to the product's cost.

mass customization the ability of a company to meet each customer's requirements

master brand situation in which the parent brand is already associated with multiple products through brand extensions.

materials and parts goods that enter the manufacturer's product completely.

media selection finding the most cost-effective media to deliver the desired number and type of exposures to the target audience.

megatrends large social, economic, political, and technological changes that are slow to form, and once in place, have an influence for seven to ten years or longer.

membership groups groups having a direct influence on a person.

memory encoding how and where information gets into memory.

memory retrieval how and from where information gets out of memory.

mental accounting the manner by which consumers code, categorize, and evaluate financial outcomes of choices.

microsales analysis examination of specific products and territories that fail to produce expected sales.

microsite a limited area on the Web managed and paid for by an external advertiser/company.

mission statements statements that organizations develop to share with managers, employees, and (in many cases) customers.

mixed bundling the seller offers goods both individually and in bundles.

motive a need aroused to a sufficient level of intensity to drive us to act.

multichannel marketing a single firm uses two or more marketing channels to reach one or more customer segments.

multitasking doing two or more things at the same time.

N

negative demand consumers who dislike the product and may even pay to avoid it.

net price analysis analysis that encompasses company list price, average discount, promotional spending, and co-op advertising to arrive at net price.

noncompensatory models in consumer choice, when consumers do not simultaneously consider all positive and negative attribute considerations in making a decision.

nonexistent demand consumers who may be unaware of or uninterested in the product.

O

opinion leader the person in informal, product-related communications who offers advice or information about a specific product or product category.

ordering ease how easy it is for the customer to place an order with the company.

organization a company's structures, policies, and corporate culture.

organizational buying the decision-making process by which formal organizations establish the need for purchased products and services and identify, evaluate, and choose among alternative brands and suppliers.

overall market share the company's sales expressed as a percentage of total market sales.

overfull demand more consumers would like to buy the product than can be satisfied.

P

packaging all the activities of designing and producing the container for a product.

paid search marketers bid on search terms, when a consumer searches for those words using Google, Yahoo!, or Bing, the marketer's ad will appear on the results page, and advertisers pay only if people click on links.

parent brand an existing brand that gives birth to a brand extension.

partner relationship management (PRM) activities the firm undertakes to build mutually satisfying long-term relations with key partners such as suppliers, distributors, ad agencies, and marketing research suppliers.

pay-per-click ads *see* paid search.

penetrated market the set of consumers who are buying a company's product.

perceived value the value promised by the company's value proposition and perceived by the customer.

perception the process by which an individual selects, organizes, and interprets information inputs to create a meaningful picture of the world.

performance marketing understanding the financial and nonfinancial returns to business and society from marketing activities and programs.

performance quality the level at which the product's primary characteristics operate.

personal communications channels two or more persons communicating directly face-to-face, person-to-audience, over the telephone, or through e-mail.

personal influence the effect one person has on another's attitude or purchase probability.

personality a set of distinguishing human psychological traits that lead to relatively consistent responses to environmental stimuli.

place advertising (also **out-of-home advertising**) ads that appear outside of home and where consumers work and play.

point-of-purchase (P-O-P) the location where a purchase is made, typically thought of in terms of a retail setting.

points-of-difference (PODs) attributes or benefits that consumers strongly associate with a brand, positively evaluate, and believe they could not find to the same extent with a competitive brand.

points-of-parity (POPs) attribute or benefit associations that are not necessarily unique to the brand but may in fact be shared with other brands.

positioning the act of designing a company's offering and image to occupy a distinctive place in the minds of the target market.

potential market the set of consumers who profess a sufficient level of interest in a market offer.

potential product all the possible augmentations and transformations the product or offering might undergo in the future.

price discrimination a company sells a product or service at two or more prices that do not reflect a proportional difference in costs.

price escalation an increase in the price of a product due to added costs of selling it in different countries.

primary groups groups with which a person interacts continuously and informally, such as family, friends, neighbors, and coworkers.

principle of congruity psychological mechanism that states that consumers like to see seemingly related objects as being as similar as possible in their favorability.

private label brand brands that retailers and wholesalers develop and market.

product anything that can be offered to a market to satisfy a want or need, including physical goods, services, experiences, events, person, places, properties, organizations, information, and ideas.

product adaptation altering the product to meet local conditions or preferences.

product assortment the set of all products and items a particular seller offers for sale.

product concept proposes that consumers favor products offering the most quality, performance, or innovative features.

product invention creating something new via product development or other means.

product map competitors' items that are competing against company X's items.

product mix *see* product assortment.

product-mix pricing the firm searches for a set of prices that maximizes profits on the total mix.

product-penetration percentage the percentage of ownership or use of a product or service in a population.

product system a group of diverse but related items that function in a compatible manner.

production concept holds that consumers prefer products that are widely available and inexpensive.

profitable customer a person, household, or company that over time yields a revenue stream that exceeds by an acceptable amount the company's cost stream of attracting, selling, and servicing that customer.

prospect a purchase, a vote, or a donation by a prospective client.

prospect theory when consumers frame decision alternatives in terms of gains and losses according to a value function.

psychographics the science of using psychology and demographics to better understand consumers.

public any group that has an actual or potential interest in or impact on a company's ability to achieve its objectives.

public relations (PR) a variety of programs designed to promote or protect a company's image or its individual products.

publicity the task of securing editorial space—as opposed to paid space—in print and broadcast media to promote something.

pull strategy when the manufacturer uses advertising and promotion to persuade consumers to ask intermediaries for the product, thus inducing the intermediaries to order it.

purchase probability scale a scale to measure the probability of a buyer making a particular purchase.

pure bundling a firm only offers its products as a bundle.

pure-click companies that have launched a Web site without any previous existence as a firm.

push strategy when the manufacturer uses its sales force and trade promotion money to induce intermediaries to carry, promote, and sell the product to end users.

Q

quality the totality of features and characteristics of a product or service that bear on its ability to satisfy stated or implied needs.

questionnaire a set of questions presented to respondents.

R

reference groups all the groups that have a direct or indirect influence on a person's attitudes or behavior.

reference prices pricing information a consumer retains in memory that is used to interpret and evaluate a new price.

relationship marketing building mutually satisfying long-term relationships with key parties, in order to earn and retain their business.

relative market share market share in relation to a company's largest competitor.

reliability a measure of the probability that a product will not malfunction or fail within a specified time period.

repairability a measure of the ease of fixing a product when it malfunctions or fails.

representativeness heuristic when consumers base their predictions on how representative or similar an outcome is to other examples.

retailer (or retail store) any business enterprise whose sales volume comes primarily from retailing.

retailing all the activities in selling goods or services directly to final consumers for personal, nonbusiness use.

risk analysis a method by which possible rates of returns and their probabilities are calculated by obtaining estimates for uncertain variables affecting profitability.

role the activities a person is expected to perform.

S

sales analysis measuring and evaluating actual sales in relation to goals.

sales budget a conservative estimate of the expected volume of sales, used for making current purchasing, production, and cash flow decisions.

sales promotion a collection of incentive tools, mostly short term, designed to stimulate quicker or greater purchase of particular products or services by consumers or the trade.

sales quota the sales goal set for a product line, company division, or sales representative.

sales-variance analysis a measure of the relative contribution of different factors to a gap in sales performance.

satisfaction a person's feelings of pleasure or disappointment resulting from comparing a product's perceived performance or outcome in relation to his or her expectations.

scenario analysis developing plausible representations of a firm's possible future that make different assumptions about forces driving the market and include different uncertainties.

secondary groups groups that tend to be more formal and require less interaction than primary groups, such as religious, professional, and trade-union groups.

selective attention the mental process of screening out certain stimuli while noticing others.

selective distortion the tendency to interpret product information in a way that fits consumer perceptions.

selective distribution the use of more than a few but less than all of the intermediaries who are willing to carry a particular product.

selective retention good points about a product that consumers like are remembered and good points about competing products are forgotten.

selling concept holds that consumers and businesses, if left alone, won't buy enough of the organization's products.

served market all the buyers who are able and willing to buy a company's product.

served market share a company's sales expressed as a percentage of the total sales to its served market.

service any act or performance that one party can offer to another that is essentially intangible and does not result in the ownership of anything.

share penetration index a comparison of a company's current market share to its potential market share.

shopping goods goods that the consumer, in the process of selection and purchase, characteristically compares on such bases as suitability, quality, price, and style.

short-term memory (STM) a temporary repository of information.

social classes homogeneous and enduring divisions in a society, which are hierarchically ordered and whose members share similar values, interests, and behavior.

social marketing marketing done by a nonprofit or government organization to further a cause, such as "say no to drugs."

specialty goods goods with unique characteristics or brand identification for which enough buyers are willing to make a special purchasing effort.

sponsorship financial support of an event or activity in return for recognition and acknowledgment as the sponsor.

stakeholder-performance scorecard a measure to track the satisfaction of various constituencies who have a critical interest in and impact on the company's performance.

status one's position within his or her own hierarchy or culture.

straight extension introducing a product in a foreign market without any change in the product.

strategic brand management the design and implementation of marketing activities and programs to build, measure, and manage brands to maximize their value.

strategic business units (SBUs) a single business or collection of related businesses that can be planned separately from the rest of the company, with its own set of competitors and a manager who is responsible for strategic planning and profit performance.

strategic group firms pursuing the same strategy directed to the same target market.

strategic marketing plan laying out the target markets and the value proposition that will be offered, based on analysis of the best market opportunities.

strategy a company's game plan for achieving its goals.

style a product's look and feel to the buyer.

sub-brand a new brand combined with an existing brand.

subculture subdivisions of a culture that provide more specific identification and socialization, such as nationalities, religions, racial groups, and geographical regions.

subliminal perception receiving and processing subconscious messages that affect behavior.

supersegment a set of segments sharing some exploitable similarity.

supplies and business services short-term goods and services that facilitate developing or managing the finished product.

supply chain management (SCM) procuring the right inputs (raw materials, components, and capital equipment), converting them efficiently into finished products, and dispatching them to the final destinations.

supply-side methods approximating the amount of time or space devoted to media coverage of an event, for example, the number of seconds the brand is clearly visible on a television screen or the column inches of press clippings that mention it.

T

tactical marketing plan marketing tactics, including product features, promotion, merchandising, pricing, sales channels, and service.

target costing deducting the desired profit margin from the price at which a product will sell, given its appeal and competitors' prices.

target market the part of the qualified available market the company decides to pursue.

target-return pricing determining the price that would yield the firm's target rate of return on investment (ROI).

telemarketing the use of telephone and call centers to attract prospects, sell to existing customers, and provide service by taking orders and answering questions.

total costs the sum of the fixed and variable costs for any given level of production.

total customer benefit the perceived monetary value of the bundle of economic, functional, and psychological benefits customers expect from a given market offering because of the product, service, people, and image.

total customer cost the bundle of costs customers expect to incur in evaluating, obtaining, using, and disposing of the given market offering, including monetary, time, energy, and psychic costs.

total customer value the perceived monetary value of the bundle of economic, functional, and psychological benefits customers expect from a given market offering.

total market potential the maximum sales available to all firms in an industry during a given period, under a given level of industry marketing effort and environmental conditions.

total quality management an organization-wide approach to continuously improving the quality of all the organization's processes, products, and services.

tracking studies collecting information from consumers on a routine basis over time.

transaction a trade of values between two or more parties: A gives X to B and receives Y in return.

transfer in the case of gifts, subsidies, and charitable contributions: A gives X to B but does not receive anything tangible in return.

transfer price the price a company charges another unit in the company for goods it ships to foreign subsidiaries.

transformational appeal elaborates on a nonproduct-related benefit or image.

trend a direction or sequence of events that has some momentum and durability.

two-part pricing a fixed fee plus a variable usage fee.

tying agreements agreement in which producers of strong brands sell their products to dealers only if dealers purchase related products or services, such as other products in the brand line.

U

unsought goods those the consumer does not know about or does not normally think of buying, like smoke detectors.

unwholesome demand consumers may be attracted to products that have undesirable social consequences.

V

value chain a tool for identifying ways to create more customer value.

value-delivery network (supply chain) a company's supply chain and how it partners with specific suppliers and distributors to make products and bring them to markets.

value-delivery system all the expectancies the customer will have on the way to obtaining and using the offering.

value network a system of partnerships and alliances that a firm creates to source, augment, and deliver its offerings.

value pricing winning loyal customers by charging a fairly low price for a high-quality offering.

value proposition the whole cluster of benefits the company promises to deliver.

variable costs costs that vary directly with the level of production.

venture team a cross-functional group charged with developing a specific product or business.

vertical integration situation in which manufacturers try to control or own their suppliers, distributors, or other intermediaries.

vertical marketing system (VMS) producer, wholesaler(s), and retailer(s) acting as a unified system.

viral marketing using the Internet to create word-of-mouth effects to support marketing efforts and goals.

W

warranties formal statements of expected product performance by the manufacturer.

wholesaling all the activities in selling goods or services to those who buy for resale or business use.

Y

yield pricing situation in which companies offer (1) discounted but limited early purchases, (2) higher-priced late purchases, and (3) the lowest rates on unsold inventory just before it expires.

Z

zero-level channel (direct-marketing channel) a manufacturer selling directly to the final customer.

Image Credits

page 331: Courtesy of Zippo Manufacturing Company; page 332: Courtesy of Digicel Group; page 334: ICP/Alamy Images; page 336: Courtesy of AB Electrolux; page 340: Reproduced by kind permission of Sainsbury's Supermarkets Ltd.; page 341: Courtesy of General Electric Company. Photograph by Benedict Redgrove; page 343: Adriano Castelli/Shutterstock; page 344: Scott Prokop/Shutterstock

Chapter 12
page 346: Feng Li/Getty Images, Inc.-Getty News; page 349: Courtesy of Jamestown Container Companies; page 351: Sean Gallup/Getty Images, Inc.-Getty News; page 352: Monica Rueda/AP Wide World Photos; page 354: UpperCut Images/Superstock Royalty Free; page 355: Courtesy of Bang and Olufsen; page 357: Courtesy of Sub-Zero, Inc.; page 358: Courtesy of Michelin North America, Inc.; page 364: Michael Perez/Philadelphia Inquirer/MCT/Newscom; page 365: Matt Cardy/Getty Images, Inc.-Getty News; page 367: Courtesy Mohawk Industries. Carpet made with DuPont™ Sorona®; page 369: Courtesy of Sara Lee Corporation; page 370: Mary Altaffer/AP Wide World Photos; page 372: Woodsy/Shutterstock; page 374: Jose Gil/Shutterstock

Chapter 13
page 376: Holandaluz Vincent de Vries/Alamy Images; page 378: Courtesy of Zipcar; page 381 (left): Michael Caulfield/Getty Images-WireImage.com; page 381 (right): Kevin Mazur/Getty Images/Time Life Pictures; page 361: John Raoux/AP Wide World Photos; page 384 (top): Eric Piermont/Getty Images, Inc. AFP; page 384 (bottom): MajaPhoto/Dreamstime LLC-Royalty Free; page 385: Courtesy of JetBlue Airways Corporation; page 391: Courtesy of Schneider National, Inc.; page 392: Karen Ballard/Redux for Fast Company; page 393: Courtesy of USAA; page 401: Kristoffer Tripplaar/Alamy Images; page 402: Frank Huster/Photolibrary

Chapter 14
page 404: Dorothea Schmid/laif/Redux; page 407: Sandra Hoyn/laif/Redux; page 410: © Corbis All Rights Reserved; page 411 (top, left): Andre Jenny/Alamy Images; page 411 (top, right): Kristoffer Tripplaar/Alamy Images; page 411 (bottom, left): Stu/Alamy Images; page 411 (bottom, right): Chuck Franklin/Alamy Images; page 412: Alex Segre/Alamy Images; page 416: Hiroko Masuike/The New York Times; page 419: Courtesy of Parker Hannifin Corporation; page 421: Courtesy of Kenworth Truck Company; page 423: © Sergej Razvodovskij-Fotolia.com; page 429: Chris Warde-Jones/Bloomberg via Getty Images; page 433: goldenangel/Shutterstock; page 434: Carlos E. Santa Maria/Shutterstock

Chapter 15
page 436: Justin Sullivan/Getty Images, Inc.-Getty News; page 439: Courtesy REI; page 440: Courtesy of Nautilus, Inc.; page 443 (top): Courtesy of RedEnvelope®; page 443 (bottom): Courtesy of WM GreenOps LLC.; page 444: Philip Scalia/Alamy Images; page 446: Jackson Lowen/The New York Times; page 447: Courtesy of STIHL Incorporated; page 452: Hemis/Alamy Images; page 453: Graham Jepson/Alamy Images; page 456: Bloomberg/Getty Images; page 458: Paul Sakuma/AP Wide World Photos; page 462: Tomohiro Ohsumi/Getty Images, Inc-Bloomberg News; page 465: NetPics/Alamy Images; page 466: © ICP/Alamy

Chapter 16
page 468: Brad Swonetz/Redux Pictures; page 470: Charles Krupa/AP Wide World Photos; page 473: Tannen Maury/Getty Images, Inc.-Bloomberg News; page 475: Steven Senne/AP Wide World Photos; page 477: Courtesy of Aéropostale, Inc.; page 478 (upper): © Tim Scrivener/Alamy; page 478 (lower): Bloomberg/Getty Images; page 479: Courtesyof Bass Pro, Inc.; page 482: JB Reed/Getty Images, Inc.-Bloomberg News;

page 487: Courtesy of ConMed, Inc.; page 468: Courtesy of Cameron Hughes Wine; page 492: CuboImages srl/Alamy Images; page 493: Kristoffer Tripplaar/Alamy Images

Chapter 17
page 496: Courtesy of Ocean Spray Cranberries, Inc.; page 499 (top): © Corbis All Rights Reserved; page 499 (bottom): Courtesy of Motorola, Inc.; page 502: Courtesy of Philips Consumer Lifestyle; page 505: Courtesy of General Electric Company. Photographer: Kai Uwe Gundlach; page 506: Jin Lee/Getty Images, Inc.-Getty News; page 509: Courtesy of Priceline.com Incorporated; page 510: Courtesy of Deere & Company; page 511: Getty Images, Inc.; page 515: Reprint Courtesy of International Business Machines Corporation, © 2010 International Business Machines Corporation; page 520: Copyright DeepGreen/Shutterstock; page 521: Kristoffer Tripplaar/Alamy Images

Chapter 18
page 524: © The Procter Gamble Company. Used by permission; page 528: PRNewsFoto/Body by Milk; page 529: Courtesy of T-Mobile Limited; page 530: Courtesy of Aflac Incorporated; page 537: © 2010 Geico. All rights reserved. Used with permission; page 536: Snickers is a registered trademark of Mars, Incorporated and its affiliates. This trademark is used with permission. Mars, Incorporated is not associated with Pearson. Advertisement printed with permission of Mars, Incorporated; page 544: Courtesy of Coupons.com Incorporated; page 546: Michael Schmelling; page 549: "The Crayola FACTORY® Tour" Photo provided courtesy of Crayola LLC and used with permission. © 2010 Crayola. The Crayola FACTORY, "TIP" character and Serpentine Design are trademarks of Crayola LLC; page 550: Mike Derer/AP Wide World Photos; page 551: Dreyer's Grand Ice Cream; page 553: Caro/Alamy; page 554:

mediablitzimages (uk) Limited/Alamy Images

Chapter 19
page 556: Pepsi-Cola Company. Photographer: Martin Wonnacott; page 559: Courtesy of L.L.Bean Inc.; page 560: Lucy Gauntlett; page 563: The BURGER KING® trademarks and advertisements are used with permission from Burger King Corporation; page 566: Trademarks are use with permission of Volkswagen Group of America, Inc.; page 569: © Intuit Inc. All rights reserved; page 570: Courtesy of Treehugger; page 571: Courtesy of Pistachio Consulting; page 572: Courtesy of Blendtec; page 574: Courtesy of Ford Motor Company; page 575: Jin Lee/Getty Images, Inc.-Getty News; page 575: 1000 Words/Shutterstock; page 586: © David Cunningham/Alamy

Chapter 20
page 588: Ryan Collerd/The New York Times/Redux Pictures; page 591: Courtesy of W. L. Gore & Associates, Inc.; page 594: Maurizio Gambarini/Newscom; page 597: Jessica Rinaldi/Reuters Limited; page 598: Buzz Pictures/Alamy Images; page 600: Martin Oeser/Getty Images, Inc. AFP; page 603: PRNewsFoto/Marriott International, Inc.; page 608: Jose M. Osorio/Chicago Tribune/Newscom; page 609: © Corbis All Rights Reserved; page 611: Jim Wilson/The New York Times/Redux Pictures; page 613: John Baran/Alamy Images Royalty Free; page 615: PSL Images/Alamy Images

Chapter 21
page 616: Joerg Boethling/Alamy Images; page 618: Ron Heflin/AP Wide World Photos; page 620: Used with permission from Microsoft; page 621: Ícaro Messias/Wikimedia Commons; page 625: Anita Back/laif/Redux Pictures; page 627: Matthew Ashton/Alamy Images; page 628: Miquel Gonzalez/laif/Redux Pictures; page 629: Indiapix/Alamy Images; page 631: Getty Images, Inc.; page 634: Getty Images, Inc.; page 636: Gold/Miller Productions/Album/Newscom; page 637:

Imaginechina/AP Wide World Photos; page 640: Sandy Young/Alamy Images Royalty Free; page 641: Lou Linwei/Alamy Images

Chapter 22
page 642: Courtesy of The Timberland Company;

page 644: Journal Times, Scott Anderson/AP Wide World Photos; page 647: © Corbis All Rights Reserved; page 649: Adam Rountree/Bloomberg/Getty Images-Bloomberg; page 652: Courtesy of Procter & Gamble; page 654: Irwin

Fedriansyah/AP Wide World Photos; page 657: Courtesy of British Airways Plc; page 658: Allsport Concepts/Getty Images; page 660: Ali Burafi/AP Wide World Photos; page 661: Courtesy of the World Wildlife Fund;

page 665: Matt Rourke/AP Wide World Photos; page 671: Alistair Ruff/Alamy Images Royalty Free; page 672: Leabrooks Photography/Alamy Images Royalty Free.

Index

Name

Company, Brand, and Organization